METALWORKING SCIENCE AND ENGINEERING

McGraw-Hill Series in Materials Science and Engineering

METALWORKING SCIENCE AND ENGINEERING

Edward M. Mielnik

Associate Professor Emeritus
Department of Industrial Engineering
University of Iowa

McGraw-Hill, Inc.

New York   St. Louis   San Francisco   Auckland   Bogotá   Caracas
Hamburg   Lisbon   London   Madrid   Mexico   Milan   Montreal
New Delhi   Paris   San Juan   São Paulo
Singapore   Sydney   Tokyo   Toronto

This book was set in Times Roman.
The editors were B. J. Clark and John M. Morriss;
the production supervisor was Friederich W. Schulte.
The cover was designed by Rafael Hernandez.
Project supervision was done by Harley Editorial Services.
R. R. Donnelley & Sons Company was printer and binder

METALWORKING SCIENCE AND ENGINEERING

1234567890 DOC DOC 9543210

ISBN 0-07-041904-3

Library of Congress Cataloging-in-Publication Data

Mielnik, Edward M.
    Metalworking science and engineering / Edward M. Mielnik.
        p.   cm.—(McGraw-Hill series in materials science and engineering)
    Includes bibliographical references.
    ISBN 0-07-041904-3
        1. Metal-work.   I. Title.   II. Series.
TS205.M52   1991
671—dc20   90-31561

Dedicated to my hardworking, long-suffering parents
who could not read or write in any language

Honor to the Ironworker

When the temple at Jerusalem was completed, King Solomon gave a feast to the artificers
employed in its construction. On unveiling the throne it was found that a smith had usurped
the seat of honor at the right of the King's place not yet awarded. Whereupon the people
clamored and the guard rushed to cut him down. "Hold, let him speak!" commanded Solomon.
"Thou has, O King, invited all craftsmen but me. Yet how could these builders have raised
the temple without the tools I have fashioned?" "True," decreed Solomon, "the seat is his of
right. All honor to the iron worker."

Anonymous legend accompanying a painting by Schuessele.

CONTENTS

3 Stress-Strain Curves and Related Mechanical Properties and Related Phenomena 125

4 Methods for Analyzing Metalworking Processes 219

Part II Classification of Metalworking Processes and Massive or Bulk Deformation Processes

5 Classification of Metalworking or Metalforming Processes

6 Rolling

7 Bar Drawing, Extrusion and Allied Processes

8 Classification of Forging Processes and Open-Die Forging

9 Closed-Die Forging Processes and Related Operations

Part III Sheetmetal Forming Processes

11 Deep Drawing Considerations and Evaluation of Formability

PREFACE

Metalworking probably started in prehistoric times by the imaginative and enterprising people who found clumps of metallic materials in the free form in nature such as gold and meteoric iron, or metals such as silver, tin, zinc, copper, iron, etc., that were reduced under natural conditions or accidentally by means of a camp or forest fire.

The main aspects of metalforming were developed as an art in countless metalworking shops over the centuries. Much of the knowledge was passed down from father to son, or from artisan to apprentice, usually as trade secrets.

The techniques of science and engineering were gradually introduced to the various metalworking operations, but much of materials processing continues to remain largely as an art. In recent years, however, great strides have been made to convert materials processing into an engineering discipline.

This textbook emphasizes the engineering aspect of metalworking. Because most metalworking processes are so very complex, because of the massive amount of information that is presently available, and because of recent developments, the time is right to treat metalforming as a unified field of engineering based on the basic science and mathematics that underlies it. Also, because of the developments in computer-aided design/manufacturing/engineering (CAD/CAM/CAE), much attention must be paid to systematizing the materials processes. Consequently, much attention has been devoted in this book to the systematic classification of the metalworking processes.

A variety of analytical and computer analysis tools have been introduced to give the reader a good idea of what is available.

Whenever convenient both the modern metric and the customary English units have been used. Although it would be very desirable to have only one set of units for all disciplines world-wide, it appears that this goal will not be achieved for a long time to come, especially since the advocates of metrication have backed off some. It appears that humankind will have to suffer with a dual set of units for many years.

The reason why this book is devoted to only one area of manufacturing or materials processing, metalworking, is that the whole field is becoming so large that to cover it adequately would make the book voluminous. Consequently, separate books will have to be used for metalworking, welding, metal cutting, metal casting, etc. The traditional descriptive courses in manufacturing or materials processing, containing many case histories for the use of the various processes, are good for acquainting the engineering student with what is available and what can be done. However, the teaching of manufacturing or materials processes has to be restructured to conform with the very limited course time available to the student. Rather than citing case histories of the various and sundry manufacturing processes, case histories of computer applications to metalworking are cited instead. The fundamental and engineering aspects of the subject should be covered in the college environment, so that the student is able to apply the background that he has received in the engineering core such as in mathematics, chemistry, physics, materials science, computer science, mechanics, etc. The subject matter that can best be presented in college should be covered there, and the remainder should be covered in on-the-job training.

A laboratory course demonstrating the underlying engineering principles on which the various materials processes are based is most desirable, so that the embryo engineer will not avoid the practical aspects of the field.

Although some of the computer analysis programs presented in this book may not be the latest ones that have been developed, they do give a good idea of how much of the information on metalworking, that has been available for a long time, can now be utilized. The basic procedures for the different computer techniques remain basically the same.

This textbook is intended for engineering students at the senior-graduate level. It is assumed that the student has had a good course (subject) in materials science. Although a course in the mechanics of deformable bodies is most desirable as a prerequisite, it should not be required.

It is hoped that the book can also be used as a tutorial or reference book for practicing engineers working in the various industries involved with materials processing such as forging, sheetmetal forming, etc.

Much of the material contained in this book has been taken freely from the literature, and it would not be possible to give credit to everyone. An attempt was made, however, to give credit wherever possible. It is hoped that some important references were not overlooked. Some of the material was also obtained by attending various conferences and seminars. Many ideas also came from attending college-level courses such as taught by W. A. Backhofen and E. Orowan.

Some of the referenced authors who should be mentioned are T. Altan, B. Avitzur, R. Caddell, G. E. Dieter, S. S. Hecker, M. T. Higashi, R. Hill, A. L. Hoffmanner, W. F. Hosford, S. Kobayshi, G. D. Lahoti, V. Nagpal, S. I. Oh, R. N. Parkins, W. L. Roberts, G. W. Rowe, J. A. Schey, S. L. Semiatin, and E. G. Thomsen.

I should here like to thank M. A. Bhatti, H-C Wu, T. F. Smith, and J. M. Trummel for reading parts of the manuscript. I also want to thank Joe Fortier,

Penny Smith, and especially Djoko Luknanto for working on the drawings and Susanto Teng for checking the problems.

I hereby acknowledge the support that I received from the Department of Industrial Engineering and especially from Robert G. Hering, Dean of the College of Engineering of the University of Iowa, in the preparation and duplication of the manuscript. The contribution of the Forging Industry Educational and Research Foundation, Cleveland, Ohio toward defraying some of the cost of publication is gratefully acknowledged.

McGraw-Hill and I would like to thank Michael Bever, one of my past instructors, Massachusetts Institute of Technology, and H. Thomas McClelland, Arizona State University, for their reviews of the manuscript.

Edward M. Mielnik
Iowa City

METALWORKING SCIENCE AND ENGINEERING

PART
I

CLASSIFICATION OF MATERIALS PROCESSES AND TECHNICAL BACKGROUND

CHAPTER

1

SCOPE AND CLASSIFICATION OF MATERIALS PROCESSES

1.1 INTRODUCTION

There are two sources of wealth: (a) raw materials; and (b) the creativity and the industry of the people [1.1]. The United States is an example of a country that prospered because of both the availability of raw materials and the productivity of its people. Japan is an example of a country that has prospered in spite of the lack of raw materials because of the productivity of its people. It can import steel scrap from the United States, process it, and ship it back in the form of finished products at a lower or, at least, competitive price.

One of the ways of creating wealth is to convert raw materials into finished products through materials processing or manufacturing. Manufacturing is an honorable endeavor, which is essential to a people's standard of living and way of life [1.1]. The United States in recent years has been losing the competitive edge in production, not so much because its productivity has declined, but because the productivity of other industrial nations has increased proportionately more. The scientific and technical capability of the people involved with manufacturing in industrial countries other than the United States is very high, and it should not be underestimated. Unless the United States can channel more of its capable people into manufacturing and increase the productivity of both management and labor, it will continue to lose its competitive edge.

A distinction is made here between materials processing and manufacturing processes or manufacturing engineering. Materials processing, in its broadest sense, is defined as the conversion of raw materials into finished products possessing useful shapes and properties such as forgings, stampings, castings, and weldments. It is one of the most interdisciplinary of engineering activities, involving the contributions from chemical, electrical, industrial, manufacturing, mechanical, and metallurgical engineering and materials and polymer sciences, as well as from other fields [1.2].

Materials processing is a more restricted term than manufacturing engineering. Manufacturing engineering has been defined as that specialty of professional engineering which requires such education and experience as is necessary to understand, apply, and control engineering procedures in manufacturing processes and methods of production of industrial commodities and products and requires the ability to plan the practices of manufacturing, to research and develop the tools, processes, machines and equipment, and to integrate the facilities and systems for producing quality products with optimal expenditures [1.2]. Materials processing is used for operations closer to the raw material end of the processing sequence. It is a term preferred by chemical, materials, metallurgical, and mechanical engineers. The term *manufacturing processes* usually applies to operations closer to the product end of the processing sequence. It is a term preferred by industrial engineers and those mechanical engineers involved with manufacturing.

It is clear that a realistic understanding of materials processing involves much more than a consideration of materials behavior under specific processing conditions. As Fig. 1.1 illustrates, consideration of the materials processing system requires the understanding of the inputs to the process of such diverse factors

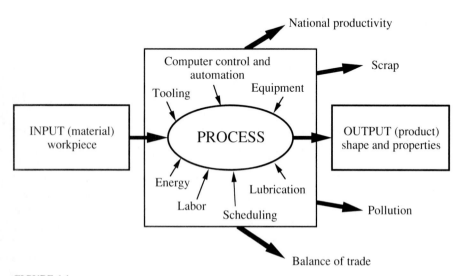

FIGURE 1.1
The global materials processing system. (*After Lahoti and Altan.*)

as the design of equipment and tooling, the consumption of energy, the lubrication appropriate for the process, the appropriate computer control and automation, and the aspects of scheduling and operations research appropriate to minimize cost or maximize the production rate. The outputs of a process involve such important social issues as pollution to the environment, generation of nonbiodegradable scrap, the consumption of raw materials which may not be retrievable and many of which may have to be imported resulting in an unfavorable balance of trade, etc. Although many of the above peripheral occupations may not be the primary endeavors of the materials processor, he must be aware of them in regard to the way they affect his process and his environment.

A good representation of the way materials processing fits into the total manufacturing enterprise is shown in Fig. 1.2 of the computer-integrated manufacturing (CIM) wheel [1.3].

The main focus of this textbook is what occurs in the central ellipse in Fig. 1.1 labelled PROCESS, as regards metalworking. It is based on the premise that in this CAD/CAM age, the traditional separation of design and manufacturing is no longer viable. It will be restricted primarily to metalworking processes. Its approach will be based largely on the mechanics of deformable bodies and

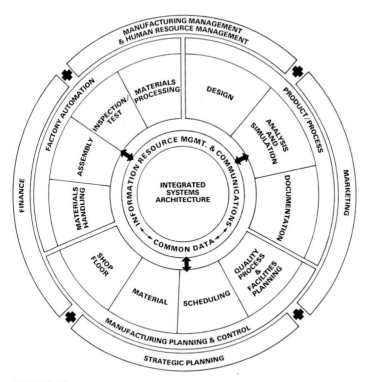

FIGURE 1.2
The computer-aided manufacturing wheel showing how the materials processing segment fits into the big picture of total manufacturing [1.3].

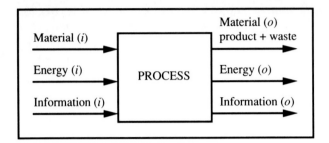

FIGURE 1.3
The general process model as a flow system after Alting [1.4]. Here *i* designates inputs and *o* outputs.

mathematical plasticity. Only that coverage of materials will be used that is necessary for the understanding of the subject matter, since materials are covered extensively in undergraduate courses in engineering such as in materials science.

1.2 A GENERAL MATERIALS PROCESS CLASSIFICATION MODEL [1.4]

According to Alting [1.4], a process can in general be defined as a change in the shape and/or properties (or qualities) of a material including mechanical behavior, state, information content, etc. To produce any change in the shape and properties (or qualities), three agents must be available: (1) material, (2) energy, and (3) information. In this textbook only materials processes will be considered.

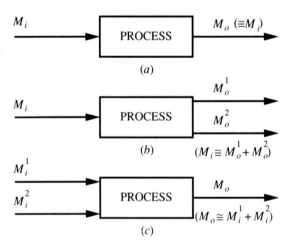

FIGURE 1.4
Black box diagrams depicting the three main types of material flow: (*a*) mass-conserving processes ($dM = 0$), (*b*) mass-reducing processes ($dM < 0$), and (*c*) assembly or mass-increasing processes ($dM > 0$). Here M means mass of material, i input, and o output. The numbers 1 and 2 refer to the number of material elements [1.4].

The general process model, as shown in Fig. 1.3, involves three flow systems: (1) material flow, (2) energy flow, (3) information flow.

The above three flow processes may be divided into three main types as follows:

1. *Through flow*, corresponding to mass-conservation processes such as forging and extrusion, as shown in Fig. 1.4(*a*).
2. *Diverging flow*, corresponding to mass-reduction processes such as metal cutting, as shown in Fig. 1.4(*b*).
3. *Converging flow*, corresponding to mass-increasing processes such as assembly or joining, e.g., welding, as shown in Fig. 1.4(*c*).

The above three types of material flow refer only to the work material but, depending on the process, they may include auxiliary flow materials such as lubricants, coolants, filler materials, etc.

Based on the above three flow systems, a complete model of a material process is shown in Fig. 1.5.

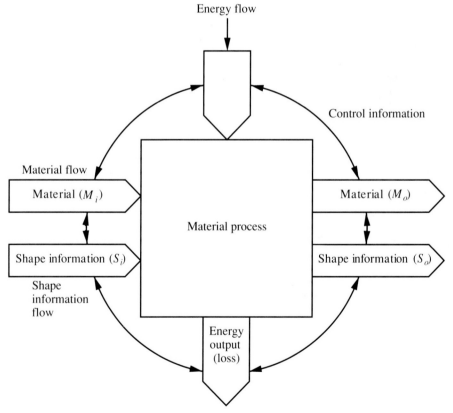

FIGURE 1.5
A complete model of a material process showing the inputs and outputs [1.4].

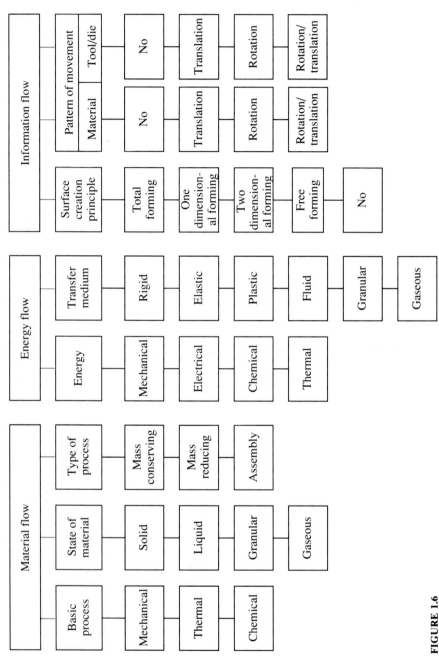

FIGURE 1.6
The morphological structure of material processes [1.4].

The energy flow associated with a process may be characterized as (1) energy supply, (2) energy transmission to the workpiece, and (3) removal or loss of energy.

Information flow includes (1) shape-change information, and (2) property-change information. Shape-change information results in the conversion of the initial shape into the desired, final shape. This change in geometry impressed on a material can be carried out in one or more steps as represented by the following equation:

$$I_f = I_i + I_{p1} + I_{p2} + \cdots + I_{pn} \tag{1.1}$$

where I_f is the final desired geometry, I_i the initial shape information of the material, and I_{pn} the shape-change information for a single process. The number of processes necessary is determined partly by technical and partly by economical considerations. Similarly, the property information flow, such as of hardness, strength, etc., involves the sum of the properties of the initial material and the changes in properties produced by the various processes [1.4].

The fundamental elements and their characterizing parameters, in the shape and structure (morphological) model of materials processes involving shape and/or property changes as shown in Fig. 1.6, are

1. *Material flow*
   (a) Basic processes: mechanical, thermal, or chemical.
   (b) State of the material: solid, granular, or gaseous.
   (c) Type of flow or process: mass-conserving, mass-reducing, or mass-increasing or assembly.
2. *Energy flow*
   (a) Type of energy: mechanical, electrical, chemical, or thermal.
   (b) Transfer medium (tooling): rigid (solid), or nonrigid; elastic, plastic, granular, fluid, or gaseous. (The transfer medium is the material or agent through which energy and/or information are transmitted to the workpiece.)
3. *Information flow*
   (a) Surface creation or generation principles or modes, which may be classified as
      (1) *Tool forming.* In this case, the transfer (tooling) contains the entire surface of the desired geometry as shown in Fig. 1.7(a), which means that no relative motion is necessary, such as in coining or closed-die forging.
      (2) *One-dimensional forming.* Here the medium of transfer contains the surface generating element (a line or a surface area along the line) of the desired surface as shown in Fig. 1.7(b), which means that one relative motion is required to produce the surface, such as in direct or indirect extrusion or cogging.
      (3) *Two-dimensional forming.* Here the medium of transfer contains a point or surface element of the desired geometry as shown in Fig.

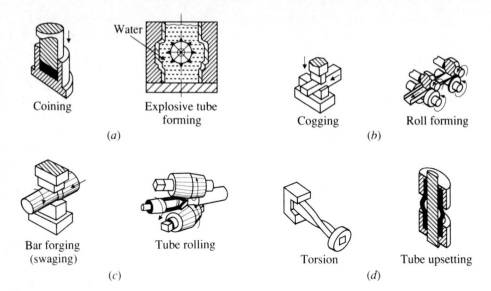

FIGURE 1.7
Examples of information utilization by mass-conserving processes with solid materials: (*a*) total forming, (*b*) one-dimensional forming, (*c*) two-dimensional forming, and (*d*) free forming [1.4].

1.7(*c*), which in turn means that two relative motions are required to produce the surface, such as in swaging (defined elsewhere) or bar forming.

(4) *Free forming*. Here the transfer medium does not contain the desired geometry, such as in upsetting where the workpiece is unsupported as shown in Fig. 1.7(*d*).

(*b*) Pattern of movement either of the material or tool and/or dies (tooling) which may have no movement, rotation, or translation and rotation.

The primary basic, material-flow processes as shown in Fig. 1.6 that change the geometry are

1. *Mechanical.* Elastic deformation, plastic deformation, brittle fracture, ductile fracture, flow, mixing, separation, placing, transporting, etc.
2. *Thermal.* Heating, cooling, melting, solidifying, evaporating, condensing, etc.
3. *Chemical.* Solution or dissolution, combustion, hardening, precipitation, phase transformation, diffusion, etc.

The characteristic classifying parameter for materials processes are tabulated in Fig. 1.8 as follows:

1. *Type of material.* Metals, polymers, ceramics, or composites.
2. *State of material.* Solid, granular, liquid, or gaseous.

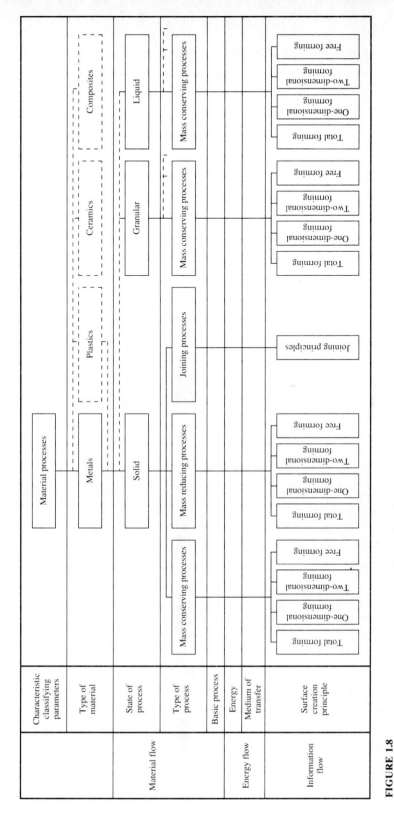

FIGURE 1.8

Classification of the technological manufacturing processes into groups having common features [1.4].

11

3. *Type of process.* Mass-conserving, mass-reducing, or mass-increasing.
4. *Basic process.* Mechanical (M), thermal (T), or chemical (C).
5. *Energy.* Mechanical (Me), electrical (magnetic) (El), thermal (Th), or chemical (Ch).
6. *Transfer media.* Rigid (solid) (Ri), elastic (rubber) (Ea), plastic (Pl), gaseous (Ga), or fluid (F).
7. *Principles or modes of surface creation or generation.* Total forming (TF), one-dimensional forming (ODF), two-dimensional forming (TDF), or free-forming (FF).

The above rational classification of materials (or manufacturing) processes as developed by Alting [1.4] has been presented in the foregoing. A more detailed classification of metalforming will be given in the Chap. 5 and chapters dealing with specific metalworking processes.

An attempt was made in this short chapter to put the entire field of materials processes into proper perspective. If the flowchart in Fig. 1.8 is followed, one can readily pinpoint the classification of a particular material process being discussed in this book. First of all, the processes deal with metallic materials: in the solid state; involving primarily a mass-conservation, mechanical process; utilizing primarily mechanical energy; involving a rigid, energy-transfer medium; and being generated by total forming such as closed-die forging or one-dimensional forming such as extrusion or upsetting. In the reading of this book, one should continually attempt to classify the particular process under discussion according to the classification presented in this chapter and in Chap. 5.

ACKNOWLEDGMENT

The material and some of the illustrations in this chapter were adapted from the references as indicated in the text and in the legends by the numbers of the references enclosed in square brackets pursuant to all copyrights.

REFERENCES

1.1 Schey, J. A., *Introduction to Manufacturing Processes*, McGraw-Hill Book Co., New York, 1977.
1.2 Workshop on Materials Processing, Oct. 30, 31, 1975, Sponsored by NSF, Organized by Carnegie-Mellon Univ., G. E. Dieter, Workshop Director.
1.3 Society of Manufacturing Engineers (SME) and the Computer and Automated Systems Assoc. of SME.
1.4 Alting, L., *Manufacturing Engineering Processes*, Marcel Dekker, Inc., New York, 1982.

CHAPTER 2

FUNDAMENTALS OF ELASTICITY AND PLASTICITY

2.1 ELASTICITY

The term *elasticity* can refer to either a property (quality) or a discipline. As a property or quality, it is the capability of a strained body to recover its size and shape after deformation in any way. The theory of elasticity is concerned with the study of the response of elastic bodies to the action of forces. It deals with the methods of calculating the stresses and strains in deformed perfectly elastic solids. A material is perfectly elastic if, when forces are applied to it, the resulting strains appear instantaneously and if, when they are removed, the initial size and shape of the body are instantaneously recovered. The body is sometimes said to be partially elastic if the deformation produced by external forces does not disappear completely after unloading. In the linear theory of elasticity, the stress produced in the body is less than the yield stress of the material, and the stress σ and strain ε are mutually proportional, which is expressed by Hooke's law, $\sigma = E\varepsilon$. The proportionality constant E is called the *modulus of elasticity*. Time-independent deformation which disappears on the release of the load is called *elastic deformation*. This section deals with elastic deformation. The difference between elastic and plastic deformation is discussed subsequently.

2.1.1 Definition of Stress and Strain

Since all metalworking processes involve the application of loads to a body or workpiece which result in a deformation or change in shape, a brief review of load-deformation relationships is a good point at which to begin.

As shown in Fig. 2.1(*a*), the external forces that act on a body are called *loads,* and the internal reactive forces per unit area, which resist the external forces, are called *stresses.* Stress therefore is defined as the *intensity of force per unit area.* The external forces may be surface forces distributed over a portion of the surface as caused by the action of the end of a punch on the surface of a steel plate, or body forces distributed over the volume of the body such as

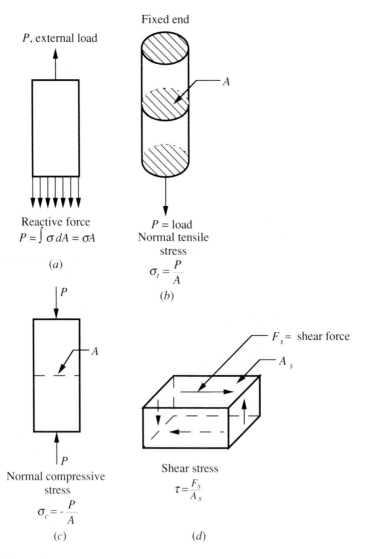

FIGURE 2.1
Definition of (*a*) reactive force, (*b*) normal tensile stress, (*c*) normal compressive stress, and (*d*) shear stress.

gravitational forces or forces due to a strong magnetic field as in electromagnetic forming. The accompanying deformations or changes in the lengths of lines and the angles between them are called *strains*. The normal component of a force per unit area of a plane on which it acts is called *normal stress*, and the tangential component of a force per unit area of a plane on which it acts is called *shear stress* as shown for uniaxial tension, compression, and "simple" shear in Fig. 2.1(*b*), (*c*), and (*d*). Stress and strain may also be defined according to the direction of the application of the force or stress, resulting in a corresponding strain, as (1) tensile (positive) or (2) compressive (negative) as shown in Fig. 2.1(*b*) and (*c*). One of the ways that, for uniaxial loading, the longitudinal, extensional, normal strain may be defined is as the change in length over the original length, $\Delta l / l_o$, and the lateral or transverse strain as the change in width over the original width as $\Delta w / w_o$, and the negative of the ratio of the lateral to the longitudinal strain as $-\varepsilon_{yy} / \varepsilon_{xx}$ is called the Poisson ratio as shown in Fig. 2.2(*a*). The Poisson ratio ν is a measure of the resistance of a material to elastic deformation at right angles or transversely to an applied longitudinal load, and varies for metallic materials between about 0.25 and 0.35.

Engineering or "simple" shear strain is defined here as the change in a unit right angle, which for small strains reduces to $\gamma = \Delta x / y$ as shown in Fig. 2.2(*b*). Pure or tensor shear strain ε_{xy} is defined as the change in angle between two line segments within or scribed on the surface of a body, which were mutually perpendicular or at right angles in the undeformed state as shown in Fig. 2.2(*c*). It is assumed here that lines that are initially straight remain straight and lines that are initially parallel remain parallel. Because in Fig. 2.2(*c*) the sum of tan α and tan β is equal to γ, it turns out that "simple" shear strain is equal to twice the pure shear strain, or $\gamma = 2\varepsilon_{xy}$.

More generally, the change of the dimensions or the shape of a body as a result of external forces is related to strain. When a body is deformed by external forces, points in the body may be displaced from their initial, no-load positions. Strain is related to any such displacement. Pure rigid body motions such as translation or rotation, do not cause the body to change its shape or be strained. For example, assume that in the body in Fig. 2.3 a line of initial length *AB*, denoted as l_o, is displaced to *CD* of length l_1 due to external forces. In the figure, *u* is the displacement of point *A* in the *x* direction and *v* is its displacement in the *y* direction. For a three-dimensional case, *w* would denote the displacement in the *z* direction. The partial derivatives, $\partial u / \partial x$, $\partial v / \partial y$, and $\partial w / \partial z$ denote the change in displacement with respect to *x*, *y*, and *z*, respectively. If l_o is equal to l_1 and parallel to it, no strain has occurred, only rigid body translation. If l_o is equal to l_1 but not parallel to it, both rigid body translation and rotation have occurred. Longitudinal strain is only induced when l_o and l_1 are unequal.

As indicated for uniaxial tension and compression above, changes in the length of a line, whether by extension or shortening, are called normal strains. Tensile strains caused by extension are considered positive, and compressive strains negative. In Fig. 2.2(*c*), if the angle between two normal lines such as *OA* and *OB* decreases, the shear strain is said to be positive, and if it increases negative.

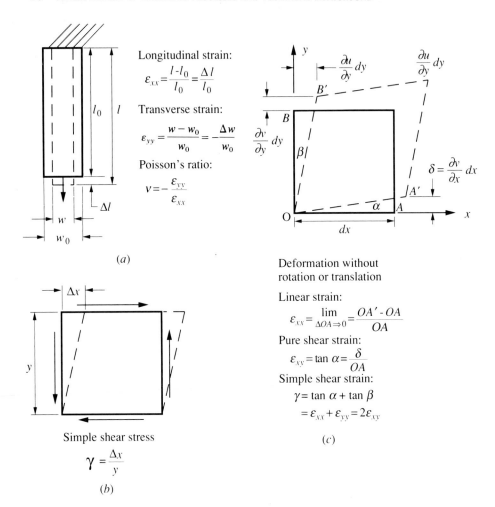

Longitudinal strain:

$$\varepsilon_{xx} = \frac{l - l_0}{l_0} = \frac{\Delta l}{l_0}$$

Transverse strain:

$$\varepsilon_{yy} = \frac{w - w_0}{w_0} = -\frac{\Delta w}{w_0}$$

Poisson's ratio:

$$v = -\frac{\varepsilon_{yy}}{\varepsilon_{xx}}$$

(a)

Simple shear stress

$$\gamma = \frac{\Delta x}{y}$$

(b)

Deformation without rotation or translation

Linear strain:

$$\varepsilon_{xx} = \lim_{\Delta OA \Rightarrow 0} \frac{OA' - OA}{OA}$$

Pure shear strain:

$$\varepsilon_{xy} = \tan \alpha = \frac{\delta}{OA}$$

Simple shear strain:

$$\gamma = \tan \alpha + \tan \beta$$
$$= \varepsilon_{xx} + \varepsilon_{yy} = 2\varepsilon_{xy}$$

(c)

FIGURE 2.2
Definition of (a) longitudinal and transverse strain and Poisson's ratio, (b) simple shear strain, and (c) linear and pure shear strains and the relationship.

There is probably no situation in physical sciences and engineering where an example of greater inconsistency can be found than assigning the sign to shear stress. The practice not only varies between engineering disciplines, but also varies within disciplines and even within single publications. The convention that will be adopted here for the shear stress, except for the construction and use of Mohr's stress circles, is that in positive shear the elongated diagonal will lie in the first and third quadrants as shown in Fig. 2.4, whereas in negative shear the elongated diagonal will lie in the second and fourth quadrants. In positive shear, the shear components are both in the positive or negative directions. In negative shear, the shear vectors are mixed plus and minus. The shear strain has the same

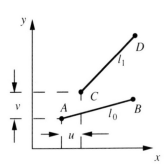

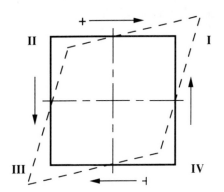

FIGURE 2.3
Displacement of an arbitrary length, l_0, to an unequal length, l_1, in a body used to define strain.

FIGURE 2.4
Free body diagram showing the convention used for positive shear stress.

sign as the shear stress. This sign convention is consistent with that used for the definition of the state of stress at a point discussed later. (In regard to Mohr's stress circle diagrams, to be discussed subsequently, it will be seen that shear stresses which cause clockwise rotation of the stress element in the physical plane are considered to be positive, while those causing counterclockwise rotation are considered negative. On the Mohr diagram, positive shear stress will be plotted upward, i.e., above the normal component, and the negative shear stress downward or below the normal component. As will be seen later all angles on the Mohr's circle are twice the corresponding angles on the surface of the body and both are positive in the counterclockwise direction.)

2.1.2 Elastic versus Plastic Deformation

Deformations may be classified as elastic, plastic, and viscoplastic. Since this chapter deals with the relatively short time deformation of metallic materials, only the first two types will be considered here. Elastic deformation disappears relatively rapidly after the forces or loads causing it cease to act. In other words, it is sensibly recoverable, and may enter into metalworking in the form of springback in cold forming or in the elastic deflection of presses or rolls during use. Plastic deformation is virtually time-independent, permanent or irreversible deformation and, of course, is of major concern in metalworking. The micro-mechanisms causing plastic deformation will be discussed later. The mathematical discipline that deals with the elastic behavior of materials subjected to external loads is called the *theory of elasticity,* and with plastic behavior, the *mathematical theory of plasticity* or the *macroscopic theory.* In elasticity, the material is usually considered to be an homogeneous, linearly elastic continuum. It is often also considered to be isotropic. An homogeneous body consists of one phase and has identical properties at all points; *isotropic* means that properties are the same in all directions; *linearly elastic* means that deformation is sensibly recoverable and the deformation is directly proportional to the applied load; and *continuum* means that the body has no voids such as shrinkage cavities or other discontinuities such as grain boundaries. The microscopic voids and discontinuities may be averaged out, and macroscopically the bulk material may be considered to be a continuum. Viscoplastic deformation is time-dependent permanent deformation.

The strains involved with plastic deformation are normally much larger than for elastic deformation depending on the materials and the methods used. It should be noted here that elasticity and plasticity refer to disciplines, whereas elastic and plastic deformation refer to processes.

Some of the many concepts involved with elastic deformation and elasticity are being covered at this point to serve as a background for the material to be covered on plastic deformation later.

2.1.3 Description of the State of Stress at a Point

Assume that an elastic body is subjected to a complex system of surface and body forces. Let an imaginary plane with an outer normal in the n-direction be passed through the body in such a way that the resultant force acting on a small area ΔA of the plane at point P can be represented by the vector $\Delta \mathbf{F}$ as shown in Fig. 2.5. The stress σ at point P on this plane is then defined as the interactive force per unit area, or

$$\sigma = \lim_{\Delta A \to 0} \frac{\Delta \mathbf{F}}{\Delta A} = \frac{d\mathbf{F}}{\Delta A} \tag{2.1}$$

Since stress depends both upon a force and the area over which it acts, it is for the general case not a vector but a symmetric, two-dimensional (second-order)

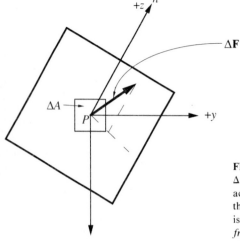

FIGURE 2.5

ΔF is a vector representing the reactive force acting on a small area ΔA on a random plane through an elastically deformed body. The z axis is taken as the outer normal to the plane. (*Adapted from G. E. Dieter, Jr., Mechanical Metallurgy, McGraw-Hill, 1961.*)

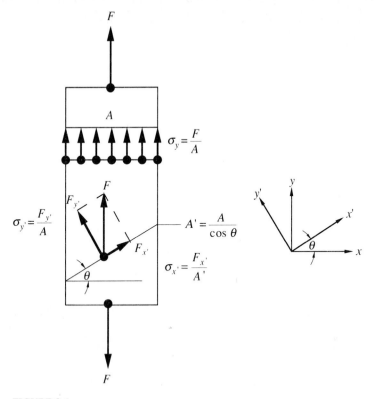

FIGURE 2.6
Forces and stresses related to different sets of axes. Since F has a component parallel to A, there is no shear stress acting on that plane [2.4].

tensor, which depends on the orientation of the axes as shown in Fig. 2.6 and as will be represented graphically by the Mohr's stress circle.

If a set of orthogonal axes is then selected so that the xy plane is coplanar with the imaginary sectioning plane and the z-axis is normal to it and parallel to n as shown in Fig. 2.5, the stress vector may then be resolved into components that are normal to the plane and parallel to it in the x and y directions. As the orientation of the plane changes, the magnitudes of the normal and shear stresses change. At some orientation of the plane both shear stresses will be zero and the normal stress σ_{zz} is then an extremum. The plane is generally inclined such that there is a normal component of stress and two shear components. The concept of the general state of stress at a point may be explained by selecting a very small, imaginary cube within the material, which is very large as compared to the size of an atom but so small that no stress gradient exists across it and is so oriented that none of the shear stress components on any of the faces are zero as shown in Fig. 2.7. The state of stress on the faces of such a small, elastic cube as it shrinks to a "point" is described as the general state of stress at the point.

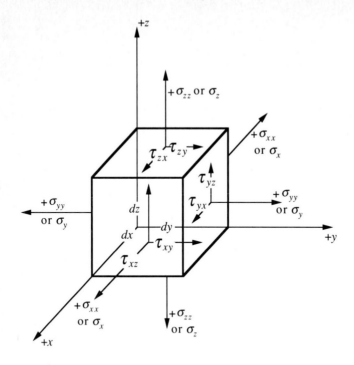

FIGURE 2.7
State of stress at a point. The shear stresses on the back faces are not shown. Since $\tau_{xy}(dy\,dz)(dx) = \tau_{yx}(dx\,dz)(dy)$, $\tau_{xy} = \tau_{yx}$.

In Fig. 2.7, the axes are designated as x, y, and z; the normal stresses are designated by σ_{xx}, etc.; and the shear stresses by τ_{xy}, etc. The first subscript designates the plane or face on which the stress acts since the orientation of a plane can be designated by the direction of its normal to the plane, and the second subscript designates the direction in which it acts. In contracted form the normal and shear components of stress may be written as σ_{ii} or $\sigma_{(plane)(direction)}$ and τ_{ii} or $\tau_{(plane)(direction)}$ respectively. It will be noted that for the normal stresses both subscripts are the same, but for the shear stresses they are always different, which fact can be used to differentiate normal stresses from shear stresses. Since, for a normal stress, the direction of the axis designates both the direction of the stress and the normal to the plane, the normal stresses may simply be designated as σ_x, σ_y, and σ_z as shown in Fig. 2.7. The shear stresses are shown only on the three visible faces of the cube. Equal and opposite shear stresses on the opposite three faces of the cube must exist so as to maintain the cube in static equilibrium, otherwise it would rotate.

All of the nine components of stress on the six faces of the volume element may be represented by the stress tensor **T** in the form of a symmetric matrix as

$$T = \begin{bmatrix} \sigma_{xx} & \tau_{xy} & \tau_{xz} \\ \tau_{yx} & \sigma_{yy} & \tau_{yz} \\ \tau_{zx} & \tau_{zy} & \sigma_{zz} \end{bmatrix}$$ (2.2)

For use with suffix notation, the coordinate axes are designated as follows: $x = x_1$, $y = x_2$, and $z = x_3$, and the components of the above symmetric stress tensor are designated as

$$T = \begin{bmatrix} \sigma_{11} & \sigma_{12} & \sigma_{13} \\ \sigma_{21} & \sigma_{22} & \sigma_{23} \\ \sigma_{31} & \sigma_{32} & \sigma_{33} \end{bmatrix}$$ (2.3)

In suffix notation, this stress tensor may be written as σ_{ij} $(i, j = 1, 2, 3)$.

By summation of the moments about each axis of the axes, it can be shown that $\tau_{xy} = \tau_{yx}$, $\tau_{yz} = \tau_{zy}$, and $\tau_{zx} = \tau_{xz}$. Therefore only six stress components are needed to describe the most general state of stress at a point for an isotropic material: σ_{xx}, σ_{yy}, σ_{zz}, τ_{xy}, τ_{yz}, and τ_{zx}. Although six stress components are needed to describe the most general state of stress at a point in elasticity, the number of stresses required may be reduced by proper selection of the axes. For example, if the axes are rotated so that the shear stresses on each face of the elemental cube are all zero, the normal stresses remaining are called the principal stresses and are designated σ_1, σ_2, and σ_3. By convention these stresses are selected so that $\sigma_1 > \sigma_2 > \sigma_3$. Some of the states of stress involving the principal stresses that are of interest are

1. General state of stress: $\sigma_1 \neq \sigma_2 \neq \sigma_3$
2. Hydrostatic state of stress: $\sigma_1 = \sigma_2 = \sigma_3 = -p$
3. Biaxial state of stress: $\sigma_1 \neq 0$, $\sigma_2 \neq 0$, $\sigma_3 = 0$
4. Uniaxial state of stress: $\sigma_1 \neq 0$, $\sigma_2 = \sigma_3 = 0$

A state of stress that is of particular interest here is the deviatoric state of stress in which the hydrostatic stress σ_m is subtracted from the general state of stress as follows:

$$D = \begin{bmatrix} \sigma_{xx} & \tau_{xy} & \tau_{xz} \\ \tau_{yx} & \sigma_{yy} & \tau_{yz} \\ \tau_{zx} & \tau_{zy} & \sigma_{zz} \end{bmatrix} - \begin{bmatrix} \sigma_m & 0 & 0 \\ 0 & \sigma_m & 0 \\ 0 & 0 & \sigma_m \end{bmatrix}$$ (2.4a)

and

$$D = \begin{bmatrix} \sigma_{xx} - \sigma_m & \tau_{xy} & \tau_{xz} \\ \tau_{yx} & \sigma_{yy} - \sigma_m & \tau_{yz} \\ \tau_{zx} & \tau_{zy} & \sigma_{zz} - \sigma_m \end{bmatrix}$$ (2.4b)

The mean stress σ_m, which is equal to the negative of the hydrostatic pressure

p, may be written as

$$\sigma_m = -p = \tfrac{1}{3}(\sigma_{xx} + \sigma_{yy} + \sigma_{zz}) \tag{2.5}$$

Since the mean or hydrostatic stress does not contribute to deformation, it may be subtracted from the general stress tensor to give the deviatoric stress tensor as indicated above. This concept will be used later in conjunction with the definition of the effective stress and the yield criterion.

In suffix notation, the stress deviator D_{ij}, given in Eq. (2.4b) is related to the stress tensor σ_{ij} by the expression

$$D_{ij} = \sigma_{ij} - \delta_{ij}\sigma_m, \tag{2.6}$$

where

$$\sigma_{ij} = \begin{cases} 1 & \text{for } i = j \\ 0 & \text{for } i \neq j \end{cases}$$

where δ_{ij} is called the *Kronecker delta*.

2.1.4   Stress Invariants

It has been shown [2.1] that for any three-dimensional state of stress, there exists a cubic equation of the following form whose roots are the principal stresses:

$$\sigma_p^3 - I_1\sigma_p^2 + I_2\sigma_p - I_3 = 0 \tag{2.7}$$

The coefficients I_1, I_2, and I_3 are functions of the stress components and are simple expressions of the three principal stresses. Since the principal stresses are independent of the orientation of the axes, the coefficients are therefore invariant.

If the coordinate axes x, y, and z coincide with the principal directions at a specified point, the stress invariants can be expressed in terms of the principal stresses σ_i as follows:

$$I_1 = \sigma_1 + \sigma_2 + \sigma_3 = 3\sigma_m \tag{2.8a}$$

$$I_2 = \sigma_1\sigma_2 + \sigma_2\sigma_3 + \sigma_3\sigma_1 \tag{2.8b}$$

$$I_3 = \sigma_1\sigma_2\sigma_3 \tag{2.8c}$$

Since the first invariant I_1 is a function of the hydrostatic or mean stress, i.e., $I_1 = 3\sigma_m$, any acceptable yield criterion should be independent of σ_m for materials such as typical metals and alloys. The magnitude of σ_m is given by

$$\sigma_m = \tfrac{1}{3}I_i = \tfrac{1}{3}(\sigma_1 + \sigma_2 + \sigma_3) = \tfrac{1}{3}(\sigma_x + \sigma_y + \sigma_z) \tag{2.9}$$

The principal directions of the stress deviator coincide with those of the stress tensor given by Eq. (2.3). Its invariant in terms of the principal stresses have the form

$$I_1' = 0 \tag{2.10a}$$

$$I_2' = \tfrac{1}{6}[(\sigma_1 - \sigma_2)^2 + (\sigma_2 - \sigma_3)^2 + (\sigma_3 - \sigma_1)^2] \tag{2.10b}$$

$$I_3' = (\sigma_1 - \sigma_m)(\sigma_2 - \sigma_m)(\sigma_3 - \sigma_m) \tag{2.10c}$$

2.1.5 Description of the State of Elastic Strain at a Point

Just as in the case for stress, the elastic strain at a point is completely defined or described by six independent strain components. The complete description of the state of strain at a point implies that the change in the length of any line in any direction and the change in angle between any two initially perpendicular lines through a point are completely specified. The concepts of extensional and shear strains were discussed in conjunction with Fig. 2.2(c). The same approach could be used for the three-dimensional case for shear strains by use of a diamond-shaped figure obtained by distorting an elemental cube by translating the corner opposite the origin slightly away from it, which is equivalent to shearing the cube in three dimensions. The state of strain at a point is fully described by six independent strain components: the three normal or extensional components along mutually orthogonal directions, and the three shear components associated with these directions, i.e., ε_{xx}, ε_{yy}, ε_{zz}, and γ_{xy}, γ_{yz}, and γ_{zx}.

Just as in the case of stress, strain is also a second-order, symmetric tensor which depends on the orientation of the axes, as will be represented graphically later by means of a Mohr's strain circle. For simplicity, let us consider a two-dimensional or plane strain condition, where the deformation is confined in the xy plane as shown in Fig. 2.2(c), and then generalized to the three-dimensional case. By use of this figure and its three-dimensional extension, it can be shown that the components of extensional strain are equal to the displacement gradients

$$\varepsilon_{xx} = \frac{\partial u_x}{\partial x} \qquad \varepsilon_{yy} = \frac{\partial u_y}{\partial y} \qquad \text{and} \qquad \varepsilon_{zz} = \frac{\partial u_z}{\partial z} \qquad (2.11)$$

The components of the simple or engineering shear strain are

$$\gamma_{xy} = \frac{\partial u_x}{\partial y} + \frac{\partial u_y}{\partial x} \qquad \gamma_{xz} = \frac{\partial u_x}{\partial z} + \frac{\partial u_z}{\partial x} \qquad \text{and} \qquad \gamma_{yz} = \frac{\partial u_y}{\partial z} + \frac{\partial u_z}{\partial y} \qquad (2.12)$$

The components of the pure or tensor shear strain ε_{xy}, ε_{xz}, and ε_{yz} are equal to one-half of the above values, i.e.,

$$\varepsilon_{xy} = \tfrac{1}{2}\gamma_{xy} \qquad \varepsilon_{xz} = \tfrac{1}{2}\gamma_{xz} \qquad \text{and} \qquad \varepsilon_{yz} = \tfrac{1}{2}\gamma_{yz} \qquad (2.13)$$

Thus, the tensor strains ε_{ij} are the components of the symmetric strain tensor **E** whose matrix representation is

$$\mathbf{E} = \begin{bmatrix} \varepsilon_{xx} & \varepsilon_{xy} & \varepsilon_{xz} \\ \varepsilon_{yx} & \varepsilon_{yy} & \varepsilon_{yz} \\ \varepsilon_{zx} & \varepsilon_{zy} & \varepsilon_{zz} \end{bmatrix} \qquad (2.14)$$

or in suffix notation

$$\varepsilon_{ij} = \frac{1}{2}\left(\frac{\partial u_i}{\partial x_j} + \frac{\partial u_j}{\partial x_i}\right) \qquad (2.15)$$

2.1.6 Mohr's Circle Diagrams

2.1.6.1 MOHR'S STRESS CIRCLE DIAGRAM.

A rather convenient, graphical method of representing the variation in the state of stress at a point is by use of the Mohr's stress circle diagram. It is a convenient way for determining two of the three principal stresses and the stresses on a plane that forms an angle with any axis at right angles to a known principal direction of stress. However, graphical solutions for a three-dimensional stress system are rather cumbersome. Since the principal application of Mohr's diagram is for the two-dimensional case, a brief description for the case of plane stress ($\sigma_{zz} = 0$) will follow to illustrate its construction and use.

Consider that a very small piece of sheetmetal is acted upon by the principal stresses σ_1 and σ_2 as in Fig. 2.8(a), and it is desired to determine the normal and shear stresses acting on the elemental area, whose axes form an angle α with

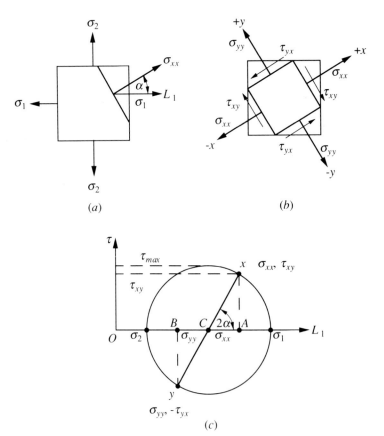

FIGURE 2.8
Stress system for illustrating the construction of Mohr's stress circle diagram for plane stress. (a) Principal stresses in plane stress; (b) rotation of the axes by an angle of α; and (c) Mohr's stress circle diagram.

the direction of the principal axis L_1 as shown in Fig. 2.8(a) and (b). Since the sum of the forces in the x and the y directions acting in the plane of the sheet must equal zero, the following expression relating the normal and shear stress in terms of the principal stresses are obtained:

$$\sigma_{xx} = \frac{\sigma_1 + \sigma_2}{2} + \frac{\sigma_1 - \sigma_2}{2}\cos 2\alpha \qquad (2.16a)$$

$$\sigma_{yy} = \frac{\sigma_1 + \sigma_2}{2} - \frac{\sigma_1 - \sigma_2}{2}\cos 2\alpha \qquad (2.16b)$$

$$\tau_{xy} = \tau_{yx} = \frac{\sigma_1 - \sigma_2}{2}\sin 2\alpha \qquad (2.16c)$$

As shown in Fig. 2.8(c), the normal stresses σ_{xx} and σ_{yy} are plotted on the abscissa, and the shear stresses on the ordinate. The axis xy is laid out in the counterclockwise direction, which will be the convention used here, at an angle of 2α, or twice the angle it makes with the principal axes in Fig. 2.8(a). The circle is defined by points $x(\sigma_{xx}, \tau_{xy})$ and $y(\sigma_{yy}, -\tau_{yx})$, which lie on opposite ends of a diameter of Mohr's circle. A point on the circle represents the normal and shear stresses on a plane whose normal makes an angle of α with the principal axis.

The procedure for laying out Mohr's stress circle for a biaxial state of stress as shown in Fig. 2.8(c) are as follows:

1. Lay out the σ, τ axes
2. Plot point x at (σ_{xx}, τ_{xy})
3. Plot point y at $(\sigma_{yy}, -\tau_{yx})$
4. Connect points x and y with a straight line, giving the center of the Mohr's circle at C
5. Construct the circle with C as the center

The general case for plane stress, in which an element is subjected to both normal and shear stress is shown in Fig. 2.9(a). By summing the forces in the x and y directions, respectively, and by making use of trigonometric identities and of the freebody diagram of Fig. 2.9(b) one obtains

$$\sigma_n = \frac{\sigma_x + \sigma_y}{2} + \frac{\sigma_x - \sigma_y}{2}\cos 2\alpha + \tau_{xy}\sin 2\alpha \qquad (2.17)$$

and

$$\tau_n = -\frac{\sigma_x - \sigma_y}{2}\sin 2\alpha + \tau_{xy}\cos 2\alpha \qquad (2.18)$$

If one constructs a Mohr's stress circle diagram that would apply in this case, similar equations to the above could be obtained from the diagram except that the angle 2α in the Mohr's circle is twice that for the stressed body, and that the

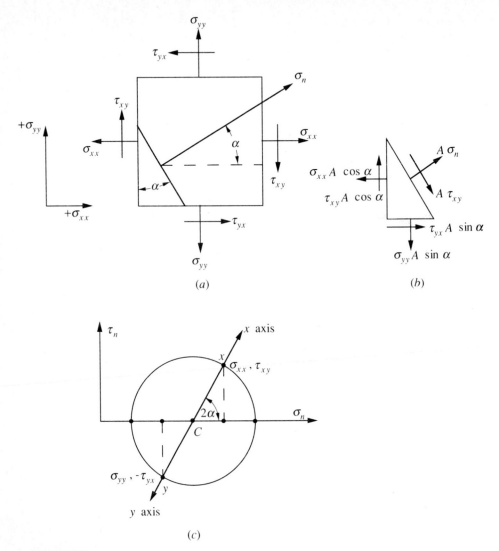

FIGURE 2.9
General case of plane stress. (a) State of stress; (b) freebody force diagram; and (c) Mohr's stress circle diagram.

sign of the last term for σ_n is negative rather than positive and the first term for τ_n is positive rather than negative. Various stratagems are used to resolve this difference between the two sets of equations. The method used depends largely on individual preference. The one used here, cited previously, is that (1) the angles on the Mohr diagram are always taken as twice the angles on the stressed body and both are positive counterclockwise, and (2) shears causing clockwise couples are treated as positive and are plotted upward on the Mohr stress circle.

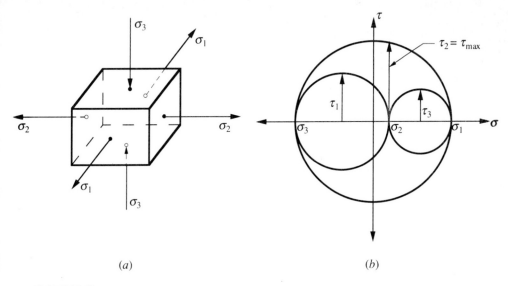

(a)   (b)

FIGURE 2.10
(a) Stress system for construction of (b) schematic Mohr's three-dimensional circle diagram.

Shears causing counterclockwise couples are negative. The foregoing sign convention for shear as mentioned previously is a lone exception to the general rule for the sign for shear. The Mohr's circle for the stress system in Fig. 2.9(c) is similar to that in Fig. 2.8(c) except for the order of plotting.

If two-dimensional analysis is applied in turn to each of the planes perpendicular to axes 1, 2, and 3 in Fig. 2.10(a) and the resulting three diagrams are superimposed, the schematic Mohr's three-dimensional stress circle diagram in Fig. 2.10(b) is obtained for the stress system in Fig. 2.10(a).

2.1.6.2 MOHR'S STRAIN CIRCLE DIAGRAM. Since $\varepsilon_{xx} = \gamma_{xy}/2$ as shown in Eq. (2.13), the Mohr's strain circle diagram may be obtained by plotting ε on the abscissa and $\gamma/2$ on the ordinate. A schematic Mohr's three-dimensional strain circle diagram is plotted in Fig. 2.11. It should be mentioned here that for small strains in hookean bodies, the principal stress axes coincide with the principal strain axes. This is not always true for large strains such as in metalworking processes, as will be pointed out later.

2.1.7 Virtual Work

(This section may be omitted at this point and covered later when dealing with the finite element method.)

There are two commonly used forms of the general principle of virtual work, those of virtual displacement and those of virtual forces [2.2]. We will mainly be concerned with the former.

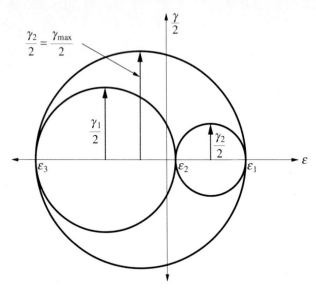

FIGURE 2.11
Schematic Mohr's three-dimensional strain circle diagram.

In the virtual displacement form of this principle, it is assumed that a body in equilibrium under body forces and applied loads is subjected to a virtual (imaginary) displacement state described by components δu_x, δu_y, and δu_z at each point. The virtual displacement must be kinematically admissible, i.e., they are continuous functions of the spatial coordinates and satisfy kinematic boundary conditions on the portion of the surface for which such conditions are prescribed.

An admissible condition may be illustrated by means of a simple, pinned beam as shown in Fig. 2.12. The admissible displacement shapes of the centerline must have a continuous variation of shape (a requirement for bending) between the end support points, where the displacement must be zero. The difference between statically and kinematically admissible conditions will be discussed elsewhere.

Under the above conditions, the principle of virtual displacement stipulates that the sum of the elastic potential (energy) of the applied loads (δV) and the stored strain energy (δU) during virtual displacement $\delta \Delta$ is equal to zero, or $\delta U + \delta V = 0$.

(a)   (b)

FIGURE 2.12
Admissible versus inadmissible virtual displacement [2.2].

The above statement can be proved by showing that the strain energy under displacement $\delta U = \int_A \sigma \, d\varepsilon \, dA$ is equal to $\int_S (F_x \, \delta u_x + F_y \, \delta u_y) \, dS = -\delta V$, or $\delta U + \delta V = 0$, by the use of (1) the strain displacement equations, (2) the concept that the terms of the equilibrium equations are equal to zero, (3) Gauss' theorem (integration by parts in the plane), and (4) the applicable boundary conditions. The minus sign is placed on $-\delta V$ to show that the potential energy of the applied loads decreases as the elastic body or structure deflects.

Imposing a virtual (imaginary) displacement field on a body while holding the stress constant is tantamount to imposing a first-order variation of the strain energy on the body, which is given by

$$dU = \int_V \sigma_{ij} \, d\varepsilon_{ij} \, dV \qquad (2.19)$$

It was mentioned above that the virtual work of the internal forces is equal to the negative of the above variation of the strain energy, i.e., $dV = -dU$.

The virtual work of the external forces acting on the body is given by

$$dV = \int_S F_i \, du_i \, dS \qquad (2.20)$$

where F_i = the components of the external forces acting on the surface of the body per unit area

   du_i = increments of displacement of the specific points of the surface

   σ_{ij} = the stress tensor at an arbitrary point of the body

   S = the external surface area of the body

Thus, the principle of virtual work can be written as

$$\int_V \sigma_{ij} \, d\dot{\varepsilon}_{ij} = \int_S F_i \, du_i \, dS \qquad (2.21)$$

as implied above.

If v_i is the components of the velocity of a surface point, and ε_{ij} is the strain rate tensor, the above equation may be written in the form

$$\int_V \sigma_{ij} \dot{\varepsilon}_{ij} \, dV = \int_S F_i \, du_i \, dS \qquad (2.22)$$

This equation simply states that the rate of storage of elastic energy inside the deforming body equals the rate at which the external forces applied to the surface do work on the velocities of their points of application.

The concept of virtual work will be used in conjunction with the calculation of the stresses in a body by the finite element method.

The variation of $U + V$, as characterized by the principle of virtual work, can be described by a well-developed branch of mathematics known as the *calculus of variations*.

Consider a one-dimensional problem described by the single function $\Delta(x)$, where x is the spatial coordinate. The fundamental problem in the calculus of variations is to determine the value of $\Delta(x)$, which results in a stationary value of the integral

$$\Pi = \int f\left(x, \Delta, \frac{d\Delta}{dx}\right) dx \tag{2.23}$$

where f is a function that takes such forms as the potential and complementary energy densities, and Π is a functional, i.e., a function of the function f. It can be shown that the functional associated with an axial member or element is a function of

$$f = \left[\frac{1}{2}\left(\frac{du}{dx}\right)^2 EA - qu\right] dx \tag{2.24}$$

and the governing (equilibrium) equation is

$$AE \frac{d^2u}{dx^2} + q = 0 \tag{2.25}$$

where A = the cross-sectional area
E = elastic modulus
u = the displacement
q = distributed load intensity

A stationary value will occur at a maximum, minimum, or a neutral (inflection) point as shown in Fig. 2.13. The function f must be twice differentiable, to contain a form possessing a minimum. At a stationary point the following condition prevails: $d\Pi/d\Delta\ (\Delta_o) = 0$, where Δ_o is the value of Δ at the stationary point, i.e., maximum, minimum, or neutral point (depending on whether the second derivative of $\Pi(\Delta_o)$ with respect to Δ is less, greater, or equal to zero). Δ represents the displacement field in terms of the full set of coordinate displacements u_x, u_y, and u_z. In matrix notation, the transformation of nodal point or joint displacement to displacement field is

$$\Delta = [N]\{\Delta\} \tag{2.26}$$

where $[N]$ = matrix of the shape function
$\{\Delta\}$ = vector of the nodal point displacement

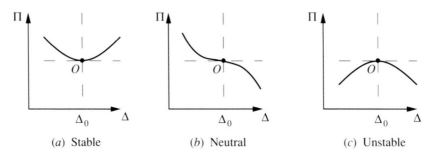

(a) Stable   (b) Neutral   (c) Unstable

FIGURE 2.13
Types of stationary points [2.2].

By application of the pertinent strain-displacement equations, one obtains

$$\boldsymbol{\varepsilon} = [D]\{\Delta\} \tag{2.27}$$

where $[D]$ is the matrix relating nodal point or joint displacements to the strain field.

For the case of the distribution of the virtual displacements $\delta\Delta$ and virtual strains, $\delta\varepsilon$, one obtains

$$\delta\boldsymbol{\Delta} = [N]\{\delta\Delta\} \tag{2.28}$$

$$\delta\boldsymbol{\varepsilon} = [D]\{\Delta\} \tag{2.29}$$

These relationships will be used in the finite element discretization of virtual work.

2.1.8 Stress-Strain Relationships in Elasticity for Small Strains

To solve problems in either elasticity or plasticity, stress and strain must be related in some way, either by some assumed constitutive relationship or by means of an experimental stress-strain curve.

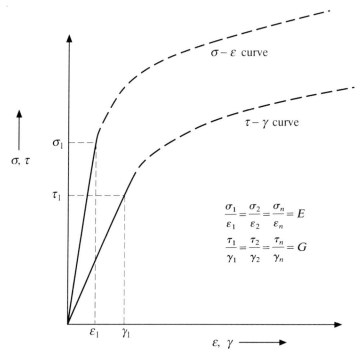

FIGURE 2.14
Initial portion of schematic stress-strain curves (solid lines) for uniaxial tension and shear for a medium carbon steel (showing no yield point).

In linear elasticity, Hooke's law is assumed to apply, which means that stress is linearly proportional to strain, which is approximated very well by the initial linear portion of the stress-strain curves of many materials such as medium carbon steel as shown in Fig. 2.14 for uniaxial tension and for simple shear. The ratio of stress to strain is a constant in this case and is given by

$$\frac{\sigma_1}{\varepsilon_1} = \frac{\sigma_2}{\varepsilon_2} = \frac{\sigma_n}{\varepsilon_n} = E \tag{2.30}$$

and called the *modulus of elasticity* or *Young's modulus E* for tension. The shear modulus or modulus of rigidity *G* for shear is given by

$$\frac{\tau_1}{\gamma_1} = \frac{\tau_2}{\gamma_2} = \frac{\tau_n}{\gamma_n} = G \tag{2.31}$$

Hooke's law for uniaxial tension may be expressed in terms of the modulus, E, as $\sigma_n = E\varepsilon_n$ or in terms of the compliance S, as $\varepsilon_n = S\sigma_n$.

Cauchy suggested that Hooke's law may be generalized to give components as a superposition of terms proportional to each independent strain component. The normal strains obtained by the application of the three normal stresses σ_{xx}, σ_{yy}, and σ_{zz} as shown in Fig. 2.15 to a linearly elastic, isotropic body are given in the following stress-strain matrix:

	Strain		
Stress	ε_{xx}	ε_{yy}	ε_{zz}
σ_{xx}	$\dfrac{\sigma_{xx}}{E}$	$-\dfrac{\nu\sigma_{xx}}{E}$	$-\dfrac{\nu\sigma_{xx}}{E}$
σ_{yy}	$-\dfrac{\nu\sigma_{yy}}{E}$	$\dfrac{\sigma_{yy}}{E}$	$-\dfrac{\nu\sigma_{yy}}{E}$
σ_{zz}	$-\dfrac{\nu\sigma_{zz}}{E}$	$-\dfrac{\nu\sigma_{zz}}{E}$	$\dfrac{\sigma_{zz}}{E}$

By superposition of the normal strain components by algebraic addition of the vertical columns of the above matrix, the following constitutive equations for normal or extensional strain are obtained:

$$\varepsilon_{xx} = \frac{\sigma_{xx}}{E} - \frac{\nu\sigma_{yy}}{E} - \frac{\nu\sigma_{zz}}{E} = \frac{1}{E}[\sigma_{xx} - \nu(\sigma_{yy} + \sigma_{zz})] \tag{2.32a}$$

$$\varepsilon_{yy} = -\frac{\nu\sigma_{xx}}{E} + \frac{\sigma_{yy}}{E} - \frac{\nu\sigma_{zz}}{E} = \frac{1}{E}[\sigma_{yy} - \nu(\sigma_{xx} + \sigma_{zz})] \tag{2.32b}$$

$$\varepsilon_{zz} = -\frac{\nu\sigma_{xx}}{E} - \frac{\nu\sigma_{yy}}{E} + \frac{\sigma_{zz}}{E} = \frac{1}{E}[\sigma_{zz} - \nu(\sigma_{xx} + \sigma_{yy})] \tag{2.32c}$$

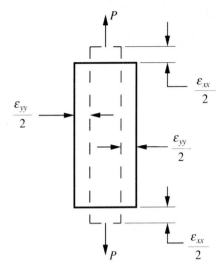

FIGURE 2.15
Gauge length of an uniaxial tension specimen showing the deformations for which the shown linear strains are calculated.

If the shear stresses τ_{xy}, τ_{yz}, and τ_{zx} act simultaneously with the normal stresses σ_{xx}, σ_{yy}, and σ_{zz}, they will produce the following shear strains:

$$\gamma_{xy} = \frac{1}{G}\tau_{xy} \tag{2.33a}$$

$$\gamma_{yz} = \frac{1}{G}\tau_{yz} \tag{2.33b}$$

$$\gamma_{zx} = \frac{1}{G}\tau_{zx} \tag{2.33c}$$

Note that a shear stress on one plane does not affect the strain on perpendicular planes. Since for an elastic, isotropic material G, E, and ν are related by the equation $G = E/2(1+\nu)$, only two of these parameters need be known.

The most generalized expression for Hooke's law (for a material that is anisotropic, linearly elastic, etc.) may be expressed in terms of

1. Moduli as

$$\sigma_{ij} = \sum_{k=1}^{3} \sum_{l=1}^{3} C_{ijkl}\varepsilon_{kl} \tag{2.34}$$

2. Compliances as

$$\varepsilon_{ij} = \sum_{k=1}^{3} \sum_{l=1}^{3} S_{ijkl}\sigma_{kl} \tag{2.35}$$

The former relationship is called a *rigidity tetror* and the latter a *compliance tetror*, of which each have 81 constants, i.e., moduli or compliances. Because of such considerations as isotropy, reversibility of elastic strains, etc., the above constants usually reduce to a small number. As the symmetry of the material increases, the independent, elastic constants reduce to two for an isotropic (hookean) material as indicated in the foregoing.

2.1.9 Plane Strain and Plane Stress

There are two important classes of problems that commonly arise in metalworking: plane strain and plane stress. In the former, a stress condition exists in which one of the normal strains and the two related shearing strains are equal to zero as shown in Fig. 2.16. In this case, the material is compressed in the y-direction and elongated in the x-direction. If $\varepsilon_{zz} = 0$, then the above equations for the generalized Hooke's law reduce to $\sigma_{zz} = \nu(\sigma_x + \sigma_y)$. For the plane stress condition, as already mentioned, a biaxial state of stress exists, as in a sheetmetal stretching operation, in which one of the normal stresses and the two associated shear stresses are equal to zero. If $\sigma_{zz} = 0$, Eqs. (2.32) reduce to

$$\varepsilon_{xx} = \frac{1}{E}(\sigma_{xx} - \nu\sigma_{yy}) \tag{2.36a}$$

$$\varepsilon_{yy} = \frac{1}{E}(\sigma_{yy} - \nu\sigma_{xx}) \tag{2.36b}$$

$$\varepsilon_{zz} = \frac{1}{E}[-\nu(\sigma_{xx} + \sigma_{yy})] \tag{2.36c}$$

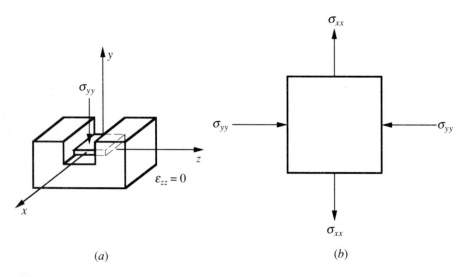

(a)   (b)

FIGURE 2.16

Example of (a) plane strain in which the workpiece is compressed in the y direction and elongates in the x direction, and $\varepsilon_{zz} = 0$; and (b) plane stress, in which $\sigma_{zz} = 0$.

2.1.10 Uniaxial Tension

For the case of uniaxial tension, in which σ_{xx} is the only nonzero stress, Eqs. (2.32) reduce to the elementary form for Hooke's law

$$\varepsilon_{xx} = \frac{\sigma_{xx}}{E} \tag{2.37a}$$

$$\varepsilon_{yy} = -\frac{\nu}{E}\sigma_{xx} \tag{2.37b}$$

$$\varepsilon_{zz} = -\frac{\nu}{E}\sigma_{xx} \tag{2.37c}$$

2.1.11 Basic Relationships of Elastic Theory

2.1.11.1 INTRODUCTION. Three systems of relationships comprise elastic theory: (1) the differential equations of equilibrium, (2) the strain-displacement and compatibility differential equations, and (3) the material constitutive equations. In any finite body, these systems are supplemented by the boundary conditions. Equilibrium must not only exist everywhere within the stressed body, but also between the internal stresses and the surface stresses.

2.1.11.2 EQUATIONS OF STATIC FORCE EQUILIBRIUM. If a solid, differential element of a body is in a varying stress field, equilibrium considerations limit the distribution of stresses possible.

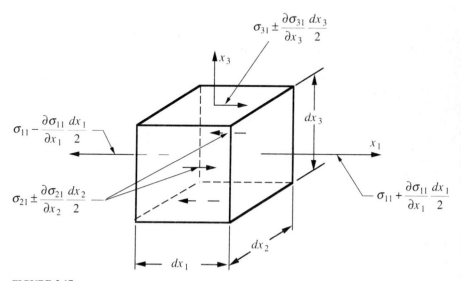

FIGURE 2.17
Element considered in the derivation of the equations of equilibrium. Force equilibrium shown in the $\pm x_1$ directions.

Let us assume that we have a stress system as shown in Fig. 2.7, and we consider for simplicity only those components of stress resulting from forces in the x_1 direction using the suffix notation as shown in Fig. 2.17. By multiplying the stress components by their respective areas to obtain forces, equilibrium can be expressed by equating the sum of the forces in the x_1 direction (and other directions, if desired) to zero as follows:

$$\sum \sigma_{ij} A_i = 0 \quad \text{or} \quad \sum F_{11} = 0 \tag{2.38}$$

If one ignores the body forces, the above summation gives the equation

$$\left(\sigma_{11} + \frac{\partial \sigma_{11}}{\partial x_1} \frac{dx_1}{2}\right) dx_2 \, dx_3 - \left(\sigma_{11} - \frac{\partial \sigma_{11}}{\partial x_1} \frac{dx_1}{2}\right) dx_2 \, dx_3$$

$$+ \left(\sigma_{21} + \frac{\partial \sigma_{21}}{\partial x_2} \frac{dx_2}{2}\right) dx_1 \, dx_3 - \left(\sigma_{21} - \frac{\partial \sigma_{21}}{\partial x_2} \frac{dx_2}{2}\right) dx_1 \, dx_3 \tag{2.39}$$

$$+ \left(\sigma_{31} + \frac{\partial \sigma_{31}}{\partial x_3} \frac{dx_3}{2}\right) dx_1 \, dx_2 - \left(\sigma_{31} - \frac{\partial \sigma_{31}}{\partial x_3} \frac{dx_3}{2}\right) dx_1 \, dx_2 = 0$$

By simplifying and clearing the above equation, one obtains the following equilibrium equation in suffix notation in the x_1 direction:

$$\frac{\partial \sigma_{11}}{\partial x_1} + \frac{\partial \sigma_{21}}{\partial x_2} + \frac{\partial \sigma_{31}}{\partial x_3} = 0 \tag{2.40a}$$

Proceeding as above in the x_2 and x_3 directions, we obtain the following equilibrium equations:

$$\frac{\partial \sigma_{12}}{\partial x_1} + \frac{\partial \sigma_{22}}{\partial x_2} + \frac{\partial \sigma_{32}}{\partial x_3} = 0 \tag{2.40b}$$

$$\frac{\partial \sigma_{13}}{\partial x_1} + \frac{\partial \sigma_{23}}{\partial x_2} + \frac{\partial \sigma_{33}}{\partial x_3} = 0 \tag{2.40c}$$

The above three equations can be written more concisely as follows by letting j denote any of the three directions:

$$\sum_{i=1}^{3} \frac{\partial \sigma_{ij}}{\partial x_i} = 0 \tag{2.40d}$$

Equations (2.40) for static force equilibrium can be written in *engineering* notation as

$$\frac{\partial \sigma_{xx}}{\partial x} + \frac{\partial \tau_{xy}}{\partial y} + \frac{\partial \tau_{xz}}{\partial z} = 0 \tag{2.41a}$$

$$\frac{\partial \sigma_{yy}}{\partial y} + \frac{\partial \tau_{xy}}{\partial x} + \frac{\partial \tau_{xz}}{\partial z} = 0 \tag{2.41b}$$

$$\frac{\partial \sigma_{zz}}{\partial z} + \frac{\partial \tau_{xz}}{\partial x} + \frac{\partial \tau_{yz}}{\partial y} = 0 \tag{2.41c}$$

2.1.11.3 STRAIN-DISPLACEMENT AND COMPATIBILITY. In three dimensions, the six strain parameters of Eqs. (2.11) and (2.12), as expressed in suffix notation as space derivatives of the three displacement parameters, u_1, u_2, and u_3 are as follows:

$$(a) \quad \varepsilon_{11} = \frac{\partial u_1}{\partial x_1} \qquad (d) \quad \gamma_{12} = \frac{\partial u_1}{\partial x_2} + \frac{\partial u_2}{\partial x_1}$$

$$(b) \quad \varepsilon_{22} = \frac{\partial u_2}{\partial x_2} \qquad (e) \quad \gamma_{23} = \frac{\partial u_2}{\partial x_3} + \frac{\partial u_3}{\partial x_2} \qquad (2.42)$$

$$(c) \quad \varepsilon_{33} = \frac{\partial u_3}{\partial x_3} \qquad (f) \quad \gamma_{31} = \frac{\partial u_3}{\partial x_1} + \frac{\partial u_1}{\partial x_3}$$

These equations usually will not possess a unique solution if the strains are arbitrarily prescribed. The condition of compatibility imposes a requirement that the displacement components must be single-valued, continuous functions. In order to ensure single-valued, continuous solutions for u_i, we must impose certain restrictions on the strain functions ε_{ij}. Even though actual elastic deformations are single-valued, and those of interest are continuous, we cannot take any tensor field ε_{ij} and expect it automatically to be associated with a single-valued, continuous displacement field.

Furthermore, if a stressed elastic body is divided into small elements, such as cubes, these cubes will distort into parallelepipeds of different proportions according to the prescribed strain condition. For those various parallelepipeds to fit their neighbors perfectly (without plastic flow or void formation), the prescribed strain components must be of a particular type satisfying certain conditions. The strains that give compatible parallelepipeds are called compatible strains as opposed to incompatible ones. The condition that strains must satisfy in order to be compatible is called the *compatibility condition*, which is expressed mathematically by the compatibility equations.

If one differentiates Eqs. (2.42a) and (2.42b) for ε_{11} and ε_{22} with respect to x_2 and to x_1 twice, and adds the result, and also if one takes the mixed derivative of Eq. (2.42c) with respect to x_1 and x_2, interchanges the order of partial differentiation assuming all derivatives are continuous, and solves all of the above equations simultaneously, one obtains one of the compatibility equations

$$\frac{\partial^2 \varepsilon_{11}}{\partial x_2^2} + \frac{\partial^2 \varepsilon_{22}}{\partial x_1^2} = \frac{\partial^2 \gamma_{12}}{\partial x_1 \, \partial x_2} \qquad (2.43)$$

Performing the same operations on ε_{22} and ε_{33}, and ε_{33} and ε_{11}, one can obtain two more similar equations.

Using somewhat the same approach, one can obtain three additional compatibility equations of the form

$$2 \frac{\partial^2 \varepsilon_{11}}{\partial y \, \partial z} = \frac{\partial}{\partial x} \left(-\frac{\partial \gamma_{23}}{\partial x} + \frac{\partial \gamma_{23}}{\partial y} + \frac{\partial \gamma_{12}}{\partial z} \right) \qquad (2.44)$$

In compact suffix notation, the six compatibility equations can be expressed as

$$\varepsilon_{ij,kl} + \varepsilon_{kl,ij} - \varepsilon_{ik,jl} - \varepsilon_{jl,ik} = 0 \tag{2.45}$$

The system consists of 81 equations, but some of these are identically satisfied, and some are repetitions because of the symmetry in indices ij and kl. Only 6 of the 81 equations are essential. They are given by Eqs. (2.43) and (2.44).

In general, the solution of a problem in elasticity involves 15 unknown quantities to be determined: 6 stress components, 6 strain components, and 3 displacement components, requiring 15 equations: 3 equilibrium equations (2.40), 6 constitutive equations (2.32) and (2.33), and 6 displacement equations, whose strain state must conform to the 6 compatibility equations similar to Eqs. (2.32) and (2.33).

2.2 PLASTICITY

The theory of plasticity deals with the methods of calculating stresses and strains in a deformed body after part of the body has yielded. The difference between elastic and plastic deformation has been discussed previously. Plastic deformation, as opposed to viscoplastic deformation, is essentially time-independent (permanent) deformation. A perfectly plastic material is one that does not strainharden, i.e., in which $d\sigma/d\varepsilon = 0$. Viscoplastic deformation is time-dependent, permanent deformation that is not only a function of the strain ε but is also a function of a time-dependent variable, the strain rate $\dot{\varepsilon}$ and temperature T as expressed by the equation for the flow stress: $\sigma = \sigma(\varepsilon, \dot{\varepsilon}, T)$. Various models for plastic material will be discussed in the next chapter in conjunction with the stress-strain curve. The remainder of this chapter and this book deals primarily with plastic deformation.

2.2.1 Conditions of Yielding

In metalworking operations, one is often interested in the stress at which yielding will occur in a material, because (1) this is the stress at which plastic or permanent deformation in the material to be formed begins, and (2) the materials used for the tools and dies yield or fail at their respective yield stress.

In uniaxial tension, yielding will occur at the point at which the yield-point stress or the yield strength σ_Y is exceeded. However, most metalforming operations involve combined states of stress, in which the stresses in certain directions may be much higher than σ_Y before yielding occurs. The question that must then be answered is, "At what stress level will yielding occur for different complex stress conditions?" To resolve this problem, an arbitrary, but logical, criterion for yielding must be established for a combined state of stress.

For a complex state of stress one can expect an isotropic material to yield plastically if a certain relation between the invariant of the stress tensor is satisfied. Thus the yield condition may generally be written in the form: $F(I_1, I_2, I_3) = 0$

[2.3]. Since the hydrostatic component does not affect yielding, the first invariant of the stress deviatoric is zero, and therefore the yield condition may be written as $F(I_2', I_3') = 0$. This condition may be represented as a certain surface in stress space as I_2' and I_3' are functions of stresses which are given by Eqs. (2.10). Therefore a yield criterion may be established in the form of equations involving stresses for different assumptions or postulates. This approach gives us the different yield criteria such as the Tresca and von Mises criteria to be discussed later.

Any mathematical expression [2.4] that attempts to predict the state of stress that will induce yielding, or the onset of plastic deformation, is therefore called a *yield criterion*. A generalized form of such an equation is

$$f(\sigma_x, \sigma_y, \sigma_z, \tau_{xy}, \tau_{yz}, \tau_{zx}) = C \qquad \text{(a constant)} \qquad (2.46)$$

A more simplified form, in terms of the principal stresses is

$$f(\sigma_1, \sigma_2, \sigma_3) = C \qquad (2.47)$$

In dealing with yielding and with plasticity, the following simplifying assumptions are usually made:

1. The material is a homogeneous, isotropic continuum
2. The onset of yielding in tension and compression is identical, i.e., there is no Bauschinger effect
3. The volume remains constant, i.e., $\Delta V/V$ and the sum of the plastic strain increments is zero, or

$$d\varepsilon_1 + d\varepsilon_2 + d\varepsilon_3 = 0 \qquad (2.48)$$

   for plastic deformation
4. A hydrostatic state of stress σ_m does not influence yielding
5. Effects of strain rate are here neglected
6. Temperature effects are not considered here

The two criteria that are most generally used to predict yielding in isotropic materials are (1) the maximum shear stress or Tresca criterion, and (2) the octahedral shear stress or von Mises criterion. They will be discussed in the following two sections.

2.2.2 Maximum Shear Stress or Tresca Criterion

This criterion postulates that yielding will occur when some function of the maximum shear stress reaches a critical value. The convention for the hierarchy of the stresses that will be used here is that $\sigma_1 > \sigma_2 > \sigma_3$. This ranking of the stresses, however, is not always known beforehand. This criterion predicts that yielding will occur when

$$\sigma_{max} - \sigma_{min} = C \qquad \text{or} \qquad \sigma_1 - \sigma_3 = C$$

If the above criterion applies, the constant C can readily be obtained from the following simple, standard tests:

1. For uniaxial tension, yielding will occur when σ_1 reaches the yield strength in tension, σ_Y, i.e., when $\sigma_1 = \sigma_Y$ and $\tau_{max} = \frac{1}{2}\sigma_Y$, or $|\sigma_1 - 0| = C = \sigma_Y$

2. For pure shear, yielding will occur when

$$\tau_{max} = \sigma_1 = -\sigma_3 \quad \text{and} \quad \sigma_2 = 0 \quad \text{or}$$

$$|\sigma_1 - (-\sigma_1)| = C = 2\sigma_1 = 2\tau_Y = 2k \tag{2.49}$$

If this criterion is observed, then $\tau_Y = \frac{1}{2}\sigma_Y$ is predicted, or the yield strength in pure shear, τ_Y or k, is predicted to be equal to $\frac{1}{2}\sigma_Y$, i.e., to one-half the yield strength in tension. Since the symbol k is used extensively for the yield strength in pure shear throughout the metalworking literature, it will also be used here interchangeably with τ_Y.

2.2.3 von Mises Criterion

The von Mises criterion postulates that yielding will occur when some value of the root mean shear stress reaches a constant or

$$[(\sigma_1 - \sigma_2)^2 + (\sigma_2 - \sigma_3)^2 + (\sigma_3 - \sigma_1)^2]^{1/2} = C_1 \tag{2.50a}$$

or

$$(\sigma_1 - \sigma_2)^2 + (\sigma_2 - \sigma_3)^2 + (\sigma_3 - \sigma_1)^2 = C_2 \tag{2.50b}$$

A more general form of this expression is

$$(\sigma_x - \sigma_y)^2 + (\sigma_y - \sigma_z)^2 + (\sigma_z - \sigma_x)^2 + 6(\tau_{xy}^2 + \tau_{yz}^2 + \tau_{zx}^2) = C_3 \tag{2.51}$$

One interpretation of the von Mises criterion, called the *distortion energy theory*, is that yielding occurs when the elastic energy causing distortion in the body reaches a critical value. (Some authorities consider this concept to be fortuitous.) Another interpretation, called the *octahedral shear stress theory*, occurs when the shear stresses acting on the octahedral planes formed by the body diagonal (111) planes, as shown in Fig. 2.18 in each octant of the orthogonal axes, reach a critical value.

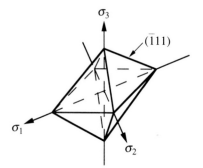

FIGURE 2.18
Regular octahedron formed by eight octahedral shear planes {111} passing through the corners of a principal cube. σ_1, σ_2, and σ_3 are normal to the surface of the cube. (See Fig. 2.54.)

The constant $C_1 = C_2^{1/2}$ in Eq. (2.50) may be determined for the following cases:

1. Uniaxial tension when

$$\sigma_1 = \sigma_Y \qquad \sigma_2 = \sigma_3 = 0$$
$$2\sigma_1^2 = C_2 = 2\sigma_Y^2 \tag{2.52}$$

2. Pure shear when

$$\sigma_1 = -\sigma_3 = \tau_Y \qquad C_2 = 0$$
$$\sigma_1^2 + \sigma_1^2 + 4\sigma_1^2 = C_2' = 6\sigma_1^2 \tag{2.53}$$

According to the von Mises criterion, the tensile and shear yield stresses are related as follows:

$$\sigma_Y = \sqrt{3}\tau_Y = \sqrt{3}k \qquad \text{or} \qquad \tau_Y = \frac{\sigma_Y}{\sqrt{3}} \tag{2.54}$$

2.2.4 Effective Stress and Strain

As indicated in the foregoing, because metalworking operations are usually performed under conditions other than uniaxial tension, some method must be devised to extend the material behavior determined in uniaxial tension to that existing in more complex loading situations. This general approach is attempted through the concept of effective stress, $\bar{\sigma}$ and effective strain, $\bar{\varepsilon}$.

The effective stress is defined in terms of the yield locus, which is the locus of all possible combinations of states of stress that will initiate yielding or plastic flow in a material characterized by a given set of strength properties. The yield loci most often used for isotropic materials are the Tresca and von Mises yield loci, which were discussed in the previous two sections. The one most often used for anisotropic (orthotropic) materials is Hill's locus, which is discussed in a later section in conjunction with anisotropy.

An expression for the effective stress $\bar{\sigma}$ may be written as a function of the applied stresses for either of the above criteria. As a result of the variations of the applied state of stress, yielding will occur when the effective stress reaches a critical value. For the von Mises criterion, $\bar{\sigma}$ is given as

$$\bar{\sigma} = \frac{1}{\sqrt{2}}[(\sigma_1 - \sigma_2)^2 + (\sigma_2 - \sigma_3)^2 + (\sigma_3 - \sigma_1)^2]^{1/2} \tag{2.55}$$

and for the Tresca criterion, it is

$$\bar{\sigma} = \sigma_1 - \sigma_3 \qquad \text{when} \qquad \sigma_1 > \sigma_2 > \sigma_3 \tag{2.56}$$

Effective plastic strain is defined so that the incremental work per unit volume is

$$dW_z = \bar{\sigma}\, d\bar{\varepsilon} = \sigma_1\, d\varepsilon_1 + \sigma_2\, d\varepsilon_2 + \sigma_3\, d\varepsilon_2 \tag{2.57}$$

which is the sum of the products of the stresses in the principal directions by the change in the plastic strain in each direction. The elastic strain components are neglected. By use of the flow rule to be discussed later and the von Mises expression for effective stress, Eq. (2.55), the effective plastic strain increment for the von Mises criterion in simplified form is

$$d\bar{\varepsilon} = [\tfrac{2}{3}(d\varepsilon_1^2 + d\varepsilon_2^2 + d\varepsilon_3^2)]^{1/2} \tag{2.58}$$

The total effective plastic strain, where applicable, is given by

$$\bar{\varepsilon} = [\tfrac{2}{3}(\varepsilon_1^2 + \varepsilon_2^2 + \varepsilon_3^2)]^{1/2} \tag{2.59a}$$

and the effective strain rate is

$$\dot{\bar{\varepsilon}} = [\tfrac{2}{3}(\dot{\varepsilon}_1^2 + \dot{\varepsilon}_2^2 + \dot{\varepsilon}_3^2)]^{1/2} \tag{2.59b}$$

For the Tresca criterion, the effective plastic strain is

$$d\bar{\varepsilon} = |d\varepsilon_i|_{max} \tag{2.60}$$

where i refers to the principal directions.

2.2.5 The Yield Surface

As mentioned in the foregoing, $\bar{\sigma}$, in Eq. (2.55), is the effective or significant stress for the von Mises criterion at which yielding begins. It is also called the

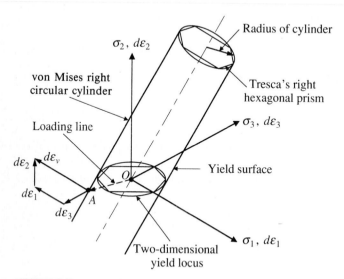

FIGURE 2.19
The cylinder represents the three-dimensional yield surface according to the von Mises criterion, and the inscribed hexagonal prism represents the yield surface for the maximum shear stress or Tresca criterion in stress space. If the material is loaded to yielding at A, the resulting plastic strain increment may be represented by the vector $d\varepsilon_v$, which is normal to the yield surface and is the vector sum of $d\varepsilon_1$, $d\varepsilon_2$, and $d\varepsilon_3$ [2.4].

flow stress. It will plot as a right cylinder of infinite length in three-dimensional space, when the three principal stresses are used as the stress axes as shown in Fig. 2.19. The yield surface for the maximum shear stress criterion will plot as a right hexagonal prism inscribed in the cylindrical yield surface of the von Mises criterion. The significance of the yield surface is that yielding will not occur as long as the path of stresses acting on the body remains within the confines of the yield cylinder or the hexagonal prism depending on the yield criterion used. The longitudinal axis or centerline of the cylinder and prism makes equal angles of 54.73° with the principal stress axes. Along the path of the centerline of the yield cylinder or prism, a hydrostatic state of stress exists, for which no plastic deformation occurs. Thus, a body that is subjected to equal triaxial tension or compression will not deform plastically, but only elastically.

If a plane coplanar with any two of the principal axes intersects the yield cylinder and prism, the trace of the cylinder on the plane will be an ellipse and of the prism will be an inscribed, elongated hexagon as shown in Fig. 2.19. These boundaries represent the yield boundaries for a biaxial stress condition. Since the yield locus is the boundary of the elastic domain, it is therefore path-independent in the sense that any point on it may be approached by many different stress paths within the elastic region as shown in Fig. 2.20 for the two-dimensional case.

Strainhardening due to cold working enlarges the cross section of the yield loci as shown in Fig. 2.21.

As mentioned above, the yield criterion such as of Tresca or von Mises determines the stress level at which plastic deformation begins, and can be written in the general form

$$f(\sigma_{ij}) = \sigma'_Y(n') \qquad (2.61)$$

where f is some function of σ_{ij}, and σ'_Y is a material parameter to be determined experimentally. The term σ'_Y may be a function of a hardening parameter n'. Moreover, the progressive development of the yield surface as shown in Fig. 2.21 can be defined by relating the yield stress σ'_Y to the plastic deformation by means of n'.

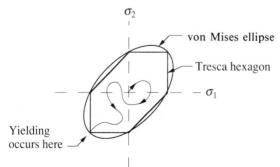

FIGURE 2.20
Yield ellipse and hexagon for a biaxial stress condition. The path independence of elastic deformation is illustrated.

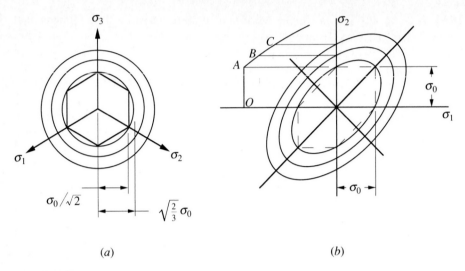

(a)   (b)

FIGURE 2.21

The effect of strainhardening on (a) the yield surface (end view) and (b) the yield ellipse for a biaxial stress condition. The enlarged yield cylinder and the ellipse are due to successive amounts of cold work. The maximum difference between the von Mises and the Tresca criteria is

$$\frac{\sqrt{\frac{2}{3}}\sigma_o}{\sigma_0/\sqrt{2}} = \frac{2}{\sqrt{3}} = 1.15 \text{ or } 15 \text{ percent.}$$

(*Adapted from N. H. Polakowski and E. J. Ripling, Strength and Structure of Engineering Materials, Prentice-Hall, 1966.*)

The strainhardening behavior of a metallic material is commonly described according to the response of the yield surface to plastic deformation as (1) perfectly plastic, (2) isotropic strainhardening, and (3) kinematic strainhardening as shown in Fig. 2.22. A perfectly plastic material as shown in Fig. 2.22(a) does not depend on the amount of plastic deformation in any way. If the yield surface enlarges as shown in Figs. 2.21 and 2.22(b) without any translation, it is said to be isotropic. On the other hand, if the subsequent yield surfaces preserve their shape and orientation but translate in stress space as a rigid body as shown in Fig. 2.22(c), kinematic strainhardening is said to take place.

The equation for the effective strain increment is given by Eq. (2.58). If the stress and strain axes coincide, the principal strain increments, or the principal strains if applicable, can be plotted on the same coordinate axes as shown in Fig. 2.19. As indicated in the foregoing, the vector sum of the incremental strains $d\varepsilon_v$, will then give the total strain increment. Each incremental strain is normal to the yield surface as shown in Fig. 2.19.

If a plastic stress-strain curve, called the *flow curve*, is plotted in terms of $\bar{\sigma}$ and $\bar{\varepsilon}$, the same stress-strain curve will be obtained regardless of the state of stress. Since the effective stress and effective strain reduce to the axial component of the true stress and the true strain for uniaxial tension, this curve approximates the $\bar{\sigma} - \bar{\varepsilon}$ curve for uniaxial tension.

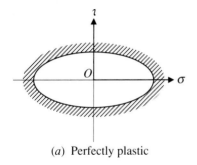

(*a*) Perfectly plastic

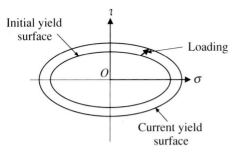

Initial yield
surface

Loading

Current yield
surface

(*b*) Isotropic strainhardening

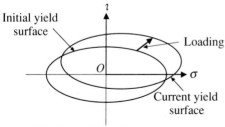

Initial yield
surface

Loading

Current yield
surface

(*c*) Kinematic strainhardening

FIGURE 2.22
Mathematical models for the representation of
strainhardening behavior. (*Adapted from D. R.
J. Owens and E. Hinton, Finite Elements in Plasticity, Pineridge Press, 1980.*)

2.2.6   State of Plastic Strain

Since the elastic strain is usually so small as compared to the total strain, it will
usually be considered to be negligible in all further consideration of plastic
deformation. Also, since plastic strains are so large, the strain increments $d\varepsilon_x$,
$d\varepsilon_y$, and $d\varepsilon_z$ are used for strain between the consecutive instants of the process
of plastic flow.

A direct parallel exists between the strain equations for elasticity, Eqs. (2.11)
to (2.15), and those for plasticity. The only difference is that the strains ε_{ii}, γ_{ij},
and ε_{ij} are replaced by the strain increments $d\varepsilon_{ii}$, $d\gamma_{ij}$, and $d\varepsilon_{ij}$. Making use of
the suffix notation, one can write the relations between components of the plastic
strain increments tensor, and the components (u_x, u_y, u_z) of a small displacement

vector **u** in the form

$$d\varepsilon_{ij} = \frac{1}{2}\left(\frac{\partial u_i}{\partial x_j} + \frac{\partial u_j}{\partial x_i}\right) \tag{2.62}$$

which are analogous to the relations given in Eq. (2.15) for small elastic strains.

Also, the equations involving the strain increment deviatoric have their counterparts in the elastic stress deviatoric equations (2.8(a), (b), and (c)). If incompressibility is assumed, the strain increment deviatoric coincides with the strain increment tensor, and the first invariant is given by

$$I_1' = d\varepsilon_x + d\varepsilon_y + d\varepsilon_z = 3d\varepsilon_m = 0 \tag{2.63}$$

The invariants of the deviatoric of the plastic strain increments may then be written as

$$I_1' = 0 \tag{2.64a}$$

$$I_2' = \frac{1}{6}[(d\varepsilon_1 - d\varepsilon_2)^2 + (d\varepsilon_2 - d\varepsilon_3)^2 + (d\varepsilon_3 - d\varepsilon_1)^2] \tag{2.64b}$$

$$I_3' = (d\varepsilon_1 - d\varepsilon_m)(d\varepsilon_2 - d\varepsilon_m)(d\varepsilon_3 - d\varepsilon_m) \tag{2.64c}$$

The above second invariant of the deviatoric is among the fundamental concepts in the theory of plastic flow. It represents the square of a magnitude called the *increment of the distortion intensity* or *increment of equivalent strain*, $d\varepsilon_i = \sqrt{I_2'}$. $d\varepsilon_i$ represents the increment of distortion intensity accumulated in a particle of material in a short period of time between two consecutive stages of the advancing process of plastic flow [2.3]. The total intensity itself characterizing the state of strain accumulated from the beginning of the deformation process can be obtained by means of the following summation:

$$\varepsilon_i = \int d\varepsilon_i = \int \left[\frac{1}{6}(d\varepsilon_1 - d\varepsilon_2)^2 + (d\varepsilon_2 - d\varepsilon_3)^2 + (d\varepsilon_3 - d\varepsilon_1)^2\right]^{1/2} \tag{2.65}$$

For uniaxial tension $d\varepsilon_1 = d\varepsilon$ and, by assuming incompressibility of the material, $d\varepsilon_1 + d\varepsilon_2 + d\varepsilon_3 = 0$, $d\varepsilon_2 = d\varepsilon_3 = -0.5\,d\varepsilon$. Therefore, $\varepsilon_i = \int \frac{1}{2}\sqrt{3}\,d\varepsilon = \frac{1}{2}\sqrt{3}\,\varepsilon$. For pure shear $d\varepsilon_1 = d\varepsilon$, $d\varepsilon_2 = -d\varepsilon$ and $d\varepsilon_3 = 0$, and therefore the distortion intensity is $\varepsilon_1 = \int d\varepsilon = \varepsilon$, the strain in uniaxial tension.

2.2.7 Plastic Strain Rate

The plastic flow velocity of the material at a given point is determined by a vector **v** with components v_x, v_y, and v_z parallel to the coordinate axes [2.3]. If δt is a short time increment, within which velocities may be assumed to preserve the constant values, then the displacements can be determined as follows:

$$u_x = v_x\,\delta t \qquad u_y = v_y\,\delta t \qquad \text{and} \qquad u_z = v_z\,\delta t \tag{2.66}$$

Similarly, as the plastic strain increments have been expressed by means of the displacement vector **u** the strain rates can be related to the components of the velocity vector **v** as follows:

$$\dot{\varepsilon}_x = \frac{\partial v_x}{\partial x} \qquad \dot{\varepsilon}_y = \frac{\partial v_y}{\partial y} \qquad \text{and} \qquad \dot{\varepsilon}_z = \frac{\partial v_z}{\partial z}$$

$$\dot{\varepsilon}_{xy} = \frac{1}{2}\left(\frac{\partial v_x}{\partial y} + \frac{\partial v_y}{\partial x}\right) \qquad \dot{\varepsilon}_{yz} = \frac{1}{2}\left(\frac{\partial v_y}{\partial z} + \frac{\partial v_z}{\partial y}\right) \tag{2.67}$$

$$\dot{\varepsilon}_{zx} = \frac{1}{2}\left(\frac{\partial v_z}{\partial x} + \frac{\partial v_x}{\partial z}\right)$$

These relations can be expressed in suffix notation as

$$\dot{\varepsilon}_{ij} = \frac{1}{2}\left(\frac{\partial v_i}{\partial x_j} + \frac{\partial v_j}{\partial x_i}\right) \tag{2.68}$$

In terms of plastic strain rate the condition of incompressibility (constancy of volume) of the materials is given by

$$\dot{\varepsilon}_x + \dot{\varepsilon}_y + \dot{\varepsilon}_z = 0 \tag{2.69}$$

2.2.8   Stress-Strain Relationships in Plasticity

A generalized mathematical theory of plasticity is not nearly as well developed as the theory of elasticity, because of the inherent complexities involved. First of all, in linearly elastic deformation, Hooke's law applies, that is, the material is assumed to be an isotropic, linearly elastically recoverable continuum; while in plastic deformation, the deformation is an irreversible process, strainhardening usually occurs as a result of the deformation, and anisotropy may occur with continued deformation. Elastic deformation depends only on the initial and final state of stress and strain, whereas plastic deformation also depends on the stress-strain path and may be inhomogeneous. For a complete reversal of strain path, the total strain may not be the sum of that in tension and compression because of the Bauschinger (reverse loading) effect. Also for cyclic loading, the strainhardening effect may saturate producing greater error in determination of the strain. In elastic deformation usually small strains are involved, and the principal axes for stress and strain coincide. In spite of the formidability of the discipline much progress has been made in the mathematical theory of plasticity over the years.

In this brief treatment of plasticity some of the concepts of continuum elasticity are extended to plasticity to give a simplified approach that may be called *continuum plasticity*. To facilitate mathematical treatment in continuum plasticity, the material is often assumed to be isotropic, rigid-plastic, and non-strainhardening with no reverse loading (Bauschinger) effects. Although metals and alloys cannot be strictly considered as continua, they do exhibit this macro-scopic (large-scale) behavior when their basic microstructural features are much less in extent than the dimensions of the deforming specimens.

There are two theories of plasticity that are commonly used: (1) the *flow or incremental theory* as expressed by the Levy-Mises equations, and (2) the *deformation theory*, in which proportional loading is assumed. The former will be presented first.

Stress-strain relationships that describe the path of plastic deformation of a material are called *flow rules*. Flow rules for any yield criterion may be obtained by the use of

$$d\varepsilon_{ij} = \frac{\partial f(\sigma_{ij})}{\partial \sigma_{ij}}(d\lambda) \tag{2.70}$$

where $f(\sigma_{ij})$ is here the isotropic yield function. For the von Mises criterion, by use of Eq. (2.50), the flow rule obtained is

$$\frac{d\varepsilon_1}{\sigma'_1} = \frac{d\varepsilon_2}{\sigma'_2} = \frac{d\varepsilon_3}{\sigma'_3} = d\lambda \tag{2.71}$$

where σ'_i are the deviatoric stress components

$$\sigma'_x = \sigma_x - \sigma_m$$

$$\sigma'_y = \sigma_y - \sigma_m \tag{2.72}$$

$$\sigma'_z = \sigma_z - \sigma_m$$

Equation (2.71) is the Reuss assumption that the plastic strain-increment is proportional to the deviatoric stress, that is, $d\varepsilon_x = d\lambda\sigma'_x$, etc.

By use of the relationship in Eq. (2.71), one can obtain the commonly used Levy-Mises equations for an isotropic material

$$\frac{d\varepsilon_x}{\sigma_x - \sigma_m} = \frac{d\varepsilon_y}{\sigma_y - \sigma_m} = \frac{d\varepsilon_z}{\sigma_z - \sigma_m} = \frac{d\gamma_{xy}}{2\tau_{xy}} = \frac{d\gamma_{yz}}{2\tau_{yz}} = \frac{d\gamma_{zx}}{2\tau_{zx}} = d\lambda \tag{2.73}$$

where $d\lambda$ is an instantaneous, positive, varying, proportionality factor called the *plastic compliance*, and σ_m is the mean or hydrostatic stress, so that is $\sigma_i - \sigma_m = \sigma'_i$, the deviatoric stress. The implication is that the ratio of the current incremental plastic strain to the current deviatoric stress is a constant.

In suffix notation, Eq. (2.73) becomes

$$(d\varepsilon_{ij})_p = \sigma'_{ij}\, d\lambda \tag{2.74}$$

Differential strains or strain increments are used in plasticity since the strains are large and may vary appreciably from point to point within the material being deformed in a metalworking process such as extrusion, and the axes of elemental volumes may rotate, resulting in the stress and the strain axes not to coincide.

In the above equation, a rigid (nonelastic), isotropic, strainhardening, plastically incompressible material is assumed, so that the elastic strains are assumed negligible. The straining condition is such that the principal stress axes coincide with the principal axes of strain at all times.

The above equation states that during plastic deformation at any instant of time, the plastic strain increments for given directions and given shear planes are proportional to the instantaneous stress deviators or to the shear stresses. As mentioned in the foregoing, the instantaneous, nonnegative proportionality factor $d\lambda$ varies continuously throughout the deformation process.

An alternate form of the above equation, in which σ is expressed by the three normal components of the principal stress, is

$$d\varepsilon_1 = d\lambda[\sigma_1 - \tfrac{1}{2}(\sigma_2 + \sigma_3)] \tag{2.75a}$$

$$d\varepsilon_2 = d\lambda[\sigma_2 - \tfrac{1}{2}(\sigma_1 + \sigma_3)] \tag{2.75b}$$

$$d\varepsilon_3 = d\lambda[\sigma_3 - \tfrac{1}{2}(\sigma_1 + \sigma_2)] \tag{2.75c}$$

It can be shown that in terms of the effective stress $\bar{\sigma}$ and the effective strain $\bar{\varepsilon}$, that $d\lambda = d\bar{\varepsilon}/\bar{\sigma}$.

Another form of the flow rule therefore is

$$d\varepsilon_1 = \frac{d\bar{\varepsilon}}{\bar{\sigma}}[\sigma_1 - \tfrac{1}{2}(\sigma_2 + \sigma_3)] \tag{2.76a}$$

$$d\varepsilon_2 = \frac{d\bar{\varepsilon}}{\bar{\sigma}}[\sigma_2 - \tfrac{1}{2}(\sigma_1 + \sigma_3)] \tag{2.76b}$$

$$d\varepsilon_3 = \frac{d\bar{\varepsilon}}{\bar{\sigma}}[\sigma_3 - \tfrac{1}{2}(\sigma_1 + \sigma_2)] \tag{2.76c}$$

Comparing the analogous constitutive equations for elastic deformation, one can see that $d\bar{\varepsilon}/\bar{\sigma}$ replaces $1/E$, and $\tfrac{1}{2}$ replaces Poisson's ratio, ν.

Let us now look at the expression for the *deformation theory*, in which *proportional loading* is assumed and the strain increment $d\varepsilon_i$ is replaced by the total strain ε_i.

For proportional loading, i.e.,

$$\frac{d\sigma_1}{\sigma_1} = \frac{d\sigma_2}{\sigma_2} = \frac{d\sigma_3}{\sigma_3} \tag{2.77}$$

which is equivalent to proportional straining, in which the ratios of the strain increments remain constant at all times, that is, $d\varepsilon_2/d\varepsilon_1 = C$ constant, the integrated strains

$$\varepsilon = \int_0^\varepsilon d\varepsilon \quad \text{and} \quad \bar{\varepsilon} = \int_0^\varepsilon d\bar{\varepsilon}$$

can replace the strain increments to give

$$\varepsilon_1 = \frac{\bar{\varepsilon}}{\bar{\sigma}}[\sigma_1 - \tfrac{1}{2}(\sigma_2 + \sigma_3)] \tag{2.78a}$$

$$\varepsilon_2 = \frac{\bar{\varepsilon}}{\bar{\sigma}}[\sigma_2 - \tfrac{1}{2}(\sigma_1 + \sigma_3)] \tag{2.78b}$$

$$\varepsilon_3 = \frac{\bar{\varepsilon}}{\bar{\sigma}}[\sigma_3 - \tfrac{1}{2}(\sigma_1 + \sigma_2)] \tag{2.78c}$$

The integrated strains can replace the strain increments, provided that no change in the directions of the principal strain increments occurs during plastic deformation and provided that the ratio of the strain increments remains constant at all times. This substitution can be rationalized as follows: If $d\varepsilon_2/d\varepsilon_1 = C$, then by use of the Eq. (2.48) for the constancy of volume and Eq. (2.59) for the effective strain written in terms of the strain increments, it can be shown that

$$d\bar{\varepsilon} = C' \, d\varepsilon_1 \tag{2.79a}$$

$$\int_0^{\bar{\varepsilon}} d\bar{\varepsilon} = C' \int_0^{\varepsilon_1} d\varepsilon_1 \tag{2.79b}$$

$$\bar{\varepsilon} = C'\varepsilon_1 \tag{2.79c}$$

so that $d\bar{\varepsilon} = d\varepsilon_1$, the strain increments, can be replaced by $\bar{\varepsilon}$ and ε_1, etc., the integrated strains.

If $\bar{\varepsilon}/\sigma$ in the equations (2.78) for plasticity is replaced by $1/E_p$, their similarity to their counterparts in elasticity is obvious, in which the Poisson's ratio ν is $\frac{1}{2}$ for all metallic materials. E_p may be considered to be the plastic modulus which, by way of emphasis, is not a constant for a given material such as is the modulus of elasticity, but a variable depending on the stress and strain. If straining is proportional, E_p may be evaluated in two ways: (1) by use of an experimental stress-strain curve, and (2) by assuming that stress and strain are related by an approximate empirical equation.

E_p may be evaluated from the effective stress versus effective strain curve, which may be equivalent to the experimental true stress versus true strain curve in uniaxial tension as shown in Fig. 2.23.

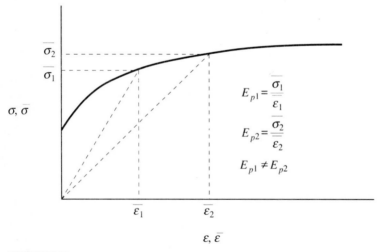

FIGURE 2.23
Effective stress-effective strain curve for an elastically rigid, strainhardening, plastic, metallic material, which is also equivalent to the true stress–true strain curve for uniaxial tension. Determination of E_p is illustrated.

If the stress-strain curve in the foregoing figure can be approximated reasonably well by an equation such as the Ludwik-Hollomon power law

$$\bar{\sigma} = K\bar{\varepsilon}^n \tag{2.80a}$$

which is equivalent to the equation for uniaxial tension

$$\sigma = K\varepsilon^n \tag{2.80b}$$

then E_p may be evaluated as follows:

$$E_p = \frac{\bar{\sigma}}{\bar{\varepsilon}} = \frac{\bar{\sigma}}{(\bar{\sigma}/K)^{1/n}} = \frac{K^{1/n}}{\bar{\sigma}^{(1/n)-1}} \tag{2.81}$$

The value of $\frac{1}{2}$ for Poisson's ratio in the above equations may be rationalized by use of the constancy of volume or incompressibility condition for which

$$\varepsilon_1 + \varepsilon_2 + \varepsilon_3 = 0 \tag{2.82}$$

For uniaxial tension $\varepsilon_2 = \varepsilon_3 = \nu\varepsilon$, substituting $\nu\varepsilon_1$ for ε_2 and ε_1, in the constancy of volume condition, one obtains $\varepsilon_1 - 2\nu\varepsilon_1 = 0$, or $\nu = \frac{1}{2}$.

2.2.9 Micromechanisms of Plastic Deformation and the Microscopic-to-Macroscopic Transition

2.2.9.1 INTRODUCTION. Most of the discussion so far regarding plastic deformation has been concerned with macroplasticity at a large scale or macroscopic level. Microplasticity, to be covered here, is concerned with the mechanical behavior of materials at a much smaller-scale level that approaches the atomic level. Since this subject matter lies primarily in the domain of materials science, only a short review will be covered here. Also, only the microplasticity of metallic materials will be discussed. The structure and the molecular deformation of polymeric materials, for example, will not be discussed.

2.2.9.2 STRUCTURE OF METALLIC MATERIALS. We may begin by stating that all metals and their alloys are polycrystalline, i.e., made up of many very small crystals or crystalline grains or, simply, grains. A material is said to be crystalline if its atoms are arranged in a definite, geometric pattern. If one surface of a small piece of metal or single-phase alloy is polished and etched, it will appear under the light microscope as shown in Fig. 2.24(a), showing many irregular grains outlined by grain boundaries. Most alloys, however, consist of two or more phases as shown in Fig. 2.24(b) and (c). Since the atoms in the boundaries (phase interfaces) are somewhat disorganized as shown in Fig. 2.25, they consequently have a higher free energy, and are not bonded as strongly as those within the grains. They are therefore removed by the etching solutions to form grooves that absorb or scatter the transmitted light of the microscope and thus appear darker than the exposed surface of the grains, which reflect much more of the light as shown in Fig. 2.26. Since the grain boundaries are as strong or nearly as strong as the grains themselves and also are irregular, fractures are transcrystalline.

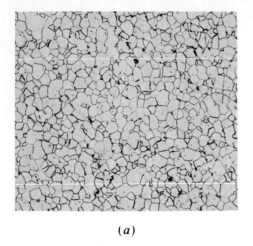

(a)

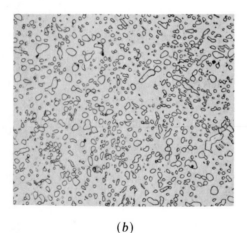

(b)

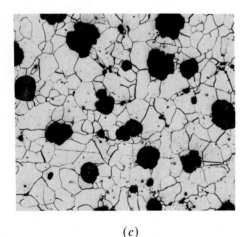

(c)

FIGURE 2.24

(a) Microstructure of a single phase (ferrite) of an annealed commercially pure iron, 0%C, polished and etched, such as with 3 percent solution of HNO_3 in ethyl alcohol (3% nital), showing grain boundaries at a magnification of 100×. (b) Microstructure of an eutectoid steel, 0.80%C, containing two phases: particles of carbide in a matrix of ferrite at 750×. The grain boundaries of the ferrite were not revealed in the etching procedure used. (c) Microstructure of annealed nodular (ductile) cast iron, containing two phases, ferrite and graphite, etched in nital and showing the ferrite grain boundaries at 100×.

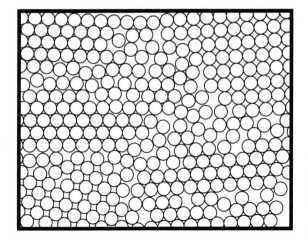

FIGURE 2.25
Schematic representation of grain boundaries showing them as regions of atomic disorder. Note that the grain boundaries are only a few atoms thick. (*After C. W. Mason, Introduction to Physical Metallurgy, ASMI.*)

Much discussion of microplasticity is concerned with the deformation of single crystals that are specially made, usually by growth from a liquid or by recrystallization of slightly deformed specimens by the strain-anneal method. A logical extension of microplasticity is the deformation of many grains in concert, the interaction of grains across their boundary surfaces, the rotation of grains to form a preferred orientation or texture, the sliding of grains relative to each other as during creep, etc. Since the grains of metals, and also the various phase, of alloys, are crystalline, we need some method conveniently and uniquely to describe this ordered, geometric arrangement called a *crystal structure*. To accomplish this end, the concept of a space lattice and methods of defining and

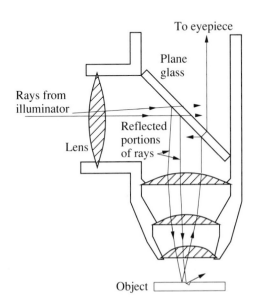

FIGURE 2.26
Drawing of the lower end of a vertical metallurgical microscope showing the illuminating system and the objective lenses. Note that the light beam from the grain boundary is reflected outside the objective whereas the light beam from the surface of the grain is reflected into the objective, which then transmits it up through the eyepiece (not shown) for viewing or photographing. (*From B. Rogers, The Nature of Metals 2nd ed., ASMI and Iowa State Press.*)

describing points, planes, and directions in a space lattice or a crystal structure were developed.

2.2.9.3 SPACE LATTICE. A space lattice is defined as a regular or periodic array of points in space over large intervals as compared to the distance between the points, and each point is so arranged that it has identical surroundings. Each point has identical surroundings when it has the same number of nearest neighbors that have the same spacing and the same angular relationship as any other point in the lattice. It has been proved mathematically by Bravais that there are only 14 ways in which points can be arranged in space so that each point has identical surroundings. These particular lattices established by Bravais are called *Bravais space lattices* or simply *Bravais lattices*. The term *space lattice* has a more general connotation. The space lattice can be described by three noncoplanar vectors, **a**, **b**, and **c**.

The basic unit of the space lattice is a unit cell, which is not uniquely determined. Usually a simple or primitive cell, which contains on the average only one point per cell, is selected. When it is evident that one can gain geometric advantage by including additional points per cell, it is convenient to use a nonprimitive cell containing more than one point per cell. In practice, the unit cell is chosen that is the smallest and is convenient in visualizing the symmetry of the crystal and in making mathematical calculations. The unit cell must be selected so that the entire lattice can be built up by translation of the cell without rotation, as shown in Fig. 2.27(a).

Once a proper unit cell has been selected, it is next necessary to construct a set of linear reference axes by means of which this cell may be conveniently described as shown in Fig. 2.27(b). In this figure, a, b, and c may or may not be equal and α, β, and γ may or may not be equal to each other or to 90°. The various systems of axes give us the seven crystal systems. The two most commonly used ones in metallic materials are (1) cubic, in which $a = b = c$ and $\alpha = \beta = \gamma = 90°$, and (2) hexagonal, in which $a = b \neq c$ and $\alpha = \beta = 90°$ and $\gamma = 120°$.

As has already been stated, some of the axes of the seven crystal systems can be simplified by adding additional points per cell such as in the center of the cell or in the center of the faces of the cell, which gives us the 14 Bravais lattices. For example, the cubic system consists of the simple cubic (SC), body-center cubic (BCC) and face-centered cubic (FCC) cells as shown in Fig. 2.28(a), (b), and (c), which make up three of the 14 Bravais lattices. The hexagonal system contains only the simple cell as shown in Fig. 2.29. The hexagonal close-packed (HCP) cell as shown in Fig. 2.28(d) is a crystal structure cell, in which two atoms (or groups of atoms) are associated with each simple lattice cell at the origin at the 000 position and at a point within the cell at the $\frac{2}{3}\frac{1}{3}\frac{1}{2}$ position as shown in Fig. 2.30. A crystal structure is formed by associating with each point of a space lattice an atom or a unique group of atoms as a basis. The difference between a space lattice and a crystal structure is that a space lattice represents a regular array of points in space having identical surroundings, whereas a crystal structure represents an array of atoms or groups of atoms in

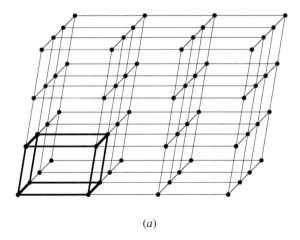

(a)

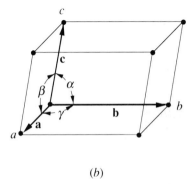

(b)

FIGURE 2.27
(a) A portion of a space lattice, with a unit cell outlined. (b) Description of the unit cell in terms of the lattice vectors **a**, **b**, **c**. The lattice constants a, b, c, and the interaxial angles α, β, and γ are shown. (*Adapted from B. D. Cullity, Elements of X-ray Diffraction, Addison-Wesley Pub. Co., 1956.*)

space referenced to a space lattice. The space lattice is a mathematical abstraction that serves only as a reference function. The crystal structure represents an array of atoms in space.

2.2.9.4 DESIGNATION OF POINTS, DIRECTIONS, OR PLANES IN A SPACE LATTICE OR CRYSTAL STRUCTURE. Points within a cell are expressed in terms of fractional coordinates such as the point within a body-centered cell that is designated as being in the $\frac{1}{2}\frac{1}{2}\frac{1}{2}$ position, and the atoms located in a hexagonal close-packed crystal structure cell are assigned to the 000 and the $\frac{2}{3}\frac{1}{3}\frac{1}{2}$ positions. All the remaining apparent points of the cell are duplicated by translation of the cell. Usually equivalent points that lie within the cell are designated, and whole numbers are avoided in point indices as they lie outside the reference cell.

The (Miller) *indices of directions* are specified by drawing a vector from the origin through a point in the desired direction and giving the coordinates of the point in terms of the lowest integers. For example, the direction of the vector drawn from the origin at 000 to either a point located at $\frac{1}{2}\frac{1}{2}\frac{1}{2}$ or a point at 111 would be designated as the [111] direction as shown in Fig. 2.31. A direction

	Lattice structure	Unit cell schematic	Ping-pong ball model	Number of nearest neighbors	Packing efficiency	Typical metals
(a)	Simple cubic	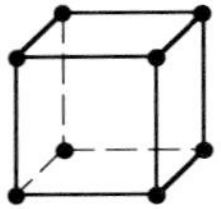		6	52%	None
(b)	Body-centered cubic	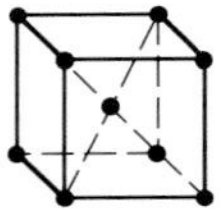		8	68%	Fe, Cr, Mn, Cb, W, Ta, Ti, V, Na, K
(c)	Face-centered cubic	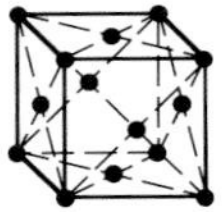	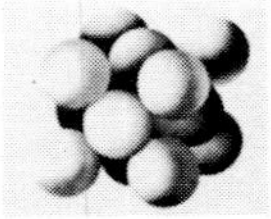	12	74%	Fe, Al, Cu, Ni, Ca, Au, Ag, Pb, Pt
(d)	Hexagonal close-packed	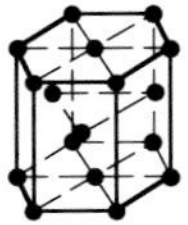		12	74%	Be, Cd, Mg, Zn, Zr

FIGURE 2.28

Comparison of some crystal structures: simple cubic, body-centered cubic, face-centered cubic and hexagonal close-packed showing the point models and hardball models of the unit cells. The number of nearest neighbors is the number of contacting neighbors each atom has, and the packing efficiency is the volume of spherical atoms occupied by the unit cell over the volume of the cell expressed in percent [10.6].

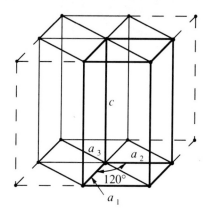

FIGURE 2.29
Relation of the (Bravais lattice) unit cell in the hexagonal three-axes system (shown in heavy lines) to that of the four-axes system. (*Adapted from C. S. Barrett and T. B. Massalski, Structure of Metals, McGraw-Hill, 1966.*)

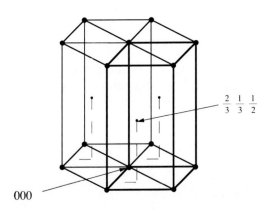

FIGURE 2.30
Crystal structure unit cell of a hexagonal close-packed crystal for the three-axes system (shown in heavy lines) and the four-axes system. In the former cell, the atoms may be assigned to the 000 position and the $\frac{2}{3}\frac{1}{3}\frac{1}{2}$ position. (*Adapted from C. S. Barrett and T. B. Massalski, Structure of Metals, McGraw-Hill, 1966.*)

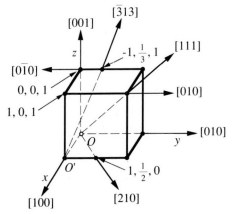

FIGURE 2.31
Indices of some common directions. To find a direction between two given points, take the coordinate difference. To find a direction from other than the indicated origin, move the origin such as from O to O'.

may be designated by a vector expressed as $t = ua + vb + wc$, where u, v, w are the smallest integers satisfying this equation. Any direction parallel to "t," regardless of its point of origin, is the same direction. If the coordinates of two points are given, the indices of direction may be obtained as the smallest integers proportional to coordinate difference of the indices of the points. For example, the indices of direction from a point 101 to a point 111 would be $(1-1)$, $(1-0)$, $(1-1)$ or the [010] direction.

The orientation of a plane in space can be designated by a system of notation called the *Miller indices of planes*. The Miller indices merely give the orientation and not the location of a specific plane in a space lattice. The Miller indices of a plane can be determined as follows:

1. Find the intercepts of the plane on the axes
2. Take the reciprocals of the intercepts
3. Reduce to the smallest whole numbers having the same ratio
4. Enclose in parentheses (   )

Some common planes in the cubic system are shown in Fig. 2.32. Following the above steps, one can obtain the (023) plane as follows: intercepts: $\infty, \frac{1}{2}, \frac{1}{3}$; reciprocals: $0, 2, 3$; lowest whole numbers: $0, 2, 3$; and enclosure: (023). Note that a plane parallel to an axis has an intercept of ∞ on that axis and a reciprocal of 0. Planes that would intersect the three axes of any (three-axes) system at $\frac{1}{2}, \frac{1}{2}, \frac{1}{2}$; 1, 1, 1; or 2, 2, 2 would be the (111) plane as shown in Fig. 2.33. Planes whose indices are negative of one another are parallel and lie on the opposite side of an arbitrary origin, for example, (210) and ($\bar{2}\bar{1}0$). Note that negative indices are designated by means of an overbar. The planes (*nh nk nl*) are parallel

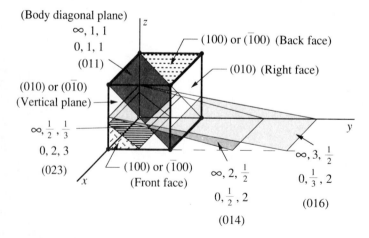

FIGURE 2.32
Miller indices of some common planes. Note that Miller indices of planes through the origin cannot be determined, so move either the plane or the origin.

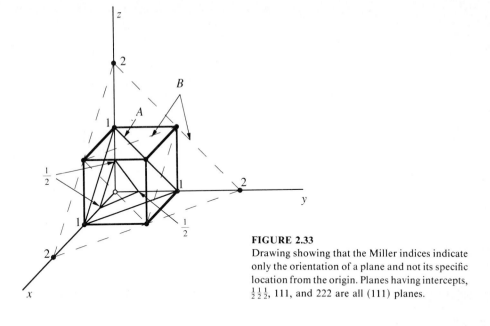

FIGURE 2.33
Drawing showing that the Miller indices indicate only the orientation of a plane and not its specific location from the origin. Planes having intercepts, $\frac{1}{2}\frac{1}{2}\frac{1}{2}$, 111, and 222 are all (111) planes.

to the plane (hkl) and have $1/n$ the spacing. The spacing (distance) between planes in the cubic system is given by

$$d = \frac{a}{\sqrt{h^2 + k^2 + l^2}} \tag{2.83}$$

where $a =$ the lattice constant (parameter). The angle between two planes in the cubic system is given by

$$\cos^2 \phi_{12} = \frac{(h_1 h_2 + k_1 k_2 + l_1 l_2)^2}{(h_1^2 + k_1^2 + l_1^2)(h_2^2 + k_2^2 + l_s^2)}, \tag{2.84}$$

where ϕ_{12} is the angle between the planes $(h_1 \, k_1 \, l_1)$ and $(h_2 \, k_2 \, l_2)$.

General points, directions, and planes may be designated as uvw, $[hkl]$, and (hkl), respectively. Directions and planes that belong to the same family are designated as $\langle hkl \rangle$ and $\{hkl\}$, respectively. All directions that have the same positive and negative permutations and have the same vector length in the unit cell belong to the same family as shown in Fig. 2.34. Likewise, planes that have the same positive and negative permutations and that have the same shape in the unit cell belong to the same family. For example, the family of planes $\{100\}$ in the cubic system consists of the following planes: $(100), (010), (001),$ $(\bar{1}00), (0\bar{1}0),$ and $(00\bar{1})$. In the hexagonal (three-axes) system, $(100), (010), (\bar{1}00),$ and $(0\bar{1}0)$ planes would belong to the $\{100\}$ family, and (001) and $(00\bar{1})$ planes would belong to the $\{001\}$ family. The former have a rectangular shape in the unit cell and the latter have a shape of a parallelogram.

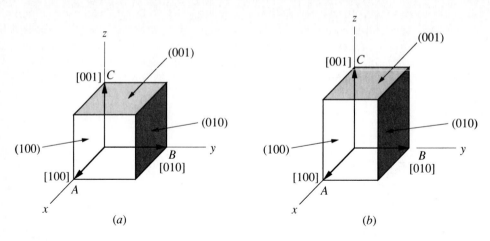

FIGURE 2.34
(*a*) Directions in the cubic system, such as **OA, OB, OC**, in which vector lengths *OA*, *OB*, and *OC* are equal, and directions of opposite sense belong to the same family, that is, ⟨100⟩ = [100]+[010]+[001]+[$\bar{1}$00]+[0$\bar{1}$0]+[00$\bar{1}$]. All the faces of the cube are squares and belong to the {100} family of planes. (*b*) Directions in non-cubic cells, much as the hexagonal (three-axes) cell, having the same lattice vector length belong to one family such as **OA** and **OB** and **AO** and **BO**, which have equal lengths, but vectors of different lengths from *OA* belong to another family, that is ⟨100⟩ = [100]+[010]+[$\bar{1}$00]+[0$\bar{1}$0], and ⟨001⟩ = [001]+[00$\bar{1}$]. The vertical faces are rectangles and belong to the {100} family of planes, whereas the top and bottom faces are regular parallelograms and belong to the {001} family of planes.

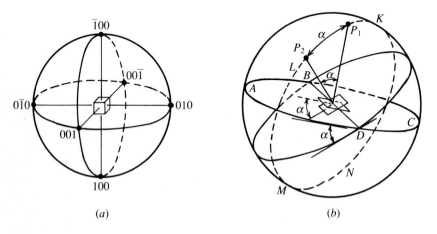

FIGURE 2.35
(*a*) Intersection of the poles and the traces of the {100} planes of a cubic crystal with the surface of a sphere. (*b*) The angle between two planes can be measured by measuring either the angle between their poles on a great circle or the angle between the traces of the planes. (*Adapted from B. D. Cullity, Elements of X-ray Diffraction, Addison-Wesley Pub. Co., 1956.*)

2.2.9.5 STEREOGRAPHIC PROJECTION. It is rather difficult to represent various planes and directions by drawing them in a sketch of a unit cell. Also, the angles between various planes usually cannot be measured in such a drawing. It is difficult, if not impossible, to represent such phenomena as the movement of dislocations and twinning by use of such a drawing. A useful tool for readily determining angles between various crystal planes and directions and representing the above phenomena is the stereographic projection.

Planes can be represented on a surface of a sphere by means of (1) the intersection of their poles with the surface or (2) the trace of the planes with the surface of the sphere as shown in Fig. 2.35(*a*). The angles between the planes can be determined by measuring the angle between the poles or between the traces of the planes on a great circle on the surface of the sphere as shown in Fig. 2.35(*b*). Since it is inconvenient to work with a sphere, a two-dimensional stereographic projection is used for this purpose instead.

To produce a stereographic projection, a small unit cell or crystal is placed in the center of a sphere as shown in Fig. 2.36. The poles of the desired planes

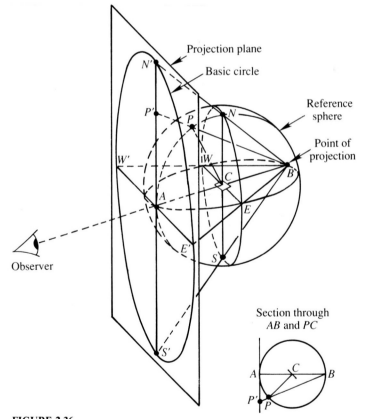

FIGURE 2.36
A graphical construction showing the stereographic projection. (*Adapted from B. D. Cullity, Elements of X-ray Diffraction, Addison-Wesley Pub. Co., 1956.*)

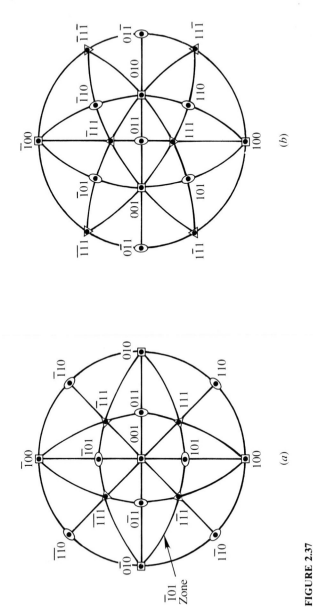

FIGURE 2.37

(*a*) Standard 001 projection of a cubic crystal, and (*b*) standard 011 projection of a cubic crystal. The 011 projection can be obtained from the 001 projection by rotating the latter 45° to the left on a Wulff net to be discussed later. (*Adapted from B. D. Cullity, Elements of X-ray Diffraction, Addison-Wesley Pub. Co., 1956.*)

are projected onto the surface of the sphere. A projection plane is placed normal to the diameter and at a point usually tangent to the surface of the sphere as shown in Fig. 2.36. The projection plane may be placed at some other convenient location instead, such as through the center of the sphere. The diameter AB may be taken colinear with some important axis of the unit cell such as the z axis. The poles are then projected from the opposite end of the diameter from point B from the surface of the sphere onto the plane such as projecting pole P to P'. The projection is viewed from the side of the plane opposite to the point of projection as shown in Fig. 2.36. Certain standard stereographic projections are made to an important plane normal to the axis of projection such as the (001) or (011) planes as shown in Fig. 2.37. The standard projections is oriented so that an important pole lies on the vertical axis such as the 100 pole at the bottom, as in Fig. 2.37. Then, in the cubic system, the 010 pole will lie at the right end of the horizontal axis. The poles at the opposite ends of the axes of the projection are just the negatives of the chosen poles since they lie on the opposite side of the origin or the center. The poles in between may be found by vector addition, such as the 110 pole is the algebraic sum of the indices in turn of the 100 and 010 poles, and in the cubic system they are 45° apart. Similarly, the 111 pole is the sum of the 110 and 001 poles, and it lies 35.3° from the 110 pole and 54.7° from the 001 pole.

To facilitate plotting of a standard projection, the poles lying on a zone are grouped together. Planes that are parallel to one line, such as an axis, belong to the same zone as shown in Fig. 2.38, and their normals or poles lie 90° from the line. For example, all the poles on the periphery of the stereographic projection in Fig. 2.37(a) have planes parallel to the [001] direction or the z axis and are 90° from it and lie in the [001] zone. In Fig. 2.37(a), poles $0\bar{1}0$, $1\bar{1}1$, 101, 111, and 010 lie in the [$\bar{1}01$] zone and are 90° from it. After a rough sketch is made of the projection, the poles can be located accurately by use of a graphing device called a *Wulff net*, such as is shown in Fig. 2.39. (The relationship of the Wulff net to the ruled projection sphere is shown in Fig. 2.40.) First, a plotting aid may be made to show the poles of a particular zone, which lie on a great circle. Only a few interplanar angles need to be found because the zone is symmetric. The interplanar angles may be calculated from Eq. (2.84) or they may be obtained

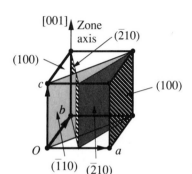

FIGURE 2.38
All shaded planes in a cubic lattice which are parallel to the [001] direction belong to the [001] zone. Note that the origin is placed at the lower left corner to the front. (*Adapted from B. D. Cullity, Elements of X-ray Diffraction, Addison-Wesley Pub. Co., 1956.*)

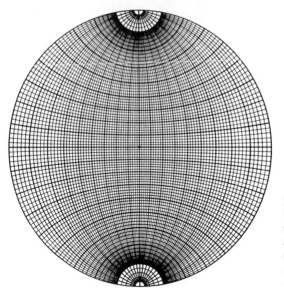

FIGURE 2.39
Wulff net with large divisions drawn to 10° and small divisions to 2°. Angles as measured on the net are angle true. (*Adapted from C. S. Barrett and T. B. Massalski, Structure of Metals, McGraw-Hill, 1966.*)

from a table such as abbreviated Table 2.1. A sheet of transparent paper placed over the Wulff net may be used to facilitate the plotting of the pole figure. Note that the pole designations are not enclosed in parentheses and that the poles lying only in one hemisphere are plotted. To obtain poles in the opposite hemisphere such as the $00\bar{1}$ pole, the poles are projected from the opposite end of the z axis, from point A in Fig. 2.36 in this case.

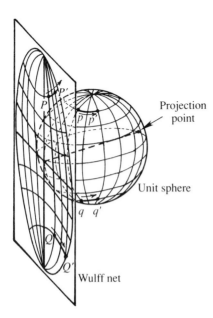

FIGURE 2.40
The relationship of the Wulff net to the ruled projection sphere. An angle as measured (1) by arc PP' on the Wulff net, (2) by arc pp' on the ruled sphere, and (3) between the crystal planes, are equal. (*Adapted from A. G. Guy, Introduction to Materials Science, McGraw-Hill, 1968.*)

TABLE 2.1
Interplanar angles (in degrees) in cubic crystals between planes of the form $\{h_1 k_1 l_1\}$ and $\{h_2 k_2 l_2\}$

$\{h_2 k_2 l_2\}$	$\{h_1 k_1 l_1\}$						
	100	110	111	210	211	221	310
100	0						
	90						
110	45	0					
	90	60					
		90					
111	54.7	35.3	0				
		90	70.5				
			109.5				
210	26.6	18.4	39.2	0			
	63.4	50.8	75.0	36.9			
	90	71.6		53.1			
211	35.3	30	19.5	24.1	0		
	65.9	54.7	61.9	43.1	33.6		
		73.2	90	56.8	48.2		
		90					

Largely from R. M. Bozorth, *Phys. Rev.* **26**, 390 (1925); rounded off to the nearest 0.1°.

2.2.9.6 POLE FIGURES. The crystalline grains of a metal or alloy may not be randomly oriented crystallographically, but may be clustered, to a greater or lesser degree, about a particular orientation called a *preferred orientation* or *texture* as discussed in the next section. Texture can be formed as a result of directional growth during casting or plating, due to rotation of the grains during plastic deformation such as cold rolling or wire drawing, and during preferred growth during recrystallization annealing.

An example of a preferred orientation or texture may be that of a wire produced by drawing a wire bar through a die. The annealed wire bar prior to drawing may have a more or less random orientation of its grains. During drawing the grains, such as for silver, for example, rotate so that the ⟨100⟩ directions become nearly parallel to the axis of the wire and the {100} planes develop a rotational symmetry about the axis of the wire. This preferred orientation or texture may be presented by showing the scatter of some convenient type of pole such as the 100, 110, 111, etc. Any pole may be selected that best portrays the texture or that is a matter of personal preference. This texture may be presented as shown in Fig. 2.41. If the vertical axis represents the axis of the wire and if the wire were a perfect crystal, the orientation of the crystal could be represented by either stereographic projections showing the 100, 110, and 111 poles as shown in Fig. 2.41(a), (b), and (c), or any other poles of interest. The wire, however,

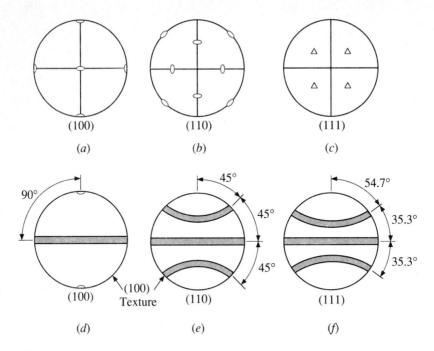

FIGURE 2.41

(*a*), (*b*), and (*c*) show projections of the 100, 110, and 111 poles of a cubic crystal respectively. (*d*), (*e*), and (*f*) show pole figures obtained by the rotation of each of the above projections about the vertical axis and rocking slightly about the horizontal axis to show a common wire texture. Each pole figure represents the same [100] texture but by use of different poles. (*Adapted from R. W. Hertzberg, Deformation and Fracture Mechanics of Engineering Materials, John Wiley & Sons, 1976.*)

will not have a perfect or ideal texture, but the orientation of the grains will be scattered about the axis of the wire with a symmetric rotation as shown in Fig. 2.41(*d*), (*e*), and (*f*). These pole figures may be generated by rotating the respective projections about the vertical axis and at the same time rocking them back and forth slightly about the horizontal axis.

Pole figures are usually obtained experimentally by use of x-ray diffraction techniques, which will not be discussed here. Preferred orientation or texture will be discussed further in another section in conjunction with anisotropy.

The three main differences between the standard stereographic projection and the (direct) pole figure are as follows:

1. The specimen in the pole figure is polycrystalline rather than a single crystal
2. The reference axes in the pole figure are oriented with respect to the external shape of the specimen
3. In the pole figure, only one crystallographic form of the pole is projected but for many crystals

2.2.9.7 SLIP AND TWINNING. Crystals and crystalline grains making up a metal or alloy usually deform plastically primarily by slip and to a lesser extent by twinning. Metals and alloys usually deform in shear regardless of the system of stresses applied.

Slip is defined as the ultimate shear displacement of discrete sections of a crystal relative to other adjacent sections. It usually takes place on the densest or closest-packed atomic planes and in the densest atomic direction as shown in Fig. 2.42. The densest planes are those of widest separation and the densest directions are those having the shortest Burgers vector (to be defined later). A slip plane and a slip direction in that plane constitute a slip system such as (111)[110] in Fig. 2.42(a) for the FCC crystal. The dominant slip systems formed

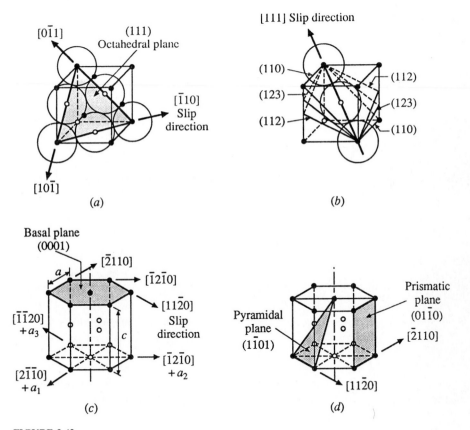

FIGURE 2.42
(a) Combined point and hardball model of a FCC metal showing one slip plane, (111), and three slip directions in that plane; (b) combined model of a BCC metal showing one close-packed direction, [111], with three potential slip planes of almost the same density of packing, (110), (112), and (123), which rotate about the slip direction (the indices refer to the type of plane and the type of direction only without regard to the origin); (c) probable slip plane, (0001), for a HCP metal having a $c/a > 1.633$; (d) probable slip planes for an HCP metal having a $c/a < 1.6333$. The c/a ratio for spheres is 1.6333 [3.6].

TABLE 2.2
Observed slip systems in crystals

Structure	Slip plane	Slip direction	Number of slip systems	
FCC Cu, Al, Ni, Pb, Au, Ag, γFe, ...	{111}	$\langle 1\bar{1}0 \rangle$	$4 \times 3 = 12$	
BCC αFe, W, Mo, β Brass	{110}	$\langle \bar{1}11 \rangle$	$6 \times 2 = 12$	
αFe, Mo, W, Na	{211}	$\langle \bar{1}11 \rangle$	$12 \times 1 = 12$	
αFe, K	{321}	$\langle \bar{1}11 \rangle$	$24 \times 1 = 24$	
HCP Cd, Zn, Mg, Ti, Be, ...	{0001}	$\langle 11\bar{2}0 \rangle$	$1 \times 3 = 3$	
Ti	{10$\bar{1}$0}	$\langle 11\bar{2}0 \rangle$	$3 \times 1 = 3$	
Ti, Mg	{10$\bar{1}$1}	$\langle 11\bar{2}0 \rangle$	$6 \times 1 = 6$	
NaCl, AgCl	{110}	$\langle 1\bar{1}0 \rangle$	$6 \times 1 = 6$	

in crystal structures commonly possessed by metals and alloys are shown in Table 2.2. (The procedure for determining the Miller-Bravais indices of planes and directions for the four-axis system shown in Fig. 2.42(c) and (d) is somewhat different from that used for the three-axis system presented earlier, and will not be discussed here.)

The density of packing of planes in a crystal can best be described by the hard-ball model of a crystal, which is built up by the stacking of dense layers of spheres. The densest packed layer of spheres is the closest-packed hexagonal array as shown in Fig. 2.43, which occupies 90.7 percent of the projected area. Both the FCC and HCP crystal structure of metals can be constructed by stacking this type of layer. The direction of stacking in FCC crystals is in the body-diagonal

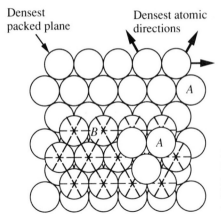

Densest packed plane

Densest atomic directions

FIGURE 2.43
Stacking of spheres to a form hexagonal close-packed structure. (1) First (bottom) layer; (2) second layer; and (3) third layer. (*Adapted from D. S. Clark and W. S. Varney, Metallurgy for Engineers, 1961.*)

or [111] type direction, and of the HCP crystal, it is in the direction of the z axis, or the [0001] direction in the four axis system as shown in Fig. 2.44. If the spheres in the third layer are directly over those in the first layer, the HCP crystal structure results as shown in Figs. 2.43 and 2.44(a). On the other hand, if the spheres in the third layer are over the voids of the first layer that were not used in placing the second layer, and the fourth layer is directly over the first layer, an FCC crystal structure results, as shown in Figs. 2.44(b) and 2.45. The densest packed directions in the FCC are the [110] type directions and for the HCP are [11$\bar{2}$0] type directions.

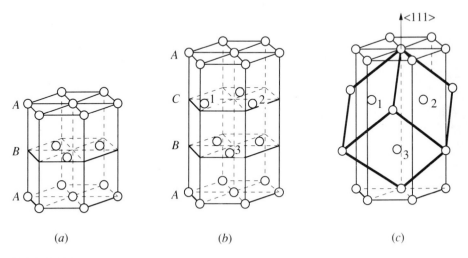

(a) (b) (c)

FIGURE 2.44
Stacking sequence for and relation between crystal structures: (a) HCP with stacking sequence ABABA...; (b) FCC with stacking sequence ABCABCA...; (c) position of the FCC unit cell relative to the hexagonal prism cell shown in (b) showing the direction of stacking. (*Adapted from W. Boas, Physics of Metals and Alloys, John Wiley & Sons, 1947.*)

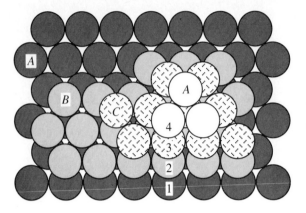

FIGURE 2.45
Stacking of spheres to form a face-centered cubic structure. (1) First (bottom) layer; (2) second layer; (3) third layer; and (4) fourth layer. (*Adapted from D. S. Clark and W. S. Varney, Metallurgy for Engineers, 1961.*)

The BCC crystal does not possess the densest packed structure. The densest packed plane in a BCC crystal of a metal is the oblique layer as shown in Fig. 2.46, which can be formed by skewing a square array until the angles shown in the figure are obtained. This layer forms the [110] type planes in the BCC crystal. The densest packed directions are the ⟨111⟩ directions. The (112) and (123) type planes are nearly as dense packed as the (110) type planes, so that slip can also readily take place on them. Consequently, this phenomenon is often called *multiplane* or *noncrystallographic slip*. These planes can be formed by rotating a plane around the [111] type direction to yield the slip systems shown in Fig. 2.42(*b*) and Table 2.2.

Twinning is of two types: mechanical and annealing (faulted growth). Mechanical twinning is the ultimate irreversible shear displacement of planes of a section of a crystal in the same direction and in an amount proportional to the distance of the plane from the twin plane and in such a manner so as to cause the twinned portion to be the mirror image of the untwinned portion as shown in Fig. 2.47. The twin systems in common crystal structures for metals are: in FCC {111}⟨11$\bar{2}$⟩, in BCC {112}⟨11$\bar{1}$⟩, and in HCP {10$\bar{1}$2}⟨$\bar{1}$011⟩. Since the amount of gross deformation produced by twinning is small, it will not be discussed here at length. The maximum extension when an entire zinc crystal is converted into a twin on the (10$\bar{1}$2) type planes is only 7.39 percent. The important role of

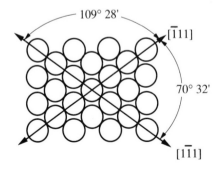

FIGURE 2.46
The densest packed plane in a BCC metal, {110}, and the densest-packed atomic direction, ⟨111⟩. The {110} planes are not formed by the closest-packed hexagonal layer of spheres but by the oblique (skewed square) array. (*Adapted from R. E. Reed-Hill, Physical Metallurgy Principles, 2nd Ed., Van Nostrand, New York, 1973.*)

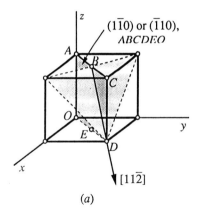

$(1\bar{1}0)$ or $(\bar{1}10)$,
ABCDEO

$[11\bar{2}]$

(a)

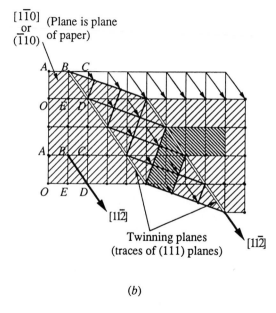

$[1\bar{1}0]$
or (Plane is plane
$(\bar{1}10)$ of paper)

$[11\bar{2}]$

Twinning planes
(traces of (111) planes)

$[11\bar{2}]$

(b)

FIGURE 2.47
(a) Unit cell showing a suggested twinning plane, (111), and a twinning direction, $[11\bar{2}]$, in FCC metals. (b) Schematic drawing illustrating the twinning process in an FCC metal. (*Adapted from J. Wulff et al., Metallurgy for Engineers, John Wiley & Sons, 1952.*)

twinning in plastic deformation comes not from the strain produced, but from the fact that orientation changes resulting from twinning may place new slip systems in a more favorable orientation with respect to the stress axis, so that additional slip can occur. Thus, twinning is important in HCP metals.

2.2.9.8 DISLOCATIONS. For many years scientists were not able to explain why the yield strengths of metallic materials were so low as compared to theoretical calculations. On the basis of the bonding forces between atoms, a much higher stress should be required to shear a crystal simultaneously over the entire slip plane analogous to sliding a deck of cards. It was first postulated, and then proved much later, that line defects called *dislocations* exist in all crystals. It requires a relatively small force to cause a dislocation to move across a crystal. When a dislocation moves from one side of a crystal to another, the crystal shears about one atomic dimension. The two conceptions of slip therefore are (1) simultaneous or homogeneous slip, in which slip occurs over the entire slip plane at once and which concept is now obsolete, and (2) consecutive slip, in which slip occurs gradually over the slip plane by movement of a dislocation and thereby requires much less stress. However, by the postulation of a dislocation, scientists overshot the goal. Now crystals were much weaker than they should be. To provide the necessary strength to a crystal, it was then necessary to provide barriers to impede the movement of dislocations such as other dislocation, precipitation particles, etc.

Two different types of dislocation models have been proposed: (1) macroscopic dislocations as shown in Fig. 2.48, which have their basis in continuum mechanics and which were proposed by Volterra and others about 1900–1910, and (2) microscopic crystalline dislocations, which were proposed by Orowan, Taylor, and Polanyi in 1934, as shown in Fig. 2.49. Both the continuum model and the crystalline model of dislocations may be of two types: (1) edge dislocations, and (2) screw dislocations as shown in Figs. 2.48 and 2.49. Burgers introduced the screw crystalline dislocation in 1939.

The continuum edge and screw dislocations can be formed by partially slitting a cylinder with a small axial hole as shown in Fig. 2.48(a) and (b), distorting it, and welding it back together. The amount of offset is called the *Burgers vector*. This model is convenient to use in the calculation of the elastic strain energy of a dislocation. The elastic strain energy, E_S, around a screw dislocation per unit length is

$$E_S = \frac{Gb^2}{4\pi} \ln \frac{R}{r_o} \tag{2.85}$$

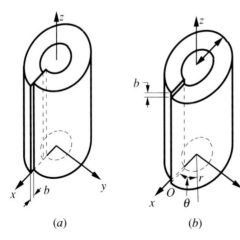

(a)　　　　　　　　(b)

FIGURE 2.48
Continuum mechanics models of (a) an edge dislocation, and (b) a screw dislocation simulating the distortion produced by the dislocations consisting of rejoined elastically distorted rings. (*Adapted from D. Hull, Introduction to Dislocations, Pergamon Press, 1965.*)

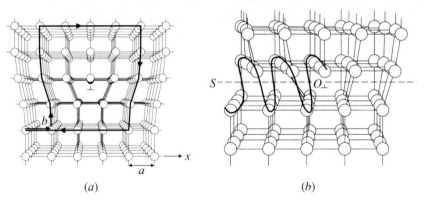

FIGURE 2.49
Simple cubic crystalline models of (a) an edge dislocation showing the line defect that extends through the crystal and in which the coordination differs from that of a perfect crystal. The edge dislocation shows a Burgers circuit yielding the Burgers vector (b). The helical arrangement of atoms is shown in the screw dislocation, which ends in an edge dislocation in this example. (*Adapted from A. G. Guy, Elements of Physical Metallurgy, Addison-Wesley, Pub. Co., 1959.*)

and the elastic strain energy around an edge dislocation per unit length is

$$E_S = \frac{Gb^2}{4\pi(1-\nu)} \ln \frac{R}{r_0} \qquad (2.86)$$

where G = shear modulus
  b = length of the Burgers vector
  ν = Poisson's ratio
  R = radius of cylinder (crystal), say, 10 mm
  r_o = radius of hole or plastic core = 30 nm

According to the above equations, the strain energy is proportional to b^2, so that slip will occur in the direction having the shortest Burgers vector, which is the densest packed direction.

The formation of an edge dislocation in a crystal may be formed by partially shearing a long crystal one atomic dimension edgewise as shown in Fig. 2.50. A line defect, called an *edge dislocation*, will form across the depth of the crystal at the terminus of the extra plane formed. If the end of the crystal is partially sheared one atomic dimension sidewise as shown in Fig. 2.51, a screw dislocation will be formed in the crystal. The name derives from the fact that the atoms along the dislocation are arranged in the form of a helical screw as shown in Fig. 2.49(b).

In view of the above discussion, two definitions of a dislocation may be formulated. A dislocation may be defined as a boundary between the slipped and the unslipped sections of a crystal. They consequently must possess many of the characteristics of other boundaries such as on a map, i.e., they cannot terminate within a crystal but must be continuous or terminate on other dislocations or on a surface. A dislocation may also be defined as a line defect in a

Extra plane

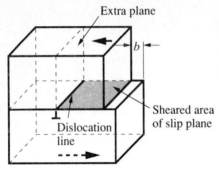

Dislocation line

Sheared area of slip plane

FIGURE 2.50
Schematic three-dimensional drawing showing how an edge dislocation might be hypothetically formed by partially shearing a crystal one-atom spacing resulting in an extra plane of atoms which terminates in an edge dislocation represented by the symbol ⊥. According to this orientation of the crystal this is a positive edge dislocation. One in the lower part of the crystal would be considered to be negative. (*Adapted from R. E. Reed-Hill, Physical Metallurgy Principles, 2nd Ed., Van Nostrand, New York, 1973.*)

crystal, in which the coordination differs systematically from the regular or ideal arrangement of atoms.

In both the edge and screw dislocations, the displacement vector is called the Burgers vector. The Burgers vector may be determined by traversing a Burgers circuit as shown in Figs. 2.49(a) and 2.51(b). The vectorial error of closure constitutes the Burgers vector. In a perfect crystal without a dislocation, a closed circuit is obtained. Note that in case of the edge dislocation the Burgers vector is perpendicular to the dislocation line, whereas in case of the screw dislocation, it is parallel to the dislocation line.

In order to explain the movement of dislocations in densely packed crystals such as FCC metals, the concept of a partial dislocation was introduced. Because the stacking planes in FCC and HCP metal crystals are offset and set in the interstices, the atoms move in a zigzag fashion so as to take the valley route as shown in Fig. 2.52, which requires less energy to move them.

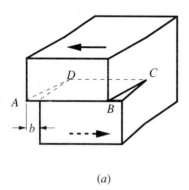

(a)

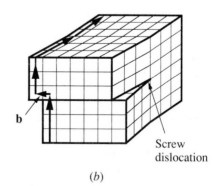

Screw dislocation

(b)

FIGURE 2.51
(a) Schematic drawing showing how a (left-hand) screw dislocation may be created by partially shearing a crystal sidewise one-atomic spacing equivalent to the Burgers vector (b). A Burgers circuit would yield the Burgers vector, which is parallel to the dislocation line. As the dislocation moves to the back of the crystal the entire top part of the crystal will have moved one atomic dimension to the left. (*Adapted from R. E. Reed-Hill, Physical Metallurgy Principles, 2nd Ed., Van Nostrand, New York, 1973.*)

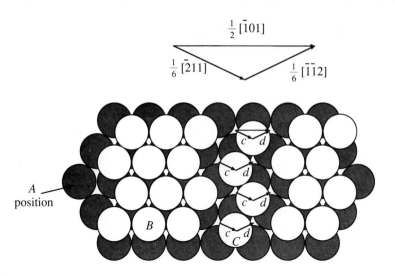

FIGURE 2.52

Bottom view of Fig. 2.49(a), but for an FCC crystal, with one (110) plane of atoms removed perpendicular to a (111) plane, the plane of the paper, and with one string of atoms shifted into a C position. (*Adapted from R. E. Reed-Hill, Physical Metallurgy Principles, 2nd Ed., Van Nostrand, New York, 1973.*)

The movement of a partial dislocation may be expressed by means of a vector equation such as follows:

$$\tfrac{1}{2}[\bar{1}01] = \tfrac{1}{6}[\bar{2}11] + \tfrac{1}{6}[\bar{1}\bar{1}2] \tag{2.87}$$

This equation means that in moving of an atom or a dislocation line from one equilibrium or slip position to another, which is $\tfrac{1}{2}$ of the distance to an equivalent void in the $[\bar{1}01]$ direction, the atom or dislocation line moves first $\tfrac{1}{6}$th of the distance to a stable void in the $[\bar{2}11]$ direction and then moves back $\tfrac{1}{6}$th the distance to an equivalent void in the $[\bar{1}\bar{1}2]$ direction. In other words, the atoms do not move directly from one equilibrium position to another, but they take the lower-energy, valley route as discussed above.

In terms of the lattice parameter a_0 the unit cell distance in a [110] type direction, which is a face diagonal, is $\sqrt{2}a_0$ and that in the [112] type direction is $(\sqrt{3}/2)a_0$ or $(\sqrt{6}/2)a_0$. In the movement of a dislocation, the atom moves 1/2 of the [110] distance or $\tfrac{1}{2}\sqrt{2}\,a_0$, or 1/2 of the equivalent distance from the origin to a point such as 1, 1, 0, and that in the [112] type direction is $\tfrac{1}{3}[(\sqrt{6}/2)\,a_0]$ or $(\sqrt{6}/6)a_0$, that is, 1/6 of the equivalent distance from the origin to a point such as 1, 2, 2.

Since partial dislocations repel each other, they tend to separate to form a stacking fault as shown in Fig. 2.53. Metals such as aluminum, that have high stacking fault energy, do not form stacking faults. However, metals such as copper, that have a low stacking fault energy, have stacking faults of about 10 atom widths.

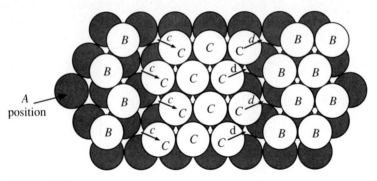

FIGURE 2.53
An extended dislocation formed by the separation of two partial dislocations creating a stacking fault as the atoms in the C positions are not in their regular equilibrium positions. (*Adapted from R. E. Reed-Hill, Physical Metallurgy Principles, 2nd Ed., Van Nostrand, New York, 1973.*)

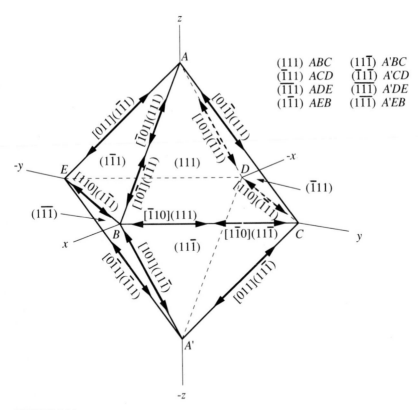

(111) *ABC*	(11$\bar{1}$) *A'BC*
($\bar{1}$11) *ACD*	($\bar{1}$1$\bar{1}$) *A'CD*
($\bar{1}\bar{1}$1) *ADE*	($\bar{1}\bar{1}\bar{1}$) *A'DE*
(1$\bar{1}$1) *AEB*	(1$\bar{1}\bar{1}$) *A'EB*

FIGURE 2.54
Octahedron formed by the {111} planes showing the 12 slip systems {111}⟨110⟩ of an FCC crystal. The slip systems of nonparallel planes forming mainly the forward tetrahedron (*BACA'E*) are shown. (Planes *ACD* (hidden) and *BA'E* (shown) are parallel and equivalent.) (Note that in the figure the directions are placed in front of the planes, that is, ⟨110⟩{111}.) (*Adapted from L. H. VanVlack, Elements of Materials Science and Engineering, Addison-Wesley Pub. Co., 1980.*)

TABLE 2.3
Four slip systems for FCC and their partial dislocation reactions

	Slip systems	Partial dislocation reactions
1.	$(111)[\bar{1}01]$	$\frac{1}{2}[\bar{1}01] = \frac{1}{6}[\bar{1}\bar{1}2] + \frac{1}{6}[\bar{2}11]$
	$(111)[0\bar{1}1]$	$\frac{1}{2}[0\bar{1}1] = \frac{1}{6}[\bar{1}\bar{1}2] + \frac{1}{6}[1\bar{2}1]$
	$(111)[\bar{1}10]$	$\frac{1}{2}[\bar{1}10] = \frac{1}{6}[\bar{2}11] + \frac{1}{6}[\bar{1}2\bar{1}]$
or	$(111)[1\bar{1}0]$	$\frac{1}{2}[1\bar{1}0] = \frac{1}{6}[1\bar{2}1] + \frac{1}{6}[2\bar{1}\bar{1}]$
2.	$(\bar{1}\bar{1}1)[101]$	$\frac{1}{2}[101] = \frac{1}{6}[2\bar{1}1] + \frac{1}{6}[112]$
	$(\bar{1}\bar{1}1)[011]$	$\frac{1}{2}[011] = \frac{1}{6}[112] + \frac{1}{6}[\bar{1}21]$
	$(\bar{1}\bar{1}1)[\bar{1}10]$	$\frac{1}{2}[\bar{1}10] = \frac{1}{6}[\bar{1}21] + \frac{1}{6}[\bar{2}1\bar{1}]$
or	$(\bar{1}\bar{1}1)[1\bar{1}0]$	$\frac{1}{2}[1\bar{1}0] = \frac{1}{6}[2\bar{1}1] + \frac{1}{6}[1\bar{2}\bar{1}]$
3.	$(1\bar{1}1)[011]$	$\frac{1}{2}[011] = \frac{1}{6}[\bar{1}12] + \frac{1}{6}[121]$
	$(1\bar{1}1)[\bar{1}01]$	$\frac{1}{2}[\bar{1}01] = \frac{1}{6}[\bar{2}\bar{1}1] + \frac{1}{6}[\bar{1}12]$
	$(1\bar{1}1)[110]$	$\frac{1}{2}[110] = \frac{1}{6}[121] + \frac{1}{6}[21\bar{1}]$
or	$(1\bar{1}1)[\bar{1}\bar{1}0]$	$\frac{1}{2}[\bar{1}\bar{1}0] = \frac{1}{6}[\bar{2}\bar{1}\bar{1}] + \frac{1}{6}[\bar{1}\bar{2}1]$
4.	$(\bar{1}11)[101]$	$\frac{1}{2}[101] = \frac{1}{6}[11\bar{2}] + \frac{1}{6}[211]$
	$(\bar{1}11)[0\bar{1}1]$	$\frac{1}{2}[0\bar{1}1] = \frac{1}{6}[\bar{1}\bar{2}1] + \frac{1}{6}[11\bar{2}]$
	$(\bar{1}11)[110]$	$\frac{1}{2}[110] = \frac{1}{6}[211] + \frac{1}{6}[12\bar{1}]$
or	$(\bar{1}11)[\bar{1}\bar{1}0]$	$\frac{1}{2}[\bar{1}\bar{1}0] = \frac{1}{6}[\bar{2}\bar{1}\bar{1}] + \frac{1}{6}[\bar{1}\bar{2}1]$

The following four different tools will now be used to illustrate the slip systems and the movement of dislocations in a FCC crystal: (1) the point model of a unit cell, (2) the hard-ball model of the slip plane, (3) the stereographic projection showing the slip systems, and (4) the Thompson tetrahedron showing the slip systems and the partial dislocation equations.

Since the FCC crystal of a metal has four nonparallel slip planes and three directions that lie in each plane as shown in Fig. 2.42(a), it has a total of 4 times 3 or 12 slip systems, which are shown on the octahedron in Fig. 2.54 and in Table 2.3. It is not convenient to work with such a representation as Fig. 2.54 when dealing with the movement of dislocations.

If we take a (111) plane of a FCC crystal as shown in Figs. 2.42(a), 2.45, and 2.55, its layer of atoms can be represented as shown in Fig. 2.56, and the directions of a movement of an atom of a dislocation is shown and the various directions of interest are indicated. The vectors showing the movement of the dislocation are for an atom that lies in the plane of atoms just above the one shown.

The twelve slip systems and the [112] type directions in which dislocations move can be easily represented by use of a stereographic projection, in which the traces represent the planes and the poles the directions as shown in Fig. 2.57. The traces of the (111) plane as an example can be visualized as a plane cutting down through the projection sphere at an angle. Simultaneous slip can be simulated by sliding the (111) plane up at an angle out of the page in the [$\bar{1}$01] direction represented by the $\bar{1}$01 pole. Slip in the [0$\bar{1}$1] direction can be simulated the same way. Slip in the [$\bar{1}$10] and in the [1$\bar{1}$0] directions may be simulated by sliding the angled (111) plane in their directions. Since they are colinear but of

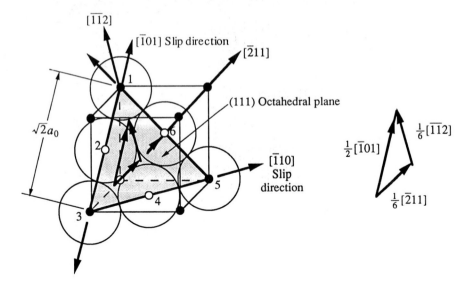

FIGURE 2.55
Combined hardball and point model showing the path of the atoms during slip on a (111) plane in an FCC metal by the movement of dislocations.

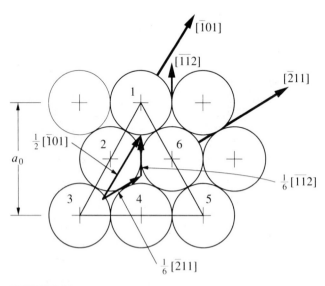

FIGURE 2.56
Closest-packed layer of atoms forming the (111) slip plane in an FCC metal showing the partial dislocation reaction, $\frac{1}{2}[\bar{1}01] = \frac{1}{6}[\bar{1}\bar{1}2] + \frac{1}{6}[\bar{2}11]$. The numbering of the atoms is the same as in Fig. 2.55.

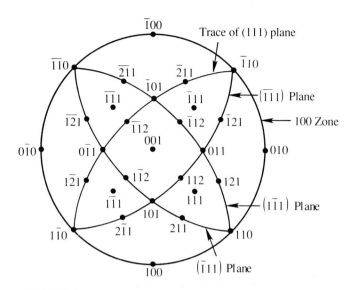

FIGURE 2.57

A 001 stereographic projection showing all 12 slip systems of a FCC metal, in which the (111) type traces represent the slip planes and the 110 type poles represent the slip directions. The [112] type directions for the movement of partial dislocations lie on each side of the [110] type slip directions such as [$\bar{2}$11], and [$\bar{1}\bar{1}$2] directions lie on each side of 101. Cross slip occurs in the directions at which the traces intersect.

opposite sense, this operation represents only one slip system. By selecting the slip directions from the other three (111) type planes all twelve slip systems can be readily obtained as shown in Table 2.3 along with their partial dislocation equations.

The [112] type directions occurring in dealing with partial dislocations may be located between the [110] type directions by vector addition. For example, the [$\bar{2}$11] direction may be obtained by the vectorial addition of $\bar{1}$01 and $\bar{1}$10, which lies 30° between them. The movement of the dislocation represented by Eq. (2.87) can be simulated by sliding the angled (111) plane up in the [$\bar{2}$11] direction a distance of $(\sqrt{6}/6)a_0$ and then back again parallel to the [$\bar{1}\bar{1}$2] direction a like distance to end up in the [$\bar{1}$01] direction for a distance of $(\sqrt{2}/2)a_0$. The foregoing may be presented much more easily by rotating the (111) type plane about the [$\bar{1}$10]-[1$\bar{1}$0] axis into the plane of the paper to form a 111 standard projection as shown in Fig. 2.58. If we consider that the center of the circle is at the origin and that $a_0 = 1$, we can represent the movement of this dislocation by laying off a distance of $\sqrt{6}/6$ to a convenient scale in the [$\bar{2}$11] direction and the same distance parallel to the [$\bar{1}\bar{1}$2] to give a distance of $\sqrt{2}/2$ in the [101] direction as shown in Fig. 2.58.

Another convenient method of representing the slip system and the movement of dislocations is by use of the Thompson tetrahedron in a unit cell as shown in Fig. 2.59(a) labelled *ABCO*. (The plane designated by *ABC* is the

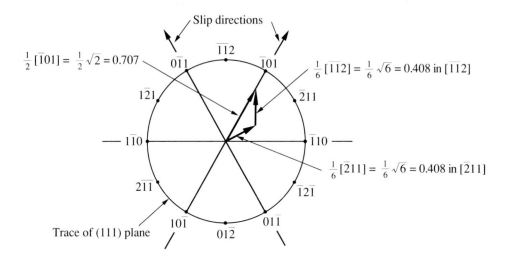

FIGURE 2.58

The 111 stereographic projection showing the 110 type slip directions and the 112 type directions for the movement of partial dislocations. The construction showing the path of the partial dislocation reaction, $\frac{1}{2}[\bar{1}01] = \frac{1}{6}[\bar{2}11] + \frac{1}{6}[\bar{1}\bar{1}2]$, where $a_o = 1$.

second (111) plane from the origin O.) The Thompson tetrahedron is a convenient graphical representation used for describing all the important dislocations and partial dislocation equations in *FCC* metals. The edges of the tetrahedron are parallel to the $\langle 110 \rangle$ slip direction, and the partial dislocations will move along directions from the corners to the midpoints of the faces of the tetrahedron shown in Fig. 2.59. If we unfold the tetrahedron, we obtain the various slip systems and dislocation equations for a *FCC* metal crystal as shown in Fig. 2.59(b). The caret symbol or arrowhead $>$ on the directions represents the sense of the direction. To go in the opposite directions take the negatives of the indices given.

2.2.9.9 SCHMID'S LAW OF CRITICAL RESOLVED SHEAR STRESS. The onset of plastic deformation in a single crystal takes place when the shear stress acting on the most favorable slip plane and in the most favorable slip direction reaches a critical value. The shear stress required to produce slip on a crystal plane in a slip direction at an appreciable rate is called the *critical resolved shear stress* (CRSS). (The time or rate variable must be introduced to take care of creep and of the effect of the rate of loading on the stress-strain curve.) For loading under a proper system of stress in the proper direction, slip may occur on several slip systems at the same time if they are available.

How can one determine the CRSS experimentally by use of a tension or compression specimen? Also, for example, on which one of the 12 slip systems would slip occur in a FCC specimen when loaded in uniaxial tension or compression?

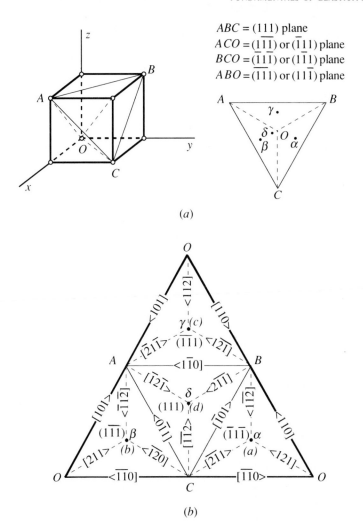

$ABC = (111)$ plane
$ACO = (1\overline{1}\overline{1})$ or $(\overline{1}11)$ plane
$BCO = (\overline{1}1\overline{1})$ or $(1\overline{1}1)$ plane
$ABO = (\overline{1}\overline{1}1)$ or $(11\overline{1})$ plane

(a)

(b)

FIGURE 2.59
(a) Thompson tetrahedron, $ABCO$, inscribed in a FCC unit crystal cell. (b) Developed view of a Thompson tetrahedron unfolded at corner O. One possible set of indices for the same planes and directions is presented. The caret $>$ indicates the sense of direction. To go in the opposite direction, take the negatives of the indices. (*Adapted from J. P. Hirth et al., Theory of Dislocations, McGraw-Hill, 1968.*)

Let us first take a HCP crystal system such as possessed by Zn, Cd, etc., that has only one prominent slip plane, the basal plane. Suppose that a HCP single crystal of zinc was grown in the shape of a round bar as shown in Fig. 2.60. The axial load in tension or compression that is required to produce slip depends not only on the critical shear stress for this particular material, but also on the orientation of the applied load with respect to the viable slip system as

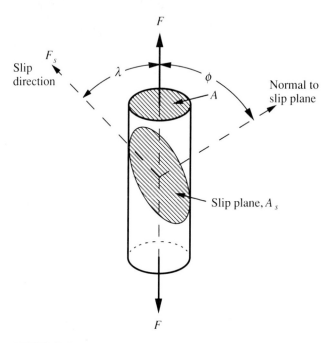

FIGURE 2.60
A drawing showing the orientation of the plane and the slip direction in a crystal relative to the loading axis for use in the determination of the critical resolved shear stress.

shown in Fig. 2.60. Also, the cross-sectional area of the slip plane, A_s, is not equal to that of the specimen, A. If ϕ is the angle between the axis of the single crystal rod and the normal to the slip plane then

$$A_s = \frac{A}{\cos \phi} \tag{2.88}$$

Furthermore, the axial load or force P must be resolved into the slip plane and in the slip direction. If λ is the angle between the load axis and the slip direction, the resolved force is, F_s

$$F_s = P \cos \lambda \tag{2.89}$$

The resolved shear stress (RSS), then is

$$\tau_{RSS} = \frac{F_s}{A_s} = \frac{P \cos \lambda}{\dfrac{A}{\cos \phi}} = \frac{P}{A} \cos \lambda \cos \phi = \sigma \cos \lambda \cos \phi \tag{2.90}$$

Equation (2.90) is called *Schmid's law*, which relates the resolved shear stress τ_{RSS} to the axial normal stress $\sigma = P/A$. According to this law for short-time yielding in single crystals, slip begins on that system which first sustains the critical value of the resolved shear stress, that is, $\tau_{RSS} = k$. Schmid's law, therefore, states that a single crystal yields on any particular slip system if the shear stress resolved on that slip plane and direction reaches a critical value on that slip system.

If the applied shear stress for any stress state under static equilibrium is specified by the tensor σ_{ij}, and the yield strength on system s as τ^s, Schmid's law may be expressed as

$$m_{ij}^s \sigma_{ij} \leq \tau^s \qquad (i, j = 1, 2, 3) \qquad (2.91)$$

where m_{ij}^s is the generalized Schmid factor and where the superscript s runs through all slip systems, positive and negative.

For the case of single slip in system $s = 1$ in a single crystal under pure tension in the z direction, m_{ij}^s degenerates into the Schmid factor

$$m = m'_{zz} = \cos \lambda \cos \phi \qquad (2.92)$$

The total incremental strain $d\varepsilon_{12}^s$ in a crystal in which the equality in Eq. (2.91) is fulfilled in any number S of systems s (using $\sigma_{ij} = \sigma_{ji}$)

$$d\varepsilon_{ij} = \tfrac{1}{2}(m_{ij}^s + m_{ji}^s)\, d\gamma^s \qquad (s = 1, \ldots, S), \qquad (2.93)$$

where $d\gamma^s$ = increment of shear strain on the crystal slip system s. Equation (2.91) is merely a special form of the general yield criterion

$$f(\sigma_{ij}) \leq C \qquad (2.94)$$

commonly used in the mathematical theory of plasticity. Similarly, Eq. (2.93) would follow from Eq. (2.91) by use of the associated flow rule

$$d\varepsilon_{ij} = \frac{\partial f}{\partial \sigma_{ij}}\, d\gamma \qquad (2.70)(2.95)$$

which is equivalent to the statement that the function f in the yield criterion in Eq. (2.94) is also the plastic potential.

If one inverts m in Eq. (2.91) and then multiplies the applied shear stress σ_{ij} $(= \sigma_{ji})$ by the incremental strain as $d\varepsilon_{ij}$ expressed by Eq. (2.93), one can see that the work done by the external forces equals the work done in the slip system [2.5].

The orientation factor $(\cos \gamma \cos \phi)$ is called the *Schmid factor*, which applies for the case of single slip systems in a single crystal under pure tension or compression in the z direction. If the axial yield stress, σ_Y, for a single crystal with only one prominent slip plane such as magnesium is plotted against the Schmid factor, a curve such as shown in Fig. 2.61 is obtained. The solid line represents the relationship given by Eq. (2.90) when $\tau_{RSS} = 434\ \text{kPa}$ (63 ksi). It should be noted that the axial stress necessary for yielding varies greatly with the Schmid factor, while the critical resolved shear stress τ_{CRSS} remains unchanged. When $\cos \gamma \cos \phi = 0$, for a slip plane normal to the axis, that is, $\phi = 0°$, or for a slip plane parallel to the axis, that is, $\phi = 90°$, for both of which $\sigma_y \to \infty$. The axial stress, σ, will be a minimum when λ and $\phi = 45°$ or $\cos 45° \cos 45° = 0.5$. A convenient statement of the yield condition, then, is that the normal stress $\sigma = \pm k$, the yield stress in shear.

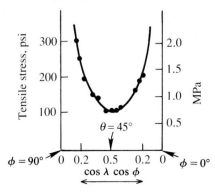

FIGURE 2.61
Axial yield stress in tension for single crystals of HCP magnesium of different orientation versus respective Schmid factors, cos λ cos ϕ. The smooth curve is for an assumed constant critical resolved stress of 434 kPa (63 psi). (*Adapted from R. E. Reed-Hill, Physical Metallurgy Principles, 2nd Ed., Van Nostrand, New York, 1973.*)

When a FCC crystal, on the other hand, is stressed to τ_{CRSS}, the crystal will yield on the most favorable slip system, i.e., the one possessing the greatest Schmid factor, and begins to rotate. When $\phi_o > 45° > \lambda_o$, then crystal rotation will bring about a reduction in the Schmid factor, thereby causing an increase in the load necessary for further deformation on the initial slip system, say, $(111)[\bar{1}01]$ with $\lambda_0 \cong 30°$ and $\phi_0 \cong 50°$. When the Schmid factor becomes less than that for another slip system that has rotated into a favorable position for slip, such as the $(\bar{1}\bar{1}1)[011]$ slip system, lattice rotation may occur between these two slip systems until the load axis is parallel to the $[\bar{1}12]$ direction in this case, when slip occurs on both slip systems.

If a full stress tensor σ_{ij} is impressed on a FCC crystal, any of the twelve $\{111\}\langle110\rangle$ slip systems can be activated. If all σ_{ij}'s are referred to the cubic axes, that is, $x = 11 = [100]$, $y = 22 = [010]$, and $z = 33 = [001]$, a generalized statement of Schmid's law can be given such as the following typical equation for one of the 12 slip systems $(111)[011]$:

$$\sigma = \frac{1}{\sqrt{6}}(\sigma_{22} - \sigma_{33} + \sigma_{12} - \sigma_{31}) \tag{2.96}$$

This generalized Schmid's law can be used for the construction of a yield locus.

2.2.9.10 RELATION BETWEEN SINGLE-CRYSTAL AND POLYCRYSTALLINE STRESS-STRAIN CURVES. The general (composite) shear-stress–shear-strain curve for a single crystal to cover all metals shown in Fig. 2.62 consists of three stages [2.6]:

I. Initial region of elastic response, which may be considered negligible, and the region of easy glide involving a very low rate of crystallographic hardening

II. Region of so-called linear hardening involving a greatly increased rate of crystallographic hardening

III. Region of dynamic recovery or parabolic crystallographic hardening

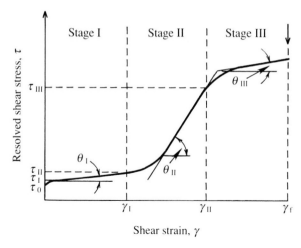

FIGURE 2.62
Schematic shear stress-strain for a single crystal loaded in tension showing the three stages of plastic deformation. $\tau_0 = \tau_{CRSS}$ and θ_1, θ_{11}, and θ_{111} are an indication of the rate of strainhardening [2.6].

All these stages are not always present for a given set of testing conditions. The presence of a given stage depends on a large number of factors such as crystal structure, crystal orientation, temperature, rate of straining, surface effects, alloying, etc. Stage III, which comprises in many cases most of the curve for a single crystal, closely resembles the stress-strain curve of the polycrystal for the same material.

Prior to studying the plastic deformation of polycrystals, one might first study bicrystals and specimens made up of a small number of crystals, called multicrystals, to determine the effect of grain boundaries and of different grain orientation. Polycrystals consist of specimens containing a large number of randomly oriented grains, usually more than 20 grains per specimen cross section.

A number of attempts have been made to relate the tensile stress-strain curve of the polycrystal to stage III of its single crystal. One of the early models that is both simple and applicable, is the one based on the work of Taylor [2.7]. According to this model, for a randomly oriented FCC polycrystal, one can relate the macroscopic stress σ to the critical resolved shear stress for slip τ_c and the macroscopic strain ε to the accumulated shear strain on all activated slip systems γ_c through the average Taylor factor $\bar{M}$ as follows:

$$\sigma = \bar{M}\tau_c \tag{2.97a}$$

$$d\varepsilon = \frac{\sum d\gamma_i}{\bar{M}} \tag{2.97b}$$

$$\varepsilon = \int_0^\gamma \frac{\sum d\gamma_c}{\bar{M}} \tag{2.97c}$$

In the original Taylor proposal, elastic strains were neglected and the strain in each grain was set exactly equal to the macroscopic average strain: $d\varepsilon = d\bar{\varepsilon}$ [2.8].

Inasmuch as volume strains cannot be imposed onto such a plastic-rigid material, five independent slip systems are necessary to satisfy any arbitrary prescribed strain. All possible combinations of five slip systems (except for some he overlooked) in FCC crystals were then considered by Taylor. He selected from among them any one of the combinations, which gives the lowest algebraic sum of shear, using a hypothesis based on an analogy of sliding rigid bodies. In other words, to permit any desired change in shape, such as will let grains fit together as in the aggregate as a whole, Taylor used the von Mises criterion that there must be at least five independent slip systems that must operate simultaneously. The principle of least work governs the choice of the systems that must operate. This principle states that the minimum of slip systems will function which can produce the required change of shape. This minimum number is five, except for special orientations. Furthermore, that group of five that will be chosen is the one for which the total internal work of deformation will be less than for any other group. It is now recognized that Taylor's minimum shear-sum criterion is in fact equivalent to fulfilling the yield criterion.

Using the principle of virtual work, Taylor considered a set of n shears that can satisfy the continuity conditions at a grain boundary. The energy expended, E_V, during a small strain of a unit volume of a grain on either side of the boundary is given by

$$E_V = \sum_{i=1}^{n} \tau_i \, d\gamma_i \tag{2.98}$$

where τ_i and $d\gamma_i$ refer to the resolved shear stress and the increment of shear strain on the ith system, respectively. This energy, E_V, must equal the work done, W_V, by the external tensile stress in producing an extension $d\varepsilon$ as follows:

$$W_V = E_V = \sigma \, d\varepsilon = \sum_{i=1}^{n} \tau_i \, d\gamma_i \tag{2.99}$$

In the restricted case, where τ_i has the same value in every slip system, then

$$\sigma \, d\varepsilon = \tau \sum_{i=1}^{n} |d\gamma_i| \tag{2.100}$$

which gives, by use of Eq. (2.97b),

$$\frac{\sigma}{\tau} = \frac{\sum\limits_{i=1}^{n} |d\gamma_i|}{d\varepsilon} = \bar{M} \tag{2.101}$$

or

$$\sigma = \bar{M}\tau \tag{2.102}$$

where $\bar{M}$ is the average Taylor factor.

To calculate the stress-strain curve for a polycrystal from the curve for a single crystal for a given orientation, the following relations are used:

$$\sigma = \bar{M}\tau \quad \text{and} \quad \varepsilon = \frac{\gamma}{\bar{M}} \tag{2.103}$$

which leads to

$$\frac{d\sigma}{d\varepsilon} = \bar{M}\frac{d\tau}{d\varepsilon} \quad \text{and} \quad d\varepsilon = \frac{d\gamma}{\bar{M}}$$

$$\frac{d\sigma}{d\varepsilon} = \bar{M}^2\frac{d\tau}{d\gamma}$$

(2.104)

where $d\sigma/d\varepsilon$ is the strainhardening rate. For a FCC polycrystal, it should be about 3.06^2 or 9.4 times the crystallographic hardening rate for the single crystal.

Comparison of an experimental stress-strain curve of FCC polycrystalline aluminum with those calculated from a single crystal with an orientation in the center of a stereographic triangle and one with an $\langle 111 \rangle$ orientation is shown in Fig. 2.63. Since the latter orientation has a greater number of slip systems operating, which is typical of a polycrystal, better agreement is observed.

A relationship similar to Eq. (2.102) can be obtained by rearranging Eq. (2.90)

$$\sigma = \frac{\tau}{\cos\phi\cos\gamma} = \tau\bar{M}'$$

(2.105)

Taylor computed $\bar{M}$ by finding the combination of slip systems that gives the minimum value of $\sum |d\gamma_i|$ and yet leads to the required external strain. All other combinations of slips that satisfy the conditions of continuity at the grain boundaries would require a higher value of σ than (τ/de) times the minimum value of $\sum |d\gamma_i|$ to produce the deformation [See Eq. (2.100).] Taylor assumed homogeneous deformation in all grains and thus, from von Mises' argument, that exactly five slip systems operated in each grain. Out of all the irreducible sets in FCC crystals, this set of systems is now the one that gives the lowest value of $M = \sum d\gamma_i/de$. [See Eq. (2.101).] Taylor calculated the value of $M = 3.1$.

More recent analyses determined that for the case of $\{111\}\langle 110 \rangle$ slip in FCC metals and $\{110\}\langle 111 \rangle$ slip in BCC metals, M is equal to 3.06. The lower limit of M for BCC crystals was determined to be 2.65. [2.8]

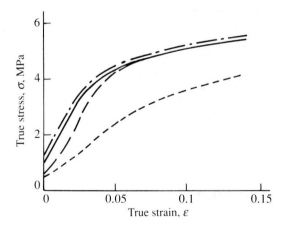

FIGURE 2.63

Comparison of an experimental (——) strain-strain curve for aluminum polycrystal with those calculated from a single crystal of center orientation (- - -) and from a single crystal of $\langle 111 \rangle$ orientation (— —). In the latter case subtraction of the initial transition region gives better fit to the experiment (— - —) [2.6].

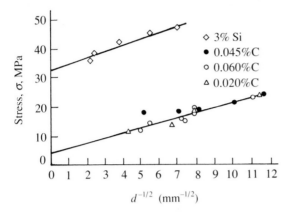

FIGURE 2.64
Relation between the lower yield stress and the grain diameter of iron alloys. (*Adapted from J. C. Suits and B. Chalmers, "Plastic Microstrain in Silicon–Ion," Acta Metallurgica, Vol. 9, Sept. 1961, p. 856.*)

2.2.9.11 RELATION OF GRAIN SIZE TO PLASTIC PROPERTIES. The treatment of polycrystalline deformation discussed in the previous section takes no account of the effect of grain size, but it simply assumes that the grain size is fine enough to ensure reasonably homogeneous deformation. At low and intermediate temperatures, where diffusion does not play a major role in the deformation of a polycrystal, the presence of grain boundaries strengthens both pure and alloy polycrystals. Part of the strengthening results from polyslip in various grains while another part results from the fact that in general grain boundaries are obstacles to the passage of slip (dislocations) across the boundaries. The size of the grains can therefore markedly affect the mechanical properties.

As shown in Fig. 2.64, the flow stress or yield strength, σ_Y, measured at constant strain for polycrystals depends at relatively low temperatures on the average grain diameter d, according to the Hall-Petch relationship

$$\sigma_Y = \sigma_i + k_y d^{-1/2} \tag{2.106}$$

where σ_i = the overall resistance of the lattice to dislocation movement other than due to grain size such as precipitation, solid solution, etc.

k_y = "locking parameter," which is a measure of the relative hardening contribution of grain boundaries

d = average grain diameter

The original mechanism proposed by Hall involved a blockage of the slip bands by the grain boundaries or the pile-up of dislocations against a grain boundary. This phenomenon is called the barrier effect. The flow stress is the external stress which, with the help of the pile-up, creates a critical stress concentration at a certain small distance r ahead of the pile-up as shown in Fig. 2.65. In this case r is equated to the average distance from the end of the slip plane and the nearest dislocation source in the adjacent grain. The Hall-Petch slope k can be expressed as

$$k = \bar{M}'^2 r^{1/2} \tau_{CRSS} \tag{2.107}$$

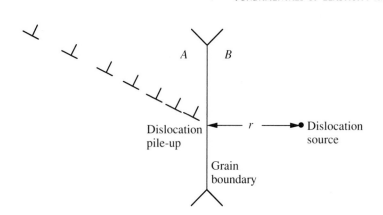

FIGURE 2.65
Slip in grain A is held up by the barrier effect of the grain boundary from propagating to grain B until the stress concentration at the average distance to the dislocation source is sufficient to generate dislocations, which will produce slip in grain B.

where τ_{CRSS} = critical resolved shear stress required to nucleate slip in the adjacent grain in the neighborhood of the boundary
$\bar{M}'$ = average Schmid orientation factor

2.2.10 Plastic Anisotropy

2.2.10.1 INTRODUCTION. Most materials used in metal forming are anisotropic, i.e., have different properties in different directions. Anisotropy may be of two kinds (1) mechanical and (2) crystallographic. Mechanical anisotropy or fibering is important in dealing with fracture, whereas crystallographic anisotropy or preferred orientation is more important in dealing with yielding and plastic deformation phenomena. Mechanical fibering may be due to the orientation and distribution of nonmetallic inclusions such as a silicate slag in steel. For example, the slag inclusion may be elongated in the direction of rolling and flattened out parallel to the surface of the sheet or plate. The steel may therefore have an ultimate tensile strength, say, 30 percent lower in a direction transverse to the direction of rolling than in the direction of rolling. Crystallographic anisotropy on the other hand is due to the preferred orientation of the crystalline grains that make up a polycrystalline material, due to processing. During cold rolling, for example, the grains of the metal rotate in a certain way so that certain crystal directions rotate parallel to the direction of rolling and certain planes rotate so as to be parallel to the surface of the sheet as shown schematically in Fig. 2.66. This alignment of certain preferred crystallographic directions and planes is called *preferred orientation* or *crystallographic texture* or merely *texture*. Since metal crystals have different properties in different directions, the textured material is anisotropic. On the other hand, if the grains of a polycrystalline metallic material are randomly oriented, the material is quasi-isotropic, and it is usually considered

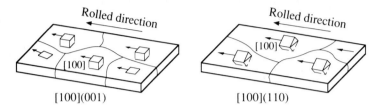

[100](001) [100](110)

FIGURE 2.66
Preferred orientation of commercially pure iron transformer sheets showing (*a*) a cube-on-face texture (100)[100], in which the {100} planes are predominantly parallel to the surface of the sheet and the ⟨100⟩ directions are predominantly parallel to the direction of rolling (R.D.), and (*b*) a cube-on-edge texture (110)[100], in which the {110} planes are predominantly parallel to the surface of the sheet and the ⟨100⟩ directions are predominantly parallel to the rolling direction. (*Adapted from L. A. VanVlack, Materials Science for Engineers, Addison-Wesley Pub. Co., 1970.*)

to be isotropic. The recrystallization of a cold-worked material by annealing usually does not remove the crystallographic texture, but it may even produce a different texture. The cold-worked texture is never perfect, but a distribution about a certain ideal texture usually exists as shown in Fig. 2.67. It may even have a mixed texture of two or more different ideal textures. The textures of different degrees of complexity have been represented for years by pole figures such as the one shown in Fig. 2.68 for a heavily cold-rolled iron-silicon alloy showing scatter about the (100)[110] ideal texture. The theory of how the crystalline grains rotate during certain simple cold-forming operations is fairly well developed, and computer programs have been developed to predict the texture expected.

Crystallographic texture is discussed elsewhere in regard to how the effect of texture or anisotropy affects the deformation of a sheet during forming by the

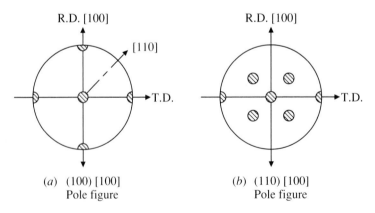

(*a*) (100) [100]
Pole figure

(*b*) (110) [100]
Pole figure

FIGURE 2.67
(*a*) A schematic (100)[100] pole figure for the texture shown in Fig. 2.66(*a*). (*b*) A schematic (110)[100] pole figure for the texture shown in Fig. 2.66(*b*). (*Adapted from B. D. Cullity, Elements of X-ray Diffraction, Addison-Wesley Pub. Co., 1956.*)

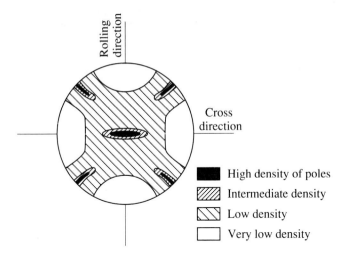

FIGURE 2.68
A {100} pole figure for heavily cold-rolled iron-silicon alloy. The ideal texture would be equivalent to that shown in Fig. 2.67 with a [110] type direction parallel to the direction of rolling. This figure can be obtained by oscillating Fig. 2.67(a) slightly about the [110] direction. (*Adapted from C. S. Barrett and T. B. Massalski, Structure of Metals, McGraw-Hill, 1966.*)

determination of the anisotropic, plastic strain ratio r. At this point, anisotropy will be discussed from the point of view of continuum plasticity without regard to its origin.

2.2.10.2 ANISOTROPIC CONTINUUM PLASTICITY THEORY. The continuum theory of plasticity (continuum mechanics) attempts to describe the stress-strain behavior of a continuum on the basis of postulated yield criteria without regard to internal structure. Crystal plasticity on the other hand is based on the slip and twinning behavior in individual grains of a polycrystalline metal, and it attempts to synthesize the polycrystalline behavior on this basis. The difference between the two approaches is most apparent in the analysis of anisotropic plastic behavior. Continuum mechanics also bypasses all of the details involved with dislocation mechanics.

Mathematical modeling of sheetmetal forming operations requires a yield criterion that describes the anisotropic yielding behavior of the sheetmetal.

Plasticity continuum theory was originally developed for an isotropic material as given by Eq. (2.73) in the section on "Stress-strain relationships in plasticity." The theory was then modified such as by Hill to explain the effects of anisotropy on the forming processes by incorporating the "parameters of anisotropic plasticity" or the "coefficients of anisotropy" [2.9].

Of the various theories of anisotropic plasticity without regard to origin and based on the modification of the von Mises yield criterion and its associated flow rule, the one postulated by Hill is the simplest to understand and the most used. Hill's theory of anisotropy is based on the following assumptions: (1) the anisotropic parameters increase in strict proportion as straining proceeds; (2) the effective stress is a function only of the total plastic work; (3) the state of anisotropy possesses three orthogonal axes of anisotropy, x, y, and z about which the properties have twofold symmetry; (4) the hydrostatic state of stress does not influence yielding; and (5) there is no Bauschinger effect, i.e., the stress-strain curves in tension and compression are mirror images [2.4].

In a rolled sheet, it is conventional to take the x, y, and z axes in the rolling, transverse, and through-thickness directions, respectively.

If the x, y, and z axes are chosen coincident with the axes of anisotropy, the anisotropic yield criterion can be written in the form [2.10]

$$2f(\sigma_{ij}) = F(\sigma_y - \sigma_z)^2 + G(\sigma_z - \sigma_x)^2 + H(\sigma_x - \sigma_y)^2$$
$$+ 2L\tau_{yz}^2 + 2M\tau_{zx}^2 + 2N\tau_{xy}^2 = 1 \tag{2.108}$$

where $f(\sigma_{ij})$ is an anisotropic yield function, and F, G, H, L, M, and N are constants, which characterize the current state of anisotropy, and are called the coefficients of anisotropy. If $F = G = H$, and $L = M = N = 3F$, the von Mises criterion obtains. In regard to the above equation, it is assumed that there is no Bauschinger effect and that the hydrostatic stress does not influence yielding. If σ_x, σ_y, and σ_z are the tensile yield strengths of specimens taken in the x, y, and z directions, respectively, and because the normal stresses in the other directions and the shear stresses are zero, the yield stresses of tensile specimens taken in the anisotropic directions in terms of the coefficients of anisotropy are

$$\sigma_x^2 = \frac{1}{G+H} \qquad \sigma_y^2 = \frac{1}{H+F} \qquad \text{and} \qquad \sigma_z^2 = \frac{1}{F+G} \tag{2.109}$$

The constants L, M, and N can be evaluated from shear tests.

Calculations of the yield loci shapes, based on the upper bound analyses by Bishop and Hill, have been computed for FCC and BCC metals with crystallographic textures that are relatively symmetric about the sheet normal z, that is, $r_{0°} = r_{45°} = r_{90°} \neq 1$ [2.4]. (The r value, or plastic strain ratio r_i, and the significance of this relationship are discussed subsequently and in Chaps. 10 and 11. The plastic strain ratio $r_i = \varepsilon_w / \varepsilon_t$ is measured from tensile test specimens cut at 0, 45, and 90 degrees to the direction of rolling of the sheet prior to forming.) Such calculations for a wide range of textures indicate that the Hill yield criterion tends to overestimate the effects of the r value on the shape of the yield loci. For loading conditions in which x, y, and z are the principal stress axes, the trends of the above calculations are better represented by a generalization of Hill's criterion of the form

$$F|\sigma_2 - \sigma_3|^a + G|\sigma_3 - \sigma_1|^a + H|\sigma_1 - \sigma_2|^a = 1 \tag{2.110}$$

where the exponent a is much larger than the value 2 of Hill's criterion.

For a planar isotropic material and for plane stress loading, the yield criterion is

$$|\sigma_1|^a + |\sigma_2|^a + r|\sigma_1 - \sigma_2|^a = (r+1)\sigma_y^a \tag{2.111}$$

The exponent a has been estimated to be approximately 6 for BCC metals and 8 to 10 for FCC metals. With increasing values of a, the yield loci approach the Tresca locus.

Hill, as discussed by Mellor and Parman [2.11], proposed a new yield criterion for planar isotropy of the form

$$(1+2r)|\sigma_1 - \sigma_2|^{m'} + |\sigma_1 + \sigma_2|^{m'} = 2(1+r)\sigma_Y^{m'} \tag{2.112}$$

where σ_Y is the yield strength in uniaxial tension, r is the usual anisotropic, plastic strain-ratio measured in uniaxial tension, and m' is a new parameter, which is analogous to the exponent a in Eqs. (2.110) and (2.111), and which is also determined experimentally. For this yield locus to be convex $m' \geq 1$. When $m' < 2$, the yield locus is elongated in the direction of equal biaxial tension as shown in Fig. 2.69.

The flow rules may be developed by using

$$d\varepsilon_{ij} = \frac{\partial f(\sigma_{ij})}{\partial \sigma_{ij}} (d\lambda) \tag{2.70}$$

where $f(\sigma_{ij})$ is the anisotropic yield function, Eq. (2.108). Differentiating Eq. (2.108) gives the following flow rules for a rigid-plastic material (see Fig. 3.1) [2.4]:

$$d\varepsilon_x = d\lambda[H(\sigma_x - \sigma_y) + G(\sigma_x - \sigma_z)] \qquad d\varepsilon_{yz} = d\varepsilon_{zy} = d\lambda L\tau_{yz} \tag{2.113a}$$

$$d\varepsilon_y = d\lambda[F(\sigma_y - \sigma_z) + H(\sigma_y - \sigma_x)] \qquad d\varepsilon_{zx} = d\varepsilon_{xz} = d\lambda M\tau_{zx} \tag{2.113b}$$

$$d\varepsilon_z = d\lambda[F(\sigma_z - \sigma_y) + G(\sigma_z - \sigma_x)] \qquad d\varepsilon_{xy} = d\varepsilon_{yx} = d\lambda N\tau_{xz} \tag{2.113c}$$

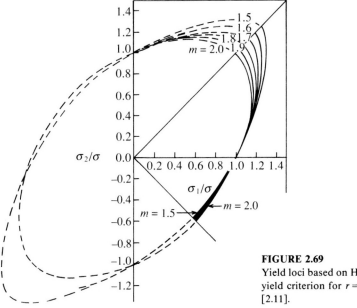

FIGURE 2.69
Yield loci based on Hill's new anisotropic yield criterion for $r = 1.0$. (See Fig. 2.71.) [2.11].

If an uniaxial tensile specimen is taken from a sheet lying in the (x, y) plane with its axis in the x-direction, then the stress components $\sigma_x \geq \sigma_y = \sigma_z = 0$ and, from Eq. (2.113), the ratios of the plastic strain increments are

$$d\varepsilon_x : d\varepsilon_y : d\varepsilon_z = G + H : -H : -G \qquad (2.114)$$

where $d\varepsilon_x$, $d\varepsilon_y$, and $d\varepsilon_z$ are the plastic strain increments in the longitudinal, width, and thickness directions respectively. In sheetmetal forming, the ratio of the width to thickness strain increments, known as the *r value* or *plastic strain ratio*, is a much used parameter for assessing the anisotropy of sheet material. Since the x-axis is taken in the direction of rolling, i.e., makes an angle of $0°$ with the direction of rolling as shown in Fig. 2.70, the r value is expressed in terms of Hill's coefficients of Eq. (2.108) as

$$r = r_o = \frac{H}{G} = \frac{\varepsilon_w^{0°}}{\varepsilon_t^{0°}} \qquad (2.115)$$

Similarly for an in-plane, uniaxial tensile specimen cut in the y-direction or $90°$ from the direction of rolling

$$d\varepsilon_x : d\varepsilon_y : d\varepsilon_z = -H : F + H : -F$$

$$r_y = r_{90°} = \frac{H}{F} = \frac{\varepsilon_w^{90°}}{\varepsilon_t^{90°}} \qquad (2.116)$$

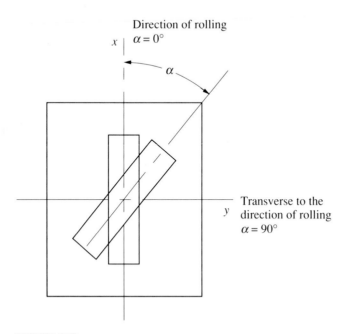

FIGURE 2.70
Method of taking tensile specimens from a sheet relative to the direction of rolling for use in determining the plastic strain ratio r_α. (See Fig. 10.2.)

If during the deformation of sheetmetal, the forces act only in the plane of the sheet, the only possible components are σ_x, σ_y, and τ_{xy}. The components normal and tangential to the surface of the sheet, σ_z, τ_{yz}, and τ_{zx}, will be zero. Then the yield criterion given in Eq. (2.108) reduces to

$$(G+H)\sigma_x^2 - 2H\sigma_x\sigma_y + (H+F)\sigma_y^2 + 2N\tau_{xy}^2 = 1 \qquad (2.117)$$

To obtain N, it is necessary to cut an in-plane, uniaxial tensile specimen at an angle α to the x-direction as shown in Fig. 2.70, so that

$$\sigma_x = \sigma_\alpha \cos^2 \alpha \qquad \sigma_y = \sigma_\alpha \sin^2 \alpha \qquad \tau_{xy} = \sigma_\alpha \sin \alpha \cos \alpha \qquad (2.118)$$

By substituting these values into Eqs. (2.113) one obtains the equations for the increment strains. The following expression for r_α can then be obtained:

$$r_\alpha = \frac{d\alpha + \pi/2}{d\varepsilon_2} = \frac{H + (2N - F - G - 4H)(\sin^2 \alpha \cos^2 \alpha)}{F \sin^2 \alpha + G \cos^2 \alpha} \qquad (2.119)$$

If $\alpha = 45°$, then

$$r_{45°} = \frac{2N - (F + G + 3H)}{2(F + G)} \qquad (2.120)$$

By substituting and rearranging, one obtains

$$\frac{N}{G} = \left(r_{45°} + \frac{1}{2}\right)\left(H + \frac{r_{0°}}{r_{90°}}\right) \qquad (2.121)$$

In the above derivations of the ratios of the parameters, it was assumed that the ratios remain constant with plastic straining, which means that the initial state of anisotropy remains unchanged by plastic straining. Also, material initially isotropic remains so during plastic straining.

2.2.10.3 MEASUREMENT OF THE PLASTIC ANISOTROPY STRAIN RATIO, r. The plastic anisotropy strain ratio r is usually determined manually as will be illustrated in Problem 3.13 in Chap. 3. It can, however, be measured more or less automatically. In one of these, a tensile specimen is inserted into the tensile testing machine and the initial and final lengths are monitored using a linear displacement transducer. All the measurements are stored electronically, and the r value is calculated by an analog computer. The r value can also be measured conveniently and rapidly by a specially designed magnetostrictive oscillator. This method is based on the principle that the magnetic and mechanical properties of crystals vary in different crystallographic directions. Since the r value depends on the variation of properties in different directions in the sheet due to the preferred orientation of the crystalline grains as a result of cold working, it is possible to measure r by use magnetostrictive properties.

2.2.10.4 EFFECTIVE STRESS AND EFFECTIVE STRAIN RELATIONS FOR AN ANISOTROPIC MATERIAL. Expressions for effective (generalized or equivalent) stress $\bar{\sigma}$, and effective strain increment, $d\bar{\varepsilon}$, can be written for an anisotropic material by use of a theory proposed by Hill as discussed by Hasek [2.12] as

$$\bar{\sigma} = \left\{ \frac{3}{2} \frac{1}{F+G+H}[F(\sigma_y - \sigma_z)^2 + G(\sigma_z - \sigma_x)^2 \right.$$

$$\left. + H(\sigma_x - \sigma_y)^2 + 2L\tau_{yx}^2 + M\tau_{zx}^2 + 2N\tau_{xy}^2] \right\}^{1/2} \quad (2.122)$$

$$d\bar{\varepsilon} = [\tfrac{2}{3}(F+G+H)]^{1/2}$$

$$\times \left\{ \left[\frac{F(G\,d\varepsilon_y - H\,d\varepsilon_z)^2 + G(F\,d\varepsilon_y - H\,d\varepsilon_z)^2 + H(F\,d\varepsilon_x - G\,d\varepsilon_y)^2}{(FG + GH + HF)^2} \right. \right.$$

$$\left. \left. + \frac{2d\gamma_{zy}^2}{L} + \frac{2d\gamma_{zy}^2}{N} + \frac{2d\gamma_{xy}^2}{N} \right] \right\} \quad (2.123)$$

where F, G, H, L, M and N are the coefficients of anisotropy.

Equation (2.122) reduces to the von Mises yield criterion when anisotropy is negligible, i.e., for $F = G = H$ and $L = M = N = 3F$ [2.10].

For *simple tension* along the rolling direction $\sigma_x = \sigma_{0°}$, $\sigma_z = \sigma_y = 0$, $\tau_{xz} = \tau_{zx} = \tau_{xy} = 0$, and Eqs. (2.122) and (2.123) reduce to

$$\bar{\sigma} = \sqrt{\frac{3}{2}} \left[\frac{1 + r_{0°}}{1 + r_{0°} + r_{0°}/r_{90°}} \right]^{1/2} \sigma_{0°} \quad (2.124a)$$

$$\bar{\varepsilon} = \sqrt{\frac{2}{3}} \left[\frac{1 + r_{0°} + r_{0°}/r_{90°}}{1 + r_{0°}} \right]^{1/2} \varepsilon_{0°} \quad (2.124b)$$

where $\sigma_{0°}$ and $\varepsilon_{0°}$ are the axial stress and strain, respectively, in the rolling direction. The similar equations for simple tension in the transverse direction are

$$\bar{\sigma} = \sqrt{\frac{3}{2}} \left[\frac{1 + r_{90°}}{1 + r_{90°} + r_{90°}/r_{0°}} \right]^{1/2} \sigma_{90°} \quad (2.125a)$$

$$\bar{\varepsilon} = \sqrt{\frac{2}{3}} \left[\frac{1 + r_{90°} + r_{90°}/r_{0°}}{1 + r_{90°}} \right]^{1/2} \varepsilon_{90°} \quad (2.125b)$$

For normal anisotropy and planar isotropy, i.e., where there is rotational isotropic symmetry about the z-axis (normal to the sheet) so that $r_{0°} = r_{45°} = r_{90°} \neq 1$ and r is the normal anisotropic index, Eqs. (2.124) and (2.125) reduce to

$$\bar{\sigma} = \sqrt{\frac{3}{2}} \left[\frac{1 + r}{2 + r} \right]^{1/2} \sigma \quad (2.126a)$$

$$\bar{\varepsilon} = \sqrt{\frac{2}{3}} \left[\frac{2 + r}{1 + r} \right]^{1/2} \varepsilon \quad (2.126b)$$

where σ and ε are the axial stress and strain, respectively. Note that, on this basis, $\bar{\sigma}$ is equal to the axial stress σ and $\bar{\varepsilon}$ is equal to the axial strain ε only when $r = 1$.

More generally, *for the biaxial deformation* of a sheet having rotational symmetry, Eqs. (2.122) and (2.123) reduce to

$$\bar{\sigma} = \sqrt{\frac{3}{2}\left[\left(\frac{1+r}{2+r}\right)\left\{\sigma_x^2 + \sigma_y^2 - \left(\frac{2r}{1+r}\right)\sigma_x\sigma_y\right\}\right]^{1/2}} \qquad (2.127)$$

and for the case where the *volume is also constant*

$$d\bar{\varepsilon} = \sqrt{\frac{2}{3}\left[\frac{(2+r)(1+r)}{(1+2r)}\left\{d\varepsilon_x^2 + d\varepsilon_y^2 + \left(\frac{2r}{1+r}\right)d\varepsilon_x\,d\varepsilon_y\right\}\right]^{1/2}} \qquad (2.128)$$

The yield locus can be referred to the uniaxial tensile stress σ by equating Eqs. (2.126) and (2.127) to obtain, for the case of *plane stress* ($\sigma_z = 0$),

$$\sigma_x^2 + \sigma_y^2 - \left(\frac{2r}{1+r}\right)\sigma_x\sigma_y = \sigma^2 \qquad (2.129)$$

By dividing by σ^2, substituting, and rearranging, one obtains

$$\frac{\sigma_x^2}{\sigma^2} = \left(1 + \alpha^2 - \frac{2\alpha r}{r+1}\right)^{-1} \qquad (2.130)$$

where $\alpha = \sigma_y/\sigma_x$ [2.4].

This yield criterion plots as shown in Fig. 2.71, where $r = 1$, the yield locus is that for an isotropic material in which $r_{0°} = r_{45°} = r_{90°} = r = 1$, and the standard von Mises ellipse results.

The higher values of r lead to increased resistance to yielding under biaxial tension, which may form the basis for appreciable texture hardening. For example,

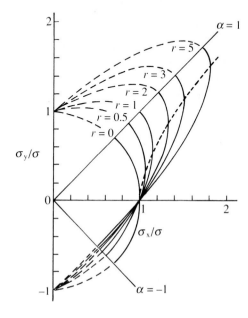

FIGURE 2.71
Plot of the normalized stresses for plane-stress ($\sigma_z = 0$) (solid lines) of the yield loci for materials with rotational symmetry about the z axis, i.e., with planar anisotropy, according to the simplified Hill criterion of Eq. (2.129). Note that in biaxial tension or biaxial compression the effect of increasing r is to increase the biaxial yield stress relative to the uniaxial yield stress. The dashed line is the locus condition for plane strain $\varepsilon_y = 0$ [2.4].

for balanced biaxial tension, where $\sigma_x = \sigma_y$ and $\alpha = 1$ and $r = 5$, $\sigma_y/\sigma_x = \sqrt{3} = 1.732$, or a 73 percent increase over that which would be expected from an isotropic material, where $r = 1$ [2.4].

From the yield criterion given in Eq. (2.112), the effective stress $\bar{\sigma}$ is given by

$$\bar{\sigma} = \left[\frac{1}{2(1+r)} \{ (1+2r)|\sigma_1 - \sigma_2|^{m'} + |\sigma_1 + \sigma_2|^{m'} \} \right]^{1/m'} \tag{2.131}$$

and from the assumption of the equivalence of plastic work, the generalized strain increment is [2.10]

$$d\bar{\varepsilon} = \frac{[2(1+r)]^{1/m'}}{2} \left\{ \frac{1}{(1+2r)^{1/(m'-1)}} |d\varepsilon_1 - d\varepsilon_2|^{m'/(m'-1)} + |d\varepsilon_1 + d\varepsilon_2|^{m'/(m'-1)} \right\}^{(m'-1)/m'} \tag{2.132}$$

where m' is Hill's new parameter used in conjunction with Eq. (2.112).

2.2.11 Stress and Strain Relations in Sheetmetal Forming

The interrelated relations involving stress and strain that are here being considered are

1. Those involving the yield criterion and the associated flow rule
2. Those involving the generalized or effective stress and strain functions equivalent to the stress system under consideration
3. The constitutive equations that relate stress to strain and to other variables of interest for different materials irrespective of whether they are an isotropic continuum or an anisotropic polycrystalline aggregate.

In order to relate σ to ε or to $\dot{\varepsilon}$ some type of material model or constitutive equation is needed. Also, some relations of the plastic flow rules and equivalent stress and strain that stem from continuum mechanics are needed. The phenomenological, constitutive equations of continuum mechanics provide a model or framework for the various deformation phenomena that must be explained by fundamental theory. It provides a unifying effect for dealing with theory and experimental data in an orderly way. It also provides a framework for organizing and critically examining experimental data more efficiently.

If strains that limit formability in a complex forming process are to be calculated accurately, it is necessary to use a mathematical material model consisting of constitutive equations that take all of the important factors into consideration. The material model describes the flow behavior of the material under the influence of external forces. It is essentially some type of constitutive relation between effective stress $\bar{\sigma}$, effective strain $\bar{\varepsilon}$, effective strain rate $\dot{\bar{\varepsilon}}$, temperature T, and macro and microstructure S of the material as given by

$$\bar{\sigma} = \bar{\sigma}(\varepsilon, \dot{\varepsilon}, T, S) \tag{2.133}$$

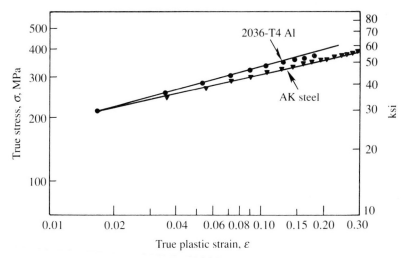

FIGURE 2.72
Plot of log of true stress versus log of true strain for 2036-T4 Al alloy and aluminum-killed (AK) steel. The deviation from a straight line for the aluminum alloy indicates that $\sigma = K\varepsilon^n$ does not hold at large strains [2.14].

This material model is used as an input into the process model to take into account the influence of material properties on the stress and strain distribution during forming of a part [2.13].

For example, the steels generally obey the Ludwik-Hollomon power law, $\sigma = K\varepsilon^n$, Eq. (2.80), very well as shown in Fig. 2.72, whereas the fit for 2036-T4 aluminum alloy does not persist to larger strains [2.14].

The following equation for equivalent stress and strain for an aluminum-killed, low-carbon sheet steel (with a normal anisotropy coefficient of $r = 1.18$) is reported as an example: $\sigma = 530\varepsilon^{0.28}$ MPa.

One group of researchers, for example, found that their data for 2024-O and 7075-O aluminum alloys at constant temperature fit the following equations presented elsewhere:

$$\bar{\sigma} = K\bar{\varepsilon}^n \tag{2.80}$$

$$\bar{\sigma} = K(\bar{\varepsilon}_o + \bar{\varepsilon})^n \tag{2.134}$$

where K, n, and $\bar{\varepsilon}_o$ are material constants. The average fit of Eq. (2.134) to the experimental data for the strain rate range of 10^{-5} to 10^{-1} s^{-1} for 2024-O aluminum alloy at 25°C (77°F) is [2.13]

$$\bar{\sigma} = 265.7(-0.023 + \bar{\varepsilon})^{0.134} \qquad \text{for} \qquad \bar{\varepsilon} > 0.05 \tag{2.135}$$

where $\bar{\sigma}$ is in MPa. This equation is for the large strain region ($\bar{\varepsilon} > 0.05$).

Although the sheet possessed planar anisotropy (different properties in different directions in the surface of the sheet), the equation is restricted to a single orientation, in this case, in the direction of rolling. In modeling the

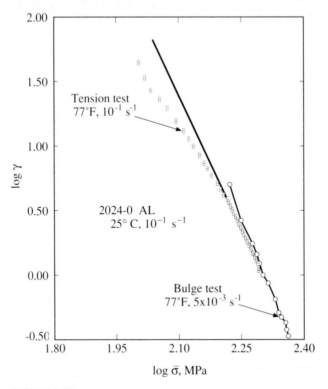

FIGURE 2.73

Plot of the log of the strainhardening coefficient γ versus the log of the effective stress $\bar{\sigma}$ showing the strainhardening behavior of 2024-O aluminum alloy in the tension and bulge tests [10.18].

strainhardening behavior, the experimental data was plotted as shown in Fig. 2.73, in which log γ was plotted against log $\bar{\sigma}$. The explicit choice of the variable, $\gamma = \gamma(\sigma\dot{\varepsilon})$, was based on Hart's concept embodied in his constitutive equation of state, (2.136), which postulates that the variables involved are state variables, which describe the current and future properties of the material at constant temperature and in the absence of recovery or recrystallization [2.15]:

$$d \ln \sigma = \gamma\, d\varepsilon + v\, d \ln \dot{\varepsilon} \tag{2.136}$$

where γ is the strainhardening coefficient and v is the stain rate sensitivity, both of which are functions of σ and $\dot{\varepsilon}$. The strainhardening coefficient γ may be expressed by

$$\gamma = \left(\frac{\partial \ln \sigma}{\partial \varepsilon}\right)_{\dot{\varepsilon}} \tag{2.137}$$

and the strain rate sensitivity v by

$$v = \left(\frac{d \ln \sigma}{d \ln \dot{\varepsilon}}\right)_{\varepsilon} \tag{2.138}$$

The explicit choice of the variables γ and ν is based on Hart's concept that these are state variables, which describe prior and present deformation history. (The use of the symbol ν rather than the more conventional m is to emphasize that the strain rate sensitivity is not necessarily a constant independent of ε and $\dot{\varepsilon}$. ν and m would be identical if the log σ and log $\dot{\varepsilon}$ plot is a straight line obtained for a constant strain. Also, the choice of $\ln \sigma$ and $\ln \dot{\varepsilon}$ as the basic variables rather than σ and ε is to simplify experimental application and because of the nondimensional nature of γ and ν. Also, σ and $\dot{\varepsilon}$ are more indicative of the mechanical state of the specimen than σ and ε.

For the small strain regime $(0.005 < \bar{\varepsilon} < 0.05)$, for the same conditions as above for the large strain regime as expressed by Eqs. (2.134) and (2.135), it was found that ε_o was nearly zero and the stress-strain relation was of the Ludwik-Hollomon form for one lot of 2024-O aluminum alloy at room temperature, namely [2.13]

$$\bar{\sigma} = 339\bar{\varepsilon}^{0.241} \tag{2.139}$$

where $\bar{\sigma}$ is the stress in MPa.

The following relation proposed by Voce fits the strainhardening behavior of brass and copper quite well [2.14]:

$$\sigma = \sigma_s - (\sigma_s - \sigma_Y)\, e^{-\varepsilon/n} \tag{2.140}$$

where σ_s is the saturation (asymptotic) flow stress, σ_Y is the initial yield strength of the material, n is the strainhardening exponent, and e is the base of natural logs (2.718). An interactive computer program has been developed to analyze the experimental data [2.13]. This program is called STRSTN and is used to (1) digitize the load-displacement or load-elongation graphs of the tensile tests, (2) convert the digitized tensile test data into true stress–true strain data and then into true effective stress true effective strain data, (3) fit a number of constitutive relations to these data, and (4) generate theoretical forming limit curves (FLC) using the parameter values of the fitted constitutive relation. FLCs are discussed elsewhere.

2.2.12 Strain Rate and Temperature Effects

Another variable that is often very important in metalworking processes is the strain rate $d\varepsilon/dt$ or $\dot{\varepsilon}$. Strain rate should not be confused with loading or deformation velocity v. Strain rate is the instantaneous deformation velocity, i.e., the crosshead or ram velocity, divided by the instantaneous gauge length or height of the test specimen or workpiece being deformed, or

$$\dot{\varepsilon} = \frac{v}{l} \quad \mathrm{s}^{-1} \tag{2.141}$$

Therefore, the $\dot{\varepsilon}$ is dependent on the instantaneous gauge length or workpiece height being deformed. For example, if the crosshead speed of a tensile testing machine is 1 mm/s and the gauge length is 50 mm ($\sim$2 in), the strain rate is 0.02 s^{-1}; whereas for a gauge length of 200 mm (~8 in), the strain rate is only 0.005 s^{-1}.

In many applications, the flow stress σ and the strain rate $\dot{\varepsilon}$ for constant temperature and strain are related by the following strain-rate, power-law equation:

$$\sigma = C\dot{\varepsilon}^{m}\big|_{T,\varepsilon} \tag{2.142}$$

where $C =$ the strength coefficient
 $m =$ the strain-rate sensitivity exponent

Because, at elevated temperature, recovery (annealing or restoration) pro-cesses involving the annihilation, climbing, and rearrangement of dislocations to a more stable configuration are important and are time dependent, strain rate effects are much more pronounced for hotworking than for coldworking. This is shown in Fig. 2.74 by use of true stress-engineering compressive strain curves. (Stress-strain curves will be discussed later.) The variation of the strain-rate sensitivity exponent m of different materials with homologous temperature is shown in Fig. 2.75.

The parameters C and m can be determined for ductile materials by use of the following three techniques: (1) By determining several stress-strain curves in separate tests at different strain rates and/or with different length specimens, (2) by changing the crosshead speed incrementally during loading, and (3) by use of the ring compression test.

Fig. 2.76 shows typical schematic true stress–true strain curves (to be discussed later) taken at constant temperature, which are used to illustrate how the parameters C and m are obtained. If Eq. (2.142) is expressed in log form,

$$\log \sigma = \log C + m \log \dot{\varepsilon} \tag{2.143}$$

it can be seen that it is the equation of a straight line on the log–log plot, whose

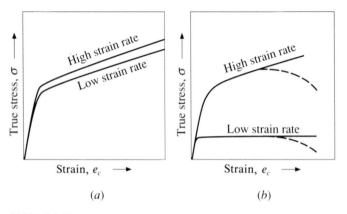

FIGURE 2.74
Schematic true stress–true strain curves for (a) coldworking, and (b) hotworking [2.15].

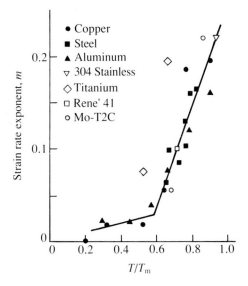

FIGURE 2.75
Variation of the strain-rate sensitivity of different materials with homologous temperature T/T_M [2.4].

slope is equal to m and whose intercept at $\dot{\varepsilon} = 1$ is equal to C. The curve can be plotted as in Fig. 2.76(b) by obtaining the stress from the different strain-rate curves for some constant value of strain, such as $\varepsilon = 0.6$. As shown in Fig. 2.76(b), the strain-rate sensitivity exponent m may be defined as the ratio of the incremental change in log σ to the resultant incremental change in log $\dot{\varepsilon}$ at a given strain and temperature, or

$$m = \frac{\log \sigma_2/\sigma_1}{\log \dot{\varepsilon}_2/\dot{\varepsilon}_1} = \frac{\Delta \log \sigma}{\Delta \log \dot{\varepsilon}} \tag{2.144}$$

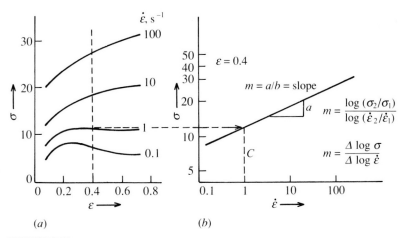

(a)   (b)

FIGURE 2.76
(a) Schematic true stress–true strain curves for constant temperature but different strain rates, and (b) plot of the flow stress at $\varepsilon = 0.4$ versus strain rate on the log–log scale for use in determining C and m [1.1].

If sufficient ductility is available, the incremental strain-rate method may be used by suddenly changing the crosshead speed, thus obtaining a recorded load-time graph as shown in Fig. 2.77. By extrapolating the lower curve for v_1 beyond the point at which a steady state load is obtained at v_2, a common strain for both speeds is obtained. The strain-rate sensitivity exponent can be calculated from

$$m = \frac{\log (P_A/P_B)}{\log (v_2/v_1)} \tag{2.145}$$

By calculating the true stress σ at one of the speeds and substituting σ and m into Eq. (2.143), C can be calculated.

(The ring compression test method for the determination of C and m is similar to the above except that the flow stress σ is obtained by use of Fig. 3.45 for two or more loading speeds from which the strain-rate is determined. The stress is plotted for the corresponding strain on log–log paper, and C and m are determined as in Fig. 2.76(b).)

The first two methods for obtaining m may be simplified in terms of σ–ε curves as shown in Fig. 2.78. The basis for this approach is as follows: If two flow stresses σ_1 and σ_2, at two corresponding strain rates $\dot{\varepsilon}_1$ and $\dot{\varepsilon}_2$, are computed at the same strain by use of Eq. (2.142), one obtains

$$\frac{\sigma_2}{\sigma_1} = \left(\frac{\dot{\varepsilon}_2}{\dot{\varepsilon}_1}\right)^m \tag{2.146}$$

or

$$\ln \frac{\sigma_2}{\sigma_1} = m \ln \left(\frac{\dot{\varepsilon}_2}{\dot{\varepsilon}_1}\right) \tag{2.147}$$

If σ_2 is not much greater than σ_1, such as at low temperature, Eq. (2.147) can be simplified to

$$\frac{\Delta\sigma}{\sigma} \cong m \ln \frac{\dot{\varepsilon}_2}{\dot{\varepsilon}_1} = 2.3m \log \frac{\dot{\varepsilon}_2}{\dot{\varepsilon}_1} \tag{2.148}$$

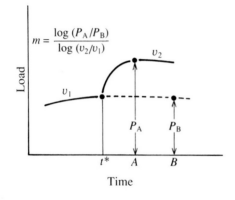

FIGURE 2.77
Schematic load-time diagram showing the variation of velocity with time for a sudden change in load.

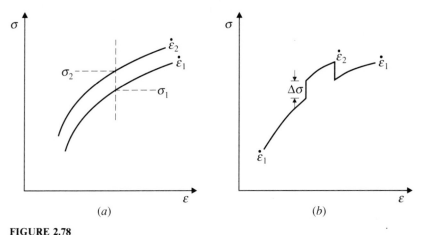

FIGURE 2.78

Two methods of determining m; (a) two continuous stress-strain curves at different strain-rates are compared at the same strain and $m = \ln\,(\sigma_2/\sigma_1)/\ln\,(\dot{\varepsilon}_2/\dot{\varepsilon}_1)$; ($b$) abrupt strain-rate changes are made during a tension test and $m = (\Delta\sigma/\sigma)/\ln\,(\dot{\varepsilon}_2/\dot{\varepsilon}_1)$ [2.4].

Since increased strain rates may cause strainhardening, the use of continuous stress-strain curves usually yields somewhat larger values of m than the abrupt strain rate change method, which compares the flow stresses for the same microstructure.

The strength coefficient C, like K, is an index of the strength level of the material. The significance of m is that it is a measure of how much harder a metal specimen must be pulled to make it stretch a certain amount faster at a given level of strain and temperature. On the other hand, the significance of $n = (\Delta \log \sigma)/(\Delta \log \varepsilon)$, the strainhardening exponent, is that it is a measure of how much harder a metal specimen must be pulled to make it stretch a certain amount more at a given strain rate.

Since tensile stresses are the main deformation stresses in some metalforming processes, in which the necking is the limiting factor and is to be avoided, the strainhardening and the strain-rate sensitivity exponents n and m are material parameters that are important in judging the formability of the material in the particular operation. Both of these parameters should be high for good formability. A large n means a greater resistance to necking, because the material in the neck or groove will harden more rapidly than the adjacent material in the nonnecked or nongrooved regions. The harder and stronger material in the localized or grooved region would then have a tendency to shift the deformation to the softer and thicker adjacent material. Likewise, the localized region or forming groove will cause the material in the groove to deform at higher rates than the adjacent portions of the material. A high value of m will require a higher stress to deform the more rapidly deforming material in the groove than the adjacent portions, which will tend to shift the deformation to them. The groove therefore tends to spread or diffuse over the entire length rather than to persist to be concentrated in a very narrow region that leads to early fracture.

The above phenomenon can be explained quantitatively by use of Eq. (2.142) as follows:

$$\sigma = C\dot{\varepsilon}^m = \frac{P}{A} \tag{2.149}$$

where P is the load on a tensile specimen of cross-sectional area A. If the volume remains constant, the expression for the strain rate can be written as

$$\dot{\varepsilon} = \frac{1}{l}\frac{dl}{dt} = \frac{1}{A}\frac{dA}{dt} \tag{2.150}$$

Solving the two equations for the cross-sectional area shrinkage rate, one obtains

$$-\frac{dA}{dt} = \left(\frac{P}{C}\right)^{1/n}\left[\frac{1}{A^{(1-m)m}}\right] \tag{2.151}$$

If $P = C$, then

$$-\frac{dA}{dt} \propto \frac{1}{A^{1/[(1-m)m]}} \tag{2.152}$$

The dependence of the cross-sectional area shrinkage rate on A is shown in Fig. 2.79. When $m = 1$ and $n = 0$, the flow is newtonian and $-dA/dt$ is independent of the area, so that any incipient necks or cross-sectional variations, even if present initially, are preserved during loading. If $m = 0$, all deformation will cease outside the neck after the maximum load, because the true stress in this region would fall.

Further discussion on the phenomenon of necking on instability is discussed in conjunction with the tensile test elsewhere in this book.

Often both the strainhardening effect and the strain-rate sensitivity effects appear together as in hotworking. A slightly more complicated power law that may be used is

$$\sigma = A\varepsilon^n\dot{\varepsilon}^m \tag{2.153}$$

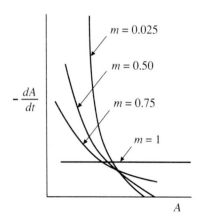

FIGURE 2.79
Schematic graph showing the dependence of the cross-sectional area shrinkage rate on the area for different strain rate sensitivity exponents [3.15].

This equation can also be solved graphically by use of the log form of the equation

$$\log \sigma = \log A + n \log \varepsilon + m \log \dot{\varepsilon} \tag{2.154}$$

If $\dot{\varepsilon}$ is constant, then

$$\log \sigma = C + n \log \varepsilon \tag{2.155}$$

A log-log plot of σ and ε will yield n as the slope and C as the intercept at $\varepsilon = 1$. On the other hand, if ε is constant, then

$$\log \sigma = D + m \log \dot{\varepsilon} \tag{2.156}$$

A log-log plot of σ and $\dot{\varepsilon}$ will yield m as the slope and D as the intercept at $\dot{\varepsilon} = 1$. Then A can be calculated from C or D.

Coleman et al. [2.16] simulated necking by use of a tapered specimen and a computer. They calculated the effect of varying n on the load deformation curve when m was held constant, and vice versa. The value of A in Eq. (2.153) was chosen so that the 0.2 percent yield strength was 166 MPa (24 ksi) for the zirconium material simulated. The load P_n, deformation e_n, curves for a variable n but with m held constant at $m = 0.05$ are shown in Fig. 2.80, and the load P_m, deformation e_m, curves for a variable m but with n held constant at $n = 0.15$ are shown in Fig. 2.81.

To emphasize neck development rather than neck initiation, the gauge length of the tensile specimen used to obtain the above figures was tapered 5 percent to minimum diameter for about 2/3 of the gauge length. Specimens with taper up to 5 percent behave similarly to untapered ones up to the maximum load; however, after the maximum load the elongation to fracture is significantly reduced. In Fig. 2.80, the load $P_{n\,\mathrm{max}}$ and the elongation $e_{n\,\mathrm{max}}$ at maximum load increase appreciably with n, while the elongation $\Delta e_{n\,\mathrm{max}-f}$ between the maximum

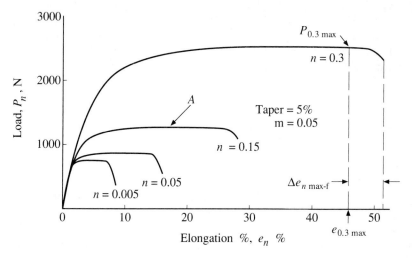

FIGURE 2.80
Simulated load-deformation curves showing the effect of n with m kept constant at 0.05 [2.16].

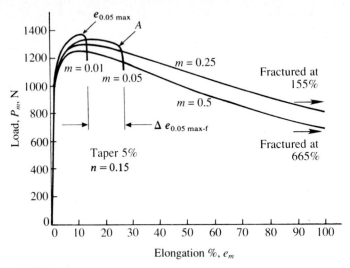

FIGURE 2.81
Simulated load-deformation curves showing the effect of m with n kept constant at 0.15. (Note the difference in scale in Figs. 2.80 and 2.81. Curve A is the same in both graphs.) [2.16].

load and fracture increases only slightly. On the other hand, in Fig. 2.81, when n is held constant, the effect of m on $P_{m\,max}$ and $e_{m\,max}$ in this case is only slight, but $\Delta e_{m\,max-f}$ increases greatly with increasing m.

Strain rate sensitivity m of Eq. (2.142) has been suggested as a measure for ductility since, for a variety of materials, the total elongation, $e_{m\,tot}$ and m correlate very well, as shown in Fig. 2.82 [2.17].

From the above analysis it was concluded that a high value of m is more effective in retarding neck development than a high value of n for this case and in general. Materials exhibiting large strain-rate sensitivity m, such as superplastic materials, can therefore undergo large plastic deformation before necking than other materials having comparable strainhardening characteristics.

A slightly more complicated equation used to describe the stress-strain relationship for a metallic material is

$$\sigma = \beta(\varepsilon_o + \varepsilon)^n \dot{\varepsilon}^m \qquad (2.157)$$

in which the additional parameter ε_o is the effective strain at fracture. Since coldworking usually reduces n, the above equation will provide a more accurate determination of n than the foregoing power law equations. It permits a more accurate analysis of spring back in cold forming of sheetmetal. The role of $\dot{\varepsilon}^m$ in this and the preceding equation is essential to understanding the high total elongation involved in superplasticity.

Which of the above equations should be used? It depends on (1) the process, and (2) the amount of information available. If sufficient information is available, the more general equation should give the best answer; however, the less general equation may give an acceptable answer with the information and time available.

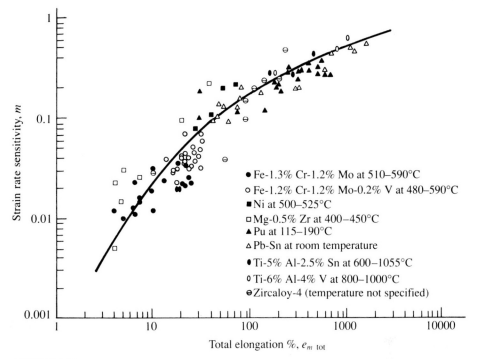

FIGURE 2.82
Correlation between strain-rate sensitivity and total elongation for a variety of materials [2.17].

When coldworking, the stress required is not too sensitive to the strain rate, so that m is small as shown in Fig. 2.80 and may be considered to be equal to zero, and Eq. (2.80) applies. For hotworking, especially at the higher temperatures at which the true stress–true strain curve is flat, n may be considered to be zero, and Eq. (2.142) applies. For warmworking between, say, $0.3 T_M$ and $0.5 T_M$, where T_M is the melting temperature, n and m are not zero, and Eq. (2.153) applies. The general approximations in Table 2.4 may be used in this text for convenience.

TABLE 2.4
Convenient approximations of n and m

Process	n	m
Coldworking (Most metallic materials)	0.25	0
Coldworking (Highly strainhardening materials)	0.45	0
Hotworking	0	0.25
Warmworking	0.15	0.15
Superplastic material	0	0.50–0.80
Ideally plastic material	0	0

The most complex equation generally applied to hotworking at high strain rates, which relates strain rate $\dot\varepsilon$ to stress and temperature, is the Garofalo [2.18] creep equation

$$\dot\varepsilon_s = A \left[\sinh\left(\alpha\sigma\right)\right]^{n'} e^{-Q/RT} \tag{2.158}$$

This equation can be written in the form

$$Z = \dot\varepsilon_s \, e^{Q/RT} = A'' \left[\sinh\left(\alpha\sigma\right)\right]^{n'} \tag{2.159}$$

where $\dot\varepsilon_s$ = secondary (steady state) creep rate as shown in Fig. 2.83
      Z = the temperature-corrected strain rate
      R = gas constant
      Q = activation energy
      T = absolute temperature, K
      A'' = temperature dependent material constant

A, α, and n' are temperature-independent material constants determined by finding the best fit to experimental data by use of a computer program. Typical values of these parameters are shown in Table 2.5. (Solving Eq. (2.142) for $\dot\varepsilon$, one obtains the following equivalents for A and n': $A = C^{-1/m}$ and $n' = 1/m$.)

Equation (2.158) may be used in conjunction with an equation such as (2.142) to obtain the flow stress in a hotworking process such as hot forging.

Usually this equation will fit the data, if the plot of the data as log ε_s versus log σ yields linear and parallel lines with a slope of n' at low stress values for different temperatures as shown in Fig. 2.84(a) for austenitic stainless steel. A plot of log ε versus σ will show linearity with a slope equal to $n'\alpha$ at high stress, as shown in Fig. 2.84(b). A plot of log $\dot\varepsilon$ versus log $\sinh(\alpha\sigma)$ will show linear and parallel lines also with a slope of n' over the entire stress range as shown in Fig.

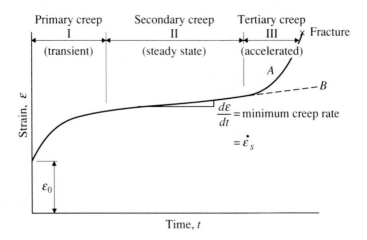

FIGURE 2.83
Typical idealized creep curve showing the three stages of creep. Curve A is for a constant load test, and curve B is for a constant stress test. (*Adapted from G. E. Dieter, Jr., Mechanical Metallurgy, McGraw-Hill, 1961.*)

TABLE 2.5

Computed values of A, α, and n'. (*Adapted from F. Garofalo, "An Empirical Relation Defining the Stress Dependence of Minimum Creep Rate in Metals," Trans. Met. Soc. of AIME, Vol. 227, April 1963, pp. 351–355.*)

Material	Test temperature K	$1, s^{-1}$	α, cm²/kg	α, m²/M	n'
Copper	673	6.80×10^{-6}	1.57×10^{-3}	1.60×10^{-8}	3.57
Copper	723	7.80×10^{-6}	2.00×10^{-3}	2.04×10^{-8}	3.36
Copper	773	6.10×10^{-6}	2.79×10^{-3}	2.84×10^{-8}	3.39
Copper	823	7.20×10^{-6}	3.26×10^{-3}	3.32×10^{-8}	3.38
Copper	903	4.70×10^{-6}	5.71×10^{-3}	5.82×10^{-8}	2.66
Copper	973	8.30×10^{-6}	9.35×10^{-3}	9.53×10^{-8}	2.26
Aluminum	477	2.78×10^{-6}	5.65×10^{-3}	5.76×10^{-8}	5.00
Aluminum	533	1.94×10^{-5}	7.28×10^{-3}	7.42×10^{-8}	4.55
Aluminum	920	2.67×10^{-8}	1.78×10^{-3}	1.83×10^{-8}	1.24
Aluminum— 3.1% magnesium	531	4.17×10^{-6}	2.96×10^{-3}	3.02×10^{-8}	2.26
Austenitic	977	1.47×10^{-8}	1.11×10^{-3}	1.13×10^{-8}	3.64
Stainless steel	1089	1.67×10^{-8}	1.51×10^{-3}	1.54×10^{-8}	3.50

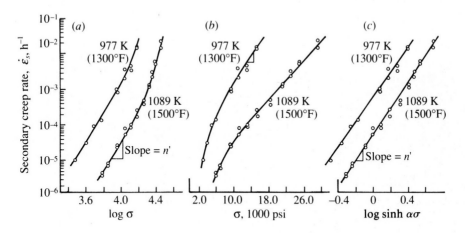

FIGURE 2.84

Variation of steady-state creep rate $\dot{\varepsilon}_s$, with various parameters for austenitic stainless steel tested at 977 and 1089 K as follows: (*a*) plot of log $\dot{\varepsilon}_s$ versus log σ yielding parallel, straight lines for the different temperatures at low stress with a slope of n; (*b*) plot of log $\dot{\varepsilon}_s$ versus σ yielding straight lines for the different temperatures at high stress with a slope of $n'\alpha$, (*c*) plot of the log $\dot{\varepsilon}_s$ versus log of the hyperbolic sine function, sinh ($\alpha\sigma$) yielding parallel, straight lines for the different temperatures over the entire operating stress range with a slope of n'. (*Adapted from F. Garofalo, "An Empirical Relation Defining the Stress Dependence of Minimum Creep Rate in Metals," Trans. Met. Soc. of AIME, Vol. 227, April 1963, pp. 351–355.*)

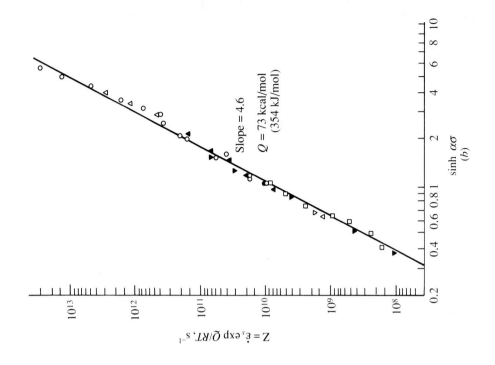

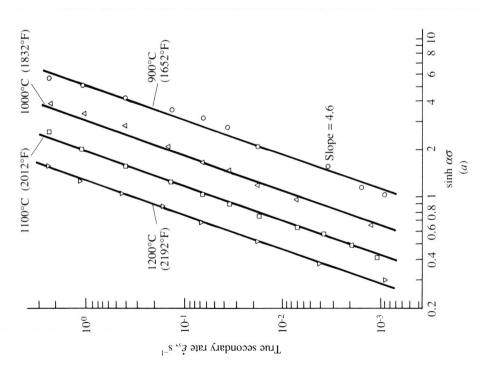

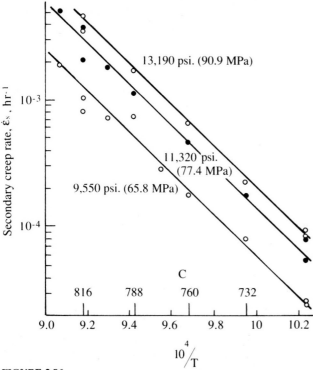

FIGURE 2.86
Dependence of log of the secondary creep rate on reciprocal of temperature for austenitic stainless steel $Q = 75,000$ cal/mol. (*Adapted from F. Garofalo, O. Richmond, W. F. Domis, and F. von Gemminger, Joint International Conference on Creep: The Institution of Mechanical Engineers, pp. 1-31.*)

2.84(c) for austenitic stainless steel and in Fig. 2.85(a) for 0.25%C steel. Replotting the data of Fig. 2.85(a) in terms of Z versus log sinh ($\alpha\sigma$), one obtains a straight line with a slope of n' for the data taken at the different temperatures as shown in Fig. 2.85(b) for 0.25%C steel [2.19]. The segment of the curve in Fig. 2.85(b) is in the range of deformation for hot working. The range of deformation for creep would extend to a much lower value. If it is assumed that the microstructure is independent of temperature during secondary or steady-state creep, Eq. (2.159) may be written in the form

$$\ln \dot{\varepsilon}_s = \ln Z - \frac{Q}{RT} \tag{2.160}$$

which gives a linear plot between $\dot{\varepsilon}_s$ and $1/T$ with a slope of Q/R as shown in

FIGURE 2.85
(a) Plot of data showing the power relationship of Eq. (2.160) between secondary strain rate and the hyperbolic sine function of the flow stress observed in hot torsion experiments on 0.25 percent carbon steel. (b) Replot of the data in (a) as the log of the temperature corrected strain rate Z versus log sinh ($\sigma\alpha$) yielding a single straight line of slope of n for different temperatures over the entire range [2.19].

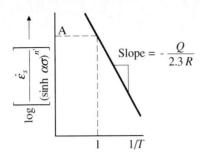

$$\text{Slope} = -\frac{Q}{2.3R}$$

FIGURE 2.87

Schematic curve showing the plot of the log of a composite parameter of $\dot{\varepsilon}_s/[\sinh(\alpha\sigma)]^{n'}$ versus the reciprocal of the absolute temperature, $1/T$, for use in determining the activation energy, Q.

Fig. 2.86. The plot of $\log \dot{\varepsilon}_s/[\sinh(\alpha\sigma)]^n$ versus $1/T$ will also plot as a straight line with a slope equal to $-Q/2.3R$ as shown schematically in Fig. 2.87.

To evaluate the parameters in the above equations, and to check the correlation of the data, n' and α are obtained as in Fig. 2.84(a) and (b) then curves such as in Fig. 2.85 can be plotted, and Q and A can then be obtained from Fig. 2.87.

Several submicro- and microprocesses may be involved during hotworking that may affect the hardness and strength of the material. First of all, the hardness usually increases due to strainhardening as a result of the increase in the dislocation density. This strainhardening may be counteracted by a softening process due to dynamic recovery as a result of the elimination of dislocations and due to dynamic recrystallization as a result of the continuous nucleation and growth of new grains. If dynamic recovery proceeds rapidly enough, the flow stress increases progressively up to a steady state value at which the stress-strain curve levels off. When dynamic recrystallization also occurs the strain-strain curve may exhibit a maximum, which may be eventually followed by the steady state stress as shown schematically in Fig. 2.88 [2.20]. The principal effect of Z (the Zener-Hollomon parameter, s^{-1}) is that the strain to the peak, $\varepsilon_{(max)}$, increases with Z as shown in Fig. 2.88. The same effect is seen entering into the shape of the stress-strain curves in Fig. 2.76(a).

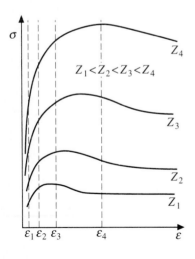

FIGURE 2.88

The effect of increasing Z on the shape of $\sigma(\varepsilon)$ when restoration is by dynamic recovery plus dynamic recrystallization [2.20].

2.2.13 Deformation Efficiency and Redundant Deformation

2.2.13.1 INTRODUCTION. The total amount of work or energy W_t required in a plastic deformation process involving a change in shape may be broken down into the following components:

$$W_t = W_h + W_r + W_f + W_s \qquad (2.161)$$

where W_h = work required for the change in shape only or the homogeneous deformation

W_r = redundant or unnecessary work or work required for the useless internal macroshear (large-scale shear)

W_f = work required to overcome external friction losses

W_s = energy stored in the material

Since W_s varies between 5 and 10 percent even in coldforming, it is usually omitted from calculation of the efficiency and is usually neglected. Also the effect of the heat generated on the yield strength of the material is usually neglected. W_s may be estimated by dissolving the deformed metal in a chemical solution such as an acid solution. (In this section, large-scale shear in the bulk metal called macroshear will be differentiated from microshear occurring in slip within the crystalline grains.)

W_h, the homogeneous deformation, is the work required to make a change in shape if the deformation is perfectly homogeneous or uniform and lossless. In other words, the plastic deformation conforms to the so-called law of minimum work, which states that the amount of lossless work is the same regardless of the system of stresses used to make the change in shape. It is equal to the area under the effective stress-strain curve up to some value ε_H, or its equivalent, multiplied by the total volume of the metal deformed, or

$$W_h = V \int_0^{\varepsilon_H} \bar{\sigma} \, d\bar{\varepsilon} \qquad (2.162)$$

The homogeneous work per unit volume, w_h, is shown by the cross-hatched area in Fig. 2.89 [2.21]. The efficiency of the deformation process is expressed as

$$\eta = \frac{W_h}{W_t} \qquad (2.163)$$

Almost all, if not all, metalworking processes involve some inhomogeneous plastic deformation. Homogeneous deformation would occur if a cylindrical block of an isotropic material is compressed axially between frictionless, over-hanging dies (anvils), so that each small, imaginary grid element on the diametral or meridian plane would deform the same way as any other element and also proportionately the same way as the entire diametral cross section as shown in Fig. 2.90(a). Inhomogeneous deformation occurring in drawing and extrusion, and rolling are compared by use of the simple grid method shown in Fig. 2.90(b) and (c).

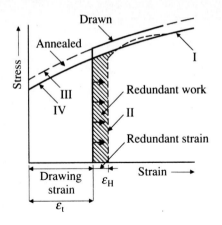

I. σ–ε curve after plastic deformation with 0 at ε_H

II. Curve fitted to original curve to show equivalent redundant work

III. Effect of redundancy on the σ–ε curve

IV. σ–ε curve prior to plastic deformation

$$w_H = \int_0^{\varepsilon_H} \sigma \, d\varepsilon$$

FIGURE 2.89
Schematic true stress–true strain curve for a material prior to plastic deformation and the curve subsequent to plastic deformation superimposed onto the above curve and translated so as to show the redundant work and strain of a cold work material. (Frictionless drawing dies are assumed.) [2.21].

To illustrate the concept of redundant work, suppose we reduce a bar of rectangular cross section to a thinner, longer bar as shown in Fig. 2.90. The work required to make the change in shape, or the work required for homogeneous deformation, would be the same regardless of whether the bar was drawn through a die, rolled between rolls, or extruded through a die. The total work, however, may be much different, because the efficiency of each of the processes is different. The only work of deformation that is necessary is that required to reduce the thickness from t_0 to t_1 or to move point A toward point B and elongate the elements. The relative shearing of point A relative to B results in internal macroshearing or internal friction losses. As a matter of fact, an element during the process of deformation may shear forward, then backward again, resulting in energy loss. This unnecessary work is called redundant work.

The redundant work is sometimes considered to consist of two components: the friction component which causes macroscopic shearing of the outer layers of the material relative to the inner layers but does not include surface sliding, and the geometric component which causes shearing and unshearing, because of the difference in the velocities of metal flow from one section to another. Extrusion through a frictionless die would still involve redundant work. Redundancy would include any unnecessary straining such as bending and unbending such as in deep drawing or reverse deep drawing of a cup from sheetmetal. Bending and unbending, which is really shearing and unshearing, is shown schematically for extrusion in Fig. 2.90(b).

It is often convenient to divide the deformed body into zones. The normal components of velocity across a boundary between two zones should be continuous such as v_{n1} and v_{n2} as shown in Fig. 2.91 [2.22]. The tangential components of velocity v_{t1} and v_{t2} need not be continuous. The difference between the two

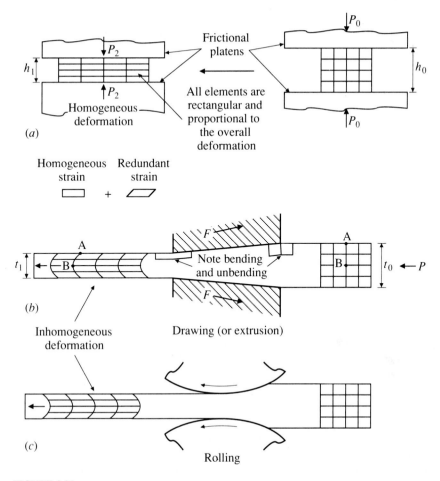

FIGURE 2.90

Illustration comparing (*a*) homogeneous deformation by compression between frictionless anvils, (*b*) inhomogeneous (redundant) deformation by bar drawing or extrusion, and (*c*) inhomogeneous deformation by rolling. Note that straight lines bend in the direction of the frictional force on passing through the dies or rolls [4.9].

tangential velocities $\Delta v = v_{t2} - v_{t1}$ is called the *velocity discontinuity* and may give rise to useless shears within the metal being deformed.

The maximum resistance to shear τ_Y that the material can develop according to the von Mises criterion is

$$\sigma_Y = \sqrt{3}\,\tau_Y = \sqrt{3}\,k \tag{2.54}$$

where σ_Y = yield strength in uniaxial tension. If the power consumption is integrated over the surface of the body (as indicated by the all-around integral

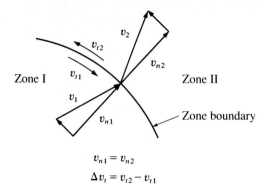

$$v_{n1} = v_{n2}$$

$$\Delta v_t = v_{t2} - v_{t1}$$

FIGURE 2.91
Tangential velocity discontinuity across a zone boundary between two deformation zones [7.3].

sign), the shear power loss is

$$P_s = \oint \tau \, |\Delta v| \, ds \qquad (2.164)$$

where ds is an increment of surface area.

One of the ways for approximately evaluating redundant work is illustrated in Fig. 2.89. The useless, internal macroshearing taking place within the material during coldworking will increase the hardness and flow strength of the material but decrease its ductility due to strainhardening, provided that the operation is performed below the recrystallization temperature of the material being deformed. If it is assumed that no recovery and recrystallization occur, the amount of redundant work may be evaluated. If a stress-strain curve is obtained after deformation and plotted as shown in Fig. 2.89, it will lie above the original or base-curve for the material. If the curve then is translated so that it coincides with the original base-curve, the area swept out under the original curve will be equivalent to the redundant work for the deformation process per unit volume.

The energy liberated due to internal and external friction losses is largely dissipated as heat. External friction is not entirely objectionable in some processes such as rolling, for example, as some friction is necessary to pull the material into and partially through the rolls. Also, the heat generated by the losses will contribute to recrystallization of the coldworked material.

2.2.13.2 MEASURE OF REDUNDANCY. It has been proposed [2.23] that the assessment of the levels of redundancy be made by means of a redundancy factor, which relates the ideal or lossless deformation to the actual.

The redundancy factor can be associated either (1) with the effect of the total strain on the magnitude of the operative stress produced in the system, or (2) with the total strain imposed, i.e., with the increase in the actual strain over and above the value of the homogeneous strain. The respective redundancy factors are defined as

$$\sigma = \Phi \sigma_H \qquad (2.165)$$

$$\varepsilon_T = \phi \varepsilon_T \qquad (2.166)$$

where Φ is the stress redundancy factor, ϕ is the strain redundancy factor, σ and ε are the equivalent or representative stress and strain, and the subscripts T and H refer to the total and homogeneous values.

If a specimen is deformed by imposing on it a strain of ε, the strain can be related to the mean yield stress as follows:

$$\sigma_{Y_m} = \frac{1}{\varepsilon} \int_0^{\varepsilon} \sigma(\varepsilon)\, d\varepsilon \qquad (2.167)$$

To include the effect of redundancy, Eq. (2.167) can be integrated between the limits of $\varepsilon = 0$, and $\varepsilon = \varepsilon_T$, where ε_T can be determined from Eq. (2.166).

In the absence of redundant effects both σ and ε_T would be numerically equal to the homogeneous stress σ_H and homogeneous strain ε_H, respectively, and $\Phi = \phi = 1$. Experimental results, however, indicate that the stress and strain redundancy factors are not generally numerically equal. Since ϕ does not depend on any arbitrarily chosen relationship between stress and strain its use is preferred to Φ.

2.2.13.3 TEMPERATURE RESULTING FROM DEFORMATION. As indicated in the foregoing, the work expended in deformation appears largely in the form of heat energy generated in the workpiece. Since about 90 to 100 percent of the work expended appears as heat [2.24], its effect on the operation may be significant. The lower value in the foregoing is for extensive coldworking, and the higher value is for hotworking.

The mechanical energy per unit volume w expended in deformation is equal to the area under the stress-strain curve [2.4]

$$w = \int_0^{\varepsilon} \bar{\sigma}\, d\bar{\varepsilon} \qquad (2.168)$$

If the deformation is adiabatic, i.e., no heat is transferred to the surroundings, the temperature rise is given by

$$\Delta T = \frac{\alpha \int \bar{\sigma}\, d\bar{\varepsilon}}{\rho c} = \frac{\alpha \bar{\sigma}_a \bar{\varepsilon}}{\rho c} \qquad (2.169)$$

where σ_a is the average value of σ over the strain interval of 0 to ε, ρ is the density of the material, c is the mass heat capacity of the material, and α is the fraction of energy stored. Equation (2.169) will be discussed in greater detail in Chap. 4 in regard to the temperature rise due to velocity discontinuities.

The problem of evaluating the local temperature existing at a particular point in a material being plastically deformed may be resolved into two steps: (1) static conduction of heat to adjacent material and die surfaces, and (2) transport of heat by plastic flow of the material. In the hotrolling of aluminum alloy slabs and plates, for example, the amount of deformation may have to be curtailed or the material has to be cooled in order to reduce the maximum temperature developed to prevent localized melting of the material. Incipient melting, however, during initial stages of hotworking, can be a problem in any alloy.

2.2.13.4 EFFECTS OF REDUNDANT SHEAR. The practical significance of the redundant macroshears varies from process to process and from cold to hot forming operations [2.25]. In most engineering materials, the shearing and unshearing that takes place as the workpiece is being deformed in coldworking directly effects the level of the yield stress by strainhardening of the material beyond the value that would result from the change in shape alone as associated with homogeneous deformation only. Additional brittleness due to the reduction of ductility is introduced unnecessarily, which may require an annealing operation or a higher quality material of greater ductility. Also, the additional concentrated deformation may cause excessive grain growth during the recrystallization annealing operation. The coarse grain microstructure may cause failure during subsequent deformation. The build-up of residual stresses at points of macroshear may predispose the material to cracking during further deformation.

The need for avoiding redundancy is very real from the point of view of the efficient and satisfactory operation of an industrial metalworking process. The solution lies in proper design of the tooling used, such as the dies for bar drawing or extrusion. The use of properly designed dies that facilitate the flow of metal through a metalforming pass can reduce the levels of inhomogeneity by as much as 25 to 50 percent in compression as compared to that obtained with the tooling usually used in industry.

ACKNOWLEDGMENT

The material and some of the illustrations in this chapter were adapted from the references as indicated in the text and in the legends by the numbers of the references enclosed in square brackets pursuant to all copyrights.

REFERENCES

2.1. Ford, H., *Advanced Mechanics of Materials*, John Wiley & Sons, New York, 1963, pp. 22-23.
2.2. Gallagher, R. H., *Finite Element Analysis Fundamentals*, Prentice-Hall, Inc., Englewood Cliffs, New Jersey, 1975, p. 136.
2.3. Szczepinski, W., *Introduction to the Mechanics of Plastic Forming of Metals*, Sijthoff & Noordhoff Inst. Pub., Netherlands, 1979, p. 24.
2.4. Hosford, W. F., and R. M. Caddell, *Metal Forming*, Prentice-Hall, Inc., Englewood Cliffs, New Jersey, 1983, p. 28, p. 100, pp. 266-269.
2.5. Kocks, U. F., "The Relation Between Polycrystal Deformation and Single-Crystal Deformation," AIME & ASM Met. Trans., vol. 1, no. 5, May 1970, pp. 1121-43.
2.6. Tegart, W. J. M., *Elements of Mechanical Metallurgy*, The Macmillan Co., New York, 1966, p. 130, p. 171.
2.7. Taylor, G. I., *J. Inst. Met.*, vol. 62, 1938, pp. 307-324.
2.8. Kocks, U. F., "Constitutive Relations for Slip", in *Constitutive Equations in Plasticity*, A. S. Argon (ed.), MIT Press, Cambridge, Massachusetts, 1975.
2.9. Hill, R., *Mathematical Theory of Plasticity*, Oxford University Press, London, 1971.

2.10. Mellor, P. B., "Forming of Anisotropic Sheet Metal" in *Engineering Plasticity: Theory of Metal Forming Processes*, vol. 1, H. Lippman (ed.), Springer-Verlag, Wein, New York, 1977, pp. 67 and 146.

2.11. Mellor, P. B., and A. Parman, "Plasticity Analysis of Sheet Metal Forming" in *Mechanics of Sheet Metal Forming*, D. P. Koistinen and N-M Wang (eds.), Plenum Press, New York, 1978, p. 67.

2.12. Hasek, V. V., "An Evaluation of the Applicability of Theoretical Analyses to the Forming Limit Diagram," *Fracture 1977*, vol. 2, p. 476, Proc. of 4th Int. Conf. on Fracture, June 1977, D. M. R. Taplin (ed.), University of Waterloo, Ontario, Canada.

2.13. Nagpal, V., T. L. Subramanian, and T. Altan, Technical Report AFML-TR-79-4168, ICAM Mathematical Modeling of Sheet Metal Formability Indices and Sheet Metal Forming Processes, November 1979, AFML/LTC, W-PAFB, Ohio, p. 66.

2.14. Hecker, S. S., "Experimental Studies of Sheet Stretchability" in Formability: Analysis Modeling, and Experimentation, Proc. of Symp., October 1977, S. S. Hecker, A. K. Ghosh, and H. L. Gegel (eds.), Pub. of AIME, p. 165.

2.15. Hart, E. W., C. Y. Li, H. Yamada, and G. L. Wire, "Phenomenological Theory: A Guide to Constitutive Relations and Fundamental Deformation Properties," *Constitutive Equations in Plasticity*, A. S. Argon (ed.), MIT Press, Cambridge, Massachusetts, 1975.

2.16. Coleman, C. E., R. A. Holt, and R. R. Hosbons, "Numerical Calculation of Plastic Instability During Tensile Deformation", Nucl. Metall., vol. 20, pt. 1-2, 1976, Proc. of the Int. Conf. on Comput. Simul. for Mat. Appl., Gaithersburg, Md., Apr. 19-21, 1976, pt. 2, pp. 807-815.

2.17. Woodford, D. A. "Strain-Rate Sensitivity as a Measure of Ductility," *ASM Trans. Quart.*, vol. 62. no. 1, March 1969, pp. 291-292.

2.18. Garofalo, F., *Fundamentals of Creep and Creep-Rupture in Metals*, The Macmillan Co., New York, 1965.

2.19. Sellers, C. M., and W. J. M. Tegart, "Hot Workability," *International Metallurgical Review*, vol. 17, 1972, pp. 1-24.

2.20. Roberts, W., "Dynamic Changes That Occur During Hot Working and Their Significance Regarding Microstructural Development and Hot Workability," Deformation Processing and Structure, 1982 ASM Materials Science Seminar, G. Krauss (ed.), ASM, Metals Park, OH, pp. 109-184.

2.21. Parkins, R. N., *Mechanical Treatment of Metals*, American Elsevier Publishing Co., Inc., New York, p. 1968, 159.

2.22. Avitzur, B., *Metal Forming: Processes and Analysis*, McGraw-Hill Book Co., New York, 1968, p. 59.

2.23. Blazynski, T. Z., *Metal Forming-Tool Profiles and Flow*, John Wiley & Sons, New York, 1976, pp. 7-18.

2.24. Bishop, J. F., "An Approximate Method for Determining the Temperatures Reached in Steady Motion Problems of Plane Strain," *Quart. Jour. of Mechanics and Applied Math.*, vol. 9, 1956, pp. 236-246.

2.25. Blazynski, T. Z., "Inhomogeneity of Deformation and Tool Design," Metal Forming Plasticity, IUTAM Symp., Tutzing, Germany, 1978, H. Lippmann (ed.), Springer-Verlag, Berlin, p. 202.

PROBLEMS

2.1. For the state of stress given below

$$\sigma_{ij} = \begin{bmatrix} 7.5 & 2 & 0 \\ 2 & 5 & 0 \\ 0 & 0 & 2.5 \end{bmatrix}$$

calculate the mean stress σ_m, the deviatoric stresses in the normal direction, and the sum of the deviatoric stresses. What conclusion might one draw from the sum of these stresses?

2.2. By use of the geometrical construction found in Mohr's stress circle for biaxial stress with shear shown in Fig. 2.9(c), derive the expressions for the principal stresses σ_1 and σ_2 and the shear stress τ_{xy}.

2.3. A thin-walled tube is subjected to a torque, which gives a shear stress of 55 MPa in the cross section, and it is also simultaneously subjected to an axial tensile stress of 55 MPa. Determine the maximum shear stress, the maximum tensile stress, and the angle between the planes in which they occur and the tube axis both (1) by use of Mohr's stress circle and (2) analytically. Also, indicate in a rough sketch the stress state showing the position of the principal stress axes and the values of the corresponding principal stresses.

2.4. A square of sheetmetal is subjected to a uniform stress field without buckling by a system of biaxial stresses shown in Fig. P2.4.1.

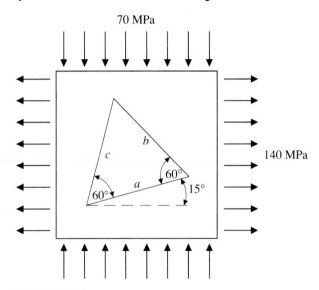

FIGURE P2.4.1

(a) Find the stresses on a, b, and c by using both (1) Mohr's stress circle and (2) analytically.

(b) Determine the stress resultants on a, b, and c.

2.5. The state of stress in a plane stress system is given by $\sigma_x = 800$ MPa (N/mm²), $\sigma_y = 200$ MPa, $\sigma_z = 0$, and $\tau_{xy} = 250$ MPa.

(a) Find the magnitude and directions of the principal stresses.

(b) Calculate the possible uniaxial yield stress, σ_Y, of the material when the stress system just causes yielding according to the Tresca and von Mises criteria.

2.6. The following state of stress exists in the plastic region:

$$\sigma_1 = 1000 \text{ MPa} \qquad \sigma_2 = 700 \text{ MPa} \qquad \sigma_1 = 0 \qquad \varepsilon_1 = 0.1$$

(a) What are the values of ε_2 and ε_3?

(b) What are τ_{max} and γ_{max}?

2.7. (*a*) Assuming that the maximum shear stress theory and proportional loading apply, by use of Eqs. (2.78) and (2.80) and by use of the data given below, determine ε_1, ε_2, and ε_3 for the following state of stress

$$\sigma_1 = 100{,}000 \text{ psi} \qquad \sigma_2 = 100{,}000 \text{ psi} \qquad \sigma_3 = 0$$

(*b*) Write a computer program in Basic (or some other convenient programming language) to calculate K and n by use of the data given below.

Experimental tensile data

P, lbf	d_0, in	d, in	R, in	A	A_0/A
9,000	0.475	0.455	0.74	0.1626	1.090
15,000	0.475	0.387	1.00	0.1176	1.506
12,000	0.475	0.230	0.14	0.0415	4.270

where $P = $ load
$d = $ final diameter
$R = $ radius of curvature of the neck
$A_0 = $ initial cross-sectional area
$A = $ final cross-sectional area

2.8. (*a*) With the aid of the stereographic projection shown in Fig. 2.57, determine the resolved shear stress on all 12 of the $\{111\}\langle110\rangle$ slip systems shown in Table 2.3 of one FCC single crystal. Assume that the crystal is loaded in tension below its critical resolved shear stress to a stress of 10 Pa along the [321] direction (which lies between the [211] and the [110] directions). Use Eqs. (2.84) and/or Table 2.1 to obtain angles ϕ and λ.

(*b*) In a unit cell, draw in all of the above pertinent directions. (If difficulty is experienced in visualizing these directions in the stereographic projection, this part might be done first.)

(*c*) On which slip system would slip initiate first?

2.9. Individual single crystals of zinc, having a normal cross-sectional area of $122 \times 10^{-6} \text{ m}^2$ and only one slip system at different orientation to the crystal axis, are loaded in tension as in Fig. 2.60 until yielding begins at an appreciable rate to give the data for ϕ, λ, and P given in Table P2.9. ϕ is the angle between the axis of

TABLE P2.9
Data for loading a single crystal of zinc

ϕ^0	λ^0	P, N
83.5	18	203.1
70.5	29	77.1
60	30.5	51.7
50	40	45.1
29	62.5	54.9
13	78	109.0
4	86	318.5

loading and the slip plane in degrees, λ is the angle between the loading axis and the slip direction in degrees, and P is the axial load in newtons.

(a) Make up a table for calculating the cosines of ϕ and λ, their products (the Schmid Factor), the axial stress, the resolved shear stress τ_{RSS}, in Pa, and the stress normal to the slip plane, σ_n, in Pa.

(b) What is the slip system for this metal?

(c) Which stress controls yielding, τ_{RSS}, or σ_n, and why?

(d) Plot the Schmid factor versus the axial stress σ_P. This plot is similar to what figure in the book?

2.10. A thin sheet of sheetmetal is subjected to unequal biaxial tension. The principal strains in the plane of the sheet are $\varepsilon_2 = -1/5\varepsilon_1$, and $\varepsilon_3 = \sigma_3 = 0$. Use the principle of normality to determine the stress ratio σ_2/σ_1 using the von Mises criterion. [See Eqs. (2.70) and (2.95).]

2.11. After a deep-drawing operation, a circle 0.50 in diameter that had been etched onto the surface of a thin steel sheet prior to drawing, changed into an ellipse with its major and minor axes being 0.650 and 0.575 in, respectively. (1) Calculate the effective strain $\bar{\varepsilon}$ at the location of ellipse, and (2) find the ratio of $\sigma_1/\bar{\sigma}$ by assuming that a plane stress state existed during the operation with the ratio σ_2/σ_1 being constant throughout the operation. Use $\varepsilon = \ln l_f/l_0$, which is presented in the next chapter, to calculate the principal strains.

2.12. By use of Fig. 2.85 and Eq. (2.158), determine the value of the activation energy Q for a 0.25%C steel by taking values off the curves at constant $\sinh \alpha\sigma$. Use curves for 900 and 1200°C.

2.13. Using Fig. 2.84 to determine n' from the slope of the curve at low stress and β from the slope of the curve at high stress at 977 K, determine approximately the stress that would be required to produce a secondary (minimum) temperature corrected strain rate Z of 1.2×10^{-5} s^{-1} at 977 K.

2.14. From a test performed on a stainless steel at 1100 K, it was found that at a temperature corrected strain rate Z of 1.2×10^{-5} s^{-1}, the stress was 167 MN/m^2. The values of n' and β, that were obtained from the experimental curves as above, were found to be equal to 3.5 and 5.3×10^{-8} m^2/N respectively. Calculate the parameter A'' by use of Eq. (2.159), and compare the result with that given in Table 2.5.

2.15. (a) Determine the expression for (1) the elastic work and (2) the ideal or lossless work due to homogeneous plastic deformation done during the tensile test. Assume the Holomon-Ludwig power law expressed by Eq. (2.80) applies.

(b) Assume that for elastoplastic deformation, the plastic deformation occurs entirely by homogeneous deformation (without necking) of a round tensile specimen 0.5 in (12.7 mm) in diameter by 2 in (50.8 mm) long. Assume that the material is AISI 1015 steel having a yield strength of 300 MPa, $K = 620$ MPa, $n = 0.18$, and $E = 30 \times 10^6$ psi (208 GPa (kN/mm^2)). Calculate (1) the elastic work, and (2) the plastic work in SI units. [See Eq. (2.162)].

CHAPTER
3

STRESS-STRAIN CURVES AND RELATED MECHANICAL PROPERTIES AND RELATED PHENOMENA

3.1 INTRODUCTION

In this chapter the following topics will be discussed:

1. Idealized stress-strain curves and their empirical equations
2. Typical experimental tensile stress-strain curves
3. Unnotched, uniaxial, monotonic tensile test and engineering versus true stress and strain
4. Notched-bar tensile test and ductile fracture initiation
5. True stress–true strain curve, corrected for the triaxial state of stress occurring in the neck
6. Plastic instability and necking
7. Ductility and reduction in area
8. Mathematical material models
9. Some tests other than conventional unnotched and notched tensile tests for determining stress-strain relationships
10. Workability

3.2 IDEALIZED STRESS-STRAIN CURVES AND THEIR EMPIRICAL EQUATIONS

Probably the most important relationship in metalworking or metalforming is the relationship between stress and strain. As yet there is no fundamental method of relating stress to strain other than by means of idealized and experimental stress-strain curves or by some similar assumed relationship such as Hooke's law or an empirical equation for the stress-strain curve.

In many problems and operations in plasticity, it is useful to use simplified forms of stress-strain curves and/or empirical constitutive equations of varying degrees of complexity to describe them. One type of idealized stress-strain curve that has already been discussed is the linearly elastic curves shown in Fig. 2.14. The idealized curves differ essentially (1) in whether the elastic portion is included and (2) in whether strainhardening is taken into consideration during plastic deformation. If elastic deformation is not included, the corresponding materials are described as rigid, i.e., with a modulus of elasticity of infinity. If strainhardening is not included during plastic deformation as shown in Fig. 3.1(*a*) and (*b*), the materials are designated as perfectly or ideally plastic materials.

The idealized stress-strain curves for a constant strain rate and their equations that are commonly used in plasticity are as follows [3.1]:

1. Rigid–perfectly plastic curve as shown in Fig. 3.1(*a*) and described by

$$\sigma = \sigma_0 \tag{3.1}$$

where σ_0 = yield stress.

2. Linearly elastic–perfectly plastic curve as shown in Fig. 3.1(*b*) and described by

$$\sigma = E\varepsilon \quad \text{for 0 to } \sigma_0,$$
$$\sigma = \sigma_0 \quad \text{from } \sigma_0 \text{ onward,} \tag{3.2}$$

where E is the modulus of elasticity.

3. Rigid–linearly strainhardening plastic curve as shown in Fig. 3.1(*c*) and described by

$$\sigma = \sigma_0 + K\varepsilon \quad \text{or} \quad \sigma = \sigma_0 + K'\sigma_0\varepsilon \tag{3.3}$$

4. Linearly elastic–linearly strainhardening plastic (plastic–plastic) curve as shown in Fig. 3.1(*d*) and described by

$$\sigma = E\varepsilon \quad \text{for 0 to } \sigma_0$$
$$\sigma = \sigma_0 K\varepsilon \quad \text{from } \sigma_0 \text{ onward,} \tag{3.4}$$

5. Nonlinear-strainhardening plastic curve shown in Fig. 3.1(*e*) and described by

$$\sigma = K\varepsilon^n \quad \text{where } 0 < n < 1 \tag{3.5}$$

This relationship, called the Hollomon-Ludwik power law, is the most used, and it will be discussed elsewhere.

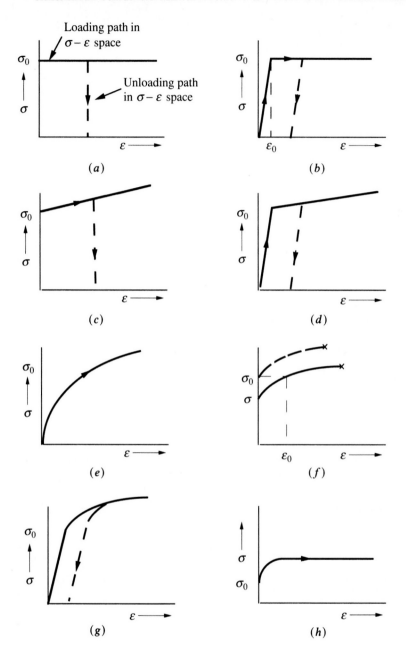

FIGURE 3.1
Schematic stress-strain curves for the following idealized materials: (*a*) rigid–perfectly plastic; (*b*) elastic–perfectly plastic; (*c*) rigid–linearly strainhardening plastic; (*d*) linearly elastic–linearly strainhardening plastic; (*e*) nonlinear strainhardening plastic; (*f*) rigid nonlinear strainhardening plastic; (*g*) linearly elastic–nonlinear strainhardening plastic (elastic–plastic); (*h*) elastic–steady state plastic.

6. Rigid-nonlinear strainhardening, plastic curve with no initial coldworking as shown in Fig. 3.1(f) (solid curve) and described by

$$\sigma = \sigma_0 + K\varepsilon^n \tag{3.6}$$

This curve ignores the elastic deformation, which is very small as compared to the plastic deformation. In Eq. (3.6), K and n are considered to be material constants (i.e., they are constant for a given material but vary from material to material) and the strain rate is assumed to be constant. K and n are determined from a specimen that has had no prior strainhardening.

7. Rigid–nonlinear strainhardening plastic curve, in which the material has been strained ε_0 by prior coldworking as shown in Fig. 3.1(f) (dashed curve), and as described by Swift's equation

$$\sigma = K(\varepsilon_0 + \varepsilon_i)^n \qquad \text{where } 0 \le n \le 1 \tag{2.134)(3.7}$$

where $\varepsilon_0 =$ strain due to prior coldworking
$\varepsilon_i =$ strain due to subsequent plastic deformation.

8. Linearly elastic–nonlinear strainhardening plastic (elastic–plastic) curve as shown in Fig. 3.1(g) and described by

$$\sigma = E\varepsilon \qquad \text{from 0 to } \sigma_0 \tag{3.8)(a}$$

$$\sigma = K\varepsilon^n \qquad \text{from } \sigma_0 \text{ onward} \tag{3.8)(b}$$

where $0 < n < 1$.

9. Elastic–steady state plastic deformation at high strains and/or temperature as shown in Fig. 3.1(h) and as described by

$$\sigma = \sigma_0 + C[1 - e^{-D\varepsilon}]^n \tag{3.9}$$

where σ_0, C, D, and n are constants depending on the strain rate and temperature. This equation reduces to Eq. (3.1) at small strains.

Other more complex equations [3.2] for the stress-strain curve have been proposed, but they will not be discussed here. In many cases in metalworking, the actual, experimental stress-strain curve is used.

In some cases after the experimental data are obtained, a curve is fitted to the data, most conveniently by use of a digital computer. Once the constants of the equation have been determined at a series of temperatures, strain rates, etc., it is possible to estimate values for intermediate temperatures, strain rates, etc., and to generate the desired flow curve on the computer printout.

3.3 TYPICAL EXPERIMENTAL STRESS-STRAIN CURVES FOR TENSION

Usually the relationship between stress and strain is obtained by means of an experimental stress-strain curve obtained by uniaxial tension for certain fixed conditions of temperature and strain (loading) rate. Experimental stress-strain curves, as will be discussed later, may be obtained by other means such as by uniaxial compression, plane strain compression, and torsion. The different methods have their advantages and disadvantages, but probably the simplest, most convenient method, the one that yields the most information and is the most used, is the one in uniaxial tension. The stress-strain curves discussed here are called *monotonic stress-strain curves*, as they are obtained by continuous loading rather than by cyclic loading as used in fatigue testing. They may also be called quasi-static, stress-strain curves as they are obtained at a rather low strain rate such as about $10^{-3}/s$, which is typical of a slow speed testing machine. The three common types of experimental, stress-strain curves for different metallic materials, shown in Fig. 3.2, that are of interest here are type I, linearly elastic curve; type II, elastic, homogeneous plastic curve; and type III, elastic, plastic curve with discontinuous yielding, i.e., with a yield point.

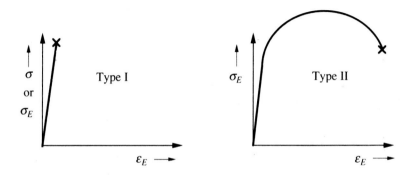

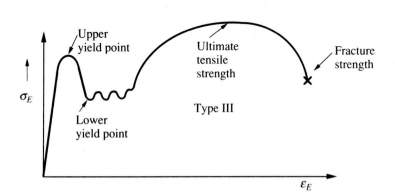

FIGURE 3.2
Common types of experimental engineering stress-strain curves for metallic materials: type I, linearly elastic; type II, elastic, plastic; and type III, elastic, plastic with discontinuous yielding.

Most metallic materials have a type II stress-strain curve; however, a very commonly used material, low-carbon steel, has a type III stress-strain curve. The load or stress at which the sudden drop occurs is called the *upper yield point* at which a discrete band of localized yielding forms at some stress concentration, such as a fillet for some materials, typically low-carbon steel. As the band or bands, called Luders bands, spread along the gauge length of the test specimen, the yield-point elongation occurs giving the lower yield point. The yield point has been attributed to two mechanisms: (1) unlocking of pinned dislocations (Cottrell) and (2) rapid multiplication of dislocations (Hahn), the more acceptable one. (See Figs. 2.48–2.52.) After the Luders bands have completely traversed the gauge length of the test specimen, further homogeneous deformation continues until necking begins. If hot-rolled, mild or low-carbon steel is deformed plastically such as in a temper-pass mill, the yield point disappears and the steel will have a type II stress-strain curve. However, the yield point will gradually return over a week or two unless the steel has been killed with aluminum, i.e., aluminum is added to the ingot mold just prior to the pouring of the ingot.

3.4 DEFORMATION AT LARGE PLASTIC STRAINS [3.3]

One of the big differences between stress-strain considerations in mechanical and structural design and in metalforming is that in the former the deformation results in only small strain in the elastic and small plastic range at the most, whereas in metalforming deformation occurs in large plastic strain. Strainhardening descriptions at large strain are inferred rather inadequately from uniaxial tensile tests, which are restricted to moderately plastic strain of less than 0.5 by plastic instability or necking.

Experiments show that strainhardening, rather than saturation or strain-softening, is more common at large strains. The power law equations (3.5), (3.6), (3.7), and (3.8b) predict continued strainhardening for large strain, whereas other model equations (such as by Voce and Kocks) predict saturation. Figs. 3.3 and 3.4 show the strainhardening behavior of annealed 1100 aluminum deformed under several different modes. As shown in Fig. 3.4, strainhardening does not saturate at high stresses but persists at slow strainhardening rates of $\theta = d\sigma/d\varepsilon$. This behavior may be the result of texture development or of microstructural effects such as different deformation mechanisms, deformation banding, or shear banding. Texture development plays a minor role at strains less than about 0.3.

Armstrong et al. [3.4] compared monotonic uniaxial compression with interruptions for machining (to be discussed later) with sequential, multidirectional compression of aluminum. The multidirectional compression was conducted on a cube by compressing sequentially by identical strain increments of 7.5% across the x, y, and z faces of the cube. The flow stress was measured and plotted as a function of cumulative plastic strain. This composite flow curve is compared with the monotonic compression curve in Fig. 3.5, which shows that when loading is changed from monotonic to multidirectional or vice versa, the flow curves tend

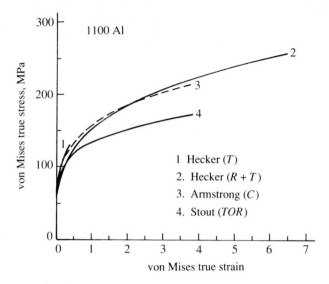

FIGURE 3.3
Comparison of torsion with other deformation modes in annealed 1100 aluminum. Torsion was performed on rod specimens using the method of Nadai to reduce torque-twist to stress-strain. All comparisons were made on the basis of von Mises effective stress and strain. (Test techniques: Tension (T), Rolling plus Tension (R + T), Compression (C), and Torsion (TOR).) [3.3].

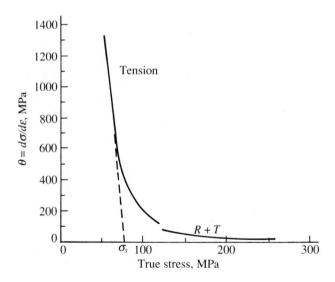

FIGURE 3.4
Strainhardening rate θ, as a function of stress for the flow curves 1, 2, and 3 in Fig. 3.3. Extrapolation of tensile data to a meaningful saturation stress is not possible (R + T stands for rolling plus tension.) [3.3].

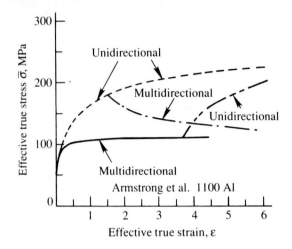

FIGURE 3.5
Stress strain curves for 1100 aluminum in unidirectional (dashed line) versus multidirectional (solid line) compression. The dash-dot curves represent changes in deformation mode from unidirectional to multidirectional and vice versa [3.3].

toward the current mode of loading. The transition from one type of strain-hardening to the other is very gradual. These results show that significant changes occur in strainhardening with changes in deformation modes, which often occurs in metalforming.

3.5 UNNOTCHED, UNIAXIAL, MONOTONIC TENSILE TEST AND ENGINEERING VERSUS TRUE STRESS AND STRAIN

In the elastic range and for small strain, less than about 0.2, the method of computing stress and strain is not important, because the methods commonly used give the same results. However, for large strains in the plastic range, the method of calculation may make a significant difference. The two methods yield what is called (1) engineering, conventional, or nominal stress or strain, and (2) true stress and true, natural, or logarithmic strain. The former will be referred to here as *engineering stress and engineering strain,* and the latter as *true stress and true strain.*

A number of different types of test specimens may be used in uniaxial tension, but the two most often used are (1) the unnotched, reduced-section, cylindrical specimen with threaded ends and (2) the reduced-section, flat specimens with vise-grip ends as specified by ASTM Standard E10, as shown in Fig. 3.6(*a*) and (*b*). Geometrically similar threaded test bars as shown in Fig. 3.6(*c*) have a constant ratio of $l_0/\sqrt{A_0}$ for the gauge section, where A_0 is the original cross-sectional area in the gauge section and l_0 is the original gauge length. This ratio for round specimens is l_0/d_0, and for Fig. 3.6(*c*), is 0.25. The rationale for proportionate sizes of specimens is discussed elsewhere.

As the specimen is loaded, the load P and the corresponding extension Δl of the gauge length is obtained either by recording the data manually at various points or by recording the information continuously on a chart of an x-y plotter,

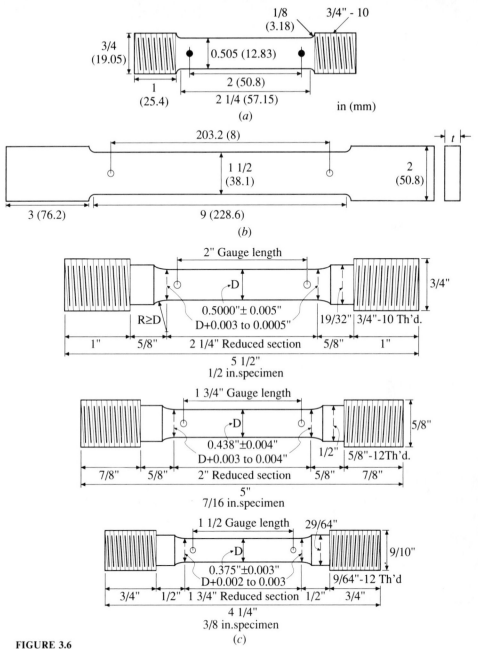

FIGURE 3.6
Common types of tension test specimens for metallic materials: (*a*) reduced-section round with threaded ends; (*b*) reduced-section flat with vise-grip ends; and (*c*) round proportional-sized with threaded ends. Smaller round specimens of the following nominal diameters, *D*, would have the following gauge lengths, G.L., and the total lengths T.L.: (*d*) $\frac{5}{16}$ in. D—$1\frac{1}{4}$ in. G.L. and $3\frac{3}{4}$ in. T.L. (*e*) $\frac{1}{4}$ in. D—1 in. G.L. and 3 in. T.L. (*f*) $\frac{3}{16}$ in. D—$\frac{3}{4}$ in. G.L. and $2\frac{3}{4}$ in. T.L., and (*g*) $\frac{1}{8}$ in. D—$\frac{1}{2}$ in. G.L. and $2\frac{1}{8}$ in. T.L. (*a*) (*Adapted from J. Wulff et al., Metallurgy for Engineers, John Wiley & Sons, 1952*), (*b*) *and* (*c*) *ASM Metals Hand Book, 1948 ed.*). (*a*) *and* (*b*) (*Adapted from E. P. deGarmo, Materials Processing in Manufacturing, 6th ed., Macmillan Pub. Co., 1985*), (*c*) *ASM Metals Handbook, 1948 ed.*)

depending on the sophistication of the available equipment. Engineering stress and strain are then calculated as follows:

$$\text{Engineering stress, } \sigma_E = \frac{\text{applied load}}{\text{original cross-sectional area}} = \frac{P}{A_0} \qquad (3.10)$$

$$\text{Engineering strain, } \varepsilon_E = \frac{\text{extension of gauge length}}{\text{original gauge length}} = \frac{l - l_0}{l_0} = \frac{\Delta l}{l_0} \qquad (3.11)$$

As the test specimen is loaded in uniaxial tension, it not only elongates, but it also contracts to give the lateral or transverse strain. As the specimen begins to neck, an appreciable amount of contraction of the diameter and area occur at the location of the neck. True stress is calculated by dividing the load P by the current, i.e., instantaneous cross-sectional area or the cross-sectional area A at the instant the load is measured as follows:

$$\sigma = P/A \qquad (3.12)$$

This method of calculating the true stress, as will be explained later, gives the average value of the stress distribution across the neck.

True strain prior to necking is obtained by referring small incremental changes in length to the instantaneous length l, i.e., the length that just preceded it, and by integrating over the total change in length as follows:

$$\varepsilon = \int_{l_0}^{l} \frac{dl}{l} = \ln \frac{l}{l_0} \qquad (3.13)$$

If the volume remains constant, $A_0 l_0 = A l$, then

$$\varepsilon = \ln \frac{l}{l_0} = \ln \frac{A_0}{A} = 2 \ln \frac{D_0}{D} \qquad (3.14)$$

where the symbols refer to the original and final lengths, areas, and diameters respectively. Since $l = l_0 + \Delta l$, true strain can be related to engineering strain as follows:

$$\varepsilon = \ln \left(\frac{l_0 + \Delta l}{l_0} \right) = \ln (1 + \varepsilon_E) \qquad (3.15)$$

The advantages of using true strain are as follows:

1. It is numerically equal in tension and compression but opposite in sign, which is not the case for engineering strain. For example, if a test specimen gauge length is elongated from 10 to 20 mm or compressed from 20 to 10 mm the following is obtained:

   (a) For true strain:

$$\varepsilon_T = \ln \frac{l}{l_0} = \ln \frac{20}{10} = 0.693$$

$$\varepsilon_C = \ln \frac{10}{20} = \ln \frac{1}{2} = -0.693$$

(b) For engineering strain:

$$\varepsilon_{E_T} = \frac{\Delta l}{l_0} = \frac{20-10}{10} = 2$$

$$\varepsilon_{E_C} = \frac{\Delta l}{l_0} = \frac{10-20}{10} = -\frac{1}{2}$$

Also, the compression of a specimen to zero thickness would give an engineering strain of -1, but a true strain of $-\infty$, which would indicate a much less realizable feat.

2. True strain is additive if done in successive stages. If a specimen gauge length is elongated from l_0 to l_1 and then to l_2, the total true strain is given by

$$\varepsilon_{l+2} = \varepsilon_1 + \varepsilon_2 = \ln\frac{l_1}{l_0} + \ln\frac{l_2}{l_1} = \ln\frac{l_2}{l_0} \tag{3.16}$$

whereas the engineering strain is given by

$$\varepsilon_{E_1} = \frac{l_1-l_0}{l_0} \qquad \varepsilon_{E_2} = \frac{l_2-l_1}{l_1} \qquad \varepsilon_{E_{1+2}} = \frac{l_2-l_0}{l_0} \tag{3.17}$$

Therefore

$$\varepsilon_{E_1} + \varepsilon_{E_1} \neq \varepsilon_{E_{1+2}} \tag{3.18}$$

A schematic true stress–true strain curve is plotted in Fig. 3.7, in which it is superimposed onto an engineering stress–engineering strain curve.

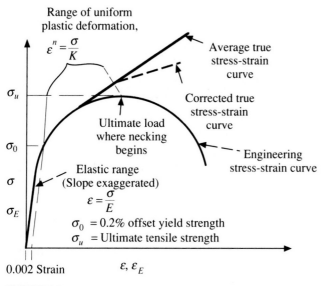

FIGURE 3.7
True stress–true strain curve superimposed onto a schematic engineering stress-engineering strain curve showing the former curve corrected for triaxial necking. (*Note:* The initial portions of the curves are exaggerated so that the elastic portion of the curves do not fall on the ordinate.)

In addition to the advantages for the use of true strain cited above, true stress, true strain, and the resulting true stress–true strain curve are very convenient and are extensively used in the literature for applications involving large deformations such as in plastic deformation. For example, the true stress–true strain curve for uniaxial tension has been shown to be equivalent to the stress–strain curve for effective stress $\bar{\sigma}$, and effective strain $\bar{\varepsilon}$, as stated previously.

One of the disadvantages of the true stress–true strain curve is that it is more difficult to obtain. Also, as normally obtained, the portion of the curve between the ultimate tensile strength and the fracture stress represents only the average stress across the neck and does not take into consideration the triaxial (spherical) state of stress resulting from the restraint caused by the neck. However, the Bridgman correction [3.5] may be applied as will be explained later to yield the corrected true stress–true strain curve as shown by the dashed line in Fig. 3.7. Because of the different assumptions and approximations made in the application of plasticity techniques to materials processing, this correction is largely academic and is seldom used.

The three common methods of obtaining the true stress–true strain curve are as follows:

1. Method of lateral dimensions, in which the reduction in the diameter D is obtained by a micrometer or a lateral "strain gauge." The true stress is calculated in the usual manner, that is, $\sigma = P/A$. The true strain is calculated as follows:

$$\varepsilon = \ln \frac{A_0}{A} = 2 \ln \frac{D_0}{D} \tag{3.14}$$

2. Method of axial strain, in which ε and σ are obtained from the engineering stress and strain data as follows:

$$\varepsilon = \ln \frac{l}{l_0} = \ln \frac{A_0}{A} = \ln (1 + \varepsilon_E) \tag{3.19}$$

$$\frac{A}{A_0} = 1 + \varepsilon_E \qquad A = \frac{A_0}{1 + \varepsilon_E} \qquad \sigma = \frac{P}{A} = \frac{P}{A_0}(1 + \varepsilon_E) = \sigma_E(1 + \varepsilon_E)$$

The determination of the true stress–true strain curve in this manner is very approximate, especially after necking begins.

3. Two-load or MacGregor method, in which σ and ε are determined at the ultimate load P_u, and at the load at fracture P_f, on a specimen whose gauge length has an hourglass shape cut to a radius of 305 mm (12 in). The approximate true stress–true strain curve is then plotted between these two points.

Equations (2.80) and (3.5) describe adequately the behavior of a tensile specimen from the point of initial yielding at σ_0 to the point of application of the ultimate load as in Fig. 3.7 for a typical, fully annealed, metallic material. To account for the effect of cold working, that may have been introduced prior to testing, Swift introduced Eq. (3.7). To indicate that this is the equivalent or effective stress, this equation has been written previously as

$$\bar{\sigma} = K(\bar{\varepsilon}_0 + \bar{\varepsilon}_i)^n \tag{2.134}$$

If a certain amount of cold work is induced in a metal, it corresponds to a particular fractional reduction in area R. The strain equivalent to this reduction can be obtained by use of Eq. (3.14) as follows:

$$R = \frac{A_0 - A}{A_0} = \left(1 - \frac{A}{A_0}\right) \qquad \frac{A_0}{A} = \frac{1}{1-R} \qquad \varepsilon = \ln \frac{A_0}{A} = \ln \left(\frac{1}{1-R}\right) \tag{3.20}$$

It should be pointed out here that K and n are constant for a material in a certain specific condition. These parameters, of course, would be different for an annealed, heat-treated specific steel, and for an annealed, precipitation hardened and overaged aluminum alloy.

3.6 THE RELEVANT FLOW STRESS [3.6]

From a practical standpoint the flow stress is the stress at which plastic deformation can be initiated and maintained at the significant strain, strain rate, and temperature prevailing in the deformation process. It should be emphasized that the tabled values of the yield stress $\sigma_{0.2}$ found in handbooks, which is an index of the point at which plastic flow is initiated for a given set of testing conditions, is usually not a meaningful index of the flow stress. The yield stress as such is used primarily in design to indicate the load at which the deformation changes from elastic to plastic, i.e., from recoverable to permanent deformation. If the equation for the stress-strain curve, such as the power law $\sigma = C\varepsilon^n \dot{\varepsilon}^m$ is known and all of the variables and parameters are known, then the flow stress can be determined rather easily.

This situation is seldom the case, so that usually the flow stress must be estimated, which often results in appreciable error. For a nonsteady state process, such as forging, the instantaneous flow stress at the end of the stroke is used. It should be remembered that the strain rate should not be confused with the deformation velocity or press speed. The strain rate is the instantaneous deformation velocity divided by the instantaneous height of the test specimen or workpiece, that is, $\bar{\varepsilon} = v/h$. For a steady state process, such as continuous extrusion or wire drawing, the specimen or workpiece usually strain and/or strain rate hardens, so that a mean flow stress σ_{fm} may be used as shown in Fig. 3.8. It may be found by integration, or by calculating the value of the flow stress at selected strains such as $\varepsilon = 0.1, 0.2, 0.3$, etc., up to the deformation to be obtained. The curve thus obtained is then extrapolated to zero and the mean flow stress σ_{fm} is found by visual averaging as shown in Fig. 3.8(a). The conveniently determined ultimate tensile strength fortuitously gives a reasonable approximation of the mean flow stress σ_{fm} for many common metallic materials as shown in Fig. 3.8(b) for a true strain of 0.5. This is why the ultimate tensile stress appears in many rules of thumb for calculating forming loads, etc. Since the ultimate load used to determine

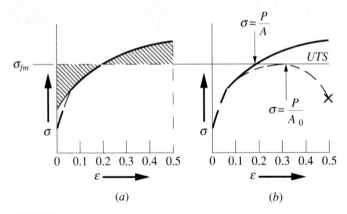

FIGURE 3.8
Determination of relevant flow stress for (*a*) steady state and (*b*) its relation to the ultimate tensile strength (UTS). (A strain of 0.5 is used for illustrative purposes.) [3.6].

the ultimate tensile strength occurs at the point of necking where $\varepsilon_u = n$, some reasonable correction can be made for smaller or larger strains.

3.7 NOTCHED-BAR TENSILE TEST AND DUCTILE FAILURE INITIATION [3.7], [3.8]

In metallic materials, plastic flow is induced by shear stresses, which may be measured by an effective stress $\bar{\sigma}$, which is proportional to the root mean square of the differences of the principal stresses as follows:

$$\bar{\sigma} = \frac{1}{\sqrt{2}} [(\sigma_1 - \sigma_2)^2 + (\sigma_2 - \sigma_3)^2 + (\sigma_3 - \sigma_1)^2]^{1/2} \tag{2.55}$$

The extent of plastic flow is usually measured by the plastic strain increment $d\bar{\varepsilon}_p$ which is proportional to the root mean square of the differences of the principal plastic strain increments as follows:

$$d\bar{\varepsilon}_p = \frac{\sqrt{2}}{3} [(d\bar{\varepsilon}_{p1} - d\bar{\varepsilon}_{p2})^2 + (d\bar{\varepsilon}_{p2} - d\bar{\varepsilon}_{p3})^2 + (d\bar{\varepsilon}_{p3} - d\bar{\varepsilon}_{p1})^2]^{1/2} \tag{3.21}$$

This equation is similar to Eq. (2.58) for the simplified form of the effective plastic strain increment for the von Mises criterion. Both $\bar{\sigma}$ and $\bar{\varepsilon}_p$ are not affected by a third parameter, the mean or hydrostatic tensile stress, $\sigma_m = (\sigma_1 + \sigma_2 + \sigma_3)/2$, because plastic flow is produced by shear stresses which are proportional to the difference in the principal stresses.

The above two stress parameters may be combined into a single non-dimensional parameter $\sigma_m/\bar{\sigma}$, which characterizes the stress state and is a measure of its triaxiality. For example, for a stress state in which all the principal stresses are all tensile and nearly equal, having the ratio, say, $5:4:3$, $\sigma_m/\bar{\sigma}$ is equal to 2.3 as compared to 0.57 for a stress state having the ratio $2:1:0$.

In uniaxial tension, in which $\sigma_2 = \sigma_3 = 0$ before the neck forms

$$\bar{\sigma} = \sigma_1 \qquad \text{and} \qquad \sigma_m = \frac{\sigma_1}{3} \qquad \frac{\sigma_m}{\bar{\sigma}} = \frac{1}{3} \tag{3.22}$$

Also, in uniaxial tension for small reductions of diameter, the transverse plastic strain increments are equal and, if constancy of volume applies, by use of Eq. (3.21)

$$\bar{\varepsilon}_p = 2 \int d\varepsilon_{p2} \tag{3.23}$$

$$\bar{\varepsilon}_p = 2 \ln \frac{d_0}{d} \tag{3.24}$$

where $\bar{\varepsilon}_p$ = the effective plastic strain, which is constant across the neck
 d_0 = the original diameter
 d = the final diameter of the specimen at the neck

(The radii a_0 and a may be substituted for d_0 and d in the above equation as the factor 1/2 will cancel out.)

Bridgman's analysis for a necked, originally unnotched or smooth specimen (to be discussed in the next section) has been extended to prenotched specimens. The value of $\sigma_m/\bar{\sigma}$ at the neck or notch will rise from 1/3 at the outer surface of the neck to a maximum value on the longitudinal axis or at the center of the neck of the specimen as follows:

$$\left(\frac{\sigma_m}{\bar{\sigma}}\right)_{\max} = \frac{1}{3} + \ln\left(\frac{a}{2R} + 1\right) \tag{3.25}$$

where $a = d/2$, the radius of the neck
 R = the profile radius as shown in Fig. 3.9

The dimensions of the notch of a typical specimen that has been used are shown in Fig. 3.9.

A photograph of cracks formed in the center of the neck on the axis of a sectioned specimen at the location of the maximum tensile stress is shown in Fig. 3.10.

Typical stress-strain curves for a high-strength, low-alloy (HSLA) steel equivalent to a USS steel HY80 for a series of notched tensile specimens with different notch radii R, and for an unnotched specimen, are shown in Fig. 3.11. The stress was calculated here by dividing the load by the current cross-sectional area, and the strain was calculated by use of Eq. (3.24).

The strain ε_f, at which the stress begins to fall off sharply, has been defined as the *strain at failure initiation*. Examination of a longitudinal section of each specimen taken through the axis has shown that the sudden drop-off of stress as shown in Fig. 3.11 resulted from a coalescence or linking up of voids or holes, as shown in Fig. 3.12, that formed prior to the drop-off. Since this linking-up of the voids or holes results in a sudden loss of load-bearing cross section, it is

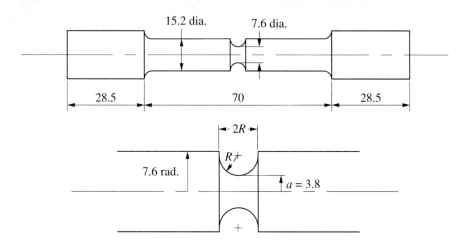

Specimen	R, mm
A	3.80
B	2.54
C	1.90
D	1.27
E	6.34

FIGURE 3.9
The geometry and dimensions of typical notched tensile specimens [3.7].

considered to be a unique occurrence in the failure process and has therefore been called *failure initiation.*

In Fig. 3.11, the specimens were taken from a hot rolled plate, in which the longitudinal axis of each specimen was parallel to the width and perpendicular to the direction of rolling. This type of specimen may be called a *long transverse* (LT) specimen. Specimens taken parallel to the edge and perpendicular to the rolled surfaces may be called *short transverse* (ST) specimens. Since the non-

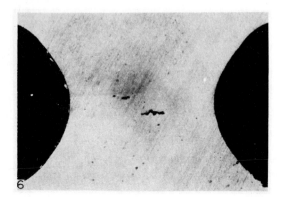

FIGURE 3.10
Photograph of the neck of a sectioned, notched specimen, showing the cracks at the location of the maximum tensile stress along the axis of the specimen [3.7].

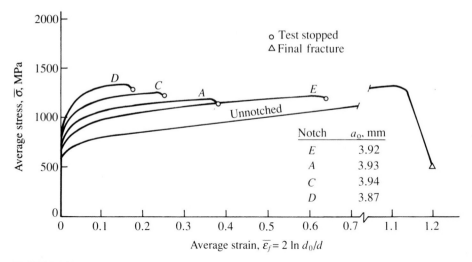

FIGURE 3.11
True stress–true strain curves for USS HY80 high strength low alloy (HSLA) steel. Specimens A to E are notched. All specimens are taken in the long traverse direction, i.e., with the axis of the specimen parallel to the width of the plate [3.7].

metallic inclusions, etc., have a tendency to roll out flat to give a greater projected area in planes parallel to the surface of rolling of plates, as expected, the short transverse specimen had, in this example, a significantly lower strain of failure initiation than their long transverse counterparts.

The results of the above tests have been correlated in terms of the stress state parameter $\sigma_m/\bar{\sigma}$ as calculated by use of Eq. (3.25) and the effective plastic strain $\bar{\varepsilon}_{pf}$ at failure initiation as shown in Fig. 3.13 for both orientations of specimens of the USS HY80 steel. A similar curve for annealed 1018 steel is also shown in Fig. 3.13. Failure initiation strains depend less strongly on $\sigma_m/\bar{\sigma}$ for annealed 1018 steel than they do for the high strength steels.

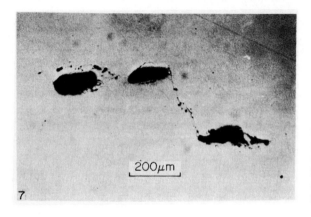

FIGURE 3.12
Photomicrograph showing the coalescence or link-up of voids or holes resulting in a sudden drop off of stress due to the loss of load-bearing cross section [3.7].

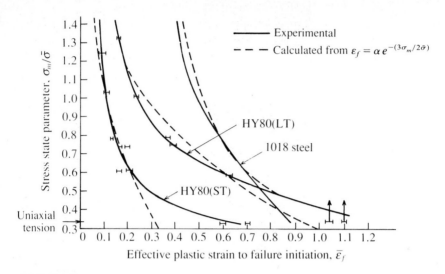

FIGURE 3.13

Failure initiation curves for hot-rolled USS 80 HSLA steel and annealed AISI/SAE 1018 steel showing the strong dependence of the effective plastic strain to failure, $\bar{\varepsilon}_f$, on the stress state parameter, $\sigma_m/\bar{\sigma}$, for specimens taken in the long and short traverse directions. Note that for a highly triaxial stress state, failure of HY(ST) occurs at a strain of about 0.1; whereas for uniaxial tension, it occurs at a strain of about 0.7 [3.8].

If it is assumed that the failure strain is inversely proportional to hole or void growth-rate within the material of the neck containing minute spherical voids, the strain for failure initiation for relatively low ductility (rigid, non-strainhardening) materials such as approximated by HSLA steels can be expressed as

$$\bar{\varepsilon}_f = \alpha \, e^{-(3\sigma_m/2\bar{\sigma})} \tag{3.26}$$

where α is a material constant. α, determined for one stress state, may possibly be used to predict failure strain at other stress states. For materials in which appreciable plastic flow occurs before voids nucleate, the above equation may be modified to

$$\bar{\varepsilon}_f = \bar{\varepsilon}_n + \alpha \, e^{-(3\sigma_m/2\bar{\sigma})} \tag{3.27}$$

where $\bar{\varepsilon}_n$ is the void nucleation strain, which may or may not be dependent on the stress state. The strain to failure initiation of high ductility materials should be much less dependent on the stress-state than the lower ductility material such as HSLA steels. (It should be noted here that the theory of ductile fracture investigated by Kobayashi and coworkers, discussed elsewhere, is based on a void growth model.)

From the above discussion, it appears that the strain to initiate failure in notched cylindrical specimens may be used as a criterion of workability of a metallic material, but at the present state of the art it must be on the basis of some arbitrary notch geometry such as the one used here with an initial notch radius R of 6.34 mm (0.250 in). The index of workability would then be the strain to initiate failure, $\bar{\varepsilon}_f$ for the material by use of the foregoing specimen. Since the test specimens can usually be taken in different directions in the material, this approach could also take mechanical anisotropy into account (see Sec. 2.2.10.1).

3.8 CORRECTED TRUE STRESS

In review, there are three ways for calculating the stress in an unnotched, cylindrical tensile specimen after localized or pronounced necking begins on monotonic loading:

1. By dividing the load by the original, cross-sectional area or P/A_0, which is called engineering or conventional stress
2. By dividing the load by the current or instantaneous area at the neck, which gives the average value of the stress distribution across the neck and which erroneously is called the "true" stress
3. By correcting the true stress for the triaxial state of stress occurring at the neck by multiplying it by the Bridgman correction factor to give the "corrected" true stress or the uniform flow stress

Due to the restraint caused by the large sections of the specimen adjacent to the neck, a triaxial or hydrostatic state of stress is developed in the neck of a cylindrical specimen as shown in Fig. 3.14. The nonuniformity at the neck causes a stress distribution as shown in Fig. 3.15. The stress at the outside surface of the neck is the corrected true stress or the uniform flow stress. At other points across the neck, the uniform flow stress is found by subtracting off the hydrostatic component, $\bar{\sigma}_r - \bar{\sigma}_{hyd}$. The remainder is the corrected true stress or the uniform flow stress as shown in Fig. 3.15. The corrected true stress or uniform flow stress, σ_t or σ_{corr}, may be found by multiplying the average stress across the neck σ_{ave}, the so-called true stress, by the Bridgman correction factor or

$$\sigma_{corr} = B\sigma_{ave}$$

and

$$B = \frac{1}{(1 + 2R/a) \ln (1 + a/2R)} \tag{3.28}$$

where a = radius of the neck cross section
$\quad\quad\quad R$ = the profile radius as shown in Fig. 3.15 [3.9]

The correction factor can also be obtained from Fig. 3.16. The value of R can be conveniently obtained by use of a jeweler's ring gauge, by photography, or by use of an optical comparator.

The maximum stress σ^*, i.e., the stress on the axis or centerline of the neck, can be obtained to a good approximation by use of Table 3.1, which gives the factor $C = \ln [1 + \frac{1}{2}(a/R)]$, by which the corrected true stress, i.e., flow stress σ_{corr}, can be multiplied to obtain the hydrostatic tension for a specimen pulled

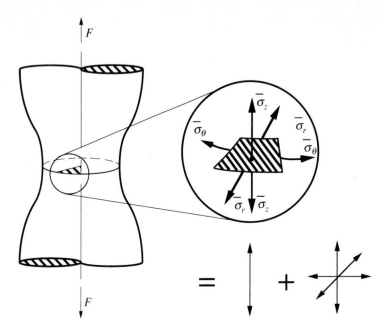

FIGURE 3.14
The necked portion of a tensile specimen showing the directions of the normal, radial, and tangential stresses and the triaxial state of stress.

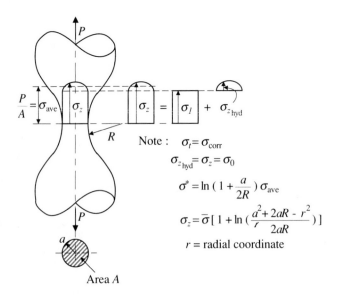

Note : $\sigma_l = \sigma_{corr}$

$\sigma_{z_{hyd}} = \sigma_z = \sigma_0$

$\sigma^* = \ln\left(1 + \dfrac{a}{2R}\right)\sigma_{ave}$

$\sigma_z = \bar{\sigma}\left[1 + \ln\left(\dfrac{a^2 + 2aR - r^2}{2aR}\right)\right]$

r = radial coordinate

FIGURE 3.15
Stress distribution in the neck of a tensile specimen showing the graphical determination of the corrected true stress, σ_{corr} [3.9].

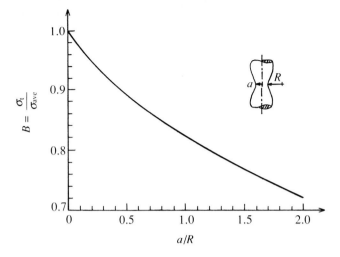

FIGURE 3.16
Variation of the Bridgman correction factor B with the ratio of radius of the neck a to the radius of the curvature of the contour or profile at the neck R. $\sigma_t = \sigma_{corr}$ [3.9].

to a true strain of $\ln A_0/A = 2 \ln d_0/d$. The stress on the axis σ^* can be calculated by use of Table 3.1 as follows:

$$\sigma^* = B\sigma_{ave} + BC\sigma_{ave} = \bar{\sigma}_{corr} + C\bar{\sigma}_{corr}$$

$$\sigma^* = B\sigma_{ave} + D\sigma_{ave} = \bar{\sigma}_{corr} + \bar{\sigma}_{hyd} \tag{3.29}$$

where B = Bridgman correction factor given in Eq. (3.28)
σ_{ave} = true or average stress
and C and D are also as defined in Table 3.1

TABLE 3.1
Correction factors for the calculation of σ_{corr} and σ^* for a given true strain

$\varepsilon = \ln A_0/A$	B Bridgman correction factor	C $\ln(1+a/R)$	$D = BC$ σ_{hyd}/σ
0.1	1.000	0.000	0.000
0.5	0.920	0.165	0.152
1.0	0.852	0.325	0.277
1.5	0.803	0.448	0.360
2.0	0.776	0.533	0.414
2.5	0.752	0.601	0.451
3.0	0.736	0.649	0.477
3.5	0.724	0.690	0.499
4.0	0.715	0.718	0.513

Table 3.1 may be used to calculate a small amount of data, or during the progress of a test by use of a hand calculator. A computer would be used to calculate a large amount of data more precisely using the following equations:

$$\bar{\sigma}_{\text{corr}} = \bar{\sigma}_{\text{ave}}\left[\left(1+\frac{2R}{a}\right)\ln\left(1+\frac{a}{2R}\right)\right]^{-1} \tag{3.30}$$

$$\sigma^* = \bar{\sigma}_{\text{corr}}\left[1+\ln\left(\frac{a^2+2aR}{2aR}\right)\right] \tag{3.31}$$

$$\bar{\sigma}_{\text{ave}} = \frac{\text{axial load}}{\text{instantaneous area}} = \frac{P}{A} \tag{3.32}$$

where $\bar{\sigma}_{\text{corr}} =$ the corrected effective true stress
  $\sigma^* =$ the axial stress at the center of the test specimen
  $\bar{\sigma}_{\text{ave}} =$ the average effective stress

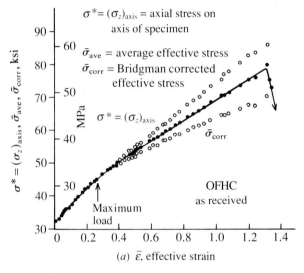

(a) $\bar{\varepsilon}$, effective strain

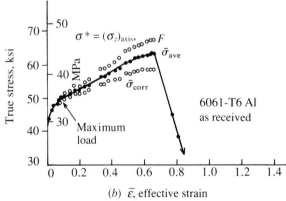

(b) $\bar{\varepsilon}$, effective strain

FIGURE 3.17
Plot of stress-strain data showing the axial stress, the average effective stress, and the corrected effective stress for (a) OFHC copper and (b) 6061-T6 aluminum [3.10].

These parameters as obtained by Thomsen et al. [3.10] for OFHC copper and 6061-T6 aluminum alloy are shown in Fig. 3.17(a) and (b), respectively.

3.9 PLASTIC TENSILE INSTABILITY AND NECKING

3.9.1 Definition of Instability

Deformation with a continuously rising load is considered here to be stable, so that deformation involved with a yield point or that following the maximum load on a specimen, on the basis of which the ultimate strength is calculated, is unstable. In the tension test, necking begins at the maximum load that can be supported by the specimen. Another criterion for instability is: if a difference in area of two cross sections of a tensile specimen increases, the deformation is unstable, and if it remains constant or decreases it is stable. As the name implies during a condition of instability, the material deforms in a relatively uncontrolled manner. Under certain conditions of state of stress and material properties, additional, useful deformation may continue to occur.

3.9.2 Necking in General

Necking, or the transverse reduction in area in general may be classified as shown in Fig. 3.18 as (1) diffused necking for which the reduction in cross-sectional area extends over an appreciable length of the specimen and is not affected appreciably by the adjacent elements of the specimen, and (2) localized or pronounced necking, in which appreciable interaction between adjacent elements of the specimen occurs leading to a superimposed triaxial state of stress and to a gradual departure from uniaxiality of loading.

Since necking begins at the maximum load, the condition of plastic instability (necking) is defined by the condition that $dP = 0$. Since $P = \sigma A$, then

$$dP = \sigma \, dA + A \, d\sigma = 0$$

and
$$(3.33)$$

$$-\frac{dA}{A} = \frac{d\sigma}{\sigma}$$

Physically, the foregoing means that the increase in strength due to strain-hardening just balances the decrease in area. Further, strain causes instability leading to the formation of a neck, and finally to fracture. If the constancy of volume condition holds, i.e.,

$$V = Al = C$$

$$(3.34)$$

$$dV = A \, dl + l \, dA = 0$$

or

$$-\frac{dA}{A} = \frac{dl}{l} = d\varepsilon$$

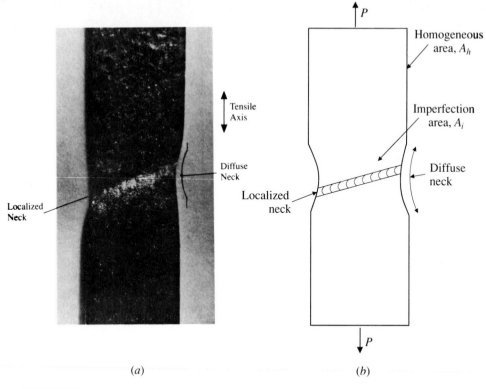

(a) (b)

FIGURE 3.18
(a) Photograph and (b) sketch of a diffuse and a localized neck in a 1100 aluminum sheet tensile specimen. (See Fig. 3.19.) [3.16].

Substituting in Eq. (3.33) for dA/A, one obtains

$$\frac{d\sigma}{\sigma} = d\varepsilon \qquad \text{or} \qquad \frac{d\sigma}{d\varepsilon} = \sigma = \sigma_u \qquad (3.35)$$

where σ_u is the ultimate tensile strength.

If $\sigma = K\varepsilon^n$ and Eq. (3.35) applies, then

$$\frac{d\sigma}{d\varepsilon} = nK\varepsilon^{n-1} = \sigma = K\varepsilon^n$$

$$nK\varepsilon^{n-1} = K\varepsilon^n$$

$$\frac{n}{\varepsilon} = 1 \qquad (3.36)$$

and necking occurs when $\varepsilon = n$ [3.11].

A comparison of two materials, 1100-O aluminum and 18-8 stainless steel with low and high K and n values, respectively, are shown in Table 3.2.

TABLE 3.2
Stress-related properties and parameters for 1100-0 aluminum and 18-8 stainless steel

Property or parameter	1100-0 Al	18-8 stainless steel
Yield strength, σ_Y	24 MPa (3.5 ksi)	275 MPa (40.1 ksi)
Ultimate strength, σ_u	48 MPa (7.0 ksi)	725 MPa (105.6 ksi)
Elongation	45%	55%
n and ε_u at necking	0.20	0.51
Engineering strain at point of necking, σ_{uE}	0.22	0.67
Engineering strain at fracture, ε_{Ef}	9.0	1.9
True strain at fracture, ε_f	2.3	1.1

If σ is function of ε and $\dot{\varepsilon}$ at constant T, Eq. (3.33) leads to

$$0 = \sigma \, dA + A\left(\frac{\partial \sigma}{\partial \varepsilon}\right)\Bigg|_{\dot{\varepsilon} T} d\varepsilon + A\left(\frac{\partial \sigma}{\partial \dot{\varepsilon}}\right)\Bigg|_{\varepsilon T} d\dot{\varepsilon} \tag{3.37}$$

Using Eq. (3.34) and letting

$$\gamma = \frac{1}{\sigma}\left(\frac{\partial \sigma}{\partial \varepsilon}\right)\Bigg|_{\dot{\varepsilon} T} \tag{3.38}$$

$$m = \frac{\dot{\varepsilon}}{\sigma}\left(\frac{\partial \sigma}{\partial \dot{\varepsilon}}\right)\Bigg|_{\varepsilon T} \tag{3.39}$$

and

$$\alpha = \frac{1}{\dot{\varepsilon}}\frac{d\dot{\varepsilon}}{d\varepsilon} \tag{3.40}$$

one obtains from Eq. (3.37)

$$0 = -1 + \gamma + m\alpha \qquad \text{or} \qquad \alpha = \frac{1 - \gamma}{m} \tag{3.41}$$

where γ = dimensionless strainhardening coefficient
 m = strain-rate hardening (sensitivity) exponent
 α = localized flow parameter

When $\alpha = -1$ for uniform flow at the maximum load at uniform crosshead speed, Eq. (3.41) becomes

$$\gamma = 1 + m \tag{3.42}$$

The necking process can then be expressed in terms of the following two phenomenological parameters:

1. A dimensionless strainhardening coefficient [3.12]:

$$\gamma = \frac{1}{\sigma}\left(\frac{\partial \sigma}{\partial \varepsilon}\right)\Bigg|_{\dot{\varepsilon}} \tag{3.43}$$

2. The strain-rate sensitivity:

$$m = \frac{d \ln \sigma}{d \ln \dot{\varepsilon}}\bigg|_{\varepsilon} = \frac{\dot{\varepsilon}}{\sigma}\left(\frac{\partial \sigma}{\partial \dot{\varepsilon}}\right)\bigg|_{\varepsilon} \tag{3.44}$$

The criterion, therefore, for stable, uniform *tensile* deformation is

$$\gamma + m \geq 1 \tag{3.45}$$

As indicated above, necking involves an interplay between the applied stress and the resistance to flow of the material. As the specimen elongates under a given load, the area decreases and the stress increases. If necking is not to occur, the flow strength of the material must increase through strainhardening and strain-rate hardening as expressed by γ and m.

At room temperature m approaches 0, and the instability criterion reduces to $\gamma \geq 1$, and from Eq. (3.43), the stable tensile deformation occurs for

$$\frac{\partial \sigma}{\partial \varepsilon} \geq \sigma \tag{3.46}$$

Both material and dimensional inhomogeneities, which may influence necking, may occur in a test specimen or workpiece. Materials possess variations in composition and microstructure such as grain size, shape, and orientation, etc. The specimen or workpiece may also contain variations in the diameter or thickness due to uneven machining or metalworking; it may contain grooves, notches, etc.

It has been shown that Eq. (3.45) attributed to Hart is not a valid stability criterion for geometric imperfections, i.e., initial cross-sectional variations; rather the criterion may more accurately be expressed as

$$\gamma \geq \left[\frac{1 - m}{1 - \dfrac{\delta \ln A_0}{\delta \ln A}} \right] \tag{3.47}$$

where A_0 is the initial cross section, A is the current cross section, and δ refers to fluctuations inside and outside the geometric imperfection [3.13].

To simplify analysis, a physically homogeneous tensile specimen may be considered with a dimensional inhomogeneity consisting of a slightly reduced cross section as shown in Fig. 3.19. The severity of the inhomogeneity may be defined by the dimensional inhomogeneity factor or ratio as follows:

$$f = \frac{A_{i0}}{A_{h0}} = \frac{\text{original area of the inhomogeneity (neck)}}{\text{original area of the homogeneous specimen}} \tag{3.48}$$

where $A_{i0} < A_{h0}$. $f = 1$ for complete homogeneity.

In some cases a material inhomogeneity may be expressed in terms of an equivalent dimensional inhomogeneity.

Since the regions inside and outside the geometric imperfections are coupled in series, they must support the same tensile load, that is, $P_i = P_h$ or $A\sigma_i = A_h\sigma_h$,

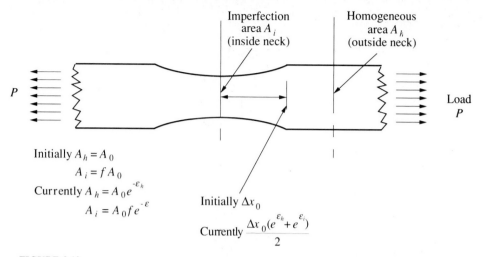

FIGURE 3.19
A schematic representation of a preexisting geometric imperfection, i.e., dimensional inhomogeneity, in an otherwise homogeneous tensile specimen [3.13].

but they may differ in the strain induced. If one lets $A_j = A_{j0} \, e^{-\varepsilon_j}$, where the subscript j refers to the initial section, the load equilibrium yields

$$A_{i0} \, e^{-\varepsilon_i} \sigma_i = A_{h0} \, e^{-\varepsilon_h} \qquad (3.49)$$

where σ_i, σ_h, and ε_i, ε_h are stresses and strains, respectively, inside and outside the inhomogeneity, and A_{i0} and A_{h0} are the original cross-sectional areas inside and outside the inhomogeneity (neck).

Numerical solution of Eq. (3.49) may be obtained by use of a constitutive equation such as one of the following:

$$(1) \quad \sigma = K\varepsilon^n \qquad (3.5)$$

$$(2) \quad \sigma = K\varepsilon^n \dot{\varepsilon}^m \qquad (3.50)$$

$$(3) \quad \sigma = K\left(\varepsilon^n + m' \ln \frac{\dot{\varepsilon}}{\dot{\varepsilon}_0} \right) \qquad \text{for} \qquad \dot{\varepsilon} \le \dot{\varepsilon}_0 \qquad (3.51)$$

where K refers to a strength coefficient, n = the strainhardening exponent, m and m' = strain rate sensitivity indices, and ε_0 = reference strain at which strain-rate hardening is negligible [3.13].

Using Eqs. (3.48) and (3.49) and the power law Eq. (3.5), one can show that

$$f \, e^{-\varepsilon_i} \varepsilon_i^n = e^{-\varepsilon_h} \varepsilon_h^n \qquad (3.52)$$

Equation (3.52) can be solved numerically for given values of f and n to give ε_h as a function of ε_i up to the value of $\varepsilon_i = n$, where necking begins as shown in Fig. 3.20 for $n = 0.25$ and $m = 0$. It should be noted that in Fig. 3.20 ε_h lags behind ε_i for $f < 1$ and saturates at a level of $\varepsilon_h^* = n$ or 0.25 in this case, which is the critical true strain for necking to be discussed in the next section.

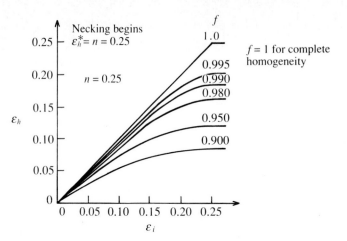

FIGURE 3.20
Comparison of strains induced in tensile specimens for different inhomogeneity factors f, assuming $n = 0.25$. Figure 3.19 indicates regions i and h [2.4].

On the other hand, if one uses Eq. (3.50) instead of Eq. (3.5), one can obtain

$$f e^{-\varepsilon_i} \varepsilon_i^n \dot{\varepsilon}_i^m = e^{-\varepsilon_h} \varepsilon_h^n \dot{\varepsilon}_h^m \tag{3.53}$$

The rate of growth of diffused necking is strongly influenced by n, m, f, and also by the fracture properties of the material.

The rate of growth, calculated numerically, of the diffused neck using Eq. (3.51) increases with n as shown in Fig. 3.21 for $m = 0.1$, $f = 0.99$ and $\varepsilon_0 = a$ constant at some negligible value [3.13].

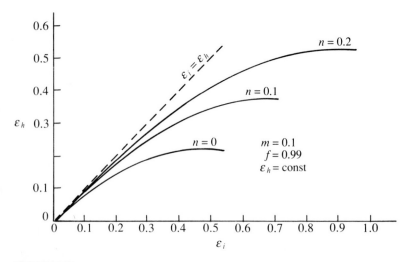

FIGURE 3.21
The influence of the strainhardening exponent n on the strain inside the neck ε_i [3.13].

The strain-rate hardening exponent m has a more pronounced effect than n in slowing the growth of the diffused neck. The calculated growth rate of the diffused neck, using the differential form of Eq. (3.50), increases with m as shown in Fig. 3.22 for $n = 0.1$ and $f = 0.99$. The pronounced effect of m on decreasing the growth of the diffused neck as compared to n can be seen by comparing the curve for $m = 0$ in Fig. 3.22 to that of $n = 0.1$ in Fig. 3.21.

By use of Eq. (3.5), the calculated effect of n, as a result of a departure from uniaxiality for localized necking on the engineering stress-strain curves for the case of $f = 0.996$, $m = 0$, r (the anisotropic plastic strain ratio discussed elsewhere) $= 1$, and $K = 510.16$ MPa (74.0 ksi) for the following values of n: 0.05, 0.10, 0.20, 0.30, and 0.40, is shown in Fig. 3.23. Since K has the same value for all cases, and a true strain of 1 would represent a relatively large strain and an extrapolation of the true stress–true strain curve, a drop in the engineering stress level occurs with increasing values of n.

The calculated influence of m for localized necking, using Eqs. (3.49) and (3.51) for $f = 0.996$, $n = 0.1$, $r = 1$, $K = 510.16$ MPa (74.0 ksi) and $\dot{\varepsilon}_0 = 0.003 \text{ s}^{-1}$ on the engineering stress-strain curves for $m = 0$ to 0.05, is shown in Fig. 3.24. It should be noted that the uniform strain occurring after the maximum load increases strongly with m and to a much lesser extent with n, as can be seen by comparing Figs. 3.23 and 3.24, and that m enhances n so that the combined influence of n and m is significantly greater than that of either n or m alone, as shown in Fig. 3.25 [3.13]. [Compare Figs. 3.23 and 3.24 to Figs. 2.80 and 2.81.]

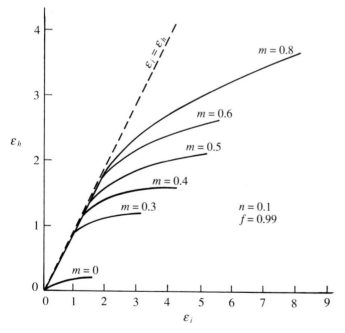

FIGURE 3.22
The influence of strain-rate sensitivity m on the strain inside the neck ε_i [3.13].

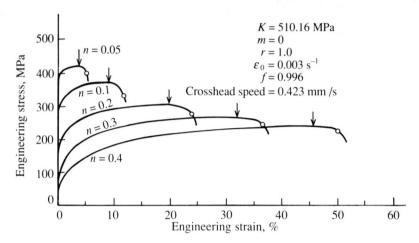

FIGURE 3.23
Engineering stress-strain curves calculated for $m = 0$ and $f = 0.996$ for hypothetical materials [3.13].

3.9.3 Necking in Sheetmetal

For a biaxial state of stress where the major strain is positive and the minor strain is negative, localized necking is recognized as the failure mechanism. Hill and others have analyzed this type of instability for anisotropic materials using Hill's theory of anisotropy. The plastic instability criterion is expressed analytically by the equation

$$\frac{d\bar{\sigma}}{d\bar{\varepsilon}} \leq f(F, G, H, \bar{\sigma}, \bar{\varepsilon}, \dot{\bar{\varepsilon}}, \alpha, T) \leq \frac{\bar{\sigma}}{Z} \tag{3.54}$$

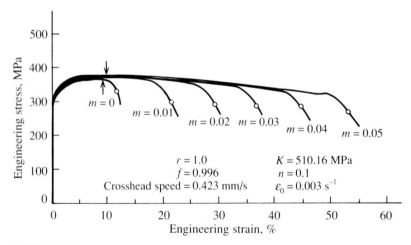

FIGURE 3.24
Engineering stress-strain curves calculated for $n = 0.1$ and $f = 0.996$ for hypothetical materials [3.13].

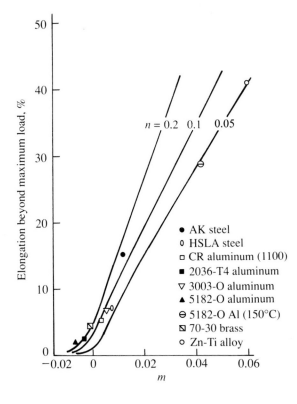

FIGURE 3.25
Postuniform strain (i.e., the engineering strain beyond the maximum load) for tensile tests of sheets. The solid curves are calculated as a function of m with n held constant at 0.2, 0.1, and 0.05. Points represent experimental data for materials shown on the graph [3.13].

where F, G, and H are anisotropy parameters, $\bar{\sigma}$ is the effective stress, $\bar{\varepsilon}$ is the effective strain, $\alpha = \sigma_2/\sigma_1$ is the ratio of the principal stresses, and ε and T are the strain rate and temperature which are here held constant [3.14]. F, G, and H are related to the anisotropic plastic strain ratios by

$$\frac{G}{H} = \frac{1}{r_{0°}} \tag{2.115}$$

and

$$\frac{F}{H} = \frac{1}{r_{90°}} \tag{2.116}$$

where $r_{0°}$ = the anisotropic plastic strain ratio of a specimen cut in the direction of rolling

$r_{90°}$ = the strain ratio cut at 90° to the direction of rolling

Another simplified way of expressing the above condition for diffused necking for pure uniaxial tension is

$$\frac{1}{\sigma}\left(\frac{d\sigma}{d\varepsilon}\right) \leq 1 \tag{3.55}$$

which is just another statement of Eq. (3.46).

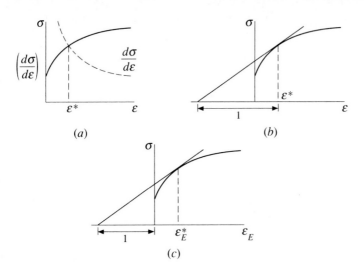

FIGURE 3.26
Graphical means of finding the necking strain. In relating (b) and (c), $\varepsilon = \ln(1 + \varepsilon_E)$ [3.15].

The critical true strain, ε^* for necking can be found graphically by plotting $d\sigma/d\varepsilon$ versus ε on a σ-ε plot as shown in Fig. 3.26(a) for diffused necking. ε^* can also be found, by trial and error, by moving a unit length ($\varepsilon = 1$) of the abscissa until a line from the left terminus is tangent to the σ-ε curve exactly above the right terminus as shown in Fig. 3.26(b). The above construction can be simplified by replacing ε with ε_E, where

$$\varepsilon_E = \frac{l - l_0}{l} = \frac{l}{l_0} - 1$$

$$\frac{l_0}{l} = 1 + \varepsilon_E$$

$$\varepsilon = \ln\left(\frac{l}{l_0}\right) = \ln(l + \varepsilon_E) \qquad (3.56)$$

The plot of σ versus ε_E will give the construction attributed to Considere shown in Fig. 3.26(c) [3.15].

A sheetmetal specimen in uniaxial tension may also acquire both a diffused and a localized neck, as shown in Fig. 3.18. The growth of a diffused neck is terminated either by fracture or by localized, through-thickness necking. Inasmuch as localized necking is used as the failure criterion in many sheetmetal forming operations such as stretching and deep drawing, it will be discussed here further. In this discussion it will be assumed that the stress-strain curve for tension will not have a yield point, such as is caused by the formation of Luders bands, and that the material is isotropic ($r = 1$).

In localized necking the sheetmetal specimen is thinned along a narrow band inclined at an angle ϕ to the axis of loading as shown in Fig. 3.27 [3.15].

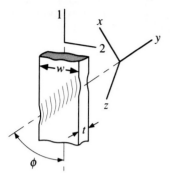

FIGURE 3.27
Local neck in a strip tension specimen. (Normal strain ε_{yy} along y axis must be zero.) (If $\varepsilon_{yy} \neq 0$, a diffused neck forms.) [3.15].

The orientation of the band, as designated by ϕ, is governed by the need for the normal strain along the neck $d\varepsilon_y$ to be zero, i.e., it must conform to the condition of plane strain. If $d\varepsilon_y$ is not zero, adjoining material will deform and the band will spread out to form a diffused neck.

Local instability is expected to occur when the current rate of strain-hardening in the diffused neck is just balanced by the rate of decrease in the cross-sectional area in a potential localized neck, as expressed by Eq. (3.33).

The state of strain during uniaxial tension of an anisotropic sheetmetal is shown in Mohr's strain circle diagram, Fig. 3.28 [3.16].

If $d\varepsilon_1$, $d\varepsilon_2$, and $d\varepsilon_3$ are the incremental strains for the axial width and thickness strains, respectively, and the anisotropic plastic strain ratio is given by $r = d\varepsilon_2/d\varepsilon_3$, by use of constancy of volume, $d\varepsilon_2$ and $d\varepsilon_3$ may be expressed as

$$d\varepsilon_2 = -\left(\frac{r}{1+r}\right) d\varepsilon_1 \tag{3.57}$$

$$d\varepsilon_3 = -\left(\frac{1}{1+r}\right) d\varepsilon_1 \tag{3.58}$$

The center of the Mohr's strain circle is located at

$$d\varepsilon = \frac{d\varepsilon_1 + d\varepsilon_2}{2} = \left(\frac{1}{2(1+r)}\right) d\varepsilon_1 \tag{3.59}$$

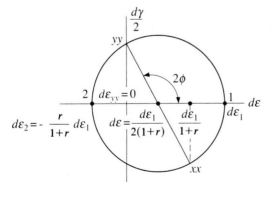

FIGURE 3.28
Mohr's circle representation of strain state during uniaxial tension testing of anisotropic sheetmetals [3.16].

If the x, y, and z axis system contains the zero-width strain as is shown in Fig. 3.27, the normal strain increments in this orientation of the axes can be obtained from the Mohr strain circle diagram as

$$d\varepsilon_{xx} = \left(\frac{1}{1+r}\right) d\varepsilon_1 \tag{3.60}$$

$$d\varepsilon_{yy} = 0 \tag{3.61}$$

$$d\varepsilon_{zz} = -d\varepsilon_{xx} = -\left(\frac{1}{1+r}\right) d\varepsilon_1 \tag{3.62}$$

The quantity dA/A, along the zero-width strain direction yy, is

$$\frac{dA}{A} = -d\varepsilon_{xx} = -\left(\frac{1}{1+r}\right) d\varepsilon_1 \tag{3.63}$$

By use of this equation in conjunction with relations for strainhardening and geometric softening, the following condition for local instability is obtained

$$\frac{\partial \sigma}{\partial \varepsilon} = \frac{\sigma}{1+r} \tag{3.64}$$

From Fig. 3.28, the angle ϕ between the tensile axis and the localized neck can be obtained as

$$\cos(180 - 2\phi) = -\cos 2\phi = \frac{1}{1+2r} \tag{3.65}$$

or

$$\tan \phi = \left(\frac{1+r}{r}\right)^{1/2} \tag{3.66}$$

For an isotropic material $r = 1$, $\tan \phi = \sqrt{2}$, and $\phi = 54° \, 44'$ [3.16].

A Mohr stress circle for localized necking in plane strain for an isotropic material is shown in Fig. 3.29.

Since localized necking results in the reduction of the specimen to carry a load, it can be considered analogous to geometrical softening, which cancels strainhardening. The rate of strain-induced hardening is still $d\sigma/d\varepsilon$ as for diffused necking, but the rate of softening is different.

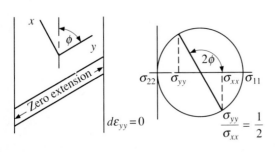

FIGURE 3.29
Plane strain in a localized neck [3.15].

Since at any stage of strain, $P = \sigma A$, the rate of change of the load P with strain ε per unit area is

$$\frac{1}{A} \frac{dP}{d\varepsilon} = \frac{\partial \sigma}{\partial \varepsilon} \tag{3.67}$$

For a condition of plane strain, the cross-sectional area changes only in thickness t, and not in width w, that is, w remains constant. Since $dA = w \, dt$, Eq. (3.67) can be written as

$$\frac{1}{A} \frac{dP}{d\varepsilon} = \frac{1}{A} \left(-\frac{\sigma w \, dt}{d\varepsilon} \right) = -\frac{\sigma w \, dt}{wt \, d\varepsilon} = \frac{\sigma(dt/t)}{d\varepsilon} \tag{3.68}$$

where

$$d\varepsilon = d\varepsilon_1 \quad \text{and} \quad \frac{dt}{t} = d\varepsilon_3 = -\frac{d\varepsilon_1}{2} \tag{3.69}$$

up to the point of necking. Substituting Eq. (3.69) for dt/t in Eq. (3.68), one obtains

$$\frac{1}{A} \frac{dP}{d\varepsilon} = \frac{\sigma}{2} \tag{3.70}$$

The condition for localized necking can, therefore, be obtained from Eqs. (3.67) and (3.70) as

$$\frac{\partial \sigma}{\partial \varepsilon} = \frac{\sigma}{2} \tag{3.71}$$

In contrast to the above, the condition for diffused necking is given by Eqs. (3.35) and (3.55) as

$$\frac{\partial \sigma}{\partial \varepsilon} = \frac{\sigma}{1} \tag{3.35}$$

These criteria for localized and diffused necking are shown graphically in Fig. 3.30 for uniaxial loading of an isotropic material in pure tension. A more general condition of biaxial loading in plane stress as shown in Fig. 3.31 is [3.17]

$$\frac{d\bar{\sigma}}{d\bar{\varepsilon}} = \frac{\bar{\sigma}}{Z_i} \tag{3.72}$$

where $\bar{\sigma}$ and $\bar{\varepsilon}$ are the effective stress and strain, Z is a function of the principal stress ratio, $\alpha = \sigma_2/\sigma_1$ (the intermediate to largest principal stress ratio),

$$\bar{\sigma} = \sigma_1(1 - \alpha - \alpha^2)^{1/2} \tag{3.73}$$

and

$$\bar{\varepsilon} = \varepsilon_1 \left[\frac{2(1 - \alpha + \alpha^2)^{1/2}}{2 - \alpha} \right] \tag{3.74}$$

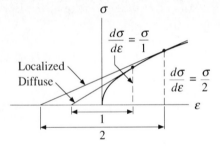

FIGURE 3.30
The criteria of localized and diffuse necking in pure tension [3.15].

The graphical solution to Eq. (3.72) is illustrated in Fig. 3.32. Z_i in Eq. (3.72) is known as the *subtangent,* and Z_d and Z_l for diffused and for localized necking, respectively, are called the *critical subtangents* [3.17].

The critical subtangent assuming planar anisotropy for local necking is given by [3.17]

$$Z_l = \frac{[\frac{2}{3}(r+2)]^{1/2}[(r+1)\alpha^2 - 2r\alpha + (r+1)]^{1/2}}{\alpha+1} \qquad (3.75)$$

or

$$Z_l = \frac{[A]^{1/2}[B]^{1/2}}{\alpha+1}$$

where $r =$ anisotropic plastic strain ratio
$\alpha =$ principal stress ratio, σ_2/σ_1 $(\sigma_3 = 0)$

The mathematical description of stress-strain curves allows the strainhardening of the whole strain range to be treated by simple parameters. If one applies the general instability condition expressed by Eq. (3.72) to equation $\bar{\sigma} = K\varepsilon^n$, the effective strain of instability, $\bar{\varepsilon}_i = nZ_i$ is obtained. The principal tangential and radial strains, respectively, at local necking ($\varepsilon_3 \leq 0$) ε_{1i} and ε_2 such as in a

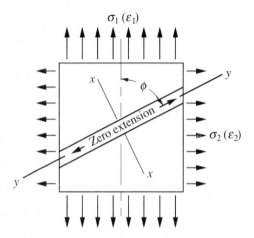

FIGURE 3.31
A localized neck at angle ϕ. No extension occurs along the neck. The angle ϕ is determined by the stress ratio. For uniaxial tension in an isotropic material, $\phi = 54°44'$, which increases to 90° for $\sigma_2/\sigma_1 = \frac{1}{2}.(d\varepsilon_2 = 0.)$ [3.17].

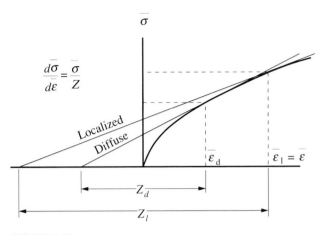

FIGURE 3.32
Graphical determination of instability strain in a sheet uniformly loaded by biaxial loading in plane stress. Z is a function of the principal stress ratio σ_2/σ_1 ($\sigma_d = 0$). Z_d relates to the beginning of diffuse and Z_l to the beginning of localized necking. For uniaxial tension, $\bar{\sigma} = \sigma$, $\bar{\varepsilon} = \varepsilon_1$, $Z_d = 1$, and $Z_l = 2$ [3.17].

hole expansion test are

$$\varepsilon_{1i} = \frac{[(r+1) - r\alpha]\bar{\varepsilon}_i}{[A]^{1/2}[B]^{1/2}} \tag{3.76}$$

$$\varepsilon_2 = \frac{[(r+1)\alpha - r]\bar{\varepsilon}_i}{[A]^{1/2}[B]^{1/2}} \tag{3.77}$$

$$\varepsilon_{1i} = n - \varepsilon_2 \qquad \frac{\varepsilon_2}{\varepsilon_1} = \frac{(r+1)\alpha - r}{(r+1) - r\alpha} \tag{3.78}$$

where ε_{1i} and ε_2 are the major and minor strains at necking, A and B are defined in Eq. (3.75), and r is the anisotropic plastic strain ratio [3.18].

The foregoing concept of the subtangent can be incorporated with the concept of the anisotropic plastic strain ratio r, and its effect on the forming limit diagram in conjunction with the hole expansion test.

In the hole expansion test, a circular blank with a central hole is stretched by a flat-bottomed punch into a die until necking and/or fracture occurs at the edge of the hole. If the sheetmetal has directional properties, i.e., if it has planar anisotropy, the hole does not remain round during its expansion. The ability of a material to resist necking or fracture at the edge of the hole is termed its *edge formability*. In evaluating test results such criteria as hole enlargement, depth (height) of the cup drawn, ovality of the hole, orientation of the neck and/or fracture, and the surface condition of the deformed zone, are used.

According to the von Mises theory, the equivalent stress in a hole expansion test may be defined by [3.19]

$$\bar{\sigma} = (\sigma_\theta^2 - \sigma_\theta\sigma_r + \sigma_r^2)^{1/2} \tag{3.79}$$

and the equivalent strain increment may be defined as

$$\overline{d\varepsilon} = \frac{2}{\sqrt{3}}(d\varepsilon_\theta^2 - d\varepsilon_\theta\, d\varepsilon_r + d\varepsilon_r^2)^{1/2} \tag{3.80}$$

The equivalent stress may be related to the equivalent strain by use of

$$\bar{\sigma} = \sigma_Y + k\bar{\varepsilon}^n \tag{3.81}$$

and the equivalent strain of the hole expansion test can then be evaluated as follows:

$$\bar{\varepsilon} = \int \overline{d\varepsilon} = \int \frac{2}{\sqrt{3}}(d\varepsilon_\theta^2 - d\varepsilon_\theta\, d\varepsilon_r + d\varepsilon_r^2)^{1/2} \tag{3.82}$$

3.10 DUCTILITY AND REDUCTION IN AREA

Two items of information that can be obtained from tensile test data in addition to the stress-strain curve are the percent elongation or ductility and the reduction in area. Ductility is the percent elongation to fracture for a certain, specified gauge length such as 50.8 mm (2 in), and the reduction in area is the percent reduction in cross-sectional area at the neck at the point of fracture and are calculated as follows:

$$\% \text{ ductility} = \left(\frac{l_f - l_0}{l_0}\right) 100 \tag{3.83}$$

and

$$\% \text{ reduction in area} = \left(\frac{A_0 - A_f}{A_0}\right) 100 \tag{3.84}$$

Although both parameters may be used as a measure of ductility and are an index of the ability of a material to flow plastically, they do not measure the same property or quality. Some materials have a rather low ductility but neck down greatly, and vice versa. These parameters may be a good index of ductility for uniaxial loading but not for multiaxial loading. In case of the latter, some criterion for ductile fracture, such as the Cockcroft-Latham criterion, might have to be used.

Often one wants to use the tensile elongation to compare the ductility of the same material, but of a different size or thickness than the standard specimen normally used. One can accomplish the foregoing approximately by holding the $l_{0i}/\sqrt{A_{0i}}$ ratio constant. The rationale involved in this technique follows [3.12].

The total extension to fracture in a tension test consists of two components as shown in Fig. 3.33: (1) the uniform extension up to the inception of necking and (2) the localized extension after the inception of necking, which can be expressed by

$$\Delta l_f = l_f - l_0 = \Delta l_2 + e_u l_0 \tag{3.85}$$

where Δl_2 is the local necking extension, $e_u l_0$ is the uniform extension, and e_u is

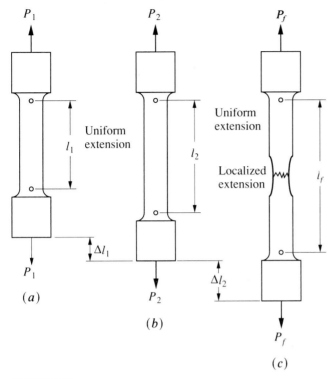

FIGURE 3.33
Three sketches showing a tensile specimen (*a*) before loading, (*b*) loading up to the inception of necking, and (*c*) loading after the point of necking and up to fracture.

the uniform extension factor. The total elongation to fracture, or ductility, may then be expressed as

$$e_f = \frac{l_f - l_0}{l_0} = \frac{\Delta l_2}{l_0} + e_u \qquad (3.86)$$

If geometrically similar specimens develop geometrically similar necks, it may be assumed that the local extension is proportional to the linear dimension of the cross-sectional area, or $\Delta l_2 = \alpha\sqrt{A_0}$. The total elongation may then be expressed as

$$e_f = \frac{\alpha\sqrt{A_0}}{l_0} + e_u \qquad (3.87)$$

The above equation for elongation gives the rationale for use of fixed ratios of the gauge length l_0 to the square root of the cross-sectional area $\sqrt{A_0}$ or, for round bars, D_0 in specifying the dimensions of tensile specimens.

If the dimensions, such as the thickness, of a piece of material is such that a standard size specimen cannot be used, and also if one wants to compare the ductility at different thicknesses as expressed by the elongation, then one can use the concept suggested by Eq. (3.87) that a constant elongation is obtained if $l_{0i}/\sqrt{A_{0i}}$ remains constant, i.e., [3.12]

$$\frac{l_{01}}{\sqrt{A_{01}}} = \frac{l_{02}}{\sqrt{A_{02}}} = \frac{l_{0i}}{\sqrt{A_{0i}}} \tag{3.88}$$

For the special case of round specimens

$$\frac{l_{01}}{d_{01}} = \frac{l_{02}}{d_{02}} = \frac{l_{0i}}{d_{0i}} \tag{3.89}$$

The main difficulty with the use of the percent elongation to fracture as a measure of ductility arises from the necking of the specimen. Although tensile ductility is commonly required in metallurgical specifications for materials, the occurrence of uniform and localized deformation often makes the percent elongation to fracture of questionable value as a quantitative measure of ductility.

A better indication of the plastic flowability of the material is the engineering stress-strain curve in tension as shown schematically in Fig. 3.34. This is especially

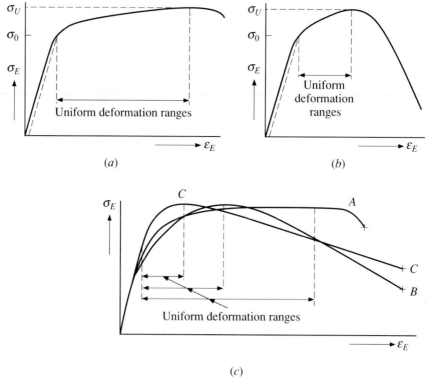

(a)

(b)

(c)

FIGURE 3.34
Schematic engineering stress-strain curves in tension showing a material having (a) a broad, uniform deformation range, and (b) a narrow, uniform deformation range; and (c) a narrow, an intermediate, and a broad uniform deformation range, curves C, B, and A, respectively. (See Fig. 3.24.)

true for metalworking operations, in which tensile stresses are developed such as in deep drawing. In these operations most of the deformation occurs between the yield strength and the ultimate tensile strength as shown in Fig. 3.34(a). The material shown in Fig. 3.34(b) would not draw well, because most of the deformation would be localized; however, it would form well in a forming operation utilizing compressive stresses in accordance to the compressive stress-strain curve. Although in Fig. 3.34(c) materials B and C have a greater ductility and reduction in area, material A would perform much better in many metalforming operations. This aspect of flowability will be discussed later when basic ductility, workability, and formability are defined.

Some of the reasons for using the reduction in area are as follows:

1. It is the most structure-sensitive parameter used in the tension test. It is sensitive, for example, to hydrogen embrittlement
2. It is a good index of the quality of steel such as to the non-metallic inclusion content
3. It is relatively independent of the specimen dimensions
4. It reveals the transition temperature in body-center cubic metals for notch impact

3.11 MATHEMATICAL MATERIAL MODELS

An equation that describes the flow behavior of a material under the influence of external forces is called a *mathematical material model.* This equation is the constitutive relationship between the flow stress $\bar{\sigma}$ and such variables as strain $\bar{\varepsilon}$, strain rate $\dot{\bar{\varepsilon}}$, temperature parameters T, microstructure S_i, anisotropic parameter r, etc. It may be represented by

$$\bar{\sigma} = f(\bar{\varepsilon}, \dot{\bar{\varepsilon}}, T, S_i, r) \tag{3.90}$$

The two constitutive equations, containing the strain rate, that have already been applied to plastic instability [3.13], are

$$\sigma = K\varepsilon^n \dot{\varepsilon}^m \tag{3.50}$$

and

$$\sigma = K\left(\varepsilon^n + m' \ln \frac{\dot{\varepsilon}}{\dot{\varepsilon}_0}\right) \qquad \text{for } \dot{\varepsilon} \geq \dot{\varepsilon}_0 \tag{3.51}$$

where $\dot{\varepsilon}_0$ = reference strain rate at which strainhardening is negligible.

The most commonly used empirical, model equation in plastic deformation, that does not include the strain rate and that was mentioned in regard to the idealized stress-strain curves, is the strainhardening power law or the Ludwik-Hollomon equation

$$(1) \quad \sigma = K\varepsilon^n \big|_{T, \dot{\varepsilon}} \tag{3.5}$$

where K is the strength coefficient and n is the strainhardening exponent. The subscripts T and $\dot{\varepsilon}$ indicate that the temperature and strain rate remain constant throughout the loading of the test specimen. K is the index of the strength level of the material. It is the value of the yield strength or flow strength when the material is plastically deformed to a true strain of 1, which in a tensile specimen would correspond to an increase in length, not of 100 percent, but of 171.8 percent or a reduction in area of 63.2 percent as shown below:

$$\ln \frac{l_f}{l_0} = \ln \frac{A_0}{A_f} = 1$$

$$\frac{l_f}{l_0} = e = 2.718 \qquad \frac{A_0}{A_f} = 2.718$$

$$l_f = 2.718 l_0$$

$$\% \, E = \left(\frac{l_f - l_0}{l_0}\right) 100 = \frac{(2.718 l_0 - l_0)100}{l_0} = 171.8\%$$

$$R_E = 2.178 l_0 \qquad R_E = \left(\frac{A_0 - A_f}{A_0}\right) = 1 - \frac{A_f}{A_0}$$

$$R_E = 1 - \frac{1}{2.718} \qquad R_E = \frac{(2.718 - 1)100}{2.718} = 63.2\%$$

K may be obtained approximately by coldworking a material to a 63.2 percent reduction in area and obtaining the yield strength in a tension test. The higher the value of K, the higher the yield or flow strength of the material. The exponent n is an index of the capability of a material to strainharden. The higher n is, the steeper is the slope of the plastic portion of the stress-strain curve, and the harder the material will become on coldworking or plastic deformation. The stainless steel shown in Fig. 3.35 may theoretically have a flow strength lower than low carbon steel when both are in the annealed condition; however, the stainless steel shown would be expected to have a higher flow strength in the strainhardened or coldworked condition. Since K and n vary with the amount of coldwork, i.e., with the microstructure, it is more meaningful to list their values for the annealed condition. However, because K and n vary so much for a given class of material and since σ is so sensitive to n, it is recommended that they be determined experimentally for each batch of material rather than using handbook values.

Some typical values for common metallic materials are given in Table 3.3.

If Eq. (3.5) is obeyed, a straight line is obtained on a log-log plot, whose slope is n and whose ordinate at $\varepsilon = 1$ is equal to K according to the equation

$$\log \sigma = \log K + n \log \varepsilon \tag{3.91}$$

as shown in Fig. 3.35 for stainless steel, 1018 steel, copper, and aluminum. It was shown in Eq. (3.36) that the true strain at the inception of necking or onset of tensile instability, ε_u, is equal to the strainhardening exponent n. (This is the basis of the two-point method of plotting the true stress-true strain curve.)

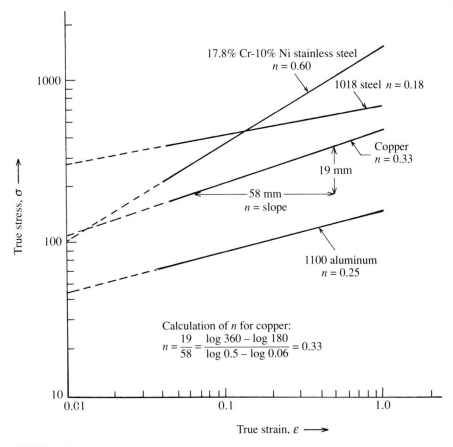

FIGURE 3.35
Log-log plot of true stress versus true strain for four common metallic materials.

Since $\varepsilon_u = n$ at the point of necking, the homogeneous or uniform deformation range is greater for a material such as stainless steel, for which $n = 0.60$, than for 1100 aluminum, for which $n = 0.25$, even though the true strain to fracture is 1.08 and 2.30, respectively.

TABLE 3.3
Typical values of K, n, and ε_f for common annealed metallic materials

Material	K_{annealed}	n	ε_f
18-10 stainless steel	1450 Mpa (210,000 psi)	0.60	1.08
Copper	450 MPa (65,000 psi)	0.33	1.21
1100 aluminum	140 MPa (20,000 psi)	0.25	2.30
1018 steel	620 MPa (90,000 psi)	0.18	1.05

3.12 DETERMINATION OF FORMING LIMIT STRAINS FOR AN ANISOTROPIC MATERIAL BY MEANS OF NECK GROWTH

3.12.1 Introduction

The information presented in the foregoing in conjunction with the discussion of corrected true stress and the Bridgman correction factor (see Figs. 3.14, and 3.15) and with diffused and localized necking (see Figs. 3.18, 3.19, 3.27, 3.29, 3.31, and 3.33) will now be used to determine the limiting strains to incipient necking, up to which sheetmetal may be considered to be safely loaded in biaxial plane stress. The limiting strains serve as a boundary region between a successfully formed part and failure, which in itself is subject to different interpretations. The plot of the forming limit strains, in strain space, for different types of biaxial loading is called a *forming limit diagram* (FLD), which will be discussed in some detail at different points later. A method has been proposed by which an entire FLD can be constructed on the basis of the limiting conditions and the mode of growth of the neck as shown in Fig. 3.36, which will be discussed here [3.20].

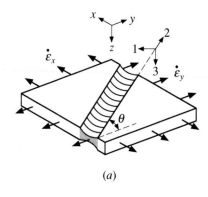

(a)

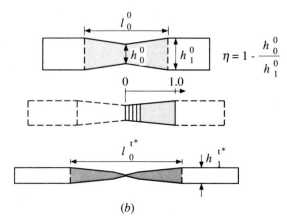

$$\eta = 1 - \frac{h\,^0_0}{h\,^0_1}$$

(b)

FIGURE 3.36
(*a*) A schematic drawing of the specimen with initial geometric inhomogeneity under a biaxial loading condition, and (*b*) designation of various cross-sectional dimensions viewed normal to the 2 axis. Two sets of cartesian axes are also defined [3.20].

3.12.2 Plasticity and Constitutive Relations Involving Anisotropy

Under multiaxial loading, the two main features of an anisotropic material are (1) the variation of the yield stress with orientation due to texture, and (2) the difference between the tensile and compressive strengths and the development of a "back stress" due to prior loading, i.e., the Bauschinger effect.

An anisotropic yield function f, similar to the isotropic yield function in Eq. (2.70), may be expressed by the Levy-Mises equation

$$d\varepsilon_{ij}^{p} = \frac{\partial f}{\partial \sigma_{ij}} \, d\lambda \tag{3.92}$$

where f is the yield function (plastic potential or loading function). A general yield function for an anisotropic material may be written as

$$f(\sigma_{ij}, \alpha_i, M_{ij}, k, \ldots) = 0 \tag{3.93}$$

where σ_{ij} = stress tensor
$\quad\ \alpha_i$ = orientation and back stress vector
$\quad\ M_{ij}$ = anisotropy matrix
$\quad\ k$ = the equivalent magnitude of the yield surface

In Eq. (3.93), M_{ij} describes the variation of the yield stress with orientation or the distortion of the yield surface, and α_i describes the strength differential between the tensile and compressive yield stresses or the offset of the origin of the yield surface. The effective size of the yield surface is given by the parameter k. α_i may describe both the initial strength difference and the back stress due to the Bauschinger effect. The structure of M_{ij} and α_i from symmetry arguments are as follows [3.21]:

$$M_{ij} = \begin{bmatrix} M_{11} & M_{12} & M_{13} & 0 & 0 & 0 \\ M_{21} & M_{22} & M_{23} & 0 & 0 & 0 \\ M_{31} & M_{32} & M_{33} & 0 & 0 & 0 \\ 0 & 0 & 0 & M_{44} & 0 & 0 \\ 0 & 0 & 0 & 0 & M_{55} & 0 \\ 0 & 0 & 0 & 0 & 0 & M_{66} \end{bmatrix} \tag{3.94}$$

$$\alpha_i = \begin{bmatrix} \alpha_1 & \alpha_2 & \alpha_3 & 0 & 0 & 0 \end{bmatrix} \tag{3.95}$$

The yield function f may be expressed in terms of the distortion (anisotropy) matrix M_{ij}, which describes the variation of the yield stress with respect to the orientation in the specimen only, and k, the effective size of the yield surface, as follows:

$$f = M_{ij}\sigma_i\sigma_j - k^2 = 0 \tag{3.96}$$

where σ_i and σ_j denote the stress vectors corresponding to the appropriate stress tensor σ_{ij}. [Compare with Eq. (3.90).] Therefore, the equivalent stress $\bar{\sigma}$ may be defined as

$$\bar{\sigma} = (M_{ij}\sigma_i\sigma_j)^{1/2} \tag{3.97}$$

For the case of plane stress loading condition ($\sigma_3 = 0$) and materials with planar isotropy, the above equation in the 1-2-3 coordinate system as shown in Fig. 3.36 may be expressed as

$$\bar{\sigma}^2 = M_{11}\sigma_1^2 + 2M_{12}\sigma_1\sigma_2 + M_{22}\sigma_2^2 + M_{44}\sigma_{12}^2 \tag{3.98}$$

[Compare with Eqs. (2.122) and (2.131).]

For material with planar isotropy, the distortion parameter M_{11} is identical to M_{22}, and they are independent of direction in the 1-2 plane. In addition, $\sigma_{12} = 0$ when $\theta = 0$.

If one assumes that the corresponding inelastic strain rate $\dot{\varepsilon}_i$ may be expressed in terms of the flow potential of the yield function f and the scalar multiplier λ, one obtains

$$\dot{\varepsilon}_i = \lambda \left[\frac{\partial f}{\partial \sigma_i} \right]_\lambda \tag{3.99}$$

Based on the yield function, Eq. (3.96), the flow rule, Eq. (3.99), and the incompressibility condition, it can be shown, for example, that

$$M_{11} + M_{12} + M_{13} = 0$$
$$M_{12} + M_{22} + M_{23} = 0 \tag{3.100}$$
$$M_{13} + M_{23} + M_{33} = 0$$

By combining Eqs. (3.96) and (3.99) for the case of plane stress loading, one obtains the relationship for the strain-rate ratio

$$r_\varepsilon = \frac{\dot{\varepsilon}_2}{\dot{\varepsilon}_1} = \frac{M_{12}\sigma_1 + M_{22}\sigma_2}{M_{12}\sigma_2 + M_{11}\sigma_1} \tag{3.101}$$

The stress ratio r_σ can be obtained as

$$r_\sigma = \frac{\sigma_2}{\sigma_1} = \frac{r_\varepsilon M_{11} - M_{12}}{M_{22} - r_\varepsilon M_{12}} \tag{3.102}$$

Two other useful ratios can also be obtained as

$$r_{\dot{\varepsilon}_{12}} = \frac{\dot{\varepsilon}_{12}}{\dot{\varepsilon}_1} = \frac{3M_{44}\sigma_{12}}{M_{11}\sigma_1 + M_{12}\sigma_2} \tag{3.103}$$

$$r_{\sigma_{12}} = \frac{\sigma_{12}}{\sigma_1} = \frac{r_{\varepsilon_{12}}}{3M_{44}}(M_{11} + r_\sigma M_{12}) \tag{3.104}$$

The well known transverse, anisotropic, plastic strain ratio r can be related to the M_{ij} matrix by use of Eqs. (3.96) and (3.99) to give

$$R_1 = \frac{2}{M_{33}} - 1 \tag{3.105}$$

When the material is completely isotropic, $M_{11} = M_{22} = M_{33} = 1$ and $M_{12} = M_{23} = M_{31} = -\frac{1}{2}$.

By rewriting Eq. (3.98), one can express the equivalent stress in terms of the stress ratios r_σ and $r_{\sigma_{12}}$ as

$$\bar{\sigma} = (M_{11} + 2M_{12}r_\sigma + M_{22}r_\sigma^2 + M_{44}r_{\sigma_{12}}^2)^{1/2}\sigma_1 \qquad (3.106)$$

The corresponding equivalent strain rate is defined by assuming that the specific plastic work rate $\dot{W}$ is comparable to $\overline{\sigma\varepsilon}$ and is equal to

$$\dot{W} = \sigma_1\dot{\varepsilon}_1 + \sigma_2\dot{\varepsilon}_2 + \sigma_{12}\dot{\varepsilon}_{12} \qquad (3.107)$$

By rearranging Eq. (3.101), one obtains

$$\dot{\bar{\varepsilon}} = \frac{\sigma_1}{\bar{\sigma}}\left[1 + \frac{r_{\dot{\varepsilon}}(r_{\dot{\varepsilon}}M_{11} - M_{12})}{M_{11} - r_{\dot{\varepsilon}}M_2} + \frac{r_{\dot{\varepsilon}_{12}}^2}{3M_{44}}\left(M_{11} + \frac{M_{12}(r_{\dot{\varepsilon}}M_{11} - M_{12})}{M_{11} - r_{\dot{\varepsilon}}M_{12}}\right)\right]\dot{\varepsilon}_1 = \beta\dot{\varepsilon}_1$$

$$(3.108)$$

The constitutive equation used here is

$$\bar{\sigma} = k_0(\varepsilon_0 + \bar{\varepsilon})^n\left(\frac{\dot{\bar{\varepsilon}}}{\dot{\varepsilon}_0}\right)^m \qquad (3.109)$$

where $k_0 =$ reference strength of the material (strength coefficient)
  $\varepsilon_0 =$ offset strain, a material constant
  $\dot{\varepsilon}_0 =$ reference strain rate, a material constant

3.12.3 Angular and Limiting Equations

The painstaking derivation of the expressions for the limiting strains is presented by Lee and Zaverl [3.20]. It is quite involved and will not be discussed here. Only the equations for the normal and shear strain rates and the final equations for the limiting strains will be given here.

The equations for the normal and shear strain rates in terms of the principal strain rates and $r_{\dot{\varepsilon}_{xy}}$, which show the angular relationship, are

$$\dot{\varepsilon}_1 = \frac{\dot{\varepsilon}_x}{2}[(1 + r_{\dot{\varepsilon}_{xy}}) + (1 - r_{\dot{\varepsilon}_{xy}})\cos 2\theta] \qquad (3.110)$$

$$\dot{\varepsilon}_2 = \frac{\dot{\varepsilon}_x}{2}[(1 + r_{\dot{\varepsilon}_{xy}}) - (1 - r_{\dot{\varepsilon}_{xy}})\cos 2\theta] \qquad (3.111)$$

and

$$\dot{\varepsilon}_{12} = \frac{\dot{\varepsilon}_x}{2}[-(1 - r_{\dot{\varepsilon}_{xy}})\sin 2\theta] \qquad (3.112)$$

The equations for the limiting strains are

$$\varepsilon_x^* = \frac{1}{(1 + r_{\dot{\varepsilon}_{xy}})} \cdot \frac{1}{\beta}[mP^{-1}(\phi, z) - \varepsilon_0] \qquad (3.113)$$

and

$$\varepsilon_y^* = \frac{r_{\dot{\varepsilon}_{xy}}}{(1 + r_{\dot{\varepsilon}_{xy}})} \cdot \frac{1}{\beta}[mP^{-1}(\phi, z) - \varepsilon_0] \qquad (3.114)$$

where $r_{\dot{\varepsilon}_{xy}} = \dot{\varepsilon}_y / \dot{\varepsilon}_x$ (see Fig. 3.36 for orientation of axes)

β = function relating $\bar{\dot{\varepsilon}}$ and $\dot{\varepsilon}_1$ as in Eq. (3.108)

m = the strain-rate sensitivity exponent

$P(\phi, z)$ = external load per unit width, which is a function of ϕ, a material constant ($\phi = (n/m) + 1$), and z, which is a function describing a set of incomplete gamma functions as shown below

ε_0 = offset strain

$$z = (1 - \eta)^{1/m} \left[1 - P\left(\phi, \frac{\varepsilon_0}{m} \right) \right] + P\left(\phi, \frac{\varepsilon_0}{m} \right)$$

where η is the initial *geometric* inhomogeneity (nonuniformity) index, which is equal to

$$\eta = \left[1 - \frac{h_A^0}{h_B^0} \right]$$

where h refers to the specific thickness, the superscript refers to time t and the subscript to location, i.e., initial thicknesses at adjacent locations A and B in the uniform and necking locations respectively, at $t = 0$

3.12.4   Generation of a Forming Limit Diagram by Neck Growth Simulation

The forming limit diagram (FLD), which is shown in Fig. 3.37, can be generated by making a number of neck growth simulations under the proportional straining conditions. (FLDs are discussed elsewhere.) The right-hand side of the FLD is computed for $r_{\dot{\varepsilon}_{xy}}$ ranging from 0.05 to 1.0, or from a total of 20 simulations, by use of Eqs. (3.113) and (3.114). The computed points are least squares fit to a sixth order polynomial and the final plot is made. The left-hand side of the FLD is determined by using the above equations for 20 different values of $r_{\dot{\varepsilon}_{xy}}$ covering the range from plane strain to uniaxial tensile loading conditions as shown in Fig. 3.37. The computed points are also fitted by the same least squares method. The material parameters in this case are not loading history-dependent. For loading history-dependent material parameters, a more generalized constitutive equation must be used in lieu of Eq. (3.109) for dealing with the inelastic (plastic) behavior of the material, if at all.

3.12.5   Summary and Conclusions

An analytical model has been developed to describe the neck growth behavior of sheetmetal under various combined in-plane stress loading conditions. The material is assumed to harden by strain and strain rate and has a through thickness plastic anisotropy. The model assumes that necking develops from the initial geometric inhomogeneity. The computed forming limit diagram based on the rate-dependent flow theory of plasticity is shown to be sensitive to the specific magnitude of material parameters, such as n, m, and M_{33}, and to the value of the initial inhomogeneity index η. Constant material parameters are used to

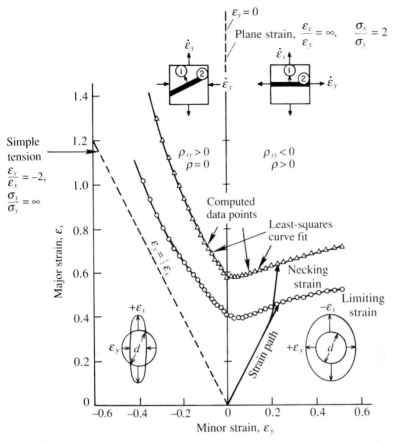

FIGURE 3.37
A schematic diagram showing the method used to compute the forming limit diagram [3.20].

predict an FLD, which is in reasonable agreement with experimental results for aluminum killed (AK) relatively thin sheet steel.

3.13 OTHER PROPERTY TESTS

The stress-strain curves and/or certain mechanical properties can be obtained by test methods other than by the conventional tension tests involving smooth unnotched (or notched) specimens subjected to uniaxial monotonic loading. Although the unnotched tension test is the most used, other tests have some distinct advantages. For example, since necking does not occur in the solid cylinder compression test, the stress-strain curve can be obtained to much larger strains.

Some of the tests other than the tension test that will be briefly discussed here are (1) variations of the solid cylinder axially symmetric (axisymmetric) test, (2) the axisymmetric ring test, (3) the plane-strain tension test, (4) the plane-strain compression test, and (5) the tension-squeeze test.

3.13.1   Conventional Solid Cylinder Axisymmetric Compression Test

Inasmuch as many metalforming operations are compressive in nature, involving friction between surfaces, and in which large strains or reductions in height are obtained, the axisymmetric compression test more nearly simulates the actual conditions of compressive production operations. One of the main objections to the conventional tension test is that necking occurs, which limits the total amount of deformation in most cases.

In the conventional compression test, the specimen is compressed axially between two polished, well-lubricated parallel platens. Because friction usually occurs between the specimen-platen interfaces, radial shear stresses set up in the vicinity of the interfaces resulting in bulging or barreling.

The average stress is calculated by dividing the load by the area obtained from the average diameter.

The engineering strain is calculated as follows [3.12]:

$$\varepsilon_E = \frac{h - h_0}{h_0} = \frac{\Delta h}{h_0} \tag{3.115}$$

The logarithmic (true) strain may be calculated as follows:

$$\varepsilon = \int_0^h \frac{dh}{h} = \ln \frac{h}{h_0} = -\ln \frac{h_0}{h} \tag{3.116}$$

For the purpose of completeness, the strain rate in compression will be discussed here briefly.

The true strain rate in a compression test is

$$\dot{\varepsilon} = \frac{d\varepsilon}{dt} = \frac{-dh/h}{dt} = -\frac{1}{h}\frac{dh}{dt} = -\frac{v}{h} \tag{3.117}$$

where v is the velocity of the platen and h is the height of the specimen at time t. Because h is continuously decreasing with time, the velocity must increase in proportion to $-h$ if $\dot{\varepsilon}$ is to be held constant. In a normal test, if v is held constant the engineering strain rate $\dot{\varepsilon}_E$ will also remain constant, since

$$-\dot{\varepsilon}_E = \frac{de}{dt} = \frac{-dh/h_0}{dt} = -\frac{1}{h_0}\frac{dh}{dt} = -\frac{v}{h_0} \tag{3.118}$$

but the true strain rate will not be constant. A special compression testing machine, called a *cam plastometer,* can compress the specimen at a constant true strain rate to a strain limit of $\varepsilon = 0.7$; however, only a few of these machines exist. Essentially constant strain rates up to $20\,\mathrm{s}^{-1}$ have been achieved on a standard closed-loop servocontrolled hydraulic testing machine [3.12].

When a constant true strain rate cannot be obtained, the mean strain rate may be used. The mean true strain rate, for an initial velocity v_0, when the specimen is reduced from the initial height of h_0 to the current height h is given by [3.12]

$$\dot{\bar{\varepsilon}} = \frac{v_0}{2} \frac{\ln (h_0/h)}{(h_0 - h)} \tag{3.119}$$

The main objections cited for the compression tests are (1) buckling occurs for initial specimen height over initial diameter h_0/d_0 (aspect) ratios greater than 2 to 2.5, (2) because of friction at the platen (die)-specimen interface, bulging or barreling of the cylindrical surface occurs causing inhomogeneous deformation. Dead-zone formation occurs at each end of the specimen, and an imbalance between the lateral transverse stress distribution supplied by the load occurs causing deformation and heat from the resistance of the material to deformation as shown in Fig. 3.38. Bulging, or barreling, is shown in Fig. 3.38(a) for a previously undeformed specimen. A straight or a concave specimen may be obtained as shown in Fig. 3.38(b) and (c), if the original specimen is first precompressed and then machined prior to loading.

Different techniques have been attempted to overcome the objections to the compression test such as placing short cylinders or blocks of the same material at each end of the specimen and also cone-ended specimens and anvils. The

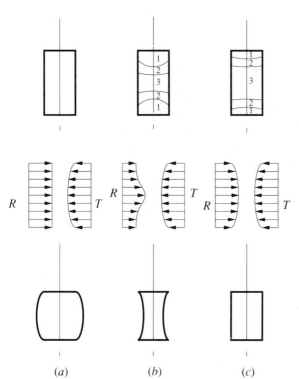

FIGURE 3.38
Relationship in compression between the variation in the hardness distribution of the sectioned specimen, the approximate transverse stress pattern T, the resistance to transverse deformation R, and the final shape of the specimens (a) showing barreling or a convex shape to the final specimen without any prior deformation of the original specimen, (b) showing a concave specimen after precompressing the original specimen to 35 percent and machining prior to testing, and (c) showing a straight final specimen after precompressing the original specimen to 20 to 25 percent, and machining prior to testing [3.22].

(a) $\qquad$ (b) $\qquad$ (c)

technique that will be presented here is the one proposed by Polakowski [3.22], in which the specimens are compressed in successive stages to 20 percent to 25 percent in height and remachined to give the same h/d ratio of 2.0 to 2.5.

3.13.2 Polakowski's Compression Test [3.22]

The steps in performing the test are as follows:

1. Machine the original test specimens for a h_0/d_0 ratio of 2 to 2.5 such as specimens 12.7 mm in diameter × 25.4 mm high (0.5 in in diameter × 1.0 in high) or 20.3 mm in diameter × 50.8 mm high (0.8 in in diameter × 2.0 in high)
2. Using smooth platens and a dry graphite lubricant, load the specimen in compression to 20 percent or 25 percent reduction in height to give a current height of 20.3 mm or 38.2 mm (0.80 in or 1.5 in), respectively, and determine the final diameter
3. Remachine the specimen to the same h/d ratio of 2.0 to 2.5
4. Repeat the above loading procedure to give a reduction of 20 percent or 25 percent to give a height of 16.26 mm (0.64 in) or 28.6 mm (1.125 in), respectively, which would yield a cumulative total reduction of about 36 percent or 43.8 percent, respectively.
5. Continue the above procedure to obtain the desired total reduction of 60 to 90 percent
6. Calculate the stress, taking into consideration the progressive increase in the area of the specimen during deformation
7. Calculate the strain by use of Eqs. (3.115) or (3.116)
8. Plot the appropriate stress-strain curve

An example of experimental stress-strain curves for mild steel, copper, and aluminum determined in the above manner, using the Polakowski technique, is shown in Fig. 3.39 [3.23]. The correlation obtained by use of the ring compression technique is also shown in Fig. 3.39.

3.13.3 Bulge Correction Factor Method

In Polakowski's compression test [3.22], the effect of friction and non-homogeneous deformation can be eliminated by good lubrication and good interface finish, and hence the deformation pressure is essentially equal to the basic flow stress of the material. This test, although accurate, is rather tedious and can be performed only at ambient temperatures and low strain rates. It also requires special facilities for machining of the specimens between stages of deformation, which may alter the strainhardened condition of the material. Another disadvantage of this method is that the stress and strain do not increase monotonically, and the stepwise application and release of the load may affect the derived effective true stress–true strain curve. For obtaining the flow stress

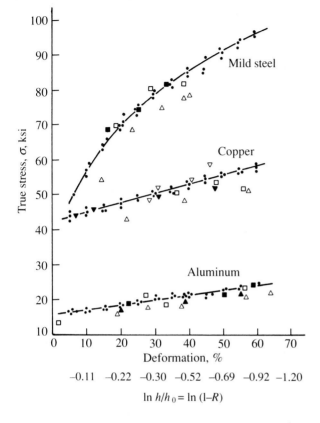

FIGURE 3.39
Flow stress measurements as a function of deformation. Solid dots ● are for data obtained by the Polakowski technique by using a 12.7 mm (0.50 in) diameter by 25.4 mm (1.0 in) high specimen in axisymmetric compression test. The remainder of the points are for the ring test using rings 19.1 mm (0.75 in) OD by 9.53 mm (0.375 in) ID having thicknesses of 6.35 mm (0.250 in), 3.18 mm (0.125 in), and 1.58 mm (0.062 in) giving the following ratios with the lubricating conditions indicated [3.23]:
▲ 6:3:2—no lubricant,
■ 6:3:1—no lubricant,
△ 6:3:2—graphite lubricant,
□ 6:3:1—Teflon lubricant,
▼ 6:3:0.5—no lubricant,
▽ 6:3:0.5—Teflon lubricant.

values at elevated temperatures and high strain rates, researchers have made attempts to minimize the effects of friction and the resulting barreling by judicious choice of specimen geometry and lubrication. Such methods, however, can lead to errors up to 30 percent in the data obtained.

In the bulge correction factor method, the flow stress of the material is determined by the analysis of the stress distribution of the midsection of the cylindrical specimen undergoing compression between parallel platens. It is assumed that the material is homogeneous and isotropic. This method accounts for the effect of the nonhomogeneous deformation and is simple to apply. It is based on Bridgman's neck correction factor method for tension described previously. A bulge correction factor for the compression test is obtained by employing the same approach used by Bridgman for necking in the tensile test.

Applying the condition of equilibrium in the r direction in Fig. 3.40 [3.24], using geometric considerations, the incompressibility condition, and the Levy-Mises plasticity equations, one can derive the following equations by mathematical manipulation [3.25]:

$$\sigma_r = \bar{\sigma} \ln \left(\frac{a^2 - 2aR - r^2}{-2aR} \right) = -\bar{\sigma} \ln \left(\frac{2aR}{2aR - a^2 + r^2} \right) \tag{3.120}$$

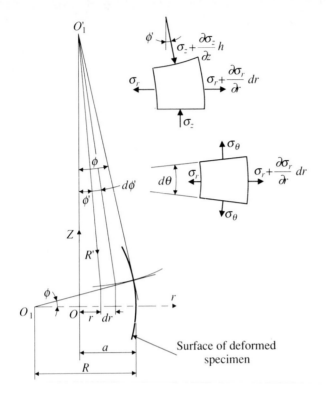

FIGURE 3.40
The geometry and the state of stress in the neighborhood of the midsection of a cylinder under compression [3.24].

$$\sigma_z = \bar{\sigma}\left[1 + \ln\left(\frac{a^2 - 2aR - r^2}{-2aR}\right)\right] = -\bar{\sigma}\left(1 - \ln\frac{2aR}{2aR - a^2 + r^2}\right) \qquad (3.121)$$

where $\qquad \bar{\sigma} =$ the effective stress

$$= \frac{1}{\sqrt{2}}\left[(\sigma_z - \sigma_r)^2 + (\sigma_r - \sigma_\theta)^2 + (\sigma_\theta - \sigma_z)^2\right]^{1/2} \text{ Pa(psi)} \qquad (3.122)$$

σ_r, σ_z, and $\sigma_\theta =$ the radial, axial, and circumferential principal stress components, respectively Pa(psi)

$a =$ radius of the midsection of the cylindrical specimen (Fig. 3.40) m(in)

$r =$ current radius of a bulged specimen (Fig. 3.40) m(in)

$R =$ radius of the bulge (Fig. 3.40) m(in)

The compressive force P across any section of the specimen is given by

$$P = \int_0^a \sigma_z \cdot 2\pi r \, dr = \pi a^2 (\sigma_z) \qquad (3.123)$$

or

$$P = \pi\bar{\sigma}(2Ra - a^2)\ln\left(\frac{2R}{2R - a}\right) \qquad (3.124)$$

The flow stress of the material then is

$$\bar{\sigma} = \frac{P}{\pi(2Ra - a^2)\ln[2R/(2R - a)]} \tag{3.125}$$

The relation between $\bar{\sigma}$ and the average axial stress $(\sigma_z)_{ave}$ may be obtained as follows:

$$\bar{\sigma} = (\sigma_z)_{ave}\left[\left(1 - \frac{2R}{a}\right)\ln\left(1 - \frac{a}{2R}\right)\right]^{-1} \tag{3.126}$$

$$\bar{\sigma} = (\sigma_z)_{ave}C' \tag{3.127}$$

where

$$C' = \left[\left(1 - \frac{2R}{a}\right)\ln\left(1 - \frac{a}{2R}\right)\right]^{-1} \tag{3.128}$$

the bulge correction factor for converting the average stress into a corrected effective stress.

Analogous to Fig. 3.16 for the neck correction factor for tension, the bulge correction factor C', as plotted as a function of the radius of curvature of the bulge at the midsection, is shown in Fig. 3.41. The bulge correction factor is of the same form as Bridgman's neck correction factor except for the sign of R. Note that if there is no friction, $R = \infty$, and $C' = 1$.

The bulge curvature R may be obtained by use of templates of known radii to measure the curvature. Also, it may be calculated by use of the following empirical formula from the measured minor and major diameters d_1 and d_2, and the current height h, as shown in Fig. 3.42

$$R = \frac{h^2 + (d_2 - d_1)^2}{4(d_2 - d_1)} \tag{3.129}$$

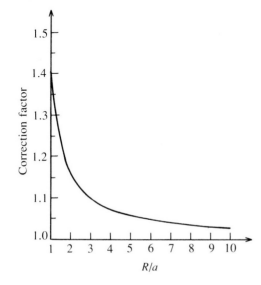

FIGURE 3.41
The correction factor as a function of the radius of curvature of the contour of the bulge of the midsection of a cylinder under compression [3.24].

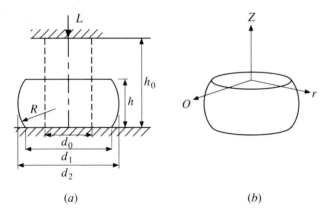

(a) (b)

FIGURE 3.42
(a) Dimensional parameters of an ordinary compression test, and (b) the three main directions [3.25].

(This expression for the bulge curvature will be used in Sec. 4.2.4 in an expression for the pressure at the surface for axisymmetric upsetting.)

A series of experiments was performed by Ettouney and Hardt [3.25] to compare the results of the zero-friction, nonbarreling compression (modified) tests with ordinary compression tests in the presence of friction and barreling with and without use of the bulge correction factor. One example of their results is shown in Fig. 3.43, in which the effective stress is plotted against effective strain. The effective stress of the zero-friction, nonbarreling modified test is calculated by dividing the load by the cross-sectional area. The effective stress in the ordinary test in the presence of friction and barreling is calculated by multiplying the average stress by the bulge correction factor C'. The average

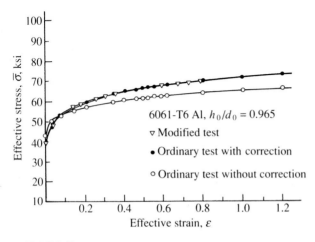

FIGURE 3.43
Compression test results for two specimens [3.25].

stress is calculated by dividing the load by the area obtained from the average diameter. The effective strain is calculated from

$$\bar{\varepsilon} = -\bar{\varepsilon}_z = \ln\left(\frac{h_0}{h}\right)$$ (3.130)

where h_0 and h are the initial and current height of the cylindrical test specimen.

In an effort to overcome the objections to the solid cylinder compression test, a considerable amount of effort has been expended to develop the axisymmetric ring compression test, which will be discussed next.

3.13.4 Axisymmetric Ring Compression Test

The ring compression test, or the changes produced in the inner and outer diameters of a short, hollow cylinder during axial compression between flat, rigid parallel platens, can be used for two purposes: (1) to evaluate the flow stress of a given material, and (2) to evaluate the Coulomb coefficient of friction, μ, or the friction shear factor, m. The former will be discussed here and the latter will be discussed later, mainly in the section dealing with friction.

When a flat ring as shown in Fig. 3.44(a) is compressed in its axial direction, outward and/or inward radial flow will occur in a way which is solely dependent on the prevailing friction condition at the platen-specimen interfaces. The lower upper-bound solution presented by Avitzur [3.26] assumes that the deformation is uniform throughout the thickness of the specimen. (Upper- and lower-bound solutions in general are discussed in the next chapter on analysis methods.) The frictional condition at the interface is described by a friction shear factor m, which is assumed constant across the interface, and is defined as

$$m = \sqrt{3}\,\frac{\tau_f}{\sigma_0}$$ (3.131)

where τ_f is the average friction shear stress at the die-ring interface, and σ_0 is the flow stress of the ring material.

There are two modes of deformation defined by the position of the neutral or no-slip radius R_n. For the case (mode 1) in which the neutral radius lies within the hole of the ring as shown in Fig. 3.44(b), both the inside and outside diameters increase. For the case (mode 2) where the neutral radius lies within the ring the flow is such that the outer radius increases and the inner radius decreases as in Fig. 3.44(c). The equations involved are relatively complex for presentation here. The two equations for the friction shear factor and for the ratio of the upsetting pressure p, and the flow stress of the ring material σ_0, are different for the two modes, but they are functions of the same variables as follows [3.23], [3.26], [3.27]:

$$\frac{mR_0}{t}\,\genfrac{}{}{0pt}{}{<1}{2>}\,f(R_i,\ R_o)$$ (3.132)

$$\frac{p}{\sigma_0} = f\left(R_i,\ R_o,\ R_n,\ \frac{mR_o}{t}\right)$$ (3.133)

where <1 applies to mode 1 only

         $2>$ applies to mode 2 only

         R_i = the inside radius

         R_o = the outside radius

         R_n = neutral or no-slip radius

         t = the ring thickness

Since the friction factor, mR_o/t is a function of R_i and R_o, p/σ_0 is independent of the thickness and dependent on the radius ratios. Unfortunately, one of the intermediate equations transforms into a quadratic, for which an analytical solution has not been found. However, numerical solutions of p/σ_0 are obtained for a certain ratio of initial specimen dimensions of $R_o:R_i:t$, for arbitrary friction factor m where $1>m>0$, and for small increments of deformation and constancy of volume conditions. From these calculations, a chart can be plotted relating the average upsetting pressure to flow stress ratio, p_a/σ_0, to the change in internal diameter for different reduction ratios as shown in Fig. 3.45, for which σ_0 can be obtained if the other parameters are known.

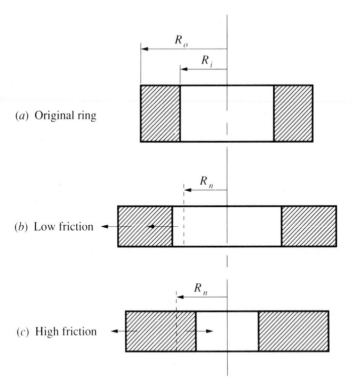

FIGURE 3.44

Deformation modes of a ring specimen and the position of the neutral or no-slip axis for various frictional levels: (a) $R_n = 0$, frictionless condition, outward flow only; (b) $R_n < R_i$, low friction, outward flow only; and (c) $R_n > R_i < R_o$, intermediate and high, friction both inward and outward flow [3.27].

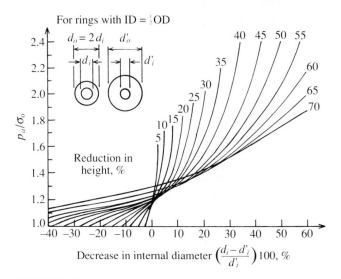

For rings with ID = $\frac{1}{2}$OD

Reduction in height, %

Decrease in internal diameter $\left(\dfrac{d_i - d'_i}{d'_i}\right)$ 100, %

FIGURE 3.45

Determination of the flow stress σ_f from the average pressure p_a measured in ring compression [3.6]. (Also, Technical Report AFML-TR-70-19, WPAFB, OH, 1970.)

A major assumption in the theoretical analysis of the deformation of a flat ring is that the interfacial friction stresses are transmitted uniformly throughout the ring thickness, resulting in little or no inhomogeneous deformation, i.e., no barreling. For this assumption to be valid for frictional conditions up to and including full sticking, the initial ring geometry should have the following ratio of outer diameter to inner diameter to thickness $(D_o : D_i : t)$ of $6:3:0.5$ or $2:1:\frac{1}{6}$, so that rings that have a $D_o : D_i$ ratio of $2:1$ and $\frac{1}{3}$ the length of D_o are commonly used.

For deformations under low friction conditions, a somewhat greater thickness of $\frac{1}{3}$ to $\frac{2}{3}D_o$ may be used to give ratios of $D_o : D_i : t$ of $6:3:1$ and $6:3:2$. For good lubrication, the thickness may be conveniently taken as $\frac{1}{3}D_o$. For use with a 22,240 N (50,000 lbf) capacity machine for annealed 1018 steel and softer materials, the following initial geometries have been used: $\frac{3}{4}$ in D_o, $\frac{3}{8}$ in D_i, and $\frac{1}{16}, \frac{1}{8}$, and $\frac{1}{4}$ in thick or 20 mm D_o, 10 mm D_i, and 1.5, 3.0, and 6.0 mm thick. For 1100 aluminum, rings of the following dimensions have also been used with good results: 1.5 in D_o, 0.75 in D_i, and 1.5 in t and 0.125 in t or 40 mm D_o, 20 mm D_i, and 12.5 mm t and 3 mm t for $D_o : D_i : t$ ratios of $6:3:2$ and $6:3:0.5$.

It is not a prerequisite that the friction factor should remain constant during the entire test, but only during each increment of deformation, which is usually about 5 percent reduction in thickness.

In this example, the flow-stress-strain curves up to logarithmic strain of 0.6 were obtained experimentally for 1100 aluminum using ring geometry ratios of $6:3:2$, and the results were compared with those obtained from tensile and compression tests up to a logarithmic strain of about 0.25. A slight underestimation of the flow or yield stress for strains less than 0.1 occurred, but very good agreement was obtained in the strain range of 0.1 and 0.25.

The incremental ring compression technique is satisfactory for use at room temperature, but it is impractical for elevated temperature use, because of the continual reheating that is required. A series-compression technique has been used for elevated temperatures, in which a series of rings of equal initial thickness are compressed to increasingly larger reductions over the deformation range required. In this technique each ring was heated only once. The data for a continuous compression stress-strain curve were also obtained by use of a special displacement transducer to receive the changes in external diameter of the ring and a conventional vertical displacement transducer to measure the corresponding change in thickness. These data were converted to flow stress and strain curves with good results.

In testing at elevated temperatures to minimize cooling of the specimen, the platens or anvils may be heated to a temperature lower than the specimen, a heat insulating lubricant used, and a testing procedure used to minimize the specimen-anvil contact time. If the temperature is relatively low, an anvil-like container for the specimen may be used that has a flow stress at least three times that of the specimen.

The incremental tests may be run by compressing the specimen to certain pre-estimated or precalculated target thicknesses or to certain predetermined, convenient load increments. The average interface pressure p_a may be calculated by dividing the load by the area of the surface of the ring, or

$$p_a = \frac{P}{\pi/4(D_o - D_i)} \tag{3.134}$$

The logarithmic strain may be calculated as follows:

$$\varepsilon = \ln \frac{t}{t_0} = \ln (1 + R) \tag{3.135}$$

where $R = (t_0 - t)/t_0$.

3.13.5   Plane-Strain Tension Test [3.11]

A plane-strain tensile specimen with deep grooves, as shown in Fig. 3.46 has been designed so as to restrict the deformation to the grooved region. If the ratio of B/L is large enough, approximately plane-strain conditions prevail in the test section. Therefore, the strain occurs in the thickness and length directions but not in the width direction. The true strain is given by

$$\varepsilon = \ln \frac{A_0}{A} = \ln \frac{w h_0}{w h} = \ln \frac{h_0}{h} \tag{3.136}$$

where h_0 is the initial thickness of the reduced section and h is the instantaneous or current thickness.

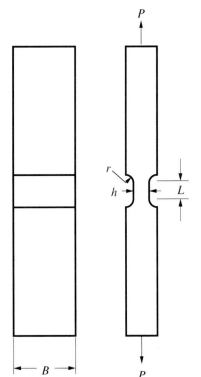

FIGURE 3.46
A plane-strain tensile specimen with deep grooves having the following dimensions: $B = 25.4$ mm (1 in), $L = 6.35$ mm ($\frac{1}{4}$ in), $h = 2.03$ mm (0.080 in), and $r = 1.59$ mm ($\frac{1}{16}$ in) [3.11].

Also, if the ratio L/h is large enough, as in Fig. 3.46, there is no notch effect, and the specimen may be considered to be an unnotched specimen. Therefore, the true stress may be determined directly by dividing the load P by the area hB.

Two disadvantages of this test are (1) it is not practicable to make the specimens from thin material, and (2) it is difficult to make axial strain measurements in the grooves. However, a special clip-on fixture allows a regular sheet specimen to be converted to a plane-strain specimen, which mitigates the first objection.

3.13.6 Plane-Strain Compression Test [3.28]

In this test, a thin sheet is indented between long narrow dies as shown in Fig. 3.47. To ensure parallelism of the accurately ground, smooth die faces and to facilitate testing, the dies are mounted in a special leader pin die set. The width of the dies b is taken between 2 to 4 times the thickness of the sheet t, and the width of the sheet w is at least 5 times the thickness. Incremental loading is used to make a 2 to 5 percent reduction in thickness each time, followed by measurement of the thickness with a micrometer and relubrication with a high pressure lubricant. By changing the dies to maintain the width-to-thickness ratio,

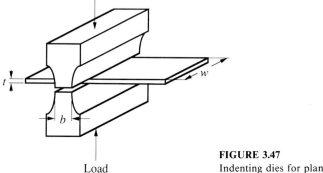

FIGURE 3.47
Indenting dies for plane-strain compression [3.12].

reductions of about 90 percent are possible. This test gives the flow stress in plane strain ($\varepsilon_w = 0$) since the strip is restrained from expansion along its width by interface friction in spite of any lubrication. It can be converted to that for uniaxial tension or compression by multiplying by $2/\sqrt{3}$ or 1.155. Because the test specimen must be incrementally loaded, removed for measurement, and relubricated, the test is slow. If less accuracy can be tolerated, simultaneous measurement of the load and the reduction in height may be measured, and the force-displacement diagram can be recorded by an xy plotter. For very high rates of loading, a cam loading device to produce a constant strain rate and an oscilloscope to present the results may be used. This instrument is known as the cam plastometer, which is capable of giving a constant strain rate for rates between $1\,\text{s}^{-1}$ and $10\,\text{s}^{-1}$.

3.13.7   Tension-Squeeze Test

To counteract the undesirable effects of necking in the uniaxial tension test, the tension-squeeze test has been developed, which combines axial tension and lateral pressure [3.10].

The dimensions of a test specimen that may be used for this test and the method of loading are shown in Fig. 3.48(a). A pressure transducer having dies 38.1×38.1 mm (1.5×1.5 in) may be used to apply the lateral pressure p, as shown in Fig. 3.48(b). For this condition of loading, the axial stress σ_z, effective stress $\bar{\sigma}$, and effective strain $\bar{\varepsilon}$, may be calculated as follows:

$$\sigma_z = \frac{P}{tw_0} \tag{3.137}$$

$$\bar{\sigma} = \frac{\sqrt{3}}{2}(\sigma_z + p) \tag{3.138}$$

$$\bar{\varepsilon} = \frac{2}{\sqrt{3}} \ln \frac{t_0}{t} \tag{3.139}$$

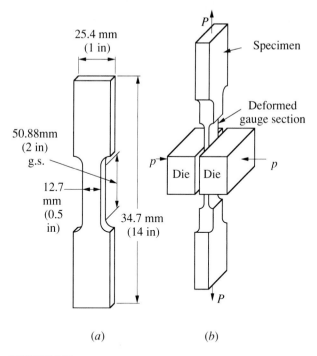

(a)   (b)

FIGURE 3.48
Drawing of (a) test specimen and (b) method of loading for the tension-squeeze test [3.10].

where w_0 = constant width of the gauge length
t_0 = initial thickness of the gauge length
t = instantaneous thickness of the gauge length
p = lateral pressure

During each test the load P, the specimen thickness t, and the lateral pressure p, may be taken at small intervals of strain so that numerical integration of the equations for the ductile fracture theories of Cockcroft-Latham and Kobayashi-Oh-Chen, to be discussed later, is to be carried out. [See Eq. (3.146).]

Suffice it to say here that these theories are expressed by the following equations:

1. Cockcroft-Latham theory:

$$\int_0^{\bar{\varepsilon}_f} \bar{\sigma}\left(\frac{\sigma_z}{\bar{\sigma}}\right) d\bar{\varepsilon} = \int_0^{\bar{\varepsilon}_f} \sigma_z \, d\bar{\varepsilon} = K_1 \tag{3.140}$$

2. Kobayashi-Oh-Chen theory:

$$\int_0^{\bar{\varepsilon}_f} \left(\frac{\sigma_z}{\bar{\sigma}}\right) d\bar{\varepsilon} = K_2 \tag{3.141}$$

where σ_z = axial true stress in uniaxial tension
   ε_f = effective strain at fracture
K_1 and K_2 = constants for the respective theories

The experimentally determined effective fracture strains $\bar{\varepsilon}_f = 2/\sqrt{3} \ln t_0/t$ for plane-strain conditions as a function of average pressure is shown in Fig. 3.49 as determined by Thomsen et al. [3.10].

  One big disadvantage of the tension-squeeze test is that lateral loading complicates the testing procedure.

3.13.8 Plane-Strain Sidepressing Test

In the sidepressing test a relatively short cylinder is compressed parallel to its axis as shown in Fig. 3.50. This convenient test is mostly used for the evaluation of the ductility of a material rather than its resistance to deformation.

  When the bar is first contacted by the platens, nearly point (line) contact occurs, so that high compressive stresses develop at the point of contact. Tensile stresses also develop along the axis of the bar. Since the ends are restrained from moving because of interfacial friction with the platen, plane-strain conditions prevail.

  Three types of deformation occur, depending on the ratio of the height of the specimen h to the width of the contact area w. When h/w is very large, localized deformation, called type I, occurs in the material only adjacent to the platens. When h/w is reduced below a critical value, a plastic zone develops in the material, which extends between the platens as illustrated by the slip-line

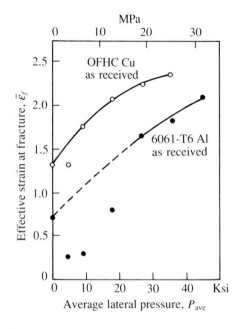

FIGURE 3.49
Fracture strains from a tension-squeeze test as a function of average pressure [3.10].

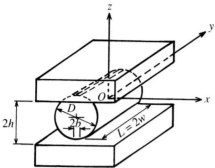

FIGURE 3.50
Sidepressing test configuration of a cylindrical specimen with machined flats ($w = 2b$) [8.5].

field (discussed in Sec. 4.4) shown in Fig. 3.51. This is called type II deformation. When h/w is less than 1, type III deformation extends to the sides of the specimen [3.12].

The plane-strain sidepressing test has been shown to be of great use in the simulation of forging operations in which the flow localizes in form of shear bands. Because it involves the lateral compression of a short bar of round (or square) cross section between flat parallel dies, the sidepressing test is simulative of forging operations such as those used to make steam and gas turbine engine blades [3.16]. This test has been performed on metals at both coldworking and at hotworking temperatures. At hotworking temperatures, it has been useful for studying flow localization under both isothermal and nonisothermal conditions. Flow localization and the flow localization parameter α is discussed elsewhere.

Even without flow localization, deformation during sidepressing of round bars is very nonuniform. Nevertheless, an average effective strain may still be calculated based on the reduction of the initial diameter of the round bar d_0 to some subsequent height h. Since $\varepsilon_{zz} = \varepsilon_{yz} = \varepsilon_{zx}$ because of plane strain, and if one assumes $\varepsilon_{xy} = 0$, from constancy of volume, $\varepsilon_{yy} = -\varepsilon_{xx}$ (where ε_{xx} is the compressive strain). For a von Mises material, $-\bar{\varepsilon}$ is equal to $(2/\sqrt{3})\varepsilon_{xx} = 1.15 \ln (h/d_0)$.

3.14 WORKABILITY DEFINITION, TESTING, AND ANALYSIS

3.14.1 Definition of Workability

There is no generally agreed-upon method for expressing workability. It is usually defined as the amount of deformation that a metallic material can undergo without cracking at a given temperature and strain rate. Three difficulties arise with this definition, as follows:

1. It is difficult unambiguously to specify a crack-initiation or fracture criterion or critical crack size

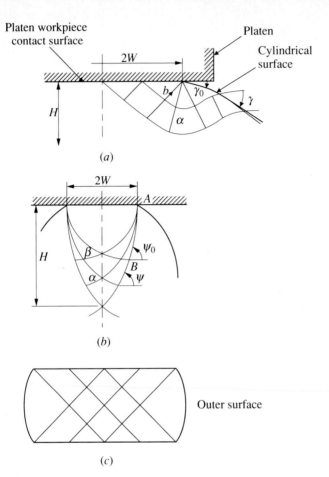

FIGURE 3.51

Schematic representations of slip-line fields for the sidepressing of cylinders with machined flats. (a) One quadrant of a slip-line field for type I mode of localized plastic deformation with $h/w \geq 8.74$; (b) one half of a slip-line field for type II mode of deformation showing plastic deformation to the center of the cylinder, in which $h/w \geq 1 \leq 8.74$; (c) full slip-line deformation extending to the outer surface of the cylinder, in which $h/w \leq 1$. (Slip-line fields are discussed in the next chapter on analysis methods.) (b) [3.12]. (a) and (c) (*Adapted from S. C. Jain and K. Kobayashi, "Deformation and Fracture of an Aluminum Alloy in Plane-Strain", Proc. 11th Int. MTDR Conf., Sept. 1970, v. B, Pergamon Press*, 1970.)

2. A method is not available to translate fracture data from the load-geometry of the workability test to that of the workpiece

3. It is difficult to correct for the effect of temperature and strain rate as these variables usually change during deformation

Another definition that has been presented is: workability is defined as the degree of deformation that can be achieved in a particular metalworking process without creating an undesirable condition [3.29]. The undesirable condition generally is cracking or fracture, but it could be another commercially undesirable condition such as poor surface finish, sheet wrinkling, or lack of die fill.

Workability is a complex property because it deals with a very complex engineering situation. In general, workability depends on the local conditions of stress, strain, strain rate, and temperature in combination with the basic resistance of the metal to ductile fracture. The material characteristics are strongly influenced by the amount, size, shape, and distribution of second-phase particles. Further complicating the measurement of workability is the fact that the states of stress and strain in a material undergoing a deformation process are not uniform, but vary from point to point. The stress and strain distributions, in turn, are determined by important process parameters such as the design of the dies, workpiece geometry, and lubrication. Workability, therefore, is a complex property that measures the basic or intrinsic ductility of the material under the stress system imposed by the process [3.29].

Since workability is a complex property, a number of different terms are used in metalworking that are associated with the ease of plastic deformation and/or the extent of plastic deformation of a material without fracture in a process. Some of these are (1) intrinsic ductility, (2) workability (of a material), (3) formability (of a material), (4) ease of working, (5) capability of the metalworking process, (6) workability (of a material-process combination), etc. Workability is also judged by such qualities as surface finish and such mechanical properties as hardness and strength of the resulting product, the latter being dependent on the final microstructure.

The general term, *workability*, as used here, will be used in conjunction with bulk working processes in which intentional, significant changes in the thickness of the workpiece are usually made. *Formability*, on the other hand, will be used in conjunction with sheetmetal working processes in which no appreciable, intentional changes in the thickness of the workpiece are usually made. There are processes that fall into the boundary region between the two such as the forging of a dome-shaped part from a thick plate, in which the thickness may not be changed a great deal, and sheetmetal stretching and ironing during deep drawing in which, in the latter case, an intentional change in thickness of the sheet is made by the close clearance provided between the punch and die. In general, *workability* will be considered here, and *formability* will be covered in conjunction with the forming limit diagram in Chapter 11 involving sheetmetal forming.

The general term workability, as applied to the material, may be used in two ways: (1) to denote both the lack of resistance of a material to deformation and the ability of the material to withstand plastic deformation without fracture, and (2) to denote only the capability of a material to undergo deformation without fracture. On the other hand, ease of working, sometimes called malleability, will be used here to denote resistance to deformation as measured in terms of the power consumed and the speed and amount of plastic deformation obtained with a given amount of power and energy.

Most bulk-forming processes such as forging, rolling, extrusion, etc. involve stress states that are primarily compressive; however, as indicated previously, induced secondary tensile stresses at specific locations in each process may interact with local microstructural features to initiate fracture. Therefore, the basic workability of a material is defined here as the maximum amount of plastic deformation as determined by the maximum true or logarithmic strain that a material can withstand, without the initiation of fracture as determined by detectable or critical cracks when subjected to an uniaxial tensile stress in the least favorable direction and at the location of interest in the workpiece (see Figs. 3.9 and 3.14). As defined here for the most severe case, it would be equivalent to the true or intrinsic ductility of a material as determined by the maximum stress above the yield stress existing on the axis of a cylindrical specimen at the neck or groove loaded in uniaxial tension, whose longitudinal axis is in the least favorable direction in the workpiece at the location of interest. This definition would eliminate purely elastic deformation, and it would take anisotropy into consideration. Basic workability may be used as a reference to which the workability of materials, processes, and material-process combinations can be compared.

The qualitative part of the definition involves the definition of "detectable or critical cracks." They may be defined as cracks (or series of cracks) that occur in the matrix material as determined by radiography or ultrasonic testing, or by subsequent examination of the sectioned test specimen by use of the scanning electron microscope (see Figs. 3.9 and 3.12). Cracks in secondary phases or in inclusions may be disregarded according to the above definition. The workability of a material without qualification may be defined as above except that the detectable cracks would be of such size, orientation, and distribution as to cause fracture or failure of the material. Workability of a process may be defined as the degree of deformation characteristic of the process that can be achieved with a particular bulk deformation metalworking process in a standard material without fracture. The standard material for ferrous materials may be a spheriodized low carbon steel such as C1018, and in aluminum alloys it may be commercially pure aluminum such as alloy 1100-0. The workability of a material-process combination may be defined as the composite of two factors: one indicating the workability of the material and the other the process as indicated by the relationship:

$$\text{Workability} = f_{1(\text{material})} \times f_{2(\text{process})}$$

where f_1 is a function of the basic ductility of the material and f_2 that of the external factors which modify the basic ductility.

In summary, the material plays an obvious role in determining workability, but the process is equally important through the control of the local tensile stresses. Thus, both must be considered in an overall evaluation of the workability of a particular system.

Since the definition of workability depends on a number of different parameters or variables, they must be defined or expressed. Some of these will have to be set more or less arbitrarily such as the strain rate, temperature, and other environmental conditions. Thus, the general term, workability, may also be subclassified as cold and hot workability. In cold workability, as in coldworking, strainhardening is an important factor. Hot workability relates to the ability of a material to deform at high temperatures ($>0.6T_M$, where T_M is the melting point in degrees K) and at relatively high strain rates.

3.14.2 Intrinsic Ductility and Ductile Fracture Criteria

3.14.2.1 INTRINSIC DUCTILITY. The determination of a basic stress-strain curve and the fundamental properties, such as true or intrinsic ductility, of a material is similar to many other goals. It is something for which we strive, but never completely achieve. Nonetheless it is the concept that is important. Every test to which we subject a material for the purpose of evaluating its mechanical behavior consists of three parts: (1) the behavior of the material in the test, (2) the system of stresses imposed on the material by the test, and (3) many test and environmental variables such as the rate of straining, temperature, etc. In many cases, we may have to define a property in terms of the test used to obtain the property such as ductility, for example, which is defined in terms of the percent elongation to fracture in the tensile test. This definition immediately raises the question as to what is meant by fracture. Is it the elongation at which a crack first appears or at total separation? Also, if we define a property such as true or intrinsic ductility, how can we be sure that a particular test will measure this property as defined? Will the making of the test influence the results? Nevertheless, it appears that there should be certain fundamental or inherent properties, obtained by certain standard, basic tests that should permit us to explain the behavior of a material when subjected to some metalworking process or to predict its behavior in some particular process being considered. Also, all of the different tests that may be performed on a material have their advantages and disadvantages regarding the information obtained as compared to the ease and cost of performing the tests.

As previously mentioned, one of the simplest and quickest tests to run, which gives much more information than the hardness test, is the monotonic uniaxial tensile test. Its true stress–true strain curve may be considered to be roughly equivalent to the flow stress-strain curve obtained by plotting the equivalent stress $\bar{\sigma}$, and equivalent strain $\bar{\varepsilon}$, for some complex state of stress.

However ductility, as defined by the tensile test as the percent elongation to fracture, does not have a fundamental significance because of the complex state of stress that exists in the neck during loading. It will not, for example, correlate well with the amount of deformation prior to fracture that can be performed on a given material in a process involving compression. On the other hand, true or intrinsic ductility may be defined as the true strain at fracture in an idealized test in which the stress system is always one of uniaxial tension. The nearest approach to uniaxial tension would be in the center of the neck of an unnotched tension specimen or in the center of a notched tension specimen. The former will be discussed here and the latter in the next section.

An approximation to the intrinsic ductility may be obtained from the unnotched tensile test by correcting for the shape of the neck by a procedure involving the remachining and reprofiling of the neck of the specimen at different stages of necking. Another approach is to apply a criterion for ductile fracture.

One of the basic problems in dealing with ductility is to explain why, for a given material, different strains are possible for different types of tests and metalworking conditions before fracture occurs. What is needed is some criterion by means of which one can predict the point at which fracture would occur. Also, it would be very desirable to establish some criterion of fracture that would make possible a rationalization of all of the data available. Ideally, such a criterion should be a general one related to deformation in a multiaxial stress system. These criteria might be in the form of either physical or mathematical models or both. Four mathematical models that have been proposed will be discussed here. Some of the more physical models will be discussed briefly, later, in conjunction with the bulk forming limit diagrams.

Over fifty years ago, Siebel [3.30] pointed out that cracking in metalworking is associated with induced tensile stresses, even for processes such as forging, which are predominantly compressive. The relative importance of tensile stress is indirectly confirmed by a large increase in ductility when a tensile specimen is deformed under hydrostatic pressure. Also, it is likely that in metalworking operations, both shear and tensile stresses play a part, since there is some evidence that localized plastic flow by shear is required to initiate cracks which are then propagated by tensile stresses. In describing the fracture of metallic materials in metalworking processes, it is therefore necessary to consider both the operative state of stress and the mechanism of fracture in conjunction with the microstructure of the material. It should be noted here that fracture is only one of the modes of failure. Failure can also be described in terms of the limit to stable flow.

The following criteria of fracture will be discussed here briefly: (1) Criterion based on McClintock's model of the strain to fracture, (2) Cockcroft-Latham criterion, (3) Kobayashi-Oh-Chen criterion, and (4) Hoffmanner criterion.

3.14.2.2 FRACTURE CRITERION BASED ON McCLINTOCK'S MODEL OF THE STRAIN TO FRACTURE.

McClintock [3.31] developed the following model of the strain to ductile fracture which occurs by void formation and void coalescence with a shear band:

$$\int_0^{\bar{\varepsilon}_f} \left[\frac{2}{\sqrt{3}(1-n)} \sinh \left\{ \frac{\sqrt{3}(1-n)}{2} \frac{\sigma_a + \sigma_b}{\bar{\sigma}} \right\} + \frac{\sigma_b - \sigma_a}{\bar{\sigma}} \right] d\bar{\varepsilon} = K \qquad (3.142)$$

and

$$K = \tfrac{4}{3}k \ln \left(\frac{l_0}{a_0} \right) \qquad (3.143)$$

where k = the strain-concentration factor in the shear band
n = the strainhardening exponent in $\sigma = K\varepsilon^n$
l_0 = the initial spacing of the voids

a_0 = the initial radius of the voids
$\bar{\sigma}$ = the effective flow stress
σ_a = the principal stress in the direction of the greatest void deformation
σ_b = the principal stress normal to σ_a

Later Oh, Chen, and Kobayashi [3.32] showed that McClintock's relationship can be expressed in the following criterion for fracture in a tension test:

$$\int_0^{\varepsilon_f} (F_1 + 1)\, d\varepsilon = \int_0^{\varepsilon_f} F_1 + \int_0^{\varepsilon_f} d\varepsilon = K \tag{3.144}$$

where $F_1 = h$ when $h > -1$, and $F_1 = -1$ when $h \leq -1$, and

$$h = \frac{2}{\sqrt{3}(1-n)} \sinh \left\{ \frac{\sqrt{3}(1-n)}{2} \left(1 + 2\frac{\sigma_r}{\bar{\sigma}} \right) \right\} \tag{3.145}$$

where σ_r is the radial stress at the necked region. If $\int F_1\, d\bar{\varepsilon}$ is plotted on the abscissa and $\bar{\varepsilon}$ on the ordinate, a straight line, with a negative slope and an $\bar{\varepsilon} = 0$ intercept equal to a value of K of 2.5, is obtained.

3.14.2.3 COCKCROFT-LATHAM DUCTILE FRACTURE CRITERION. According to Cockcroft and Latham [3.33], this criterion must be based on some combination of both stress and strain rather than on either one separately. A criterion that was proposed for the fracture of a ductile material in tension is that in which the tensile strain energy reaches a critical value for a given condition of loading

$$\int_0^{\varepsilon_f} \bar{\sigma} \left(\frac{\sigma^*}{\bar{\sigma}} \right) d\bar{\varepsilon} = C_i = K_1 \tag{3.146}$$

where
ε_f = fracture strain
$\bar{\varepsilon}$ = equivalent strain
$\bar{\sigma}$ = equivalent stress
σ^* = the maximum tensile stress attained in the specimen under axial loading
σ^*/σ = non-dimensional stress-concentration factor representing the highest tensile stress σ^*
C_i = constant for a material i at a given temperature and strain rate as determined from an uniaxial tension test.

The evaluation of Eq. (3.146) will be discussed subsequently under workability testing.

A material will fracture when it achieves a strain-energy density equal to the above integral. C_i may be determined from independent test data such as for the tensile test using Bridgman's analysis.

During necking the highest stress occurs on the centerline of the specimen at the point at which fracture begins, as shown in Figs. 3.15 and 3.52. Equation (3.146) then reduces to the following form, and the true or intrinsic ductility ε_{hf} may be determined from the true strain at fracture ε_{nf} that is observed in a

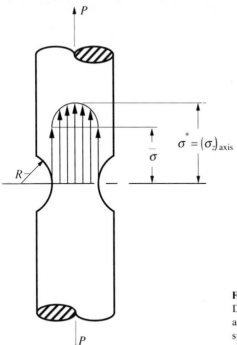

FIGURE 3.52
Drawing showing the distribution of the stress across a random plane through the axis of the specimen, where σ^* is the maximum stress and $\bar{\sigma}$ is the average stress. (See Fig. 3.11.)

conventional uniaxial tension test:

$$\int_0^{\sigma_{nf}} \sigma^* \, d\varepsilon = C = \int_0^{\varepsilon_{hf}} \sigma \, d\varepsilon \tag{3.147}$$

where σ and ε refer to the true stress and the true strain. σ^* may be calculated from an equation in which it is a function of the radius of the specimen at the neck a, and the radius of the neck profile.

In reference to Fig. 3.53, ε_{hf} may be obtained by numerical integration by use of the trapezoidal or the Simpson rule so that

$$A_{2(n)} \leq A_1 \leq A_{2(n+1)} \tag{3.148}$$

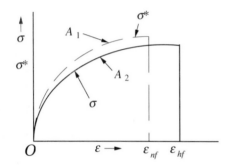

FIGURE 3.53
Schematic diagram for use in estimating ε_{hf} by numerical integration and in evaluating the Cockcroft-Latham integral. A_1 = area under curve σ^*, and A_2 = area under curve σ.

where, by use of the trapezoidal rule,

$$A_{2(n)} = \sum_{i=1}^{n} \left[\frac{(\sigma_{(ih)} + \sigma_{(i-1)}h)h}{2} \right] \cong \int_{0}^{nh} \sigma \, d\varepsilon \qquad (3.149)$$

If the size of the grid, i.e., the unit dimension on the abscissa, is h, then ε_{hf} may be calculated by linear interpolation as follows:

$$\frac{\varepsilon_{hf} - \varepsilon_{nh}}{h} = \frac{A_1 - A_{2(n)}}{A_{2(n+1)} - A_{2(n)}}$$

$$\varepsilon_{hf} = nh + \frac{h(A_1 - A_{2(n)})}{A_{2(n+1)} - A_{2(n)}} \qquad (3.150)$$

In reference to Fig. 3.53, the strain energy or plastic work is equal to the area A_1 as follows:

$$A_1 = \int_{0}^{\varepsilon_{nf}} \sigma^* \, d\varepsilon = \int_{0}^{\varepsilon_{hf}} \sigma \, d\varepsilon \qquad (3.151)$$

The Cockcroft-Latham criterion for ductile fracture permits measurement of ductility made in a torsion test to be correlated with those of the tension test. For torsion the criterion may be expressed as

$$\int_{0}^{\varepsilon_{\tau f}} \frac{\bar{\sigma}}{\sqrt{3}} \, d\bar{\varepsilon} = C \qquad (3.152)$$

where $\varepsilon_{\tau f}$ = torsional fracture strain.

The results of the torsion test predict an increase in ductility when tensile tests are carried out under hydrostatic pressure. The Cockcroft-Latham criterion also predicts the incidence of cracking at the edges of plates during rolling (Fig. 6.29(c)) and along the centerline in cold rod extrusion for small reductions, causing chevron defect formation (Fig. 7.11), and other situations where tensile stresses prevail.

Cockcroft and Latham [3.33] have applied this criterion successfully to coldworking processes as indicated above, and Sellers and Tegart [3.2] to hot-working processes. Kuhn [3.34] and Kuhn et al. [3.35] reformulated the criterion to provide a predicted fracture line for comparison with an experimental fracture line for a combination of tension and compression in the second quadrant of strain space.

3.14.2.4 HOFFMANNER FRACTURE CRITERION.

This criterion of fracture is based on the detrimental effect of a tensile stress induced in a specimen or workpiece in the most disadvantageous direction, the direction of the normal to the second phase particle or inclusion (microstructural) alignment and/or normal to the axis of mechanical texturing. Hoffmanner [3.36] proposed the following exponential relationship between the effective or flow strain at fracture and the reduced average stress transverse to the axis of mechanical texture and/or inclusion alignment:

$$\bar{\varepsilon}_f = a \exp\left[b\left(\frac{\sigma_T}{\bar{\sigma}}\right)\right] \tag{3.153}$$

where $\bar{\varepsilon}_f$ = the effective strain to fracture

σ_T = average principal tensile stress perpendicular to the above alignment or fibering

$\bar{\sigma}$ = effective flow stress

Equation (3.153) represents a linear semilog plot between the logarithm of the effective strain $\bar{\varepsilon}_f$ and the stress ratio $\sigma_T/\bar{\sigma}$, which may be expressed as

$$\ln \bar{\varepsilon}_f = b\left(\frac{\sigma_T}{\bar{\sigma}}\right)_{ave} + \ln a \tag{3.154}$$

where a = the intercept $\ln \bar{\varepsilon}_f$ when $\sigma_T = 0$

b = the slope of the line

$\sigma_T = 0$, when the second phase particles or inclusions are parallel to the axis of the tensile specimen.

According to Hoffmanner, a and b are material parameters related to the mechanical behavior of the matrix (solid solution) and mechanical texturing, respectively. It appears that the slope b depends on the alloy and the intercept a depends on the alloy condition.

The correlation between this criterion and some experimental results for tension and torsion are shown in Fig. 3.54. There is, however, a lack of correlation with surface fracture in upset tests, and it does not predict the shape of the experimental forming limit diagram. Consequently, its importance is diminishing at this time.

3.14.3 Workability Testing

When selecting a workability test, it is important to recognize that fractures initiate in localized regions where interaction between the state of stress and the macro- and/or microstructure of the material reaches a critical or limiting value. The orientation, shape, size, and volume fraction of inclusions and other inhomogeneities have a significant effect on the fracture process. It is therefore very important that workability test specimens contain material having the same macro- and microstructural features as the material in the potential, localized fracture regions of the actual metalworking process. When evaluating for surface cracking, for example, the test specimen should contain the same surface as that of the workpiece. Likewise, when evaluating for internal fractures such as central bursts (Fig. 7.11), the test specimens should be taken from the center of the workpiece where the conditions such as segregation found there prevail.

Workability tests may be grouped for the purpose of discussion into cold and hot tests. Some tests, such as the notched tension test (Fig. 3.9), may be well suited for the determination of cold workability but not as well suited for hot

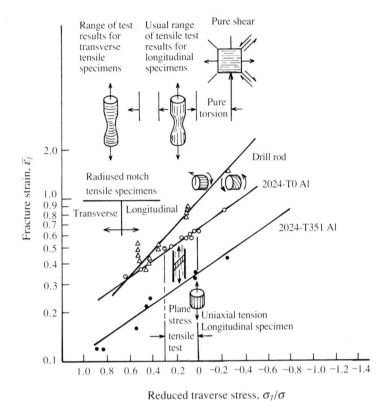

FIGURE 3.54
Hoffmanner criterion of fracture, showing the linear relationship between the log of the effective fracture strain $\log \bar{\varepsilon}_f$ and the reduced stress $\sigma_T / \bar{\sigma}$ with superposition of the ranges of $\sigma_T / \bar{\sigma}$ corresponding to different tests [3.35].

workability, whereas a simple uniaxial compression test may be suited to both, but the speed of loading would be an important factor.

The workability of a material may be evaluated by (1) conventional materials testing equipment, (2) specialized testing equipment, (3) laboratory equipment that duplicates or simulates industrial processes such as a rolling mill or an extrusion press, and (4) standard production equipment, the use of which is usually not economical for workability testing. A test may in a sense be considered to be a process which is performed for the purpose of obtaining experimental data.

Most of the equipment may be used, with certain limitations and with different accessories for both cold and hot testing. Some of the important features that may play a role in the selection of a testing machine or test method are (1) selection of the specimen, (2) the constancy of strain rate control, (3) maximum attainable strain rate, (4) temperature control, (5) ease of flow stress measurement, (6) range of maximum uniform deformation, (7) maximum attainable strain in one pass, (8) loading conditions that limit instability, (9) suitability for microstructural examination, (10) source of specimens for subsequent mechanical testing, (11) ease of multipass simulation, and (12) ease of thermal processing during cycling such as heating, holding, and cooling.

In addition to the various tension and compression tests mentioned in the foregoing, torsion and bent tests are also used, but to a lesser extent.

Reduced gauge section solid and radiused tubular specimens with very fine longitudinal and circumferential grid markings on the surface are often used for cold workability measurements. Hot twist tests of solid specimens without reduced sections are made, in which the specimen may be twisted several times during the course of the test, yielding very high strains. The nonmetallic inclusions and other features of the microstructures may change orientation during the test, thereby resulting in a change of the mechanical texturing and anisotropy of the specimen, complicating the interpretation of the results. It has been found that the transverse fracture strain, ε_T, of the tensile test, i.e., the strain normal to the particle alignment, might correlate well with the torsion strain in medium ductility alloys.

Bending of bars is another deformation test which, like the upset test, avoids necking and microstructural reorientation. Stress and strain states on the outer surface may be altered to a limited degree by changing the width-to-thickness ratio [3.37]. These stress and strain states are similar in sign and complementary in magnitude to those in the upset (compression) test. Bend tests are usually substituted for upset tests when the tensile stress orientation cannot be obtained in upset tests.

The bend specimens can be loaded as shown in Fig. 3.55. They can be carried out with a three-point bend fixture with a punch radius of 3 mm (0.118 in). Both tensile and compressive strains are measured over 3 mm (0.118 in) gauge

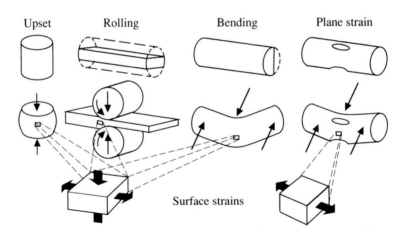

Upset   Rolling   Bending   Plane strain

Surface strains

FIGURE 3.55
Schematic illustration of upsetting, rolling, bending, and plane-strain bending tests, for which the specimens are cut so that the rod surfaces undergo strain in each test [3.35].

bands. By using a range of thickness of test specimens, a variety of stress and strain states can be produced at the free surface. The same thing applies to rolling.

Because of their suitability for evaluation of workability, the upset and bend tests were used by Kuhn [3.34] and Kuhn et al. [3.35] to determine the forming limit diagram for bulk deformation plotted in tensile-compressive strain space. The procedure and results of their work will be discussed briefly below.

3.14.4 Workability Test Procedure and Test Analysis

In axial compression of a cylinder without friction at the die-material interfaces, the test specimen undergoes uniform compression or homogeneous deformation throughout its volume. No barreling of the cylindrical surface occurs and, from the constancy of volume considerations, it can be shown that the circumferential and radial strains are tensile and equal to one-half of the magnitude of the axial compressive strain.

During axial compression with friction at the die contact surfaces, bulging or barreling of the free surface occurs, having a strain state as shown in Fig. 3.56, and the stress and strain distributions are nonuniform, and inhomogeneous deformation occurs. Increasing the friction or the aspect ratio (the height-to-diameter ratio) increases the bulge curvature and the degree of nonuniformity. The equatorial diameter and the circumferential strain are greater than they would have been for homogeneous (frictionless) compression at the same height reduction. Likewise, because of the bulge curvature in the vertical direction, the axial strain at the surface is less than it would have been in homogeneous compression.

Strains on the bulge surface may be measured by means of a 3 mm (0.118 in) grid placed on the cylindrical surface by electrochemical etching or scribing prior to the test. It has been found that the circumferential or hoop strain ε_θ, measured from the vertical grid lines, is identical to that measured from the overall equatorial diameter as shown in Fig. 3.57. Kuhn and his collaborators used specimens 12.7 mm ($\frac{1}{2}$ in) in diameter and 9.5, 12.7, 15.9, and 19.1 mm ($\frac{3}{8}$, $\frac{1}{2}$, $\frac{5}{8}$, and $\frac{3}{4}$ in) in length, giving aspect ratios of 0.75, 1.0, 1.25, and 1.5, respectively.

The following frictional conditions may be used: (1) rough knurled surfaces, (2) polished dies to 2μ surface finish, (3) polished dies with a graphite-grease

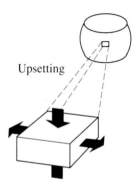

Upsetting

FIGURE 3.56
Tensile, circumferential, and compressive axial strains at the free surface of an upset cylinder [3.34].

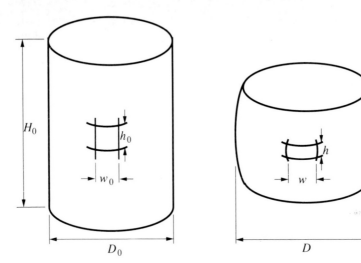

FIGURE 3.57
Schematic illustration of the upset test on cylindrical specimens. Surface principal strains are calculated from grid displacements [3.35].

lubricant, and (4) polished dies with 0.127 mm thick Teflon sheets placed on both die-contacting surfaces for each 5 percent increment of height reduction. The friction factor (the ratio of frictional shear to the shear yield strength of the material) can be determined by use of the ring test. Kuhn et al. [3.35] determined the friction factors, as obtained above, to be 0.45, 0.21, 0.085, and 0 respectively.

Using the test results for compression for cylinders having the above aspect ratios and for different frictional conditions, the above investigators obtained strain-path curves of the form as shown in Fig. 3.58. The upper ends of the curves, except for the frictionless case depicting homogeneous deformation, would represent the biaxial strain conditions at which fracture would occur. The approximate curves for plane-strain forming, bending, and rolling are also shown in Fig. 3.58. The fracture data for 1045 steel is shown in Fig. 3.59. The data for bending would fall on the lower end of the line and that for plane strain would fall on the ordinate. This line is virtually parallel to the line for the frictionless case or homogeneous deformation. The data fits a straight line of slope $\frac{1}{2}$ and of the form

$$\varepsilon_{\theta f} = a - \frac{\varepsilon_{zf}}{2} \tag{3.155}$$

where the subscript f denotes fracture and a is the intercept, the plane-strain ductility, i.e., plane-strain fracture strain.

The height or intercept of the forming limit line can be used as an index of workability and has been shown to be useful in evaluating the bulk deformation of materials as a function of material variables.

By using the Levy-Mises equations for r, θ and Z directions, and the equations for $d\bar{\varepsilon}$, the equivalent strain increment, and $\bar{\sigma}$, the equivalent stress,

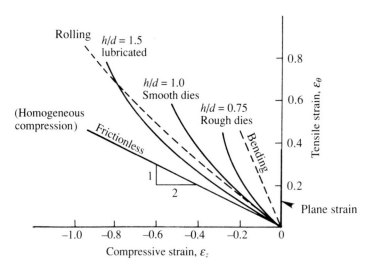

FIGURE 3.58
Variation of strains at the free surface of upset cylinders [3.34].

and the equation for constancy of volume, the following equation for the stress ratio can be obtained:

$$\frac{\sigma_\theta}{\sigma_z} = \frac{(\frac{1}{2}+a)}{(b+a/2)} \qquad (3.156)$$

where a = strain ratio, $d\varepsilon_\theta/d\varepsilon_z$
$b = \sigma_{Yz}/\sigma_{Yr}$, ratio of the axial to the radial yield strength

Note that when $a = -\frac{1}{2}$ for frictional compression, $\sigma_\theta = 0$; for $|a| > \frac{1}{2}$, σ_θ has positive values.

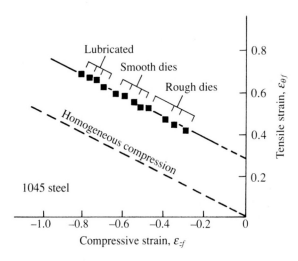

FIGURE 3.59
Strains at fracture in upset tests on cold-drawn rods of SAE 1045 steel [3.34].

The Cockcroft-Latham criterion equation (3.146) can be evaluated by (1) expressing σ^* and $d\varepsilon$ in terms of the strain ratio a, (2) performing the integration from 0 to $\varepsilon_{\theta f}$, (3) solving for $\varepsilon_{\theta f}$ in terms of C, the Cockcroft-Latham constant, and K and n of the power law $\sigma = K\varepsilon^n$. σ^* is the maximum tensile stress, which is σ_θ in this case. The results yield a ε_{zf} plot with a slope of $\frac{1}{2}$. The intercept a is obtained from the plane fracture strain developed in a specimen with a hole transverse to the axis. When the intercept is evaluated by a separate tensile test, the Cockcroft-Latham criterion gives a good agreement with experimental data.

The stress ratio $\sigma_T/\bar{\sigma}$ of the Hoffmanner criterion can also be evaluated in terms of a. Continuous curves of $\sigma_T/\bar{\sigma}$ versus $\log \bar{\varepsilon}$ can be constructed from the equations for $\sigma_T/\bar{\sigma}$ and $\bar{\varepsilon}_f$ for different values of a from 0 to 2. A linear relation expected is not obtained, which indicates an inconsistency between the Hoffmanner criterion and the experimental data.

The approach used by Kuhn et al. [3.35] has also been used to plot forming limit diagrams for bulk deformation similar to those used to plot forming limit diagrams for sheetmetal forming discussed elsewhere. Figure 3.60 shows that the fracture strain line predicted by the Cockcroft-Latham criterion equation (3.146) is in reasonably good agreement with the experimental results. The height of the predicted line, i.e., the intercept a, is determined by experiment, such as a tensile test [3.37].

There is, however, a clear discrepancy between the calculated and experimental results for the Hoffmanner criterion. This is particularly true relative to the very low finite strain to fracture, as can be seen in Fig. 3.60, predicted for

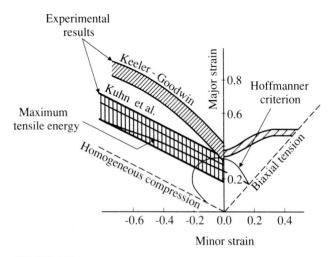

FIGURE 3.60
Comparison of the forming limit diagrams predicted by the Cockcroft and Latham criterion and by the Hoffmanner criterion with experimentally determined diagrams obtained by Keeler and Goodwin for sheetmetal forming and by Kuhn et al. for bulk deformation processes. Logarithmic or true strain is used for the major and minor strains. [In Eq. (3.128) for the Hoffmanner criterion, $a = 0.3$ and $b = 1$.] [3.37].

homogeneous compression, which should be very large. Correlation of this criterion with tension and torsion tests as in Fig. 3.54, but lack of correlation with surface fracture in upset tests as in Fig. 3.60, indicates that the major limitation of the Hoffmanner criterion may be that it does not account for stresses other than those perpendicular to the inclusion alignment of the material [3.37].

3.14.5 Workability Analysis

The height of the fracture line such as in Fig. 3.59, which gives the forming limit for bulk deformation, is chiefly a function of the composition and macro/micro-structure of the material for a given temperature and strain rate. In upsetting of a cylinder the strain path as shown in Fig. 3.58 is a function mainly of the geometric and lubrication parameters of the process, such as the aspect ratio and the lubricant used. These parameters give the relationship between tensile and compressive surface strains as deformation progresses. The geometric parameters are influenced by such factors as design of the die and the geometry of the workpiece.

Workability analysis consists of superimposing strain paths for the process of interest on the material fracture limit diagram as shown in Fig. 3.61. The intersection of the strain paths with the fracture line indicates that fracture is likely and gives the strain at fracture. Alteration of the strain paths, through modification of the geometry or lubrication, or movement of the material fracture line, by the modification of the material or by the selection of a new material, can be attempted to reach combinations for which the strain paths do not intersect the fracture line before the forming of the part is completed [3.37].

Kuhn [3.34] cited an example for the forming of a bolt head by upsetting, as shown in Fig. 3.61. If it is required to form a bolt head of diameter D on a rod of diameter d, the required circumferential, logarithmic strain ε_θ on the free surface of the head is $\varepsilon_\theta = \ln D_0/d$. Let us assume that the strain path a describes the strain state in the expanding, peripheral free surface of the bolt head for a particular friction condition, and the material being utilized has the forming limit

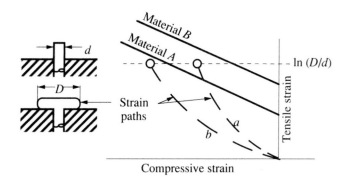

FIGURE 3.61
Illustration of the superposition of strain paths on forming limit diagrams for workability studies [3.34].

line labeled A. Before the final diameter, D, of the bolt head is formed, the strain path a of the peripheral surface must in this case cross the fracture limit line, and therefore the probability of the formation of a crack at the edge of the head is very high. Of the different options available to produce an acceptable, uncracked part, two obvious ones would be either to substitute a new material such as B with a higher fracture limit line or to lower the strain path to b by improving the lubrication. For example, a hot-rolled 1020 steel with an intercept of 0.32 may be substituted for a cold-drawn 1045 steel with an intercept of 0.28, provided that all other requirements are met. Other options might be to increase the temperature of the workpiece, to reduce the strain rate, or to superimpose a hydrostatic pressure, all of which would be expected to raise the fracture limit line [3.34].

Figure 3.62(b) shows the effect of superimposing a hydrostatic component of stress on the original stress state shown in Fig. 3.62(a). The Cockcroft-Latham criterion can be used to predict the effect of superimposing a pressure p, as shown in Fig. 3.63. The superimposed pressure ($p > 0$) increases the height of the fracture limit line and also decreases the slope slightly as shown in Fig. 3.63. On the other hand, superimposing a tension (negative pressure) decreases the height of the fracture limit line, decreases its average slope, and provides a slight downward curvature.

Internal fractures along the centerline of extruded or drawn bars causing defects called "central bursts" are well known. This type of internal defect can

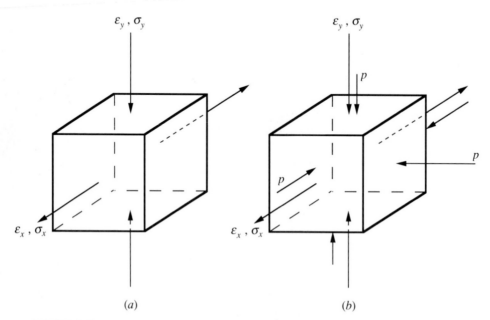

(a)   (b)

FIGURE 3.62
(a) Stress and strain state is shown at the free surface (right-hand face) of an upset cylinder, and (b) the same strain state, but the stress state is modified by additional hydrostatic pressure p [3.34].

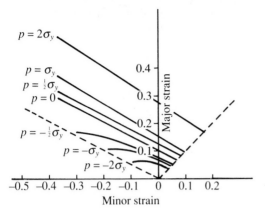

FIGURE 3.63
Effect of additional hydrostatic stress component on fracture strain lines as predicted by the Cockcroft fracture criterion. ($p = 0$ indicates a free surface fracture line.) [3.34].

be demonstrated by compressing a disc-shaped part as shown in Fig. 3.64 by compressing the edges of the disc with opposing dies having equal holes in the center, so as to allow the material to extrude into the holes. As the outer region of the disc is compressed between the dies, material flows radially inward and then vertically into opposing hubs. This flow develops a hydrostatic stress state at the center of the workpiece. Initially it is compressive, and then it reverses, becoming tensile as the flange thickness is reduced, and flow into the hubs occurs. As deformation proceeds, the strain at the center increases, but the hydrostatic pressure also increases so that the fracture limit line rises. However, as the flange thickness approaches one-half of the die-hole diameter, the hydrostatic stress becomes tensile so the fracture limit line is lowered. As the strain at the center continues to rise, the strain path eventually intersects the lowered fracture limit line, causing the central burst to occur.

3.14.6 Generalized Approach to Workability and to the Workability Utilization Factor [3.38]

3.14.6.1 GENERAL FORM OF THE WORKABILITY UTILIZATION FACTOR [3.38]. Devedzic has proposed that a workability utilization factor q be used as a general workability indicator, which is independent of the kind of working process. He also proposed a comprehensive systemization of all workability limit criteria, which may be used in each individual case of plastic working.

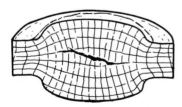

FIGURE 3.64
Example of a central burst in forging of a double-hubbed disk [3.34].

In the simplest case, the workability utilization factor is defined as

$$q = \frac{P_C}{P_L} \tag{3.157}$$

where P_L = the extreme possible (limiting) value of a workability indicator P
P_C = the value of P in the critical forming area

The possible limits of q are $0 \le q \le 1$, where $q = 1$ means that all the available workability has been completely exhausted.

The universal classification of all basic workability limit criteria has been proposed as shown in Fig. 3.65. Such a classification makes it possible to solve numerous problems in metalworking by use of a computer, not only to compute the factor q, but also to optimize it, to study the effect of the variation of some of the parameters, etc.

However, if the factors influencing P_L are changing with time t during the forming process, then one should write

$$q = \int_0^{P_C} \frac{dP}{P_L(t)} \tag{3.158}$$

To simplify the discussion of the workability limit criteria it will be divided here into (1) material fracture as a workability limit criterion and (2) all other workability criteria as a group.

3.14.6.2 FRACTURE AS A WORKABILITY LIMIT CRITERION (A IN FIG. 3.65). Since fracture is often taken as the limiting phenomenon for the workability limit, its application to the mathematical description of workability will be discussed here briefly.

Fracture, such as in the deep drawing of a cup (discussed elsewhere) or of a wire, may occur either (1) in the main deformation zone, or (2) in the transmission zone, i.e., the zone through which the load is transmitted.

The maximum or limiting value of the equivalent strain to fracture in the critical location is $\bar{\varepsilon}_L$, which is taken here as the formability indicator.

The magnitude of this strain depends primarily on (1) the characteristics of the material (S) (the flow stress σ_0, microstructure, etc.), (2) the state of stress in the critical location, (3) possible change of the basic stress model during the deformation process (i.e., the strain history), (4) temperature (T), (5) the strain rate ($\dot{\varepsilon}$), and (6) the measure of the relative position of the intermediate principal stress (σ_2) in the existing stress system by use of Lode's stress state coefficient λ, as follows:

$$\lambda = \frac{\sigma_2 - (\sigma_1 + \sigma_3)/2}{(\sigma_1 - \sigma_3)/2} = \frac{2(\sigma_2 - \sigma_3)}{\sigma_1 - \sigma_3} - 1 \tag{3.159}$$

If the indicator of the stress system is denoted by β and the change in the microstructure during the deformation process by s, the dependence of $\bar{\varepsilon}_l$ on the

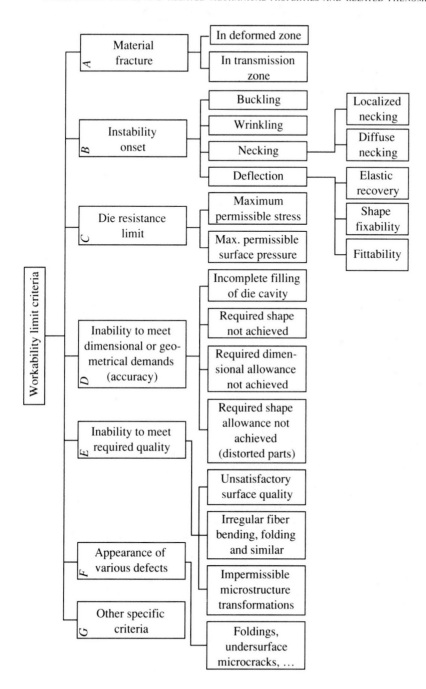

FIGURE 3.65
Flowchart for the universal classification of basic workability limit criteria [3.38].

foregoing parameters may be expressed as

$$\bar{\varepsilon}_L = \bar{\varepsilon}_L(S, \beta, T, \dot{\varepsilon}, \lambda, s) \tag{3.160}$$

[Compare this equation with Eqs. (2.133), (3.113), (3.90), and (3.114).]

The stress system indicator β may be defined as a function of the ratio of the first invariant of the stress tensor to the absolute value of the second invariant and may be expressed by

$$\beta = \frac{\tau_m}{\bar{\tau}} = \sqrt{3}\,\frac{\sigma_m}{\bar{\sigma}} \tag{3.161}$$

where τ_m and σ_m are the mean shear and normal stresses, respectively, and $\bar{\tau}$ and $\bar{\sigma}$ are the equivalent shear and normal stresses, respectively.

Because of the variation in the stress-dependence resulting from changes in the workpiece geometry (G), frictional conditions, workhardening, etc., it is often necessary to use the mean value of β:

$$\beta_m = \frac{1}{\bar{\varepsilon}_C} \int_0^{\bar{\varepsilon}_C} \beta[G(\bar{\varepsilon}), \sigma_0(\bar{\varepsilon})]\, d\bar{\varepsilon}$$

$$\beta_m = \frac{1}{\bar{\varepsilon}} \int_0^{\bar{\varepsilon}} \beta(\bar{\varepsilon})\, d\bar{\varepsilon} \tag{3.162}$$

where G is the variable geometry parameter and σ_0 is the flow stress.

If the equation for the strain rate $\dot{\varepsilon}$ and the limiting strain $\bar{\varepsilon}_L$, during the time t, are known, then the workability utilization factor q can be defined as

$$q = \int_0^{t_C} \left(\frac{\dot{\varepsilon}}{\bar{\varepsilon}_L}\right) dt \tag{3.163}$$

It is assumed that the required functions are available.

If one takes into account the relation between the accomplished strain $\bar{\varepsilon}$ and the time t, one can also write

$$q = \int_0^{\bar{\varepsilon}_C} \frac{d\bar{\varepsilon}}{\bar{\varepsilon}_L(\bar{\varepsilon})} \tag{3.164}$$

In the case of a more complicated deformation, an iterative procedure could be applied for computing a workability utilization factor.

In the foregoing documentation of q, it is assumed that the deformation process is monotonic, i.e., continuously loaded and the deformation path is linear in each step. In practice, this assumption is only approximately valid, i.e., quasi-monotonic deformation prevails.

The relationship for q for the nonmonotonic case will not be discussed here except that it is possible to use a criterion of the workability limit based on the permissible damage. Namely, from a certain value of q^*, the damage occurring in the material is no longer repairable, which can be expressed by

$$q^* < q < 1 \tag{3.165}$$

The workability utilization factor q depends mainly on the temperature, thermomechanical conditions, and the stress state rather than on the nature of the metal. For the common metallic materials in the recrystallized state, it is approximately equal to 0.2–0.3. Often larger defects are allowed, so that it can have a value of 0.6–0.7.

The Keeler-Goodwin formability limit diagram shown in the upper zone of Fig. 3.60, can be adapted for sheetmetal to this discussion by plotting the longitudinal strain $\bar{\varepsilon}_1$, versus the transverse strain $\bar{\varepsilon}_2$, as shown in Fig. 3.66. In this case, it is assumed that that the deformation is monotonic and proportional during loading showing a straight-line deformation path D as shown in the figure. However, if the deformation path deviates appreciably from the straight line as in D', the limit curve may be shifted as shown. The Keeler-Goodwin forming limit diagram (FLD) as applied to sheetmetal deformation will be discussed in detail in Chap. 11.

The right-hand side of the empirical forming limit curve in Fig. 3.66 for $\varepsilon_2 > 0$ may be expressed analytically by some such relation as

$$\varepsilon_{1L} = a_1 + a_2\varepsilon_2 + a_3\varepsilon_2^2 \tag{3.166}$$

The straight-line deformation path is easy to define as $\varepsilon_1 = (\varepsilon_{1C}/\varepsilon_{2C})\varepsilon_2$. Letting $\varepsilon_1 = \varepsilon_{1L}$ and assuming that the strains ε_{1C} and ε_{2C} at the critical location are previously empirically determined, one can obtain the strain ε_{2L} and then the workability utilization factor q.

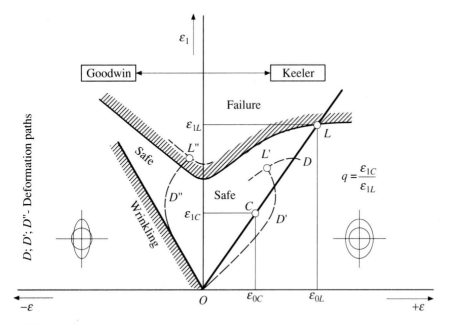

FIGURE 3.66
Keeler-Goodwin flow limit diagram (FLD) and the relevant relations of workability parameters (see Figs. 3.37, 3.60, and 11.28) [3.38].

3.14.6.3 OTHER WORKABILITY LIMIT CRITERIA (*B* TO *G* IN FIG. 3.65). The
fundamental meaning of the other workability limit criteria in Fig. 3.65 may be
deduced from the names themselves, and will not be discussed here in detail.

Generally speaking, in some instances more than one workability criterion
applies. For example, pure deep drawing of a cup can be limited by fracture in
the wall by localized deformation (necking) or by wrinkling in the flange as
shown on the left-hand side of Fig. 3.66.

The formation of a rough surface and of stretcher strains are examples of
defects resulting from the inability of an operation to meet the required quality.

3.14.6.4 THE COMPUTER IN THE EVALUATION OF THE FACTOR *q*. The
classification of the workability limit criteria proposed above may serve as the
basis for creating a general computer program and an appropriate database for
the evaluation of the workability utilization factor *q*. Such a program could give
some insight into the effects caused by the variations of certain important variables,
enabling the optimization of their interaction.

A very simplified version of the general algorithm for computer-aided
evaluation of the factor *q* is shown in Fig. 3.67.

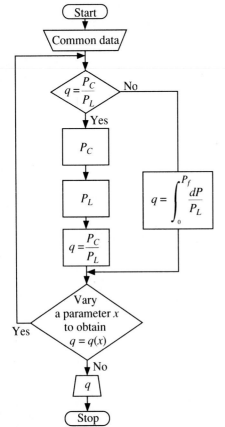

FIGURE 3.67
Flowchart for the general algorithm for the computer-aided evaluation of the workability utilization
factor *q* [3.38].

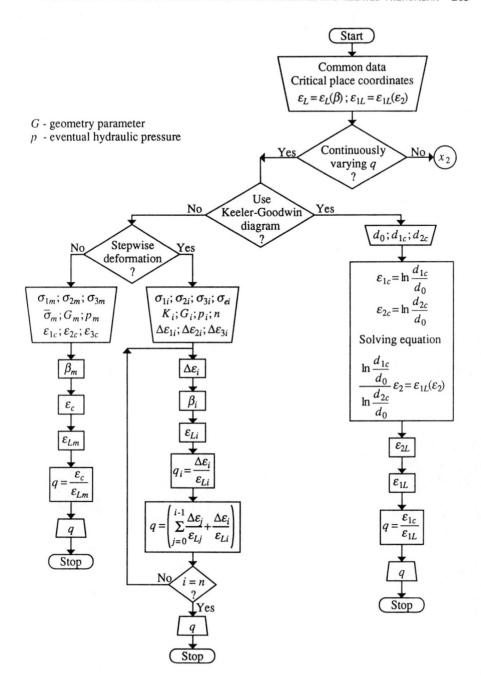

FIGURE 3.68
Flowchart of an example of the procedure used for the evaluation q, for which the workability limit criterion is based on fracture [3.38].

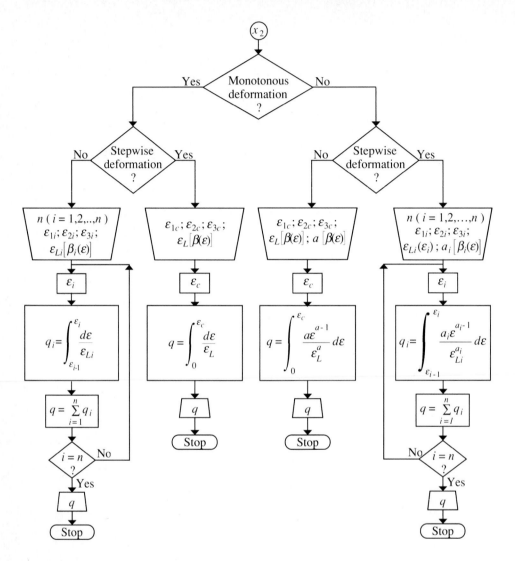

FIGURE 3.68 Continued

An example of the procedure that may be used for the evaluation of q in the case of workability limit criterion based on fracture is given by the flowchart in Fig. 3.68.

ACKNOWLEDGMENT

The material and most of the illustrations in this chapter were adapted from the references as indicated in the text and in the legends by the numbers of the references enclosed in square brackets pursuant to all copyrights.

REFERENCES

3.1. Johnson, W., and P. B. Mellor, *Engineering Plasticity*, Van Nostrand Reinhold Co., New York, 1973, p. 14.

3.2. Sellers, C. M., and W. J. Tegart, "Hot Workability," *Inter. Met. Reviews*, vol. 17, 1972, pp. 1–24.

3.3. Hecker, S. S., and M. G. Stout, "Strain Hardening of Heavily Cold Worked Metals," Deformation Processing and Structure, 1982 ASM Mat. Sc. Seminar, October 1982, ASM, Metals Park, Ohio, pp. 1–46.

3.4. Armstrong, P. E., J. E. Hockett, and O. D. Sherby "Large Strain Deformation of Polycrystalline Metals of Low Homologous Temperatures," *J. Mech. Phys. Solids*, vol. 30, 1982, pp. 37–38.

3.5. Bridgman, P. W., *Studies in Large Plastic Flow and Fracture*, McGraw-Hill, New York, 1952, pp. 9–37.

3.6. Schey, J. A., *Introduction to Manufacturing Processes*, McGraw-Hill Book Co., New York, 1977, p. 103.

3.7. MacKenzie, A. C., et al., "On the Influence of State of Stress on Ductile Initiation in High Strength Steels," *Engr. Fracture Mechanics*, 1977, vol. 9, pp. 167–188.

3.8. Hancock, V. W., and A. C. MacKenzie, "On the Mechanism of Ductile Failure in High-Strength Steels Subjected to Multi-Axial Stress-States," *J. Mech. Phys. of Solids*, 1976, vol. 24, pp. 147–169.

3.9. Marshall, E. R., and M. C. Shaw, "The Determination of Flow Stress from a Tensile Specimen," *Trans. ASM*, vol. 44, 1952, pp. 705–725.

3.10. Thomsen, E. G., A. H. Shabaik, and F. D. Negroni, "A New Method for the Study of Ductile Fractures at Large Strains," 8th NAMRC, SME, 1980, pp. 102–109.

3.11. Dieter, G. E., "Tension Testing," *Workability Testing Techniques*, G. E. Dieter (ed.), ASM 1984, pp. 21–35.

3.12. Male, A. T., and G. E. Dieter, "Hot Compression Testing," *Workability Testing Techniques*, ASM, 1984, pp. 51–72.

3.13. Ghosh, A. K., "Necking in Materials with Strain Hardening and Strain-Rate Sensitivity," Formability: Analysis Modeling and Experimentation, AIME/ASM Symposium, 1977, pp. 14–28.

3.14. Nagpal, V. et al., "Formability Models for 2024-O Aluminum Alloy Sheet Material," 7th NAMRC, SME, 1979, pp. 172–179.

3.15. Backofen, W. A., *Deformation Processing*, Addison-Wesley Pub. Co., Reading, Mass., 1972, pp. 199–207.

3.16. Semiatin, S. L., and J. J. Jonas, "Formability and Workability of Metals," ASM, 1984, pp. 29–31, pp. 191–194.

3.17. Keeler, S. P., and W. A. Backofen, "Plastic Instability and Fracture in Sheets Stretched Over Rigid Punches," *Trans. ASM*, vol. 56, 1963, pp. 25–31.

3.18. de Groot, M. "On the Interpretation of the Results of Hole Expansion Tests on Sheet Steels," Sheet Metal Forming and Energy Conversion, 9th Biennial Congress of IDDRG, October 1976, pp. 193–206.

3.19. Yamada, Y., and M. Koide, "Analysis of the Bore-Expanding Test by the Incremental Theory of Plasticity," *Int. J. Mech. Sci.*, Pergamon Press, 1968, vol. 10, pp. 1–14.

3.20. Lee, D., and F. Zaverl, Jr., "Neck Growth and Forming Limits in Sheet Metals," *Int. J. of Mech. Sci.*, vol. 24, no. 3, pp. 157–173, 1982.

3.21. Shih, C. F., and D. Lee, "Further Developments in Anisotropic Plasticity," *Journal of Engineering Materials and Technology, ASME Trans.*, vol. 100, no. 3, July 1978, pp. 294–302.

3.22. Polakowski, N. H., "The Compression Test in Relation to Cold Rolling," *J. Iron and Steel Inst.*, vol. 163, 1949, pp. 250–276.

3.23. Saul, G., A. T. Male, and V. DePierre, "A New Method for the Determination of Material Flow Stress Values under Metalworking Conditions," in *Metal Forming*, A. L. Hoffmanner, Plenum Press, 1971, pp. 293–306.

3.24 Saluja, S. S., P. C. Pandey, and S. Dalela, "A Simple Method for Flow Stress Determination under Metalworking Conditions," *9th NAMRC*, May 1981, pp. 153–157.

3.25. Ettouney, O., and D. E. Hardt, "A Method for In-Process Failure Prediction in Cold Upset Forging," *J. of Engr. for Industry*, vol. 105, August 1983, pp. 161–167.

3.26. Avitzur, B., *Metal Forming Processes and Analysis*, McGraw-Hill, New York, 1968, pp. 81–93.

3.27. Bramley, A. N., and N. A. Abdul, "Stress Strain Curves from the Ring Test," *Proc. 15th Int. Mach. Tool Design and Research Conf.*, 1974, S. A. Tobias and F. Koeningsberger (eds.), pp. 431–436.

3.28. Watts, A. B. and H. Ford, *Proc. Inst. Mech. Eng.*, 1952–1953, Vol. 1B, p. 448.

3.29. Dieter, G. E., "Overview of Workability," *Workability Testing Techniques*, ASM, 1984, pp. 1–20.

3.30. Siebel, E., "Plastic Forming of Metals," *Steel*, vol. 93, no. 17, pp. 37–38.

3.31. McClintock, F. A., "A Criterion for Ductile Fracture by the Growth of Holes," *J. of Applied Mechanics*, p. 363, 1968.

3.32. Oh, S. I., C. C. Chen, and S. Kobayashi, "Ductile Fracture in Axisymmetric Extrusion and Drawing," *J. of Engr. in Industry, ASME Trans.*, vol. 101, February 1977, pp. 36–43.

3.33. Cockcroft, M. C., and D. J. Latham, "Ductility and Workability of Metals," *J. Inst. of Metals*, vol. 96, pp. 33–39, 1968.

3.34. Kuhn, H. A., "Workability in Hot and Cold Deformation Processes—Test Methods, Criteria, and Applications," *Formability Analysis Modeling and Experimentation*, *Proc. AIME and ASM Symposium*, 1977, S. S. Hecker, A. K. Ghosh, and H. L. Gegel (eds.), pp. 259–280.

3.35. Kuhn, H. A., P. W. Lee, and T. Erturk, "A Fracture Criterion for Cold Forming," *J. of Engr. Materials and Technology, Trans. of ASME*, October 1973, pp. 213–218.

3.36. Hoffmanner, A. L., "The Use of Workability Test Results to Predict Processing Limits," *Metal Forming: Interrelation Between Theory and Practice*, A. L. Hoffmanner (ed.), Plenum Press, New York, 1971, pp. 349–391.

3.37. Kuhn, H. A., "Forming Limit Criteria—Bulk Deformation Processes," *Advances in Deformation Processing*, Plenum Press, J. J. Burke and V. Weiss (eds.), 1978, pp. 159–186.

3.38. Devedzic, B., "Evaluation of the Plastic Workability of Metals—Possible Approaches and Specific Problems," in *Proc. of the 26th Interl. Mach. Tool Design and Research Conf.* B. J. Davies (ed.), Macmillan Publishers Ltd., September 1986, pp. 443–451.

PROBLEMS

3.1. If the state of stress at a point P in the elastic range is given by the matrix σ_{ij} below, determine the principal stresses.

$$\sigma_{ij} = \begin{bmatrix} 40 & 0 & 0 \\ 0 & 60 & 80 \\ 0 & 80 & -60 \end{bmatrix} \text{MPa}$$

3.2. After a deep-drawing operation, a circle 0.50 in in diameter, that had been etched onto the surface of a thin steel sheet prior to drawing, changed into an ellipse with its major and minor axes being 0.650 in and 0.575 in, respectively. (1) Calculate the effective strain $\bar{\varepsilon}$ at the location of ellipse, and (2) find the ratio of $\sigma_1/\bar{\sigma}$ by assuming that a plane stress state existed during the operation with the ratio σ_2/σ_1 being constant throughout the operation.

3.3. The ultimate tensile strength of a steel part has been determined to be 520 MPa, and the strainhardening coefficient is believed to be 0.1. Estimate the equivalent true flow stress in compression at the point of necking. What assumption is made regarding the stress-strain curves?

3.4. (*a*) The stress-strain curve of an annealed, aluminum-killed, low-carbon steel is represented by the power relation, $\bar{\sigma} = 530\bar{\varepsilon}^{0.28}$ MPa. A bar of this steel is initially cold worked 15 percent, followed by an additional cold deformation of 25 percent. What is the probable yield (flow) strength of the bar?

(b) Another bar of the same material is initially cold worked some unknown amount. It is then given an additional cold deformation of 20 percent, which resulted in a yield strength of 400 MPa. Calculate the amount of cold work induced initially.

3.5. A 12 mm diameter wire bar is drawn through a die to reduce its diameter to 11.5 mm. Using the power law equation (2.139), and Eqs. (2.162) and (2.163), determine the following:

(a) The drawing stress, assuming an ideal process, i.e., homogeneous deformation.

(b) Calculate the actual drawing stress, if the overall drawing and deformation efficiency is 65 percent.

3.6. If, in the plane-strain compression test as shown in Fig. 3.47, the direction of loading is 1, the width direction is 2, and the length direction is 3, answer the following questions:

(a) What is the effective stress?

(b) What is the effective strain as a function of stress and strain in the loading direction?

(c) What is the ideal work per unit volume dw in terms of the effective stress and strain?

(d) If the power law in Eq. (2.80) applies, what is the stress in the loading direction in terms of ε_1, K, and n?

3.7. If r, in Eq. (3.75) for a plane stress condition, is taken as the mean value, $\bar{r}$, and the principal strain ratio is 0.5, calculate Z_1 if $r_{0°} = 0.84$, $r_{45°} = 0.80$, $r_{90°} = 0.85$.

3.8. A cylindrical steel specimen, having $d_0 = 15$ mm, $h_0 = 18$ mm, and $h = 14.40$ mm, as shown in Fig. 3.42, was compressed with a load of 126.49 kN, using a collodial graphite lubricant. The bulge radius R, as shown in Fig. 3.40, was measured with a toolmaker's microscope to be 136 mm. The radius at the midsection a was measured to be 8.34 mm.

(a) Calculate the flow stress in MPa.

(b) Calculate the average stress.

(c) Calculate the correction factor, and check it against the above results.

3.9. A tensile test was performed on SAE 4140 steel yielding the following computed data:

ε	σ (ksi)	a/R	B	σ_{corr}
0.002	110			
0.1	142			
0.2	153			
0.4	171	0.19	0.956	163.5
0.6	190	0.38	0.918	174.4
0.8	208	0.57	0.884	183.9
1.0	221	0.76	0.855	189.0

(a) Calculate B and σ_{corr}.

(b) Plot the log-log of (1) the σ-ε curve and (2) σ_{corr}-ε curve.

(c) Determine K and n.

3.10. It is desired to study the effect of cold rolling on the mechanical properties of an expensive alloy. The original cross section is 25.4 mm (1 in) wide and 6.35 mm

(0.250 in) thick. The length of the tensile test specimen to be used is 152.4 mm (6 in) long. Assuming that the volume remains constant and the width does not increase during rolling, i.e., it is a plane-strain process ($\varepsilon_y = 0$), calculate (1) the target thickness that would give the following reductions: 5, 10, 20, and 30 percent, and (2) calculate the length of the bar that should be cut off to give a test specimen 152.4 mm long after rolling for each of the above reductions.

3.11. A hollow steel cylinder had initially an outside diameter of 30 mm and an inside diameter of 15 mm and a height of 10 mm. It was heated to 1000°C and compressed with a force of 470 kN at a velocity of 600 mm/s to yield the following final dimensions: outside diameter 38.3 mm, inside diameter 10.8 mm, and final height 5 mm. Determine the flow stress. Use Fig. 3.45, and estimate the strain rate at the end of the stroke.

3.12. If at a strain rate of 12 s^{-1} the same material under the same processing conditions as in Prob. 3.11 had a flow stress of 150 MPa, determine (1) the strength coefficient C, and (2) the strain rate sensitivity exponent m. Obtain C and m by use of a log-log plot.

3.13. A tensile test was conducted on a reduced-section specimen cut from sheetmetal. The following original gauge dimensions were used: $l_0 = 50.8$ mm (2 in), $w_0 = 6.35$ mm (0.25 in), and $h_0 = 1.02$ mm (0.040 in). The test was interrupted before the onset of yielding by necking, and the following dimensions were obtained: $l_f = 61.0$ mm (2.4 in) and $w_f = 5.69$ mm (0.224 in). Since it is difficult to measure the final thickness, h_f, with sufficient accuracy, it was decided to obtain h_f, the average thickness, by use of the constancy of volume principle. Calculate the plastic strain ratio r. Would the material be suitable for deep drawing on the basis of this test? Explain.

3.14. A tensile specimen as shown in Fig. 3.6(b) has a gauge length of 100 mm, a width of 12 mm, and a thickness of 4 mm. It is desired to compare to it the ductility of a specimen 2 mm thick.
(a) What gauge length should be used?
(b) Are the specimens in Fig. 3.6(c) geometrically similar?

3.15. If, in using the tension squeeze test shown in Fig. 3.48, a tensile load P of 300 N and a lateral pressure of 20 MPa are applied, calculate the effective stress $\bar{\sigma}$, and effective strain $\bar{\varepsilon}$, from the following data: $w_0 = 12.7$ mm, $t_0 = 3.25$ mm, and $t = 2$ mm.

CHAPTER

4

METHODS
FOR
ANALYZING
METALWORKING
PROCESSES

4.1 INTRODUCTION

Plasticity theory, which serves as a basis for metalforming processes, is a macroscopic, phenomenological theory based on mathematically described, large-scale behavior of a material continuum during plastic deformation, as has been discussed previously. The various analysis methods, that are presently used to analyze metalworking processes are shown in Fig. 4.1 [4.1]. Rather exact equations may be written to describe a particular metalforming process; however, their solutions are usually quite formidable. The elementary theory of plasticity circumvents these mathematical difficulties by making a number of simplifying assumptions regarding the mode of deformation and the states of stress occurring in the metalworking process.

In the elementary theory of plasticity or the slab method, it is assumed that the deformation is homogeneous; i.e., sections that are plane remain plane during the course of deformation. Metalforming processes are by nature non-homogeneous, in which the principal axes of deformation and stress have different directions at different points in the workpiece. The fundamental equations must be formulated in such a manner that they are independent of the orientation of the coordinate system.

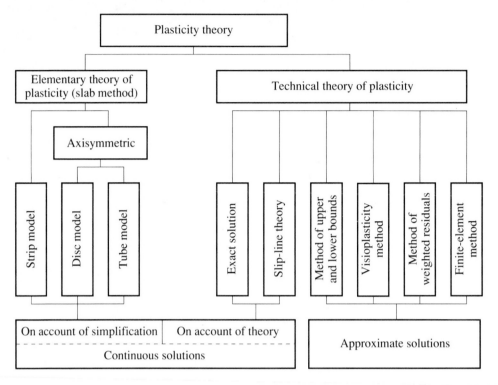

FIGURE 4.1
Flowchart showing various theoretical solution methods for metalforming problems [4.1].

Even in the more exact, so-called technical theories, some simplification must be made, such as in regard to the material model. In case of the von Mises theory of plasticity, rigid–perfectly plastic material as in Fig. 3.1(a) is assumed as opposed to an elastic–perfectly plastic material as in Fig. 3.1(b) as in the case of the Prandtl-Reuse theory.

The fundamental equations of the von Mises theory are the equilibrium equations (2.40a), (b), and (c), the continuity equations (2.44) and (2.45), the yield criterion (2.51), and the constitutive relations, i.e., the Levy-Mises equations (2.73), (2.74), and (2.75) or the flow rules. Exact solutions of the von Mises theory equations can only be found for certain special, simple problems.

A brief simplified summary of the most commonly used methods of analysis is given in Table 4.1 [4.2]. Of the ones listed, the following methods will be discussed here in some detail: (1) the slab or equilibrium method; (2) the bounding methods; (3) the slip-line field method; (4) the finite element method; (5) the system approach and process modeling; and (6) the coupled analysis of plastic deformation and heat transfer. A greater discussion of these methods will take place in relation to their application to specific forming processes such as extrusion, rolling, etc.

TABLE 4.1
Summary of various analysis methods [4.2]

Method	Input			Output				Comments
	Flow stress	Friction†	Velocity field	Stress field	Temperature field	Stresses on tools		
Slab	Average	a, b	No	Yes	No	Yes		Ignores redundant work
Uniform energy	Average	b	No	No	No	Average		Redundant work can be included aproximately
Slip line	Average	a, b	Yes	Yes	No	Yes		Valid for plane-strain problems
Upper-bound	Distribution	b	Yes	No	No	Average		Gives upper bound loads, can determine free boundaries
Hill's	Distribution	a, b	Yes	No	No	Average		Can treat 3D problems
Finite difference	Distribution	a, b	Yes	Yes	Yes	Yes		Requires considerable computer time
Finite element	Distribution	a, b	Yes	Yes	Yes	Yes		Requires considerable computer time
Matrix	Distribution	a, b	Yes	Yes	Yes	Yes		Treats rigid–plastic material
Weighted residuals	Distribution	a, b	Yes	Yes	Yes	Yes		Very general approach

† a: $\tau = \mu\sigma_n$; b: $\tau = (m/\sqrt{3})\bar{\sigma}$

The following methods, listed in Table 4.1, will not be discussed here: (1) uniform-energy method; (2) Hill's general method; (3) matrix method; and (4) weighted residuals method.

4.2 THE CLASSICAL SLAB OR EQUILIBRIUM METHOD

4.2.1 Introduction

In the classical slab method pioneered by Sachs [4.3], Siebel [4.4], and von Karman [4.5], which is also called the freebody equilibrium method, the friction-hill method, and the elementary slab method, the equilibrium of a slab of the deformed body is considered, in which a simplified stress distribution such as plane strain is assumed for the slab. The governing equilibrium equations in the direction of the principal stresses are solved, and an approximate solution for the forming forces and stresses is obtained. The slab method neglects the effect of friction stress upon the internal stress distribution and thereby introduces errors of an unknown magnitude. It has been successfully applied to many practical problems, especially by using modular and numerically interactive computer techniques. Although approximate, it is a very powerful tool in predicting forming stresses, loads, and, in some cases, even metal flow. (The word "slab" as used here has a somewhat different connotation than when it is normally used to describe a semifinished rolled shape, in which the width is greater than twice the thickness. It refers here to a very thin imaginary slice chosen as a freebody in a slab-like shape, as will be discussed subsequently. In this discussion, the word "strip" will be analogous to the conventional "slab." The context of the discussion will indicate which meaning of "slab" is being used.)

In the slab or equilibrium method, a representative volume element in the body of the material or workpiece undergoing plastic deformation is isolated and the behavior of this element is observed as it moves along the work zone of the pass. Since the element continues to form an integral part of the body or workpiece, in conjunction with the rigid dies or tools, it must remain constantly in the state of force equilibrium throughout its entire period of deformation. The behavior of the element reflects the whole of the workpiece and can therefore be analyzed by considering the equilibrium of the forces acting at any instant of deformation. Essentially, this method requires that conditions of force equilibrium are established in the three directions, i.e., that the sum of the forces is zero in the x, y, and z directions or

$$\sum F_x = \sum F_y = \sum F_z = 0 \qquad (4.1)$$

The above analysis usually leads to the formulation of one or more differential equations involving the stress system produced in the body of the material. The friction effect at the die-workpiece interface is incorporated through the friction force involving either the coefficient of friction μ or friction shear parameter, m. Stress is related to strain rate by a suitable constitutive relationship. Finite values of the operative stresses are obtained by integrating the differential equations between the conditions occurring at the entry to and exit from the working zone of the pass or, if this is of a complex nature, by splitting the pass into a number of interconnected zones as in forging and summing the effect in the individual zones [4.6].

4.2.2 The Classical Slab Method in Plane-Strain Upsetting Using the Strip Model

The simplest approach in applying slab analysis in plane-strain upsetting is to consider the homogeneous deformation of a long strip of material between overhanging dies or platens as shown in Fig. 4.2 , showing the initial and the final (current) positions of the dies [4.7].

In estimating the stress distribution at the die-strip interface in plane-strain upsetting, a slab of infinitesimal thickness is selected perpendicular to the direction of metal flow as in Fig. 4.3(a). The analysis can be simplified by assuming that the interface pressure p is a principal stress; that σ_x is independent of the z direction; that the thickness of the slab h is less than the width b, and the deformation is homogeneous so that no bulging occurs; that the friction is uniform at the die-material interface; that a unit depth of the strip is being considered or a depth of 1; and that an incompressible, rigid–perfectly plastic material is being used.

If a force balance is performed on the above slab, a simple differential equation of stable equilibrium is obtained. Summation of the forces in the x

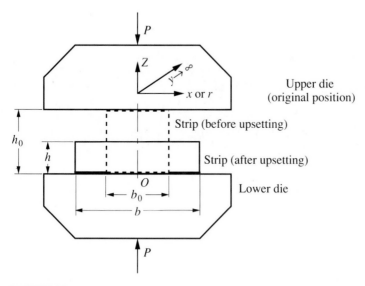

FIGURE 4.2
End view of the upsetting of a long strip in plane strain between overhanging dies showing the original shape in dashed lines and the final shape in solid lines. For right, circular cylinders, $b_0 = 2R_0$ and $b = 2R$.

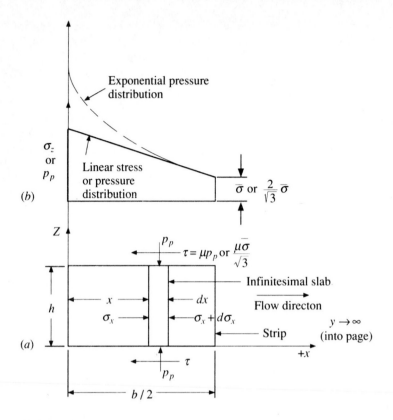

FIGURE 4.3
(*a*) Schematic equilibrium stress diagram for plane strain, homogeneous upsetting (double scale); and (*b*) pressure (*p*) or stress (σ_z) distribution at the die-material interface.

direction yields:

$$\sum F_x = \sigma_x h - (\sigma_x + d\sigma_x)h - 2\tau \, dx = 0$$

or

$$d\sigma_x = -\frac{2\tau \, dx}{h}$$

(4.2)

Integration of Eq. (4.2) yields

$$\sigma_x = -\int_0^{b/2} \frac{2\tau \, dx}{h} = -\frac{2\tau}{h}x + C$$

(4.3)

where C is the constant of integration. Since, in slab analysis, it is assumed that the stresses in the metal flow direction and in the direction perpendicular to the metal flow direction are principal stresses

$$\sigma_z = \sigma_1 \qquad \sigma_x = \sigma_3 \qquad \sigma_y = \sigma_2$$

(4.4)

If the Tresca maximum shear stress criterion of yielding applies, which is usually used in the elementary slab theory, it gives

$$\sigma_1 - \sigma_3 = \sigma_z - \sigma_x = \bar{\sigma}$$

or

$$\sigma_z = \sigma_x + \bar{\sigma}$$

(4.5)

Substituting Eq. (4.3) for σ_x one obtains

$$\sigma_z = -\frac{2\tau}{h} x + C + \bar{\sigma}$$

(4.6)

From the boundary condition at $x = b/2$, where $\sigma_x = 0$, from Eq. (4.3) one obtains

$$\sigma_x = -\frac{2\tau}{h}\left(\frac{b}{2}\right) + C = 0$$

or

$$C = \frac{\tau b}{h}$$

(4.7)

and Eq. (4.6) becomes

$$\sigma_z = -\frac{2\tau}{h} x + \frac{\tau b}{h} + \bar{\sigma}$$

$$= \frac{2\tau}{h}\left(\frac{b}{2} - x\right) + \bar{\sigma}$$

(4.8)

If the von Mises criterion applies, then as discussed below

$$\sigma_1 - \sigma_3 = \sigma_z - \sigma_x = \left|\frac{2\bar{\sigma}}{\sqrt{3}}\right|$$

(4.9)

and

$$\sigma_z = \frac{2\tau}{h}\left(\frac{b}{2} - x\right) + \frac{2\bar{\sigma}}{\sqrt{3}}$$

(4.10)

This relationship may be obtained as follows:

The Levy-Mises plasticity equations (2.73) give

$$\dot{\varepsilon}_2 = \dot{\varepsilon}_y = \lambda(\sigma_2 - \sigma_m) = 0$$

or

$$\sigma_2 = \sigma_m$$

(4.11)

Since, by definition, $\sigma_m = (\sigma_1 + \sigma_2 + \sigma_3)/3$, then

$$\sigma_m = \sigma_2 = \frac{\sigma_1 + \sigma_3}{2}$$

(4.12)

For plane strain $\sigma_2 = \sigma_m$, the von Mises criterion (2.55) gives

$$3[(\sigma_1 - \sigma_m)^2(\sigma_3 - \sigma_m)^2 - 0] = 2\bar{\sigma}^2$$

(4.13)

so that

$$\sigma_1 - \sigma_3 = \sigma_z - \sigma_x = \frac{2\bar{\sigma}}{\sqrt{3}} \tag{4.14}$$

By following the above procedure involving Eqs. (4.6), (4.7), and (4.8), one can obtain Eq. (4.10).

In Eqs. (4.8) and (4.10), τ can be taken equal to μp_p or $m\bar{\sigma}/\sqrt{3}$. By integrating Eqs. (4.8) and (4.10) over the entire width b, that is, from $-b/2$ to $+b/2$, of the strip for a unit depth, one obtains the upsetting load per unit depth for the Tresca and von Mises criteria, respectively:

$$P = \bar{\sigma}\left(1 + \frac{\sqrt{3}\,\mu b}{4h}\right)b \tag{4.15}$$

or

$$P = \frac{2\bar{\sigma}}{\sqrt{3}}\left(1 + \frac{mb}{4h}\right)b \tag{4.16}$$

Equation (4.2) can also be solved for the die-material pressure distribution by assuming, say, Coulomb friction ($\tau = \mu p_p$) and by noting that at $x = +b/2$, $\sigma_x = 0$ and $p = \bar{\sigma}$ for the Tresca criterion. The resulting pressure or interfacial stress distribution for the slipping friction case is

$$p_p = \bar{\sigma}\exp\left[\frac{\mu(b \pm 2x)}{h}\right] = \bar{\sigma}\exp\left[\frac{2\mu}{h}\left(\frac{b}{2} \pm x\right)\right] \tag{4.17}$$

where h = thickness of the slab

        b = strip width

        μ = Coulomb coefficient of friction

        $p_p = \sigma_z$ = normal pressure or interfacial stress at the die-material interface

        $\bar{\sigma}$ = effective flow strength of the material equal to $2\tau_Y = 2k$

        $\exp = e^{[\ ]}$ is the exponential e

The $+$ sign refers to the left portion and the $-$ sign to the right portion of the strip.

Equations (4.8), (4.15), and (4.17) have die-material pressure distributions as shown in Fig. 4.3(b).

The mean or average pressure or interfacial stress may be obtained from

$$p_m = \frac{\displaystyle\int_0^{b/2} p\,dx}{A} \tag{4.18}$$

to give

$$\frac{p_m}{\bar{\sigma}} = \frac{h}{\mu b}(e^{\mu b/h} - 1) \tag{4.19}$$

Equation (4.17) gives the pressure distribution over the face of the strip, which is in contact with the anvil or platen, as shown in Fig. 4.4(a). This pressure

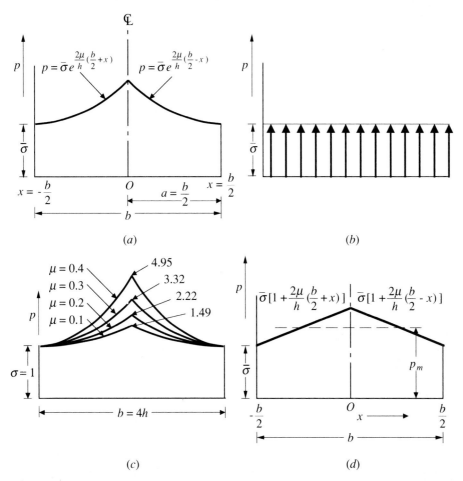

FIGURE 4.4
Schematic diagrams showing the variation of the pressure at the die-strip interface (*a*) for sliding friction μ for the general case; (*b*) for frictionless case $\mu = 0$ of a perfectly plastic material; (*c*) for selected values of μ for the case where $b = 4h$, and (*d*) for the simplified linear case [4.22].

distribution is called the *friction hill,* which indicates that when there is friction at the platen-strip interface, the pressure at the edge of the strip is equal to the flow stress of the nonstrainhardening metal, and it is a maximum at the centerline. The fact that the friction causes a lateral stress σ_{xx} increases the surface pressure and causes the friction hill. The maximum value at the centerline for slipping friction, at $x = 0$, is

$$p_{\max} = \bar\sigma e^{\mu b/h} \qquad (4.20)$$

For the frictionless case, assuming homogeneous deformation of a perfectly plastic (nonstrainhardening) metal, the stress would be uniform and equal to the flow stress of the metal across the interface as shown in Fig. 4.4(*b*). The relative shape of the friction hill according to Eq. (4.17), for different values of $\mu < 0.577$ for $\bar{\sigma} = 1$ and $b = 4h$, is shown in Fig. 4.4(c).

The variation of the horizontal stress σ_{xx} with x may be obtained from

$$\sigma_{xx} = \bar{\sigma} - p = \bar{\sigma}[1 - e^{[2\mu/h(b/2 \pm x)]}] \tag{4.21}$$

where the $-$ sign applies to the right side and $+$ to the left side of the centerline.

Since the curvature of the two sides of the curves is usually small if μ is low as in sliding friction, they may be replaced by straight lines tangent to the exponential curves at the ends of the strip as shown in Fig. 4.4(d). The higher μ is, the greater the slope. If the expansion

$$e^{y} = 1 + y + \frac{y^2}{2} + \cdots \tag{4.22}$$

is used to simplify the above equation (4.17), it becomes

$$p = \bar{\sigma}\left[1 - \frac{\mu}{h}(b \pm x)\right] \tag{4.23}$$

where the $-$ sign applies to the right and the $+$ sign to the left of the centerline.

If the width of the strip is b, the maximum pressure at the centerline is

$$p_{max} \cong \bar{\sigma}\left(1 + \frac{\mu b}{h}\right) \cong \bar{\sigma}\left(1 + \frac{2\mu a}{h}\right) \tag{4.24}$$

and the mean pressure is

$$p_m = \bar{\sigma}\left(1 + \frac{\mu b}{2h}\right) = \bar{\sigma}\left(1 + \frac{\mu a}{h}\right) \tag{4.25}$$

The total compressive or forging load P can then be obtained from

$$P = p_m b l \tag{4.26}$$

where $l =$ the length normal to the page.

The approximate expressions for the variation in pressure p along the face of the die, the maximum and the mean pressures, are obtained for the case where sticking friction occurs, i.e., in which $\mu = 0.5$ as for hot compression or the hot forging of a strip, by substituting this value of μ in Eqs. (4.23), (4.24), and (4.25) to give

$$p = \bar{\sigma}\left(1 + \frac{b \pm x}{2h}\right) = \bar{\sigma}\left(1 + \frac{a \pm x}{h}\right) \tag{4.27}$$

$$p_{max} \cong \bar{\sigma}\left(1 + \frac{b}{2h}\right) \cong \bar{\sigma}\left(1 + \frac{a}{h}\right) \tag{4.28}$$

and

$$p_m \cong \bar{\sigma}\left(1 + \frac{b}{4h}\right) \cong \bar{\sigma}\left(1 + \frac{a}{h}\right) \tag{4.29}$$

where $b =$ width of the strip
$\quad\quad a = b/2$
$\quad\quad h =$ the current height or thickness of the strip

Slightly different-appearing equations for this problem may be obtained depending on where the origin for x is taken and whether the Coulomb coefficient of friction μ, or the friction factor m, is used. For example, we may select $x = 0$ at each edge of the strip and measure x from each edge to the centerline as shown in Fig. 4.5(a) for Coulomb friction. Then $\sum F_x = 0$ gives

$$(p' + dp')h = p'h + 2\mu(p' + 2\mu(p' + \bar{\sigma}))\,dx$$

$$\frac{2\mu}{h}\,dx = \frac{dp'}{p - \bar{\sigma}} \tag{4.30}$$

The solution of this differential equation for slipping friction is

$$p' = Ce^{2\mu x/h} - \bar{\sigma}$$

At $x = 0$, $p' = 0$, and $C = \bar{\sigma}$, then

$$p' = \bar{\sigma}e^{2\mu x/h}$$

Since $p = p' + \bar{\sigma}$

$$p = \bar{\sigma}(1 + e^{2\mu x/h}) \tag{4.31}$$

If the frictional force is assumed to be a constant factor m of the yield strength, as seen in Fig. 4.5(b), then $\sum F_x = 0$ gives

$$(p' + dp')h = p'h + 2m\bar{\sigma}\,dx$$

and

$$\frac{dp'}{dx} = \frac{2m\bar{\sigma}}{h} \tag{4.32}$$

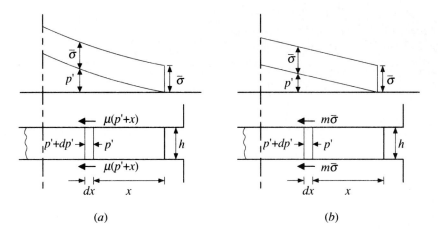

(a)   (b)

FIGURE 4.5
Stress distribution in a strip in plane-strain compression (a) for Coulomb coefficient; and (b) for constant friction factor m [9.8].

The solution of this differential equation gives

$$p' = \frac{2m\bar{\sigma}x}{h} + C \tag{4.33}$$

At $x = 0$, $p = 0$, and $C = 0$, so

$$p' = \frac{2m\bar{\sigma}x}{h} \tag{4.34}$$

Since $p = p' + \sigma$, then

$$p = \bar{\sigma}\left(1 + \frac{2mx}{h}\right) \tag{4.35}$$

In summary, in deriving Eq. (4.8), it was assumed that the friction is uniform over the entire surface at the die-material interface. Another similar solution in plain strain, called the (*classical*) *elementary slab method*, may be obtained if it is assumed that the die surfaces are so rough that the metal adheres perfectly to them. This limiting case is known as *sticking friction*, for which the shearing stress at the interface is constant and equal to the shearing strength of the material, $\tau = \tau_Y = k = \bar{\sigma}$ for the Tresca criterion (or $2/\sqrt{3}\,\bar{\sigma}$ for the von Mises criterion). Equation (4.8) may then be written as

$$\sigma_z = p_p = \bar{\sigma}\left(1 + \frac{b - 2x}{2h}\right) \tag{4.36}$$

Equation (4.8) for sticking friction predicts that the pressure distribution over a plate of breath b is linear with a maximum pressure at the center as shown in Fig. 4.3(b) by the solid line. On the other hand, if the shearing stresses at the die-material interfaces are related to the normal pressure on the interface by Coulomb's law of sliding friction, Eq. (4.17) is obtained.

4.2.3   The Classical Slab Method in Homogeneous Axisymmetric Upsetting with Friction Using the Tube Model [4.7]

The analysis procedure is similar to that used in plane-strain upsetting.

By summation of the forces in the r direction in Fig. 4.6, one obtains

$$\Sigma\, F_r = \sigma_r(d\theta)rh - (\sigma_r + d\sigma_r)(r + dr)h\, d\theta + 2\sigma_\theta \sin\frac{d\theta}{2} h\, dr - 2\tau r\, d\theta\, dr = 0 \tag{4.37}$$

Since angle $d\theta$ is very small, $\sin d\theta/2 = d\theta/2$, and Eq. (4.37) reduces to

$$-\sigma_r = \frac{d\sigma_r}{dr}r + \sigma_\theta - \frac{2\tau}{h}r = 0 \tag{4.38}$$

Since, in axisymmetric deformation, $\dot{\varepsilon}_r = \dot{\varepsilon}_\theta$, by use of the Levy-Mises plasticity equations (2.73) one obtains

$$\sigma_r = \sigma_\theta \qquad \frac{d\sigma_r}{dr} + \frac{\tau}{h} = 0 \tag{4.39}$$

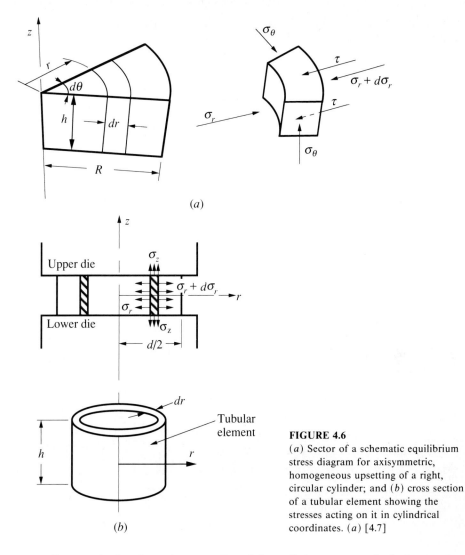

(a)

(b)

FIGURE 4.6
(a) Sector of a schematic equilibrium stress diagram for axisymmetric, homogeneous upsetting of a right, circular cylinder; and (b) cross section of a tubular element showing the stresses acting on it in cylindrical coordinates. (a) [4.7]

Since at the free boundary, $r = R$ and the radial stress, $\sigma_r = 0$, the integration of Eq. (4.39) gives

$$\sigma_r = \frac{2\tau}{h}(r - R) \tag{4.40}$$

By applying the von Mises flow rule for axisymmetric-symmetric upsetting $(\sigma_z - \sigma_r = |\bar{\sigma}|)$, one obtains

$$\sigma_z = \frac{2\tau}{h}(r - R) - \bar{\sigma} \tag{4.41}$$

which illustrates that the surface stress or pressure for homogeneous deformation with friction increases linearly from the edge toward the center of the circular surface of the cylinder in contact with the die.

If τ is taken as $m\bar{\sigma}/\sqrt{3}$, the load for axisymmetric homogeneous upsetting with friction can now be obtained by integrating the above stress distribution equation over the circular surface of the cylinder being upset which gives

$$P = \int_0^R \sigma_z 2\pi r \, dr = \bar{\sigma}\pi R^2 \left(1 + \frac{2mR}{3h\sqrt{3}} \right) \qquad (4.42)$$

4.2.4   Modified Slab Method for Axisymmetric Upsetting

In the foregoing classical, Sachs-Siebel slab method, the equilibrium of a slab of the deforming body is considered for a simplified stress distribution for the slab. The governing equilibrium equations in the direction of principal stresses are solved, and an approximate solution for the forming forces and stresses is obtained. By neglecting the influence of the frictional forces on the internal stress distribution in the slab method, one introduces errors of unknown magnitude. In the modified slab method being considered here, these errors are minimized [4.8].

In the classical slab method, the theoretical results show that the distribution of pressure across the die-material interface is always convex as shown in Fig. 4.3(a) irrespective of the aspect ratio h_0/d_0, that is, the ratio of the initial height to the initial diameter. This distribution is commonly called the *friction hill of normal pressure distribution.*

As indicated in the foregoing, the following assumptions are generally made in the classical slab method [4.8]:

1. The material is isotropic and incompressible
2. Elastic deformation is neglected, i.e., the material is rigid
3. Inertial forces are small and neglected
4. Plane surfaces in the material remain plane
5. The flow stress $\bar{\sigma}$ is constant and is not a function of z and r
6. Friction is constant
7. The material flows according to the von Mises flow rule

It can be shown, by theoretical and experimental analysis, that the distribution of normal pressure over the interface is convex, i.e., greater at the center of the interface than at the edge only when the h_0/d_0 ratio is small, i.e., less than 0.4. The normal pressure distribution, however, starts changing to concave when it becomes large, i.e., when $h_0/d_0 > 0.4$ as shown in Fig. 4.7.

One explanation of this phenomenon is that when the aspect ratio is small, the distance of separation between the two interfaces is relatively small, so that the mutual interference of the friction forces acting on both interfaces is great enough to prevent the growth of a bulge on the free cylindrical surface. The

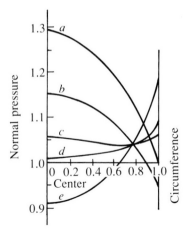

	h_0/d_0
a	0.25
b	0.40
c	0.75
d	1.00
e	1.25

FIGURE 4.7
Theoretical results showing the distribution of normal pressure on the die-material interface of a compressed cylinder [4.8].

deformation of the cylinder, therefore, becomes more uniform, and the normal pressure distribution becomes convex, similar to the classical distribution of Sachs and Siebel, in which nonuniform deformation is neglected. When h_0/d_0 is large, the mutual interference of friction forces from the two interfaces is weak, and the bulge grows readily. The normal pressure distribution becomes concave as shown in Fig. 4.7(c, d, and e).

Physically speaking, the normal pressure distribution becomes convex when h_0/d_0 is small, because the hydrostatic pressure at the center becomes large by mutual interference of the friction acting on both interfaces. On the other hand, when h_0/d_0 is large, the internal hydrostatic pressure decreases and the forces, which pull the side surface of the cylinder outward, increase. This interaction causes a concave distribution of pressure as shown in Fig. 4.7(c, d, and e) [4.8].

The expression for the pressure on the interface surface in nonuniform upsetting of a cylinder can be found by combining the bulge correction factor approach, shown in Figs. 3.40 and 4.8, with the curved slab method.

In Fig. 4.8, it is assumed that a cylindrical specimen is being plastically deformed between two parallel dies. As the thickness of the specimen is reduced, its major radius increases. It is further assumed that the material is homogeneous and isotropic in its mechanical properties. Also, the stresses near the surfaces are not principal stresses, since shear stresses act on the element faces as shown in Fig. 4.8 [4.8].

The following expression for the pressure at the surface has been derived [4.8]:

$$\frac{p}{\bar{\sigma}} = \left(\ln \frac{-2r_2 R'}{r_2^2 - r'^2 - 2r_2 R'} - 1 \right) \exp \left(\frac{-\mu(r_1 - r')h'}{2r_1 r'} \right) \tag{4.43}$$

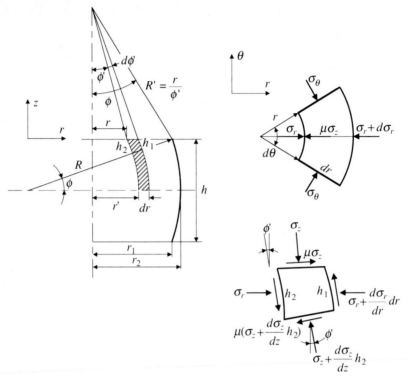

FIGURE 4.8
Approximate state of stress on an element near the surface of a compressed cylinder [4.8].

where

$$r' = \frac{h^2}{8R'} + r$$

and

$$R' = \frac{h^2 + (d_2 - d_1)^2}{4(d_2 - d_1)} \tag{3.129}$$

and where r_1, r_2 = the minimum and maximum radii of a bulged specimen as shown in Fig. 4.8, m (in)

r, r' = the instantaneous (current) minimum and maximum radii of a bulged specimen, m (in)

R' = the radius of the bulge as shown in Fig. 4.8

h' = length of the height of the bulged cylinder, m (in)

h = current height of the specimen, m (in)

The importance of the bulged height h', and the bulge radius R should be noted. As R approaches infinity, the expression for the classical solution is obtained.

By integrating Eq. (4.43) between 0 and r, one can obtain the equation for the average pressure at the interface, which will not be presented here [4.8].

It is claimed that the above mathematical model is accurate enough to be used for the real time adaptive control of the upset forging of cylinders [4.8].

Since, in most of the metalforming processes, the aspect ratio h_0/d_0 is less than 0.4, the classical solutions, having a convex friction-hill curve of normal pressure, will be used in this book.

4.3 BOUNDING METHODS AND LIMIT ANALYSIS

4.3.1 Introduction and Background

It is not always possible to determine precisely the load to cause plastic deformation to begin or proceed for a given metalworking operation [4.9]. However, an acceptable solution may be obtained by bounding the load, i.e., by finding one which is too large called the *upper bound* and another which is too small called the *lower bound*. Fortunately, theorems have been available for obtaining the upper and lower bounds to forming loads for many years. The upper bound is based on a possible velocity field. The lower bound, while ensuring that there is everywhere stress equilibrium and that a yield criterion is not exceeded, gives a load that is inadequate to perform the metalworking operation.

Two separate solutions are obtained: (1) the upper bound solution, which gives a value of the rate of work done or the power required equal to or greater than the actual power required, and (2) the lower bound solution, which provides a value of power equal to or lower than the actual power. Since the actual value is bracketed between two limits, this type of analysis is called *limit analysis*. The gap between the upper- and lower-bound solutions may be narrowed by selecting the lowest upper bound solution and the highest lower bound solution of the several that may be calculated. The exact solution would lie somewhere in between [4.10].

The exact solution must satisfy completely the following predetermined set of conditions [4.10]:

1. The differential equations of equilibrium for the stress tensor must be satisfied throughout the deforming body. If one disregards the body forces, these equations in compacted form may be written as

$$\frac{\partial \sigma_{ij}}{\partial x_i} = 0 \tag{4.44}$$

2. Continuity of flow must be maintained, i.e., the constancy of volume must be satisfied as expressed by

$$\varepsilon_{ii} = \varepsilon_{11} + \varepsilon_{22} + \varepsilon_{33} = 0 \tag{4.45}$$

or

$$\dot{\varepsilon}_{ii} = \dot{\varepsilon}_{11} + \dot{\varepsilon}_{22} + \dot{\varepsilon}_{33} = 0 \tag{4.46}$$

3. A yield criterion, such as the von Mises yield criterion, must be obeyed
4. The geometric and static boundary conditions must be satisfied

The von Mises yield criterion postulates that plastic flow begins when a certain combination of the components of the stress deviatoric tensor reaches a characteristic value as expressed by

$$J_2 = \tfrac{1}{2} S_{ij} S_{ij} = \tfrac{1}{2}(S_{11}^2 + S_{22}^2 + S_{12}^2 + S_{23}^2 + S_{31}^2) \leq \frac{\sigma_0^2}{3} \tag{4.47}$$

where J_2 = the second invariant of the stress tensor
$$S_{ij} = \sigma_{ij} - \delta_{ij} S$$
$$S = \tfrac{1}{2}(\sigma_{11} + \sigma_{22} + \sigma_{33}) \tag{4.48}$$
$$\delta_{ij} = \begin{cases} 1 & \text{where} \quad i = j \\ 0 & \text{where} \quad i \neq j \end{cases}$$
σ_0 = flow stress of the material being formed

The components of the stress deviatoric tensor are related to the strain rate components by

$$S_{ij} = \pm \frac{\sigma_0}{\sqrt{3}} \frac{\dot{\varepsilon}_{ij}}{[(\tfrac{1}{2})\dot{\varepsilon}_{kl}\dot{\varepsilon}_{kl}]^{1/2}} \tag{4.49}$$

A hypothetical material conforming to these relations is called a *von Mises material.*

Exact analytical solutions for metalforming processes are usually very complex, so simplifying assumptions, approximations, and such techniques as limit analysis are usually used.

The lower-bound theorem (theorem I) may be stated as follows: The rate of work done by the actual surface forces with certain prescribed velocities is greater than or equal to the rate of work done or power required by the surface forces corresponding to any other statically admissible stress fields. A lower bound of the limit load may be found from any statically admissible stress field assumed in the body. This stress field must satisfy equations of internal equilibrium, static boundary conditions and ensure that the yield criterion is nowhere violated. Kinematic boundary conditions and compatibility conditions may not be satisfied [4.11].

Specifically, the lower-bound theorem states that in a rigid–perfectly plastic material or an elastic–plastic material in a steady state process, there can be no plastic deformation under loads for which a stress distribution can be found which (1) everywhere satisfies the equilibrium equations, (2) is in equilibrium with external loads, and (3) is everywhere within the yield locus (surface) [4.12].

The limit load is the load to which the load-deformation curve approaches asymptotically, i.e., becomes nearly horizontal. It is analogous to the ultimate strength for a flat engineering stress-strain curve for a rigid–plastic material. The power of the theorem lies in the fact that the stress distribution chosen need not be the correct one.

How high the limit load may be is still not known from the lower bounds. Therefore, it is necessary to have a technique for estimating a load that is certain to cause plastic deformation. This estimate can be provided by the upper-bound theorem (theorem II): The rate of work done or power required by the actual surface forces with certain prescribed velocities is less than or equal to the rate of work done or power required by the surface forces corresponding to any other kinematically admissible velocity field. An upper bound on the limit load may be found from any kinematically admissible deformation mechanism. This mechanism must satisfy conditions of compatibility Eq. (2.45) and incompressibility Eqs. (2.48), (2.69), and (2.82) and the kinematic boundary conditions [4.11].

This theorem states that in a rigid–plastic continuum, deformation must occur under any system of loads, P_k, for which a distribution of displacements can be found such that (1) the displacement boundary conditions, if any, are satisfied, (2) the displacements can be differentiated to give a strain, with no change in volume anywhere, and (3) the resulting plastic work done throughout the material, found from the resulting equivalent strain, is less than the work done by the external loads P_k acting through the assumed displacements dp_k, as follows [4.12]:

$$\sum_\kappa P_k \, dp_k > \int_V \bar{\sigma}_y \, d\bar{\varepsilon}_p \, dV \tag{4.50}$$

where $\bar{\sigma}_y$ = the equivalent flow stress
   $d\bar{\varepsilon}_p$ = the equivalent plastic strain increment
   dV = incremental volume of the material

The power of this theorem lies in the fact that the assumed displacement need not be the correct one.

The upper-bound method considers a kinematically admissible velocity field (a velocity field to be defined later which satisfies the incompressibility condition and the velocity boundary conditions) for describing the metal flow [4.2]. Based on this velocity field, the deformation, the shear (if tangential velocity discontinuities are present), and the friction energy rates are computed to give the total forming power and forming load. The forming load, thus calculated by use of the limit theorems, is necessarily higher than the actual load required by the process; thus, it represents an upper bound to the actual forming load. As indicated above, the lower the upper-bound load, the better the prediction.

As inferred above, a kinematically admissible field (in more technical matrix language) may be defined as a set of velocity components v_i which satisfy the strain rate-velocity relations, the constancy of volume condition, and the boundary kinematic constraints or compatibility conditions. On the other hand, a statically admissible field is a set of stress components σ_{ij} which satisfy the equilibrium equations and the boundary relations, and does not violate the yield criterion of the material [4.13]. (See Sec. 4.5.1.)

In general, there are an infinite number of kinematically admissible velocity fields for a particular forming process [4.2]. Therefore, often a class of admissible velocity fields containing one or more parameters is considered. The best number of this class is determined by minimizing the total energy rate, including deformation and friction energies, with respect to unknown parameters. Thus, the exact values of the parameters involving the field are determined, and a lower upper bound to the forming load is obtained. Obviously, with an increasing number of parameters in the considered class of velocity fields, the calculated result improves, but the computations become more complex. Consequently, for practical use of the upper-bound method, compromises are made in selecting an admissible velocity field.

The basis of an upper-bound analysis [4.14] is:

1. The assumed flow field must account for the required shape change and be geometrically self-consistent. Many such fields can be proposed, but the closer such a field is to the true flow field, the closer the upper-bound prediction approaches the exact solution.
2. The energy consumed internally in the deformation field is calculated by use of the appropriate strength properties of the workpiece material.
3. The external forces or stresses are calculated by equating the external work to the internal energy consumption.

The following assumptions are made in applying the upper-bound method to metalworking operations [4.14]:

1. The material of the workpiece considered here is a homogeneous, isotropic, rigid–perfectly plastic continuum such as a von Mises material.
2. There are no strainhardening or strain-rate effects in the usual analysis.
3. Either frictionless or constant shear stress conditions are assumed to prevail at the tool-workpiece interface.
4. Usually two-dimensional, plane strain flow is considered or assumed with all deformation occurring by shear on a few discrete planes. Everywhere else the material is considered to be rigid.

4.3.2   Principles of the Bounding Method

In metalworking, the emphasis is on the smallest upper bound that can be found since the load then ensures that the desired plastic deformation occurs without excess press capacity. Since we are here interested in operations in which the body or workpiece is deformed plastically, only the upper bound will be considered in detail.

Limit analysis, on which the bounding method is based, utilizes the extremum principle involving the method of virtual work, which is discussed elsewhere. In this method, a virtual (hypothetical) displacement field is imposed on the body while the stress is maintained constant. This procedure is tantamount to imposing a first-order variation (no variable with a power greater than one) of the strain energy of the body, which is given by

$$dE = \int_V \sigma_{ij} \, d\varepsilon_{ij} \, dV \qquad (4.51)$$

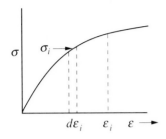

FIGURE 4.9
True stress-true strain curve in uniaxial tension.

In the above equation the product $\sigma_{ij}\,d\varepsilon_{ij}$ is the variation of the external energy expended per unit volume over all ij permutations of stress and strain variations. The integral is merely the summation of the strain energy variations over the entire volume to give the change or variation in strain energy, dE, due to an assumed external loading. For pure uniaxial tension, this energy would be equivalent to the area under the true stress-true strain curve up to a strain of ε_i as shown in Fig. 4.9.

It can be shown that the virtual work of the internal forces is equal to the negative of the above variation of the strain energy, that is, $dW_E = -dE$. The virtual work of the external forces acting on the surface of the body is given by

$$dW_E = \int_S F_i\,du_i\,dS \qquad (4.52)$$

where F_i = the components of the external forces acting on the surface of the body per unit original area
du_i = increments of displacement of the specific points of the surface
σ_{ij} = the stress tensor at an arbitrary point of the body
S = the external surface area of the body

Equation (4.52) is merely the summation of the product of the forces and displacements (distances) taken over the surface involved, S.

Thus, the principle of virtual work can be written as

$$\int_V \sigma_{ij}\,d\varepsilon_{ij}\,dV = \int_S F_i\,du_i\,dS \qquad (4.53)$$

If v_i is the components of the velocity of a surface point, and ε_{ij} is the strain rate tensor, the above equation may be written in the form

$$\int_V \sigma_{ij}\,d\dot\varepsilon_{ij}\,dV = \int_S F_i v_i\,dS \qquad (4.54)$$

This equation simply states that the rate of change of elastic energy inside the deforming body equals the rate at which the external forces applied to the surface do work on the velocities at their points of application. It provides only the portion of energy related to homogeneous deformation. Equation (4.53) in this simplified form is equivalent to a potential energy functional derived from a variational principle to be discussed later.

The steps in applying the upper-bound method to deformation processes are as follows [4.7]:

1. Describe a family of admissible velocity fields, which satisfy the conditions of incompressibility, continuity, and velocity boundaries
2. Calculate the energy rates for (*a*) homogeneous deformation, (*b*) internal shear (redundant deformation), and (*c*) friction shear
3. Calculate the total energy rate, and minimize it with respect to the unknown parameters of velocity field formulation

The load is then obtained by dividing the energy rate by the relative velocity between the die and the deforming material [4.7].

The total energy rate, or the upper bound of power $\dot{E}_T$, is given by the load multiplied by the die (ram) velocity v_D, as follows:

$$\dot{E}_T = P v_D = \dot{E}_D + \dot{E}_S + \dot{E}_F$$

or

$$\dot{E}_T = \int_V \bar{\sigma}\dot{\bar{\varepsilon}}\, dV + \int_{SS} \tau |\Delta v|\, dS + \int_{SF} \tau_i v_i\, dS$$

(4.55)

where $\dot{E}_D$, $\dot{E}_S$, and $\dot{E}_F$ are the energy rates for plastic deformation, internal shear, and external friction, respectively; P is the forming load; V is the volume of deforming material; v is the relative velocity between two zones of material, when the velocity field has internal shear surfaces of velocity discontinuity; S indicates the surface (internal shear SS, or frictional SF at the die-material interface); v_i is the die-material interface velocity in the i portion of the deforming material $\tau = \bar{\sigma}/\sqrt{3}$; and $\tau_i = m_i\bar{\sigma}/\sqrt{3} =$ the interface shear stress at the i portion of the deforming material. τ is the tangential or shear stress exerted by the tool surface on the workpiece surface SF. m is usually assumed constant over SF during forming. $\bar{\sigma}$ is the flow stress of the workpiece material in tension or compression.

The load calculated by Eq. (4.55) is necessarily higher than the actual load and therefore represents the upper bound to the actual forming load.

4.3.3   Application of the Bounding Method to Axisymmetric Upsetting [4.10]

4.3.3.1   UPPER BOUND. Let us now apply the upper-bound method to the homogeneous upsetting of a disk, in which no bulging occurs.

The velocity field for homogeneous upsetting as shown in Fig. 4.2, is given by the following:

1. The velocities that describe the kinematically admissible field:

$$v_r = \frac{v_D r}{2h} \qquad v_z = -\frac{v_D z}{h} \qquad v_\theta = 0$$

(4.56)

2. The strain rates:

$$\dot{\varepsilon}_r = \dot{\varepsilon}_\theta = \frac{v_D}{2h} \qquad \dot{\varepsilon}_z = -\frac{v_D}{h} \qquad \dot{\gamma}_{\theta z} = \dot{\gamma}_{r\theta} = 0 \qquad (4.57)$$

3. The effective strain rates:

$$\dot{\bar{\varepsilon}} = \sqrt{\tfrac{2}{3}(\dot{\varepsilon}_\theta^2 + \dot{\varepsilon}_r^2 + \dot{\varepsilon}_z^2)} = |\dot{\varepsilon}_z| \qquad (4.58)$$

If one assumes that the flow stress $\bar{\sigma}$ remains constant, the deformation energy rate is:

$$\dot{E}_D = \int_V \bar{\sigma}\dot{\bar{\varepsilon}}\, dV = h\pi R^2 \bar{\sigma}\frac{v_D}{h} = \pi R^2 \bar{\sigma} v_D \qquad (4.59)$$

Since homogeneous deformation is assumed, the internal shear energy rate or redundant energy rate $\dot{E}_S = 0$, because there are no internal velocity discontinuities in the homogeneous velocity field.

The friction energy rate is

$$\dot{E}_F = 2\int_{SF} \tau_i v_i \, ds \qquad (4.60)$$

where v_i is the radial velocity, given in Eqs. (4.56), and $ds = 2\pi r\, dr$. $\dot{E}_F$ includes the external friction energies on both the top and the bottom surfaces of the deforming part as follows:

$$\dot{E}_F = 2\int_0^R \tau_i \frac{v_D}{2h} r 2\pi r\, dr = \frac{4\pi\tau_i v_D}{2h}\int_0^R r^2\, dr \qquad (4.61)$$

or, with $\tau_i = m\bar{\sigma}/\sqrt{3}$,

$$\dot{E}_F = \frac{2}{3}\pi m \frac{\bar{\sigma}}{\sqrt{3}}\frac{v_D}{h} R^3 \qquad (4.62)$$

Therefore, the total energy rate is

$$\dot{E}_T = \dot{E}_D + \dot{E}_F$$

or

$$\qquad\qquad(4.63)$$

$$\dot{E}_T = \pi R^2 \bar{\sigma} v_D + \frac{2}{3}\pi m \frac{\bar{\sigma}}{\sqrt{3}}\frac{v_D}{h} R^3$$

The equivalent load then is

$$P = \frac{\dot{E}_T}{v_D} = \pi R^2 \bar{\sigma}\left(1 + \frac{2}{3\sqrt{3}} m \frac{R}{h}\right) \qquad (4.64)$$

which is the same as that obtained in Eq. (4.42) for the slab method for homogeneous deformation.

In inhomogeneous deformation, a parameter β is introduced to represent the severity of the bulge. The exact value of β is determined from the minimization condition

$$\frac{\partial \dot{E}_T}{\partial \beta} = 0 \tag{4.65}$$

This value of β is used to calculate the velocities and strain rates which then give the minimum value for the energy rate $\dot{E}_{min}$, which is used in turn to calculate the load as follows: $P = \dot{E}_{min}/v_D$.

One may rewrite Eq. (4.55) (in which the power to overcome inertial forces, environmental pressure, void opening energy, and surface energy are neglected) for a von Mises material (see Eqs. (4.47)–(4.49)) as follows [4.10]:

$$\dot{E}_T = \frac{2}{\sqrt{3}} \sigma_0 \int_V \left(\frac{1}{2}\dot{\varepsilon}_{ij}\dot{\varepsilon}_{ij}\right)^{1/2} dV + \int_{SS} \tau |\Delta v|\, dS - \int_{SF} \tau_i v_i\, dS \tag{4.66}$$

where $\dot{E}_T$ = calculated upper bound of power

   σ_0 = flow stress of the material being formed

   $\dot{\varepsilon}_{ij}$ = components of the strain-rate tensor

   τ = shear stress

   $|\Delta v|$ = absolute value of the velocity discontinuity

   τ_i = externally applied stress

Equation (4.66) is, of course, equivalent to Eq. (4.55).

In review, using Eq. (4.66) to obtain the upper bound of power for upsetting of a disk of radius R and thickness h between two parallel platens, one can proceed as follows [4.10]:

1. Select the kinematically admissible field, which is given by Eqs. (4.56):

$$v_r = \frac{v_D r}{2h} \qquad v_z = -\frac{v_D z}{h} \qquad v_\theta = 0 \tag{4.56}$$

2. Find the strain-rate components, which are given by Eq. (4.57):

$$\dot{\varepsilon}_r = \dot{\varepsilon}_\theta = \frac{v_D}{2h} \qquad \dot{\varepsilon}_z = -\frac{v_D}{h} \qquad \dot{\gamma}_{\theta z} = \dot{\gamma}_{r\theta} = 0 \tag{4.57}$$

3. Compute the internal power of deformation from

$$\dot{E}_D = \frac{2}{\sqrt{3}} \sigma_0 \int_V \left[\frac{1}{2}(\dot{\varepsilon}_r^2 + \dot{\varepsilon}_\theta^2 + \dot{\varepsilon}_z^2)\right]^{1/2} dV \tag{4.67}$$

which may be obtained for the upsetting of a disk as follows:

Since, by the use of Eqs. (4.56) and (4.57),

$$\dot{\varepsilon}_r = -\tfrac{1}{2}\dot{\varepsilon}_z \qquad \text{and} \qquad \dot{\varepsilon}_\theta = +\tfrac{1}{2}\dot{\varepsilon}_z$$

$$\dot{E}_D = \frac{2}{\sqrt{3}} \sigma_0 [\tfrac{1}{2}(\tfrac{1}{4}+\tfrac{1}{4}+1)\dot{\varepsilon}_z^2]^{1/2} \int_V dV \tag{4.68}$$

$$\dot{E}_D = \sigma_0 \frac{v_D}{h}(\pi R^2 h) = \pi R^2 \sigma_0 v_D$$

4. Compute the friction losses on the top and bottom surfaces assuming a constant friction factor m as follows:

$$\tau = \frac{m\sigma_0}{\sqrt{3}}$$

$$\Delta v = \dot{v}_r\big|_{z=0,h} = \frac{1}{2}\frac{r}{h}\dot{v}_D$$

$$\dot{E}_F = \int_S \tau|\Delta v|\, dS = 2\int_{r=0}^{R}\left(\frac{m\sigma_0}{\sqrt{3}}\right)\left(\frac{1}{2}\frac{r}{h}\dot{v}_D\right)(2\pi r\, dr)$$

$$\dot{E}_F = \frac{2}{3}\pi m\frac{\sigma}{\sqrt{3}}\frac{\dot{v}_D}{h}R^3$$

(4.69)

5. Compute the upper bound of power from

$$\dot{E}_T = \dot{E}_D + \dot{E}_F$$

$$\dot{E}_T = \pi R^2\sigma_0\dot{v}_D\left(1+\frac{2}{3}\frac{m}{\sqrt{3}}\frac{R}{h}\right)$$

(4.70)

6. Compute the total upsetting form P from

$$\dot{E}_T = P\dot{v}_D = \pi R^2 p_{av}\dot{v}_D = \pi R^2\sigma_0\dot{v}_D\left(1+\frac{2}{3}\frac{m}{\sqrt{3}}\frac{R}{h}\right)$$

(4.71)

The relative die pressure is given by

$$\frac{p_{av}}{\sigma_0} = 1+\frac{2}{3}\frac{m}{\sqrt{3}}\frac{R}{h}$$

(4.72)

where p_{av} is the average interface pressure.

Since the p_{av}/σ_0 is never greater than that given in Eq. (4.72), the total upsetting force for the simplifying assumptions made is never greater than

$$P = \pi R^2\sigma_0\left(1+\frac{2}{3}\frac{m}{\sqrt{3}}\frac{R}{h}\right)$$

(4.73)

which is the upper bound. (The term mR/h combines the effect of friction and geometry.) [4.10].

4.3.3.2 LOWER BOUND [4.10]. As mentioned in the foregoing, lower-bound solutions are those which are lower than or equal to the actual value in each case. The lower-bound solution is more complex, and consequently much less work has been done on it, and it has not been developed to the same extent as the upper-bound solution.

The first step in the lower-bound solution is to formulate a statically admissible stress field which is much harder to conceive than the velocity field for deforming the body in the upper-bound approach. Among all statically admissible stress fields the actual one minimizes the expression

$$I = \int_{S_V} \tau_i v_i \, dS \qquad (4.74)$$

where I is the computed power applied by the die over the surfaces over which the velocity is prescribed, τ_i is the applied stress on the surface for which the velocity is prescribed, S_V is the surface of the velocity discontinuity, and v_i is the die or ram velocity.

In case of the upsetting of a disk for which the friction is assumed constant over the entire die-material interface $\sigma_r = \sigma_\theta$, and the von Mises yield criterion applies, the following lower-bound approximation for the relative die pressure p_{av}/σ_0 is obtained:

$$\frac{p_{av}}{\sigma_0} = (1 - m^2)^{1/2} + \frac{2}{3}\frac{m}{\sqrt{3}}\frac{R}{h} + \frac{P}{\sigma_0} \qquad (4.75)$$

where m is the constant shear stress friction factor, p_{av} is the average interface pressure, σ_0 is the flow stress of the material being formed, p is the variable pressure over the surface, R is the radius of the disk, and h is its height.

A graphical comparison between the upper- and lower-bound solutions for the upsetting of a disk is shown in Fig. 4.10, in which the relative pressure, p_{av}/σ_0, is plotted against the diametral ratio R_0/h. In this case, the gap between the two is very narrow.

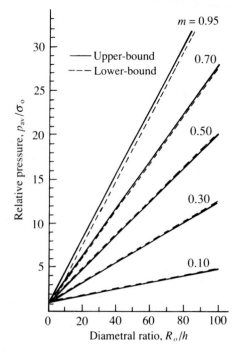

FIGURE 4.10
Graphical comparison of the upper- and lower-bound solutions for the upsetting of a disk [4.10].

4.3.4 Temperature Rise Due to Velocity Discontinuities

Upper bounds for plane-strain processes using systems of tangential velocity discontinuity (Figs. 2.91 and 4.11) have achieved much popularity because of their simplicity and ease of application. The existence of these discontinuities is well established, especially when temperature jumps occur during plane-strain deformation processes. This temperature rise, ΔT, across a plane of shear discontinuity is proportional to the shear strain γ, as can be shown by the simple model of plane-strain, narrow-band flow across a plane of intense shear discontinuity shown in Fig. 4.11 [4.14].

Figure 4.11(a) shows an element $ABCD$ of a rigid–ideally plastic material deformed under conditions of plane strain to $A'B'C'D'$ after crossing a plane

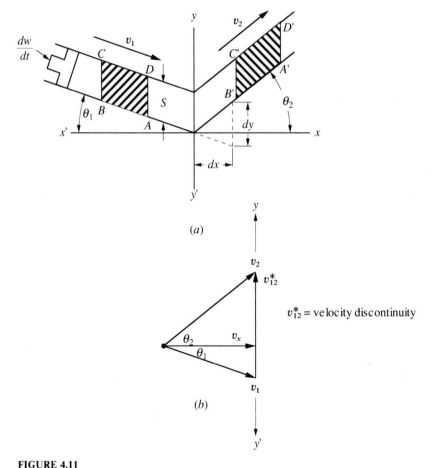

(a)

$v_{12}^* = $ velocity discontinuity

(b)

FIGURE 4.11
(a) Basis for analysis of energy dissipation along a plane of intense shear discontinuity; and (b) the hodograph or velocity vector diagram [4.14].

with its edge at yy'. For element $ABCD$ to deform to element $A'B'C'D'$, it will not only have to be sheared upward in crossing yy', but it will also have to be compressed somewhat. The forming operation involved may be compared to the extrusion of a plate between two V-shaped dies having the geometrical arrangement shown in Fig. 4.11(a).

The rate at which external work is done is

$$\frac{dW}{dt} = kSv_{12}^{*} \tag{4.76}$$

where k is the shear strength of the material, S is the length of yy' involved, and v_{12}^{*} is the vector difference between v_1 and v_2 and is the velocity discontinuity parallel to yy' as shown in Fig. 4.11(b), which is the velocity vector diagram or hodograph for the conditions shown in Fig. 4.11(a). v_1 and v_2, the absolute velocities on each side of yy', must have a horizontal component v_x, otherwise the material entering and leaving yy' would differ in volume, which of course would violate the concept of incompressibility. The engineering shear strain $\gamma = dy/dx$ may be made equal to v_{12}^{*}/v_x by use of similar triangles shown in Fig. 4.11(a) and (b) which, when combined with the volume of flow across yy' per increment of time dt, yields Eq. (4.76).

For deformation fields involving more than one plane (line) of discrete shear, that is, i number of planes, the rate at which work is done to effect this shear deformation is

$$\frac{dW}{dt} = \sum_{1}^{i} kS_i v_i^{*} \tag{4.77}$$

where S_i and v_i pertain to each individual ith plane. This equation is the form used in most problems involving upper-bound calculations. It implies that an element deforms in a way that offers maximum plastic resistance [4.14].

For the adiabatic case, where all the work done on an element is converted into heat and none is lost, the temperature rise is given by

$$\Delta T = \frac{k}{J\rho c} \cdot \frac{v_{12}^{*}}{v_x} = \frac{k}{J\rho c} \cdot \gamma \tag{4.78}$$

where J = mechanical equivalent of heat in appropriate units
ρ = density of the material
c = specific heat of the material
k = shear strength of the material
γ = shear strain

According to the first law of thermodynamics, heat energy and mechanical energy are mutually convertible, which may be expressed in equation form as

$$J \oint \delta Q = \oint \delta W \tag{4.79}$$

The first term is the cyclic integral of the heat transfer, and the second term the cyclic integral of the network. J is the proportionality factor, depending on the units used. In customary units, it is 778 ft-lb/Btu. In SI units it equals 1 and is not necessary.

4.3.5 Kinematic Element Method for Analyzing Plastic Flow [4.15]

Courtois et al. [4.15] have presented a generalized method based on the upper-bound approach, called the *kinematic element method*, for obtaining an acceptable velocity field by minimizing the power dissipated during plastic deformation. By use of this method the forging load, etc., can be predicted for the plane strain and the axisymmetric forging processes.

This method can be described as follows: A cross section of the workpiece for a plane or axisymmetrical strain is divided into kinematic elements which can be rectangular, triangular or trapezoidal. Each kind of element requires a single kinematically admissible and plastically acceptable formulation of the plastic flow, which depends on the element's dimensions and the uniform velocities on each boundary. The calculation of the dissipated power for each element establishes a linear relation with uniform velocities at the boundaries. The dissipated power function is expressed using surface variables which are the boundary velocities of the constituent elements. The minimization of the dissipated power is obtained by using Simplex procedures. The dissipated power calculation is available for isotropic, isothermal, rigid, perfectly plastic materials.

From the velocity calculations, the hodograph of the plastic flow into the cross section, the global effect, and the pressure on the moving interfaces can be obtained. Then, the parameters that define the forming operation such as the forging load can be determined.

The mathematical formulation of kinematic elements in plane strain for the following shaped elements, accompanied by test results and final comments, is as follows:

1. *Rectangular kinematic elements.* The normal velocities are V_1, V_2, V_3, and V_4 on the boundaries, the dimensions are a and b as shown in Fig. 4.12. The velocity components u and v are assumed to vary linearly within the element

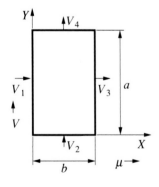

FIGURE 4.12
Rectangular kinematic element [4.15].

as follows:

$$u = u(x) \qquad \text{and} \qquad v = v(y)$$

so that

$$u = \left(\frac{V_3 - V_1}{b}\right) x + V_1 \tag{4.80a}$$

and

$$v = \left(\frac{V_4 - V_2}{a}\right) x + V_2 \tag{4.80b}$$

The internal dissipated power (which always must be positive, thereby complicating the problem) in this element is equal to

$$\dot{W}_i = \frac{2\sigma_0}{\sqrt{3}} b |V_2 - V_4| \tag{4.81}$$

and the frictional functions are defined at boundaries as

$$E_1 = \bar{m}_1 \frac{\sigma_0}{\sqrt{3}} a \left(\frac{V_2 + V_4}{2}\right) \tag{4.82}$$

where $\bar{m}_1$ = the Tresca friction factor on face 1
σ_0 = the flow strength of the material

When this element is contiguous with another one or with the die surface, the dissipated power resulting from velocity discontinuities at a boundary is defined by

$$\dot{W}_f = |E_{kl} - E_{jm}| \tag{4.83}$$

where k and j are the boundary numbers and l and m the adjacent element numbers.

2. *Triangular kinematic elements.* The reference velocities on the boundaries of the element as shown in Fig. 4.13 are V_{Xr}, V_{Yr}, and V_S which makes an angle ϕ with the normal n to the sloping boundary, which has a slope of θ with the x axis. The continuity of velocity through this boundary is expressed by

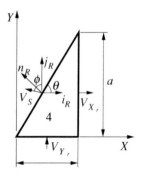

FIGURE 4.13
Reference velocities on the boundaries of a triangular element [4.15].

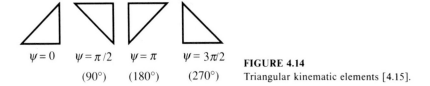

$\psi = 0$ $\psi = \pi/2$ $\psi = \pi$ $\psi = 3\pi/2$
(90°)   (180°)   (270°)

FIGURE 4.14
Triangular kinematic elements [4.15].

the condition:

$$vA - uB = V_S(AC + BD) \tag{4.84}$$

where $A = \cos\theta$, $B = \sin\theta$, $C = \cos\phi$, $D = \sin\phi$

The constant velocity field given by Eq. (4.85), in which $u = V_{Xr}$ and $v = V_{Yr}$, verifies the incompressibility condition

$$u = V_y\left(\frac{b}{a}\right) - V_S(AC + BD)\left(\frac{\sqrt{a^2+b^2}}{a}\right)$$
$$v = V_Y \tag{4.85}$$

This equation simply means that the triangular region is rigid, and the power is dissipated only at the boundaries.

Three other triangular elements can be obtained by rotating the reference triangle by angles of 90, 180, and 270° as shown in Fig. 4.14. Modifications of the velocity field and dissipated power equations are obtained by multiplying them by a rotation matrix.

3. *Kinematic trapezoidal element.* This reference element is shown in Fig. 4.15. The velocities are V_1, V_2, V_3, and V_4, which make an angle of ϕ with the normal n to the boundary, which slopes at an angle of θ with the x axis. The velocity field is given by

$$u = a\left[\frac{\left(V_1 - \dfrac{A}{B}V_2 + DV_4 + \dfrac{AC}{B}V_4\right)}{\dfrac{B}{A}x + a}\right] + \frac{A}{B}V_2 - DV_4 - \frac{AC}{B}V_4 \tag{4.86a}$$

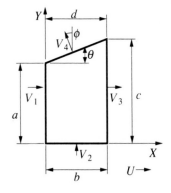

FIGURE 4.15
Trapezoidal kinematic element [4.15].

$$v = a\left[\frac{\left(\dfrac{B}{A}V_1 - V_2 + \dfrac{DB}{A}V_4 + CV_4\right)}{\left(\dfrac{B}{A}x + a\right)^2}\right]y + V_2 \qquad (4.86b)$$

The formulation of the kinematic elements in axisymmetric strains will not be discussed here.

4. *Test of the kinematic element method.* This method has been tested to observe material flow during plane strain and axisymmetric loading of plasticine at ambient temperature. For forging in plane strain the Lyapunov-Kobayashi test, using the open-ended die geometry shown in Fig. 4.16, was used. The tool velocity was 1.27 mm/min and the constant friction factor $\bar{m}$ was taken equal to 0.3.

The forging process was simulated by use of the computer program called GALOPIN. All three elements for plane strain plus two for axisymmetric strain are utilized in the GALOPIN software and can be automatically generated by a preprocessor. The minimization of dissipated power in the plastic flow is that performed by means of the Simplex algorithm. (The Simplex procedure is a special mathematical procedure used for solving any problem in linear programming.)

By use of a postprocessor, one can then study the plastic flow by viewing the instantaneous hodographs at each step of forging and the forging force history.

Figure 4.17 gives the flow pattern shown by stream lines indicating the velocity distribution for plane strain deformation of plasticine at ambient temperature for a tool velocity of 1.27 mm/min. Figure 4.18 compares the variations of the height and width of both the calculated and experimental workpiece during deformation.

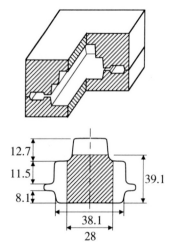

12.7

11.5

8.1

39.1

38.1

28

FIGURE 4.16
Configuration of the test setup: (*a*) Cross section of a long die; (*b*) end view showing the work geometry [4.15].

$\Delta H = 6$ mm

$\Delta H = 12$ mm

$\Delta H = 14.1$ mm

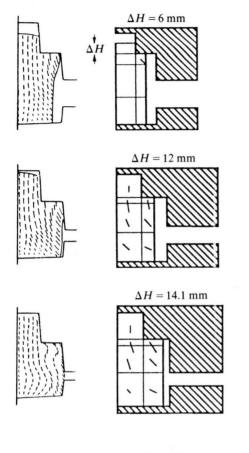

$\Delta H = 14.1$ mm

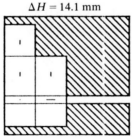

FIGURE 4.17
Flow pattern shown by slip-lines indicating the velocity distribution for plane-strain deformation of plasticine at ambient temperature for different depths of penetration ΔH and for a tool velocity of 1.27 mm/min. (*Courtesy of Laboratoire de Genie Mecanique U.V.H.C.-C.I.S.I., and Informatique Internationale, which supports the GALOPIN computer program.*) [4.15].

5. *Final comments*: The equations for the dissipation of power internally and at the boundaries, if any, were not presented for the different elements. The economic function, which has to be minimized, is the sum of all the dissipated powers for each element.

These comments conclude the discussion of the bounding methods. The slip-line field method will be discussed next.

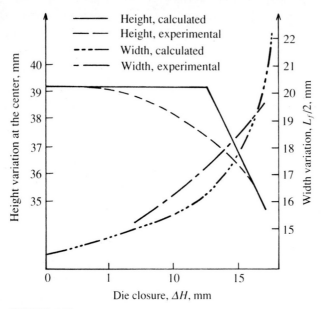

FIGURE 4.18
Variation of the height and width of the workpiece with die closure (calculated results were done with the GALOPIN program) [4.15].

4.4 SLIP-LINE FIELD METHOD

4.4.1 Introduction

In the upper-bound approach as applied to plane strain discussed in the foregoing, it was assumed that the deformation (flow localization) occurred along lines or planes (narrow regions) of intense shear. Material inside each polygon or polyhedron was considered to move more or less as a rigid block shearing only along its boundary. To portray a more realistic picture, a plastic slip-line field theory was developed to show the flow pattern throughout the region being deformed. (The term slip-line in this sense has a different connotation from that used by the metallurgist to describe the region along which slip has occurred in a metal crystal.)

Slip-line analysis is based upon a deformation field that is geometrically consistent with the change in shape of the region being deformed. Although equilibrium conditions are observed within the field being considered, equilibrium outside the field is ignored and may not apply. Thus, such a solution may be an upper bound [4.14]. Often, the severe restrictions that are imposed by the required assumptions, make the method nonunique and very difficult to apply to actual forming problems [4.2].

Most of the assumptions made in the common approach to the slip-line field method are similar to those for the upper-bound method, i.e., the material is a homogeneous, isotropic, rigid–perfectly plastic continuum; there are no temperature, strain-rate, or time effects; and there is a constant shear stress at the tool-material interface, which is either frictionless or shears just beneath the surface of the material with a constant shear stress due to sticking friction. However, localized shear may take place throughout the field and is not restricted to a few discrete planes.

Despite the above limitations the slip-line field theory, as applied to plane strain, is claimed to be perhaps the most successful, detailed, and useful technique for analyzing models of metalforming processes [4.9]; however, because of the advances in the computer matrix methods, its use is declining.

Although Hill [4.16] showed how a slip-line field could be developed numerically, graphical methods have been used almost exclusively until recent years. Several computer techniques have been utilized to analyze such problems as extrusion [4.17], forging [4.18], etc. With the rapid increase in the use of computer-aided design, in which an interactive graphics terminal is used, a much greater use of this method to analyze metalworking processes will undoubtedly take place. The application of the computer to the slip-line field method will be discussed briefly later.

4.4.2 Slip-Line Field Theory

A *slip-line field* (or better *maximum shear-plane field*) is a two-dimensional vector diagram which shows the direction of the maximum (or minimum) shear stress at any point along the line. These lines have the property of satisfying static equilibrium, the prevailing yield condition, and a possible flow field everywhere in the plastic zone of the metal being deformed without any reference to the plasticity equations and strain rates. Slip-lines have the property that the shear strain is a maximum and the linear strain is zero tangent to their direction. As indicated previously, the term "slip-lines" as used in this sense should not be confused with slip-lines, bands, or markings that might be seen in the surface of a plastically deformed metal resulting from crystallographic slip. These surface lines or markings are essentially macroscopic in nature and physically related to Luders (localized yielding) lines in some low carbon steels.

Since shear stress is always accompanied by a complementary shear stress at 90° to preserve rotational equilibrium as shown in Fig. 2.7, the slip-line field is always a network of lines crossing each other at right angles, as shown in Fig. 4.19(a) and (b) for a two-dimensional slab of a rigid perfectly plastic material being compressed between two frictionless, overhanging anvils. It is conventional to designate these lines as α and β, so that the line of action of the algebraically greatest principal stress lies in the first and third quadrants as shown in Fig. 4.19(c). The α line is taken here as the abscissa (x) and the β line as the ordinate (y) according to the sign convention adopted here for shear, i.e., in which the diagonal of the free-body diagram is elongated in the first (I) and third (III) quadrants as shown in the above figure.

As will be illustrated here for the flat indentation punch problem, although slip-line theory is mathematically rigorous, the slip-line field is generally construc-

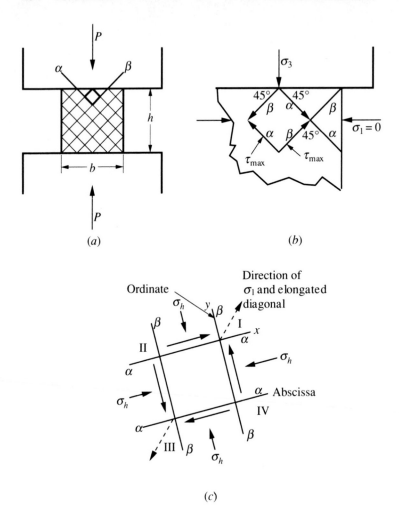

FIGURE 4.19

(a) Slip-line field for the homogeneous deformation of a perfectly plastic material for a two-dimensional strip being compressed in plane strain between two frictionless, overhanging dies or platens; (b) sketch of an elemental block of the slip-line grid showing α and β lines as direction of the shear stress so that the block is in rotational equilibrium; and (c) sketch of an elemental grid block showing the convention used in labeling the slip-line field.

ted by a trial-and-error procedure based on previous experience. One starts with the knowledge of the equilibrium conditions at the boundaries and proceeds to satisfy the continuity and velocity conditions within the deformed metal. Because the deformation is caused by pure shear stress at the instant of yielding, the shear stress along the slip-line has the value of $\tau_{max} = k$ equal to the flow stress measured in a pure shear test. The stress system at any point in the zone of plastic deformation can be considered as a combination of this stress with a hydrostatic

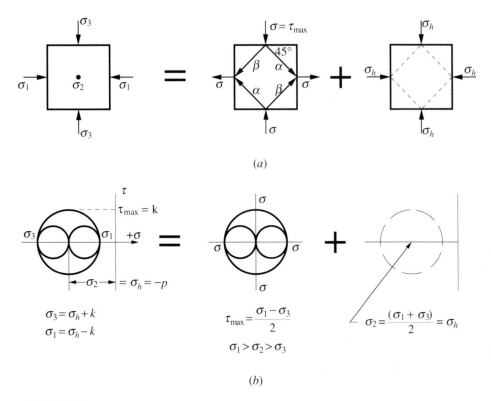

FIGURE 4.20
Equivalence of principal, applied stress in plane-strain compression to the shear stress plus a hydrostatic component, which is compressive and equal to $\frac{1}{2}(\sigma_1 + \sigma_2)$.

component, $\sigma_h = -p$, which does not influence the flow stress. As shown in Fig. 4.20, the principal stresses σ_1 and σ_3 have the values $\sigma_h + k$ and $\sigma_h - k$, respectively, and act at 45° to the direction of the slip-lines. Therefore, if σ_h can be determined, the magnitude and direction of both principal stresses can be found from the slip-line field and a knowledge of the flow stress.

Considerations of equilibrium conditions and an application of Mohr stress circles show that the change in σ_h between two points is directly related to the angle between the slip-line tangents at these points as shown in Fig. 4.21. In the above simple, compression example in Fig. 4.19, the slip-lines are straight and, for this condition, σ_h is everywhere constant. For most metalworking operations, however, the slip-line field is more complex and involves lines of both constant and varying curvature as shown in Fig. 4.21. Note that ϕ is the angle between the tangent of the α slip-line and the x axis measured in the counterclockwise direction in radians.

Slip-line field solutions are always referred to plane strain for which the principal stresses for an incompressible, perfectly plastic material, and nearly so

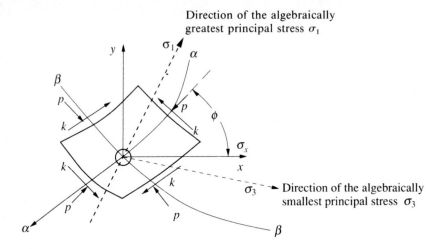

FIGURE 4.21
A small curvilinear element showing that the change in σ_h between two points is directly related to the angle between the slip-line tangents at these points [4.20].

for real metals, are related as seen in Fig. 4.20 as follows [4.19].

$$\sigma_2 = \tfrac{1}{2}(\sigma_1 + \sigma_3) \tag{4.87}$$

The Mohr stress circle for plane strain may be drawn with a radius of

$$\tau_{max} = k = \tfrac{1}{2}[-\sigma_3 - (-\sigma_1)] = \tfrac{1}{2}(\sigma_1 - \sigma_3) \tag{4.88}$$

and centered on σ_2 as shown for the above case in simple compression. From this figure, it can be seen that the principal stresses are equal to

$$\sigma_1 = \sigma_2 - k \tag{4.89a}$$

$$\sigma_2 = \sigma_h = -p \tag{4.89b}$$

and

$$\sigma_3 = \sigma_2 + k = -p + k \tag{4.89c}$$

If all of the principal stresses are expressed in terms of the hydrostatic pressure, they are

$$\sigma_1 = \sigma_h - k = -p - k \tag{4.90a}$$

$$\sigma_2 = \sigma_h = -p \tag{4.90b}$$

and

$$\sigma_3 = \sigma_h + k = -p + k \tag{4.90c}$$

The complete stress system in plane strain can therefore be considered to be pure shear with a superimposed hydrostatic pressure. From Fig. 4.22, the values of

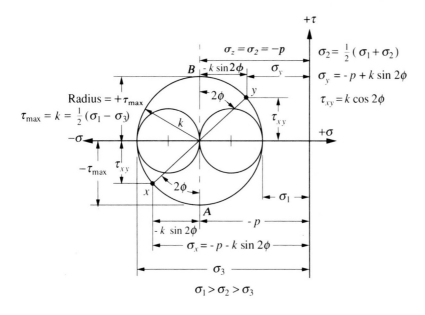

FIGURE 4.22
Mohr's stress circle diagram for stress in plane plastic strain. A and B represent the stress states
$(-p, \pm k)$ at a point on planes parallel to the slip-lines through that point [4.20].

the stresses on the x and y planes can be obtained as

$$\sigma_x = -p - k \sin 2\phi \qquad (4.91a)$$

$$\sigma_y = -p + k \sin 2\phi \qquad (4.91b)$$

and

$$\tau_{xy} = k \cos 2\phi \qquad (4.91c)$$

where p is the normal or hydrostatic stress or pressure, and the axial and angular
arrangement is shown in Fig. 4.21.

If Eqs. (4.91) are differentiated and substituted into the Eqs. (4.92) for
equilibrium for plane strain, by summation of the forces in the x-y plane, one
obtains [4.20]

$$-\frac{\partial p}{\partial x} - 2k \cos 2\phi \frac{\partial \phi}{\partial x} - 2k \sin 2\phi \frac{\partial \phi}{\partial y} = 0 \qquad (4.92a)$$

$$-2k \sin 2\phi \frac{\partial \phi}{\partial x} - \frac{\partial p}{\partial y} + 2k \cos 2\phi \frac{\partial \phi}{\partial y} = 0 \qquad (4.92b)$$

The angle ϕ is defined in Figs. 4.21 and 4.22 and also below.

Also, if the α and β slip-lines are taken to coincide with the x and y axes for which $\phi = 0$, the following equations are obtained

$$-\frac{\partial p}{\partial x} - 2k\frac{\partial \phi}{\partial x} = 0 \tag{4.93a}$$

$$-\frac{\partial p}{\partial y} + 2k\frac{\partial \phi}{\partial y} = 0 \tag{4.93b}$$

By integrating the above equations, one obtains

$$p + 2k\phi - f_1(y) + C_\alpha = 0 \tag{4.94a}$$

$$p - 2k\phi - f_2(x) + C_\beta = 0 \tag{4.94b}$$

However, $f_1(y)$ and $f_2(x) = 0$ when $\phi = 0$, so that Eqs. (4.94) become

$$p + 2k\phi = C_\alpha \tag{4.95}$$

$$p - 2k\phi = C_\beta \tag{4.96}$$

where Eq. (4.95) is for the α lines and Eq. (4.96) is for β slip-lines, and C_α and C_β are constant along the α and β lines, respectively, ϕ is the counterclockwise rotation of the tangent to the respective slip-lines in radians, and k is the flow stress in shear.

Since these equations were first applied to deformation in metals by Hencky, they are known as *Hencky slip-line equations*. They can be used to determine the hydrostatic pressure $p = \sigma_h$ at any point in a deforming body from the curvature of the slip-lines, provided that the value of the constant is known. The constant can be found from the equilibrium conditions at one of the boundaries. In general, the values of C_α and C_β vary from one slip-line to another, but numerical evaluation of these constants is generally unnecessary. In effect, as indicated above, Eqs. (4.95) and (4.96) are the equilibrium equations expressed along a slip-line, and therefore the inclusion of equilibrium considerations is one of the major differences between slip-line theory and the upper-bound approach [4.14].

The state of stress at any point can be completely determined if the magnitude of p and the direction of k can be found. The latter is given by the direction of the slip-lines. The changes in p can be obtained from the angular rotation of the tangent to the slip-lines between two points in the field, as discussed below. The absolute value of p can be found by starting at some point on a boundary where p is known from the boundary conditions.

Since C_α is constant along the α line, by use of Eq. (4.95) and Fig. 4.22 [4.20],

$$p_A + 2k\phi_A = p_B + 2k\phi_B$$

$$\Delta p = \Delta\sigma_h = p_A - p_B + 2k\phi_A - 2k\phi_B \tag{4.97}$$

$$\Delta p = 2k\Delta\phi$$

A slip-line net of α- and β-lines must be so constructed that the change in ϕ is the same along a given family of lines moving from one intersection with

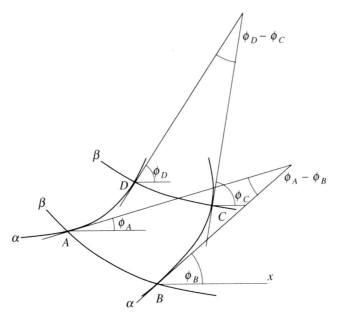

FIGURE 4.23
Two pairs of α- and β-lines for analyzing the change in the mean normal stress by traversing two different paths [4.20].

the opposite family to another such intersection. In other words, in Fig. 4.23 the difference between ϕ at A and C can be established by traversing two paths, from A to D to C and from A to B to C, which gives the following change in ϕ:

$$\phi_A - \phi_B = \phi_D - \phi_C$$

and   (4.98)

$$\phi_A - \phi_B = \phi_B - \phi_C$$

This equivalence in the change in ϕ is in addition to the orthogonality requirement, and it indicates that the angular change, rather than the actual length traversed, is of sole importance [4.14].

Since slip-lines are directions of maximum shear stress, and the deformations along them are in pure shear, the dimensions of the elements lying along them distort but do not elongate or compress. Because the material is assumed incompressible, the superimposed hydrostatic pressure will not affect the dimensions of the elements. Therefore, there cannot be any change in velocity along the slip-lines, arising from any extension of the elements. Since normal strain is not permitted in either direction, displacement or velocity components normal to a slip-line must be the same on both sides of the line as shown in Fig. 2.91, otherwise separation would occur. Displacement and velocity discontinuities tangential to a slip-line are allowed, so long as the different components on either side of the slip-line are constant along its length. However, if there is a change in the

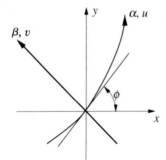

FIGURE 4.24
Component velocities of a particle in a plastically deforming body. Note that ϕ is the angle between the tangent to an α slip-line and the x axis measured in the counterclockwise direction in radians [4.20].

directions of the slip-lines, there may be a change in velocity due to the change in the component perpendicular to the lines. If the curvature of an α line to a fixed direction x is ϕ, as shown in Fig. 4.24, it may be shown that the following Geiringer equations relating the change in velocity with the angular change of slip-lines may be obtained:

$$du - v\,d\phi = 0 \qquad \text{along an } \alpha \text{ line} \tag{4.99}$$

$$dv + u\,d\phi = 0 \qquad \text{along a } \beta \text{ line} \tag{4.100}$$

where u and v are the components of the velocity of a point along the α and β slip-lines, respectively. These equations may be used to verify whether the velocities predicted by the slip-line field are compatible with the imposed velocity boundary conditions. For example, there cannot be a change in velocity normal to a slip-line unless separation occurs, and the tangential velocity difference must be constant along the slip-line so that an extension along the slip-line would not occur.

In summary, the governing equations for plane-strain, plastic flow of rigid perfectly plastic materials are hyperbolic [4.19]. The characteristics form an orthogonal net of lines called slip-lines which follow maximum shear stress directions. One family of slip-lines is called α lines and the other family β lines. By convention the labels are determined by requiring the maximum principal stress direction to be in the first and third quadrants of a right-handed curvilinear coordinate system with an α line as the abscissa. The following relations must be satisfied as one moves

(1) along α lines

$$p + 2k\phi = C_\alpha$$

$$du - v\,d\phi = 0 \tag{4.101}$$

$$\frac{dy}{dx} = \tan \phi$$

(2) along β lines

$$p - 2k\phi = C_\beta$$

$$dv - u\,d\phi = 0 \tag{4.102}$$

$$\frac{dy}{dx} = -\cot \phi$$

where ϕ is the angle between the tangent to the α line and the x direction of a cartesian coordinate system measured in the counterclockwise direction in radians, p is the hydrostatic pressure, u and v are the velocities in the α and β directions, respectively, and k is the maximum shear stress τ_{max}.

The velocities in the x and y directions are

$$u_x = u \cos \phi - v \sin \phi$$
$$v_y = u \sin \phi + v \cos \phi \tag{4.103}$$

and the stresses in the x-y plane are

$$\sigma_x = -p - k \sin 2\phi$$
$$\sigma_y = -p + k \sin 2\phi \tag{4.104}$$
$$\tau_{xy} = k \cos \phi$$

By use of the concept, discussed previously, that the gradients of stresses along and perpendicular to a slip-line are equal to zero, i.e.,

$$\frac{d\sigma_\alpha}{d\alpha} = \frac{d\sigma_\beta}{d\beta} = 0 \tag{4.105}$$

where $d\alpha$ and $d\beta$ are incremental distances along the α and β slip-lines, respectively, it was shown that along an α slip-line

$$p + 2k\phi = C_\alpha \tag{4.95}$$

and along a β slip-line

$$p - 2k\phi = C_\beta \tag{4.96}$$

4.4.3 Procedure for Solving Plastic Deformation Problems by Use of the Slip-Line Field Method

In general the steps in solving a plastic plane-strain problem by use of the slip-line field method are

1. Construct the slip-line field, which satisfies all the given boundary conditions in stresses, starting from certain boundary surfaces of the metal and from the assumed rigid–plastic boundary slip-lines

2. Obtain the velocity distribution by means of the given boundary conditions in velocities and examine whether the remainder of the velocity boundary conditions are fulfilled

3. Inspect whether the rate of plastic work in the deforming region is everywhere positive

4. Ensure that the yield criterion in the assumed nondeforming or rigid region is not violated [4.21]

In construction of a slip-line field, it should be noted that the slip-lines are normal to each other and that they make an angle of 45° with (1) a stress-free surface, (2) a frictionless boundary in contact with a tool surface, and (3) with an axis of symmetry.

We shall now look specifically at the plotting of slip-line fields for two different classical problems involving slabs (strips) of different, finite thicknesses: (1) the indentation of slabs of different thickness, h, to width of punch, b, ratios, by two opposing narrow punches as shown in Fig. 4.25(a), having frictionless punch-material interfaces, and (2) the compression of a slab with different width, b, to thickness, h, ratios by means of overhanging platens (anvils), having sticking friction at the platen-material interfaces. In the former, the normalized indentation pressure $p_p/2k$ will be plotted against h/b, and in the latter the normalized average pressure will be plotted against b/h. (See Figs. 4.27 and 4.34.)

4.4.4 Slip-Line Field Analysis of an Indentation as a Function of the Relative Slab Thickness to Punch Width

Let us first examine the slip-line fields for slabs (workpieces) of an isotropic, nonstrainhardening material of finite thickness being compressed by opposing frictionless punches for the following cases:

1. *Where the slab or workpiece thickness h equals the punch breadth b or $h/b =$* 1. The slip-line field for this simple case is shown in Fig. 4.25(a). Since the punch-material interfaces are assumed to be frictionless, the slip-lines intersect the interface surfaces at 45°. At any point A on a slip-line, the horizontal principal stress $\sigma_1 = 0$ (since there is no lateral restraint due to the frictionless punch), so that for $\sigma_1 = -p - k = 0$ and so $p = -k$.

Since the principal vertical stress σ_3, as seen in the Mohr stress circle diagram in Fig. 4.25(b), is given by

$$\sigma_3 = p_p = -p + k = 2k \qquad (4.106)$$

it must therefore be equal to $2k$, or

$$\frac{p_p}{2k} = 1 \qquad (4.107)$$

where p_p is the punch or tool pressure and p is the hydrostatic pressure.

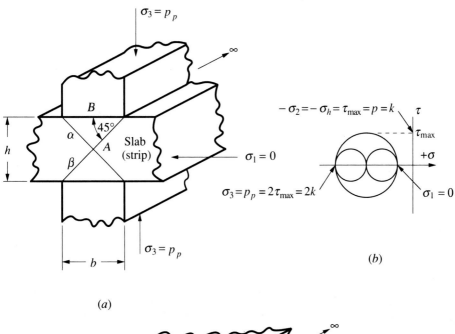

(a)

(b)

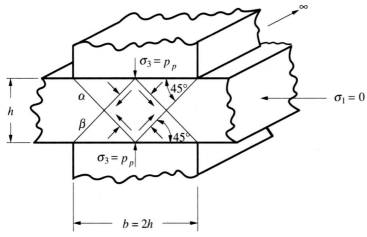

(c)

FIGURE 4.25
Schematic slip-line fields for indentation by opposing, frictionless punches in a rigid, perfectly plastic material for the following strip thickness to punch width ratios, h/b of (a) $h/b = 1$, (c) $h/b = \frac{1}{2}$; and (b) Mohr's stress circle diagram for (a), that is, $h/b = 1$. p_p is the punch or tool pressure.

2. *Where the punch breadth is an integral multiple of the slab* (*workpiece*) *thickness, or* $b/h = 1, 2, 3, 4$, *etc.* In this case the $h/b < 1$ and is equal to $\frac{1}{2}, \frac{1}{3}, \frac{1}{4}$, etc. The slip-line field for the case for which $b/h = 2$ or $h/b = \frac{1}{2}$ is shown in Fig. 4.25(*c*). For this ratio and for any other integral multiple ratio, $\sigma_3 = 2k$ as shown in the Mohr circle diagram in Fig. 4.25(*b*).

3. *Where* $h/b > 1 < 8.75$. As h/b increases, a different field must be used to satisfy field requirements. This is illustrated for $h/b = 5.43$ shown in Fig. 4.26, which is a net having angular increments ($\Delta\phi$) of 15° or $\pi/12$ radians [4.14]. The coordinates of the points of a 15° net for a two-centered fan are also shown.

In triangle AOO',

$$\sigma_y = -p_p \qquad \sigma_{2\text{ at }A} = \sigma_y + k = -p + k \qquad (4.108)$$

where σ_y is the downward axial compressive stress, p_p is the punch or tool

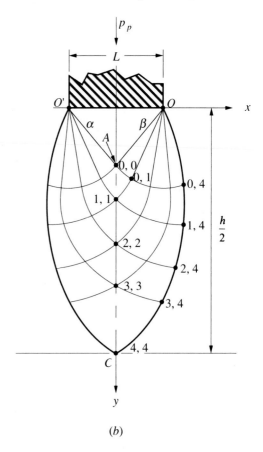

m, n	Δφ	y	x
0, 0	0	1.0	0
0, 1	π/12	1.225	0.2930
0, 2	π/6	1.366	0.6380
0, 3	π/4	1.414	1.000
0, 4	π/3	1.366	1.366
1, 1	0	1.605	0
1, 2	π/12	1.915	0.404
1, 3	π/6	2.120	0.904
1, 4	π/4	2.195	1.471
2, 2	0	2.440	0
2, 3	π/12	2.885	0.584
2, 4	π/6	3.195	1.335
3, 3	0	3.640	0
3, 4	π/12	4.306	0.870
4, 4	0	5.43	0

(*a*) (*b*)

FIGURE 4.26
(*a*) Coordinates of the points (*m, n*) of a 15° net for a two-centered fan; (*b*) appropriate slip-line field for indentation when $b/h = 5.43$ [4.14].

pressure, and σ_2 is the mean stress. If in Fig. 4.26(b) one moves along an α line from point $(0, 0)$ at A to point $(0, 1)$,

$$\sigma_{2 \text{ at } (0, 1)} = \sigma_{2 \text{ at } A} + 2k \, \Delta \phi_\alpha \tag{4.109}$$

If one then moves back along a β line from $(0, 1)$ to $(1, 1)$, then

$$\sigma_{2 \text{ at } (1, 1)} = \sigma_{2 \text{ at } (0, 1)} - 2k \, \Delta \phi_\beta$$

$$\sigma_{2 \text{ at } (1, 1)} = \sigma_{2 \text{ at } A} + 2k(\Delta \phi_\alpha - \Delta \phi_\beta) \tag{4.110}$$

$$\sigma_{2 \text{ at } (1, 1)} = -p_p + k + 2k(\Delta \phi_\alpha - \Delta \phi_\beta)$$

Since $\sigma_{x \text{ at } (1, 1)} = \sigma_{2 \text{ at } (1, 1) + k}$, then

$$\sigma_{x \text{ at } (1, 1)} = -p_p + 2k + 2k(\Delta \phi_\alpha - \Delta \phi_\beta) \tag{4.111}$$

where σ_x is the horizontal compressive stress. Since $\Delta \phi_\alpha = +\pi/12$ or $15°$ and $\Delta \phi_\beta = \pi/12$, at any point (n, n) along the centerline of the punch, that is, $(1, 1)$, $(2, 2)$, etc.,

$$\Delta \phi_\alpha = \frac{n\pi}{12} \quad \text{and} \quad \Delta \phi_\beta = -\frac{n\pi}{12} \tag{4.112}$$

so that

$$\sigma_{x(n, n)} = -p_p + 2k(1 + \Delta \phi_a - \Delta \phi_\beta) = -p_p + 2k(1 + 2\Delta \phi)$$

For the case where the slab is not constrained in the x direction, the net force,

$$F_x = 0 = \int_0^{h/2} \sigma_x \, dy$$

If Eq. (4.112) is substituted for σ_x, then

$$p_p = 2k + \frac{4k}{h} \int_0^{h/2} 2 \, \Delta \phi \, dy \tag{4.113}$$

The integral can then be evaluated graphically by first plotting $2 \, \Delta \phi$ versus y, or numerically by use of the trapezoidal rule [4.14].

The results of such calculations are shown in Fig. 4.27, where $p_p/2k$ is plotted versus h/b, and acceptable slip-line fields are shown for various h/b ratios. Note that indentations that cause plastic deformation to the center of the slab have values of $h/b < 8.75$.

Let us now examine the nonpenetrating case for which $h/b > 8.75$.

4.4.5 Slip-Line Field Analysis of a Single-Punch Indentation of a Semi-Infinite Slab

As shown in Fig. 4.27, when the slab (workpiece) is very thick relative to the punch width, i.e., when the ratio of the slab thickness h to the width of the punch b is greater than about 8.75, the zones of plastic deformation do not extend completely through the slab, and the deformation involved becomes one of

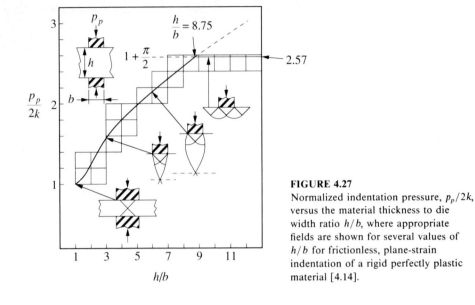

FIGURE 4.27
Normalized indentation pressure, $p_p/2k$, versus the material thickness to die width ratio h/b, where appropriate fields are shown for several values of h/b for frictionless, plane-strain indentation of a rigid perfectly plastic material [4.14].

single-sided indentation by one punch. Beyond $h/b = 8.75$, the reduction of the die width has no further influence on the load required and $p_p/2k = 2.57$.

One might intuitively assume that the greatest concentration of stress would occur at the edges of the punch, and the plastic deformation would occur there first immediately upon the application of the load. Upon continued indentation the plastic deformation would be expected to spread out in a fanlike shape consisting of a straight line net and a fan net as shown in Fig. 4.28. Just such a slip-line field was suggested by (*a*) Prandtl (1920) for the sticking friction case and (*b*) Hill (1950) for the frictionless case as shown in Fig. 4.28(*a*) and (*b*), respectively. The former will be used here, which is a composite of a straight line net and two centered fan nets.

The general state of stress at a point in plane shear, assumed in this problem, is shown in Fig. 4.29(*a*), and the corresponding Mohr three-dimensional stress circle and strain-rate circle diagrams are shown in Fig. 4.29(*b*) and (*c*) [4.14]. Arbitrarily, the three normal stresses have been chosen as compressive with $\sigma_z = \sigma_2$, the intermediate stress. It can be seen from Fig. 4.29(*b*) that the normal stresses acting on the planes upon which the shear stress k acts is the mean stress σ_2.

In Fig. 4.30(*a*) and (*b*), along *OC*, $\sigma_y = \sigma_1 = 0$, $\sigma_x = \sigma_3$ and is compressive, and $\sigma_z = \sigma_2 = \frac{1}{2}\sigma_3$. Since triangle *OBC* is assumed to be a net of straight lines, everywhere in *OBC*, $\sigma_1 = 0$, $\sigma_2 = -k$, and $\sigma_3 = -2k$, as seen from Fig. 4.30(*b*) [4.14]. In moving through an angle $\Delta\phi_\alpha = -\pi/2$ from *B* to *A* along an α line (Hencky), Eq. (4.95) gives

$$\sigma_{2A} = \sigma_{2B} + 2k\,\Delta\phi_\alpha \tag{4.114}$$

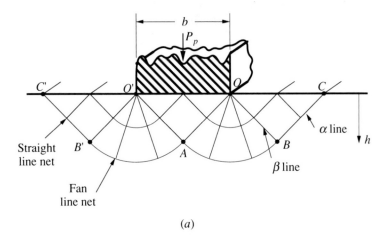

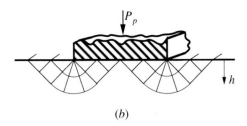

FIGURE 4.28
Slip-line fields for flow under a flat, nonpenetrating punch in plane strain of a semi-infinite slab (a) for the sticking friction case according to Prandtl, in which material sticks onto the end of the punch forming a dead zone; and (b) for the frictionless case according to Hill, in which the material slides along the face of the punch with a velocity v_{AB} [4.14].

Since

$$\sigma_{2B} = -k \quad \text{and} \quad \Delta\phi_\alpha = -\frac{\pi}{2}$$

$$\sigma_{2A} = -k + 2k\left(-\frac{\pi}{2}\right) = -k(1 + \pi)$$

(4.115)

where σ_{2A} is the intermediate principal stress σ_2 at A, normal to the end of the punch and satisfying the condition of plane strain. The shear stress k acts along the slip-lines, while the mean stress σ_2, acts normal to these lines. This is also the value of σ_2 throughout AOO', as can be seen in Fig. 4.30(c).

To determine the pressure of the punch or tool, p_p, on the surface of the slab, which from Fig. 4.30(c) is equal to $-\sigma_y = -\sigma_3$, one may use the following

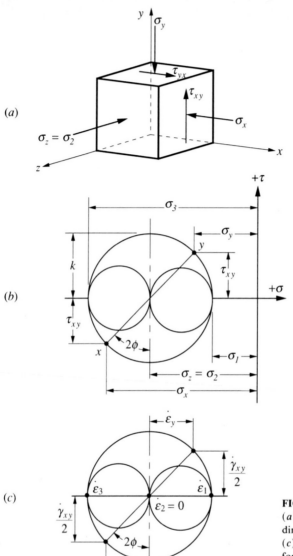

FIGURE 4.29
(a) Stress element; (b) Mohr's three-dimensional stress circle diagram; (c) Mohr's strain-rate circle diagram for the general state of stress at a point in plane strain [4.14].

relationships by use of Fig. 4.30(c) and Eq. (4.115):

$$-p_p = \sigma_{3 \text{ at } OO'} = (\sigma_{2A} - k) = -k(1 + \pi) - k$$

$$p_p = 2k\left(1 + \frac{\pi}{2}\right)$$

then

$$\frac{p_p}{2k} = 1 + \frac{\pi}{2} = 2.57 \tag{4.116}$$

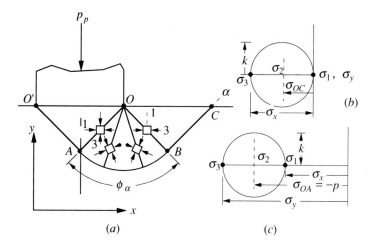

FIGURE 4.30
A detailed development of a portion of the slip-line field of Fig. 4.20(a) showing (a) the changing stress field in sector OAB; (b) Mohr's stress circle for triangle OBC; and (c) Mohr's stress circle for triangle AOO' [4.14].

which is the limiting value of the normalized pressure for the Tresca criterion as shown in Fig. 4.27. For the von Mises criterion, $2k = 1.15\sigma_y$, so that $p_p = 2.97\sigma_y$.

In Fig. 4.30(a), the regions OBC and OAO' are subjected to a constant mean stress σ_2, but of different magnitude. The sector OAB deforms gradually into OBC, and σ_2 decreases from OAO' to OBC. Energy is dissipated during the gradual deformation of OAB.

The construction of a velocity vector diagram (hodograph) in slip-line field analysis is necessary for the following reasons [4.14]: (1) to ensure that the field is kinematically admissible, (2) to determine the relative amount of energy dissipated by gradual deformation as opposed to intense shear, and (3) to predict the approximate change in shape of initially straight lines as they proceed through the deformation zone to exit.

Figure 4.31(a) and (b) shows the partial field and the associated vector velocity diagram (hodograph) for the above sticking-friction, punch-indentation problem. The dead-zone ODA moves downward at the punch speed $V_0 = 1$. At OA, a velocity discontinuity V^*_{OA}, parallel to OA, occurs. A point just inside OAB sector at A must have an absolute velocity V^*_{OA}, tangent to arc AEB at A. Since the magnitude of a velocity discontinuity is constant along a slip-line, the magnitude of V^*_A is constant along arc AEB. V^*_E has the same magnitude as V^*_A, but its direction represents a line tangent to E on arc AEB. The direction of the velocity only in this case changes gradually through sector AOB, and there is no abrupt velocity discontinuity across OB. (In entering or leaving a region where σ_2 will gradually change, an abrupt discontinuity may or may not occur.) The velocity everywhere in triangle OBC is V^*_B, which is parallel to BC [4.14].

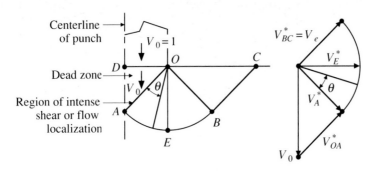

FIGURE 4.31
(*a*) A partial field and (*b*) an associated vector velocity diagram (hodograph) for Fig. 4.22(*a*) for the case of sticking friction [4.14].

Intense shear (flow localization) occurs along AO at a velocity of V^*_{OA}, along AEB at $V^*_A = V^*_E = V^*_B$, etc., and along BC at $V^*_B = V^*_{\text{exit}}$. Here, velocity magnitudes are implied. Shear (flow localization) always occurs at the boundary between the field and the undeformed metal outside the field, and most of the energy is dissipated at these locations.

In the foregoing, the indentation of a slab between opposing punches, having a constant shear stress at the interfacial boundary, was discussed. Let us now look at the plotting of slip-line fields for slabs of different width-to-thickness ratios, b/h, with overhanging platens (anvils). (See Fig. 4.34.)

4.4.6 Slip-Line Field Analysis of Plane-Strain Compression with Overhanging Platens

In this case, the platens overhang the slab or workpiece to distinguish this operation from punching where the width of the punch is less than the width of the slab. Let us look at the following two cases: (1) the compression of a slab of a perfectly plastic material in plane-strain between two frictionless overhanging platens; and (2) the compression under similar conditions except that sticking friction exists at the two material-platen interfaces.

The above two cases will be discussed in the following:

4.4.6.1 PLANE-STRAIN COMPRESSION WITH FRICTIONLESS OVERHANGING PLATENS.
In the absence of friction at the platen-material interface, there will be no tangential, frictional stress at the interface and consequently no resultant normal stress at the free surface, so that $\sigma_2 = 0$. The slip-lines must therefore make an angle of 45° with the free faces and the platen faces and be straight lines as shown in Fig. 4.25(*a*) and (*c*) and in Fig. 4.32. From Eqs. (4.106) and (2.49)

$$\sigma_1 = -p - k = 0 \quad \text{and} \quad -p = k$$

$$\sigma_3 = p_p = -p + k = 2k = \bar{\sigma} \tag{4.117}$$

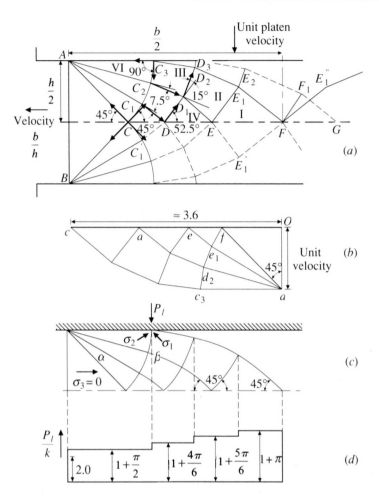

FIGURE 4.32
An approximate slipline field solution, using a 15° network, for plane-strain compression between overlapping platens with sticking friction showing the following: (*a*) The initial stages in the construction of the field for $b = 3.6h$; (*b*) the hodograph construction for one-quarter of the field; (*c*) the final smoothed slip-line field; (*d*) the pressure distribution [4.22].

This is the expected result, since the normal stress to initiate plastic flow in compression is equal to the yield or flow stress of the material.

4.4.6.2 PLANE-STRAIN COMPRESSION WITH OVERHANGING PLATENS HAVING STICKING FRICTION AT THE PLATEN-MATERIAL INTERFACE. It may be helpful to illustrate this case by means of a graphical construction.

For sticking friction assumed here, the slip-lines must meet the platen surfaces at 0 and 90° [4.22]. They must also meet the central plane of the slab at 45° as shown in Fig. 4.32 to avoid resultant shear on the plane of symmetry.

These two conditions are fulfilled by two equal circular-type fans centered at A and B and extending to the centerline, each having a radius of $h/(2 \sin 45°)$, as shown in Fig. 4.32 for a $15°$ incremental field. In the construction of the slip-line field graphically, D is found by drawing the chord C_1D from C_1 at $15/2°$ or $7\frac{1}{2}°$ to the direction AC_1. Likewise, to obtain point D_1, a chord is drawn from C_1 at $15/2°$ or $7\frac{1}{2}°$ to the direction AC_2 to intersect at $52\frac{1}{2}°$ to the central plane. Using a similar approach, one can extend the graphical solution regardless of the width of the platens. Since, in this case, b/h is taken as 3.6, the last interior solid slip-line is $C_3D_2E_1F$. On the other hand, if the b/h ratio is increased to 4.5, this portion of the slip-line field would be extended to $D_3E_2F_1G$ shown by the dashed line.

It should be noted that the region of the slab, bounded by the platen and the solid slip-line $C_3D_2E_1F$ (and its mirror image) remains rigid and moves with the platen and can be regarded as a dead (rigid) zone.

The compatibility of the graphically constructed slip-line field with the velocity boundary conditions may be checked by construction of a velocity vector diagram (hodograph) as shown in Fig. 4.32(b). This task is most easily accomplished by first drawing chords and then joining them with smooth curves.

In this example, the velocity solution is begun at point F. Each platen is assumed to move vertically toward the central plane with a unit velocity as represented by length Oa in Fig. 4.32(b). As metal from the rigid zone adjacent to the upper platen crosses the boundary E_1F near F, it is sheared parallel to the slip-line at $45°$ to the central plane so as to yield a velocity of af. Since the tangential velocity does not change along the slip-line, the velocity everywhere along the slip-line $AC_3D_2E_1F$ will be equal but of different direction. The velocities ae_1, ad_2, and ac_3 are therefore drawn equal to af and parallel to their respective slip-line segment.

The remainder of the velocity vector diagram is constructed in a similar manner, until the position of c is found. The velocity of the boundary ACB must be compatible with the rigid metal to the left and have a velocity horizontally outward equal to Oc. In this case, it is equal in magnitude to b/h times the platen

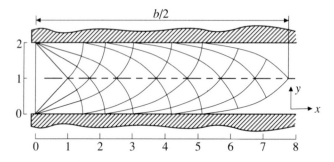

FIGURE 4.33
A slipline field for compression with sticking friction showing smooth, curved slip-lines [4.14].

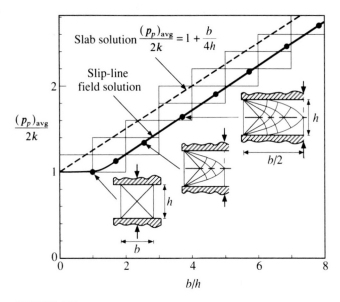

FIGURE 4.34
Normalized average indentation pressure versus width/height ratio b/h, for compression with sticking friction, using the approximate portion of the slip-line field in Fig. 4.33 and the slab-force analysis given by $p_p/2k = 1 + b/4h$ [4.14].

velocity, which is assumed here to be unity. Since b/h is taken here to be 3.6, $V_{OC} = 3.6$ [4.22].

The foregoing example, involving sticking friction and overhanging platens, is approximated by hot open-die forging. With sticking friction, as indicated above, the slip-lines must be parallel or perpendicular to the surfaces at points where they meet the surface. They do not, however, meet the surface at the rigid or dead zone. An example of such a slip-line field with smooth, curved slip-lines is shown in Fig. 4.33.

The extent of this field depends upon the h/b ratio. As in the punch indentation problem, the boundary condition is $\sigma_x = 0$ along the left-hand side of the field, and the value of $p_p = -\sigma_y$ can be found along the centerline. $F_y = \int s_y\, dx$ can be determined by graphical and numerical integration and $(p_p)_{av} = F_y/b$ [4.14].

The results are shown graphically in Fig. 4.34 for one-half of the field, where $p_p/2k$ is plotted as a function of b/h. The slab solution of $p_p/2k = 1 + b/4h$ is also shown for comparison.

4.4.7 Developments Needed in Plotting of Slip-Line Fields

Although the basic equations and questions of uniqueness are well understood in the slip-line field method, there are still inherent difficulties in constructing the solution to any real, metalworking problems [4.23]. These difficulties arise from the decoupling of the stress and deformation behavior, through the indeterminate form of the flow rule for a perfectly plastic material and the fact that the boundary conditions usually encountered in forming processes are mixed, in the sense that they involve both velocity and traction (surface loading) components. Thus, although the governing equations are hyperbolic, there are seldom enough data specified on any boundary arc to enable the stress and/or velocity solution to be constructed by the usual analytical procedures.

Usually the effect of deformation on the mechanical behavior of the material and the effects of changes in variables such as temperature, strain rate, etc., are not taken into consideration in the slip-line field method.

Most of the early solutions using this method, such as for plane-strain drawing through short, frictionless or constant shear dies, consisted of regions containing, at least in part, straight lines, and the boundary conditions at the die-material interface that were frictionless with a shear stress of zero or with constant shear, implying that the slip-lines must meet the die surface at 45°, and with the normal velocity component equal to zero. Solutions such as these are said to be of the "direct" type, since the complete slip-line field and its associated velocity vector diagram can be constructed in a straightforward, step-by-step manner outward from the constant state or simple wave regions.

Another type of solutions of more complicated metalworking processes is called "*indirect*" *solutions*, in which there is not a sufficient number of curves of known shape for the complete solution to be determined in a step-by-step manner.

It is very laborious and time-consuming to draw manually indirect slip-line fields by a trial-and-error procedure and also to draw progressive slip-line fields using the velocity vector diagrams to determine the shape after each incremental deformation. The digital computer, however, can reduce the amount of labor and time required, and improve the accuracy of the plotted fields. Also, it can increase the capability of dealing with more complex processes and include other variables such as friction, material properties, etc.

4.4.8   Use of a Digital Computer for Drawing Slip-Line Fields

The first main development, utilizing the computer for facilitating the construction of slip-line fields, was the one presented by Ewing [4.24]. In this method, the radii of curvature of a pair of slip-lines through a chosen origin are expressed as a power series in terms of rotation along these lines. This method increases the accuracy over the manual and computerized manual chord methods reduces errors, and requires little computer time. The only errors that arise are from power-series termination and the accumulated roundoff. The errors inherent in the finite-difference approximation disappear here.

The second development by Collins [4.25] was a matrix operational method for the construction of complete fields. This method greatly helps to overcome the problem of the indirect type of solution when no initial slip-line is known at

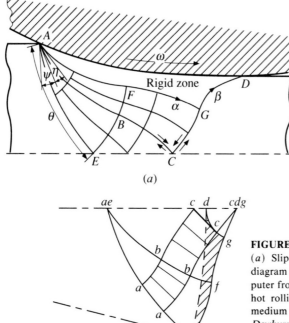

(a)

(b)

FIGURE 4.35
(a) Slip-line field and (b) velocity vector diagram (hodograph) drawn by a digital computer from mathematical formulation for the hot rolling of a strip (slab) with small-to-medium diameter rolls. (*Adapted from P. Dewhurst, I. F. Collins, and W. Johnson, "A Class of Slipline Field Solutions for the Hot Rolling of Strip", J. Mech. Engr. Sci., 15, 1973, p. 440.*)

the outset such as in the case of rolling. The point has now been reached where the slip-line field and the corresponding velocity vector diagram (hodograph) can be drawn by the computer as shown in Fig. 4.35(a) and (b) for rolling with small-to-medium diameter rolls.

Let us now discuss briefly the computerization of the manual method for constructing the slip-line field for the plane-strain compression of the slab with overhanging platens involving sticking friction. Then we shall look briefly at the matrix operational method for constructing complete slip-line fields.

4.4.9 Computerized Drawing of a Slip-Line Field for Plane-Strain Compression

As in the manual solution presented in the foregoing, in this computerized chord method the intersections of the slip-line nets (the nodal points) are found by drawing a series of chords to replace the curved slip-lines as shown in Fig. 4.36 [4.22]. Smaller angles may easily be used here to improve the accuracy.

The point M on the horizontal centerline (plane) may be selected as the origin of the (x, y) coordinates. The corner point A has the coordinates $(0, +h/2)$ and the first intersection C of the slip-line field and the centerline, (x_{00}, y_{00}), is at $(+h/2, 0)$. The intersection at $C_1(x_{01}, y_{01})$ is defined by the incremental angle

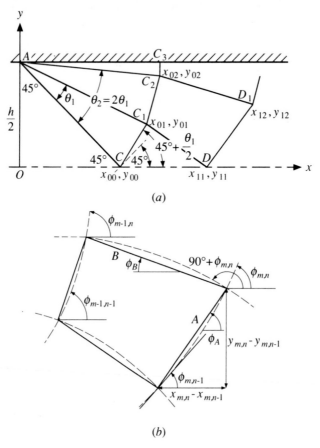

FIGURE 4.36
(a) Part of a slip-line field, showing chords and nodal points, drawn by a digital computer for plane-strain compression (note $OA = OC = h/2$); (b) the coordinates of the nodal points of an element of a general slip-line network such as shown in (a) [4.22].

θ_1. The tangent to the slip-line on the centerline at C must be 45°, so that the angle of the chord CC_1 to the centerline will be $(45 + \theta_1/2)°$. The coordinates of C_1 are therefore

$$x_{01} = \frac{h}{2} + AC\theta_1 \cos\left(45° + \frac{\theta_1}{2}\right) \tag{4.118a}$$

$$y_{01} = AC\theta_1 \sin\left(45° + \frac{\theta_1}{2}\right) \tag{4.118b}$$

where $AC = \sqrt{2}h/2$.

The coordinates of C_2 and D are found similarly, but to find D_1 it is necessary to solve a pair of simultaneous equations relating to the lines DD_1 and C_2D_1. The general case for such a solution is shown in Fig. 4.36(b).

From Fig. 4.36(b) it can be seen that the slope of the chord A is equal to the mean of the slopes of the tangents as follows:

$$y_{m,n} - y_{m,n-1} = (x_{m,n} - x_{m,n-1}) + \tan \phi_A \tag{4.119}$$

where $\phi_A = \frac{1}{2}(\theta_{m,n} + \theta_{m,n-1})$.

The slope of chord B is equal to the mean of the slopes of the tangents to the slip-line of the other family, which is orthogonal to the first as follows:

$$\theta_B = 180° - \frac{1}{2}(90° + \phi_{m,n} + 90° + \phi_{m-1,n}) \tag{4.120a}$$

$$\phi_B = 90° - \frac{1}{2}(\phi_{m,n} + \phi_{m-1,n}) \tag{4.120b}$$

$$y_{m-1,n} - y_{m,n} = (x_{m,n} - x_{m-1,n}) \tan \phi_B \tag{4.120c}$$

$$y_{m,n} - y_{m-1,n} = -(x_{m,n} - x_{m-1,n}) \cot \frac{1}{2}(\phi_{m,n} + \phi_{m-1,n}) \tag{4.120d}$$

In this way the coordinates of all the points in the quadrant can be found. The calculations are performed in sequence for small increments of angle along each slip-line, starting with $C - C_3$. After each calculation the question is asked whether y has reached the value of $h/2$ at the platen surface. When this point is reached, the next line $D - D_1$ is calculated, and so forth. The slip-line field is completed when x reaches the value of $b/2$ at the centerline.

A suitable flowchart [4.22] for the calculations is shown in Fig. 4.37. Instructions to the plotter will cause it to begin plotting the field at centerpoint F, and to ignore all points above F as seen in Fig. 4.38.

The velocity vector diagram (hodograph) can be produced from the computer solution of the slip-line field as shown in Fig. 4.38. Since corresponding elements of the two diagrams are perpendicular to each other, that is, fe_1 and FE_1, e_1e, and E_1E, etc., the velocity vector diagram may be considered as an inverted mirror image of the slip-line diagram with a normalized scale. The former is started with coordinates $(0, -1)$ at a and $(-1, 0)$ at f, and the point e_1 is found from the condition that fe_1 is perpendicular to FE_1 and the discontinuity ae_1 is parallel to AF at E, giving a pair of simultaneous equations.

After e_1 is located, the construction proceeds by noting that e_1e is perpendicular to E_1E of the slip-line field, and e has the y coordinate of zero. The point d_1 is next found using the conditions that ed_1 is perpendicular to ED_1, and d_2d_1 is perpendicular to D_2D_1 of the slip-line field. The coordinates are then determined from trigonometric simultaneous equations similar to Eqs. (4.119) and (4.120) for plotting of the slip-line field.

The velocity vector diagram is completed when all of the nodal points of the slip-line field have been used. The final exit velocity can be printed out as Od.

By use of the foregoing approach, a slip-line field solution of a plane-strain compression problem with variable friction has been obtained [4.22]. Also, it has been used for the slip-line solutions of nonsteady-state conditions and for progressive deformation with sticking friction. However, the capability of this approach is limited, and a more powerful slip-line field computer technique must be used such as, for example, the computerized matrix technique proposed by Collins [4.23], which is discussed next.

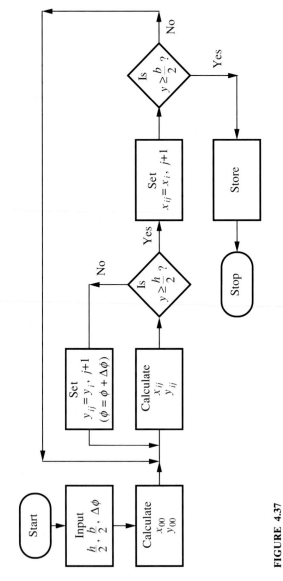

FIGURE 4.37

A flowchart for drawing a slip-line field for compression. See Figs. 4.32(*a*) and 4.36(*a*) for definition of $h/2$ and $b/2$, and Eqs. (4.119) and (4.120) for definition of the coordinate system [Also see Figs. 12.23(*b*).] [4.22].

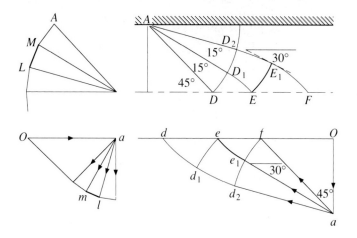

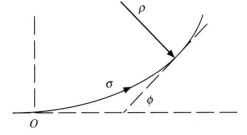

FIGURE 4.38
Diagrams showing orthogonality of elements of the slip-line field and the hodograph [4.22].

4.4.10 Computerized Matrix Technique for Constructing Slip-Line Field Solutions [4.23]

As indicated in the foregoing, a complete slip-line field is a network of lines made up of a finite number of subregions in each of which the solution is analytic [4.23]. The curvature (or perhaps some derivative of it) of the slip-line is discontinuous across the boundary between any two subregions. The solution in Fig. 4.36(a) has six such subregions. The radius of curvature ρ of any slip-line in a subregion is an analytic function of ϕ, the angle turned through by the tangent, measured from a suitable base point O as shown in Fig. 4.39. Hence, this function can be expanded as a convergent power series in ϕ.

$$\rho(\phi) = \sum_{n=0}^{\infty} a_n \frac{\phi^n}{n!} \tag{4.121}$$

A given curve is specified by a set of coefficients (a_n, $n = 1, 2, \ldots$) which may be written in the form of an infinite dimensional column vector denoted by

FIGURE 4.39
The relation of the radius of curvature ρ is shown relative to the angle of rotation ϕ [4.23].

a boldface $\boldsymbol{\sigma}$, where

$$\boldsymbol{\sigma} = \begin{Bmatrix} a_1 \\ a_2 \\ a_3 \\ \vdots \end{Bmatrix} \tag{4.122}$$

Thus, for example, an arc of a circle with a unit radius, as shown in Fig. 4.39, may be denoted by the vector

$$\boldsymbol{c} = \begin{Bmatrix} 1 \\ 0 \\ 0 \\ 0 \\ 0 \end{Bmatrix} \tag{4.123}$$

Various basic algebraic operations can be given simple geometric interpretations. For example, to obtain a curve represented by $-\boldsymbol{\sigma}$ from $\boldsymbol{\sigma}$, one merely reflects the curve in the tangent line at the base point O. $\lambda\boldsymbol{\sigma}$ means that the radius of curvature has been scaled up by a factor of λ at all points of the curve. $\boldsymbol{\sigma}_1 + \boldsymbol{\sigma}_2$ is the sum of the radii of curvature of two curves at this angular distance.

The construction of a complete slip-line field is accomplished by the successive use of a few basic matrix operators as follows: (1) shift (Fig. 4.40(a)) used to displace the base point of a curve from O to O' through an angular distance of θ, which can be expressed in terms of a shift matrix S_θ; (2) reversion (Fig. 4.40(b)), used to reverse the direction on the curve in terms of the angle turned through in the opposite direction from the previous one, which can be expressed in terms of a reversion matrix R_θ; (3) differentiation and integration, used to

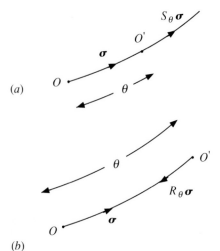

(a)

(b)

FIGURE 4.40
Definition of the (a) shift operator; and (b) reversion operator [4.23].

perform these operations; and (4) basic slip-line P and Q operators, used to construct a complete slip-line field where two slip-lines, one of each family, are given and expressed by the following equations in matrix notation:

$$\sigma_3 = P_\psi^* \sigma_1 + Q_\psi^* \sigma_2 \tag{4.124}$$

$$\sigma_4 = P_\theta^* \sigma_2 + Q_\theta^* \sigma_1 \tag{4.125}$$

where P_ψ and Q_ψ are matrix operators illustrated graphically in Fig. 4.41. P_ψ^* and Q_θ^* can be seen in Fig. 4.41(b) to be operators which generate curves in a singular field on the convex side of a given slip-line [4.23].

Various identities exist between basic operators in matrix formulation, which produce a great simplification in analysis.

The matrix method introduced very briefly above enables a slip-line field of the indirect type to be formulated mathematically. One promising slip-line curve, say, σ, is arbitrarily selected as the base curve and the other principal curves in the field are then expressed in terms of σ. By using the basic operators and working systematically through the slip-line field, and if necessary through the velocity vector diagram, one proceeds until the final consistent condition is

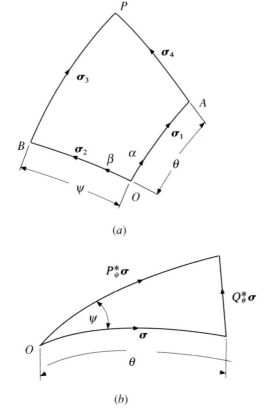

(a)

(b)

FIGURE 4.41
Definition of P^* and Q^* operators showing (a) OA, OB, BP, and AP being denoted by σ_1, σ_2, σ_3, and σ_4; and (b) P^* and Q^* operators for the special case in which $\sigma_3 = 0$, so that the base curve OB degenerates into a single point, so that the field is singular at O [4.23].

reached. This procedure gives an equation in σ which is usually of the form

$$A\sigma = Bc \tag{4.126}$$

where A and B are composite matrices made up of various combinations of the six basic operators, and c is the circle vector.

The complexity of this basic equation depends to some extent on the choice of the base curve σ. Even here the question as to which particular choice leads to the simplest algebraic formulation is a matter for experience and experiment at this point in time.

In applying the above matrix procedure, not many numerical difficulties have been encountered. The convergence of the series is extremely rapid and usually only six terms need to be retained. The only place where numerical difficulties have occurred is where a nonlinear optimization subroutine for solving a system of nonlinear algebraic equations has been used, either to ensure that certain rigid regions are in equilibrium or to construct solutions for a given tool geometry, or both. In steady-state forming processes such as rolling and extrusion, a good check on the accuracy of the calculations can be obtained by using the slip-line and velocity diagram geometries to compute and compare the mass fluxes at exit and entry. Once it becomes necessary to use a digital computer to solve a given problem, it can be argued that a finite element method to be discussed next would be more appropriate, since it is possible to improve the constitutive model of the material by including elastic, hardening, and rate effects, for example. The slip-line approach still has many advantages. Firstly, the scales of the two types of programs differ by several orders of magnitude. The subroutines involved here only require the inversion of a very small matrix and, even when using auxiliary optimization subroutines, it has proved possible to calculate all cases of practical interest in a few seconds computing time [4.23]. This is particularly true of steady-state processes where one includes hardening effects as a succession of incremental deformations. As will be seen later, the solution of some finite element problems may require a matter of hours on a high speed computer.

4.5 FINITE ELEMENT METHOD

4.5.1 Introduction

For many years the upper-bound method has been used for predicting the load and the metal flow in metalforming operations. The method is based on the upper-bound theorem, discussed previously, which states that among all the given admissible velocity fields, the best approximation to the actual one minimizes the upper-bound functional or the energy rate. (A functional is a function of a function.) The theorem provides a mathematically sound approximation in the sense that the convergence of the computed solution to the actual one can be achieved for a sufficiently wide class of admissible velocity fields [4.26].

The classical method of solution by the upper-bound method involves the selection of an admissible velocity field which can describe the metal flow reasonably well. The admissible velocity field must satisfy the incompressibility condition (2.48), (2.69), and (2.82) and the velocity boundary conditions. Such a velocity field is usually formulated on the basis of the metal flow pattern obtained by experiments. This procedure, however, becomes extremely difficult when the workpiece geometry or the flow pattern is complicated. The selected admissible velocity field in general includes parameters to reflect the influence of process conditions on metal flow. The optimum values of these parameters are determined to minimize the upper bound functional.

The use of the upper-bound method has been limited to simple metalworking problems, mainly because of the difficulties involved in finding a sufficiently broad class of admissible velocity fields or to describe complicated metal flow problems. Furthermore, once a class of admissible velocity fields is chosen, the solution accuracy becomes fixed.

The rigid–plastic or rigid–viscoplastic finite element method (FEM), to be discussed later, utilizes basically the same mathematical principle as that for the upper-bound method. What is different is the choice of the trial functions. In the FEM, the workpiece is divided into subregions called *elements* as shown in Fig. 4.42. The elements are assumed to be interconnected at a discrete number of nodal points located on their boundaries. Then, at each element, a set of trial functions (or admissible velocity fields) are usually assigned with constant parameters which are identified to the nodal point velocities. The trial functions in each region are combined to form an admissible velocity field which satisfies the

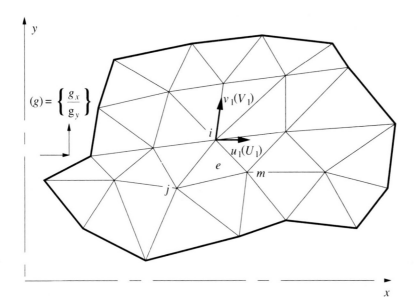

FIGURE 4.42
A plane stress region divided into finite elements [4.28].

necessary requirements except the volume constancy requirement. The latter is enforced by the variational principle, which also allows the calculation of the mean stress [4.26].

First, in order to get a feel for the variational method, let us consider a functional expressed as

$$\Pi = \int_{x_1}^{x_2} F\left(x, u, \frac{\partial u}{\partial x}, \frac{\partial^2 u}{\partial x^2}, \ldots\right) dx \tag{4.127}$$

where the dependent variable u is a function of x, the independent variable. The integral in Eq. (4.127) is defined in the closed two-dimensional region or domain $[x_1, x_2]$ as shown in Fig. 4.43. (Note that in the literature and in this book Π and Φ are used interchangeably as well as other symbols that are used interchangeably for variational functionals.) [4.27].

Functionals are functions of other functions. In mechanics, the functional usually has some physical meaning such as the potential energy of a deformed body.

In the variational method, a tentative solution is tried for a given problem, and the functional is expressed in terms of the tentative solution. From all such possible solutions satisfying the boundary conditions, the solution which satisfies the variational principle governing the behavior will be the one which makes the functional Π stationary, i.e., existing at its maximum or minimum state. The mathematical procedure used to select the correct solution from a number of tentative solutions is called the *calculus of variations*.

Any tentative solution $\bar{u}$ in the vicinity of the exact solution may be represented by the sum of the exact solution u and a variation of u, δu, as shown in Fig. 4.44 and as follows:

$$\bar{u} = u + \delta u \tag{4.128}$$

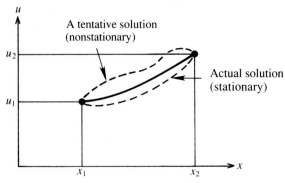

Actual solutions

Tentative solutions

FIGURE 4.43
A closed two-dimensional region or domain $[x_1, x_2]$ used to define the variational functional given in Eq. (4.127) [4.27].

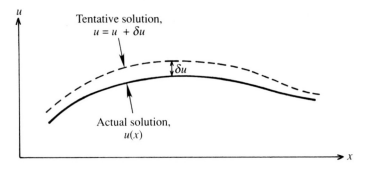

FIGURE 4.44
Variational notation defining the variation of a tentative solution from the exact solution [4.27].

The variational of $u = u(x)$ is defined as an infinitesimal arbitrary change in u for a fixed value of the dependent variable x, that is, for $\delta x = 0$. The symbol δ of the variational notation δx can be treated as an operator, similar to the differential operator d [4.27].

Small changes or variations in this functional correspond to variations in the solution. Therefore, to extremize (maximize or minimize) a functional one merely makes the first variation of the functional Π vanishing small, so that its trace will not move from its position, i.e., is stationary. This condition can be expressed as

$$\delta\Pi = \int_{x_1}^{x_2} \partial F\, dx = 0 \tag{4.129}$$

A variational principle may specify a scalar quantity or functional, which is defined by an integral of the form

$$\Pi = \int_{\Omega} F\left(u, \frac{\partial u}{ux}, \ldots\right) d\Omega + \int_{\Gamma} E\left(u, \frac{\partial u}{\partial x}, \ldots\right) d\Gamma \tag{4.130}$$

where Π = scalar quantity or stationary functional [4.28], u = unknown function, which can be in matrix form such as $u = \sum N_i a_i$ where a_i are the nodal parameters and where F and E are functions of $u(x, \ldots)$ and its derivatives, and Γ is the curve bounding the closed region or domain Ω.

One can attempt to make Π stationary with respect to variations in u among the admissible set of functions satisfying the following general boundary conditions,

$$B_1(u) = 0 \quad \text{on} \quad \Gamma_1 \tag{4.131a}$$

$$B_2(u) = 0 \quad \text{on} \quad \Gamma_2 \tag{4.131b}$$

where $\Gamma_1 + \Gamma_2 = \Gamma$.

For small admissible variations in u, the first variation in Π may be expressed as

$$\delta\Pi = \int_{\Omega} A(u)\, \delta u\, d\Omega \tag{4.132}$$

then the stationary requirement states that

$$\delta\Pi = 0$$

or

$$A(u) = 0 \quad \text{in} \quad \Omega$$

since δu is arbitrary.

The solution to the continuum problem is a function of u which makes Π stationary with respect to small changes, δu. Thus, for a solution to continuum problems, the variation is $\delta\Pi = 0$ [4.28].

In general, the mathematical formulation of a variational principle is such that the integral of some typical function has a smaller (or larger) value for the actual performance of the system than any virtual performance subject to the general conditions of the system.

The concepts of elements and trial function provide several advantages over the upper-bound method. The solution procedure is free of geometrical restrictions since any workpiece can be subdivided into a finite number of elements. Also, the construction of the variational functional, and/or its derivatives (stiffness-matrix) at the elemental level, follows the same procedure throughout the workpiece. This property of the FEM makes it possible to treat a wide class of boundary value problems in a unified way.

The major advantage of the finite element method is its ability to generalize, i.e., it can be applied to a wide class of boundary conditions value problems with little restriction on the workpiece geometry [4.29]. In practical, massive metal-working processes, a number of preforming operations are usually required to transform the initial, simple geometry of the blanks or slugs into the complex geometry of the final shape, while achieving the desired tolerance and properties. The desired workpiece shapes, in general, are obtained by using dies of various shapes. Therefore, a method of analysis which can treat the boundary conditions of dies is necessary in order to utilize fully the advantages of the FEM in metalworking analysis. Such a method, which is suitable to analyze the practical metalforming process, has been proposed and programmed into a computer code ALPID (Analysis of Large Plastic Incremental Deformation), which will be discussed briefly later. Some proponents of the FEM are of the opinion that this method will supersede the slip-line field and the upper-bound techniques, because of its greater versatility and because the degree of complexity that can be introduced is limited only by the size of the digital computer available.

The major disadvantages of the FEM in upper-bound solutions is the great amount of computer time required and the need of a large computer. New techniques for simplifying calculations and making them more efficient are continually being presented in the literature.

4.5.2 Preview of Finite Element Methods Used in Forming Processes [4.30]

4.5.2.1 INTRODUCTION. Many numerical methods are available, some of which are shown in Fig. 4.45, for the analysis of metalforming processes, that are aimed

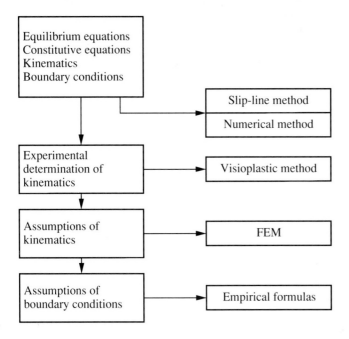

FIGURE 4.45
Flowchart showing the methods for calculation of metalforming processes. (See Fig. 4.1.) [4.30].

to predict stress and strain fields and material flow. The classical approximate methods that have been found to be particularly effective are (1) the slip-line field method for plane-strain problems, (2) the elementary theory which reduces a three-dimensional problem to a one-dimensional problem by means of kinematic restrictions, and (3) the upper- and lower-bound theorems [4.30]. If the shape of the formed part and the regions of localized flow are complex, it is expedient to use a computer-oriented, numerical method like the finite element method (FEM) rather than to use the foregoing classical methods, i.e., the slip-line field, the elementary theory, and the bound methods. The FEM has a wide range of applications from the analysis of simple plane-strain processes to complex 3D and sheetmetal forming processes.

In comparison with the other methods, the FEM has its advantages in solutions of problems with complex shapes, in treatments of nonsteady-state processes, and in obtaining detailed stress and strain fields.

4.5.2.2 SUMMARY OF THE FINITE ELEMENT METHODS [4.30]. A number of FE methods now exist that have been developed in different ways, depending on the material model used; namely, elastic–plastic and rigid–plastic as shown in Fig. 4.46, and also on the theory of plasticity used, i.e., flow theory or the deformation theory (not shown in the figure). The deformation theory used in FE analyses is often referred to as the J_2 *deformation theory* since, for an isotropic,

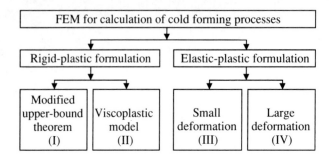

FIGURE 4.46
Flowchart showing some finite element methods for analyzing cold forming processes [4.30].

incompressible material, the yield criterion with the third order term neglected may be expressed as $f(J_2) = 0$, where $J_2 = -(\sigma_1\sigma_2 + \sigma_2\sigma_3 + \sigma_3\sigma_1)$. Since the deformation theory assumes proportional loading, the flow theory is more accurate for large plastic strains.

The rigid–plastic formulation is, therefore, preferred for the development of the FEM to calculate forming processes with very large plastic deformation. However, some problems, such as sheetmetal forming involving elastic deformation, can be simulated better by elastic–plastic modeling as shown in Fig. 4.47.

FEM Processes	Rigid-plastic formulation		Elastic-plastic formulation	
	(I)	(II)	(III)	(IV)
Indentation	x	x	x	x
Forging	x	x	x	x
Extrusion	x	x	x	x
Drawing	x			x
Rolling	x	x		x
Stretching		x		x
Deep drawing		x		x
Radial drawing	x		x	x
Hydraulic bulging			x	x
3D forming	x	x		x

FIGURE 4.47
Chart showing the applications of FEM in metal cold-forming industries [4.30].

Following is a summary of different FE methods, listing the formulation used and some advantages and disadvantages [4.30].

1. Elastic–plastic (E-P) FEM

(a) *Material laws.* Hooke's law for the elastic region:

$$d\varepsilon^e_{ij} = \frac{1+\nu}{E}\left(d\sigma_{ij} - \frac{\nu}{1+\nu}\delta_{ij}\,d\sigma_{kk}\right) \tag{4.133}$$

Prandtl-Reuss equations (which includes plastic strain) with von Mises criterion for the plastic region:

$$d\varepsilon_{ij} = d\varepsilon^e_{ij} + d\varepsilon^p_{ij} \tag{4.134}$$

$$d\varepsilon^p_{ij} = d\lambda\sigma'_{ij} \quad \text{with} \quad \sigma'_{ij}\sigma'_{ij} = \tfrac{2}{3}\bar{\sigma}^2, \tag{4.135}$$

$$d\sigma_{ij} = 2G\left[d\varepsilon_{ij} + \delta_{ij}\frac{\nu}{1-2\nu}d\varepsilon_{kk} - \sigma'_{ij}\frac{\sigma'_{kl}\,d\varepsilon_{kl}}{S}\right] \tag{4.136}$$

where σ'_{ij} = the stress deviator
  ν = Poisson ratio
  G = shear modulus
  δ_{ij} = Kronecker delta (when $i=j$, $\delta_{ij}=1$; when $i \neq j$, $\delta_{ij}=0$)
  S = material dependent value
  $\bar{\sigma}$ = the equivalent stress

(b) *Formulation of E-P FEM.* (1) Lagrangian reference system is used (where subsequent deformation is referred to the original undeformed configuration); (2) the formulation is in stress or strain space; (3) the unknown quantity is displacement; (4) the basic functionals are based on the variational principle or the principle of virtual work; and (5) the incremental solution method for large plastic deformation is used.

(c) *Advantages of E-P FEM.* (1) Consideration of the transition between the elastic and plastic region is taken; (2) both the elastic and plastic regions can be handled; (3) geometric nonlinearity and instability are considered; and (4) residual stresses, springback, and friction can be handled.

(d) *Disadvantages of E-P FEM.* (1) Complicated solution method for nonlinear material behavior may be needed; (2) high computational time may be required, especially if the flow theory of plasticity is used; and (3) numerical errors may accumulate.

2. Rigid–plastic (R-P) FEM

(a) *Material law.* The Levy-Mises material law applies:

$$\sigma'_{ij} = \frac{2}{3}\frac{\bar{\sigma}}{\dot{\bar{\varepsilon}}}\dot{\varepsilon}_{ij} \tag{4.137}$$

with

$$\begin{cases} \bar{\sigma} < \sigma_Y & \text{rigid material} \\ \bar{\sigma} = \sigma_Y & \text{plastic region} \end{cases}$$

$$\dot{\varepsilon}_{ii} = 0 \qquad \dot{\bar{\varepsilon}} = \sqrt{\tfrac{2}{3}\,\dot{\varepsilon}_{ij}\dot{\varepsilon}_{ij}} \qquad\qquad (4.138)$$

$\sigma_Y =$ the yield strength, and $\dot{\bar{\varepsilon}} =$ the equivalent strain rate.

(*b*) *Formulation of R-P FEM.* (1) Eulerian reference system is used (in which the deformation is always referred to the current configuration, i.e., the coordinate system is attached to the particle); (2) the unknown is the velocity field; (3) basic functionals with boundary value problems have the incompressibility conditions added in the variational principle using either the penalty functions or the lagrangian multipliers; and (4) analysis of the instationary forming processes are achieved by means of many small steady-state deformation steps.

(*c*) *Advantages of R-P FEM.* (1) Linearized relationship between stress and strain rate is done in each iteration step; (2) quasi-steady-state solution method is used for unsteady-state problems; (3) easier linkage is achieved with a rezone procedure; and (4) low computational time may be realized, depending on the theory of plasticity used.

(*d*) *Disadvantages of R-P FEM.* (1) It is not able to take into account the elastic loading or plastic unloading; and (2) no solutions for geometric nonlinearity and instability are feasible.

3. Rigid–viscoplastic (R-V) FEM

(*a*) *Material law.* The continuum is considered to be a non-newtonian fluid, to which the von Mises criterion is adapted.

(*b*) *Formulation of R-V FEM.* Same as for rigid–plastic.

(*c*) *Advantages of R-V FEM.* (1) Simulation of hot-forming processes is possible; and (2) every iteration step has a physical meaning of the unsteady state process.

(*d*) *Disadvantages of R-V FEM.* (1) Elastic deformation is neglected; and (2) nonlinear system of equations becomes sensitive due to the viscosity coefficient.

4. Other FE methods

FEM for 3D problems is being developed for use in analyzing geometrically complex parts involving three-dimensional metal flow. Although the extension of FEM to 3D problems is needed, it presently requires a considerable amount of computer effort and time. One of the FEM codes that has been developed is ALPID-3D, which is based on rigid–viscoplastic formulation [4.31].

There are still other variations of FEM, which will not be discussed here. Some of these procedures are designed to deal with certain specific problems such as (1) friction, (2) thermomechanical behavior, (3) irregular shapes having regions of localized deformation, (4) strain and fracture limits, and (5) hot forging.

Applications of a number of the above FE methods will be given throughout the remainder of this book.

In closing, it should be said that the developments in computers, with the accompanying graphics capabilities, from the personal, desk-top computer to the supercomputer, with modern vector and parallel computing techniques, are having a great impact on the use of FEM. The former is relatively inexpensive and readily available, and the latter is much less accessible and extremely expensive. Examples of the use of both of these computers are also cited in what follows.

4.5.3 Fundamentals of FEM Analysis [4.28]

Many problems may be modeled by using a finite number of well-defined components or elements. Such problems are called *discrete*. Others are continuous, that may be subdivided indefinitely and that may be defined by using infinitesimal subdivisions. The solution of the latter leads to the use of differential equations, which imply an infinite number of elements.

To deal with continuum problems, various methods of discretization have been proposed that approximate the true continuum solution. Reasonably good solutions to a continuum problem can be obtained by subdividing the continuum into small portions, called elements, and by applying a standard procedure in the solution applicable to discrete systems. One definition of the finite element method is given as a general discretization procedure of continuum problems expressed by mathematically defined statements.

The basis of the FEM is the representation of the body (or structure) by a contiguous assembly of subdivisions or subregions as shown in Fig. 4.42 called *finite elements*. In a continuum, the body is divided into a finite number of such elements in such a manner as to provide ease of calculation and the required information. This process of selecting only a discrete number of points by dividing the body into elements is called *discretization*. One of the ways to discretize a body or structure is to divide it into an equivalent system of smaller bodies or units. The assemblage of such units then represents the original body. Instead of solving the problem for the entire body in one operation, the solutions are formulated for each constituent unit and combined to obtain the solution for the original body or structure. This approach is known as going from the part to the whole. Although the analysis procedure is thereby considerably simplified, the amount of data to be handled is dependent upon the number of smaller bodies or elements into which the original body is divided. For a large number of subdivisions or elements, it is a formidable task to handle the large volume of data, requiring a relatively large amount of computer time and a large digital computer [4.27].

If a finite element representation were to meet all equilibrium (2.40) and compatibility (2.45) conditions, then the exact solution would be obtained and further grid refinement would produce no further improvement in the results. All numerical solution procedures, whether series representations, finite element, finite difference, or whatever, should produce improved results with grid refinement, because they do not meet all of the basic conditions for an exact solution.

The above elements are considered to be interconnected at the joints which are called nodes or nodal points. Simple functions are chosen to approximate the distribution or variation of the actual displacements over each finite element. Such assumed functions are called *displacement functions* or *displacement models*, and this approach is known as the *displacement formulation*. The unknown magnitudes or amplitudes of the displacement functions are the displacements or their derivatives at the nodal points. Hence, the final solution will yield the approximate displacements at discrete locations in the body, the nodal points. A displacement model can be expressed in various simple forms such as polynomials and trigonometric functions. Since polynomials offer ease in mathematical manipulation, they are often used in finite element applications [4.27].

A variational principle of mechanics, such as the principle of minimum potential energy, is usually used to obtain the set of equilibrium equations of each element. The potential energy of a loaded elastic body or structure, for example, is represented by the sum of the internal energy stored as a result of the deformations and potential energy of the external loads. If the body is in a state of equilibrium, this energy is a minimum. This is a simple statement of the principle of minimum potential energy. The application of this principle to the FEM will be discussed later.

The following six steps summarize the finite element procedure in setting up and solving any equilibrium problem [4.27]:

1. *Discretization of the continuum.* The continuum broadly is the physical body, structure, or solid being analyzed. As indicated above, discretization may be simply described as the process in which the given body is subdivided into an equivalent system of finite elements. For a two-dimensional continuum, the finite elements may be triangular, groups of triangles, or quadrilaterals. Figure 4.42 shows an arbitrary, two-dimensional body discretized into a system of triangular finite elements. For three-dimensional analysis, the finite elements may be tetrahedra, rectangular prisms, or hexahedra. Although some efforts have been made to automate the processes of subdivisions, it remains essentially a judgmental process on the part of the engineer. He must decide what number, size, and arrangement of finite elements will give an effective representation of the given continuum for the particular problem being considered. Only the significant portion of such a continuum need be considered and discretized.

2. *Selection of the displacement models.* The assumed displacement functions or models represent only approximately the actual or exact distribution of the displacements. For example, a displacement function is commonly assumed to be a polynomial, and practical considerations limit the number of terms

that can be retained in the polynomial. Consequently, the first approximation of the finite element method is introduced at this stage.

There are three interrelated factors which influence the selection of a displacement model: (1) the type and degree of the displacement model; (2) the particular displacement magnitudes that described the model selected; and (3) the requirements that the model should satisfy.

3. *Derivation of the element stiffness matrix using the variational principle.* The stiffness matrix consists of the coefficients of the equilibrium equations derived from the material and geometric considerations and obtained by use of the principle of minimum potential energy discussed elsewhere. The stiffness matrix relates the nodal displacements to the nodal forces. The equilibrium relation between the rectangular stiffness matrix $\{k\}$, nodal force vector $\{F\}$, and the nodal displacement vector $[x]$ is expressed in matrix notation as a set of simultaneous linear algebraic equations,

$$[k]\{x\} = \{F'\} \tag{4.139}$$

The stiffness matrix for an element depends upon (1) the displacement model, (2) the geometry of the element, and (3) the local material properties and constitutive relations. For an isotropic, elastic material, the material properties may be defined by Young's modulus E, and the Poisson ratio v.

4. *Assembly of the algebraic equations for the overall discretized continuum.* This process includes the assembly of the overall or global stiffness matrix for the entire body from the individual element stiffness matrices, and the overall or global force or load vector from the element nodal force vectors. In general, the basis for an assembly method is that the nodal interconnections require the displacements at a node to be the same for all elements adjacent to that node. The overall equilibrium relations between the total stiffness matrix $[K]$, the total load vector $\{R\}$, and the nodal displacement vector for the entire body $\{U\}$ is again expressed as a set of simultaneous equations

$$[K]\{U\} = \{R\} \tag{4.140}$$

The above equations cannot be solved until the geometric boundary conditions are taken into consideration by appropriate modification of the equations. A geometric boundary condition arises from the fact that displacements may be prescribed at the boundaries or edges of the body or structure.

5. *Solution for unknown displacements.* The algebraic equations assembled in step 4 above are solved for the unknown displacements. In linear equilibrium problems, this is a rather straightforward application of matrix algebra techniques. For nonlinear problems, however, the desired solutions are obtained by a sequence of steps, each step involving the modification of the stiffness matrix and/or load vector.

6. *Computation of the element strains and stresses corresponding to the calculated nodal displacements.* In certain cases the magnitudes of the primary unknowns, the nodal displacements, will be all that are required for an engineering

solution. More often, however, other quantities derived from the primary unknowns, such as strains and/or stresses, must be determined.

In general, the stresses and strains are proportional to the derivatives of the displacements as shown (directly or indirectly) in equations (2.11) to (2.15) and (2.27), (2.32), and (2.34). Some average value of the stress or strain is taken at the center of the element.

An alternate, but a much less common, procedure to the above would be to convert the displacements into stresses prior to setting up of the stiffness matrix. In summary the procedure in this case would be: (1) divide the body or structure into a finite number of elements; (2) write equations for the displacements of the nodes; (3) convert the displacements into strains and, by use of moduli, into stresses; (4) determine the stiffness matrix from the above equations, relating the displacements at the nodes to the forces acting there; and (5) obtain an expression for the stiffness of the entire whole body preserving strain compatibility of each element with its neighbors.

4.5.4   Simple Elastic, Plane-Stress and Plane-Strain Examples [4.28]

The procedure for use of the FEM for analyzing a continuum has been presented in the foregoing in general terms. Now we will apply the procedure to two specific cases: (1) that of the elastic analysis of a thin slice of the body, which is in plane stress; and (2) that in which the dimensions of the body or structure change only in two directions, say x and y, but not in the z direction, that is, τ_{xz} and τ_{yz} and $\varepsilon_{zz} = 0$, which is the condition of plane strain. Both of these are two-dimensional problems as shown in Fig. 2.16(a) and (b).

The steps of analysis [4.28] are therefore as follows:

1. *Divide the body (slice) into elements* as shown in Fig. 4.42. A typical finite element e is defined by nodes i, j, m, etc., and straight line boundaries.
2. *Define the displacements* at any point within the element as a column vector $\{f(x,y)\}$:

$$\{f\} = [N]\{\delta\}^e = [N_i N_j N_m \cdots] \begin{Bmatrix} \delta_i \\ \delta_j \\ \delta_m \\ \vdots \end{Bmatrix} \tag{4.141}$$

in which the components $[N]$ are, in general, functions of position, and $\{\delta\}^e$ represents a listing of nodal displacements for a particular element e, denoted by the superscript.

In the case of plane stress, for instance,

$$\{f\} = \begin{Bmatrix} u(x, y) \\ v(x, y) \end{Bmatrix} \tag{4.142}$$

represents horizontal and vertical movement of a typical point within the element and

$$\{\delta_i\} = \begin{Bmatrix} u_i \\ v_i \end{Bmatrix} \tag{4.143}$$

represents the corresponding displacements of node i.

The functions N_i, N_j, N_m have to be so chosen as to give appropriate nodal displacements when the coordinates of the appropriate nodes are inserted in Eq. (4.141). For this particular case, $N_i(x_i, y_i) = I$ (identity matrix), and $N_i(x_i, y_i) = N_i(x_m, y_n) = 0$, etc., which is simply satisfied by suitable linear functions of x and y.

3. Convert the displacements within the element into strains by use of the following general relationship written in matrix notation

$$\varepsilon = \{\varepsilon\} = [B]\{\delta\}^e \tag{4.144}$$

where, for plane strain $\{\varepsilon\}$ is the strain vector,

$$\varepsilon = \{\varepsilon\} = \begin{Bmatrix} \varepsilon_x \\ \varepsilon_y \\ \gamma_{xy} \end{Bmatrix} = \begin{Bmatrix} \dfrac{\partial u}{\partial x} \\[2mm] \dfrac{\partial v}{\partial y} \\[2mm] \dfrac{\partial u}{\partial y} + \dfrac{\partial v}{\partial x} \end{Bmatrix} \tag{4.145}$$

and $[B]$ is a matrix consisting of a set of numbers, which relates strain to the displacements such as $b_i = y_i - y_m$ for the triangular case only and the multiplier $\frac{1}{2}\Delta$ composed of position coordinates of the apices of the triangular element and contained

$$\varepsilon_x = \frac{\partial u}{\partial x} = \frac{b_i u_i + b_j u_j + b_m u_m}{2\Delta} \tag{4.146}$$

where $u =$ the displacements and

$$\Delta = x_i y_m + x_m y_i + x_i y_i - (x_m y_i + x_i y_m + x_i y_i) \tag{4.147}$$

which is the area of the triangular element [4.22]. The matrix $[B]$ is obtained from Eq. (4.144) when the functions N_i, N_j, and N_m are determined.

4. *Convert the strain to the local stress* by use of

$$\{\sigma\} = [D]\{\varepsilon\} \tag{4.148}$$

or in equivalent notation

$$\boldsymbol{\sigma} = \boldsymbol{D}\boldsymbol{\varepsilon} \tag{4.149}$$

For the elastic, plane-stress case, this may be done by use of Eqs. (2.32) and (2.33) with τ_{xz} and τ_{yz} and $\varepsilon_{zz} = 0$, and $G = E/2(1 - v)$. These equations can be written as

$$\sigma_x = \frac{E}{1-\nu^2}\,\varepsilon_{xx} + \frac{E\nu}{1-\nu^2}\,\varepsilon_{yy} + 0 \tag{4.150}$$

$$\sigma_y = \frac{E\nu}{1-\nu^2}\,\varepsilon_{xx} + \frac{E}{1-\nu^2}\,\varepsilon_{yy} + 0 \tag{4.151}$$

$$\tau_{xy} = 0 \qquad\qquad +0 \qquad\qquad + \frac{E}{2(1-\nu)}\,\varepsilon_{xy} \tag{4.152}$$

In matrix notations, these equations may be written in the form of Eq. (4.148), where $\{\sigma\}$, $[D]$, and $\{\varepsilon\}$ are defined below:

$$\sigma = \begin{Bmatrix} \sigma_x \\ \sigma_y \\ \tau_{xy} \end{Bmatrix} = \begin{Bmatrix} \dfrac{E}{1-\nu^2} & \dfrac{E\nu}{1-\nu^2} & 0 \\[2mm] \dfrac{E\nu}{1-\nu^2} & \dfrac{E}{1-\nu^2} & 0 \\[2mm] 0 & 0 & \dfrac{E}{2(1-\nu)} \end{Bmatrix} \begin{Bmatrix} \varepsilon_x \\ \varepsilon_y \\ \varepsilon_{xy} \end{Bmatrix} \tag{4.153}$$

$[D]$ is the elasticity matrix containing the appropriate material constants, namely, E and ν. $[D]$ can also be expressed as

$$D = [D] = \frac{E}{1-\nu^2} \begin{bmatrix} 1 & \nu & 0 \\ \nu & 1 & 0 \\ 0 & 0 & \dfrac{(1-\nu)}{2} \end{bmatrix} \tag{4.154}$$

For an isotropic, elastic material, the constitutive equations for plane strain are

$$\varepsilon_x = \frac{\sigma_x}{E} - \frac{\nu\sigma_y}{E} - \frac{\nu\sigma_z}{E} \tag{4.155}$$

$$\varepsilon_y = \frac{\sigma_y}{E} - \frac{\nu\sigma_x}{E} - \frac{\nu\sigma_z}{E} \tag{4.156}$$

$$\varepsilon_z = \frac{\sigma_z}{E} - \frac{\nu\sigma_x}{E} - \frac{\nu\sigma_y}{E} = 0 \tag{4.157}$$

Solving Eq. (4.157) for σ_z and substituting into Eqs. (4.155) and (4.156), with the addition of the $\varepsilon_{xy} - \tau_{xy}$ equation, one obtains for plane strain the following equations in matrix form:

$$\varepsilon = \begin{Bmatrix} \varepsilon_x \\ \varepsilon_y \\ \varepsilon_{xy} \end{Bmatrix} = \frac{1-\nu^2}{E} \begin{bmatrix} 1 & \dfrac{-\nu}{1-\nu} & 0 \\[2mm] \dfrac{-\nu}{1-\nu} & 1 & 0 \\[2mm] 0 & 0 & \dfrac{2}{1-\nu} \end{bmatrix} \begin{Bmatrix} \sigma_x \\ \sigma_y \\ \tau_{xy} \end{Bmatrix} \tag{4.158}$$

By inversion, one obtains for plane strain

$$\boldsymbol{\sigma} = \left\{ \begin{array}{c} \sigma_x \\ \sigma_y \\ \tau_{xy} \end{array} \right\} = \frac{E}{(1+\nu)(1-2\nu)} \left[\begin{array}{ccc} 1-\nu & \nu & 0 \\ \nu & 1-\nu & 0 \\ 0 & 0 & \dfrac{(1-2\nu)}{2} \end{array} \right] \left\{ \begin{array}{c} \varepsilon_x \\ \varepsilon_y \\ \varepsilon_{xy} \end{array} \right\} \qquad (4.159)$$

(The inverse of a square matrix is defined as a matrix which, when multiplied by itself, results in an identity matrix, i.e., one which has unity on each diagonal position and zero on all off-diagonal positions. A special procedure is followed to determine an inverse matrix.)

Since strain is related to displacement by Eq. (4.144), the stresses can be related directly to displacements by the following matrix equation:

$$\{\sigma\} = [B][D]\{\delta\}^e \qquad (4.160)$$

5. *Determine the force applied to the element from the displacement.* Assume that the force is linearly related to the displacement and the deformation is elastic only as before. If a force f_i is applied to vertex i of the element e in Fig. 4.42, giving a linear displacement u_i, the force can be related to the displacement by

$$\{f'\} = [C]\{u_i\} \qquad (4.161)$$

It is assumed that all forces act at the nodes of the mesh of triangular elements. Now the stresses are found by dividing the force acting at each of two nodes by the projected area of the element, for example, $(x_j - x_i)t$, where t is the thickness of the element, constant according to the original assumption. In general terms:

$$2\{f'\} = t[A]\{\sigma\} \qquad (4.162)$$

where $[A]$ is a matrix dependent upon the differences of the positional coordinates of the nodes i, j, and m of Fig. 4.42. In fact, it is the transpose of the matrix $[B]$ of Eq. (4.160), excluding the multiplier $\frac{1}{2}\Delta$, which is composed of position coordinates of the nodal points. Δ is the area of the element expressed in terms of the positional coordinate values x_i, x_j, x_m, y_i, y_j, and y_m.

The matrix force relation is then given by

$$\{f'\} = [B]^T[D][B]t\Delta\{\delta\} \qquad (4.163)$$

or simply by

$$\{f'\} = [k]\{\delta\} \qquad (4.164)$$

where $[k]$ is the stiffness matrix for the element.

6. *Determine the external forces acting on the whole system.* The force-displacement relationship for the whole system is given by

$$\{F'\} = [K]\{\delta\} \qquad (4.165)$$

where F represents the external forces acting on each node of the triangular-mesh network, $\{\delta\}$ represents the displacements at each node, and

$$[K] = [k]_N = [B]_N^T [D]_N [B]_N t\Delta \tag{4.166}$$

where $[k]_N$ are the components of the individual stiffness matrices which are assembled to give the master or global stiffness matrix $[K]$. (The superscript T stands for transpose. The transpose of a matrix simply contains the same matrix components written with the rows and columns transposed.)

If the forces are known, the deflection can be calculated from

$$\{\delta\} = [K]^{-1}\{F'\} \tag{4.167}$$

where $[K]^{-1}$ denotes the inverse of $[K]$.

4.5.5 Application of FEM to Plasticity [4.28]

Elastoplastic behavior in one dimension is characterized by an initial elastic material response on to which a linearly plastic deformation is superimposed after a certain level of stress has been reached, as shown in Fig. 3.1(g). Plastic deformation is essentially irreversible on unloading. The onset of plastic deformation or yielding is governed by a yield criterion [4.32].

As discussed elsewhere, yielding or plastic flow occurs when the system of stresses satisfies a general yield criterion such as

$$F'(\boldsymbol{\sigma}, H) = 0 \tag{4.168}$$

where H is the strainhardening (or softening) parameter. (The boldface print indicates that the symbol represents a vector or matrix such as in two dimensions

$$\boldsymbol{\sigma} = \left\{ \begin{array}{c} \sigma_x \\ \sigma_y \\ \sigma_z \end{array} \right\} \tag{4.169}$$

where in tensor notation, $\boldsymbol{\sigma} = \sigma_{ij}$.) The yield condition can be expressed by Eq. (4.168) visualized as a surface in n-dimensional stress space with the position of the surface dependent on the instantaneous value of the parameter H.

With reference to Fig. 4.48, the strainhardening parameter H given in Eq. (4.168) may be defined as

$$H' = \frac{d\sigma}{d\varepsilon_p} = \frac{d\sigma}{d\varepsilon - d\varepsilon_e} = \frac{E_T}{1 - E_T / E} \tag{4.170}$$

where E_T is the slope of the plastic portion of the stress-strain curve, which may be called the tangential modulus.

The plastic strain increment $d\varepsilon_p$ can be related to the yield surface by

$$d\varepsilon = \lambda \frac{\partial F'}{\partial \boldsymbol{\sigma}} \tag{4.171}$$

where λ is a proportionality constant.

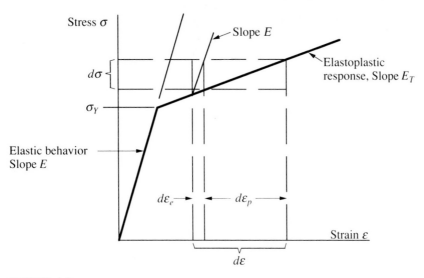

FIGURE 4.48
Elastic, linear strainhardening stress-strain behavior for the uniaxial case. (See Fig. 3.1(d).) [4.32].

The total incremental strain therefore consists of the elastic and plastic strain portions as follows:

$$d\varepsilon = d\varepsilon_e + d\varepsilon_p \tag{4.172}$$

Equation (4.172) may also be written as

$$d\varepsilon_{ij} = d\varepsilon_{ij}^e + d\varepsilon_{ij}^p \tag{4.173}$$

and

$$d\{\varepsilon\} = d\{\varepsilon\}^e + d\{\varepsilon\}^p \tag{4.174}$$

where e and p indicate elastic and plastic strain.

Since the elastic strain increments are related to the elastic stress increments by the symmetric matrix $\mathbf{D}$, the total strain increment can be expressed as

$$d\varepsilon = \mathbf{D}^{-1}\,d\boldsymbol{\sigma} + \frac{\partial F'}{\partial \boldsymbol{\sigma}}\lambda \tag{4.175}$$

When plastic flow occurs, the stress state is on the yield surface given by Eq. (4.168), which can be continuously varying depending on H.

Differentiating Eq. (4.168), one can write

$$dF' = \frac{\partial F'}{\partial \sigma_1}\,d\sigma_1 + \frac{\partial F'}{\partial \sigma_2}\,d\sigma_2 + \cdots + \frac{\partial F'}{\partial H}\,dH = 0 \tag{4.176}$$

or

$$\left\{\frac{\partial F'}{\partial \boldsymbol{\sigma}}\right\}^T d\sigma - A\lambda = 0 \tag{4.177}$$

in which the following substitution is made

$$A = -\frac{\partial F'}{\partial H} dH \frac{1}{\lambda} \tag{4.178}$$

When employing the Levy-Mises equations (2.73) and (2.78), it can be shown that

$$\frac{\partial F'}{\partial \sigma} = \frac{3}{2\bar{\sigma}} \{\sigma\}^T \tag{4.179}$$

where $A = n$, the slope of the $\bar{\sigma}-\bar{\varepsilon}$ curve. Equations (4.175) and (4.177) can be written in a single symmetric matrix form as

$$\begin{Bmatrix} d\varepsilon \\ 0 \end{Bmatrix} = \begin{bmatrix} D^{-1} & \dfrac{\partial F'}{\partial \sigma} \\ \left(\dfrac{\partial F'}{\partial \sigma}\right)^T & -A \end{bmatrix} \begin{Bmatrix} d\sigma \\ \lambda \end{Bmatrix} \tag{4.180}$$

The constant λ can be eliminated, which results in an explicit expansion that determines the stress change in contracted matrix notation as

$$d\sigma = D^*_{e,p} \, d\varepsilon \tag{4.181}$$

where

$$D^*_{e,p} = D - D\left\{\frac{\partial F'}{\partial \sigma}\right\}\left\{\frac{\partial F'}{\partial \sigma}\right\}^T \cdot D \cdot \left[A + \left\{\frac{\partial F'}{\partial \sigma}\right\}^T D \left\{\frac{\partial F'}{\partial \sigma}\right\}\right]^{-1} \tag{4.182}$$

The combined elasticity-plasticity matrix, $D^*_{e,p}$ is analogous to the elasticity matrix D in elastic analysis given in Eq. (4.154).

4.5.6 FEM Computer Programs [4.28]

4.5.6.1 ELEMENTARY MODULAR FEM COMPUTER PROGRAM. Many complex and efficient programs are available for finite element method analysis. A number of these are proprietary such as ANSYS [4.33]. The more complex the program, the more difficult it usually is to update. The R. L. Taylor elementary modular FEM computer program to be discussed very briefly here is a relatively simple, flexible one, in which various modules can be changed or added at will [4.28].

A finite element computer program in general can be separated into two basic parts: (1) the data input module and preprocessor; and (2) the solution and output modules or postprocessor to carry out the actual analysis.

To have a generally applicable finite element computer program, a macro programming language may be used, which is associated with a set of compact subprograms each designed to compute one or only a few basic steps in the finite element solution process such as to form a global stiffness matrix, solve equations, print results, etc.

The solution of a finite element problem using the above computer program begins with a sketch of a probable mesh covering the region to be analyzed. In

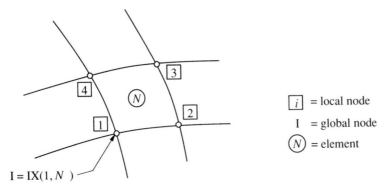

$I = IX(1, N)$

FIGURE 4.49
Typical labeling of a typical four-node element [4.28].

sketching the mesh, the type (triangular, quadrilateral, etc.) and order (linear, quadratic, etc.) must be taken into consideration.

After a sketch of a mesh is prepared, the elements and nodes are designated as illustrated in Fig. 4.49. The user of the program can then proceed with the preparation of the data for the program.

An analysis requires at least the following:

1. A coordinate data set which follows a macro-command such as COOR and which contains the mode number, the generator increment, and the value of the coordinates for the nodes.
2. An element data set which follows a macro-command such as ELEM and which contains the element number, material set number, and the sequence of modes connected to the element.
3. A material data set which follows a macro-command such as MATE and which contains the material set number, element type number, and the alphanumeric information to be outputted.

In addition, most analyses require specifications of nodal boundary restraint conditions (BOUN), the corresponding nodal force or displacement values (FORC), and nodal temperature (TEMP).

The data input module must transmit sufficient information to the other modules so that the problem can be solved.

One of the first steps is to establish the nodal coordinate input data and to prepare it for inputting to the computer. For a very large mesh, the preparation of each piece of mesh data would be very tedious and time-consuming; so a program should have the capability to generate much of nodal coordinate data. For example, certain key, easily-established boundary points may be inputted, so that the program can then generate by some scheme, such as linear interpolation, all of the required interior points.

Each element has material properties associated with it, which must be entered. For example, for a linear isotropic elastic material, the modulus of elasticity E and Poisson's ratio ν describe the material for an isothermal state.

In most solutions, several elements have the same material properties, so that it is not necessary to specify the properties for each element individually, but they need to be specified only once. In case of a solution involving temperature dependence, the temperature must be entered.

The listing of the above finite element Fortran computer program may be broken down into three routines:

1. The control and data input modules, which provide (1) for control of the problem solution, the data input, and the mesh parameters and arrays, (2) the generation of missing data by linear interpolation, and (3) the monitoring of the available memory.

2. The solution and output modules, which control problem solutions and output algorithms by specifying macro commands.

3. The element routines such as for linear elastic–linear strainhardening, in which we are interested, linear heat transfer, and a steady state fluid flow element. The element routine for linear analysis inputs the material properties, computes the stiffness parameter, and shape functions.

4.5.6.2 GENERALIZED MODULAR PROGRAM FOR NONLINEAR ANALYSIS.
The modular scheme shown in Fig. 4.50 has been presented [4.32], in which separate subroutines are employed to perform the various operations required in nonlinear finite element analysis. Generally each program consists of nine modules, each with a distinct operational function. Each module in turn is composed of one or more subroutines relevant only to its own needs and, in some cases, of subroutines which are common to several modules. Control of the modules is accomplished by the main or master segment. The main purpose of this segment is to call the above modules and to control the load increments and the iteration procedure according to the solution algorithm being employed and the convergence rate of the solution process.

4.5.6.3 ALPID PROGRAM. A user-oriented, general purpose program (see end of Sec. 4.5.1) called ALPID (Analysis of Large Plastic Incremental Deformation) [4.34], has been presented to improve computational efficiency. The main features of the program include (1) use of higher-order elements, (2) general description of the die and of the automation of die boundary condition which enable the user to use any number of arbitrarily shaped dies with different friction types and coefficients, and (3) automatic initial guess generation by which input data requirements are reduced to the level of those for simple elastic analysis and the solution efficiencies are improved markedly.

The FEM code of ALPID is capable of handling both rigid–plastic and rigid–viscoplastic materials, and it can treat both constant friction shear stress or Coulomb type friction at the tool-material interface. The program uses higher-

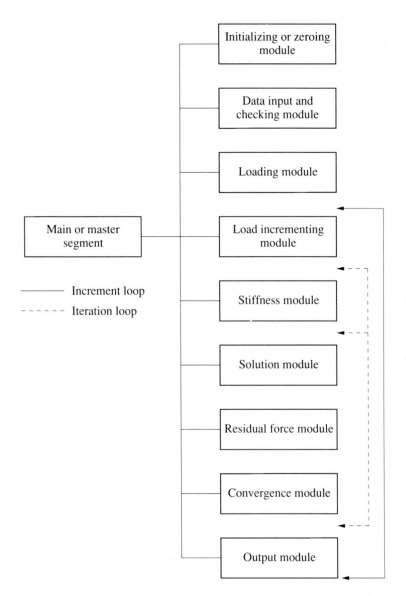

FIGURE 4.50
Program modules for performing the various operations in nonlinear finite element analysis [4.32].

order elements, in addition to linear elements, such as quadratic and cubic elements of the lagrangian and serendipity families. The basis of this program is the variational principle functional for rigid-viscoplastic material. The rigid-viscoplastic formulation used here is just an extension of the rigid-plastic formulation used previously.

The constitutive equation for the rigid–viscoplastic finite element formulation used here may be represented by

$$\sigma'_{ij} = \frac{2}{3} \frac{\bar{\sigma}}{\dot{\bar{\varepsilon}}} \dot{\varepsilon}_{ij} \qquad (4.183)$$

where σ'_{ij} is a component of deviatoric stress, $\dot{\varepsilon}_{ij} = \frac{1}{2}(v_{i,j} + v_{j,i})$ is a component of strain rate, v_i is a velocity component, (,) denotes differentiation, and $\bar{\sigma}$ and $\dot{\bar{\varepsilon}}$ are the effective stress and the effective strain rate, respectively. The strain rate, of course, would be a factor in the analysis of strain-rate sensitive sheetmetal.

The effective stress, $\bar{\sigma}$, for rigid–viscoplastic deformation is in general a function of both the total strain and the strain rate, whereas for rigid–plastic deformation it is a function of strain only.

The variational principle functional (see Sec. 4.5.1) for rigid–viscoplastic material can be written as

$$\Phi = \int_V E(\dot{\varepsilon}^*) \, dV - \int_{S_F} \boldsymbol{F} \cdot \boldsymbol{v}^* \, dS + \int_V \frac{1}{2} K(\dot{\varepsilon}_{KK})^2 \, dV \qquad (4.184)$$

where the starred quantities are kinematically admissible ones, and where the following symbols have the following connotations:

Φ = variational functional related to the total potential energy
dV = volume increment undergoing plastic deformation
S_F = surface area of the body on which the surface force vector $\boldsymbol{F}$ acts
$\boldsymbol{F}$ = external force vector acting on the surface of the body (note that F and T are used interchangeably for the traction forces)
v^* = kinematically admissible velocity vector of a surface point
dS = area increment of the external surface of the body
$\dot{\varepsilon}^*$ = strain rate tensor
$\bar{\sigma}$ = effective stress (given below), which is a function of the total effective strain (2.59a) and the effective strain rate (2.59b) given typically by

$$\bar{\sigma} = \frac{2}{3} \sigma_Y(\bar{\varepsilon}) \left[1 + \left(\frac{\dot{\varepsilon}}{\gamma} \right)^m \right] \qquad (4.185)$$

where $\sigma_Y(\bar{\varepsilon})$ is the static yield stress, and γ and m are material constants.

The first term on the right of Eq. (4.184) represents the distortional strain energy, the second term represents the rate of work due to the external tractions (forces), and the third term represents the rate of strain energy.

Here the work function $E(\dot{\varepsilon})$ can be expressed as

$$E(\dot{\varepsilon}) = \int_0^{\dot{\varepsilon}} \bar{\sigma} \, d\dot{\bar{\varepsilon}} \qquad (4.186)$$

and K in Eq. (4.184) is a large positive constant which penalizes the dilational strain rate component. It can be readily shown that the mean stress is $\sigma_m = K\varepsilon_{kk}$. The above functional reduces to that of rigid–plastic material if $\bar{\sigma}$ is a function of $\bar{\varepsilon}$ only. If Eq. (4.185) is substituted into Eq. (4.186) for $\bar{\sigma}$, the term $E(\bar{\varepsilon})$ will also contain the effective strain $\bar{\varepsilon}$.

The discretization of this functional follows the standard procedure of the FEM. If one substitutes the distribution functions and the strain rate expression into Eq. (4.184), the variational functional Φ becomes a set of nonlinear algebraic equations with unknown constants u_i, which are the velocity components of the nodal points. The solution of the highly nonlinear algebraic simultaneous equations is obtained iteratively by the Newton-Raphson method.

ALPID is supported by an interactive graphic program called FEMGRA, for pre- and postprocessing of FEM analysis. Both of these programs are general purpose programs, which can be used for the analysis of two-dimensional forming problems without any restrictions on the geometries of the dies and workpiece. The structures and the interactions of the two programs are shown in Fig. 4.51.

FEMGRA is capable of displaying the load-displacement relation, the FEM grid distortion, the relative position of the dies, the velocity vector fields, and the contour plots of stress, strain, and strain rates including their effective quantities at any stage of deformation. The plots obtained by FEMGRA can be displayed either on a CRT terminal for quick viewing or on a CALCOMP plotter as hard copies.

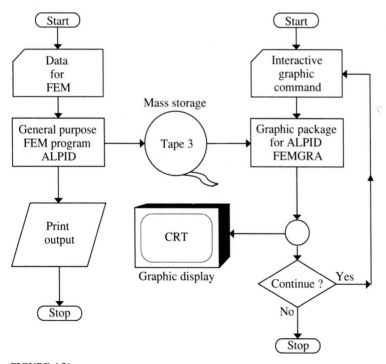

FIGURE 4.51
Structure and interaction of Analysis of Large Plastic Incremental Deformation program (ALPID) and interactive FEM Graphics program (FEMGRA) [4.34].

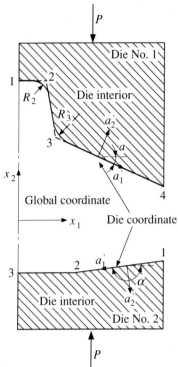

FIGURE 4.52
Description of an arbitrarily shaped spike forging die and the sequential die surface coordinate system [4.34].

The implementation of the die boundary conditions is based on a formulation that allows the unified treatments of the die boundary conditions without the die shape restrictions. The die shape is described by the coordinates of the corner points and the associated corner radii in sequential order, as shown in Fig. 4.52.

An example solution obtained by the use of the ALPID program is shown in Fig. 4.52, in which metal is extruded up into the die cavity in so-called spike forging. Figure 4.53(a) shows the undeformed workpiece geometry with a 16-element grid system, when the top and bottom dies are in their initial positions. Figure 4.53(b) shows the deformed grid distortion at a die stroke of $0.50H_0$. The calculations in this case were made for a Ti alloy at 954°C (1750°F), a shear factor of 0.3, die velocity of 25.4 mm/s (1.0 in/s), and at steps of 0.02 times the original workpiece height, H_0. Figure 4.54 shows the effective strain contour lines plotted by FEMGRA.

4.5.6.4 FINITE ELEMENT ANALYSES OF METALWORKING PROCESSES [4.35].
4.5.6.4.1 Introduction. In Sec. 4.5.4 the finite element method (FEM) was applied to elastic problems, and in Sec. 4.5.5 it was extended to elastic–plastic problems, where large scale plastic flow predominates. In each case, it was assumed that a large mainframe computer was available. As a matter of fact disadvantages, that were cited in Sec. 4.5.1 for FEM, were that a great amount

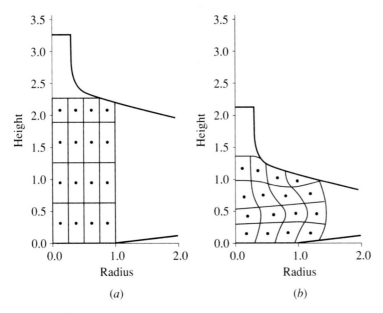

FIGURE 4.53
Axisymmetric spike forging of a titanium alloy. (*a*) Undeformed, initial, 16-element FEM grid; (*b*) distorted grid after a die stroke $0.50H_0$, where H_0 is the initial billet height [4.34].

of computer time and the need of a large computer were required. The high capital cost and the computer-time cost of these large computers has restricted finite element plasticity program development. Research, however, has been done (1) to design more efficient programs to reduce the computer time and (2) to adapt the FEM to smaller computers. The application of the FEM to microcomputers has been furthered by their rapid recent development. Although the computer time is significantly longer on the microcomputer, the turnaround time may be significantly less, coupled with acceptable accuracy.

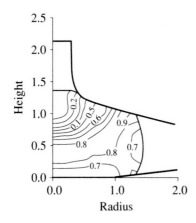

FIGURE 4.54
Effective strain contour lines plotted of a spike forging by the FEMGRA program for a die stroke of $0.5H_0$ [4.34].

4.5.6.4.2 FEM in metalworking using a mainframe computer [4.35]. The first stage in FEM is to input all initial data, i.e., the mesh details, the constitutive relationship, and the boundary conditions. The second stage, the processing part of the program, involves establishing for each element the stress-strain matrix [D] and the strain-displacement matrix [B], so that the local stiffness matrix for an element $[k]_e$ may be evaluated using the following equation:

$$[k]_e = [B]^T[D][B]V \qquad (4.187)$$

where V is the element volume.

The global stiffness matrix [K] must then be determined to the form of a banded matrix, and the simultaneous equations solved to obtain the incremental displacement $\{\Delta\delta\}$ from

$$\{\Delta\delta\} = [K]^{-1}\{\Delta F\} \qquad (4.188)$$

[See Eqs. (4.163) and (4.164) for the evaluation of the stiffness matrix for the elastic case and Eq. (4.166) for the corresponding master or global matrix, which are analogous to Eqs. (4.187) and (4.188) for the plastic case. The thickness t is replaced here with the volume V, and δ and F' are replaced by the incremental values $\Delta\delta$ and ΔF.]

Figure 4.55 shows the metal flow pattern as predicted by FEM for the axial compression (upset forging) of a cylinder with flat, parallel, overhanging platens (dies) with (a) low and (b) high friction. To solve this problem, 842 elements were used and about 500 nodal points, which required about 2.5 s of computing time per increment of deformation with the use of a mainframe (CDC 7600) computer.

A much smaller number of elements must be used, so that a microcomputer can cope with this problem. A finite element model containing only eight elements was therefore processed on the mainframe and a microcomputer as described later. The mesh, using constant strain axisymmetric triangles and representing one quadrant of a meridian plane, is shown in Fig. 4.56. This mesh was run on both computers, so that a comparison of the results could be made.

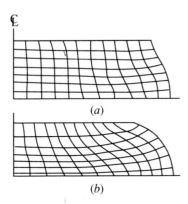

(a)

(b)

FIGURE 4.55
Distorted grids for upset forging of a cylinder with (a) low friction; and (b) high friction, as predicted by use of FEM elastic-plastic equations for an 842-element mesh [4.35].

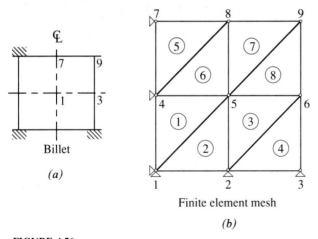

FIGURE 4.56
(*a*) Meridian plane of a solid cylindrical billet in compression; and (*b*) a finite eight-element mesh representing one quadrant of a meridian plane [4.35].

4.5.6.4.3 Restructuring of the finite element program for use with a micro-computer. As the geometry of the billet and the distribution of the material properties are changing nonlinearly throughout the deformation process, an incremental type of analysis must be used. An elastic–plastic finite element technique is used here. The flowchart, shown in Fig. 4.57, illustrates the stages into which the finite element technique is divided for plasticity problems.

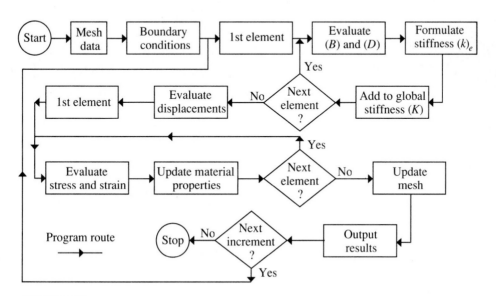

FIGURE 4.57
Flowchart for a FORTRAN finite element program used on a mainframe (CDC 7600) computer [4.35].

The original Fortran program, on which the software for the microcomputer was based, was rewitten in Basic and restructured to accommodate the different operating system of the microcomputer. The flowchart for the microcomputer is shown in Fig. 4.58.

The great limitation for the use of a microcomputer in finite element analysis is the small random access memory (RAM). A small computer may be used by using a much smaller number of elements and much longer computer run times. The example shown in Fig. 4.55 of axisymmetric upsetting was processed on a small microcomputer, a Tektronix 4051 microcomputer possessing only a 32K random access memory supplemented with a 300K data cartridge. To operate the microcomputer with maximum efficiency of RAM usage, any part of the program that has been used, but not required for further processing was immediately deleted from the memory of the machine as is illustrated by the flowchart in Fig. 4.58.

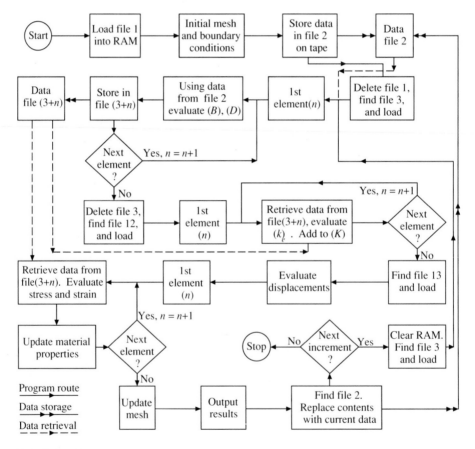

FIGURE 4.58
Flowchart for a Basic finite element program used on a TEKTRONIX microcomputer [4.35].

The cartridge contained the complete program for the specified upsetting problem, which consisted of a series of files, some with subroutines equivalent to those of the original program and other empty files, ready to receive data at a specified point in the run. In the example used here, the number of empty files was set equal to the number of elements in the mesh. One file contained all the information necessary to set up the computer model. This initial generation of data may be accomplished with a small predetermined program or interactively. In either case, the data must be transferred to a specified file location loaded into the RAM. This file contains the instruction to construct the $[B]$ and $[D]$ matrices for each element. This file must therefore recall the relevant mesh and property data from the tape, evaluate the above matrices, then store this information on the tape at predetermined locations. This process is continued until all the elements in the mesh have been considered, at which point the RAM is cleared. The program is then directed to the next file, and after retrieving the data previously set up for each element in turn evaluates the element stiffness matrix $[k]_e$, and finally the global stiffness matrix $[K]$. Once again this information is transferred back to the tape and the RAM cleared. The final file is then loaded for retrieval of the stiffness matrix. The displacement of each nodal point is evaluated, again using the Gauss elimination method, from which the strain and the stress in each element are determined. The material properties and mesh geometry are then updated ready for the next increment. Although this approach has been described as one of interchange between machine and cartridge, at no time is any of the program detail deleted from the tape.

This microcomputer is on the small end of the microcomputer scale. With the recent developments in microcomputers with larger and larger memories and with increased speeds, this approach is made more and more viable.

4.5.6.4.4 Computer results. The results of the 8-element mesh are shown in Fig. 4.59. The decimal fractions give the predicted strains (those in parentheses are for the microcomputer). The grid in Fig. 4.59(a) for zero friction shows homogeneous deformation throughout the billet without any redundant deformation. (This terminology is discussed in Sec. 2.2.13.) When the interface friction is zero, the effective strain can be calculated by taking the natural log of the ratio of the initial height to the current height, which for a 20 percent reduction would be 0.22314. The strains in Fig. 4.59(a) predicted by the mainframe show a range of values between 0.2217 and 0.2223, giving a maximum error of -0.645 percent. For the microcomputer, the predicted strain is 0.2209 in each element, giving an error of -1 percent.

As is discussed elsewhere, with high friction, the pattern of deformation is quite different. The billet material in contact with the platens is prevented from sliding, which results in a conical zone of rigid material beneath the punch and a barreling on the free cylindrical surface. These results are clearly identifiable on the earlier results shown in Fig. 4.55, but are much less obvious with the much smaller number of elements in the 8-element mesh shown in Fig. 4.59(b). However, the barreling on the free surface can be seen and the high strains, that are evident

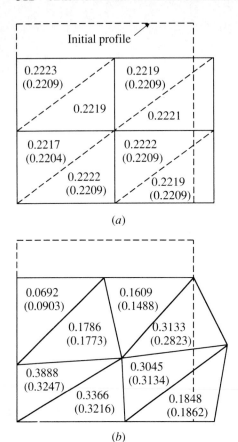

(a)

(b)

FIGURE 4.59

Distorted grids and generalized strain distribution values at a 20 percent reduction in height for (a) zero friction and homogeneous deformation; and for (b) high friction. Unenclosed results are for a CDC 7600 computer and results enclosed in parentheses are for a TEKTRONIX microcomputer, both for an eight-element mesh [4.35].

on a diagonal band from the top right corner to the center of the billet, are clearly in general accordance with the earlier theoretical results and with experimental results as discussed elsewhere in a number of places in this book. The predicted strains, using the 842 elements, for high friction conditions as compared to experimental results, were found to correlate within 4 percent. Both the predicted strains and the work done in deforming the billet, from which the forging force may be calculated, compare closely in each of the three cases.

In summary, although the results from each computer displayed a good correlation, the major difference was in the computing times (0.03 s per increment of deformation for eight elements versus 270 s). The large number of tape movements and file transfers contributed to a large part of the computer time used on the microcomputer.

4.6 SYSTEMS APPROACH—PROCESS MODELING

Materials processes are generally so complex that it is impossible to define them in simple relationships involving only one or two parameters. Multi-parameter models must be created to deal with them in design, analysis, and control. To

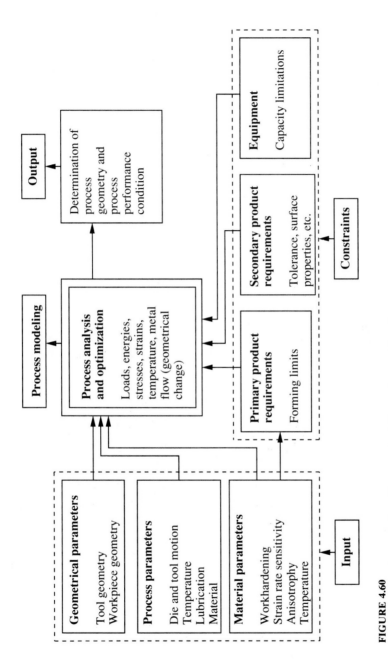

FIGURE 4.60
Block diagram of an overview of process modeling and control [4.37].

313

many, such a scientific approach connotes a mathematical model which permits, for example, the prediction and description of the flow fields that occur during metalforming as a function of materials properties, initial and final geometry, die design, temperature effects, heat transfer, rate of deformation, lubrication, etc. For most industrial processes such mathematical descriptions can be extremely complex, and closed form solutions are not attainable. Approximate solutions must be used that are feasible on a relatively small computer [4.36].

Process modeling may be defined as methods of analyzing and solving materials processing problems by use of mathematical modeling and computer simulation for the purpose of designing, optimizing, and controlling materials processes by use of a combination of scientific and engineering principles and empirical data.

In general, the goals of materials processing are:

1. To achieve the desired geometry (size, shape, and tolerance) of a part or component with adequate defect control
2. To develop a controlled microstructure to yield the desired properties and performance in service
3. To optimize the economic aspects of production [4.36]

In the design and application of a materials process, it must be examined critically both globally and locally. An overall view of process modeling is shown in the block diagram for process design and control in Fig. 4.60 [4.37].

The modeling of forming processes requires the consideration of the process as a system. The application of the system approach to massive or bulk deformation, for example, is illustrated (1) in Fig. 4.61 as applied to rolling and (2) in Fig. 4.62 as applied to a single-blow impression die forging operation [4.38].

This system approach allows the study of the input-output relationships and the effect of process variables upon product quality and process economics. The significant variables of a massive forming process are given in Table 4.2. As

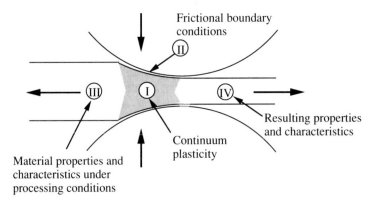

FIGURE 4.61
Rolling as an example of a bulk deformation processing system [3.15], [4.38].

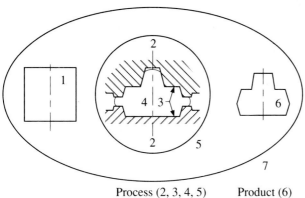

Process (2, 3, 4, 5)   Product (6)

FIGURE 4.62
One-blow impression die forging as an example of a deformation processing system consisting of following entities: (1) billet, (2) tooling, (3) tool-material interface, (4) deformation zone, (5) forming equipment, (6) product, and (7) plant and environment [4.38].

TABLE 4.2
Significant variables in a deformation process [4.38]

Billet material	Tooling	Conditions at tool-material interface
Flow stress as function of strain rate, temperature and microstructure (constitutive equations)	Geometry of tools	Lubricant type and temperature
Workability as function of strain rate, temperature and microstructure (forming limit curves)	Surface conditions	Insulation and cooling characteristics of the interface layer
Surface conditions	Material/heat treatment/hardness	Lubricity and friction shear stress
Thermal/physical properties	Temperature	Characteristics related to lubricant application and removal
Initial conditions (composition, temperature, history/microstructure)	Stiffness and accuracy	
Effect of changes in microstructure and composition upon flow stress and workability		

Deformation zone	Equipment used	Product
Deformation mechanics, model used for analysis	Speed/production rate	Geometry
Metal flow, velocities, strain rates, strains (kinematics)	Force/energy capabilities	Dimensional accuracy/tolerances
Stresses (variation during deformation)	Rigidity and accuracy	Surface finish
Temperature (heat generation and transfer)		Microstructure, mechanical and metallurgical properties

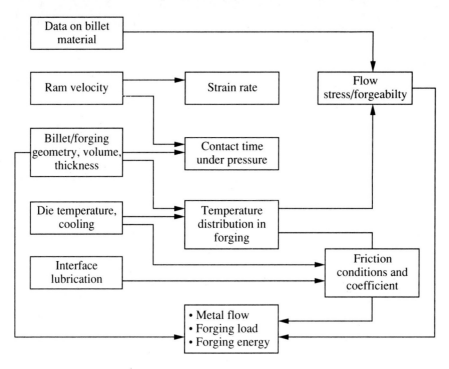

FIGURE 4.63
Block diagram showing the interaction of the most significant system variables in impression die forging [4.38].

an example, the interaction of the most significant process variables in die forging is shown in Fig. 4.63 in a simplified manner. In this example, the direction of metal flow, the magnitude of deformation, and the temperature greatly influence the properties of the forged components. The metal flow determines the mechanical properties related to local deformation, and the formation of defects such as cracks or folds on the external surface or interior. The local metal flow is in turn influenced by the process variables [4.38].

4.7 COUPLED ANALYSIS OF PLASTIC DEFORMATION AND HEAT TRANSFER [4.39]

4.7.1 Introduction

In industrial deformation processes, most of the deformation energy is transformed into thermal energy, which manifests itself as heat generation. This heat generation causes the temperature to increase within the workpiece and results in a varying thermomechanical behavior of the material. In an inhomogeneous deformation process, the external friction losses also raise the temperature at the die-workpiece interface. Therefore, the influence of these temperature increases on the behavior of the material and on the load of deformation must be taken into account in any mathematical simulation.

The thermomechanical behavior of the material is treated here by means of a coupled analysis using the finite element method (FEM) for the plastic deformation analysis and the finite difference method (FDM) for the heat transfer analysis. The processes of heat generation and heat conduction are calculated separately using FEM for the former and FDM for the latter. By combining the finite element and the finite difference methods in this manner, one uses less computer memory than by a coupled analysis of FEM alone. The method of calculation presented here is carried out by means of a computer program called the *F*inite Element *A*nalysis of *R*igid-Plastic *M*etal Forming (FARM). This program deals with both the steady and unsteady state.

FEM has been discussed at some length in Sec. 4.5. A brief discussion is made here of FDM as applied to heat conduction, as an example, showing how the FDM numerical solution relates to the analytical one.

In order to circumvent the mathematical difficulties that preclude a useful solution of an analytical equation such as for heat flow, a numerical method may be used as a good approximation. For an analytical solution the differential equation, which is valid for every point in the conduction region, is solved for the temperature distribution throughout the region. The numerical methods use, on the other hand, an algebraic equation that applies to only a network of points in the conduction region, to estimate the temperature at these points as shown in Fig. 4.64(a).

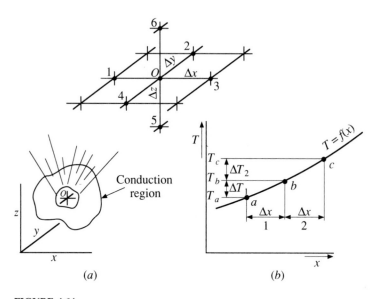

FIGURE 4.64
(a) Coordinate system for the time stepping scheme; (b) iteration method for calculating the stresses and temperature fields [4.40].

In FARM, the finite element model has two types of linear elements: triangular and quadrilateral. The latter is a combination of triangular elements. The use of linear elements means that a linear function for velocities for plastic metal flow is used and the mean stress and strain rates are constant in each element. This method analyzes the plastic deformation of an unsteady state (transient) process by using several small steady state (i.e., invariant with time) deformation steps. After each step, the finite element mesh is updated by new nodal coordinates calculated by multiplying the velocity by the time increment. In this way, the material flow and the stress and strain fields are determined step-by-step from the beginning to the end of the forming process. The shear stress τ due to external friction, is calculated on the basis of the constant friction factor concept: $\tau = m\sigma/\sqrt{3}$, discussed elsewhere.

The heat generation by external friction losses and redundant deformation, as discussed later, and the concomitant heat transfer are analyzed in each time

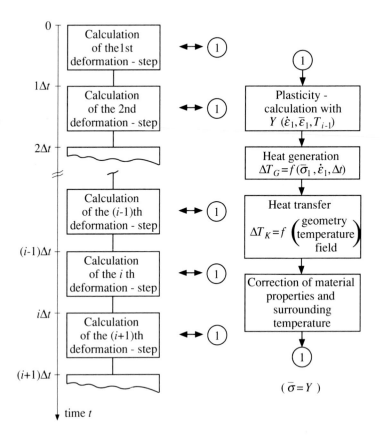

FIGURE 4.65
Iteration scheme for the calculation of a temperature field during an unsteady forming process [4.39].

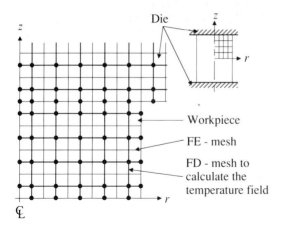

FIGURE 4.66

Meshes of one quadrant for the FDM and FEM analysis at the workpiece and the workpiece-die interface [4.39].

increment to obtain the temperature distribution. The material behavior is continually updated just subsequent to each predicted temperature field. The FDM is modified in such a way as to be compatible with the FARM program.

Quantities such as stresses, forces, and displacements are predicted at the fixed points designating the nodes and elements by the FEM after a time step of Δt. The resulting generation of heat is computed from the expended forming and frictional forces for the relevant time step. The results of this computation show an inhomogeneous temperature field with a time dependent temperature compensation, which is analyzed for the same time step Δt by the FDM. By use of a constitutive equation containing the relationship expressed by Eq. (2.133): $\bar{\sigma} = \bar{\sigma}(\varepsilon, \dot{\varepsilon}, T, S)$, the coupling of the mechanical deformation with temperature is achieved as shown in Fig. 4.65.

For the heat transfer calculations, it is necessary to assign the temperatures of the elements to discrete reference points, which are taken at the midpoints of the finite element polygons. To calculate the temperature at the boundary of the workpiece, additional points are needed at the boundary such as the midpoints at the sides of the elements. Figure 4.66 shows the mesh structures on an axial plane for the FEM and the FDM for the axisymmetric upsetting of a cylinder.

Both the FEM and the FDM used here have many numerical simplifications in order to save computer time. The FEM, for example, includes a rigid–plastic material model, linear elements, single point integration [4.39].

4.7.2 Generalized Heat Conduction Equation

The three-dimensional heat-flow (Poisson) equation for a homogeneous, isotropic material with constant properties is

$$\frac{\partial^2 T}{\partial x^2} + \frac{\partial^2 T}{\partial y^2} + \frac{\partial^2 T}{\partial z^2} + \frac{\dot{q}}{k} = \frac{1}{\alpha} \frac{\partial T}{\partial t} \tag{4.189}$$

where $\alpha = \text{thermal diffusitivity} = \dfrac{\text{thermal conductivity}}{(\text{density})(\text{specific heat capacity})}$ m^2/s

$T = \text{temperature, }^\circ\text{C}$

$t = \text{time, s}$

$\dot{q} = \text{volumetric heat generation, W/m}^3$

The volumetric heat generation $\dot{q}$ in the above equation accounts for the temperature rise due to deformation. By specifying the boundary conditions, one completes the problem statement. It should be noted that the friction energy is dissipated at the boundary between the workpiece and tool. One should consult any standard heat transfer book for additional discussion of the above equations [4.40].

It is necessary to convert Eq. (4.189) into a system of algebraic equations for a numerical solution. This conversion is accomplished by obtaining expressions for the second spatial derivative and the first-order time derivatives in terms of nodal temperatures.

The second-order derivative can be estimated in terms of six nodal temperatures adjacent to node O at temperature T_0, as can be seen in Fig. 4.64(a) [4.41].

An indication of the derivatives of the above expressions is shown in terms of the discussion that follows. The central estimate based on both the right and the left intervals, 1 and 2, identified in Fig. 4.64(b) is

$$\frac{dT}{dx} \cong \frac{\Delta T_1 + \Delta T_2}{2\Delta x} \cong \frac{T_c - T_a}{2\Delta x} \tag{4.190}$$

Two "one-sided" estimates are possible: one based on the backward interval in x, 1, called the *backward difference*, and one based on the forward interval in x, 2, called the *forward difference*, as follows:

$$\frac{dT}{dx} \cong \frac{\Delta T_1}{\Delta x} \cong \frac{T_b - T_a}{\Delta_x} \tag{4.191}$$

and

$$\frac{dT}{dx} \cong \frac{\Delta T_2}{\Delta x} \cong \frac{T_c - T_b}{\Delta x} \tag{4.192}$$

From Fig. 4.64, if values T_a, T_b, and T_c are replaced with T_1, T_2, and T_3, the second derivative used to replace the derivatives in Eq. (4.189) is [4.41]

$$\frac{\partial^2 T}{\partial x^2} \cong \frac{(T_3 - T_0)/\Delta x - (T_0 - T_1)/\Delta x}{\Delta x} \cong \frac{T_1 - T_3 - 2T_0}{(\Delta x)^2} \tag{4.193}$$

In terms of multiple subscripts as shown in i, j, k for the x, y, z coordinates, respectively, the equations for the first-order derivatives for the forward, central, and backward finite difference approximations are, respectively [4.41],

$$\left(\frac{\partial T}{\partial x}\right)_{i,j,k} = \frac{T_{i+1,j,k} - T_{i,j,k}}{\Delta x} \tag{4.194a}$$

$$\left(\frac{\partial T}{\partial x}\right)_{i,j,k} = \frac{T_{i+1,j,k} - T_{i-1,j,k}}{\Delta x} \tag{4.194b}$$

$$\left(\frac{\partial T}{\partial x}\right)_{i,j,k} = \frac{T_{i,j,k} - T_{i-1,j,k}}{\Delta x} \tag{4.194c}$$

Similar expressions can be written for the y and z coordinates.

The order of the term that is neglected in the first and third of the above equations is Δx, and of the second equation is $(\Delta x)^2$.

The three-dimensional heat-flow equation can be approximated as above or more rigorously by use of a Taylor series expansion to give

$$\left(\frac{\partial^2 T}{\partial x^2}\right)_{i,j,k} = \frac{T_{i-1,j,k} - 2T_{i,j,k} + T_{i+1,j,k}}{(\Delta x)^2} \tag{4.195}$$

The order of the terms neglected in the above equation is $(\Delta x)^2$.

The time derivative may be expressed in an explicit or an implicit mode. Here, the implicit mode is used and is stated as follows:

$$\frac{\partial T}{\partial t} = \frac{T_O^{t+\Delta t} - T_O^t}{\Delta t} = f(T^{t+\Delta t}) \tag{4.196}$$

where the function f contains the temperature terms for the considered and adjacent nodes that are evaluated at the future time of $t + \Delta t$, where Δt is the time step.

The overall change in temperature of each node is due to (1) the heat generated due to external friction loss, (2) the heat generated due to plastic deformation, and (3) the heat transferred from each element. The heat transfer from the element occurs by conduction for interior elements and conduction, convection, and radiation for elements on the boundary surfaces. Each of these phenomena, affecting the calculation of the temperature of an element, is discussed below.

4.7.3 Numerical Solution of the Temperature Field

Analogous to Eq. (4.189), the temperature increase of element O is obtained from the energy balance as represented schematically in Fig. 4.67 as follows:

$$(\Delta \dot{Q}_f + \Delta \dot{Q}_D) + \Delta \dot{Q}_O = \Delta \dot{Q} = c\rho \, \Delta V_O \frac{\Delta T_O}{\Delta t} \tag{4.197}$$

where $\Delta \dot{Q}_f$ = rate of heat generated due to external friction
$\Delta \dot{Q}_D$ = rate of heat generated due to plastic deformation
$\Delta \dot{Q}_C$ = rate of heat transferred to element O from adjacent elements
c = specific heat capacity of the material
ρ = density of the material
V = volume of the element

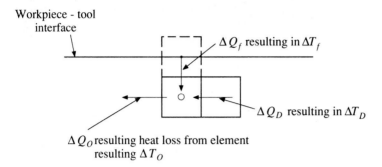

FIGURE 4.67
An approximate schematic diagram showing the energy balance for an element O.

The relationship for heat transfer can be obtained by establishing an energy balance by forward difference, taking both heat conduction and heat convection into consideration as shown in Fig. 4.68 and yielding the following generalized equation:

$$(\rho c)\,\Delta V_0\!\left(\frac{T_0^{\Delta t}-T_0}{\Delta t}\right)=\sum k_{Oj}(T_j^{\Delta t}-T_0^{\Delta t})+\Delta \dot{Q}_f+\Delta \dot{Q}_D \tag{4.198}$$

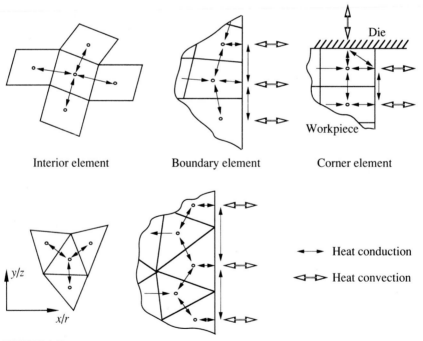

FIGURE 4.68
Scheme of a coupled analysis of plastic deformation and heat transfer [4.39].

where $T_O^{\Delta t}$ = temperature after time increment Δt, °C

V_O = volume of the element O, m^3

k_{Oj} = heat transfer conductors (factors) between the inner element O and adjacent elements, W/m^2-C

Expressions for $\Delta \dot{Q}_f$ and $\Delta \dot{Q}_D$ are given later.

The resulting three-dimensional equation will not be written here. However, equations such as the following in matrix notation are available:

$$[C]_t \frac{(\{T\}_{t+\Delta t} - \{T\}_t)}{\Delta t} = [K]_t \{T\}_{t+\Delta t} + \{F\}_t \qquad (4.199)$$

where $[C]$ is an n-by-n matrix for n nodes containing the functions of heat capacitance, $\{T\}$ is a column vector containing the temperatures for n nodes, $[K]$ is an n-by-n matrix containing the functions of thermal conductivity and convective boundary conditions, and $\{F\}$ is a column vector containing the functions of convective boundary conditions, heat flux boundary conditions, and internal heat generation terms. In expressing Eq. (4.199), an implicit scheme for the time derivative of temperature is used.

4.7.4 Calculation of Heat Generation

(1) The heat generation due to friction between the workpiece and the die (tool) is obtained from the following relations:

$$\Delta \dot{Q}_f = \frac{\Delta Q_f}{\Delta t} = \Delta \dot{W}_f = F \frac{\Delta s}{\Delta t} = \tau \, \Delta A \left(\frac{\Delta s}{\Delta t} \right) = \frac{m\sigma}{\sqrt{3}} \Delta A v \qquad (4.200)$$

where $\tau = m\sigma/\sqrt{3}$ and $v = \Delta s/\Delta t$.

With the use of Eq. (4.197), the temperature increase due to external friction, where the other heat transfer mechanisms are neglected, is estimated by

$$\Delta T_f = \frac{2m\sigma \, \Delta A v \, \Delta t}{\Delta V (c_w \rho_w + c_t \rho_t)\sqrt{3}} \qquad (4.201)$$

where

m = the constant friction factor (0.65)

σ = the flow stress of the material, N/m^2

v = slide velocity of the node at the workpiece-tool interface, m/s

ΔA = contact area increment, m^2

Δt = time increment, s

ΔV = volume of the friction element divided into two equal parts spanning the workpiece and the tool interface, m^3

c_w and c_t = specific heat capacities of the workpiece and tool materials, respectively, kJ/kg-C

ρ_w and ρ_t = densities of the workpiece and tool materials, respectively, kg/m^3

(Note that the product ρc in Eq. (4.197) is expressed by $\rho c = \rho_w c_w + \rho_t c_t$ when the element contains portions of the tool and the workpiece.)

(2) The heat generation due to dissipation of deformation energy is calculated as follows:

$$\Delta \dot{Q}_D = \frac{\Delta Q_D}{\Delta t} = \Delta \dot{W}_D = \eta \sigma \dot{\bar{\varepsilon}} \, \Delta V_w \qquad (4.202)$$

The resulting temperature increase, neglecting other heat transfer mechanisms, is

$$\Delta T_D = \eta \frac{\sigma \dot{\bar{\varepsilon}} \, \Delta t}{c_w \rho_w} \qquad (4.203)$$

where η = the thermal efficiency for conversion of mechanical energy to thermal energy ($0.85 \leq \eta \leq 0.95$)

$\dot{\bar{\varepsilon}}$ = the equivalent strain rate, s^{-1}

4.7.5   Results

This method was tested by analyzing the upsetting of a cylindrical billet (slug) of steel 20 mm (0.8 in) in diameter and 30 mm (1.2 in) in height for a reduction in height of 33 percent, which is divided into 10 deformation steps. The billet and tool were initially at an ambient temperature of 20°C (68°F). The upsetting process was simulated using a structure with 48 quadrilateral linear elements for performing the coupled analysis using FEM for plastic deformation and FDM for the heat transfer. Table 4.3 summarizes the computational parameters used for the calculations. The steel is equivalent to an AISI 1015 steel.

TABLE 4.3
Computation parameters for a coupled analysis of plastic deformation and heat transfer [4.39]

Workpiece	Dimension: $h_0/d_0 = 30/20$ mm/mm
	Density: 7.9 kg/dm³
	Specific heat capacity: 0.4772 kJ/kg-°C
	Heat conductivity coefficient: 36 W/m-°C
	Thermal efficiency: 0.865
	Initial temperature: 20°C
Contact layer	Contact conductance data: 4 kW/m²-°C
	Thickness: 0.001 mm
Air	Density: 0.001 kg/dm³
	Specific heat capacity: 0.24 kJ/kg-°C
	Heat transfer coefficient: 0.003 kW/m²-°C
Die	Density: 7.9 kg/dm³
	Specific heat capacity: 0.4772 kJ/kg-°C
	Heat conductivity coefficient: 19 W/m-°C
	Velocity: top die with 20 mm/s
	bottom die with 0 mm/s

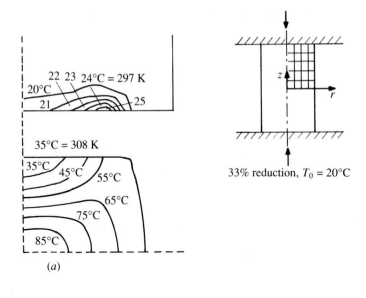

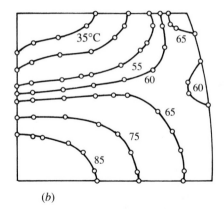

(b)

FIGURE 4.69
(a) Experimental results of Rebelo and Kobayashi [4.42] using coupled FEM for both the plastic deformation analysis and the heat transfer analysis with the following data: $\eta = 0.865$; $\bar{m} = 0.65$; $h_0/d_0 = 1.5$; and a die velocity of 10 mm/s. (b) Predicted temperature distribution after 33 percent reduction in height for considering the heat transfer during an upsetting test of a small cylindrical steel billet 20 mm in diameter by 30mm high for a reduction in height of 33 percent [4.39].

Figure 4.69(b) shows the isotherms on one-quarter of the central plane of the predicted temperature distribution as calculated by the FARM program. This figure shows excellent agreement with the more cumbersome Rebelo and Kobayashi coupled FEM method and good agreement with experimental data [4.42]. From Fig. 4.69 it can be seen that, for this relatively small cylinder (30×20 mm in diameter), compressed a relatively small amount (10 mm) at a relatively slow speed (20 mm/s), the maximum temperature rise is about 45°C (112°F). It should be noted that the greatest rise in temperature is at the center of the cylinder and the lowest is at the dead zone at the center of the tool-workpiece interface.

4.8 CONCLUSION

The application of the engineering approach utilizing the methods of analysis discussed in the foregoing may be done in the following steps [4.43]:

1. Select one of the methods of analysis such as the slab method, upper-bound method, slipline-field method, finite element method, etc.
2. Make a certain number of fundamental assumptions and idealizations depending on the material, the method of analysis selected, and the application being considered. Such assumptions and idealizations can, for example, be homogeneity, isotropy, incompressibility, yield criterion, flow rule, friction law, plane sections remain plane, plane strain, perfectly plastic material, rigid tools, etc. (Some of these decisions may be made for the engineer as default values built into the computer program being used.)
3. Carry out the analysis using the developed methods, computer programs, etc., and arrive at the desired solution.
4. Transform these answers to useful information for the tool engineer, production engineer, etc. (Much of this work may be done by a CAD/CAM system.)

ACKNOWLEDGMENT

The material in this chapter was adapted from the references as indicated in the text and in the legends by the numbers of the references enclosed in square brackets pursuant to all copyrights.

REFERENCES

4.1. Lange, K. (ed.), *Handbook of Metal Forming*, McGraw-Hill, 1985, English Edition, pp. 5.1–5.32.
4.2. Altan, T., and G. D. Lahoti, "Limitations, Applicability and Usefulness of Different Methods in Analyzing Forming Problems," *CIRP Annals*, vol. 28, 1979, pp. 473–478.
4.3. Sachs, G., *Z. Metallk.*, vol. 16, p. 55.
4.4. Siebel, E., "Forces and Material Flow in Plastic Deformation" (in German), *Stahl u Eisen*, vol. 45, 1925, pp. 1563–1566.
4.5. von Karman, T., "Contribution to the Theory of Rolling" (in German), *Z Angew. Math. Mech.* vol. 5, 1925, pp. 139–141.
4.6. Blazynski, T. Z., *Metal Forming*, John Wiley & Sons, 1976, p. 20.
4.7. Altan, T., S. I. Oh, and H. L. Gegel, "Metal Forming," ASM, pp. 136–141.
4.8. Ettouney, O. M., and K. A. Stelson, "A Modified Slab Method for Axisymmetric Upset Forging," 12th NAMRC, SME, May 1984, pp. 133–140.
4.9. Johnson, W., "Continuum Mechanics and Deformation Processing," *Advances in Deformation Processing*, J. J Burke and V. Weiss (eds.), Plenum Press, 1978, p. 9.

4.10. Avitzur, B., *Metal Forming, The Application of Limit Analysis*, Marcel Dekker, Inc., New York, 1980, pp. 137, 152, and 160.

4.11. Szczepinski, W., *Introduction to the Mechanics of Plastic Forming of Metals*, Sijthoff & Noordhoff Int Pubs., Warsaw, 1979, pp. 59-63.

4.12. McClintock, F. A., and A. S. Argon, *Mechanical Behavior of Materials*, Addison-Wesley Pub. Co., 1966, pp. 365-367.

4.13. Shabaik, A. H., "Analysis of Forming Processes: Experimental and Numerical Methods," *Applications of Numerical Methods to Forming Processes*, AMD-vol 28, ASME Winter Meeting, December, 1978, pp. 15-25.

4.14. Hosford, W. F., and R. M. Caddell, *Metal Forming Mechanics and Metallurgy*, Prentice-Hall, Inc., p. 115.

4.15. Courtois, P., et al., "The Kinematic Element Method in Plane and Axisymmetric Forging Process Design," in *Proc. of the Internl. Mach. Tool Design and Research Conf.* September 1986, B. J. Davies (ed.), Macmillan Publishers Ltd., pp. 459-466.

4.16. Hill, R., *The Mathematical Theory of Plasticity*, Clarendon Press, Oxford, 1950.

4.17. Venter, R. D., et al., "Application of the Matrix Inversion Technique to Extrusion and Drawing Problems," *Applications of Numerical Methods to Forming Processes*, AMD-vol. 28, ASME Winter Meeting, December 1978, pp. 143-154.

4.18. Dewhurst, P., I. F. Collins, and W. Johnson, "A Class of Slipline Field Solutions for the Hot Rolling of Strip," *J. Mech. Eng. Sci.*, vol. 15 (1973), pp. 439-447.

4.19. Bachrach, B. I., and S. K. Samanta, "Plane Strain Sheet and Tube Extrusion Through Cosine-Shaped Dies with Friction," *NAMRC II*, SME, 1974, p. 180.

4.20. Johnson, W., and P. B. Mellor, Van Nostrand-Reinhold Co., New York, 1973, pp. 383-387.

4.21. Harris, N. H., *Mechanical Working of Metals*, Pergamon Press, New York, 1983, p. 184.

4.22. Rowe, G. W., *Principles of Industrial Metalworking Processes*, Edward Arnold, 1977, pp. 260-262, 359-362, 387-392.

4.23. Collins, I. F., "Integral Equation Formulation of Slipline Field Problems," Applications of Numerical Methods to Forming Processes, H. Armen and R. F. Jones, Jr (eds.), AMD-vol. 28, ASME, 1978, pp. 129-153.

4.24. Ewing, D. J. F., "A Series Method for Constructing Plastic Slipline Fields," *J Mech. Phys.*, vol. 15, 1967, pp. 105-114.

4.25. Dewhurst, P., and I. F. Collins, "A Matrix Technique for Constructing Slip-line Field Solutions to a Class of Plane Strain Plasticity Problems," *Inst J. Num. Methods Engr.*, vol. 7 (1973), pp. 357-378.

4.26. Oh, S. I., G. D. Lahoti, and T. Altan, "Application of a Rigid-Plastic Finite Element Method to Some Metalforming Operations," *Process Modeling Tools*, ASM, 1981, pp. 196-197.

4.27. Desai, C. S., and J. F. Abel, *Introduction to the Finite Element Method*, van Nostrand-Reinhold Co., New York, 1972.

4.28. Zienkiewicz, O. C., *The Finite Element Method*, 3d ed., McGraw-Hill, 1977, pp. 461-463, 683, 691-693.

4.29. Oh, S. I., G. D. Lahoti, and T. Altan, "Application of FEM to Industrial Metal Forming Processes," *Numerical Methods in Industrial Forming Processes*, J. F. T Pittman et al. (eds.), Pineridge Press Ltd., Swansea, U.K., 1982, pp. 145-153.

4.30. Mahrenholtz, D., and N. L. Dung, "Mathematical Modelling of Metal Forming Processes by Numerical Methods," in *Advanced Technology of Plasticity*, 1987, vol. 1, K. Lange (ed.), *Proc. of the 2d Intl. Conf. on Technology of Plasticity*, Stuttgart, August 1987, Springer-Verlag, New York, pp. 3-10.

4.31. Park, J. J, and S. I. Oh, "Application of Three-Dimensional Finite Element Analysis to Metal Forming Processes," in *1987 Mfg. Tech. Rev., 15th NAMRC Proc.*, SME, pp. 296-303.

4.32. Owen, D. R. J., and E. Hinton, *Finite Elements in Plasticity*, Pineridge Press Ltd., Swansea, U.K. 1980, pp. 27, 222.

4.33. ANSYS, a commercially available general purpose finite element analysis program available from Swanson Analysis Systems, Inc., Houston, Pa.

4.34. Oh, S. I., G. D. Lahoti, and T. Altan, "ALPID–A General Purpose FEM Program for Metal Forming," *9th NAMRC Proceedings*, 1981, SME, pp. 83–88.

4.35. Fadzil, M. et al., "Metal-Forming Analysis on Desk-Top Microcomputer Using Non-Linear Elastic–Plastic Finite Element Techniques," in *Proc. of the 22nd International Machine Tool Design and Research Conf.*, September 1981, B. J. Davies, (ed.), Macmillan Press Ltd., pp. 533–539.

4.36. Bute, H. M., and H. L. Gegel, "The Role of Process Modeling in the Future of Materials Science and Technology," *Process Modeling, Proceedings of ASM Process Modeling Sessions, Materials and Processing Congresses*, 1978 and 1979, ASM, pp. 2 and 4.

4.37. Kobayashi, S., "Metalworking Process Modeling and the Finite Element Method," *9th NAMRAC*, 1981, SME, p. 16.

4.38. Altan, T., G. D. Lathoti, and V. Nagal, "Application of Process Modeling in Massive Forming Processes," op. cit., ref. 4.36, pp. 77–83.

4.39. Marten, J., et al., "A Coupled Analysis of Plastic Deformation and Heat Transfer," in vol. 27, *Proc. of the 27th International MATADOR Conf.*, 1988, (ed. B. J. Davies), Macmillan Education Ltd., pp. 397–403.

4.40. Gebhart, B., *Heat Transfer*, 2d ed., McGraw-Hill, 1971, pp. 49–51.

4.41. Incropera, F. P., and D. P. DeWitt, *Fundamentals of Heat and Mass Transfer*, 2d ed., John Wiley & Sons, New York, 1985.

4.42. Rebelo, N., and S. Kobayashi, "A Coupled Analysis of Viscoplastic Deformation and Heat Transfer," in Pts. I and II, *Int. J. Mech. Sci.*, vol. 22, 1980, pp. 699–707.

4.43. Wanheim, T. et al., "Physical Modelling of Metal Forming Processes," op. cit., ref. 4.36, p. 146.

PROBLEMS

4.1. Plane-strain compression is performed on a slab of a metal whose yield strength in shear, $\tau_Y = k$, is 70 MPa. The width of the slab is 150 mm and its thickness (height) is 25 mm. Assume the average coefficient of friction at each die-metal interface is 0.20 and the von Mises yield criterion applies.
  (*a*) What is the approximate maximum pressure at the inception of plastic flow?
  (*b*) What is the approximate average pressure at this point?
  (*c*) What would be the above results for sticking friction?

4.2. By use of Eq. (4.78), calculate the temperature rise for the intense shear discontinuity of Fig. 4.11 for low-carbon steel using the following data for steel: k, the shear yield strength, $= 140$ MPa; $\rho = 7871$ kg/m^3; and $c = 481$ J/kg K. Assume $\theta_1 = 20°$, $\theta_2 = 40°$, and $v_x = 1$ in/s.

4.3. For the triangular element shown in Fig. P4.3, calculate the strain when the horizontal and vertical displacements at each node are known. The [B] matrix for the triangular

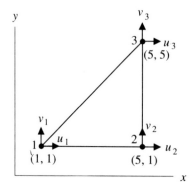

FIGURE P4.3

element, whose coordinates are expressed with respect to global coordinates, is given in Fig. P4.3

$$[B] = \frac{1}{\det} \begin{bmatrix} y_2 - y_3 & 0 & y_3 - y_1 & 0 & y_1 - y_2 & 0 \\ 0 & x_3 - x_2 & 0 & x_1 - x_3 & 0 & x_2 - x_1 \\ x_3 - x_2 & y_2 - y_3 & x_1 - x_3 & y_3 - y_1 & x_2 - x_1 & y_1 - y_2 \end{bmatrix}$$

where $\det = x_2 y_3 - x_3 y_2 + x_1(y_2 - y_3) + y_1(x_3 - x_2) = $ twice the area of the triangle.

4.4. The triangle in Fig. P4.3 is strained according to the following nodal-displacement values.

$$u_1 = v_1 = v_2 = 0 \qquad u_2 = 0.01 \qquad u_3 = 0.015 \qquad v_3 = 0.005.$$

Calculate the stresses induced in the triangular element. Assume the material is steel with $E = 30 \times 10^6$ psi and $\nu = 0.3$, and the deformation is linearly elastic.

4.5. Develop the general procedure for calculating stress and strain by FEM. For the purpose of illustration use the square sheet divided into two triangular elements as shown in Fig. P4.5.

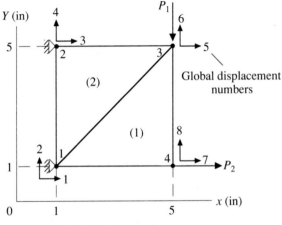

(a) Global numbering

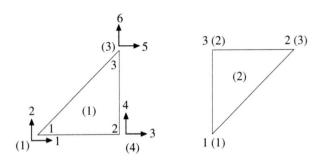

(b) Local numbering

FIGURE P4.5

4.6. Write a computer code in Fortran 77 (or some other convenient programming language) for the calculating $[B]$ matrix.

4.7. A portion of a meridional plane of a cylindrical steel billet such as is shown at the right side of Fig. 4.69(a) and in Fig. P4.7. By use of the parameters given in Table 4.3, calculate the increase in temperature in element 1 due to friction between the workpiece and the die. Take a time step of 0.01 s. When necessary, assume that the strain rate and the stress are uniform throughout the workpiece.

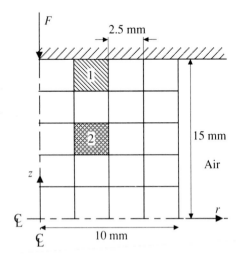

FIGURE P4.7

4.8. By use of the information in Probs. 4.7, calculate the increase in temperature in element 1 due to deformation.

4.9. Calculate the increase in temperature in element 2 shown in Fig. P4.7. Use the same parameters as those used in Probs. 4.7 and 4.8. Assume for simplicity that the initial temperature in element 2 is at 20°C and those in the surrounding elements are at 35°C throughout. For calculating the temperature increase due to plastic deformation in element 2, use the value obtained for element 1 in Prob. 4.7.

4.10. Repeat the procedure given in example Probs. 4.7 and 4.8 for a cylindrical billet of 1050 aluminum. Use the values listed below.

Workpiece: Dimensions $h_0/d_0 = 30/20$ mm/mm
Density $= 2.705$ Mg/m^3
Specific heat capacity $= 900$ J/kg $\cdot$ K
Thermal conductivity coefficient $= 231$ W/m $\cdot$ K
Thermal efficiency $= 0.865$
Initial temperature $= 20$°C

Die material: Use the values listed in Table 4.3.

4.11. Calculate the increase in temperature for an interior node of Prob. 4.10 in the same manner as that shown in Prob. 4.7.

PART

II

CLASSIFICATION OF METALWORKING PROCESSES AND MASSIVE OR BULK DEFORMATION PROCESSES

CHAPTER
5

CLASSIFICATION OF METALWORKING OR METALFORMING PROCESSES

5.1 INTRODUCTION

With the rapid advance of CAD/CAM, increased pressure will continue to be exerted to classify the various metalworking processes as well as other materials of manufacturing processes. To take full advantage of the various computer techniques, the various processes will have to be categorized and systematized.

In Chap. 1 metalworking processes as compared to other processes were classified as through-flow processes, in which virtual conservation of mass is retained as a result of the process. Although an extensive amount of plastic deformation occurs in the formation of a chip during metal cutting, this process will not be considered here as a metalworking process, but as a divergent-flow, mass-reducing process.

Metalworking or metalforming is therefore defined here as an operation in which the change in shape of the processed workpiece or preform is not accompanied by an extensive amount of metal removal as the principal method of altering the shape. It is true that some processes such as shearing, shaving, blanking, piercing, etc., may involve some metal cutting or chip formation and may therefore fall in the boundary area between chipforming and metalforming processes. They nonetheless will be included here as metalforming, as the major part of the operation involves metalforming or else it is an important first step for a subsequent process such as making a blank for a deep-drawing operation.

Although some primary forming operations are very important, such as the rotary piercing of billets, they will not be discussed in this chapter, because they are specialized operations with which the average engineer in the manufacturing industries would seldom come in contact.

A number of criteria or mechanisms have been proposed and are being used for the classification of metalworking processes. Some of these methods are as follows:

1. Whether or not strainhardening occurs as in cold- or hotworking
2. Type or state of stress involved at a certain point in the workpiece during metalworking
3. Whether or not an appreciable change in thickness occurs during deformation as in bulk working or sheetmetal forming
4. Size of the deformation zone, whether local or general
5. Mode of deformation, whether steady or nonsteady state
6. Rate of deformation, whether low, intermediate, or high
7. Primary process such as rolling of plates and sheets; secondary forming processes such as deep-drawing, etc.
8. Continuous processes such as rolling and extrusion and batch processes such as closed die forging
9. Whether or not chip formation is involved

There is no single method that serves all purposes. The traditional, and still common method, of major classification of hot- and coldworking has outgrown its usefulness. The forging of steel has been traditionally classified as a hotworking process but we now have cold forging and warm extrusion. Cold-, warm-, and hotworking form essentially a continuous spectrum with temperature. Strain rate usually has a relatively strong effect during warm- and hotworking.

For the purpose of discussing the basic theory of the metalworking processes, they may conveniently be classified as bulk working and sheetmetal working processes, because they represent two different classes of work being done. The classification of these processes according to the state of stress or stress system involved is very useful in that it distinguishes between the complexity of the stress system required to produce the desired change in shape and the types of stresses involved.

Probably, at some particular location, at some stage, in some type of metal-working process, all states of stress from uniaxial tension or compression to triaxial tension or compression, and all combinations in between, result in plastic deformation.

The state of stress or stress system method of classifying metalworking processes will be discussed in greater detail in the next section.

Using some of the foregoing criteria, Boulger [5.1] has classified metalforming operations or processes as follows:

1. According to the *type of workpiece*:
   (*a*) *Massive or bulk forming processes*—the starting material is in the form of semifinished shapes, bars, etc.; the workpiece has a small surface to volume ratio; forming causes large changes in shape and cross section; the elastic recovery is usual negligible.
   (*b*) *Sheetmetal processes*—the starting material is rolled sheet; the workpiece has a large surface to volume ratio; forming causes large changes in shape but small changes in thickness; the elastic recovery is usually significant.
2. According to the *effect of deformation and temperature* on mechanical properties:
   (*a*) *Hot working*—dynamic recovery occurs, no strainhardening, deformation temperature range is $0.7 < T_M < 0.8$ where $T_M = $ incipient melting temperature.
   (*b*) *Warm working*—some strainhardening and/or precipitation hardening may occur, deformation temperature range is $0.3 < T_M < 0.5$.
   (*c*) *Cold working*—strainhardening occurs, deformation temperature range is $< 0.3 T_M$.
3. According to the *mode of deformation*:
   (*a*) *Steady state*—continuous wire drawing,
   (*b*) *Non-steady state*—die forging, and
   (*c*) *Mixed or transitory*—extrusion.
4. According to the *system of stresses* imposed on the workpiece:
   (*a*) Compression.   (*d*) Bending.
   (*b*) Tension.   (*e*) Torsion.
   (c) Tension and compression.   (*f*) Shear.

5.2 CLASSIFICATION BY STRESS SYSTEMS

One of the main systems for the classification of the plastic-deformation processes on the basis of a stress system is the one presented by Kienzle [5.2], who classified the processes on the basis of six types of stress systems as shown in Fig. 5.1(*a*) and (*b*). Subdivisions are made according to (1) the movement of the tool relative to the workpiece, (2) the tool geometry, (3) the workpiece geometry, and (4) the interrelation between the tool and workpiece geometry.

   In Fig. 5.1(*a*), drop forging and coining are in the same group, because they are distinguished only by the temperature of working Power spinning and spinforging are found in two different places depending on whether the predominant force is compressive or shear.

   The geometrical shapes which can be produced by a particular process vary within limits determined by the properties of the material, condition of lubrication, temperature of the material, and the velocity of deformation. There are many shapes that can be produced by more than one process. There is, also, a trend toward widening the capabilities of particular processes. The shape of the part and of any preforms are important when various processes are combined as

Mode		Process	
Compression	1	Upsetting	
	2	Drawing out	
	3	Drop forging coining	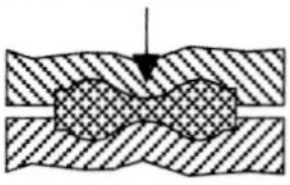
	4	Pressing in closed die	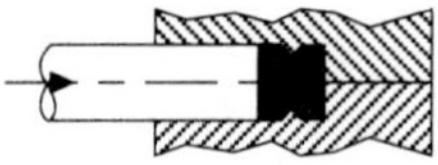
	5	Extrusion	
	6	Reducing	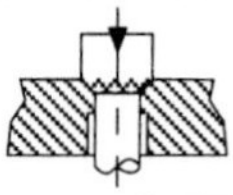
	7	Swaging	
	8	Rolling	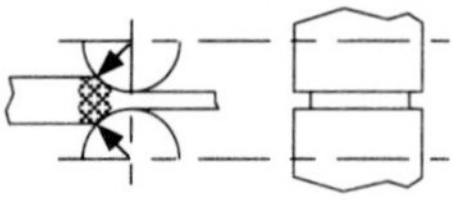
	9	Reducer rolling	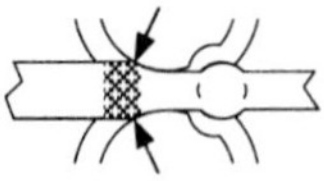
	10	Spinning (conventional)	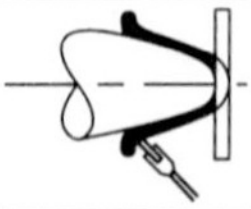
	11	Power spinning	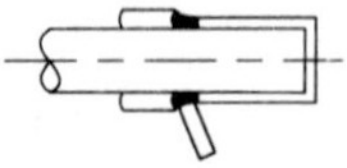

FIGURE 5.1

(*a*) Classification of plastic-forming processes on the basis of six system of stresses: Compression, tension, tension and compression, bending, shear, and torsion. (Double crosshatching and black areas indicate zoned deformation.) [5.2]

Mode		Process		
Tension	12	Expanding		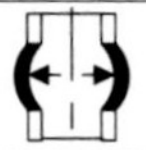
Tension	13	Stretch forming		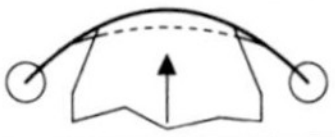
Tension	14	Embossing		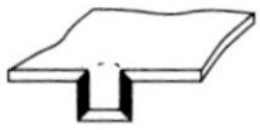
Tension and compression	15	Wire drawing		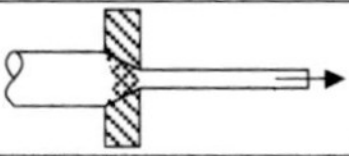
Tension and compression	16	Deep drawing	With blank-holder	 
Tension and compression	16	Deep drawing	Without blank-holder	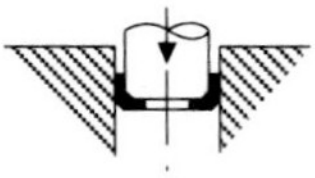
Tension and compression	17	Ironing		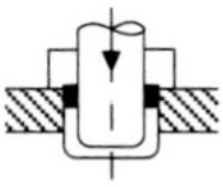
Bending	18	At straight axis		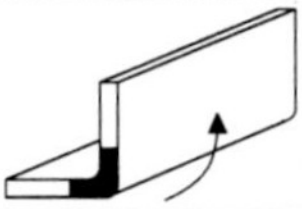
Bending	19	At curved axis		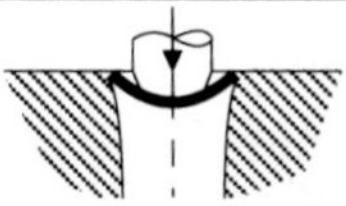 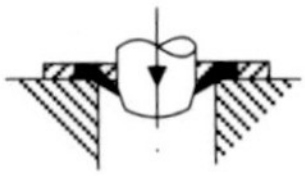
Shear	20	Shear spinning		
Shear	20	Shear pressing		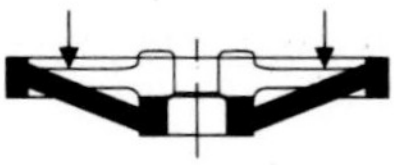
Torsion	21	Setting		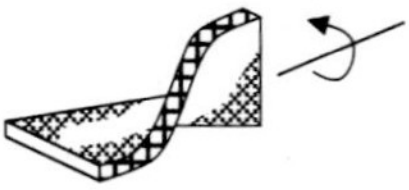

FIGURE 5.1
(*b*) Classification of plastic-forming processes on the basis of six system of stresses. (Double crosshatching and black areas indicate zoned deformation.) (Continued.) [5.2]

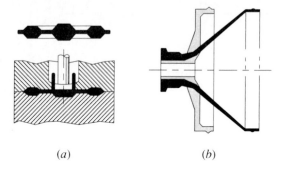

(a)   (b)

FIGURE 5.2
Combinations of forming processes:
(a) forging and extrusion combined,
and (b) forging and shear spinning
combined [5.2].

shown in Fig. 5.2(a) for forging and extrusion and in Fig. 5.2(b) for forging and spinning.

Kienzle indicated that insights into the flow of material during the metal-working processes can be gained from theory and/or experiment. The theory of plasticity, as cited elsewhere, gives some hints for designing slip-lines which give the direction of maximum shear stress at every point in a plane-forming process. Additional geometrical data are to be found in stream lines, which give the direction of movement of all points at a certain instant, and path lines which represent the path of a particular point throughout the entire process. Stream lines and path lines are identical in stationary processes such as extrusion, but they are not identical in nonstationary processes such as die forging. The difference between path lines and stream lines may be seen in Fig. 5.3 for the upsetting of a cylinder.

Experimental information can be obtained regarding the flow of material by means of the following experiments: (1) inserting small hard pins into the workpiece and observing their movements during the course of deformation; (2) using layers of clay of different colors and observing the flow of the clay after deformation; (3) using grid patterns on the surface or cross section of the workpiece and observing the change in the pattern after deformation; and (4) macroetching of a cross section of the deformed part. Some of these experimental techniques will be discussed in greater detail elsewhere in conjunction with the discussion of the individual processes. (For example, grid lines and markings are shown in Figs. 2.90, 3.57, 11.51, and 11.67. A macroetching of a connecting rod is shown in Fig. 9.52.)

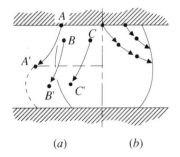

(a)   (b)

FIGURE 5.3
(a) Path lines, and (b) stream lines indicating the motion
of particles during upsetting [5.2].

5.3   CLASSIFICATION BY MULTIPLE CATEGORIES

Methods for classifying metalworking processes other than by stress have been proposed. One such system has been presented by Kudo [5.3], in which several different categories are used in addition to the state of stress such as the premises (purpose and given requirements) of the operations, mode of deformation, mode of deformation sequence, type of tooling and equipment, etc. These categories and their associated characteristics are shown in Table 5.1 (top). The application of this classification system is also shown in Table 5.1 (bottom). As may be noted, the purpose of the operation may include "re-forming," which involves only localized plastic deformation such as straightening, bending, roll-leveling of sheets, etc.

The "shape of the starting workpiece" and the "shape of the product" are key categories in this classification system. Both the shape of the starting workpiece and product include such shapes as bars of different cross section such as rounds, squares, tees, etc.; tubes with different cross section such as rounds, squares, fin-shaped, etc.; strips such as flat, curved, and angled cross section, etc.; and blocks, plates, and rings. Transitions between characteristic shapes are not as yet clearly defined.

One of the characteristics listed under the purpose of the operation is "property modification." One of the purposes for plastic deformation is to enhance the mechanical properties of the product. Kienzle [5.2] has cited a good example of how the starting shape affects the final properties of a cold-headed bolt or cap screw as shown in Fig. 5.4. As shown, the bolt can be formed for a slug with (1) a diameter of the head a, (2) a diameter of the body b, or (3) with some intermediate diameter. In the first case, essentially all the strainhardening occurs in the shaft, in the second case it occurs in the head, and in the third case it occurs in both the head and shaft.

The workpiece material has not as yet been utilized in this system as one of the categories of forming processes. It only determines what category will be used and what procedures will be followed in a forming process.

It should be noted that the category for the "mode of deformation" involving the state of strain and the extent of deformation is a separate category from the "state of stress." It should also be noted that in Table 5.1 the "state of strain" may be designated according to the direction as 1, 2, and 3, which represent the three main directions of the workpiece or product in order of decreasing length such as for a plate: 1, length; 2, width; and 3, thickness. The "extent of deformation" zone within a workpiece may also be designated by 1, 2, and 3, where 1 represents total or through deformation, 2 partial deformation, and 3 a minute amount of deformation.

As mentioned previously, the state of stress is the primary classification category in a number of classification systems for materials processes or operations, even though stresses are normally invisible during the deformation process and are dependent on the strains. Kudo suggests the categories and characteristics for the classification of metalforming processes on the basis of

TABLE 5.1
Kudo's classification system for forming operation [5.3]

Characteristic notation	PREMISES OF OPERATION — Purpose	Workpiece material	Shape of starting workp.	Shape of product	Workg. temperature	Workg. speed	MODE OF DEFORMATION — State of strain (1 2 3)	Extent of deformation zone (1 2 3)	STATE OF STRESS — Direct stress (1 2 3)	Auxiliary stress (1 2 3)	Hydrostatic stress	MODE OF DEFORMATION SEQUENCE — Direction of working of neighbg. part	Transfer of workg. to Ng. part	Successive workg. of a part	Workg. of separate parts	TYPE OF TOOL — Shape & size determining tool	Workp. pressing tool	Type of power transmission to workp.
(0)	general		general				general	general	general		general	general	general	general	general	general		general
(1)	deformation		bar & wire				tension	whole	tension		> 0	1	intermt.	intermt. w/ same tool	simultan. w/ same tool	shapeless		gas & fluid pressure
(2)	separation		Tube & hollow bar				compression	partial	compression		ca 0	2	contin.	intermt. w/ diff tool	simultan. w/ diff tool	shaped punch & die		mechanism
(3)	joining		strip				bending	minute	bending		0 ~ k_f	3	contin. & intermt.	contin. w/ same tool	progress w/ same tool	plain punch & die		gravity
(4)	reforming		solid block	ditto			shearing		shearing	ditto	< - k_f	simultan. combined 1 & 2		contin. w/ diff tool	progress w/ diff tool	non-cicular roll	ditto	man power
(5)	surface finishing		hollow block									one after another				cicular roll		fuel & explosive
(6)	property modification		plate & thin flat piece									at random				chuck & drum		heat conduction
(7)			ring & plate w/ hole													support & anvil		electro magnetic force
(8)																other		other
(9)							none		none			none	none	none	none	none		

Application of Kudo's classification system to some typical forming operation:

	Purpose	Shape of starting workp.	Shape of product	State of strain	Extent	Direct stress	Auxiliary stress	Hydrostatic	Direction	Transfer	Successive	Separate parts	Shape & size tool	Workp. pressing tool
A	(1)	(3)	(3)	(192)	(111)	(992)	(199)	(3)	(1)	(2)	(4)	(12)	(5)	(5)
B	(1)	(1)	(1)	(192)	(111)	(992)	(999)	(3)	(1)	(2)	(9)	(9)	(4)	(4)
C	(1)	(4)	(4)	(912)	(111)	(992)	(999)	(4)	(9)	(9)	(9)	(9)	(2)	(2)
D	(1)	(6)	(5)	(2/3 99)	(111)	(992)	(999)	(2)	(9)	(9)	(9)	(9)	(2)	(2)

Operations : A Continuos strip rolling, B Reducer rolling, C Die forging of a billet, D Deep drawing

340

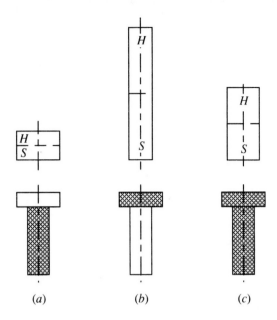

FIGURE 5.4
Example of how the starting shape affects the final properties of a cold-headed bolt or cap screw. Different strainhardening effects in parts formed by (a) heading, (b) extrusion, and (c) combination of heading and extrusion. The origin of the material is designated by H for head and S for shaft. Crosshatching indicates predominantly strainhardened material [5.2].

(a)   (b)   (c)

TABLE 5.2
Categories and characteristics for classification of state of stress [5.3]

Category	Direction	Characteristic	Remarks
State of direct stress	1 2 3	Tension, compression, bending, shearing and none	E.g., tension along can wall in deep drawing
State of main deformation stress	1 2 3		E.g., radial compression in wire drawing
State of auxiliary stress	1 2 3		E.g., back tension in wire drawing
State of induced stress	1 2 3		E.g., circumferential tension in deep drawing
Hydrostatic stress		Tension compression and none	Scalar quantity

stress as given in Table 5.2. In this table, "direct" stress is the stress generated by the main working force (or torque) exerted by the forming press or machine. The "main deformation" stress is the stress that results in the major deformation of the operation. The "auxiliary" stress is a secondary stress applied to the workpiece by the equipment to assist the main deformation stress. The "induced" stress is secondarily generated by other stresses.

The term "direction of working of neighboring part" refers to the direction in which the workpiece is fed, if at all, such as in the longitudinal direction in the roll forming of an angle iron and in the circumferential direction for ring rolling. These directions obey the same definition of direction as for deformation and stress. The "transfer of working to neighboring part" refers to the mode of transfer of working such as simultaneous, continuous, intermittent, or combined. Most multicavity die-forging processes are characterized as intermittent. Rolling of a strip under a single roll is classified as continuous. Tandem rolling or wire drawing, in which the material is under or in successive rolls at the same time, is denoted here as "overlapping with tools of the same type."

The tool or transfer medium may be rigid (solid), elastic (rubber), plastic, gaseous, granular, or fluid. The means of exerting a force on a tool are pneumatic pressure, fluid pressure, mechanical force, gravity, explosive force, heat, electromagnetic force, human power, and others.

Using the foregoing approach, Kudo presented the tentative classification system shown in Table 5.1. As he indicated, much more work needs to be done on this system to make it viable. One of the disadvantages of this system is that some 22 to 24 digits would be needed to code a process for computer use, whereas only 9 digits are practicable as an upper limit for a coding system.

REFERENCES

5.1. Boulger, F. W., "Metal Forming: Status and Challenges," Towards the Factory of the Future, PED-Vol. 1, Winter Annual Meeting, Nov. 16–21, 1980, p. 18, ASME.

5.2 Kienzle, O., "Classes and Characteristics of Plastic-Deformation Processes," *Machine Design*, pp. 200–207, Nov. 7, 1963.

5.3 Kudo, H., "An Attempt for Classification of Metal Forming Operations," Annals, CIRP, vol. 29, p. 2, 1980.

CHAPTER

6

ROLLING

6.1 ROLLING THEORY AND PRACTICE

6.1.1 Introduction

In the section on the classification of metalworking processes, they were classified as primary and secondary processes. The function of the primary processes is to provide the semifinished shapes that have the necessary configuration, dimensions, and properties that will be suitable for the subsequent, secondary processing whether by additional forming, welding, machining, heat treating, or whatever. The secondary metalworking processes are subsequent processes that will produce the final configuration of the desired part.

Since the term "primary" has the connotation of "first," hot rolling of a steel or an aluminum alloy to a slab or plate may be considered as the primary process for subsequent hot and cold rolling to sheets, which might provide the stock for a deep-drawing operation, for example. One simplification is to adopt the classification used by the process engineer of (1) originating process or operation and (2) the principal process or operation. The originating process is one that produces the general configuration of the workpiece. The originating process of a steel forging may be a hot-rolled bar, whereas the originating process for the machining of a connecting rod for an internal combustion engine may be either a forging or a nodular (ductile) cast-iron casting. The principal or main process by which the connecting rod is produced would be metal cutting or machining.

One very important primary metalworking process, that is used for both hot- and cold-working, is rolling. Rolling is a mechanical process whereby the plastic deformation of the metal is achieved by passing it between rotating rolls. It is the most widely used of all metalworking processes. About 90 percent of all

343

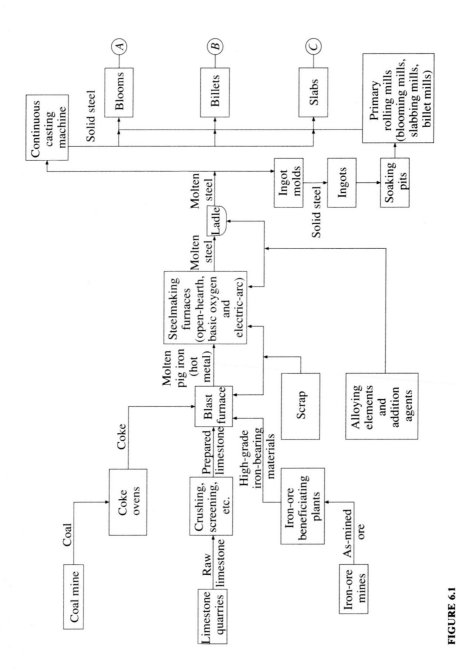

FIGURE 6.1
Flow diagram of steelmaking processes. The diagram shows the principal processes involved in converting raw materials into mill products (excluding coated products). (*Adapted from ASM Metals Handbook, 8th Ed., Vol. 5, Forging and Casting, T. Lyman, Ed., 1970, p. 110.*)

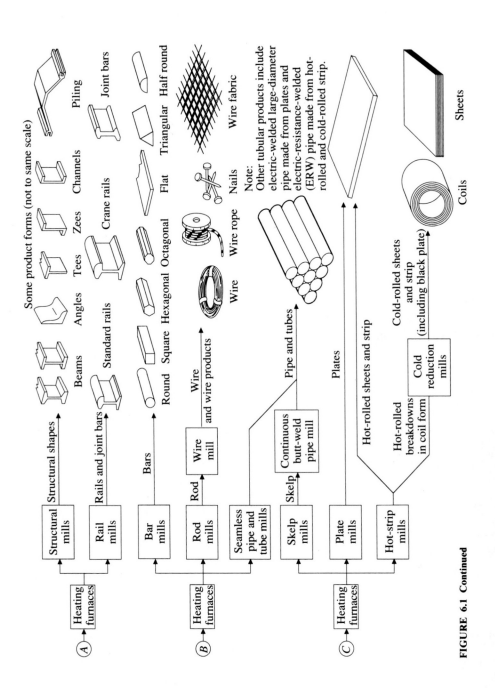

FIGURE 6.1 Continued

steel, aluminum, and copper produced annually in the world is rolled. It would be difficult to imagine how our present-day society could exist without rolled plates, sheets, bars, and structural shapes. The primary steelworking processes are those that are performed first to provide the semifinished shapes such as blooms, billets, slabs, plates, bars, structural shapes, etc., with acceptable mechanical properties, etc., for subsequent use in subsequent secondary processes or a series of processes.

An overall flow diagram showing the principal processes involved in converting raw materials into mill products is shown in Fig. 6.1. The steelmaking aspects of the overall process are discussed in other books, whereas the theory and practice of metalworking aspects are discussed here.

As can be seen from Fig. 6.1 all the semifinished shapes and many large tonnage products such as structural shapes, rails, bars, pipe, plates, hot-rolled sheets and strip are hot rolled. Some hot-rolled sheets in turn are pickled and otherwise processed and then cold rolled to produce cold-rolled sheet such as for automobile bodies and cans. The semifinished shapes, plates, and bars for nonferrous metals are also hot rolled; however, a much greater percentage of nonferrous, finished products are cold rolled. The difference between hot and cold rolling is essentially the same as the difference between other metalworking processes discussed elsewhere.

The main difference between hot and cold rolling is that in hot rolling the workpiece is initially at, or is heated to, some temperature appreciably above room temperature, and in some cases to near the solidus temperature (the temperature of incipient melting). As contrasted to cold rolling, the workpiece is initially at ambient temperature. In case of hot rolling of plain, low-carbon steel, it may be heated to 2350°F (1288°C). Medium carbon steel may be heated to 2000–2100°F (1093–1148°C), and high carbon steel to a temperature of 1950–2050°F (1006–1121°C). On the other hand aluminum alloys may be heated to a temperature of 850–1200°F (450–650°C). At elevated temperatures the metal will have an appreciably lower flow stress, and it is usually much less prone to cracking as a result of rolling.

Hot rolling is much more dependent on the temperature of the workpiece and the strain rate. During hot rolling the metal is continuously being annealed.

Strainhardening does not occur in hot rolling as in cold rolling, although a lag in the development in strainhardening during cold rolling may exist. Also, a much higher coefficient of friction exists, as expected, in hot rolling which results in a larger angle of bite or draft during hot rolling. The workpiece and the work rolls in cold rolling may be lubricated such as with substitute palm oil, so that the type of friction in cold rolling is described as sliding in contrast to sticking friction in hot rolling.

6.1.2 The Rolling Mill

Rolling is done with a device called a *rolling mill.* The rolls, whose periphery may be flat or grooved, are mounted in a housing such as is shown in Fig. 6.2.

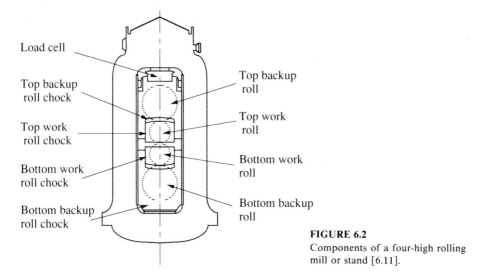

Load cell

Top backup
roll chock

Top work
roll chock

Bottom work
roll chock

Bottom backup
roll chock

Top backup
roll

Top work
roll

Bottom work
roll

Bottom backup
roll

FIGURE 6.2
Components of a four-high rolling
mill or stand [6.11].

The assembly of rolls and housing is called a *stand.* A rolling mill may consist
of one stand or a series of stands. Typical arrangements of rolls in a stand are
shown in Fig. 6.3. A stand having two rolls is called a *two-high mill.* A *three-high
mill* has three rolls, a *four-high mill* four rolls, etc. The rolls in contact with the

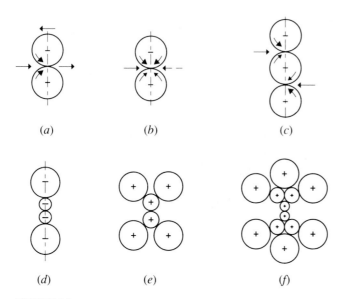

(a)   (b)   (c)

(d)   (e)   (f)

FIGURE 6.3
Typical arrangements of rolls in a stand for a rolling mill. (*a*) 2-high single pass or pull over; (*b*)
2-high reversing mill; (*c*) 3-high; (*d*) 4-high; (*e*) and (*f*) 6- and 12-high roll cluster mills. A 20-high
Sendzimir cluster mill is available. (*Adapted from J. A. Schey, The More Common Fabrication Processes,
in Techniques of Metals Research, R. F. Bunshah, Ed., Vol. 1, Part 3, Interscience Publishers, 1968,
p. 1448.*)

steel are called the *work rolls*, while those that idle against and support the work rolls are called *backup rolls*. As will be seen later, there are definite advantages for using small diameter work rolls; however, they lack rigidity and may deflect vertically and/or laterally, so that the backup rolls are necessary to provide support to counteract this deflection. A four-high mill would counteract only vertical deflection, whereas a six-high mill would counteract both vertical and lateral deflection. Some mills also have vertical rolls, so as to roll the metal at the sides or edges, and are called *universal mills*. Such a mill may produce *universal plate* as opposed to *sheared-edge plate*, which is cross-rolled and sheared, so as to have more uniform directional properties, and sharper edges and more accurate width dimensions.

The rolling procedure and sequence depends on a number of factors such as the type and amount of metal to be rolled, the amount of reduction, the shape to be rolled, the type and arrangement of equipment available, the mechanical properties desired, etc.

The working rolls rotate at the same speed but in opposite directions. If the metal to be rolled is placed at one side of a mill and if it is rolled through to the other side, this operation is called a *pass*. Some mills, called *reversing mills*, can be reversed after each pass, so that the metal can be rolled back and forth decreasing the distance of separation between the rolls when necessary. An

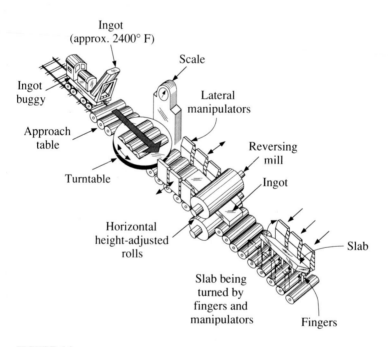

FIGURE 6.4
Reversing mill arrangement for the rolling of a steel ingot into a slab. (*Adapted from J. Wulff et al., Metallurgy for Engineers, John Wiley & Sons, New York, 1952, p. 532.*)

example of the use of a reversing mill is the breaking down or reducing of a steel *ingot* into a *bloom, billet,* or *slab* after it is taken from the *soaking pit* as shown in Fig. 6.4 in slab rolling. In case of a nonreversing, two-high mill the stock, if heavy, must be passed back over top of the rolls to the rear of the mill for each subsequent pass, if any. Metal can be rolled back and forth through a three-high mill without reversing it. Tilting tables on each side of the mill lift or lower the metal for each pass.

Another factor that affects the rolling procedure is the arrangement of the stands and the ancillary equipment such as in tandem and continuous mills. Tandem mills as shown in Fig. 6.5 consist of a series of stands arranged in a straight line and connected with roller conveyors for transporting the metal from one stand to the next, which may or may not be reversible. The first few stands, where the major reduction occurs, are called *roughing stands,* while the last group are called *finishing stands.* When the metal such as a continuous strip in either hot or cold rolling is under more than one stand at the same time, it is called a *continuous mill.* Cylindrical rolls, of course, are used for flat rolling of plates and sheets, and grooved rolls are used for rolling of a variety of shapes such as round bars, structural shapes, rails, etc., as shown in Fig. 6.1.

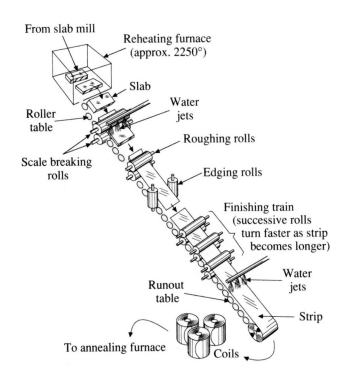

FIGURE 6.5

Tandem mill for rolling of a hot-rolled steel strip. (*Adapted from J. Wulff et al., Metallurgy for Engineers, John Wiley & Sons, New York, 1952, p. 530.*)

Slab

Always oblong
Mostly 2 to 9 in thick
Mostly 24 to 60 in wide

Bloom

Square or slightly oblong
Mostly in the range 6 x 6 in to 12 x 12 in

Billet

Mostly square
Mostly in the range 2 x 2 in to 5 x 5 in

FIGURE 6.6
Relative shapes and sizes of slabs, blooms, and billets for steel, primarily. The nomenclature and dimensions differ somewhat for different metals. (All corners are rounded and the dimensions are usually given to the nearest whole number.) [6.11].

The terminology used to describe semifinished rolled products is fairly loose and is overshadowed by that used in steelmaking. The molten steel is cast into a shape, in the conventional process, that is suitable for rolling or forging, called an *ingot*. In steelmaking terminology, as seen in Fig. 6.6, a *bloom* is the first reduction of an ingot, and it is a square or rectangular semifinished shape that is 6×6 in (152.4×152.4 mm), or larger or equivalent. A further reduction yields a *billet*, which is a square, rectangular, or round semifinished shape that ranges from $1\frac{1}{2} \times 1\frac{1}{2}$ in (38.1×38.1 mm) to 6×6 in (152.4×152.4 mm), or equivalent. A billet, in nonferrous terminology such as for aluminum, may be a casting such as for extrusion. A *slab* is a semifinished shape, in which the width is at least twice the thickness with a minimum thickness of $1\frac{1}{2}$ in (38.1 mm) and with a cross-sectional area greater than 16 in^2 (0.01 m^2). A *plate* is a finished product, in which the thickness is equal to or greater than $\frac{1}{4}$ in (6.4 mm), and its width greater than 6 in (152.4). For widths over 48 in (1.2 m), its thickness is over $\frac{3}{16}$ in (4.8 mm). A *sheet* has a thickness less than $\frac{1}{4}$ in (6.4 mm) and a width greater than 12 in (305 mm). Widths of 12 in (305 mm) or less are called *strips*. Secondary rolling processes such as roll forming, roll bending, roll forging, and roll threading will be covered elsewhere.

6.1.3 Planetary Mill

A different concept in the deformation of metal by the use of a rolling mill, which was patented by Sendzimir in 1948, is the *planetary mill*. As seen in Fig. 6.7, this

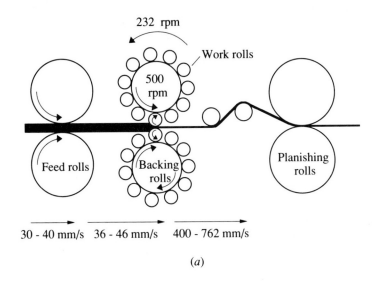

232 rpm

Work rolls

500 rpm

Feed rolls

Backing rolls

Planishing rolls

30 - 40 mm/s   36 - 46 mm/s   400 - 762 mm/s

(a)

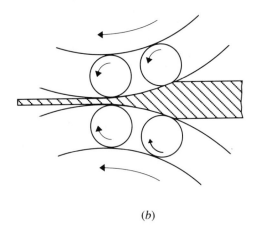

(b)

FIGURE 6.7
(a) Planetary mill, showing feed rolls required to push the workpiece into the mill; (b) action of planetary rolls [6.10].

device has a pair of heavy backing rolls at the periphery of which there are a large number of small working rolls. The action is not one of true rolling as may be seen from the direction of rotation of the planetary rolls. As there is no true rolling action, no force exists that tends to draw the workpiece into the rolls. The planetary rolls are, therefore, preceded by a pair of feed rolls, which give a small preliminary reduction and push the stock into the planetary rolls.

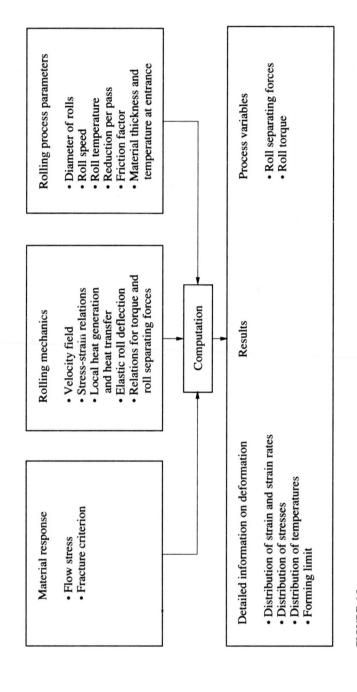

FIGURE 6.8
The overall technical approach for the analysis of the rolling process [6.1].

The advantage of the planetary mill is that it can roll slabs directly into strip with less heat loss and scaling, thus replacing three or four roughing stands and a six-stand finishing mill and perhaps a preheat furnace of the conventional rolling method. For example, a 50 mm (2 in) thick slab can be hot-rolled to 2.0 mm (0.080 in) thick strip in a single operation. Because of the action of the work rolls, tensile stresses are suppressed, so that relatively brittle metals can be rolled which normally cannot be rolled by the conventional rolling process. The planetary mill is well adapted to a continuous casting plant. Early application of the planetary mill encountered many operating and maintenance difficulties, which have been largely solved.

6.2   OVERALL TECHNICAL APPROACH TO ROLLING

6.2.1   Introduction

In the analysis and investigation of the rolling process, the overall, technical approach used may be outlined as shown in Fig. 6.8 [6.1]. This outline will in general be followed in this discussion of rolling.

For determining the flow stress in characterization of the material response listed in the outline, the flow stress may be determined by use of some such test as the upset compression test. The friction factor may be obtained by use of the ring test.

In conjunction with the flow stress, a concept that is used in connection with rolling, is the constrained yield strength of the workpiece material. This concept will be discussed later. Another very important parameter listed in Fig. 6.8 is friction. It will also be discussed in greater detail later in conjunction with the calculations of the coefficient of friction in cold rolling from measurement of the rolling force.

The mechanics of the rolling process may be analyzed by one of the theories or mathematical models for rolling such as presented by Orowan [6.2], Alexander [6.3], etc. The goals of the mathematical models of the rolling process are as follows: (1) to improve the rolling process, (2) to assist rolling mill designers and builders, (3) to guide rolling mill operators, and (4) to serve as a basis for the computer control of rolling mill operations.

The rolling process involves the interaction of (1) the work rolls, (2) the lubricant, if any, and (3) the workpiece. The exact behavior of each of these components is too complex to treat rigorously in a model, so various simplifications are made involving many assumptions, which result in a number of different theories of rolling. Because of the complexity of the problem, the development of a universal theory of rolling is extremely challenging.

Although to some people in the field of metalworking, rolling theory and its mathematical modeling may appear to be in a rather imperfect state, however, the progress that has been made over a period of some 60 years has been made due to the hard work of some very capable and distinguished people. Among those that might be mentioned, with the dates indicating chronological order and rather than references, are Siebel (1924), von Karman (1925), Ekelund (1927), Hitchcock and collaborators (1935), Orowan (1943), Bland and Ford (1948), Smith (1952), Cook and Parker (1953), Stewartson (1954), Sims (1954), Ford (1957), Jortner (1959), Cosse (1968), and others.

The analytical method for determining the roll separating force and torque follows.

6.2.2 Estimation of Rolling Pressure and Roll Separating Force on the Basis of Homogeneous Deformation

Some of the terminology involved with rolling is shown in Fig. 6.9. Simplified drawings illustrating the rolling process and the pressure distribution in the rolling of metallic materials involving homogeneous and inhomogeneous deformation with and without strainhardening are shown in Fig. 6.10(*a*) and (*b*).

A simple estimate of the roll pressure and separating force or load for the rolling of sheetmetal may be obtained by the homogeneous compression of a strip between well-lubricated overhanging anvils or platens. The area of the strip is taken as the area of contact of the rolls projected onto a horizontal plane as shown in Fig. 6.10(*a*) and (*b*). It will be shown later that the projected length

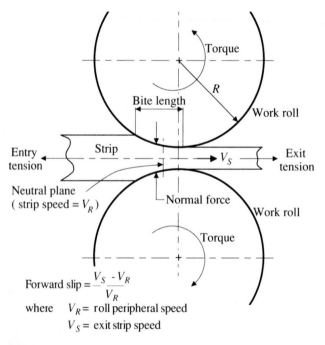

FIGURE 6.9
Some of the terminology used in rolling [6.15].

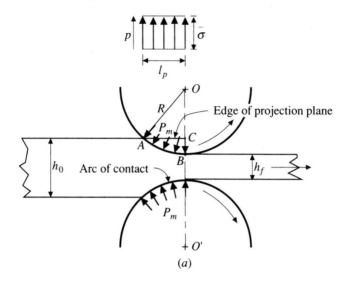

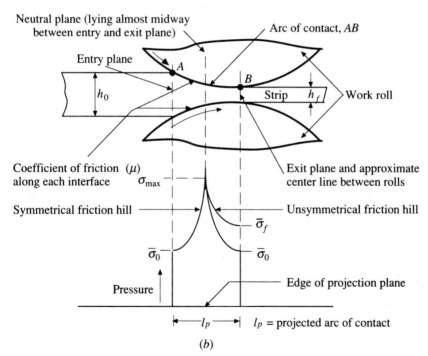

FIGURE 6.10
Schematic diagrams of (*a*) roll pressure distribution over the area of contact for a perfectly plastic material excluding external and internal shear losses, and (*b*) roll pressure distribution illustrating the external friction hill for case (1) where no strainhardening occurs as in hot rolling, and (2) where strainhardening occurs as in cold rolling (*b*) [6.11].

of the arc of contact of a roll with the metal l_p is given approximately in terms of the radius of the rolls R and the decrease in thickness Δh (called the draft) by

$$l_p = \sqrt{R\,\Delta h} \qquad (6.1)$$

The projected area of contact, therefore, is equal to $l_p w$, where w is the length of the strip, which is equivalent to the width of the sheet being rolled.

If the effect of external friction and internal shear losses are neglected, the mean pressure distribution is equal to the flow stress of perfectly plastic (non-strainhardening) material, $\bar{\sigma}$, as shown in Fig. 6.10(a).

Since

$$p_m = \frac{P}{A} = \frac{P}{l_p w} = \bar{\sigma}$$

$$\qquad (6.2)$$

$$\frac{P}{w} = \bar{\sigma} l_p = \bar{\sigma}\sqrt{R\,\Delta h}$$

Since external friction is ignored in the above equation, Orowan suggested that 20 percent be added to the above equation to allow for friction as follows:

$$\frac{P}{w} = 1.2\bar{\sigma}\sqrt{R\,\Delta h} \qquad (6.3)$$

where $\bar{\sigma}$ = mean yield stress in plane strain.

This is a very convenient equation for estimating roll separating forces or loads, and it will be used later to compensate for roll flattening during rolling.

It can also be shown from Fig. 6.10(a), that the roll separating load (force) is given by

$$P = p_m(l_p)(\overline{AB}) \qquad (6.4)$$

If it can be assumed that $(\overline{AB}) = (\overline{AC})$, then

$$\overline{OA}^2 = \overline{AC}^2 + \overline{OC}^2 = \overline{AC}^2 + (OB - CB)^2 \qquad (6.5)$$

$$R^2 = \overline{AC}^2 + \left(R - \frac{\Delta h}{2}\right)^2 = \overline{AC}^2 + R^2 - R\,\Delta h + \frac{\Delta h^2}{4} \qquad (6.6)$$

Since Δh is small, Δh^2 can be neglected, and

$$\overline{AC} = \overline{AB} = l_p = \sqrt{R\,\Delta h} \qquad (6.1)(6.7)$$

Substituting into Eq. (6.4), one obtains the separation load or force,

$$P = p_m l_p \sqrt{R\,\Delta h} = \bar{\sigma}\sqrt{R\,\Delta h} \qquad (6.8)$$

Equation (6.3) gives a good approximation if the deformation can be considered to be homogeneous rather than plane strain. If the ratio of the arc of contact, $\overline{AB} \approx l_p \approx \sqrt{R\,\Delta h}$, to the thickness h is small, the deformation may be considered to be homogeneous, and if it is large, it is plane strain.

6.2.3 Stress or Roll Separating Force Evaluation by the Classical Slab Method

Since, as indicated above, rolling is essentially a direct compression operation, it is similar in many respects to simple compression between flat anvils or platens such as in regard to the restriction of the friction to the flow of metal, for example. The effect of friction between the platen and the ends of the solid cylinder in restricting the outward flow of metal during plastic compression was considered previously in conjunction with the slab method of analysis. Since, in rolling, the width of the plate or sheet is usually much greater than four to eight times the thickness, the conditions of plane strain apply, and there is no spreading of the plate or sheet along its width.

The approximate expressions for the variation in pressure along the face of the die, the maximum and the mean pressure obtained for the case where sticking friction occurs, i.e., in which $\mu \cong 0.5$ as for hot compression or hot forging of a strip, were presented in Chap. 4 as

$$p = \bar{\sigma}\left(1 + \frac{b \pm x}{2h}\right) = \bar{\sigma}\left(1 + \frac{a \pm x}{h}\right) \tag{4.27}$$

$$p_{\max} \cong \bar{\sigma}\left(1 + \frac{b}{2h}\right) \cong \bar{\sigma}\left(1 + \frac{a}{h}\right) \tag{4.28}$$

and

$$p_m \cong \bar{\sigma}\left(1 + \frac{b}{4h}\right) \cong \bar{\sigma}\left(1 + \frac{a}{2h}\right) \tag{4.29}$$

where $b =$ the width of the strip
$\quad\quad a = b/2$
$\quad\quad h =$ the height or thickness of the strip

The equation for the variation in pressure for slipping friction was given as

$$p = \bar{\sigma}(1 + e^{2\mu x/h}) \tag{4.31}$$

If a constant friction factor m is used instead of μ, the variation in pressure then becomes

$$p = \bar{\sigma}\left(1 + \frac{2mx}{h}\right) \tag{4.35}$$

6.2.4 Application of the Friction Hill to Rolling

The concepts of a neutral point and friction hill covered in Chap. 4 may readily be applied to rolling. If there is no spreading of the width of the metal along the rolls then, because the material must elongate to preserve the constancy of volume as its thickness is reduced as it passes through the rolls, its velocity must increase. If the metal enters at the same speed as the surface of the rolls, it must leave faster, or if it leaves at the same speed as the rolls, it must enter slower. The actual speed conditions are somewhere between these extremes, in which the speed of the metal entering the rolls will be slower than the surface speed of the rolls, and it will leave faster than that of the rolls. This change in the relative speed means that at some point along the contacting area of the rolls, the speed of the rolls and of the metal is the same. This point or line is the neutral or no-slip point or line. Just as in the case of plane-strain compression of a strip, the metal before it reaches the neutral point will slip toward the entry side of the rolls, and when it passes the neutral point, it will slip toward the exit side of the rolls. Since at the neutral point or line no relative motion takes place between the material and the rolls, the frictional forces act toward the neutral or no-slip point both from the exit and entry sides resulting in a friction hill similar to that occurring in plane-strain compression of a strip as shown in Figs. 4.3 and 4.4(a).

6.2.5 Contact Surface Pressure Distribution in Rolling

The derivation and the general solution of the differential equation for the pressure distribution along the arc of contact in strip rolling without external tension on the ends of the sheet is very much more involved than that for the plane-strain compression analogy, and it consequently will not be presented here in full. The procedure used is similar, however, to that contained in Chap. 4 on hot compression and hot forging, and it will be outlined here very briefly [6.4].

As shown in Fig 6.11(a) two slices or segments on each side of the neutral or no-slip point are taken, freebody diagrams are drawn, and the summation of forces for equilibrium are made similar to what was done in the plane-strain compression problem. Essentially, the same assumptions are made, i.e., plane-strain compression, homogeneous deformation, rigid–perfectly plastic material, constant coefficient of friction and arc of contact, and no elastic deformation of the rolls.

The following additional assumptions are made: the principal stresses lie in the x and y directions, the radial and vertical pressures are the same, and the rate of strainhardening is low.

In Fig. 6.11, the longitudinal resolution of the forces acting on an element A, of unit width, in the deformation zone, on the exit side of the neutral point gives the following forces:

$$(\sigma_x + d\sigma_x)(h + dh) - h\sigma_x \qquad \text{due to longitudinal stress}$$

$$2\left(p_r \frac{dx}{\cos \alpha}\right) \sin \alpha \qquad \text{due to radial pressure on both rolls}$$

$$2\mu\left(p_r \frac{dx}{\cos \alpha}\right) \cos \alpha \qquad \text{due to friction against both rolls}$$

For steady-state rolling, these forces must be in equilibrium:

$$h \, d\sigma_x + \sigma_x \, dh + 2p_r \, dx \tan \alpha + 2\mu p_r \, dx = 0 \qquad (6.9)$$

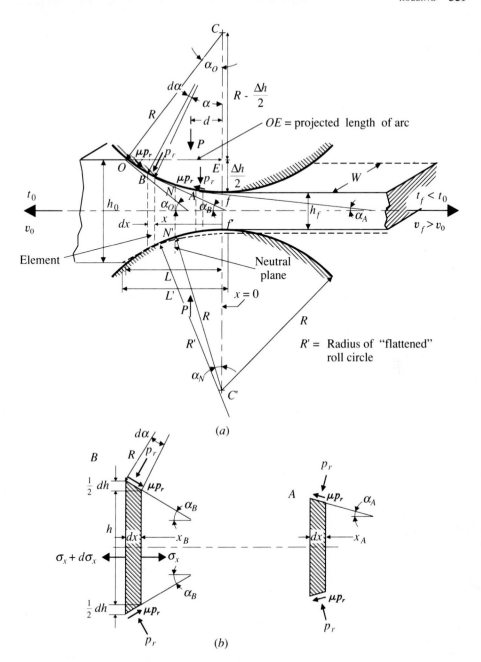

(a)

(b)

FIGURE 6.11

(*a*) Diagram showing the material being rolled through rolls of radius R from an initial thickness of h_0 to final thickness of h_f. Tension in the forward direction t_f, and backwards t_0, may or may not be applied. (*b*) Freebody diagrams of slices or segments taken on either side of the neutral or no-slip point or line [6.4].

The equilibrium of a similar element B in Fig. 6.11, on the entry side of the neutral point, gives a similar equation, but with the frictional force in the opposite direction:

$$h \, d\sigma_x + \sigma_x \, dh + 2p_r \, dx \tan \alpha - 2\mu p_r \, dx = 0 \tag{6.10}$$

It is convenient to combine these two equations:

$$h \, d\sigma_x + \sigma_x \, dh + 2p_r \, dx \tan \alpha \pm 2\mu p_r \, dx = 0 \tag{6.11}$$

The upper sign refers to the exit side of the neutral point, and the lower sign to the entry side. Substituting from Fig. 6.11(b) $dh = 2dx \tan \alpha$, one obtains

$$h \, d\sigma_x + \sigma_x \, dh + p_r \, dh \pm \mu p_r \, dh \cot \alpha = 0 \tag{6.12}$$

or

$$d(h\sigma_x) = -p_r(1 \pm \mu \cot \alpha) \, dh \tag{6.13}$$

By some simplification and manipulation, Eq. (6.13) in terms of the dimensionless ratio $p/\bar{\sigma}$ becomes

$$\frac{d}{d\alpha}\left[h\bar{\sigma}\left(1 - \frac{p}{\bar{\sigma}}\right)\right] = -2Rp \sin \alpha (1 \pm \mu \cot \alpha) \tag{6.14}$$

$$h\bar{\sigma}\frac{d}{d\alpha}\left(1 - \frac{p}{\bar{\sigma}}\right) + \left(1 - \frac{p}{\bar{\sigma}}\right)\frac{d(h\bar{\sigma})}{d\alpha} = -2Rp(\sin \alpha \pm \mu \cot \alpha) \tag{6.15}$$

where $\bar{\sigma}$ is the mean yield stress in plane strain $= 1.55\sigma_Y$.

By use of the simplification suggested by Bland and Ford [6.5], the second term in Eq. (6.15) can be neglected in comparison with the first, so that Eq. (6.15) becomes

$$h\bar{\sigma}\frac{d}{d\alpha}\left(\frac{p}{\bar{\sigma}}\right) = 2Rp(\sin \alpha \pm \mu \cot \alpha) \tag{6.16}$$

Since the angle of contact is small, $\sin \alpha \approx \alpha$, $\cos \alpha \approx 1 - \alpha^2/2 \approx 1$, the following equation is obtained:

$$\frac{d(p/\bar{\sigma})}{p/\bar{\sigma}} = \frac{2\alpha \, d\alpha}{h_\alpha/R + \alpha^2} \pm \frac{2\mu \, d\alpha}{h_\alpha/R + \alpha^2} \tag{6.17}$$

Integrating both sides of this equation and introducing the following symbol

$$H = 2\sqrt{\frac{R}{h_f}} \tan^{-1}\left(\sqrt{\frac{R}{h_f}}\,\alpha\right)$$

for the case of no front and back tension, the constant of integration can be evaluated and the following equations for the variation in the vertical roll pressures are obtained:

1. On the exit side of the neutral point,

$$p_f = \bar{\sigma}\frac{h}{h_f} e^{\mu H} \tag{6.18}$$

2. On the entry side of the neutral point,

$$p_0 = \bar{\sigma}\left(\frac{h}{h_0} e^{\mu(H_0 - H)}\right) \tag{6.19}$$

where h_f and h_0 = the final and initial thickness or height of the strip, respectively

h = the height of the intermediate slice, segment, or element

In Eqs. (6.18) and (6.19), H and H_0 are functions in the Bland and Ford solution [6.5] and are defined as

$$H = 2\sqrt{\frac{R}{h_f}} \tan^{-1}\left(\sqrt{\frac{R}{h_f}}\,\alpha\right) \tag{6.20}$$

$$H_0 = 2\sqrt{\frac{r}{h_f}} \tan^{-1}\left(\sqrt{\frac{R}{h_f}}\,\alpha_0\right) \tag{6.21}$$

where α = the angular position of any point on the arc of contact measured from the centerline between the roll centers

α_0 = the angular position of the surface entry point as measured above

Siebel and Lueg [6.6] first verified the existence of the friction hill by measuring the pressures in the roll gap using radially drilled holes in one roll which contained steel pins pressing against piezoelectric quartz crystals.

By use of the above equations, the theoretical vertical pressure distribution along the arc of contact may be plotted as shown in Fig. 6.12(a) for a low

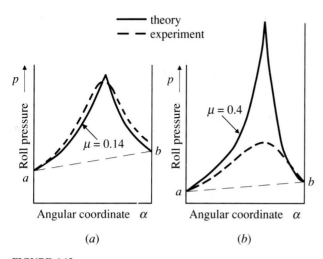

FIGURE 6.12
Comparison of experimentally determined variation of roll pressure along the arc of contact with the results of Orowan's theory for (a) low friction and (b) high friction conditions [6.4].

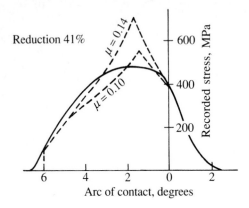

FIGURE 6.13
Pressure distribution curves with transverse displacements of the measuring pin across the strip for a 45 percent reduction in thickness by cold rolling of an annealed high conductivity copper strip 40 mm wide and 2 mm thick [6.7].

coefficient of friction. The experimental distribution is plotted by means of a dashed line. The theoretical pressure distribution is plotted in Fig. 6.12(*b*) for a modified, improved theory for high friction, and the corresponding experimental curve is shown by a dashed line. The fact that the experimental pressure distribution does not rise to a sharp peak, as for the theoretical solution, mainly indicates that the neutral "point" is not really a line but an area due to roll deformation, etc. The area above *ab* bounded by the curves represents the force required to overcome friction between the rolls and the sheet, whereas the area under the

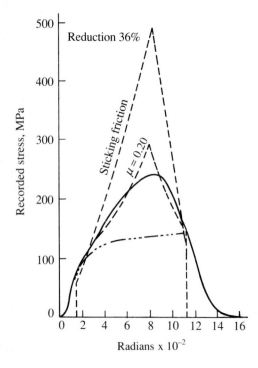

FIGURE 6.14
Comparison of the experimental stress distribution along the arc of contact at the center of the strip in cold rolling of an annealed high conductivity copper strip for a 40 percent reduction in thickness [6.7].

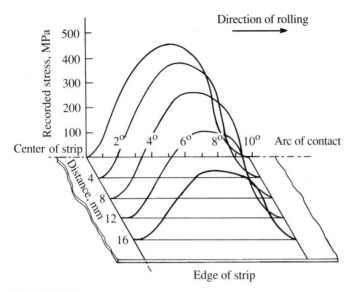

FIGURE 6.15
Comparison of the experimental pressure distribution in hot rolling of high conductivity copper with theoretical calculations by the Orowan method [6.7].

dashed line *ab* represents the force required to deform the metal in plane-strain homogeneous deformation.

Smith et al. [6.7] used a photoelastic dynamometer, inside the lower roll, to measure the normal force exerted on a small radial pin inset into the roll. Fig. 6.13 shows the pressure distribution curve with transverse displacement of the measuring pin across the strip for a 45 percent reduction in thickness by cold rolling of an annealed high conductivity copper strip 40 mm wide by 2 mm thick. Fig. 6.14 [6.7] compares the experimental stress distribution along the arc of contact at the center of the strip in cold rolling of an annealed high conductivity copper strip for a 40 percent reduction in thickness and no back tension, with theoretical calculations for two different assumed coefficients of friction, by the Orowan method [6.2]. Figure 6.15 compares the experimental pressure distribution in hot rolling of high conductivity copper with theoretical calculations by the Orowan method for sticking and slipping friction.

6.2.6 Calculation of Rolling Load and Torque

Anyone involved with rolling usually wants to know the load or torque required to make a particular reduction by rolling under a given set of conditions. Because of the importance of rolling, much effort has been expended to provide the relationships for calculating or determining the load and torque required that are simple, accurate, and generally applicable. Many approaches have been proposed, that have their advantages and disadvantages, some being better than others. A distinction must always be made as to whether the approach applies to cold rolling, for which strainhardening is important, or to hot rolling, for which the strain rate effect is important, or to both. Only a few approaches will be presented here such as by Ekelund [6.8] and by Orowan and Pascoe [6.9] for hot rolling, and by Bland and Ford [6.5] for cold rolling.

6.2.7 Separating Force, Torque, and Work in Hot Rolling

6.2.7.1 PLANE STRAIN COMPRESSION ANALOGY.
The rolling load or force is, of course, the force with which the rolls press against the metal being rolled. Because this force is equal and opposite to a force trying to separate the rolls, it is commonly called the *roll separating force*. If it is expressed as roll load or force divided by the area of contact between the roll and the strip, it is called the *mean specific roll pressure*.

Since an analogy was made between plane-strain compression and rolling and since the coefficient of friction in hot rolling can be approximately taken as $\mu = 0.5$, without introducing too great an error, Eq. (4.29) may be used to estimate the rolling load or roll separating force from the mean pressure p_m:

$$p_m \cong \bar{\sigma}\left(1 + \frac{b}{4h_f}\right) \tag{4.29}$$

In the derivation of the above expression, it was assumed that plane sections remain plane, but in rolling, an inhomogeneous stress distribution obtains. Orowan demonstrated that the effect of the foregoing situation results in reducing the pressure by a factor of 0.8. The above expression is therefore written as

$$p_m \cong \bar{\sigma}\left(0.8 + \frac{x}{4h_f}\right) \tag{6.22}$$

where h_f is taken as the thickness of the sheet after rolling [6.10].

If $w =$ the width of the sheet and $x = l_p$, the projected length of the arc of contact, which is given by

$$l_p = \left[R(h_0 - h_f) - \frac{(h_0 - h_f)^2}{4}\right]^{1/2}$$

and

$$l_p \cong [R(h_0 - h_f)]^{1/2} \cong \sqrt{R\,\Delta h} \tag{6.1)(6.23}$$

may be used to obtain the rolling load P. [The projected length of the arc of contact was given previously by Eq. (6.7).]

Then P, the approximate rolling load or roll separating force, is obtained by use of Eqs. (6.22) and (6.23) as

$$P = w l_p p_m$$

or

$$\tag{6.24}$$

$$P = w\sqrt{R\,\Delta h}\,\bar{\sigma}\left(0.8 + \frac{l_p}{4h}\right)$$

where $w =$ width of the sheet; $l_p =$ length of the projected arc of contact.

The above expression applies for the plane-strain condition, in which the sheet width is at least six to eight times the thickness. Where the sheet width is less than that, the effect of the spreading of the sheet must be taken into consideration.

6.2.7.2 EKELUND'S EQUATION. Ekelund [6.8] developed the following equation first for hot rolling in 1927, in which he took into account the influence of strain rate on the mean yield stress:

$$\frac{P}{w} = \left[\sigma + \frac{2v\eta\sqrt{\Delta h/R}}{h_0 + h_f} \right] \sqrt{R\,\Delta h} \left(1 + \frac{1.6\mu\sqrt{R\,\Delta h} - 1.2\,\Delta h}{h_0 + h_f} \right) \tag{6.25}$$

where v is the peripheral speed of the rolls in mm/s, and σ is the yield stress. η, the so-called viscosity of hot steel, and μ, the coefficient of friction are defined below:

$$\eta = 1373 - 0.098\,T \qquad \text{and} \qquad \mu = 0.84 - 0.0004\,T$$

(for billet temperatures T in excess of 700°C).

The temperature is in °C, and the yield stress is in kN/mm^2. It is now desirable to determine the mean yield stress directly for the existing temperature and strain-rate conditions.

If the term in the square brackets is replaced by $\bar{\sigma}$ and R is replaced R', which takes roll flattening into consideration and which will be discussed later, Ekelund's equation for cold rolling results. This equation, although based on a very simplified method of stress analysis, gives very good predictions of roll loads over a wide range of sizes and redundancy, and it is recommended for general purpose use [6.4].

6.2.7.3 ROLL TORQUE. The torque or twisting moment on the rolls may be obtained from the roll separating force P. Since it is spread out along the arc of contact as indicated by the friction hill, its effect on the torque is the same as if it were concentrated at a single point on the arc of contact at a distance d from the line through the center of the rolls. The product of the force P and the lever arm d, gives a torque on each roll, which must be overcome if the material is to be rolled. The lever arm d is often taken as one-half of the length of the projected arc of contact or $l_p/2$. Since the roll separating force acts on both rolls, by use of Eq. (6.7) the total torque is equal to

$$T = Pl_p \cong P\sqrt{R\,\Delta h} \qquad (\text{N} \cdot \text{m}) \tag{6.26}$$

During one revolution of each roll, P moves along the circumference of a circle equal to $(2\pi)(l_p/2)$, so that the total work for two rolls is

$$W = 2\left(2\pi\frac{l_p}{2} \right) P = 2\pi l_p P = 2\pi\sqrt{R\,\Delta h}\,P \qquad (\text{N} \cdot \text{m}) \tag{6.27}$$

6.2.8 The Effect of Tension and Roll Flattening in Cold Rolling

Since, in cold rolling, to keep the strip flat and also to control the thickness, front and/or back tension, t_f and t_0 is applied. Such tension also has a further advantage of reducing the rolling load. Also, in cold rolling, more roll flattening is expected and the metal strainhardens as it is rolled, so that allowance should be made for these factors.

To take external tension into consideration, Eqs. (6.18) and (6.19) for the pressure with *no* external tension are modified as follows:

1. On the exit side of the neutral axis

$$\frac{p_f}{\bar{\sigma}} = \left(1 - \frac{t_f}{\bar{\sigma}_f}\right)\frac{h}{h_f}\, e^{\mu H} \tag{6.28}$$

2. On the entry side of the neutral axis,

$$\frac{p_0}{\bar{\sigma}} = \left(1 - \frac{t_0}{\bar{\sigma}_0}\right)\frac{h}{h_0}\, e^{\mu(H_0 - H)} \tag{6.29}$$

where h is the thickness of an element (see Fig. 6.11). t_f and t_0 are the front and back tensions on the exit and entry side of the neutral axis, respectively. The subscripts 0 and f refer to the entry and exit side of the neutral point, respectively. These equations are similar to those in the absence of tension except the right term is multiplied by the factor $(1 - t_i/\bar{\sigma}_i)$.

H and H_0 in the above equations are defined by Eqs. (6.20) and (6.21), and are written here to include the effective radius R', called the *Hitchcock radius*, which is a larger radius of the rolls to which they flatten but retain their circular profile (which Orowan [6.2] showed was far from circular):

$$H = 2\sqrt{\frac{R'}{h_f}}\tan^{-1}\left(\sqrt{\frac{R'}{h_f}}\,\alpha\right) \tag{6.30}$$

$$H_0 = 2\sqrt{\frac{R'}{h_0}}\tan^{-1}\left(\sqrt{\frac{R'}{h_0}}\,\alpha_0\right) \tag{6.31}$$

The value for R' suggested by Hitchcock is [6.4]

$$R' = R\left(1 + \frac{16(1 - \nu^2)P}{\pi E\,\Delta h}\right) \tag{6.32}$$

where R = undeformed roll radius
  ν = Poisson's ratio of the work rolls
  P = specific force applied to the rolls per unit of length of rolls, lbf/in (N/m)
  E = modulus of elasticity of the roll material
  Δh = the total reduction in thickness of the workpiece called the draft
   = $h_0 - h_f$

The roll separating force per unit width, P/w, is obtained by integrating the vertical roll pressure p_f and p_0 over the area of contact through an angle equal to $\alpha_n + (\alpha_0 - \alpha_n)$ as follows:

$$\frac{P'}{w} = R' \int_0^\alpha p \, d\alpha = R' \left(\int_0^{\alpha_N} p_f \, d\alpha + \int_{\alpha_N}^\alpha p_0 \, d\alpha \right) \tag{6.33}$$

where $P' =$ rolling load based on R'

$$R' = R \left(1 + \frac{CP'}{(h_0 - h_f)w} \right) = R \left(1 + \left(\frac{C}{\Delta h} \right) \left(\frac{P'}{w} \right) \right) \tag{6.34}$$

$w =$ width of the sheet being rolled, mm

$C =$ a constant depending on the elastic constants of the rolls (E and ν)

($C \cong 0.022$ mm^2/kN or 1.52×10^{-7} in^2/lbf for steel)

C for the Hitchcock approximation given in Eq. (6.32), is given by

$$C = \frac{16(1 - \nu^2)}{\pi E} \tag{6.35}$$

The solution to the above equation to obtain the rolling load P may be obtained by use of the digital computer. It may also be obtained by manual calculation by integrating graphically appropriate values of the vertical pressure p versus α according to Eqs. (6.28), (6.29), (6.30), (6.31), (6.32), and (6.33), since

$$\frac{P}{w} = R' \int_0^\alpha p \, d\alpha = R'(\Delta A) \qquad \left(\frac{\text{kN rad}}{\text{mm}} \right) \tag{6.36}$$

where ΔA is the area under the p versus α curve as shown in Fig. 6.16.

For calculation of R', Orowan's approximate equation

$$\frac{P}{w} = 1.2\bar\sigma \sqrt{R \, \Delta h} \tag{6.3)(6.37}$$

may be used in conjunction with Eq. (6.35). $\bar\sigma$ may be found from the true stress–true strain curve, using the area up to $\varepsilon = \ln h_0/h_f$. α may be found from

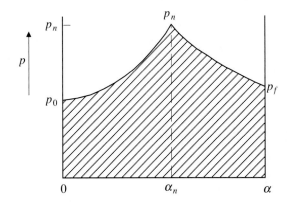

FIGURE 6.16
Schematic diagram showing method of obtaining the value of $\int_0^\alpha p \, d\alpha = \Delta A$ from p versus α plot, where ΔA is the hatched area.

the relation

$$h_0 - h_f = \Delta h = R'\alpha^2 \quad \text{or} \quad \alpha = \sqrt{\frac{\Delta h}{R'}} \tag{6.38}$$

The rolling load or roll separating force may be calculated from

$$P = w(\text{mm}) R'(\text{mm}) \int_0^\alpha p \, d\alpha \quad \frac{\text{kN}}{\text{mm}^2} \tag{6.39}$$

To evaluate P, p_0 and p_f of Eqs. (6.18) and (6.19) are plotted against α from p_0 to p_n and from p_n to p_f as shown in Fig. 6.16. The area under the curve has usually been obtained manually, but a computer program in Basic has been devised to do this tedious task (see Prob. 6.6).

6.2.9 Strain Rate in Rolling

As in other hot-metalworking processes, the flow stress $\bar{\sigma}$ is a function of strain rate $\dot{\varepsilon}$, which depends on the speed of rolling. In practice, it is usually satisfactory to determine merely the mean rate of strain $\dot{\varepsilon}_{st}$ for sticking friction from

$$\dot{\varepsilon}_{st} = v \left[\frac{2}{D(h_0 - h_f)} \right]^{1/2} \ln \frac{h_0}{h_f} \tag{6.40}$$

where v = surface speed of the rolls, D = diameter of the rolls, and h_0 and h_f are the initial and final thicknesses, respectively.

The above mean strain rate for sticking friction, where the velocity of the material is equal to the velocity of the working rolls, is obtained by first obtaining the rate at which an element under the rolls, as shown dashed in Fig. 6.11, is deformed. If the angle α, formed by the radius of a work roll to any deformation element in the workpiece between the rolls along the arc of contact, and if the peripheral speed is v and the element height is h, the rate at which it is compressed is $2v \sin \alpha$. The strain rate at which each element is deformed is $2v \sin \alpha / h$. If the height (thickness) of the exiting strip is h_f and the diameter of the work rolls is D, then [6.12]

$$h = h_f + D(1 - \cos \alpha) \tag{6.41}$$

The strain rate of each element under conditions of sticking friction is

$$\dot{\varepsilon}_{h\alpha} = \frac{2v \sin \alpha}{h_f + D(1 - \cos \alpha)} \tag{6.42}$$

When slipping friction occurs the velocity of the workpiece cannot be assumed to be equal to the peripheral velocity of the work rolls. There is only one point (line) where they are the same and that is at the neutral point (line).

For slipping friction, therefore, the neutral angle α_N must be taken into consideration. The mean deformation rate is derived similar to that for sticking friction to give

$$\dot{\varepsilon}_{sl} = \left[\frac{vh_\alpha \cos \alpha_N}{h_0 h_f}\right]\left[\frac{2(h_0 - h_f)}{D}\right]^{1/2} \tag{6.43}$$

which may also be written as

$$\dot{\varepsilon}_{sl} = \left[\frac{vh_\alpha \cos \alpha_N}{h_0^2(1-r)}\right]\left[\frac{2(h_0 - h_f)}{D}\right]^{1/2} \tag{6.44}$$

If $h_\alpha \approx h_f$, then for the case of slipping friction, the mean strain rate may be approximated by

$$\dot{\varepsilon}_{sl} = \frac{v}{h_0}\left[\frac{2(h_0 - h_f)}{D}\right]^{1/2} \tag{6.45}$$

where v, D, h_0, and h_f are defined above in conjunction with Eq. (6.40). In general, the rate of deformation with slipping friction for equal conditions will be lower than for sticking friction.

A more exact solution is

$$\dot{\varepsilon}_{sl} = \left[\frac{v(3h_f + h_0)}{4h_0 h_f(2h_0 - h_f)}\right]\frac{2(h_0 - h_f)}{D^{1/2}} \cos \alpha_N \tag{6.46}$$

where v = the surface speed of the rolls
h_α = thickness of the workpiece at the neutral plane as shown in Fig. 6.17
α_N = neutral plane-exit plane angle
h_o = entry workpiece thickness
h_f = final thickness as rolled
D = work roll diameter
r = the reduction expressed as a decimal fraction [6.11]

If the neutral plane is assumed to coincide with the exit plane, i.e., no forward slip occurs, and the effective deformed diameter of the work rolls is

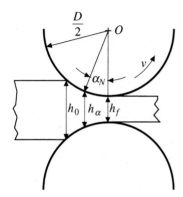

FIGURE 6.17
Sketch showing the roll bite for strain rate computation [6.12].

assumed to be 2.5 times their actual diameter, the following equation ensues

$$\dot{\varepsilon} \approx 0.0358v\left(\frac{4}{Dh_0}\right)^{1/2} \tag{6.47}$$

where v is in mm/s, and D and h_0 are in mm.

It should be remembered that the above expressions represent the average strain rate occurring in the roll bite. In reality, the strain rate varies along the entire length of the arc of contact, decreasing continually from a maximum value at the entry.

The effect of the strain rate on the roll load may be taken into consideration by correcting the flow stress by some such relationship as $\bar{\sigma} = C\dot{\varepsilon}^m$, and using this value of the flow stress in the calculations. Typically, strain rates in cold rolling are in the range of 10 to 1000 s^{-1}, which may result in dynamic yield strengths of twice the yield strength as usually measured.

6.2.10   Constrained Yield Strength of the Workpiece [6.12]

In rolling operations, in addition to pulling the workpiece into the rolls, friction is necessary both to impart deformation energy from the rolls to the strip and to prevent the lateral spread of the strip as it is rolled. It is still desirable to determine the pressure or stress that must be exerted by the work rolls on the strip to deform it plastically in the absence of frictional forces acting parallel to the direction of rolling. This is a problem in plane strain. The frictional constraint in the transverse direction gives rise to the principal compressive stress σ_2 that will permit no change in width of the strip in the roll bite when the strip is subjected to the other principal stresses σ_1 and σ_3. If proportional loading is assumed, Eq. (2.78b) applies,

$$\varepsilon_2 = \frac{\bar{\varepsilon}}{\bar{\sigma}}[\sigma_2 - \tfrac{1}{2}(\sigma_1 + \sigma_3)] \tag{2.78b}$$

Since, in plane strain, $\varepsilon_2 = 0$, then

$$\sigma_2 = \tfrac{1}{2}(\sigma_1 + \sigma_3) \tag{6.48}$$

When this value for σ_2 is substituted in the expression representing the von Mises yielding criterion, one obtains

$$\sigma_1 - \sigma_3 = \frac{2}{\sqrt{3}}\sigma_Y = 1.155\sigma_Y = \sigma_C \tag{6.49}$$

where σ_Y is the yield strength in uniaxial tension, and σ_C is the so-called "constrained yield strength."

One expression for the constrained yield strength as affected from the constraint to the sideways flow of the strip in the roll bite, that has been presented [6.12], is

$$\sigma_C = 1.155(\sigma_Y + a \log_{10} 1000\dot{\varepsilon}) \tag{6.50}$$

where σ_Y is the yield strength as conventionally measured at low strain rates. $\dot{\varepsilon}$ is the strain rate during rolling, and a is the strain rate effect which is constant with a value of about 6250 psi (43.1 MPa) per decade change in strain rate.

6.2.11 Calculating the Coefficient of Friction in Cold Rolling [6.12]

If the strip tensions and the dynamic yielding characteristics of the strip are known, it is possible to calculate the coefficient of friction solely from measurements of the rolling force The ease with which this can be done depends on the mathematical rolling model used. The overall rolling model used consists basically of the following relationships:

1. The strain rate $\dot{\varepsilon}$, such as Eq. (6.47)

$$\dot{\varepsilon} \approx 0.0358 v \left(\frac{r}{Dh_0} \right)^{1/2} \tag{6.47}$$

2. The constrained yield stress σ_C, such as Eq. (6.50)

$$\sigma_C = 1.155(\sigma_Y + a \log_{10} 1000\dot{\varepsilon}) \tag{6.50}$$

3. The deformed roll diameter of radius R', such as Eq. (6.32)

$$R' = R \left(1 + \frac{16(1 - \nu^2) P}{\pi E \, \Delta h} \right) \tag{6.32}$$

4. The coefficient of friction μ, whose equation is given below.

The equation for μ may be obtained by equating the product of the frictional force exerted by the roll surface ahead and after the neutral point to the spindle torque. One such expression so obtained is given as

$$\mu = 2\sqrt{\frac{2h_0}{D'r}} \left[\frac{P(1-r)}{\sigma_C - \sigma_1} \sqrt{\frac{2}{D'h_0 r}} - 1 + \frac{5r}{4} \right] \tag{6.51}$$

where r is the fractional reduction in thickness, and σ_1 is the average of the tensile stresses in the strip on the entry into and exit from the roll bite [6.12]. From a set of rolling data, the value of the strain rate determined by Eq. (6.47) can be substituted in Eq. (6.50) to yield the constrained yield stress, which in turn can be used in Eq. (6.51). The simultaneous solution of Eqs. (6.32) and (6.51) therefore yields the coefficient of friction μ. This solution has been presented in graphical form, but it is more convenient to use the computer for the solution (see Prob. 6.8).

6.2.12 Friction Angle and the Angle of Bite

As shown in Fig. 6.18, the forces acting on any point along the arc of contact, between the rolls and the sheet or plate may be resolved into two components,

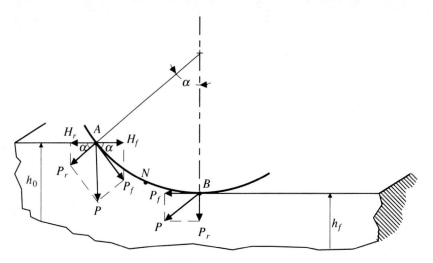

FIGURE 6.18
Forces acting at the point of entry A and the point of exit B during rolling.

the radial force P_r and the friction force P_f, as shown for the point of entry A and the point of exit B. The radial force at all points along the arc of contact except point B, act at an angle toward the entry and consequently has a horizontal component $H_r = P_r \sin \alpha$, which acts opposite to the rolling direction of the roll surface velocity at all points between the entry point A and the neutral or no-slip point N, and it acts opposite to the direction of the roll velocity at all points between N and the exit point B.

A sheet or plate of thickness h_0, brought in contact with the rolls at point A, will be drawn into the rolls if the horizontal forward force H_f is equal to or slightly greater than H_r, the backward force. Since $H_f = P_f \sin \alpha$ and $H_f = P_f \cos \alpha$, then the plate will be drawn into the rolls when

$$P_r \sin \alpha \leq P_f \cos \alpha$$

or

$$\frac{P_f}{P_r} \geq \frac{\sin \alpha}{\cos \alpha} = \tan \alpha$$

Since $\mu = P_f / P_r$,

$$\mu = \frac{P_f}{P_r} = \tan \theta = \tan \alpha \qquad (6.52)$$

where θ is the friction angle.

Clearly the material cannot be drawn into the rolls when the contact angle α is greater than the friction angle θ. Therefore, the coefficient of friction μ controls the maximum thickness or bite which the rolls can take without assistance. Since the contact angle at entry is determined by the diameter of the rolls and the amount of reduction to be made, to obtain large reductions with smooth rolls, i.e., low μ, large diameter rolls must be used. It is apparent that it may not always be desirable to reduce the coefficient of friction. In hot rolling, high values of μ are usually used with large diameter rolls to obtain large reductions in thickness, but with resulting high roll separating forces. In cold rolling, where smooth rolls are used to yield a good surface finish on the metal and where the yield strength of the metal is high, low values of μ and small diameter working rolls may be necessary.

6.2.13 Effect on the Roll Force by the Rolling Variables [6.9]

6.2.13.1 EFFECT OF THE MEAN FLOW STRESS. As can be seen from Eqs. (6.18), (6.19), and (4.29), the roll pressure, p (and the roll force) is directly proportional to $\bar{\sigma}$ and raises the friction hill as shown schematically in Fig. 6.19, provided that the other parameters are held constant.

6.2.13.2 EFFECT OF INTERFACIAL FRICTION. As was seen in the derivation for the pressure distribution across the arc of contact of the roll during rolling, the coefficient of friction μ has a decided effect on the roll pressure and the roll load. The experimental results, showing the effect of interfacial friction on the roll face pressure in the rolling of aluminum with 178 mm (7 in) diameter rolls to a reduction of about 50 percent in thickness by use of smooth and rough rolls, are presented in Fig. 6.20 [6.10].

6.2.13.3 EFFECT OF INITIAL THICKNESS FOR THE SAME REDUCTION. Increasing the initial thickness for the same reduction not only affects the maximum or mean roll force or pressure but also it influences the arc of contact, and the arc of contact to thickness ratio as shown in Fig. 6.21 for a 254 mm (10 in) wide, mild steel strip rolled with 610 mm (24 in) diameter rolls to a reduction of 30 percent from the initial thickness of 10.2 mm (0.4 in) and 2.54 mm (0.1 in). Since the contact area for the thinner strip is smaller than that for the thicker one, 3.9×10^3 mm^2 (6 in^2) versus 7.7×10^3 mm^2 (12 in^2), it is expected that the rolling load would be less, 5.27 MN (592 tons) versus 3.26 MN (366 tons). Although the

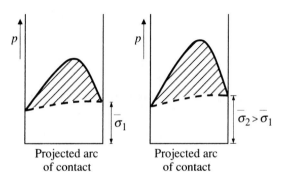

Projected arc of contact   Projected arc of contact

FIGURE 6.19
Schematic diagrams showing the effect of increase in the flow stress or roll face pressure p, and consequently of the roll force P.

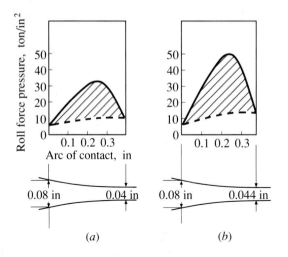

FIGURE 6.20
The effect of interfacial friction on the roll face pressure illustrated by rolling of aluminum using 178 mm (7 in) diameter rolls to about 50 percent reduction in thickness by use of (*a*) smooth rolls and (*b*) rough rolls. (*From E. C. Lake, The Rolling of Strip, Sheet, and Plate, Champman and Hall, London, 1963.*)

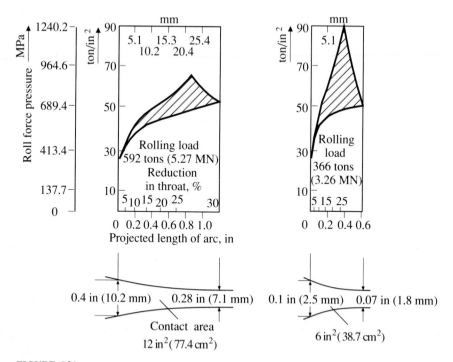

FIGURE 6.21
The effect of the initial strip thickness on the roll face pressure for a 30 percent reduction of mild steel with 610 mm (24 in) diameter rolls. (*From E. C. Lake, The Rolling of Strip, Sheet, and Plate, Champman and Hall, London, 1963.*)

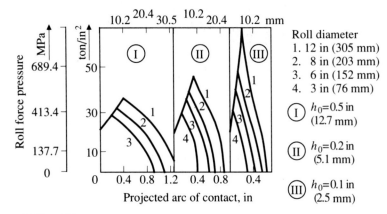

FIGURE 6.22
The effect of roll diameter on the roll face pressure in the rolling of copper. (*From M. Cook and E. C. Lake, J. Inst. Metals, 1945, Vol. 71, p. 371.*)

contact areas differ by 50 percent, the rolling loads differ by only 36 percent because of the zones of restrained deformation are closer together and play a greater role in the overall deformation.

6.2.13.4 EFFECT OF THE ROLL RADIUS. The effect of reducing the roll diameter is to reduce the roll pressure and load as shown in Fig. 6.22 for the rolling of copper [6.10].

6.2.13.5 EFFECT OF BACK AND FRONT TENSION. Back and front tension has already been discussed in regard to the pressure on the exit and entry sides of the neutral point in conjunction with Eqs. (6.28) and (6.29). It has also already been seen that external friction during rolling causes longitudinal stresses which increase with friction up to sticking friction and which act toward the neutral point producing the so-called friction hill. Any external opposing stress in the form of front and back tension by the coiler and decoiler, respectively, would therefore decrease the friction hill as shown in Fig. 6.23 and would also affect

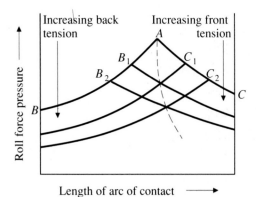

FIGURE 6.23
Effect of back tension (B_1 and B_2) and front tension (C_1 and C_2) on the height of the friction hill and the movement of the neutral point. Dashed line represents the movement of the neutral point for both back and front tension [6.10].

the location of the neutral point. If only back tension is used, the neutral point A moves toward the entry along the curve AB to positions B_1, B_2, etc., as the back tension is increased. With only front tension, the neutral point moves toward the exit to positions C_1, C_2, etc., as the front tension is increased. If equal back and front tension are applied simultaneously, the entire friction hill is depressed and the neutral point moves toward the exit side as shown by the dashed line, because of the greater effect of the front tension.

From the foregoing discussion, it is seen that, for a given metal of given dimensions, in order to decrease the roll load, rolling should be done under conditions of low friction, with rolls of small diameter and with front and back tension. There are, however, other considerations that may influence these conclusions.

6.2.14 Minimum Thickness in Cold Rolling

When thin hard strip is rolled, it is found that it is not possible to reduce the thickness below a certain minimum. Tightening the rolls together in an attempt to do so, results in greater elastic deformation of the rolls and mill housing without any further plastic deformation of the strip. The higher the modulus of elasticity of the rolls, the less the roll flattening. The less the roll flattening, the smaller the limiting thickness. As the roll radius is reduced, the area of roll contact is less for a given reduction, and the smaller is the limiting thickness. The higher the hardness of the metal being rolled, the greater the minimum thickness.

It has been found that the limiting, minimum thickness is a function of the above parameters as follows:

$$h_{min} = f(C, \mu, R, \bar{\sigma}) \tag{6.53}$$

One expression for h_{min} is

$$h_{min} = \frac{C\mu R}{E'}(\bar{\sigma} - \sigma_t) \tag{6.54}$$

where C is the elastic deformation parameter for roll flattening, and it may be expressed by

$$C = \frac{16(1 - v^2)}{\pi E} \tag{6.55}$$

The other parameters in [Eq. (6.54)] are defined as follows:

$\mu = $ coefficient for friction
$R = $ radius of the work rolls, mm
$E' = \dfrac{E}{(1 - v^2)}$
$\bar{\sigma} = $ average plane-strain flow stress (MPa) $= (\sigma_1 + \sigma_2)/2$ where σ_1 and σ_2 are the flow stress at the entry and exit of the rolls
$\sigma_t = (\sigma_{ft} + \sigma_{bt})/2 = $ the mean forward and backward tension

For steel rolls *only* for $E = 201$ GPa, h_{min} may be expressed as

$$h_{min} = 22.234 \mu R \bar{\sigma} \quad (\text{mm}) \tag{6.56}$$

Consequently, to obtain the thinnest possible strip, the material used for making the rolls should have a high modulus of elasticity such as tungsten carbide, the coefficient of friction should be as low as possible by using polished rolls and a good lubricant, and small diameter rolls, and the metal being rolled should be soft. Front and back tension would decrease the limiting thickness, but tearing and distortion of the thin foil would result. Thinner foil may be cold rolled by stacking two or more sheets on top of each other prior to rolling, as is done in rolling of aluminum foil; however, the surface finish of the interfaces not in contact with the rolls will be dull.

6.2.15   Inhomogeneous Deformation in Rolling

In comparison with other metalworking processes, the deformation produced by rolling for heavy reductions, in which the plastic zone penetrates to the centerline of the workpiece, rolling is a relatively uniform or homogeneous process. However, investigations with grid-lines have shown that the surface layers are not only in compression but also in shear. During homogeneous deformation, straight lines scribed or marked vertically on the central vertical plane of a workpiece should remain straight during and after rolling as shown in Fig. 6.24(*a*). In practice, some backward extrusion results in the entry zone, which bends the straight lines backward, and some forward extrusion occurs in the exit zone, which straightens them up again slightly as shown in Figs. 6.24(*b*) and 2.90(*c*). The difference between inhomogeneous and homogeneous deformation under similar conditions gives rise to redundant deformation, which decreases the efficiency of rolling. The foregoing equilibrium analysis does not take redundancy into consideration; however, it can be taken into consideration in the slip-line field method.

Another type of nonuniform deformation results when the plastic deformation is not uniform throughout the thickness, as shown in Fig. 6.25(*a*). Since, in this case, the surface of the strip may also deform laterally while the center remains unchanged in width, an overhang may result. In subsequent passes, the

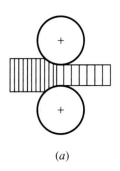

(*a*)

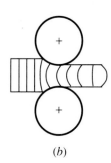

(*b*)

FIGURE 6.24
Distortion of vertical lines in the central vertical section during rolling in case of (*a*) homogeneous deformation and (*b*) for inhomogeneous deformation in which the lines first bend backward and then straighten slightly. (*Adapted from J. A. Schey, The More Common Fabrication Processes, in Techniques of Metals Research, R. F. Bunshah, Ed., Vol. 1, Part 3, Interscience Publishers, 1968, p. 1442.*)

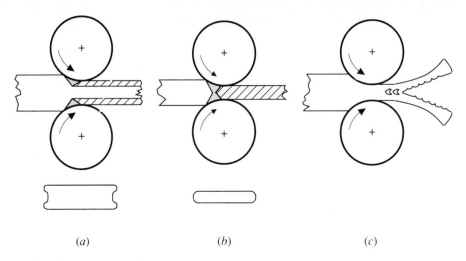

(a) (b) (c)

FIGURE 6.25
Nonuniform deformation which may result in cracking from (a) overhang, (b) barreling, or (c) central defect formation and alligatoring. (*Adapted from J. A. Schey, The More Common Fabrication Processes, in Techniques of Metals Research, R. F. Bunshah, Ed., Vol. 1, Part 3, Interscience Publishers, 1968, p. 1454.*)

overhang may not be compressed directly but is forced to elongate by the neighboring material. Higher tensile stresses may be set up, which may lead to edge cracking. A sequence of heavy passes may cause barreling in narrow strips as shown in Fig. 6.25(b), which in production may be controlled by use of vertical edge rolls. Nonuniform deformation in metal of limited ductility may cause alligatoring as shown in Fig. 6.25(c), especially if it contains a coarse cast microstructure or laminations. Alligatoring is usually caused by ductile metal surfaces, more than the center, being deformed in rolling, thereby leading to cracking, particularly if center defects are present.

6.2.16 Slip-Line Field for the Hot-Rolling Process

Although the foregoing approach for setting up equilibrium equations for the forces acting on a slice or segment of material under the rolls in the rolling process gives a good estimate of the magnitude and distribution of the roll face pressure, it does not give a good description of the way the metal flows during rolling. Also, it is difficult to formulate a physical picture of the concept of a neutral or no-slip point and to reconcile the rounding of the friction hill at its peak. One of the ways to get a better appreciation of the rolling process is to construct a slip-line field and a velocity diagram or hodograph for it. The slip-line field type of solution is of more importance in hot rolling than cold rolling, because the amount of distortion, and consequently the redundant work, is greater.

Alexander [6.3] presented a slip-line field solution for hot rolling for a rigid–perfectly plastic material during which sticking friction occurs. He presented his results in the form of three diagrams: (*a*) the physical plane diagram showing the slip-line field; (*b*) the stress plane diagram representing the state of stress at any point along a slip-line in a physical plane; and (*c*) the velocity diagram or hodograph. The effect of rotation of the rolls is accounted for by taking into consideration the effect of rotation on a velocity diagram. Because of space limitations and complexities involved, only the first of these will be considered here.

The slip-line field diagram shown in Fig. 6.26 is for the solution of a problem in hot rolling for the conditions in which the roll radius is 381 mm (15 in), the entry thickness h_0, is 6.6 mm (0.259 in), the exit thickness h_f is 4.4 mm (0.173 in) giving a $33\frac{1}{3}$ percent reduction in thickness, and the arc of contact is assumed to remain circular and equal to that of the undeformed roll radius. Since the slip-line

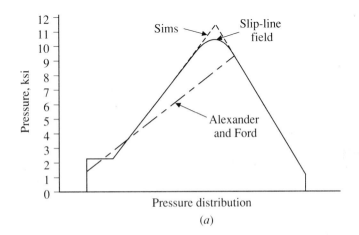

(a)

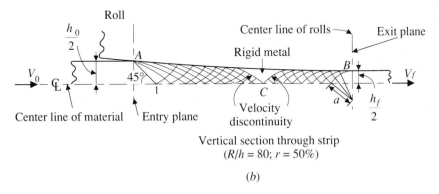

Vertical section through strip
$(R/h = 80;\ r = 50\%)$

(b)

FIGURE 6.26
(*a*) Pressure distribution along the arc of contact and (*b*) upper half of a symmetric slip-line field diagram for hot rolling of material with an entry thickness of 6.6 mm (0.259 in), exit thickness of 4.4 mm (0.173 in) and a circular arc of contact of 29.0 mm (1.14 in), using rolls of 127 mm (15 in) radius [6.5].

field is symmetric about the centerline of the material being rolled, only the upper half of the diagram is shown in Fig. 6.26(b). The length AB is taken so that the radius of the roll is equal to 13.16 times the distance AB. The metal enters at a velocity v_0 and leaves at v_f.

Point A is a singular point, and the entrance slip-line A1 is nearly straight and meets the roll surface at 45°. A curved slip-line is tangent to the roll surface at point B. The dead or rigid metal is shown as the labeled clear zone with point C on the centerline of the material. The plastic metal at the singular point C splits into two parts moving in opposite directions. The dead metal should rotate about point B relative to the remainder of the material with the angular velocity of the rolls, and there should be a constant tangential velocity discontinuity along the boundary between the dead-metal zone and the deformed metal.

Some of the contributions of this treatment are as follows:

1. The neutral point in the foregoing treatment is replaced by a neutral zone of rigid or dead metal.

2. A very thin surface layer or zone of rigid material adjacent to the roll surface starting at the entry point A is predicted to exist. A large velocity discontinuity exists between the boundary of this layer and the deformed metal underneath, which would correspond in the real metal to a band of intense shearing (localized flow) and which might contribute to "roll-pickup" of metal.

3. The curved slip-line, which is tangent to the roll surface at the exit point B, leads to a high ratio of the shear stress to normal stress of 1.9 at this point, for this example.

6.2.17 Bending and Crowning of Rolls

A mathematical analysis of work-roll bending has been carried out by Stone and Gray [6.13] from the viewpoint of a beam on an elastic foundation, which gives the deflection of the roll along its length transverse to the direction of rolling, called *cambering*. The crown is the barreling of the roll, which may not be uniform along its length but may be greater at the quarter points, for example. The difference in diameter as measured at the center of the roll and at one end is called a *crown*. A roll with a larger center diameter is said to have a *positive crown*, whereas a hollow-ground roll surface is said to have a *negative crown*. Rolls that are used cold are usually given a positive crown of constant curvature, but to avoid the work rolls touching each other beyond the edges of the strip, the curvature may be less at the center of the roll than at the ends. Back-up roll bending and the horizontal roll deflection might also be taken into consideration.

To counteract the effects of roll bending or cambering, the rolls usually are bowed or cambered as shown in Fig. 6.27 [6.14]. The degree of camber varies with the width of the sheet, the flow stress of the metal being rolled, and the reduction per pass. Insufficient amount of camber results in a thicker center as shown in Fig. 6.27(a) and Fig. 6.28(a), which means that the edge would be

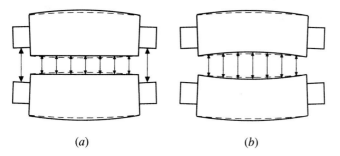

(a)   *(b)*

FIGURE 6.27
(*a*) Use of cambering to compensate for roll bending; (*b*) uncambered rolls result in a crown in the strip [6.14].

plastically elongated more than the center, resulting in tension at the centerline and compression along the edges. Such a stress pattern may cause centerline cracking, edge wrinkling, etc. Overcambering, as shown in Fig. 6.29(*a*), results in compression along the centerline and tension along the edges as in Fig. 6.29(*b*), resulting in edge cracking, splitting, and centerline wrinkling as in Fig. 6.29(*c*), (*d*), and (*e*) [6.14].

The effect of temperature gradients in the rolls must also be taken into consideration. A graphical energy balance model shown in Fig. 6.30 is designed to determine the partition of rolling energy among the various components, which may include the effects of strip quenching [6.1].

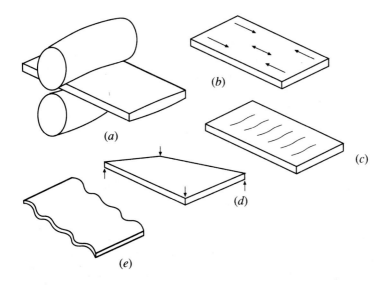

FIGURE 6.28
Possible detrimental effects of (*a*) insufficient amount of camber resulting in (*b*) undesirable stress pattern, (*c*) centerline cracking, (*d*) warping, and (*e*) edge wrinkling [6.14].

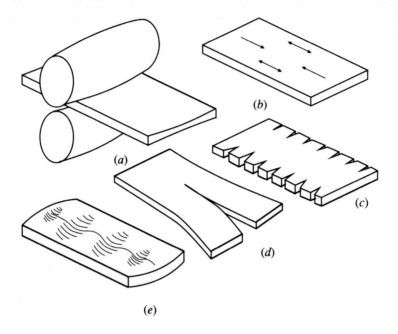

FIGURE 6.29
Possible detrimental effects of (a) over-camber resulting in (b) undesirable stress pattern, (c) edge cracking, (d) splitting, and (e) centerline wrinkling [6.14].

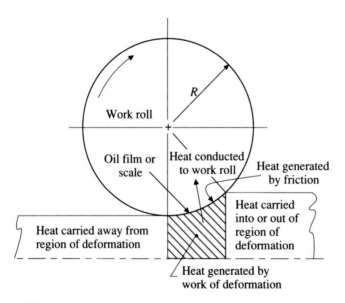

FIGURE 6.30
Graphical energy balance model for strip rolling [6.1].

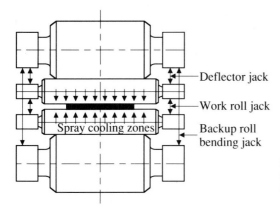

FIGURE 6.31
Cambering jack control system for four-high mill [6.15].

The roll thermal camber is due to the fact that the surface of the middle of the rolls runs warmer than the ends. The thermal camber must be equal and opposite to the mechanical deflection of the rolls. The roll gap and strip shape model is used to calculate, by iteration, the mechanical deflection of the rolls.

As shown in Fig. 6.31 for a four-high mill stand, hydraulic roll jacks may be used to push apart the chocks at the end of the work rolls to alleviate edge wave unflatness, and deflection jacks may be placed between the work and back-up roll chocks to counteract the formation of center buckles. Chocks are the bearing supports as shown in Fig. 6.2, for the ends of the rolls; the upper ones are usually movable to adjust the roll gap, etc., and the lower ones are usually fixed. Roll pairs and their chocks are often removed and replaced in the stands as an assembly.

Recent developments in steelmaking practice have resulted in changes in the conventional rolling practice used over the years. Two of these changes are the strand process of steelmaking involving continuous casting of the semifinished shapes and the computer analysis and control of the rolling process. These newer developments will be discussed here.

6.2.18 Computer Analysis of Rolling

The rolling of metallic materials involves a very complex application of independent and dependent mechanical, thermal, and physical parameters as shown in Fig. 6.8. Because of its complexity, the rolling process and the rolling mill can best be analyzed by means of mathematical models in conjunction with a computer. Rather than analyzing rolling operations and designing of rolling mills by use of historical and experimental data, a computer model may be used to simulate the operation of an existing mill or of a proposed new mill. The primary purposes of a computerized modeling are to aid in optimizing performance of existing mills, in the design of new mills, and in devising open- and closed-loop, automatic shape and flatness control systems. These programs are used primarily for the analysis of the rolling process and should not be confused with the computer

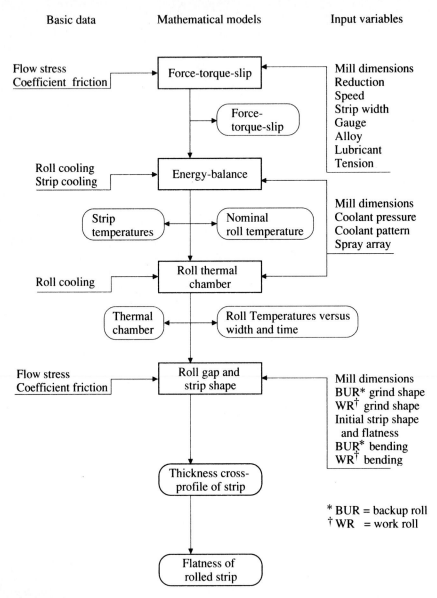

FIGURE 6.32
Simplified flowchart for the overall model for cold rolling in a single rolling mill stand [6.15].

programs for the on-line, automatic computer control and sequencing of rolling mills, some of which use adaptive or corrective feedback control.

A simplified flowchart of the overall model for cold rolling in a single rolling mill stand is shown in Fig. 6.32 [6.15]. The force-torque-slip model, shown in the chart, is used to predict the force normal to the plane of the sheet being rolled, the torque required to turn the rolls, and the forward slip. Forward slip is defined as the percentage increase of the strip exit speed over the roll speed. The main purpose of the roll-gap-and-strip shape model is to predict the exit strip thickness profile and flatness, entry and exit strip tensile stresses, roll bending jack pressures, and the mechanical grind or roll surface contour and thermal camber profiles of the work and backing rolls. The flowchart of this model is shown in Fig. 6.33 [6.15].

The term "shape" as applied to rolled strip refers either (1) to the cross-sectional profile of the strip or (2) to the ability of the strip to lie flat on a

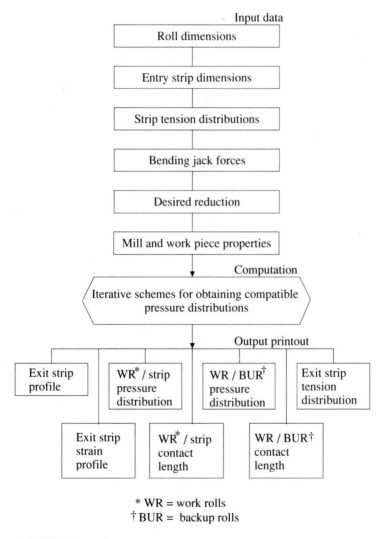

* WR = work rolls
† BUR = backup rolls

FIGURE 6.33
Flowchart of roll-gap-and-strip shape model [6.15].

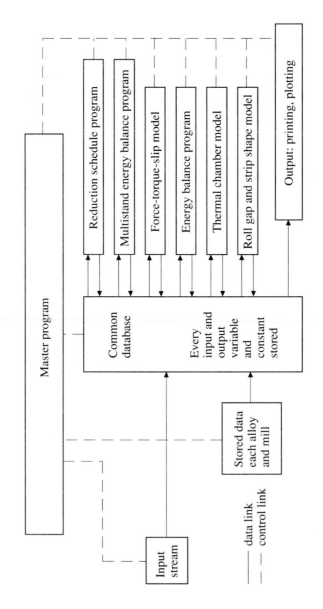

FIGURE 6.34
Master program and common data base [6.15].

horizontal planar surface. According to the former definition, the strip may contain a defect such as a crown whereas, according to the latter, it may contain such defects as longitudinal or cross bow, twist, edge waviness, center or quarter buckles, etc., as seen in Figs. 6.28 and 6.29.

The flowchart in Fig. 6.32 is for cold rolling in a single rolling mill stand. This model can be extended to multistand or multipass processing into a master program as shown in Fig. 6.34 [6.15]. One of these programs is the reduction schedule program, and the other is the multistand energy balance program. These are the mass and energy conservation programs that track these factors through a tandem mill or multiple passes through one or several mills.

The master computer program shown in Fig. 6.34 controls the sequence of analysis. It has a stored data file for the metal and the rolling mill and a common database, which reduces to a minimum the amount of information input.

The models used in the master program together with its flexibility make possible the following: (1) the analysis of production problems; (2) the identification and quantification of parameters for new mill design; and (3) the design of automatic control systems.

6.2.19 Computer Control of Rolling

Various degrees of process control are available for rolling mills from manual setting, to automatic decelerating and stopping equipment for reversing mills, to preprogrammed control systems, and finally to on-line computer control systems. A preprogrammed control system for a reversing mill, for example, may actuate or set the following: (a) the rolls per pass; (b) the thickness gauges; (c) the front and back tension per pass; (d) the speed per pass; (e) the auxiliary equipment such as spraying; and (f) the starting and stopping operation [6.12]. On-line computer control may be achieved by use of either a digital computer or an analog computer. An on-line computer control system is one in which a computer is connected to a process and the computer system responds to external stimuli as they occur. The input information in conjunction with the mathematical models describing the various aspects of the process determine what control of the operating conditions must be made by the computer to yield the desired results.

Digital computers used for control purposes may be able to do the following [6.12]:

1. Scan the sensors, transducers, and contact devices for data
2. Store the necessary information for control purposes
3. Perform the necessary computation
4. Make the necessary decisions or perform the necessary logic operations
5. Communicate with peripheral devices such as printers
6. Produce the output signals to control the rolling operation

Some use of analog computers has been made to control tandem mills, utilizing adaptive control, but these will not be discussed here.

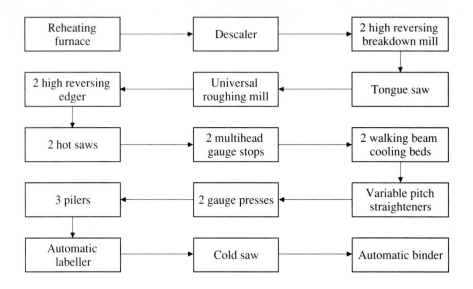

FIGURE 6.35
Layout of a fully computerized, wide-flange beam mill at Sumitomo's Kashima Works [6.11].

A fully computerized wide-flange I-beam rolling mill was put into production at Sumitomo's Kashima Works in Japan in 1975 [6.11]. It can also roll narrow flange beams and U-shaped piling with a projected capacity of 66,700 tonnes (66.7 Mg) per month. The flowchart for the layout of the mill is shown in Fig. 6.35.

The rolls are changed in the roughing and finishing mills by stand shifting. The edgers are stands that usually have horizontal rolls for rolling the web and vertical rolls for rolling the outer surfaces of the two flanges, which may or may not be driven. For automatic control purposes and minimizing labor costs, this mill utilizes 2 large process computers, 6 minicomputers, and 18 computerized sequence controllers.

The layout of Phoenix Steel's 160 in (4.1 m) plate mill is shown in Fig. 6.36 [6.11].

Figure 6.37 shows a flowchart of the automatic computer control system for a slabbing mill. This system controls (a) the scheduling of soaking (temperature control) pits associated with both a slabbing and a blooming mill, (b) information processing and process control for both mills, and (c) the automatic control of the slabbing mill operations [6.11].

After cold rolling, sheets are cleaned, annealed, and temper rolled as shown in the layout in Fig. 6.38 for low-carbon steel. Temper or skin-pass rolling is a very light reduction (0.1–1 percent) given to annealed stock in order to flatten the material, and to prevent stretcher strains (Luder's bands) in subsequent drawing operations [6.12].

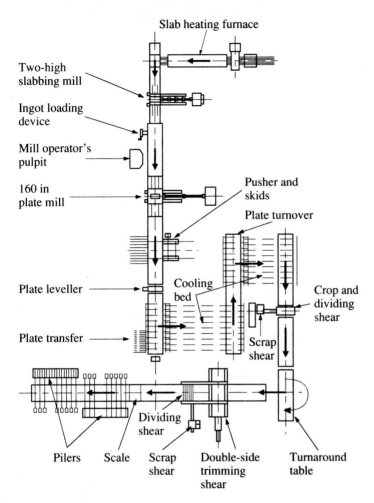

FIGURE 6.36
Layout of Phoenix Steel's 160 in (4.1 m) plate mill showing equipment location and material flow [6.11].

The overall processing cycle for the rolling of stainless steel sheets and strip is given in Fig. 6.39 as an example of the variety of operations that are involved in the production of sheet and strip [6.12].

6.2.20 Continuous (Strand) Casting of Semifinished Shapes

The continuous, direct casting of slabs, blooms, or billets, often called *strand casting*, is a newer method by which many steps in the traditional operations of steelmaking are bypassed. In this process, the molten steel from a melting furnace

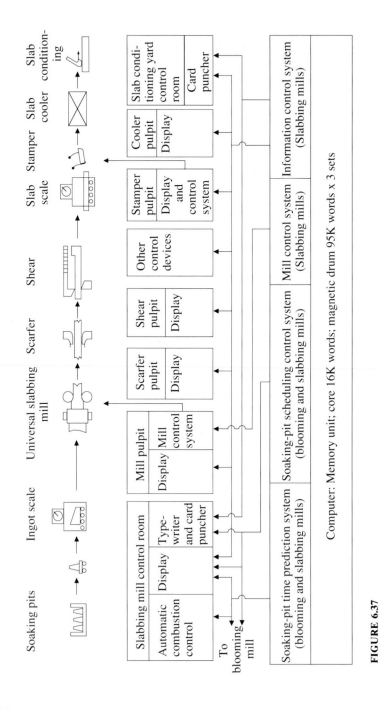

FIGURE 6.37
A computer control system for slabbing mill [6.11].

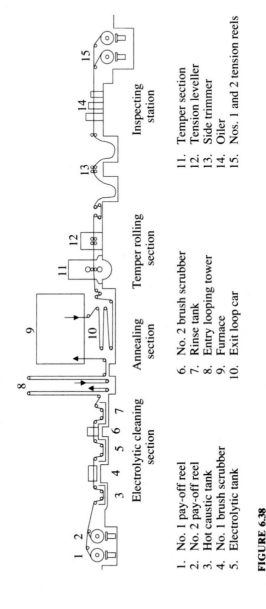

Electrolytic cleaning
section

Annealing
section

Temper rolling
section

Inspecting
station

1. No. 1 pay-off reel
2. No. 2 pay-off reel
3. Hot caustic tank
4. No. 1 brush scrubber
5. Electrolytic tank

6. No. 2 brush scrubber
7. Rinse tank
8. Entry looping tower
9. Furnace
10. Exit loop car

11. Temper section
12. Tension leveller
13. Side trimmer
14. Oiler
15. Nos. 1 and 2 tension reels

FIGURE 6.38
Layout of the continuous annealing and processing line for low-carbon steel sheet [6.12].

391

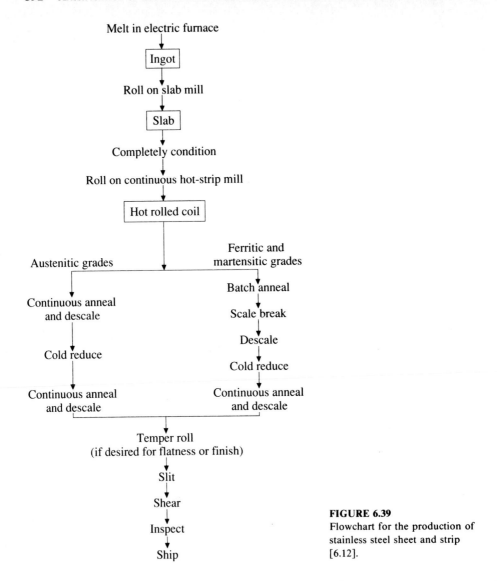

FIGURE 6.39
Flowchart for the production of stainless steel sheet and strip [6.12].

is lifted in a ladle to the top of the strand caster, where it is poured into a tundish, which feeds the molten steel into an oscillating mold to produce either slabs, blooms, or billets, depending upon its design. In the case of a slab caster, the solidified metal descends through pinch rolls, turned into a horizontal position, fed through a slab straightener and finally to a traveling-torch, cut-off table. A slab caster at the Gary Works of U.S. Steel is shown in Fig. 6.40 [6.11]. The semifinished shape is then transferred to the hot rolling facilities required for the desired mill forms just as in the traditional process. This particular single-strand unit is capable of producing about 2 million tons (1.8 Gg) of slabs per year in

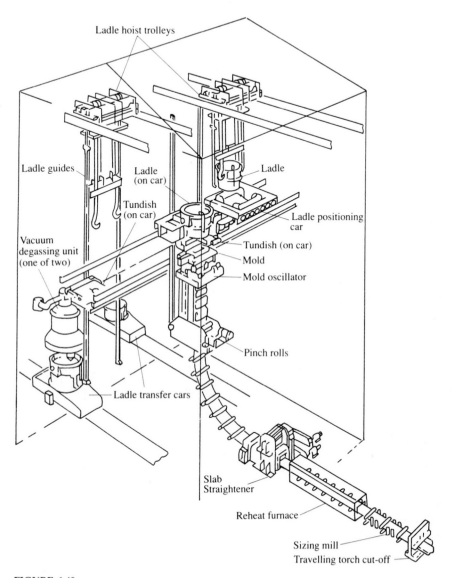

Ladle hoist trolleys

Ladle guides

Ladle
(on car)

Ladle

Tundish
(on car)

Ladle positioning
car

Vacuum
degassing unit
(one of two)

Tundish (on car)

Mold

Mold oscillator

Pinch rolls

Ladle transfer cars

Slab
Straightener

Reheat furnace

Sizing mill

Travelling torch cut-off

FIGURE 6.40
Slab caster at the Gary Works of U.S. Steel Corp. (circa late 1960s. Caster was redesigned 1984.)
[6.11]. [*Sketch courtesy of Connie Reasoner, Des Moines, Iowa.*]

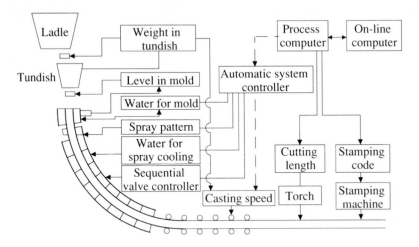

FIGURE 6.41
Automatic control system for a slab caster at Kashima Works of Sumitomo Metal Industries, Ltd. [6.11]

sizes up to 10 in (254 mm) thick and 76 in (1.9 m) wide required by an 84 in (2.1 m) continuous hot-strip mill. The successful operation of a slab caster is dependent upon the use of extensive instrumentation and automatic controls, as shown in Fig. 6.41 [6.11].

ACKNOWLEDGMENT

The material and most of the illustrations in this chapter were adapted from the references as indicated in the text and in the legends by the numbers of the references enclosed in square brackets pursuant to all copyrights.

REFERENCES

6.1. Lahoti, G. D. et al., "Application of Process Modeling to Hot Isothermal Rolling of Titanium Alloy Strips," *Formability Analysis Modeling and Experimentation*, S. S. Hecker et al. (eds.), Proceedings Symposium, Oct. 24-25, 1977, AIME, pp. 125-149.

6.2. Orowan, E., "The Calculation of Roll Pressure in Hot and Cold Flat Rolling," *Proc. Inst. Mech. Engrs.*, vol. 150, pp. 140-167, 1943.

6.3. Alexander, J. M., "A Slip-line Field for Hot Rolling Process," *Proc. Inst. Mech. Engrs.*, London, vol. 169, 1021-1030, 1955.

6.4. Rowe, G. W., *Principles of Industrial Metalworking Processes*, Edward Arnold, London, 1977, pp. 208-259.

6.5. Bland, D. R., and H. Ford, "The Calculation of Roll Force and Torque in Cold Strip Rolling with Tension," *Proc. Inst. Mech. Engrs.*, vol. 159, pp. 144-153, 1948.

6.6. Siebel, E., and W. Lueg, *Mitteilungen aus dem Kaiser-Wilhelm Inst.*, 1933, vol. 15, pp. 1-14.

6.7. Smith, C. L., F. H. Scott, and W. Sylwestrowicz, "Pressure Distribution Between Stock and Rolls in Hot and Cold Flat Rolling," *J. Iron and Steel Inst.*, 1952, vol. 152, pp. 347-359.

6.8. Ekelund, S., "The Analysis of Factors Influencing Rolling Pressure and Power Consumption in the Hot Rolling of Steel," *Steel*, vol. 93, nos. 8-14, 1933 (Translated from Jerkontorets Ann., Feb. 1927 by Blomquist.)

6.9. Orowan, E., and K. J. Pascoe, "A Simple Method of Calculating Roll Pressure and Power Consumption in Hot Flat Rolling", *Iron and Steel Inst., Special Report No. 34*, p. 124, 1946.

6.10. Parkins, R. N., *Mechanical Treatment of Metals*, Amer. Elsevier Pub. Co., Inc., New York, 1968, pp. 107–113. (Taken over by Unwin Hyman Ltd., London.)

6.11. Roberts, W. L., *Hot Rolling of Steel*, Marcel Dekker, Inc., New York, pp. 109, 111, 356–359, 437, and 930.

6.12. Roberts, W. L., *Cold Rolling of Steel*, Marcel Dekker, Inc., New York, 1983, pp. 234–236, 731–774.

6.13. Stone, T. A., and R. Gray, "Theory and Practical Aspects in Crown Control", Iron and Steel Engineer Year Book, 1966, pp. 519–522.

6.14. Hosford, W. F., and R. M. Caddell, *Metal Forming*, Prentice-Hall, Englewood Cliffs, New Jersey, 1983, pp. 135–137.

6.15. McPherson, D. J., "Contributions to the Theory and Practice of Cold Rolling," *Met. Trans.*, vol. 5, December 1974, pp. 2479–2799.

PROBLEMS

6.1. Explain briefly why small-diameter work rolls, such as in Fig. 6.3(f), are used and why the cluster back-up rolls are necessary? On the other hand, why are large-diameter rolls used in the rolling of semifinished shapes such as slabs in a steel mill?

6.2. (a) Determine the roll separating force when a carbon steel plate 900 mm wide, 25 mm thick, is reduced 30 percent by hot rolling in a mill with roll diameter of 750 mm. The flow stress of the steel is 70 MPa (N/mm^2).

(b) Would the assumption of homogeneous deformation be a good approximation?

(c) Would the speed of rolling be a factor in the roll separating force?

6.3. (a) By successive approximation, determine the deformed radius of curvature of steel rolls 600 mm in diameter, which are to be used to roll an aluminum alloy strip 915 mm wide and 50 mm thick, that is to be reduced by 15 percent. The yield stress of the aluminum is 75 MPa. The Poisson's ratio of steel is 0.35 and Young's modulus of steel is 207 GPa. Since the strip does not widen perceptibly, the reduction may be considered as a reduction in thickness.

(b) Determine the minimum thickness of foil that can be rolled if $\mu = 0.20$.

6.4. Determine and plot the rate of deformation of individual elements where a slab 150 mm thick is reduced to 100 mm in one pass by hot rolling with work rolls that are 750 mm in diameter and that are operating at a peripheral speed of 3500 mm/s, and in which total sticking friction is involved whereby the velocity of workpiece and the work rolls are the same. Obtain values of elements for angles at intervals of 2° and end with the angle of contact.

6.5. Compare the maximum possible reduction of a steel slab 150 mm thick (a) during hot rolling when $\mu = 0.8$, and (b) during cold rolling when $\mu = 0.1$, if the diameter of the working rolls is (1) 500 mm, and (2) 1000 mm.

6.6. (a) Calculate the roll load required to roll 250 mm wide annealed copper strip from 2.50 mm to 2.00 mm thick using 350 mm diameter rolls with a coefficient of friction μ of 0.05. Use Eqs. (6.34) and (6.3) to calculate R', and Eq. (6.36) to calculate the load P. K and n for copper are 450 MPa and 0.33, respectively.

(b) Write a computer program in the Basic programming language to calculate P in part (a) above by use of Eqs. (6.18) and (6.19).

6.7. Repeat the above calculations for the cold rolling of AISI 1015 low-carbon steel for a strip 150 mm wide to be reduced from 3.0 mm to 2.25 mm using 500 mm diameter rolls and with $\mu = 0.07$. K and n for the steel are 620 MPa and 0.18, respectively.

6.8. By use of Eqs. (6.32) and (6.51), calculate the coefficient of friction μ from the following cold rolling data:

$$E = 69480 \text{ MN/m}^2 \text{ (MPa)}$$
$$\nu = 0.28$$
$$R = 0.1778 \text{ m} \quad (7 \text{ in})$$
$$h_0 = 2.54 \text{ mm} \quad (0.1 \text{ in})$$
$$h_f = 1.524 \text{ mm} \quad (0.06 \text{ in})$$
$$P = 3.8 \text{ MN/m}$$

The constrained yield stress may be approximated by the following version of Swift's power law:

$$\sigma_C = \sigma_Y = \sigma_{Y_0}(1 + B\bar{\varepsilon})^n$$

where

$$B = 727.65$$
$$\bar{\varepsilon} = \frac{2}{\sqrt{3}} \ln \frac{h_0}{h_f}$$
$$n = 0.23$$
$$\sigma_{Y_0} = 85.46 \text{ MN/m}^2 \text{ (MPa)}$$
$$\sigma_1 = \frac{\sigma_Y - \sigma_{Y_0}}{2}$$

6.9. Repeat the above calculations for hot rolling in which the following parameters are changed: $B = 0$, $h_0 = 15.24 \text{ mm}$, $h_f = 2.54 \text{ mm}$, and $P = 25 \text{ MN/m}$.

BAR DRAWING, EXTRUSION AND ALLIED PROCESSES

7.1 INTRODUCTION

The different common processes by which a bar (or wire) might be reduced by flow through a converging die are bar and wire drawing, direct or forward extrusion, indirect or backward extrusion, hydrostatic extrusion, and impact extrusion. All of these processes may be classified as indirect compression processes, in which the major forming stress results from the compressive stresses as a result of the direct tensile or compressive stresses exerted in drawing or extrusion as shown in Fig. 7.1 for drawing and for direct or forward extrusion. Here, the converging die surface in the form of a truncated cone is used, but die surfaces of other geometries might also be used. An important distinction of these metal-working processes is that the plastic deformation may be done by hot-, warm-, or coldworking according to the definition of these deformation processes as given elsewhere. Prototypes of the direct, indirect, and impact or backward extrusion processes are shown in Fig. 7.2. A drawing of the die assembly for the pressure-to-pressure hydrostatic extrusion process is shown in Fig. 7.3. Methods of extruding hollow shapes using internal and spider mandrels are shown in Figs. 7.4 and 7.5. Tube thinning and elongation by drawing with internal support provided by a moving mandrel, a plug, and a floating plug; and without internal support by sinking is shown in Fig. 7.6.

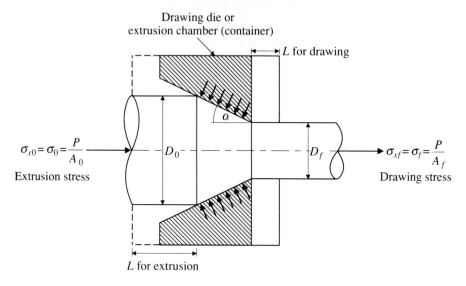

FIGURE 7.1
Composite drawing showing the indirect compressive stresses generated in drawing and extrusion through a converging die [7.1].

The existing solutions for calculating the drawing or extrusion stress or pressure may be divided into the four groups: (1) analytical, (2) numerical, (3) semiempirical, and (4) empirical.

Exact analytical solutions for metalworking problems such as extrusion are very difficult to obtain because of the complexity of the problems. A number of simplifying assumptions must be made. As mentioned previously, exact or complete solutions must satisfy the following requirements:

1. Equilibrium conditions, i.e., must satisfy the three equilibrium equations
2. Continuity of flow, in which the material is incompressible and no voids are formed, etc., i.e., it must satisfy the equations of compatibility
3. Stress-strain relations and the yield criterion used
4. Boundary conditions, including the effect of friction

For analytical upper- and lower-bound solutions, for example, some of the above conditions are relaxed for the process being considered. For example, a von Mises material may be used as a good approximation, which is a rigid (nonelastic), homogeneous, isotropic, nonstrainhardening continuum, that obeys the von Mises yield criterion.

One would expect a blending of the theoretical and empirical solutions to provide semiempirical solutions. Pragmatically, the proponents of the theoretical solutions attempt to fit them to practical, every-day production problems, and

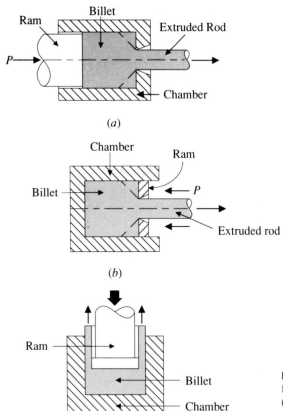

(a)

(b)

(c)

FIGURE 7.2
Prototypes of extrusion processes:
(a) Direct extrusion with a flat-faced
die; (b) indirect extrusion with a flat-
faced die; and (c) impact extrusion
with a flat ram [7.3].

the technologists who rely on empirical equations or formulas based on experimental and production data attempt to utilize theoretical solutions for the purpose
of simplification and rationalization in an effort to understand the process and
to place it on a sound foundation.

The analytical or mathematical solutions to be discussed here are obtained
by one of the following methods of analysis:

1. Drawing or extrusion without friction or redundancy losses
2. Freebody equilibrium or slab technique.
3. Upper-bound solution
4. Slip-line field analysis, which is limited to plane strain conditions.

The freebody equilibrium solutions assume homogeneous deformation
throughout the deformation zone and include external friction effects, but do not
include internal shear losses or redundant work, which is an important factor

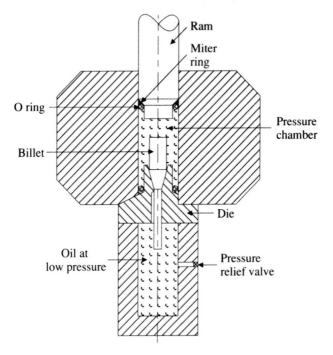

FIGURE 7.3
Schematic drawing of a ram-type extrusion chamber for the pressure-to-pressure hydrostatic extrusion process [7.3].

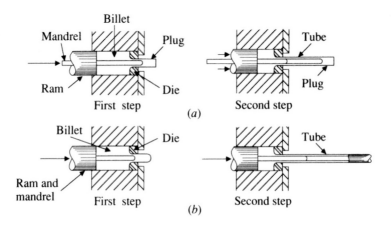

FIGURE 7.4
Two methods of extruding hollow shapes using internal mandrels [8.6].

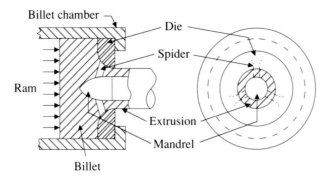

FIGURE 7.5
Extrusion of a hollow shape using a spider mandrel [8.6].

for die angles above the optimal amount commonly used in practice. Consequently the solutions predict drawing and extrusion stresses or pressures that are below those actually required and may therefore represent lower-bound solutions. All the important factors are taken into consideration in the computer design of flat-face die extrusion to be discussed later.

The upper-bound solutions assume a kinematically admissible velocity field and provide solutions which predict drawing or extrusion pressures that are expected to be above those actually required. Since the main concern in metal processing is usually to ensure adequate power requirements, these solutions of the theoretical ones are usually preferred.

The semiempirical solutions may include a wide variety of solutions of different degrees of empiricism such as the slip-line field method, visioplasticity, etc.

The empirical solutions are primarily based on experimental and production data, in which an equation is fitted to the data by regression analysis or some

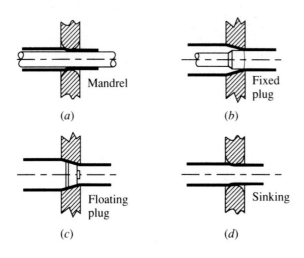

FIGURE 7.6
Tube thinning and elongation by drawing with internal support provided by (a) a moving mandrel, (b) a plug, and (c) a floating plug; and (d) without internal support by sinking [7.1].

other form of curve-fitting. These methods would include the various graphical methods that have been proposed to predict the drawing or extrusion pressures.

After a brief discussion of the energy required for homogeneous deformation and for the various losses, the application of the above approaches to the solution of converging-die drawing and extrusion problems will now be illustrated as examples of their application to metalworking problems.

7.2. DRAWING AND EXTRUSION OF ROUND BARS AND FLAT STRIPS

From the standpoint of the state of stress causing deformation, bar drawing and forward extrusion with conical dies are quite similar and will be discussed here together.

If external friction and internal shearing losses are excluded, the stress required for drawing or extrusion is simply that required for homogeneous deformation:

$$\sigma = \bar{\sigma} \ln \frac{A_0}{A_f} = \bar{\sigma} \ln \left(\frac{1}{1-r} \right) \tag{7.1}$$

where σ = drawing or extrusion stress or pressure
A_0 = entry or initial area
A_f = exit or final area
r = fractional reduction in area $(A_0 - A_f)/A_0$
$\bar{\sigma}$ = flow stress for a nonstrainhardening material or the mean true flow stress σ_{fm} for a strainhardening material as is shown in Fig. 3.8

To correct for external friction and internal shearing redundancy losses, the above value for the drawing stress may be divided by the efficiency $\eta = w_h/w_t$, or multiplied by two correction factors, one to compensate for the external friction loss $C_f(\alpha)$, which is a function primarily of the die half-angle α, and the other to compensate for the internal shear redundancy loss $C_i(\alpha, r)$, which is a function not only of the die half-angle α, but also of the fractional reduction of area r. The correction factors also depend on the process, i.e., drawing, extrusion, etc. The die half-angle α is the angle that the die surface makes with the axis of the workpiece.

The above equations may therefore be written as

$$\sigma = C_f(\alpha) C_i(\alpha, r) \bar{\sigma} \ln \frac{A_0}{A_f} \tag{7.2}$$

and

$$\sigma = C_f(\alpha) C_i(\alpha, r) \bar{\sigma} \ln \left(\frac{1}{1-r} \right) \tag{7.3}$$

If the fractional reduction in area, r, and the lubrication practice are fixed, a graph showing schematically for a limited range of α, the variation of the various relative stress and work terms, is shown in Fig. 7.7. As stated previously the total work per unit volume is given as

$$w_t = w_h + w_f + w_i \tag{7.4}$$

The homogeneous deformation w_h is not a function of α and is therefore constant. The optimal die half-angle is given by α^*. To the left of the minimum of w_t on the graph, i.e., of α^*, external friction predominates. A very large stress and much work would be theoretically required to draw or extrude a workpiece through a very long die with a very small α and consequently with a very large surface area. As α is increased, w_f decreases and w_i increases until it predominates. During extrusion, as the die half-angle is increased a dead zone may develop, which essentially limits the value of α, as will be discussed later. As external friction increases to the extreme of sticking, α^*, the optimal die half-angle, also increases. Friction is high in hot-working operations, and α is made larger than the optimal value to ensure better surface quality and safe tool loading. The optimal die half-angle α^* increases with the amount of reduction from about $3\frac{1}{2}°$ for about 10 percent reduction to $8\frac{1}{2}°$ for a 45 percent reduction.

Once the equation for the total drawing or extrusion stress or the total work is written in terms of the die half-angle, the optimal angle may be found by differentiating the equation and equating to zero.

As shown in Fig. 7.7, if one calculates only the relative drawing or extrusion stress or the work of deformation W_h, while neglecting the external friction and redundancy losses, appreciable error may occur. One of the next stages in the development, therefore, is to determine a drawing or extrusion stress equation in which external friction is included in the analysis, but redundancy is neglected, that is, $w_i = 0$. This is one of the oldest approaches to drawing and extrusion. The freebody equilibrium or slab approach for the drawing of a cylindrical bar with a conical die will be used here as a typical example of the equilibrium solution. In this case α, μ, and $\bar{\sigma}$ will be assumed to be constant. The extension of the resulting equation to forward extrusion and tube drawing will then be discussed.

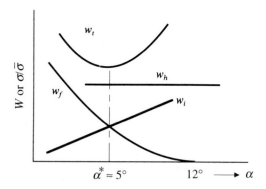

FIGURE 7.7
Schematic curves showing the effect of die half-angle on the relative drawing or extrusion stress and work balance for a constant reduction ratio and lubrication condition. α^* is the optimal die half-angle.

7.3 FREEBODY, SLAB, OR EQUILIBRIUM APPROACH TO DRAWING AND EXTRUSION

Figure 7.8 shows a cylindrical rod being drawn through a conical die and a freebody equilibrium diagram of an element of the rod in the process of being reduced.

The sum of the forces in the axial (and in the radial) direction should be zero. If the freebody is in static equilibrium, the axial components of the forces in the x direction consist of those due to the following stresses:

1. Longitudinal stress, σ_x
2. Die pressure, p, that is, normal pressure at the die surface
3. Frictional drag, μp, on the extrusion chamber, die surface, and/or die land L, as shown in Fig. 7.1, where μ is the Coulomb coefficient of friction

Summing the forces in the x direction, one obtains

$$\Sigma F = (\sigma_x + d\sigma_x)\frac{\pi}{4}(D + dD)^2 - \sigma_x \frac{\pi}{4}D^2$$

$$+ p\left(\pi D \cdot \frac{dx}{\cos \alpha}\right)\sin \alpha + \mu p\left(\pi D \frac{dx}{\cos \alpha}\right)\cos \alpha = 0 \qquad (7.5)$$

where D is any cone diameter and α is the die half-angle as shown in Fig. 7.8.

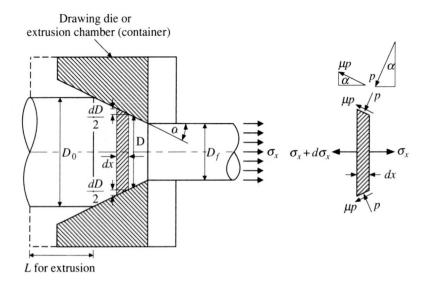

Drawing die or extrusion chamber (container)

L for extrusion

FIGURE 7.8
Cylindrical rod being drawn through a conical die and a freebody equilibrium diagram at an element in the reduced section [7.1].

If one ignores the products of the infinitesimal quantities and simplifies, one obtains

$$D\,d\sigma_x + 2[\sigma_x + p(1 + \mu \cot \alpha)\,dD] = 0 \qquad (7.6a)$$

$$2r\,dr\,\sigma_x + r^2\,d\sigma_x + 2pr\,dr + \frac{2r\,dr\,\tau}{\tan \alpha} = 0 \qquad (7.6b)$$

where $\tau = $ the friction shear stress $= m\bar{\sigma}/\sqrt{3}$.

Likewise, summing the forces in the radial direction, one obtains the radial or die-breaking stress σ_r

$$\Sigma\,F_r = \sigma_r(\pi D\,dx) + \left(\pi D\frac{dx}{\cos \alpha}\right)\cos \alpha - \mu p\left(\pi D\frac{dx}{\cos \alpha}\right)\sin \alpha = 0 \qquad (7.7)$$

and

$$\sigma_r = -p(1 - \mu \tan \alpha) \qquad (7.8)$$

For small angles, $\mu \tan \alpha$ may be ignored, and $\sigma_r = -p$ [7.1].

By combining the yield criterion with Eq. (7.6) for the axial force, letting $B = \mu \cot \alpha$, integrating the resulting differential equation, and simplifying, one obtains the following equation for the average drawing stress:

$$\frac{\sigma_x}{\bar{\sigma}} = \frac{1 + B}{B}\left[1 - \left(\frac{D_f}{D_0}\right)^{2B}\right] \qquad (7.9)$$

where $\bar{\sigma}$ is the mean flow stress, B is equal to $\mu \cot \alpha$, and D_0 and D_f are the original and final diameters.

The same approach can be used to yield equations of essentially the same form for such similar operations as drawing of a wide strip through a wedge-shaped die, mandrel and plug drawing and sinking (drawing with no internal support) of tubing (Fig. 7.6), and extrusion of bars and strips.

For frictionless drawing and extrusion, where $\mu = 0$, both external friction and redundancy are neglected, so the equation for homogeneous deformation must be used.

The following is a listing of other similar slab or equilibrium equations for drawing and extrusion, which excludes the effect of friction and redundancy:

1. Drawing of a strip through a wedge-shaped die in plane strain [7.1]:

$$\frac{\sigma_x}{S} = \frac{1 + B}{B}\left[1 - \left(\frac{h_f}{h_0}\right)^{B}\right] \qquad (7.10)$$

where $S = 2/\sqrt{3}\,\sigma_0$ or $1.15\sigma_0$ and is the yield (flow) stress in a plane-strain compression test according to the von Mises criterion and σ_0 is the yield stress in uniaxial tension, and h_0 and h_f are the initial and final thickness.

2. Close-pass plug and straight mandrel drawing with a conical die as in Fig. 7.6(a), (b), and (c):

$$\frac{\sigma_x}{S} = \frac{1 + B^*}{B^*}\left[1 - \left(\frac{h_f}{h_0}\right)^{B^*}\right]$$ (7.11)

where $B^* = \dfrac{\mu_1 \pm \mu_2}{\tan \alpha - \tan \beta}$ and $S = \dfrac{2}{\sqrt{3}}\sigma_0$ as above

> (The plus sign is used for plug drawing and the minus sign for mandrel drawing.)
> α = outside die half-angle
> β = inside die half-angle
> μ_1 = coefficient of friction at the die-workpiece interface
> μ_2 = coefficient of friction at the plug or mandrel-workpiece interface
> h_f = final tube thickness
> h_0 = initial tube thickness

In mandrel drawing, if $\mu_1 = \mu_2$, the equation (7.1) for homogeneous deformation applies. If $\mu_2 > \mu_1$, the drawing stress for mandrel drawing may be less than for frictionless drawing for the same reduction in area.

3. Tube sinking (tube drawing with no internal support) as in Fig. 7.6(d):

$$\frac{\sigma_x}{1.1\sigma_0} = \frac{1 + B}{B}\left[1 - \left(\frac{D_f}{D_0}\right)^{B}\right]$$ (7.12)

4. Round-bar extrusion through a conical die

$$\frac{\sigma_x}{\sigma_0} = \frac{1 + B}{B}\left[1 - \left(\frac{D_0}{D_f}\right)^{2B}\right]$$ (7.13)

where σ_x = extrusion pressure on the end of the billet
  $B = \mu \cot \alpha$

Note that the entry and exit conditions for extrusion versus drawing inverts the diameter ratio.

5. Extrusion of flat strip through constant angle dies:

$$\frac{\sigma_x}{S} = \frac{1 + B}{B}\left[1 - \left(\frac{h_s}{h_f}\right)^{B}\right]$$ (7.14)

As the above simple solutions represent lower-bound solutions, the next stage in the development is to consider upper-bound solutions.

As applied to hot forward extrusion through conical dies, one can convert equation (7.5) by expansion, simplification, and manipulation to the form

$$-\sigma_{x0} = \bar{\sigma}\ln\left(\frac{A_0}{A_1}\right) + \frac{\tau \ln(A_0/A_1)}{\sin \alpha \cos \alpha}$$ (7.15)

where $\quad -\sigma_{xo}$ = pressure at the extrusion end of the die
$$\ln (A_0/A_1) = 2 \ln (r_0/r_1)$$
A_0 and A_1 = cross-sectional area of the billet and of the extrusion respectively,
r_0 and r_1 = their radii, respectively
α = die half-angle

The first term of Eq. (7.15) represents the homogeneous deformation or lossless work, and the second term the external friction loss [7.2].

7.4 UPPER-BOUND SOLUTIONS TO DRAWING AND EXTRUSION PROBLEMS

As mentioned in the foregoing, exact mathematical solutions for stresses (or forces) for such complex metalforming operations as bar drawing or extrusion through conical converging dies are not available. Another approach, in addition to the semiempirical solutions such as the slip-line theory and visioplastic analysis to be discussed later, is to use one of the upper-bound solutions, which provides a value known to be higher or equal to the actual stress, as opposed to the lower-bound solution, which provides a value equal to or less than the actual stress. For example, in Fig. 7.9, the drawing stress/flow stress ratio $\sigma_{xf}/\bar{\sigma}$ is plotted as the ordinate versus the die cone half-angle α as the abscissa for the upper- and lower-bound solutions for sound metal flow as obtained by Avitzur

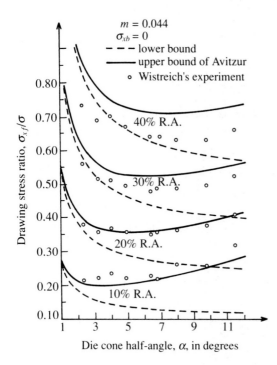

FIGURE 7.9
Drawing stress ratio, i.e., drawing stress/flow stress versus die half-angle for various reductions in area, $r = (A_f - A_0)/A_0$ for sound metal flow. The circles are for experimental data for electrolytic copper. $\mu = 0.02 - 0.03$ ($m = 0.044$). σ_{xf} is the final, axial, front-pull stress. The back-push stress, σ_{xb}, is zero [4.10], [7.5].

[7.3] together with the corresponding experimental values obtained by Wistreich [7.4]. The experimental values were obtained for electrolytic copper annealed at 450°C and then at 400°C for $2\frac{1}{2}$ h, and drawn through truncated conical dies at 0.21 mm/s (6 ft/min) with a coefficient of friction $\mu = 0.02$ to 0.03. Since the effect of external friction loss drops off very rapidly as the optimal die angle is approached and exceeded slightly, consequently for die angles above the optimum, internal shear losses or redundancy are of primary importance as shown in Fig. 7.10. Because of the occurrence of such phenomena as the fracture of the wire in drawing and central-burst formation and shaving in extrusion to be discussed later, the curves in the above figure may not be applicable. The reader should compare Figs. 7.7, 7.9, and 7.10.

In the derivation of Eq. (7.9) for drawing and extrusion for a constant shear factor, neither a back push stress σ_{xb} nor the redundant work were included. These terms may be added, respectively, to give the following equation for the front pull stress σ_{xf} for drawing

$$\frac{\sigma_{xf}}{\sigma} = \frac{1+B}{B}\left[1 - \frac{d_f^{2B}}{D_0}\right] + \frac{\sigma_{xb}}{\bar{\sigma}}\left(\frac{D_f}{D_0}\right)^{2B} + \left(\frac{2}{\sqrt{3}}\right)\left(\frac{\alpha}{\sin^2 \alpha} - \cot \alpha\right) \qquad (7.16)$$

where $B = \mu \cot \alpha$.

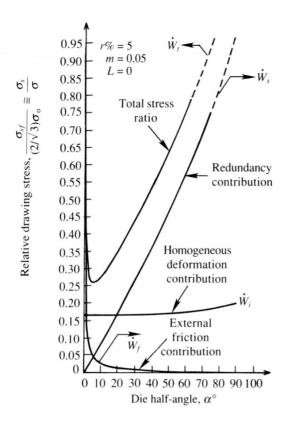

FIGURE 7.10

Contribution of the three power requirements to the relative drawing stress ratio. $\dot{W}_t$, $\dot{W}_i$, and $\dot{W}_s$ represent the total power (work per unit time): the redundant power associated with internal shear; the internal power associated with homogeneous deformation; and the power associated with external friction, respectively [7.5].

By use of the upper-bound theory, which gives the upper bound on energy consumption, Avitzur [7.3] derived the following equations for the drawing (+) or forward (−) extrusion stresses of rounds for a constant frictional shear factor with no backward tension in drawing or forward tension in extrusion:

$$\frac{\sigma_x}{\bar{\sigma}} = \pm 2f(\sigma) \ln \frac{R_0}{R_f} \pm \frac{2}{\sqrt{3}} \left[\frac{\alpha}{\sin^2 \alpha} - \cos \alpha + m(\cos \alpha) \ln \frac{R_0}{R_f} + m \frac{L}{R_L} \right] \quad (7.17)$$

where
σ_x = back push stress for extrusion or front pull stress for drawing
$\bar{\sigma}$ = flow stress of the perfectly plastic metal assuming the von Mises yield criterion applies
α = the die half-angle or the dead-zone cone half-angle for flat-die extrusion
R_0 and R_f = the initial and final radii of the cylindrical workpiece, respectively
$R_L = R_f$ for drawing and R_0 for extrusion
L = length of the cylindrical surface in contact
m = constant frictional shear factor
$f(\alpha)$ = complex function involving $\sin^2 \alpha$ and $\cos \alpha$, which varies from 1 to 1.666 as α^0 varies from 0 to 90°. (For 30, 45, and 60°, $f(\alpha)$ = 1.000625, 1.0159, and 1.0343, respectively.)

If in drawing backward tension or in extrusion forward tension is exerted, the term σ_{xb}/σ_0 or σ_{xf}/σ_0, respectively, would be added to Eq. (7.17).

The derivation of Eq. (7.17) involves minimizing the energy or power consumed (1) in causing the reduction in cross section, (2) in shear at the surfaces of tangential velocity discontinuity, and (3) in overcoming friction at the interfaces.

The first term of Eq. (7.17) represents the internal energy of deformation, which is here slightly angular dependent; the first two terms in the square brackets represent the shear losses at the spherical surfaces of the tangential velocity discontinuities to be discussed subsequently; the third term in the brackets represents the external friction loss over the conical die surface; and the fourth term in the brackets represents the external friction loss of any cylindrical surface of length L either at the entry or exit of the die. The plus sign is used for drawing and the minus sign for extrusion. The angular dependence of the internal deformation is rather involved and will not be presented here [7.3].

7.5 CENTRAL-BURST FORMATION AND SHAVING IN EXTRUSION

In forward extrusion the primary mode of failure is *center-burst* or *chevron formation*, also called *cupping*. Although this defect does not occur with great frequency, it is insidious because it is usually not visible from the surface but, because of its seriousness, 100 percent nondestructive testing such as by x-ray radiography or ultrasonic testing may be required. Central bursts, or chevrons,

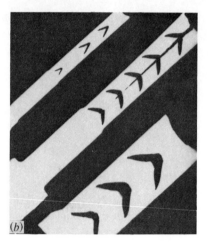

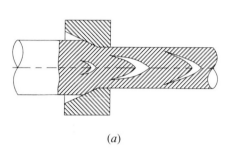

(a)   (b)

FIGURE 7.11
(a) Sketch showing central bursts or chevrons in the process of formation in cold extrusion.
(b) Photograph of center bursts formed in forward cold extrusion of steel. (a) [7.3]. (b) (*Courtesy of Bethlehem Steel Corp.*)

are internal defects that appear on the longitudinal cross section of the workpiece as arrowhead- or chevron-shaped voids that point in the direction of metal flow, as seen in Fig. 7.11. It usually results from small reduction of nonstrainhardening metals such as severely cold-worked metal, since cold-working reduces the strain-hardening exponent. In multistep operations, chevroning, therefore, usually occurs when a light reduction follows a heavy one.

They are caused by periodic tensile stresses that result from non-homogeneous deformation which requires an abrupt acceleration of the metal in the extrusion die. They occur with relatively small reductions, relatively large die angles, relatively high surface friction, and subsequent to previous severe cold working. These defects can therefore be prevented by (1) increasing the reduction, (2) decreasing the die half-angle, (3) decreasing the friction, and (4) increasing the strainhardening capability of the material by annealing or material selection. The foregoing criteria for the prevention of central bursting is summarized in Fig. 7.12 [7.5], where β gives the prorated slope of the true stress–true strain curve of a rigid, linearly strainhardening material in the plastic range or the tangent to the σ-ε curve of a nonlinearly strainhardening metal. The true stress–true strain curve or a segment in the plastic range may be defined by the relationship [7.6]:

$$\sigma = \sigma_n(1 + \beta\varepsilon_n) \tag{7.18}$$

If the stresses at ε_1 and ε_2 are σ_1 and σ_2, the solution of the above equations simultaneously for β yields

$$\beta = \frac{\sigma_2 - \sigma_1}{\sigma_1(\varepsilon_2 - \varepsilon_1)} \tag{7.19}$$

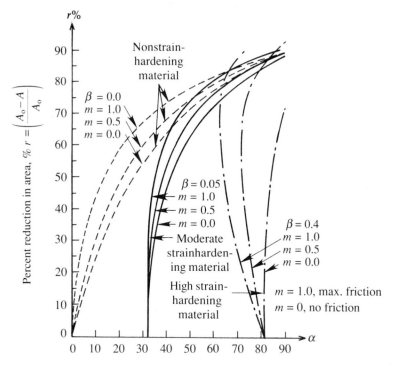

FIGURE 7.12
Graph summarizing the criteria for the occurrence of central bursts for drawing and forward extrusion on the basis of die half-angle α, percent reduction, friction factor m, and material strainhardening capability β. The area to the left or above any curve represents a safe zone for the conditions indicated by that curve. For example, for $r = 40\%$ and $m = 0$, an α of 18° can be used safely. [4.10], [7.5].

In Fig. 7.12, m is the friction shear factor. The region to the left of any curve represents the safe zone in which no central bursting is expected for the conditions indicated by the particular curve. Arrows show that central-bursting is expected for the conditions indicated by the particular curve. Arrows show that central-bursting may be prevented by either reducing the die half-angle or increasing the percent reduction. Sound metal flow therefore does not occur for all combinations of die angle, percent reduction, and friction values.

In addition to probable central-burst formation, there are other limitations in regard to how large a die half-angle α can be used in drawing and/or extrusion in order to obtain sound metal flow. These are (1) dead-zone formation, (2) shaving, and (3) the breaking of the wire or rod on the exit side in case of drawing.

As shown in Fig. 7.10, as the die half-angle increases from 0° to the optimal half-angle α^*, the external friction losses drastically decrease, and the drawing or extruding energy or stress decreases to a minimum at which sound flow of metal occurs. Beyond this point, an increase in the die half-angle causes the drawing or extrusion stress to increase, because the internal shear losses or redundancy increases rather rapidly as shown in Fig. 7.10. This rise in the drawing or extrusion stress will not, of course, increase indefinitely, but at some die half-angle called the first critical angle, α_{cr1}, dead-zone formation begins as shown in Fig. 7.13 [7.5]. At this point, internal shearing of the metal next to the die surface occurs forming a dead-metal zone, which no longer participates in the flow process but instead adheres to the surface of the die as a built-up surface and acts much like the extended surface of the die, virtually limiting the size of the die half-angle. The first critical die half-angle is a function of the percent reduction in area and the shear factor. The drawing or extrusion stress remains constant, as shown in Fig. 7.13 in the dead-zone formation region.

As the die half-angle increases further, the second critical die half-angle, α_{cr2}, is reached, at which the dead-zone metal ceases to adhere to the die and begins to move backward forming metal chips somewhat the same as one would peel or shave off a chip from a wooden stick, with a knife. As the wire or rod proceeds through the die, the outer surface is shaved off and the core moves

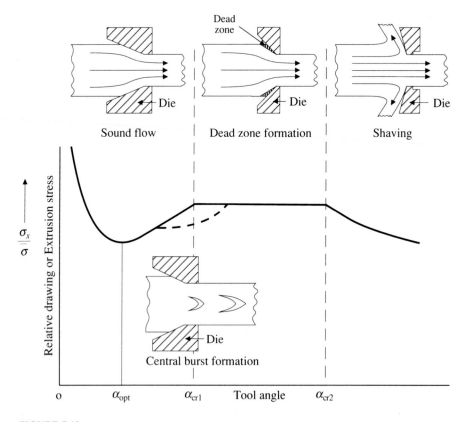

FIGURE 7.13
Schematic diagram showing the effect of die half-angle on the mode of metal flow and on the drawing stress. This graph is drawn for relatively small drawing stress so as to obviate necking and fracture at the exit of the die [7.3], [7.5].

through the die without plastic deformation with equal entrance and exit velocities. The drawing or extrusion stress is found to decrease with an increase in α as shown in Fig. 7.13 in the shaving region. The critical die half-angle for shaving, α_{cr2}, is dependent on the percent reduction in area, the sharpness of the tool and whether or not a built-up edge occurs, and the type of process, i.e., drawing or extrusion.

If conditions are favorable for center-burst formation, as shown in Fig. 7.13, then at some angle α_{cr1}, as determined by the criterion for central-burst formation, this internal defect will form and, if sufficiently severe, total fracture of the workpiece will result.

7.6 CAUSE OF CENTRAL-BURST FORMATION

An explanation of the cause of central-burst or chevron formation in wire drawing and extrusion and the limitations placed on these processes has been presented by Avitzur [7.5].

For his upper- and lower-bound solutions, Avitzur included a term in the upper-bound theorem that involved a surface of tangential velocity discontinuity, and he divided the metal in the vicinity of the die into three zones as shown in Fig. 7.14(a), as follows: zone I, in which the velocity vector of the metal flow is parallel to the longitudinal axis of the workpiece and equal to the ram velocity, v_0; zone II, in which the direction of the velocity vector is toward the apex of the cone of the die; and zone III, in which the direction of the velocity vector is again parallel to the longitudinal axis of the workpiece. The two transition regions between zones I and II and between zones II and III, in which the direction of flow changes gradually, have been successfully replaced by two spherical boundaries B_1 and B_2, of tangential velocity discontinuities, with their centers at the apex of the die angle and with radii r_0 and r, respectively. During deformation, as soon as a material point reaches the first boundary, a change in the direction of metal flow occurs as it starts to move faster and faster toward the apex of the die. As the material point reaches the second boundary, a change in the direct metal flow occurs once again, restoring it to its original direction parallel to the longitudinal axis. The tangential discontinuities in velocities parallel to the surfaces B_1 and B_2 and of the magnitude $v_0 \sin \theta$ and $v_f \sin \theta$, result. [These velocity discontinuities result in the shear losses mentioned in conjunction with Eq. (7.17).] The velocity components tangent to the boundary surfaces cause a shear stress over the surfaces. It should be emphasized that to preserve constancy of volume, no discontinuity of velocity occurs normal to the surfaces, where the normal components of velocity are continuous, as shown in Fig. 7.14(b).

In zone II, the material point near the center of the rod moves somewhat faster than a corresponding point closer to the surface in order to preserve constancy of volume, i.e.,

$$\frac{v_0}{v_f} = \frac{V_f}{V_0} = \left(\frac{R_f}{R_0}\right)^2 = \left(\frac{D_f}{D_0}\right)^2 \tag{7.20}$$

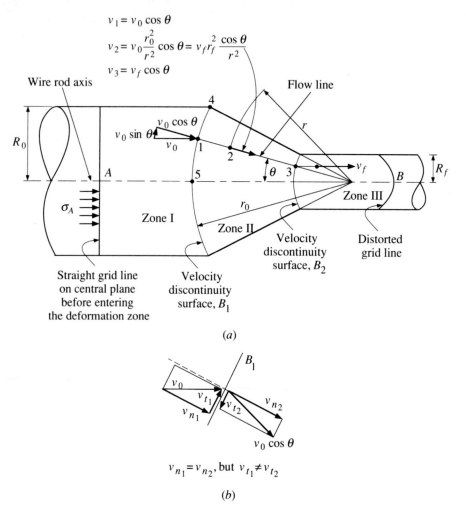

$$v_1 = v_0 \cos \theta$$

$$v_2 = v_0 \frac{r_0^2}{r^2} \cos \theta = v_f r_f^2 \frac{\cos \theta}{r^2}$$

$$v_3 = v_f \cos \theta$$

(a)

$$v_{n_1} = v_{n_2}, \text{ but } v_{t_1} \neq v_{t_2}$$

(b)

FIGURE 7.14

(a) Schematic representation showing (1) a continuous, kinematically admissible velocity field for steady-state direct extrusion, (2) a directional flow line, (3) distorted grid lines (surfaces) of boundaries of the deformation zone, and (4) zones I, II, and III of undeformed metal, the deformation region, and final deformed metal, respectively. (b) Velocity polygon showing a discontinuity in the tangential but not in the normal velocity (ν and v are used here interchangeably with v) [7.3].

The velocity of a material point entering the plastic zone (zone II) at the spherical boundary B_1 is equal to $v_0 \cos \theta$, where v_0 is the initial velocity or that of the ram end. θ is the angular position of the point from the centerline. The angle θ varies from zero at the center to α at the surface of the die, so that the velocity of the material point will vary from v_0 at the centerline at the boundary B_1 to $v_0 \cos \alpha$ at the surface of the die at the periphery of B_1.

As the material point travels through the deformation zone (zone II) from boundary B_1 toward boundary B_2 along a flow line, its angular position θ does not change; however, its radial distance r from the apex decreases. As r decreases, the velocity v increases, so as again to preserve the constancy of volume since the flow cavity is narrowing. The velocity of the material point along the flowline in zone II is given by

$$v_2 = v_0 \left(\frac{r_0}{r}\right)^2 \cos \theta = v_f \left(\frac{r_f}{r}\right)^2 \cos \theta \qquad (7.21)$$

as shown in Fig. 7.14(a). A straight transverse grid line in the diametral plane through the longitudinal axis of the workpiece will distort as shown in Fig. 7.14(a) on moving from point A to point B. This distortion will increase as α increases, and for high values of α ($\alpha > 30°$) will extend back into zone I, which indicates that the internal shear loss or redundancy increases with α.

The central burst may be explained by means of the distortion of the spherical velocity field as shown in Fig. 7.15(a) and (b). This distorted deformation zone is also compatible with the formation of grid patterns with double maxima as is represented in Fig. 7.15 and discussed in the section on visioplasticity. Undistorted deformation zones will have grid patterns with only a single maximum, as shown in Fig. 7.14(a).

The boundaries of velocity discontinuities B_1 and B_2, which are spherical for optimal die half-angles, tend to distort as the die half-angle increases and tend to approach each other. For some drawing or extrusion conditions, they touch each other and their area of contact expands. Since the exit velocity v_f is greater than the entrance velocity v_0, a velocity discontinuity normal to a plane occurs. An internal crack or burst initiates along the centerline, and grows until

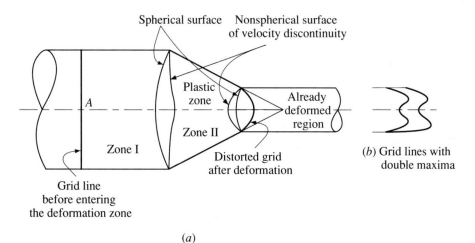

(*a*)

FIGURE 7.15
(*a*) Schematic representation of distorted nonspherical surfaces of horizontal velocity discontinuities, and (*b*) schematic grid lines showing double maxima [7.5].

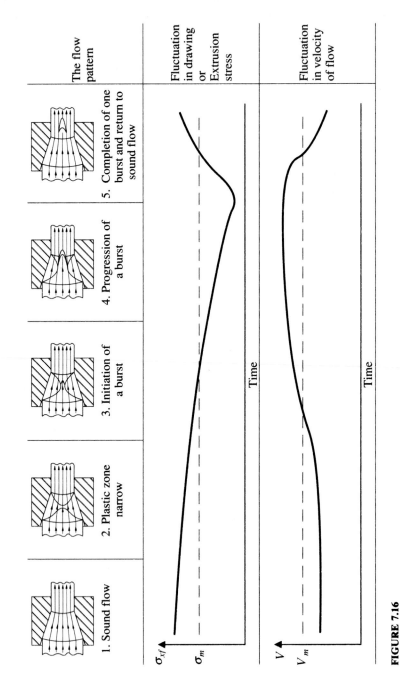

FIGURE 7.16

(*a*) Sequence of drawings showing the periodic variation at the exit in the boundaries of horizontal velocity discontinuities resulting in central-burst or chevron formation. (*b*) and (*c*) Schematic curves showing the periodic variation at the exit in the drawing (or extrusion) stress and the velocity of metal flow associated with central-burst formation [7.5].

it departs from the die. Nonsteady-state flow occurs, and the sequence of crack initiation, crack growth, and the departure of a single crack or burst from the die cavity becomes a periodic event yielding a series of central bursts or chevrons along the centerline of the drawn or extruded rod as shown in Fig. 7.16. The periodic variation of the drawing or extrusion stress and the velocity of flow are also shown schematically in the foregoing figure. Note how the front pull stress σ_{xf} and the velocity at exit of the die v vary below and above the mean velocity, respectively, with the initiation, growth, and departure of a single central-burst defect.

The material characteristics that cause susceptibility to central bursting will be discussed by use of the slip-line field method, after its use is illustrated for determination of the extrusion pressure for backward and forward extrusion.

7.7. APPLICATION OF THE SLIP-LINE FIELD METHOD TO EXTRUSION

7.7.1 Slip-Line Field Solution for a Special Case [7.7]

The general geometry used for the special case occurs when the fractional reduction in area (thickness) r is chosen so that $r = 2 \sin \alpha / (1 + 2 \sin \alpha)$, where α is the die half-angle. The general arrangement for this type of extrusion (or drawing) is shown in Fig. 7.17 where, for convenience, the half-thickness of the slab $h_0/2$ is taken as unity. The half-thickness h_f, at the exit of the die, is equal to $1 - r$, where r is the fractional reduction in area. Since the width is assumed not to change in the process, this reduction is equal to the reduction in thickness,

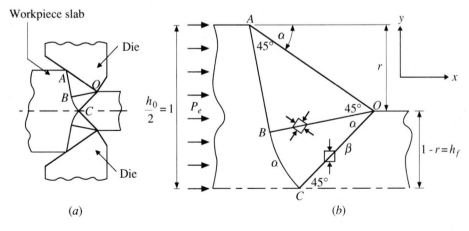

(a) (b)

FIGURE 7.17
The general geometry for an acceptable field used in plane-strain extrusion of drawing where the reduction r, and the half-die angle α, are related by $r = 2 \sin \alpha / (1 + 2 \sin \alpha)$. (a) Overall view, and (b) enlargement of half of the upper field. (The straight line net and the fan net lines are not shown.) Intense localized shear occurs along $ABCO$ [7.7].

or $r = (h_f - h_0)/h_0$. In reference to Fig. 7.17, the relationship between the reduction r and the die half-angle α, is shown below [7.7].

$$\overline{OC} = \frac{(1-r)}{\sin 45°} = \sqrt{2}(1-r)$$

$$\overline{OB} = \overline{AB} = \overline{OC} = \sqrt{2}(1-r)$$

$$\overline{AO} = \overline{OB}\sqrt{2} = 2(1-r) \tag{7.22}$$

$$\sin \alpha = \frac{r}{\overline{AO}} \frac{r}{2(1-r)}$$

$$r = \frac{2 \sin \alpha}{(1+2 \sin \alpha)}$$

This expression represents the maximum reduction for which this type of slip-line field is valid for geometric reasons alone. It should be mentioned here that the broken line $ABCO$ in Fig. 7.17 represents a line of intense localized shear.

If the relation in Eq. (7.22) is obeyed, a simple field consisting of a straight-line net and one-fan net, as shown in Fig. 7.17, is applicable. If r is less than the α term, the field has to be extended to contain another radial fan centered on B also.

By use of Mohr's stress circles, it can be shown that the pressure perpendicular to the die surface, $p_{\perp \text{d.s.}}$, along AO is

$$p_{\perp \text{d.s.}} = 2k(1+\alpha) \tag{7.23}$$

By summing the forces in the extrusion (x) direction, the expression for the extrusion pressure p_e can be found to be

$$\frac{p_e}{2k} = r(1+\alpha) = (1+\alpha)\frac{2 \sin \alpha}{1+2 \sin \alpha} \tag{7.24}$$

If the reduction occurs by drawing rather than by extrusion, a similar analysis would yield

$$\frac{\sigma_d}{2k} = r(1+\alpha) = (1+\alpha)\frac{2 \sin \alpha}{1+2 \sin \alpha} \tag{7.25}$$

where σ_d is the drawing stress at the exit from the die. α_d, however, must be below the ultimate tensile strength of the material being drawn as the exiting bar or wire will neck and break.

7.7.2   Construction of the Slip-Line Field for Inverted (Indirect), Steady-State, Plane-Strain Extrusion

The slip-line field for inverted (indirect), steady-state, plane-strain extrusion with a reduction of 50 percent or a reduction ratio of 2 by means of a 90° (square-faced) die with no lubrication is shown in Fig. 7.18(a). Since this is a simple problem, the slip-line field will be drawn by inspection. The standard slip-line net to be discussed in the next section could also be used.

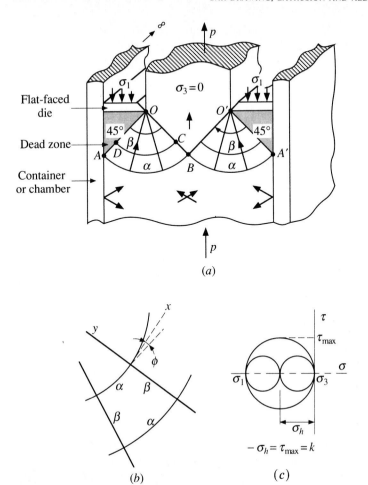

FIGURE 7.18
Inverted (indirect), steady-state, plane-strain extrusion to a reduction ratio A_0/A_f of 2, (*a*) showing the extrusion process and the slip-line field, (*b*) showing convention for labeling slip-lines, and (*c*) Mohr stress circle for the extrusion process.

The construction of the slip-line field must conform to the following three conditions:

1. Since there is no friction between the billet and the container in inverted extrusion, the slip-lines must meet the container wall at 45°
2. The centerline of the billet and the extrusion is an axis of symmetry, therefore all the slip-lines must meet the centerline at 45° with no resultant shear stress along this axis.
3. Since the die shoulder is not lubricated, a dead-metal zone will exist there. Although the dead-zone boundary is usually curved, a good approximation is that it is straight and meets the centerline at 45° [7.8].

The two corners of the die cross section may readily be identified as two points of stress singularity at which a solution for the stress is indeterminant. Since, in the inverted plane-strain extrusion being considered here, there is no motion of the undeformed billet relative to the container, the slip-line field will be assumed to make an angle of 45° with the container wall. As a matter of fact the exact angle of this boundary will not affect the results appreciably. Since the extrusion is symmetrical, the slip-line field will intersect the centerline at A at 45°. From the foregoing it can be deduced that the slip-line field will consist of two radial fans centered at O and O' as shown in Fig. 7.18(a). The α and β lines are labeled as shown in Fig. 7.18(b). Further examination will show that the slip-line field also satisfies the following boundary conditions involving velocities:

1. That the normal velocity across AB and BA' must everywhere be compatible with the relative velocity of the rigid billet, i.e., the normal component of the velocity across the slip-line must be equal
2. That the velocity component along the β-line, u, is zero, since there is no flow across OA and $O'A'$
3. That the velocity component along OB and BO' must be compatible with the rigid extruded strip leaving the die

7.7.3   Stress Evaluation by Use of the Slip-Line Field for Inverted (Indirect), Steady-State, Plane-Strain Extrusion

Since there is no externally applied force on the strip being extruded in Fig. 7.18(a), a convenient place to start is at some point C along slip-line OB, at which the principal stress in the direction of extrusion is zero.

By use of the Mohr stress circle diagram in Fig. 7.18(c), the hydrostatic pressure $\sigma_h = -p$ at the free surface is equal to $\tau_{max} = k$.

By use of Hencky's equation

$$p - 2k\phi = C_\beta \tag{4.96}$$

it can be seen that since OB is a straight line, ϕ does not vary between O and B, and $-p$ is constant and equal to k between these points. Starting at point C, one can see that the tangent along an α line rotates clockwise through an angle of 90° or $\pi/2$ to point D, so that ϕ for any point D on OA is equal to $-\pi/2$. The Hencky equation for the α line at point C is

$$p + 2k\phi = C_\alpha \tag{4.95}$$

Then, at point D,

$$p + 2k\left(-\frac{\pi}{2}\right) = k \tag{7.26}$$

or

$$p = k(1 + \pi) \tag{7.27}$$

Thus, the major principal stress at point D is

$$\sigma_1 = p + k$$

or

$$\sigma_1 = k(2 + \pi)$$

(7.28)

Because OA is straight, σ_1 is constant all along OA, which is transmitted through the dead zone and acts on the movable die.

The extrusion pressure p which must be applied by means of the container base, acts over the entire area. For a 50 percent reduction, the reduction (extrusion) ratio is $R = A_0/A = 2/1$, and $A_0 = 2A$, that is, the area of the billet is twice that of the die, so

$$p = \frac{\sigma_1}{2} = k\left(1 + \frac{\pi}{2}\right)$$

(7.29)

or

$$\frac{p}{2k} = \frac{1}{2} + \frac{\pi}{4} = 1.29$$

(7.30)

which falls in the range for extrusion in Fig. 4.27 at which point the plastically deformed zones penetrate to the centerline. [See Fig. 7.23.]

Very good agreement has been obtained in calculating the $p/2k$ ratio for different reduction (extrusion) ratios and the experimental values obtained by *plane-strain* extrusion of lead as can be seen in Fig. 7.19, if the von Mises criterion for yielding is used, i.e.,

$$\bar{\sigma} = \sqrt{3}\,\tau_{max} = \sqrt{3}\,k$$

(7.31)

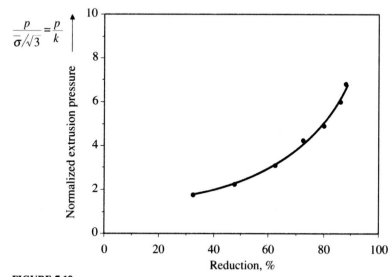

FIGURE 7.19

Comparison of the results obtained from the use of slip-line field theory and experiment in plane-strain extrusion of lead. (*From N. W. Purchase and S. J. Tupper, J. Mechanics and Physics of Solids, 1952, Vol. 1, p. 277.*)

7.7.4 Velocity Evaluation by Use of the Slip-Line Field for Inverted (Indirect), Steady-State, Plane-Strain Extrusion

The velocity of this inverted, plane-strain extrusion process can be analyzed by constructing a velocity-vector diagram or hodograph. For this purpose, let us redraw one-half of the slip-line field of Fig. 7.18(a) as shown in Fig. 7.20(a) [7.8].

Let us assume that to the left of AB, the metal of the billet moves with a velocity of 1, which is represented by Oa on the hodograph. A velocity discontinuity occurs at AB as was shown in Fig. 7.14 because, as a metal particle crosses this line, it undergoes a sudden shearing parallel to the tangent to AB at the point of crossing. This change in velocity is represented by a vector drawn parallel to the tangent at that point. For a point close to A, the vector is parallel to the tangent at A. The metal element itself must slide along a line given by AO since it is constrained by the dead metal as shown in Fig. 7.20(a). Line ab must be parallel to the tangent to AB at A, and Ob must be parallel to the shear plane AO. The velocity discontinuity along AB must have a constant magnitude equal to ab. A particle crossing AB at any other point will undergo a velocity change parallel to the tangent at the point of crossing, and it will be equal to ab. At B the tangent will have revolved through 90°, and the velocity vector for B is given by ac. The metal particle now crosses OB and leaves the deformation zone to

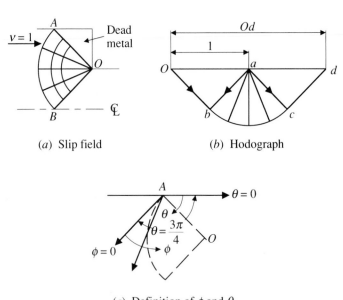

(a) Slip field   (b) Hodograph

(c) Definition of ϕ and θ

FIGURE 7.20
(a) One-half of the slip-line field, (b) the velocity vector diagram (hodograph) for an inverted, plane-strain extrusion process, and (c) the reference line for measurement of ϕ is chosen to coincide with the tangent of the α line AB at A measured counterclockwise and θ is measured clockwise from the centerline [7.1], [7.8].

emerge at a velocity cd, which is parallel to BO. The final velocity of the extrusions is in the direction of Oa and is given by Od. The bottom half of the extrusion will contribute to the final extrusion velocity Od equal to 2 [7.8].

Now that the slip-line field and hodograph have been constructed, let us see whether the slip-line field satisfies the velocity conditions, which are as follows:

1. The velocity horizontal across AB must be the velocity of the billet, assumed to be 1.
2. The horizontal velocity across OB must be the velocity of the extrusion. (In practice this is related to the billet velocity by the reduction achieved.)
3. The velocity across OA must be zero, since the metal across this boundary is dead and does not move.

Since it has been stipulated that the velocity of the billet is 1, then any point on AB must conform to

$$u^2 + v^2 = 1 \tag{7.32}$$

Also, since $\sigma_1 = 0$, as there is no applied stress on the extruded metal, and σ_3 must be compressive or negative, the circumferential line must be α and the radial line β. The velocity of any radial line making an angle of θ to the centerline then is $v = (1) \cos \theta = \cos \theta$.

To find the velocity on a curved α line, one usually starts at the boundary such as at A. The velocity u across OA must be zero, since it is the boundary of a dead-metal zone. If ϕ is measured from A, then the tangent to OA at A is designated as $\phi = 0$. Since θ is measured in radians from the direction of the centerline in a clockwise direction as shown in Fig. 7.20(c), $\theta = 3\pi/4$. Therefore, the general equation of any position on AB is

$$\theta + \phi = \frac{3\pi}{4} \tag{7.33}$$

The Geiringer equation for an α line is

$$du - v\, d\phi = 0 \tag{4.73}{(7.34)}$$

Since at A,

$$\frac{du}{d\phi} = \cos \theta = \cos \left(\frac{3\pi}{4} - \phi \right) \tag{7.35}$$

By integrating, one obtains

$$u = -\sin \left(\frac{3\pi}{4} - \phi \right) + \text{constant at } \phi = 0 \qquad u = 0 \tag{7.36}$$

$$\text{constant} = \sin \left(\frac{3\pi}{4} \right)$$

$$u = -\sin \left(\frac{3\pi}{4} - \phi \right) + \sin \left(\frac{3\pi}{4} \right) \tag{7.37}$$

Condition 2 above indicates that the horizontal velocity across OB is the velocity of the extrusion. Point A on the α-line AB must rotate through $\pi/2$ in a counterclockwise direction to B, and this value of ϕ can be used to calculate the extrusion velocity as follows:

$$u_B = -\sin\left[\frac{3\pi}{4} - \left(-\frac{\pi}{2}\right)\right] + \sin\frac{3\pi}{4}$$

$$u_B = \frac{1}{\sqrt{2}} + \frac{1}{\sqrt{2}} = \sqrt{2}$$

(7.38)

The same result is obtained for any point on OB. There is therefore a downward flow of metal across OB with a velocity of 2 compared to a velocity of 1 for the billet. The velocity of the extrusion is the horizontal component of this velocity across OB for the top half of the extrusion process. The bottom half, which is a mirror image of the top half, also contributes metal flow across $O'B$. The resultant horizontal flow will therefore be twice the flow across OB or

$$2u_B \cos\frac{\pi}{4} = 2\sqrt{2}\,\frac{1}{\sqrt{2}} = 2$$

(7.39)

which is the result to be expected for a 50 percent reduction. Therefore, the solution is correct from both a slip-line and a metal velocity point of view [7.8].

7.7.5 Slip-Line Field Nets and Forward Large-Ratio Extrusion

To facilitate the plotting of slip-line fields, standard slip-line field nets may be made for typical forming problems. Thomsen et al. [7.9] have plotted a standard two-centered fan net, which may be used for plotting the slip-line fields for punch penetration and extrusion problems. First, the die and container are drawn on transparent paper to the same scale as the distance between the points of singularity of the net. The drawing is then placed over the net, and only the slip-lines that fall within the boundaries of the die-container setup are used. If the slip-lines at the boundary do not fit exactly, the x and y coordinates of the nodal points of the net as calculated by a digital computer are given in tabular form, which may be used to sketch readily the appropriate boundary slip-lines.

If the standard net were used in the preceding problem, only the circular slip-lines near the points of singularity would fall within the boundaries of the container. Thomsen et al. [7.9] applied the standard net to a plane-strain extrusion problem, in which the extrusion ratio is large (12.5) as shown in Fig. 7.21 and obtained the following values for σ_x/k ratio, where σ_x is the axial stress, for the points indicated:

Point	A	D	E	F	G	N
σ_x/k	0	−5.14	−5.71	−8.87	−7.28	−5.14

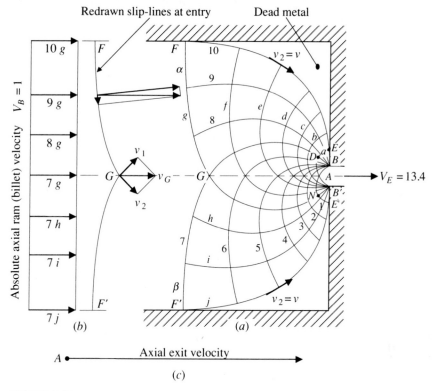

FIGURE 7.21
(*a*) A slip-line field for a plane-strain direct extrusion with an extrusion ratio of 12.5. The absolute velocity vectors taken (*b*) at $V_B = 1$ at various points on the billet at entry, and (*c*) at point A at the exit at $V_E = 13.4$ are shown. (*b*) Velocity components, v_1 and v_2, tangent to two slip-lines intersecting at a point (ν and v are used here interchangeably with v) [7.9].

7.7.6 Velocity Field Diagram
for Large-Ratio Extrusion [7.9]

After a probable slip-line field is constructed, to satisfy the boundary conditions a velocity field is usually constructed to check whether a velocity field exists that will satisfy equilibrium conditions and whether the rigid material surrounding the slip-line field can support the stresses without yielding. Since the slip-lines are not extensible, the instantaneous velocity components along them cannot change, that is, $dv/ds = 0$, and the normal velocity components across a slip-line must be equal, that is, $v_1 = v_1'$.

The velocity field diagram as shown in Fig. 7.22, may be constructed from a slip-line field diagram. The lines of the velocity diagram are transformed slip-lines and are parallel to the instantaneous components, v_1 and v_2, of the velocity vectors. v_1 and v_2 are tangent to two slip-lines intersecting at a point as shown in Fig. 7.21(*b*). The absolute velocity vector, giving its magnitude and

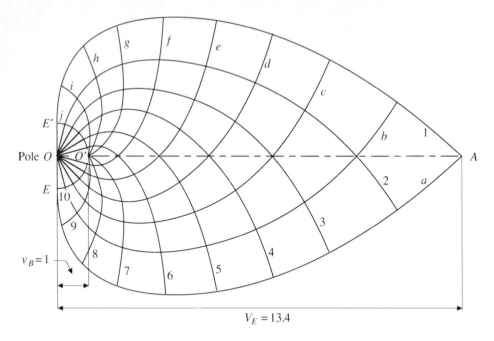

FIGURE 7.22
Complete velocity field diagram of the slip-line field of Fig. 7.21 [7.9].

direction, can be found for any point given by the intersection of two slip-lines by connecting the so-called pole of the transformed slip-line diagram to its corresponding numbered intersection. It will be noted that the shapes of the two diagrams are entirely different. The closely spaced lines on one are widely spaced on the other, and vice versa. The points that fall above the centerline on one generally fall below it on the other. It should be noted that the velocity of all the points on the rigid–plastic interface FGF' in Fig. 2.21(a) have the same vector and consequently have a velocity of the same magnitude and direction, which is equal to the velocity of the ram. Also, the absolute velocity, V_E, of point A in the slip-line diagram, will have the velocity of OA, equal to $V_E = 13.4$, which is the absolute velocity of the extruded material leaving the die as shown in Figs. 7.21 and 7.22 [7.9].

The complete graphic procedure for the construction of the velocity field diagram will not be discussed, but some brief remarks will be made.

Briefly, the absolute velocity vector V_B, for the billet which in this case is unity, is laid out from pole O, which represents a stationary reference point such as the dead-metal region. The relative exit velocity V, which can be calculated from the fact that the volume is assumed to remain constant ($R = 12.5$, $(12.5A_f)(1)(1) = A_f V$, $V = 12.5$), is laid off as $O'A$ along the centerline as shown in Fig. 7.22. The velocity v_2 tangent to line 10 at F and to line j at F' is equal to v. To preserve continuity, the velocity must be tangent to slip-lines 10 and j and equal to v, and must therefore terminate a semicircle with a radius equal to v and with the pole as the center as shown in Fig. 7.22.

We will now return to explaining the susceptibility of some material to central bursting by use of the slip-line field method. (See Sec. 7.5.)

7.7.7 Central-Bursting Susceptibility and the Slip-Line Fields

In addition to the process parameters in drawing and extrusion, i.e., the die half-angle α, the fractional reduction in area per pass r, the friction shear factor m, and the capacity of the metal to strainharden as expressed by β or n as expressed by Eqs. (7.19) and (3.5), there are other material characteristics that are an index of the metal's susceptibility to structural damage such as by central bursting (Figs. 7.11, 7.13, and 7.16) and other crack formation during processing. Metallic materials that have nonmetallic inclusions and hard secondary phase particles such as carbides, that will nucleate voids or cracks, are prone to structural damage. Structural damage during wire drawing and extrusion for a given microstructure has been found generally to correlate well with the amount of hydrostatic stress that develops within the material. As discussed elsewhere, a stress system at any point within a solid body subjected to external forces can be described in terms of three deviatoric stresses and a hydrostatic component. The deviatoric stresses act to alter the shape of the body, while the hydrostatic component acts to change its volume. A high hydrostatic tensile component will tend to nucleate voids or cracks in a body and will enhance their growth.

The flow processes in drawing and extrusion can be extremely non-homogeneous. One of the few methods that is amenable to dealing with non-homogeneous deformation is the semiempirical, plane-strain slip-line field method, which can be practically extrapolated to the axisymmetric case.

One of the restrictions placed on the solution is concerned with the maximum reduction for a given die angle beyond which the solution approaches that for the homogeneous deformation case, in which the plastically deformed zone extends over a finite range along the centerline. In other words, the solution is one applicable to the case for which the slip-line field intersects the centerline of a drawn strip, or its axisymmetric analog, at a single point as shown in Fig. 7.23 for the frictionless case [7.10]. Another restriction is that for a given die half-angle, a minimum reduction exists below which metal flow occurs ahead of the die in the form of upsetting or bulging. The above two limitations have been expressed by Green and Hill as presented by Rogers [7.10] as

$$\alpha\left(0.230+\frac{\alpha}{9}\right) < r < \frac{2 \sin \alpha}{(1+2 \sin \alpha)} \tag{7.40}$$

where α is the die half-angle and r is the fractional reduction in area. The closer the reduction is to the lower limit, i.e., the lighter the allowable reduction relative to the die half-angle, the more inhomogeneous the deformation and the greater the hydrostatic tension and the probable structural damage.

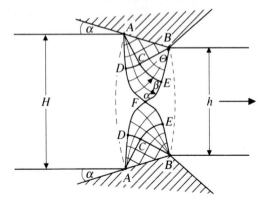

FIGURE 7.23
Slip-line field and plastic zone for drawing a strip through a frictionless, wedge-shaped die. (*From R. Hill, The Mechanical Theory of Plasticity, Oxford Press, 1950.*)

In partial explanation of the foregoing equation (7.40), the maximum reduction for which the slip-line field is valid, for geometrical reasons alone, is

$$r = 1 - \frac{h}{H} = \frac{2 \sin \alpha}{1 + 2 \sin \alpha} \tag{7.41}$$

where h, H, and α are defined in Fig. 7.23.

If the available techniques of slip-line field theory and practice are used, the ratio of the hydrostatic pressure, σ_h, to the flow stress of the material, $\bar{\sigma}$, is obtained at various points within a strip drawn through a die, in which $\alpha = 15°$ and the reduction in area is 8.5 percent, as presented by Rogers [7.10] and as shown in Fig. 7.24. It will be noted that the highest value of hydrostatic compres-

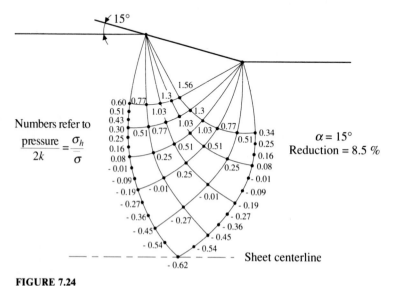

FIGURE 7.24
Distribution of hydrostatic pressure-to-flow stress ratio, $\sigma_h/\bar{\sigma}$, for one set of strip drawing conditions [7.10].

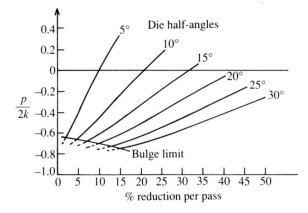

FIGURE 7.25
Hydrostatic stress-to-flow stress ratio versus percent reduction in area per pass at the centerline for strip drawing through frictionless dies having various die half-angles [7.10].

sion, which is positive, is directly under the die, whereas the highest value of hydrostatic tension, which is negative, is at the centerline, where the structural damage would therefore be expected to occur. For each die half-angle, the highest hydrostatic tension exists for the least possible reduction before bulging occurs for the frictionless case, and lower reductions are required for the lower angle dies than for the higher angle dies, as shown in Fig. 7.25. The effect of friction makes the hydrostatic component of stress more negative than would be expected under the same conditions for the frictionless case.

It was shown that, as in other forms of ductile fracture, such material characteristics as cleanliness (no nonmetallic inclusions), low strainhardening capability, brittleness, etc., play a major role in the amount of structural damage produced; however, pearlitic 4340 steel suffered substantial amount of damage during drawing with poor correlation to the prevailing stress state. It was also found that structural damage is also cumulative, increasing with successive draws.

Another very useful, semiempirical method for obtaining solutions to metal-working problems such as extrusion is the visioplastic method, which will be discussed next.

7.8 STRESS DISTRIBUTION UNDER PLANE STRAIN BY USE OF THE VISIOPLASTIC METHOD

7.8.1 Introduction

An important experimental method for determining stress, strain, and strain rate, and to get a good idea of how the metal flows during deformation, and the amount of redundancy existing, is the visioplastic method. It provides a means of obtaining the stress field and the flow field that describe the mechanics of the process. It is a method by which the velocity vector field is established experimentally and the strain rates, strains, and stresses are calculated from it. This is accomplished by placing a grid pattern onto the median plane of an axisymmetric body or workpiece, i.e., on a plane at right angles to the metal flow, as in a plane-strain problem, and observing its rate of distortion. For steady-state flow problems such as for extrusion, after the initial stage, etc., for which the flow field does not vary with time, the steady-state flow pattern is obtained by deforming the metal sufficiently in one step. For nonsteady-state flow problems such as forging, etc., incremental deformation must be used and the rate of grid distortion must be recorded. Photographs of the distorted grid pattern may be taken for different stages of deformation and the grid distortion is analyzed as a function of time. The coordinate points after distortion may be tracked by a scanning machine and the distortion grid plotted out by a computer.

Only the steady-state stage of the forward extrusion process will be considered here. In this case a cylindrical billet is pointed by swaging and then split longitudinally in half prior to extrusion and a square grid is placed on one of the polished, split faces by etching or by a photographic and etching process, as shown in Fig. 7.26. The grid consists of a set of lines parallel to the billet axis, called *flow lines*, and a set initially perpendicular to the first, called *transverse lines*. The two halves are put back together, the pointed billet is placed in the extrusion container and partially extruded, removed from the die, separated, and the resulting deformation of the grid lines observed. [See Fig. 2.90(*b*).]

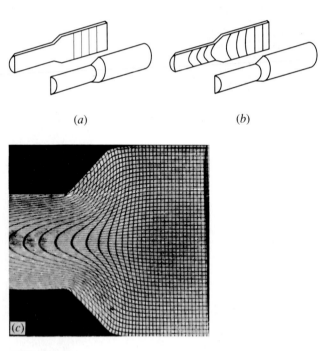

(*a*)   (*b*)

(*c*)

FIGURE 7.26
Sketches illustrating the procedure followed for making and using a grid pattern to study metal flow as a result of extrusion, in which (*a*) the cylinder is pointed, split longitudinally, and gridded, and (*b*) the two halves are assembled, partially extruded, and disassembled; and (*c*) a photograph of a distorted grid pattern in an axisymmetric extrusion of a lead-tin alloy with $R = 4$, and with a molykote lubricant [7.12].

7.8.2 Solution of the Stress Equation

Two common methods of analysis may be used: (1) graphical method, and (2) flow function method. The elementary definitions of strain and strain rate as the gradients of displacement and velocity components serve as a basis of the analysis. Since the part is cylindrical in this example, it is convenient to use cylindrical coordinates as shown in Fig. 7.27.

The following is a brief discussion of the above two methods of analysis:

7.8.2.1 GRAPHICAL METHOD [7.1]. Four graphs are drawn (1) of the axial velocity v against the axial distance z, (2) of the radial velocity u against the radial distance r, (3) of v against r, and (4) of u against z. If one lets the velocity of a particular grid-line intersection (o, a) in Fig. 7.27 be given by V_0, u and v will now represent velocities and not displacements. The slopes of the curves at each of the desired points gives the strain rates:

$$\dot{\varepsilon}_r = \frac{\partial u}{\partial r} \qquad \dot{\varepsilon}_z = \frac{\partial v}{\partial z} \qquad \text{and} \qquad \dot{\gamma}_{zr} = \frac{\partial u}{\partial z} + \frac{\partial v}{\partial r} \qquad (7.42)$$

where v = velocity component along the longitudinal axis of the cylinder or the z direction

u = velocity component in the r direction as shown in Fig. 7.27, and $\dot{\varepsilon}_r$, $\dot{\varepsilon}_z$, and $\dot{\varepsilon}_\theta$ are the normal strain rate components in the r, z, and tangential directions, respectively, and γ_{zr} is the shear strain component in an rz plane.

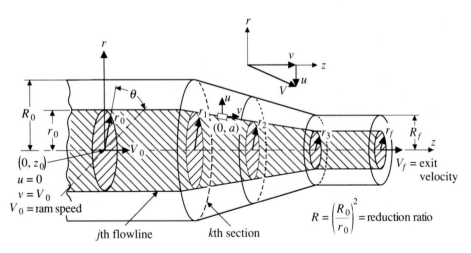

FIGURE 7.27
Diagrammatic representation of the flow function envelope. The shaded tubular envelope represents a surface of constant ϕ. The volume flow rate is constant past any transverse section. The components of particle velocity are u and v for a material point moving along a flow line in the r and z directions, respectively (v and v are used here interchangeably with v) [7.11].

The next step is to evaluate the effective strain rates, $\bar{\dot{\varepsilon}}$, using the equation,

$$\bar{\dot{\varepsilon}} = (\tfrac{2}{9}[(\dot{\varepsilon}_z - \dot{\varepsilon}_r)^2 + (\dot{\varepsilon}_r - \dot{\varepsilon}_\theta)^2 + (\dot{\varepsilon}_\theta - \dot{\varepsilon}_r)^2 + \tfrac{1}{3}\dot{\gamma}_{zr}^2])^{1/2} \qquad (7.43)$$

and then to integrate this equation along a flow line to find the effective strain $\bar{\varepsilon}$, from which the effective stress $\bar{\sigma}$ can be deduced by use of an equation for the flow stress such as

$$\bar{\sigma} = K\bar{\varepsilon}^n \qquad \bar{\sigma} = C\dot{\bar{\varepsilon}}^m \qquad \text{or} \qquad \bar{\sigma} = A\bar{\varepsilon}^n\dot{\bar{\varepsilon}}^m \qquad (7.44)$$

where K, C, A, n, and m are material constants defined elsewhere.

7.8.2.2 FLOW FUNCTION METHOD [7.11]. The graphical method is of course tedious, involves a considerable amount of manual operations, requires questionable smoothing of the results, and is largely of historical interest. An alternate procedure is the flow function solution, in which the experimental data is first fitted, usually by a sixth- (2 to 8) order polynomial that is used for the remaining calculations. This method will also be illustrated for the cylindrical extrusion.

The flow function $\phi_{(r,z)}$ is defined with reference to Fig. 7.27 as the rate of axial volume flow through a circular cross section of radius r as

$$\phi = 2\pi \int_0^r vr\, dr \qquad \left(\frac{\text{mm}^3}{\text{s}}\right) \qquad (7.45)$$

Here, as above, v is the axial component of particle velocity and u is the radial component in cylindrical coordinates, r, θ, and z [7.1]. ϕ measures the volume flow rate through an area of radius r centered on the axis of symmetry and depends on both r and z as shown in Fig. 7.27. This figure illustrates schematically the envelope of all circles passing material at one particular volume flow rate. This envelope is a surface of constant ϕ, and a diametral plane through the centerline intersecting this envelope is a flow line. Two important assumptions are that the material is incompressible and that the shape of the ϕ surface does not change with time.

Differentiating Eq. (7.45) with respect to r and rearranging, one obtains for the radial velocity component

$$u = \frac{1}{2\pi r}\left(\frac{\partial\phi}{\partial r}\right) \qquad (7.46)$$

Also, since along any flow line, the flow function is constant, $d\phi = 0$, and by use of the slope of the flow line $dr/dz = v/u$, it can be shown that the axial velocity component is

$$v = -\frac{1}{2\pi r}\left(\frac{\partial\phi}{\partial z}\right) \qquad (7.47)$$

It is possible to determine ϕ as a function of r and z from the form of a given flow line, starting with the velocity V_0 that the ram imparts to all elements of the workpiece upstream from the die at some point (O, a). For any chosen starting flow line j of radius r_j

$$\phi_j = \pi r_j^2 |V_0| \tag{7.48}$$

where ϕ_j = the value of the flow function along the jth line
   r_j = the radius of the jth flow line at the entry section
   V_0 = the ram speed taken as unity

It is convenient to measure $r_j(k)$ at equally spaced intervals along the z axis. A sixth-order polynomial expression can then be fitted to the variation of ϕ with r at each individual section k along the axis

$$\phi = \sum_{m=1}^{6} A_m r^m \qquad \text{at } k = \text{constant} \tag{7.49}$$

Smoothing of ϕ may be carried out in both the r and z directions. Note that j is the number of the flow line, and k is the number of the section or station [7.1].

The shape of a flow line may be approximated by a sixth-order polynomial mentioned in the foregoing

$$r_{j(z)} = \sum_{n=0}^{6} b_{jn} z^n \tag{7.50}$$

in which coefficient b_{jn} can be established by the least squares fitting of the measured point (z, r) corresponding to flow line j [7.11].

The axial and radial velocities v and u are then found by numerical differentiation of ϕ according to Eqs. (7.46) and (7.47), and these can be processed as strain rates, as for the graphical method, but using the basic polynomial.

The complete calculation of velocities, strain rates, strains, and stresses for axisymmetric extrusion using the known values of the flow function ϕ can be obtained.

From the experimentally determined steady-state flow pattern, the radial and axial velocity components (u, v) can be calculated from known values of ϕ as follows:

$$u = \frac{1}{2\pi r}\left(\frac{\partial \phi}{\partial z}\right) \tag{7.46)(7.51}$$

and

$$v = -\frac{1}{2\pi r}\left(\frac{\partial \phi}{\partial r}\right) \tag{7.47)(7.52}$$

When the velocity components are known at all points in the deformation zone, the strain-rate components and the total effective strain rate can be determined as follows [7.12]:

$$\dot{\varepsilon}_r = \frac{\partial u}{\partial r} = -\frac{1}{2\pi r^2}\frac{\partial \phi}{\partial z} + \frac{1}{2\pi r}\frac{\partial^2 \phi}{\partial r\, \partial z} \tag{7.53}$$

$$\dot{\varepsilon}_z = \frac{\partial v}{\partial z} = -\frac{1}{2\pi r}\frac{\partial^2 \phi}{\partial r\, \partial z} \tag{7.54}$$

$$\dot{\varepsilon}_\theta = \frac{u}{r} = \frac{1}{2\pi r^2}\frac{\partial \phi}{\partial z} \tag{7.55}$$

$$\dot{\gamma}_{zr} = \frac{\partial u}{\partial z} + \frac{\partial v}{\partial r} = \frac{1}{2\pi r}\left[\frac{\partial^2 \phi}{\partial z^2} - \frac{\partial^2 \phi}{\partial r^2} + \frac{1}{r}\frac{\partial \phi}{\partial r}\right] \tag{7.56}$$

$$\dot{\bar{\varepsilon}} = \sqrt{\tfrac{2}{3}}(\dot{\varepsilon}_r^2 + \dot{\varepsilon}_\theta^2 + \dot{\varepsilon}_z^2 + \tfrac{1}{2}\dot{\gamma}_{rz}^2)^{1/2} \tag{7.57}$$

The total effective strain $\bar{\varepsilon}$ can then be calculated by the integration of $\dot{\bar{\varepsilon}}$ with respect to time along the flow lines from

$$\bar{\varepsilon} = \int_0^t \dot{\bar{\varepsilon}}\, dt \tag{7.58}$$

The stress components at any point in the deformation zone can be evaluated by considering the equilibrium equations ($\partial\sigma_{ij}/\partial x_i = 0$), the constitutive equations ($\dot{\varepsilon}_{ij} = \lambda\sigma_{ij}$), and the strain-rate velocity relations ($\dot{\varepsilon}_{ij} = \frac{1}{2}(\partial u_i/\partial x_j + \partial u_j/\partial x_i)$), resulting in the following [7.12]:

$$\sigma_{z(r,z)} = \int_0^a \left[\frac{\partial}{\partial r}\left(\frac{\dot{\gamma}_{rz}}{2\lambda} + \frac{\dot{\gamma}_{rz}}{2r\lambda}\right)\right] dz + \int_0^r \left[\frac{\partial}{\partial r}\left(\frac{\dot{\varepsilon}_z - \dot{\varepsilon}_r}{\lambda}\right)\right]$$

$$-\frac{\partial}{\partial r}\left[\frac{\dot{\gamma}_{rz}}{2\lambda} - \frac{\dot{\varepsilon}_z - \dot{\varepsilon}_\theta}{r\lambda}\right]_{z=a} dr + \sigma_{z(0,a)} \tag{7.59}$$

$$\sigma_{r(r,z)} = \sigma_{z(r,z)} + \frac{2}{3}\bar{\sigma}\left(\frac{\dot{\varepsilon}_z - \dot{\varepsilon}_r}{\dot{\bar{\varepsilon}}}\right) \tag{7.60}$$

$$\sigma_{\theta(r,z)} = \sigma_{z(r,z)} + \frac{2}{3}\bar{\sigma}\left(\frac{\dot{\varepsilon}_\theta - \dot{\varepsilon}_z}{\dot{\bar{\varepsilon}}}\right) \tag{7.61}$$

$$\tau_{rz} = \frac{1}{2}\frac{\dot{\gamma}_{rz}}{\lambda} \quad \text{and} \quad \sigma_h = \frac{1}{3}(\sigma_r + \sigma_\theta + \sigma_z) \tag{7.62}$$

In the equations for $\sigma_{z(r,z)}$ and τ_{rz},

$$\lambda = \frac{3}{2}\frac{\dot{\bar{\varepsilon}}}{\bar{\sigma}} = \frac{3}{2}\frac{\dot{\bar{\varepsilon}}}{\bar{\varepsilon}^n} \tag{7.63}$$

and $\sigma_{z(0,a)}$ is the axial stress at a reference point (O, a), which is selected inside the deformation zone. $\sigma_{z(0,a)}$ can be evaluated at point (O, z_0) as follows:

$$\sigma_{z(0,a)} = \int \sigma_{z(r,z)}(2\pi r\, dr) = 0 \tag{7.64}$$

as the resultant force is zero at the exit.

Computer programs have been developed to perform the computation associated with flow-line analysis such as the one presented by Medrano et al. for the calculation of the velocity, strain components, and strain rate [7.11]. The data are taken off a visioplastic grid pattern as shown in Figs. 7.28 and 7.29.

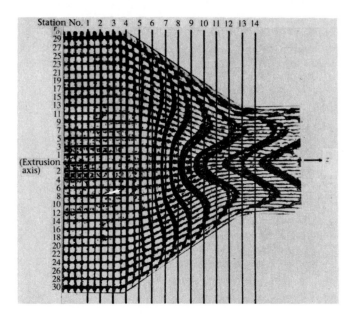

FIGURE 7.28
Illustration of the procedure used to take data from a grid pattern for the flow function analysis [7.11].

These data are processed by the computer. The value of the flow function for each line is computed from its upstream radius using Eq. (7.48). The shape of the line may then be approximated by use of Eq. (7.50). These polynomials may be used to obtain interpolated data points by subdividing the interval Δz between axial stations and evaluating all of the $r_j(z)$ for the original and the intermediate stations by use of the polynomials. From the measured and interpolated data, the flow function is approximated by use of Eq. (7.49). The calculation of the velocity, strain components, and strain rate is based on Eqs. (7.42).

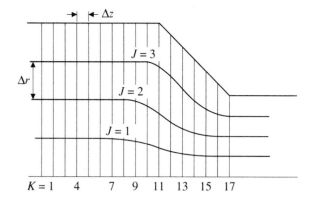

FIGURE 7.29
Computational mesh formed by the intersection of flow lines having initially equal spacing Δr in the region upstream from the die and radial lines having equal axial spacing Δz (*From R. E. Medrando and P. P. Gillis, J. Strain Analysis, Vol. 7, No. 3, 1972, p. 173.*)

The following observations may be made regarding the results of a computer analysis of extrusion similar to the above:

1. Axial and radial velocity distributions for different flow lines, $k = l$ to n, are plotted out

2. If the velocity components are added vectorially, the resultant velocities along the centerline and along the die boundary are obtained

3. Calculated flow lines are plotted out, which can be compared as a check with the experimental ones

4. If one of the smooth, intermediate flow lines is selected as the die boundary, the velocity gradient between the centerline and the boundary would be very much reduced, and the velocity field would approach that of uniform deformation, assuming no change in friction

5. The total effective strain distribution with r, for different k lines, shows a sudden rise near the boundary

6. Axial stress distribution with r is plotted for different k lines, which shows that an axial tensile stress exists in the central portion, which may cause centerline bursts or chevrons

7. Selection of a proper die boundary will eliminate these defects and produce less residual stress

7.9   GRAPHICAL METHODS FOR OBTAINING THE EXTRUSION PRESSURE IN COLD EXTRUSION

For equations such as the above to be useful to the tool designers and production personnel, they must be placed in a form such as nomographs so as to be readily applied. One such graphical method has been proposed by Drake and Throop [7.13] for predicting the pressures for forward and backward cold extrusion of 14 steels commonly used in cold extrusion such as SAE 1008, 1010, etc. This method is based on the results of extruding lead. The ram (punch) pressure for forward, p_F, and backward, p_B, extrusion of the above steels in units of lbf/in^2 are [7.13]

$$p_F = 37.9\,Fr^{0.787}\alpha^{0.375} \qquad lbf/in^2 \qquad (7.65a)$$

and

$$p_B = 38.2\,Fr^{0.855}\alpha^{0.355} \qquad lbf/in^2 \qquad (7.65b)$$

$$p_F = 261.3\,Fr^{0.787}\alpha^{0.375} \qquad MPa \qquad (7.65c)$$

and

$$p_B = 263.4\,Fr^{0.855}\alpha^{0.355} \qquad MPa \qquad (7.65d)$$

where α = total die angle
$\quad r$ = percent reduction in area
$\quad F$ = a conversion factor, which relates the values of pressure for the extrusion of steel to that for lead

Since the strainhardening exponent n is approximately the same for lead and the above steels, F in the above equations turns out to be the ratio of the strength coefficients, K, for the steel to that of lead or

$$F = \frac{K_{steel}}{K_{lead}} \tag{7.66}$$

For example, lead, 1020 steel, and 1050 steel having K values of 3165, 91,786, and 142,133 would have F values of 1, 29.0 and 44.91, respectively. The above information has been plotted in the form of a nomograph (not presented here), which is easy to use.

It can be noted in Fig. 7.19 that the extrusion pressure increases slowly until the percent reduction, $\%r = (A_0 - A_f)/A_0(100)$, of 80 to 90 percent and then rises more sharply. If the ratio of the extrusion pressure p, to the flow stress $\bar{\sigma}$, is plotted against the natural log of the extrusion ratio R, a straight line is obtained having an equation of the form

$$\frac{p}{\bar{\sigma}} = a + b \ln R \tag{7.67}$$

where a and b are constants dependent on the die friction and redundant work, and R is the extrusion ratio.

Sometimes a third term is added, cl, where c is a constant and l is the length of the billet to take care of the frictional forces in direct extrusion.

Since, in industrial practice, axisymmetric extrusions rather than plane-strain extrusions are made, data for this type of extrusion is empirically fitted to an equation of the above form. One such equation that has rather wide application is

$$\frac{p}{\bar{\sigma}} = 0.9 + 1.5 \ln R \tag{7.68}$$

which is plotted in Fig. 7.30. This equation was obtained for a 90° die, and the data points that are plotted for Pb, Al, Sn, and mild steel were obtained from different sources and show good agreement, within about 10 percent for R values < 4, with the equation for the line.

The extrusion pressure is not markedly different for products of different shapes such as rounds, structural shapes, tubes, etc., as long as the extrusion ratio remains constant. Also, the extrusion pressure for several smaller holes in a multiple-hole die is not much greater than for a one-hole die with a cross-sectional area equal to the sum of the areas of the smaller holes.

Experimental extrusion data can also be fitted to an equation of the form

$$p = A (\ln R)^N \tag{7.69}$$

where A and N are constants that depend on the material and extrusion conditions. The two variables that have been considered to be of prime importance are the material factor and the reduction ratio. The above relationship may

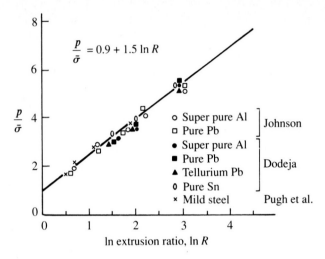

FIGURE 7.30
Effect of extrusion ratio upon the extrusion pressure required to extrude various materials through a 90° die. (*From R. J. Wilcox and P. W. Whitton, J. Inst. Metals, 1960, Vol. 88, p. 200.*)

therefore be expressed as follows [7.14]:

$$p = a' H^{m'} (\ln R)^{n'} \tag{7.70}$$

where

$p = P/A_0$, the maximum extrusion pressure
$R = A_0/A_f$, the extrusion ratio
H = Brinell (BH) and Vickers hardness (VH) [for Eq. (7.71)] in conventional units
a', m', and n' are material and process constants [see Eq. (7.72)]
P = maximum extrusion force N
A_0 and A_f = billet and product cross-sectional area

A typical example of this relationship for the cold extrusion of fully annealed cold-forging steel is

$$p = 35.5 HV^{0.78} (\ln R)^{0.72} \qquad N/mm^2 \text{ (MPa)} \tag{7.71}$$

The die entry angle, 2α, and the billet length to the diameter ratio, L/D, are correction factors included in the constant a'. If the natural logarithm, $\ln R$, is converted to log to the base 10, and the log is taken of both sides of the above equation, the following is obtained

$$\log p = A + m' \log H + n' \log (\log R) \tag{7.72}$$

where

$$A = \log a' + \log 2.3 \tag{7.73}$$

The above equation (7.72) is the equation of a plane when plotted on log p, log H, and log (log R) as axes, so that the plot of log p and log H, and log p and log (log R) would be straight lines. The slope of the former plot would yield m' and the slope of the latter n'. Rearranging the above equation (7.72), one obtains

$$\log \frac{p}{H^{m'}} = A + n' \log (\log R) \qquad (7.74)$$

where the intercept at $R = 1$ yields A, from which a' can be calculated by use of Eq. (7.72). The slope of this line is also equal to n'.

From experimental data obtained from various sources, for a billet diameter ratio D of 1 and for a square entry die, i.e., one in which $2\alpha = 180°$, the following values were obtained for the above constants for cold forging steel rods: $a' = 47$, $m' = 0.75$, and $n' = 0.8$. These values are applicable to a range of Brinell or Vickers hardness from 80 to 240 and for R ratios of 1.11 to 6.5. Within these limits, Eq. (7.70) may be written as

$$p = 47 H^{0.75} (\ln R)^{0.8} \qquad (7.75)$$

This equation has been incorporated into a convenient nomograph as the International Cold Forging Group (ICFG) Data Sheet No. 1/70 for the cold forward extrusion of steel [7.14]. By use of this nomograph (not presented here), the extrusion load can be obtained from the container diameter, die diameter, the billet length/diameter ratio, and the die angle. A similar nomograph is also available for the cold extrusion of a can as ICFG Data Sheet No. 2/70 [7.15].

The less significant factors, which are believed to have an effect of less than ±5 percent, are

1. The type, capacity, and speed of the press
2. Tool material and design other than the die angle
3. Nature and condition of the work material other than the hardness
4. Billet characteristics such as exact size, method of preparation, effect of die fitting tapered nose L including parallel portion only
5. Small variations in lubrication from that used to obtain the basic data, i.e., zinc phosphate coating with Bonderlube 235

7.10 CAD/CAM FOR EXTRUSION

7.10.1 Introduction

In recent years, a considerable amount of work has been conducted on the improvement of the extrusion process for producing shapes from aluminum, titanium, and high-temperature alloys and steel. This work has resulted in the development of some new extrusion techniques, such as the extrusion of steel and high-strength alloys with glass lubrication. However, the overall extrusion technology still remains to be largely based on empirical methods. Most of the extrusion die design and manufacturing work is still considered to be an art rather than a science. This situation can be explained by the inherent complexity of the extrusion process. The difficult-to-predict metal flow pattern, the simultaneous heat generation and transfer which takes place during the process, the friction at the material-tool interfaces, and the metallurgical variations make the extrusion process very difficult to analyze from an engineering point of view. Consequently, there remains still considerable development work to be done in order to upgrade the extrusion technology to the level of an advanced manufacturing process, for producing sound parts at moderate costs [7.16].

Since current practices for the extrusion of aluminum alloys are quite different from those for the extrusion of steel, titanium, and high-temperature alloys, they are usually discussed separately.

In the unlubricated extrusion of aluminum, the billet is extruded through a flat-faced or shear-faced die as shown in Fig. 7.31 for direct and indirect extrusion. With this technique, however, very high extrusion forces are required because of the great amount of internal shearing between the flowing and the stationary metal along the container surface and at the die corners as seen in Fig. 7.31. The energy dissipated by internal shearing, or redundant work, represents energy that is converted into heat, and results in a gradual increase of the product temperature as the extrusion proceeds. If not controlled, this adiabatic heating can be sufficient to cause hot shortness (brittleness) and melting in the extruded material.

Since the metal flows by internal shear and not by sliding along the die surfaces, the resulting extrusion has a bright surface finish; however, as mentioned

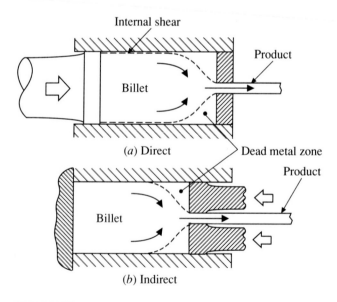

FIGURE 7.31
Schematic representation of direct and indirect extrusion through a flat-faced die without a lubricant showing the dead or nonmoving zone [7.16].

above, this type of extrusion has the following disadvantages:

1. Because of nonuniform metal flow, the redundant work and the extrusion pressure are high
2. To reduce the amount of heat generation, lower extrusion speeds must be used, which reduces the production rate
3. Nonuniform metal flow results in anisotropy across the section of extruded material

The extrusion speeds for the unlubricated extrusion of soft aluminum alloys with flat-faced dies are reasonably high and the extrusion pressure is relatively low. These factors, coupled with the fact that flat-faced dies are more economical to manufacture than streamlined dies, suggest that the extrusion of soft aluminum alloys by use of lubricated streamlined dies does not offer any significant advantage. However, in the extrusion of hard alloys, much can be gained through lubricated extrusion with streamlined dies. Higher extrusion speeds can be obtained because of the smaller temperature increase due to friction and redundant work. Also, lower capacity presses can be used since the required specific extrusion pressures are less than in unlubricated extrusion through flat-faced dies.

Titanium alloys, alloy steels, stainless steels, and tool steels are hot extruded on a commercial basis with streamlined dies and a variety of graphite and glass base lubricants. In extruding titanium alloys and steel, billet temperature is usually 1800 to 2300°F (982 to 1260°C) whereas the maximum temperature that the tooling can withstand is usually 900 to 1000°F (482 to 538°C), so that appropriate lubricants, insulative die coatings and ceramic die inserts are used with proper die design to minimize wear.

Possible die designs for the extrusion of aluminum alloys, steel, and titanium alloys are shown in Fig. 7.32.

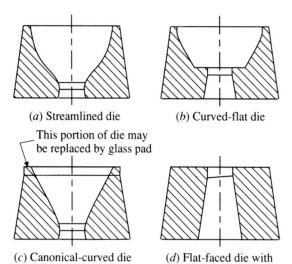

(a) Streamlined die

(b) Curved-flat die

This portion of die may be replaced by glass pad

(c) Canonical-curved die

(d) Flat-faced die with variable land

FIGURE 7.32
Possible die designs for the extrusion of aluminum alloys, steel, and titanium alloys [7.16].

Three different systems of computer programs were developed by Battelle's Columbus Laboratories for the CAD/CAM of extrusion of aluminum alloys, steel, and titanium alloys: (1) ALEXTR; (2) EXTCAM; and (3) SHAPE [7.17, 7.18]. ALEXTR allows the CAD/CAM of flat-faced dies for unlubricated extrusion of aluminum alloy structural shapes. EXTCAM is used in conjunction with ALEXTR and uses the data developed by ALEXTR to produce other sets of data for numerically controlled (NC) machining of the extrusion template and die. SHAPE allows the CAD/CAM of streamlined dies for the lubricated extrusion of aluminum, steel, and titanium alloys.

7.10.2   ALEXTR/EXTCAM Computer Program Systems [7.18]

ALEXTR is an interactive system of computer programs which are written to follow certain logical design procedures as outlined in Fig. 7.33. It operates interactively with a user to produce designs of flat-faced dies for the extrusion of aluminum alloy shapes. The system uses a graphic display unit to show the extrusion section and die layout to the user. This feature gives the user immediate, visual feedback as to what the programs are doing. The system will arrange the openings of a multihole die based on simple design rules. The user has complete freedom, however, to modify the arrangement. This is done by identifying the particular hole to be changed with the light pen, and then entering the parameters to be changed through the keyboard.

The following conventions have been used to structure the ALEXTR system: (a) ANSI FORTRAN IV standards are followed as much as is practical; (b) the extrusion shapes are described in a cartesian coordinate system; (c) the program is for interactive operation only.

An overview of the program operation is given in Fig. 7.34. The interaction between the user and the computer is shown in Fig. 7.35.

The program begins with the description of the shape of the extrusion, which is plotted on the terminal screen and on a x-y plotter. Information regarding the press capacity, etc., is stored previously in a data file. Next the die opening positions or holes are laid out, which are then corrected for thermal shrinkage and die deflection under load. The tool-strength analysis is performed, and the die-bearings are designed.

EXTCAM is a series of computer programs which generate punched tapes for the NC manufacturing of dies for extruding of aluminum alloys [7.18]. These dies are of flat-faced design conventionally used in the aluminum extrusion industry. In contrast to the ALEXTR die design system, EXTCAM makes no graphic display on the terminal screen, and it only interacts with the user to the extent necessary to determine what machining operation is to be calculated and what cutter size is to be used.

The operation and options of the EXTCAM system are shown in Fig. 7.36. A root-segment subprogram of the EXTCAM system is also called EXTCAM. It does little data processing of its own. Instead, it handles the reading of the

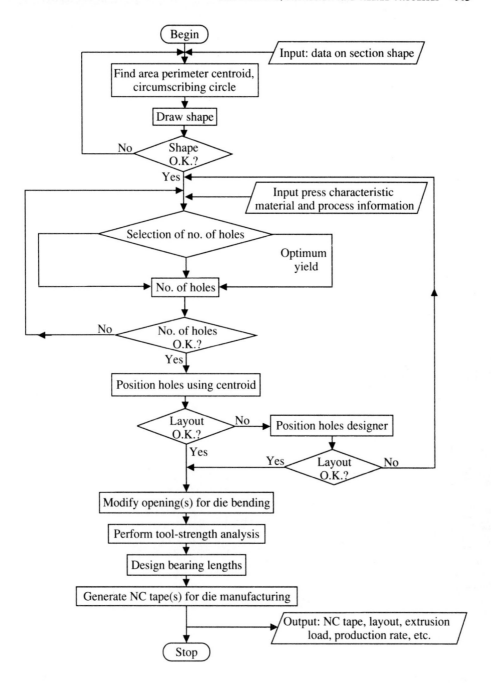

FIGURE 7.33
Flowchart of ALEXTR and EXTCAM interactive systems of computer programs for extrusion die design and manufacture [7.17].

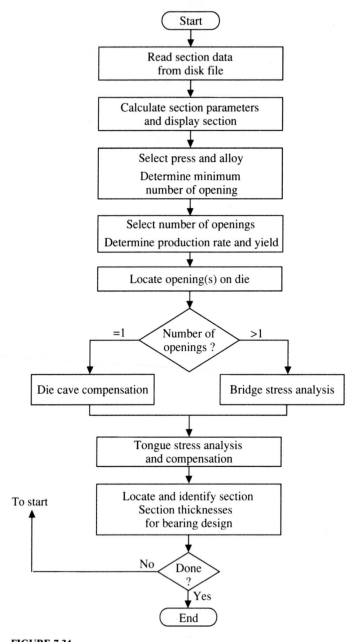

FIGURE 7.34
Flowchart showing the general operation of ALEXTR. (A tongue is a cantilever portion of a die and/or of its supports (backer or bolster) of a die stack.) [7.18]

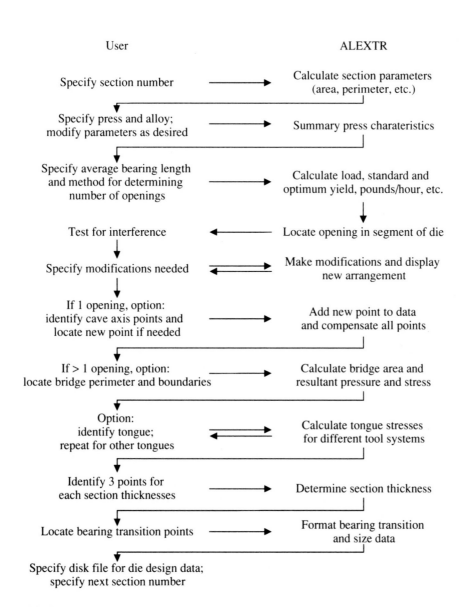

FIGURE 7.35
Flowchart illustrating user/program interaction [7.18].

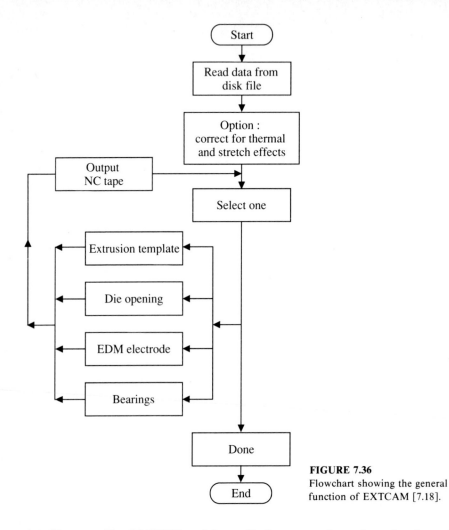

FIGURE 7.36
Flowchart showing the general function of EXTCAM [7.18].

data file created by ALEXTR and then calls the appropriate subroutine depending on the indication of the operator of what is to be done.

When first started, EXTCAM asks the user to enter the data file name to be used. This file, an output of ALEXTR, is then opened and read. The user is next asked if the die dimensions are to be expanded due to thermal and stretch considerations. The expansion coefficient is calculated and used by the user.

The user is then asked what machining operation tool path is to be generated from the options: (*a*) template for the finished extrusion; (*b*) front and back die profile; (*c*) EDM electrode to cut the die opening; and (*d*) bearings (die land) in back of the die.

After a cutter path is generated as requested by the user, EXTCAM loops back and rereads the input file. The user may then specify a different machining operation or cutter size.

7.10.3 Calculation of the Extrusion Load for Flat-Faced Dies

In unlubricated extrusion of shapes through flat-faced dies, the deforming material shears internally during the initial stages and forms dead or nonmoving zones on the flat face of the die. The formation of dead zones generates a new pseudo-die surface for subsequent flow of the material during the extrusion process as seen in Fig. 7.37. To analyze the steady-state extrusion process, the shape of the dead zones must be predicted, based on the principle that the material deforms such that the rate of energy dissipation is a minimum. In analyzing the conventional extrusion of round shapes, the shape of the dead zone can be predicted by calculating the rate of energy dissipation in extrusion through an arbitrarily shaped die, or through dies of different configurations. The die, which requires the minimum extrusion pressure, yields the shape of the shear surface.

The basic equation for the calculation of the extrusion load in ALEXTR is just an extension of the stress equation (7.17) derived by the upper-bound method. It can also be derived specifically for the extrusion of a circular section through a symmetric, single-hole, flat-faced die by minimizing the rate of energy supplied by the ram, i.e., the ram power $\dot{E}_t$.

At any instance, $\dot{E}_t$ must be equal to the sum of the rates of energy dissipation as follows [7.18]:

$$\dot{E}_t = \dot{E}_{fc} + \dot{E}_i + \dot{E}_{sh} + \dot{E}_{fd} + \dot{E}_{fl} \tag{7.76}$$

where $\dot{E}_t = P_t \cdot v_R = A\bar{p}v_R$
P_t = total extrusion load
v_R = speed of the ram
A = cross-sectional area of the billet
$\bar{p}$ = average extrusion pressure
E_{fc} = rate of energy dissipated due to friction at the container wall
E_i = rate of energy dissipated due to plastic deformation

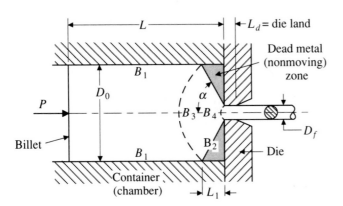

FIGURE 7.37
Unlubricated extrusion through a single-hole, flat-faced die [7.18].

E_{sh} = rate of energy dissipated due to shearing caused by tangential velocity discontinuities

E_{fd} = rate of energy dissipated due to friction at the die surface if any

E_{fl} = rate of energy dissipated due to friction at the die land

If the values of $\dot{E}_t$ and the energy dissipation terms (not given here) are substituted into this equation, and the equation is solved for P, the following equation is obtained:

$$\frac{P}{\bar{\sigma}} = \frac{1}{\sqrt{3}} \pi D \left[L - \left(\frac{D - D_f}{2} \right) \cot \alpha \right]$$

$$+ A \left[f(\alpha) \cdot \ln \left(\frac{A}{A_f} \right) + \frac{2}{\sqrt{3}} \left(\frac{\alpha}{\sin^2 \alpha} - \cot \alpha \right) + \frac{1}{\sqrt{3}} \cot \alpha \ln \left(\frac{A}{A_f} \right) + \frac{1}{\sqrt{3}} \frac{l_c - L_d}{A_f} \right]$$

$$(7.77)$$

where P = total extrusion load

$\bar{\sigma}$ = average flow stress

D_0 = diameter of the billet (see Fig. 7.37)

D_f = diameter of the extrusion

A_0 = cross-sectional area of the billet

A_f = final area of the extrusion

α = angle that the pseudo-die surface makes with the extrusion axis given below

$f(\alpha)$ = complex function involving $\sin^2 \alpha$ and $\cos \alpha$, which varies from 1 to 1.666,

l_c = perimeter of a circular section of equivalent cross-sectional area

L_d = length of the die land (see Fig. 7.37)

The dead zone cone angle α is an unknown parameter which can be determined by the upper-bound theorem from the condition:

$$\frac{\partial P}{\partial \alpha} = 0 \qquad (7.78)$$

If one neglects $(\partial L_1 / \partial \alpha)$ in the differentiation in Eq. (7.78), the value of α for various reductions can be derived. α can be approximated by the following relationships for the ranges of r given:

$$\begin{array}{ll} \text{For} \quad 0 \le r \le 5 & \alpha = 3r \\ \text{For} \quad 5 \le r \le 80 & \alpha = 15.0 + 0.56 \, (r - 5.0) \\ \text{For} \quad 80 < r < 100 & \alpha = 57.0 + 0.9 \, (r - 80.0) \end{array}$$

where $r = (A - A_f)/A$.

Equation (7.77) has been modified [7.17] to give expressions for the loads for the extrusion of nonsymmetric sections through single- and multihole flat-faced dies, but these equation are not presented here.   .

A practical method of estimating extrusion pressures for shapes is to use a shape factor C

$$P = P_0 C \qquad (7.79)$$

where P is the extrusion load for the shape under consideration, P_0 is the extrusion load for a round bar of equivalent cross-sectional area, and C is a shape factor that is a function of the perimeter of the extruded shape and of an equivalent round:

$$C = f\left(\frac{L_e}{L_0}\right) \tag{7.80}$$

where L_e is the perimeter of the extruded shape and L_0 is the perimeter of a round bar of the same cross-sectional area. The variation of C with various perimeter ratios is shown in Fig. 7.38 for a number of extrusion conditions. For

Symbol	Material	Load	Lubricant	ε_h
$-\cdot-\cdot-$ $-\!-\!-\;-\!-$	Lead	$\dfrac{P_{max}}{P_{min}}$	None	2.15
$-\!-\!-\!-\!-$ $-\!-\!-\!-$	Al 99.5 Al MgSi	P_A	Oil Graphite	4.3
$\triangle$	Al alloy	P_{min}		
$\diamond$	Al 99.5	$\dfrac{P_{max}}{P_{min}}$	None	
$\bullet$	Pure lead	P_{min}	Not given	3.7
$\circ$	Tin	$\dfrac{P_{max}}{P_{min}}$	None	1.4

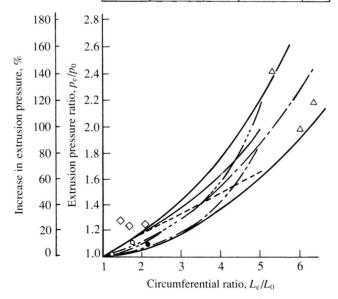

FIGURE 7.38
Comparison of various experimental data showing the increase in extrusion load as a function of the perimeter ratio, L_e/L_0, in direct extrusion of sections [7.2].

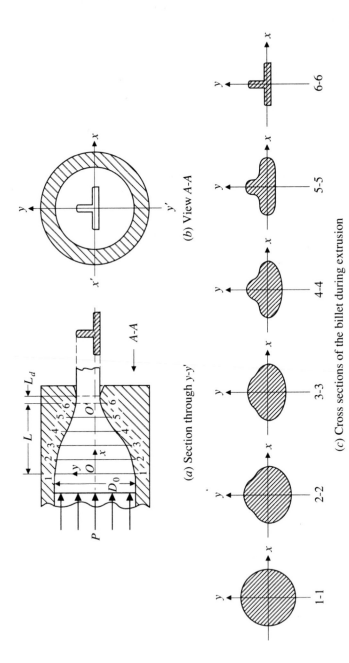

(a) Section through y-y'

(b) View A-A

(c) Cross sections of the billet during extrusion

FIGURE 7.39

Schematic of a streamlined die for extruding a T-shaped section [7.17].

hollow sections and multihole dies, the extrusion pressure may be 2 to 3.2 times higher to overcome friction and internal shear stresses [7.2].

7.10.4 SHAPE Computer System for CAD/CAM of Streamlined Dies for the Lubricated Extrusion of Simple Structural Shapes [7.16, 7.17]

SHAPE allows the determination of (1) optimal length and shape of the die in lubricated extrusion, (2) shear-zone configuration in unlubricated extrusion, (3) extrusion load and die-pressure distribution, and (4) cutter paths in NC machining of EDM electrodes. SHAPE can be used in both the batch and the interactive mode.

In lubricated extrusion of relatively complex shapes, such as U, L, I, T, and others, it is required to use streamlined dies which provide a smooth metal flow from the circular container, or billet, to the shaped-die exit.

The design of a streamlined die for extruding a T shape from a round billet is schematically shown in Fig. 7.39. The geometry of this die and the variables of the extrusion process should be optimized to (1) give a defect-free extrusion requiring minimum postextrusion corrective operations such as twisting and straightening, (2) require minimum load and energy, and (3) yield maximum throughput at minimum cost.

As mentioned previously, in lubricated extrusion, the die should provide a smooth transition from the circular billet to the final extruded shape. In addition, the die surface contour should be such that the metal undergoes minimum redundant deformation and also exits from the die without bending or twisting. To select the shape of the optimal die, metal flow through dies of different shapes must be analyzed. The optimal die geometry can then be determined by selecting the die configuration which gives the minimum rate of energy dissipation during extrusion. This approach requires that, as a first step, the surface contour of the streamlined die be defined in a general and arbitrary manner. Again, for structural shapes such as T, L, U, I and others, it is not possible to describe analytically a die surface which provides a smooth transition from a round billet to the desired shape, so a numerical approach is necessary as in the case of unlubricated extrusion with a flat-faced die.

As indicated above, a numerical technique for determining the geometry of a streamlined die is used to provide a smooth flow from a round billet to a T shape without its twisting or bending. The latter is satisfied if the die shape is such that the extruded material at the die exit has a uniform velocity across its cross section in the axial direction. Therefore, each segment of the original cross section must undergo an equal reduction in area as it progresses through the die.

The initial circular cross section of the billet is then divided into a number of sectors such a 012, 023, etc., as shown in Fig. 7.40. The final cross section is divided into the same number of segments such as 01'2', 02'3', etc. This is done while keeping the extrusion ratios (the area of a sector in the billet/area of the corresponding segment in the product) equal to the overall extrusion ratio A_0/A_f,

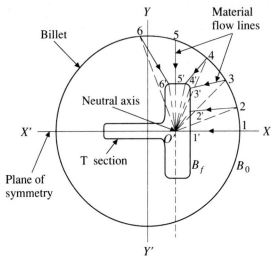

FIGURE 7.40
Top view showing the division of the initial circular cross section of the billet and the final cross section of the T-shaped extrusion into segments, which are connected by proposed flow lines. The unprimed numbers refer to the initial section and the primed numbers to the final section [7.17].

as follows:

$$\frac{\text{Area } 012}{\text{Area } 01'2'} = \frac{\text{area } 023}{\text{area } 02'3'} \cdots = \frac{\text{area } 056}{\text{area } 05'6'} = \frac{A_0}{A_f} \quad (7.81)$$

A wooden model of an EDM electrode made by NC machining along the flow lines is shown in Fig. 7.41. The actual electrode would be cut from graphite and then hand polished.

To compare the metal flow, the surface of a billet of 7075 aluminum alloy was gridded with circumferential and longitudinal lines approximately $\frac{1}{4}$ in (6.4 mm) apart and 0.015 in (0.381 mm) deep, and was partially extruded. Fig. 7.42 shows the theoretical and experimental gridlines for this extrusion.

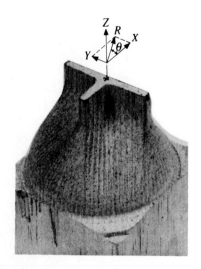

FIGURE 7.41
Wooden model of an EDM carbon electrode machined by numerical control along the flow lines of a streamlined die [7.17].

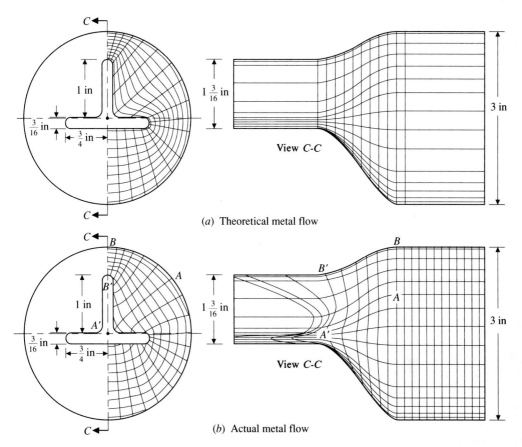

FIGURE 7.42
Comparison of the actual flow pattern with that predicted from a theoretical deformation model [7.17].

The difference between the actual and the predicted metal flow is attributed to frictional effects. In Fig. 7.42 it is seen that the metal moved faster along the outer edges of the T sections compared to the inner fillet areas. This flow difference is attributed to the difference in distance traveled by the material points to reach the exit die plane.

The load required to extrude the above $1\frac{1}{2}\times1\times\frac{3}{16}$ in $(38.1\times25.4\times4.8$ mm) T section of 7075 aluminum from a $2\frac{7}{8}$ (73 mm) $\times6$ in (152.4 mm) diameter billet at 600°F (315°C) with the die and container at 550°F (288°C) and Felpro C300 lubricant was 220 tons (1.96 MN) and 180 tons (1.6 MN) for extrusion. The container was 3 in (76.2 mm) in diameter, and the ram speed was 80 ipm (34 mm/s). The load required to extrude this same shape and material through a flat-faced die without lubrication for a billet temperature of 790°F (421°C) and die and container temperature of 700°F (371°C) was 360 tons (3.2 MN) for breakthrough and 230 tons (2.1 MN) for extrusion. However, the surface finish of the former was described only as fair and for the latter excellent.

7.10.5 Calculation of Extrusion Pressure and Load for Streamlined Dies

A simple method which is basically an extension of Siebel's method [7.16] is used to calculate (1) the total extrusion load and the various components that make up this load, and (2) the distribution of the mean pressure along the die surface in the axial direction.

The total extrusion pressure, P_{av}, is given as the sum of its components

$$P_{av} = P_{fc} + P_i + P_{sh} + P_{fd} + P_{fl} \tag{7.82}$$

where the various subscripted terms are analogous to those of the energy rates of Eq. (7.76) except here they refer to the components of pressure rather than the energy rate.

From the total extrusion pressure, the total extrusion load is determined by the relation

$$P_t = \frac{\pi}{4} D_0^2 P_{av} \tag{7.83}$$

where D_0 is the initial diameter of the billet.

The derivation of the total extrusion pressure given by Eq. (7.82) parallels that for the unlubricated, flat-faced die discussed previously, involving Eqs. (7.76) and (7.77). By substituting the expressions for the various energy terms in terms of their corresponding pressures, the total extrusion pressure can be evaluated by summing as in Eq. (7.82). The mean extrusion pressure and the distribution of pressure on the dies are expressed as a function of the process variables, such as initial billet diameter, initial billet length, speed of extrusion, final extrusion shape, area reduction, type of die, friction of the container and die surfaces, temperature, and flow properties of the metallic material being extruded. For given values of these process variables, the extrusion load is calculated numerically. The system of computer programs developed for this purpose comprise those called SHAPE.

7.10.6 Structure of SHAPE [7.16]

The computer programs developed to obtain the optimum die shape, to calculate the extrusion and die pressures, and to obtain coordinate data for NC machining of extrusion die are grouped under the name SHAPE. This software package can be used in either batch or interactive mode. It is written in Fortran IV language.

SHAPE is written in an overlay structure as shown in Fig. 7.43. It has a main overlay and three primary overlays. Each of the overlays perform functions during the execution of the program.

The main overlay, SHAPE, 0, 0, assigns default values to unspecified variables, reads values of variables specified by the designer, and controls the other overlays. The subroutines in this overlay are all utility routines and are called by routines in other overlays. The input of the variables, specified by the designer, is accomplished via a namelist.

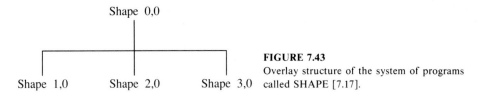

FIGURE 7.43
Overlay structure of the system of programs called SHAPE [7.17].

The primary overlay, SHAPE, 1, 0, performs the following tasks: (1) reads the coordinate data for describing the product shape, (2) fits the radii to the corners and fillets of the product shape defined as a polygon, (3) moves the shape with respect to the billet center, if desired, and (4) defines the die shape as a set of points in 3-D space.

The second primary overlay, SHAPE, 2, 0, performs the load calculations. For given values of extrusion-process variables specified in the namelist, the total extrusion pressure and its components, total extrusion load and die pressure distribution are determined. In addition, such parameters as cross-sectional area of the shape, extrusion ratio, perimeter of the shape, and the surface area of the die are computed.

The third primary overlay, SHAPE, 3, 0, calculates the coordinates of the cutter paths for NC machining of the EDM electrode. The overlay checks for undercutting or gouging by the tool. In the interactive mode, if it is determined that the specified tool will undercut, the designer is warned and given the option to change the size of the cutter.

7.10.7 Conclusions Drawn from Trial Runs of Battelle's CAD/CAM Systems

From the results of extrusion trials in the laboratory with use of production type equipment, the following conclusions were drawn [7.17]:

1. The ALEXTR and EXTCAM systems of computer programs for the design and manufacture of flat-faced dies can be applied successfully to the unlubricated extrusion of both low and high strength aluminum alloy structural shapes such as T sections.

2. The SHAPE system of computer programs can be used for the design and manufacture of streamlined dies for the lubricated extrusion of simple structural shapes of titanium and steel. However, further development work on suitable lubricants and process conditions was needed at that point in time to make lubricated extrusion of aluminum alloys a viable process.

7.10.8 BNF CAD/CAM System for Extrusion Die Design

A set of CAD/CAM packages utilizing design rules based entirely on empirical principles and data has been developed. One set of such design packages

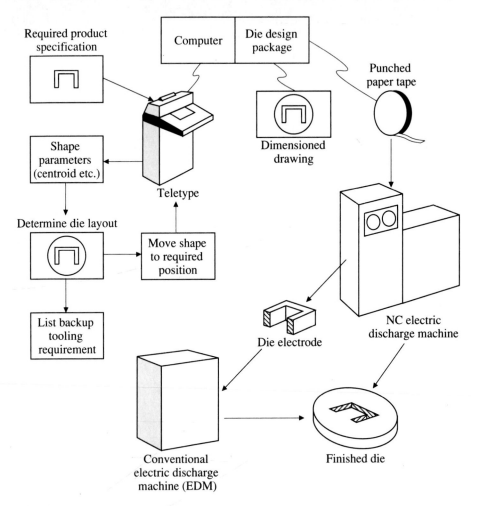

FIGURE 7.44
BNF system of computer-aided design of extrusion dies [7.19].

developed at BNF Metals Technology Centre in England is shown graphically in Fig. 7.44. In this system, the profile and the required specifications for the extrusion are input into the system. The dimensional allowances are applied automatically, and the bearing lengths, etc., are calculated. The output of the system is a dimensioned drawing and a punched paper tape, which can be used on a wire electric discharge machine for cutting out of the finished die [7.19].

7.10.9 Advantages of a CAD/CAM Extrusion System

Some of the advantages of a CAD/CAM extrusion system such as the above are as follows [7.17]:

1. Improve precision in cost estimating

2. Improve accuracy in die manufacture, thereby producing extrusions with closer dimensional tolerance

3. Provide a scientific basis for die design

4. Reduce requirements for skilled manpower

5. Reduce costs and lead times for die design manufacture

6. Optimize extrusion process variables to improve productivity and to increase material utilization

7.10.10 CAD/CAM of Three-Dimensional Dies for Optimized Extrusion of Arbitrary Shapes

7.10.10.1 INTRODUCTION. In addition to the advantages cited in the foregoing, the design of three-dimensional dies for optimal direct extrusion of complicated shapes from initially round billets has some other advantages: (1) an optimal die surface eliminates the dead zone in the flow and thus improves the quality of the product by yielding a better surface and fewer defects due to less heat generation, and (2) an optimal design may eliminate the twist and/or bending of the emerging extrusion, besides saving energy [7.20]. It should be pointed out, however, that various mathematical optimization procedures, which are usually based on minimum energy, do not always yield the best mechanical properties of the resulting product. Optimization results are usually a good place to start. Some computer systems have incorporated within themselves methods for checking the results against forming limits.

Most of the methods of designing extrusions discussed in the foregoing are based on the assumption of constant axial velocity either on the whole cross section or in the radial direction, and some have limitations in geometrical representation of the die surface. In this section a new die design method is used, which utilizes surface blending and Fourier series in order to give solutions in detail of three-dimensional extrusion of arbitrarily shaped sections [7.21]. In one version of this method, the description of the die surface is given conveniently in a parametric form with spline segments [7.20].

7.10.10.2 ANALYTICAL EXPRESSION OF A 3-D SURFACE FOR EXTRUSION DIES [7.20]. When the cross-sectional shapes of the entrance and exit are arbitrarily shaped contours, the analytical expression of connecting die surface between the two cross sections can be provided by using parametric Bezier curves discussed elsewhere. However, in this case it is difficult to obtain a continuous function for the whole die surface in cylindrical coordinates because of the parametric expression of sectional shapes. It is desirable to find an analytic expression of the three-dimensional die surface, that is given by a single continuous function. As shown in Fig. 7.45, one can define the contour of the inlet and the outlet of the die of length L as a function of θ as $R(\theta, 0)$ and $R(\theta, L)$, respectively. As shown in Fig. 7.46. when the cross-sectional shapes of both the

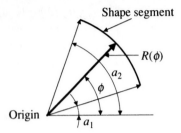

FIGURE 7.45
Definition of $R(0)$ on a segment [7.20].

entrance and exit are given by these analytic functions, any intermediate cross-sectional contour, $R(\theta, z)$ can be blended by using a blending function $\nu(z)$ as follows [7.21]:

$$R(\theta, z) = R(\theta, 0)\nu(z) + R(\theta, L)(1 - \nu(z)) \qquad (7.84)$$

where $\nu(z)$ is a continuous function subjected to the following boundary conditions (and other constraints): $\nu(0) = 1$ and $\nu(L) = 0$. In order to satisfy these conditions and constraints, the blending function of the least polynomial can be selected as the third-order polynomial as follows:

$$\nu(z) = 2\left(\frac{z}{L}\right)^3 - 3\left(\frac{z}{L}\right)^2 + 1 \qquad (7.85)$$

When the cross-sectional shape cannot be expressed in exact analytic form, an approximate analytic function, $T(\theta)$, for the sectional contour can be represented by a finite number of terms in a Fourier series

$$T(\theta) = \frac{A_0}{2} + \sum_{n=1}^{M} (A_n \cos \theta + B_n \sin \theta) \qquad \text{for} \qquad 0 \le \theta \le 2\pi \qquad (7.86)$$

where
$$A_n = \frac{1}{\pi} \int_0^{2\pi} t(\theta) \cos n\theta \, d\theta \quad \text{(Fourier coefficient)} \qquad (7.87a)$$

$$B_n = \frac{1}{\pi} \int_0^{2\pi} t(\theta) \sin n\theta \, d\theta \quad \text{(Fourier coefficient)} \qquad (7.87b)$$

M = number of terms in the Fourier series
$t(\theta)$ = data points along the sectional contour

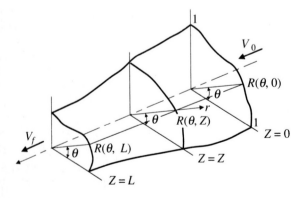

FIGURE 7.46
General kinematically admissible velocity field for three-dimensional extrusion of arbitrarily shaped sections through a continuous die [7.21].

Any arbitrarily contoured section can, therefore, be expressed by Eq. (7.86), by means of which the analytical expression for the three-dimensional die surface can be completely determined.

In order to find an analytical function for the final section contour and to apply it to the developed method, Eq. (7.86) can be reduced to the following form because of the symmetry of the given final section:

$$R(\theta, L) = \frac{A_0}{2} + \sum_{k=1}^{M} A_k \cos kN_s\theta \qquad \text{for} \qquad 0 < \theta < 2\pi \qquad (7.88a)$$

where
$$A_k = \frac{N_s}{\pi} \int_0^{2x/N_s} \frac{2}{N} t(\theta) \cos kN_s\theta \, d\theta \quad \text{(the Fourier coefficient)} \quad (7.88b)$$

N_s = number of axes of symmetry for a given section
M and $t(\theta)$ are defined above.

Since the initial cross section has a constant value of R_0, equation (7.84) can be rewritten to give the die profile function for the extrusion of a section having N_s axes of symmetry from a round billet as

$$R(\theta, z) = R_0 \nu(z) + R(\theta, L)(1 - \nu(z)) \qquad (7.89)$$

7.10.10.3 GENERALIZED KINEMATICALLY ADMISSIBLE VELOCITY FIELD
[7.22]. If the plastic zone is assumed to be bounded by two planes which are perpendicular to the z axis at the entrance and exit of the cavity as shown in Fig. 7.46, and if the billet material is assumed to be incompressible, the three-dimensional flow is given by

$$\frac{1}{r} \frac{\partial}{\partial r}(rV_r) + \frac{\partial V_z}{\partial z} + \frac{\partial V_\theta}{\partial \theta} = 0 \qquad (7.90)$$

The general solution of Eq. (7.90) is expressed as a function of the cylindrical coordinates r, θ, and z to give the equations of the radial, tangential, and axial velocities, respectively, $V_r(r, \theta, z)$, $V_\theta(r, \theta, z)$, and $V_z(r, \theta, z)$. The equations for these general kinematically admissible velocities are rather involved and will not be presented here. They may be found in the original references [7.20, 7.21, 7.22].

The velocity field that has been derived from incompressibility conditions, and which satisfies the velocity boundary conditions, is a generalized kinematically admissible velocity field which has no velocity discontinuity at the entrance and exit. The velocity discontinuity along the die surface ΔV_3 is given by

$$\Delta V_3 = [V_r^2 + V_\theta^2 + V_z^2]^{1/2}_{r=R(\theta, z)} \qquad (7.91)$$

From the determined velocity field, the strain rate components can be computed as follows:

$$\dot{\varepsilon}_r(r, \theta, z) = \frac{\partial V_z}{\partial r} \qquad (7.92a)$$

$$\dot{\varepsilon}_\theta(r, \theta, z) = \frac{1}{r} \frac{\partial V_\theta}{\partial \theta} + \frac{V_r}{r} \qquad (7.92b)$$

$$\dot{\varepsilon}_z(r, \theta, z) = \frac{\partial V_z}{\partial z} \tag{7.92c}$$

$$\dot{\varepsilon}_{r\theta}(r, \theta, z) = \frac{1}{2}\left(\frac{1}{r}\frac{\partial V_r}{\partial \theta} + \frac{\partial V_\theta}{\partial r} - \frac{V_\theta}{r}\right) \tag{7.92d}$$

$$\dot{\varepsilon}_{\theta z}(r, \theta, z) = \frac{1}{2}\left(\frac{\partial V_\theta}{\partial \theta} + \frac{1}{r}\frac{\partial V_z}{\partial \theta}\right) \tag{7.92e}$$

$$\dot{\varepsilon}_{rz}(r, \theta, z) = \frac{1}{2}\left(\frac{\partial V_r}{\partial z} + \frac{\partial V_z}{\partial r}\right) \tag{7.92f}$$

7.10.10.4   UPPER-BOUND SOLUTION [7.22]. The upper bound on total power consumption J^* can be expressed by the following conditional terms:

$$J^* = \dot{W}_i + \dot{W}_f + \dot{W}_s \tag{7.93}$$

where $\dot{W}_i$, $\dot{W}_f$, and $\dot{W}_s$ are the power dissipations due to homogeneous deformation, external friction loss, and internal shear loss. Since there is no velocity discontinuity at the entrance and exit, the shear power consumption $\dot{W}_s$ vanishes. In Eq. (7.93), the internal power of deformation $\dot{W}_i$ is calculated from Eqs. (7.92a) to (7.92f), as follows:

$$\dot{W}_i = \int_v \bar{\sigma}\dot{\bar{\varepsilon}} \, dv \tag{7.94}$$

$$\dot{W}_i = \frac{2}{\sqrt{3}}\bar{\sigma}_m \int_0^L \int_0^{2\pi} \int_0^{R(\theta, z)} \left(\frac{1}{2}\dot{\varepsilon}_{ij}\dot{\varepsilon}_{ij}\right)^{1/2} r \, dr \, d\theta \, dz \tag{7.95}$$

In the foregoing equation, $\bar{\sigma}_m$ represents the mean effective stress for strainhardening materials and is approximated by the following equation:

$$\bar{\sigma}_m = \int_0^{\bar{\varepsilon}_{fav}} \frac{\bar{\sigma} \, d\bar{\varepsilon}}{\bar{\varepsilon}_{fav}} \tag{7.96}$$

where $\bar{\varepsilon}_f = \int_0^t \dot{\bar{\varepsilon}} \, dt$ is integrated along a constant streamline.

The frictional power dissipated along the internal surface of the die is given by

$$\dot{W}_f = \frac{m}{\sqrt{3}}\bar{\sigma}_m \int_0^{2\pi} \int_0^L [V_r^2 + V_\theta^2 + V_z^2]_{r=R(\theta, z)}^{1/2} \left[1 + \frac{1}{R^2}\left(\frac{\partial R}{\partial \theta}\right)^2 + \left(\frac{\partial R}{\partial z}\right)^2\right]^{1/2} R \, d\theta \, dz \tag{7.97}$$

where R is the abbreviation of $R(\theta, z)$ and m is the friction factor at the die-material interface discussed elsewhere. The upper bound on the extrusion pressure is then determined to be

$$P_{av} = \frac{J^*}{\pi V_0} \tag{7.98}$$

where $V_0 = $ incoming velocity of the billet.

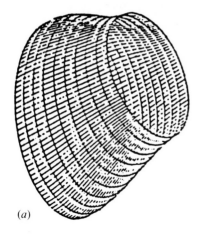

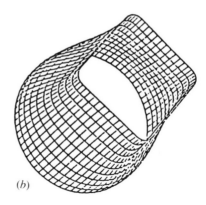

(a)   (b)

FIGURE 7.47
Configuration of the die geometries constructed by the design method discussed here for (a) an elliptical outlet and a circular inlet, and (b) a rectangular outlet and a circular inlet [7.21].

7.10.10.5 COMPUTATIONAL EXAMPLES AND RESULTS. As computational examples for arbitrarily shaped products, extrusions with elliptic and rounded rectangular cross sections are chosen. Figure 7.47(a) and (b) shows the die configurations of the internal surfaces of the dies of an elliptic section and a rectangular section with rounded corners when extruded from round billets by this method of design using a blending function and a Fourier series. In this case a blending function is employed as described in Eq. (7.85). The die surfaces are shown to have smooth transitions throughout the whole region. When the number of terms is 5 and 13, respectively, for an elliptic and a rounded rectangular section, the error of approximation by the Fourier series can be within 10^{-4} for a billet of unit radius. This error is negligible in the design of a die of complex cross section.

Annealed aluminum alloy 2024 having the following stress-strain relationship is used:

$$\sigma = 357.7\bar{\sigma}^{0.156} \quad (\text{MPa}) \tag{7.99}$$

The deformation patterns are obtained by use of the grid-marking technique discussed elsewhere, in which the billet is split prior to extruding and a square grid is scribed onto one of the flat meridional planes. The two halves are first placed together and then extruded with the split surfaces positioned in two different directions to the plane of symmetry. The grid distortion patterns, of a partially extruded billet for two areas of reduction of 60 and 80 percent for a rectangular section as extruded from a round billet, are shown in Fig. 7.48.

If the internal surface of the die is defined in parametric form, the optimal die surface may be represented by the spline method as shown in Fig. 7.49 of some nonaxisymmetric dies. These optimal die surfaces are obtained in a computerized interactive fashion. The output of such a CAD program is a set of

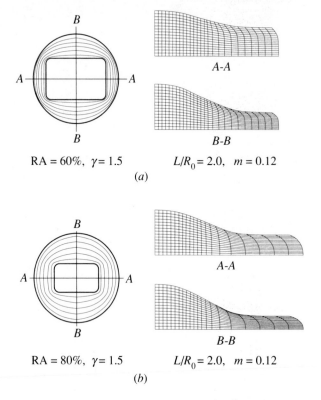

RA = 60%, $\gamma = 1.5$ $L/R_0 = 2.0$, $m = 0.12$

(a)

RA = 80%, $\gamma = 1.5$ $L/R_0 = 2.0$, $m = 0.12$

(b)

FIGURE 7.48
Grid distortion patterns for two area reductions of 60 and 80 percent in the extrusion of rectangular sections [7.21].

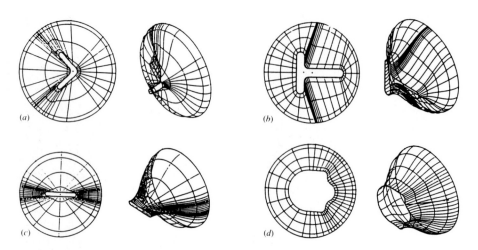

FIGURE 7.49
Examples of 3-D surfaces as obtained by the method discussed [7.20].

coordinates of the die surface, readily accessible to CAM. The manufacturing process can be implemented by means a CNC machine to generate the EDM electrode to produce the die, or to machine directly the die itself.

ACKNOWLEDGMENT

The material and the illustrations in this chapter were adapted from the references as indicated in the text and in the legends by the numbers of the references enclosed in square brackets pursuant to all copyrights.

REFERENCES

7.1. Rowe, G. W., *Principles of Industrial Metalworking Processes*, Edward Arnold, London, 1977, pp. 105-118.

7.2. Altan, T., S.-I. Oh, and H. L. Gegel, *Metal Forming: Fundamentals and Applications*, ASM, Metal Park, Ohio, 1983, pp. 189-217.

7.3. Avitzur, B., *Metal Forming: Processes and Analysis*, McGraw-Hill, New York, 1968, pp. 153-258. Revised edition reprinted by Robert Krieger Publishing Co., Inc., Huntington, N.Y., 1979.

7.4. Wistreich, J. G., "Investigation of the Mechanics of Wire Drawing," *Proc. Inst. Mech. Engrs. (London)*, vol. 169, pp. 654-55, 1955.

7.5. Avitzur, B., "Study of Flow Through Conical Converging Dies," *Metal Forming*, A. L. Hoffmanner (ed.), Plenum Press. New York, 1971, pp. 1-46.

7.6. Zimerman, Z. et al., "Selection of Operating Parameters to Prevent Central Bursting Defects During Cold Extrusion," *Metal Forming*, A. L. Hoffmanner (ed.), Plenum Press, New York, 1971, pp. 47-62.

7.7. Hosford, W. F., and R. M. Caddell, *Metal Forming Mechanics and Metallurgy*, Prentice-Hall, Englewood Cliffs, New Jersey, pp. 181-183.

7.8. Harris, J. N., *Mechanical Working of Metals*, Pergamon Press, New York, 1983, pp. 178-197.

7.9. Thomsen, E. G. et al., *Mechanics of Plastic Deformation in Metal Processing*, Macmillan Co., New York, 1965, pp. 193-198.

7.10. Rogers, H. C., "Prediction and Effects of Material Damage During Deformation Processing," *Metal Forming*, A. L. Hoffmanner (ed.), Plenum Press, New York, 1971, pp. 453-474.

7.11. Medrano, R. et al., "Application of Visioplasticity Techniques to Axisymmetric Extrusions," pp. 85-113, *Metal Forming*, A. L. Hoffmanner (ed.), Plenum Press, New York, 1971.

7.12. Shabaik, A. H., "The Effect of Material Properties on Tension Zone and Boundary Shear Stress in Extrusion," Ibid., pp. 63-69.

7.13. Drake, R. J., and J. W. Throop, "How to Predict Cold Extrusion Forces," *Metal Progress*, May 1971, vol. 99, no. 5, p. 72. Also, Source Book on Cold Forming, ASM, pp. 212-215, 1975.

7.14. ICFG Data Sheet No. 1/70, Prepared by the International Cold Forging Group, "Calculation of Pressures for Cold Forward Extrusion of Steel Rods," Source Book on Cold Forming, ASM, pp. 292-293, 1975.

7.15. Ibid, Data sheet no. 2/70, pp. 294-295.

7.16. Nagpal, V., and T. Altan, "CAD/CAM for Extrusion of Al, Ti, and Steel Structural Parts—Phase I, AMMRC TR 76-6, Final Report, Battelle's Columbus Labs., 1976, DTIC, ADA 023946.

7.17. Nagpal, V., C. F. Billhardt, and T. Altan, Ibid, Phase II, Vol. I, AMMRC TR, 72-76, Final Report, Battelle's Columbus Labs., 1978, pp. 1-2 to 1-7, 1-12, 2-6 to 2-7, 3-37 to 3-38.

7.18. Ibid, Vol. II, pp. 4-9, 25-26, and I-6 to I-8.

7.19. Sessions, T. M. B. et al., "Extrusion," T. Z. Blazynski (ed.), *Design of Tools for Deformation Processes*, Elsevier Applied Science Publishers, New York, p. 133.

7.20. Shafry, D., J. Tirosh, and A. Ber, "Cad-Cam of Three-Dimensional Dies for Optimized Extrusion," *Manufacturing Review*, ASME, vol. 2, no.1, March 1989, pp. 60-65.

7.21. Yang, D. Y., C. H. Han, and M. U. Kim, "A Generalized Method for Analysis of Three-Dimensional Extrusion of Arbitrarily-Shaped Sections," *Int. J. of Mech. Sci.*, vol. 28, no. 8, 1986, pp. 517–534.

7.22. Han, C. H., D. Y. Yang, and M. Kiuchi, "A New Formulation for Three-Dimensional Extrusion and its Application to Extrusion of Clover Sections," *Int. J. of Mech. Sci.*, vol. 28, no. 4, 1986, pp. 201–218.

PROBLEMS

7.1. It is desired to produce a 0.5 mm diameter copper wire with an ultimate tensile strength of 350 MPa from a copper wire bar of 15 mm in diameter. To what diameter would the wire have to be hot worked or cold worked and annealed before the final cold drawing. Experimental data shows that an annealed copper bar would have to be reduced 50 percent in area to yield an ultimate tensile strength of 350 MPa.

7.2. A strip of an annealed steel 10 mm wide and 0.45 mm thick is drawn to a thickness of 0.35 mm through a die of 20° included angle at 2.0 m/s. Calculate the total work done to draw a length of wire 2×10^3 m long if the flow stress before and after drawing is 350 and 650 MPa (N/mm²), respectively, and $\mu = 0.10$.

7.3. (a) If, for a homogeneous deformation, the lossless work done is $W = V\bar{\sigma}_Y \ln(l_1/l_2)$, what is the expression for the load (force) required to draw a wire through a die in terms of original and final areas? It is assumed that the volume of the metal being deformed, V, remains constant.

   (b) Calculate the minimum drawing load to draw a 2.50 mm diameter annealed brass wire to a 2.15 diameter, which has a flow stress of 0.30 kN/mm².

7.4. (a) Construct one-half of a symmetric slip-line field for the plane-strain, frictionless bar-drawing (or forward extrusion) of a flat strip from a thickness of 40 mm to a thickness of 25 mm, using a wedge-shaped die with a 20° included angle, similar to that shown in Fig. 7.23, and using a 10° net.

   (b) How would the appearance of the field change in case of forward extrusion if a dead zone occurred at the die and sticking friction occurred at the container wall.

7.5. Cold extrusion is performed on a steel billet 25 mm in diameter to obtain one 22 mm in diameter. The flow strength of the steel is 620 MPa. Calculate the extrusion pressure.

7.6. Convert Eqs. 7.65(a) and (b) into SI units and calculate the forward and backward extrusion pressures, p_F and p_B, required to extrude a 3 in (diameter) SAE 1020 steel billet. A conversion factor of 29.0 can be used to relate the extrusion pressure for the steel to that for lead. The die angle is known to be 90°, and the diameter of the billet is 5 in.

7.7. A continuous die has a circular entrance with a radius of 1 unit and an elliptic exit of 0.75 and 0.50 units as the major and minor axes, respectively. Obtain the expression for the entire die surface. Use a blending function of a polynomial of the order 3. Take the length of the die to be 2 units long.

CHAPTER 8

CLASSIFICATION OF FORGING PROCESSES AND OPEN-DIE FORGING

8.1 DEFINITION AND CLASSIFICATION OF FORGING PROCESSES

Quite a number of different definitions may be found in the literature or in use for the term "forging." Obviously it means different things to different people. Forging is here broadly defined as a bulk, plastic deformation process of a metallic material, either hot or cold, to some predetermined shape primarily by compressive forces usually exerted by a hammer or press.

It is called a *bulk deformation process* because a significant change in the thickness of the workpiece usually occurs as compared to a sheetmetal process. When the term is used in a general sense, forging will include all bulk deformation processes of this class. When specific processes are meant, they will be referred to as hot, warm, or cold forging. When the forging of steel is mentioned without classification, hot forging will be meant.

Forging processes will here be classified as (1) typical or conventional production forging processes and (2) special or miscellaneous forging processes. The first category will include all hot-working processes, which are done above the recrystallization temperature and for carbon and alloy steels, in the austenite range, and by use of forging hammers, presses, and/or upset forging machines. The second category will include all cold-working operations such as warm and cold forging, and forging done by the less common types of forging equipment such as roll forging, ring and wheel forging, rotary forging and swaging, shear forming, typical extrusion processes, etc.

Forging in the conventional sense may be classified as (1) open-die (flat-tool) or smith forging, and (2) closed-die or impression-die forging, sometimes called drop forging; however, both of these categories are subject to some confusion. *Open-die forging* is the term applied to all forging operations, in which there is no lateral constraint except for friction and consequently no three-dimensional confinement. *Closed-die forging* is the term applied to all forging operations involving three-dimensional control. Sometimes the distinction between open- and closed-die forging is not too clear, such as, for example, in swaging and edging operations, in which a considerable amount of lateral confinement may occur. In these cases, however, the nature of the forging operations and the equipment used will definitely place them in one category or the other.

Open-die or smith forging, which will be discussed first in subsequent sections, is done with a hand hammer, a power hammer (Fig. 8.1), or a power press (Fig. 8.2) by use of tools or dies that are flat or nearly flat (Fig. 8.3), in which the manipulation of the workpiece is done by hand or by a mechanical manipulator.

This process is used (1) when the desired shape is simple, (2) when the quantity of forgings required is too small to justify the time and cost of making closed dies, (3) as a preliminary operation to closed-die forging to produce a forging multiple or preform of the required shape and size, (4) where the forging is too large to be forged in closed dies (Fig. 8.4), and (5) when, in some cases,

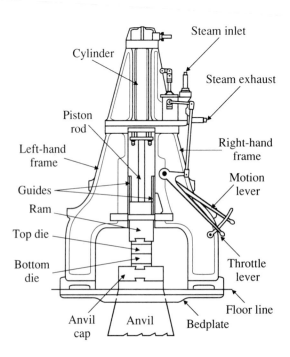

FIGURE 8.1
A typical, double-frame, steam-driven, open-die forging power hammer. Small hammers are single frame. The guides, etc., are not accurate enough for use with drop-forging dies. The anvil sets on a rather massive base consisting of a steel subbase, a select oak timber cribbing, and a large, reinforced concrete footer. (*Courtesy of Forging Industry Association.*)

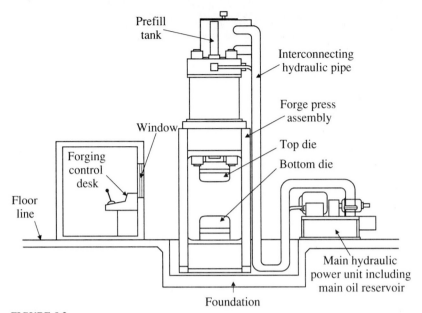

FIGURE 8.2
A typical hydraulic press with a remote hydraulic power unit and control room. Fast-acting, electric-motor powered, V-belt driven, mechanical presses are also available. (*Courtesy of Forging Industry Association.*)

the delivery date is too close, i.e., the lead time is too short to make the closed dies needed.

In some cases, the open-die forging is used in its final form as forged such as a crane hook or a clevis for farm equipment with perhaps only a scale removal and/or painting operation, or it may be rough machined, finished machined, heat treated, and finished ground to the final shape as shown in Fig. 8.5. Often, not only a considerable amount of machining is eliminated by open-die forging, but also much superior mechanical properties are imparted to the metal by breaking up the coarse, dendritic, cast microstructure; by welding voids; and by proper metal flow.

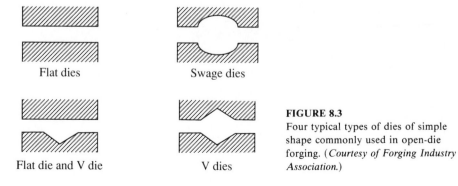

Flat dies

Swage dies

Flat die and V die

V dies

FIGURE 8.3
Four typical types of dies of simple shape commonly used in open-die forging. (*Courtesy of Forging Industry Association.*)

FIGURE 8.4
A large open-die forging positioned in a lathe preparatory to machining. Typical open-die forgings of this type are rotors and spindles for large, motor-generator sets. (*Courtesy of Forging Industry Association.*)

The stock or forging multiple is usually cut by cold shearing or cold sawing. Often only one end of a long workpiece is inserted into the furnace for heating to the proper forging temperature, and the other cooler end is held with the hands or with tongs for forging and for shearing off after forging.

The following topics pertaining to open-die (flat-tool) forging will be discussed next: (1) open-die forging operations, (2) cogging or drawing out by

FIGURE 8.5
A large eight-throw crankshaft, such as for a large marine engine, finished machined from an open-die forging involving a minimum of machining and possessing properties superior to those made some other way. (*Courtesy of Forging Industry Association.*)

flat-tool forging, (3) axisymmetric compression of a short cylinder or disc between flat, overhanging anvils, (4) role of friction in metalworking processes, (5) interface pressure in open-die forging, (6) upsetting of a rectangular slab in plane strain, (7) plane strain slip-line field analysis for sidepressing, (8) flow localization, and (9) axisymmetric open-die, extrusion forging—an upper-bound approach.

8.2. OPEN-DIE HOT-FORGING PROCESSES

8.2.1 Open-Die (Flat-Tool) Forging Operations

Some of the typical, principal open-die forging operations as shown in Fig. 8.6 are as follows:

1. Cogging or drawing out, involving compression between narrow dies
2. Upsetting, involving compression between flat, overhanging dies
3. Heading, involving localized upsetting of the end of a workpiece between a confining or gripping die and a flat or contoured upsetting die
4. Swaging, involving compression between longitudinal, semicircular or semi-contoured dies
5. Fullering, involving compression between rounded or convex dies to reduce a middle section of a bar
6. Edging, involving compression with concave dies to form an enlarged middle section of a bar and to distribute the metal to the desired shape

Some of the open-die forging ancillary operations as shown in Fig. 8.7 are as follows:

1. Punching, involving indenting (as in center punching) or perforating with mating dies
2. Piercing, involving impressing an indentation into the workpiece
3. Shearing, involving severing with off-set dies
4. Extrusion forging or ring extrusion, involving the extrusion of a projection or spike into a die containing a hole or cavity
5. Bending of a workpiece between mating dies
6. Twisting, as of a flat bar or V-eight crankshaft

Cogging is the systematic forging of an ingot to reduce it to a bloom as shown in Figs. 8.8 and 8.9, whereas drawing out is the elongation of any shape by systematically reducing its cross section as shown in Figs. 8.10 and 8.11. Upsetting is a compression operation usually parallel to the longitudinal or cylindrical axis of the workpiece. When an enlarged section is upset on the end of a smaller section, the operation is called heading. Swaging is radial compression operation by shaped dies for finishing, i.e., sizing and truing, a round or semiround workpiece after it has been drawn out or forged nearly to size. Fullering is the making of grooves or reduced sections in a bar yielding shoulders on both ends.

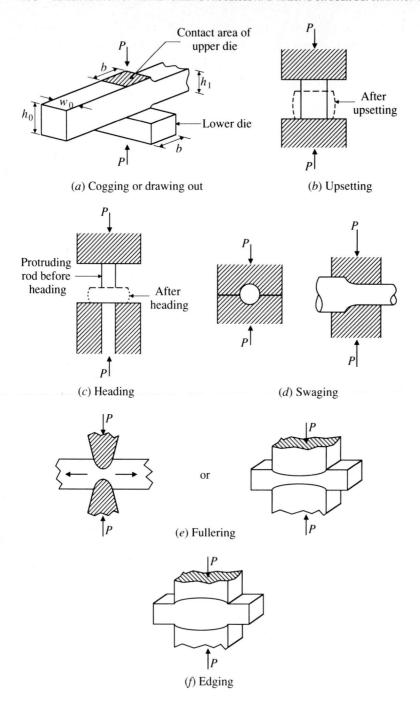

(a) Cogging or drawing out

(b) Upsetting

(c) Heading

(d) Swaging

(e) Fullering

(f) Edging

FIGURE 8.6
Typical operations performed with open-die forging.

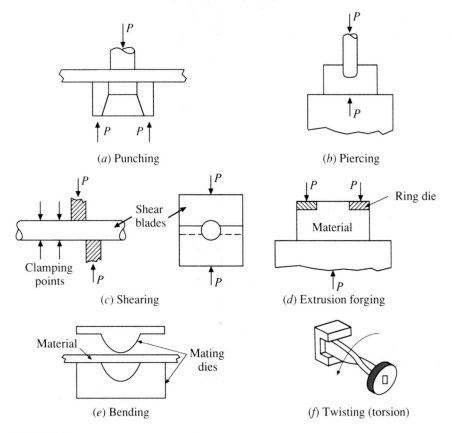

(a) Punching

(b) Piercing

(c) Shearing

(d) Extrusion forging

(e) Bending

(f) Twisting (torsion)

FIGURE 8.7
Some typical ancillary operations associated with open-die forging.

8.2.2   Cogging or Drawing Out by Flat-Tool Forging

The object of cogging or drawing out is to reduce the cross section of the workpiece in a stepwise sequence by moving the ingot, billet, or bar from one end toward the other during forging in what is called a *pass*. To reduce the workpiece in one pressing operation may require a very large force and/or also a very large press platen width, and consequently may be impracticable. Both the reduction in height Δh and the bite b shown in Fig. 8.12, should be as large as possible without causing such defects as laps. Several passes alternating on each pair of faces are usually required to complete the operation. Usually the forging procedure is left up to the experienced operator or forgemaster; however, with recent emphasis on increasing production and automation, each operation must be programmed, i.e., examined and preplanned from an engineering point of view in order to optimize results.

Each compression or squeeze operation, resulting in a reduction in thickness, will cause the workpiece not only to elongate in length but also to spread in

FIGURE 8.8
A 275 ton (255 Mg), fluted ingot
being cogged with a 7500 ton
(67 MN) hydraulic press.
(*Courtesy of Forging Industry
Association.*)

width as shown in Fig. 8.12. These two dimensional changes may be expressed
in terms of the coefficient of spread, S, and the coefficient of elongation, $1 - S$,
as follows:

$$S = \frac{\text{width elongation}}{\text{thickness reduction}} = \frac{\ln (w_1/w_0)}{\ln (h_0/h_1)} \tag{8.1}$$

$$1 - S = \frac{\text{length elongation}}{\text{thickness reduction}} = \frac{\ln (l_1/l_2)}{\ln (h_0/h_1)} \tag{8.2}$$

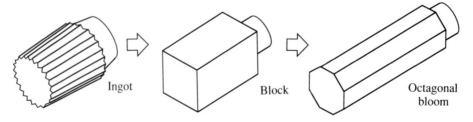

FIGURE 8.9
Forging sequence in open-die forging of an octagonal bloom from a fluted ingot. (*Courtesy of Forging
Industry Association.*)

FIGURE 8.10
A vintage photograph and a sketch of a 110 ft (33.5 m) section of a press column being drawn out to a rectangular shape. The part is forged to the final length in several stages. (*Courtesy of Bethlehem Steel Co.*) (*Sketch courtesy of Connie Reasoner, Des Moines, Iowa.*)

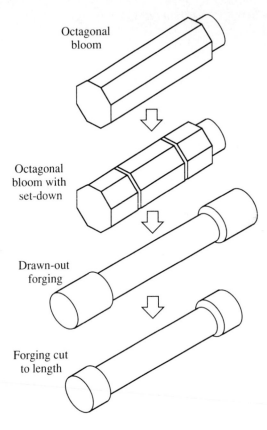

Octagonal bloom

Octagonal bloom with set-down

Drawn-out forging

Forging cut to length

FIGURE 8.11
Sequence of operations in open-die forging of an octagonal bloom to a drawn-out forging. (*Courtesy of Forging Industry Association.*)

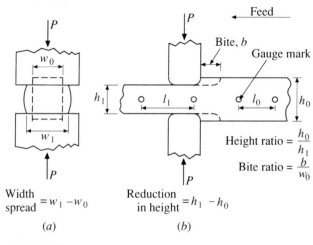

$$\text{Height ratio} = \frac{h_0}{h_1}$$

$$\text{Bite ratio} = \frac{b}{w_0}$$

$$\frac{\text{Width}}{\text{spread}} = w_1 - w_0 \qquad \frac{\text{Reduction}}{\text{in height}} = h_1 - h_0$$

(a) (b)

FIGURE 8.12
Nomenclature for cogging and drawing out of a rectangular workpiece (*a*) end view, and (*b*) side view [8.11].

The above parameters may be obtained from the expression for the constancy of volume

$$\frac{h_1 w_1 l_1}{h_0 w_0 l_0} = 1 \tag{8.3}$$

If the natural logarithms are taken of both sides of the above expression ($\ln l = 0$) and rearranged then

$$\frac{\ln (w_1/w_0)}{-\ln (h_1/h_0)} + \frac{\ln (l_1/l_0)}{-\ln (h_1/h_0)} = 1 \tag{8.4}$$

The equations (8.1) and (8.2) may also be written as

$$\frac{w_1}{w_0} = \left(\frac{h_0}{h_1}\right)^S \quad \text{and} \quad \frac{l_1}{l_0} = \left(\frac{h_0}{h_1}\right)^{1-S} \tag{8.5}$$

If the first term in Eq. (8.4) is set equal to S, then the second term is equal to $1 - S$. (In sheetmetal forming, S is analogous to the r ratio or r value.)

Tomlinson and Stringer [8.1] found empirically that for hot, low-carbon steel, the bite ratio was the main factor influencing S as shown in Fig. 8.13, although the height ratio h_1/h_0, also exerted a small but statistically significant effect. The spread coefficient S as a function of the bite ratio b/w_0, as shown in Fig. 8.14, is given by

$$S = 0.14 + 0.36\left(\frac{b}{w_0}\right) - 0.054\left(\frac{b}{w_0}\right)^2 \tag{8.6}$$

Their analysis indicated that the coefficient of spread, S, derived for a bar forging depends mainly on the shape of the tool contact area as defined by the bite ratio. Their analysis also showed no effects attributable to forging temperatures or cross-sectional shape and indicated that there are no other factors to consider. Their experimental data revealed that less spreading occurs during the forging of a bar than during the compression of a comparable rectangular block between

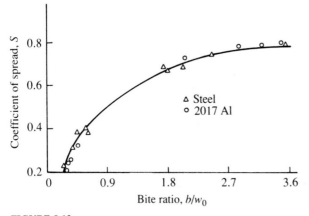

FIGURE 8.13
Relation between the coefficient of spread and the bite ratio for open-die forging of rectangular blocks [8.1].

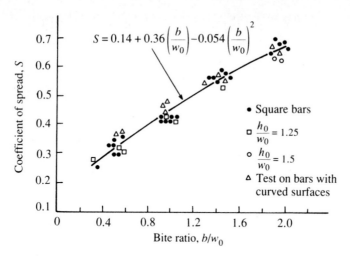

FIGURE 8.14
Relation between the coefficient of spread and the bite ratio in cogging [8.1].

overhanging platens, presumably due to the absence of the constraint of the bar material extending outside of the dies in drawing out. They showed that the spread coefficient for blocks can be predicted as shown in Fig. 8.13 by the simple equation

$$S = \frac{b}{b + w_0} \tag{8.7}$$

The longitudinal expansion per squeeze or stroke increases with both the bite and the height ratio as given by

$$x = \frac{b}{w_0}\left[\left(\frac{h_0}{h_1}\right)^{1-S} - 1\right] \tag{8.8}$$

Schutt [8.2] carried out experimental work in this regard by making indentations in plasticine bars of square and rectangular sections and suggested that the equation (8.9) given below involving the ratios b/w_0 and h_0/w_0 fitted the experimental data better than any linear regression equation. If ε_h and ε_l are the true strains in the height and width direction, respectively, the equation proposed is

$$\frac{\varepsilon_h}{\varepsilon_l} = 1 + \frac{b}{w_0}\left(1.789 - 0.321\frac{h_0}{w_0}\right) \tag{8.9}$$

where b in this case is half the width of the indentation.

The first successful theoretical attempt to obtain the sidewise spread and forging pressure in flat-bar forging is due to Hill [8.3], whose formula for the spread coefficient is given by

$$S = \frac{1}{2}\left[1 - \frac{1}{2\sqrt{3}\,(b/w_0)} + \tan h\left(2\sqrt{3}\,\frac{b}{w_0}\right)\right] \tag{8.10}$$

The effect of frictional constraint was neglected in the analysis, so that Eq. (8.10) gives reasonable predictions for small bites only. Also, since the variations in stress and strain throughout the thickness were neglected in the analysis, Eq. (8.10) is probably acceptable only when $b/h_0 > 1$.

Baraya and Johnson [8.4] used an analytical velocity field and also the concept of rigid sliding blocks for calculating the theoretical upper bounds to the loads in flat-tool forging. They also reported the specific forging pressure, coefficient of sidewise spread, bulge profile, elongation, and maximum amount of spread for various forging geometries from experimental work under the conditions of maximum constriction between the tool and workpiece. They concluded that the coefficient of spread, S, as evaluated by Hill fits experimental results fairly well, especially for $0.5 \leq b/w_0 \leq 1.5$, even though his analysis neglected the effect of frictional restraint. Based on these experiments, they have also suggested an empirical formula for spread given as below:

$$S = a_0 + a_1 \frac{b}{w_0} + a_2 \left(\frac{b}{w_0}\right)^2 + a_3 \left(\frac{b}{w_0}\right)^3 \tag{8.11}$$

where a_0, a_1, a_2, and a_3 are constants dependent on material properties and are determined by fitting a curve to experimental results by regression analysis [8.5].

By use of the upper-bound approach, Lahaoti and Kobayashi [8.5] obtained the following relationship by theoretical analysis for the average specific forging load:

$$\frac{P}{2Af} = 1 - \frac{1}{2b} \int_0^b \alpha(x)\, dx - \frac{\mu}{4bh} \alpha'(b) \int_0^h z\phi(z)\, dz \tag{8.12}$$

where
$P =$ the forging load, lb (kN)
$A =$ the area of the tool-workpiece interface
$f = \frac{2}{3}\sigma_y$ for moderate to large bites $(b/w_0 > \frac{1}{2})$
$f = 2/\sqrt{3}\sigma_y$ for small bites $(b/w_0 \leq \frac{1}{2})$
$\sigma(x)$ and $\phi(z) =$ fairly involved functions describing the bulge in the x and z directions, respectively
$\alpha'(b) =$ the derivative of $\alpha(b)$ (see [8.5])
$\mu =$ a variable coefficient of friction at the tool-workpiece interface

Experimental data was obtained for 1100-F aluminum [8.5]. The predictions for sidewise spread, elongation, and bulge in thickness compared reasonably well with experiment for small to medium bites. However, for large bites the correlation was not good, since a single class of velocity fields would not be expected to describe the deformation patterns for all geometrical ratios in a complex pattern such as flat-bar forging.

8.2.3 Axisymmetric Compression of a Short Cylinder or Disc Between Flat, Overhanging Platens

This problem has already been dealt with directly in conjunction with the compression test and indirectly with the analytical analysis of the friction in

(a)

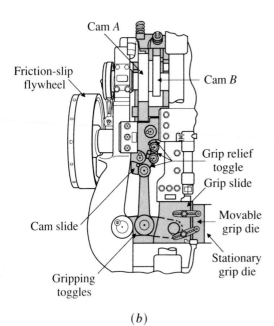

(b)

(c)

FIGURE 8.15
(a) A cutaway side view of an upset forging machine showing a three-position movable gripper die.
(b) Cutaway top view of the forging machining. Cam A closes the movable grip die and cam B opens
it. The heading tools are not shown. (c) Set of upset forging dies having four positions to which the
workpiece is transferred successively. ((a) *Courtesy The National Machinery Company.* (b) *Courtesy
of American Machinist, 1947, McGraw-Hill.*)) (c) *Courtesy of the Ajak Manufacturing Company.*)

plane strain for rolling. It will be extended here to the estimation of the average or mean pressure by first estimating the Coulomb coefficient of friction for a short cylinder or thin disc.

In the compression of a ductile cylindrical specimen with overhanging flat dies or platens, in addition to the extent of inhomogeneous deformation that may occur that was considered in the previous section for the case of compression of a long workpiece with narrow anvils or dies, the question of whether or not buckling will occur and the amount and type of friction that exists must also be considered. Let us first dispense briefly with the problem of buckling.

The maximum, initial height-to-diameter ratio that can be successfully used in upsetting is important in conjunction with the operation of the horizontal upset forging machine or upsetter shown in Fig. 8.15. Suffice it to say at this point that this ratio should not exceed two or two and one-half at the most, when an unsupported cylindrical specimen or workpiece is compressed with flat dies, otherwise lateral buckling or skewing will occur as shown in Fig. 8.16. The actual maximum limit that may be used may be found experimentally, and it depends on such factors as the accuracy with which the ends are cut, the parallelism of the die surfaces, the surface finish and lubricity of the faces, etc.

Since in an upsetter the stock is gripped firmly at one end and may be enclosed in a cavity which modifies buckling at the other, somewhat greater lengths can be upset than by flat, parallel die upsetting. The following three design rules illustrated in Fig. 8.17 should be followed in designing parts that are to be upset forged [8.6]:

1. The limiting length of unsupported metal that can be upset in one blow without buckling is three times the diameter of the bar
2. Lengths of stock greater than three times the diameter may be upset successfully provided that the diameter of the die cavity is not more than $1\frac{1}{2}$ times the diameter of the bar

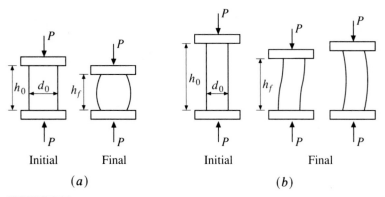

Initial   Final   Initial   Final

(a) (b)

FIGURE 8.16
The effect of the maximum height-to-diameter ratio (aspect ratio) on the mode of upsetting of a right, circular cylinder in compression between flat, parallel, overhanging anvils. (a) If $h_0/d_0 \leq 2$ to 2.5, the cylinder upsets successfully, and (b) if $h_0/d_0 \geq 2$ to 2.5, the cylinder skews or buckles as shown.

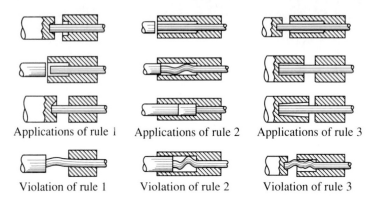

Applications of rule 1   Applications of rule 2   Applications of rule 3

Violation of rule 1   Violation of rule 2   Violation of rule 3

FIGURE 8.17
Design rules governing upset forging. (*Courtesy The National Machinery Company.*)

3. In an upset requiring stock with a length greater than three times the diameter of the bar and where the diameter of the upset is less than $1\frac{1}{2}$ times the diameter of the bar, the length of unsupported metal beyond the face of the die must not exceed the diameter of the bar

Even though the foregoing upsetting operations are constrained and would therefore be classified as closed-die forging, they are included here to complete the discussion of buckling.

The amount and nature of the localized deformation or flow localization resulting from the inhomogeneous deformation may be analyzed by use of a number of different macroscopic methods to study the sectioned specimen such as by measuring the distortion of a grid pattern, obtaining the hardness gradient, etching of the cold-worked metal, etching of the recrystallized cold-worked metal, etc.

In the grid or visioplastic method, fine ductile wires may be threaded through small axial and/or diametral holes equally, or regularly spaced so as to form a grid on the diametral, axial plane of the specimen. Also, a higher melting-point wire grid may be cast into a lower-melting-point metal such as, for example, a copper grid in an aluminum alloy.

After deformation the specimen is sectioned along a diametral plane and ground on a fine abrasive belt or wheel to expose the wires. A schematic representation of such a grid pattern before and after deformation is shown in Fig. 8.18. As is illustrated in the figure, the material adjacent to the platens in region *A* remains virtually undeformed and behaves as a rigid metal "cone" or dead zone as it penetrates into the specimen. The cones approximately coincide with the surfaces of maximum shear, but their base angles are between 35 and 40° rather than 45°, and decrease as the height of the specimen becomes less than the diameter. The bulk of the deformation or flow localization occurs in region *C* with the greatest deformation occurring at the center of the cylinder and a lesser amount in region *B*.

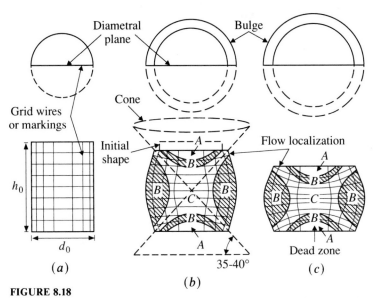

FIGURE 8.18

Illustration of inhomogeneous deformation and flow localization in compression of a right, circular cylinder with overhanging anvils and with interface friction showing a cross section of a diametral plane of (a) the undeformed cylinder, (b) the distortion of the grid pattern and the region of variable deformation (region A the least and C the most), and (c) the final cylinder showing barreling. (*Adapted from "Principles of Forging Design", prepared by Illinois Institute of Technology Research Institute and published by the Committee of Hot Rolled and Cold Finished Bar Products American Iron and Steel Institute.*)

As the specimen is deformed, because of the interfacial friction between the metal and the platen, the material located in the central part of the specimen flows more readily than that in the immediate vicinity of the platen or die, causing the cylinder to become barrel-shaped. The degree of barreling developed for a given reduction of height increases with the frictional resistance at the material-platen interface. For sticking friction, if the h_0/d_0 ratio and the reduction are high enough, the cylindrical surface folds over or is inverted so as to become a peripheral-ring on the ends of the deformed specimen. If the cylindrical surface is tarnished or oxidized and the ends are polished prior to deformation, a dark peripheral ring can be seen on the ends of the specimen after deformation as shown in Fig. 8.19.

The size of the slip zone goes through a maximum during the compression of a tall cylinder, i.e., one with a h_0/d_0 ratio of 1.5 to 2.2. During initial compression, the slip zone first grows by inversion as discussed above. Then, as compression is continued the specimen begins to deform as a short rather than a tall cylinder. As the cylinder slides over the platen, the slip cone shrinks in size. The metal at the center flows outward and the center is in tension until the upper and lower dead-metal zones begin to interact, then they begin to deform and the stresses at the center become entirely compressive as shown graphically in Fig. 8.20.

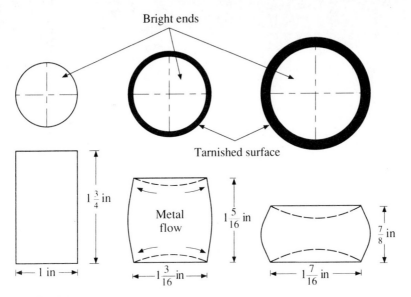

FIGURE 8.19
Schematic drawings showing the flow of metal by inversion during compression of a tall cylinder with sticking friction at the platen-workpiece interface. The tarnished, peripheral ring on the ends is maximum for sticking friction and decreases with the reduction in friction until it disappears for the frictionless case [3.22].

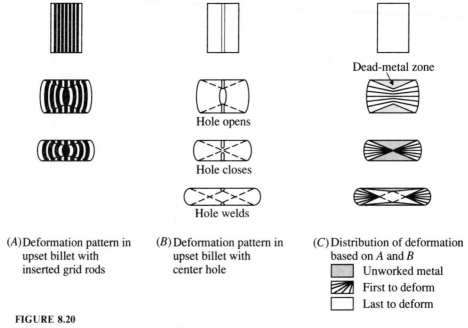

(A) Deformation pattern in upset billet with inserted grid rods

(B) Deformation pattern in upset billet with center hole

(C) Distribution of deformation based on A and B

FIGURE 8.20
Deformation patterns in cylindrical billet upset forged between flat, parallel dies.

As the h_0/d_0 ratio is progressively decreased, the dead zones do not meet and interpenetrate as is sometimes thought, but they progressively flatten. In very short cylinders, they not only flatten but also begin to decrease in diameter when the h/d ratio falls below a certain minimum value.

If the hardness is taken of the cross section shown in Fig. 8.18 of a cold-forged cylinder, the strainhardening will be nil in zone A, it will increase through the intermediate zone B, and it will be a maximum in zone C. When care is taken to reduce the friction to a minimum at the platen-metal interface, so that the deformation is practically homogeneous, the difference in strainhardening is virtually absent.

A good picture of the degree of deformation that takes place in different regions of a cylindrical specimen upon axial compression may be obtained by drawing an isostrain contour map. Kobayashi [8.7] used the finite element method to obtain a solution for axisymmetric upsetting of a solid cylinder having a h_0/d_0 ratio of 0.8 under conditions of sticking friction such as of an aluminum alloy. The computed distribution of the effective plastic strain $\bar{\varepsilon}$ and the bulge profile for a 20 percent reduction in height are shown in Fig. 8.21(a). It should be noted that the effective strain is about 40 times greater in the vicinity of the corners of the specimen than at the center of its ends, and that the strain rises somewhat exponentially across the contact surface of the specimen from the center of the end to the similar point at the corner as in Fig. 8.21(b). A Rockwell superficial 15T hardness traverse across the contact surface shows a similar distribution as in Fig. 8.21(c).

The effect of tangential stresses on the average interface pressure in the compression of thin cylindrical specimens between overhanging platens has been investigated by Schroeder and Webster and presented in their classic paper [8.8]. Their work has been extended by Bishop [8.9].

In general, the average or mean pressure required for forging depends upon (1) the significant, inherent flow stress of the metallic material, (2) the strain pattern determined by the configuration or geometry of the part, and (3) the effect of friction at the die-material interface.

In analyzing the effect of friction of thin circular discs, Schroeder and Webster [8.8] considered three cases:

1. Where relative sliding motion or sliding occurs between the blank and the die surfaces at all points except at the geometric center of the blank
2. When sticking friction occurs with no relative sliding motion at the interface and with the spreading action resulting from shearing of the metal below the surface of the blank parallel to the die surfaces
3. The intermediate condition, where sliding takes place in an annular zone near the edge, and sticking results in the central core

Schroeder and Webster categorized the above three cases in terms of the k/μ ratio, where $k = 1/\sqrt{3} = 0.577$ for the von Mises criterion and μ is the coefficient of friction, which follows from the fact that the tangential, frictional

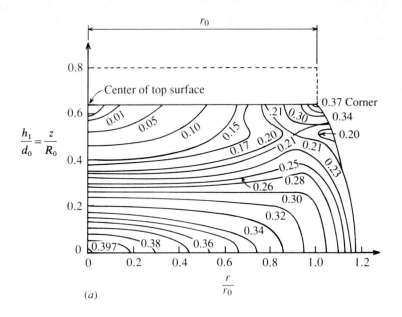

$$\frac{h_1}{d_0} = \frac{z}{R_0}$$

(a)

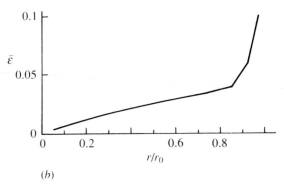

(b)

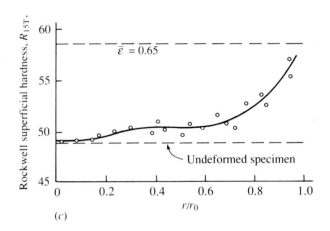

(c)

shear stress at the interface for sticking friction is limited to a value of the flow stress in shear, τ_0. According to the von Mises criterion, τ_0 is related to the flow stress in uniaxial tension or compression by $2\tau_0 = 2\bar{\sigma}/\sqrt{3}$.

Since

$$\tau_0 = 0.577\bar{\sigma} = k\bar{\sigma},$$

$$k = \frac{1}{\sqrt{3}} = 0.577 \tag{8.13}$$

If one follows the same procedure as was used for obtaining Eq. (4.42) for the friction hill for the axial compression of a cylinder by the elemental slab method and as was followed in obtaining Eq. (4.19) for the plane-strain deformation of a strip or slab, the following axisymmetric equation for the pressure distribution at the platen-cylinder interface for which no sticking occurs, i.e., sliding friction occurs over the entire surface, is obtained:

$$\frac{p}{\bar{\sigma}} = e^{2\mu/h(d/2-r)} \tag{8.14}$$

where p = normal interfacial pressure at a point
$\quad d$ = the diameter of the cylinder or workpiece
$\quad r$ = the radial distance from the center to any point on the face of the cylinder
$\quad h$ = the height or thickness of the cylinder or disc
$\quad \bar{\sigma}$ = flow stress of the workpiece
$\quad \mu$ = coefficient of friction

The above nomenclature is also used in the discussion that follows.

The ratio of $p/\bar{\sigma}$ is called the *intensity* or *constriction factor* Q_a, to be discussed later. The subscript in this case means that this factor is for the axisymmetric case.

The analytical expression for the critical radius r_c at which sticking ceases and sliding begins for the intermediate case can be found by equating the frictional drag μp for sliding friction to that for sticking friction $\bar{\sigma}/\sqrt{3}$ as follows:

$$\mu p = \frac{\bar{\sigma}}{\sqrt{3}}$$

$$p = \frac{\bar{\sigma}}{\sqrt{3}\,\mu} \tag{8.15}$$

FIGURE 8.21
(*a*) Isostrain contour maps and bulge profile of the FEM computed effective strain distribution at 10 percent reduction in height. (*b*) Computed strain distribution across the contact surface. (*c*) HR15T superficial hardness distribution across the contact surface r is the radial distance from the cylinder's axis to any point along the radius [8.7].

By substituting p into equation (8.14), one obtains

$$\frac{\bar{\sigma}}{\sqrt{3}\,\mu} = \bar{\sigma}e^{2\mu/h(d/2-r_c)} \tag{8.16}$$

Taking the natural logs of both sides one obtains

$$\ln\left(\frac{1}{\sqrt{3}}\,a\right) = \frac{2\mu}{h}\left(\frac{d}{2}-r_c\right)$$

$$r_c = \frac{d}{2} - \frac{h}{2\mu}\ln\left(\frac{1}{\sqrt{3}\,\mu}\right) \tag{8.17}$$

The average or mean pressure may then be obtained from

$$p_m = \frac{\displaystyle\int_0^{d/2} p\,dr}{A} \quad\text{and}\quad p_m = \frac{P_m}{A} \tag{8.18}$$

The above cases may now be classified, and the expression for the pressure intensity, multiplying, or constraint factor given as follows:

Case 1 applies when both μ and r/h are small, i.e., sliding friction applies, and

$$\frac{p}{\bar{\sigma}} < \frac{k}{\mu} < \frac{1}{\sqrt{3}\,\mu} \quad\text{or}\quad \frac{d}{2h} < \frac{1}{2\mu}\ln\frac{k}{\mu} \tag{8.19}$$

The pressure intensity multiplying factor Q_a, for this case, is equal to

$$Q_a = \frac{p_m}{\bar{\sigma}} = \frac{2(e^{\mu d/h} - \mu d/h - 1)}{(\mu d/h)^2} \tag{8.20}$$

Case 2 applies when $\mu \geq k$, that is, sticking friction occurs. The pressure intensity multiplying factor Q_a, for this case, is equal to

$$Q_a = \frac{p_m}{\bar{\sigma}} = 1 + \frac{kd}{3h} \cong \left(1 + \frac{d}{3\sqrt{3}}\right) \tag{8.21}$$

Case 3 applies when $\mu < k$ but $p/\bar{\sigma} = k/\mu$, or

$$\frac{h}{d} > \frac{1}{\mu}\ln\frac{k}{\mu} \tag{8.22}$$

The pressure intensity multiplying factor Q_a is complex, and its function may be expressed as

$$Q_a = \frac{p_m}{\bar{\sigma}} = f(\mu, d, h, k, \text{ and } r_c) \tag{8.23}$$

where r_c is the critical value of r at which the average pressure p_c is equal to the critical pressure p_m at which the transition from sliding to sticking type of friction results.

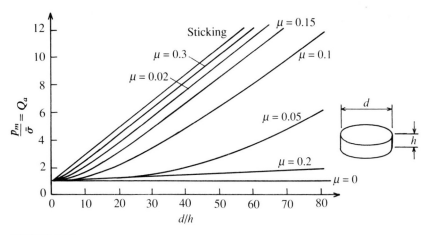

FIGURE 8.22
Nondimensional plot showing the combined effect of the disc geometry factor d/h and the Coulomb coefficient of friction μ on the average interface pressure-to-flow ratio $p_m/\bar{\sigma}$ for case 1—sliding friction, case 2—sticking friction, and case 3—combined sliding and sticking friction for the axial upsetting of short cylinders or thin discs at room temperature [8.11].

The equations as formulated above are essentially functions of three non-dimensional ratios:

$$\frac{p_m}{\bar{\sigma}} \qquad \frac{h}{d} \qquad \text{and } \mu$$

which relate the average pressure required to the flow stress of the material, the geometry of the workpiece, and the effects of friction. Therefore, the solution for one value of d/h and μ provides a value of $p_m/\bar{\sigma}$ for all geometrically similar circular blanks with the same d/h ratio. The pressure intensity multiplying factor for axisymmetric upsetting Q_a may be plotted against the diameter-to-thickness ratio for a constant value of μ for each of the above three cases in the non-dimensional graph shown in Fig. 8.22. (The frictional shear factor m may be substituted for μ for the case of sticking friction, as will be seen in the next section.) Figure 8.22 shows the extreme importance of maintaining a low coefficient of friction for forging when the ratio d/h is relatively large.

Since the coefficient of friction μ enters significantly into the above formulation, it will be discussed next.

8.2.4   Friction in Metalworking Processes

A very important variable that enters into almost all phases of metalworking, but with which we cannot as yet fully cope, is the phenomenon of friction. Since in metalworking relative motion occurs between the tools or dies and the workpiece, except for a few isolated cases such as dieless wire drawing, friction is an inherent part of the process. In most cases it is undesirable, but in some rare cases such as in rolling, it is a necessary part of the process, which could not proceed without it. Although a tremendous amount of work and discussion has gone into the subject of friction, much of it in conjunction with metalworking processes, it is still not very well understood.

There are presently two different parameters that attempt to define quantitatively the amount of friction existing between two contacting surfaces: (1) Coulomb's coefficient of friction μ, and (2) friction factor m.

There are three major effects of friction between the workpiece and the tools or dies in metalforming operations: (1) it results in an increase in the power required, because of the external friction loss; (2) it affects the surface finish; and (3) it causes wear of the tools and dies.

Usually a discussion of the subject of friction begins with a definition of Coulomb's coefficient of friction and Coulomb's law. If P is the normal force as shown in Fig. 8.23 and F is the lateral force necessary to slide one body over another for certain given conditions, then the Coulomb coefficient of friction μ is defined as

$$\mu = \frac{F}{P} = \frac{F/A}{P/A} = \frac{\tau_i}{p_i} \tag{8.24}$$

where τ_i = the tangential shear stress at the interface
  p_i = the normal pressure at the interface

Even though the surface contact is often limited to only a few high points or asperities on the surface, the area A is usually taken as the total area of

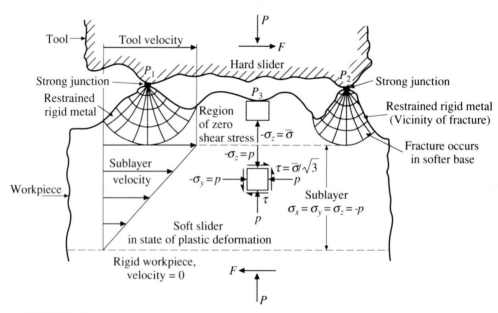

FIGURE 8.23
Microscopic model of sliding friction of two sliders showing sublayer plastic flow [7.9].

apparent contact. μ is usually assumed constant for a given die, workpiece, and lubricant.

As will be seen later, since in metalworking processes when the tangential or interfacial shear stress τ_i equals the flow strength in shear of the workpiece material $\tau_i = \tau_{max} = k$, the softer and weaker workpiece refuses to slide over the harder and stronger tool, but instead it shears beneath the surface inside the workpiece material, so that the coefficient of friction μ reaches a maximum value of 0.577, 0.5, or 0.39 depending on the yield criterion or flow model used.

A number of different models for the contacting surfaces have been assumed to explain the frictional resistance to relative motion. Shaw et al. [8.10] proposed the following description of the contacting surfaces that are typical of the surfaces in metalworking at the different levels of surface pressure: (1) at light loads, region I in Fig. 8.24, the two surfaces contact only at the asperities and the actual area of contact is small, (2) at higher pressures, region II, localized plastic flow of the asperities occurs increasing the area of contact and friction becomes load-dependent, and (3) at still higher pressures, region III, total conformity of the surfaces is achieved, and plastic flow with the bulk material is initiated, and the interfacial shear stress is limited to that of the shear stress of the material.

Models of the contacting surfaces usually involve such concepts as (1) the mechanical interlocking of asperities, (2) plowing of the softer surfaces, and (3) the pressure welding and subsequent strainhardening of the asperities. According to the latter model, wear of tools and dies may be explained by the fracture of the asperities at their softer and weaker base or roots as shown in Fig. 8.23.

However, during metalworking at high loads and poor lubrication during which "sticking" friction occurs, the subsurface of the softer and weaker workpiece material may shear, and consequently no relative motion between the surfaces of the workpiece and the tools or dies is assumed to occur. Therefore, the interfacial shear stress τ_i cannot rise above the maximum flow stress in shear, $\tau_{max} = k$, of the softer workpiece material. The condition at which no relative motion of the interfaces occurs is called *sticking friction*, even though no sticking or actual adhesion of the surfaces occurs.

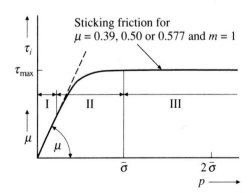

FIGURE 8.24
Schematic curve showing the variation of the frictional shear stress τ_i and the coefficient of friction μ with normal pressure p. μ is assumed to be constant above $p = \bar{\sigma}$ [7.9].

Three criteria or theories can be used to evaluate the maximum value of μ: (1) slip-line field, channel-flow theory for friction; (2) the maximum shear stress theory; and (3) the von Mises theory.

The slip-line, channel-flow model for dealing with friction was presented by Thomsen et al. [7.6]. In the development of this model, let Fig. 8.25(a) represent channel flow through rigid, parallel boundaries for plane-strain conditions. The metal is assumed to be rigid upon exit from the slip-line field as it flows from the left as shown in the figure.

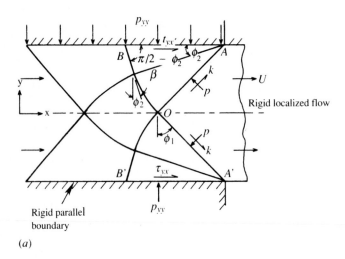

(a)

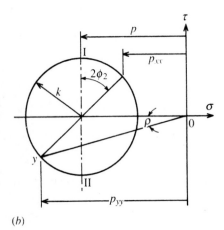

(b)

FIGURE 8.25
Slip-line field for maximum friction in channel flow. (a) Physical plane, and (b) stress plane shown in a Mohr stress diagram [7.9].

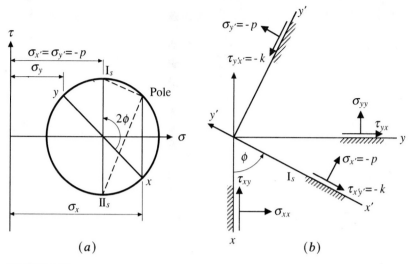

FIGURE 8.26
Rotation of the x and y planes to coincide with the planes of maximum shear. (a) Stress plane shown in a Mohr stress diagram, and (b) physical plane [7.9].

If a general plane x is rotated through an angle ϕ into the plane of maximum shear stress as shown in Fig. 8.26, the following Hencky-type equations (8.25) and (8.26) are obtained giving the stresses for any angle ϕ:

$$\sigma_{xx} = -p_{x'x'} = -p + k \sin 2\phi \tag{8.25}$$

$$\sigma_{yy} = -p_{y'y'} = -p - k \sin 2\phi \tag{8.26}$$

$$\tau_{x'y'} = k \cos 2\phi \tag{8.27}$$

where σ_{xx} and σ_{yy} = the normal stress on the x and y planes and in the x and y directions, respectively
$p_{x'x'}$ and $p_{y'y'}$ = the mean pressure on the maximum shear planes x' and y'
$\tau_{x'y'}$ = shear stress on the $x'y'$ plane
$k = \tau_{\max}$ = maximum shear stress of the material

Other parameters relating to the slip-line field are defined in Fig. 8.25(a).

The coefficient of friction on boundary AB in Fig. 8.25(a), where $\phi = \phi_2$, is given by use of Eq. (8.24) and Figs. 8.25(b) and 8.26(b) as

$$\mu = \tan \rho = \frac{\tau_{x'y'}}{p_{y'y'}} = \frac{k \cos 2\phi_2}{p + k \sin 2\phi_2} \tag{8.28}$$

For the frictionless case for $\mu = 0$, $\phi_1 = 45°$ and the slip-line makes angles of $45°$ at A and B with the surface. For the case of maximum friction, $\phi_2 = 0°$ and the slip-line at B is normal to the surface.

To determine the state of stress along OA', one can substitute the boundary conditions, $\sigma_{xx} = 0$ and $\phi_1 = 45°$, into Eq. (8.25), which results in $p = \tau_{\max} = k$;

however, from Eq. (4.95)

$$p + 2k\phi = C_\alpha \qquad\qquad (4.95)(8.29)$$

along an α slip-line. Substituting $p = k$ and $\phi_2 = 45° = \pi/4$ rad into Eq. (8.29), one obtains

$$C_\alpha = k\left(1 + \frac{\pi}{2}\right) = 2.57k \qquad\qquad (8.30)$$

The condition of maximum shearing stress at AB for $\phi_2 = 0$ gives

$$p = p_{yy} = 2.57\tau_{max} = 2.57k \qquad\qquad (8.31)$$

The coefficient of friction μ_{max}, for a maximum shearing stress, is given by

$$\mu_{max} = \frac{(\tau_{xy})_{max}}{p_{yy}} = \frac{k}{2.57k} = 0.39 \qquad\qquad (8.32)$$

Since, according to the maximum shear stress theory, the flow stress in shear is equal to one-half that for tension or compression, μ will in this case assume the maximum value of

$$\mu_{max} = \frac{k}{\bar\sigma} = 0.5 \qquad\qquad (8.33)$$

For the von Mises theory, it will assume the value of

$$\mu_{max} = \frac{k}{p_{yy}} = \frac{\bar\sigma/\sqrt{3}}{\bar\sigma} = \frac{1}{\sqrt{3}} = 0.577 \qquad\qquad (8.34)$$

It is therefore necessary to select for sticking friction a reasonable value of μ_{max} from 0.577, 0.5, or 0.39. Fortunately, the difference in the predicted load for most metalworking operations is not great if the higher or the lower value for μ is selected for sticking friction or sublayer flow. In this text, when $\mu = 0.577$, 0.5, or 0.39, it is assumed that the von Mises, maximum shear stress, or the slip-line criterion applies respectively.

In the foregoing, it is assumed that the shear stress is constant and equal to that of the workpiece material. The mean interfacial or frictional shear stress for metalforming then may be expressed as

$$\tau_i = \frac{m\bar\sigma}{2} \quad \text{or} \quad \frac{m\bar\sigma}{\sqrt{3}}$$

and

$$\tau_i = mk = \frac{\mu p_1}{\sqrt{3}} \quad \text{and} \quad \mu_{max} = \frac{m}{\sqrt{3}}$$

$\qquad\qquad (8.35)$

where m is the frictional shear factor. This factor may be taken as constant for a given surface and temperature condition in a given metalforming process. Usually m is considered to be constant over the entire surface and independent of the velocity. If no friction exists, m is zero, and as the friction increases, it will assume the maximum value of 1 at the point that sticking friction occurs.

The concept of μ breaks down at the point at which sticking friction occurs, since the normal interface pressure may exceed the uniaxial flow strength by several factors because of the system of stresses that are acting on the surface. Values of p and $\bar{\sigma}$ would indicate that either μ would have to decrease or τ_i would have to increase as p increases above $\bar{\sigma}$. Since τ_i remains constant at a value of τ_0, which is unaffected by pressure, it appears that the use of the shear factor m is a more rational choice for use in describing frictional phenomena. It also is not completely adequate, so that at the present time there is no completely satisfactory way for representing frictional conditions mathematically. Also, neither μ nor τ_i gives any information about the conditions at the interface.

Although the study of frictional effects in metalworking and other engineering applications involving sliding surfaces is very difficult, the concept of the coefficient of friction (or the friction shear factor) is a good one. It indicates that some sort of allowance must be made for the frictional force F, which varies with μ and which is related to the actual normal force, the condition at the interface, and operating conditions in some way. μ in metalforming has been found experimentally to vary between about 0.03 to 0.4. For many operations with the typical lubricants used, μ varies between about 0.1 to 0.2. For the purpose of simplicity, the following values will be used for μ and m in this textbook: (1) for cold working at room temperature, $\mu = 0.1$ and $m = 0.173$; (2) for warm working, $\mu = 0.2$ and $m = 0.346$; and (3) for hot working, $\mu = 0.4$ and $m = 0.693$. However, in some cases such as for extrusion, for example, it may be preferred to estimate the actual interfacial shear stress τ_i and use it in calculating the extrusion load or force.

In most metalforming operations μ will be assumed to be constant over the entire surface of contact. However, by embedding tiny pressure-sensitive pins into one of the dies or platens, Pearsall and Bockhofen showed that in the axial compression of an aluminum cylinder with $d_0 = 2$ in (50.8 mm) and $h_0 = 0.5$ in (12.7 mm) to a reduction of 20 percent without a lubricant, μ varied from about 0 at the center of the face of the cylinder to 0.5 at its periphery.

Friction is an important factor in some processes. It causes an increase in (1) the pressure on the dies and consequently in general die wear, (2) the forces and energy required for deformation, (3) the inhomogeneity of deformation, and (4) the temperature generated in the process. It is an important variable in rolling and deep drawing. One of the ways of controlling friction is by use of lubrication. The subject of lubrication and how the coefficient of friction and lubrication are evaluated experimentally by means of the ring test will be discussed later.

8.2.5 Interface Pressure in Open-Die Forging

The calculation of the average or mean pressure p_m, the force or load P, and the amount of deformation in open-die forging by the *multiplying or constriction factor method* will be covered in this section.

The approach used for the calculation of the interface pressure and the force of deformation will be covered for the following typical operations performed in open-die forging: (1) cogging or drawing out as in Fig. 8.12; (2) upsetting of an axisymmetric, right, circular cylinder with overhanging platens as in Fig. 8.18; and (3) upsetting of a rectangular slab or plate with overhanging platens to be covered later (see Fig. 8.31). The solutions for the pressure and force obtained for open-die forging can be applied with only minor changes to the final or finishing operation for closed-impression-die forging, to be covered later also. This method of calculation would yield the maximum force since it is determined by the total projected area of the die cavity and of the flash land (the flow-controlling, narrow, landed restriction at the periphery of the die cavity in

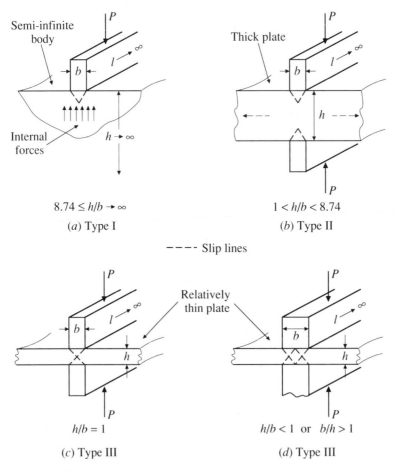

FIGURE 8.27
Modes of deformation in plane strain with long ($l = \infty$), narrow dies for the case of (a) a semi-infinite body resulting in inhomogeneous deformation when $Q_i \cong 3$ (type I deformation), (b) a thick plate resulting in inhomogeneous (non-through) deformation where $1.15 < Q_i < 3$ (type II deformation), (c) a relatively thin plate resulting in essentially homogeneous deformation where $Q = 1.15$ or 1 (type III deformation) [see Fig. 4.25(a) and (b)] and (d) a relatively thin plate and wide-dies for which friction predominates [8.11].

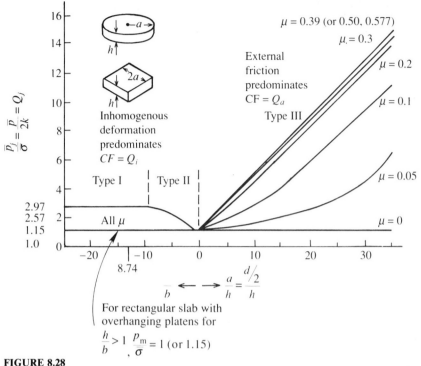

FIGURE 8.28
Variation of mean pressure with a/h ratio for cylindrical and square billets. (*After J. F. M. Bishop, J. Mechanics and Physics of Solids, 1958, Vol. 6, p. 132.*)

closed-die forging). It is assumed that other more complex shapes can be treated as composites of the above shapes.

In analyzing a general open-die forging operation, it must first be determined on the basis of the ratio of the workpiece thickness to the interface width, h/b, whether the predominant factor is due to inhomogeneous deformation as shown in Fig. 8.27 or to frictional effects. (Inhomogeneous deformation in this case means that it is localized near the punches or dies and does not extend through the thickness of the plate. It is non-through thickness deformation.) Then, the average interface pressure-to-flow stress ratio $p_m/\bar{\sigma}$ can be determined from semiempirical curves such as in Fig. 8.28. This ratio can be considered as an intensity multiplying factor Q_j, by means of which the flow stress can be multiplied to obtain the average interface pressure, that is, $\bar{p}_j = Q_j\bar{\sigma}$. Since it also represents the amount that the material is constricted from flowing freely by adjacent metal or by friction, it is also called a *constriction factor*.

The practice presented by Schey [8.11] is followed here, in which the following subscripts are used to differentiate the three multiplying or constriction factors as shown in Table 8.1.

The curves shown on the right side of Fig. 8.28 for Q_a versus d/h are also shown in Fig. 8.22. The curve shown on the left side of Fig. 8.28 for Q_i versus

TABLE 8.1
Constriction (intensity multiplying) factors

Operation	Q_j factor
Inhomogeneous deformation such as cogging or drawing out	Q_i
Plane-strain upsetting of a rectangular plate or slab	Q_p
Axisymmetric upsetting of a cylinder	Q_a

h/b for the plane-strain indentation compression of a slab is presented as Fig. 8.29. The curves showing the variation of the interface pressure multiplying or constriction factor for plane-strain compression of a rectangular slab are presented later as Fig. 8.30.

After the operation being considered is classified as to its type, i.e., inhomogeneous, axisymmetric, cylinder upsetting, or plane-strain, slab upsetting, and the proper constriction factor Q_j determined; the next step is to evaluate the flow stress $\bar{\sigma}$ for the prevailing conditions such as for the type of deformation—whether steady state or nonsteady state, and the amount of strain, strain rate, temperature, and strainhardening, etc., involved. Since most open-die forging operations are nonsteady state as compared to extrusion, wire-drawing, etc., the

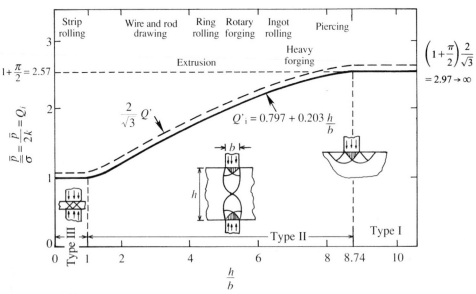

FIGURE 8.29
Relationship between frictionless, plane-strain indentation pressure and the h/b ratio for a block (slab) of nonstrainhardening material of thickness h indented by a flat rigid indenter of width b. The solid curve is for the maximum shear stress criterion and the dashed curve is for the von Mises criterion for yielding. (Note: Here b refers to the width of the punch and h to the thickness of the slab.) (*Adapted from W. Johnson, and A. G. Mamalis, "A Survey of Some Physical Defects Arising in Metal Working Processes"*, *Proc. 17th Int. Mech. Tool Design and Res. Conf.*, *S. A. Tobias* (*ed.*), *Vol. 17th, 1976, p. 607.*).

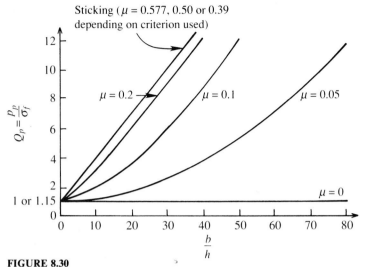

FIGURE 8.30

Interface pressure-muliplying factor Q_p versus b/h for the plane-strain compression of a rectangular slab. (Note the difference in ratio with preceding figure.) [8.11].

instantaneous flow stress occurring at the end of deformation is the controlling stress. Since the open-die forging is here classified as a hot-working process, strainhardening is not a factor, but the strain rate is. If the strain-rate coefficient C and the strain sensitivity exponent m are available, the flow stress $\bar{\sigma}$ may be calculated for the prevailing strain rate from the relationship $\bar{\sigma} = C\dot{\varepsilon}^m$, or from a similar relationship. If the above information is not available, the flow stress will have to be obtained experimentally, because it would be too risky to extrapolate low strain-rate conventional, tensile test data for this purpose. In addition to the interface pressure or force of deformation, the amount of deformation per stroke, or the change of shape during the foregoing operations is also of interest.

8.2.6 Inhomogeneous Plastic Deformation with Narrow Indenters

The inhomogeneous (nonuniform) deformation produced by deforming a thick workpiece with narrow, flat anvils or dies has already been covered briefly in Chap. 4 on Analysis Methods, which culminated in Fig. 4.27. This figure was replotted here for convenience as Fig. 8.29, where $\sigma_0 = \bar{\sigma} = 2k = 2\tau_{\max}$ for the case of the maximum shear stress criterion for yielding and $\bar{\sigma} = 2/\sqrt{3}\,\sigma_0$ for the case of the von Mises criterion for yielding. σ_0 is the flow stress of the material in uniaxial tension.

Wistreich and Shutt [8.12] give the following expression for the curve in Fig. 8.29 for the case where the maximum shear-stress criterion applies:

$$Q_i' = 0.797 + 0.203\,\frac{h}{b} \tag{8.36}$$

which applies in the range $1 \le h/b \le 8.74$ and which was obtained on the basis of a slip-line field solution. For the case where the von Mises criterion for yielding applies, the above function would be multiplied by $2/\sqrt{3}$.

When narrow compression dies are used as in cogging and drawing out, since $b/h < 1$ or $h/b > 1$, it can be assumed that the process is frictionless and $\mu \cong 0$, and inhomogeneous plastic deformation predominates. If $h = b$, as in Fig. 8.28, and $h/b = b/h = 1$, neither inhomogeneous deformation nor external friction effects are factors and $p/\bar{\sigma} = 2/\sqrt{3} = 1.15$ (or 1 depending on the yield criterion used) as seen in Fig. 8.28. If $1 < h/b < 8.74$ as shown in Fig. 8.28, then Q_i should be obtained from Fig. 8.29, and $p = Q_i\bar{\sigma}$. If $h/b \ge 8.74$ as shown in Fig. 8.29, then $p/\bar{\sigma} = 2.97 \cong 3$, and $p \cong 3\bar{\sigma}$. If $b/h > 1$ $(h/b < 1)$, then external friction effects predominate and the right portion of Fig. 8.28 or else Fig. 8.22 for the upsetting of a cylinder should be used, or Fig. 8.30 for the plane-strain compression of a rectangular slab, which will be discussed subsequently.

After the operation under consideration has been classified as an inhomogeneous, plastic deformation process and Q_i has been determined from Fig. 8.29, the next step is to evaluate $\bar{\sigma}$ for the prevailing condition of strain, strain rate, temperature, etc.

8.2.7 Upsetting of a Rectangular Slab (Block) in Plane Strain

In the deformation of a long slab $(l > 6 \text{ to } 8b)$ by compression, frictional constraint prevents elongation or spreading in the length direction, so that this process may be considered as being one of plane strain. The lateral stress that prevents spreading in the width direction increases the compressive stress or pressure at the die-material interface over that for the frictionless case, forming a friction hill as shown in Fig. 8.31(a). The dashed lines at each end of the pressure surface represent the truncation of the friction hill due to an opposing transverse friction hill resulting from the elongation of the ends of the slab.

Equation (4.17) developed for the mean or average interface pressure for the plane-strain compression problem by the elemental slab (equilibrium) method of analysis will be used here to obtain the intensity, multiplying, or constriction factor Q_p, for the upsetting of a slab.

The equation for the mean pressure p_m, for the case for which sliding friction occurs over the entire surface as obtained by the slab method of analysis is

$$\frac{p_m}{\bar{\sigma}} = \frac{h}{\mu b}\left(e^{\mu b/h} - 1\right) \tag{8.37}$$

where $\bar{\sigma}$ is the flow stress in uniaxial tension.

The equation for the intermediate case for which sticking friction occurs to the critical location of x_c from the centerline and slipping friction to the edge of the slab $b/2$ is given by

$$\frac{p_m}{\bar{\sigma}} = \frac{h}{\mu b}\left[\frac{(1 + 2\mu x_c/2)^2 + 1}{4\mu} - 1\right] \qquad \text{for} \qquad 0 \le x_c \le \frac{b}{2} \tag{8.38}$$

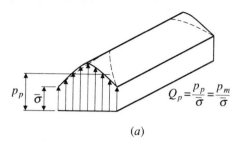

$$Q_p = \frac{p_p}{\bar{\sigma}} = \frac{p_m}{\bar{\sigma}}$$

(a)

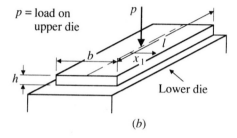

$p = $ load on upper die

Lower die

(b)

FIGURE 8.31
(a) Variation of the pressure at the interface at the die-material interface as a result of (b) upsetting a flat, rectangular workpiece with friction in plane strain by use of overhanging platens. (Note: b here refers to the width of the slab not the punch.) [8.11].

The equation for sticking friction over the entire interface is

$$\frac{p_m}{\bar{\sigma}} = \left(1 + \frac{\mu b}{2h}\right) \tag{8.39}$$

If $\mu = 0$, $p_m/\bar{\sigma} = 1$ or 1.15, which gives the lowest curve in Fig. 8.30. If Eq. (8.37) is used for lower values of μ, for which sliding friction is expected to occur, curves such as for $\mu = 0.05$ in Fig. 8.30 can be obtained. If the preferred value for μ for sticking friction is used in Eq. (8.37), that is, $\mu = 0.577$, 0.5, or 0.39, the highest curve labeled "sticking friction" can be obtained. If for intermediate values for μ, with some criterion for choosing x_c, such as was used for developing a similar graph for short cylinders or discs, the intermediate curves can be obtained.

8.2.8   Plane-Strain Slip-Line Field Analysis for Sidepressing

A better understanding of the foregoing plane-strain deformation may be obtained by resorting to slip-line field analysis covered elsewhere. The experimental work cited by Kobayashi [8.7] in the deformation and fracture obtained by sidepressing of cylindrical specimens as shown in Fig. 3.50 with machined flats of various widths provides a good insight to the different modes of deformation. (In regular open-die, sidepressing operations, the initial flats are, of course, forged onto the cylindrical surface.)

In this example, the cylinders used were 25.4 mm (1 in) in diameter by 25.4 mm (1 in) long of a relatively nonductile 7075-T6 aluminum alloy. The cylinders were compressed in plane strain in a special jig between platens with smooth and with rough surfaces.

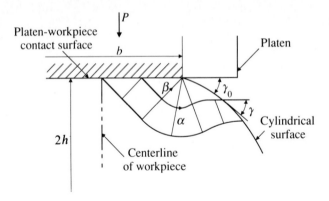

FIGURE 8.32

Schematic drawing of one quadrant of a slip-line field for type 1 mode of deformation for which $h/b \geq 8.74$ and in which the plastic deformation has not as yet spread to the free surface of the cylinder [see Fig. 3.51(a)]. (*Adapted from S. C. Jain, and K. Kobayashi, "Deformation and Fracture of an Aluminum Alloy in Plain-Strain", Proc. 11th Int. MTDR Conf., Sept. 1970, v. B, Pergamon Press, 1970, p. 1137-1154.*)

As was stated previously, when the material height to punch width ratio is high enough, that is, $h/b \geq 8.74$, the deformation occurs in the material adjacent to the surface of the dies as shown in Fig. 8.29 and is called type I mode of deformation. The slip-line field for this type of deformation shown in Fig. 8.32 was presented earlier for a semi-infinite body in Fig. 8.51(a) and for an intermediate geometry between a very thick infinite plate and a rectangular slab in Fig. 8.51(b). For a relatively large radius of curvature of the free surface of the flattened cylinder in comparison with the width of the die-workpiece contact surface, the mean forging pressure or the stress p_m, at which yielding or flow will ensue, can be approximated by

$$\frac{p_m}{\bar{\sigma}} = 1 + \frac{\pi}{2} - \gamma_0 \qquad (8.40)$$

where $\bar{\sigma}$ = effective or flow stress of the material

γ_0 = angle between the face of the die and the free surface of the cylinder

If $\gamma_0 = 0$, $p_m/\bar{\sigma} = 2.57$, and $h/b = 8.74$. The value of $h/b = 8.74$ is the critical value for type I mode of deformation, and it is the boundary value between type I and type II modes. For the rectangular slab, $\gamma_0 = \pi/2$, and $p_m/\bar{\sigma} = 1$ for all values of $h/b > 1$, that is, for both type I and type II modes as shown in Fig. 8.29. It should be noted that the slip-line field, and therefore the mean die pressures, are independent of friction conditions at $h/b \geq 1$.

When the h/b ratio decreases below the critical value of 8.74 and is in the range of $8.74 > h/b > 1$, type II mode of deformation obtains and the two sides of the specimen move apart laterally as rigid masses. A fractured sidepressed specimen and the slip-line field of this type of deformation are shown in Fig. 8.33(a) and (b). From this figure it can be seen that the fracture occurred along

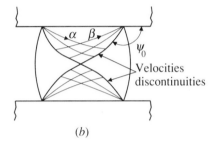

FIGURE 8.33
(*a*) Fractured specimen, and (*b*) slipline field for type II mode deformation with velocity discontinuities shown in heavy line along one of which fracture occurred. Rough parallel dies were used in this case in a sidepressing operation. (*(a) Adapted from S. C. Jain, and K. Kobayashi, "Deformation and Fracture of an Aluminum Alloy in Plain-Strain", Proc. 11th Int. MTDR Conf., Sept. 1970, v. B, Pergamon Press, 1970, p. 1137–1154.*) (*b*) [8.7].

the velocity discontinuity line characterized by ψ_0, which is the angle between the contact and fracture surfaces and which is about 45° in this case. Although rough surface dies were used in this case, type II deformation was found to be independent of friction conditions.

For h/b ratios less than one, that is, $h/b < 1$ or $b/h > 1$, the plastic deformation extends to the lateral sides of the sidepressed specimen and type III mode of deformation obtains. Slip-line field solutions for this mode of deformation are dependent on the friction conditions at the die-workpiece interface.

The fractured sidepressed specimens and the schematic slip-line fields for different b/h ratios and for both smooth and rough die surfaces are shown in Fig. 8.34 for different values of b/h. It should be noted that for Fig. 8.34(*a*), the fracture occurred along the slip-lines of velocity discontinuity or flow localization, which is also the boundary slip-line. In Fig. 8.34(*b*) and (*c*), the fracture also occurred along the boundary slip-lines.

8.2.9 Flow Localization

The ability to form metals into useful shapes is often limited by the occurrence of flow localization or fracture as indicated in the foregoing. In flow localization, regions of limited deformation of varying degree are separated from each other by thin regions of much higher than normal deformation as shown in Fig. 8.35. Flow localization or fracture modes, that limit the capacity of deformation

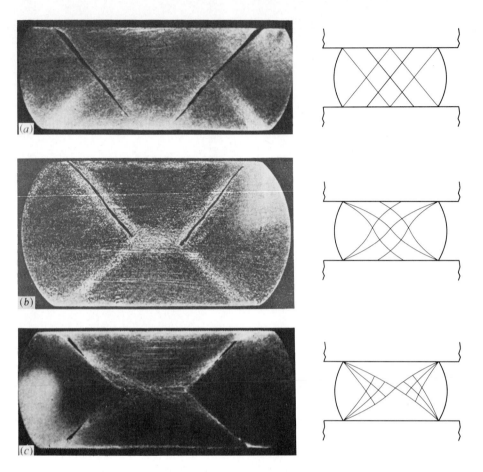

FIGURE 8.34
Fractured specimen (left) and schematic slip-line fields (right) for type III mode of deformation for sidepressing of cylinders with machined flats. (*a*) Smooth dies and $b/h \cong 2$ (integral); (*b*) Smooth dies and $b/h \cong 1.3$ (non-integral); (*c*) Rough dies and $b/h \cong 1.34$. (*Adapted from S. C. Jain, and K. Kobayashi, "Deformation and Fracture of an Aluminum Alloy in Plain-Strain", Proc. 11th Int. MTDR Conf., Sept. 1970, v. B, Pergamon Press, 1970, p. 1137–1154.*)

processes to be carried out on a metallic material, are greatly affected by the forming temperature, deformation rate, and stress state. Perhaps the most important of these factors is the forming temperature [8.13]. In general, flow localization and flow instability may be attributed to one or more of the following causes [8.13]:

1. The destabilizing influence of area reduction during tensile deformation, which was covered in conjunction with the tensile test
2. The accentuation of strain gradients by frictional effects
3. Flow softening, that occurs following exhaustion of strainhardening capacity
4. Die-chilling of portion of the workpiece

FIGURE 8.35
Transverse section of a upset steel cylindrical specimen deformed at room temperature under conditions of high friction. The dark dead-metal zones on the top and bottom of the specimen are separated from the deformed bulk by narrow regions of high deformation or shear bands, which etched lighter in the above macrograph [8.13].

During bulk forming at cold working temperatures, friction may cause (1) plastic deformation to localize within the workpiece, as well as cause (2) free surface bulging, which can generate secondary tensile stresses and thus tensile instability and flow localization at the surface of the workpiece. In the former instance, friction causes zones of limited deformation, often called dead-metal zones, to be generated in the area of the workpiece in contact with the dies. Separating these regions of limited deformation from the deforming bulk material are thin regions of much higher than normal deformation crossing many grains, commonly known as shear bands, as shown in Fig. 8.35 [8.13].

As was indicated in the discussion of the compressive test, several types of instabilities can be developed in this test. The first type is associated with a maximum in the true stress–true strain curve. The second type deals with shear-band formation. The former was discussed in conjunction with the compressive test, and the latter will be discussed here.

It has been observed that the mode of flow localization due to flow softening varies in a manner depending on the deformation state or strain path followed. Under conditions of axisymmetric deformation, such as uniaxial compression, flow concentration takes the form of localized (as opposed to uniform) bulges, which are analogous to necks in the tension testing of sheetmetal specimens as shown in Fig. 3.18. By contrast, when a plane-strain loading path is followed, the localization is free to become more concentrated, leading to the formation of macroscopic shear bands. Shear bands are narrow regions of internally localized plastic flow crossing many grains. Because they are essentially planar or two-dimensional regions, as mentioned previously shear bands are usually not observed under axisymmetric conditions of flow such as during upsetting of a cylinder unless friction, tool misalignment, or other effects produce a shift in the strain state. Flow localization in the form of shear bands can be evaluated by examining the shear stress and shear strain along the slip-lines, since (1) shear bands have been shown experimentally to initiate along slip-lines, and (2) geometric hardening effects (which are flow stabilizing) vanish along these lines [8.13].

In the process of defining the flow localization parameter for sidepressing, α_τ, the following assumptions are made: (1) that the slip-lines have no curvature, so that the cross-sectional area subjected to the maximum shear stress A_τ, and α itself, do not vary with x' as defined below, that is, $dA_\tau\, dx' = 0$ and $d\tau/dx' = 0$; and (2) that similar strainhardening and strain-rate sensitivity coefficients γ'_τ and m, as defined for tensile and compressive deformation, apply to deformation in shear. The following equation, analogous to a similar equation in tension, can then be applied to shear (see Eqs. (2.136)–(2.138), and (3.37)–(3.40)):

$$\left(\frac{\partial \ln \tau}{\partial x'}\right)\bigg|_\tau = \gamma'_\tau\left(\frac{\partial \gamma_\tau}{\partial x'}\right)\bigg|_t + m\left(\frac{\partial \ln \dot{\gamma}_\tau}{\partial x}\right)\bigg|_t, \tag{8.41}$$

where τ = shear stress on the shear-band planes
  x' = displacement coordinate perpendicular to the shear-band planes
  γ_τ = shear strain attributable to τ
  $\dot{\gamma}_\tau$ = shear strain rate attributable to τ

$$\gamma'_\tau \equiv \frac{\partial \ln \tau}{\partial \gamma}\bigg|_{\dot{\gamma}}$$

$$m \equiv \frac{\partial \ln \tau}{\partial \ln \dot{\gamma}_\tau}\bigg|_{\gamma, T}$$

For $d\tau/dx' = 0$, the above equation becomes

$$0 = \gamma'_\tau\, \delta\gamma_\tau + m\gamma_\tau \ln \dot{\gamma}_\tau \tag{8.42}$$

From this expression, the flow localization parameter can be defined as

$$\alpha_\tau \equiv \frac{\delta \ln \dot{\gamma}_\tau}{\delta\gamma_\tau} = -\frac{\gamma'_\tau}{m} \tag{8.43}$$

If one assumes that the material is isotropic and that the von Mises criterion applies, so that

$$\tau = \frac{\bar{\sigma}}{\sqrt{3}} \qquad \gamma_\tau = \sqrt{3}\,\bar{\varepsilon} \qquad \dot{\gamma}_\tau = \sqrt{3}\,\dot{\bar{\varepsilon}}$$

Eq. (8.43) reduces to an expression for the flow localization parameter, α [8.13]:

$$\alpha \equiv \frac{\delta \ln \dot{\bar{\varepsilon}}}{\delta\bar{\varepsilon}} = \frac{(\partial \ln \bar{\sigma}/\partial\bar{\varepsilon})|_{\dot{\bar{\varepsilon}}}}{m} = \frac{\gamma'_c}{m} \tag{8.44}$$

In Eq. (8.44), γ'_c is the normalized flow-softening rate in compression, for which $\varepsilon = -\bar{\varepsilon}$, and is identical to the γ'_c in the following equation for compression:

$$\alpha = -\frac{\delta \ln \dot{\varepsilon}}{\delta\varepsilon} = \frac{\gamma'_c - 1}{m} \tag{8.45}$$

Note that in Eqs. (8.44) and (8.45)

$$\frac{\delta \ln \dot{\bar{\varepsilon}}}{\delta \bar{\varepsilon}} = -\frac{\delta \ln \dot{\varepsilon}}{\delta \varepsilon}$$

becomes $\varepsilon = -\bar{\varepsilon}$ for deformation in compression (see Eq. (3.41)).

Equations (8.43) and (8.44) specify that the rate at which shear strain-rate concentrations develop in plane strain is proportional to the ratio of the normalized flow-softening rate to the strain-rate sensitivity exponent. When Eq. (8.44) is compared to (8.45), it can be seen that in plane-strain deformation, the tendency for shear-band formation is greater than that for localized bulging because of the absence of the cross-sectional area term, that is, $\gamma'_c/m > (\gamma'_c - 1)/m$, where -1 represents the area term. It is, therefore, not surprising that shear bands commonly develop under plane-strain conditions during mechanical working. It is, therefore, preferable to determine the effect of material properties on the occurrence of shear bands from deformation investigations carried out under plane-strain conditions of testing [8.13].

When shear bands are observed in metallographic sections, their morphology usually follows identical patterns, which are a function of reduction as shown in Fig. 8.36. At reductions close to that at which they are initiated, two complementary shear bands intersect at about 90° at the center of sidepressing. At this reduction, they appear to be similar in form to the slip-lines for sidepressing. With increasing reduction, the legs of the X rotate away from the primary compression axis, which indicates that the shear bands are primarily associated with material, not spatial, elements; that is, they only form on planes of maximum shear stress when material coefficients adopt certain critical values in Eq. (8.43). With still further deformation, the intersection of the shear bands lead to the formation of a flat region of intense deformation at the center of the specimens, which eventually bows toward one or the other of the die surfaces with increasing deformation.

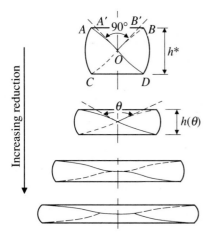

FIGURE 8.36

Schematic representation of the mechanism of shear-band formation in isothermal sidepressing of a cylinder. h^* is the height of initiation and $h(\theta)$ is the height of first metallographic detection of shear bands (see Figs. 8.20 and 8.56) [8.13].

A simple technique has been developed to determine the reduction at which shear bands are initiated in sidepressing. It makes use of metallographic observations and the fact that, in plane strain, shear bands initiate along the zero-extension directions or slip-lines of plasticity theory. The method assumes that true initiation takes place before it is visible metallographically. Therefore, the height h^* associated with true initiation, which corresponds to the moment when the slip-lines are perpendicular, can be found by back extrapolation from the earliest moment at which they are visible metallographically. The extrapolation technique employs a construction based on the assumption that, once shear bands are initiated, deformation proceeds more or less by block shear. In Fig. 8.36 the block AOB has deformed into the shape shown, which may be approximated by $A'OB'$. By measuring the angle θ_h and the height $h(\theta_h)$ at which shear bands are first observed metallographically, the height at initiation, h^*, may be estimated [8.13]:

$$h^* = h(\theta_h)\sqrt{\tan\left(\frac{\theta_h}{2}\right)} \tag{8.46}$$

In the foregoing discussion, flow localization was discussed on the basis of flow softening during plane-strain deformation by sidepressing. Let us now briefly examine flow softening arising from adiabatic (no heat added or lost) heating due to deformation at high stress levels at coldworking temperatures.

The strain for instability, at which the flow curve passes through a maximum under adiabatic conditions, along the maximum shear direction in plane strain can be calculated from

$$d\bar{\sigma} = 0 = \left(\frac{\partial\bar{\sigma}}{\partial\bar{\varepsilon}}\right)\Bigg|_{\dot{\bar{\varepsilon}},T} d\bar{\varepsilon} + \left(\frac{\partial\bar{\sigma}}{\partial\dot{\bar{\varepsilon}}}\right)\Bigg|_{\bar{\varepsilon},T} d\dot{\bar{\varepsilon}} + \left(\frac{\partial\bar{\sigma}}{\partial T}\right)\Bigg|_{\bar{\varepsilon}\dot{\bar{\varepsilon}}} dT \tag{8.47}$$

The critical strain $\bar{\varepsilon}_c$ for flow localization can then be calculated by use of isothermal flow curve expressed by $\bar{\sigma} = K\bar{\varepsilon}^n$ as follows:

$$\bar{\varepsilon}_c = -\frac{\rho cn}{0.95(\partial\bar{\sigma}/\partial T)|_{\bar{\varepsilon},\dot{\bar{\varepsilon}}}} \tag{8.48}$$

where ρ is the density of the metal and c is its specific heat. In the above equation, it is assumed that 95 percent of the heat generated by plastic deformation is retained by the workpiece, which represents a departure from adiabatic conditions (see Eqs. (2.169) and (4.78).

Metals with a relatively large strainhardening exponent n, such as normalized 1006 steel ($n = 0.24$), annealed 304 stainless steel ($n = 0.50$), and 6061-O aluminum ($n = 0.24$) require a large amount of strain before the onset of instability and flow localization. In contrast, quenched and tempered steels such as 4340 ($n = 0.055$) can be deformed only a small amount before the initiation of flow localization. For the above class of materials, γ' is defined as

$$\gamma' = -\left(\frac{d\ln\bar{\sigma}}{d\bar{\varepsilon}}\right)\Bigg|_{\dot{\bar{\varepsilon}}} = -\left(\frac{d\ln\bar{\sigma}}{d\bar{\varepsilon}}\right)\Bigg|_{\dot{\bar{\varepsilon}},T} - \left(\frac{\partial\ln\bar{\sigma}}{\partial T}\right)\Bigg|_{\bar{\varepsilon},\dot{\bar{\varepsilon}}}\frac{dT}{d\bar{\varepsilon}} \tag{8.49}$$

It is instructive to determine the amount of quasi-stable postuniform deformation beyond $\bar{\varepsilon}_c$ that can be expected. This can be done by determining the strain $\bar{\varepsilon}$ at which the flow localization parameter α reaches an arbitrary critical value such as 5 or 10. It can be shown by use of Eqs. (8.44), (8.48), and (8.49) that the normalized strain $\bar{\varepsilon}/\bar{\varepsilon}_c$ at which flow localization may be expected to initiate can be found from the following equation by setting α equal to 5:

$$\frac{\bar{\varepsilon}}{\varepsilon_c} = \left(1 - \frac{\alpha m \rho c}{0.95(|\partial \bar{\sigma}/\partial T|)|_{\bar{\varepsilon},\dot{\bar{\varepsilon}}}}\right)^{-1} \tag{8.50}$$

From Eq. (8.50), it can be seen that a large m and a large ρc tend to increase the amount of quasi-stable deformation and a large $(|\partial \sigma/\partial T|)|_{\bar{\varepsilon}\dot{\bar{\varepsilon}}}$ tends to decrease it. A 1006 steel with a small $\partial \bar{\sigma}/\partial T = 625$ kPa/°C can be expected to undergo large quasi-stable deformation prior to shear band initiation at $\alpha = 5$, whereas quenched and tempered 4340 steel with $\partial \bar{\sigma}/\partial T = 1925$ kPa/°C can be expected to form shear bands almost immediately after $\bar{\varepsilon}_c$ is exceeded [8.13]. As was seen in chap. 7, much localized flow occurs in extrusion (see Fig. 7.17).

8.2.10 Axisymmetric, Open-Die Extrusion Forging —an Upper-Bound Approach

Prior to the analysis of the more complex closed-die forging operation, it may be helpful to consider the simpler, axisymmetric extrusion(spike)-forging process as shown in Fig. 8.37, which is classified as an open-die forging process, since no lateral confinement other than by friction and no three-dimensional confinement of the metal is realized, and also since no flash is formed. As shown in Fig. 8.37, in this problem a cylindrical workpiece is forged in its axial direction between two flat parallel overhanging dies, the top one of which contains a

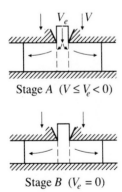

Stage A $(V \leq V_e < 0)$

Stage B $(V_e = 0)$

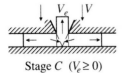

Stage C $(V_e \geq 0)$

FIGURE 8.37
Axisymmetric extrusion forging showing the metal flow and velocity fields for three states A, B, and C [8.14].

central, circular hole. This type of ring-extrusion forging involves symmetric flow about an axis called *axisymmetric flow* as opposed to flow in a plane, called *plane-strain flow*.

If the size of the central hole is small and the friction is low, the deformation may be considered to occur in three stages, *A*, *B*, and *C*, having velocity and metal flow fields as shown in Fig. 8.37(*a*). The velocity fields and the metal flow fields are essentially the same for each of the three stages. The velocity field determines the instantaneous velocity of small volume elements, both in direction and magnitude. The streamlines of the velocity field designate those lines which have velocity vectors as tangents. The actual paths of volume elements traversed during deformation are called *path lines* or *flow lines*. The parameters involved with the three stages are shown in Fig. 8.38.

During the initial stage of compression, especially when the frictional constraint at the die-workpiece interface is small or negligible and the configuration and dimensions of the die are not favorable, extrusion of the material through the central hole of the upper die does not take place. As a matter of fact, the total height of an initial, central projection as expressed by the H/H_0 ratio decreases. In other words, a disc without a projection in the initial stages of compression in stages *A* and *B*, behaves much as though the hole was not there. In stage *B*, the current-to-initial height ratio of the top of an existing central hole extrusion H/H_0 levels off, and then increases again in stage *C*. Although the H/H_0 ratio or H/H_0 percent decreases during deformation in stage *A*, the net extruded height, $H - h$, increases monotonically throughout the deformation

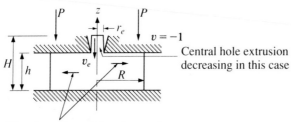

Direction of metal flow (stage *A*)

(*a*) $v_e \le 0$

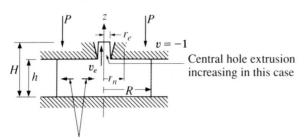

Direction of metal flow (stage *C*)

(*b*) $v_e \ge 0$

FIGURE 8.38
Two modes of deformation for extrusion forging: (*a*) no-extrusion mode when μ is small or negligible and when $v_e < 0$, and (*b*) extrusion mode when μ is large and $v_e > 0$ [8.14].

process, as can be seen in Fig. 8.39(a), in which the relative change in height of the extrusion is plotted against the relative reduction in flange height.

A number of different approaches may be used to deal with this problem depending on what information is desired. The upper-bound approach is presented here to establish the relationship between the friction of the interface and the changes in the shape of the workpiece.

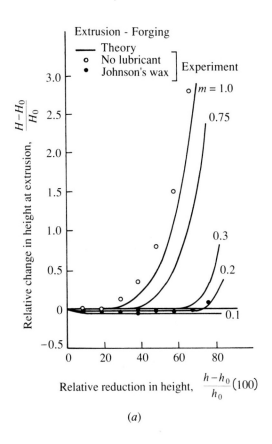

(a)

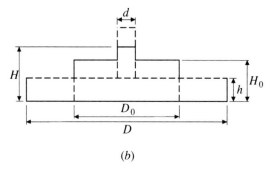

(b)

FIGURE 8.39
(a) Relative change in height of the central-hole extrusion as a function of the relative reduction in the flange height. (b) Nomenclature of the total height of the extrusion H, and of the initial and current height of the flange H_0 and h, respectively. ((a) Y. Saida, C. H. Lee, and S. Kobayashi, "Some Aspects of Friction in Forging Problems", in Material Technology I, II Interamerican Conf. on Materials Technology, ASME, Aug. 1970.)

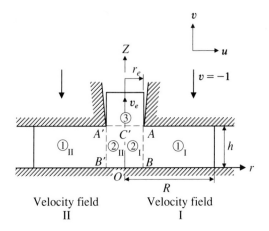

Velocity field II   Velocity field I

FIGURE 8.40
Two types of velocity fields assumed in extrusion forging, type I and type II, involving three workpiece zones 1, 2, and 3 [8.14].

The theoretical analysis presented here after Jain et al. [8.14] uses an assumed velocity field, which approximates the actual flow of the material during compression, even though the field contains velocity discontinuities. The workpiece is divided into three zones, 1, 2, and 3, as shown in Fig. 8.40. Two types of velocity fields, I and II, are considered here. In both types, the radial and axial velocity components, u_1 and v_1, in zone 1 are defined by

$$u_1, I = u_1, II = \frac{1}{2} h \left[r - (1 - v_e) \frac{r_e^2}{r} \right]$$

and   (8.51)

$$v_1, I = v_1, II = -\frac{1}{h} z$$

for a unit downward velocity of the upper die, that is, $v = 1$, where r and r_e are the instantaneous radius in zone 1 and the radius of the central-hole extrusion, respectively, and h is the current height of the flange. v_e is the vertical velocity of the central-hole extrusion. The parameters of the velocity equations are given in Fig. 8.40. In zone 2, the velocity components for the type I field are

$$u_1, I = -\frac{r_e}{2h} v_e \quad \text{and} \quad v_2, I = \frac{r_e}{2h} (v_e) \left(\frac{z}{r} \right)$$ (8.52)

In zone 2, the velocity components for the type II velocity field are

$$u_2, II = -\frac{v_e}{2h} r \quad \text{and} \quad v_2, II = \frac{v_e}{2h} z$$ (8.53)

Zone 3 is assumed to move as a rigid body with an axial component of v_e. The boundaries between the zones, that is, AB and AO for type I velocity field and $A'B'$ and $A'C'$ for the type II field, represent surfaces across which the tangential velocity components are discontinuities. For the extrusion mode of deformation given in Fig. 8.38(b), when $v_e > 0$, the neutral cylindrical surface of radius r_n, at which the radial velocity component u is zero, appears in zone 1. The neutral radius r_n in this case is given by

$$r_n = \sqrt{1 + v_e}(r_e) \tag{8.54}$$

where v_e is the upward velocity and r_e is the radius of the central-hole extrusion, respectively.

The total forging load or force for a unit downward die velocity, $v = -1$, is equal to the total energy dissipation rate, which can be obtained by adding (1) the deformation energy rate in zones 1 and 2, (2) the frictional energy dissipation rate at the die-workpiece interface, and (3) the energy rate due to the velocity discontinuities.

With reference to Fig. 8.40, the deformation energy rates, $\dot{E}_1$ and $\dot{E}_2$, in zones 1 and 2, respectively, are given by

$$\dot{E}_1 = 2\pi \int_0^h dz \int_{r_e}^R \bar{\sigma} \dot{\varepsilon} r \, dr \tag{8.55}$$

and

$$\dot{E}_2 = \int\int \bar{\sigma} \dot{\varepsilon} 2\pi r \, dr \, dz \tag{8.56}$$

where $\bar{\sigma}$ = the effective flow stress of the material
$\dot{\varepsilon}$ = effective strain rate = $\sqrt{\frac{2}{3}(\dot{\varepsilon}_r^2 + \dot{\varepsilon}_\theta^2 + \dot{\varepsilon}_z^2 + \frac{1}{2}\dot{\gamma}_{rz}^2)}$

The frictional energy dissipation rate $\dot{E}_{f0}$, due to friction at the top die-workpiece interface over the region $r_e \leq r \leq R$ can be expressed by

$$E_{f0} = m \int_{r_e}^R k|\Delta u| 2\pi r \, dr \tag{8.57}$$

where m is the shear friction factor, k is the shear flow strength $\sigma/\sqrt{3}$ of the material, and Δu is the relative radial velocity at the interface. Δu has two solutions for $v_e \leq 0$ and $v_e > 0$.

The frictional energy dissipation rate $\dot{E}_{f0}$, due to friction at the bottom die-workpiece interface over the region $0 \leq r \leq r_e$ for the type I velocity field and over the region $r_e \leq r \leq R$ for the type II velocity field, is given by

$$\dot{E}_{fc} = \frac{m\pi k}{h}\left(\frac{|v_e|r_e^3}{n}\right) \tag{8.58}$$

where h = the current height of the flange of the forging
$n = 2$ for the type I velocity field and 3 for the type II velocity field and the other parameters are defined above

The energy dissipation rate $\dot{E}_{sa}$ along the discontinuity AB is

$$\dot{E}_{sa} = \frac{\pi\bar{\sigma}}{\sqrt{3}} r_e\left(1 + \frac{v_e}{2}\right)h \tag{8.59}$$

for the type I velocity field, and it is similar in form to the above relation for boundary $A'B'$ of the type II velocity field except that the factor $\frac{1}{2}$ is omitted from the v_e term.

The energy dissipation rate along AO in the type I velocity field is given by

$$\dot{E}_{sb} = 2\pi k \int_0^{r_e} |\Delta s| \frac{r\,dr}{\cos\theta} \tag{8.60}$$

where $|\Delta s| = \frac{1}{2}|v_e| \sqrt{1 + \left(\frac{r_2}{h}\right)^2}$

θ = angle of the slope of $AO = \tan^{-1}(h/r_e)$.

The energy dissipation rate along $A'C'$, which appears after the central projection is formed, for the type II velocity field is given by

$$\dot{E}_{a0} = \frac{\pi\bar{\sigma}}{\sqrt{3}} \cdot \frac{1}{3} \frac{|v_e|r_e}{h} \tag{8.61}$$

As stated previously, the total energy dissipation rate, from which the total forging load or force for a unit downward die velocity is calculated, is the sum of the above energy terms for the type I and for the type II velocity fields. Since these two equations for the load or force are rather involved, they will not be presented here [8.14].

After the variables and parameters in the above equation are established or evaluated, the forging load or force can be calculated. Also the unknown parameter v_e can be determined, so that the total energy dissipation rate becomes a minimum. Once this parameter is known, the velocity field can be defined completely at any configuration during the operation.

On the basis of the above theoretical analysis, the effect of friction and of the hole size on the total height of the extrusion, as expressed in terms of the ratio of the current total height to the initial total height in percent, H/H_0 percent, as a function of the percent relative reduction of the flange height to the initial total height, $(H_0 - h)/H_0$, is shown in Figs. 8.41 and 8.42. Also, the effect of the workpiece size on the total height is shown in Fig. 8.43. It should be noted here that the initial stage, stage A, is not detected in term of the net extruded height $(H - H_0)$ as shown in Fig. 8.39, in which the relative change is monotonic throughout. In spite of the assumptions made in this analysis, the dimensional changes predicted theoretically are very close to those observed experimentally, as will be discussed subsequently. It should also be pointed out, however, that the assumptions must be made carefully and other judgments made on the basis of experience in order to get accurate results.

At the start of the forging operation, H_0 is equal to h and the total height H is equal to the initial height H_0. Thus, in Fig. 8.41 the reduction in flange height plotted on the abscissa starts at $(H_0 - h)/H_0 \times 100 = 0$, while on the ordinate at $H/H_0 \times 100 = 100$. When the reduction is still small, for example <15 percent for $m = 1$, the frictional constraint at the die-workpiece interface is relatively small and extrusion through the central hole of the upper die does not occur; therefore, the height of the apparent extrusion decreases with a reduction in the

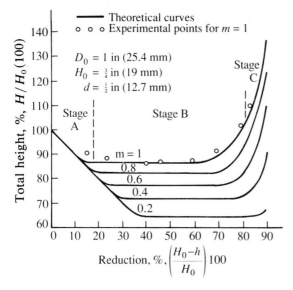

FIGURE 8.41
Theoretical effect of friction on total height of the extrusion in extrusion forging [8.14].

height of the forging. This is the reason why the initial portions of the curves in Figs. 8.41, 8.42, and 8.43 decrease for small reductions. When forging is continued, the frictional constraint increases and extrusion through the hole begins. The flat portions of the curves indicate that further reduction in height is accompanied simultaneously by an increase in the height of the extrusion of the same magnitude, thereby causing the total height to remain constant. Frictional constraint increases

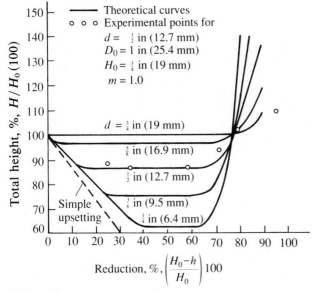

FIGURE 8.42
Theoretical effect of the hole size on the total height of the extrusion in extrusion forging [8.14].

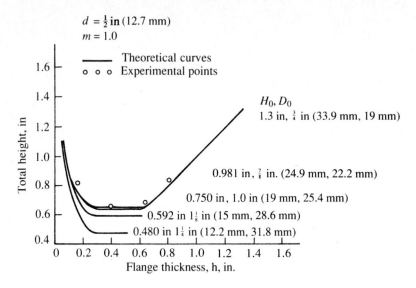

FIGURE 8.43
Theoretical effect of the billet size on the total height of the extrusion in extrusion forging [8.14].

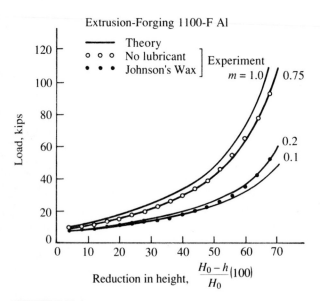

FIGURE 8.44
Comparison of the theoretical and experimental results of the load-displacement relationship in extrusion forging. (*Y. Saida, C. H. Lee, and S. Kobayashi, "Some Aspects of Friction in Forging Problems", in Material Technology I, II Interamerican Conf. on Materials Technology, ASME, Aug. 1970.*)

significantly with further forging, and the height of extrusion through the hole increases much faster than the reduction of the flange. This phenomenon occurs, for example, in Fig. 8.41 at about 70 percent reduction for $m = 1$.

Figure 8.44 gives a comparison of the theoretical and experimental compression load-displacement relationship for the extrusion forging of 1100-F aluminum with no lubricant and with a wax as a lubricant. It is seen that the friction factor for the lubricated condition is what might be expected, but for nonlubricated condition $m = 0.75$, which is above the limiting value of, say, 0.577. The value of m estimated from the geometrical shape is even higher ($m > 1$) as can be seen in Fig. 8.41, which would indicate that for high frictional constraint the mathematical model to predict the geometrical changes deviates more as friction increases.

In the experimental work done to check the validity and applicability of the theoretical analysis, the effect of the following variables as defined in Fig. 8.45 were investigated:

1. Degree of deformation—up to 90 percent reduction in the flange thickness
2. Forging speed—low speed 0.07 ft/s (0.0213 m/s) and high speed 15-50 ft/s (4.6–15.2 m/s), which are equivalent to nominal low and high strain rate ranges of 1 s^{-1} to $10^{2.5} \text{ s}^{-1}$ respectively
3. Frictional conditions—poor (dry) to good lubrication (Copaslip, a mixture of Cu and Pb powder in a bentone)
4. Workpiece initial aspect ratio range—$H_0/D_0 = 1.78$ to 0.38
5. Extrusion hole diameter, d, range—$\frac{1}{4}$ in (6.35 mm) to $\frac{7}{8}$ in (22.23 mm)
6. Extrusion hole draft angle—$q = 0$ and 5 degrees, respectively
7. Extrusion hole corner radius—$s = 0$ and $\frac{1}{4}$ in (6.35 mm)

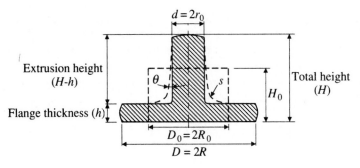

$$\text{Reduction} \quad \% = \frac{H_0 - h}{H_0} \times 100, \quad \theta = \text{taper angle}$$

$$\text{Total height} \quad \% = \frac{H}{H_0} \times 100$$

FIGURE 8.45
Nomenclature used for the experimental forging-extrusion operation. Note that although a flange is formed, no flash as such is formed [8.14].

To reduce the amount of testing, the effect of each variable was compared to the results obtained for a given set of conditions. The value of the variables for the datum condition are as follows: $H_0 = 20$ mm (0.75 in), $D_0 = 25.5$ mm (1.0 in), $d = 12.7$ mm (0.50 in), θ and $s = 0$, and high speed was used with no lubrication.

In general, the experimental curves agreed with the theoretical curves as shown in Figs. 8.41, 8.42, and 8.43. The experimental results for the datum condition only appear in the above figures as open circles. As can be seen in Fig. 8.41, for the datum condition the total height was reduced by about 12 percent up to about 30 percent flange reduction in stage A. In stage B, from 30 percent to 70 percent flange reduction, the total height remained constant, and beyond 70 percent reduction in stage C, the total height increased. The experimental results taken in conjunction with Fig. 8.41 appear to be consistent with those obtained by theoretical analysis.

As indicated by the theoretical curves in Fig. 8.42 and also by the experimental results relating to it, the reduction in the extruded hole size d, for a constant workpiece height, showed the following effects:

1. Stage A increases and stage B decreases with hole reduction. Stage A vanishes at 20 mm ($\frac{3}{4}$ in) hole size
2. In stage C, the curves cross each other. The total height for the experimental data appears to be a maximum for hole sizes of 10 to 30 mm ($\frac{3}{8}$ to $\frac{3}{4}$ in).

As can be seen in Fig. 8.43, in general, the taller the initial cylinder, i.e., the higher the aspect ratio, the greater the total height for a given flange thickness, h. In case of the shorter cylinders, i.e., those with $H_0/D_0 = 0.526$ and 0.384, stage C is absent.

It is concluded from this presentation that, in order to achieve a maximum amount of extrusion with a minimum load and energy, a workpiece with a high aspect ratio should be used in conjunction with no lubricant and with a hole in the upper die that has a generous radius at the bottom and a taper as shown on the forging in Fig. 8.45. The maximum loads and energies are seen to be solely dependent upon the annular flange area surrounding the extruded portion of the workpiece, and they show a strong correlation with the axisymmetric upsetting of an equivalent simple cylinder. The foregoing conclusion should supply a clue as to what should be expected in initial stages of the closed-die forging of a similar part.

8.2.11 Upper-Bound Elemental Technique [8.15]

8.2.11.1 INTRODUCTION. A knowledge of metal flow in forging processes is of importance, so that the optimum size and shape of the billet (slug, multiple) can be determined, and the material waste and the power required can be minimized by proper preform design.

A generalized technique for the prediction of the load and metal flow in extrusion forging is presented here. The method is based on the upper-bound elemental technique (UBET) and simulates the process in an incremental way similar to the kinematic element method discussed in Section 4.3.5. The upper-bound technique, despite its simplifications, offers useful predictions of load requirements, and it should be possible to extend the method to accommodate flow prediction in single and compound metal flow problems. A computer program has been written in order to simulate the process in incremental steps via a computer graphics terminal [8.15].

The concept of generalized elements, consisting of three basic elements, as shown in Fig. 8.46, is used here. Each element is treated independently using the parallel velocity field and allowing the flow of any magnitude or direction on all boundaries of the element. (This concept of basic elements is also used in conjunction with closed-die forgings in the next chapter.)

The velocity across the boundary is assumed to be both constant and uniform along the region surface. On the other hand, when a cylindrical extrusion forging is considered, and the division is achieved, the generated elemental rings are connected together with surfaces of velocity discontinuity where a continuous velocity field over the cross section is obtained. This field ensures a smooth transition of flow and satisfies volume constancy through any line of the imposed orthogonal mesh. The forging power is then obtained by summation of the shear losses along the discontinuities, the external friction losses at the die-billet interface, and the deformation energy generated over the deforming volume. The basic elements used in this analysis are shown in Fig. 8.46(a), (b), and (c). Regions (d) and (e) are treated following the same procedure. The difference between (b), (c), and (d), (e) types of triangular rings is found to be in the difference of the shear losses with their neighbors.

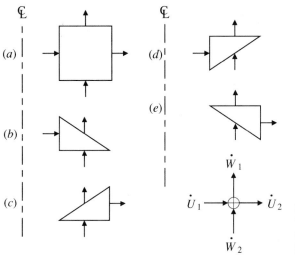

FIGURE 8.46
The basic generalized elements consisting of three basic elements [8.15].

The upper-bound technique has been used to give good approximations to the forging power of a given configuration by choosing a velocity field which may become similar to the actual one. In order to obtain the best velocity field, which gives a lower upper-bound load and describes the actual flow, some considerations of the physical nature of the process need to be imposed.

From the following it will be seen that the proposed technique is valid for metal flow prediction, and it is in agreement with the criterion that material tends to flow in the direction which requires minimum power.

8.2.11.2 INCREMENTAL SOLUTION. A computer simulation technique has been developed, in which the forging process, from start to finish, is analyzed in an incremental manner [8.15]. To maintain continuity in the simulation, the initial dimensions of the process are given through a set of coordinates which describes the cavity outlines, the size, and the position of the billet at the instant when the process begins. The billet may take any preform shape with straight line contours describing its cross section. The other process parameters such as the friction factor at the die-billet interface, the flow stress, and the die velocity are considered to be constant. Variable flow stress due to strainhardening and to strain rate effects could also be introduced if the relevant constitutive equation is known. Therefore, the effect of the preform (billet) on the forging load can be studied and the required number of stages for a forming process can be investigated. In order to maintain continuous simulation of the process the shape coordinates at any stage will be linked together with straight lines. The billet coordinates are then fed into an automatic subdividing technique, written specifically for such type of process to achieve an acceptable subdivision at each stage and successful incrementation from one stage to another. After the elemental subdivision is generated the number and position of the free boundaries are identified and the velocity across them is obtained. However, when the number of those boundaries is greater than the total number of equations of the imposed conditions of compressibility on each element, the difference gives the number of surfaces with undefined velocities. These are given approximate initial values. In order to cause plastic deformation, the forging load P may be expressed as

$$P = \frac{1}{\dot{u}} (\dot{E}_i + \dot{E}_s + \dot{E}_f) \tag{8.62}$$

where $\dot{u}$ = ram velocity
  $\dot{E}_i$ = the internal rate of deformation energy
  $\dot{E}_s$ = the energy rate required to overcome shear losses along the discontinuities
  $\dot{E}_f$ = the energy rate required to accommodate friction forces at the die-billet interface

Minimum load is obtained by optimizing the velocity field with respect to those undefined velocities.

After successful optimization is achieved, the resultant velocity field determines the mode of deformation at that stage. The velocity across the free boun-

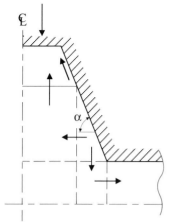

FIGURE 8.47
Metal flow across the free boundary during extrusion forging
[8.15].

daries defines the direction and the amount of flow per unit time across the surfaces. For a unit time increment, such velocity will represent the admissible displacement field of the free boundaries for material flow in a cavity of constant area. When the cavity area is decreasing, the flow is directed to follow the surface of the tool as shown in Fig. 8.47, where the material is extruded through the die with a draft angle of α. The procedure is applied to all the free boundaries of the shape under consideration. Therefore, the displacement field is defined, and the material is advanced through to fill the cavities in proportion to the degree of flow in each direction. The billet volume is maintained constant considering that, in axisymmetric forgings, the axial flow is proportional to the axial displacement while the radial flow is a function of the radial position of the surface. The velocity field once established, remains unchanged for a small increment of time during which the displacement field advances through the billet. The obtained shape coordinates are passed to the next increment and connected with straight lines. The incremental procedure flowchart is illustrated in Fig. 8.48.

8.2.11.3 EXTRUSION-FORGING PROCESS. As discussed in the previous subdivision, the extrusion-forging process is a compound flow process where the material may flow radially through the gap between the upper and lower die and/or extrude into the cavities as shown in Fig. 8.40.

The effects of the billet and die shape on the metal flow obtained by Jain have been presented in the previous subsection [8.14]. His results, together with the theoretically predicted results using the incremental technique with different frictional conditions, are shown in Fig. 8.49, showing good agreement. It can be seen that the radial flow takes place as the process is started and the total billet height decreases. At this stage the material deforms radially including the metal under the punch face, so that the total height of the component decreases considerably. However, this stage ends when the energy required to overcome the frictional forces at the die-billet interface become greater than that for the

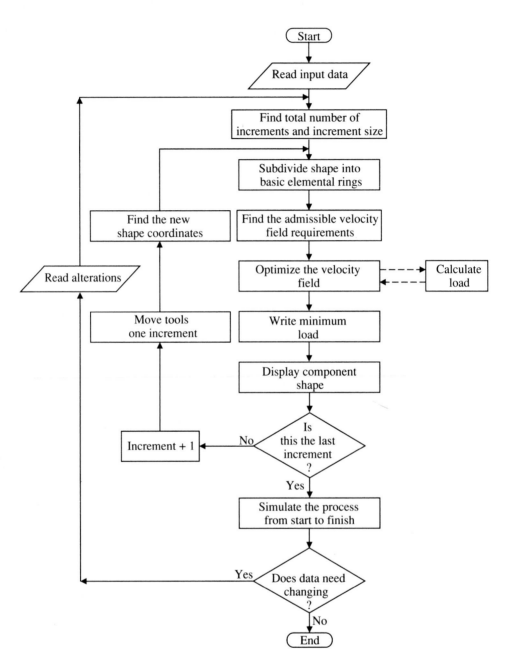

FIGURE 8.48
Flowchart for the incremental procedure [8.15].

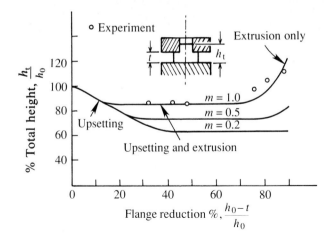

FIGURE 8.49
Theoretical and experimental results for metal flow in extrusion-forging. (Compare to Fig. 8.4.1.) [8.15].

material to extrude through the die. At this point, the extrusion starts and the total height remains constant as the process proceeds, thus indicating that both upsetting and extrusion are occurring. A point may also be reached at which the radial flow stops, and the extrusion continues.

With the aid of a visual display, this incremental technique may be used as a method of bridging the gap between the design and the production processes. Several cavities and preform boundaries can be examined and modified as needed to optimize the process.

Lubrication, which is a very important topic, has been mentioned several times in the foregoing. It will finally be discussed in the next section.

8.3   LUBRICATION IN METALWORKING PROCESSES

8.3.1   Introduction

Lubrication for metalworking is usually classified as (1) hydrodynamic, (2) boundary, (3) extreme pressure, and (4) solid film, although the distinction between the classes is not always clear.

Commercial lubricants may also be classified into two broad categories: (1) wet and (2) dry.

Wet lubricants include

1. Pure vegetable or mineral oil
2. Oils with fatty acids and extreme pressure additives
3. Oil, or water-based solid-phase lubricants

Dry lubricants include

1. Solid-phase lubricants carried in volatile solvents
2. Polymeric materials
3. Waxes

In hydrodynamic lubrication a liquid lubricant such as mineral oil may be "dragged" into the interface between workpiece and die by their rapid relative motion such as in wiredrawing and extrusion, thereby effecting a full separation between them. Some lubricants such as fatty acids like oleic that form solid metallic soaps with the metal, are remarkably effective as very thin films. Since under certain conditions they are worn away, they are called *boundary lubricants*. Some of these lubricants are compounds that contain S, Cl, and P, such as chlorinated paraffin (50% Cl), and can withstand very high pressures during operation and are called *extreme pressure lubricants*. Any solid film, that has a lower shear strength than the metallic workpiece, can be used as a solid lubricant such as copper, lead, graphite, molybdenum disulphide (MoS_2) (trade name Molykote).

Some of the functions of a good lubricant in metalworking are (1) reduce friction, (2) reduce die wear, (3) prevent metal pickup on the tool surfaces or seizing, (4) provide thermal insulation between the workpiece and the die surface in order to prevent excessive heat loss of the former and excessive heating of the latter, (5) cool the workpiece in some cases to prevent overheating of the workpiece due to the heat generated during working, and (6) control surface finish of the workpiece.

Some of the requirements of a lubricant in metalworking are (1) they must withstand the working conditions of pressure and temperature, (2) they must not deteriorate in service and storage, (3) they must be easy to apply and remove and not leave an objectionable residue, and (4) they must be safe, nontoxic, and not otherwise objectionable for use.

Since the cost of the dies is 10 to 20 percent of the cost of the forgings, lubrication is an important factor in hot forging and similar processes.

8.3.2 Evaluation of Friction and Lubricity

The ring compression test can provide a sensitive indication of the frictional conditions of the end-faces of the ring or hollow cylinder. This test can therefore be used to determine the coefficient of friction μ or the friction shear factor m between surfaces and can also be used to evaluate lubricants. Probably the correlation for the effectiveness of the lubricant in the ring test and that for the service application will depend on whether or not the same mode of lubrication applies.

As was explained in the discussion of the ring test, when a short, hollow cylinder is compressed axially between flat, parallel, rigid platens, the diameter of the hole may instantaneously increase, decrease, or remain constant as shown in Fig. 3.44 according to the amount of frictional constraint imposed by the platen-cylinder interface. Under frictionless conditions, the diameter of the hole increases proportionately to the outer diameter and the cylinder compresses as would the corresponding portion of a solid cylinder. With an increase in friction, the rate of expansion of the hole decreases and eventually the compressive circumferential or hoop stress developed at the inner surface of the hole is sufficient to cause the hole to contract.

Based on some important and analytical work by others, Hawkyard and Johnson [8.16], derived straightforward equations establishing the relationship between the coefficient of friction μ and the change of the inside or bore diameter ΔD_i, with the percent axial reduction of the cylinder ΔH. The derived values of the percentage change in the internal diameter may be plotted against the percentage axial compression for convenient values of μ or m between the limits of $\mu = 0.577$ ($m = 1$) and $\mu = m = 0$ as shown in Fig. 8.50. The constraint of $\mu = 0.577$ ($m = 1$) is, of course, for the condition for which sticking friction occurs and no relative motion occurs at the interface and shearing occurs in the subsurface of the softer material in which the frictional shear stress is equal to the shear stress of the ring material or

$$\tau_i = m\tau_0 = \mu\frac{\bar{\sigma}}{\sqrt{3}} \tag{8.63}$$

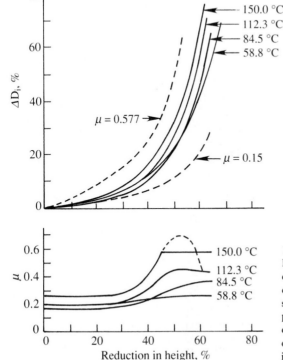

FIGURE 8.50
Ring compression test results at four die temperatures spray lubricated with colloidal graphite for EN8 (AISI 1040) steel at 1100°C (2012°F) showing (a) percentage decrease in internal diameter, and (b) Coulomb coefficient of friction versus percentage reduction in height [8.18].

In the above derivation, it is assumed that μ or m remains constant over the interface and that there is no nonuniform distortion or barreling of the cylinder. Since the theoretical calculations agree generally quite well with various experimental results reported, the curves in Fig. 8.51 will be used to estimate μ and m in this textbook.

Figure 8.52 gives the typical curves for the evaluation of the relative lubricity by means of the ring test of certain selected lubricants, having the descriptions given in Table 8.2 [8.17].

The rings used in the experimental work resulting in Fig. 8.52 were made of mild steel of the following initial dimensions: $D_0 = 2.00$ in (50.8 mm), $D_i = 1.00$ in (25.4 mm), and $H_0 = 0.667$ in (16.7 mm).

Rooks [8.18] performed ring compression tests using rings having the following dimensional ratio: $2:1:0.667$, which were made of EN8 (AISI 1040) steel and which were heated to 1100°C (2012°F). The dies were heated to temperatures whose means were 84.5°C (184°F), 112.4°C (234°F), and 150°C (302°F), and lubricated by spraying with a colloidal graphite suspension in water.

The results showed that as the bulk die temperature is increased, μ also increases as shown in Fig. 8.50. It was found that for any one mean temperature

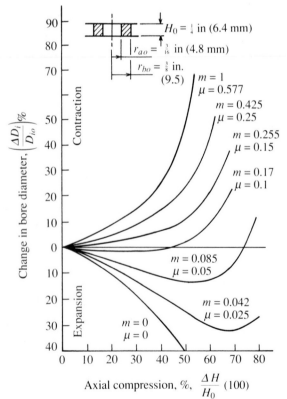

Axial compression, %, $\dfrac{\Delta H}{H_0}$ (100)

FIGURE 8.51
Theoretical curves for the variation of the internal diameter of a hollow cylinder with its reduction in height when compressed axially for certain selected values of μ or m for a ring ratio of 6:3:4 [8.16].

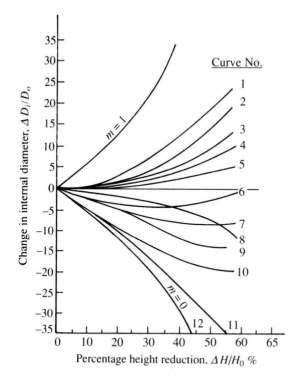

FIGURE 8.52
Relative lubricity of various typical lubricants used in metalforming obtained by use of the ring test. (See Table 8.2 for description of the lubricant.) [8.17].

group, the results could be expressed by the following empirical equation:

$$\log a(\Delta H) = a(\Delta D_i) + b \qquad (8.64)$$

where ΔH = percentage reduction in the height of the ring
ΔD_i = percentage decrease in the internal diameter of the ring
$a = 0.06$ to 0.07
$b = -0.003$ to -0.72, depending on the die temperature

TABLE 8.2

Curve no.	Description of lubricants
1	None
2	Chlorinated, paraffin in hydrocarbon containing 63 percent chlorine
3	Zinc phosphate
4	Rocol Ultracut (wet type)
5	Suspension of MoS_2 in a solvent with an epoxy bonding resin
6	Dry MoS_2 resin-bonded antiscuffing spray
7	Greasy, dry-type MoS_2 running-in spray
8	Wet type of lubricant with water-soluble soap
9	Zinc phosphate base with reactive sodium stearate
10	PTFE 0.012 in (0.30.mm) sheet
11	MoS_2, dry inorganic-bonded antiscuffing spray

In upset tests involving 1 in (25.4 mm) in diameter × 1.125 in (28.6 mm) long cylinders of the same material under similar conditions, it was concluded that an increase in the bulk die temperature caused an increase in the coefficient of friction and a decrease in the amount of metal sliding over the die, resulting in a decrease in wear with increase in the bulk die temperature.

As shown in Fig. 8.53, the application of a lubricant caused an increase in die wear, which decreased as it became less effective. The increase in die wear with the application of the lubricant was shown to be due to the increase in the amount of metal sliding over the surface of the die.

Male and Cockcroft [8.19] obtained an empirical system of curves, that are quite similar to the derived curves. They obtained their calibration curve for a range of μ of 0.055 to 0.57 and of deformation of 20 to 60 percent by use of a ring of a different material having a D_0 of 0.750 in (19.1 mm), a D_i of 0.375 in (9.5 mm), and an H_0 of 0.250 in (6.35 mm). This system of curves may be expressed by

$$\Delta D_i = a \ln \left(\frac{\mu}{0.055} \right) \tag{8.65}$$

where ΔD_i = the percentage decrease in the internal diameter of the ring
μ = Coulomb coefficient of friction
ΔH = the percentage decrease in the height of the ring

In Eq. (8.65), a is given by

$$\ln a = (0.44)(\Delta H) + 10.6 \tag{8.66}$$

Since μ cannot be conveniently calibrated by use of the derived relationships, μ (or m) may be either obtained graphically from Fig. 8.51 or calculated by use of the above empirical equation (8.65).

A computer program was developed at Battelle's Columbus Laboratories that simulates the ring-upsetting process for given friction shear factors m by including the bulging of the free surface [8.20]. Calibration curves generated by this program are shown in Fig. 8.54. This program can also be used to estimate the average flow stress of the ring material, provided that the forging load is

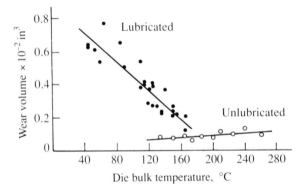

FIGURE 8.53
Effect of the bulk die temperature on the wear volume of H.50 steel spray lubricated with colloidal graphite and unlubricated [8.18].

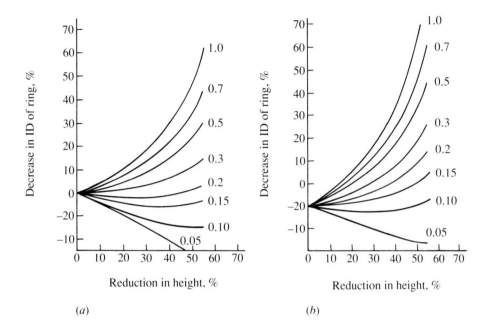

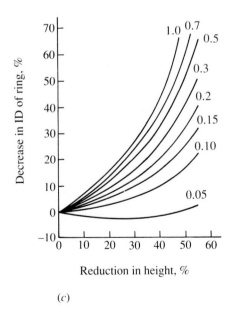

FIGURE 8.54
Theoretical calibration curves for upsetting rings with different OD:ID thickness ratios [8.20].

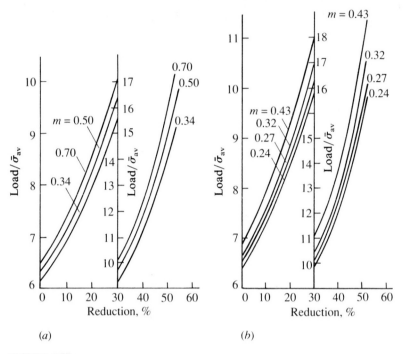

FIGURE 8.55

Load/$\bar{\sigma}_{av}$ data calculated at various shear factors m: (a) ring ratio $6:3:2$, and (b) ring ratio $6:3:1$. (Note the folded scale.) [8.20].

measured during the test. The ratio of the forging load to the average instantaneous flow stress $P/\bar{\sigma}_{av}$, as shown in Fig. 8.55, was calculated from a ring of $6:3:2$, $6:3:1$ and $6:3:0.5$ (not shown). (See also the ring test in Chap. 3.)

8.4 PROCESS MODELING OF OPEN-DIE FORGING

8.4.1 Introduction [8.21]

In recent years the need to conserve raw materials and to make manufacturing production more economical has led to the development of a scientific approach to the design and understanding of metalworking processes such as forging. This approach, being scientific in nature, depends not so much on the design rules and observations based on experience, but rather on the development of detailed mathematical and experimental models of the deformation process itself.

Such process models as mentioned above include a synthesis of information describing (1) the workpiece material and its properties, (2) the characteristics of the tooling-workpiece interface, and (3) the mechanics of plastic deformation in the particular process of interest.

The workpiece material model includes descriptions of the flow stress as a function of strain, strain rate, and temperature; the workability of the material;

and the effects of processing conditions on the final microstructure and service properties. The deformation model allows metal flow and forming loads to be predicted using mathematical techniques such as the upper-bound or finite element methods. These methods, when applied to actual metalworking processes, often rely on high-speed digital computers and peripheral graphics capabilities to perform actual process simulations and to present the final results.

Integration of the material model, the interface model, and the deformation model results in a system from which information on metal flow, defect development, and die loading can be derived.

These data, therefore, are useful tools in the design of dies and preforms (preforged workpiece shapes), in the prediction of final microstructure and properties in the finished part, and in the economics of alternate processing sequences. All of this analysis, design, and planning, can be done without actually constructing the necessary tooling, which is usually very costly and which may not be satisfactory in production of the desired part.

Examples of this approach in regard to a deformation model that predicts metal flow will be given for (1) the sidepressing of a cylindrical bar, and (2) spike forging.

8.4.2 Mathematical Modeling of Deformation [8.22]

Mathematical modeling has been applied successfully to metalworking processes by use of the finite element method (FEM) in addition to the upper-bound method. The major advantage of the FEM is its ability to generalize, i.e., it can be applied to a wide class of boundary-value problems without restrictions of the workpiece geometry or die shape. Rigid plastic and rigid viscoplastic materials have been used in the analyses (see Fig. 3.1) [8.21].

The general approach to mathematical modeling of plastic deformation to predict the manner of material flow and the distribution of effective strain in the workpiece follows.

The deformation of a body of volume V is characterized by the following field equations [8.22]:

1. *Equilibrium equation (body forces neglected)*

$$\sigma_{ij,j}n = 0 \tag{8.67}$$

where σ_{ij} is the stress component and the comma denotes the differentiation.

2. *Strain rate-velocity relation*

$$\dot{\varepsilon}_{ij} = \tfrac{1}{2}(v_{i,j} + v_{j,i}) \tag{8.68}$$

where $\dot{\varepsilon}_{ij}$ and v_i are the strain rate and velocity components, respectively.

3. *Constitutive relation*

$$\sigma'_{ij} = \frac{2\bar{\sigma}}{3\dot{\bar{\varepsilon}}}\dot{\varepsilon}_{ij} \tag{8.69}$$

where σ'_{ij} is the deviatoric stress component, and $\bar{\sigma}$ and $\dot{\bar{\varepsilon}}$ are defined by $\sqrt{(\frac{3}{2}\sigma'_{ij}\sigma'_{ij})}$ and $\sqrt{(\frac{2}{3}\dot{\varepsilon}_{ij}\dot{\varepsilon}_{ij})}$, respectively. The flow stress $\bar{\sigma}$, in general, is a function of total strain, strain rate and temperature.

4. Boundary condition

$$\sigma_{ij}n_i = F_j \text{ on } S_F \tag{8.70a}$$

$$v_i = U_i \text{ on } S_U \tag{8.70b}$$

$$|f_s| = \text{given, sign } (f_s) = -\text{sign } (\Delta v_s) \text{ on } S_C \tag{8.70c}$$

where σ_{ij} = stress tensor component
n_i = component of unit normal to the surface
F_j = prescribed boundary traction
S_F = portion of the surface on which F_i acts
v_i = velocity component
U_i = prescribed boundary velocity
S_U = portion of the surface on which U_i acts
f_s = frictional traction
Δv_s = slipping velocity
S_C = remainder of the surface where the frictional stress acts

The above field equations can be put into a variational functional such as is expressed by Eq. (4.184), for which the work function can be expressed by use of Eq. (4.186). When one substitutes Eq. (4.186) and the expression for the velocity component in the x_1 and x_2 directions (for the two-dimensional case) into an equation of the type (4.184), a linearized form of the variation functional Φ is obtained

$$\left[\frac{\partial \Phi}{\partial u_i}\right]_{u=u_0} + \left[\frac{\partial^2 \Phi}{\partial u_j\, \partial u_i}\right]_{u=u_0} \cdot \Delta u_j = 0 \tag{8.71}$$

Solving the above equation with respect to Δu_j, the node velocity increment, the forces at each node are obtained by an iterative process.

The above procedure corresponds to that given in the six steps summarized in Sec. 4.5.3, in which the continuum is divided into elements interconnected at a finite number of nodal points. The variational functional Φ is then approximated by a function of nodal point values. In the displacement method, these nodal point values are the displacement or velocity components.

The discretization of the variational problem is performed on the elemental level by approximating the functional with respect to the mth element by a function of the mth-element nodal point values. This approximation is accomplished by replacing the actual distribution with an approximation velocity distribution in each element. When an approximate operator is applied to the approximated velocities, the strain-rate components in the element are derivable and the stress-rate components can be expressed in terms of strain-rate components. For isotropic materials the stress-rate and strain-rate components are associated by the Levy-Mises equations (2.73) during continuous loading in the plastic region. The variational functional Φ, summing the functionals of sub-regions, is then approximated by the function of nodal point variables. Applying the variational principle to this approximating function results in simultaneous equations for the unknown velocity components at the nodes of the region in the form

$$K\dot{u} = \dot{R} \tag{8.72}$$

where $\dot{u}$ is the nodal point velocity vector, K is the stiffness matrix, and $\dot{R}$ is the equivalent nodal point force-rate vector. The solution of the simultaneous equations for the nodal point velocities and elemental distributions then provide the approximate solution to the actual velocity distribution. For mixed boundary conditions, where the velocity vectors over a part of the surface are described, the matrix equations for the unknown nodal point vectors are obtained by using the submatrices of the global stiffness matrix K [8.7].

8.4.3 Sidepressing of a Cylindrical Bar

Process-modeling techniques have been applied successfully to predict the localiz-ation of metal flow into shear bands as depicted by Figs. 8.18, 8.20, 8.33, 8.34, and 8.35. The predicted relative effective strain distribution as shown in the cross section of an isothermal sidepressed cylindrical bar of a Ti alloy is shown in Fig. 8.56. The effective strain is an indication of the degree of deformation. The rationale for the isostrain contour map and bulge profile in Fig. 8.21(a) can now be seen.

Figure 8.56 explains why the localized flow pattern or shear bands have the appearance that they do and why defects may occur in these regions.

8.4.4 Spike-Forging FEM Analysis [8.22]

Solutions of the spike-forging process were obtained by using the finite element method discussed in Chap. 4 and above. As may be recalled in the spike-forging process, a cylindrical billet is forged vertically in a die containing a central hole

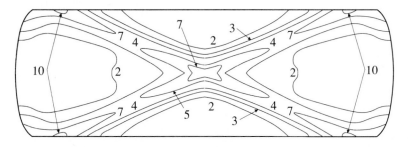

FIGURE 8.56
Specimen cross section and simulated metal flow for isothermal sidepressing of a bar of Ti-6Al-2Sn-4Zr-2Mo-0.1Si alloy. The starting microstructure was alpha Widmansätten, $T = 1675°F$ (913°C), and the strain rate $= 10\,\text{s}^{-1}$ (see Figs. 8.20 and 8.36) [8.21].

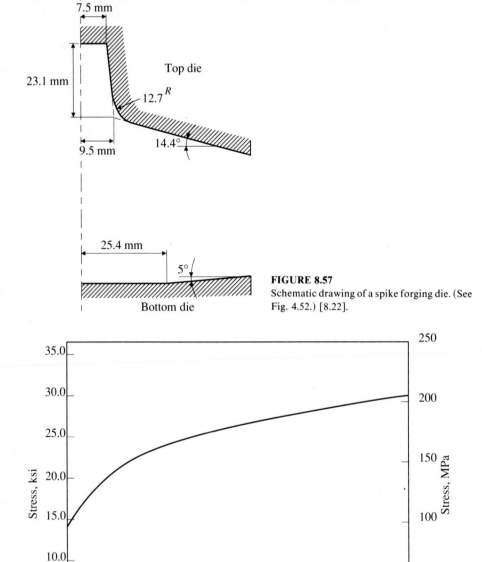

FIGURE 8.57
Schematic drawing of a spike forging die. (See Fig. 4.52.) [8.22].

FIGURE 8.58
Stress-strain rate relation of an $\alpha + \beta$ microstructure for a Ti-6242-0.1Si alloy at 954°C (1750°F) [8.22].

or cavity as shown in Fig. 8.57. This die is beginning to approach the geometry of the closed-impression dies to be discussed in the next chapter. The material flow, which is characterized by spike height variation, depends on the interface friction as well as on the geometries of the die and the billet used.

Analysis of isothermal spike forging was performed by Oh [8.22] for two different frictions, $m = 0.3$ and $m = 0.6$, which simulate lubricated and unlubricated hot-forging operations, respectively. The material at a temperature of 954°C (1750°F) was a Ti alloy having a stress-strain rate curve shown in Fig. 8.58. The

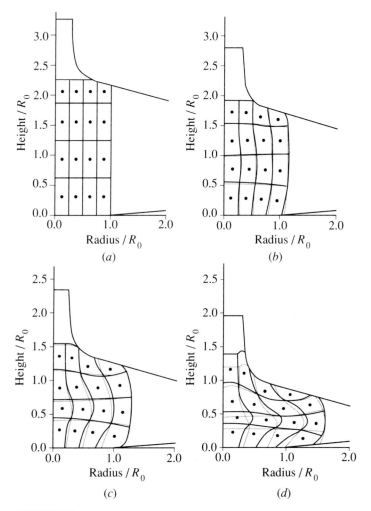

FIGURE 8.59
Calculated FEM grid distortions at die displacements of (a) $0.0H_0$, (b) $0.2H_0$, (c) $0.4H_0$, and (d) $0.58H_0$. Solid lines are for $m = 0.6$ and dashed lines are for $m = 0.3$. Units are multiples of the undeformed radius (see Fig. 4.53) where R_0 and H_0 are the initial workpiece radius (25.4 mm) and height (52.2 mm) respectively [8.22].

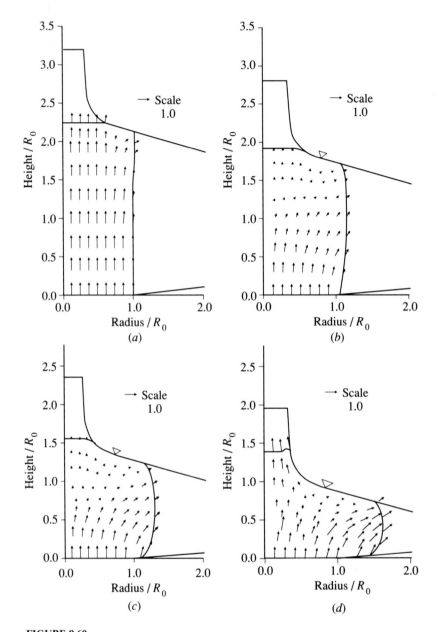

FIGURE 8.60
Relative velocity distributions at die displacements of (a) $0.0H_0$, (b) $0.2H_0$, (c) $0.4H_0$, and (d) $0.58H_0$ when $m = 0.6$. The symbol ∇ denotes the location of the neutral point [8.22].

shape and dimensions of the dies is shown in Fig. 8.57. The velocity of the upper die used for analysis was 25 mm/s (1.0 in/s), and the lower die was stationary.

Figure 8.59 shows the undeformed FEM grid used for analysis and the calculated grid distortions at the die displacements of 0.2, 0.4, and $0.58H_0$, with both frictional cases superimposed for comparison. (Since H_0 is the original height, the fractional values represent the aspect ratios.) As can be seen from Fig. 8.59, the solution shows that, at an early stage, the deformation is concentrated near the right upper corner of the workpiece where it touches the top die, while the rest of the workpiece undergoes virtually no deformation. Because of this concentration, folding of the top surface starts to take place during the early stage. As the deformation progresses, the deformation zone spreads throughout the workpiece, forming the side surface bulge. The material near the center of

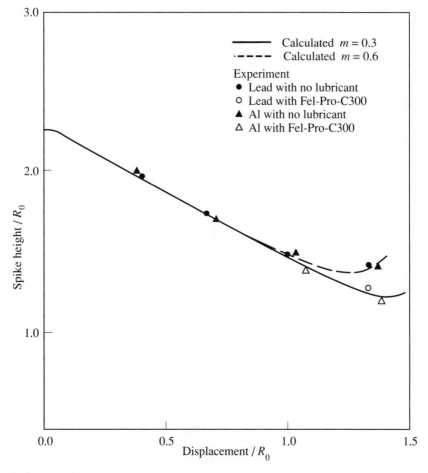

FIGURE 8.61
Variation of spike heights from the base line when $m = 0.3$ and $m = 0.6$ (compare to Figs. 8.41, 8.42, and 8.49) [8.22].

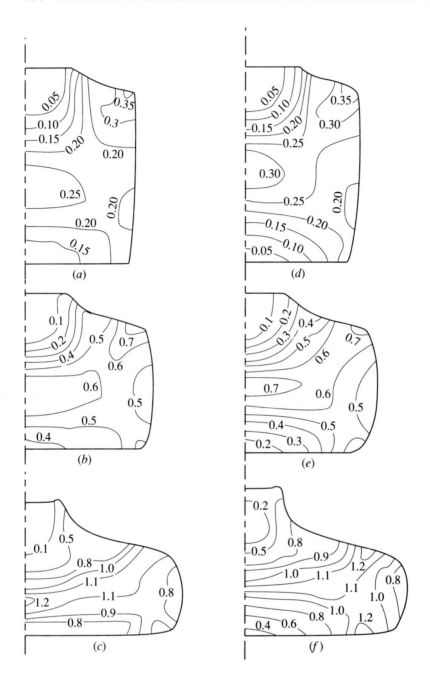

FIGURE 8.62
Effective strain distributions at die displacements of (a) $0.2H_0$, (b) $0.4H_0$, and (c) $0.58H_0$ when $m = 0.3$, and (d) $0.2H_0$, (e) $0.4H_0$, and (f) $0.58H_0$ when $m = 0.6$ (compare isostrain contours to those in Figs. 4.54 and 8.21) [8.22].

the upper surface virtually undergoes no deformation. The spike height is not affected by the friction during the early stages of deformation; however, the higher spike is formed with the higher friction, with the difference being largest at the largest displacement.

Figure 8.60 shows the local velocity distributions for die displacements of 0.02, 0.2, 0.4, and $0.58H_0$ and for $m = 0.6$. The velocities shown in the figure are relative quantities with respect to that of the upper die of V_D. At a displacement of $0.58H_0$, the relative velocity of the spike tip is about $1.25V_D$ when $m = 0.6$, and $0.465V_D$ when $m = 0.3$.

As can be seen from the relative velocity patterns, a part of the workpiece flows into the central cavity while the rest of the material flows radially. Because of these different directions of flow, a neutral point forms on the upper die-workpiece interface where the relative movement between the die and material becomes zero. The data at two frictions shows that the neutral point forms earlier for the higher friction and that its location is farther away from the center axis.

Figure 8.61 shows the change of spike height as a function of die displacement, which is in general agreement with experimental results.

In the finite element method the local information such as strains, stain rates, and stresses can be easily obtained. The information can be used not only to investigate the effect of flow stress on the overall deformation but also to predict defect formation in metalforming such as central bursts. Figure 8.62 shows the effective strain distribution for the example cite here. The figure shows that almost no deformation occurs near the spike tip with the highest strain concentration occurring along the band joining the upper right corner of the specimen and the middle of the height near the center. It should be noted that the strain gradient is higher for the higher friction and that the deformation is more uniform for the lower friction.

ACKNOWLEDGMENT

The material and most of the illustrations in this chapter were adapted from the references as indicated in the text and in the legends by the numbers of the references enclosed in square brackets pursuant to all copyrights.

REFERENCES

8.1. Tomlinson, A., and J. D. Stringer, "Spread and Elongation in Flat-Tool Forging," *J. Iron and Steel Inst.*, 1959, vol. 193, p. 157.

8.2. Schutt, A., "A Note on Spreading in Indenting," *Appl. Scientific Research, Sec. A*, 1960, vol. 9, p. 389.

8.3. Hill, R., "A General Method of Analysis for Metal-working Processes," *J. Mech. Phys. Solid*, 1963, vol. 11, p. 305.

8.4. Baraya, G. L., and W. Johnson, "Flat-bar Forging," *Proc. 5th Int. Conf. MTDR*, 1964, p. 449.

8.5. Lahaoti, G. D., and S. Kobayashi, "Flat-Tool Forging," *Proc. 2nd NAMRC II*, 1974, pp. 73–87.

8.6. DeGarmo, E. P., J. T. Black, and R. A. Kohser, *Materials and Processes in Manufacturing*, 6th ed., 1984, Macmillan Pub. Co., New York, p. 355.

8.7. Kobayashi, S., "Theories and Experiment on Friction, Deformation, and Fracture in Plastic Deformation Processes," *Proc. AIME: Metal Forming: Interrelation Between Theory and Practice,* A. L. Hoffmanner (ed.), Plenum Press, 1971, pp. 325–347.

8.8. Schroeder, W., and D. A. Webster, "Press-Forging Thin Sections: Effect of Friction, Area, and Thickness on Pressures Required," *Trans. ASME, J. of Applied Mech.,* vol. 71, pp. 289–294, 1949.

8.9. Bishop, J. F. M., "On the Effect of Friction on Compression Indentation Between Flat Dies," *J. Mech. and Phys. of Solids,* 1958, vol. 6, pp. 132–144.

8.10. Shaw, M. C. et al, "Friction Characteristics at Sliding Surfaces Undergoing Subsurface Plastic Flow," *MIT Report P-5,* pp. 101–17, June 1939.

8.11. Schey, J. A., *Introduction to Manufacturing Processes,* McGraw-Hill, 1977, pp. 108–111.

8.12. Wistreich, J. G., and A Shutt, "Theoretical Analysis of Bloom and Billet Forging," *J. Iron and Steel Inst.,* 1959, vol. 193, p. 161.

8.13. Semiatin, S. L., and J. J. Jonas, *Formability and Workability of Metals,* ASM, 1984, pp. 1–4, 31–32, 70–72, and 109–111.

8.14. Jain, S. C., A. N. Bramley, C. H. Lee, and S. Kobayashi, "Theory and Experiment in Extrusion Forging," *Proc. 11th Int. MTDR Conf.,* Sept. 1970, vol. B, Pergamon Press, 1970, pp. 1097–1115.

8.15. Osman, F. H., and A. N. Bramley, "Metal Flow Prediction in Forging and Extrusion Using UBET", in *Proc. of the 18th International Machine Tool Design and Research Conf.,* Sept., 1977, J. M. Alexander (ed.), Dept. of Mech. Engr., The Imperial College, London, Macmillan Press Ltd., pp. 51–59.

8.16. Hawkyard, J. B., and W. Johnson, "An Analysis of the Changes in Geometry of Short Hollow Cylinders During Axial Compression," *Int. J. Mech. Sci.,* 1967, vol. 9, no. 163, pp. 163–182.

8.17. Abdul, N. A., "Assessment of Lubrication for the Cold Extrusion of Steel," *Proc. 17th Inter. Mach. Tool Design and Res. Conf.,* S. A. Tobias (ed.), vol. 17, 1976, pp. 401–409.

8.18. Rooks, B. W., "The Effect of Die Temperature on Metal Flow and Die Wear During High-Speed Hot Forging," *Proc. 15th Inter. Mach. Tool Design and Res. Conf.,* S. A. Tobias and F. Koenigsberger, (eds.), vol. 15, 1974, pp. 487–494.

8.19. Male, A. T., and M. G. Cockcroft, "A Method for the Determination of the Coefficient of Friction of Metals under Conditions of Bulk Plastic Deformation," *Journal of the Institute of Metals,* vol. 93, pp. 38–46, 1964–65.

8.20. Douglas, J. R., and T. Altan, "Characteristics of Forming Presses: Determination and Comparisons," *Proc. 13th Int. Mach. Tool Design and Res. Conf.,* S. A. Tobias (ed.), pp. 535–545.

8.21. Semiatin, S. L., "Material Characteristics," in *Forging Handbook,* T. G. Byrer, S. L. Semiatin, and D. C. Vollmer (eds.), FIA/ASM, 1985, pp. 115–119.

8.22. Oh, S. I., "Finite Element Analysis of Metal Forming Processes with Arbitrarily Shaped Dies," *Inter. J. of Mech. Sci.,* 1982, Vol. 24, no. 8, pp 479–493.

PROBLEMS

8.1. A process of cogging or drawing out is performed on a large rectangular workpiece. The width and thickness of the piece are both 4 in. The bite is 2 in long and 0.5 in deep. (See Fig. 8.12.) The final width is 4.5 in. Calculate the new length of the workpiece as a result of one blow of the forging hammer.

8.2. Solve Prob. 8.1 by using Eq. (8.6) for calculating S.

8.3. A part is to be made of 410 stainless steel whose flow–stress-strain rate relationship is given by $\sigma_f = 140\dot{\varepsilon}^{0.08}$ for hot-working operations. A billet 75 mm in diameter and 70 mm in height is hot upset at 1050°C to a height of 20 mm. The speed of the press is 250 mm/s. Assuming no lubricant is used, calculate the press load (force) at the end of the stroke.

8.4. A stainless steel cylinder of 45 mm in diameter and 10 mm high is to be subjected to an axial pressure so as to obtain a diameter of 48 mm and a height of 6 mm. A lubricant is provided to reduce the coefficient of friction to $\mu = 0.1$. Calculate the required axial (1) pressure and (2) load (force) to perform this upsetting operation. Use the stress-strain relation $\sigma = 650\bar{\varepsilon}^{0.24}$ MPa.

8.5. It is desired to produce a flat pin from a square wire of an A302 stainless steel, whose original dimensions are 0.35 by 0.35 by 9 in long. 5 in of the 9 in long wire is flattened to a thickness of 0.10 and a width of 0.75 in. Determine by use of Fig. 8.30 the required load in kips when no lubricant is used. The stress-strain relation of the steel is given by $\bar{\sigma} = 190\bar{\varepsilon}^{0.3}$ ksi.

8.6. A relationship for an α parameter for bulging is similar to the one for flow localization as expressed by Eq. (8.45). If bulging occurs when α is of the order of 5, would a Ti alloy, in which $m = 0.134$, $\gamma' = 1.67$, have a tendency to bulge?

8.7. Determine the critical strain $\bar{\varepsilon}_c$ for flow localization of a SAE 1006 steel whose density is 7.86 g/cm^3, specific heat is 0.11 cal/g · C, strainhardening exponent n is 0.24, and the flow-stress-temperature gradient is 625 kPa/C.

8.8. By use of the same data as in Prob. 8.7, what would be the effective strain $\bar{\varepsilon}$ at which flow localization would occur for $\alpha = 5$ and $m = 0.01$?

CHAPTER

9

CLOSED-DIE
FORGING
PROCESSES
AND RELATED
OPERATIONS

9.1 INTRODUCTORY DESIGN AND ANALYSIS ASPECTS

As defined previously, closed-die forging as opposed to open-die forging is the term applied to all forging operations ultimately involving three-dimensional confinement and control.

In the course of the design of a part that may be produced by closed-die forging, the following steps may, in general, be followed:

1. The design of the part itself, which in many cases is a finished machined part such as a connecting rod for an internal combustion engine. This stage in the design process provides the required geometry and the necessary mechanical properties. The design may originally have been made with or without a forging in mind. With perhaps some redesign, the part may finally be made from a ductile (nodular) cast iron or even from a heavy metal stamping, for example, instead of a forging.
2. Once the decision is made to make the part by the hot-forging process, the finished forging and its dies are designed by the addition of the machining allowance and the necessary taper or draft so that the part may be readily removed from the die during the forging operation. At this stage, the forging

and its die are designed so as to fill the die cavity completely (by the addition of some extra metal that overflows to form the flash) and to forge the part without any defects such as folds or overlaps. The power and energy requirements for making the finished forging are also determined at this stage.

3. If the forging is complex at all, it may have to be made in stages, so that the necessary preform or blocker dies may have to be designed to distribute the metal adequately. The geometry of the forging slug (stock) or multiple is determined.

Most of the following discussion will be involved with steps (2) and (3) of the above and is usually referred to as the "design of the forging."

Closed-die forging at best is a very complex forming process from the point of view of the mechanics of deformation or of metal flow. It is difficult to analyze, because of such factors as nonsteady state and nonuniform metal flow, the variable interface friction, and the unsteady state of heat flow between the material being deformed and the dies, all of which present a real challenge to evaluation. Also, the mean strain rate and temperature are not constant during forging and vary from one zone of deformation to another, and in addition they change continuously as the deformation proceeds. Due to the value of the surface-to-volume ratio the heat loss from the flash occurs at a much greater rate than in the die cavity. Because of the difference in volume and in the incremental energy input, the heat generated in different zones is different.

There are four basic analytical approaches used in the analysis of the forging process involving different degrees of simplification: (1) various modifications of the elementary slab (equilibrium) method, which involves more experience and a greater amount of approximation; (2) the upper-bound method; (3) the slip-line field method; and (4) the finite element method (FEM), which is covered in the section on the finite element method. Although the main emphasis here will be on the application of the slab method, two examples of the upper-bound method will be presented. The slip-line field method requires a considerable amount of expertise and experience on the part of the designer and is not adaptable to a wide range of forgings, so it will not be discussed here.

The slab method is the most widely used method for closed-die forging. All of the foregoing methods have been computerized and are in the process of being refined. Three examples of computation using the slab technique will be discussed briefly later. One of these utilizes a programmable calculator, and the other a digital computer in the interactive mode.

The slab and upper-bound method will be considered here for the analysis of the forging process and in the design of an axisymmetric closed-die forging. In the presentation of the slab method, the work of Dean [9.1], Biswas and Rooks [9.2], Altan [9.3], and Altan and Fiorentino [9.4], among others, will be cited. In the presentation of the upper-bound method, the work of McDermott and Bramley [9.5] will be cited.

To be useful, the analysis of the forging process by any method must include such factors as the estimation of the maximum load required by the equipment,

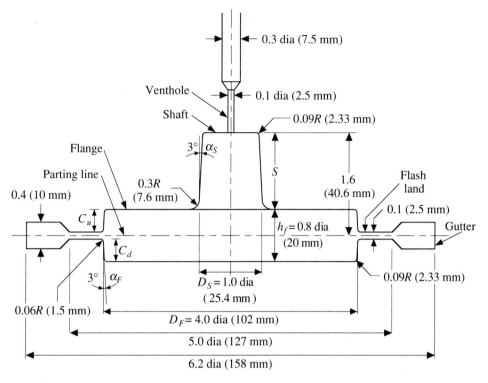

FIGURE 9.1
Drawing of the axisymmetric die cavity under discussion [9.41].

the maximum stress distribution on the surfaces of the dies, and the total energy necessary to complete the deformation. The stages of deformation and the load-displacement will be discussed first as applied to the closed-die forging of a circular, axisymmetric part such as would be forged by use of the die shown in Fig. 9.1. Approximately 65 percent of the parts being closed-die forged are circular.

The three main stages of deformation and the load-displacement curve during the forging cycle of such a part are shown in Fig. 9.2 as follows:

1. *Upsetting*, in which the forging slug is initially compressed resulting (*a*) in outward flow of metal to form the flange, and (*b*) inward and upward flow to extrude the boss or shaft, as was discussed in extrusion forging
2. *Die filling*, in which the lower cavity is essentially filled, except perhaps for the upper portion of the shaft, and the flash begins to form
3. *End of forging*, in which the dies are completely filled as the load and the pressure within the die cavity rapidly rises due to the restriction of the metal flow to form the colder, thinner flash with any excess metal flowing into the flash gap and gutter

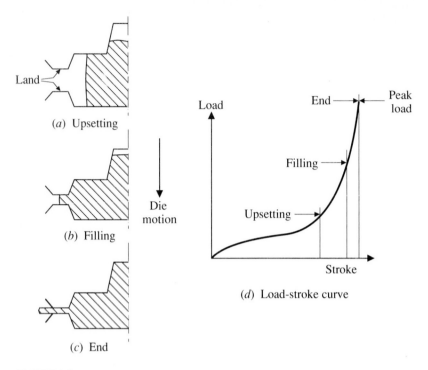

FIGURE 9.2
(*a*) to (*c*) Illustration of metal flow and (*d*) the load-stroke curve in forging with the die shown in Fig. 9.1 [9.41].

The purpose of the land of the die, as shown in Figs. 9.1 and 9.2, is to restrict the flow of metal into the gutter and thereby control the back pressure to the flow of metal in the die and thus promote the filling of the die. The longer the effective land and the thinner and colder the flash, the greater the back pressure.

It is important to keep the amount of flash formed to a minimum for two reasons: (1) excess flash increases the peak die loads as shown in Fig. 9.2 and therefore reduces die life, and (2) it increases the loss of material, which is economically significant. According to one estimate, on the average 50 percent of the total cost of forgings is made up of material cost, as shown in Fig. 9.3.

The material yield in closed-die forging can vary between 50 to 70 percent of the original workpiece material, with the average yield of 70 percent. A 10 percent decrease in the material, which results in a 5 percent decrease in the cost, may be appreciable. The dies, therefore, should be designed so that the dimensions of the flash and stock are just sufficient to fill the die cavity completely. The stock, however, must be cut to provide an excess of metal (1) because of the variation in the dimensions of the forging blank, and (2) because of the wear that occurs in the die cavity. Material wastage due to the latter effect may be reduced if all of the blanks are not cut at once.

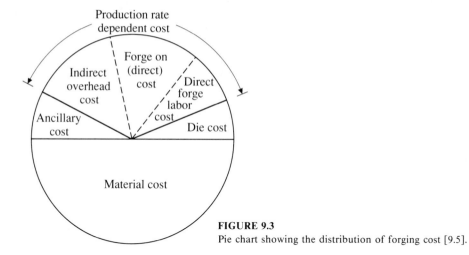

FIGURE 9.3
Pie chart showing the distribution of forging cost [9.5].

The degree of filling of the die cavity just prior to the initiation of the flash formation is a good indication of the optimum blank geometry. In order to determine the degree of filling of the die cavity quantitatively, a coefficient of filling, $k = V_m / V_d \times 100$ has been used [9.6], where V_m is the volume of the metal in the die cavity, as shown in Fig. 9.4, and V_d is the volume of the die cavity. Figure 9.5 shows the variation of the coefficient of die-filling, k, as a function of the aspect ratio, height/width, h_0 / b_0, of the workpiece. This curve was obtained experimentally for metal flow in plane strain of a long workpiece having the cross section shown in Fig. 9.4.

Since the volume of the workpiece remains constant, the portion of the metal in the flash can also be considered as a measure of the die-filling. The volume of the flash can be determined readily from the flash thickness and width. All of the metal not in the flash is in the die cavity. The smaller the volume of the flash and the later its formation begins, the better is the die-filling capacity.

9.2 PREDICTION OF FORCES AND ENERGY REQUIREMENTS

In addition to applied experience, the different techniques for estimating the forces and/or energy requirements in closed-die forging, which will be briefly

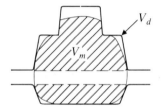

FIGURE 9.4
Cross section showing the volume of the die cavity V_d, and the volume of the metal V_m [9.6].

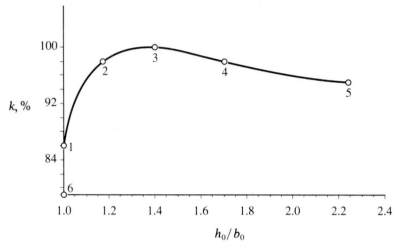

FIGURE 9.5
Graph showing the variation of the coefficient of die-filling, k, as a function of the aspect ratio h_0/b_0.
[9.6]

discussed here, are:

1. Shape complexity or multiplying factor, empirical formula method
2. Empirical regression equation method
3. Elemental upper-bound method
4. Variations of the slab method such as the
   a. Constant flash stress method
   b. Programmable calculator method
   c. Modular slab method for stress analysis of an axisymmetric forging
5. Computer methods in forging design
   a. Computer simulation of the modular slab method
   b. Modular sequential simulation computer method for an axisymmetric forging
   c. Biswas-Knight method for hot forgings and dies
   d. Desk-top computer interactive design of axisymmetric forgings
   e. Computer-aided design of hot forgings and dies
   f. Computer, upper-bound modeling of hammer forging operations
   g. Computer-aided forging design systems
      (1) Battelle's Die Forge CAD/CAM system
      (2) A CAD/CAM system for axisymmetric forgings
      (3) Proprietary CAD/CAM/CAE forging systems

A varying degree of approximation and understanding of the forging process is obtained with each of the above methods. For some of the above methods only a simple or a programmable calculator is used. For the more involved ones, a digital computer is required.

9.3 SHAPE COMPLEXITY METHOD [9.7]

A rough estimate may be quickly obtained of the maximum load or force required in close-die forging by use of the following empirical formula:

$$P = S_1 \bar{\sigma}_m A_p \tag{9.1}$$

where S_1 = a shape complexity factor (to be discussed elsewhere) for calculation of the load depending on the complexity of the forging and which might be obtained from Table 9.1, from empirical data, or from an empirical equation

$\bar{\sigma}_m$ = the estimated mean flow stress of the material at a given forging temperature and strain rate

A_p = the projected area of the forging, including the effective flash, which may or may not include the flash in the gutter

In estimating the value of $\bar{\sigma}_m$, the strain ε and strain rate $\dot{\varepsilon}$ must first be estimated from

$$\varepsilon = \ln \frac{h_1}{h_0} = \ln \frac{V}{A_p h_0} \tag{9.2}$$

where V is the appropriate volume of the forging, and from $\dot{\varepsilon} = v/h \text{ s}^{-1}$, where v is the instantaneous speed of the die (press), and h is the appropriate thickness.

The energy requirement may be estimated from

$$E = S_2 V \varepsilon \bar{\sigma}_m \tag{9.3}$$

where S_2 = shape factor for calculation of energy

ε = average strain (Eq. (9.2)), and

$\bar{\sigma}_m$ = mean flow stress at the given forging temperature and average strain rate.

Empirical formulas such as in the foregoing do not generally contribute very much to a better understanding of the forging process since they are not

TABLE 9.1
Multiplying factors for estimating the force and energy requirements in forging

Mode of deformation	Factors	
	S_1	S_2
Compression of cylinder between flat platens		
$\varepsilon_E = 0.5$	1.2	1.2
$\varepsilon_E = 0.8$	1.5–2.5	1.5
Impression die forging of simple shape		
without flash formation	3–5	2.0–2.5
with flash formation	5–8	3.0
Impression die forging of complex shapes (tall webs) with		
flash formation	8–12	4.0

based on the fundamental phenomena of metal deformation and flow. To provide a better understanding of the forging process, one of the analytical methods such as the slab method is needed.

9.4 EMPIRICAL REGRESSION EQUATION METHOD [9.8]

In an effort to eliminate bias and the reliance on the memory of the experienced forging designer, laboratory and shop data may be analyzed statistically by the use of regression analysis. Data for the main parameters, such as the cross-sectional area of the forging excluding the flash A, the forging shape complexity factor S, temperature of the forging T, etc., may be obtained.

The equation for the best fit to the data is then obtained by regression analysis. The regression equation for the first- and second-order dependence and interaction $(A'B')$ is of the general form

$$P = a + bA' + cB' + dA'B' + eA'^2 + \cdots \tag{9.4}$$

If a power equation is desired as in the case of the Drop Forging Research Association (DFRA) equations, regression equations for the log of equations similar to the above equation may be obtained for the forging load in tonf.

Balogun, as cited by Thomas and Bannister [9.8, 9.9] presented the following equations for

1. *Axisymmetric forging*

$$P = 362 + 32.78A - 565.66S - 0.53T \tag{9.5}$$

2. *Elongated forging*

$$P = 786 + 35.73A - 57.85S - 0.30T \tag{9.6}$$

where A = the projected area of a forging excluding the flash
S = the forging shape complexity factor defined as the weight of the forging divided by the weight of an enveloping prism or cylinder
T = the forging temperature, °C

The DFRA equations are based on the slab method and have the general form for the load P

$$P = a(h_m)^p \left(\frac{w}{h}\right)^q (A_t)^r \tag{9.7}$$

where h_m = mean height of forging excluding the flash, in
w = flash width, in
h_f = flash thickness
A_t = total projected area of the forging including the flash, in^2
a, p, q, and r are constants

In the foregoing equation, $P = f(\sigma_y, A_t)$, where σ_y is a function of $w/(h_f)(h_m)$. The DFRA equations obtained by regression analysis are presented in the following form:

1. *For simple forgings*

$$P = \sigma_y A_t = 21.06 \left(\frac{w}{(h_f)(h_m)} \right)^{0.025} \tag{9.8}$$

2. *For complex forgings*

$$P = \sigma_y A_t = 33.45 \left(\frac{w}{(h_f)(h_m)} \right)^{0.009} \tag{9.9}$$

3. *For axisymmetric forgings*

$$P = \sigma_y A_t = 8.391 h_m^{-0.1154} \left(\frac{w}{h_f} \right)^{0.5082} A_t^{1.178} \tag{9.10}$$

In the latter case, it was found that very little precision was lost by ignoring h_m to give

$$P = 9.309 \left(\frac{w}{h_f} \right)^{0.4696} A_t^{1.162} \tag{9.11}$$

In the above DFRA equations, P is the total load on the forging in tonf, σ_y is the mean flow stress, A_t is the total projected area of the forging including the flash in in^2, w and h_f are the flash-land width and thickness in in, and h_m is the mean height of the forging excluding the flash in in.

The objections to the regression analysis method are that (1) it requires experimental or shop data for application to a particular situation, (2) it requires some statistical and computer expertise to determine the equations, and (3) it is not sufficiently general for application to a variety of different forging situations.

Its major advantage is that it is custom-designed for a particular forging operation.

9.5 ELEMENTAL UPPER-BOUND METHOD [9.10]

As opposed to most of the other methods used in the calculation of the forging load and the optimum flash geometry, which are based on the slab method, this method is based on the upper-bound approach. It has been applied to the analysis of axisymmetric forgings. In this approach, the forging is broken down into basic, elemental regions or rings. (See Sections 4.3.5 and 8.2.11.1 for other applications of the upper-bound elemental technique.) Figure 9.6 shows how an extrusion forging was broken down into two rectangular rings by Kudo. In the extension of this method by McDermott and Bramley [9.5, 9.10], the forging may be divided into eight basic rings as shown in Fig. 9.7. The eight regions or rings are divided in such a manner so that, as the top surface descends vertically, as a result of an external force of unit velocity, the inner and outer surfaces of the rings move inward or outward from the centerline as shown in Fig. 9.7. The boundaries of these regions may be considered as either rigid tools or as rigid parts of adjacent elements of the workpiece.

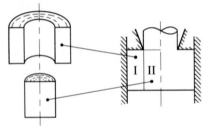

FIGURE 9.6
Breakdown of an extrusion forging into a ring and cylinder for the purpose of analysis by the elemental upper method as proposed by Kudo [9.5].

For each of these eight regions shown, a general admissible velocity field, i.e., one which is a distribution of particle velocities which is kinematically compatible within itself and with the externally applied forces, is considered as shown in the example shown in Fig. 9.8 for the inward flow of a triangular region. In obtaining the velocity fields for each of the above basic regions, it is assumed that the radial velocity $\dot{u} = du/dt$ is independent of the axial direction Z (in order to facilitate calculation of the internal rate of energy dissipation and to allow connection with neighboring deforming regions) and that the inlet and outlet velocities from any region boundary are constant along the boundary.

The velocity fields for rectangular and triangular flow, both inward and outward, are given below. The fields for convex and concave circular flow are

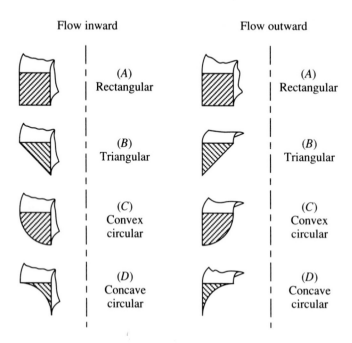

FIGURE 9.7
Drawings showing the cross sections of eight basic elemental "rings" [9.5].

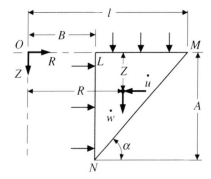

FIGURE 9.8
Diagram used for the definition of the parameters and for the derivation of the rate of internal energy dissipation $\dot{E}$ [9.5].

not given for the sake of brevity. The parameters A, B, R, z, and α are defined in Fig. 9.8. $\dot{u} = du/dt$ and $\dot{w} = dw/dt$ are the radial and axial velocities, respectively.

Rectangular flow inward

$$\dot{u} = \frac{-(1-R^2)}{2AR} \qquad \text{also} \qquad \dot{u} = \frac{-(1-B)(1-R)}{2AR} \qquad (9.12)$$

$$\dot{w} = \frac{-z}{A} \qquad \text{also} \qquad \dot{w} = \frac{(1-B)z}{2AR} \qquad (9.13)$$

Rectangular flow outward

$$\dot{u} = \frac{R^2 - B^2}{2AR} \qquad \text{also} \qquad \dot{u} = \frac{(1-B)(B+R)}{2AR} \qquad (9.14)$$

$$\dot{w} = \frac{-z}{A} \qquad \text{also} \qquad \dot{w} = \frac{(1-B)z}{2AR} \qquad (9.15)$$

Triangular flow inward

$$\dot{u} = -\frac{\cot \alpha}{2}\left(1 + \frac{1}{R}\right) \qquad (9.16)$$

$$\dot{w} = \frac{\cot \alpha}{2}\left(\frac{z}{R}\right) + 1 \qquad (9.17)$$

Triangular flow outward

$$\dot{u} = \frac{\cot \alpha}{2}\left(1 + \frac{B}{R}\right) \qquad (9.18)$$

$$\dot{w} = -\frac{\cot \alpha}{2R}z + 1 \qquad (9.19)$$

Once the velocity components for any of the eight basic regions are known, then by definition [9.5]

$$\dot{\varepsilon}_R = \frac{\partial \dot{u}}{\partial R} \qquad \dot{\varepsilon}_z = \frac{\partial \dot{w}}{\partial R} \tag{9.20}$$

$$\dot{\varepsilon}_\theta = -(\dot{\varepsilon}_R + \dot{\varepsilon}_z) \tag{9.21}$$

$$\dot{\gamma}_{Rz} = \left(\frac{\partial \dot{u}}{\partial z} + \frac{\partial \dot{w}}{\partial R}\right) \tag{9.22}$$

The rate of internal energy dissipation can be calculated for that particular field according to Hill [9.11] from

$$\dot{E} = \frac{\sqrt{2}}{3} \sigma_y \int_V \left(\dot{\varepsilon}_R^2 + \dot{\varepsilon}_\theta^2 + \dot{\varepsilon}_z^2 + \frac{1}{2}\dot{\gamma}_{Rz}^2\right) dV + \sigma_y \int_s m\dot{S}\, ds \tag{9.23}$$

where $\dot{E}$ = the rate of internal energy dissipation
  σ_y = the flow stress of the metal being forged
  $\dot{\varepsilon}_R$ = the strain rate in the radial R direction
  $\dot{\varepsilon}_z$ = the strain rate in the axial Z direction
  $\dot{\varepsilon}_\theta$ = the strain rate in the circumferential θ direction
  $\dot{\gamma}_{Rz}$ = the shear strain rate in the R-Z plane
  m = the friction factor at the region boundaries
  $\dot{S}$ = the rate of relative slip at the boundaries
  s = surface of the velocity discontinuity
  V = volume of the workpiece [9.5]

The first integral $\int_V$ in Eq. (9.23) is carried out throughout the entire volume of the workpiece which is deformed continuously, and the second integral $\int_s$ is carried out over all surfaces of velocity discontinuity on the workpiece-tool and the inter-region boundaries. The value of $\dot{E}$ for any particular region, i, can now be expressed nondimensionally by dividing by the product of the flow stress, surface area of pressing, and the pressing speed of that unit region, $\sigma_y A_i V_i$, giving what might be called "the coefficient of internal energy dissipation." When considering the total rate of energy dissipation for a certain velocity field in some given forging consisting of many such unit regions, the total rate of energy dissipation, $\dot{E}_t$, can be represented by [9.5]

$$\dot{E}_t = \sigma_y \sum_{i=1}^{i=n} e_i A_i V_i \tag{9.24}$$

where e_i = the coefficient of internal energy dissipation for region i
  A_i = the pressing area of region i
  V_i = the pressing speed of region i
  n = the total number of unit regions comprising the total forging

Now the upper bound for the mean extrusion pressure, for example, over the whole cross-sectional area of the billet could be expressed by

$$\frac{P}{\sigma_y} = \frac{\dot{E}_t}{(\pi D_i^2 / 4) V_t} \tag{9.25}$$

where $\pi D_i^2 / 4$ is the total pressing area of the forging, and V_t is the speed of die closure.

The solutions of Eqs. (9.23) and (9.24) are not simple additions of the terms shown in the equations. In determining a general admissible velocity system at any point inside and along the boundaries of each region, the mathematics becomes very involved to determine the strain rate terms in Eq. (9.23), and it becomes impossible to perform the volume integration with them by direct mathematical methods. Computer analysis is therefore used to simplify the solution. In order to obtain the load directly in tons (kN) to deform any of the eight regions or rings, all that is required is to input the following data into the computer: (1) type of region, (2) flow stress of the material being deformed, (3) press speed at which the metal is being deformed, (4) internal and external radii, and (5) friction factors m_1 [9.5].

The analysis of a complex forging can now be completed by dividing the forging into basic, elemental shapes, entering the data for each shape, and summing to find the total load. It should be emphasized here that this method of analysis is such that it considers the forging only at the end of the process

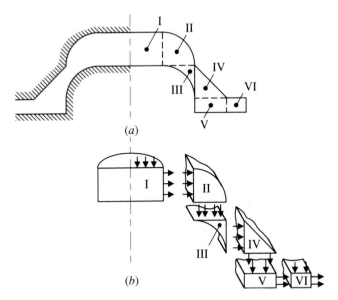

FIGURE 9.9
(*a*) Drawing showing the cross section of a hypothetical axisymmetric forging, and (*b*) subdivision of the forging into elemental shapes for analysis at the end of the forging operation at the point that the space in the die cavity is just filled [9.5].

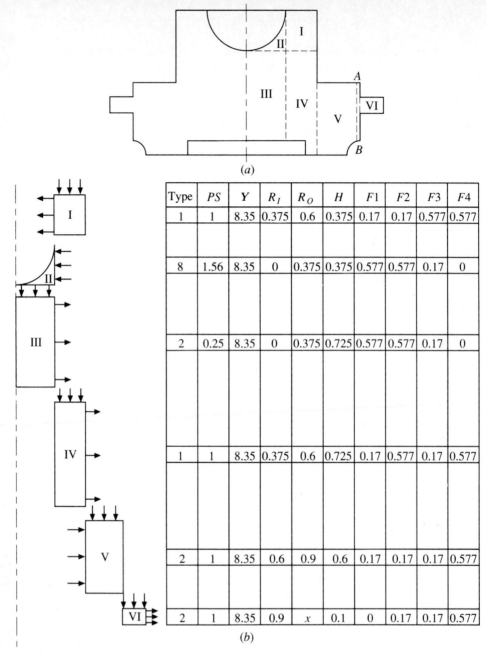

Type	PS	Y	R_I	R_O	H	F1	F2	F3	F4
1	1	8.35	0.375	0.6	0.375	0.17	0.17	0.577	0.577
8	1.56	8.35	0	0.375	0.375	0.577	0.577	0.17	0
2	0.25	8.35	0	0.375	0.725	0.577	0.577	0.17	0
1	1	8.35	0.375	0.6	0.725	0.17	0.577	0.17	0.577
2	1	8.35	0.6	0.9	0.6	0.17	0.17	0.17	0.577
2	1	8.35	0.9	x	0.1	0	0.17	0.17	0.577

FIGURE 9.10

(a) Cross section of a forging, for which all the composite regions do not link onto one another to produce a smooth transition of flow on an interelemental scale. Cyclic type flow exists in regions I to IV. An infinitesimal elemental gap, AB, allows Region V to flow outward to maintain continuity of analysis. (b) Subdivision of the forging into elemental shapes and the values of their associated parameters. (PS = press speed (in/sec), Y = yield stress of the material being forged (ton/in²), R_I = internal radius (in), R_O = outside radius (in), H = height of the element (in), and F_i = friction coefficients on the region boundaries [9.5]).

554

when all the space in the die cavity is filled, i.e., at maximum load. It is therefore only suited for press forging as hammer forging requires energy calculations for the full process.

Figure 9.9 shows a cross section of a hypothetical, axisymmetric forging, which produces a smooth transition of flow between the basic elemental regions. Figure 9.10(*a*) and (*b*) show a smooth transition of flow in regions I to IV, but not V and VI. To include these regions, the material is considered to fill an infinitesimal elemental gap, *AB*, as shown at the right edge of Fig. 9.10(*a*), to maintain a continuity of analysis. At the moment of filling the die cavity, the metal in region V would flow outward to close this gap [9.5].

The analysis was completed in the above manner to produce the elements for the forging shown in Fig. 9.10(*a*) and their associated parameters. The flash thickness was kept constant while the flash width varied. The theoretical results are compared to those obtained experimentally in Fig. 9.11, which shows poor agreement for flash width to flash thickness ratios less than 2.5. A computer flowchart illustrating the analysis procedure is shown in Fig. 9.12.

This method of analysis can also be used to predict the dimensions of a flash as shown in the computer flow diagram in Fig. 9.13. It predicts the dimensions of the flash that is just sufficient to ensure complete die filling. It therefore optimizes flash wastage and also increases die life as a result of a reduced peak die load.

The procedure for the foregoing is based on the fact that at the point of minimum die separation, the largest contributing factor to the total load is that from the flash itself. Consider the die closing incrementally. For each step of the

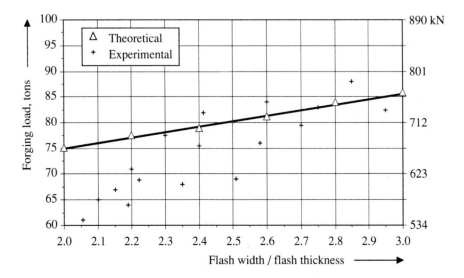

FIGURE 9.11
Graph comparing the theoretical calculations using Eq. (9.25) with the experimental results of the load, tons (kN) versus the flash width to thickness ratio [9.5].

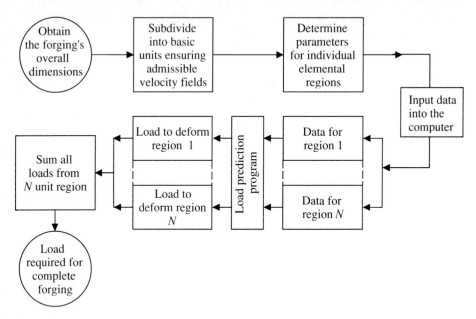

FIGURE 9.12
Computer flowchart illustrating the analysis procedure used in the elemental upper-bound method [9.5].

closure process, assuming that all regions inside the die cavity are fully filled, certain parameters such as the height H of each of the elements making up the whole forging would change with the load at this point. At some stage in this closure process, there comes a point when the load contribution from the flash would be greater than that from all the other regions combined. At this point it could be said that less energy is required to complete the filling of the die cavity than to expand the flash through another increment of growth. At the point of balance, when the load to deform the flash equals the load to deform the rest of the forging, the energy required is a minimum. By noting the die separation distance at this point and using constancy of volume, one can determine the complete flash geometry to achieve the optimum flash size and minimum wastage of material [9.5].

9.6 VARIATIONS OF THE SLAB METHOD

9.6.1 Introduction

The elementary slab or equilibrium method is an approximate method for analyzing plastic deformation problems and was originally applied by Siebel in 1934 to various types of forming processes. A considerable amount of effort has been expended in recent years by a number of people in the application of this method to forging. Much of this effort has already been used throughout the

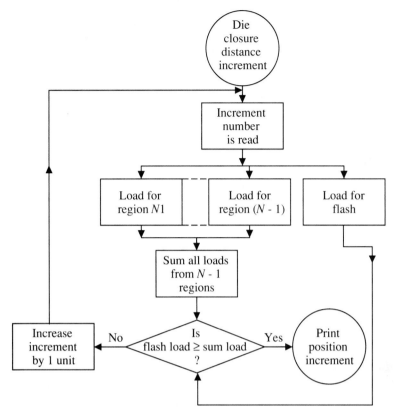

FIGURE 9.13
Flow diagram showing flash prediction procedure [9.5].

material presented on compressive deformation and metalworking processes such as in the compression of slabs, cylinders, rings, and thin discs. This background material is necessary for understanding better the mechanics of the foregoing processes. Some of these concepts will be reviewed here.

The slab method assumes that the stresses on a plane perpendicular to the direction of metal flow are in the directions of the principal stresses (i.e., contain no shear stresses) and that the deformation is homogeneous throughout each deformation zone studied [9.3]. A slice or slab of infinitesimal thickness is selected and a force balance is made as was done in Fig. 4.3 for obtaining the expression for the friction hill.

When applying the slab method, as may be recalled, the following assumptions are usually made [9.4]:

1. The material is isotropic and incompressible
2. The elastic deformation is neglected
3. The inertial forces are small and can be neglected

4. Plane surfaces remain plane
5. The effective flow stress $\bar{\sigma}$ is constant in a specific deformation zone, but it may have different values in different zones
6. The frictional shear stress is related to the normal stress by the Coulomb coefficient μ or the constant friction factor m
7. The effective flow stress $\bar{\sigma}$ of the material obeys the von Mises criterion as follows:
   a. For plane strain

$$-\bar{\sigma} = \frac{\sqrt{3}}{2}(\sigma_y - \sigma_x) \tag{9.26}$$

   where σ_y is in the upsetting and σ_x is in the flow direction.
   b. For axisymmetric flow

$$-\bar{\sigma} = \sigma_z - \sigma_r \tag{9.27}$$

   where σ_z is in the axial (upsetting) direction and σ_r is in the radial (flow) direction

9.6.2 Constant Flash Stress Slab Method

In this version of the axisymmetric slab method, it is assumed that the axial stress across the die cavity is the same as the stress developed in the flash as shown in Fig. 9.14(a). By use of the equation for the friction hill for the axisymmetric case similar to Eq. (8.14), one obtains the following equation for the distribution of the pressure or stress, σ_{f+c}, across the forging for both the flash and die cavity:

$$p = \sigma_{f+c} = \bar{\sigma}_f[1 + e^{(2\mu/h)(\bar{r}_f - r_c)}] \tag{9.28}$$

and the total forging load is given by

$$P = A_t\sigma_{f+c} \tag{9.29}$$

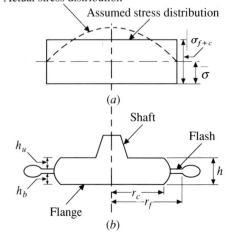

Actual stress distribution

Assumed stress distribution

σ_{f+c}

σ

(a)

Shaft

Flash

h_u

h_b

h

Flange

r_c

r_f

(b)

FIGURE 9.14
Constant flash stress model for predicting the forging load. (a) The stress distribution in (b) an axisymmetric forging.

where the stresses and dimensions are defined in Fig. 9.14(a), and A_t is the total cross-sectional area of the forging including the flash.

9.6.3 Programmable Calculator Slab Method for Estimating Forging Loads [9.12]

9.6.3.1 INTRODUCTION. Most forging engineers must often have to estimate forging loads. There is a need for simple but accurate methods of load estimation which can be applied on the shop floor where mathematical capability and computational facilities are limited. Many existing formulas for estimating the forging load, derived from experimental data, are simple to use, but they are not sufficiently general to consider the effects of critical properties, part geometry, and strain rate on the forging load. A simple but effective programmable calculator slab method to calculate the forging stresses and loads has been presented by Subramanian and Altan [9.12]. The main advantage of the slab method is that it allows the division of a complex forging into some basic deformation units, or blocks, which can be analyzed separately. The results can then be put together in a building block manner to obtain the load required for the deformation of a rather complex forging.

The method consists of dividing a forging into various plane strain and/or axisymmetric portions, in which the metal is assumed to occur (1) either in a plane, called *plane-strain flow*, or (2) symmetrically about an axis, called *axisymmetric flow*, as shown in Figs. 9.15 and 9.16. Simple equations can then be used

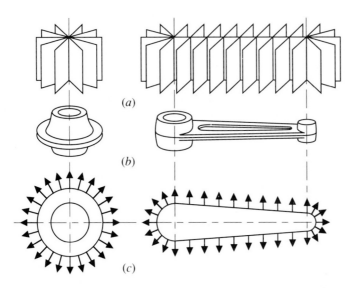

FIGURE 9.15
Planes and directions illustrating plane strain and axisymmetric metal flow during the forging of two simple shapes. (*Adapted from T. Altan, "Computer-Aided Design and Manufacturing (CAD/CAM) of Hot Forging Dies", COMMLINE, Aug. 1983, pp. 10–13.*)

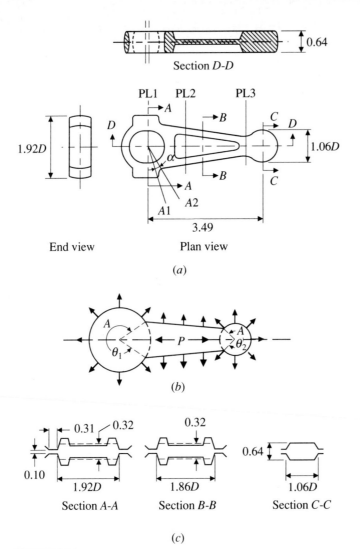

FIGURE 9.16
Geometry, direction of metal flow, and representative cross sections of a connecting rod forging. (*a*)
Cross-sectional and plan views of the connecting rod (PL1, PL2, and PL3 = planes giving the plane
strain cross sections, and α = a segment angle for giving locations of axisymmetric cross sections).
(*b*) Directions of metal flow: A = axisymmetric, P = plane strain. (*c*) Representative cross sections
and their simplification. (The depth of the plane strain cross section is taken as the average depth
between two successive cross sections.) [9.12].

to predict the pressure and the load for each portion, before adding the loads of
all the components together to obtain the total load for forging. Originally the
calculations were programmed in machine language for use on an HP 67 calculator, but it was modified and simplified for use on an available HP 41C calculator
at the University of Iowa, Iowa City. The user does not have to know the equations

but must be able to follow the instructions on how to use the calculator and must input the data on part geometry, material properties, and friction.

In order to estimate the forging load for a given part, it is necessary to know (1) the part geometry, (2) the type of metal flow, (3) the flow stress of the deforming material under forging conditions, and (4) the friction at the die-material interface.

The part geometry and type of material are obtained from the working, detailed drawing of the part, which is modified or "figured" to give the finish forging, from which one or more preforms may be obtained as needed. The flow model is then determined as in Fig. 9.17. The flow stress, σ_f may be calculated from the strain rate and temperature as discussed later. The friction factor m is estimated or obtained from a ring test. It is usually between 0.30 to 0.50 for steel.

The procedure in general is that the approximate flow stress of the material σ_{fi} for the conditions of forging are calculated for the flash and for the body of the forging (the cavity portion) separately. They are then converted into loads by use of $P_i = \sigma_{fi} A_i$, where A_i is the area of the flash or the cross-sectional area of the forging cavity without the flash. The total load on the cross section including the flash is obtained by adding the two loads such as for axisymmetric forging or a portion thereof:

$$P_{ta} = P_{fa} + P_{ca} \tag{9.30}$$

9.6.3.2 ESTIMATION OF THE FLOW STRESS. Forging stresses and the loads obtained from them in a forging operation are directly influenced by the instantaneous flow stress of the material being forged in the critical locations of the

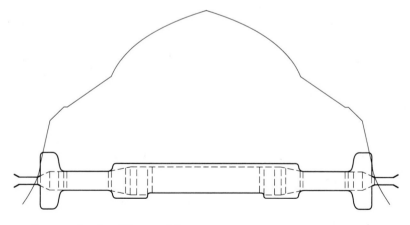

Cross section 1 — Flow model —
Scale factor = 1.180   X length 6.6330   Z length 0.900
Do you want to modify the flow model? Enter Y or N.

FIGURE 9.17
Geometry of the cross section, the theoretical flow model, and the stress distribution obtained by computer analysis [9.12].

die such as in the flash and the body of the forging. Because conditions differ in the flash and the die cavity portion, the flow stress is different in the flash and in the die cavity portion of the forging. For a given composition and microstructure, the flow stress of a metal depends on (1) the part geometry, (2) the type of metal flow, (3) the flow stress of the deforming material under forging conditions, and (4) the friction of the die-material interface, or

$$\sigma_{fi} = f(\varepsilon, \dot{\varepsilon}, T) \tag{9.31}$$

During forging, different portions of the part undergo different amounts of deformation depending upon the stock or preform configuration and on the finish forging. The effect of strain in hot forging of most common metallic materials upon the flow stress can be neglected and only enters into the calculations indirectly. The rate of deformation or strain rate is determined (1) by the speed of the ram and (2) by the initial and final thickness of the forging. The temperature of the forging at the end of the forging stroke depends upon (1) the stock temperature, (2) the die temperature, (3) speed of deformation, and (4) the frictional conditions. The temperature varies across the forging due to die chilling and also due to heat generation by friction and by deformation. In a simple analysis using a programmable calculator, the flow stress should be estimated on the basis of some reasonable approximation of temperature and strain rate.

The equation for estimating the flow stress at a constant strain ε and temperature T is as follows:

$$\bar{\sigma} = C\dot{\varepsilon}^m \big|_{\varepsilon, T} \tag{9.32}$$

where $\bar{\sigma}$ = flow stress

$\dot{\varepsilon}$ = average strain rate = ram velocity/average thickness

C, m = material constants obtained from uniform compression tests, or from a table found in a handbook

C and m are functions of strain and temperature. In cold forging, flow stress is largely influenced by the strain. Whereas in warm or hot forging, the strain rate and temperature have the predominant effect on the flow stress, so the temperature of the deforming material should be known. If one neglects the temperature gradients and considers the forging as a thin plate of uniform temperature cooled symmetrically from both sides, the average temperature of the forging in the cavity or in the flash can be expressed as

$$T = T_1 + (T_s - T_1) e^{-\alpha t/cph} \tag{9.33}$$

where T = instantaneous average temperature of the forging

T_1 = initial die-surface temperature

T_s = initial stock temperature

α = heat transfer coefficient at the forging-die interface (0.0039 Btu/in² °F for steel)(11.48 kJ/m² °C)

t' = time of contact estimated from the press speed

c = specific heat of the material being forged (0.109 Btu/lb°F) (0.456 kJ/Kg°C)

ρ = density of the forged material $(0.285\ \text{lb/in}^3)(7.89 \times 10^3\ \text{kg/m}^3)$
h = average thickness of the forging

To estimate the duration of contact, the average velocity of the ram during forging should be determined. It is the ram velocity at the time it touches the workpiece. For a mechanical press with a crank-slide mechanism, for example, the ram velocity with respect to the ram position is

$$V = d\frac{\pi n}{30}\sqrt{\frac{S}{d} - 1} \tag{9.34}$$

where d = the average distance of the ram from bottom dead center
n = rpm of the crank
S = length of the stroke, in (mm)

The duration of contact t' can then be obtained from the billet or workpiece average thickness h_b and the forging average thickness h_f as follows:

$$t' = \frac{h_b - h_f}{V} \tag{9.35}$$

The temperature increase due to plastic deformation is given by

$$\Delta T = \frac{A\bar{\sigma}_a \bar{\varepsilon}_a}{c\rho} \tag{9.36}$$

where A = factor to convert mechanical energy to heat energy $(1.07 \times 10^{-4}\text{Btu/in lb})(1.0\ \text{J/m-N})$ [see Eq. (4.79)]
$\bar{\sigma}_a$ = average flow stress in the material
$\bar{\varepsilon}_a$ = average strain, estimated from the initial and final thickness

$$\bar{\varepsilon}_a = \ln\frac{h_0}{h_f} \tag{9.37}$$

The model used in this analysis is based on a simplified model shown in Fig. 9.18. In this analysis, it is assumed that the die cavity has a rectangular shape

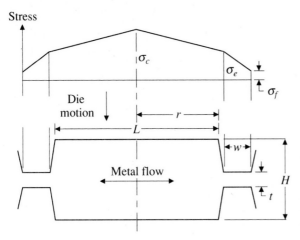

FIGURE 9.18
Schematic drawing showing that the shape of the die cavity and of the flash for the closed-die forging of a simple part. The distribution of the stress across the forging is superimposed on the drawing [9.12].

and has a flash geometry as shown in Fig. 9.18. In actual practice, where the die cavity is not a rectangle, the cross section is simplified to conform to this model.

In most practical forging operations, the friction shear factor m is reduced as much as possible by lubricating the dies and sometimes also by precoating the stock or workpiece. The most common experimental method for estimating the friction shear factor under forging conditions is the ring test (see Sec. 8.3.2). When any such data are not available, then an estimated value of 0.30 to 0.50 is used. When the friction is due to internal shearing of the metal, the value of m is 1.

9.6.3.3 FORGING LOAD ESTIMATION.

As mentioned in the foregoing, the stresses required to deform a forging preform are estimated, from which the loads are in turn estimated. The relationship for estimating the stress σ_i on (1) the axisymmetric and/or (2) the plane-strain sections of a forging by what is known as the slab method for a constant friction factor may be obtained from Fig. 9.19 as indicated below.

A stress balance across the element dx gives

$$(p + dp)h = ph + 2\mu\sigma_y \, dx \tag{9.38}$$

$$\frac{dP}{dx} = \frac{2\mu\sigma_y}{h} \tag{9.39}$$

The solution of this differential equation is

$$P = \frac{2\mu\sigma_y x}{h} + C \tag{9.40}$$

At $x = 0$, $P = 0$ and $C = 0$, so

$$P = \frac{2\mu\sigma_y x}{h} \tag{9.41}$$

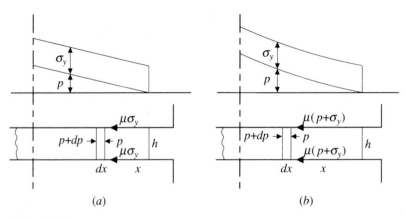

(a)   (b)

FIGURE 9.19
Stress and load distribution for a slab loaded in compression in plane strain, (a) in which a constant friction factor is assumed, and (b) in which Coulomb friction is assumed, i.e., the frictional force is assumed to be a constant proportion of the yield strength of the material σ_y [9.8].

and since $\sigma_i = P + \sigma_y$, then

$$\sigma_i = \sigma_y \left(\frac{2\mu x}{h} + 1 \right) \tag{9.42}$$

where σ_y is the flow stress of material. Since $\tau = \mu\sigma = m\sigma/\sqrt{3}$,

$$\mu = m/\sqrt{3}. \tag{9.43}$$

If $\mu = m/\sqrt{3}$, $x = w$, the flash width, $h = R - r$, the flash thickness, and $\sigma_f =$ the flow stress in the flash region, the flow stress σ_{ea} at the entrance from the die cavity into the flash of (1) an axisymmetric cross section is given by use of Eq. (9.42) as

$$\sigma_{ea} = \sigma_f \left(\frac{2}{\sqrt{3}} m \frac{w}{h} + 1 \right) \tag{9.44}$$

By integrating the stress, one obtains the forging load acting on the flash region as follows:

$$P_{fa} = 2\pi\sigma_f \left[-\frac{2}{3} \frac{m}{\sqrt{3}} \frac{1}{h} (R^3 - r^3) + \left(1 + \frac{2m}{\sqrt{3}} \frac{R}{h} \right) \left(\frac{R^2 - r^2}{2} \right) \right] \tag{9.45}$$

where $w = R - r$ the flash width.

Similarly, the load acting on the die cavity portion of the workpiece can be obtained as

$$P_{ca} = 2\pi r^2 \left(\frac{m}{\sqrt{3}} \frac{\sigma_c}{3} \frac{r}{H} + \frac{\sigma_{ea}}{2} \right) \tag{9.46}$$

where σ_c is the flows stress in the cavity portion, σ_{ea} is defined above, and H is the overall height of the workpiece as shown in Fig. 9.18. Because of rapid chilling and high deformation rate, the flow stress in the flash region is considered to be different from that in the die cavity. Therefore, two different flow stresses are used for flash and cavity regions. The total load on the axisymmetric cross section of the forging, if any, is

$$P_{ta} = P_{fa} + P_{ca} \tag{9.30)(9.47}$$

For plane-strain flow in (2) the plane-strain sections of the forging, if any, the equations corresponding to Eqs. (9.44), (9.45), and (9.46) are

$$\sigma_{ep} = \frac{2}{\sqrt{3}} \sigma_f \left(m \frac{w}{h} + 1 \right) \tag{9.48}$$

$$P_{fp} = \frac{2}{\sqrt{3}} w\sigma_f \left(m \frac{w}{h} + 2 \right) \tag{9.49}$$

and

$$P_{cp} = \left(\sigma_{ep} + \frac{L}{2H} \frac{m}{\sqrt{3}} \sigma_c \right) L \tag{9.50}$$

where L is the width of the die cavity, that is, $L = 2r$ in Fig. 9.18 and σ_{ep} is the stress at the cavity-boundary interface as shown. Equations (9.48), (9.49), and (9.50) are used to estimate the loads in the flash and in the die cavity portion for a unit depth of the workpiece for the plane-strain sections of the forging, if any. In this section it is assumed that there is no elongation in the longitudinal direction, that is, $\varepsilon_l = 0$. The total load of the plane-strain sections of the forging, if any, is

$$P_{tp} = P_{fp} + P_{cp} \tag{9.51}$$

The total load on a forging is the cumulative sum of the loads acting on individual cross sections of the forging, whether axisymmetric or plane strain, and is

$$P = \sum P_{ta} + \sum P_{tp} \tag{9.52}$$

The calculator program utilizes Eqs. (9.44) to (9.47) for axisymmetric flow, and (9.48) to (9.51) for the plane-strain flow. The total load is the cumulative sum of the loads acting on the individual cross sections of the workpiece. The program consists of a series of label, store, recall, and mathematical operation entries that will solve the above equations for the different variables in the equations. A magnetic strip can be made for reuse of the program.

9.6.3.4 CONCLUSIONS FOR THE PROGRAMMABLE CALCULATOR METHOD. Experimental analysis [9.12] indicated that the results of the simplified analysis of the programmable calculator method are within practical engineering accuracy. For simple to moderately complex forgings, this analysis can be effectively used for die material selection, for press selection, and for cost estimating. This analysis is very simple to understand and can be used on the shop floor by forging die designers who are not familiar with the computer methods. However, it should be noted that the accuracy of the final results depends largely upon the proper estimation of the flow stress and the friction shear factor. Some experience and knowledge of the forging analyses are necessary to make these estimates with acceptable accuracy. If the capabilities of a large high speed computer are available, then detailed calculations of the flow stress, forging stress, and forging load can be made more accurately and with less effort than is possible with a programmable calculator.

9.6.4 Modular Slab Method for Stress Analysis for Axisymmetric Forging [9.3], [9.41]

9.6.4.1 INTRODUCTION. As shown in Fig. 9.20(a), (b), and (c), the entire forging may be divided into deformation units or zones for the three stages of forging. The diameter of the neutral surface in Fig. 9.20(a) and (b) is designated by D_n. The stresses and loads can be calculated for each zone by considering that the strain distribution must be continuous, i.e., the value of the normal stress must be equal at the interface of two adjacent zones. The procedure used for the calculation of the stresses and loads will be presented in some detail for the

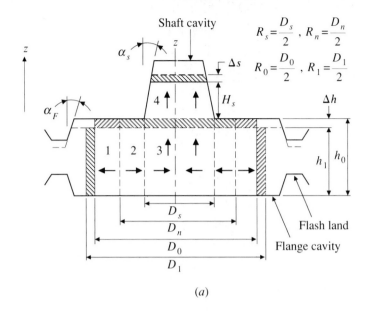

(a)

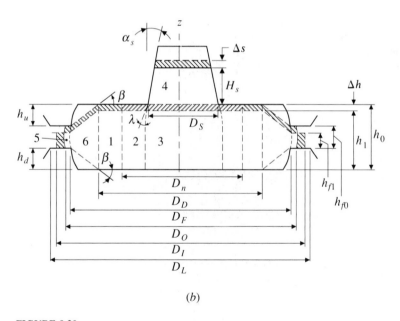

(b)

FIGURE 9.20
(a) Upsetting stage during forging in the die cavity shown in Figs. 9.1 and 9.2; (b) deformation zones and metal flow during the filling stage of the die cavity and the definition of the symbols used; and (c) deformation zones and metal flow during the end stage (D_S = diameter of shaft, D_n = diameter of neutral zone, D_D = diameter of deformation zone, D_F = diameter of start of land, D_O = diameter of blank, D_I = diameter of end of land). (Note that on the left side of (c) metal flow is by shear and on the right side by slip.) [9.41].

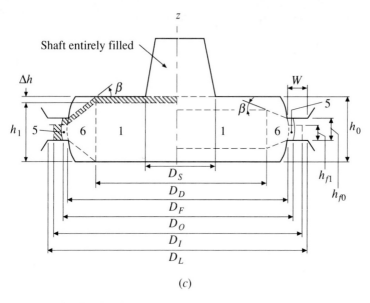

(c)

FIGURE 9.20. Continued.

upsetting stage only as shown in Fig. 9.20(a). The procedure for the calculation of the total load for the die-filling stage and the end-of-forging stage will be discussed subsequently in less detail.

9.6.4.2 UPSETTING STAGE ANALYSIS. The stress calculations for upsetting may be initiated for the case in Fig. 9.20(a) by starting from the free boundaries at zone 4 in the shaft and at zone 1 in the flange, outside of the neutral surface. The symbols shown in Fig. 9.20(a) will be used. The stresses and loads for metal flow for the following zones and directions for stage 1 may be calculated as follows:

1. **Converging and diverging flow in the longitudinal direction.**
   This type of converging flow occurs in zone 4 of Fig. 9.20(a) for which the axial stress distribution is given by

   $$\sigma_{z4} = K_4 \ln \frac{R_s - z \tan \alpha_s}{R_s - H_s \tan \alpha_s} \tag{9.53}$$

   where

   $$K_4 = \frac{2\bar\sigma_4[m_4(1 + \tan^2 \alpha_s) + \tan \alpha_s]}{\tan \alpha_s} \tag{9.54}$$

   and $z = 0$ at the entrance to the shaft. The subscript 4 refers to zone 4, and α_s is the angle of taper of the shaft. The load $P_4 = P_s$ at the upper surface of the flange necessary to extrude the shaft is

   $$P_4 = P_s = \pi R_s^2 K_4 \ln \left(\frac{R_s}{R_s - H_s \tan \alpha_s} \right) \tag{9.55}$$

To obtain a similar equation for divergent flow one can substitute $-\alpha_s$ for $+\alpha_s$ in the above equation.

2. **Parallel flow in the longitudinal direction.**
   This type of flow occurs in zone 3 in Fig. 9.20(a), for which the axial stress increases toward the lower die according to

$$\sigma_{z3} = \sigma_{zB} + \frac{4\bar{\sigma}_3 z}{\sqrt{3}\, D_s} \tag{9.56}$$

where σ_{zB} is the axial stress at the upper surface of the deformation zone at which $z = 0$

$\bar{\sigma}_3 = $ flow stress inside the deformation zone

$D_s = $ the diameter of the deformation zone

The average value of σ_{z3} will be used to calculate σ_{z2} for use in calculating P_2.

3. **Parallel flow in the lateral direction.**
   a. *Inward flow.* This type of flow occurs in zone 2 of the flange of Fig. 9.20(a), for which the axial stress is given by

$$\sigma_{z2} = \frac{2\bar{\sigma}_2 m_2}{h_0}(r - R_s) + \sigma_{z3(\mathrm{av})} \tag{9.57}$$

where $\bar{\sigma}_2$ is the flow stress inside zone 2, $\sigma_{z3(\mathrm{av})}$ is the average axial stress at the boundary of zones 2 and 3 and m_2 is the constant friction factor for zone 2-die interface. The axial load over zone 2 is obtained by integrating

$$P_2 = 2\pi \int_{R_s}^{R_n} r\sigma_{z2}\, dr \tag{9.58}$$

where $R_n = $ radius of the neutral surface

$R_s = $ radius of shaft

$\sigma_{z2} = $ axial stress inside zone 2

   b. *Outward flow.* This type of flow occurs in zone 1 of the flange of Fig. 9.20(a), for which the axial stress is

$$\sigma_{z1} = \frac{2\bar{\sigma}_1 m_1}{h_0}(R_0 - r) + \bar{\sigma}_1 \tag{9.59}$$

where m_1 is the constant friction factor at the zone 1-die interface

$\bar{\sigma}_1 = $ flow stress of the material inside zone 1

$R_0 = $ original radius of the blank

$h_0 = $ original height of the blank

The axial load is obtained by integrating

$$P_1 = 2\pi \int_{R_n}^{R_0} r\sigma_{z1}\, dr \tag{9.60}$$

The total forging load, therefore, for the upsetting stage, stage 1, is the sum of the loads to upset zones 1 and 2, and to extrude the shaft, $P_5 = P_4$, as follows:

$$P = P_1 + P_2 + P_4 \tag{9.61}$$

The foregoing completes the discussion of the upsetting stage for producing an axisymmetric forging. The determination of the position of the neutral surface and the analysis of the die-filling stage will now be discussed.

9.6.4.3 DETERMINATION OF THE POSITION OF THE NEUTRAL SURFACE.

To determine the position of the neutral surface by evaluating its radius R_n, it is necessary to estimate the stresses acting upon the different zones of the forging. Since the peak of the friction hill will occur at the neutral surface, the axial stresses in the flange area will have their maximum value at $r = R_n$, as shown in Fig. 9.21. The neutral surface in this case is the boundary between zones 1 and 2, at which the axial stresses σ_{z1} and σ_{z2} must be equal. By equating these stresses, one obtains the following expression for R_n for stage 1:

$$R_n = \frac{1}{\bar{\sigma}_1 m_1 + \bar{\sigma}_2 m_2} \left[\bar{\sigma}_1 m_1 R_0 + \bar{\sigma}_2 m_2 R_s + \frac{h_0}{2} (\bar{\sigma}_{z1} - \bar{\sigma}_{z3(av)}) \right] \tag{9.62}$$

The symbols are defined in the foregoing. R_n establishes the location of the boundary between zones 1 and 2 [9.3], [9.41].

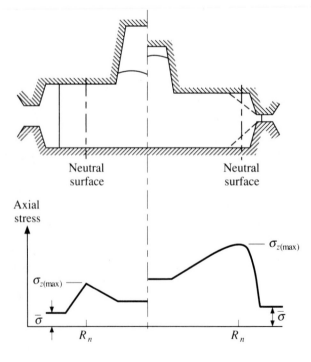

FIGURE 9.21
Drawing of the extent of the metal flow at two different penetrations of the die showing the neutral axes and the axial stress distribution across the die cavity [9.41].

It is now necessary to establish the boundary between zones 2 and 3 for stage 1. As the material being forged is compressed, the metal in zone 3, called the transition zone, changes its velocity and direction to flow from the flange into the shaft. In Figs. 9.20(a) and 9.22(a), the boundary of the shear surface between zones 2 and 3 was arbitrarily placed at $D_c = D_s$ ($R_c = R_s$), where D_c is the diameter of the cylindrical shear surface and D_s is the diameter of the shaft. Two other flow models are also shown in Fig. 9.22(b) and (c). The boundary of zone 3 depends upon the resistance to the outward flow of metal at the interface

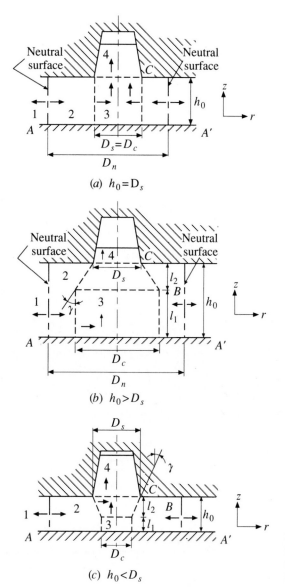

(a) $h_0 = D_s$

(b) $h_0 > D_s$

(c) $h_0 < D_s$

FIGURE 9.22
Flow models illustrating the possible modes of metal flow into the shaft (spike) cavity [9.41].

between the metal and the lower die surface caused by the axial stress σ_{zA}. The actual flow is the one which minimizes the amount of deformation energy. Therefore, at a given forging stage, the actual flow can be approximated with a flow model that results in a minimum axial stress, σ_{zA}, acting at the surface of the lower die cavity at surface AA' in Fig. 9.22. The geometry of the transition zone, zone 3, is defined by R_c and the angle γ. The stress σ_{zA} is calculated by adding the axial stresses calculated in the two adjacent zones. If σ_{zA} is minimized with respect to $\tan \gamma$, that is, $\partial \sigma_z / \partial (\tan \gamma) = 0$, one obtains

$$\tan \gamma = \pm \left(1 - \frac{\delta - 1}{\delta \ln \delta} \right)^{1/2} \tag{9.63}$$

where $\delta = D_c / D_s$, when $\tan \gamma \geq 0$
$\quad \delta = D_s / D_c$, when $\tan \gamma \leq 0$

The expression for σ_{zA} cannot be minimized with respect to h_0, the instantaneous flange height, so the relation D_c / D_s is obtained numerically as

$$\frac{D_c}{D_s} \cong 0.8 \left(\frac{h_0}{D_s} \right)^{0.92} \quad \text{for} \quad \frac{h_0}{D_s} \geq 2 \tag{9.64}$$

and

$$\frac{D_c}{D_s} \cong 0.333 + 0.584 \frac{h_0}{D_s} \quad \text{for} \quad 0.5 \leq \frac{h_0}{D_s} < 2 \tag{9.65}$$

as shown graphically in Fig. 9.23 [9.13].

The foregoing completes the discussion of the upsetting stage for producing an axisymmetric forging. Now the procedures for calculating the total load for the die-filling stage and the end-of-forging stage are discussed briefly.

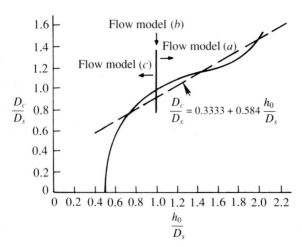

FIGURE 9.23
Determination of the cylindrical shear-surface diameter D_c shown in Fig. 9.22(a), (b), and (c) for a given instantaneous height h_0 and for a known shaft diameter D_s. Flow models labeled (a), (b), and (c) refer to the flow models shown in Fig. 9.22(a), (b), and (c) [9.41].

9.6.4.4 DIE-FILLING STAGE ANALYSIS. In the filling stage or stage 2, as shown in Fig. 9.20(b), the metal flows into the flash by shearing along a tapered surface, defined by the angle β. The angle β must be such that the axial stress σ_n, at the neutral surface, must be a minimum, that is, $\partial \sigma_n / \partial (\tan \beta) = 0$. This minimization yields

$$\tan \beta = \left[1 - \frac{(R-1)\sqrt{3}\, m_1}{R \ln R} \right] \tag{9.66}$$

where $R = h_0 / h_{f0}$
m_1 = the friction factor at the flange
h_0 = instantaneous height of the flange
h_{f0} = instantaneous flash thickness (Fig. 9.20(c)).

The location of the tapered surface R_D is given by

$$R_D = R_F - \frac{h_u}{\tan \beta} \tag{9.67}$$

where R_D = radius of the start of the tapered surface (Fig. 9.20(c))
R_F = radius of flange
h_u = depth of upper die flange cavity (Fig. 9.20(b))
β = angle of tapered surface with horizontal [see Fig. 9.20(b) and (c)]

The location of the neutral surface R_n is again determined for the condition that $r = R_n$ at $\sigma_{z1} = \sigma_{z2}$ to give

$$R_n = \frac{1}{\bar{\sigma}_1 m_1 + \bar{\sigma}_2 m_2} \left[\bar{\sigma}_1 m_1 R_D + \bar{\sigma}_2 m_2 R_S + \frac{h_0}{2} (\sigma_{z6}(r = R_D) - \sigma_{z3\,\mathrm{av}}) \right] \tag{9.68}$$

where $\quad R_n$ = radius of the neutral surface
r = instantaneous radius
$\bar{\sigma}_1$ and m_1 = the flow stress and friction factor in zone 1, respectively
$\bar{\sigma}_2$ and m_2 = the same for zone 2
R_D = radius of deformation zone
R_S = radius of shaft
h_0 = height of deformation zone (flange)
σ_{z6} = axial (vertical) stress in zone 6
σ_{z3} = average value of axial stress in zone 3 (boundary condition for calculating the stress in zone 2)

The stresses and loads can now be calculated in the same way as was done for the upsetting stage in stage 1 but not done here.

The total forging load in the filling stage (Fig. 9.20(b)) is obtained by adding the forging loads acting on each deformation zone as follows:

$$P = P_1 + P_2 + P_{34} + P_5 + P_6 \tag{9.69}$$

The individual loads, P_1, P_2, etc., are obtained by integrating the respective axial stress distributions (P_{34} denotes P_4 in stage 3) [9.3], [9.41].

9.6.4.5 END-OF-FORGING STAGE ANALYSIS. At the last stage, stage 3, of the forging operation, the die cavity is completely filled, the neutral surface moved to the center of the forging, and the excess metal present in the die cavity is being extruded into the flash and/or gutter.

There are two possible types of metal flow in this stage: (1) complete shearing in the cavity as shown at the right side of Fig. 9.20(c), and (2) shearing only along the tapered surfaces as shown at the left side of the figure [9.3], [9.41].

In case of complete shearing, the geometry is given by

$$\tan \beta = \left[1 - \frac{R-1}{R \ln R} \right]^{1/2} \tag{9.70}$$

where

$$R = \frac{h}{h_{fo}} \quad \text{and} \quad \frac{h}{h_{fo}} = 0.8 \left(\frac{R_F}{h_{fo}} \right)^{0.92} \frac{h_0}{h_{fo}}$$

where h = shear zone height (Fig. 9.20(c))
h_{fo} = instantaneous flash thickness (Fig. 9.20(c))

The total load for the end-of-forging stage (Fig. 9.20(c)) is given by

$$P = P_1 + P_6 + P_5 \tag{9.71}$$

This completes the discussion of the deformation mechanics of the modular slab method of stress analysis for an axisymmetric forging. The computer program for this method will be discussed in the next section of computer methods in forging [9.3], [9.41].

9.7 COMPUTER METHODS IN FORGING

9.7.1 Computer Simulation of the Modular Slab Method [9.13]

To perform all of the calculations of the stress distribution and forging loads for the simplified, three-stage, modular slab analysis method presented in the last section by use of a hand calculator would be very tedious. (A simplified model for use of a programmable calculator was presented earlier.) Computer programs, therefore, have been developed in the form of subroutines, or modules, for calculating the stress distribution and the deformation loads for each deformation unit or zone. These subroutines have been coded in a unified fashion in Fortran language. A flow diagram for one such computer program is shown in Fig. 9.24. Some of the symbols used in the flowchart are defined in Fig. 9.25 and in conjunction with the preceding equations. Some additional symbols are as follows:

H_0 = original height of the forging blank
R_0 = original radius of the forging blank
H_S = final height of the shaft from the base line
S = final height of the shaft

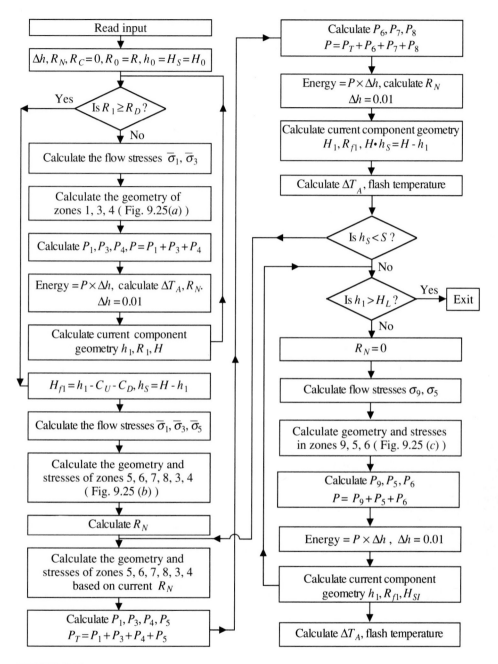

FIGURE 9.24
Flowchart of a computer program for estimating the load and energy in axisymmetric closed-die forging. (See Fig. 9.25(a), (b), and (c) for symbols.) [9.13]

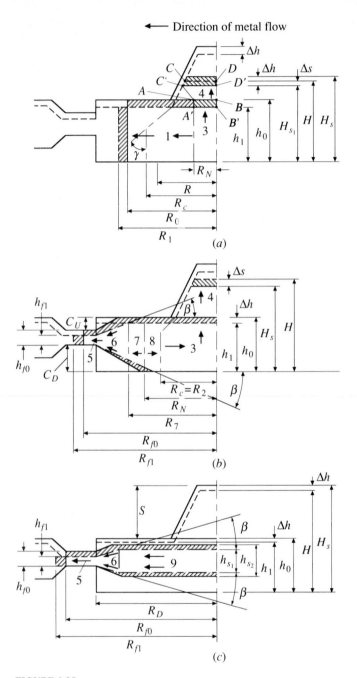

FIGURE 9.25
Flow models showing deformation zones: (*a*) stage I, (*b*) stage II, and (*c*) stage III [9.13].

H_L = final height of the flange
H = instantaneous (current) forging height
h_1 = current flange height
h_S = current shaft height
Δh = amount of platen (die) descent

Some of the relationships that may be used in making calculations in the foregoing flowchart are as follows:

1. *Flow strain rate*

$$\dot{\varepsilon}_i = A_2 \left(\sinh \alpha \bar{\sigma}_i \right)^{n_2} e^{-Q/RT} \tag{9.72}$$

where i denotes the zone of deformation, A_2, α, n_2, and Q are structural constants of the deforming material, and R is the universal gas constant. This equation is similar to Eq. (2.158) for steady-state creep.

2. *Adiabatic temperature rise due to deformation*

$$\Delta T = \frac{\Delta E / V}{C_p \rho} \left(\frac{1}{J} \right) \tag{9.73}$$

ΔE = incremental energy input for a deformation of Δh
V = volume of the specimen
C_p and ρ = the specific heat and density of the material
J = the mechanical equivalent of heat (see Eq. (4.79))

3. *Cooling of the flash*

$$T_{fi} = T_d + \left(T_{f0} - T_d \right) e^{-At'2w/bt} \tag{9.74}$$

where T_{fi} and T_{f0} = new and original flash temperatures, °C
T_d = die temperature
A = thermal diffusivity
t' = contact time of metal with die
w = flash land width
b = actual flash width
t = thickness of flash

(See Eq. 9.33.) (The flow chart shown in Fig. 9.24 should be studied at this point.)

In the foregoing method, an unsteady-state problem is solved by use of a computer simulation technique that utilizes the slab method to determine the stress distribution and forging load for a complex part by estimating the stress distribution and by summing the loads for deformation units (zones) at incremental steps of the deformation stroke. Also, since this technique can be used for only one part at a time requiring a separate program, it does not lend itself to general application. A more general program will be discussed later. This method also has other practical limitations in that the designer has to assume the existence of certain flow models to describe the deformation of a particular component and has to determine the optimum geometry at each incremental stage of the deformation. This approach requires specialized skill and a large computer. To overcome some of these difficulties, a simplification of the slab technique has been presented [9.13]. With the latter technique, a general approach can be made to estimate load and energy so that a wide range of parts can be analyzed from one basic program. Each part is broken down into modules of deformation such as upsetting, extrusion, etc., which are deformed sequentially, as shown in Fig. 9.26, rather than simultaneously. Although this technique required some additional development, because of its simplicity and general applicability it would be more attractive to industrial application.

Figure 9.27 shows a comparison of the experimental load-displacement curve with the curve predicted by computer simulation in forging 6061 aluminum alloy [9.2]. The flow stress of the metal in the die cavity $\bar{\sigma}_c$ was determined experimentally at 430°C (806°F) and at a ram speed of 33.9 mm/s (80 in/min) to be 48.3 MPa (7000 psi). The average flash temperature was determined to be 342°C (648°F) by use of Eq. (9.74), and the flow stress in the flash, $\bar{\sigma}_f$, was estimated to be 75.8 MPa (11,000 psi) for a friction factor of $m = 0.5$. Although the agreement is good at low loads, the predicted maximum load is 27 percent

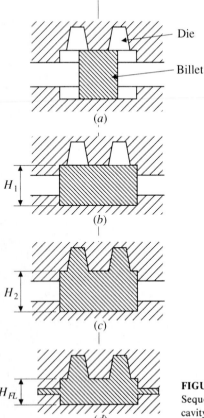

FIGURE 9.26
Sequences for the modular filling of the axisymmetric die cavity: (a) positioning of billet; (b) upsetting; (c) extrusion ($H_2 < H_1$); and (d) flash formation [9.2].

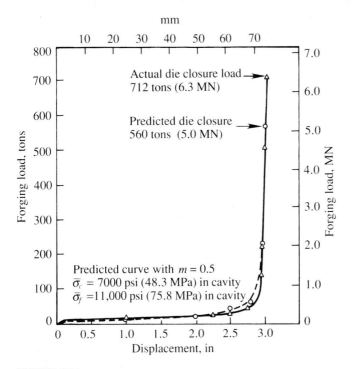

FIGURE 9.27

Comparison of the experimental load-displacement curve with predictions from computer simulation in forging a 6061 aluminum alloy. (The specimen is 2 in (50.8 mm) in diameter by 3.8 in (97 mm) high. The specimen temperature is 350°F (427°C), and the die temperature is 350°F (177°C) [9.41]).

lower than the experimental value. Because of the steep ascent of the curve at relatively displacements, it is difficult to determine the temperature and the flow stress of the flash and the friction factor to give close agreement.

Although the incremental modular simulation method of analysis gives a good approximation of the stress distribution and loads required for making relatively simple forgings and its use has been extended to predict the configuration of the preforms and to include computer-aided design and manufacture of forging dies, it does not utilize a detailed flow of metal during deformation. This is a simple, practical method that provides a good example of one way that the many concepts that have been presented earlier may be utilized.

9.7.2 Modular Sequential Simulation Computer Method for Axisymmetric Forging [9.2]

This process will be considered here as a closed-die forging process, as a flash is formed in the last stage of filling out of the die cavity and lateral or three-dimensional confinement of the metal is realized.

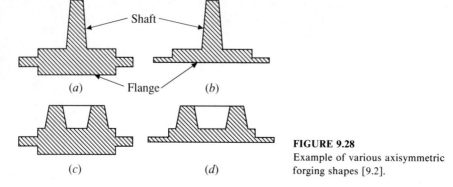

FIGURE 9.28
Example of various axisymmetric
forging shapes [9.2].

    In this simplification of the slab simulation technique, each forging, such
as shown in Fig. 9.28, is broken down into modules of deformation such as
upsetting (module 1), central (shaft) extrusion (module 2), and annular extrusion
(module 3), as shown in Fig. 9.29. A computer subroutine has been developed
for each of these modules to calculate the peak load and the total energy for
deforming each module. The function of the basic computer program is to string
these modules together in a sequential manner and to calculate the load-deformation characteristic and the total energy required to produce each forging. The

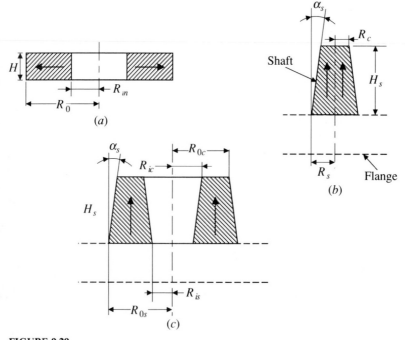

FIGURE 9.29
Deformation modules showing flow patterns that can be used to forge the shapes in Fig. 9.28: (a)
upsetting (module 1); (b) central extrusion (module 2); and (c) annular extrusion (module 3) [9.2].

forging at any stage is assumed to consist of zones of characteristic metal flow as shown in Fig. 9.29. This technique differs from other slab techniques in that the deformation is simulated by deforming the modules sequentially, as shown in Fig. 9.26, rather than simultaneously. The sequential order of filling of the die cavity is (1) stage 1, lateral filling of the flange cavity (module 1), (2) stage 2, filling of the annular extrusion cavity (module 3), and stage 3, lateral filling out of the flash (module 1).

Stage 1 is completed with the filling of the flange of height H_1 (Figs. 9.26(b) and 9.29(a)) and a load of P_1, as shown in Fig. 9.30, calculated as follows:

$$P_1 = 2\pi \left[\frac{A_1}{3} (R_0^3 - R_{in}^3) + \frac{B_1}{2} (R_0^2 - R_{in}^2) \right] \tag{9.75}$$

where $A_1 = -2\bar{\sigma}_1 m_1 / H$

$\quad\quad B_1 = -A_1 R_0 + \bar{\sigma}_1$

$\quad\quad \bar{\sigma}_1 = $ flow stress in module 1

$\quad\quad m_1 = $ module 1 die-material interface friction factor

The dimensions R_0, R_{in}, and H are defined in Fig. 9.29(a)

The energy absorbed in stage 1 (E_1) is given by the area of the triangle *OAB* in Fig. 9.30.

Stage 2 is completed with the filling of the annular extrusion cavity when the flange height is equal to H_2 (Figs. 9.26(c) and 9.29(c)) and the load is P_2, where

$$P_2 = P_{21} + P_{22} \tag{9.76}$$

and where the first subscript denotes the stage and 1 or 2 denotes the load.

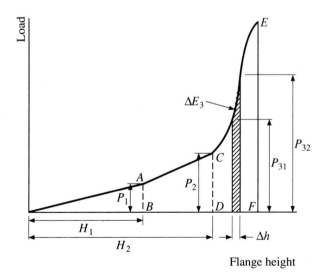

FIGURE 9.30
A typical deformation curve obtained by the application of the modular method. (Compare with Fig. 9.2(d) [9.2].)

P_{21} is the load required to extrude metal into the extrusion cavity and is given by

$$P_{21} = \pi(R_{0s}^2 - R_{is}^2)\frac{K_3}{K_4}\ln\frac{K_2}{K_2 + K_3 H_s}$$ (9.77)

where $K_2 = R_{0s}^2 - R_{is}^2$
$\quad\quad K_3 = -2\tan\alpha(R_{0s} + R_{is})$
$\quad\quad K_4 = -2(R_{0s} + R_{is})\sigma_3(m_3 + \tan\alpha + m_3\tan^2\alpha)$

$\bar{\sigma}_3$ = flow stress in module 3, and the symbols for the dimensions are given in Fig. 9.29(c).

P_{22} is the load required to reduce the flange height in Fig. 9.26 from H_1 to H_2, and it is calculated similar to that of P_1 by use of Eq. (9.75). The average energy absorbed in stage 2 (E_2) is given by area $ABCD$ in Fig. 9.30. The total energy absorbed at the end of stage 2 is equal to $E_1 + E_2$.

Stage 3, the final stage of the deformation sequence, reduces the flange height in Fig. 9.26 from H_2 to the final flange height H_{FL}, during which the excess metal is extruded into the flash gap. The total load involved in this stage is the sum of that required to deform the flange P_{F1} and to form the flash P_{F2}. The total load after descent of the die by an increment of Δh, as indicated in Fig. 9.30, is given by

$$P_{32} = P_{F1} + P_{F2}$$ (9.78)

The energy absorbed during the die descent of Δh is shown by the shaded area in Fig. 9.30 and is equal to

$$E_3 = \tfrac{1}{2}\Delta h(P_{32} - P_{31})$$ (9.79)

where the subscript 3 denotes the stage and 1 or 2 denotes the load.

The accuracy for the above results for simple shapes is sufficient for industrial applications provided that the variables can be controlled sufficiently accurately. Two problems are involved: (1) the choice of modules, and (2) the acquisition of the input data such as the dimensions, material parameters, temperature, velocity, friction factor, etc.

This simplified approach for the application of the slab method to forging will be used in the integrated programs utilized in the Biswas-Knight computer-aided design method for forgings and forging dies.

9.7.3   Biswas-Knight CAD Method
for Hot Forgings and Dies

9.7.3.1   INTRODUCTION. Using the simplified modular slab method discussed previously, Biswas and Knight [9.14, 9.15] have developed a computer software system for designing axisymmetric and elongated forgings and the dies to produce them. The computer programs involved have been combined as subprograms to form one integrated CAD system.

Three main stages must be completed before a forging is put into production: (1) the appropriate forging must be designed from the machined part required as above; (2) the method and sequence of operations to produce the forging, and the approximate amount of material must be determined; and (3) the appropriate dies required, including those for all preforming operations, must be designed.

The design of forging shapes and dies can be facilitated by use of the concept of group technology, in which forged parts may be classified into families of forgings that are related by similar design and manufacturing requirements. One family may consist of axisymmetric forging, another of elongated forgings, etc., as shown in simplified form in Fig. 9.31. Associated with each class may be a number of alternative standard processing sequences with variations mainly in the number and type of preforming operations used. Additional discussion of the classification systems for closed-die forgings will be presented in a later section.

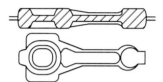

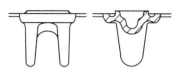

A. Axisymmetric forging with
     external flash only

B. Essentially axisymmetric
     forging with noncentral
     boss or other feature

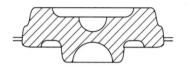

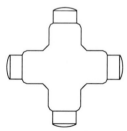

C. Axisymmetric forging with
     external and internal flash

D. Pseudocircular forging
     with essentially radial flow

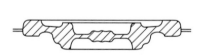

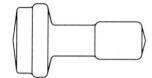

E. Elongated forging of
     complex cross section

F. Elongated forging of
     simple cross section

FIGURE 9.31
Examples of forgings belonging to different families or groups, in each of which the forgings are related by similarity of design and/or manufacture [9.8].

9.7.3.2 CAD OF AXISYMMETRIC HOT FORGINGS AND THEIR DIES. The first stage in the design procedure of a pulley-type forging, for example, from a detail drawing of the machined part shown in Fig. 9.32 involves the following:

1. Selection of the die parting lines
2. The assigning of machining allowances such as British Standards (BS) 4114 to the various surfaces to be machined (see *ASM Handbook*, 9th ed., 1978, Vol. 1, p. 369)
3. The selection of the draft angles
4. The addition of edge and fillet radii
5. The allocation of tolerances

Once the forging is designed, it must be converted into the shape of the finished die cavity of the finishing die and any required preform shapes designed. The cavity of the finishing die, such as is shown in Fig. 9.32(*b*), consists of the final forging shape, with a suitable flash land and gutter around the parting line. The purpose of the flash land is to restrict the lateral flow of metal to facilitate die filling without subjecting the die to excessive loading. Figure 9.32(*a*) shows in dashed lines the various modifications that are made to the final, machined part to produce the forging.

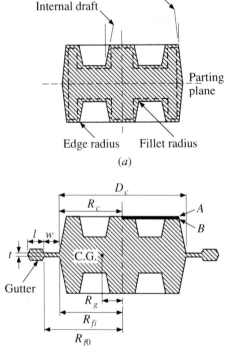

(a)

(b)

FIGURE 9.32
(*a*) Typical axisymmetric forging, (*b*) Forging cavity, including the flash land and gutter. The finished machined part is shown in dashed lines in (*a*) [9.14].

An outline block diagram for the system program is shown in Fig. 9.33. The design procedure starts with the input of a geometric description of the required machined part, in the form of the coordinates of the change points of the cross section profile and the selected parting plane of the die. Additional entries made are the material of the forging, and the forging conditions such as forging speed and temperature, which enable the data in a material file to be accessed at various stages in the execution of the program.

The machined part profile is converted by the computer into an appropriate forging design by the addition of machining allowances, draft angles, and edge and fillet radii, using the design rules provided. A drawing of the forging, superimposed on the original machined part, is plotted out automatically. Logic is included to omit small steps and recesses in the machined part when determining the forging profile. The weight of the forging, the flash geometry, the bar or billet size are then calculated. The computer program selects the diameter of the ejector

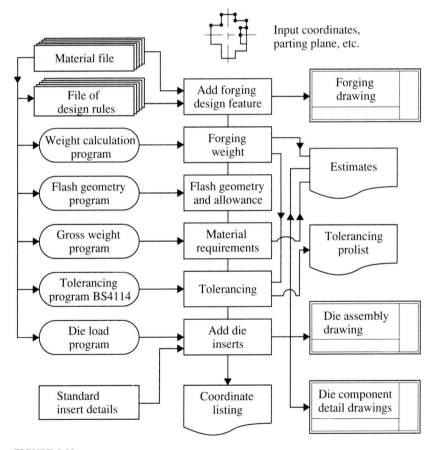

FIGURE 9.33
Outline flow diagram of the computer diagram (BS stands for British Standard) [9.14].

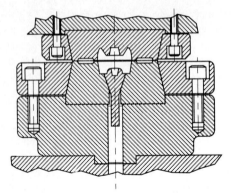

FIGURE 9.34
Interchangeable forging die inserts assembled in a custom-built die set [9.14].

pin and plots the detail drawings of the die components and the die assembly as shown in Fig. 9.34. (The original computer program system was written in Fortran IV and required a relatively long computer time of 30 minutes to run.)

The weight of the forging is calculated by multiplying the volume by the density of the material. The center of gravity with respect to the y axis, R_g, is calculated from

$$R_g = \frac{1}{4} \sum_1^n (x_{i+1}^2 y_i - x_i^2 y_{i+1}) \tag{9.80}$$

The following empirical expressions are used to design the flash dimensions:

1. The flash thickness t is given by

$$t = 0.017 D_c + \frac{1}{(D_c + 5)^{1/2}} \tag{9.81}$$

where t and D_c, the diameter of the forging without the flash, are in mm.

2. The flash width w is given by

$$\frac{w}{t} = 0.02 + 0.0038 S \left(\frac{D_0}{t}\right) + \frac{4.93}{(W/2.2)^{0.2}} \tag{9.82}$$

where D_c is the diameter of the material rough stock, w and t are expressed in mm, W is the forging weight in lb, and S is the shape difficulty factor and is defined as

$$S = \alpha \beta \tag{9.83}$$

α is the shape complexity factor given by

$$\alpha = \frac{P^2 H_c D_c}{F4(H_c + D_c)^2} \tag{9.84}$$

where P = perimeter of the axial cross section

F = area of the axial cross section and the other dimensions are given in Fig. 9.32(b)

β is the lateral shape factor given by

$$\beta = 2\frac{R_g}{R_c}$$

Typical approximate flash thickness, width, and net weight in lb/in (g/mm) are given in Table 9.2 [9.14]. The gross weight of the forging is obtained by adding a proportion of excess metal, which is lost in the form of flash and scale, to the actual forging weight. The loss of weight due to scaling (oxide formation) is 7.5 percent for small forgings up to 10 lb (4.5 kg) for large forgings.

In this approach the fictitious disc, slab method, is used. In this method, the shear zone is treated as a disc of a diameter and thickness equal to that of the flash. The peak load P is given for a dry friction condition by

$$P = 2\pi\left[\frac{A}{3}(R_{f0}^3) + \frac{B}{2}(R_{f0}^2)\right] \tag{9.85}$$

where

$$A = -\frac{2\bar{\sigma}}{\sqrt{3}t} \quad \text{and} \quad B = -AR_{f0} + \bar{\sigma}$$

$\bar{\sigma}$ is the flow stress, which can be calculated from Eq. (9.72) for the strain rate

$$\dot{\varepsilon} = A_1(\sinh A_2\bar{\sigma})^{A_3}\, e^{(-A_4/RT)} \tag{(2.158)(9.72)(9.86)}$$

where A_1, A_2, A_3, and A_4 are strain rate, temperature and strain insensitive material constants, $\dot{\varepsilon}$ and T are the mean strain rate and temperature, K, of the deforming material, and R is the universal gas constant. (Compare Eqs. (9.85) and (9.75).)

A big objection to this software system in present-day terms is that it was not interactive. This object was overcome by Lui and Das [9.16], who made it interactive, which will be discussed in the next section.

TABLE 9.2
Approximate flash thickness and width for hot trimmed steel forgings
[9.16]

Net weight lb (kg)	Thickness in (mm)	Width in (mm)	Weight of flash lb/in (g/mm)
Up to 1 ($\frac{1}{2}$)	$\frac{1}{8}$ (3.2)	$\frac{3}{4}$ (19.1)	0.0266 (0.475)
1 to 5 ($\frac{1}{2}$-$2\frac{1}{4}$)	$\frac{1}{8}$ (3.2)	1 (25.4)	0.0354 (0.632)
5 to 10 ($2\frac{1}{4}$-$4\frac{1}{4}$)	$\frac{5}{32}$ (4.0)	$1\frac{1}{4}$ (31.8)	0.0553 (0.988)
10 to 15 ($4\frac{1}{2}$-$6\frac{3}{4}$)	$\frac{3}{16}$ (4.8)	$1\frac{3}{8}$ (34.9)	0.0730 (1.30)
15 to 25 ($6\frac{3}{4}$-$11\frac{1}{3}$)	$\frac{7}{32}$ (5.6)	$1\frac{1}{2}$ (38.1)	0.0941 (1.68)
25 to 50 ($11\frac{1}{3}$-$22\frac{2}{3}$)	$\frac{1}{4}$ (6.4)	$1\frac{3}{4}$ (44.5)	0.125 (2.23)
50 to 100 ($22\frac{2}{3}$-$45\frac{1}{3}$)	$\frac{5}{16}$ (8.0)	2 (50.8)	0.1790 (3.20)
100 to 200 ($45\frac{1}{3}$-$90\frac{2}{3}$)	$\frac{3}{8}$ (9.5)	$2\frac{1}{2}$ (6.35)	0.2670 (4.77)

9.7.4   Interactive Design of Axisymmetric Forging Dies Using a Desk-Top Computer

9.7.4.1   INTRODUCTION. Lui and Das [9.16] presented an interactive computer method for the designing of dies for axisymmetric forging by use of a low-cost, desk-type computer. With an integral data base, this computer system does the following: (1) receives the dimensional coordinates of the finished part as input; (2) helps in the decision-making process involving the forging parameters; (3) produces drawings of the final forging, of the forging dies with the appropriate flash-land and gutter, and of the ejector; and (4) provides the NC tape for machining the EDM electrode for use in fabricating the dies.

9.7.4.2   STAGES OF FORGING DESIGN WITH A DESK-TOP COMPUTER. The basic design of the forging is carried out in four stages as shown in profile form in Figs. 9.35 and 9.36, which are similar to that of the conventional method of design. In the course of the design process, the dimensional coordinates of the finished part are fed into the computer, along with information concerning the machining allowance, location of the parting-line, draft angle, and fillet and edge radii. The die impression for the forging is shown in Fig. 9.35(d) after the foregoing changes have been made. The forging after the flash-land and gutter impressions have been added is shown in Fig. 9.36. The cross-hatched area represents the excess metal that was added to make a successful forging.

The (Teterin) shape complexity (difficulty) factor approach is used in the design of the flash and gutter. The shape difficulty factor S is given by Eq. (9.83) as

$$S = \alpha\beta \qquad (9.83)$$

where α is the longitudinal shape factor comparing any shape to its circumscribed cylinder, and β is the lateral shape factor. The thickness of the flash and the

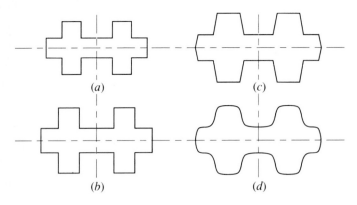

FIGURE 9.35
Profiles showing the four stages of axisymmetric forging design: (a) basic shape of the final part; (b) machining allowance added to the basic shape; (c) draft added; (d) fillet and edge radii added. (Two-dimensional sections taken from the center.) [9.16]

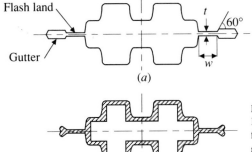

Flash land

Gutter

t

60°

w

(*a*)

(*b*)

FIGURE 9.36
Profiles showing the die impressions of the forging: (*a*) die cavity showing flash land and gutter, and (*b*) material added to the basic shape of the part. (Two-dimensional section taken from the center.) [9.16]

ratio of the flash-land width to flash thickness, w/t, are given by equations similar to Eqs. (9.81) and (9.82) as follows:

$$t = 1.13 + 0.89\sqrt{W} - 0.017\,W \tag{9.87}$$

and

$$\frac{w}{t} = 0.02 + (0.0038\,S)\left(\frac{D}{t}\right) + 4.93\,W^{-0.2} \tag{9.88}$$

where t and w are in mm, D is the diameter of the round forging billet (slug) in mm, and W is the forging weight in kg.

9.7.4.3 THE DESK-TOP COMPUTER PROGRAM. The flowchart of the computer program is shown in Fig. 9.37. The stored files shown at the right side contain various physical constants, forging design rules, and standard conventions. The main functions in the center of the chart coordinate the various activities and allow the user to interact with the computer to modify the results that appear on the screen of the terminal, etc. The output from the computer is shown on the left side, and the operator can request any desired output either on the screen or in the form of a printout.

Since the information concerning the forging and the dies is already stored in digital form, a set of NC tapes can easily be prepared to assist in the making of the dies. Such a set may consist of the following:

1. Tapes for direct machining of the forging into a finished part by use of an NC machine
2. Tapes for machining the die inserts and the ejector, if required
3. Tape for machining the EDM electrode for sinking the die cavities

The computer program is also capable of calculating an estimate of the peak total forging load P_t as follows:

$$P_t = P_f + P_b \tag{9.89}$$

where $P_f = $ the flash forging load, and $P_b = $ the body forging load.

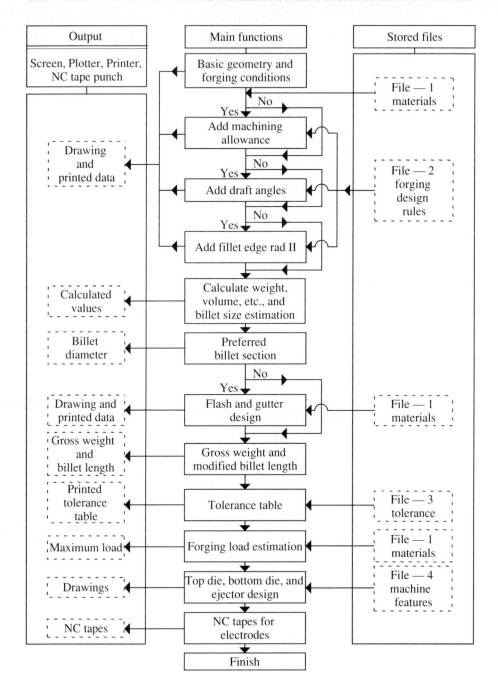

FIGURE 9.37
Flowchart of the computer program for the desk-top computer (compare to Fig. 9.33) [9.16].

P_f may be estimated as follows:

$$P_f = \bar{\sigma}_f A_f \sqrt{\frac{w}{t}} \tag{9.90}$$

where A and w are the area and the width of the flash-land, respectively, and t is the thickness of the flash. $\bar{\sigma}_f$ can be obtained from the simultaneous solution of Eq. (9.86) and the following equation for the strain rate: (see Eq. (3.117))

$$\dot{\varepsilon} = \frac{v}{L} \tag{9.91}$$

where v is the forging velocity, and L is the initial slug height.

P_b may be estimated from

$$P_b = \bar{\sigma}_b A_b \sqrt{\frac{w_b}{t_b}} \tag{9.92}$$

where A_b is the projected area of the plan view of the body, and w_b and t_b are the average width and thickness of the body. $\bar{\sigma}_b$, the effective stress for the body, may be expressed as

$$\bar{\sigma}_b = \bar{\sigma}\left(1 + \frac{2\mu w}{t}\right) \tag{9.42)(9.93}$$

where $\bar{\sigma}$ is the flow stress of the material, μ is the friction factor and $\bar{\sigma}_b$ is taken at the boundary of the body and the flash.

A conclusion that was drawn from this presentation is that the foregoing CAD program for a desk-type computer for the interactive design of simple, axisymmetric forgings and their dies should be ideally suited for the small forge shop.

9.7.5 CAD of Elongated Hot Forgings and Dies [9.15]

9.7.5.1 INTRODUCTION. A high proportion of forgings, such as connecting rods, etc., have a long straight axis. Usually elongated forgings are made from bar stock and normally require several preforming stages, the number employed being determined by process limitations and economic considerations of the quantity required. If the cross-sectional area varies appreciably, the metal must be distributed along the length of the workpiece by drawing down the bar at various locations. For hammer forging this is achieved by fuller and edging (roller) dies, but for press forging these dies are replaced by reducer rolls as shown in Fig. 9.38. These initial preforming stages result in a rough forged workpiece with metal distributed axially in a manner similar to the final forging so as to facilitate the flow of metal into the dies without the formation of forging defects or die lock. The size and volume of the forging of the initial forging blank used is dependent on the largest cross-sectional area of the forging and on the total volume of the forging including the estimated flash.

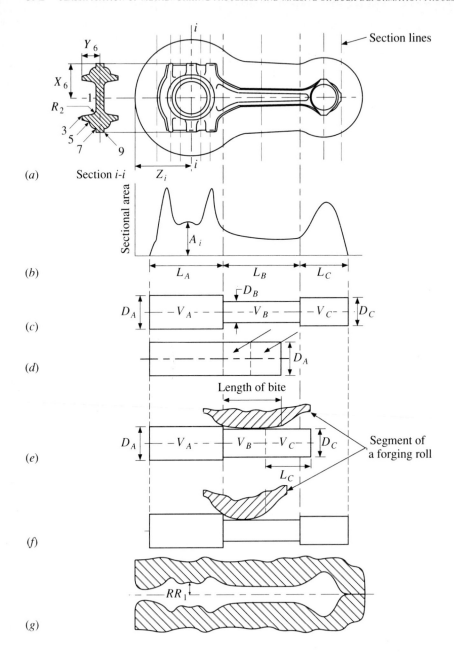

FIGURE 9.38
General design procedure for mass distribution in the preforms: (a) final forging including the flash; (b) mass distribution diagram for the final forging; (c) block form of the mass distribution of the preform (idealized fullered stock); (d) equivalent bar stock or forging multiple; (e) first fuller stage formed by roll forging; (f) second fuller stage formed by roll forging; and (g) longitudinal roller die profile for forming the final preform for the blocker die impression [9.15].

The basis for the design of the fuller and edging (roller) dies, and for the determination of the stock size, is the mass distribution diagram of the forging as shown in Figs. 9.38(*b*) and 9.39(*b*). These diagrams are plots of the cross-sectional area of the forging and of the flash at various critical points along the axis of the forging. The area under the curve gives the total volume of the material required to produce a sound forging. Enough cross sections of the forging must be chosen as shown in Fig. 9.38(*a*) to determine this diagram with sufficient accuracy.

The mass distribution diagram can be reduced to a block form, correspond-ing to major changes in the cross-sectional area of the forging as shown in Fig. 9.38(*c*). The stock size is then determined from the volume of the largest sectioned block of material divided by its length. The bar may generally be round or square as appropriate.

The block form of the mass distribution represents the idealized form of the stock after the fullering operation is completed, without any radii, etc., omitted. The length of bar required is determined by reducing the smaller sectioned blocks of material to the bar size as shown in Fig. 9.38. During the forging operation, the stock form is then altered to the idealized block form shown in Fig. 9.38(*c*), by one or more fullering operations, to reduce the bar down to the next largest section size, and so forth. It is unusual for more than two fullering stages to be used.

As indicated above, the object of fullering is to reduce the cross-sectional area of the stock in various regions while at the same time increasing the length of the drawn down portion. In hammer forging, this is accomplished by giving repeated blows to the bar between the horizontal faces of the fuller dies, while rotating the bar, usually by 90°, after each blow. For hammer forging, the mass distribution preforming is done largely by open-die forging techniques as described above, whereas for press forging preforming is usually done by the use of reducer rolls as shown in Fig. 9.38(*e*) and (*f*). An alternate procedure to obtain the preforming mass distribution is by use of forging rolls as shown in Fig. 9.40(*a*) and (*b*).

One of the purposes of using a blocking impression in a forging operation is to control the flow of material in the individual cross sections of the final die. Also, optimum die design should ensure die filling with a minimum of stock and of die wear. Large radii are used to promote good metal flow.

9.7.5.2 OUTLINE OF THE CAD PROCEDURE FOR ELONGATED FORGINGS. The general flow of information for a series of computer-aided die design procedures for elongated forgings is shown in Fig. 9.41. Since forging die cavities are relatively simple volumetric shape elements such as truncated cones, cylinders, etc., these elements may be combined to build up forgings of various types. Thus, it may be more convenient to describe the finished forging geometry as a combination of these simple shapes rather than to use a programming language such as APT, which might be considered as an overkill, in this case.

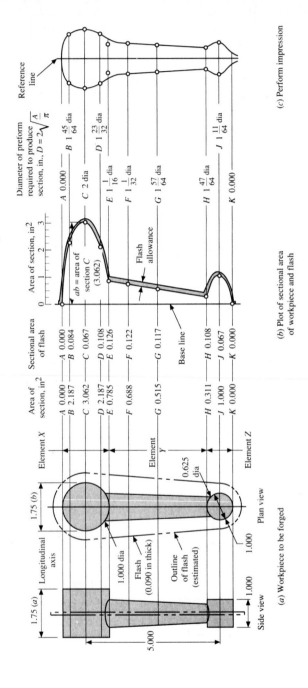

FIGURE 9.39

Example of a layout procedure of a forging to determine the shape of the preform impression and the equivalent stock or blank diameters. (*After L. G. Drabing.*) [9.25]

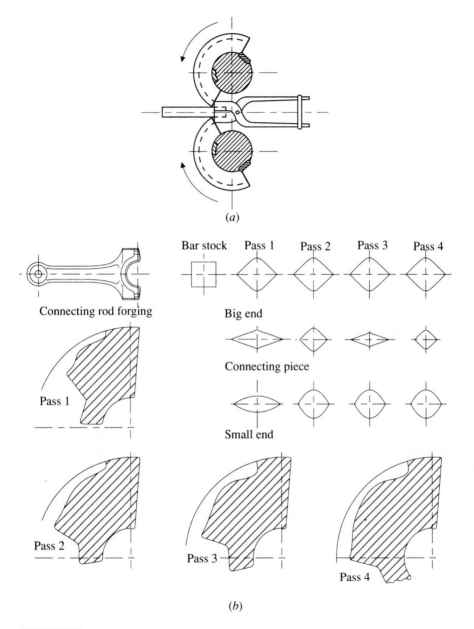

FIGURE 9.40
(*a*) Positioning of bar stock in forging rolls. (*b*) Cross sections of the workpiece at three different locations for each pass and the corresponding roll design for each pass [9.18].

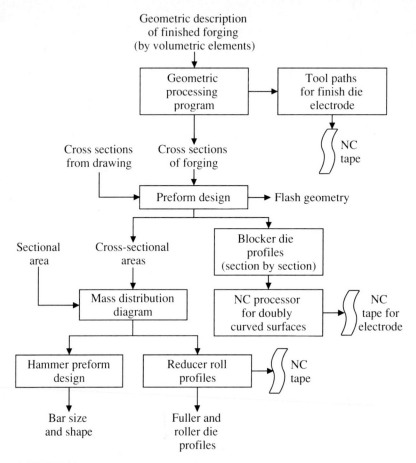

FIGURE 9.41
Flowchart showing the general information flow in a computer program for the design of "long" hot forging preforms from the input of such information as the mass distribution diagram [9.18].

A computer program using this approach has been developed. It can be used to provide input information for preform design programs in the form of selected sections of the forging, and also to generate the tool paths for the machining of the EDM electrode on an NC machine to produce the die cavities [9.16].

A computer program has been developed for the design of hammer preforms, which from an input of the mass distribution diagram of the forging enables the profiles of the fuller and edging (roller) dies to be generated, together with the details of the appropriate bar stock size and length required for forging. Up to six fullering stages can be covered in the program, but in practice more than two such stages are rarely used. Empirical design rules in current industrial use have been incorporated in this program. A related program for reducer roller profiles has been developed as indicated in Fig. 9.41 [9.17].

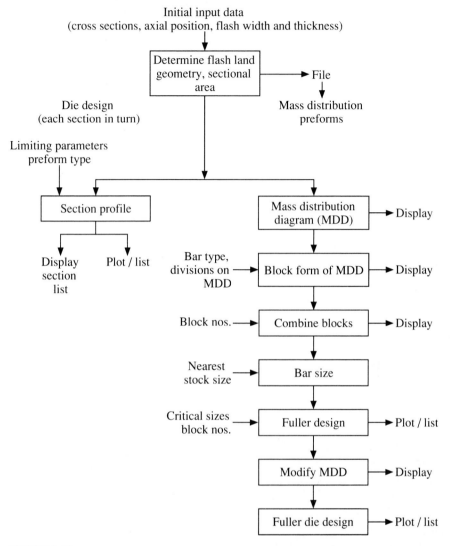

FIGURE 9.42
General information flow diagram for the generation of the mass distribution diagram (MDD) and the fuller die design directly from the input of the data of the final impression design [9.15].

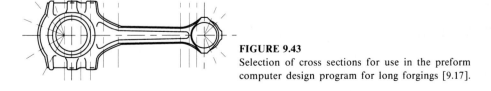

FIGURE 9.43
Selection of cross sections for use in the preform computer design program for long forgings [9.17].

In accordance with Figs. 9.42 and 9.43 the computer design procedure is as follows [9.17 and 9.18]:

1. A selected number of cross sections as in Fig. 9.43 is entered in terms of the change points and radii in the profiles, together with the width and thickness of the expected flash and the axial positions of the cross sections to be considered.

2. From the input data, the areas of the cross sections and the width and thickness of the flash lands are calculated. The separate elements are merged together in producing the EDM electrode to produce the finished forging dies.

3. If required, the profile of the blocker impression is developed by modifying the selected cross sections of the finished forging as shown in Fig. 9.43.

4. The general design procedure for mass distribution preforms for hammer forging is as follows:

    a. The mass distribution diagram of Fig. 9.38(b) is divided at various points corresponding to the major changes in cross-sectional area of the forging, from which the volume of material in each length section is determined.

    b. A block form of the distribution diagram is then displayed as shown in Fig. 9.38(c). The designer may then combine any blocks of stock to a workable number of fullers, usually not more than two.

    c. The bar size and volume are then determined as in Fig. 9.38(d).

    d. The designer now enters the sequence of fullering operations and designs the fullering die cavities. Extra material and features may be added in order to conform to the empirical design rules and limitations. (For example, the flash gap or thickness h is assumed constant, while the flash land width varies as follows: $b_F = 63h/w$, when w is the width of the cross section at the die line.)

    e. The edging (roller) die profile is then obtained by reducing the areas on the mass distribution diagram to diameter equivalents to obtain the longitudinal profile of the edging die, as shown in Fig. 9.38(g) and other views of the die.

Thus, from the same input data, the profiles of the various dies are obtained, together with the bar or billet size, flash geometry, etc.

The above brief description is of a system of programs that has been developed for the CAD of the preforms of certain classes of long forgings produced on drop hammers. The profiles of the fuller, edging, and blocking impression dies may be determined from the input data for the forging cross sections, along with the size and volume of the bar or billet stock required to produce the forging.

9.7.6 Computer Upper-Bound Modeling of Hammer Forging Operations [9.19]

The design of hammer forging operations and dies is still being done largely empirically by experienced forging designers. In recent years, the design process has been quantified to a greater extent to calculate the forging loads and energies for use in the selection of the hammer size and the number of blows required to produce a given forging. Programs have been developed for programmable calculators and minicomputers to facilitate the calculations and the design process. An example of a programmable calculator method is discussed in Sec. 9.6.3. An example of an interactive computer method presented by Reynolds and Fuller is briefly presented here [9.19].

This preliminary computer model consists of three algorithms for the calculation of the geometry of the part, and the force and energy required as can be seen in Fig. 9.44. (An algorithm is a set of well-defined procedures for the solution of a problem on a computer by a programmed sequence of instructions.) These three programs can be, of course, combined into one large program if so desired. Figure 9.44 illustrates a general flowchart of the three computer programs used. The flow of information is similar to that used in hand calculation except for one important respect. Instead of going in a single step from the starting geometry to the final configuration, the programs calculate the pressure distribution and load at different steps as the die is being filled during the closing operation. The number of steps depends on the number requested.

Figure 9.45 is a more detailed flowchart of program A, which calculates the geometry of the part during die closure. Manual input of the geometry at the terminal is accomplished by responding to the following series of questions by the computer: What are the number of sections and the width and thickness of each section? Whether an automatic starting distance calculation is desired and the number of steps of die closure for monitoring the progress of the operation? The program then runs and follows automatically the rest of the flowchart from α to the end and creates a data file of the geometry at each step of die closure.

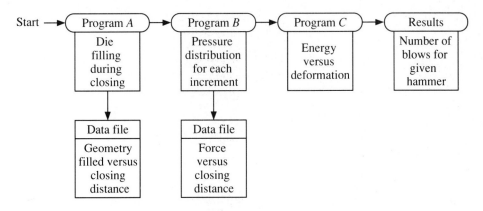

FIGURE 9.44
General flowchart listing three interactive computer programs, A, B, and C for the calculation of the die-filling capacity, the forging loads, and energy requirements for the selection of the hammer size and the number of blows required to produce a given forging [9.19].

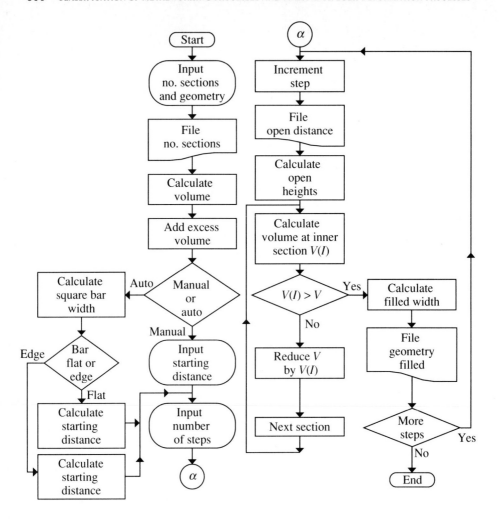

FIGURE 9.45
Flowchart of program *A* in Fig. 9.44 for the calculation of the die-filling behavior in multiple blow hammer forging [9.19].

Program *B* follows the algorithm of Fig. 9.46 after the following data is entered: the striking velocity *V*, strain rate sensitivity *C*, strain rate hardening exponent *M*, friction factor *m'*, and whether the section is long or round. (See the relationships and assumptions below.) The force required at each step of deformation (die closure) is calculated and presented on the terminal screen and also printed out. The program utilizes the fictitious disc slab method for calculating the load. Only the plane strain type of flow is discussed here.

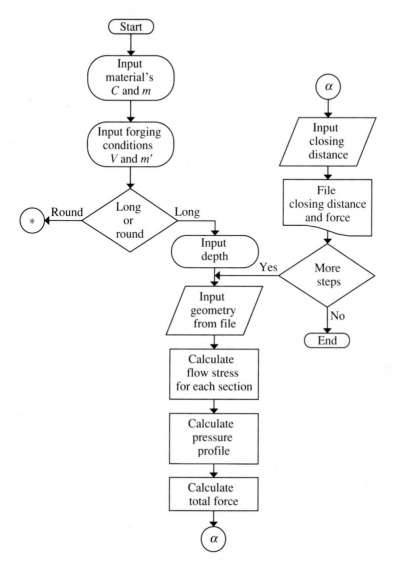

FIGURE 9.46
Flowchart of program B in Fig. 9.44 for calculating the force requirement or load at each incremental distance (see Eqs. (9.94) and (9.95) for significance of C, m, V, and m') [9.19].

Program C follows the algorithm of Fig. 9.47 after the following data is entered: the spring constants for the ram and anvil in million lbf/in (MN/mm), the weight of the ram, and the striking velocity. The program calculates and presents the elastic, plastic, and total energy for each step of die closure and the number of blows. The difference between a "soft" and a "hard" blow is shown in Fig. 9.48.

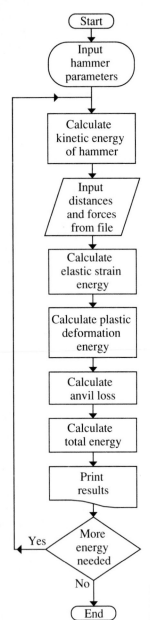

FIGURE 9.47
Flowchart of program C in Fig. 9.44 for calculating the energy requirements versus deformation for use in hammer selection [9.19].

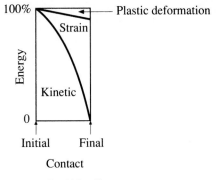

(a) "Hard blow"

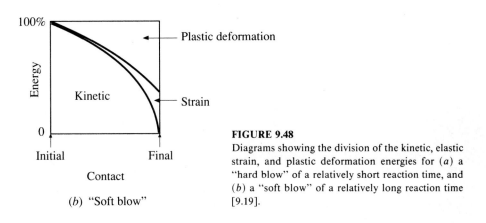

(b) "Soft blow"

FIGURE 9.48
Diagrams showing the division of the kinetic, elastic strain, and plastic deformation energies for (a) a "hard blow" of a relatively short reaction time, and (b) a "soft blow" of a relatively long reaction time [9.19].

The relationships and assumptions used in the above algorithms are as follows:

1. Assumption: $\bar{v} = \frac{2}{3}V$, where $\bar{v}$ is the average velocity and V is the striking velocity.

2.
$$\sigma_f = C(\dot{\varepsilon})^m = C\left(\frac{V}{h}\right)^m \qquad (9.94)$$

where σ_f is the flow stress, C is the strain rate sensitivity, $\dot{\varepsilon}$ is the strain rate, m is the strain rate hardening exponent, and h is the height of the workpiece.

3. Assumption: p versus w_N is linear for plane strain, where p is the pressure and w_N is the width of section N.

4.
$$p_N = p_{N-1} + \frac{2}{\sqrt{3}}\sigma_N(m')\left(\frac{w}{h}\right) \qquad (9.95)$$

where m' is the friction shear factor and N is the section number.

5. Elastic strain energy in the ram and anvil

$$= \frac{F^2}{2} \left(\frac{1}{R_1} + \frac{1}{R_2} \right)$$

where F is the force and R_1 and R_2 are the spring rate of the ram and anvil.

6. Plastic deformation energy

$$= \sum \frac{F(I-1) + F(I)}{2} (\Delta h)$$

where (I) is the Ith step.

7. Assumption: Anvil momentum loss plasticity factor

$$= 1 - \frac{F(\Delta h)}{E_a}$$

where E_a is the available energy.

8. $$E_a = \frac{F^2}{2} \left(\frac{1}{R_1} + \frac{1}{R_2} \right) + \Sigma F(\Delta h) + \left(\frac{M_r + M_a}{2} \right) \left(\frac{M_r V_r}{M_r + M_a} \right)^2 \left(1 - \frac{F(\Delta h)}{E_a} \right)$$

$$(9.96)$$

where M_r is the mass of the ram and M_a is the mass of the anvil.

9. Assumption: Anvil ratio is 20 to 1.

   With additional developments such as that for the constant velocity, the above assumptions may be relaxed.

9.7.7   Computer-Aided Design of Forgings

9.7.7.1   INTRODUCTION. Traditionally, the shapes for hot-forging operations have been designed by experienced designers, spending many hours of valuable engineering time. Recent advances in computer-aided design and manufacturing (CAD/CAM) have shown how the experience-based intuition and skill of the designer can be enhanced by computer-aided analysis and design [9.20].
   One of the disadvantages of the computer simulation slab techniques involved with forging, discussed in the foregoing, is that a new computer program has to be written for each new cross section of all but the simplest forgings. In recent years, interactive computer programs have been developed, in which the shape to be forged can be defined in terms of a series of selected cross sections that can be divided into certain basic, standard, modular shapes, so that all analyses and calculations can be made by a generalized program without the necessity for writing a new program for each cross section.
   Recent developments for simulating forging operations indicate that CAD/CAM can also increase considerably the productivity of the die designer. This increase is accomplished primarily by making a large database available to the designer, by computerizing such tedious calculations as area and volume, by simulating metal flow during forging, and by calculating stresses and forging

loads. A block diagram showing the integrated CAD/CAM approach to hot, closed-die forging is shown in Fig. 9.49.

9.7.7.2 BATTELLE'S DIE FORGE CAD/CAM SYSTEM.
9.7.7.2.1 Description. One computer system, that has been developed by Battelle's Columbus Laboratories for the Air Force Materials Laboratory, Wright-Patterson AFB, in cooperation with Wyman-Gordon Company and McDonnell Aircraft Company for use in forging design, is called DIE FORGE [9.21]. This program was written by Battelle in Cyber Fortran for use with the CDC-6400 computer in conjunction with a Tektronix graphic display terminal. DIE FORGE was converted to Fortran 77 at The University of Iowa, Iowa City for use with a PRIME 750 computer and any graphic display terminal for which TEKCOM works such as a Tektronix with a baud rate of 1200 bps. In this brief description of DIE FORGE the block diagram in Fig. 9.49 will be followed.

DIE FORGE is a system of computer programs for the design and analysis of the closed-die forging processes for rib-web type structural parts. This system can be used for (1) designing forging cross sections from the machined-part data, (2) designing blocker and preblocker dies from the finish forging data, and/or (3) estimating loads and stresses, and designing the flash geometry for the finish forging dies. The DIE FORGE computer software system, which contains a main program and 84 subprograms and function subroutines, has four major sections: (1) preprocessing, (2) load analysis, (3) preform design, and (4) display. The abbreviated tree structure of the DIE FORGE computer software is shown in Fig. 9.50. As seen in this figure, this system consists of a main program, called DIEFRG, and four main subprograms: preprocessor, stress analyzer, preform designer, and terminal display.

The sole purpose of DIEFRG is (1) to initialize a number of input variables by a data statement, (2) to initialize the error recovery commands, and (3) to call the Monitor (MONITR) routine, which monitors the functions of all other routines in the DIE FORGE system except DIEFRG. The input variables include the material code, flow stress in the cavity and flash, flash thickness and width, friction factor for the cavity and flash, die and preform temperature, heat-transfer coefficient at the die-material interface, press speed, etc. DIE FORGE has default values for all these inputs, and the designer assigns values only to those variables for which his choices differ from those of the default values. The recovery package prevents premature termination of the program execution as a result of any unintentional mistakes in inputting the data. Although the flowchart for the DIE FORGE system is very instructive, because it is very extensive, it will not be shown here for the sake of brevity.

Starting with a set of coordinate data describing the various cross sections of the forging, DIE FORGE processes, analyzes, and designs the various forging shapes, i.e., blocker and preblocker preform geometries, to the specifications of the designer.

The CAD of preform and finish dies are based on a set of data developed from the geometric definitions of the finish forgings. The data normally available,

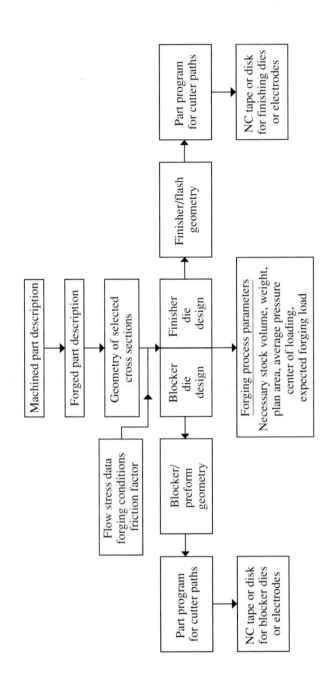

FIGURE 9.49

A block diagram showing the integrated CAD/CAM approach to hot, closed-die forging. (*Adapted from T. Altan, "Computer-Aided Design and Manufacturing (CAD/CAM) of Hot Forging Dies", COMMLINE, Aug. 1983, pp. 10-13.*)

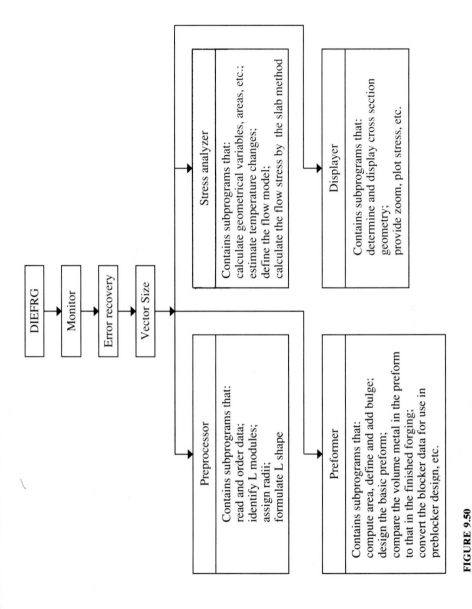

FIGURE 9.50
An abbreviated tree structure diagram of the DIE FORGE system [9.21].

however, are those for the finish part which is machined from the finish forging. Hence, one of the basic tasks in a forging design procedure is the conversion of the machined part data into forged part data. For this purpose, the necessary forging envelope, fillet and corner radii, and draft angles are added to the machined part surfaces. In addition, difficult-to-forge deep recesses and holes are eliminated and thin and tall ribs are thickened. The conventional conversion of machined part data into forging data requires a large amount of valuable engineering time.

The objective of die design for hot forging is to fill the die cavity efficiently and completely with a minimum amount of die wear and of loading in such a manner so as to prevent the formation of forging defects such as folds or overlaps as shown in Fig. 9.51. The forging blank or workpiece must be of such a size and shape as to fill readily the die cavity without any defects or excess flash, and with the optimum flow pattern or fiber structure to provide the necessary directional strength and toughness to the forging. In many cases the forging blank or multiple has to be preshaped to have the required metal distribution so that it can flow readily into the die cavity without the formation of any forging defects or die lock due to premature filling of any of the die impressions.

In the case of the drop hammer forging of a connecting rod, for example, as shown in Fig. 9.52, the forging blank is first preformed by fullering and edging

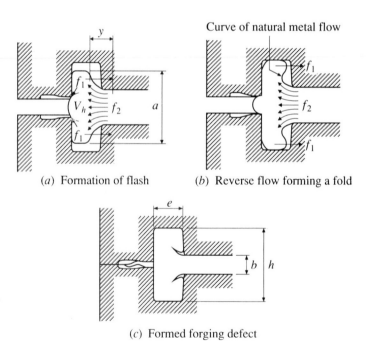

(a) Formation of flash   (b) Reverse flow forming a fold

(c) Formed forging defect

FIGURE 9.51
Sequential metal flow in die filling resulting in the development of a forging defect due to improper proportioning of the material in the preform [9.21].

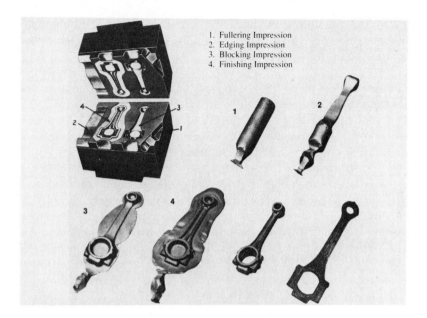

1. Fullering Impression
2. Edging Impression
3. Blocking Impression
4. Finishing Impression

FIGURE 9.52

Impression drop-forging dies for use in hammer forging of an automobile connecting rod one-at-a-time and the product resulting from each impression. The flash is trimmed from the finished connecting rod in a separate trimming die. The sectional view at the extreme right is a macroetching, which shows the flow pattern resulting from the forging process. The die impressions are as follows: 1. fullering, 2. edging, 3. blocking, and 4. finishing. (The forging blank 1 at the right is first used in impression No. 1.) (*Courtesy of the Drop Forging Association, Cleveland, Ohio.*)

by open-die forging on the face of the die block to proportion the metal correctly for the filling of the shaping or blocker die cavity. The die is designed in such a manner that most of the flow, and consequent wear, occurs in the blocker cavity. The finisher cavity is used to impart accurate dimensions to the forging and the fine detail. Generally a minimum amount of flow occurs in the finisher cavity, so as to reduce the load and wear, in order to preserve its accuracy and fine detail. In case of the connecting rod, four different forging blanks or workpieces are involved: (1) the initial forging blank cut from the bar or billet, (2) the preblocker preform, (3) the blocker preform, and (4) the finish forging, which is normally machined to produce the required part. (This example showing the various cavities at a forging die was not, of course, designed by the use of the Die Forge System.)

As the geometry of the part being forged becomes more complex, more than one preforming or preblocking operation become necessary to forge defect-free parts starting from stock having a relatively simple shape. The die design sequence is the reverse of the forging sequence. In the design sequence the dimensions and geometry of the finished part are modified to yield the shape of the finish forging and its die cavity. The geometry of the blocker is then used to design the preform or preblocker and its cavity, and so on. In case of the computer software system being discussed here, essentially the same set of computer subroutines are used to design the preform and blocker geometries.

9.7.7.2.2 Geometry of selected cross sections. The most critical information necessary for forging die design and equipment specification for a given material is the geometry of forging to be produced. DIE FORGE is basically a two-dimensional system, in which only one cross section at a time is analyzed just as is done in conventional die design for hot forging.

First, two-dimensional cross sections are taken through the part at different, strategic locations that can be used to describe the geometry of the three-dimensional part and the model for the flow of metal in the die cavity, completely, as shown in Fig. 9.16. To avoid the necessity of writing a separate computer program to design each new cross section of a preform, the computer-aided cross-sectional design procedure is based on a modular approach. In the modular approach, each cross section of a rib-web type forging is first divided into a number of modular, basic-L, stepped-L, and/or tapered-L shapes as shown in Fig. 9.53. In case of one of the cross sections of a preform, the geometry is designed for each module using the same generalized subprogram, and the modular preform L-shapes are assembled in a building-block manner to obtain the design parameters of the whole cross section.

Whenever preforms cannot be designed for a complicated cross section by the regular procedure, the designer divides the cross section into subsections

To continue enter *C*
To redefine the origin of L shapes, enter *R*
To design preform by subsections, enter *S*

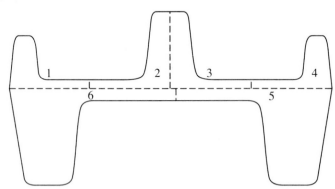

Cross section 2 — L identification —
Scale factor = 546   *X* length 12.704   *Z* height 6.988

FIGURE 9.53
Reproduction of the computer screen display of the cross section with L separation and identification numbers for the L modules in the DIE FORGE system [9.21].

To specify the window, position cross-hair at the ends of the diagonal
and hit any key after each positioning

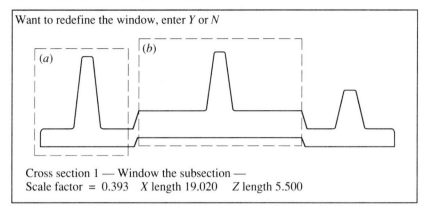

FIGURE 9.54
(*a*) Finished shape geometry and the first window outlined by the printer by dotted lines for dividing the cross section into subsections for preform design in DIE FORGE system. (*b*) The second window is superimposed by dashed lines [9.21].

using a built-in graphical technique as shown in Fig. 9.54. The subsections are designed one by one, assembled automatically, and displayed along with the original cross section. Modifications, if necessary, are made by editing the assembly geometry. For complex shapes the designer elects to design by the use of subsections while inputting data for the process variables.

Additional features of this program correct for forging defects and design irregularities that may occur during the design process. For example, when a relatively deep rib is forged on one side of the web, the metal at the base of the rib has a tendency to be drawn in or "sucked in." To eliminate the resulting defect, a bulge is added at the base of the rib as shown in Fig. 9.55. Also, in the course of the above modular design procedure, mismatches in the rib and web heights, as shown in Fig. 9.56, might occur. In the course of the design process, these mismatches are recognized and eliminated by blending the different modular shapes.

In designing the finisher and blocker dies for hot forging, it is convenient to consider critical cross sections of a forging workpiece, where metal flow is either (1) plane-strain flow or (2) axisymmetric flow, as shown schematically in Fig. 9.16(*a*) and (*b*). This is also the same procedure used in conventional, manual design. The selected series of two-dimensional cross sections approximates the complex, three-dimensional geometry and metal flow of actual forging as shown in Fig. 9.16. It also shows how the depth of planes in plane strain analysis and segment angles in axisymmetric analysis are specified. The depth of the plane-strain cross section is the average distance between two successive cross sections as shown.

For central L

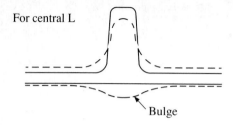

Bulge

For terminal L

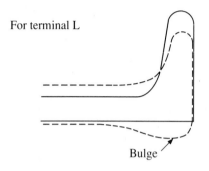

Bulge

FIGURE 9.55
In the DIE FORGE system a linear bulge is placed opposite the base of a tall, thin rib or rim of a preform to compensate for "suck-in." [9.21]

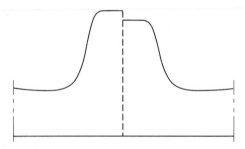

(*a*) Mismatch at rib height

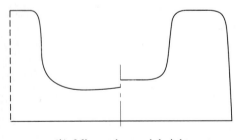

(*b*) Mismatch at web height

FIGURE 9.56
Drawings showing mismatches that may occur between different modular shapes and which are recognized and eliminated in the DIE FORGE system by blending during the course of computer processing [9.21].

9.7.7.2.3 Determination of the flow model. In DIE FORGE, metal-flow analysis is performed by dividing the forging into a number of basic deformation units or zones (see Fig. 9.20). Each unit is analyzed separately. The results of the separate units are then combined to obtain the total analysis of the entire forging.

In putting together the units of deformation, flow models are formed to represent the actual metal flow for purposes of analysis. When the metal flow is not restricted by the die-material interface, it is necessary to determine the surfaces in the material where shear occurs. This shearing boundary, where metal flows from the die cavity into the flash by shearing internally, is shown in Fig. 9.57. The flow model is determined by calculating the vertical stress σ_{yA} at vertical plane A-A (Fig. 9.57) and by minimizing the mathematical expression which gives that stress σ_{yA} with respect to angle α, and height h, defining the flow model. (A similar approach can be used for longitudinal flow into a shaft or a rib.) After the forging is divided into L shapes, the metal-flow pattern for each individual L shape is determined by minimizing the vertical stress at the neutral plane. The separate flow models for each modular L are then arranged to obtain the flow model for the entire cross section. The flow models of the various cross sections are combined to give the flow model for the entire three-dimensional forging workpiece. It should be emphasized here that the purpose for dividing the shape to be forged into modules is so that a generalized computer subroutine can be used to analyze each module, the result of which can be assembled with other modules to make the shear boundaries of each cross section. This shear boundary information can then be used to divide the forging into deformation units or zones that constitute the flow model. For a typical modular L shape shown in Fig. 9.58, it is logical to assume that the neutral plane is at its origin at plane

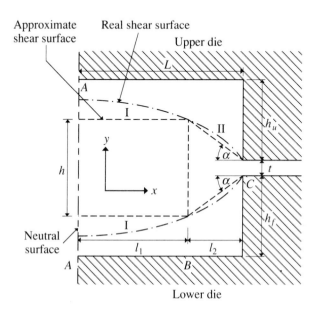

FIGURE 9.57
Flow model in the DIE FORGE system for analyzing the stresses and loads for metal flow into the flash (see Figs. 9.20 and 9.25) [9.21].

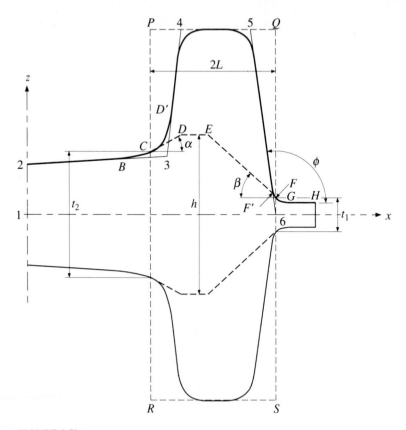

FIGURE 9.58
Flow-model geometry for typical L shapes used in the DIE FORGE system [9.21].

1-2. At the beginning of forging, metal flow starts by sliding to the right along the die surface $2B$. As the forging operation progresses, metal flow by sliding continues until it reaches point C, the midpoint of the arc BCD'. Beyond point C, metal flow occurs only by shearing along line CD and then along line DE. This shear path occurs because beyond point C, the slope of the arc BCD' is greater than 45 degrees, the nominal slope of the shear plane.

Similarly, on the flash side of the preform, metal flow starts by sliding along plane GH and continues up to point F, the midpoint of arc $F'FG$. During the later stages of metal deformation, metal flow is by shearing along line FE where FE has a slope of tan β. Thus, the metal flow by internal shear is confined to the rectangular region $PQSR$ shown by the dashed lines in Fig. 9.58.

Using the slab method of analysis, one can calculate the vertical stress at plane 1-2 of Fig. 9.58 as a function of the flow model geometry and the average flow stress of the material. The geometry of the flow model in the zone where metal flows by sliding is fixed and is given by the die surface. Hence, for the vertical stress at plane 1-2 of Fig. 9.58 to be a minimum, the stress induced by the shear deformation of the material in rectangle $PQSR$, shown by dashed lines, should be a minimum.

In Fig. 9.58, the vertical stress at point C can be obtained (in terms of the dimensions shown) using the slab method of analysis, as follows:

$$\sigma_{yc} = \bar{\sigma} \left[\frac{2m}{h} \left(2L - \frac{h-t_2}{2\tan\alpha} - \frac{h-t_1}{2\tan\beta} \right) + \left(Y - \frac{m(1+\tan^2\alpha)}{\tan\alpha} \right) \ln\left(\frac{t_2}{h} \right) \right.$$

$$\left. + \left(Y - \frac{m(1+\tan^2\beta)}{\tan\beta} \right) \ln\left(\frac{h}{t_1} \right) \right] + \sigma_{yf} \tag{9.97}$$

where σ_{yc} = vertical stress on the vertical plane passing through point C
σ_{yf} = vertical stress on the vertical plane passing through point F
m = shear friction factor (0.577, the default value)
$\bar{\sigma}$ = average flow stress in the deforming material
Y = factor related to the yield condition; it is equal to $2/\sqrt{3}$ for plane strain flow and to 1 for axisymmetric flow

Equation (9.97) can be minimized with respect to h, α, and β by rearranging and equating the partial derivatives of the equation

$$\frac{\partial}{\partial(A)} \left[\frac{\sigma_{yc} - \sigma_{yf}}{\bar{\sigma}} \right] = 0 \tag{9.98}$$

where $A = \tan\alpha$, $\tan\beta$, or h/t_1.

This step yields three equations. Solving them simultaneously, one obtains

$$\tan\alpha = \sqrt{1 - \frac{h/t_1 - t_2/t_1}{(h/t_1)\ln(h/t_2)}} \tag{9.99}$$

$$\tan\beta = \sqrt{1 - \frac{h/t_1 - 1}{(h/t_1)\ln(h/t_1)}} \tag{9.100}$$

$$\frac{h}{t_1} = \frac{(4L/t_1)\tan\beta + 1 + (t_2/t_1)(\tan\beta/\tan\alpha)}{(1+\tan\beta)^2} \tag{9.101}$$

Since these equations cannot be solved analytically, they are solved by numerical methods.

The flow model, showing the shear surfaces for the above forging example, is shown in Fig. 9.59(a). This flow model, originally defined in the form of a polygon, is connected into a set of rectangular and/or trapezoidal "slabs" or deformation units as shown in Fig. 9.59(b).

DIE FORGE is set up so as to permit the designer to edit the flow-model geometry by adding, deleting, or modifying the points defining it.

9.7.7.2.4 Stress calculations. The stress calculations for each forging cross section are done interactively by use of the slab method of analysis. During the design analysis, the stress distribution may be displayed on the screen of the terminal together with the average forging pressure as shown in Fig. 9.60.

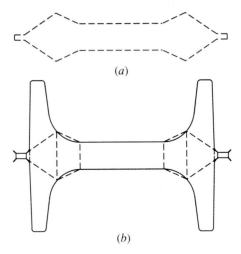

(a)

(b)

FIGURE 9.59
Separation of the flow model into deformation elements in the DIE FORGE system [9.21].

If the stresses on any cross section exceed allowable levels, the die will either crack or deform permanently. To avoid any such adverse effects, the shapes are modified either by increasing the forging temperature or by changing the flash geometry. A thicker flash or a short flash land will result in lower peak stresses. Changes in the flash geometry affect the stresses in the flash, but they do not affect the shape of the stress distribution in the cavity. Whenever the flash geometry is modified, the stresses in the cavity are increased or decreased proportionately, as shown in Fig. 9.61.

Maximum stress = 72549.275 psi

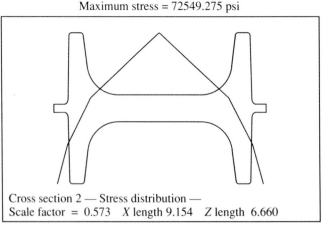

Cross section 2 — Stress distribution —
Scale factor = 0.573   X length 9.154   Z length 6.660

Flash thickness = 0.300   Flash width = 0.400   Finish area = 22.217
Load = 437697.0 lb acting at $x = -0.600$ Forging pressure = 58376.1 psi

FIGURE 9.60
Reproduction showing the stress distribution across of a cross section of a large aircraft connecting link as displayed on the terminal screen in the DIE FORGE system [9.21].

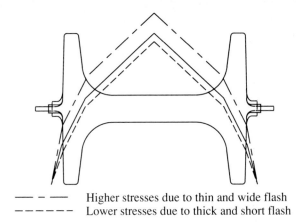

——— – ——— Higher stresses due to thin and wide flash
————— – ——— Lower stresses due to thick and short flash

FIGURE 9.61
Reproduction of the changes in stress distribution due to change in flash geometry as displayed on the terminal screen of the DIE FORGE system. [9.21]

Therefore, by modifying (1) the flash dimensions, (2) the material temperature, (3) the die temperature, (4) the press speed, and (5) the friction factor, the die designer by the use of DIE FORGE is able to evaluate the influence of these factors upon the forging stress and load. Thus, he is able to select the combination of conditions which appear to be the most favorable to him. After the forging stresses and loads are estimated for each selected cross section, the loads are added and the center of loading for the forging is determined.

9.7.7.2.5 Empirical guidelines. Also, because of the extreme complexity of the analysis in forging die design and because of the large number of process variables involved, it is not possible, and in some cases not desirable, to develop a completely analytical procedure for preform design. DIE FORGE is structured to use design parameters based on empirical guidelines found in the available literature as *default values*. These guidelines depend on the material and forging machine used, and are summarized as follows:

1. The blocker forging is slightly narrower than the finisher forging. The difference in width is about 0.5 to 1 mm on each side, so that the blocker forging can fit into the finisher die.
2. The blocker has usually larger fillet and corner radii to enhance metal flow.
3. The cross-sectional areas of the blocker are slightly larger than those of the finisher.
4. For forging high ribs in the finisher, it is often necessary to use lower ribs in the blocker. At the same time, the web thickness in the blocker is larger than the finisher. In steel forgings, whenever possible, the ribs of the blocker sections should be narrower but slightly higher than those in the finisher sections, to reduce die wear.
5. In order to increase metal flow toward the ribs in forging, it is useful to provide an opening taper from the center of the web to the ribs.

9.7.7.2.6 Advantages and disadvantages. Some of the advantages cited for the DIE FORGE system are:

1. The system possesses a fundamental, rational basis and the potential for revision and development.
2. The cross-sectional areas and volume are rapidly and accurately calculated.
3. Empirical and proven design data can be easily incorporated into the system and can be used as default values.
4. The system can generate alternate designs very quickly.
5. The system allows quick estimation of forging stresses and loads.

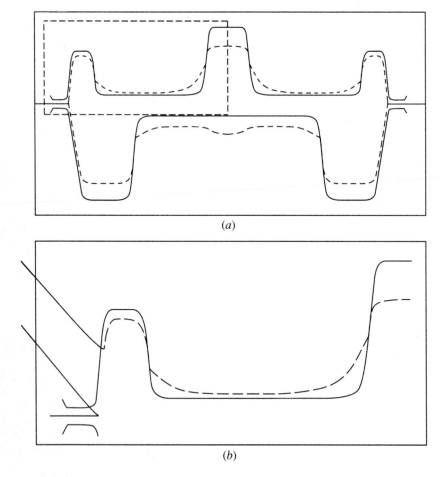

(*a*)

(*b*)

FIGURE 9.62
(*a*) A typical forging cross section and a possible blocker design displayed on a computer graphics terminal in the DIE FORGE system. (*b*) Zooming to examine a small portion of the blocker/finisher cross section outlined by a dashed rectangle in (*a*) [9.21].

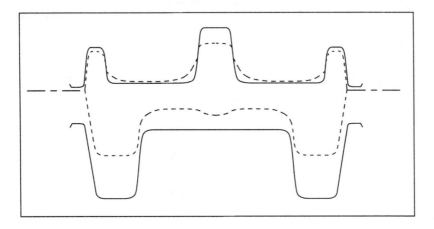

FIGURE 9.63
Blocker die profile, designed by the computer in the DIE FORGE system, shown with the finisher dies in a separated position. (*Adapted from T. Altan, "Computer-Aided Design and Manufacturing (CAD/CAM) of Hot Forging Dies", COMMLINE, Aug. 1983, pp. 10–13.*)

6. The system is very much user oriented and can readily be adapted to the designer's own system. A stand-alone, turnkey system is not needed.

7. The design data can be readily used to produce numerical control (NC) tape for machining EDM electrodes or the actual die cavities.

8. The designer can zoom to investigate a given small portion of a forging as shown in Fig. 9.62. If necessary, he may view the blocker forging position in the finisher dies at various openings to study the initial die contact point as shown in Fig. 9.63.

Some of the disadvantage or limitations of DIE FORGE are:

1. The system is basically two-dimensional, i.e., only one section at a time is analyzed as is done in conventional, manual design.

2. Presently, the system is primarily suited to rib-web structural parts.

3. The system cannot give or select the optimum preform design automatically.

4. An experienced designer is required.

In brief the DIE FORGE software basically modifies a forging cross section by using various multiplication factors applied to an L-shaped substructure of the entire cross section. Any modification made to one of these factors is applied to every L-shape component, thus making minor modifications at different cross section locations difficult. In addition, the software is fairly intolerant to changing the way in which these multiplication factors are applied to the design [9.22].

Although the designing of a forging by cross sections provides an opportunity to visualize the changes that take place during the forging operation, the transitions between the cross sections cannot be controlled in this two-dimensional approach. Therefore, additional work should be done to develop a general purpose, fully operational computer-aided system which can generate forging designs automatically from machined part geometry.

In summary, DIEFORG is an interactive Fortran computer program that combines the tools of computer-aided design, graphics, user interaction, etc., with classical techniques of forging design. The program consists of three modules:

1. *Input/processing module.* This module performs the following functions:
   a. It permits the user to set the program control parameters interactively through a NAMELIST input.
   b. It reads in the input geometry of the desired forging from the keyboard or from an existing data file.
   c. It displays the input geometry on the screen and allows the user to modify the input if necessary.
   d. It allows the conversion of machined part data into forging data.
   e. It automatically locates the parting line and divides the cross section into L-shaped modules.
   At every stage, the user is given an opportunity to modify any parameters that he feels are unsatisfactory. Only when the user is fully satisfied with the current set of parameters does the program proceed to the next step.
2. *Stress and loads estimating module.* After the preprocessing is completed, the program executes this module to estimate the forging stresses and required loads. The main features of this module are:
   a. It allows the user to set the forging parameters: the material, stock temperature, press speed, etc., through a NAMELIST input.
   b. The temperature and flow stress in the die cavity and in the flash are calculated by an interative process.
   c. A flow model of the metal flow during the forging process is derived and displayed.
   d. The forging stresses and loads are calculated based on the flow model. The stress distribution is then displayed on the screen along with the maximum stress.
   Within this module, the user also has the option of repeating any phase of the analysis with new parameters if the results of that particular phase are unacceptable.
3. *Preform design module.* This module designs the preform geometry for the forging that is being considered. The user can set the preform design parameters interactively through NAMELIST. The program then designs the preform and displays the preform geometry. Die separation and zoom features are also provided to give the user a better visualization of the preform. This feature is particularly important when the forgings are complex. In this module, the user also is given some control over the design process and can redesign the preform with a different set of parameters if the present design is not acceptable.

After the three modules have been successfully executed, DIEFORG prints a summary of the foregoing design on the screen. In addition, a more detailed listing of the results is saved on a disk file. Also, a copy of the die geometry is written to a separate file that can be used as input to an APT program which in turn can be used to drive a numerically controlled machine that can actually produce the dies.

9.7.7.3 A CAD/CAM PACKAGE FOR AXISYMMETRIC FORGING DIES [9.23].
9.7.7.3.1 Introduction. Two main disadvantages of the computer-aided software systems to closed-die forging as developed by Subramanian, Akgerman, and Altan [9.21], and as extended by Biswas and Knight [9.14] as discussed in the foregoing are (1) they required a relatively large computer, CDC 6400 (or PRIME 750) and IBM 1130, respectively, and (2) they were not interactive. (The former has a limited amount of interactivity and the latter is essentially not interactive.) As discussed previously, Lui and Das [9.16] repeated Biswas and Knight's work on a desk-top computer, structured their program in modular form, and made it interactive. Yu and Dean expanded on the foregoing work and developed a commercially viable package as will be discussed here [9.23]. In designing their computer program their objectives were as follows:

1. To ease the shape input format, so as to avoid manual calculation as much as possible
2. To include finishing die design for hollow parts as machined
3. To design any preform cavities, if needed
4. To construct the program in an interactive mode, so as to enable the user to override computer decisions, if necessary
5. To plot out dimensioned drawings
6. To generate NC tapes for the cutting of die cavities

9.7.7.3.2 Program structure. The program was implemented on a 64K Tektronix 4052 microcomputer and the software was programmed in Basic computer language, which allows for its easy transfer between microcomputers. The program is constructed as a combination of subroutines, so that it can be easily updated. It can be used for the design of both press and hammer dies.

The flowchart of the system at this stage of development is shown in Fig. 9.64. It begins with a manual preparation of the numerical profile data to be input into the computer. When the correct shape has been described, the design rules are retrieved sequentially from the program files, to design the finishing cavity initially. Upon completion, NC tapes, dimensioned drawings, and other forging data such as the gross volume, the bar size, and the load or energy estimates are produced. These data are then stored permanently in files for the use of the preform design routines, whenever these are used. The NC tapes and dimensioned preform profile are prepared in the same manner as for the finishing cavity.

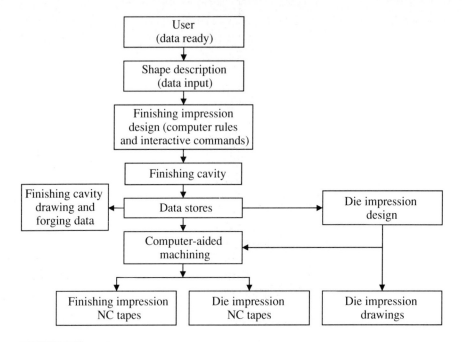

FIGURE 9.64
System flowchart showing the adaptation of a forging design system to the interactive mode of operation to form a CAD/CAM system for the design of dies for axisymmetric forgings [9.23].

9.7.7.3.3 Example of the use of the program. Figure 9.65 is a drawing of a machined spur gear blank, the example part, that is to be forged. The required input data relating to the right-hand half of the diametrical section is listed in Table 9.3. The shape is described by assigning coordinates to the intersection points of the surfaces of the shape, together with an intersection radius. These are labeled 1 through 12 in Fig. 9.65. The Y axis is always the centerline of the shape, while the X axis may be chosen by the user and, in this case, it is the lowest surface in the forging. Points are numbered in a counterclockwise direction starting from the one nearest the Y axis on the lower part of the section. A machining index of 1 or 0 is used to indicate whether or not a surface needs machining after forging. A machining allowance conforming to built-in program rules is allocated to those surfaces given a machining index of 1. Each surface is specified by the lowest of the two point numbers defining its ends. The parting line position, where the die surfaces meet, also needs to be specified. Other required input data are dimensional units, machine type, tolerance range, and initial draft angles. The latter can be altered in the design stage, if required. All the above data are input to the computer by means of the keyboard. Mistakes due to errors in typing and miscalculation can be rectified directly on the screen. A suitable scale factor is chosen to display the input shape if it is larger than the screen size.

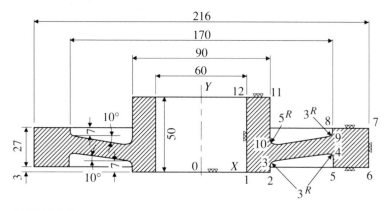

FIGURE 9.65

Drawing of a machined spur gear blank used as an example part showing the numerical data preparation prior to shape input [9.23].

After the data have been input, the computer program executes the following sequences in designing the finishing cavity as shown by the rectangles in the flowchart in Fig. 9.66: (1) adds the web, if the input shape has a central hole; (2) allocates the machining allowance; (3) adds the draft angles; (4) adds the corner or fillet radii; (5) designs the flash-land and gutter; (6) calculates the gross

TABLE 9.3
Full listing of the input data for the shape in Fig. 9.65

No. of point	X coordinate	Y coordinate	Inherent radius	Machining index
1	30	0	0	1
2	45	0	0	0
3	45	7	3	0
4	110	190	3	0
5	85	3	0	1
6	108	3	0	1
7	108	30	0	1
8	85	30	0	0
9	85	23	3	0
10	110	190	5	0
11	45	50	0	1
12	30	50	0	1

Input 12 points
Parting line ordinate, 15.00 mm
Forcing machine, mechanical press
Normal forging tolerance
Metric unit
Internal draft, 6 (degrees)
External draft, 4 (degrees)

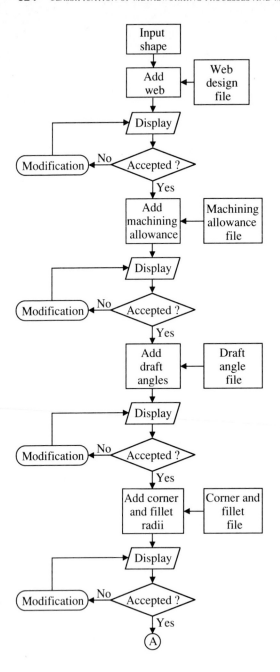

FIGURE 9.66
Flowchart of the interactive CAD/CAM program showing the development of the final drawings
and the machining data by the modification of the basic shape by addition of the web, machining
allowance, draft, etc. [9.23].

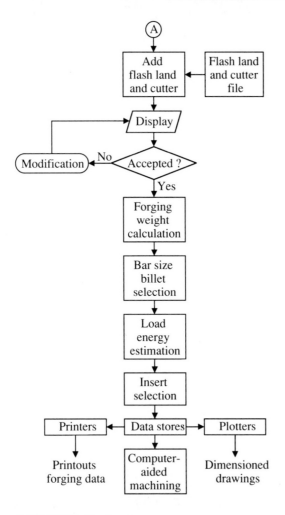

FIGURE 9.66. Continued.

forging volume; (7) selects the bar (billet) size and geometry; (8) estimates the load or energy required; and (9) selects the inserts of the top and bottom die.

The interactive nature of the computer program can be seen from Fig. 9.66. The empirical design rules are built into the program. Figure 9.67(a) to (d) shows the profile of the central section of the forging showing a step-by-step design of the above sequences. The current shape, shown by solid lines, is displayed on the computer screen and superimposed with the input shape, shown by dashed lines and indicating the machining allowance. (Note that the flat web in the center will be machined out of the forging to form the central hole in the part.) The designer can alter the shape at will until he obtains the desired shape. Figure 9.68 shows the cross section of the die inserts.

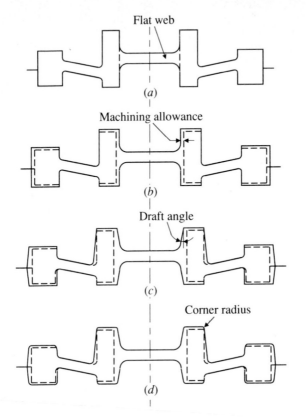

FIGURE 9.67

Computer generated drawings of profiles of central sections produced by the CAD/CAM system depicted in the flowchart shown in Fig. 9.66 representing (*a*) addition of a flat web at the midheight of the central hole (which will eventually be machined out), (*b*) the addition of the machining allowance, (*c*) inclusion of the draft angles, and (*d*) introduction of radii at the sharp fillets and corners. [9.23]

The program can plot out dimensioned drawings of the finishing die cavities and of the preform profile. Table 9.4 shows the printout of the required forging data. A listing of the tolerance specifications can also be printed out.

Based upon the profile of a finishing cavity and its volume plus the flash, a subroutine executes the design of the preform die impression. In addition to

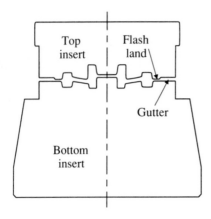

FIGURE 9.68

Profiles of the die inserts showing the flash land and gutter [9.23].

TABLE 9.4
Computer printouts of forging data for Fig. 9.69(*a*)

```
FORGING MACHINE IS MECHANICAL PRESS
FORGING MATERIAL EN8
FORGING TEMPERATURE 1250 (C)
PRESS LOAD 2480 (TDNf)
SQUARE BAR SIDE 90 (MM)
BAR LENGTH 132.5 (MM)
FLASH THICKNESS: 3.7 (MM)
FLASH WIDTH: 14.7 (MM)
FLASH WIDTH/FLASH THICKNESS RATIO: 4.0
STOCK MATERIAL WEIGHT 8.42 (KG)
FORGING WEIGHT (WITHOUT FLASH): 7.09 (KG)
```

having two design methods available within the program, a user can interactively construct a particular shape. Preform die cavities are designed by modifying the finishing profile in the following three respects, assuming no flash is formed in the operation: (1) the preform profile is made with a smaller diameter than the finishing profile to allow for ease of location of the preform in the finishing die cavity; (2) generous radii are introduced at die corners and fillets to facilitate metal flow; (3) web thickness and rib heights are adjusted to facilitate insertion while maintaining volume equivalence.

A preform produced by the first method is shown located inside the finishing cavity in Fig. 9.69(*a*). A plot of its dimensioned profiles is shown in Fig. 9.69(*b*).

After the finishing or preform die impression design is completed, NC tapes can be generated for the cutting of the dies or of the EDM electrodes as shown in the flowchart in Fig. 9.70. The cutting sequence is completed in the rough and finish cuts. Cutter paths, spindle speeds and feed rates are calculated by the program. Before generating the NC tapes, the cutter paths are simulated on the video display screen to avoid problems during actual machining.

The program is rather user friendly, and the time required to run it on the average is usually less than one hour.

9.7.7.4 PROPRIETARY CAD/CAM/CAE FORGING SYSTEMS. The forging industry is taking advantage of the computer-aided design/manufacturing/engineering (CAD/CAM/CAE) technology to meet customer demands for higher quality, lower cost forgings.

Computer are used in the forging industry in three basic ways [9.24]:

1. Preparing part, die, and fixture drawings and generating the machining data
2. Using a coordinate measuring machine to control the dimensions of the part or the dies, electrodes, etc., for making them
3. Analyzing and simulating the forging process

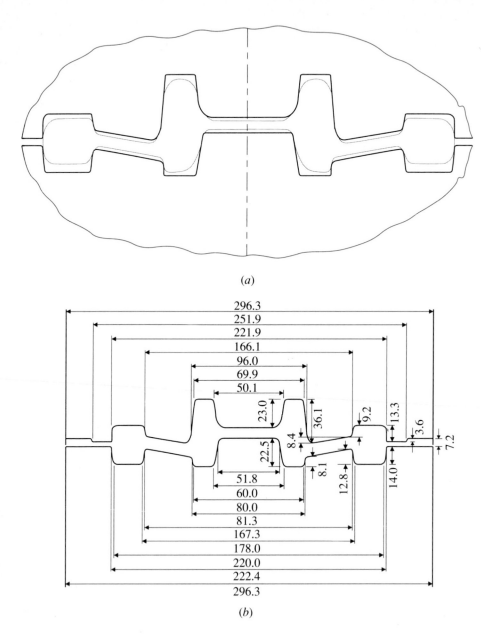

(a)

(b)

FIGURE 9.69

Reproduction of the computer printouts showing (b) the plot of the dimensioned finishing cavity profiles and (a) location of the computer designed forging in the finishing cavity [9.23].

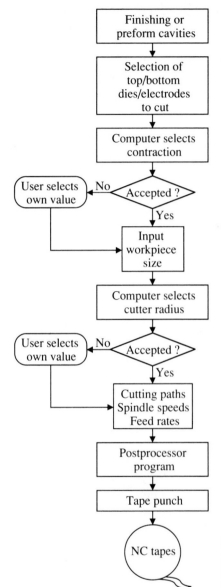

FIGURE 9.70

Flowchart showing the steps for the production of the NC tape for the machining of the finishing and/or preform cavities shown in Fig. 9.69 [9.23].

The ability to transfer graphic design data from one computer to another eliminates the need for reentering these data into the CAD/CAM system of the forging company. This electronic transfer of geometric data by use of tapes, disks, or telephone lines is referred to as Initial Graphic Exchange Specification (IGES). IGES reduces errors and the lead time before production. IGES allows dissimilar CAD systems to exchange data. It is an outgrowth of the U.S. Air Force ICAM (Integrated Computer-Aided Manufacturing) program, which has become the

ANSI standard and is directed by the National Bureau of Standards. IBM's IGES Processor is designed to transfer data between CAD systems via a series of disk files.

A flowchart showing an integrated CAD/CAM system of a modern forging company is shown in Fig. 9.71. The "Expert Systems" referred to in Fig. 9.71 are Knowledge-Based Expert Systems similar in principle to the various forging design analysis systems discussed elsewhere in this book. The U.S. Air Force, in conjunction with its Manufacturing Science Program, is in the process of developing a more sophisticated Expert System, which was to be made available in 1988 [9.24]. (The term "expert system" for computer software stems from its attempt to capture the expertise of the retiring, irreplaceable skilled expert in a systematic and logical manner. Expert systems will be discussed in greater detail in Sec. 9.15 in conjunction with their application to cold forging of steel.)

The development of reasonably accurate and inexpensive computer software to simulate metal flow during the forging process provides the ultimate advantage

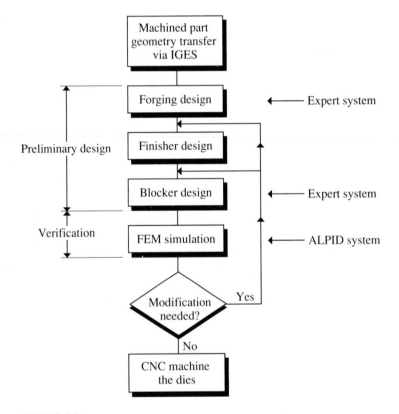

FIGURE 9.71
Flowchart of a typical commercial, stand-alone CAD/CAM system for forging die design providing graphic and drafting capabilities, 2D-load and stress estimation, metal-flow simulation, and advanced FEM modeling, which reduces the need for numerous and costly die tryout [9.24].

of computer application to forging. The forging process can continue to be simulated with this software until the optimum forging design is obtained. The finite element (FEM) simulation program called ALPID (Analysis of Large-scale Plastic Incremented Deformation) is discussed elsewhere. Two new versions of ALPID, called ALPIDT and ALPIDP, have been developed to simulate non-isothermal forging processes and the compaction of powder metal preforms, respectively.

Three Battelle-developed expert systems are: Automatic Forging Design (AFD), Blocker Initial Design (BID), and Forming Sequence Design for Flashless Forging of Axisymmetric Parts (FORMEX). Since the FORMEX program deals with forming of axisymmetric parts from rod stock, none of the DIE FORGE software is applicable to this expert system.

The major suppliers of CAD/CAM systems for the design of forgings and forging dies are shown in Table 9.5. Most of these systems do not possess preprocessing capability for FEM analysis and/or the postprocessing capability for displaying the results of the analysis for easy interpretation, so that separate software packages such as SUPERTAB or PARTRAN must be purchased.

ToolChest is an example of a very user-friendly CAD/CAM system, using an integrated menu system, developed by Battelle and was created expressly for tool and die makers and product designers. It automates all design and manufacturing phases of mold, tool, and die-making operations. It enables relatively quick design and cost-effective manufacturing of complex geometric shapes, and it increases the productivity of numerical control machining. It provides an integrated approach to the whole gamut of activities from product design to data handling, drafting, viewing, and machining. It creates NC programs for any

TABLE 9.5
Major CAD/CAM systems for die design

Software	Supplier
Anvil 5000	Manufacturing Consulting Services (MCS)
Autotrol	Auto-Trol Technology
Bravo	Applicon/Schlumberger
Cadds 4	Computervision
Camax	Camax Systems Inc.
Catia	IBM
Euclid	Datavision
Euklid	Fides
Grattek	Graphics Tech. Corp.
Intergraph	Intergraph Corp.
Patran	PDA Engineering
Supertab	CAE International
Toolchest	Batelle Columbus Laboratories
Unigraphics	McDonnel Douglas Manufacturing Systems

† Software for pre- and postprocessing for FEM. Courtesy, Taylan Altan, Center for Net Shape Manufacturing, Ohio State University

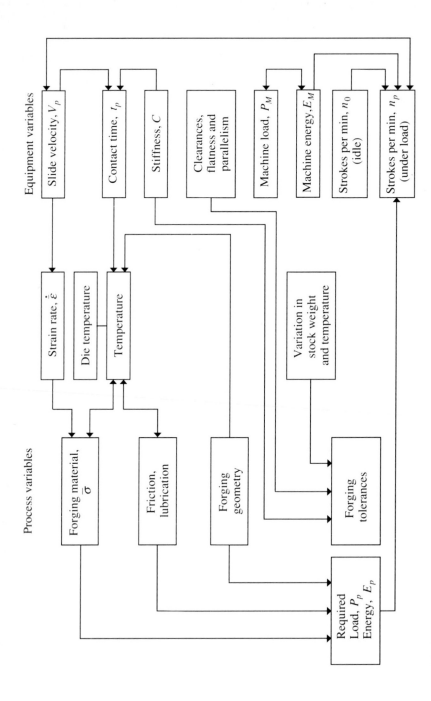

FIGURE 9.72
Relationship between process and machine variables in hot-forging processes conducted in presses. (*Adapted from T. Altan, "Selection of Forging Equipment", in Forging Handbook, T. G. Byrer et al. Editors, FIA/ASM, Metals Park, 1985, pp. 203–205.*)

available machine tool and consequently eliminates the need to master a complex NC programming language.

9.8 SELECTION OF FORGING EQUIPMENT

9.8.1 Introduction

How do the many process and material parameters (see Table 4.2) discussed thus far, such as the required load and energy, the flow stress, strain rate, temperature, geometry of forging, etc., affect the selection of forging equipment? Some clue to the interaction of the various process and material parameters and the equipment used is given in Figs. 4.60 and 4.63. The interaction between the principal *process* and *equipment* variables for hot-press forging is shown in Fig. 9.72, where a line between two blocks indicates that one variable influences the other one.

As seen on the left side of Fig. 9.72, the flow stress $\bar{\sigma}$, the interface friction conditions and the forging geometry determine both the load P_p at each position of the stroke and the energy E_p required by the forging process. The flow stress $\bar{\sigma}$ increases with increase in the deformation rate $\dot{\varepsilon}$ and with decrease in temperature T. The magnitude of these variations depends on the specific forging material. The friction of the tool material interface increases with an increase in die chilling [8.20].

As indicated by the lines connected to the temperature block for a given initial stock temperature, the temperature variations in the forging are largely influenced by the surface area of contact between the dies and the forging, the thickness or volume of the workpiece, die temperature, the amount of heat generated by deformation and friction, and the contact time under load. During deformation, the heat transfer from the hot workpiece to the cooler dies is nearly perfect with graphite-based lubricants. With glass-based lubricants, the heat transfer is greatly reduced, depending on the interface temperature and the thickness and type of glass coating [8.20].

The velocity of the slide under pressure V_p, shown in the upper right corner of Fig. 9.72, determines mainly the contact time under pressure t_p and the deformation rate ε. The number of strokes per minute n_0 under no-load conditions, the machine energy E_M, and the deformation energy E_p required by the process, influence the slide velocity under load V_p and the number of strokes under load n_p, which determines the production rate [8.19].

As indicated in Fig. 9.72, the stiffness of the press influences the contact time under load and the thickness tolerance of forged parts in mechanical press forging.

9.8.2 Description of Closed-Die Forging Equipment

9.8.2.1 CLOSED-DIE FORGING HAMMERS [9.25].

9.8.2.1.1 Board drop hammers. In the board drop hammer, the ram is lifted by one or more boards, which is keyed to it and which passes between two friction rolls at the top of the hammer as shown in Fig. 9.73. As the board is rolled upward, it is tripped mechanically allowing the ram to drop from the predetermined desired height, which cannot be altered without stopping the machine. A single stroke is obtained by depressing the treadle once and releasing it. Successive strokes are obtained by keeping the treadle depressed. The size of the hammer is rated on the basis of the weight of the ram assembly excluding the upper die. Board hammers have falling weights, or rated sizes, of 100 to 10,000 lb; however, standard sizes have falling weights of 1,000 to 5,000 lb, in increments of 500 or 1,000 lb [9.25].

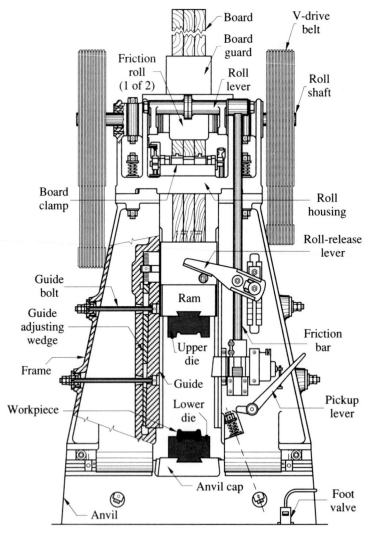

FIGURE 9.73
Principal components of a board drop hammer [9.25].

9.8.2.1.2   Air-lift gravity drop hammers. In the air-lift gravity drop hammer, the ram assembly is raised by air or steam but drops by gravity when released. The ram is held in the raised position by a piston-rod clamp. Cycling is continued while the treadle is kept depressed. The length of stroke can be controlled. The generally available size ranges from 500 to 10,000 lb on the basis of the weight of the ram assembly, which is equivalent to the range of energy per stroke of about 2,500 to 52,000 ft-lb (350 to 7,230 m-kg).

9.8.2.1.3   Power drop hammers. In the power drop hammer shown in Fig. 9.74, the force of the dropping ram assembly is supplemented by a pressure of steam or air at 90 to 125 psi (620 to 862 kPa) acting on the piston in the cylinder. Power drop hammers are rated by the weight of the striking mass, not including the upper die, and commonly range from 500 to 35,000 lb (or occasionally to 50,000 lb), which is equivalent to about 7400 to 425,000 ft-lb (1030 to 59,000 m-kg). (Note that m-kg is a nonstandard energy unit. 1 m-kg ≡ 7.23 ft-lb.) As much as 15 to 25 percent of the kinetic energy is dissipated in the anvil and foundation, which imposes a high stress on the anvil block and necessitates a very large anvil.

9.8.2.1.4   Counterblow hammers (impacters). Counterblow hammers are of two types: vertical, as shown in Fig. 9.75, and horizontal. The striking force develops from the movement of two rams from opposite directions and meeting at the midpoint. The vibration of impact is reduced and approximately full energy of each blow is delivered to the workpiece without loss to an anvil. The horizontal counterblow hammer is similar in principle and operation to the vertical hammer. Vertical hammers are rated in m-kg, and horizontal hammers are rated in ft-lb. The former are available to a capacity of 125,000 m-kg (900,000 ft-lb), and the latter have an energy rating of 3000 to 70,000 ft-lb (417 to 9722 m-kg).

9.8.2.1.5   High energy-rate forging (HERF) machines. HERF machines are of three basic types:

1. Ram and inner frame machines having capacities of 12,500 to 550,000 ft-lb (1736 to 76,389 m-kg) of impact energy
2. Two-ram machines having a maximum rating of 300,000 ft-lb (41,667 m-kg) of impact energy
3. Controlled-energy-flow machines made in two sizes, 73,000 and 400,000 ft-lb (10,139 and 55,556 m-kg)

Each type differs from the others in engineering and operating features, but all are essentially very high velocity, single-blow hammers that require less moving weight than do conventional hammers to achieve the same impact energy per blow. All the designs employ the counterblow principle to minimize foundation requirements and energy losses. All the designs use an inert gas, usually nitrogen, at high pressure, controlled by a quick-release mechanism for rapid acceleration of the ram. In none of the designs is the machine frame required to resist the

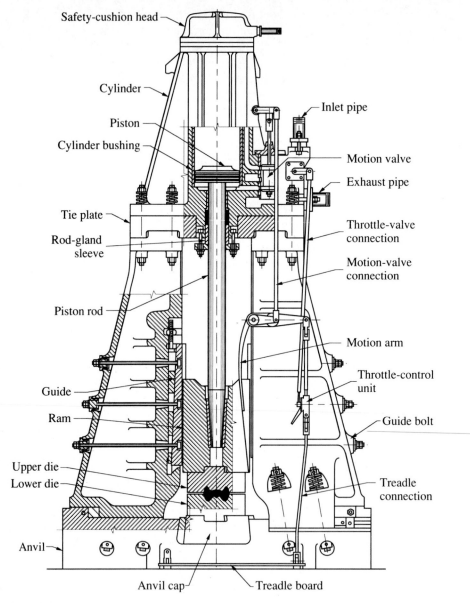

FIGURE 9.74
Principal components of a power drop hammer with foot control to regulate the force of the blow [9.25].

forging forces. The ram velocity at impact is in the range from 200 to 800 in/s (5 to 20 m/s) compared to ram velocities of 100 to 350 in/s (2.5 to 8.9 m/s) for power drop hammers. Although the finished forging generally is made in one high-speed blow, some machines can be fired two or three times before the workpiece has cooled below the forging temperature.

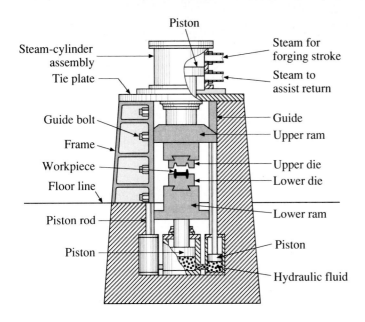

FIGURE 9.75
Essential components of a vertical counterblow hammer with a steam-hydraulic actuating system [9.25].

Accurate complex parts of low forgeability materials having thin, deep sections and a good surface finish can be forged by HERF. The process is generally limited to symmetrical parts having no sharp corners or fillets.

9.8.2.2 CLOSED-DIE FORGING PRESSES. Presses for closed-die forging may be classified as follows:

9.8.2.2.1 Mechanical presses. Mechanical presses such as shown in Fig. 9.76, having maximum force capacities of 300 to 8000 tons (2.7 to 71.2 MN), are electric motor driven, air-chuck controlled machines.

Some of the advantages cited for mechanical forging presses over drop hammers are (1) higher production rates are possible, (2) dies are less massive because of less impact, and (3) less operator skill is required.

Some disadvantages of mechanical presses over hammers are (1) higher initial cost, (2) less adapted to preforming operations such as fullering and rolling, and (3) less suitable for unsymmetrical parts.

9.8.2.2.2 Hydraulic closed-die forging presses. Hydraulic presses used in closed-die forging are similar in principle to those used for open-die forging shown in Fig. 8.2, but they are usually smaller. The basic difference between a hydraulic forging press and other forging equipment is that the pressure is applied by a squeezing action rather than by impact. They are of two basic types: (1) direct-

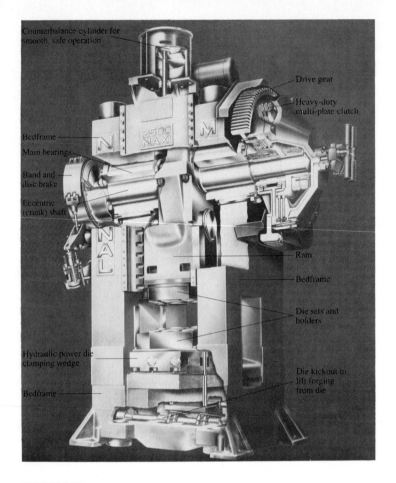

FIGURE 9.76
Cutaway photograph of a 2500 ton capacity press. It extends 21 ft above the floor and 6 ft below and weighs 200 tons. (*Courtesy National Machinery Co.*)

drive hydraulic presses, which operate with hydraulic fluid (oil or water) pressurized directly by high-pressure pumps, and (2) accumulator-drive hydropneumatic presses, which usually operate with a water-oil emulsion as the working fluid, and which use accumulators loaded with nitrogen, steam, or air to pressurize the working fluid. Many hydraulic presses are equipped with control circuits providing a rapid advance, a slow working stroke, and a dwell period, if desired. Some advantages of hydraulic presses are (1) pressure can be changed as desired at any point of the stroke, (2) rates of deformation can be controlled, (3) split dies can be used to forge complex parts, and (4) they have better die life and less die maintenance because of the gentle squeezing action. Some disadvantages are (1) high initial cost, (2) slower acting than mechanical presses, and (3) longer contact of the heated workpiece with the die, resulting in greater heat transfer and reduced die life.

9.8.2.2.3 Screw presses. Screw presses are primarily used for forging in Europe with only a few used in the United States. The screw press uses a friction, gear, electric, or hydraulic drive to accelerate a horizontal flywheel connected to a vertical screw assembly to convert the angular kinetic energy to linear energy of the slide or ram. Two common screw-press drives are (1) the friction drive and (2) the direct electric drive. In the friction-drive press, the driving discs are mounted on a horizontal shaft and are rotated continuously. For a down stroke, one of the driving discs is pressed against the flywheel by a servomotor. The flywheel, which is connected to the screw, is accelerated by the driving disc through friction. At the bottom of the stroke, the servomotor presses the upstroke disc against the flywheel, and the motion of the screw is reversed. In the direct electric drive press, the rotor of a reversible electric motor is mounted directly on the screw and the stator is mounted on the frame. The motor is reversed to change directions after each stroke. Several other types of screw drives are available, but will not be discussed here.

9.9. MANUFACTURE OF DIES AND FORGINGS

Most of the discussion thus far has been involved with the engineering design of forgings and the dies to manufacture them. Not so much discussion has been devoted to the forging procedure and the manufacture of the dies. Although the computer-aided design (CAD) function and the computer-aided manufacturing (CAM) function are usually considered together and utilize the same database, different departments are primarily interested in the two different functions. The engineering design department is, of course, primarily interested in the design of the forgings and their dies, whereas the manufacturing engineering department is primarily interested in the manufacture of the dies and the forgings. The CAD portion of the ultimate manufacture of a forging may be considered separately as shown in Fig. 9.77 [9.26], although it is often difficult to tell where CAD leaves off and CAM begins. The CAD/CAM interface shown in Fig. 9.78 [9.27] is not a sharp line of demarcation as shown, but it is an irregular, diffused zone. The big picture of the production of hot forgings by use of a hammer is summarized in the flowchart in Fig. 9.79 [9.28].

The manufacture of the forging dies may be done (1) by conventional die sinking (machining) or (2) by the use of electric discharge machining (EDM). In the former as indicated in Fig. 9.79 for hammer forging, the steel die blocks are selected, holes are drilled in the sides into which bars may be inserted to facilitate handling, the shanks for attachment to the ram or anvil cap of the hammer (Fig. 9.73) are machined, one face of each block is milled to provide an accurate surface, two matched edges are machined at right angles to serve as reference surfaces for accurate layout of the impressions, the cavities are sunk by use of a die-sinker or an NC machine, the finishing cavity is finished, a lead

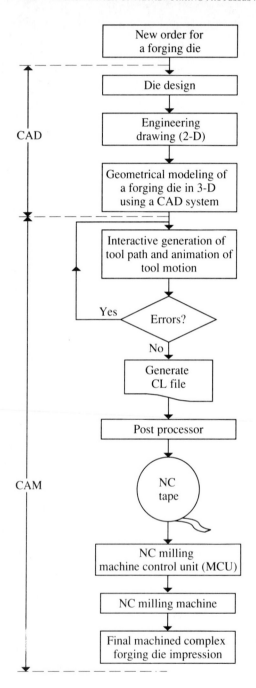

FIGURE 9.77
Flowchart showing the separation between the CAD portion and CAM portion of a CAD/CAM used in the design and manufacturing of forging dies [9.26].

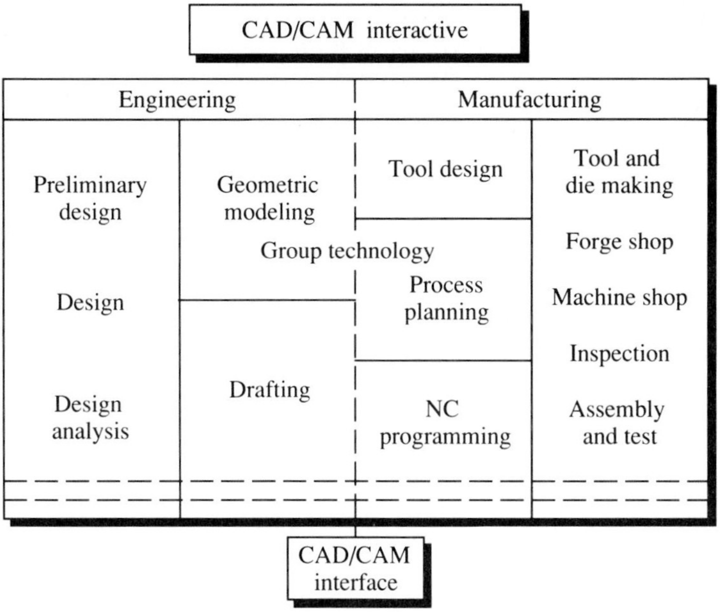

CAD/CAM interactive			
Engineering		Manufacturing	
Preliminary design	Geometric modeling	Tool design	Tool and die making
	Group technology		Forge shop
Design		Process planning	Machine shop
			Inspection
Design analysis	Drafting	NC programming	Assembly and test

CAD/CAM interface

FIGURE 9.78
Interrelationship between engineering and manufacturing functions showing the division of activities between CAD and CAM. (The vertical dashed line between CAD and CAM is a diffused zone rather than a sharp line.) (*Adapted from E. N. Nilson, "The CAD/CAM Interface: Problems and Solutions", Pratt & Whitney Aircraft.*)

proof casting is made and inspected, the remaining impressions and the flash-land and gutter are machined, and the dies are completed.

In the EDM method of sinking the die cavities, the electrodes usually are made from graphite and are machined by conventional machining or by an NC machine tool. The NC tape may be produced as part of the CAD/CAM procedure as shown in Fig. 9.77.

The forging steps in the manufacture of the closed-die forging may be achieved by following the left side of the flowchart in Fig. 9.79 as follows:

1. Inspection of the raw material (stock)
2. Shearing or cutting of the stock to form forging multiples or slugs
3. Heating the multiples for forging
4. Performing the preliminary drop forging operations
   a. Fullering—to decrease the cross section of the workpiece between the ends and lengthen it to the required working size
   b. Edging—to gather and rearrange the material so that it is properly distributed to fill the cavities
   c. Bending (if needed)—to change the axis of the workpiece

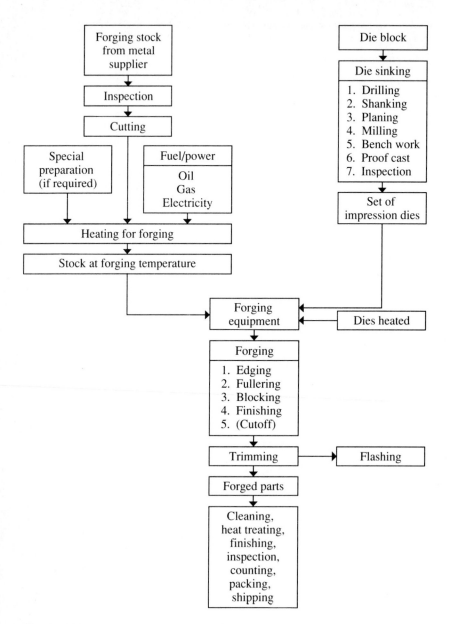

FIGURE 9.79
Flowchart of the typical operations in the production of hot forgings. (*Adapted from T. G. Byrer, S. L. Semiatin, and D. C. Vollmer, "Manufacturing of Forgings", (Ch. 4) in Forging Handbook, T. G. Byrer et al. Editors, FIA/ASM, Metals Park, 1985, pp. 149–155.*)

5. Blocking—to produce the major change in shape

6. Finishing—to give the fine detail and accuracy

7. Trimming—to remove the flash and to punch out the web-slugs

8. Coining or sizing (if required) (done cold)—to give accurate dimensions and a good finish

9.10 SHEARING (CROPPING) OF THE FORGING MULTIPLES [9.29]

9.10.1 Introduction

The cutting of the forging multiples (slugs or billets) for closed-die forging is very important. They may be cut by machining, sawing, or shearing (cropping). The latter method is usually the quickest and cheapest but least accurate process to use, which will be considered here.

If its volume is too large, the excess metal increases the flash volume, which increases the amount of material used and the die load, which in turn is not only wasteful but also causes premature die failure. Too small a volume, on the other hand, leads to rejected forgings due to incomplete filling of the die, and in extreme cases results in die clashing and die failure.

Variation in forging multiple volume ΔV arises from variations in its length ΔL and its cross-sectional area ΔA or, for round bars, its diameter ΔD.

The relative volumetric variation can be expressed for round bars by

$$\frac{\Delta V}{V} = \frac{\Delta L}{L} + 2\left(\frac{\Delta D}{D}\right) \qquad (9.102)$$

where ΔL and ΔD are the variations in the length and diameter of the multiples from their nominal values, respectively [9.29].

Since the diametral variation has the coefficient of 2, its contribution to the volumetric variation is more serious than the variation in length. If the diametral variation is small, such as for the more expensive, cold-drawn bars, a relatively simple control system having a manually adjustable bar stop is adequate. However, for large diametral variations, an adaptive system must be used that involves a computer-controlled measuring system to control variations in the length of the multiple by continually controlling the setting of the bar stop. A number of factors affect the length of the multiple such as the temperature, distortion of the ends of the multiples, condition of the surfaces of the fractures, etc. These factors depend on such things as the properties of the material, cutting speed, condition of the tooling such as the condition and clearance of the shear blades, etc. Usually these conditions are constant during an operation, so that the length of the multiple depends on the location of the bar stop. For example, the profile of the fractured surfaces of the ends of the multiple usually match. That is, they are complementary to one another, so that they do not cause too much variation of ΔL and consequently will produce volume fluctuations within an acceptable statistical range. From Eq. (9.102) it can be seen that the volumetric scatter will be less with larger multiples.

It has been shown that variations of ΔL due to the large tolerance of hot-rolled bars is 5 to 11 times that of cold-drawn bars of the same size. The volumetric variations of cold-drawn bars with large diameters are very small, being less than about 1 percent.

9.10.2 Forging Multiple (Slug or Billet) Volume Setting Systems

9.10.2.1 FIXED LENGTH APPROACH. In this method, the setting of the bar stop is adjusted periodically manually by interrupting production and adjusting the screw that is shown in Fig. 9.80. The setting is then checked by observing the variation of the weight of a few multiples. This method is slow and wasteful and is best suited for cold-drawn bars of large diameter and long length.

9.10.2.2 SPECIFIC WEIGHT APPROACH. This approach is based on determining the weight per unit length of a bar and then adjusting the bar stop position to vary the cutoff length according to the required weight or volume. The principle behind this technique can be explained by use of Fig. 9.81.

Basically, it involves measuring the reactions, due to the weight of the whole bar, at two points R_1 and R_2, with the center of gravity of the bar being located in between them as shown in Fig. 9.81(a). By noting the reactions at these points together with the fixed distances S and B, one can calculate the weight per unit length, w, of the bar as follows:

$$\frac{1}{w} = \frac{L}{W} = \frac{2B}{(R_1 + R_2)}\left(\frac{R_1}{(R_1 + R_2)} + \frac{S}{B}\right) \tag{9.103}$$

where L and W are the effective length and weight of the bar, respectively. The unknown length L_x, to which the bar stop must be adjusted to produce a required

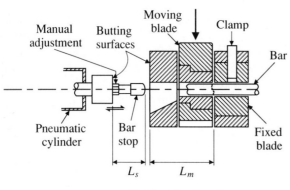

Offcut length $= L_m - L_s$

FIGURE 9.80
A schematic drawing for the fixed length approach for the continual shearing (cropping) of forging multiples or slugs [9.29].

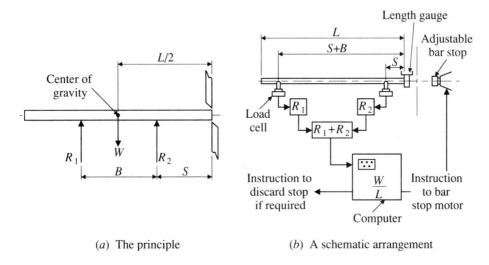

(a) The principle   (b) A schematic arrangement

FIGURE 9.81
The specific weight approach for continual shearing of forging multiples [9.29].

multiple weight W_x, is obtained by

$$L_x = \frac{W_x}{w} = \frac{2 W_x B}{(R_1 + R_2)} \left(\frac{R_1}{R_1 + R_2} + \frac{S}{B} \right) \qquad (9.104)$$

The principle of this approach is therefore relatively simple, and the process requires only a single weighing operation by use of two load cells.

This approach was tried for a cut-to-weight bar shearing system as shown schematically in Fig. 9.81(b). For rapid calculation and decision-making, a computer was used to process the data and adjust the position of the bar stop by remote control. The reliability of the system was not too satisfactory. This approach is best adapted to the production of long multiples from relatively long and heavy bars of uniform properties and cross-sectional area.

9.10.2.3 ADAPTIVE LENGTH APPROACH. This approach is based on the monitoring of the current diameter or area directly. Any deviation of the current cross-sectional area of the cutoff multiple from the reference area is compensated for by adjusting the position of the bar stop accordingly.

A schematic layout for such a system, which is controlled by a desk-top computer, is shown in Fig. 9.82.

As a safety feature, the computer controls the activation of the shearing machine to prevent damaging the controlling instruments during operation. The equipment consists of a chain-driven bar feeder, an automatic bar gauge, the shearing or cutoff machine, remote controlled bar stop, and the forging machine. These units are linked by a desk-top computer, which controls the operation as shown in the flowchart in Fig. 9.83 [9.29].

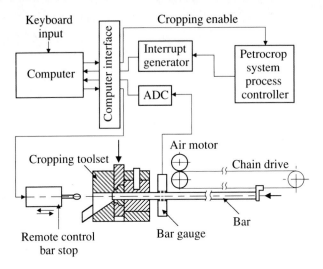

FIGURE 9.82

A schematic layout of adaptive length approach for the continual cutting-off of forging multiples controlled by a desk-top computer (ADC stands for an analogue digital converter) [9.29].

9.10.3   CAD/CAM System for a High-Speed, Cutoff Tooling [9.30]

The flowchart of a computer program for the computer-aided design and manufacture of high-speed, forging-multiple, tooling is shown in Fig. 9.84, which shows the key features of the three design modes. With the interactive mode of operation, the program produces not only the final dimensions but also simple drawings and an NC tape for machining the die inserts, if so desired [9.30].

9.11   REVIEW OF EMPIRICAL DIE DESIGN PRACTICE

In general, in addition to the engineering aspects such as the design of the flash and gutter impressions, and the estimation of the forging load required, the design of a steel forging and its dies involves the following:

1. The selection of the die parting line (plane)
2. The allocation of machining allowance and tolerance to the various surfaces
3. The selection of the draft angles
4. The addition of edge and fillet radii
5. The selection of proper rib width and web thickness, if required

   Some empirical rules for choosing a parting line are

1. The parting surface should be a plane [9.31], if possible, as shown in Fig. 9.85

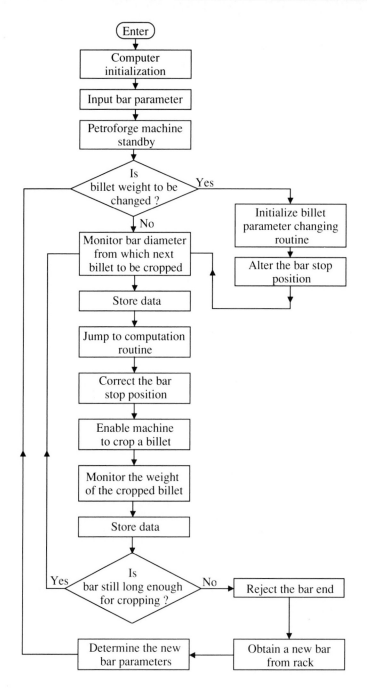

FIGURE 9.83
Flowchart for the computer-aided billet volume control system [9.29].

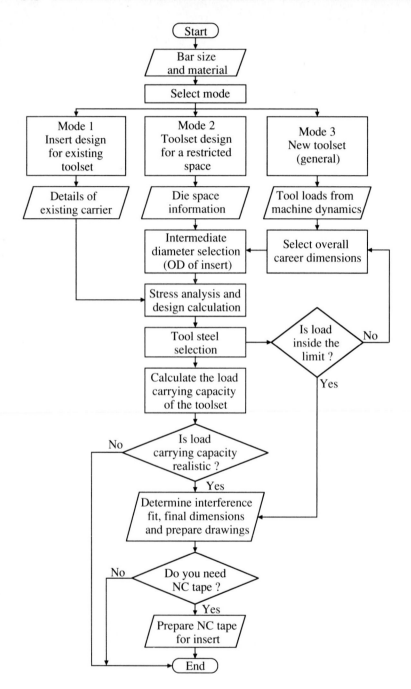

FIGURE 9.84
Flowchart of a computer program for the computer-aided design and manufacture of high-speed forging multiple tooling [9.30].

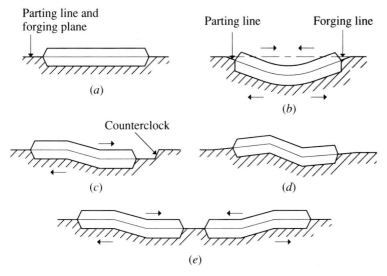

Parting line and forging plane

Parting line   Forging line

(a)

(b)

Counterclock

(c)   (d)

(e)

FIGURE 9.85
Drawings illustrating the design rules for use of straight and broken parting lines for closed impression forging dies [9.31].

2. For symmetrical parts, the parting line should divide the forging symmetrically into two equal halves as shown in Fig. 9.86(a) and (d) as opposed to (b) and (c)

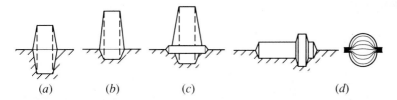

(a)   (b)   (c)   (d)

FIGURE 9.86
Drawings illustrating the design rules for positioning the die parting line on axisymmetric forgings so as to divide the forging to two equal halves as shown in (a) and (d) [9.31].

3. The parting line should be chosen to facilitate the flow of metal into the die cavity as shown in Fig. 9.87(b) as opposed to Fig. 9.87(a)

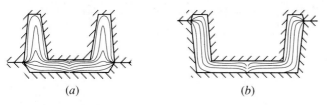

(a)   (b)

FIGURE 9.87
Drawings illustrating the design rules for positioning the die parting line to facilitate the flow of metal into the die cavity [9.31].

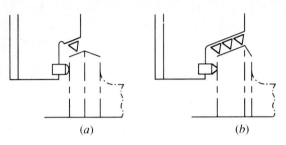

(a)　　　　　　　　　(b)

▽ Stationary surface locators

FIGURE 9.88
Drawings illustrating the design rules for the positioning the die parting line to facilitate the clamping of the workpiece for subsequent machining [9.31].

4. The parting line should be positioned to facilitate the clamping of the workpiece for subsequent machining such as to provide for a larger clamping surface, as shown in Fig. 9.88(b)

The machining allowance, such as $\frac{1}{16}$ in (1.6 mm) will include the finishing allowance, scale pitting, decarburization, shrinkage allowance, and all tolerances such as for die wear, mismatch, etc., as shown in Fig. 9.89 [9.32].

The draft angle is selected as shown in Fig. 9.90 and Table 9.6. The inside draft is greater than the outside draft since, in the case of the former, the material shrinks on cooling onto the boss of the die [9.31].

Too small die radii might inhibit metal flow during forging and might cause stress concentrations in the part. The selection of fillet and corner radii on the basis of weight is given in Fig. 9.91 and of height of a rib and boss is given in Fig. 9.92 [9.31].

The minimum achievable web and rib dimensions for steel forgings made by conventional hot forging are given in Figs. 9.93 and 9.94 [9.31].

From the working detail drawing of the part, the faces which require a machining allowance are identified and the allowances are applied on the basis of past experience and/or recognized standards. Similarly, draft angles are applied on the vertical faces to facilitate the flow of metal into the die cavities and the removal of the forging from the dies. It is customary to put the deepest cavity

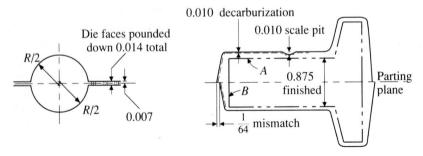

FIGURE 9.89
Drawings illustrating the various allowances included in the machining allowance [9.32].

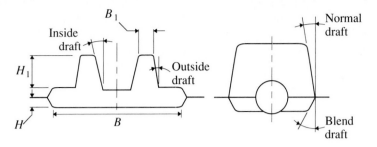

FIGURE 9.90
Nomenclature for the draft angles of closed-die forgings [9.31].

TABLE 9.6
Draft and draft tolerances for steel forgings

Height or depth of draft, in	Commercial standard		Special standard	
	Draft, deg	Tolerance† plus, deg	Draft, deg	Tolerance plus, deg
Outside draft				
$\frac{1}{4}$ to $\frac{1}{2}$	—	—	3	2
$\frac{3}{4}$ to 1	5	3		
Over $\frac{1}{2}$, up to 1	—	—	5	2
Over 1, up to 3	7	3	5	3
Over 3	7	4	7	3
Inside draft				
$\frac{1}{4}$ to 1	7	3	5	3
Over 1	10	3	10	3

† The minus tolerance is zero

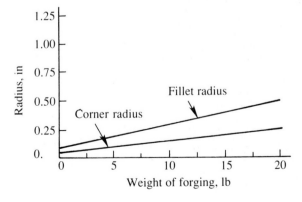

FIGURE 9.91
Graph showing the dependence of fillet and corner radii for steel forgings on the weight of the forging [9.31].

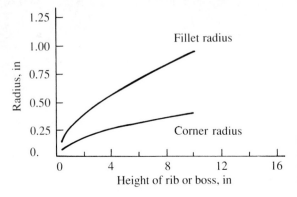

FIGURE 9.92
Curves showing the dependence of fillet and corner radii on the height of a rib or boss [9.31].

in the upper die since a downward blow tends to force the metal upward and since the falling scale can be removed more easily for the shallower lower die.

To ensure that the main die cavity is completely filled, excess metal is provided in the forging slug, and the flow of the excess metal out of the die cavity is restricted by the clearance in the flash impression. Any excess metal beyond that required for the flash flows into the gutter. The flash and gutter impressions must therefore be added to the die.

The design of a forging and the necessary dies requires a considerable amount of experience and is labor intensive. To alleviate the situation, computer-aided methods may be used.

9.12   CLASSIFICATION OF FORGING SHAPES

9.12.1   Introduction

There is no completely satisfactory system as yet for classifying the shapes of forgings that is both practical and lends itself conveniently to mathematical and computer manipulation.

It would be very desirable to have a universal classification system for use in the CAD/CAM of forgings, so that a general computer program could be used to design most any type of forging.

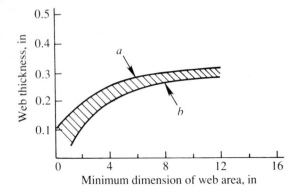

FIGURE 9.93
Recommended minimum web thickness for steels of good forgeability in relation to the web dimensions: (*a*) minimum for rapidly completed forgings; and (*b*) attainable usually at extra cost [9.31].

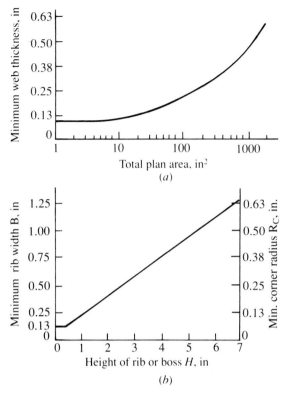

FIGURE 9.94
Recommended dimensions for web and rib thickness and corner radii of forgings with unconfined webs for steels with good forgeability [9.31].

Some of the basic requirements of the shape of a forging are (1) to facilitate the flow of metal into the die cavity without the formation of defects, (2) to facilitate the removal of the forging from the die, (3) to simplify die design and manufacture to avoid an irregular parting plane and the need for sections that move laterally, etc., (4) to facilitate the forging operation such as the prevention of die shifting, reduction of die wear, reduction of the amount of temperature control, etc. To fulfill the foregoing requirements, it may be necessary to make two or more parts from one forging multiple to form a platter, as shown in Fig. 9.95(a) and (b), to facilitate the forging operation and to lower the cost [9.28]. (Compare the design of the dies for forging automobile connecting rods in Figs. 9.52(a) and 9.95 one-at-a-time versus two-at-a-time, respectively.) Figure 9.95(c) shows a two-at-a-time platter forged in an automatic transfer die, in which the slug is fed every other stroke of the press. The workpiece is under stations 1, 3, and 5 for one stroke of the press and under 2 and 4 for the subsequent stroke. This part is an automobile connecting rod with a $5\frac{1}{2}$ in (140 mm) stroke. Here the classification is primarily of a shape of a forging itself rather than of a group of parts making up a platter. Let us return to the discussion of forging shape.

The ideal situation would be one in which the shape complexity factor of the forging is given along with other important information such as the material, equipment available, etc., and the computer program would call all the necessary

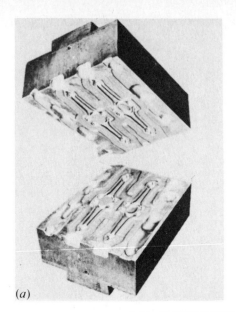

(a)

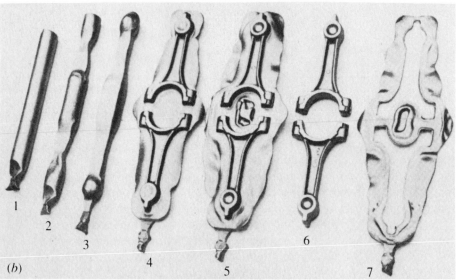

(b)

1

2

3

4

5

6

7

(c)

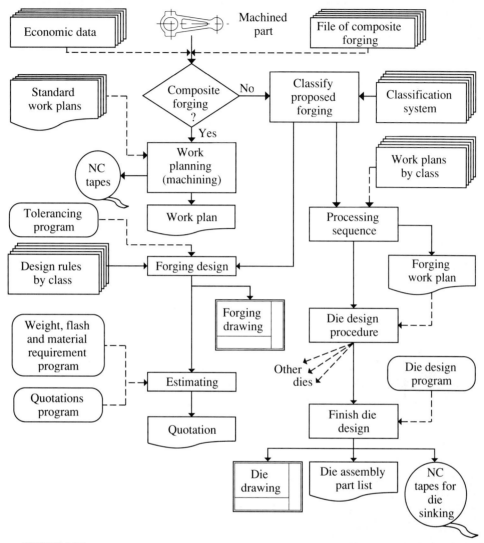

FIGURE 9.96
An example of how a classification system may be incorporated into an integrated design and process system for forging dies. (See Fig. 9.98 for an example of a composite forging.) [9.33].

FIGURE 9.95
(*a*) Closed impression dies used for hammer forging automotive connecting rods two at a time are shown at the right. (*b*) The forging blank and the workpiece at various stages of the forging sequence are shown above: (1) forging blank or multiple, forging shapes after (2) fullering; (3) edging; (4) blocking; (5) finishing; and (6) trimming; (7) shows the trimmed flash. (See Fig. 9.52 for a single forging die.) (*c*) Two-at-a-time platter forged in an automatic transfer die in a large mechanical forging press such as in Fig. 9.76. (*a*) and (*b*) [9.28], and (*c*) (*Courtesy of National Machinery Co.*).

subroutines in the order required to design the forging and its dies. Moreover, a cost analysis might be made to indicate whether the forging would be made in one of a number of forge shops or even by some other process such as precision investment casting. Figure 9.96 is an early illustration of how a classification system may be incorporated into an integrated design and process system for forging [9.33].

The two methods of classification of closed-die forgings according to shape, that have been introduced in the foregoing were (1) the simplified group technology approach such as is shown in Fig. 9.31, and (2) the shape difficulty factor method expressed by Eq. (9.83). The former will be expanded here somewhat.

9.12.2 Group Technology Approach

9.12.2.1 INTRODUCTION. The use of group technology (GT) or part family approach for machining operations is well established, but a similar approach to metalforming operations is not so well developed. Metalforming operations involve a highly specialized technology with the result that traditionally such functions as die design and manufacture are carried out with heavy reliance on

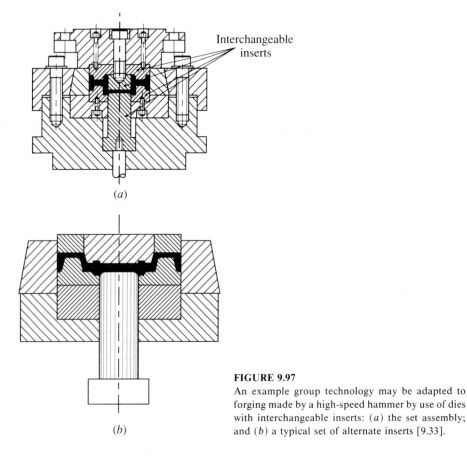

Interchangeable inserts

(a)

(b)

FIGURE 9.97
An example group technology may be adapted to forging made by a high-speed hammer by use of dies with interchangeable inserts: (a) the set assembly; and (b) a typical set of alternate inserts [9.33].

the skill of experienced personnel with poor utilization of the vast amount of available information. Considerable benefits accrue from a more rationalized approach to design and manufacture in metalforming, especially forging. Integrated systems for design, planning, and manufacture of metalformed parts such as forgings (and stampings) should be established similar to current levels in machined parts.

9.12.2.2 APPLICATION OF GT TO FORGING [9.33]. One of the methods that has been suggested to apply group technology (GT) to forging is to use dies with interchangeable inserts such as is shown in Fig. 9.97, in which standardized die inserts, ejectors, and clamping rings are used in both the upper and lower dies. Although more readily applicable in press forging, this concept can also be used in drop hammer forging operations but with increased maintenance. The use of group die sets has two main advantages: (1) the die cost for individual forgings is reduced because of the lower cost of the inserts as compared to the entire die assembly, and (2) the reduced changeover time as the main assembly is not removed for forgings belonging to the same group.

Another method, that has been suggested for the use of GT, is the use of a "composite" forging, from which all the slightly different parts belonging to the same group may be machined, but with much less machining than if the parts were machined from a round bar as shown in Fig. 9.98.

9.12.2.3 SPIES THREE-DIGIT METHOD OF CLASSIFICATION. Spies [9.34] classified forging shapes into three main groups: (1) compact shapes; (2) disc shapes; and (3) elongated or oblong shapes, which may contain subgroups and subsidiary elements, as shown in Fig. 9.99 [9.35].

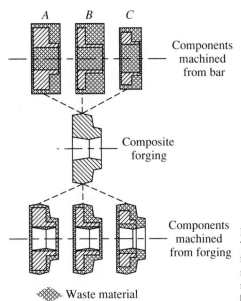

A   B   C

Components machined from bar

Composite forging

Components machined from forging

Waste material

FIGURE 9.98
The use of the principle of the composite forging for applying group technology to forging. The machining required of each forging would be much less than for machining from a round bar [9.33].

	Subgroup	101 No subsidiary elements	102 Unilateral subsidiary elements	103 Rotational subsidiary elements		104 Unilateral subsidiary elements
Shape class 1 compact shape $l = b = h$ — Spherical and cubical	Shape group / Subgroup	No subsidiary elements	With hub	With hub and hole	With rim	With rim and hub
Shape class 2 disc shape $l = b > h$ — Parts with circular, square and similar contours: crosspiece with short arms; upset heads and long shapes (flanges, valves, etc.) — 21 Disc shape with unilateral element		211	212	213	214	215
22 Disc shape with bilateral elements			222	223	224	225

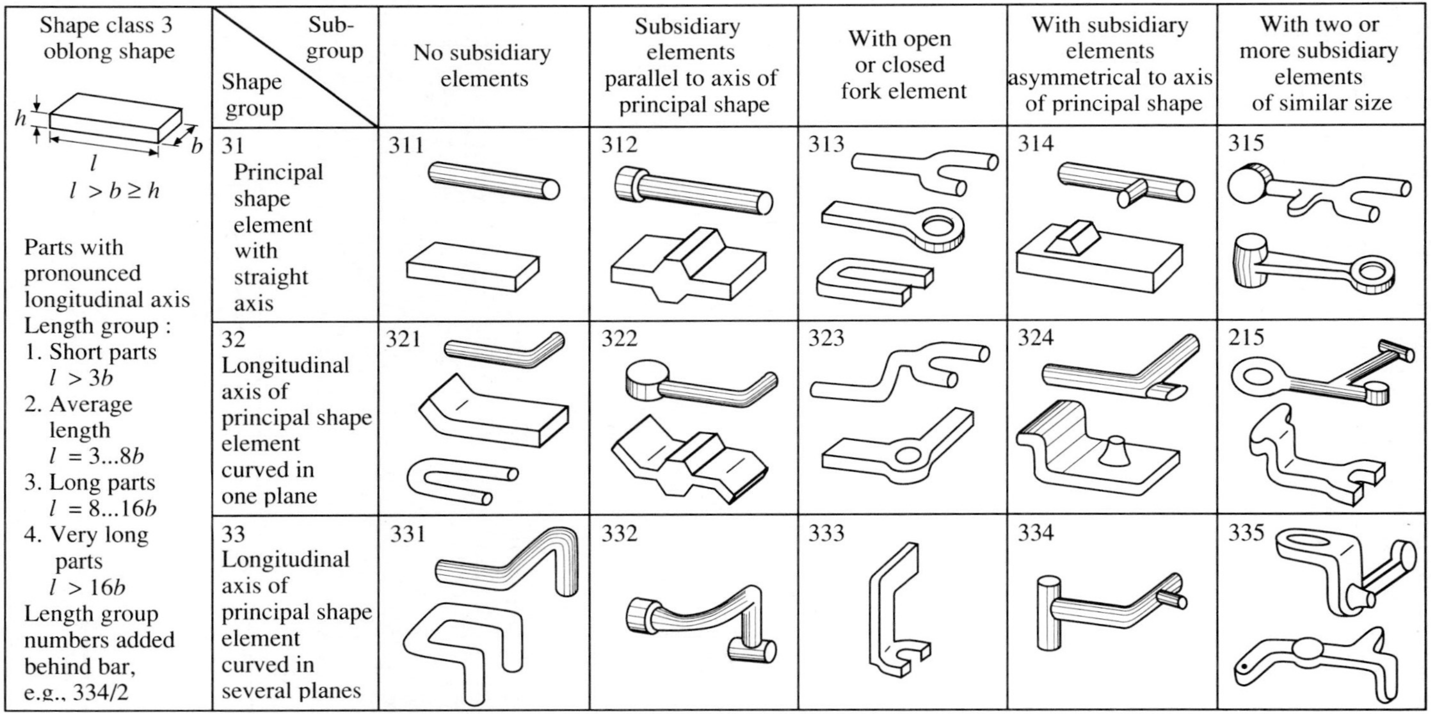
Shape class 3
oblong shape
h
b
l
$l > b \geq h$
Parts with pronounced longitudinal axis
Length group :
1. Short parts $l > 3b$
2. Average length $l = 3...8b$
3. Long parts $l = 8...16b$
4. Very long parts $l > 16b$
Length group numbers added behind bar, e.g., 334/2
Sub-group
Shape group
No subsidiary elements
Subsidiary elements parallel to axis of principal shape
With open or closed fork element
With subsidiary elements asymmetrical to axis of principal shape
With two or more subsidiary elements of similar size
31 Principal shape element with straight axis
311
312
313
314
315
32 Longitudinal axis of principal shape element curved in one plane
321
322
323
324
215
33 Longitudinal axis of principal shape element curved in several planes
331
332
333
334
335

FIGURE 9.99
Spies' system for the classification of forging shapes [9.35].

The compact shapes, or class 1 forgings, have the three major dimensions (length, width, and height) approximately equal. The disc shapes or flats, or class 2 forgings, have two dimensions approximately equal (length and width) and larger than the height. This group includes about 30 percent of the commonly used forgings. The elongated or oblong shapes, or class 3 forgings, have one dimension that is significantly greater than the other two ($l > b > h$). Examples of the numerical designation of a gear blank containing a rim and hub would be 225, and of a connecting rod would be 315 according to this system.

Although Fig. 9.99 appears to give quite a number of choices of shapes, still if one would attempt to classify a variety of closed-die forgings that have already been made, one would encounter a number of forgings to which it would be difficult to assign a classification number.

9.12.2.4 KNIGHT CLASSIFICATION SYSTEM [9.33]. The systems outlined in Figs. 9.100 and 9.101 combine some of the features of the system by Spies with those of a Soviet system and is for hot press and hammer forgings. The first three digits categorize the shape of the forging in a similar manner to Spies, but with somewhat more detail, into compact, flat, and long parts. The subsequent digits

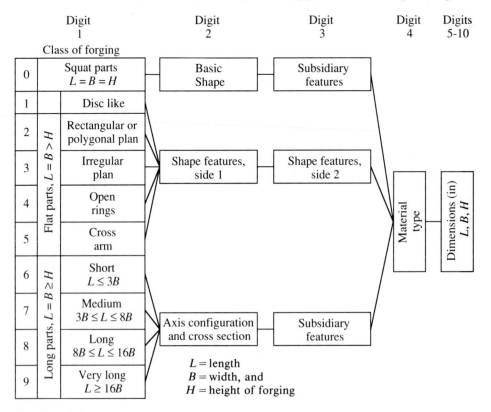

FIGURE 9.100
Outline of Knight's classification system for hot press and hammer forgings [9.33].

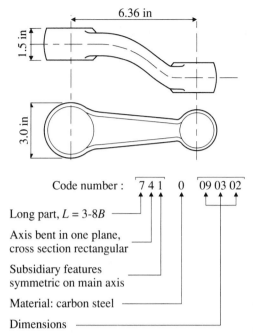

Code number :   7 4 1   0   09 03 02

Long part, $L = 3\text{-}8B$

Axis bent in one plane,
cross section rectangular

Subsidiary features
symmetric on main axis

Material: carbon steel

Dimensions

FIGURE 9.101
A typical forging coded by means of the Knight classification system for forgings [9.33].

cover the subsidiary features to the basic shape. The shape code is followed by details of the size and material of the forging. Figure 9.101 shows an example of a part coded with this system.

The ultimate objectives of such a system is to design, from the drawing of the finished machined part, all the dies and tools necessary to process the associated forging by use of a CAD/CAM system.

9.12.2.5 DESIGN-FOR-FORGING HANDBOOK SYSTEM [9.36]. The classification system described in the foregoing in conjunction with Fig. 9.100 has been expanded and integrated into a handbook [9.37], which attempts to design the forging and the forging process more systematically by considering groups of related parts. The basis of the handbook is a coding system, similar to the foregoing, which covers those features of parts which influence the forging process and which are presented in such a manner as to indicate those which are likely to cause problems in manufacture.

The handbook is divided into five sections: (1) classification of materials into their general order of forging difficulty; (2) classification of the basic shapes, subsidiary features, and the geometric complexity of the forged part in order of relative forging difficulty; (3) material data sheets for each material group with general information such as forging temperature range, flow stress, density, etc.; (4) detailed design data sheets to assist the designer in the selection of detailed design features such as parting line location, etc., of forgings belonging to the various classes of parts; and (5) the final section contains general information and terminology useful to the forging designers. The purpose of the handbook is to present forging information more systematically so that the designer is led successively through the various stages required in using it for a particular part. The major factors which influence forging difficulty in a particular case are the complexity of the part and the material used. These factors are strongly inter-related, since a shape that is relatively easy to forge in one material may be difficult or impossible to forge in another. The approach adopted in the handbook is to classify components by the basic shape features and then to rate those according to the materials used, so that the relative difficulty of the various shape-material combinations is indicated.

For the purpose of the handbook, materials have been divided into ten groups, identified by one digit code as shown in Fig. 9.102, and these groups have been ranked in general order of difficulty. The material groups include most of the materials which are forged.

The first three digits of the classification system of the handbook are similar to those of the Spies and Knight systems. The first digit code, given in Fig. 9.102,

0	Compact parts $L/B \leq 3/2, L/H \leq 3/2$ (1)		
1	Flat parts $L/B \leq 3/2$ $L/H > 3/2$ (1)	Round (disk-like) parts (2)	
2		Non-round parts (2)	
3	Long parts $L/B > 3/2$ (1)	Longitudinal axis of part straight (3)	$L/B \leq 3$
4			$3 < L/B \leq 8$
5			$L/B > 8$
6		Longitudinal axis of part bent or curved in one plane (3)	$L/B \leq 8$
7			$L/B > 8$
8		Longitudinal axis of part bent or curved in more than one plane (3)	$L/B \leq 8$
9			$L/B > 8$

FIGURE 9.102
Allocation of the first-digit value for the shape classification of forged parts by the University of Massachusetts Handbook Method [9.36].

divides parts into the basic categories of compact, flat, and long parts, as determined from the dimensions of the envelope of the (straightened) part as shown in Fig. 9.103(a). Allocation of a particular first-digit code then leads to one of a series of coding charts for the second and third digits of the classification, which

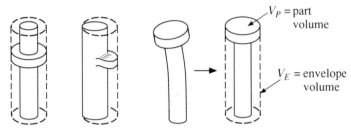

V_P = part volume

V_E = envelope volume

(a) Cylindrical envelopes for upset forgings
for allocation of first and third digit values

$$F_C = \frac{V_E}{V_P}$$

Straight axisymmetric parts	$L \leq D$	Part with same transverse cross section along axis of part	Part with circular transverse cross sections	0
			Part with polygonal transverse cross sections only	1
		Part with combinations of circular and polygonal transverse cross sections		2
		Part with noncircular and/or nonpolygonal transverse cross sections (including gears, splines, etc.)		3
	$L > D$	Part with same transverse cross section along axis of part	Part with circular transverse cross sections	4
			Part with polygonal transverse cross sections only	5
		Part with combinations of circular and polygonal transverse cross sections		6
		Part with noncircular and/or nonpolygonal transverse cross sections (including gears, splines, etc.)		7
Parts with non-axisymmetric and twofold features and/or parts with a bent or curved axis			$L \leq D$	8
			$L > D$	9

(b) Shape classification for upset forgings —
allocation of first digit values

FIGURE 9.103
Shape complexity factor for forged part as determined by the envelope method [9.36].

covers the subsidiary features which are important to the different classes categorized under the first digit. There are six of these coding charts for the second and third digits, corresponding to first digit codes of 0, 1, 2, 3-5, 6-7, and 8-9, respectively. The coding chart for main class 1 forgings is for flat round parts, as an example. The second digit value increases as the general level of forging difficulty increases. The third digit gives an indication of the complexity, by means of the shape complexity factor F_c, illustrated in Fig. 9.103(a), and the size of the part. F_c is the ratio of the volume of the envelope over the volume of the part. For long parts, F_c is obtained with the axis of the part first straightened out.

As an illustration for the use of the above coding system, Fig. 9.104 shows a flat round forging, together with the code number (102) allocated to it. This is a simple part which has a low valued code number and is consequently relatively straightforward to produce as a forging. If radial ribs were added on the hub side, the part would be increased in complexity, which would be difficult to produce by forging, requiring additional forming stages, with reduced die life and greater material losses. This ribbed part, therefore, would be allocated a higher valued code number within the classification of 181 as opposed to 102 for the former.

This classification system has been applied to more specialized upset forgings. The first digit divides the upset forging into broad categories depending on its proportions, cross-section type, and symmetry as shown in Fig. 103(b). The

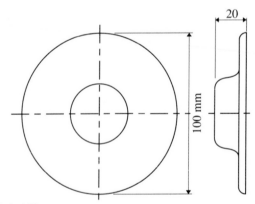

Code 102

First digit :   Envelope dimensions : $L = 100$, $B = 100$
$H = 20$. $L/B = 1$, $L/H = 5$. Plan profile is
round. The first coding digit is 1.

Second digit : The part has a boss only. Second coding
digit is 0.

Third digit : $L = 100$. Part volume $= 58$ cm^3.
Envelope volume $= 157$ cm^3. $F_c = 2.7$.
Third coding digit is 2

FIGURE 9.104
Example of a simple part along
with its allocated code number
[9.36].

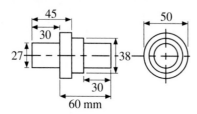

Code 476

First digit : Straight axisymmetrical part with circular
transverse cross sections only. The
dimensions of the basic envelope of the
part are $L = 130$ mm and $D = 80$ mm,
i.e. $L > D$.
The first coding digit value is 4.

Second digit : This part has a profile which is stepped
discontinuously with no axial holes.
The second digit value is 7.

Third digit: The part has six parallel stepped portions
and the profile is stepped discontinuously.
The smallest section circumscribing
diameter (38 mm) is smaller than $0.5\,D$
(40 mm). The third digit's value is 6.

FIGURE 9.105
Example of a simple upset
forging along with its allocated
code number [9.36].

first eight classed, 0 to 7, are devoted to axisymmetric parts which make up most
of the parts in upset forging, and the last two classes, 8 and 9, are for nonaxisymmetric parts. The second digit designates the basic form of the axial profile and
the presence of axial holes. It indicates whether a part is stepped down continuously from one or both ends, or stepped up to both ends. The third digit
categorizes the form of the axial profile in more detail. It differentiates between
parts with axial portions parallel to the axis only or those with conical and/or
curved portions. It also indicates the proportion of the part to be upset and the
variations in cross-sectional area. Coding sheets are available to simplify the
coding. An example of an upset forging, together with its code number, is shown
in Fig. 9.105 [9.28].

The design procedure for upset forging is in the process of being computerized.

9.13 COMPUTER-AIDED SEQUENCE DESIGN FOR HOT UPSET FORGINGS

9.13.1 Introduction

In Chap. 8, Sec. 8.2.3, axisymmetric compression of a short cylinder or disc
between overhanging platens (anvils) was discussed. Since this operation is akin
to upsetting or heading, the upset forging machine and the three simple design

rules for upset forging were introduced (see Figs. 8.15 and 8.17). In Chap. 8, emphasis was placed on the open-die forging aspects of upsetting. Here, the emphasis will be on the closed-die forging aspects.

Components produced on upset forging machines, such as is shown in Fig. 8.15, require a sequence of operations involving combinations of upsetting (heading), extrusion and piercing, depending on the shape required. Each stage in the sequence is governed by process limitations, and the selection of the appropriate overall sequence requires both experienced judgment and the application of established design rules. The basic rules are illustrated in Fig. 9.106. These rules vary somewhat with different reference sources, but they differ only in detail and the principle involved remains the same. For example, one source considers that the limits set by the above rules are too high and suggests that for free upsetting, $l_0 \leq 2.3 d_0$ is more applicable, and the allowable upset ratio should depend on the type of heading die, together with the flatness and squareness of the end surfaces of the bar. In Figs. 9.107 and 9.108, the allowable upsetting ratios for cylindrical and taper upsetting are shown for a bar 10 mm (0.4 in) in diameter. In practice the taper upsetting method is widely used for the intermediate stages of the multistage upsetting process. Taper upsetting generally requires a lower number of operations in the sequence for a given overall upset ratio [9.38].

9.13.2   Computer-Aided Sequence Design [9.38]

In order to facilitate the development of computer-aided design systems for upset forgings by rationalization of the design process, the three-digit coding system discussed in the previous section has been used. As explained in that section, this system classifies parts by considering the general similarity of their geometric

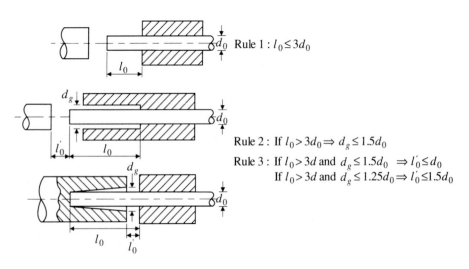

Rule 1 : If $l_0 \leq 3 d_0$

Rule 2 : If $l_0 > 3 d_0 \Rightarrow d_g \leq 1.5 d_0$

Rule 3 : If $l_0 > 3 d$ and $d_g \leq 1.5 d_0 \Rightarrow l_0' \leq d_0$
If $l_0 > 3 d$ and $d_g \leq 1.25 d_0 \Rightarrow l_0' \leq 1.5 d_0$

FIGURE 9.106
Basic design rules of upset forging (see Fig. 8.17) [9.36].

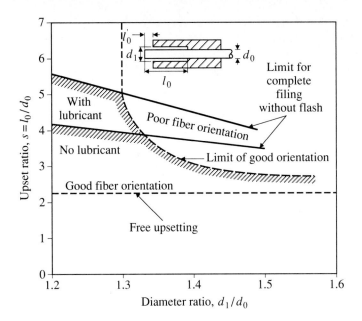

FIGURE 9.107
Relation between the maximum upset ratio and diameter ratio for cylindrical upsetting [9.36].

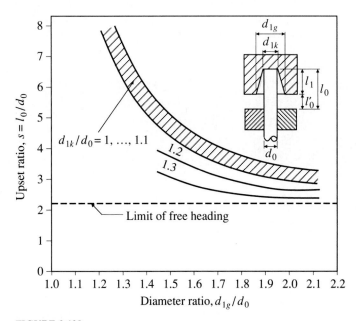

FIGURE 9.108
Relation between the maximum upset ratio and diameter ratio for taper upsetting [9.36].

shape, in terms of combinations of features which influence the processing sequence. The first digit in the handbook classification system discussed in the foregoing divides parts into broad categories depending on the proportions, cross-section type and symmetry. Eight classes (0–7) are devoted to axisymmetric parts which make up the bulk of the components produced on upset forging machines. Classes 0–3 are for axisymmetric parts with a ratio of the overall length l to the envelope diameter d of less than one; for such components deformation will take place in the whole body of the part during the various operations. Classes 4–7 are axisymmetric parts with an l/d ratio of greater than one, and for these parts deformation may take place separately at each end or possibly in a central portion independently of the ends. Classes 8 and 9 are for parts with nonaxisymmetric features. Within these groups of four classes, the parts are categorized according to the types of cross section present.

The classification system and the established design rules discussed in the foregoing, form the basis for a computer-aided process design system for upset forgings, which is under development [9.38]. With this system the appropriate code number of the part is entered and this results in requests for the detailed geometry of the part, described by a limited number of axial shape elements such as cylindrical, conical, and radiused portions. The appropriate sequence of forging stages is then determined automatically, within the applicable process limitations. The number of operations required to make a component is dependent not only on the overall upset ratio but also on the final geometry. In addition for a given overall upset ratio, the final geometry will influence the intermediate shapes. For example, Fig. 9.109 shows two components having the same overall upset ratio, but their geometries require different intermediate shapes, because the smaller upset diameter of 70 mm (2.8 in) on the right must be produced in the first operation whereas the larger one of 75 mm (3.0 in) on the left does not.

A general flowchart of the computer program for a computer-aided sequence design system for an upset forging is shown in Fig. 9.110. The geometries of the

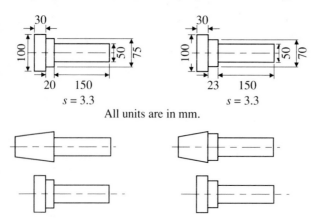

All units are in mm.

FIGURE 9.109
Effect of component shape on the intermediate stage for a given upset ratio [9.36].

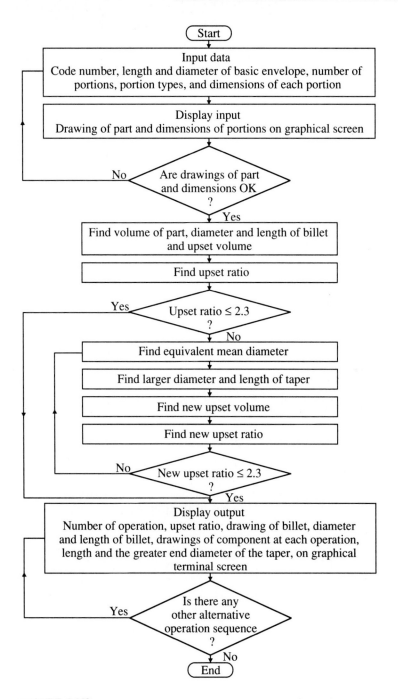

FIGURE 9.110
A general flowchart of the computer program for a computer-aided sequence design system for an upset forging [9.36].

parts are described by considering the various axial volumetric portions which make up the particular parts. The various elements for round parts consist of cylindrical portions (input code 0), conical portions (input code 1), convex and concave curved portions (input codes 2 and 3, respectively) as shown in Fig. 9.111. The characteristic dimensions of each element are input interactively in response to the following questions:

1. Code number of part?
2. Length and diameter of the basic envelope?
3. Number of portions of part?
4. Portion types (enter codes)?
5. Dimensions of each portion? (See Fig. 9.111.)

In response to this data input, the shape of the part is drawn on the screen along with its dimensions to serve as a check by the user. From this stage the appropriate processing sequence is determined, and the configuration of the component at each stage in the sequence is displayed together with the following information:

1. Number of operations
2. Upset ratio
3. Diameter and length of the required multiple
4. Length and largest diameter of each tapered upset

In conclusion it might be stated that this example of a computer-aided process design system illustrates the need for a good classification system for forging shapes. It is still in the developmental stage and offers great promise for expansion.

A software system for optimizing the sequence of operations, such as is used for cold forging of steel to be discussed in the following section, may be

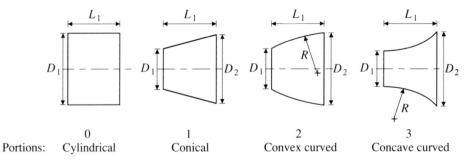

| 0 | 1 | 2 | 3 |
| Portions: Cylindrical | Conical | Convex curved | Concave curved |

FIGURE 9.111
Nomenclature and input code numbers for shape elements for the geometric description of round parts [9.36].

used in conjunction with the above sequence design program except that instead of being so concerned with the strain rate sensitivity *m*, more concern will be with strainhardening as expressed by the strainhardening exponent *n*.

9.14 OPTIMIZATION IN COLD FORGING [9.39]

9.14.1 Introduction

In Chap. 5, cold working, such as is involved in cold forging, was defined as a metalworking process, in which the material strainhardens during the working process and the deformation occurs at ambient or room temperature or appreciably below the cold-work recrystallization temperature, or below about 0.3 times the absolute melting temperature of the metal. Cold forging may involve upsetting or heading, extrusion, piercing, or a combination of these operations. The empirical equations for the determination of the pressure for cold extrusion were discussed briefly in Sec. 7.9 of Chap. 7.

The cold forging of steel can greatly reduce material waste, ensure a good surface finish and close tolerances as compared to conventional machining and/or hot forging, and increase the hardness and strength of the material. A factor that may be considered a disadvantage is the initial high cost of the tooling required. Also, the amount of deformation possible during cold working and the amount of force required are limiting factors.

In the cold forging of steel a number of alternative sequences of operations is feasible, even for a simple part. It would be desirable to consider all of the alternatives in detail, including an analysis of the sensitivity of calculations to unavoidable inaccuracies in the assumptions, to future variations in the direct and indirect costs, etc., before deciding on the "best" sequence.

Because, even for a relatively simple part, the number of feasible cold forging alternative sequences of operations, such as could be devised by an experienced process engineer, could be large. Some type of optimization technique is usually necessary, because the evaluation of all the alternatives may be prohibitively expensive and the cutting of corners may lead to the selection of a poor alternative, which may also be very expensive in the long run. Also, because the initial costs, including the tool costs, are large in cold forging of steel, even an apparently simple change in the operational sequence could be a very expensive and time-consuming exercise. A computer-aided method of optimization, based on the skills of the process planning engineer in setting up alternative sequences of operations, has been developed as represented by the flowchart in Fig. 9.112 [9.39]. The technical and economic data of a large number of alternative processing routes, together with the sensitivity of each result to changes in cost factors, can now be conveniently calculated.

Because the design of a sequence of operations in cold forging is based largely on experience and intuition, attempts to carry out this creative process by a computer would be a futile exercise. However, once the likely alternative operations are established, the subsequent laborious calculations become ideally

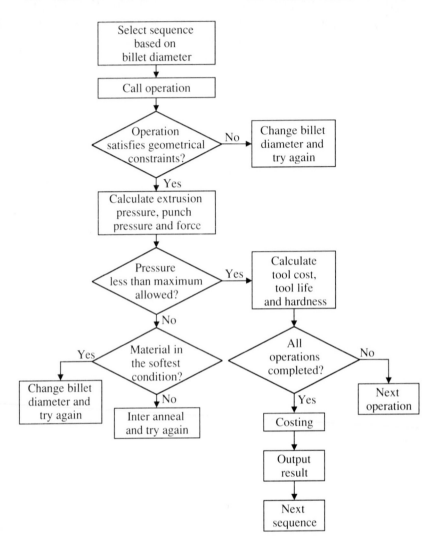

FIGURE 9.112
Steps involved in the determination of the optimum sequence of operations [9.39].

suitable for the computer. Not only can comparisons be made under prevailing conditions, but also the effect of future changes in such variables as labor and material costs, discount rates, etc., can be quickly and cheaply evaluated. Also, by relieving the process planning engineer of repetitive calculations, his experience can be utilized where it matters the most: (1) in designing an alternative sequence of operations, (2) in considering the main features of the equipment, and (3) in assessing the relative merits of the alternatives by evaluating the computer results.

9.14.2 Illustrative Cold Forging Example

The shape shown in Fig. 9.113 is used to illustrate the procedure for the optimiz-ation of the cold forging of steel. First, a number of alternative sequences of operations is devised which appear feasible for this particular shape. To retain a reasonable clarity only 13 alternatives, which is a small number of the total possible, are considered, as shown in Fig. 9.114. Many ramifications and sequences of operations enter into the selection of the "best" sequence. For example, depending on the rate of strainhardening and/or the initial hardness of the slugs, the second annealing and lubrication for alternatives 9 and 13 in Fig. 9.114 might not be necessary. Also, depending on the actual value of angle α, it might be better to extrude a preform at the optimum die angle and then obtain α by some additional operation. It can, therefore, be seen that the 13 alternatives shown in Fig. 9.114 may represent well over 100 different sequences of operations, although the difference in some cases might only be the addition of just one further operation to an already existing sequence.

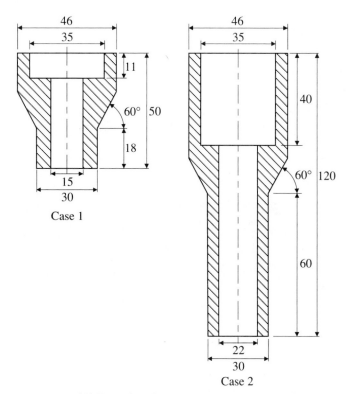

All dimensions in mm
Material 040A04 to BS 970 part 1 1972

FIGURE 9.113
Dimensions of alternate parts [9.39].

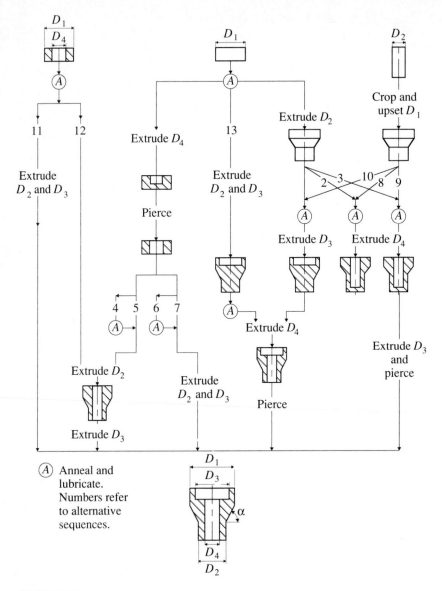

FIGURE 9.114
Alternate sequence of operations for a particular component shape [9.39].

Each sequence is characterized by a combination of operations carried out in the specific order given and no other. Every operation is subjected to a set of constraints which must be satisfied before proceeding to the next operation, such as the level of work hardening, the maximum practicable extrusion pressure, the largest length to diameter ratio, etc. The question that must be answered is whether it is possible to manufacture the part by applying a certain sequence, if at all.

After the hardness of the steel and the extrusion pressure after each operation are estimated as in Sec. 7.9 and by use of data from the literature, the type and size of the extrusion container is selected. The container, the tooling, and the labor costs are estimated for a certain amount of production. The next step is to make a comparative cost analysis for the different sequences.

Figure 9.115 shows a few of the basic results for the component with the dimensions shown in Fig. 9.113, case 1, while Fig. 9.116 shows the same for case 2 in Fig. 9.113. In order to have a reasonably small number of alternatives in the graphs, computed data are shown only for a vertical mechanical press with a single station tool, for either hand or hopper feeding. Costs are given as a function of the number of parts required per calendar month, and the production is assumed to extend over the discounting period. Figures 9.117 and 9.118 also show that changes in the dimensions of the part, while keeping the basic shape the same, not only alter the actual costs but also cause different sequences to become predominant and cause the crossover points to occur at different production levels. The cheapest sequences are Nos. 10 and 11 at large quantity production for case 1, while sequences Nos. 5 and 6 for case 2. For case 1, Fig. 9.117 shows the sensitivity of the results to a relative increase in material costs, while Fig. 9.118 shows the effect of changes in the capital cost.

One fairly general rule found for various shapes was that those sequences which require the least number of operations tend to give lower unit costs for

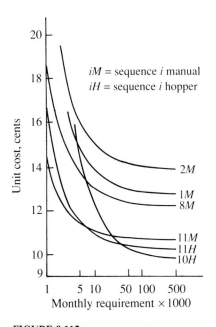

FIGURE 9.115
Present worth of costs per component for case 1 in Fig. 113 [9.39].

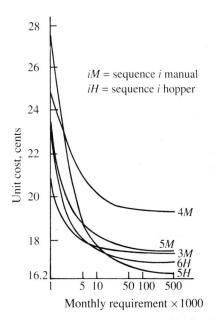

FIGURE 9.116
Present worth of costs per component for case 2 in Fig. 113 [9.39].

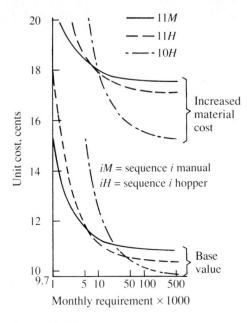

FIGURE 9.117
Doubling material cost of the component for case 1 [9.39].

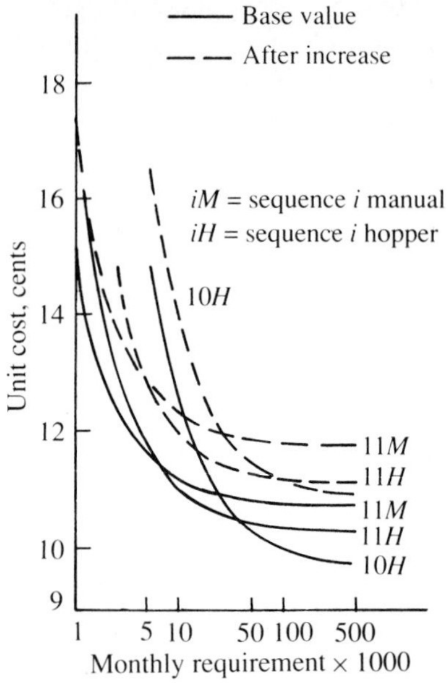

FIGURE 9.118
Doubling capital cost for case 2 [9.39].

smaller batches. In large batch production of a few items, the saving in unit costs offered by this method might be small, but the total gain could still be large due to the vast quantities involved.

In conclusion, it might be stated that this interactive method of analysis is simple and cheap, requires only a modest computing facility, and still provides as wide a range of technical and economic forecasts as are likely to be needed in most cases.

This optimization program is essentially an EXPERT system for the cold forging of steel, a more general application of which will be discussed in the next section.

9.15 EXPERT SYSTEM IN THE COLD FORGING OF STEEL

9.15.1 Introduction

The term EXPERT system was used in conjunction with a CAD/CAM system for forging die design mentioned in Sec. 9.7.7.4, Proprietary CAD/CAM/CAE Forging Systems.

Expert systems are computer programs which model human expertise and apply logical reasoning (inference) to the knowledge base in solving problems. The knowledge base itself is an organized set of information in the computer memory, obtained from people, who are experts in that particular field, i.e., domain experts such as in metalworking processes [9.40]. Any computer system developed by means of an expert system building program is considered to be an expert system, even though the system is so narrowly constrained that it would in no way rival a human expert. The term is now being used so loosely that it lacks precise meaning.

This rule-based method is applied in the expert system shell (framework program without the knowledge base): Augmented Prolog for Expert Systems implemented in LPA MicroProlog Professional, which is just a version of Prolog designed for use with the IBM PC microcomputer. Prolog is a conversational, computer programming language that is used for solving problems involving objects and relationships between objects. It is a symbolic, computer programming language based on predicate calculus, which is an extension of proportional calculus. Each elementary unit in predicate calculus is called an *object*, and statements about objects are called *predicates*. The matching and sequencing of the rules to the facts is called the *inference engine*, which contains that portion of a knowledge system that contains the inference and the control strategies, i.e., the order in which reasoning occurs.

The cold forging of steel is an ideal candidate for expert system development because of its potential. However, to make the system operable, highly specialized knowledge must be supplied in the following areas:

1. *Design for production.* Very specific cold forging design rules must be provided relating to such aspects as dimensions, shape, tolerances, surface finish, mechanical properties, etc., in order to determine whether or not cold forging might be used to produce the particular part.
2. *Process planning.* An optimizing system must be provided to select the best sequence of operations from those given that will produce the part in the quantity desired at the lowest cost.
3. *Production equipment center layout.* The proper selection, design and development, and layout of the production equipment involving such equipment as presses, tooling, annealing furnaces, lubrication systems, etc. that are essential for successful operation.

9.15.2 Cold Forging Design Rules

Cold forging design rules apply to such features as the shape and symmetry of the part, i.e., whether it is a solid or a hollow cylinder; whether it is plain, stepped, flanged, tapered, etc.; whether the holes are blind or through; whether the end faces have recesses and/or projections; whether there are undercuts; etc. Specific examples of rules dealing with cold forging are the design rules for upsetting discussed in previous sections. In backward extrusion of cans the ratio of the punch length to its diameter must be kept below a certain maximum to prevent its failure by buckling (tension stresses caused by bending of the tungsten carbide).

The ratio of the thickness of the base to that of the walls of a can should not be less than one; otherwise cracks may occur at the inside corner of the cold forging. Another important set of rules relates to the workpiece and product properties and qualities such as hardness (flow stress level), attainable dimensions, tolerances, surface finish, ease of metal flow in the die, the fiber structure of the forged part, etc.

9.15.3 System Development

As indicated in the previous section on optimization, it would be difficult to devise a comprehensive set of rules which would provide many different sequences of operations, which appear feasible for a particular shape, that would replace an experienced process planning engineer with an expert system.

As was discussed in Sec. 9.14, it is more realistic to have the process planning engineer use his ingenuity and expertise to devise various probable sequences of operations for the particular shape and allow the computer program to make all the routine deductions and checks against all of the above cold forging rules and the design details of the part.

In the method used here, the process planning engineer devised all the sequences that appeared practicable for the particular cold forging and coded them into the knowledge base. The program then checked all these sequences against the rules, selected the feasible sequences, and calculated the slug size and the loads and stresses required, while it rejected the impracticable sequences and gave the reasons for their rejection.

As this EXPERT system is written in PROLOG, each rule behaves like a procedure, it is therefore easy to add or delete rules without disturbing the rest of the system. This feature is important since it would be impossible to create a general system for cold forging that could handle all possibilities regarding shapes, materials, etc., especially within the limited memory of a microcomputer. Also, various forgers want to use their own shapes and design rules. This is one reason why it was decided to allow the process planning engineer to design the sequences of operations into the system, rather than building rules into the knowledge base for setting up the various sequences when the shape, material, and other information are provided.

9.15.4 Example Shape

The shape, possessing arbitrary dimensions within design rule limits shown in Fig. 9.119, is used here to illustrate the type of solution that is obtained from the output of this system.

Five sequences, as preselected by the process planning engineer, are shown in Fig. 9.120, in which A denotes a lubrication operation and $1A$ denotes both an annealing and lubrication operation. The critical pressure is set at 2000 MPa (290,000 psi). The extrusion pressure is calculated for an operation, and if it exceeds the critical pressure, an annealing and lubrication operation is tried, and

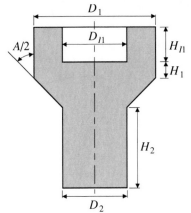

FIGURE 9.119
Shape of cold-forging sample [9.40].

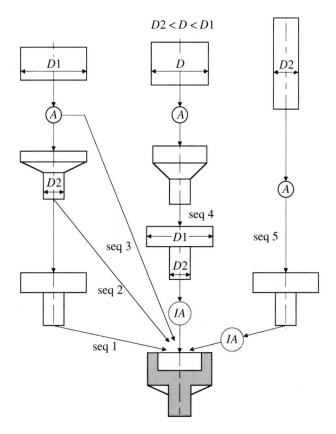

FIGURE 9.120
Various sequences of operations [9.40].

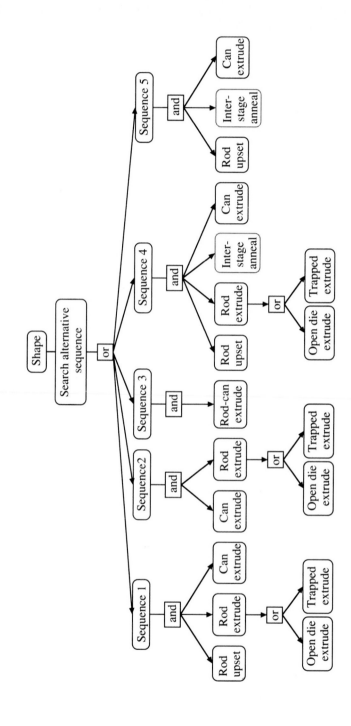

FIGURE 9.121
Simplified AND-OR tree where the basic operations appear in more than one sequence [9.40].

the pressure is recalculated. If it is less than the critical pressure, the operation is accepted and recorded. If the pressure still exceeds the critical pressure, then the operation is failed, which fails the whole sequence.

The sequences can be represented in the form of an AND-OR tree, as shown in Fig. 9.121, where the basic operations appear in more than one sequence. This suggests that the rules for these operations should be constructed as general as possible, so that they can be used in all sequences. As the slug diameter varies between sequences, the extrusion ratios used in the computations also vary, therefore the ratios have to be defined in terms of slug diameters to account for this difference.

The principal limitation for an EXPERT system used on a microcomputer is memory space, so a modular structure was used in the program. The structure developed for this software system, called the Cold Forging Expert System (COFEX), is shown in Fig. 9.122.

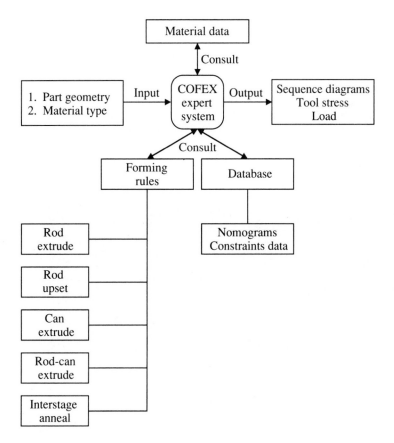

FIGURE 9.122
Structure of the Cold Forging Expert System (COFEX) [9.40].

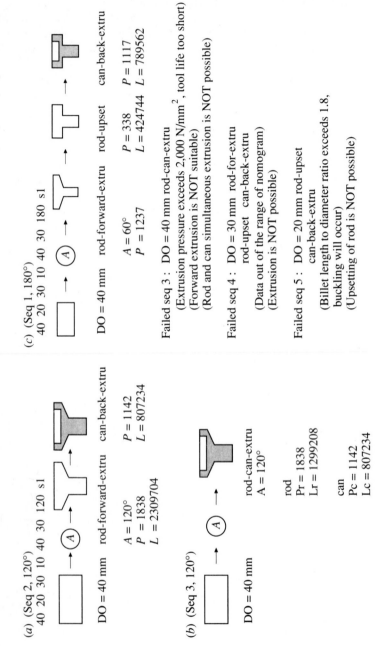

(a) (Seq 2, 120°)
40 20 30 10 40 30 120 s1

DO = 40 mm   rod-forward-extru   can-back-extru

A = 120°
P = 1838
L = 2309704

P = 1142
L = 807234

(b) (Seq 3, 120°)

DO = 40 mm

rod-can-extru
A = 120°

rod
Pr = 1838
Lr = 1299208

can
Pc = 1142
Lc = 807234

(c) (Seq 1, 180°)
40 20 30 10 40 30 180 s1

DO = 40 mm   rod-forward-extru   rod-upset   can-back-extru

A = 60°
P = 1237

P = 338
L = 424744

P = 1117
L = 789562

Failed seq 3 : DO = 40 mm rod-can-extru
(Extrusion pressure exceeds 2,000 N/mm^2, tool life too short)
(Forward extrusion is NOT suitable)
(Rod and can simultaneous extrusion is NOT possible)

Failed seq 4 : DO = 30 mm rod-for-extru
rod-upset   can-back-extru
(Data out of the range of nomogram)
(Extrusion is NOT possible)

Failed seq 5 : DO = 20 mm rod-upset
can-back-extru
(Billet length to diameter ratio exceeds 1.8,
buckling will occur)
(Upsetting of rod is NOT possible)

FIGURE 9.123
Reproduced computer printout from the Cold Forging Expert System (COFEX). (The computer print-out was folded for ease of presentation.) (A = angle in degrees, P = extrusion pressure in MPa, and L = extrusion load in N.) [9.40]

682

9.15.5 Sample Consultation with COFEX

Two examples were run with COFEX of the shape shown in Fig. 9.119, using the five sequences shown in Fig. 9.120, three of which use a starting slug (multiple or billet) diameters of $D1$, and one each use $D2$ and D, respectively, where $D2 < D < D1$.

The dimensions of the two sample forgings as indicated in Fig. 9.119 are $D1 = 40$ mm (1.6 in), $D2 = 20$ mm (0.8 in), $DI1 = 30$ mm (1.2 in), $H1 = 10$ mm (0.4 in), $H2 = 40$ mm (1.6 in), $HI1 = 30$ mm (1.2 in), with the only difference appearing in the angle, in one case $A = 180°$, in the other $A = 120°$. The steel is equivalent to AISI 1012, denoted by s1 in the program.

The sequences 1, 4, and 5 in Fig. 9.120 are for a die angle of 180°, while 2 and 3 are for die angles less than 180° down to 60°.

The computer output is shown in Fig. 9.123. The first line in the printout in Fig. 9.123 shows the forging dimensions in the same order as given above, the second line is a sketch (not to scale) showing the accepted sequence, the third line giving the slug diameter (DO) and the abbreviations for rod forward extrusion, rod upsetting, and can backward extrusion. Then the die angle (A), the respective extrusion pressures in MPa (P), and the extrusion loads (L) in Newtons are given.

The remaining output contains the messages. For the forging with $A = 180°$, only sequence 1 using a slug diameter $DO = 40$ mm (1.6 in) is acceptable (Fig. 9.123(c)). One of the rules in COFEX is that the optimum die angle must be used when feasible, so that for forward extrusion of a rod, the optimum inclusive die angle of 60° is selected. Sequence 2 is not suitable because it would not provide the required angle of 180° for the forging. Sequence 3 is rejected because the forward extrusion pressure at 180° inclusive die angle exceeds the permitted maximum critical pressure. Sequence 4 for slug diameter of $DO = 30$ mm (1.2 in) is not suitable because the backward extrusion of the can is not feasible without interstage annealing. Sequence 5 is unacceptable because for $DO = 20$ mm (0.8 in) the length/diameter ratio of the slug is too large so that plastic buckling would occur in upsetting. For forgings with $A = 120°$, sequences 2 and 3 are acceptable. In forward extrusion and in combined extrusion, a 120° inclusive die angle is used as required for the final shape of the forging. Sequences 1, 4, and 5 are not acceptable because they are suitable for forgings with $A = 180°$.

In conclusion, it might be said that the expert system is a powerful tool for use in the cold forging of steel, and its use can profitably be extended to many other metalworking processes. Furthermore, the foregoing discussion of the optimization of cold forging is a good example of the way that some of the powerful tools of engineering can be used in metalforming.

ACKNOWLEDGMENT

The material and most of the illustrations in this chapter were adapted from the references as indicated in the text and in the legends by the numbers of the references enclosed in square brackets pursuant to all copyrights.

REFERENCES

9.1. Dean, T. A., "The Mechanics of Flash in Drop Forging-Temperature and Speed Effects," *Proc. Inst. Mech. Engrs.*, vol. 190, no. 33, 1976, pp. 457-466.

9.2. Biswas, S. K., and B. W. Rooks, "Application of a Modular Approach to Estimate Load and Energy in Closed Die Forging," *Proc. 15th Int. Machine Tool Design and Research Conf.*, S. A. Tobias and F. Koenigsberger (eds.), 1974, pp. 445-453.

9.3. Altan, T., "Computer Simulation to Predict Load, Stress, and Metal Flow in an Axisymmetric Closed Die Forging," *Metal Forming*, A. L. Hoffmanner, Plenum Press, New York, 1971, pp. 249-273.

9.4. Altan, T., and R. J. Fiorentio, "Prediction of Loads and Stresses in Closed-Die Forging," *Journal of Engr. for Industry*, May 1971, pp. 477-484.

9.5. McDermott, R. P., and A. N. Bramley, "Forging Analysis—A New Approach," *Proc. 2nd NAMRC*, SME, 1974, pp. 35-47.

9.6. Lyapunov, N. I., and S. Kobayashi, "Metal Flow in Plane-Strain Closed-Die Forging," *5th NAMRC 1977*, SME, Dearborn, Michigan, pp. 114-121.

9.7. Schey, J. A., "The More Common Fabrication Processes," vol. 1, part 3, *Techniques of Metals Research*, R. F. Bunshah (ed.), Interscience Publishers, 1968, p. 1472.

9.8. Thomas, A., and I. Bannister, "The Accuracy of Forging Load Estimation in Drop Forging," *Proc. 17th Int. Mach. Tool Design and Research Conf.*, S. A. Tobias (ed.), 1976, pp. 343-353.

9.9. Balogun, S. A., "Die Load and Stresses in Press Forging," PhD Thesis, University of Aston in Birmingham, 1971.

9.10. McDermott, R. P., and A. N. Bramley, "An Elemental Upper-Bound Technique for General Use in Forging Analysis," *Proc. of 15th Mach. Tool Design and Res. Conf.* 1974, vol. M, S. A. Tobias and F. Koenigsberger, pp. 437-443.

9.11. Hill, R., *The Mathematical Theory of Plasticity*, Clarendon Press, Oxford, 1950.

9.12. Subramanian, T. L., and T. Altan, "A Practical Method for Estimating Forging Loads with the Use of a Programmable Calculator," *J. Applied Metalworking*, vol. 1, no. 2, 1980, pp. 60-68.

9.13. Biswas, S. K., and B. W. Rooks, "Application of a Computer Simulation Technique to Estimate Load and Energy in Forging," *Proc. 13th Int. Mach. Tool Design and Research Conf.*, S. A. Tobias (ed.), 1972, pp. 371-381.

9.14. Biswas, S. K., and W. A. Knight, "Computer-Aided Design of Axisymmetric Hot Forging Dies," *Proc. 15th Int. Mach. Tool Design and Research Conf.*, S. A. Tobias and F. Koenigsberger (eds.), 1974, pp. 135-143.

9.15. Biswas, S. K., and W. A. Knight, "Computer-Aided Preform Design for Long Hot Forgings," *Proc. 17th Int. Mach. Tool Design and Research Conf.*, S. A. Tobias (ed.), 1976, pp. 27-36.

9.16. Lui, S. W., and M. K. Das, "Interactive Design of Axisymmetric Forging Dies Using a Desk-Top Computer," *J. of Mech. Working Tech.*, vol. 5, nos. 1 and 2, June 1981, pp. 85-103.

9.17. Chen, Y. K., and W. A. Knight, "Computer-Aided Design and Manufacture of Dies For Long Hot Forging," *Proc. 6th NAMRC*, SME, April 1978, pp. 455-462.

9.18. Mullineux, G., and W. A. Knight, "Computer-Aided Design and Manufacture of Forging Rolls," *Proc. 7th NAMRC*, SME, 1979, pp. 315-322.

9.19. Reynolds, C. C., and G. F. Fuller, "Computer-Aided Modeling of Forging Energy and Load in Hammer Forging," *Process Modeling Tools*, ASM, 1981, pp. 173-194.

9.20. Subramanian, T. L., K. Akgerman, and T. Altan, "Computer-Aided Preform Design for Precision Isothermal Forging," *Proc. 5th NAMRC*, 1977, pp. 198-213.

9.21. Subramanian, T. L., N. Akgerman, and T. Altan, "Application of Computer-Aided Design and Manufacturing to Precision Isothermal Forging of Titanium Alloys," Battelle's Columbus Laboratories, Final Report AML-TR-77-108, vols. I, II, and III, Air Force Materials Lab., July 1977.

9.22. Kuhlman, David J., CAD/CAM Applications Engineer, Metals Processing Section, Battelle, Letter, Aug. 7, 1987.

9.23. Yu, G. B., and T. A. Dean, "A CAD/CAM Package for Axisymmetric Forging Dies," in *Proc. of the 25th International Machine Tool Design and Research Conf.*, S. A. Tobias (ed.), April 1985, Macmillan Publishers Ltd., pp. 595–464.

9.24. Kubel, Edward J., Jr., "Advances in Forging Technology," *Advanced Materials & Processes including Metal Progress*, vol. 131, no. 6, June 1987, pp. 55–59.

9.25. ASM Metals Handbook, 8th ed., 1970, T. Lyman (ed.), vol. 5, Forging and Casting, pp. 1–18.

9.26. Badawy, A., and T. Altan, "Computer-Aided Design and Manufacturing (CAD/CAM) Applications in Forging," *Forging Handbook*, T. G. Byrer et al. (eds.), FIA, ASM, Metals Park, 1985, p. 81.

9.27. Nilson, E. N., "The CAD/CAM Interface: Problems and Solutions," All Together Now ... Building for the Future, 1978, Numerical Control Society.

9.28. Forging Industry Handbook, J. E. Jenson (ed.), 1970, Forging Industry Assoc., Cleveland, Ohio, pp. 119 and 286.

9.29. Chuah, C. L., and M. K. Das, "Some Preliminary Considerations for a Computer-Aided Billet Volume Control in Bar Cropping," in *Proc. of 22d Intl. Mach. Tool Design and Research Conf.*, Sept. 1981, vol. 22, B. J. Davies (ed.), The Macmillan Press Ltd., pp. 573–579.

9.30. Lui, S. W., and M. K. Das, "Computer-Aided Design and Manufacture of High Speed Cropping Tools," in *Proc. of 22d Intl. Mach. Tool Design and Research Conf.*, Sept. 1981, vol. 22, B. J. Davies (ed.), The Macmillan Press Ltd. p. 467.

9.31. Schey, J. A., "Principles of Forging Design," American Iron and Steel Institute, Washington, DC., 1975, pp. 11, 36–39.

9.32. *Fundamentals of Tool Design*, F. W. Wilson (ed.), Prentice-Hall, Englewood Cliffs, New Jersey, 1962, p. 302.

9.33. Knight, W. A., "Part Family Methods for Bulk Metal Forming," *Int. J. Prod. Res.*, 1974, vol. 12, no. 2, pp. 209–231.

9.34. Spies, K. Von, "Preforming in Forging and Preparation of Reduced Rolling" (in German), Doctoral Dissertation, Technical University of Hanover, 1959.

9.35. Altan, T., S. Oh, and H. L. Gegel, "Metal Forming: Fundamentals and Applications," ASM, Metals Park, Ohio, 1983, p. 149.

9.36. Gokler, M. I., W. A. Knight, and C. Poli, "Classification for Systematic Component and Process Design for Forging Operations," *Proc. 9th NAMRC*, SME, 1981, pp. 158–165.

9.37. Poli, C., and W. A. Knight, "Design for Forging Handbook," University of Massachusetts at Amherst, Amherst, Massachusetts.

9.38. Glokler, M. I., and T. A. Dean, "Computer-Aided Sequence Design for Hot Upset Forgings," in *Proc. of 22d Intl. Mach. Tool Design and Research Conf.*, Sept. 1981, vol. 22, B. J. Davies (ed.), The Macmillan Press Ltd. pp. 457–465.

9.39. Lengyel, B., and T. V. Venkatasubramanian, "Optimisation in the Cold Forging of Steel," in *Proc. of 18th Intl. Mach. Tool Design and Research Conf.*, Sept. 1977, vol. 18, J. M. Alexander (ed.), The Macmillan Press Ltd. pp. 153–157.

9.40. Lengyel, B., and M. L. Tay, "Expert System in the Cold Forging of Steel," in *Proc. 27th Intl. Mach. Tool Design and Research Conf.*, Apr. 1988, vol. 27, B. J. Davies (ed.), The Macmillan Press Ltd. pp. 345–351.

9.41. Altan, T. et al., *A Study of Mechanics of Closed-Die Forging*, Final Report June 1968–June 1970 (Aug. 1970), Contract No. DAAG 46-68-C01211 (AD 711 544, AMMRC-CR-70-18).

PROBLEMS

9.1. Calculate the forging loads in lbf for the three representative sections of the connecting rod forging shown in Fig. 9.16 by use of Eqs. (9.44) to (9.47) for the axisymmetric sections and Eqs. (9.48) to (9.50) for the plane-strain section of the forging. All cavity cross sections are approximated by rectangles, whose dimensions are reflected in the data for r and L.

The data are as follows:
(1) For the axisymmetric section described by Sec. A-A:
$r = 0.96$ in, $H = 0.32$ in, $w = 0.31$ in, $h = 0.082$ in, $m = 0.7$, the flow stress for the cavity section: $\sigma_c = 14,000$ psi, and the flow stress for the flash section: $\sigma_f = 20,000$.
(2) For the plane-strain section B-B:
The data are the same as above except that $L = 0.93$ in.
(3) For the axisymmetric section described by Sec. C-C:
The data are same as for Sec. A-A except that $r = 0.53$ in and $H = 0.64$ in.

9.2. For the example Prob. 9.1 above, write a computer program for calculating the forging load for an axisymmetric section. Use Basic, Fortran 77, or Pascal.

9.3. In order to estimate the flow stress of a material accurately, the temperature of the deforming material should be known.
   (a) Calculate the temperature due to deformation by use of Eq. (9.36). (See also Eqs. (2.169) and (4.78).) Make the calculations in both the customary and SI units. Estimate the true strain from the initial and final thickness.
       Use the following values:

$$
\begin{aligned}
A &= 9.7985 \text{ J/kg-m} = 1.07 \times 10^{-4} \text{ Btu/in-lbs} \\
\sigma_a &= 124 \text{ MPa} \qquad = 18,000 \text{ psi} \\
t_0 &= 19.05 \text{ mm} \qquad = 0.75 \text{ in (initial thickness)} \\
t_f &= 452 \text{ J/kg-K} \qquad = 0.108 \text{ Btu/lb}°\text{F} \\
\rho &= 77,400 \text{ N/m}^3 \qquad = 0.285 \text{ lb/in}^3
\end{aligned}
$$

   (b) By use of Eq. (9.33) estimate the average temperature of a forging in the die cavity in °C by using the data given in this equation. Assume a thin plate of uniform thickness cooled symmetrically from both sides. Initial temperatures of the die and the workpiece are 175 and 1050°C, respectively. The average plate thickness is 8.13 mm and the time of contact is taken to be 0.0315 s.

9.4. In reference to the flowchart in Fig. 9.24 answer the following questions:
   (a) What does the first loop end up doing?
   (b) What is R_N, and how is it defined?
   (c) What does the second loop end up doing?
   (d) What does the last loop end up doing?

9.5. (a) If the length and diameter of the billet are 20 and 40 mm, respectively, and the weight of the forging is 0.1636 kg, by use of Eqs. (9.87) and (9.88) calculate the flash-land width to thickness ratio and the flash-land width. Use a shape complexity factor of 0.64.
   (b) If the overall diameter of a very small, experimental, dislike forging shown in Fig. 9.36 including the flash, is 55 mm, and the diameter of the body is 42 mm, the average thickness of the forging is 15 mm, and the shape complexity factor is 0.64, calculate the forging peak load by use of Eqs. (9.90) and (9.92). Assume that the flow stress of the flash is 200 MPa and that of the forging body is 130 MPa.
   (c) (1) Make a sketch of the carbon electrode that would be used to electrical discharge machine the die cavity, and (2) draw the schematic curve showing the variation of the load P with distance of descent of the die during the forging stroke.

9.6. (a) By use of Figs. 9.65 and 9.69(b), check approximately the load given in Table 9.4 by use of Eq. (9.10). How do the results compare?
   (b) Convert Eq. (9.10) into SI units, so that P is in kN and h_m and A_t are in mm and mm^2, and calculate the load.

PART

III

SHEETMETAL FORMING PROCESSES

CHAPTER
10

CLASSIFICATION AND ANALYSIS OF SHEARING, BENDING, STRETCH-FORMING, AND SHEETMETAL FORMING OPERATIONS

10.1 STATUS OF THE PRESS SHOP

10.1.1 Historical Perspective and Future Requirements

Historically, the evolution of a sheetmetal stamping from conception through part design to die design to the final die tryout has been a slow, cautious process based on the trial-and-error experience and the skill of the artisan [10.1]. The press-shop today is successful only because of the technological skill developed over the years by the artisans. At the present time, it would be very difficult, using the scientific approach only, even to duplicate the capability of the artisan in producing a part, not to mention the development of another part of equivalent complexity, by use of the analytical procedures. So far, we can provide only an approximate analytical solution to the anticipated process performance of sheetmetal forming of only the simplest parts, and then only in retrospect.

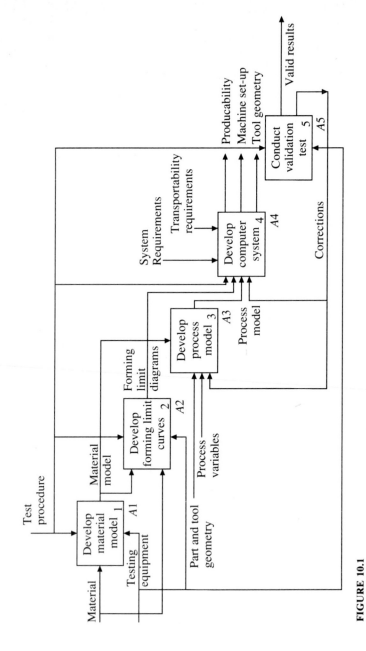

FIGURE 10.1

Flowchart for the overall development of computer systems for sheetmetal forming [10.18].

However, a breakdown of the artisan system is beginning to occur for the following reasons: (1) breakdown of the long-term apprenticeship training system, (2) the trend toward earlier retirement, (3) reduced lead time for die tryout and development, (4) increased complexity of parts, (5) introduction of new, unfamiliar materials, (6) greater emphasis on cost-effectiveness, and (7) the rapid development of computer-aided design. It would be very difficult for the average diemaker to function properly without the backup support from the process engineer. New developments are occurring at an ever-increasing rate. The typical toolmaker is no longer able to cope with these developments. There is definitely a need to replace the present experienced-based, trial-and-error techniques with cost-effective, knowledge-based, analytical techniques in sheetmetal forming. Productivity increases in sheetmetal forming can be achieved if the part geometry, the fabrication method, the die design, and the material property parameters are correctly specified at the design stage.

According to Keeler [10.1], the system of the future to replace the artisan should meet eight requirements. It must (1) be an interactive system, (2) be modeled with known and unknown variables, (3) incorporate the material properties of real materials, (4) not be biased by historical rules of thumb, (5) provide predictive capability, (6) improve the interaction between design and manufacturing functions, (7) be responsive to new in-service requirements, and (8) be attuned to end-product economy.

To meet the above requirements, computer-aided design and manufacturing (CAD-CAM) systems are being developed and applied to sheetmetal forming. To develop such a CAD/CAM software system for sheetmetal forming operations, it is necessary to develop the following [10.2]: (1) analytical models describing the material behavior under various forming conditions of temperature, strain, and strain rate, and (2) mathematical models simulating each specific sheetmetal forming process of interest. The analytical models for material behavior should enable the calculation of the limits to which the material can be deformed. The mathematical models for the processes should describe the local states of the stresses and strains in the material during forming. These two models, when integrated, will form the basis for a CAD/CAM system for sheetmetal forming [10.3]. Such a system must be capable of dealing with the material behavior, the process conditions, the process variables, and the processing equipment, considered simultaneously. An example of the overall development of an interactive computer system structured from scratch is shown in the flowchart in Fig. 10.1 [10.3].

10.1.2 Analytical Models of Material Behavior

The development of a material model will at some stage of the development involve the following: (1) the acquisition and/or measurement of the relevant material properties, i.e., the characterization of the material, and (2) the identification and verification of the constitutive equations applicable to the material and the process.

10.1.3 Characterization of the Sheetmetal [10.3], [10.18]

In attempting to use the properties of materials in forming operations, we have the inherent difficulty of utilizing the entire strain history of the material which involves both the description of (1) the limit of stable flow which the material can sustain and (2) the point of fracture of the material. This situation means that the parameters derived from a rather limited strain history available in the uniaxial tensile test is of questionable value. This situation explains why tests involving large plastic strains, such as the bulge test for sheetmetal, are now being used. Even though the effect of friction and flow rate are ignored, sheetmetal forming is still complex because the stability and the fracture processes are determined both by the stress state and the detailed microstructure.

In order to characterize the material under consideration, the following data will need to be acquired from the literature or experimentally or both as needed: (1) uniaxial tensile test data such as by constant extension rate tests, (2) stress-strain rate data at the required strain and temperature such as by load relaxation tests, (3) hydraulic bulge test data, (4) plastic anisotropy data, etc.

The uniaxial tensile test may be used to provide such data as the ultimate tensile strength, yield strength, percent elongation, etc., at different constant strain rates at constant temperature such as 25°C (75°F).

The load relaxation test may be used to determine the strain rate sensitivity exponent m. The procedure used is to load the specimen to a convenient plastic strain and allow the load to relax to obtain the load-time data for calculation of the true stress σ and the true strain rate $\dot{\varepsilon}$, at equal load intervals.

The hydraulic bulge test is performed by clamping a blank, say, 248 mm (9.76 in) in diameter, firmly in grooved ring dies and subjecting it to a fluid pressure on one side. An element at the pole of the dome of the bulge is deformed in approximately equal biaxial stress and strain. The bulge test permits the study of material behavior at strains well in excess of the maximum uniform strains in the tension test. The stress-strain relation for the material can be derived from measurements of surface extension, curvature, and pressure. Assuming some simplifying conditions such as a thin spherical shell, balanced biaxial stress and strain at the pole, no stress normal to the sheet due to fluid pressure, and no bending stress and constraint effects, one can obtain the following relations for the membrane stress σ_m and thickness strain ε_z:

$$\sigma_m = \frac{PR}{2t} = \frac{PR}{2t_0} e^{-\varepsilon_z} \tag{10.1}$$

$$\varepsilon_z = \ln\left(\frac{t}{t_0}\right) = -2\ln\left(\frac{D}{D_0}\right) \tag{10.2}$$

where R is the radius of curvature, P is the fluid pressure, D_0 is the initial reference circle diameter, and D is the instantaneous diameter of the reference circle based on extensometer displacement.

The plastic anisotropy, which will be discussed at length later, is characterized by the plastic strain ratio $r = \varepsilon_w / \varepsilon_t$, measured from tensile test specimens cut at 0, 90, and 45° to the direction of rolling of the sheet prior to manufacture

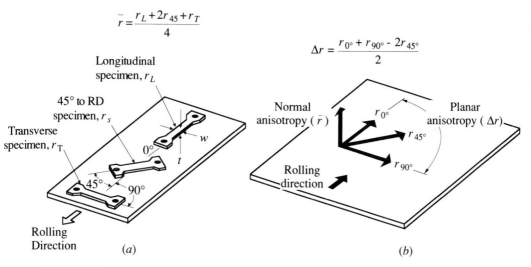

$$\bar{r} = \frac{r_L + 2r_{45} + r_T}{4}$$

$$\Delta r = \frac{r_{0°} + r_{90°} - 2r_{45°}}{2}$$

FIGURE 10.2
(a) Tensile specimen orientation for determining $\bar{r}$ and Δr. (b) Axes used in defining normal and planar anisotropy.

as shown in Fig. 10.2 [10.4]. Here ε_w and ε_t are the true (logarithmic) width and thickness strains, respectively. $\bar{r}$ is called the normal anisotropy and is expressed as the average of the anisotropy values in the plane of the sheet. Planar anisotropy Δr gives the variation of r in the plane of the sheet.

Much of the above experimental information for the characterization of a sheetmetal may be summarized graphically in a forming limit diagram (FLD). The basic theory, experimental determination, and application of the FLD will be discussed elsewhere.

10.2 CLASSIFICATION OF SHEETMETAL FORMING PROCESSES

10.2.1 Scope of Problem

Sheetmetal forming processes represent a wide range of metal flow processes that are difficult to classify precisely so that the classification is mutually exclusive. Some of these processes are shown in Table 10.1 based on the system of pressures used in the processes as presented by Kienzle in Fig. 10.3 as discussed by DeGarmo [10.6]. Since many sheetmetal parts are formed by means of a press, they may be classified as press-formed parts as opposed to nonpress-formed parts, such as those formed by form-rolling, etc., as shown in Table 10.1. Sheetmetal formed parts, especially shallow parts that are blanked out of sheetmetal with only minor forming operations done on them, are called *stampings*. Stampings will be defined later and discussed in conjunction with deep drawing. Another complication in the classification of sheetmetal forming processes is that shearing or severing processes such as blanking, piercing, shear cutting, etc., are also done on a punch press in which metalforming (deformation) is incidental.

TABLE 10.1
Classification of some forming operations [10.6]

Number	Process	Schematic diagram	State of stress in main part during forming (see Fig. 10.3 for key)
1	Rolling		7
2	Forging		9
3	Extruding		9
4	Shear spinning		12
5	Tube spinning		9
6	Swaging or kneading		7
7	Deep drawing		In flange of blank, 5 In wall of cup, 1
8	Wire and tube drawing		8
9	Stretching		2
10	Straight bending		At bend, 2 and 7
11	Contoured flanging	(a) Convex	At outer flange, 6 At bend, 2 and 7
		(b) Concave	At outer flange, 1 At bend, 2 and 7

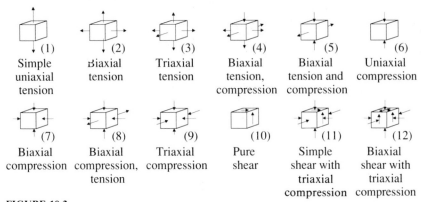

(1)	(2)	(3)	(4)	(5)	(6)
Simple uniaxial tension	Biaxial tension	Triaxial tension	Biaxial tension, compression	Biaxial tension and compression	Uniaxial compression

(7)	(8)	(9)	(10)	(11)	(12)
Biaxial compression	Biaxial compression, tension	Triaxial compression	Pure shear	Simple shear with triaxial compression	Biaxial shear with triaxial compression

FIGURE 10.3
Classification of the states of stress for use in the classification of forming processes [10.6].

Also, sheetmetal forming processes as opposed to bulk or massive deformation processes were defined as processes in which no intentional change in thickness of the material occurs. There are sheetmetal processes in which a change in thickness is intentionally made, such as in ironing, for example, which may be done as a part of a deep-drawing operation or subsequent to it. Also, thick metal stampings are made from plates up to about 19 mm ($\frac{3}{4}$ in) thick. Some typical parts made of heavy metal stampings are shown in Fig. 10.4. In sheetmetal forming processes, the stresses are usually primarily tensile, as opposed to compressive, as used in bulk or massive forming. There are, of course, quite a number of exceptions such as deep drawing, for example.

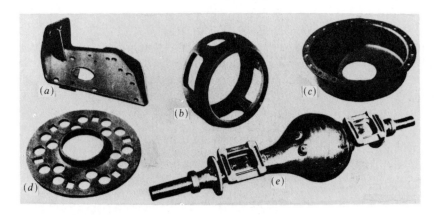

FIGURE 10.4
Examples of thick metal stampings: (*a*) truck bracket drawn from $\frac{3}{8}$ in (9.5 mm) thick steel with welded webs, (*b*) universal joint cage drawn from $\frac{7}{16}$ in (11.1 mm) thick steel with pierced side slots, (*c*) converter drive disc drawn from $\frac{1}{4}$ in (6.4 mm) thick steel, (*d*) clutch plate produced from $\frac{1}{2}$ in (12.7 mm) thick steel, and (*e*) truck rear axle housing made by welding six components, the largest of which is drawn from $\frac{3}{8}$ in (9.5 mm) thick steel. (*Adapted from Wick, C., "Heavy Metal Stampings", Manufacturing Engineering, Aug. 1977, SME, pp. 50–54*).

TABLE 10.2
Type of press working operations [10.12]

(See Fig. 10.5)

1. Shear cutting operations	
(a) Blanking	(f) Trimming
(b) Piercing (punching)	(g) Shaving
(c) Perforating	(h) Notching
(d) Shearing (cropping)	(i) Slitting
(e) Parting	
2. Drawing operations	
(a) Forming	(c) Redrawing
(b) Drawing	(d) Ironing
3. Bending operations	
(a) Air bending	(c) Channel bends
(b) V-bending	
4. Compression operations	
(a) Coining	(d) Sizing
(b) Embossing	(e) Swaging
(c) Impact extrusion	(f) Riveting

For the purpose of discussion, press-working operations may be classified as shown in Table 10.2.

Nonpress-forming operations may include such forming operations, shown in Table 10.1, as (1) roll forming, (2) thread-roll forming, (3) multiple-slide machine forming, (4) hammer forming, (5) spinning, (6) electromagnetic forming, (7) stretch forming, (9) explosive forming, etc.

10.2.2 Proposed Classification and Coding of Sheetmetal Components

Because of the rapid increase in interactive computer graphics and computer-aided-design (CAD), it is becoming more and more important to develop a precise system of classification and coding of metalworking processes as indicated in the foregoing. One such system, proposed for sheetmetal components by Fogg et al., relates to group technology (GT) and is oriented toward tool design [10.7].

The variation in the range of shapes and sizes of parts produced by sheet-metal forming is very large. Despite this vast variation in shape between components, it is usually found that, within limits, any shape can be obtained by a synthesis of several basic press-working processes (operations) as shown in Fig. 10.5 [10.7].

The first step in the above classification and coding of components for press work by Fogg et al. is to divide them into discrete areas of activity or application. The preliminary, condensed form of this classification consists of 10 classes of applications designated from 0 electronic to 9 general. The 10 classes consist of the following: electronic, electrical, instruments, business machines, automotive accessories, domestic utensils, packaging and containers, domestic appliances and equipment, automobile, and general. As an example, two of the classes

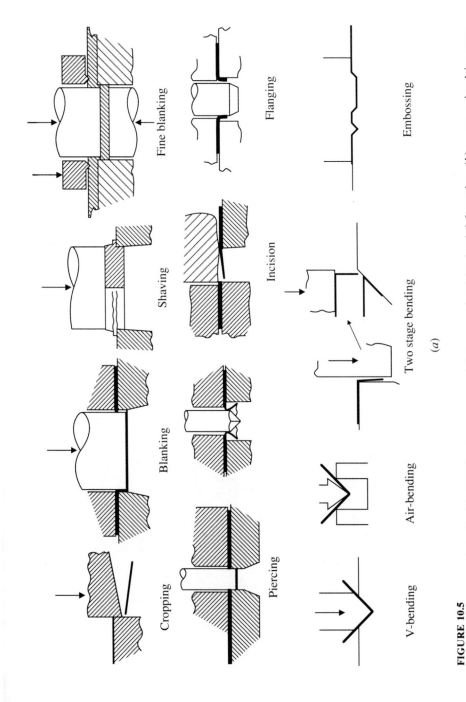

Cropping   Blanking   Shaving   Fine blanking

Piercing   Incision   Flanging

V-bending   Air-bending   Two stage bending   Embossing

(a)

FIGURE 10.5
Basic processes involved in forming sheetmetal components. (a) Processes involving local deformation; (b) processes involving more extensive area of the sheet (continued) [10.7].

697

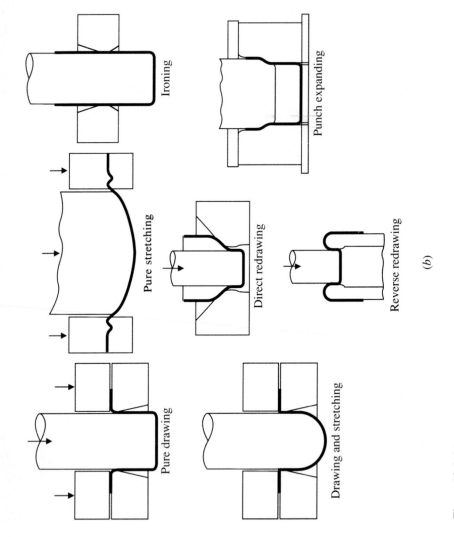

Ironing

Punch expanding

Pure stretching

Direct redrawing

Reverse redrawing

Pure drawing

Drawing and stretching

(b)

Figure 10.5 (b)

TABLE 10.3
Two classes and coding of components for presswork in the electrical industry [10.7]

Digit		Areas of activity	
0	Electronic	Group I	Metal components for valves, C.R. tubes, semi conductors; capacitor cans, valve screens, etc.
		Group II	Chassis, panels, racks, etc.
8	Automobile	Group I	Body panels, structural members, etc.
		Group II	Levers, brackets, covers, gas tanks, facia, etc.

consisting of 0 electronic, and 8 automotive applications, are shown in Table 10.3. This classification is based on the premise that sheetmetal parts for a given industry and application have a certain amount of commonality allowing for the application of group technological techniques. This system allows access to design information for metalforming on the basis of industrial categories.

The second stage in the above classification process, oriented toward die design, is to classify the equipment and tooling associated with a given area of activity for a particular industry. A list summarizing the manufacturing process or tooling classes, which accommodates groups of parts produced in the electronic and electrical industries, is given in Table 10.4. These various types of tooling will be discussed elsewhere.

The third step is to determine the variety of operations that can be produced by each class of tooling given in Table 10.4. For example, a single station die is used primarily for producing components involving simple, individual blanking, piercing, bending, drawing, and redrawing operations. A compound die, formed by use of pressure pads and other die components, permits a combination of the above different simple operations to be done with the single stroke of the press. To increase production, a progressive die involving one or more stations may be used. Complex-shaped parts produced in large quantities involving a variety of forming operations are often produced in either a single or double four-slide machine to be discussed later (see Fig. 10.25).

TABLE 10.4
Process or tooling classes for use with Table 10.3

Digit 0	Single station tool
1	Compound tool
2	Progressive tool
3	Transfer press (moving punch type)
4	Transfer press (moving die type)
5	Four-slide machine (single)
6	Four-slide machine (double)
7	Fine blanking press
8	Special
9	

I Digit 0	II 1	III 2	IV 3	V 4	VI 5	VII 6	VIII 7	IX 8	X 9

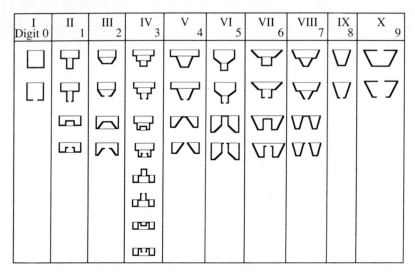

FIGURE 10.6
Groups of components produced by transfer tooling [10.7].

The fourth step is to classify the parts according to the complexity of the shape and tooling and according to the general external shape and predominant process, technological features such as flat, flat with apertures, flat with bends, hollow drawn, etc. For example, parts produced by transfer tooling have been classified on a basis of increasing complexity in terms of tooling requirements, as shown in Fig. 10.6.

A general coding method proposed for components produced in the electronic industry is shown in Fig. 10.7 [10.7].

While a general access code for press-working processes can presently be developed as indicated in the foregoing, a great deal of development and research needs yet to be done to provide the necessary discrimination required.

10.3 CLASSIFICATION OF SHEETMETAL OR PLATE SHEAR CUTTING OPERATIONS

10.3.1 Introduction

Sheetmetal shear cutting operations, other than metal cutting or machining operations, may be classified either by the purpose, or shape and extent of the cutting action, as follows [10.8]:

1. *Operations for producing blanks*
   (*a*) *Shearing* (cropping), where the shear cutting action is along a straight line.
   (*b*) *Cutoff*, where the shear cutting action is along a line, which not necessarily straight.

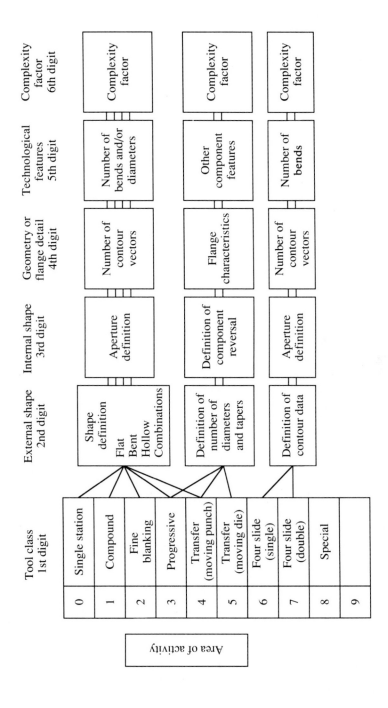

FIGURE 10.7

A general coding method for components produced in the electronic industry [10.7].

701

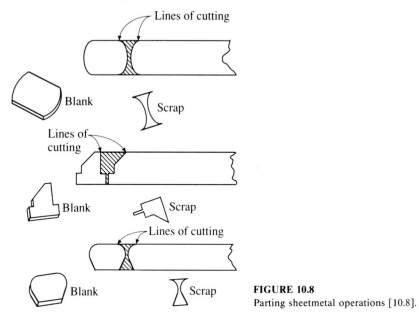

FIGURE 10.8
Parting sheetmetal operations [10.8].

(c) *Parting*, whereby the shear cutting operation produces a small, scrap section as shown in Fig. 10.8.

(d) *Blanking*, whereby a shear cutting operation produces a workpiece or part of a complete or enclosed contour with a single stroke of the press for further use or processing, as shown in Fig. 10.9.

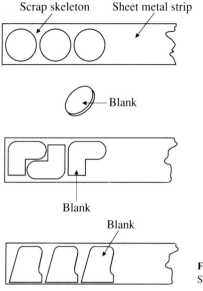

FIGURE 10.9
Sheetmetal blanking operations [10.8].

2. *Operations for shear cutting holes*
   (*a*) *Piercing* or *punching*, whereby a cutting or shearing operation produces holes of a variety of sizes and shapes in a part. In piercing or punching the slug produced is scrap. In case of blanking, the metal blanked out is saved for further use or processing, and the waste metal, sometimes called offal (or skeleton), is scrapped. (If the hole is formed with a jagged-edged, shrink flange without a slug, the operation is sometimes also called piercing. It will be referred to here as *hole flanging*.)
   (*b*) *Slotting*, where the cutting or shearing action forms elongated or square holes.
   (*c*) *Perforating*, where many holes are pierced, usually close together.
3. *Operations involving restricted or partial cutting*
   (*a*) *Notching*, where a piece of scrap metal is removed from the edge of a blank or strip to form a notch.
   (*b*) *Seminotching*, where a piece of scrap metal is removed from the central portion of a strip to facilitate subsequent bending or for providing part attachment along the edges of a skeleton for progressive forming.
4. *Operations for size control*
   (*a*) *Trimming* is the cutting off of excess or damaged metal after a forming operation such as deep drawing.
   (*b*) *Slitting* is the cutting of a wide coil into several narrow coils in a rotary shear called a slitter.
   (*c*) *Shaving* is the cutting off of metal in a chiplike fashion to remove the rough fractured edge of the sheet and to obtain accurate dimensions (see Fig. 10.5(*a*)).

10.3.2   Analysis of Cutting by Shearing

When cutting or mechanical severing of plate or sheetmetal by shearing, the forces applied to the metal are basically shear forces as shown in Fig. 10.10. These shear forces create a shear stress which causes the metal to fail or fracture.

All of the operations listed in the foregoing classification are shear cutting operations usually involving a punch and die. The manner in which sheetmetal fails when cut in a die varies considerably, depending on the spacing of these shear forces, or the clearance (gap) between the punch and die. The nomenclature of the severed edge of the metal such as low-carbon steel made with a punch and die having sharp cutting edges and proper clearance (10 to 15 percent of the metal thickness on a side) is shown in Fig. 10.11.

With proper clearance, the cracks or fractures in the metal such as low-carbon steel, emanating from the cutting edge of the punch and of the die, meet as shown in Fig. 10.12. With small clearances, particularly near 3 to 5 percent, the cracks do not meet and a secondary shear and resulting crack occur between the two cracks.

The essential characteristics of the shear cutting operation, blanking, are summarized in Fig. 10.13.

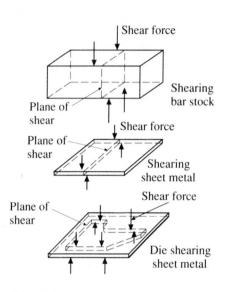

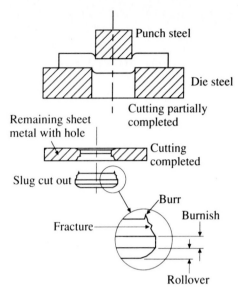

FIGURE 10.10
Representation of shearing forces employed in shearing operations [10.8].

FIGURE 10.11
Nomenclature of the severed edge resulting from punching or shearing operations [10.8].

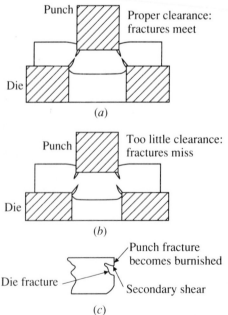

FIGURE 10.12
Examples of (a) proper and (b) improper die clearance which allows the fracture surfaces to meet as shown in (a). Improper clearance results in secondary shear and in irregular fracture surfaces as shown in (b) and (c) [10.8].

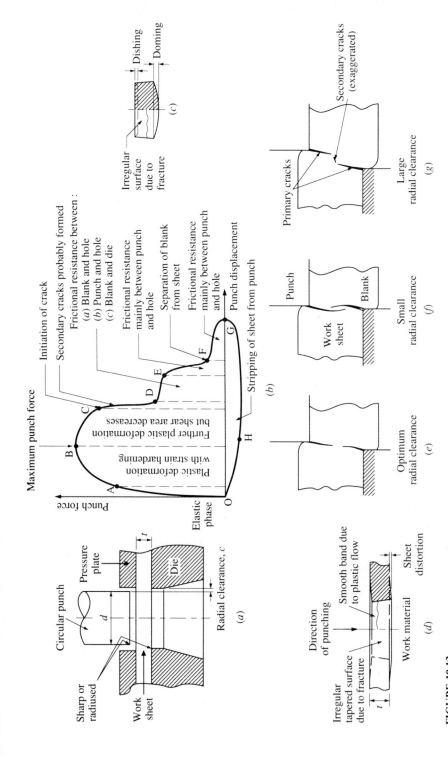

FIGURE 10.13
Essential characteristics of a blanking operation. (*a*) Diagrammatic arrangement for axisymmetric blanking. (*b*) Schematic representation of punch force versus punch displacement autographic diagram. (*c*) Cut surface of blank after blanking. (*d*) Cut surface of sheet after blanking. (*e*) Crack formation for optimum radial clearance. (*f*) Crack formation for too close radial clearance. (*g*) Crack formation for too large radial clearance.

10.3.3 Shear Forces [10.8]

When cutting during shearing progresses, the required force increases until it reaches a maximum and then decreases as shown schematically in Fig. 10.13(b) [10.9].

The force curves have been reported to fall into three categories as shown in Fig. 10.14 [10.8]: (1) normal curve, showing evidence of proper or excessive clearance, (2) hump curve, showing evidence of insufficient clearance or secondary shear, and (3) angled curve, showing evidence of extreme lack of clearance and extreme secondary shear.

The factors that affect the shearing force are:

1. The clearance between the punch and die
2. The sharpness of the cutting edges
3. The angle of shear on the punch and/or die
4. The shear strength of the material
5. The percentage penetration

The total punch force also includes any forces required for blank holding and stripping.

If it is assumed that squared-end punches and dies are used and the blank or slug is completely sheared without other resistance, the basic equation for

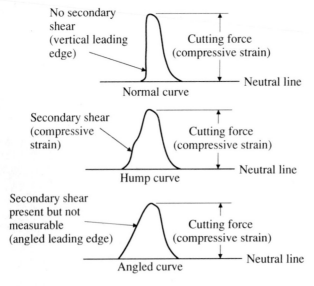

FIGURE 10.14
Schematic cutting (shearing) force curves obtained by mounting strain gauges vertically on the punch, showing (a) normal clearance, (b) insufficient clearance, and (c) extreme lack of clearance. The cutting force is plotted versus the punch travel during the punching operation [10.8].

calculating of the shear force (load) in N (lb) is

$$P = SLt \qquad \text{N (lb)} \tag{10.3}$$

and for a circular shape, it is

$$P = S\pi Dt \qquad \text{N (lb)} \tag{10.4}$$

where S = shear strength of the material, MPa (psi)
$\quad L$ = length of cut, mm (in)
$\quad t$ = thickness of the material, mm (in)
$\quad D$ = diameter of the blank or slug, mm (in)

An angle is often ground on the face of the punch or die, called a *shear*, to reduce the impact load on the punch and to distribute the load over a greater portion of the stroke. When the end of the punch and the surface of the die are parallel, i.e., with no shear, the load on the tools and the press rises rapidly after contact to a maximum and is released suddenly when the operation is completed. For blanking, the shear may be applied to the face of the die as shown in Fig. 10.15(*b*), so that the distortion occurs in the scrap or skeleton rather than in the blank. The most common type of shear used on the die is convex shear with a rounded apex to prevent initiating a crack in the material. As shown in Fig. 10.15

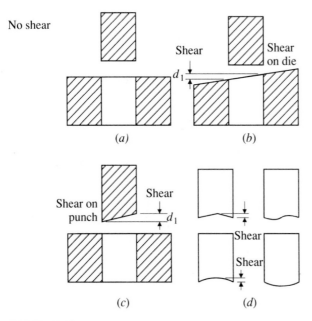

FIGURE 10.15
Types of shear: (*a*) zero shear resulting in maximum shearing force and sudden breakthrough; (*b*) shear placed on the die for blanking resulting in a distorted, scrap skeleton; (*c*) shear placed on the punch for piercing and perforating resulting in a distorted, scrap slug; and (*d*) examples of irregular shears placed on the punch [10.8].

(c), for piercing or punching, the shear is placed on the punch so that the distortion occurs in the scrap slug rather than in the workpiece. Shear reduces shock on the press, noise, and the shear force, but the amount of work required is about the same as that for dies without any shear.

The cutting force for dies without any shear can be calculated by first finding the work done in blanking or piercing by use of

$$W = Pd \qquad \text{J (in-lb)} \tag{10.5}$$

where $W =$ work done in joules (in-lb)
   $P =$ punch load or force in kN (lb)
   $d =$ distance the load acts in mm (in), which is equal to the thickness times the fraction of the penetration before fracture

The shear force is reduced by use of the angular shear of the die and can be calculated as follows:

$$P_{sh} = \frac{W}{d + d_1} \tag{10.6}$$

where $P_{sh} =$ the average cutting force, N (lb) with angular shear
   $d_1 =$ the depth of angular shear, mm (in)

W and d are defined above.

The amount of shear may be from one-third of up to the full stock thickness. The shear force decreases with the amount of shear but increases with the percent penetration before fracture.

10.3.4   Blank Layout

The factors to be considered in making a stock layout are:

1. Size, shape, and thickness of the blank
2. Material required
3. Scrap percentage
4. Direction of the texture or fiber
5. Direction of the burr
6. Type of stock: strip or coil
7. Type of production required
8. Die cost
9. Type of press used

In medium and high production of medium-sized blanks, the cost of material is 50 to 75 percent of the total cost of the blank. For large blanks, it may be more than 95 percent of the total cost of the blank. Substantial savings in net material cost often can be achieved by coordinating blank layout with the selection of the stock form and width to minimize the amount of scrap produced.

The term *utilization* or *yield* is often used to denote the complement of scrap as follows:

$$\% \text{ utilization} + \% \text{ scrap} = 100\%$$

The percentage of scrap in a strip layout can be calculated as follows:

$$\% \text{ scrap} = 100\left(1 - \frac{A_B}{A_S}\right) \tag{10.7}$$

where A_B is the area of the blank produced in one press stroke and A_S is the area of the strip consumed per stroke, or the strip width times the feed length.

Three methods of blank layout for circular blanks are shown in Fig. 10.16 [10.8]. The terminology used in blank layout is given in Fig. 10.17. The relationship of the percent scrap and the number of blanks produced per stroke is shown in Fig. 10.18 [10.10].

Nesting is the fitting together of irregular blanks in order to occupy the maximum amount of the surface area of the strip so as to increase the utilization and decrease the scrap as shown in Fig. 10.19 [10.8]. This may be done when conditions permit, such as favorable directionality of properties of the material and the location of the burr. The direction of the texture or fiber (see Sec. 2.2.10.1) may affect the strength and ductility of the workpiece or part, which may cause problems in subsequent forming and in service.

It is often desired to have the burr on one side over the other so as to be hidden or not to interfere with subsequent forming. The production required and the thickness of the metal determine the nature of the stock, i.e., its width and whether it is a straight, flat strip, or in coil form. Low production of thin material usually requires strip stock, a single-pass layout, and one or more blanks cut out at a time. Low production of thick material usually requires a single- or double-pass layout and one blank cut out at a time. High production requirements for thin material are the same as for thick materials except coiled stock is used. High

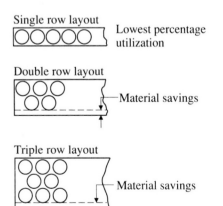

Single row layout — Lowest percentage utilization

Double row layout — Material savings

Triple row layout — Material savings

FIGURE 10.16
Examples of layouts for circular blanks to facilitate production and increase utilization of material [10.8].

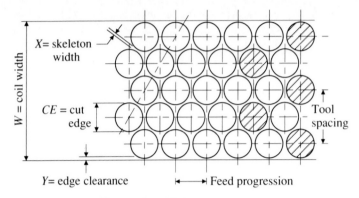

N = number of blanks out. $N = 5$ as shown
Coil width = $W = \sin 60°(N-1)(CE+X) + CE + 2Y$
Feed progression = $CE+X$
Tool spacing = $2 \sin 60°(CE+X)$

FIGURE 10.17
Terminology used in blank layout showing the method of calculating the coil width needed, the feed, and the tool spacing. The number of blanks cut out per stroke of the press N, in this case is 5. (See Figs. 12.30 and 12.31.) [10.10].

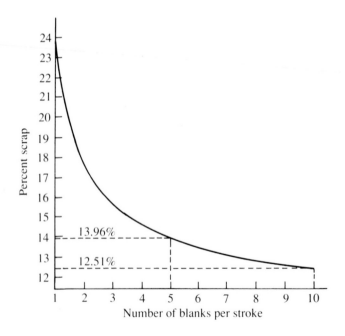

FIGURE 10.18
Relationship between the percentage of coil skeleton scrap and the number of blanks per stroke of the press [10.10].

Before tipping

After tipping

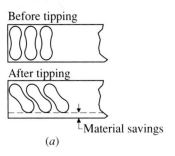

‎⌐Material savings

(a)

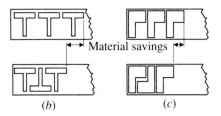

Material savings

(b)   (c)

FIGURE 10.19
Examples of nesting of irregular blanks
(a) by tipping, and (b) and (c) by
turning to increase utilization of
material [10.8].

production for thick material would require more than one blank at a time. For high production, as short a progression (advancement) as possible is used to reduce time and scrap.

The following points should be considered when comparing the cost of dies for blanking or piercing:

1. High production and multiple-cuts increase the cost of the dies
2. Double-pass dies are less expensive than two-at-a-time dies
3. Multiple-cut dies for complex or very accurate shapes are more expensive than one-at-a-time dies

10.4   FLEXIBLE MANUFACTURING SYSTEM (FMS) FOR PUNCHING AND SHEARING OF SHEETMETAL [10.11]

10.4.1   Introduction

A flexible manufacturing system (FMS) is typically defined as a set of machine tools linked by a materials handling system, all controlled by a computer system. FMS does not necessarily imply an unmanned or totally automated manufacturing system; however, one expects an FMS to be automated to some degree. They can be characterized by different degrees of four types of flexibility involving (1) the manufacturing module, (2) the materials handling system, (3) the computer system, and (4) the organizational system flexibilities.

10.4.2   Equipment Configuration of an FMS

If one ties together two or more of such items of stand-alone equipment as a CNC punch press with or without a plasma arc contour cutting option, a CNC right-angle blade shear, CNC edge bending equipment, etc., with material handling equipment and a computer, a flexible sheetmetal manufacturing system is formed.

The typical sheetmetal FMS described here includes a computer numerical control (CNC) punch press, a CNC shear, storage, and material handling devices, all communicating with a dedicated manufacturing computer, which may be linked to a mainframe computer. The manufacturing computer supervises the machine CNCs and the material handling controls, performs file management program generation, and integrates the punching information with the shear nesting pattern. This enables the automated shearing of prepunched multiple parts and realizes the benefits inherent to FMS.

Out of the many configurations which are possible in order to satisfy a particular application, a typical configuration may contain a turret punch press and a right-angle shear system of a Bendix, Wiedemann Division DNC system 1000 as an example of a typical system.

The punch press produces holes, shapes, or forms in sheetmetal, and consists of a high-speed x-y sheet positioning table, a turret with multiple tool stations, a punching head, and options such as for plasma arc contour cutting. The shear consists of a similar positioning table and a right-angle shear which shears in both the x and y directions with one stroke of the ram. This typical system can process sheet sizes up to 48 by 144 in (1.2 by 3.6 m) by $\frac{3}{16}$ inch (6.25 mm) thick, and produces the needed parts by shearing prepunched multiples.

The material handling equipment may consist of an automatic stacker crane which loads pallets of sheets onto the traverse table and removes the completed ones. The loading of a punch press is accomplished with an overhead vacuum-type loader, which carries a sheet to the machine table and locates it. Unloading sheets from the punch press and dragging them to the shear is done by an edge gripper mechanism. Once the sheet is sensed at the shear, it is located automatically. Sorting from the shear is typically done by a series of conveyors, following the unloading conveyor, which can be raised or lowered to deflect the parts to the proper bins.

10.4.3   Control Configuration

The control of the FMS, being described here, is achieved by use of a hierarchical control scheme. The highest level is typically from a main computer that is performing material requirements planning (MRP) and/or computer-aided design (CAD), and possibly other comparable tasks. This information is down-loaded to the FMS, mini- or superminicomputer, which is the central control unit of the system. At the lowest level, each machine is controlled by CNC, and the material handling equipment is either controlled by programmable controllers or a CNC cell controller, depending on the complexity of the system. The main computer can be eliminated, and these functions can be implemented on the FMS computer, which contains the production file and the other files. A short discussion of these files is given below.

The *production file* is the direct access file and contains such information as the panel file name, a description of the part, a material characteristics code, part numbers, quantity desired, etc. The *build run* program accepts data from the production file and the master parts file to build the nesting program, called *Compu-Cut, run, and part* files. The turret configuration requirements from the *master parts file* are used to group parts with compatible tooling requirements into the same nesting job within each run.

The input and output of the Compu-Cut nesting program is shown in Fig. 10.20. This program analyzes the shearing requirements, determines the number and size of panels for shearing, produces detailed layouts of parts to be sheared per panel, sequences panels for shearing, and minimizes scrap material and shearing time. The Compu-Cut program also produces management summary reports for each run, listing the scrap rate, total material used, estimated machine cycle time, total material cost, etc. It also produces a production plan, listing each shearing pattern, number of panels used, the quantity of parts and their shearing sequence, etc. The plot program plots the nesting solution developed by the Compu-Cut program on either a graphics terminal or a pen plotter.

The output of the Compu-Cut program builds the shear NC file and the solution file for the preferred nesting which, in conjunction with the part NC data files, are used to drive the integration program. The piece part programs from the part NC data files are translated and rotated to correspond to the location of each part's blank on the panel. After this is completed, the punch press file is assigned the necessary priorities and rearranged to shorten the punch time. A report on the punching (or burning cycle) time requirements can be generated. The final outputs of this process are contained in the punch and the shear NC files for each job in the run. These files, along with the material handling file, are used by the automated material handling supervisor (AMHS) to coordinate the transfer of command information to (1) the stacker crane control (if part of the system), (2) the material handling cell controller, and (3) the CNC controls on the punch press and on the shear.

When a job is started on the punch press, the AMHS program checks on materials availability by issuing a request on the stacker crane supervisor. If there is not enough material on hand to complete the job, the operator is so informed on the shop floor terminal, and the job is aborted. If the material is available, it is reserved for the job, and the job is started.

When a job is started, the AMHS enters a request in the stacker crane controller's queue to obtain the first pallet of material from storage and requests the material handling control (MHC) to drive the input traverse table to its load position. Once the material is loaded on the traverse table, it will be commanded to its unload position beside the punch press, and the manufacturing system

Programmer inputs:

Parts	Punch press program	Part size	Required quantity
1.		4.25 in × 6 in	370
2.		3.5 in × 16.5 in	140
3.		21.5 in × 24.375 in	10
4.		6.125 in × 9.875 in	160
Available material:		48 in × 72 in 48 in × 96 in	

(a)

Computer program outputs the nested punching program and shearing program

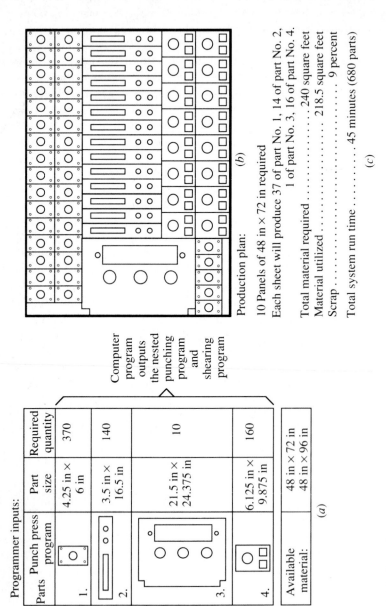

(b)

Production plan:

10 Panels of 48 in × 72 in required
Each sheet will produce 37 of part No. 1, 14 of part No. 2,
1 of part No. 3, 16 of part No. 4.

Total material required . . . . 240 square feet
Material utilized . . . . 218.5 square feet
Scrap . . . . 9 percent

Total system run time . . . . 45 minutes (680 parts)

(c)

FIGURE 10.20

Performance of the Bendix, Wiedemann Division, Compu-Cut computer blank nesting program. (a) Data input, (b) nested blank layout output, (c) production plan output, and program run time [10.11].

starts. As sheets are fed through the system, the AMHS provides sheet identification numbers to the MHC, so that individual sheets can be tracked through the system. These sheet numbers are used to determine which sheet NC file is to be accessed when down-loading information to the shear.

When the supply of raw material on the load traverse table is exhausted, the MHC drives it back to its load position and informs the AMHS that it is out of material. The AMHS enters two requests in the stacker crane controller's queue: (1) to store the empty pallet, and (2) to request a full one. When the empty pallet has been stored, its information in the storage map is cleared, freeing the cell to accept a new supply of sheets. When the load traverse table receives the full pallet from the stacker crane, it returns to its unload station at the press, and the processing continues as before.

When the run is finished, the AMHS commands the MHC to return the load traverse table to its load station. A request is entered in the stacking crane controller's queue to return the partially used pallet to storage. When the pallet is unloaded from the stacker crane, the information for that cell in the storage map is updated. The quantity is reduced by the number of sheets used from the pallet, and the reserved flag is cleared.

10.4.4 Material Handling Control

The material handling cell control coordinates the operation of all the manufacturing floor hardware. Once the direct numerical control (DNC) communication links between the machine tool CNC's and the manufacturing computer are established, system operation is started from the MHC, as follows:

1. Start of punch press line by the operator, which causes the control to drive the traverse table to its load position
2. Load a pallet onto the traverse table by the stacker crane which, upon loading, returns to its unload position
3. Request of the sheet thickness and identification by the control from the manufacturing computer
4. Pickup a sheet of material with the vacuum lifter
5. Check for double sheet condition
6. Load the sheet on the punch press
7. Start the punch press
8. Return the punched sheet to the warehouse via unload traverse table
9. If the sheet is to be sheared, grasp the sheet by the unloader/loader, and drag to and load onto the shear, where punching and shearing will occur simultaneously

Whenever a press runs out of material, the material handling control drives its traverse table to its load position and informs the AMHS that it should store the empty pallet and transfer a full pallet to the traverse table.

As sheets are moved from one station to another in the system, their positions and identification numbers are sent back to the manufacturing computer.

10.4.5   Machine Utilization Information

Complete information regarding the machine utilization will be obtained and recorded, such as the time the control is on, time spent punching and positioning, and the number of holes punched. The utilization information is transmitted over a circuit called the *DNC communication link*, which consists of 20 mA current loops, that are not sensitive to voltage spikes caused by the industrial electrical and magnetic environment. In the future, even less sensitive fiber optics may be used for this purpose according to the IEEE 802 standard.

When any machine is not operating, the system operator can enter on the shop floor terminal of the manufacturing computer the machine's ID number and the reason for its not running. When a machine is brought back on line, the manufacturing computer is so informed by the operator through the shop floor terminal. The reasons for a machine not operating are given as machine repair, tool setup, preventive maintenance, tool repair, or scheduled idle time.

The manufacturing computer maintains a log of the utilization entries and a list of total machine time by category. At the request of the system operator, the log can be printed and/or cleared. Running totals of each time category and the number of activations will be maintained even when the journal is cleared. Machine efficiency can be calculated for each machine by dividing "in cycle time" by "on" time. The total down time can be calculated and printed out.

In closing, it might be emphasized that there are many different configurations of FMS based on the machines and the material handling equipment presented here, which should satisfy most sheetmetal manufacturing applications. The key to the effectiveness of the system is the system control software. This is truly a flexible manufacturing system.

10.5   TYPES OF PRESSES

10.5.1   Classification of Presses

A comprehensive, mutually exclusive classification of presses for all purposes is rather difficult, because of the many different types and sizes available. However, a type and size of press for a particular job can usually be readily found. Usually the types of presses and supporting equipment determine the type of work taken by a sheetmetal working job shop or some other type of shop requiring press equipment. If the press equipment is not available to a particular shop, the job may have to be farmed out and a make-or-buy decision will, of course, have to be made.

A general classification of the types of presses or press-like equipment is given in Table 10.5 [10.12].

TABLE 10.5
Characterization of presses and press-related equipment
[10.12]

A. Source of power	3. Eccentric
1. Manual	4. Power screw
2. Power	5. Rack and pinion
a. Mechanical	6. Knuckle joint
b. Steam, gas, pneumatic	7. Hydraulic
c. Hydraulic	8. Toggle
B. Ram	9. Pneumatic
1. Single-acting vertical	*E.* Purpose of press
2. Double-acting vertical	1. Squaring shears
3. Multiple-slide machine	2. Circle shears
4. Special ram configuration	3. Brake
C. Design of frame	4. Punching
1. Bench	5. Extruding
2. Open back inclinable	6. Seaming
3. Inclined straight	7. Straightening
4. Gap	8. Forcing
5. Arch	9. Coining
6. Vertical straight side	10. Transfer
7. Horn	11. Nibbler
8. Deep throat	12. Stretching
D. Method of applying power to ram	13. Turret
1. Crank	14. Forging
2. Cam	

10.5.2   Selection of Presses

In selecting the type of press to use for a given job, a number of factors must be considered. Among these are the kind of operation to be performed, size of the part, power required, and speed of operation. For most blanking, piercing, and trimming operations, crank or eccentric-type presses are generally used. In these presses, the energy of the flywheel may be transmitted to the main shaft either directly or through a gear train. For coining, squeezing, or some forging operations, the knuckle-joint press is ideally suited. It has a short stroke and is capable of exerting a tremendous force. Presses for deep-drawing operations have slower speeds than for piercing and blanking. Hydraulically operated presses are especially desirable for deep drawing of large parts.

Hydraulic presses are available in many varieties and sizes. Because almost unlimited capacities can be provided, most large drawing presses are of this type. By using several hydraulic cylinders, programmed loads can be applied to the ram and any desired force and timing can be applied independently to the blankholder, as will be discussed later. Some presses can be programmed to have a fast rapid traverse for the approach and return movements, and a slow working movement with a high force for forming. Although most hydraulic presses are slow, types are available that provide up to 600 strokes per minute for high-speed blanking operations.

10.5.3 Hydraulic versus Mechanical Presses

Comparisons of the hydraulic and mechanical presses are given below [10.13]:

1. In a hydraulic press the force is constant throughout the stroke, whereas in a mechanical press the force developed varies with the position of the slide
2. The length of the stroke is easily adjusted and controlled in a hydraulic press, whereas in a mechanical press it is fixed by the throw of the crank or eccentric
3. The speed of a hydraulic press is adjustable over a wide range, whereas in a mechanical press the speed is limited by the type of drive
4. A hydraulic press cannot be overloaded, whereas a mechanical press can, and overload protection should be installed to prevent damage
5. Mechanical presses cycle faster and are better suited than hydraulic presses to high production
6. Because energy is stored in a flywheel, a mechanical press can use as much as a $2\frac{1}{2}$ times smaller motor than an equivalent hydraulic press
7. Because of higher ram velocity and better shock resistance, mechanical presses are better suited than hydraulic presses to blanking and piercing

10.5.4 Drive Mechanisms

The various drive mechanisms for presses are shown in Fig. 10.21. All of the power train of each is not shown.

In most mechanical presses, a flywheel is the major source of stored energy which is applied to the slides by the cranks, gears, eccentrics, or linkages during the working part of the stroke. During operation, the flywheel runs continuously

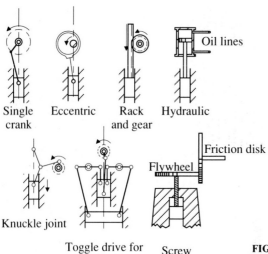

Single crank   Eccentric   Rack and gear   Hydraulic   Oil lines

Knuckle joint   Toggle drive for blankholder   Screw   Flywheel   Friction disk

FIGURE 10.21
Drive mechanisms used on presses [10.12].

and is engaged by a clutch only when a press stroke is needed. In some very large mechanical presses, the drive motor is connected directly to the press shaft, thus eliminating the need for a flywheel and clutch.

10.5.5   Characteristics of Mechanical Presses

Some of the characteristics of some of the above presses as shown in Figs. 10.22 and 10.23 are as follows:

1. *Arch press,* which has a large bed as compared to its capacity so as to take wide sheets.
2. *Gap press,* which has a C-shaped frame to provide good clearance for dies and large sheets.
3. *Open back inclinable (OBI) press,* which has an open back and can be inclined, so that the workpiece (and scrap) can readily slide out of the press by gravity into a tote (portable transporting) box.
4. *Inclined straight side press,* which is a more rigid, straight-side press permanently fixed in an inclined position for the purpose of ejecting the parts and scrap by gravity.
5. *Horn press,* which has a large, rigid cylindrical shaft or "horn" that replaces the bed of the press. This construction permits curved or cylindrical workpieces to be placed over the horn for such operations as seaming, punching, riveting, etc. In some cases a bed is provided, which may be removed or swung to one side when the horn is being used.
6. *Knuckle-joint press,* which is equipped with a knuckle-joint mechanism as shown in Fig. 10.24 to activate the slide. As the two knuckle-joint links are brought into a straight-line position a tremendous force is exerted by the slide. The knuckle causes a rapid ram approach for die closing and then a slow ram

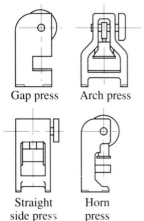

Gap press   Arch press

Straight   Horn
side press   press

FIGURE 10.22
Typical frame designs used in presses [10.12].

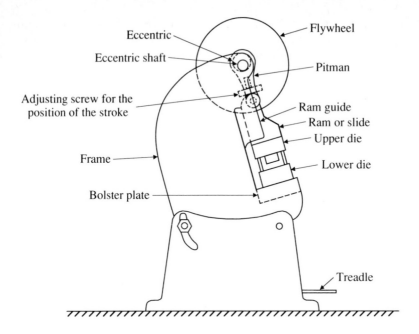

Eccentric

Eccentric shaft

Flywheel

Pitman

Adjusting screw for the
position of the stroke

Ram guide
Ram or slide
Upper die

Frame

Lower die

Bolster plate

Treadle

FIGURE 10.23
Schematic drawing showing the important features of an open back inclinable (OBI) mechanical
punch press. (*Adapted from Campbell, J. S., "Principle of Manufacturing, Materials, and Processes,
McGraw-Hill, New York, 1961.*)

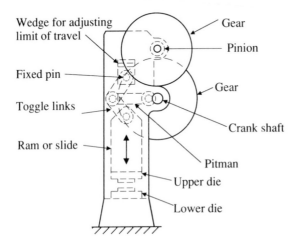

Wedge for adjusting
limit of travel

Gear

Pinion

Fixed pin

Gear

Toggle links

Crank shaft

Ram or slide

Pitman

Upper die

Lower die

FIGURE 10.24
Schematic drawing illustrating the important features of a knuckle-joint press. With one revolution
of the crankshaft, the toggle is straightened moving the ram downward with great force. It is used
when high pressures are needed, such as for coining. (*Adapted from Campbell, J. S., "Principle of
Manufacturing, Materials, and Processes, McGraw-Hill, New York, 1961.*)

travel as the metal is deformed. A small pause or dwell may be noted at the bottom of the stroke. Further rotation of the crankshaft causes a reversal of the ram to the up position. Because of the knuckle, the stroke of this press is limited to 254 mm (10 in). They are for operations with high loading requirements such as coining, cold forging, etc., and are built to well over 9.96 MN (1000 tonf) capacity.

7. *Transfer press*, which is fully automatic and is capable of performing consecutive operations simultaneously. The stock is fed automatically to the first die. After the completion of each ram stroke the part is automatically and progressively transferred to the next die station while maintaining accurate orientation of the part. The economic use of the transfer press depends upon the production rate, usually about 500 to 1500 parts per hour

8. *Multiple-slide machine*, which is a horizontal cam-operated press that contains a series of bending and forming slides located on four sides of the machine. They may be single stage or progressive. In the latter, coiled stock is fed into the machine automatically and is progressively pierced, notched, bent, or otherwise processed, and cut off at the final slide station as shown in Fig. 10.25. Its use is limited to small stampings (76 mm (3 in) wide by 356 mm (14 in) long maximum) and of large production volume.

The many other types of presses based on design, operation, and function listed in the foregoing will not be discussed here because of space limitation.

Presses may also be classified in regard to their action or the number of cams or slides on the press. The action may be single, double, or triple, depending on whether the press has one, two, or three rams or slides. In deep drawing, the inner ram may provide the drawing force, whereas the outer ram the blankholder force, as shown by the standard motion cycle in Fig. 10.26 [10.8].

The Joint Industry Conference (JIC) has developed and published standards for certain types of presses such as open-back inclinable and straight-side presses. JIC standards include bed dimensions, bolster design, T-slot and mounting hole spacing, minimum shut height, etc.

10.6 BENDING OF SHEETMETAL AND PLATE

10.6.1 Scope and Types of Bending Operations

Bending of sheetmetal and plate is one of the most used industrial processes. Only straight bending will be considered here. Form bending such as stretch and shrink flanging, as shown in Fig. 10.27, will be considered later. The emphasis will be on the bending of sheetmetal rather than plate.

Several bending operations are done on sheetmetal and plate such as shown in Fig. 10.28 and later: (1) air bending, (2) V-die bending (closed or semiclosed), (3) rubber die bending (or forming) or the Guerin process, (4) wiping, (5) U-bending, etc. [10.8]. These operations may be done by use of a press brake as shown in Fig. 10.29 or by use of a punch press as shown in Fig. 10.30. Bending

722

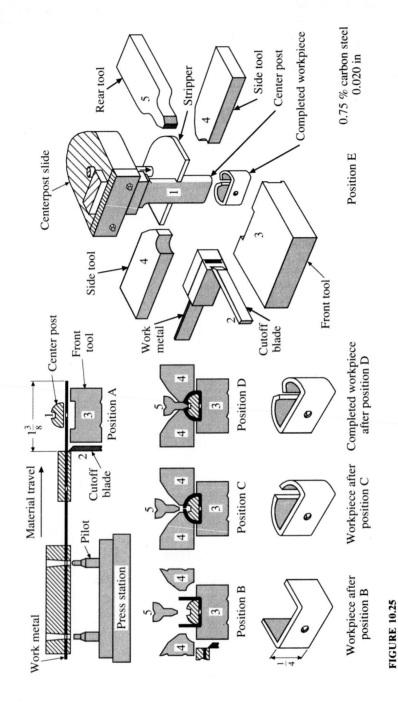

FIGURE 10.25
Tooling and sequence of operations for forming a simple clip from $\frac{1}{4}$ in (6.32 mm) wide spring steel at one level (i.e., at the same level at which the blank enters rather than one or two levels below that level) with a multiple-slide machine [10.13].

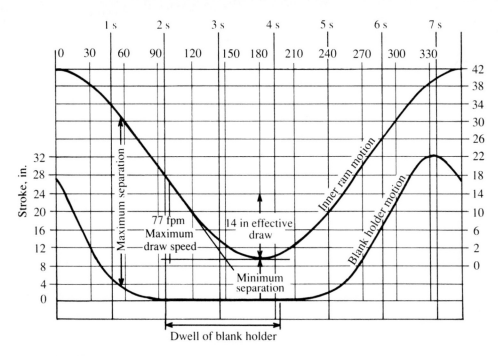

FIGURE 10.26
Standard motion cycles for the inner ram for providing the drawing force and for the outer ram for providing the blankholding force, in which the time of ram travel and rotation of the crank are plotted against the travel of each ram [10.8].

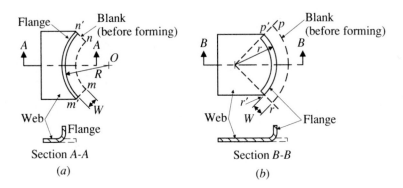

FIGURE 10.27
Two types of contoured flanges: (*a*) a stretch flange, and (*b*) a shrink flange (see Fig. 10.47). (*Adapted from Campbell, J. S., "Principle of Manufacturing, Materials, and Processes, McGraw-Hill, New York, 1961.*)

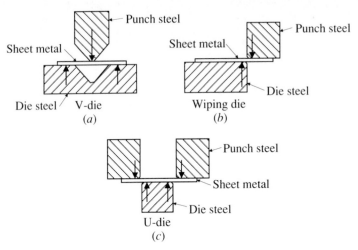

FIGURE 10.28

Examples of bending operations and the force systems involved showing (*a*) air bending in the initial stages and V-die bending in the final stages, (*b*) wiping, and (*c*) U-bending [10.8].

can also be done with a device called a bar folder as shown in Fig. 10.31. A production shop may do anywhere from 100 percent brake bending to 100 percent punch press bending depending on the type of production required. More than 99 percent of the brake formed parts, which represent over 50 percent of the formed parts, in the aircraft industry are formed by air bending. A quarter of the production may be produced by rubber die forming. These three bending operations will be discussed briefly here.

10.6.2 Stress Systems in Bending and Springback

During bending the outer surface of the bent sheet is placed in tension and the inner surface is placed in compression as shown in Fig. 10.32. If both the outer and the inner surfaces of the bend are subjected to tension during forming, the operation is called *stretch forming*, which will be discussed later.

As bending progresses, the neutral axis shifts from the center of the cross section of the sheet toward the center of curvature or the compression side as shown in Fig. 10.32. As the load is removed, springback occurs due to elastic recovery. It is often expressed in terms of angular springback error defined as

$$\text{Springback error} = \frac{\theta_1 - \theta_2}{\theta_1} \tag{10.8}$$

where θ_1 and θ_2 are the bend angles, respectively, before and after the bending load is removed.

Springback may be counteracted by overbending or by bottoming or setting (coining). For example, if a 90° bend is desired, the apex angle of the V-punch and die is made 88° as shown in Fig. 10.33, so that when the load is removed

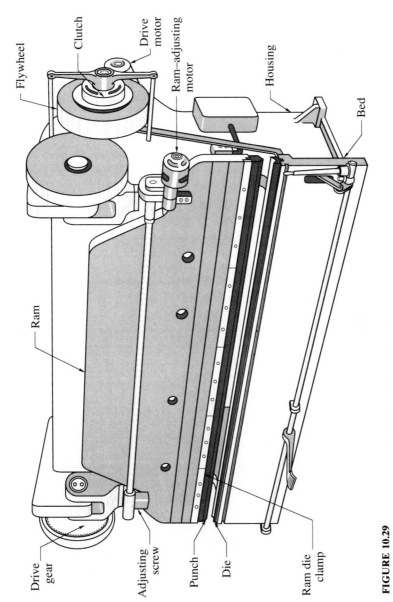

Flywheel

Clutch

Drive motor

Ram-adjusting motor

Housing

Bed

Ram

Drive gear

Adjusting screw

Punch

Die

Ram die clamp

FIGURE 10.29
Principal components of a mechanical press break [10.13].

725

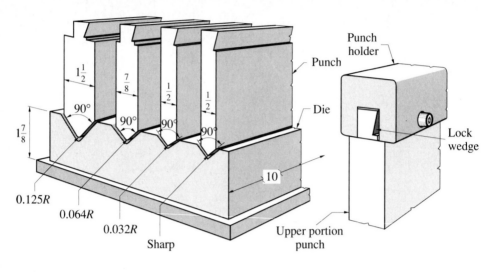

FIGURE 10.30
V-bending punch and die for making a variety of bends in a punch press [10.13].

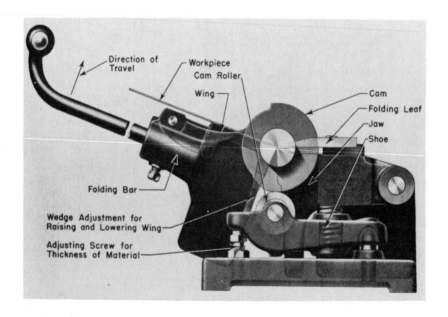

FIGURE 10.31
Phantom section of a bar folder. [Courtesy of Niagara Machine and Tool Works.]

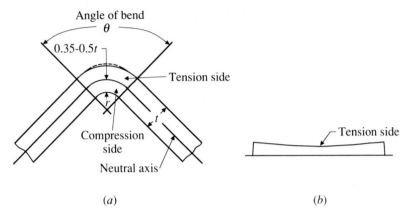

(a)   (b)

FIGURE 10.32
(a) Nature of a bend in sheetmetal. (b) Cross section through the bend of the tension side of a bent sheet metal or bar, showing variation in thickness (exaggerated) due to restraint at edges. (See Figs. 10.50(b) and 10.53(a)) [10.6].

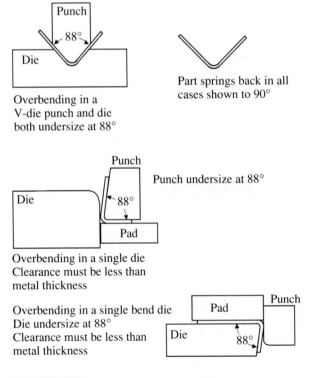

FIGURE 10.33
Methods of overbending to obtain the desired angle after springback [10.8].

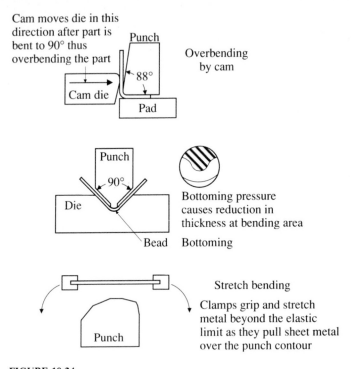

FIGURE 10.34
Springback can also be overcome (*a*) by use of a cam arrangement, (*b*) by bottoming, and (*c*) by stretch bending [10.8].

the sheetmetal springs back to the 90° angle desired. Bottoming or setting consists of striking the metal severely at the area containing the radius so as to obtain localized plastic flow. Bottoming is often accomplished by placing a bead on the apex of the punch so as to concentrate the plastic deformation at the bead as shown in Fig. 10.34. Springback can also be overcome by use of a cam and by stretch bending as shown in Fig. 10.34.

A prototype adaptive breakforming system has been developed which automatically compensates for material springback [10.14]. A direct contact built into the die, as shown in Fig. 10.35, is used to measure the angle between the sheet and die. The transducer output is subtracted from a command angle to form an error signal used to control the punch position. A microcomputer system is used to deform the sheet in a series of loading and unloading cycles. On each cycle, the sheet is loaded to a given angle, then unloaded, the point of unloading is automatically detected, the springback is measured, and a new loaded bend angle is determined. The desired unloaded angle is approached in an iterative way. Convergence to 0.2° is obtained in two or three cycles. The potential benefits derived from this system are increased part accuracy, improved quality control, insensitivity to material property variations, and improved operator safety.

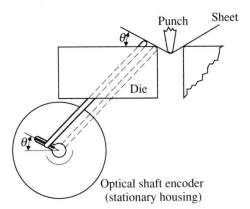

FIGURE 10.35
Schematic drawing of a measuring system suggested for use for controlling springback by adaptive control [10.18].

10.6.3   Material Length Allowance for Bend

The allowance of the length of material for a bend or the bend allowance, BA, is usually made on the basis of the length of the arc along the shifted, neutral axis, as shown in Fig. 10.32, as follows:

$$BA = \frac{\theta}{360} 2\pi(r + kt) \tag{10.9}$$

where r is the radius of the inner surface of the bend or the punch radius, and θ is the bend angle in degrees. Since the neutral axis shifts toward the center of curvature, the last term, kt, varies from $0.3t$ to $0.5t$ or $0.4t$ on the average.

10.6.4   Pure Bending versus Transverse-Force Bending [10.15, 10.16]

A distinction is made between pure bending, in which deformation is achieved by application of a constant moment, and transverse-force bending, in which a punch forces the workpiece into a die. (Although air bending may be treated as pure bending, it is not considered to be the same.) In air bending, the moment increases from zero at the die shoulders (corners) to a maximum directly underneath the punch as shown in Fig. 10.36 [10.15]. In the numerical analysis to be described later, the sheet is divided into small elements as shown in Fig. 10.36, with each element subjected to a constant but different bending moment.

Transverse-force bending falls into two major categories: air bending and V-die bending. In air bending, the desired geometry is achieved without the benefit of a die shape. Only the punch and die shoulders (corners) exert forces on the sheet during the entire process. In V-die bending, the final workpiece geometry results from the sheet being pressed into the die by the punch until it is in contact with the sides of the die to the maximum extent possible. The dies can be either closed or semiclosed. A closed die has a bottom curvature. A semiclosed die, as shown in Fig. 10.36, usually has an open bottom with which the sheet can never make contact during the bending process.

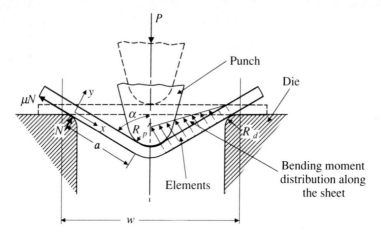

FIGURE 10.36
Schematic drawing of the deformation in air bending showing the bending moment distribution along the sheet, the division of the beam into small elements, and the geometric parameters [10.15].

V-die bending is a nonsteady process. With punch motion, the parameters that are constantly affected are workpiece geometry, bending moments and force directions, material response caused by elastic-plastic strain, and strainhardening. Several consecutive processes are involved in V-die bending as shown in Figs. 10.37 and 10.38. Initially, the workpiece passes through the air bending stage. At the outset bending is elastic. Plastic deformation sets in when the stress in the outer fibers of the workpiece exceeds the elastic limit. As the bending process continues, it reaches a stage when the legs of the bent sheet or plate become tangent to the sides of the die near both support locations. At this instant the transition from air bending and bottoming or setting begins. Further reduction of the bending span causes the ends of the workpiece to lift off from the die faces. With further downward motion of the punch, the sheet or plate opens up again. The bending angle is then forced to approach the die angle, and the inner radius of curvature of the workpiece adjusts to the curvature of the punch, if it is sufficiently large.

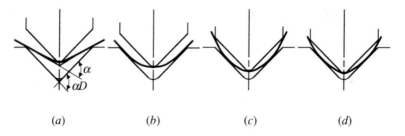

| (a) | (b) | (c) | (d) |

FIGURE 10.37
90° V-die bending with a small punch radius. (a) Air bending; (b) end of air bending; (c) end of overbending; (d) reforward bending [4.1, pp. 19-23].

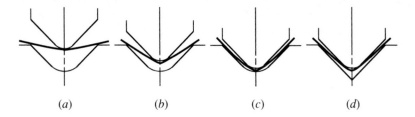

FIGURE 10.38
90° V-die bending with a large punch radius. (*a*) Air bending; (*b*) continued air bending with two-point contact at the punch curvature; (*c*) start of coining; (*d*) semiclosed-die bending [4.1, pp. 19-23].

10.6.5 Analysis of Deformation under Pure Bending

Most of the theories to date describing stresses and strains in plastic bending of a sheet or plate are based on pure bending, and assume that plane sections remain plane. It is often assumed that the thickness of the workpiece remains constant and that the material is either perfectly plastic or rigid–perfectly plastic. It is also assumed that the die width is very much greater than the workpiece thickness and that the punch radius is of the order of the sheet or plate thickness, say, less than 5 to 8 times the die width.

To develop an understanding of the mechanics of bending, a very simple case will be treated initially, which is for the bending of a flat sheet of non-workhardening material subjected to pure bending, as shown in Fig. 10.39 [10.17].

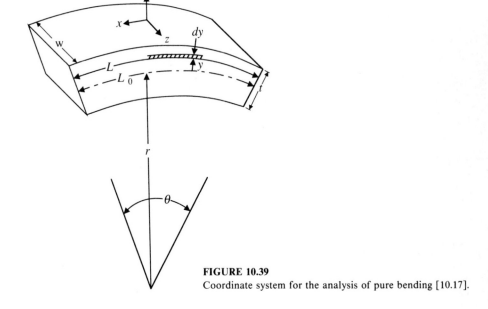

FIGURE 10.39
Coordinate system for the analysis of pure bending [10.17].

Since the arc length in the midplane L_θ does not change during bending, $L_\theta = r\theta$, where θ is the bend angle in radians. At y the arc length after bending is $L = (r+y)\theta$, so the engineering strain is

$$e_x = \frac{(L - L_0)}{L_0} = \frac{y\theta}{r\theta} = \frac{y}{r} \tag{10.10}$$

The true strain is [10.17]

$$\varepsilon_x = \ln\left(1 + \frac{y}{r}\right) \cong \frac{y}{r} \tag{10.11}$$

To calculate the bending moment M needed to produce the bend, it is assumed that there is no net external force in the x direction, that is, $\Sigma F_x = 0$. The external force dF_x, however, acting on any incremental element of cross section $w\, dy$ is $dF_x = \sigma_x w\, dy$. The total bending moment then is [10.16]

$$M = \int_{-t/2}^{t/2} w\sigma_x y\, dy = 2\int_0^{t/2} w\sigma_x y\, dy \tag{10.12}$$

For a perfectly plastic material with no elastic core, $\sigma_x = \sigma_0$, and if it is assumed that the central fiber retains a central position, the total bending moment is

$$M = 2w\sigma_0 \int_0^{t/2} y\, dy = w\sigma_0 \frac{t^2}{4} \tag{10.13}$$

where w and t are the width and thickness of the sheet or plate, and σ_0 is the flow stress of the material [10.17].

Approximate, empirical equations often found in the literature for calculating the load P in bending are based on the elastic deformation of a simple beam as shown in Fig. 10.40 as follows:

$$P = \frac{2}{3}\frac{swt^2}{L} \tag{10.14}$$

where P = bending load (force), lb (N)
s = ultimate tensile strength (which is approximately equal to the true yield strength), psi (MPa)
w = length of the beam, in (mm)
t = thickness of the sheet, in (mm)
L = width of the die, in (mm)

Usually P is taken as twice the above value or

$$P = 1.33\frac{swt^2}{L} \tag{10.15}$$

As soon as additional system parameters are taken into consideration, such as the strainhardening behavior of the material, the equation for the bending moment becomes more complex.

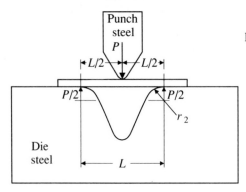

For V-dies

$$P = 1.33 \frac{swt^2}{L}$$

FIGURE 10.40
Bending of sheetmetal which, in the initial stages, is being treated approximately as elastic deformation of a simple beam.

For a rigid plastic, linearly strainhardening material (Fig. 3.1(c)), the following relation between the bending moment M and the mean radius of curvature r_m can be derived [10.15]:

$$\frac{M}{K_0 t_0^2} = t'^2 \left\{ \frac{1}{2} + \frac{1 - r'^2/4}{r'^2} (1 - e^A) \right.$$

$$\left. + \frac{K_v}{2K_0} \left[\frac{1 + r'^2/4}{r'^2} \ln\left(\frac{1 + r'/2}{1 - r'/2}\right) - \frac{1}{r'} + \frac{1}{r'} \ln\left(\frac{1 - r'^2/4}{t'^2}\right) \right] \right\} \quad (10.16)$$

where

$$r' = \frac{2(r_0 - r_i)}{r_0 + r_i} = \frac{t}{r_m} \qquad t' = \frac{r_0 - r_i}{t_0} = \frac{t}{t_0}$$

$$A = \frac{K_v}{2K_0} \ln\left(\frac{1 - r'^2/4}{t'^2}\right) \ln\left(\frac{1 + r'/2}{1 - r'/2}\right)$$

where t_0 is the initial sheet thickness, t is the instantaneous sheet thickness, r_0 is the radius of the outer surface, and r_i is the radius of the inner surface. K_0 and K_v are material constants which define the linear strainhardening behavior of the sheet material expressed by

$$\bar{\sigma} = \sqrt{3}\, K_0 + \tfrac{3}{2} K_v \bar{\varepsilon} \quad (10.17)$$

$\bar{\sigma}$ and $\bar{\varepsilon}$ are the effective stress and effective strain, respectively.

In Eq. (10.16), t' is a measure of the change in thickness and r' is a measure of the change in curvature. The relation of t' and r' in plane-strain bending of a linearly strainhardening, rigid–plastic material is [10.15] (see Fig. 3.1(c))

$$\frac{dt'}{dr'} = \frac{t'}{2r'} (e^{-A} - 1) \quad (10.18)$$

where A is defined above with Eq. (10.16).

10.6.6 Deformation in Air Bending [10.15]

At the start of the air-bending operation, the deformation of the sheet is completely elastic. However with additional bending, portions of the sheet undergo elastic-plastic deformation.

By summation of forces in the vertical direction from Fig. 10.36, one obtains

$$N = \frac{P}{2(\cos \alpha + \mu \sin \alpha)} \tag{10.19}$$

where P is the bending load per unit width, N is the normal reaction at the die radius, and μ is the coefficient of friction at the die-sheet interface. With the origin of the axis at the die-sheet contact point and the axis along the sheet, the bending moment at any point on the midthickness of the sheet is

$$M_x = N\left[x + \mu\left(y + \frac{t}{2}\right)\right] \quad \text{for} \quad x \le a$$

$$\tag{10.20}$$

$$M_x = M_a \quad \text{for} \quad x > a,$$

where $x = a$ at the location at which the sheet starts to wrap over the punch and M_a is the bending moment at the location of $x = a$ (see Fig. 10.36).

The punch load P, for air bending may be evaluated by summing the moments $\sum M = 0$ and by using Eqs. (10.16) and (10.19) to obtain [10.16]

$$P = \frac{\sigma_0 t^2 \cos \alpha \, (\cos \alpha + \mu \sin \alpha)}{W - 2(r_p + t)\sin \alpha + \mu t \cos \alpha} \quad \text{kN/mm} \tag{10.21}$$

where σ_0 = flow stress in the outer fiber, MPa (psi) = $K(\ln \sqrt{1 + t/r_p})^n$
$\quad K$ = power law strength coefficient
$\quad t$ = thickness of the sheet, mm (in)
$\quad \alpha$ = one-half of the bend ($\theta/2$) or the angle between the sheet and the die face (see Fig. 10.42)
$\quad \mu$ = coefficient of friction
$\quad W$ = width of the die, mm (in)
$\quad r_p$ = radius of the punch, mm (in)

This equation suggests that the force rises asymptotically as the sheet or plate thickness as shown by the experimental data in Fig. 10.41 [10.17].

10.6.7 Computer Models for Simulation of Bending [10.18]

Two models are available for simulation of bending: (1) finite element model (FEM) developed at the University of California and discussed in the section on the FEM, and (2) the simplified numerical model based on the pure bending analysis presented in the foregoing. The former is more rigorous and accurate, but it requires an excessive amount of computer time (1 to 2 h) and is not too adaptable to an interactive computer system. The latter method is simpler, requires much less computer time (less than 1 min), and has been adapted to an interactive

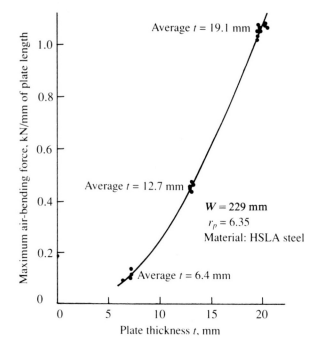

FIGURE 10.41
Graph showing the maximum reduced air bending force as a function of plate thickness for the largest ratio of die width to punch radius [10.16].

computer system. The set of computer programs that process the input information and make and interpret all the calculations is called BRKBND [10.18].

Using the supplied data on the flow and formability properties of the material being formed, the sheet thickness, the punch radius, the die width and radius, and the bend angle, BRKBND does the following: (1) simulates the entire bending process, (2) calculates the springback, and (3) predicts, by comparing the predicted maximum strain with the critical fracture strain, whether or not the sheet can be bent without fracture.

Tests were conducted in both a laboratory and a production shop to check the validity of the BRKBND computer program [10.18]. Some of the results of the laboratory tests are shown in Fig. 10.42. This figure gives the predicted and experimental load-displacement curves for a punch radius $R_p = 0.10$ in (2.54 mm) and different die widths. The predicted curves are shown for coefficients of friction of $\mu = 0.0$ and 0.1.

The predicted load-punch displacement curves are always above the measured curves, the maximum difference in the load being about 10–15 percent. This difference is attributed to (1) inaccuracies in experimental measurements, (2) differences in the actual and nominal dimensions of the tooling and specimens, and (3) errors due to the simplifying assumptions made in the mathematical model.

The predicted and measured variation of the bend angle after springback as a function of punch displacement is shown in Fig. 10.43. The predicted bend angles are larger than the measured angle for a given punch depth. When the displacement is corrected for the slack and elastic deflection of the machine and

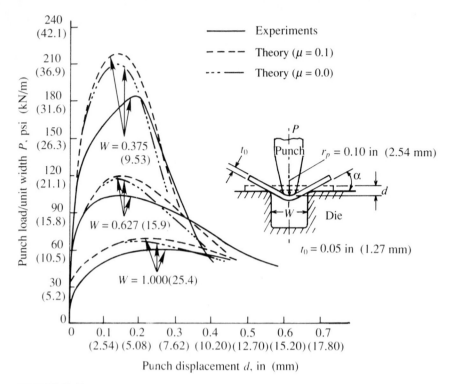

FIGURE 10.42
Graph showing the variation of the punch load/unit width with punch displacement for various die widths W [10.18].

tooling, the correlation between the predicted and actual punch displacement for a given bend angle is excellent as shown in the figure.

BRKBND analyzes two types of data: (1) given the punch radius, die width, material code, and the desired final angle, BRKBND predicts the producibility and indicates whether or not the sheet can be bent without fracture; (2) alternately, if producibility has already been established, BRKBND analyzes the process and determines how much the punch must be lowered to obtain the desired final angle and the expected springback [10.18].

When the input data are read from the data file, BRKBND analyzes each set of data successively and lists the results for each case separately. The output consists of (1) the punch displacement at full load, (2) the punch load at maximum displacement, (3) the angle of bend, and (4) the springback.

If a graphic display is requested on the screen, graphs of (1) the punch, die, and sheet geometries are shown for successive amounts of punch penetration as in Fig. 10.44(a), (2) the load-displacement plot as shown in Fig. 10.44(b), and/or (3) strain-bend angle plot as shown in Fig. 10.44(c) [10.18].

Good correlation also existed between the predicted values of punch depth and the actual measurements under production conditions.

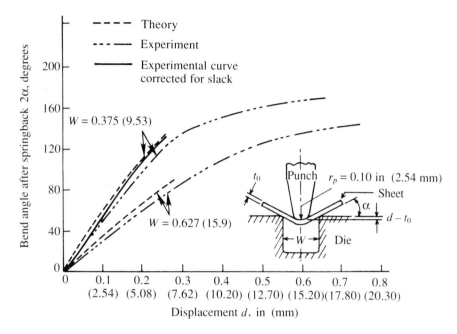

FIGURE 10.43
Graph showing the variation of the bend angle after springback with punch displacement for two die widths [10.18].

10.6.8 Rubber-Pad Forming Process [10.18]

In rubber-pad forming, also known as the Guerin process, the sheet is bent to form a straight or curved flange under pressure exerted by a rubber pad as shown schematically in Fig. 10.45. The rubber pad takes the place of the conventional female mating die. The rubber pad fills all the space around the die block and transmits pressure in all directions similar to a fluid, thereby forcing the metal blank to take the shape of the male die. A separate rubber sheet may be placed directly on the blank to take the wear rather than the relatively expensive pad.

The plane-strain rubber forming process is analyzed using a procedure similar to that for air bending except that the simple beam with three-point loading is replaced with a cantilever beam with a uniform pressure exerted by the rubber and that no sliding in of the sheet takes place as the punch descends.

In the analysis of rubber-pad forming, the following assumptions are made:

1. Deformation occurs under plane strain conditions
2. Rubber exerts a uniformly distributed pressure
3. In calculating bending moment–radius of curvature relationship, the neutral axis is assumed to lie at the center of the sheet thickness. Radial stress distribution across the sheet thickness is neglected

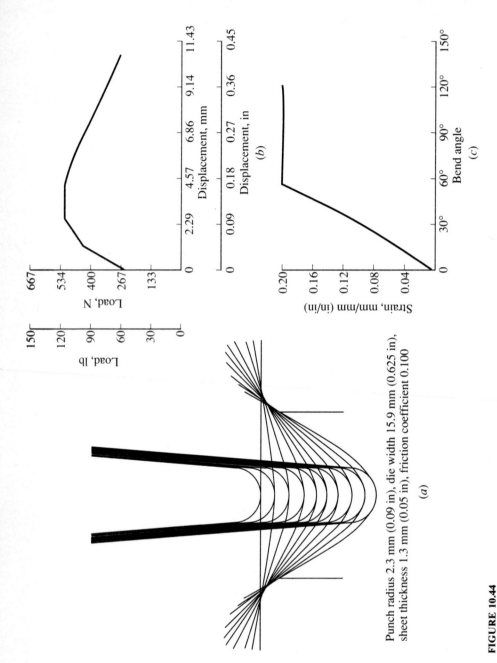

Punch radius 2.3 mm (0.09 in), die width 15.9 mm (0.625 in), sheet thickness 1.3 mm (0.05 in), friction coefficient 0.100

FIGURE 10.44
Reproduction of the graphic display of the computer simulation of brake bending: (*a*) deflection of the sheetmetal for successive amounts of punch penetration; (*b*) the load-displacement plot; and (*c*) strain-bend angle [10.18].

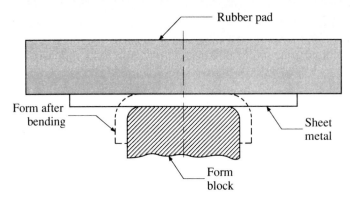

FIGURE 10.45
A schematic drawing of plane-strain rubber forming [10.18].

4. Friction at the rubber-sheet interface is neglected
5. The constitutive relation for the plastic flow of the material is given by the Swift equation:

$$\bar{\sigma} = K(\varepsilon_0 + \bar{\varepsilon}_p)^n \qquad (10.22)$$

where $\qquad \bar{\sigma} =$ the effective stress
$\qquad\qquad \bar{\varepsilon}_p =$ the effective plastic strain
$K, n,$ *and* $\varepsilon_o =$ the material constants

10.6.9 Moment versus Radius of Curvature in Pure Bending [10.18]

In conjunction with one analysis of rubber-pad bending, the approach given below was used to obtain the relation between the moment M and the radius of curvature R for pure bending [10.18].

When radial stress is neglected, the circumferential stress σ_θ in bending is approximately given by

$$\sigma_\theta = E\varepsilon_0 \qquad \text{for} \qquad \bar{\varepsilon} \le \varepsilon_y \text{ in the elastic region} \qquad (10.23)$$

$$\sigma_\theta = AK(\varepsilon_0 + \bar{\varepsilon} - \varepsilon_y)^n \qquad \text{for} \qquad \bar{\varepsilon} > \varepsilon_y \text{ in the plastic region} \qquad (10.24)$$

where

$$A = \frac{2}{\sqrt{3}} \left[\frac{(2+r)(1+r)}{2(1+2r)} \right]^{1/2}$$

r is the average plastic strain ratio for anisotropic sheetmetal, ε_y is the strain at the yield point, ε_θ is the cirumferential strain, and $\bar{\varepsilon}$ is the total effective strain. ε_θ and $\bar{\varepsilon}$ are related approximately by $\varepsilon = A\varepsilon_\theta$. The circumferential strain at any outer fiber located at a distance y radially from the neutral surface is $\varepsilon_\theta = y/R$, where R is the radius of curvature of the neutral surface.

The bending moment is given by

$$M = 2 \int_0^{b/2} \sigma_0 y \, dy \tag{10.25}$$

$$M = 2 \left[\int_0^{y_E} E \varepsilon_\theta y \, dy + \int_{y_E}^{t/2} AK (\varepsilon_0 + A\varepsilon_0 - \varepsilon_y)^n y \, dy \right] \tag{10.26}$$

where t is the shear thickness and y_E is the location of the elastic-plastic interface, as shown later.

By integrating, one obtains the following relation between M and R for pure bending:

$$\frac{M}{2R^2} = \frac{E\varepsilon_y^3}{3} + A^2 K \left\{ \frac{1}{(n+2)} \left[\left(\frac{\varepsilon_0 - \varepsilon_y}{A} + \frac{t}{2R} \right)^{n+2} - \left(\frac{\varepsilon_0 - \varepsilon_y}{A} + \varepsilon_y \right)^{n+2} \right] \right.$$
$$\left. - \frac{\varepsilon_0 - \varepsilon_y}{A(n+1)} \left[\left(\frac{\varepsilon_0 - \varepsilon_y}{A} + \frac{t}{2R} \right)^{n+1} - \left(\frac{\varepsilon_0 - \varepsilon_y}{A} + \varepsilon_y \right)^{n+1} \right] \right\} \tag{10.27}$$

This relationship will be used in the next section in calculating the radius R to the neutral axis from the moment M.

10.6.10 Deformation in Plane-Strain Rubber Bending [10.18]

The deformation of the sheetmetal during this operation can be divided into two stages: (1) bending of the overhanging (cantilevered) portion of the sheet until the free end touches the forming tool surface as shown in Fig. 10.46(a), and (2) bending of the sheet under the pressure exerted by the rubber against the tool surface as shown in Fig. 10.46(b).

The analysis of the first stage is similar to that for air bending. The bending moment at any point B located at a distance s from the free end is given by

$$M = \int_0^s pl \, ds \tag{10.28}$$

l is the perpendicular distance between B and the direction of pressure application. Knowing the moment distribution, one can determine the bend radius at the neutral surface from Eq. (10.27).

As the sheet end touches the forming tool at the beginning of stage 2, the moment distribution changes to that shown in Fig. 10.46(b). The sheet can now be treated as a beam with one end fixed and the other end movable. With increase in the rubber pressure, the movable end will slide along the forming tool surface. Whether or not any plastic deformation occurs along the corner radius (fixed end) during this stage will depend upon the magnitude of the moment $M_a \approx pL^2/8$ acting at this end, which decreases drastically when the free end touches the forming tool surface. Approximately a 400 percent increase in pressure would be required to cause further plastic deformation at the radius end. If sufficient pressure cannot be exerted, the deflection of the sheet in stage 2 will be mostly

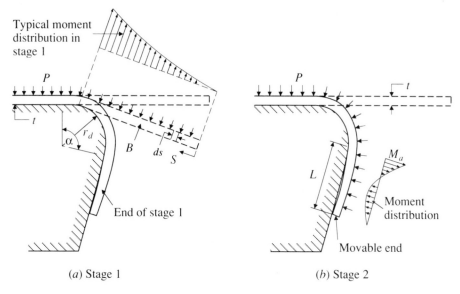

FIGURE 10.46
Schematic representation of deformation and moment distribution in plane-strain rubber forming [10.18].

elastic and thus completely recoverable upon removal of the rubber pressure. Also, after the bending operation is completed, the sheet will spring back elastically upon release of the rubber pad pressure. This springback can be estimated as was done in the air bending analysis [10.18].

10.6.11 Computer Program for Rubber Forming [10.18]

An interactive computer program called "RUBFOM" has been developed for designing rubber forming operations [10.18]. The analysis simulates the process taking into account the effects of (1) the flow and formability properties of the sheetmetal being formed, and (2) the process variables such as the sheet thickness, die radius, bend angle, and length of the sheet projecting outside the die surface. In RUBFOM, the material properties data which includes constitutive relation (i.e., the effective stress-strain equation), modulus of elasticity, yield strength, anisotropic strain ratio, and longitudinal fracture strain for a given sheetmetal are stored as a separate subroutine.

RUBFOM is designed for forming under both plane-strain and axisymmetric conditions. Under axisymmetric conditions, both shrink and stretch flanging operations as shown graphically in Fig. 10.47 are analyzed independently with different mathematical models. In RUBFOM, the three different analyses: (1) plane strain, (2) axisymmetric stretch flanging, and (3) axisymmetric shrink flanging, are performed based on the input data, and the relevant results are displayed on the output screen.

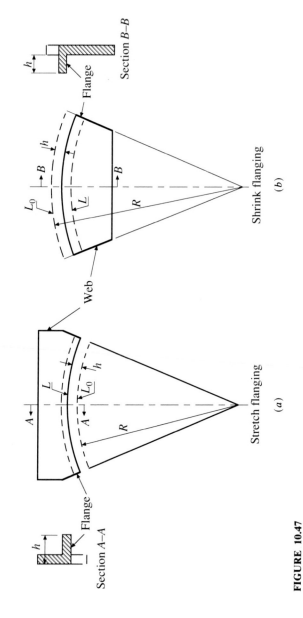

FIGURE 10.47
Schematic drawing of (*a*) stretch and (*b*) shrink flanging operations (see Fig. 10.27) [10.18].

Using the supplied data on sheet thickness, die radius, desired final bend angle, and in the case of axisymmetric forming, the center distance, RUBFOM accomplishes the following: (1) simulates the entire forming process, (2) estimates the springback, (3) predicts whether or not the sheet can be bent to the desired angle without fracture, (4) in axisymmetric forming, determines whether the sheet will buckle, and (5) in the case of axisymmetric stretch flanging, predicts whether the sheet will split or form a localized neck under the specified conditions.

10.7 STRETCH-FORMING OF SHEETMETAL

10.7.1 Scope of Stretch-Forming [10.18]

Stretch-forming is a forming process in which sheetmetal is formed by the application of tensile loads to the material in such a way as to cause permanent or plastic strains to occur in varying degree across the cross section so as to produce the required shape. The sheet is firmly clamped in serrated jaws at both ends and stretched well beyond the elastic limit over a forming tool (die) or stretch block as shown in Fig. 10.48(a). Variations of the process are stretch-leveling and stretch-wrap forming. In stretch-forming the tool moves into the clamped sheet as shown. In stretch-wrap forming, the sheetmetal is first stretched beyond the elastic limit or yield "point" and then wrapped over the form block as shown in Fig. 10.48(b). The stretch-forming process is limited to parts having gradual contours and no sharp bends. It is used for making prototype models of aircraft and automotive body parts. It is used in production for making truck and trailer bodies and rocket motor housings.

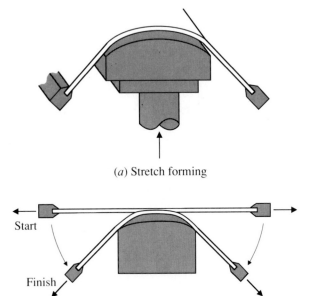

(a) Stretch forming

Start

Finish

(b) Stretch-wrap forming

FIGURE 10.48
Two methods of forming of sheetmetal by stretching: (a) stretch forming, and (b) stretch-wrap forming [10.4].

Some advantages for stretch-forming are (1) only one male stretch form (die) is needed, (2) the stretch form can be made of inexpensive material, (3) contours having compound curvatures can be made, and (4) there is little or no springback.

10.7.2 Distribution of Tension along the Sheet [10.18]

Because of friction at the die-sheet interface, the tension across the sheet thickness varies over the die (block) face shown in Fig. 10.49(a). It is a maximum at location A where the jaws hold the sheet and a minimum at the center O. This variation of the tension can be calculated by use of Fig. 10.49(b). Let R_p be the effective radius of curvature of the die surface and let ds be the length of the sheet-die interface for the element. From the equilibrium of forces in the radial direction, one obtains

$$p = \frac{T}{R_p} \tag{10.29}$$

where p is the contact pressure, and T is the tension stress. Force equilibrium in the tangential direction gives

$$\frac{dT}{T} = -\frac{\mu}{R_p} ds \tag{10.30}$$

Integrating, one obtains

$$\ln\left(\frac{T_B}{T_0}\right) = -\mu \int_A^B \left(\frac{1}{R_p}\right) ds \tag{10.31}$$

where μ is the coefficient of friction at the sheet-tool interface and T_B is the

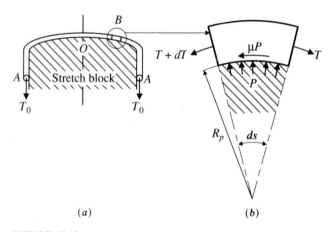

(a)   *(b)*

FIGURE 10.49
Tension variation along the punch in stretch forming: (a) location of segment B, and (b) force representation on the segment [10.18].

tension at the section B. The right-hand side of the above equation can be evaluated numerically for any given stretch-block contour.

10.7.3   Springback in Stretch-Forming [10.18]

The total strain in a small element ds of the sheet in stretch-forming is shown in Fig. 10.50. The bending strain ε_b at a fiber at a distance y from the midthickness is

$$\varepsilon_b = \frac{y}{R_p^*} \tag{10.32}$$

where R_p^* is the radius of the neutral axis, or

$$R_p^* = \left(R_p + \frac{t}{2} \right)$$

and t is the sheet thickness. The maximum value of ε_b occurs at the outermost fibers where $y = \pm t/2$. The strain ε_t due to tension can be calculated using Figs. (10.39) and (10.40) to give

$$\varepsilon_t = \left(\frac{T}{tE} \right) \qquad \text{for} \qquad \varepsilon_t \le \varepsilon_y \tag{10.33}$$

$$\varepsilon_t = \left(\frac{T}{Kt} \right)^{1/n} + \varepsilon_y - \varepsilon_0 \qquad \text{for} \qquad \varepsilon_t > \varepsilon_y \tag{10.34}$$

The magnitude of ε_t (or T) and ε_b (or M) determines if the deformation of the sheet cross section is completely plastic or partially elastic–plastic.

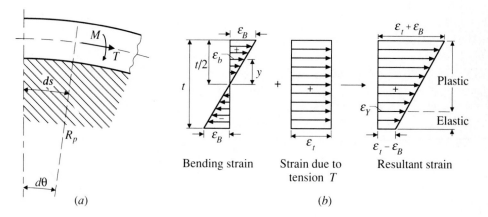

FIGURE 10.50
Strain analysis existing in sheetmetal stretch-forming: (a) tensile force and moment acting on a sheetmetal segment, and (b) the total strain resulting from the sum of the bending and tensile strains [10.18].

The explanation of why springback is practically negligible in stretch-forming may be made with the aid of Figs. 10.51 and 10.52. As shown in Fig. 10.53, as the tension is increased, the portion of the cross section deformed elastically shifts toward the inner surface. It disappears completely as the tension becomes sufficiently high so that both the outer and inner surfaces are deformed plastically in tension. The criterion for determining whether the cross section has been entirely deformed plastically is

$$\varepsilon_t - \varepsilon_b \geq \varepsilon_y \qquad (10.35)$$

where ε_y is the strain at the yield point (elastic limit).

If it is assumed that the tension and the bending moment act at the midthickness, the following equations for tension T and moment M can be derived from equilibrium considerations for the general case where the neutral axis has shifted from the midplane of the sheet and the cross section is deformed

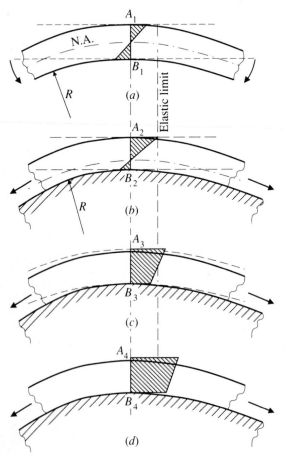

FIGURE 10.51
Successive drawings (a) to (d) show how the state of stress on the upper and lower surfaces changes from tension/compression to tension/tension, which practically eliminates springback. (*Adapted from G. G. Thomas, "Production Technology", Oxford University Press, London, 1970.*)

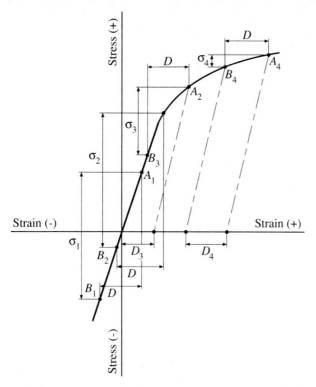

FIGURE 10.52
Stress-strain analysis of the stretch-forming operation shown in Fig. 10.51. This figure shows that both the top of the sheet at point A_4 and the bottom at point B_4 both flow plastically thereby practically eliminating any springback (*Adapted from G. G. Thomas, "Production Technology", Oxford University Press, London, 1970.*)

both elastically and plastically, as shown in Figs. 10.51(b) and 10.53(d):

$$M = \frac{KR_p^{*2}}{n+2}\left\{\left(\varepsilon_0 - \varepsilon_y + \frac{t/2+a}{R_p^*}\right)^{n+2} - \varepsilon_0^{n+2}\right\}$$

$$-\frac{K(\varepsilon_0 - \varepsilon_y + a/R_p^*)R_p^{*2}}{n+1}\left\{\left(\varepsilon_0 - \varepsilon_y + \frac{t/2+a}{R_p^*}\right)^{n+1} - \varepsilon_0^{n+1}\right\}$$

$$-\frac{E}{R_p^*}\left\{\left(\frac{ay_E^2}{2} - \frac{y_E^3}{3}\right) - \left[\frac{a}{2}\left(a - \frac{t}{2}\right)^2 - \frac{(a-t/2)^3}{3}\right]\right\} \tag{10.36}$$

$$T = \frac{E}{R_p^*}\left(\frac{y_E^2}{2} - \frac{(a-t/2)^2}{2}\right) + \frac{KR_p^*}{n+1}\left[\left(\varepsilon_0 - \varepsilon_y + \frac{t/2+a}{R_p^*}\right)^{n+1} - \varepsilon_0^{n+1}\right] \tag{10.37}$$

where E, K, ε_0, and n are defined from the constitutive relations

$$\bar{\sigma} = E\bar{\varepsilon} \qquad \text{for} \qquad \bar{\varepsilon} \le \varepsilon_y \tag{10.38}$$

$$\bar{\sigma} = K(\varepsilon_0 + \bar{\varepsilon} - \varepsilon_y)^n \qquad \text{for} \qquad \bar{\varepsilon} > \varepsilon_y \tag{10.39}$$

Resultant   Strain distribution   Stress distribution

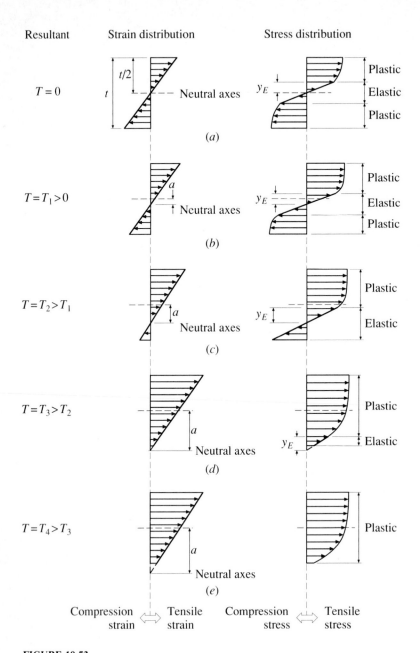

Compression Tensile Compression Tensile
strain   strain   stress   stress

FIGURE 10.53
Effect of tension on the stress and strain distributions and on the position of the neutral axis in stretch-forming of sheetmetal [10.18].

E = modulus of elasticity in tension, GPa (psi)

t = thickness of the sheet, mm (in)

ε_y = strain at the yield point (elastic limit)

$\bar{\varepsilon}$ = effective strain

R_p = effective radius of curvature of the die surface or the punch face, mm (in) (see Fig. 10.49(b))

R_p^* = radius of the neutral axis ($R_p + t/2$), mm (in)

a = distance from the center of the cross section to the neutral axis (surface), mm (in) [10.18]

When the load is removed, the material springs back elastically. The final shape of the part is therefore different than the shape of the stretch-block. It is assumed that unloading of the tension T will result in the sheet sliding on the punch without change of shape, whereas unloading the moment will change the radius of curvature of the sheet from R_p to R'_p. Since the springback is elastic, it is the result of an elastic change in curvature due to an equal and opposite moment M as follows:

$$\frac{1}{R_p} - \frac{1}{R'_p} = \frac{12M}{Et^3} \quad \text{or} \quad \frac{12M}{Et^3}(1 - \nu^2) \tag{10.40}$$

where ν is the Poisson ratio and E is the modulus of elasticity of the material. If one knows the bending moment and the R_p distribution at the time of unloading, which is the same as the punch shape, a numerical procedure can be used to calculate R'_p and the resultant change in the part shape.

10.7.4 Numerical Procedure for Calculating the Strains and the Final Shape after Stretch-Forming [10.18]

The strain distribution and the final shape of the stretch-formed part after removal of the load can be calculated by use of a numerical procedure outlined in Fig. 10.54 as follows:

1. Input process and material variables such as the sheet thickness, sheet material, stretch-block geometry, final position of the jaws, and the tension force T_0 applied at the jaws

2. Calculate the maximum tension stress σ_T in the sheet at the holding jaws by use of the relation

$$\sigma_T = \frac{T_0}{Lt} \tag{10.41}$$

where L is the length of the sheet held between the jaws

3. Check to see if the σ_T is greater than the ultimate tensile strength σ_U of the sheet causing it to tear. Reduce the process variables, such as the tension force at the jaws, so as to produce an acceptable part

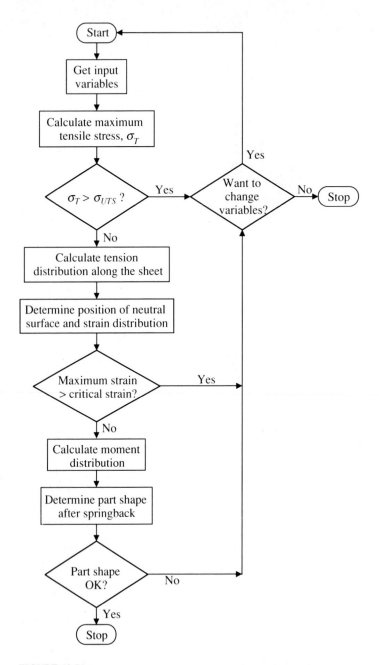

FIGURE 10.54
Flowchart for the mathematical modeling of a sheetmetal stretch-forming operation [10.18].

4. Using Eq. (10.31), calculate the tension force distribution along the die contour
5. Calculate the position of the neutral surface along the sheet under the combined action of tension and bending by use of equations such as (10.36), and (10.37)
6. Calculate the strain, which varies linearly from zero at the neutral surface to a maximum at the outer fibers, by use of the following equation:

$$\varepsilon = \frac{y}{R_p} \qquad (10.42)$$

where y is the distance from the neutral surface and R_p is the radius of the stretch block
7. Check to see if the maximum tensile strain exceeds the assumed plane-strain intercept of the forming limit curve for the material (to be discussed later). If so, the process variables, including the stretch-block geometry, must be modified to produce a sound part
8. Calculate the moment distribution along the sheet by use of relations such as Eq. (10.36)
9. Calculate the change in the radius of curvature of the part upon unloading by use of Eq. (10.40). If the resulting shape is not acceptable, change the process variables such as T_0 and the die geometry so as to obtain the desired shape

10.8 APPLICATION OF THE FEM TO SHEETMETAL FORMING [10.19]

10.8.1 Introduction

The sheetmetal forming processes basically involve a significant amount of elastic deformation, and also due to the complexities of plasticity, the exact analysis of a process is not feasible in many cases. Thus, a number of approximate methods have been suggested, with varying degrees of approximation and idealization. Among these, techniques using the FEM take precedence because of their flexibility, their ability to obtain a detailed solution, and inherent proximity of their solutions to the exact one [10.19].

A prime objective of mathematical analysis of metalworking processes is to provide necessary information for proper design and control of these processes. Therefore, the method of analysis must be capable of determining the effects of various parameters on metal flow characteristics. Furthermore, the computation efficiency, as well as solution accuracy, is an important consideration for the method to be useful in analyzing metalworking problems.

With this viewpoint in mind, the rigid–plastic FEM (sometimes called the *matrix method*) has been used successfully in analyzing various metalforming processes such as compression, extrusion, etc., as discussed elsewhere.

The formulation of the matrix method, however, cannot be extended to the sheetmetal forming analysis for the following reasons:

1. The classical variational formulation which is the basis of the matrix method does not necessarily determine a unique deformation mode
2. The kinematic assumption in the matrix method is no longer valid for the sheetmetal forming process

The classical variational formulation for the rigid–plastic solid are not appropriate for solving the sheetmetal forming problems, because of the non-uniqueness of the deformation mode under certain boundary conditions. This nonuniqueness, however, can be resolved by taking the strainhardening rate into consideration. Such an introduction of the strainhardening rate into the formulation, on the other hand, necessitates the consideration of the geometry change. The available classical formulation in which these two aspects are considered is not, however, applicable to the statically indeterminate problems, sheetmetal forming being one, because it is formulated in such a way that knowledge of the stress distribution is necessary. (See Section 4.5.1 for a discussion of the variational method.)

10.8.2   Classical Variational Formulation of a Rigid-Plastic Solid [10.19]

In this formulation, quasi-static deformation of a rigid–plastic solid body is considered [10.19]. The resulting equation is similar to Eq. (4.184) in the section on the FEM, except for the last term.

On a portion S_v of the surface S of this body are prescribed given velocities, while the remainder S_T of the surface S is subjected to given traction forces F_i. If it is assumed that these surface velocities and tractions are such that the entire body is in a state of plastic flow, the stresses σ_{ij} and strain rates $\dot{\varepsilon}_{ij}$ throughout the body can be determined.

The conventional formulation of variational principle for this problem is that among all kinematically admissible strain-rate fields $\dot{\varepsilon}_{ij}^*$, the actual one minimizes the expression

$$\pi_1 = \int \bar{\sigma}\dot{\bar{\varepsilon}}\, dV - \int_{S_T} F_i V_i^*\, dS \tag{10.43}$$

where $\bar{\sigma}$, the effective stress and $\dot{\bar{\varepsilon}}$, the effective strain rate are defined, respectively, by

$$\bar{\sigma} = \sqrt{\tfrac{3}{2}}\sqrt{\sigma_{ij}'\sigma_{ij}'} \quad \text{and} \quad \dot{\bar{\varepsilon}} = \sqrt{\tfrac{2}{3}}\sqrt{\dot{\varepsilon}_{ij}\dot{\varepsilon}_{ij}} \tag{10.44}$$

and where σ_{ij}' is the deviatoric component of σ_{ij}. Here a strain rate field $\dot{\varepsilon}_{ij}$, defined throughout the body under consideration, is called *kinematically admissible* if it is derivable from a velocity field V_i^* which satisfies the condition of incompressibility $\partial V_i^*/\partial x_i = 0$ throughout the body and the boundary conditions on S_v. The variational principle in this form has been successfully applied to the analysis of metalforming problems, such as extrusion. In general, with the variational formulation given in Eq. (10.43), there is a question regarding uniqueness of deformation mode even though the stress field is uniquely determined.

The boundary conditions used are

$$n_i \sigma_{ij} = \hat{F}_i \quad \text{on} \quad S_T$$

$$v_i = \hat{v}_i \quad \text{on} \quad S_v$$

(10.45)

where n_j is the unit normal vector to the surface of the body, and $\hat{F}_i$ and $\hat{V}_i$ are prescribed values.

The significance of these boundary conditions is that the plastic flow is unconstrained, and all or part of the body is free to deform. Mathematically, this nonuniqueness is due to the fact that the Levy-Mises theory, implied in the variational formulation of π_1 and also appearing in the constitutive equations ($\mu \sigma_{ij} = \dot{\varepsilon}_{ij}$, where μ is an arbitrary constant), does not include the viscous flow effect. This indeterminacy is resolved if the workhardening effect is taken into consideration. In proper formulation the traction rate $\dot{F}_i$ must be specified on S_T, and then from an infinite number of kinematically possible modes the actual mode can be singled out by the additional requirement that there must exist an equilibrium distribution of stress rate compatible with the given traction rate $\dot{F}_i$ on S_T. Also, the workhardening effect is explicitly brought into the constitutive equation in the form of

$$h \dot{\varepsilon}_{ij} = \frac{\sigma'_{ij}}{\bar{\sigma}} \dot{\bar{\sigma}}$$

(10.46)

where $\dot{\bar{\sigma}}$ is the time rate of charge of $\bar{\sigma}$, h is the workhardening effect of the material, which is equal to $\frac{2}{3} d\bar{\sigma}/d\bar{\varepsilon}$.

Hill showed that among all variational modes compatible with the boundary conditions for $\hat{V}_i$ on S_T and the existing stress distribution σ_{ij}, the actual mode minimizes the following expression when geometry changes are included

$$\pi_2 = \frac{1}{2} \int h(\dot{\varepsilon}_{ij}^*)^2 \, dv - \frac{1}{2} \int \sigma_{kj} v_{i,k}^* v_{j,i} v \, dv - \int_{S_T} F_i v_i^* \, dS$$

(10.47)

where the starred quantities are the kinematically admissible ones, and h is the workhardening effect, $\frac{2}{3} d\bar{\sigma}/d\bar{\varepsilon}$. In Eq. (10.47) π_2 should be normal to the yield surface at the existing stress point in the stress space due to the compatibility requirement with existing stress distributions.

10.8.3 Finite Element Formulation in Sheetmetal Forming [10.19]

The variational formulation used in the previous rigid–plastic analyses in forging, etc., is inadequate for analyzing sheetmetal forming processes, because of the nonuniqueness of deformation mode for the quasi-static deformation of a rigid–plastic solid under certain types of boundary conditions. Furthermore, out-of-plane sheetmetal forming processes involve large geometrical change during deformation [10.20]. A variational formulation of a finite element model for sheetmetal forming is presented here. (A review of the variational principle and the FEM in Sec. 4.5 and Subsec. 8.4.2 might be in order at this point.)

If the total functional is equal to the sum of the contributions of each element $\phi^{(m)}$, then finite element modeling can be achieved by approximating the functional π by ϕ as

$$\pi \cong \phi = \sum_{m=1}^{M} \phi^{(m)} \mathbf{u}^{(m)} \tag{10.48}$$

where $\mathbf{u}^{(m)}$ is the incremental displacement vector at nodes associated with the mth element.

By assuming equilibrium of stress and the principle of virtual work, and assuming that the principal axes of the true strain rate keep the same directions in the elements as in the sheet and the principal components of strain rate maintain constant ratios during a small time increment, one may obtain the functional ϕ in the following form for axisymmetric thin sheets subject to loading [10.19]:

$$\Phi = \int_{v} \bar{\sigma} \, (d\bar{E}) t \, dA + \frac{1}{2} \int H' \, (d\bar{E})(t \, dA) - \int (T + dT) \, du_j \, dA \tag{10.49}$$

where $d\bar{E} = \sqrt{\frac{2}{3} \sum (dE_p)^2}$

dE_p = logarithmic plastic strain component

$\bar{\sigma}$ = effective stress

t = local sheet thickness

dA = incremental area of the sheet element

$dV = t \, dA$

$H' = d\sigma / d\varepsilon$ = slope of the stress strain curve

T = traction force*

du_j = increment of displacement of the element

The first term in Eq. (10.49) corresponds to the volumetric strain energy of deformation, the second term represents the strain energy involved with strain hardening, and the third term represents the work of external tractions (stresses).

If the circumferential direction and the meridian direction are the principal directions and if the friction between the shell or dome being drawn and the die is negligible, the thickness direction is the third direction. The logarithmic strain increment may then be used as a measure of the strain increment, so that by definition

$$d\mathbf{E} = \begin{Bmatrix} dE_1 \\ dE_2 \end{Bmatrix} = \begin{Bmatrix} dE_r \\ dE_\theta \end{Bmatrix} = \begin{Bmatrix} \ln s/s_0 \\ \ln r/r_0 \end{Bmatrix} \tag{10.50}$$

if, during the incremental deformation, an element of undeformed length s_0 is stretched to the length s, and the point currently at the radial distance r_0 moves to the deformed radial location r. (The subscripts r and θ refer to the meridian and the circumferential direction, respectively) [10.19].

---

* Note T and F are used interchangeably for the traction forces.

To account for the fact that the actual sheetmetal has directional properties, normal anisotropy is assumed, and the corresponding stress-strain increment relation by use of Hill's criterion such as Eq. (2.108), one obtains

$$\frac{dE_r}{(1+R)\sigma_r - R\sigma_\theta} = \frac{dE_\theta}{(1+R)\sigma_\theta - R\sigma_r} = \frac{d\bar{E}}{(1+R)\bar{\sigma}} \tag{10.51}$$

where R is the planar isotropy parameter, which is the ratio of the logarithmic width strain to the logarithmic thickness strain in uniaxial tension. (Note R used here for this parameter instead of r, as r is used for the radius.) The effective stress $\bar{\sigma}$ and effective strain $d\bar{E}$ are defined as

$$\bar{\sigma} = \sqrt{\sigma_\theta^2 - \frac{2R}{1+R}\sigma_r\sigma_\theta + \sigma_r^2} \tag{10.52}$$

$$d\bar{E} = \frac{1+R}{\sqrt{1+2R}}\sqrt{dE_r^2 + \frac{2R}{1+R}dE_\theta\,dE_r + d\bar{E}_\theta^2} \tag{10.53}$$

The effective strain $d\bar{E}$ may be written in matrix form as

$$d\bar{E} = \sqrt{\tfrac{2}{3}}\,[d\mathbf{E}^T D\,d\mathbf{E}]^{1/2} \tag{10.54}$$

where $d\mathbf{E} = (dE_r, dE_\theta)^T$

$$D = \frac{3(1+R)}{2(1+2R)}\begin{bmatrix} 1+R & R \\ R & 1+R \end{bmatrix}$$

The sheet geometry is approximated by a series of frustums of a cone as shown in Fig. 10.55. Linear functions, or shape functions as they are often called in the FEM literature, are enough, because of the class of the integrand in the functional. The unknown coefficients, or nodal values, are taken to be the incremental displacement at the nodes. The incremental displacement field inside

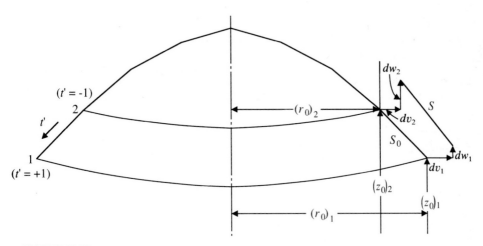

FIGURE 10.55
The drawing shows the approximation of a dome-like sheetmetal geometry by a series of conical frustums [10.20].

the element may be written as

$$\mathbf{u} = \left\{\begin{matrix} d\mathbf{v} \\ d\mathbf{w}^{\cdot} \end{matrix}\right\} = \begin{bmatrix} \dfrac{1+t'}{2} & 0 & \dfrac{1-t'}{2} & 0 \\ 0 & \dfrac{1+t'}{2} & 0 & \dfrac{1-t'}{2} \end{bmatrix} \left\{\begin{matrix} dv_1 \\ dw_1 \\ dv_2 \\ dw_2 \end{matrix}\right\} \tag{10.55}$$

$$\mathbf{u} = \mathbf{N}\mathbf{u}^{(m)} \tag{10.56}$$

where t' is the local coordinate varying from the value of -1 at node 2 to $+1$ at node 1 as can be seen in Fig. 10.55, and dv_i and dw_i are the radial and axial components of the incremental displacement of the ith node. Because of this incremental displacement field, an element of length s_0 is

$$s_0 = \sqrt{\{(r_0)_1 - (r_0)_2\}^2 + \{(z_0)_2 - (z_0)_1\}^2} \tag{10.57}$$

which is stretched to a new length s,

$$s = \sqrt{(r_1 - r_2)^2 + (z_2 - z_1)^2} \tag{10.58}$$

where $(r_0)_i$, $(z_0)_i$ are the radial and the vertical positions of the ith node at the undeformed configuration and $(r)_i$, $(z)_i$ at the deformed configuration. Since the element is straight, any point of t' in the local coordinates is shown to have a global radial position r_0 determined by

$$r_0 = \left(\frac{1+t}{2}\right)(r_0)_1 + \left(\frac{1-t}{2}\right)(r_0)_2 \tag{10.59}$$

The new position, r, of the same particle is given by

$$r = r_0 + \left(\frac{1+t}{2}\right) dv_1 + \left(\frac{1-t}{2}\right) dv_2 \tag{10.60}$$

By use of Eqs. (10.57) to (10.60), inclusive, the following expression for the strain energy increment field $d\mathbf{E}$ can be obtained:

$$d\mathbf{E} = \left\{\begin{matrix} \dfrac{1}{2}\ln \dfrac{\{(r_0)_1 - (r_0)_2 + dv_1 - dv_2\}^2 + \{(z_0)_1 - (z_0)_2 + dw_2 - dw_1\}^2}{s_0^2} \\[2mm] \ln \dfrac{r_0 + [(1+t')/2]\, dv_1 + [(1+t')/2][(1+t')/2]\, dv_2}{r_0} \end{matrix}\right\} \tag{10.61}$$

The Lagrangian strain increment is approximated, for simplicity, by the logarithmic strain during the small time increment as given by Eq. (10.50), where s_0, s, r_0, and r are expressed by Eqs. (10.57) to (10.60), inclusive.

$\phi^{(m)}$ in Eq. (10.48) can now be expressed in terms of the nodal values as

$$\phi^{(m)} = \int \bar{\sigma}\left(\sqrt{\frac{2}{3}}\right) t[d\mathbf{E}^T D\, d\mathbf{E}]^{1/2}\, dA$$

$$+ \frac{1}{2}\int H'\left(\frac{2}{3}t\right)[d\mathbf{E}^T D\, d\mathbf{E}]\, dA - \int \bar{\mathbf{T}}^T \mathbf{N}\mathbf{u}^{(m)}\, dA \tag{10.62}$$

for unit included angle of element, where $dA = r\, dt'$, t is the thickness of the sheet, and integration is performed from $t' = -1$ to $t' = +1$, and where

$$T = \begin{Bmatrix} T_1 + dT_1 \\ T_2 + dT_2 \\ T_3 + dT_3 \\ T_4 + dT_4 \end{Bmatrix} \tag{10.63}$$

Minimization of the above function can be obtained by use of the partial derivative $\partial \phi^{(m)} / \partial \mathbf{u}^{(m)}$ to give a set of simultaneous equations:

$$\frac{\partial \phi^{(m)}}{\partial \mathbf{u}^{(m)}} = \int \bar{\sigma}\left(\sqrt{\frac{2}{3}}\right) t [d\mathbf{E}^T D\, d\mathbf{E}]^{-1/2} \frac{\partial (d\mathbf{E})}{\partial \mathbf{u}^{(m)}} D\, d\mathbf{E}\, dA$$

$$+ \int H'\left(\frac{2}{3}t\right)[D\, d\mathbf{E}\, dA] \frac{\partial (d\mathbf{E})^T}{\partial \mathbf{u}^{(m)}} - \int N^T \bar{T}\, dA \tag{10.64}$$

$\partial (d\mathbf{E}) / \partial \mathbf{u}^{(m)}$ can be evaluated by use of Eq. (10.50) as follows:

$$\frac{\partial (d\mathbf{E})}{\partial \mathbf{u}^{(m)}} = Q = \left[\frac{\partial (d\mathbf{E})_i}{\partial \mathbf{u}_j^{(m)}}\right] = \begin{bmatrix} \dfrac{r_1 - r_2}{s^2} & \dfrac{1+t}{2r} \\[2ex] \dfrac{-(z_2 - z_1)}{s^2} & 0 \\[2ex] \dfrac{-(r_1 - r_2)}{s^2} & \dfrac{1-t}{2r} \\[2ex] \dfrac{(z_2 - z_1)}{s^2} & 0 \end{bmatrix} \tag{10.65}$$

Equation (10.64) may be rewritten as

$$\frac{\partial \phi^{(m)}}{\partial \mathbf{u}^{(m)}} = \int \left(\frac{2}{3}t\right) \bar{\sigma}\left[\frac{2}{3}d\mathbf{E}^T D\, d\mathbf{E}\right]^{-1/2} QD\, d\mathbf{E}\, dA$$

$$+ \int \left(\frac{2}{3}t\right) HQD\, d\mathbf{E}\, dA - \int N^T \bar{T}\, dA = 0 \tag{10.66}$$

By assembling all the elements in the finite element scheme, the following nonlinear simultaneous equations can be obtained

$$\frac{\partial \Phi}{\partial \mathbf{u}} = \Sigma \frac{\partial \phi^{(m)}}{\partial \mathbf{u}^{(m)}} = 0 \tag{10.67}$$

Equation (10.67) can be solved by the Newton-Raphson method by taking an initial guess of the solution $\bar{\mathbf{u}}$ for the true solution $\mathbf{u}_0$ and neglecting the second and higher order terms of $\Delta \mathbf{u} = \mathbf{u}_0 - \bar{\mathbf{u}}$ in the Taylor expansion to obtain the linear stiffness equation of

$$P\, \Delta \mathbf{u} = \mathbf{H} - \mathbf{f} \tag{10.68}$$

where P is the load such as on a hemispherical punch

$$P = \sum p^{(m)} \qquad H = \sum H^{(m)} \qquad f = \sum f^{(m)} \qquad (10.69)$$

The explanation of the foregoing equations follows. It can be shown that

$$\frac{\partial^2 \phi^{(m)}}{\partial u_i^{(m)} \partial u_\psi^{(\mu)}} = p^{(m)} = \frac{2}{3} \int \frac{1}{d\bar{E}} \left\{ (\bar{\sigma} + H\,d\bar{E}) \left(K - \frac{2bb^T}{3\,d\bar{E}} \right) + \frac{2}{3} \frac{Hbb^T}{d\bar{E}} \right\} t\,dA \qquad (10.70)$$

where

$$\mathbf{b} = QD\,d\bar{E} \qquad K = QDQ^T \qquad (10.71)$$

$$Q = \frac{\partial(d\mathbf{E})}{\partial \mathbf{u}^{(m)}} \qquad (10.72)$$

Also, it can be shown that

$$\frac{\partial \phi^{(m)}}{\partial u_i^{(m)}} = \mathbf{H}^{(m)} - \mathbf{f}^{(m)} \qquad (10.73)$$

where

$$\mathbf{H}^{(m)} = \frac{2}{3} \frac{1}{d\bar{E}} (\bar{\sigma} + H\,d\bar{E}) \mathbf{b} t\,dA \qquad (10.74)$$

$$\mathbf{f}^{(m)} = \int N^T \bar{\mathbf{T}}\,dA. \qquad (10.75)$$

The integrals are evaluated with the Gaussian quadrature formulas and the convergence is checked by the fractional norm.

By assembling the equations for an element, one obtains the equation for the tentative solution to Eq. (10.68):

$$P^* \Delta u = f - H^* \qquad (10.76)$$

where the starred quantities are initial guesses [10.19].

Three different sheetmetal forming processes, hydrostatic bulging of a sheet, stretching of a sheet with a hemispherical punch, and deep drawing with a hemispherical punch, have been solved by the FEM method discussed in the foregoing with good agreement with experimental results. It is concluded that the present rigid–plastic FEM can be used to treat sheetmetal forming problems with efficiency and reasonable accuracy [10.20].

10.8.4   Application of FEM to Rectangular Cup Drawing of Rate-Sensitive Sheetmetal [10.21]

An incremental rigid–plastic finite element method based on membrane theory is used to analyze a rectangular cup drawing process. The normal anisotropy, strain-hardening, strain-rate hardening, and Coulomb friction are incorporated into the analysis. The variational form of the equilibrium equation of a deforming body can be expressed as

$$\int_v \bar{S}\,(d\bar{E})\,dV - \int_s \mathbf{T} \cdot \delta\mathbf{u}\,dS = 0 \qquad (10.77)$$

where $\bar{S}$ = the effective stress
   $d\bar{E}$ = the effective Lagrangian strain increment
   dV = the volume element at the reference configuration
   $\mathbf{T}$ = the traction vector
   $\delta\mathbf{u}$ = virtual displacement vector
   dS = surface element at the reference configuration

The normal anisotropy is defined similar to Eq. (10.53) except that Cartesian are used in lieu of cylindrical coordinates, in which r and θ are replaced with x and y. It should be noted that R is the planar anisotropic strain ratio.

To accommodate the strain-rate sensitivity of sheet metallic materials the effective stress-strain curve is approximated by

$$\bar{S} = \bar{\sigma}_0 + (\tilde{h} - 2\bar{\sigma}_0)\,d\bar{E} \qquad (10.78)$$

where

$$\tilde{h}_0 = \frac{\partial\bar{\sigma}}{\partial\bar{\varepsilon}} + \frac{\partial\bar{\sigma}/\partial\dot{\bar{\varepsilon}}}{\Delta t}$$

$\bar{\sigma}$, $\bar{\varepsilon}$, and $\dot{\bar{\varepsilon}}$ are the effective true stress, effective true strain, and effective true strain rate, respectively, and Δt is the current time step. The quantities $\bar{\sigma}_0$, $\partial\bar{\sigma}/\partial\bar{\varepsilon}$, and $\partial\bar{\sigma}/\partial\dot{\bar{\varepsilon}}$ are evaluated at the reference configuration.

In this application, the true stress–true strain curve is approximated by

$$\bar{\sigma} = K(\varepsilon_0 + \bar{\varepsilon})^n \left(\frac{\dot{\bar{\varepsilon}}}{\dot{\bar{\varepsilon}}_0}\right)^m \qquad (10.79)$$

where ε_0 and $\dot{\bar{\varepsilon}}_0$ are the reference strain and strain rate, and n and m are the strainhardening exponent and strain-rate sensitivity, respectively.

The finite element discretization of the sheet domain is accomplished with the assumption of a linear displacement function for triangular elements. The assembly of elemental equations results in a system of equations which can be solved for the geometrical and tractional boundary conditions for the rectangular drawing process. The finite element domain used in the simulation is shown in Fig. 10.56. The twofold symmetry of a rectangular shape, rather than the fourfold symmetry of a square shape, complicates greatly the solution procedure.

The materials parameters are as follows

Parameter	302 stainless steel	Al-killed steel
K	248,000 psi (1710 MPa)	107,000 psi (738 MPa)
ε_0	0.06	0
n	0.64	0.228
m	0.01	0.012
R	0.94	1.6
$\dot{\varepsilon}_0$	0.001 s^{-1}	0.001 s^{-1}

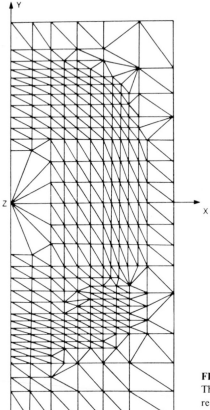

FIGURE 10.56
The finite element domain used in the simulation of a rectangular cup drawn from rate-sensitive sheetmetal [10.21].

The punch speed used in computation is 1 in/s (25.4 mm/s). The computed load-displacement curves of rectangular cup drawing for AISI 302 stainless steel and aluminum-killed (AK), plain-carbon steel sheet material is shown in Fig. 10.57.

In this application, a punch and die assembly is used as shown in Fig. 10.58. The coefficient of friction between the punch and the sheet μ_p is taken as 0.1 and that between the die and the sheet μ_d is taken as 0.05. The dimensions of the sheet are 28.5 in (723.9 mm) × 24.5 in (622.3 mm) × 0.035 in (0.899 mm) thick.

Comparison of the computed deformed flange shape with experimental results is shown in Fig. 10.59, and the predicted flow pattern is shown in Fig. 10.60.

The finite element simulation of rectangular cup drawing of strain-rate-sensitive sheetmetal, both the 302 stainless steel and the AK steel sheets, show highly nonuniform thickness strain distributions in the corner regions. The different material flow rates between the corners and the straight sides of the punch and die, as indicated in Fig. 10.56, result in localization of strain. The

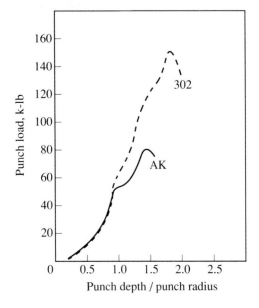

FIGURE 10.57
Computed load-displacement curves for rectangular cup drawing of AISI 302 stainless steel and aluminum-killed (AK) plain-carbon steel sheetmetal [10.21].

higher strainhardening capability of the 302 stainless steel renders a more uniform thickness strain distribution as compared to the AK steel, which, however, results in higher punch loads, as for the 302 stainless can be seen in Fig. 10.57.

A simplified three-dimensional (3D) finite element method for the analysis of sheetmetal forming has been presented as follows [10.22]. The same approach and the same assumptions, parameters, and hardware used in the foregoing analysis are used in this 3D example except for the method of simulation and for the incremental punch advancement.

In the simulation, a thin strip of sheetmetal with a finite element domain, is chosen from the undeformed sheetmetal blank as shown in Fig. 10.61. The geometrical feature of this strip is described by an inclined angle θ and a vertical height h. The variation of the inclined angle with respect to the x axis determines the location of the strip. Therefore, by varying its orientation, analytical results can be obtained at various locations for a given set of punch and die geometries. The vertical height of the strip is kept constant during changes in orientation. Thus, only one set of data is required in the analysis. Different input data can be obtained merely by changing the value of the inclined angle in the existing data file. The same data set can also be modified for different forming-tool geometries. With these minor modifications, the simplified analysis actually encompasses the entire sheetmetal domain of any arbitrary shape.

The program has automatic input-data generation built into it. Only the first and the last element data have to be provided, and the program will generate the missing data consecutively. The input of the nodal point data, however, needs some cautious judgment. For a particular forming process, nodal-point data should be provided whenever there is a change in the initial boundary condition

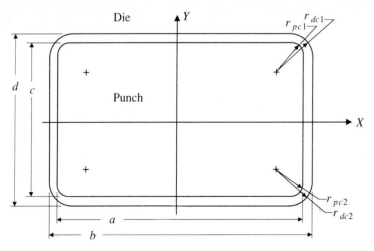

Punch corner radii	r_{pc1} = 2.35 in (59.69 mm)	a = 13.50 in (342.9 mm)
	r_{pc2} = 2.75 in (69.85 mm)	b = 14.36 in (363.22 mm)
Die corner radii	r_{dc1} = 2.75 in (69.85 mm)	c = 15.25 in (387.35 mm)
	r_{dc2} = 3.15 in (80.01 mm)	d = 16.05 in (407.69 mm)
Punch radius	r_p = 2.25 in (57.15 mm)	
Die radius	r_d = 0.5 in (12.7 mm)	

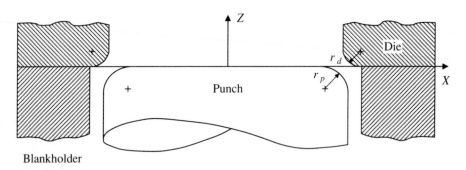

Blankholder

FIGURE 10.58
Schematic view of the rectangular punch and die assembly. (Note that clearance should be provided between the punch and disc.) [10.21].

of the sheetmetal domain. The variations of the boundary conditions during deformation is updated automatically. Uniform spacings are generated between the missing data with the same boundary condition as the last input data. Overall, the effort of preparing the input data is much less than in fully 3D analysis, and the computation time is reduced substantially to a more affordable level.

The additional geometrical and tractional boundary conditions for the cutout edges of a strip are shown in Fig. 10.62. For a membrane with unsymmetrical geometry subject to nonuniform loading, both normal force F_n and shear

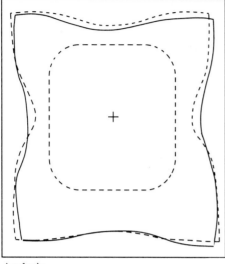

Analysis   - - -
Experiment   ———

FIGURE 10.59
Comparison of the predicted contour (dashed lines) with the experimental results (solid lines) for AISI 302 sheet material and a punch depth of 5.5 in (139.7 mm). (In the design of the production die for this rectangular cup, drawbead segments would be placed opposite the drawn-in locations at each of the four sides.) [10.21].

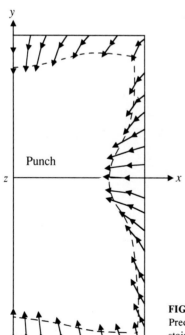

FIGURE 10.60
Predicted metal flow paths of the outer flange for AISI 302 stainless steel constructed from successive nodal point displacements [10.21].

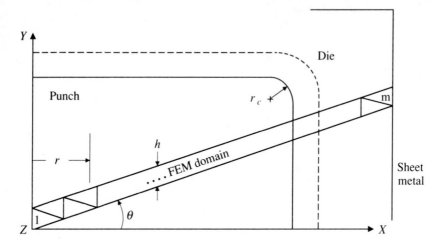

FIGURE 10.61
One quadrant of the thin sheetmetal strip and the finite element domain used in the simplified 3D analysis [10.22].

force F_s exist at the edges, whereas bending moment is absent. The resulting forces in the x and y directions can be expressed as

$$F_x = F_s \cos \theta \mp F_n \sin \theta \tag{10.80}$$

$$F_y = F_s \sin \theta \pm F_n \cos \theta \tag{10.81}$$

where the upper and lower signs in the equations refer to the upper and lower portions of the cutout edges, respectively.

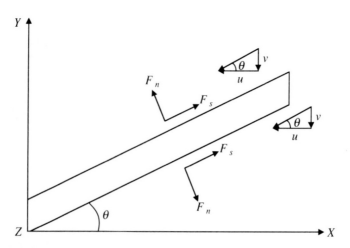

FIGURE 10.62
Supplemental boundary conditions for the cutout strip [10.22].

The material flow at the edges satisfy the following condition

$$v = u \tan \theta \qquad (10.82)$$

where u and v are the displacements in the x and y directions, respectively.

The punch speed used in the computation is the same as in the foregoing problem, that is, 1.0 in/s (25.4 mm/s); however, the deformation is induced by advancement of the punch in increments of 0.025 in (0.635 mm) for each step. Iterations take place from an initially assumed displacement field until the solutions converge. The computation is very efficient, requiring 10 to 15 iterations for convergence for a single step of punch increment for this simplified 3D method of analysis. The geometry and boundary conditions of the deformed sheetmetal are next updated, and the solution procedure is repeated until a desired punch depth is achieved.

The results obtained from the simplified method agreed favorably with the fully 3D analysis for a rectangular cup drawing process. The magnitude of the peak thickness strain and its location from the center of the die cavity varied somewhat from the fully 3D analysis as shown in Fig. 10.63. This discrepancy is attributed to the much finer mesh used in the region of the forming-tool radii in the simplified analysis as compared to that used in the fully 3D analysis.

From the above discussion, one might conclude that the simplicity and substantial saving in the computer time make the simplified method an attractive choice for the analysis of a complex sheetmetal cup drawing problem. Its application to an arbitrary geometry should be much more feasible than the fully 3D analysis [10.22].

10.8.5   Elastoplastic Finite Element Analysis of Axisymmetric Deep Drawing Based on Deformation Theory [10.23]

10.8.5.1   INTRODUCTION. When large deformation problems are examined, the results of the finite element analysis method based on the rigid–plastic material and the flow theory of plasticity are in good agreement with experimental results. However, the method does not account for elastic unloading and cannot handle such phenomena as springback and the development of residual stresses.

The approach presented here differs from other elastoplastic finite element approaches in that it is based on the deformation theory of plasticity, which is a numerical process that is very economical of computational time with reasonably accurate prediction of strain (see Eq. (2.78.)). This approach is used in the calculation of strain, stress, and deformation in the forming of an axisymmetric shape.

In this analysis, the elements are defined at three nodes: one at each end and one in the interior. Nodal locations are defined on the final geometry of the sheet, so that points of interest, such as corners and bends, will contain the proper concentration of nodes. The problem is now to find the corresponding initial locations of these nodes on the undeformed sheet. This is done through the

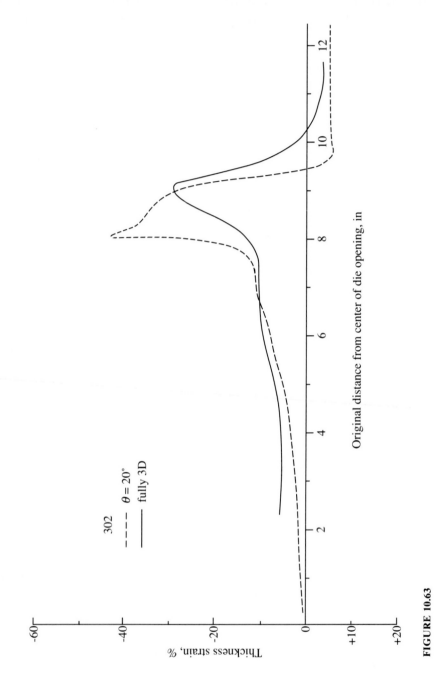

FIGURE 10.63
Comparison of the thickness strain distribution for the simplified ($\theta = 20°$) and fully 3D analyses for 302 stainless steel [10.22].

application of the finite element method by requiring that the potential energy due to deformation from the initial to the final geometry be a minimum. Once the initial locations of the nodes are determined under this requirement, the distance between the nodes, and their relative positions before and after deformation, allow a complete definition of all field quantities.

10.8.5.2 STRESS-STRAIN RELATIONSHIPS. With reference with Fig. 10.64, it is assumed (1) that the stress in the thickness direction σ_t is negligible in comparison with the radial and hoop stresses σ_r and σ_θ, respectively, (2) that the deformation theory of plasticity applies, (3) that generalized plane stress applies, and (4) that the material is isotropic. The foregoing assumptions coupled with symmetry conditions associated with an axisymmetric shape requires that the hoop strain ε_θ and the radial strain ε_r be coincident with the principal stretch directions.

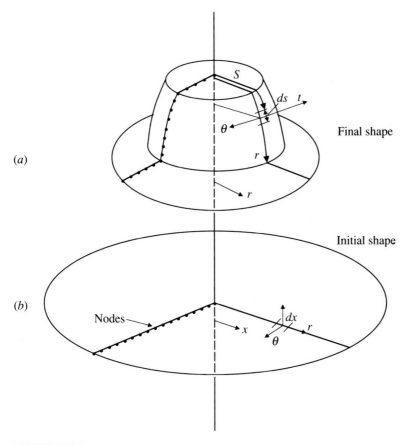

FIGURE 10.64
Drawings showing the geometry of the problem, the associated coordinate system, and the nodal points along the meridian line (a) in the deformed configuration, and (b) in the initial flat sheet [10.23].

The foregoing strains are given by

$$\sigma_\theta = \ln\left(\frac{r}{x}\right) \tag{10.83a}$$

$$\varepsilon_r = \ln\left(\frac{ds}{dx}\right) \tag{10.83b}$$

where x, r = radial coordinates of the initial and final positions, respectively, of
a given point
dx, ds = lengths of an infinitesimal increment along meridional lines in the
initial and final shapes, respectively

By replacing the strain and stress measures in the small strain (J_2) deformation theory by the logarithmic strains and the Cauchy true stresses, one obtains the following constitutive equations for the elastic strains ε^e in the radial, hoop, and thickness directions:

$$\varepsilon_r^e = \frac{1}{E}(\sigma_r - \nu\sigma_\theta) \tag{10.84a}$$

$$\varepsilon_\theta^e = \frac{1}{E}(-\nu\sigma_r + \sigma_\theta) \tag{10.84b}$$

$$\varepsilon_t^e = -\frac{\nu}{E}(\sigma_r + \sigma_\theta) \tag{10.84c}$$

where E is the elastic modulus and ν is the Poisson ratio. Likewise the plastic strains ε^p are given by

$$\varepsilon_r^p = \left(\frac{1}{E_s} - \frac{1}{E}\right)\left(\sigma_r + \frac{\sigma_\theta}{2}\right) \tag{10.85a}$$

$$\varepsilon_\theta^p = \left(\frac{1}{E_s} - \frac{1}{E}\right)\left(-\frac{\sigma_r}{2} + \sigma_\theta\right) \tag{10.85b}$$

$$\varepsilon_t^p = -\frac{1}{2}\left(\frac{1}{E_s} - \frac{1}{E}\right)(\sigma_r + \sigma_\theta) \tag{10.85c}$$

The secant modulus E_s is given by the slope of the true stress–logarithmic strain curve shown in Fig. 10.65, and it is assumed to be a function of the effective stress or strain.

The effective stress $\bar{\sigma}$ is defined by

$$\bar{\sigma} = (\sigma_r^2 + \sigma_\theta^2 - \sigma_r\sigma_\theta)^{1/2} \tag{10.86}$$

Consistent with the J_2 deformation theory, the effective strain $\bar{\varepsilon}$ is defined by

$$\bar{\varepsilon} = \frac{\bar{\sigma}}{E} + \sqrt{\frac{2}{3}}[(\varepsilon_r^p)^2 + (\varepsilon_\theta^p)^2 + \varepsilon_t^p)^2]^{1/2} \tag{10.87}$$

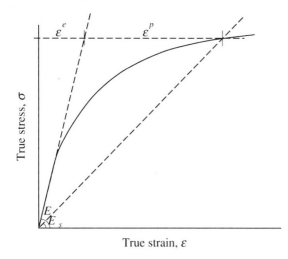

FIGURE 10.65
True stress-true strain curve showing the tangent and secant moduli (see Figs. 2.23 and 3.7) [10.23].

Based on the above definitions of effective stress and strain, the secant modulus is

$$E_s = \frac{\bar{\sigma}}{\bar{\varepsilon}} \qquad (10.88)$$

During the application of these stress-strain relationships, it will be necessary to find the stress state σ, given a known strain state ε. One can achieve this by the following iterative numerical process: (1) assuming a trial value of the secant modulus E_s, designated as E_N, and solving for σ_r and σ_θ, by using Eqs. (10.84) and (10.85), (2) computing the effective stress $\bar{\sigma}$ from Eq. (10.86), and the effective strain $\bar{\varepsilon}$ from Eq. (10.88), (3) obtaining, from the stress-strain curve at $\varepsilon = \bar{\varepsilon}$, a new estimate of the effective stress $(\bar{\sigma})_N$, and (4) computing another trial value of E_s by use of Eq. (10.88) and repeating until convergence.

10.8.5.3 APPLICATION OF THE FINITE ELEMENT METHOD (FEM). At the beginning of the numerical process, the final shape of the sheet, the nodal locations, and the outer diameter are known, but their final thickness is not. It is also known that the initial sheet is flat and its thickness is known, whereas its nodal locations and outer diameter are not known. To begin the numerical process, the trial nodal positions on the undeformed sheet are assumed. Through the application of Eqs. (10.83a and b), one can compute the hoop and radial strains in the deformed sheet that are compatible with the assumed nodal positions. The stresses in the deformed state can also be computed through the application of the constitutive equations (10.84) to (10.88). The equilibrium state is determined by minimizing the potential energy through an iterative process which is a variant of the Newton-Raphson approach. In this procedure, quadratic isoparametric elements are used, and the computations are done using Gaussian integration (numerical integration in which the base points x_i are not necessarily equally spaced).

The principle of minimum potential energy is used in this analysis. The potential energy Ψ, when one goes from the undeformed shape to the deformed shape, is defined as

$$\Psi = \int_V \left(\int_0^{\varepsilon_f} \sigma \, d\varepsilon \right) dV - \int_{S_r} Tw \, dS \qquad (10.89)$$

where ε_f = final strain
V = undeformed volume
T = surface tractions
w = boundary displacements
S_r = portion of the boundary where the surface transitions are prescribed
S = surface

The first term in Eq. (10.89) corresponds to the volumetric strain energy of deformation, and the second term represents the work of external tractions.

The volumetric strain energy is divided into two parts: Ψ_x, the potential energy associated with the sequence of trail values $\{x\}$ of the nodal locations on the undeformed sheet, and Ψ_u, the potential energy increment due to the sequence of small increments $\{u\}$ of the trial values of nodal locations as follows:

$$\Psi_x = \int_V \left(\int_0^{\varepsilon_x} \sigma \, d\varepsilon \right) dV - \int_{S_r} Tw_x \, dS \qquad (10.90a)$$

and

$$\Psi_u = \int_V \left(\int_{\varepsilon_x}^{\varepsilon_f} \sigma \, d\varepsilon \right) dV - \int_{S_r} Tw_u \, dS \qquad (10.90b)$$

where the subscript x denotes the quantities associated with the trial nodal locations $\{x\}$, and subscripts denotes quantities associated with the increments in $\{u\}$. The stress σ, and the strain ε, are expressed as linear functions of the small increments $\{u\}$ in the trial nodal locations as follows:

$$\sigma = \sigma_x + \sum_1 \frac{\partial \sigma}{\partial u_i} u_i \qquad (10.91a)$$

and

$$\varepsilon = \varepsilon_x + \sum_1 \frac{\partial \varepsilon}{\partial u_i} u_i \qquad (10.91b)$$

Then the potential energy increment due to the small increments $\{u\}$ is given by

$$\Psi_u = \frac{1}{2} \int_v \left(2\sigma_x + \sum_1 \frac{\partial \sigma}{\partial u_i} u_i \right) \left(\sum_1 \frac{\partial \sigma}{\partial u_i} u_i \right) dV - \sum_1 T_i u_i \qquad (10.92)$$

where the term $\sum_1 T_i u_i$ represents the effect of the nodal tractions, i.e., friction.

The set of nodal locations on the initial configuration which minimizes the potential energy can now be found by varying the trial values of the nodal locations by a small increment $\{u\}$ and finding the conditions where the potential energy Ψ is minimized with respect to $\{u\}$, as follows:

$$\frac{\partial}{\partial\{u\}}\Psi = 0 \tag{10.93}$$

or, since Ψ_x is independent of $\{u\}$

$$\frac{\partial}{\partial\{u\}}\Psi_u = 0 \tag{10.94}$$

The solution of Eq. (10.94) gives values of $\{u\}$, which are used to correct the trial values of $\{x\}$ in an iterative manner as follows.

The cup meridian is broken into a number of finite elements each defined by three nodes, typically denoted by the points $i, j,$ and k as in Fig. 10.66(a). The elements are projected into isoparametric spaced defined by the parameter

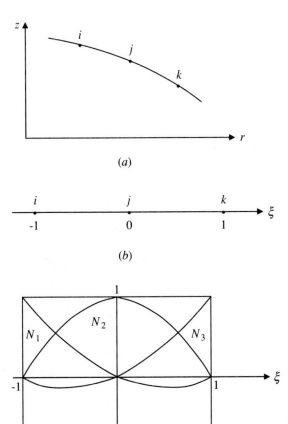

(a)

(b)

(c)

FIGURE 10.66
Elementary geometry and shape functions for axisymmetric deepdrawing. (a) Three nodal points in $z - r$ space of a finite element on the cup meridian. (b) Nodal points in isoparametric space. (c) Shape functions [10.23].

ξ as shown in Fig. 10.66(b), where the end nodes are situated at $\xi = \pm 1$ and the midnode at $\xi = 0$. The shape functions N_1, N_2, and N_3 are defined as follows:

$$N_1 = \tfrac{1}{2}(\xi^2 - \xi) \tag{10.95a}$$

$$N_2 = (1 + \xi^2) \tag{10.95b}$$

$$N_3 = \tfrac{1}{2}(\xi^2 + \xi) \tag{10.95c}$$

One can now denote any variable between $\xi = \pm 1$ as a function of the shape functions and the value that the variable takes at the nodal points i, j, and k such as for

$$r = r_i N_1 + r_j N_2 + r_k N_3 \tag{10.96a}$$

$$x = x_i N_1 + x_j N_2 + x_k N_3 \tag{10.96b}$$

$$s = s_i N_1 + s_j N_2 + s_k N_3 \tag{10.96c}$$

$$u = u_i N_1 + u_j N_2 + u_k N_3 \tag{10.96d}$$

From Eqs. (10.94) and (10.95) it can be seen that all of the above variables are functions of ξ.

Similarly, certain derivatives can be written as functions of ξ such as

$$\frac{ds}{dx} = \frac{ds/d\xi}{dx/d\xi} = \frac{[s_i(dN_1/d\xi) + s_j(dN_2/d\xi) + s_k(dN_3/d\xi)]}{[x_i(dN_1/d\xi) + x_j(dN_2/d\xi) + x_k(dN_3/d\xi)]} \tag{10.97}$$

A similar equation can be written for du/dx by substituting u for s.

By taking the derivatives of Eqs. (10.95), $dN_1/d\xi = \xi - \tfrac{1}{2}$, etc., in the above equations. Thus, the quantities that define strain, stress, displacement, etc., are now relatable to the values of x, s, r, z, and u at the nodes, and to the function ξ.

When trial nodal locations x are incremented by an amount u, then the strains in the sheet from Eqs. (10.83a and b) are given by

$$\varepsilon_\theta = \ln\left(\frac{r}{x+u}\right) \approx \ln\left(\frac{r}{x}\right) - \frac{u}{x} \tag{10.98a}$$

and

$$\varepsilon_r = \ln\left(\frac{ds}{dx+du}\right) \approx \ln\left(\frac{du}{dx}\right) - \frac{du}{dx} = \ln\left(\frac{ds/d\xi}{dx/d\xi}\right) - \frac{du/d\xi}{dx/d\xi} \tag{10.98b}$$

The numerical process is begun by computing the strain ε_θ and ε_r and the corresponding stresses σ_θ and σ_r produced by the deformation from the assumed trial nodal locations $\{x\}$. These stresses and strain are computed by use of Eqs. (10.83) to (10.88) at the Gauss points that are to be used in numerical integration of the strain energy. A three-point integration scheme is used here. These computed quantities are denoted by a subscript 0.

A numerical variant of the Newton-Raphson scheme of solving a system of nonlinear equations is now used. Each trial nodal point $\{x\}$ is given a small increment u', in turn, and the stresses and strains are recomputed using Eqs. (10.98) and accounting for this small increment. In the numerical work, u' may be taken as 0.051 mm (0.002 in), but it may be any reasonable small dimension. The result is a series of expressions for the stress and strain at each Gauss point which are linear functions of the position increment u, as was written originally in Eqs. (10.91). For example, at a given Gauss point,

$$\varepsilon_r = \varepsilon_{r_0} + (\varepsilon_{r_i} - \varepsilon_{r_0}) u_i / u' + (\varepsilon_{r_j} - \varepsilon_{r_0}) u_j / u' + (\varepsilon_{r_k} - \varepsilon_{r_0}) u_k / u' \qquad (10.99)$$

where ε_{r_i} is the total strain at the Gauss point resulting from the trail nodal positions $\{x\}$, with an increment of u' at the nodal point i. Similar definitions apply to ε_{r_j} and ε_{r_k}. Thus, the strain and stress at each Gauss point is a linear function of the so far unknown increments $\{u\}$. The potential energy increment Ψ_u is now computed according to Eq. (10.92) using Gaussian integration. Because it contains products of the type $\sigma_r \varepsilon_r$, the result is a quadratic expression in $\{u\}$. Minimization of the potential energy with respect to $\{u\}$, according to Eq. (10.94), gives a set of linear algebraic equations in $\{u\}$ which can be solved numerically. Once this is done, a new set of trial nodal positions $\{x + u\}$ on the undeformed body is obtained. Because of the highly nonlinear nature of the constitutive and geometric relationships, the correct set of the nodal positions $\{x\}$ must, in practice, be found through several iterations. Convergence can be checked by observing that the potential energy approaches a minimum when the increments $\{u\}$ vanish. The solution might be considered to have converged when $|u|/u' < 0.001$ for all nodes. About 20 or 30 iterations are generally sufficient to achieve convergence. Even with the incorporation of convergence aids into the computer program, it is sometimes slow.

10.8.5.4 FURTHER DEVELOPMENTS OF SHEET METAL FORMING ANALYSIS METHOD

10.8.5.4.1 Improvement in the iteration process. To reduce the computer time still more, while using membrane type elements and deformation theory, an improved numerical scheme is incorporated, in which an elastic stress-strain relationship is used to initiate the solution. The converged solutions, which contain information about the history of deformation, are used as starting points to initiate the actual solution schemes. The difficulty, that causes a relatively high number of iterations, originates from two sources of nonlinearities: (1) the geometrical description, and (2) the stress-strain relationship. To overcome these problems, the following alternative scheme is employed. Initially, a completely elastic material, which has the same Young's modulus as the actual material, is assumed. The iterative scheme is initiated using the stress-strain relationship for the elastic material with any arbitrary trial nodal locations $\{x\}$. The convergence is achieved quickly in about five iterations, resulting in u_i values $\leq 10^{-7}$ for the last iteration [10.24].

At the end of this cycle, the adjusted nodal values $\{x + u\}$ correspond to the equilibrium positions which are associated with the assumed elastic material. These new nodal positions, which contain information about the specific history of deformation, constitute appropriate trial values for initiating the solution with the nonlinear material model. The rate of convergence is improved and values of u_i less than 10^{-7} are achieved within 5 or 10 iterations. Therefore, with the total number of iterations for the elastic material and the real material model such as Eq. (10.79), a convergence is readily achieved and the lengthy search through $\{x\}$ domains is avoided. Moreover, the convergence is not sensitive to the assumed values of $\{x\}$ and any set of initial nodal points leads to a unique solution [10.24].

10.8.5.4.2 Description of frictional conditions and bending effects. The equilibrium of forces at the metal-punch interface in the normal direction to an infinitesimal surface element yields the following equation in final form of [10.24]

$$f = \mu_p N = \frac{\mu_p t}{\rho_p}\left[\sigma_r + \sigma_\theta\left(1 - \frac{r_p}{r}\right)\right] \qquad (10.100)$$

where μ_p = coefficient of friction at the metal-punch interface
$\quad N$ = normal reaction stress
$\quad t$ = current thickness
$\quad \rho_p$ = radius of the punch corner
$\quad r_p$ = distance between the punch radius and the axis of symmetry
$\quad \sigma_r$ = radial stress
$\quad \sigma_\theta$ = tangential stress

The equation for the metal-die interface is the same as the above except that the subscripted values for the metal-punch interface: μ_p, ρ_p, and r_p are replaced by those for the metal-die interface: μ_d, ρ_d, and r_d.

Bending at the punch radius causes the outer surface radial strain to increase. Since this bending takes place with high mean tension, the neutral axis is near the inner surface and, as a result, the added strain at the outer surface is approximately t/r_p, where t is the sheet thickness and r_p is the punch corner radius. Likewise, bending at the draw radius can be similarly corrected for [10.23].

10.8.5.4.3 Extension of analysis to multistage metal forming [10.25]. In the foregoing approach, it is assumed that the deformation takes place in a single step. In actual practice, however, the final configuration of the part is obtained in several stages, were additional changes in the shape of the part are introduced in each step. In order to simulate such processes in a realistic manner, each step of the entire process is analyzed. Moreover, by dividing the deformation history into successive steps, a proportional straining in each step may be maintained; however, greater anisotropy may exist in subsequent steps. In order to retain computational efficiency, the deformation theory of plasticity is used in the analysis.

In the multistep operation, the initial and final configurations refer to the geometry of the part at the beginning and the end of each step, respectively. As before, the magnitude of change in each nodal position is designated by u_i, where i refers to the node number. The trial nodal positions in the initial configuration

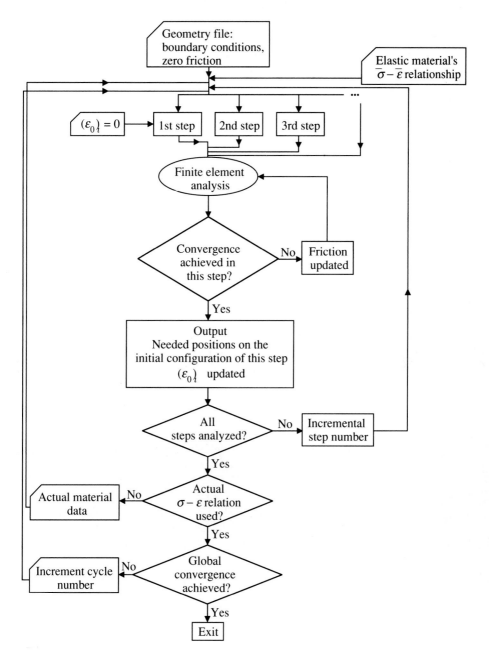

FIGURE 10.67
Flow diagram of the multistep sheetmetal forming model [10.25].

are then improved by adding the values of u_i to x_i. Distributions of the tangential and hoop components of strain in each step are then computed through several iterations from the improved initial and final positions of the nodes in the corresponding step. Generalization of such a scheme from a two- to a multistep operation is shown in Fig. 10.67, which shows the flow diagram of the entire process.

10.8.5.4.4. Comparison of analytical and experimental results. The calculated and experimental distributions for the radial and hoop strain distributions are compared in Fig. 10.68 for drawing quality enameling iron (DQEI) sheetmetal by the original approach cited earlier [10.23]. The dimensions of the cup are 33.0 mm (1.3 in) in diameter, and 22.9 mm (0.9 in) deep. The thickness of the material is 0.69 mm (0.027 in), and it is nearly isotropic. The following are some of the details of the forming operation: punch radius 4.8 mm (1.9 in), die radius 5.0 mm (0.20 in), coefficient of sliding friction 0.025 to 0.048, blankholder force 4.0 kN (0.9 lb), initial blank diameter 70.1 mm (2.76 in), final flange diameter

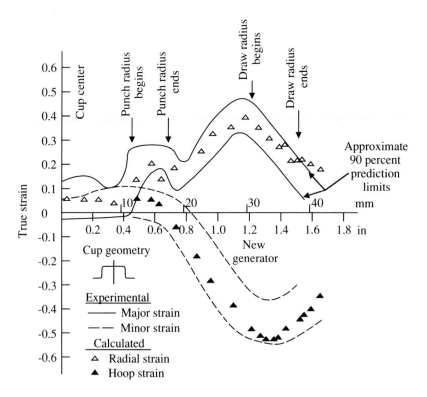

FIGURE 10.68
Strain distribution for all orientations with respect to the rolling directions for axisymmetric deep-drawing, showing a comparison of the computed major and minor true strains along the final generator with experimental data [10.23].

51.0 mm (2.01 in) [10.23]. The material constants for DQEI for Eq. (10.79) are K, 620.6 MPa (90 ksi); ε_0, 0.19; $\dot{\bar{\varepsilon}}_0$, $2.78 \times 10^{-4} \text{s}^{-1}$; n, 0.5; and m, 0.0067 [10.24]. Figure 10.68 shows experimental major and minor true strains obtained from grid circles measured on the radial and hoop directions and computer calculated radial and hoop strains along the final generator. The shapes of the curves vary appreciably with cup diameter, cup depth, and type of lubrication.

The discrepancy between the predicted and the measured results may be attributed to the following: (1) the fact that the history dependence of plastic deformation is ignored by using total strain theory may cause errors in those regions of the part where strain components are not proportional; (2) errors are introduced when stress and strain are expressed as linear functions of increments u (linear approximation of strain energy may also introduce errors unless a sufficiently small increment of strain is used); (3) the bending and unbending of the material over the die profile is neglected; and (4) there is an uncertainty about the distribution of the coefficient of friction at the metal-tool interface [10.24]. In spite of the foregoing discrepancies, it is believed that the use of the deformation theory of plasticity and the assumption of proportional loading is a significantly more economical approach than the approach based on incremental theory of plasticity.

ACKNOWLEDGMENT

The material and most of the illustrations in this chapter were adapted from the references as indicated in the text and in the legends by the numbers of the references enclosed in square brackets pursuant to all copyrights.

REFERENCES

10.1. Keeler, S. P., "Sheet Metal Stamping Technology—Need for Fundamental Understanding," *Mechanics of Sheet Metal Forming*, D. P. Koistinen and N.-M. Wang, Plenum Press, 1977, pp. 3–18.

10.2. Nagpal, V., B. S. Shabel, J. F. Thomas, Jr., and H. L. Gegel, "Formability Models for 2024-O Aluminum Alloy Sheet Material," *7th NAMRC*, 1977, SME pp. 172–179.

10.3. Nagpal, V., and T. Altan, "Mathematical Modeling of Sheet Metal Formability Indices and Sheet Metal Forming Processes," *Battelle*, AFML-TR-78-140, Oct. 1978, pp. 6, 34–45, 58–66, 84–85, 149–150, 198–199, 210–211, 245, 259–264. (Also, Ref. 10.18.)

10.4. Lindberg, R. A., *Processes and Materials of Manufacture*, 3d ed., Allyn and Bacon, 1983, p. 289.

10.5. Kienzle, O., "Classes and Characteristics of Plastic-Deformation Processes," *Machine Design*, pp. 100–207, Nov. 7, 1963.

10.6. DeGarmo, E. P., *Materials and Processes in Manufacturing*, 5th ed., Macmillan Publishing Co., New York, pp. 341–342.

10.7. Fogg, B., G. A. A. Jamison, and A. W. W. J. Chisholm, "Component Classification as an Aid to the Design of press Tools," *Annals of the C.I.R.P.*, vol. XVIV, pp. 141–151.

10.8. Eary, D. F., and E. A. Reed, *Techniques of Pressworking Sheet Metal*, 2d ed., Prentice-Hall, Inc., Englewood Cliffs, New Jersey, pp. 2–27, 42–43, 57, 65–72, 230, 452–453.

10.9. Johnson, W., and P. B. Mellor, *Engineering Plasticity*, Van Nostrand-Reinhold, Co., New York, p. 318.

10.10. Langewis, C., "Two-Piece Can Manufacturing Blanking and Cup Drawing," *Innovations in Die Design*, K. A. Keyes (ed.), SME, Dearborn, Michigan, 1982, pp. 150–151.

10.11. Schorn, G. J., and N. H. Ashworth, "Control of a Sheet Metal Flexible Manufacturing System," in *Proc. of the First Interl. Machine Tool Conf.*, Birmingham, Ed., June 26-28, 1984, IFF and North-Holland Pub. Co., p. 393-402.

10.12. Amstead, B. H., P. F. Ostwald, and M. L. Begeman, *Manufacturing Processes*, 7th ed., John Wiley & Sons, New York, 1979, p. 395.

10.13. ASM Metals Handbook, 8th ed., vol. 4, Forming, 1969, T. Lyman, Editor, Metals Park, Ohio, pp. 1-10.

10.14. Gossard, D. C., and B. T. Allison, "Adaptive Breakforming," *8th NAMRC*, 1980, SME, pp. 252-256.

10.15. Nagpal, V. et al., "Development of a Process Model for Press Brake Bending," *Process Modeling*, *Proc. Process Modeling Sessions*, 1978 and 1979, ASM, Metal Park, Ohio, pp. 287-301.

10.16. Weinmann, K. J., "Effect of Tools and Workpiece Geometries Upon Bending of HSLA Steel Plate," *6th NAMRC*, 1978, SME, Dearborn, Michigan, pp. 220-225.

10.17. Hosford, W. F., and R. M. Caddell, *Metal Forming*, Prentice-Hall, Englewood Cliffs, New Jersey, pp. 250-252.

10.18. Nagpal, V., T. L. Subramanian, and T. A. Altan, "ICAM Mathematical Modeling of Sheet Metal Formability Indices and Sheet Metal Forming Processes," Technical Report AFML-TR-79-4168, 1979, AFML/LTC, WPAFB, OH 45433, pp. 38-46, 199-201, 216-217, 257-265, 273.

10.19. Kim, J.H., S.I. Oh, and S. Kobayashi, "Analysis of Axisymmetric Sheet-Metal Forming by the Rigid-Plastic, Finite-Element Method," DTIC, Technical Report AFML-TR-78-120, September 1978, pp. 1-12.

10.20. Kobayashi, S., and J. H. Rim, "Axisymmetric Sheet Metal Forming Processes by the Rigid-Plastic Finite Element Method," *Mechanics of Sheet Metal Forming*, D. P. Koistinen and N.-M. Wang (eds.), Plenum Press, 1978, p. 344.

10.21. Toh, C. H., W. T. Carter, Jr., and L. R. Kisand, "Rectangular Cup Drawing of Strain Rate-Sensitive Sheet Materials," in *1987 Manufacturing Technology Review*, NAMRC 15 Proc., NAMRI/SME, pp. 340-345.

10.22. Toh, C. H., "A Simplified Three-Dimensional Finite Element Method for the Analysis of Sheet Metal Forming," in *1988 Manufacturing Technology Review*, NAMRC 16 Proc., NAMRI/SME, pp. 119-124.

10.23. Levy, S., C. F. Shih, J. P. D. Wilkinson, P. Stine, and R. C. McWilson, "Analysis of sheet Metal Forming to Axisymmetric Shapes," in *Formability Topics—Metallic Materials*, ASTM STP 647, B. A. Niemeier, A. K. Schmieder, and J. R. Newby (eds.), American Society for Testing Materials, 1978, pp. 238-260.

10.24. Majlessi, S. S., and D. Lee, "Further Development of Sheet Forming Analysis Method," *J. of Engng. for Industry, Trans. ASME*, vol. 109, no. 4, November 1987, pp. 330-337.

10.25. Majlessi, S. S., and D. Lee, "Analysis of Multi-Stage Sheet Metal Forming Processes," in *1987 Manufacturing Technology Review*, 15th NAMRC, pp. 330-334.

PROBLEM

10.1. Calculate the load per unit width of die required to air bend to a depth of 2.54 mm a 2024-O aluminum alloy, in which the flow stress is 90.5 MPa, the thickness of the sheet is 1.27 mm, the angle of bend is 60°, the coefficient of friction is 0.1, the width of the die is 9.53 mm, and the radius of the punch is 2.54 mm.

CHAPTER 11

DEEP DRAWING
CONSIDERATIONS
AND EVALUATION
OF FORMABILITY

11.1 DEEP DRAWING AND ALLIED PROCESSES

11.1.1 Definition of Deep Drawing

In this section conventional deep drawing of a cylindrical cup from a thin, flat, circular blank with a flat-bottom punch as shown in Fig. 11.1(a) will be discussed primarily. Redrawing operations are shown in Fig. 11.1(b), (c), and (d). Sheet-metal forming processes, broadly classified as deep drawing or stamping operations, include a wide spectrum of operations and flow conditions. At one end of the spectrum is the forming of flat-bottomed cylindrical cups by radial drawing or cupping. In this case one of the principal strains in the plane of the sheet is positive and the other is negative with the change in thickness, if any, being small. At the other end of the spectrum are operations involving biaxial stretching of the sheet, at which two principal strains are tensile, and thinning is required. The distinction between *shallow drawing* and *deep drawing* is arbitrary, although shallow drawing generally refers to the forming of a cup no deeper than one-half its diameter, with little thinning of the metal. In deep drawing, the cup is deeper than one-half its diameter, and wall thinning, although not necessarily intentional, may be more than in shallow drawing. Deep drawing is also called cupping. If the wall thickness (especially at the top of the cup) is reduced during the operation by means of a restricted clearance between the punch and the die lip, the operation is called *ironing*.

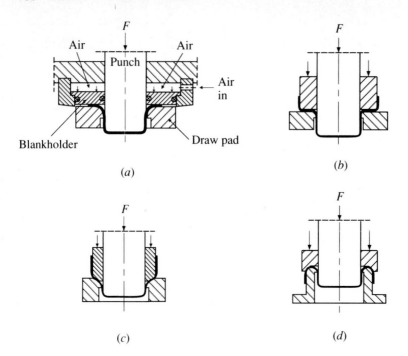

FIGURE 11.1
Various methods of deep drawing: (*a*) conventional drawing, (*b*) direct or straight redrawing, (*c*) direct inclined plane redrawing, and (*d*) reverse redrawing [10.10, p. 152].

11.1.2 Analysis of Deep Drawing

Two principal actions usually take place in deep drawing: (1) *biaxial stretching* over a punch, in which both principal strains are tensile, and (2) *drawing-in* of a flange into a die cavity in which one principal strain is tensile and the other is compressive.

For use in the analysis of deep drawing, the flat blank may be divided into three zones, X, Y, and Z, as shown in Fig. 11.2 [10.9]. The outer annular zone X consists of material in contact with the die, the inner annular zone Y is initially not in contact with either the punch or the die, and the circular zone Z is in contact with the flat bottom of the punch only.

During the course of deep drawing, the following five processes take place:

1. Pure radial drawing between the die and blankholder
2. Bending and sliding over the die profile
3. Stretching between the die and punch
4. Bending and sliding over the punch profile radius
5. Stretching and sliding over the punch nose [10.9]

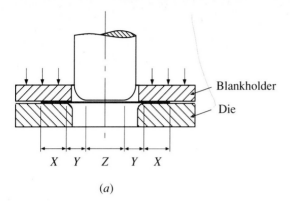

(a)

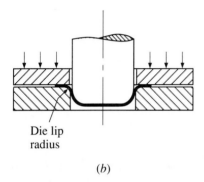

Die lip
radius

(b)

FIGURE 11.2
Initial stages of deep drawing: (a) initial contact stage,
and (b) a intermediate stage showing the outer annular
zone X, inner zone Y, and punch-end contact zone Z.
[10.9, p. 293]. In deep drawing the blank is allowed to
slip under the blank holder. Deformation is essentially
restricted to the flange area. Usually, no deformation
occurs under the bottom of the punch.

Various parts of zone X may go through some or all of the processes 1, 2,
and 3; those of Y through 2, 3, and 4; and those of Z through 3, 4, and 5. The
first process thickens the metal, and 3 and 5 thin it.

As a deep drawing operation proceeds, the outer flange portion of the blank
is subjected to a radial drawing tensile stress and an induced compressive hoop
stress, and when the magnitude of these stresses exceeds a certain critical value,
dependent on the current flange dimensions, lateral collapse into wrinkles occurs.

If the flange is not laterally supported with a blankholder, it can be shown
theoretically [10.9] that instability begins in the range

$$0.46\left(\frac{t_0}{D_0}\right) \le \frac{\sigma_\theta}{E_0} \le 0.58\left(\frac{t_0}{D_0}\right) \tag{11.1}$$

where σ_θ is the induced hoop stress, t_0 is the initial material thickness, D_0 the
initial blank diameter, and E_0 is the plastic buckling modulus given by

$$E_0 = \frac{4EP}{(\sqrt{E}+\sqrt{P})^2} \tag{11.2}$$

where E is the elastic modulus and P is the appropriate slope of the true stress–true
strain curve of the material.

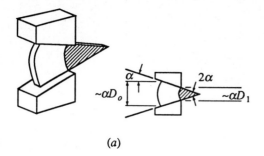

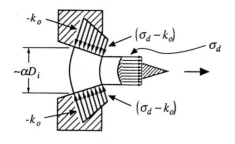

(a)

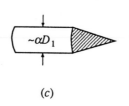

(b)

(c)

FIGURE 11.3
Analogy between deep drawing and strip (or flat wire) drawing. (Side supports are not shown.) In deep drawing the limit of deformation is reached when the load required to deform the flange becomes greater than the load capacity of the cup wall. Failure occurs in the unworked area near the bottom of the cup wall.

FIGURE 11.4
Wrinkling in the flange of a partially drawn cup due to insufficient hold-down force. (*From D. J. Meuleman, Ph.D. thesis, Univ. of Michigan, 1980.*)

Blankholders may be of one of three types: (1) spring loaded, or (2) pneumatic or hydraulic for a single-action press, and (3) outer ram action of a double-action press, the standard motion cycle of which is shown in Fig. 10.26.

An analogy can be made between deep drawing and wire drawing, in which the wire is replaced by a two-dimensional strip as shown in Fig. 11.3. The die is replaced by sectors of the blank adjacent to the one under consideration together with the blankholder and the opposing die surface. If the blankholding pressure is not sufficient at any time during the drawing operation, the flange will buckle causing flange wrinkling as shown in Fig. 11.4. Shallow draws of relatively thick material may be cupped without a blankholder.

The objective of this analysis of deep drawing is to provide the necessary knowledge to assist in the following phases of the production of a drawn part from sheetmetal [10.16]:

1. Product design of the drawn shapes
2. Process planning of the operation sequence
3. Design of the drawing dies
4. Selection of presses for drawing
5. Trying out of the drawing dies
6. Diagnosis and solving of production problems

There are two important regions to be considered in the analysis of deep drawing: the flange (rim) where most of the deformation occurs, and the wall which must support a sufficient force to cause the deformation in the flange. If the diameter of the blank is too large, the force that must be transmitted to the wall to draw the blank through the die will be excessive, and the wall will fail by necking or fracture. The formability may therefore be expressed as a *limiting drawing ratio* (LDR), which is the ratio of the largest diameter of the blank that can be drawn without failure, to the diameter of the cup or punch.

The following simplifying assumptions will be made in the following treatment of deep drawing [10.17]:

1. The work of external friction loss and internal friction loss by bending and unbending will be neglected in the initial treatment and will be accounted for later by use of an efficiency factor η. Initially the deformation efficiency is considered to be 100 percent or η is 1
2. Since the strainhardening exponent n has only a minor effect on the limiting drawing ratio (LDR), an ideally plastic material will be considered with $n = 0$
3. The thickness of the sheet remains constant
4. The material has planar isotropy, i.e., normal anisotropy, and any angular variations of R can be handled by the average anisotropic plastic strain ratio

$$\bar{R} = \frac{(R_0 + 2R_{45} + R_{90})}{4} \qquad (11.3)$$

Note that R is used here for the plastic anisotropic strain ratio $\varepsilon_w/\varepsilon_t$ to differentiate it from the current radius r (R and r for the plastic strain ratio may be used interchangeably depending upon the situation)

5. Hill's anisotropy theory of plasticity applies (see Eq. (2.108))

First let us consider the deformation occurring in the flange or rim as shown in Fig. 11.5. With the assumption of plane strain $\varepsilon_z = 0$ in the flange means that the surface area inside any element originally at radius ρ_0, and currently at radius ρ, is unchanged or remains constant as follows:

$$\pi\rho_0 = \pi\rho^2 + 2\pi r_1 h = \text{constant} \tag{11.4}$$

where ρ_0, ρ, r, and h are defined in Fig. 11.5.

Taking the derivative, one obtains

$$2\pi\rho \, d\rho + 2\pi r_1 \, dh = 0$$

or

$$d\rho = -\frac{r_1 \, dh}{\rho} \tag{11.5}$$

Since the circumference of the element is proportional to ρ, $d\varepsilon_y = d\rho/\rho$, and since $d\varepsilon_z = 0$, if one substitutes into Eq. (11.5), then

$$d\varepsilon_x = -d\varepsilon_y = -\frac{d\rho}{\rho} = \frac{r_1 \, dh}{\rho^2} \tag{11.6}$$

where r_1 is the punch radius and dh is the incremental distance moved by the punch [10.17].

The incremental work dW done on this element is equal to the volume of the element $2\pi t\rho \, d\rho$ times the incremental work per volume $\sigma_x \, d\varepsilon_x + \sigma_y \, d\varepsilon_y + \sigma_z \, d\varepsilon_z$. Since $d\varepsilon_z = 0$, $d\varepsilon_x = -d\varepsilon_y$, the work per volume is $(\sigma_x - \sigma_y)\sigma \, d\varepsilon_x$, so the work on this element is $dw = 2\pi t\rho \, d\rho (\sigma_x - \sigma_y)(r_1 \, dh)/\rho^2$.

Although the relative values of σ_x and σ_y vary with element position, the term $(\sigma_x - \sigma_y)$ should be constant and is designated by σ_f (the flow strength of the flange under the constraint $d\varepsilon_z = 0$). With $d\varepsilon_z = 0$ and $\sigma_z = 0$, $\sigma_y = -\sigma_x$, so that $\sigma_f = 2\sigma_x$. The total work W for an ideally plastic material on all elements of the flange per increment of punch travel for 100 percent deformation efficiency,

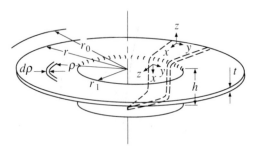

FIGURE 11.5
Schematic illustration of a partially drawn cup showing coordinate system and dimensional notation [11.1, p. 79].

i.e., for a deformation efficiency factor of $\eta = 1$, is

$$\frac{dW}{dh} = \int_{r_1}^{r_2} \frac{2\pi r_1 t\sigma_f \, d\rho}{\rho} = 2\pi r_1 t\sigma_f \ln\left(\frac{r}{r_1}\right) = F_d \tag{11.7}$$

The drawing force F_d, which must equal dW/dh, will have its largest value at the beginning of the draw, when $r = r_0$, so

$$F_{d(max)} = \frac{dW}{dh_{(max)}} = 2\pi r_1 t\sigma_f \ln\left(\frac{r_0}{r_1}\right) = 2\pi r_1 t\sigma_f \ln\left(\frac{d_0}{d_1}\right) \tag{11.8}$$

or

$$\sigma_{d(max)} = \sigma_f \ln\left(\frac{d_0}{d_1}\right) \tag{11.9}$$

where d_0 and d_1 are blank and cup or punch diameters, respectively, and σ_f is defined above as the flow strength of the flange in plane strain [10.17].

The blank diameter d_0 decreases continuously during drawing from d_0, at the start, to that of the cup or punch d_1, at the end. At any intermediate state at d_i, the drawing stress for a deformation efficiency of η would be given by

$$\sigma_d = \frac{1}{\eta} \sigma_f \ln\left(\frac{d_i}{d_1}\right) \tag{11.10}$$

or

$$F_d = \frac{1}{\eta} \pi d_i t\sigma_f \ln\left(\frac{d_i}{d_1}\right) \tag{11.11}$$

According to Eq. (11.10), the variation of σ_d (and F_d) with the punch stroke or cup depth is as shown in Fig. 11.6. However, this relationship is not exactly what is observed during cupping. Instead of being a maximum at the beginning of the stroke, F_d (and σ_d) reach a maximum shortly after some cupping has already taken place, as shown schematically in Fig. 11.7. The actual oscillograph trace showing the variation of the punch load (force) with punch travel is shown in

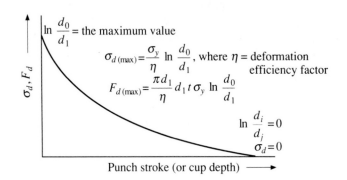

FIGURE 11.6
Schematic curve showing the variation of drawing stress (or force) versus depth of cup according to Eq. (11.10).

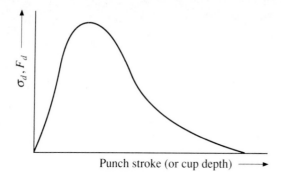

FIGURE 11.7
Schematic curve showing the actual variation of the drawing force (or stress) versus cup depth.

Fig. 11.8 for different percentage reductions $= [(d_0 - d_1)/d_0]100$. The diameter of the blank was successively increased in $\frac{1}{8}$ in (3.2 mm) increments, which explains the uneven percentage reduction. (Note that the punch travel is from right to left on each graph.) The variation of the drawing force with the percentage reduction obtained experimentally is shown in Fig. 11.9. Note that a much greater force (and work) would be required to draw the stainless steel as compared to the aluminum alloy as indicated by the heights of their respective curves. Also, the drawing quality steel outperforms the commercial quality steel in this example by only a small margin, if at all.

Let us now look at the situation in the cup wall. To avoid failure, the cross-sectional area of the cup wall must carry the force $F_{d(\max)}$. Therefore, the drawing limit will be reached when the axial stress σ_x reaches the flow strength of the wall σ_w or when

$$\sigma_x = \sigma_w = \frac{F_{d(\max)}}{2\pi r_1 t} = \sigma_f \ln\left(\frac{d_0}{d_1}\right) \tag{11.12}$$

Let us now examine the drawing limit. Since the circumference of the wall is constrained by the punch from shrinkage, plane strain prevails, where $\varepsilon_y = 0$, and so the limit drawing ratio (LDR $= d_{0(\max)}/d_1$) is governed by the ratio of the two plane-strain flow strengths, that is, σ_w of the cup wall and σ_f of the flange, as follows:

$$\beta = \frac{\sigma_w\,(\varepsilon_y = 0)}{\sigma_f\,(\varepsilon_z = 0)} = \ln\,(\text{LDR}) \tag{11.13}$$

where $\beta =$ the ratio of the plane-strain flow strength in the wall of the cup, σ_w ($\varepsilon_y = 0$), to that in the flange, σ_f ($\varepsilon_y = 0$) [10.17].

For the isotropic case where no texturing occurs during drawing and for an ideally plastic material assumed, $\sigma_f = \sigma_w$, and $\beta = 1$, and Eq. (11.13) predicts LDR $= e = 2.72$. In actual practice, LDR is nearer to 2.1 to 2.2, since friction and bending are neglected in the foregoing. Correction for these losses of work may be made by introducing a factor for the deformation efficiency η. The actual

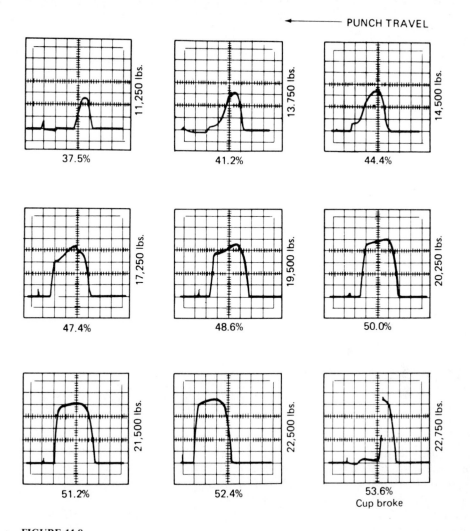

FIGURE 11.8
Oscillograph trace showing the variation of punch load (force) with punch travel for different percentage reductions, $\%R = [(d_0 - d_1)/d_0]100$. (Note that the direction of punch travel is from right to left.) [10.8, p. 122].

maximum axial drawing force and stress for an ideally plastic material would be

$$F_{d(max)(a)} = \frac{2\pi r_1 \sigma_f}{\eta} \ln \frac{d_0}{d_1}$$ (11.14)

and

$$\sigma_{x(a)} = \frac{\sigma_f}{\eta} \ln \frac{d_0}{d_1}$$ (11.15)

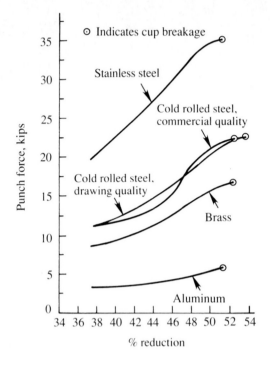

FIGURE 11.9
Experimental variation of the drawing force F with percentage reduction = $[(d_0 - d_1)/d_0]100$ in the deep drawing of cups for different sheetmetal materials [10.8, p. 122].

The corresponding relation for LDR would be given by

$$\ln(\text{LDR}) = \eta\beta \tag{11.16}$$

The efficiency η varies with lubrication, hold-down pressure, sheet thickness, and die lip radius. A typical value can be estimated from the fact that the LDR values for relatively isotropic materials with $\beta = 1$ are in the range of 2.1 to 2.2, which gives with $\eta = 0.74$ to 0.79 [10.17].

For an ideally plastic material having planar anisotropy, the Hill theory predicts that

$$\beta = \sqrt{\frac{(R+1)}{2}} \tag{11.17}$$

and so Eq. (11.16) becomes

$$\ln(\text{LDR}) = \eta\sqrt{\frac{(R+1)}{2}} \cong \eta\sqrt{\frac{(\bar{R}+1)}{2}} \tag{11.18}$$

where R = the radially symmetric plastic strain ratio $\varepsilon_w/\varepsilon_t$
   $\bar{R}$ = the average plastic strain ratio (Eq. (11.3)) [10.17]

This theory predicts a much greater dependence of LDR on $\bar{R}$ than is confirmed by experiment.

Relating R and β is a very critical use of any theory of anisotropy. R, which is measured in a uniaxial tension test, is related to the slope $\partial\sigma_y/\partial\sigma_x$ of the yield locus on that loading path. The following relation

$$\left(\frac{\partial\sigma_y}{\partial\sigma_x}\right)_{(\sigma_y=0)} = \frac{(R+1)}{R} \tag{11.19}$$

can be derived from the normality principal and constancy of volume and does not depend on the yield criterion. β, on the other hand, is the ratio of flow stresses under still two different loading paths as shown in Fig. 11.10. Small deviations of the yield locus from elliptical shape assumed in the Hill theory would cause substantial error in Eq. (11.19), and also the LDR is very sensitive to β. Therefore, even though the Hill theory may reasonably describe the shape of the yield locus, for most purposes, it may lead to serious errors in theories of drawability [11.1].

Although there is much scatter in the data mentioned above, as shown in Fig. 11.11, the following relationship for β fits better the experimental data for various symmetric textures for FCC metals than that obtained with the Hill theory:

$$\beta = \left(\frac{2R}{R+1}\right)^{0.27} \tag{11.20}$$

This relationship does not agree at all with Eq. (11.17) from Hill, which predicts $\beta \to \infty$ as $R \to \infty$ rather than $\beta = 1.23$ as $R \to \infty$ as shown in Fig. 11.11 [11.1].

The effects of strainhardening (workhardening) can be incorporated into the previous analysis by use of some constitutive equation such as the Ludwik-Hollomon power law, $\sigma = K\varepsilon^n$. Since these equations are rather complex the mathematical details will not be included here, but only the results. The plot of

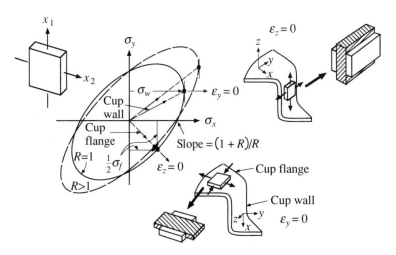

FIGURE 11.10
Schematic yield loci showing important loading paths in deep drawing. The solid figure is for an isotropic material ($R = 1$) and the dashed curve is for an anisotropic material with planar isotropy ($R > 1$) [3.15].

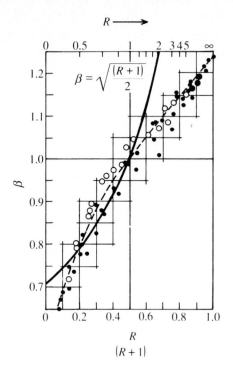

FIGURE 11.11
The calculated relation of R and β for radially symmetric sheets deforming by $\langle 110 \rangle$ [111] or $\langle 111 \rangle$ [110] slip. The solid points are for textures with a single (hkl) plane parallel to the sheet. Open circles are for textures with varying proportions of [100], [110], and [111] lying nearly parallel to the sheet. The dashed line trend through the calculated points is $\beta = [2R/(R+1)]^{0.27}$ while the solid line is from Hill's theory, Eq. (11.17) [11.1, p. 86].

the drawing (punch) force F_d, normalized by the wall strength $F_{w(max)}$ versus the normalized punch stroke $h/h_{(max)}$, is shown in Fig. 11.12 for several levels of the strainhardening exponent n, at constant deformation efficiency η of 1 or 100 percent. It can be seen that the maximum punch force is reached later in the stroke as n increases, which is more realistic as can be seen by comparing the curves in Fig. 11.12 [10.17].

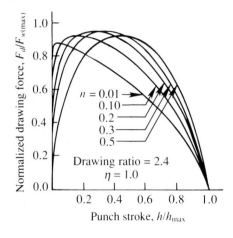

FIGURE 11.12
Calculated variation of drawing force with stroke h. The drawing force is normalized by the wall strength and the punch stroke by the final cup height. Note that the maximum punch force is reached later as the n value increases [11.1, p. 82].

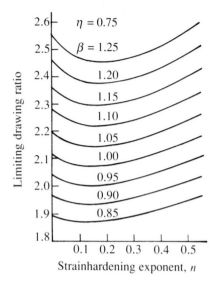

FIGURE 11.13
Calculated values of the limiting drawing ratio (LDR) for different strainhardening exponents with $\eta = 0.75$ [11.1, p. 83].

Figure 11.13 shows the calculated variation of LDR with the strainhardening exponent n for several levels of β at a constant η of 0.75. It can be seen that the effect of n is rather minor [10.17].

11.1.3 Earing

The top edges of drawn cups are usually not completely even. The edges along the perimeters of the tops of the cups are often wavy, consisting of crests and valleys as shown in Fig. 11.14. These projections along the top edge of a drawn cup are called *ears*. Four ears are most common, but occasionally two, six, or even eight ears may be found. Earing is due to planar anisotropy, and correlates well with the angular variation of R. At angular positions with low R-values, more thickening occurs, so that the wall heights are lower. At positions of high R, the walls are thinner and higher. The ear height and position correlate well

FIGURE 11.14
Earing behavior of cups made from three different copper sheets. Arrow indicates the rolling direction of the sheets. (*From D. V. Wilson and R. D. Butler, J. Inst. Met., Vol. 90, 1961–1962.*)

with the parameter called planar anisotropy defined (see Fig. 10.2) as [10.17]

$$\Delta R = \frac{R_0 + R_{90} - 2R_{45}}{2} \tag{11.21}$$

When $\Delta R > 0$, ears form at 0 and 90°, while if $\Delta R < 0$, ear formation occurs near $\pm45°$. Earing is undesirable since more metal must be trimmed. Therefore the full benefit of a higher $\bar{R}$ value on the LDR may not be realized if ΔR is too large [10.17].

It is recommended that a good drawing material should exhibit less than 4 percent earing. Earing is very undesirable as it can lead to "clipping" in drawing or ironing operations. It can occur in cupping when at the end of the draw, the full blankholding force is concentrated on the tips of the ears. These tips can then be pinched off due to the high stress developing in them. The accumulation of these clippings in the die can create a very serious problem.

11.1.4 Tooling Considerations

Of course, such items to be discussed here in the design of a deep drawing die as die clearance, radius of curvature of the die lip, punch-nose radius, lubrication, and the blank hold-down pressure play an important role in deep drawing.

Die clearance is the gap left between the punch and die to allow for flow of the metal. It is commonly measured on one side rather than overall. Usually, it is made larger than the thickness of the sheet to allow the metal to thicken during drawing. Due to excessive thickening of metal during drawing, the clearance between the die and the punch may be as high as 125 percent of the blank thickness to prevent burnishing (ironing). If the clearance is equal to or less than the blank thickness, burnishing or ironing will occur.

The *die lip radius* is the radius over the top edge of the hole of the die or of the die ring as shown in Fig. 11.2(*b*). As the die radius is increased, a 35 percent decrease in the punch load may occur, as shown in Fig. 11.15, for a drawing quality steel. The general design rule is that the die radius should fall

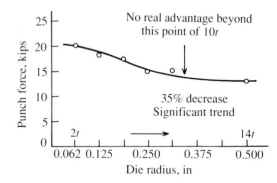

FIGURE 11.15
Graph shows the way that the punch load decreases with increase in the die lip radius in deep drawing of steel and levels off at a radius equal to about ten times the thickness of the sheetmetal [10.8, p. 115].

between $2t$ and $10t$, where t is the thickness of the metal. Any increase in the die radius beyond $10t$ does not result in a proportional decrease in the punch drawing force. The work expended in bending and unbending the sheet as it flows over the die lip increases with the ratio of the sheet thickness to radius of curvature of the die lip, causing higher drawing forces and lower LDRs. However, if the die radius is too large, wrinkling of the sheet can occur in the unsupported region between the die and the punch.

The *punch-nose radius* is the radius of the leading edge of a flat-bottomed punch. Its increase does not have a significant effect on the drawing force. It does have some effect if the die radius is also varied.

The effect of friction is twofold [10.17]. Lubrication of the flange is beneficial since it reduces the work expended to overcome external friction. On the other hand, high friction on the cylindrical surface of the punch can increase drawability. With any stretching of the wall, elements on the wall would move upward relative to the punch, causing a shear stress between wall and punch so that the bottom of the wall does not experience the full drawing force. This is important because the lower wall has not been strainhardened as much as regions further up the wall. Thus, roughened punches and differential lubrication can be used to increase drawability. With very low friction there is increased thinning of the cup bottom, and the failure site tends to shift downward into the punch radius. More viscous, heavier lubricants, however, may contribute to wrinkling of the flange.

11.1.5 Planning for Deep-Drawing Operations

The steps generally used in planning for a deep drawing operation, not necessarily in this order, are

1. Determining of the size and shape of the blank and determining the number of redraws needed
2. Designing the necessary blanking, drawing, and trimming dies as needed
3. Cutting out of the trial and final blanks
4. Selecting the presses needed
5. Making any trial runs
6. Making any necessary adjustments
7. Making out any process routing charts and issuing the production order

11.1.6 Determination of the Size and Shape of the Blank

If it is assumed that no change in thickness occurs in deep drawing, the surface area of the blank is made equal to the surface area of the cup to be formed plus any trimming allowance. For a cylindrical shaped cup made of sheetmetal with a small bottom-corner radius, no final flange and no trimming allowance, the trial diameter of a circular blank can be calculated as follows:

Circular blank area = cup bottom area + cup wall area

$$\frac{\pi D_0^2}{4} = \frac{\pi d^2}{4} + \pi dh \tag{11.22}$$

$$D_0 = \sqrt{d^2 + 4dh} \tag{11.23}$$

where D_0 = diameter of the blank, mm (in)
$\quad\quad d$ = diameter of the cup or punch mm (in)
$\quad\quad h$ = height of the cup, mm (in)

If the cup has a flange (rim) of width w, the trial diameter of the blank is

$$D_0 = \sqrt{(d + 2w)^2 + 4dh} \tag{11.24}$$

If the corner radii are large, and/or the part is irregular, the shape is broken down into areas that are easy to calculate manually, or a computer program may be used. For example, for manual calculation, a square or rectangular box might be subdivided into four quarter-cylinders and four flat panels. Allowance can also be made for thinning. The trim allowance per side varies from about 1.58 mm (0.062 in) for a 25.4 mm (1 in) cup diameter or less, to 12.5 mm (0.5 in) for a 152.4 mm (6 in) cup diameter. A 25.4 mm (1 in) trim allowance per side is used for larger cups. If a simpler, circular blank can be used with only a small loss of material, it would be used to reduce the cost of construction of the blanking die. (The blanking operation is discussed in Secs. 10.3.3 and 10.3.4.)

11.1.7   Design of a Blank for an Irregular Shaped Part by the Slip-Line Field Method [11.2, 11.3]

11.1.7.1   INTRODUCTION. The slip-line field method is discussed at some length in Sec. 4.4. The solution method, utilizing slip-line theory, comes down to determining a grid network of lines of maximum shear stress. The directions of the lines are always at right angles to each other, forming two orthogonal families of curves usually labeled α and β. As indicated in Sec. 4.4, the restrictions placed on the slip-line field method are (1) a rigid–perfectly plastic (nonstrainhardening), [see Fig. 3.1(a)], isotropic material is used conforming to the von Mises yield criterion, (2) time and strain rate do not affect the forming processes, (3) no transition exists between the plastic and the elastic material zones, and (4) only in-plane distortion occurs. A five-sided deep-drawn part with rounded corners and a flat bottom, as shown in the 3D computer graphics plot in Fig. 11.16, is used here as an example.

The examination of the plastic deformation process during deep drawing is restricted to the region between the given internal contour line and the external contour line corresponding to the outline of the blank to be determined, as shown in Fig. 11.17.

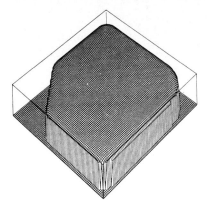

FIGURE 11.16
A five-sided deep drawn sheetmetal example part with rounded corners and a flat bottom, as shown in a three-dimensional computer graphics plot [11.3].

The internal contour line is defined by the shape of the cross section of the drawing punch, neglecting the punch radius. Taking only the actual flange into consideration seems to be justified since the deformation in the bottom and side walls is relatively small. Therefore, it is possible to reduce the three-dimensional process of deep drawing to a two-dimensional plane strain problem, so that the fundamental equations of plasticity can be applied.

11.1.7.2 FUNDAMENTAL EQUATIONS OF PLASTICITY [11.3]. In this example, the tensor of the strain rate distribution has the form

$$v = \dot{\varepsilon}_{ij} = \begin{bmatrix} \dot{\varepsilon}_x & \dot{\varepsilon}_{xy} & 0 \\ \dot{\varepsilon}_{xy} & \dot{\varepsilon}_y & 0 \\ 0 & 0 & 0 \end{bmatrix} \qquad (11.25)$$

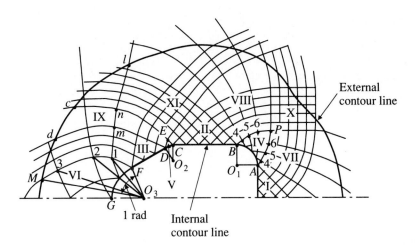

FIGURE 11.17
A slip-line field for the determination of the blank shape of the drawn part in Fig. 11.16 with the bottom shape indicated by *ABCDEFG* [11.2].

where

$$\dot{\varepsilon}_{ij} = \frac{1}{2}\left(\frac{\partial v_i}{\partial x_j} + \frac{\partial v_j}{\partial x_i}\right) \tag{2.15}$$

$$\dot{\varepsilon}_x = \frac{1}{2}\left(\frac{\partial v_x}{\partial y} + \frac{\partial v_y}{\partial x}\right) \tag{11.26}$$

Applying the von Mises yield criterion to a rigid–perfectly plastic, nonstrain-hardening material, one obtains

$$v = 0 \qquad \text{if} \qquad J_2 < k^2, \tag{11.27}$$

$$v = \lambda D \qquad \text{if} \qquad J_2 = k^2 \tag{11.28}$$

with

$$J_2 = -\sigma'_x \sigma'_y + \tau^2_{xy} \tag{11.29}$$

where $J_2 = I_2 =$ the second invariant in Hill's expression for yielding Eq. (2.8b)
$\quad k =$ yield stress in shear
$\quad \lambda =$ proportionality constant
$\quad \sigma' =$ deviatoric stress
$\quad D =$ the stress deviator is

$$D = \begin{bmatrix} \sigma'_x & \tau_{xy} & 0 \\ \tau_{xy} & \sigma'_y & 0 \\ 0 & 0 & 0 \end{bmatrix} \tag{11.30}$$

The condition of incompressibility is

$$\frac{\partial v_i}{\partial x_i} = 0 \tag{11.31}$$

and for plane strain

$$\frac{\partial v_x}{\partial x} + \frac{\partial v_y}{\partial y} = 0 \tag{11.32}$$

The equations for equilibrium are

$$\frac{\partial \sigma_x}{\partial x} + \frac{\partial \tau_{xy}}{\partial y} = 0 \tag{11.33a}$$

and

$$\frac{\partial \tau_{xy}}{\partial x} + \frac{\partial \sigma_y}{\partial y} = 0 \tag{11.33b}$$

The von Mises yield condition

$$J_2 = \tau^2_{xy} - \sigma'_x \sigma'_y = k^2 \tag{2.8b)(11.34}$$

If the diagonal terms of the stress deviator are substituted in the above equation for σ'_x and σ'_y, it takes the form

$$\tfrac{1}{4}(\sigma_x - \sigma_y)^2 + \tau^2_{xy} = k^2 \tag{11.35}$$

The yield condition of von Mises and Tresca are identical for plane strain and have the form

$$\frac{|\sigma_1 - \sigma_2|}{2} = k \tag{11.36}$$

where σ_1 and σ_2 are the principal stresses.

Since plane strain is assumed, the slip-line theory can be used as a solution method. Stresses have to satisfy the equilibrium equations (11.33) and the yield condition (11.35).

If boundary conditions for the stresses are assumed, a slip-line diagram can be constructed as shown in Fig. 11.17. If Fig. 4.22(b) is replotted in the positive σ direction, Fig. 11.18 is obtained, and with $\sigma_m = 2k\omega$, Eqs. (4.91) with the sign change become

$$\sigma_x = 2k\omega + k \sin 2\phi \tag{11.37a}$$

$$\sigma_y = 2k\omega - k \sin 2\phi \tag{11.37b}$$

$$\tau_{xy} = -k \cos 2\phi \tag{11.37c}$$

where $\omega = \sigma_m/2k$

ϕ = angle from the tangent to the α slip-line and the x axis

These expressions also satisfy the yield condition (11.35). Substituting the equations (11.37) into the equations for equilibrium (11.33), one obtains the basic set of equations in terms of unknown functions ω and ϕ. Equations (4.92a) and

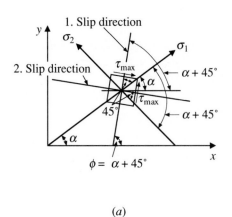

(a)

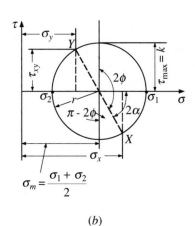

(b)

FIGURE 11.18
(a) Angle correlations between main normal stress and slip direction of a material element. (b) The state of stress as shown in a Mohr stress circle [11.2].

(*b*) become

$$\frac{\partial \omega}{\partial x} + \cos 2\phi \frac{\partial \phi}{\partial x} + \sin 2\phi \frac{\partial \phi}{\partial y} = 0 \qquad (11.38a)$$

$$\frac{\partial \omega}{\partial x} - \cos 2\phi \frac{\partial \phi}{\partial y} + \sin 2\phi \frac{\partial \phi}{\partial x} = 0 \qquad (11.38b)$$

Solving Eqs. (11.38) by means of the Method of Characteristics, one obtains

$$\frac{dy}{dx} = \tan \phi = \tan \left(\alpha + \frac{\pi}{4} \right) \qquad (11.39a)$$

$$\frac{dy}{dx} = -\cot \phi = \tan \left(\alpha - \frac{\pi}{4} \right) \qquad (11.39b)$$

where $\omega \pm \alpha = $ constant.

In review, some of the properties of slip-lines are (1) they form an orthogonal net, (2) the angle between two slip-lines of one family, where they are cut by a slip-line of the other family, remains constant and independent of the choice of the latter, and (3) any change of the state of stress can be expressed in a slip-line field by

$$\partial \sigma_m = 2k \, \partial \phi \qquad (11.40)$$

The change of the mean stress is proportional to the change of the tangent along a slip-line. If a segment of a slip-line is a straight line, the stresses along it do not change. We can then rewrite Geiringer equations (4.99) and (4.100) to give the change of the state of velocity in a slip-line field as

$$dv_1 - v_2 \, d\phi = 0 \qquad (11.41a)$$

and

$$dv_2 + v_1 \, d\phi = 0 \qquad (11.41b)$$

These equations imply that the strain rate along the shear directions is equal to zero as shown. By assuming boundary conditions, one can construct a valid slip-line field as shown in Fig. 11.17 and to derive the state of stresses and velocities.

11.1.7.3 DETERMINATION OF THE OUTLINE OF THE BLANK [11.2].

The outline of the flat bottom, as shown in Fig. 11.17, is regarded as the outline of constant velocity that is equal to the velocity of the punch movement. The tangential stress σ_t at the inside contour is zero, consequently the slip-lines cut across the outline at an angle less than 45°, so that the tangential stress $\sigma_t = 0$, the radial stress $\sigma_r = 2k$, and the shear stress $\tau = 0$.

The slip-line field is constructed by starting from the inside contour outline of the drawn part. Along the straight-line sections (zones I, II, and III opposite the straight contour lines), the slip-line field is straight-lined, and with its outline it makes an angle of 45°. Along the circular outline sections (zones IV, V, and

VI), the slip-line field consists of logarithmic spirals up to the boundary R_{max}. For zone IV (opposite AB on the right), $R_{max} = \overline{O_1 P}$. Beyond the boundary R_{max}, the slip-lines become straight lines as shown in zone X.

In zone IX (on the left) between curves c-C and d-D, the straight lines are transformèd into logarithmic spirals m-n, and then again they are transformed into straight lines n-l.

If a slip-line field is known, then the position of a point, such as point M at the left on the outer outline, can be determined. If the position of the unknown point M has been established, then the external outline can be determined. The outline of the optimum blank shape intersects the slip lines at an angle less than 45°. Along the external outline, no shear stresses are present, that is, $\tau = 0$.

11.1.7.4 DETERMINATION OF THE STRESS AND VELOCITY DISTRIBUTION IN DEEP DRAWING [11.2]. The stress distribution in the drawn part during deep drawing depends mainly on the shape of the part and the outline of the blank. The blanks of deep-drawn parts usually consist of a combination of circular arcs with different radii and of straight lines. The determination of the stresses is based on the established fact that, during deep drawing, upsetting of the material takes place in the flange.

The mean (m), tangential (t), and radial (r) stresses located at point M at the lower left of the external outline opposite the circular section on the inside contour are, respectively, $\sigma_{mM} = -k$, $\sigma_{tM} = -2k$, and $\sigma_{rM} = 0$.

By use of the stresses at point M, the stresses along the slip-line at the intersection with other slip-lines can then be found. Since, by Hencky's equation (4.91),

$$p + 2k\phi = C_\alpha = \text{constant} \tag{4.91}$$

$$\sigma_{mF} + 2k\phi_F = \sigma_{mM} + 2k\phi_M \tag{11.42}$$

$$\sigma_{mF} - \sigma_{mM} = 2k\,\Delta\phi \tag{11.43}$$

Since, in this case, $\Delta\phi = 1$ rad and $\sigma_{mM} = -k$, then

$$\sigma_{mF} + k = 2k$$

or

$$\sigma_{mF} = k,$$

the mean stress at point F.

The radial and tangential components at point F are $\sigma_{rF} = 2k$, and $\sigma_{tF} = 0$.

Since the angles subtended by $F1$, $F2$, and $F3$ are 15, 30, and 45°, the mean stresses at points 1, 2, and 3 may be established the same way as follows:

$$\sigma_{mF} - \sigma_{m1} = 2k(0.262) \qquad \sigma_{m1} = 0.476k$$

$$\sigma_{mF} - \sigma_{m2} = 2k(0.524) \qquad \sigma_{m2} = -0.048k$$

and

$$\sigma_{mF} - \sigma_{m3} = 2k(0.785) \qquad \sigma_{m3} = -0.0570k$$

TABLE 11.1
Computed stresses of the slip-line field for Fig. 11.17 [11.2]

	$\Delta\theta$ (grad)*	$\Delta\theta$ (rad)	σ_m	σ_r	σ_t
M	57.3	1.0	$-k$	0	$-2k$
F	0	0	k	$2k$	0
1	15	0.262	$0.476k$	$1.476k$	$-0.524k$
2	30	0.524	$-0.048k$	$0.952k$	$-1.048k$
3	45	0.785	$-0.570k$	$0.430k$	$-1.570k$
E	13	0.227	$0.546k$	$1.546k$	$-0.454k$
4	11.25	0.196	$0.608k$	$1.608k$	$-0.392k$
5	22.5	0.392	$0.216k$	$1.216k$	$-0.784k$
6	33.75	0.588	$-0.176k$	$0.824k$	$-1.176k$

* 1 grad $= 1.57 \times 10^{-2}$ rad $= 9.0 \times 10^{-1}$ degree

The components of stress in the various points can be obtained from Mohr's stress circle diagram as shown in Fig. 11.18. The computed stresses at some of the points of the slip-line field shown in Fig. 11.17 are listed in Table 11.1.

At the points A, B, C, D, and F along the internal outline, the stresses are identical, and the mean stresses are equal to k, that is,

$$\sigma_{mA} = \sigma_{mB} = \sigma_{mC} = \sigma_{mD} = \sigma_{mF} = k \qquad (11.44)$$

Therefore, in zones I, II, and III the tangential stresses are $\sigma_t = 0$, and the radial stresses are $\sigma_r = 2k$. A similar state of stress as at P also exists in zone X, whereas in zone XI, the state of stress is equal to E.

With the assistance of the known slip-line field, the velocity diagram (hodograph) can be drawn as shown in Fig. 11.19, the construction of which will not be discussed here.

By means of the velocity diagram and with the use of a known punch velocity, the displacement velocity of the material at any point can be determined. The radial velocity component V_P for a point P on a logarithmic spiral, for example in zones IV or VI of Fig. 11.19, can be computed from

$$V_P = v_P \left(\frac{r_i}{\rho}\right) \qquad (11.45)$$

where $v_P =$ punch velocity
$\qquad$ $r_i =$ radius of the internal contour line
$\qquad$ $\rho =$ flow radius

The next step is to obtain the stress distribution along the external outline. The mean stress can be calculated in a manner similar to the way they were calculated above for the inside contour line.

11.1.7.5 DETERMINATION OF THE DRAW BEAD REQUIREMENTS [11.3]. In addition to the determination of the size and shape of the blank, it is also possible

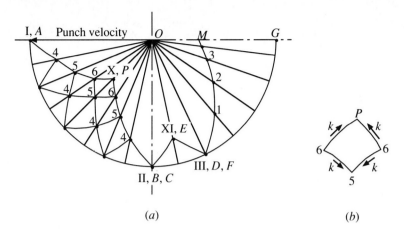

(a)

(b)

FIGURE 11.19
(a) Velocity vector diagram (hodograph) for the blank shown in Fig. 11.17. (b) An element of the blank surface [11.2].

by use of the slip-line field method to establish the position of the draw beads located in the blankholder. To reduce buckling in thin sheets, either the load on the blankholder may be increased within limits or the drawing ratio $(d_b - d_c)/d_b$ may be reduced. A more acceptable solution is to use draw bead insert sectors. (A draw bead for a circular part is shown later in Fig. 11.30.)

The mean, radial, and tangential stress distribution is shown in Fig. 11.20. By restricting the sliding of the sheet into the die, the material can be made to flow out of the round corners into the straight-lined, side-wall sections, thereby resulting in a more uniform stress in the material. From the stress distribution along the external outline of the blank as seen in Fig. 11.20 the locations, at which metal flow should be controlled, can be spotted. In sections with a relatively

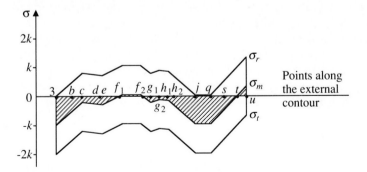

FIGURE 11.20
Distribution of the mean, radial, and tangential stresses along the external outline of the blank, which for this graph lies inside the outer contour shown in Fig. 11.17, passing through point 3 and paralleling the outer contour shown in Fig. 11.17 [11.2].

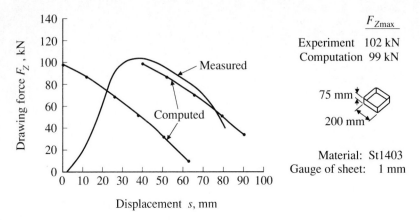

FIGURE 11.21
Load versus displacement characteristics. The fact that a rigid ideally plastic material model was used explains why the drawing force maximum is located at the beginning of the process rather than later as in the actual process [11.3].

high radial stress σ_r the flow of material should be restricted such as at the arcs b to h_2 and s to u. In the sections with high tangential stress σ_t, such as at the arcs 3 to b and h_2 to s, the material flow should be increased by increasing the die lubrication or the die clearance.

The foregoing hand-calculator method has been extended for use with a computer by use of a computer Fortran program called PLATIN2, whose use will be discussed in Sec. 12.1.4 [11.3]. By use of this program, the force of deformation can be calculated, while taking into consideration the friction and bending forces. Figure 11.21 shows a comparison of the computed and the experimental load versus displacement curve. The fact that a rigid–perfectly plastic material is used in the calculations explains why the maximum of the drawing force is located at the beginning of the drawing process, whereas in the actual process it appears later, as was shown schematically in Figs. 11.6 and 11.7.

In concluding this section, it might be said that, because of the good agreement with other methods of calculation and with experimental results, the slip-line field method can be used to determine the size and shape of blanks for deep drawing. For more complicated shapes, it is the only way to establish the blank shape, other than by employing empirical formulas or carrying out tests.

11.1.8   Redrawing

Often a single drawing operation does not produce a cup of the desired depth, so that one or more redrawing operations are required with perhaps intermediate annealing operations. Of course, if one tries to draw too deep a cup with a single draw, the bottom will be pushed out of the partially formed cup or the the cup will fracture in its wall. Also, as the material is drawn, its tensile strength and

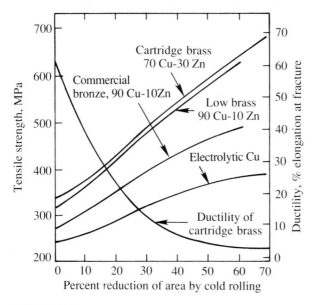

FIGURE 11.22
Tensile strength determined on sheet specimens of copper and copper-base alloys that had been previously subjected to various amounts of cold rolling as indicated on the abscissa [11.19].

hardness increase and its ductility decreases as a result of strainhardening, much as shown in Fig. 11.22 for cold rolling.

There are two common ways by means of which the redrawing operations may be accomplished, as illustrated in Fig. 11.1(b) and (d): (1) direct or conventional redrawing, and (2) reverse redrawing.

At first glance reverse redrawing seems to be a more severe metalforming operation than direct redrawing, but the opposite is true. During direct redrawing, the sheetmetal is bent in the opposite direction at the blankholder to that of the die radius, so that straightening must occur between the two radii. When reverse redrawing, the sheetmetal is bent in the same direction at both the inner and outer die radii. Often the die ring has a single 180° radius on its (top) edge, so that straightening between radii is eliminated and less workhardening occurs, with reduced punch loads and less wall thinning.

11.1.9 Calculation of Percentage Reduction in Deep Drawing

Although the drawability of a sheetmetal to form a cylindrical cup may be expressed either as the ratio of the blank diameter to the punch diameter D_0/d_0 or as the percentage reduction in area, which will be seen to be equivalent to the percentage reduction in diameter, the latter will be used here to designate the percentage reduction and the former the drawability. If $\bar{r} > 1$, the material resists thinning and has good drawability (stretchability). If $\bar{r} < 1$, the material thins easily and has poor drawability (stretchability).

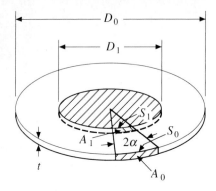

FIGURE 11.23
Drawing used for calculating the percentage reduction in area, %R, in deep drawing in which the cross-sectional area of the edge A_0 is reduced to A_1.

The percentage reduction in metalworking is calculated on the basis of the cross-sectional area. If A_0 is the cross-sectional area of the outer edge of the sector of the flange (or blank) and A_1 is the cross-sectional area of the edge of the inner sector of the flange (or the blank sector) and S_0 and S_1 are the lengths of the arcs of the outer and inner sectors as shown in Fig. 11.23, then

$$S_0 = 2\alpha r_0 = D_0\alpha \qquad (11.46)$$

and

$$S_1 = D_1\alpha \qquad (11.47)$$

where α is the apex half-angle of the sector in radians. Then $A_0 = \alpha D_0 t$ and $A_1 = \alpha D_1 t$. If the thickness t remains constant, then the percentage reduction in area is

$$\%R = \frac{(\alpha D_0 t - \alpha D_1 t)100}{\alpha D_0 t} = \left(\frac{D_0 - D_1}{D_0}\right)100 \qquad (11.48)$$

which is the same as the percentage reduction in diameter. The calculation is usually made on the basis of the cup inside diameter or punch diameter. Sometimes it is made on the basis of the mean diameter of the cup wall.

The drawing limit occurs near a reduction of 47 to 50 percent depending on the materials and conditions. The empirical drawing limits are given in Table 11.2 for single draws.

TABLE 11.2
Empirical drawing limits for some annealed common metals

Metal	Percentage reduction
Austenitic stainless steel	50
70/30 brass	50
Copper	45
Low-carbon steel	45
Aluminum	40

Cumulative reduction in area of multiple draws may be calculated as follows. Let us assume three reductions from D_0 to D_3. Then the total reduction after draw no. 3 may be obtained as follows:

$$\%R_3 = \left(\frac{D_0 - D_3}{D_0}\right)100 = \left(1 - \frac{D_3}{D_0}\right)100 = \left[1 - \left(\frac{D_3}{D_2}\right)\left(\frac{D_2}{D_1}\right)\left(\frac{D_1}{D_0}\right)\right]100$$

but

$$\frac{D_3}{D_0} = \left(\frac{D_3}{D_2}\right)\left(\frac{D_2}{D_1}\right)\left(\frac{D_1}{D_0}\right)$$

Then

$$R_1 = \left(\frac{D_0 - D_1}{D_0}\right) = \left(1 - \frac{D_1}{D_0}\right) \qquad \frac{D_1}{D_0} = (1 - R_1)$$

etc., so that

$$\%R_{\text{total}} = [1 - (1 - R_1)(1 - R_2)(1 - R_3)]100 \tag{11.49}$$

If three reductions of 40, 20, and 10 percent are assumed, the total reduction is

$$\%R_{\text{total}} = [1 - (1 - 0.40)(1 - 0.20)(1 - 0.10)]100$$
$$\%R_{\text{total}} = 56.8\% \tag{11.50}$$

The inside diameter of a cup, deep drawn from an 18 in (457.2 mm) blank, can then be calculated by use of the total reduction as follows:

$$D_3 = D_0(1 - R_3) = 18(1 - 0.568)$$
$$D_3 = 7.8 \text{ in } (198 \text{ mm})$$

11.1.10   Ironing

In conventional deep-drawing operations, the clearance between the punch and die is usually about 130 to 150 percent of the thickness of the blank. When the clearance is significantly smaller than this range, a forced reduction in the thickness of the cup wall takes place during the drawing operation, as shown in Fig. 11.24(a). This operation is regarded as simultaneous deep drawing with ironing. When the ironing is performed as a separate operation after deep drawing, as shown in Fig. 11.24(b), it is called *conventional* (or *separated*) *ironing*. It has been shown that during ironing the drawing ratio (D_0/d_0) is increased only over a narrow range of ironing reductions. When the clearance between the punch and die is less than 85 percent of the blank thickness, the limiting drawing ratio is decreased. The wall thickness of the cup is more uniform after conventional ironing than in simultaneous deep drawing and ironing [11.4]. Ironing in general yields a more uniform wall thickness and consequently an increased height. Often, only the top of the wall is ironed. This is achieved by specifying the clearance between the punch and die lip so that no ironing occurs until the thickened material on the outer part of the flange flows over the die lip. Ironing adds to

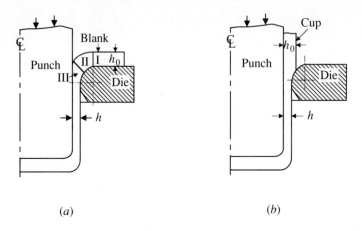

(a)   (b)

FIGURE 11.24
Difference in thickness reduction processes in (a) a simultaneous deep drawing and ironing operation, and (b) conventional ironing, in which the wall thickness is reduced by ironing after deep drawing [11.4].

the total punch load, but if it occurs only late in the draw cycle after the maximum punch force is reached, it does not affect drawability, as shown in Fig. 11.25. Excessive ironing, however, may cause a second maximum in the drawing force, thereby reducing the limiting drawing ratio.

The maximum ironing reduction per pass, $[(t_0 - t_1)/t_0]_{max}$, decreases with strainhardening exponent n as shown in Fig. 11.26, but depends only slightly on $\bar{R}$ the average plastic anisotropic strain ratio (see Eq. (11.3)). Here r_0 is the initial blank radius, r_1 is the radius of the cup being ironed, t_0 is the initial sheet thickness (which is assumed not to change during drawing and redrawing), and t_1 is the wall thickness after ironing. With high R-values, there is less wall thickening in the initial drawing and redrawing steps, so smaller ironing reductions are required to achieve the same wall thickness [10.17].

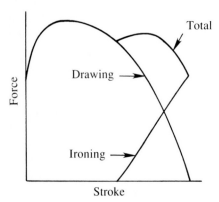

FIGURE 11.25
The graph shows the variation of drawing force with punch travel or stroke when ironing occurs late in the draw. Drawability will be decreased if so much ironing occurs that the second maximum is greater than the first [10.17, p. 289].

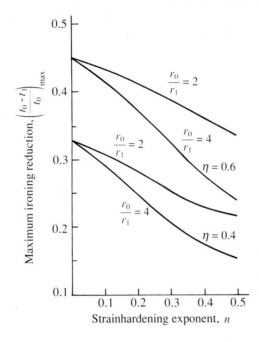

FIGURE 11.26
Calculated dependence of maximum ironing reduction per pass upon strainhardening exponent n, efficiency η, and prior drawing and redrawing reduction r_0/r_1, where r_0 is the initial blank radius and r_1 is the radius of the cup being ironed [11.1, p. 43].

11.1.11 Edge Conditions in Deep Drawing

When a blank is sheared out or cut out, two changes occur. First, the edge is strainhardened (cold workhardened) during the shearing or cutting operation, and second, a burr or ridge is formed at the edge. Since only the edge of the blank is strainhardened, its ductility is decreased, and during subsequent deformation during forming it may crack, forming a stress raiser. Burrs also act as notches at the edge of the blank, and induce cracking during forming. Dull shearing and blanking dies and improper clearance contribute to burr formation. When the burr height and the amount of cold working are kept to a minimum, the probability of producing a good part is greatly increased. Edge condition analysis is covered in Sec. 11.2.12.6.

11.2 ANALYSIS AND EVALUATION OF SHEETMETAL FORMABILITY

11.2.1 Definition and Scope

Formability has been defined as the ability of a sheetmetal to be deformed by a specific sheetmetal forming process from its original shape to a defined final shape without failure [11.5]. The three key elements of this definition are: (1) material, (2) process, and (3) shape. All three of these key elements must be considered simultaneously in any study of formability, because they all interact in the process of forming parts.

In this discussion, the following topics are to be considered: (1) introduction to forming limit diagrams (FLD), (2) methods of determining FLDs, (3) typical forming limit diagrams, (4) strain paths and strain limits for failure, (5) example of the calculation procedure for strain limits to failure, (6) superposition of severity curves on the FLD, (7) strain distribution in the forming of parts, (8) simulative cup tests, and (9) shape analysis including its application, adaptation, and optimization.

11.2.2   Introduction to Forming Limit Diagrams

In 1946 Gensamer reported that when sheetmetal is subjected to a biaxial state of stress the value of the maximum strain at instability varies with the strain ratio. During the early 1960s, Keeler collected information on the principal surface strains at the onset of fracture from a number of biaxial stretching experiments and from many industrial stampings and noted that the value of the major principal strain is a function of the minor principal strain. He plotted the values of the major strain against the minor strain and obtained what he termed the forming limit diagram (FLD). Keeler considered that the forming limit curve (FLC) represents the boundary between the strain combinations which produce instability and/or fracture and those that are permissible in forming operations. He suggested that by using the FLD it should be possible to establish, with much confidence, the proximity to failure in biaxial stretching [11.6]. (When reference is being made to the curve as such, it will be called the *forming limit curve* (FLC). However, when the entire diagram is being considered, it will be referred to as the *forming limit diagram* (FLD). When fracture is used as the criterion for failure, the diagram will be called the *fracture limit diagram*.)

Keeler's work was limited to the conditions when both the principal surface strains were positive. In 1968 Goodwin extended Keeler's work to the situations where the major principal surface strain is positive and the minor principal strain is negative. This composite diagram as shown in Fig. 11.27 is now well known as the Keeler-Goodwin forming limit diagram [11.6]. Either engineering strain represented here by e or true or logarithmic strain represented by ε may be used.

The forming limit diagram for a particular sheetmetal material is a graphic representation illustrating the limits of the principal strain, which it may suffer without failure, in a forming process. The criteria of failure or performance are (1) localized necking (grooving), (2) fracture, and (3) wrinkling. A schematic FLD, with various linear strain paths, the fracture limits and strain states for wrinkling for a square-cup, and pertinent test information superimposed, is shown in Fig. 11.28.

More realistically, because of variations in the material, testing procedure, etc., the forming limit will fall into a marginal zone as shown in Fig. 11.29; however, FLDs are usually drawn as curves rather than as zones. A linear and a nonlinear strain path are also shown in the figure, the former showing a safe limiting strain at point 3 and the latter showing a limiting strain at point D, which would have a high probability of failure according to the failure criterion being

Forming limit diagram

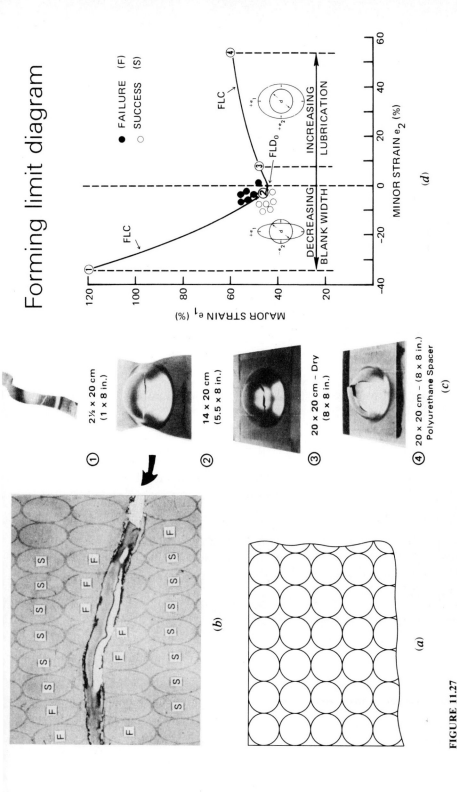

FIGURE 11.27

Method of obtaining a conventional forming (or fracture) limit diagram (FLD) showing (a) circle grid before deformation, (b) circle grid in the vicinity of the fracture after deformation, (c) the strip test specimens used, and (d) the resulting forming (fracture) limit diagram. (The major axes of the ellipses are parallel to the direction of the greater elongation. If the area of the original circle before deformation is less than the area of the ellipse after deformation, the thickness of the sheet has changed at the point since the volume remains constant during deformation (Eqs. (2.48), (2.69), and (2.82).) (*Courtesy of General Motors Research Laboratories.*)

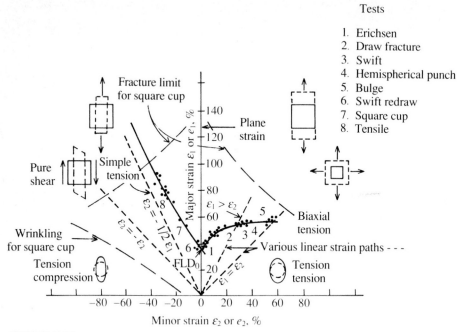

Tests

1. Erichsen
2. Draw fracture
3. Swift
4. Hemispherical punch
5. Bulge
6. Swift redraw
7. Square cup
8. Tensile

FIGURE 11.28
Schematic composite forming limit diagram (FLD) constructed from several types of laboratory tests. Each type of test provides a different range of major strain versus minor strain values. A series of strips of various widths drawn over a hemispherical punch can provide the full range of strain deformation with negative or positive minor strain [11.20].

used. As will be seen in Sec. 11.2.5, the path has a profound effect on the limit strain and the FLD.

The FLD that serves as a guide in analyzing sheetmetal deformation processes is presently the best method available for that purpose. FLDs were first obtained experimentally, and all of the ones used to analyze production problems are still obtained empirically. However, recently several attempts have been made to evaluate them on the basis of material parameters and certain criteria for failure such as the limiting strain to localized necking and to fracture. The optimum strain condition that exists at the point of failure will be known as the *limit* or *limiting strain*. A distinction is now made between the FLDs (1) based on localized thinning or necking as a criterion for failure and (2) that based on fracture, although at times the distinction is confounded. Also, a distinction is made between FLDs obtained primarily from (1) rigid hemispherical punch tests, (2) in-plane stretching tests, and (3) hydraulic bulge tests.

11.2.3 Methods of Determining FLDs and the Test Procedure Used

The FLD could be obtained by measuring at critical areas the major and minor strains from deformed circles that have been previously electoetched or imprinted

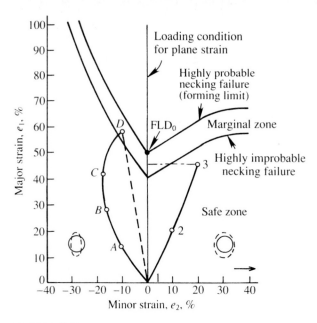

FIGURE 11.29

Forming limit diagram showing highly probable and highly improbable forming limit curves creating the marginal zone. A linear strain or slightly concave path (123) and a nonlinear strain path (*ABCD*), and grid circles before and after deformation are also shown [11.18].

on the surfaces of a number of different types of stampings possessing different drawing severity and made of the same material, but this would be a rather inefficient and time-consuming way of doing it. An engineered test method as described in the foregoing would, of course, be a very much preferred method.

The method test proposed by Nakazima and developed by Hecker, for determining experimental FLDs, is now used by many laboratories. In this method the biaxial state of stress is varied by stretching rectangular strips (blanks) of different widths, such as shown in Fig. 11.27, and with different interface lubrication over a rigid hemispherical punch with the ends of the strip being held down by flat (ungrooved) hold-down pads. After each blank is loaded to failure, the major and minor engineering strains are obtained from measurements made of the distortion of small circles (2.5 mm ≅ 0.1 in) of a circular grid etched or imprinted on the surface of the sheet beforehand as shown in Fig. 11.27. The major and minor *limiting* engineering strains are plotted to give a skewed V-shaped curve as shown in Fig. 11.27. This arrangement is typical of that now being used, and the resulting diagram will be referred to here as a *conventional forming limit diagram.*

Other methods of obtaining forming limit-type diagrams are also used. In one of these methods proposed by Hecker uses strips of different widths firmly clamped with a grooved hold-down without any drawing-in and with a hemispherical punch as shown in Fig. 11.30. Measurement is made of the limiting

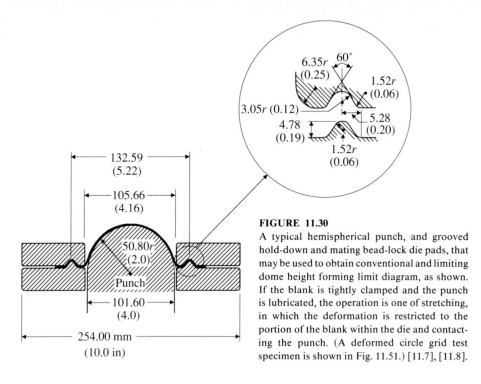

6.35r 60°
(0.25)

1.52r
(0.06)

3.05r (0.12)

4.78
(0.19)

5.28
(0.20)

1.52r
(0.06)

132.59
(5.22)

105.66
(4.16)

50.80r
(2.0)

Punch

101.60
(4.0)

254.00 mm
(10.0 in)

FIGURE 11.30

A typical hemispherical punch, and grooved hold-down and mating bead-lock die pads, that may be used to obtain conventional and limiting dome height forming limit diagram, as shown. If the blank is tightly clamped and the punch is lubricated, the operation is one of stretching, in which the deformation is restricted to the portion of the blank within the die and contacting the punch. (A deformed circle grid test specimen is shown in Fig. 11.51.) [11.7], [11.8].

dome height (LDH), and the ratio of the limiting dome height to the punch radius is plotted against the minor strain as shown in Fig. 11.31. The conveniently-measured dome height at failure, which combines the effects of the forming limit with the appropriate strain distribution for the strain-state and which is still a good measure of stretchability, may be used in lieu of the major strain. A forming limit diagram obtained in this way may be better called the *limiting dome height diagram.* Both of the above types are forming limit diagrams [11.7], [11.8]. If the strips are clamped tightly with no drawing-in and both the longitudinal and lateral strains are obtained from previously inscribed circular grids, the diagram would be classed as a *partial* forming limit diagram. Along with the LDH test, a circular grid can be inscribed on the test specimen and a partial FLD obtained. Still other FLD diagrams are obtained by biaxial stretching of flat sheets in free space. In some cases, fracture is used as the criterion as an index of the limiting strain; in others, true strain is plotted instead of engineering strain, etc. [11.7], [11.8].

The objective of an FLD test is to simulate the various states of strain that are encountered in sheetmetal press-forming operations. These strain systems might vary anywhere from balanced, biaxial tension ($e_1 = e_2$) through plane-strain loading ($e_2 = 0$) to tension-compression ($+e_1$ and $-e_2$) systems as shown in Fig. 11.28 for linear strain paths. When both strain components are tensile, the test is a measure of stretchability. When the sheet metal slips between the hold-down pad and slips or is drawn into the die as in drawing of a cup, one strain component

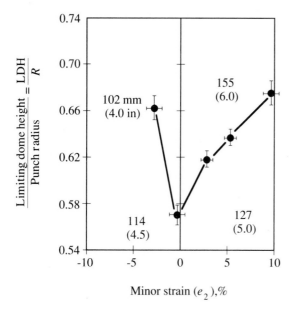

FIGURE 11.31

Limiting dome heights vary with the critical minor strain, as determined by test strips with different widths w, indicated in mm and the same length 155 mm (6.0 in). Ranges on each data point represent results of four separate tests [11.7], [11.8].

is tensile and the other is compressive. The test can be used as a measure of ductility. The drawing-in of narrow-strip test specimens can be longitudinal from the clamped ends or lateral from the unclamped longitudinal edges of the strip. When smooth, flat (ungrooved) hold-down pads are used as shown in Fig. 11.27, the drawing-in is usually both longitudinal and lateral. When a grooved, bead-lock hold-down is used, the drawing-in is expected to be only lateral. The punch is usually unlubricated in the dome-height test to minimize the lateral draw-in.

One of the disadvantages of the test procedure using smooth, flat, ungrooved hold-down pads is that it is not possible to control or reproduce accurately the relative amounts of stretching versus drawing-in; consequently, inconsistent results may be obtained. The objective of the rigid, hemispherical punch tests is to control the relative amount of lateral drawing-in by use of test strips of different widths and/or the amount of lubrication used. For many sheetmetal forming operations, the strain states for localized necking fall near the plane-strain state in the region expressed by $-10\% < e_2 < +20\%$.

11.2.4 Typical Forming Limit Diagrams

Conventional FLD for (1) an aluminum-killed, low-carbon steel, (2) a 70-30 α-brass, and (3) 2036-T4 aluminum alloy are shown in Fig. 11.32.

Keeler and Brazier have shown that the conventional forming limit diagrams for low-carbon and some other common steels have essentially the same shape. The only principal difference is its position on the e_1 axis, i.e., the intercept FLD_0 on the e_1 axis. They also showed that the intercept of the FLC with the major axis FLD_0 is a function of the sheetmetal thickness and its yield strength, as shown in Figs. 11.33 and 11.34. The variation of FLD_0 with the strainhardening

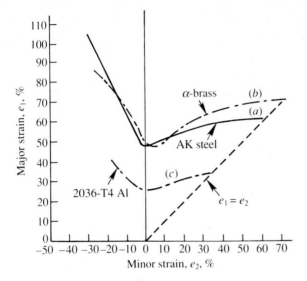

FIGURE 11.32
Forming limit curves (FLC) for
(a) aluminum-killed (AK) low-
carbon steel, (b) 70-30 α-brass,
and (c) 2036-T4 aluminum alloy.
(The higher the curve the better
the formability. Also, it should be
noted that the diagram is not
symmetric, so that a
comprehensive minor strain gives
a higher major strain than an
equal positive minor strain.)

exponent n and with the yield strength for high-strength steel for different
thicknesses is shown in Fig. 11.35. They also showed that the FLD for steel is
affected only slightly (if at all) by variables such as composition, elongation,
specimen orientation relative to the direction of rolling of the sheet, plastic strain
ratio (r), and the nature of the inclusions. However, because these variables
strongly influence the value of n, their effect on the forming characteristics is
indirect, in limiting dome height.

Partial forming limit diagrams obtained from the dome height test by plotting
major and minor strains from grid circles for some low-carbon steels and
aluminum alloys are shown in Fig. 11.36. The ratio of limiting critical dome
height (LDH) normalized with respect to the punch radius R is plotted against
the minor engineering strain e_2^* in Fig. 11.37 for low-carbon steels, brass, and
aluminum alloys. To obtain the data for Fig. 11.37, every sample is clamped
firmly to prevent longitudinal drawing-in along the strip, and the dome height
at maximum load and the critical minor strains, e_2^*, in the neck due to lateral
drawing-in are measured. The compositions of these materials are given in Table
11.3 and the tensile properties and characteristics are given in Table 11.4. In
general, LDH diagrams have much the same configuration as the conventional
FLD diagrams, in which the major strain obtained from grid circles is plotted
on the ordinate. The slopes of the former, however, are quite different as may
be seen by comparing Figs. 11.36 and 11.37, because of the strain distribution
over the dome surface. Except for 70-30 α-brass in Fig. 11.37, LDH curves show
a minimum in-plane strain $(e_2^* = 0)$ [11.7], [11.8].

Because identical blank widths do not produce identical minor strain values
for different materials, e_2^* in the stretched dome is plotted as a function of the
transverse constraint of the blank. Transverse constraint is defined as the blank

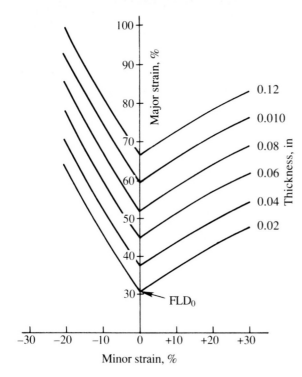

FIGURE 11.33
Variation of forming limit curves
with thickness for low-carbon steel
of constant composition [11.18].

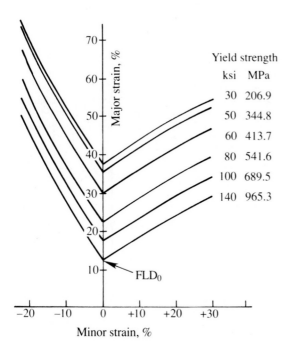

FIGURE 11.34
Variation of forming limit curves for
steels of different yield strengths for
constant thickness of 0.04 in
(1.02 mm) [11.18].

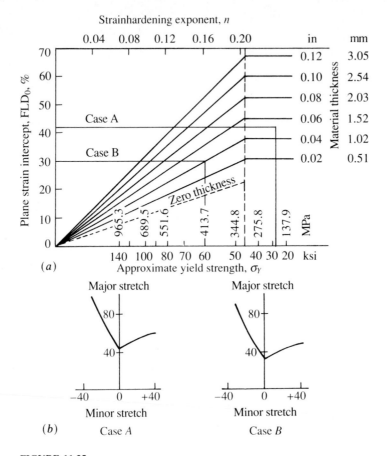

FIGURE 11.35

(*a*) Relationship between the plane-strain intercept (FLD$_0$) and *n* and the yield strength of steel as a function of metal thickness. FLD$_0$ depends only on the thickness for values of σ_Y greater than about 48 ksi (330 MPa). (*b*) Shows examples (case *A* and case *B*) of how the approximate FLDs can be obtained for steel by obtaining the FLD$_0$ for a given thickness by use of (*a*) and slipping the FLCs along the plane strain axis [11.18].

width *W* normalized with respect to the diameter of the clamping bead circle $D = 132$ mm (Fig. 11.30). Values of $W/D < 1.0$ indicate lateral drawing-in. Values of $W/D \geq 1$ indicate no lateral drawing-in and are plotted at 1.0 as shown in Fig. 11.38 for aluminum-killed steel, brass, and an aluminum alloy. A W/D ratio of 0.85 would be equivalent to a minor strain e_2 of ≈ 0 percent for Al, -2.5 percent for 60–40 brass, and -7 percent for aluminum-killed, low-carbon steel [11.7], [11.8].

To apply this approach as a quality control tool one would need, as a reference, both the LDH curve and the transverse constraint plot (e_2^* versus W/D) for a given sheetmetal material. Through circle grid analysis, e_2 for the critical area of each part would be determined, and the specific dome test for

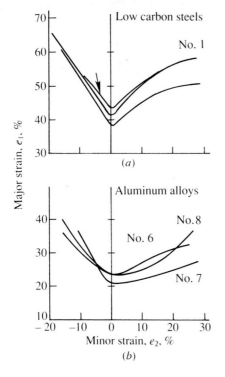

FIGURE 11.36
Partial forming limit curves showing forming characteristics of (*a*) low-carbon steels, and (*b*) aluminum alloys [11.7].

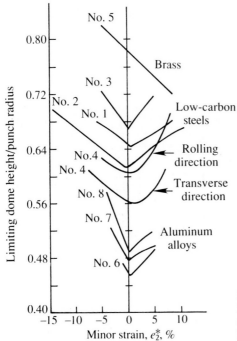

FIGURE 11.37
Limiting dome height (LDH) plots for a number of test materials indicate effects of minor strains [11.7].

TABLE 11.3
Characteristics of tested materials [11.7], [11.8]

Code	Steels*	Composition %							Thickness, mm
		C	S	P	Mn	Si	N†	Al	
1	DQ, killed	0.012	0.014	0.007	0.30	0.01	48	0.05	0.94
2	DQ, killed	0.049	0.016	0.003	0.34	0.01	246	0.05	0.81
3	DQ, rimmed	0.048	0.011	0.003	0.37	<0.01	28	0.002	0.78
4	Fe–Zn coated, killed	0.014	0.011	0.004	0.34	0.01	72	0.061	1.07

	Nonferrous alloys	Cu	Zn	Mn	Mg	Fe	Other	Thickness, mm
5	CR 70:30 brass	69.8	30.9	—	—	0.01	0.002 Al	0.95
6	2036-T4 Aluminum	2.68	0.05	0.25	0.01	0.29	0.35 Si	1.01
7	5085-O aluminum	0.06	0.02	0.04	6.16	0.19	0.07 Si	1.09
8	5182-O aluminum	0.03	0.03	0.36	3.91	0.22	0.09 Si	0.89

* DQ, drawing quality; CR, cold rolled.
† Parts per million.

TABLE 11.4
Tensile properties of tested materials [11.7], [11.8]

Code*	Yield strength, MPa (10³ psi)	Tensile strength, MPa (10³ psi)	Uniform Strain, %	Total Strain, %	n	n'(†)	m	r	ΔR(‡)	YPE,‖ %
1	106.2 (15.4)	298.5 (43.3)	28.4	48.3	0.281	—	0.010	2.23	0.65	0.0
2	172.8 (25.1)	296.2 (42.9)	24.3	43.1	0.215	—	0.016	1.84	0.69	0.0
3	213.4 (30.9)	306.4 (44.4)	26.7	44.2	0.235	—	0.016	1.20	—	1.5
4	266.0 (38.6)	337.0 (48.9)	20.4	33.9	0.172	—	0.010	0.89	-0.21	3.0
5	113.0 (16.4)	328.1 (47.6)	53.6	61.1	0.560	0.510	0.000	0.90	—	0.0
6	189.8 (27.5)	358.5 (52.0)	20.6	23.0	0.259	0.166	-0.005	0.77	-0.15	0.0
7§	139.5 (20.2)	320.3 (46.5)	25.1	27.6	0.325	0.266	0.009	0.76	-0.56	0.0
8§	142.4 (20.6)	335.3 (48.6)	22.8	25.3	0.330	0.240	-0.010	0.84	-0.52	1.2

* All properties are averaged according to $x = \frac{1}{4}(x_0 + 2x_{45} + x_{90})$; subscripts refer to 0°, 45°, and 90° to sheet rolling direction (see Fig. 10.2).
† n' terminal slope of the log σ versus log ε curve.
‡ $\Delta R = \frac{1}{4}(R_0 + R_{90} - 2R_{45})$.
§ Serrated flow curve.
‖ YPE, yield point elongation %.

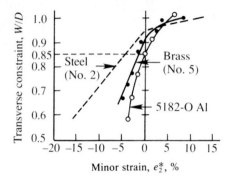

FIGURE 11.38
Critical minor strain rises with transverse constraint, defined as the blank width W normalized with respect to the diameter of the clamping bead circle D [11.7].

that part would then be designed. Blanks of appropriate size would then be cut, based on transverse constraint plots, and then punch tests would be run to check whether the incoming material meets the required LDH specifications. LDH curves and transverse constraint plots can provide guidelines for die and blank adjustments to take advantage of the effects of lateral drawing-in. This approach would significantly reduce the down-time in the shop [11.7].

11.2.5   Strain Paths and Strain Limits

Variation in the strain path has been shown to have a profound effect on the limit strain and consequently on the forming and fracture limit diagrams. A strain path may be defined as the locus of the coordinates of the major and minor strains of a small element of sheetmetal during loading. If the ratio of the major to minor strain is a constant as shown in Fig. 11.39, the strain path is said to be *proportional* or *linear*. If the strain path is parallel to the ε_1 axis, at which $\varepsilon_2 = 0$, the strain path is said to be *plane strain*. (Note that in the previous section e_1

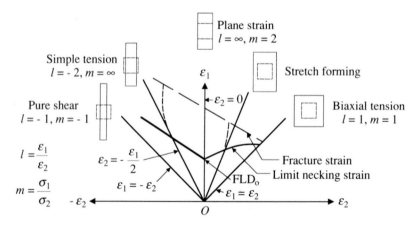

FIGURE 11.39
Schematic diagram showing the position of the forming limit strain curve and the fracture strain curve in principal strain [11.10].

and e_2 were used for the major and minor engineering strains. In this section ε_1 and ε_2 will be used for the major and minor true strains. e and ε are used more less interchangeably in conjunction with FLDs.)

Strain paths are considered here from the point of view of two applications: (1) the determination of the forming and fracture limit diagrams as shown in Fig. 11.39, and (2) the determination of the strain envelope such as for a square-cup part as shown in Fig. 11.40. Usually for single stage forming operations, strain

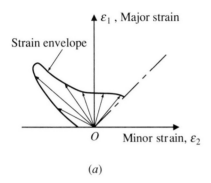

(a)

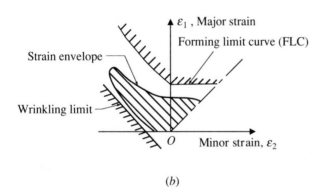

(b)

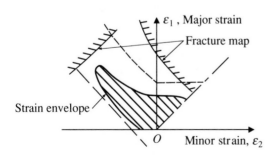

(c)

FIGURE 11.40
Schematic diagrams showing the following: (a) the envelope of the greatest achievable strains for any linear strain path for the deep drawing of a square cup, (b) the limiting strains for local necking (FLC) and for wrinkling in relation to the strain envelope, and (c) the limiting strains for fracture in relation to the strain envelope [11.21].

paths for the determination of forming and fracture limit diagrams are linear or slightly concaved toward the path of plane strain ($\varepsilon_2 = 0$) as shown in Fig. 11.29 for aluminum-killed low-carbon steel. Forming limit diagrams obtained for linear strain paths may be called *basic* FLDs as shown in Fig. 11.41(a). The limit strains for nonlinear strain paths may lie in relation to the FLC as shown in Fig. 11.41(b). The tests for all the data for the latter figure were performed on commercial quality deep-drawing low-carbon steel, and the data for the nonlinear strain paths were obtained by the Nakazima-Hecker type tests, in which rectangular specimens of varying widths were rigidly clamped at the ends and then stretched over a hemispherical punch with a sheet of PTFE as a lubricant. The limit strain for a linear plane strain path would fall at D, at which the major limit strain is 0.28, which is below 0.50 at B for the irregular strain path shown in Fig. 11.41(b). Also, for two stage straining where biaxial stretching is followed by uniaxial straining, the limit strain may fall at C, which is below the basic FLC.

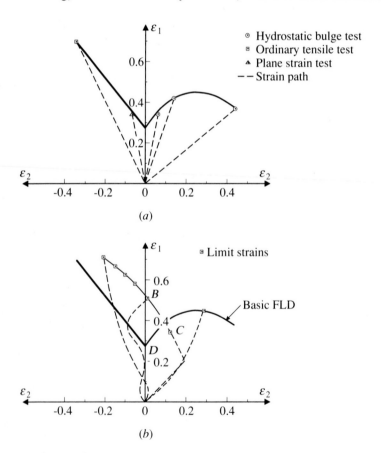

FIGURE 11.41
(a) Basic FLD obtained for linear strain paths, and (b) limit strains obtained for various, nonlinear strain paths by use of Nakazima-Hecker type tests [11.6].

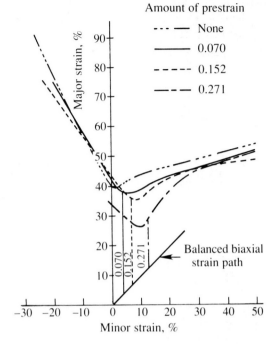

FIGURE 11.42
Forming limit diagrams for aluminum-killed steel as a function of balanced prestrain [11.20].

Prestraining by prior plastic deformation also affects the strain path and the limit strain. Stamping of sheetmetal components often involves multiple operations, which may vary from drawing-in (extension-contraction) to stretching (extension-extension). It has been found that biaxial prestraining lowers the limit strain and consequently lowers FLC for aluminium-killed low-carbon steel as shown in Fig. 11.42.

Strain paths are often nonlinear. Since in different tests the strain paths are different, the limit strains corresponding to linear strain paths have to be calculated to obtain comparative FLDs. The effective limit strain in the case of nonlinear strain path can be calculated from

$$\bar{\varepsilon}^* = \int d\bar{\varepsilon} \tag{11.51}$$

where the integral is taken over the applied strain path. If one describes the experimentally determined strain path by a mathematical expression, the effective strain increment can be calculated from the Levy-Mises equations written for plane strain as

$$\frac{d\varepsilon_1}{r_{90}(r_0 - r_0\alpha + 1)} = \frac{d\varepsilon_2}{r_0(\alpha + r_{90}\alpha - r_{90})} = \frac{-d\varepsilon_3}{r_{90} + r_0\alpha}$$

$$= \frac{d\bar{\varepsilon}}{[\frac{2}{3}(r_0 + r_{90} + r_0 r_{90})\{r_0(r_{90} + 1)\alpha^2 - 2r_0 r_{90}\alpha + r_{90}(r_0 + 1)\}]^{1/2}}$$

$$\tag{11.52}$$

where α is the stress ratio σ_2/σ_1 and r_0 and r_{90} are the anisotrophy parameters in the rolling and transverse directions. The effective limit strain $\bar{\varepsilon}^*$ is the sum of the increments as predicted by Eq. (11.51). If it is assumed that the total amount of straining depends only on the final stage of the strain path, the effective limit strain can be divided into the principal limit strains ε_1^* and ε_2^* by using Eq. (11.52). The stress ratio of the final stage of the strain path is taken from the relation

$$\alpha = \frac{(1/r_0+1)\rho+1}{1/r_{90}+1+\rho} = \frac{\sigma_2}{\sigma_1} \tag{11.53}$$

where ρ is the strain ratio $d\varepsilon_2/d\varepsilon_1$, measured from the slope of the strain path [11.9].

The limit strains for the stress states corresponding to the left-hand side of the FLD can be calculated from the condition for local instability (necking)

$$\frac{d\bar{\sigma}}{d\bar{\varepsilon}} = \frac{\bar{\sigma}}{Z_1} \qquad Z_1 \rightarrow Z_l \tag{11.54}$$

where $\bar{\sigma}$ and $\bar{\varepsilon}$ are the effective stress and strain, and Z_l is the critical subtangent (discussed elsewhere) calculated from

$$Z_1 = \frac{[\frac{2}{3}(r_0 + r_0r_{90} + r_{90})]^{1/2}[r_0(r_{90}+1)\alpha^2 - r_0r_{90}\alpha + r_{90}(r_0+1)]^{1/2}}{r_0\alpha + r_{90}} \tag{11.55}$$

[Compare Eq. (11.55) and Eq. (3.75).]

Experimental data for nonlinear strain paths obtained from aluminum-killed (AK) steel are plotted in Fig. 11.43 [11.9]. The codes and characteristics of the test specimens are given in Table 11.5. The limit strain for plotting the FLC can be obtained by fitting a polynomial equation to the strain path data by regression analysis and determining the point at which the limit strain departs from the curve. This change in strain path may be adopted as the criterion for the necking limit strain, and it can be found very accurately by the sudden change in slope of the strain path.

The equation fitted to the experimentally determined strain path is of the form

$$d\varepsilon_1 = ad\varepsilon_2^3 + bd\varepsilon_2^2 + cd\varepsilon_2 + d \tag{11.56}$$

where a, b, c, and d are constants. The subscripts identify the principal axes. The constants are solved for each strain path by using normal curve fitting. In all cases the paths could be described by a single equation up to a certain point where the experimental values deviate from the calculated curves. The strain coordinates of this point are defined to be the limit strains as indicated above.

The total effective strain along a strain path can therefore be obtained by integrating

$$\bar{\varepsilon}^* = \int d\bar{\varepsilon} \tag{11.51}$$

up to the point corresponding to the limit strains. The effective strain increment

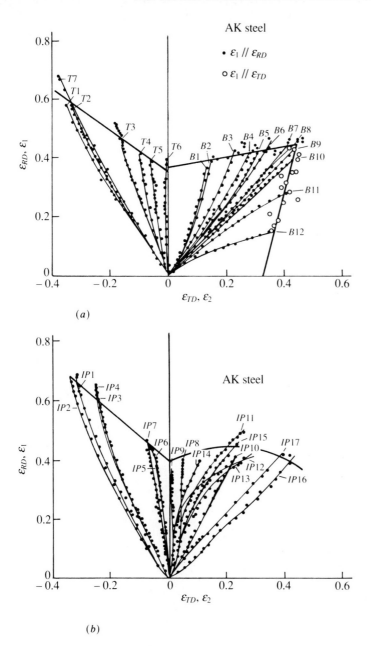

FIGURE 11.43
Limit strains and strain paths obtained by in-plane testing (*IP*), by hydraulic bulging (*b*), and tensile testing (*T*). Strain paths are indicated by numbers. Points without a strain path have been measured from fractured bulge specimens using a circle grid. *RD* = rolling direction, *TD* = transverse direction, and *AK* = aluminum killed [11.9].

TABLE 11.5
The codes and characteristics of the test specimens [11.9]

In-plane test specimens width, mm	80	100	120	130	140	150	250*
codes	IP1, IP2	IP3, IP4	IP5–IP7	IP8, IP9	IP10	IP11, IP15	IP16, IP17
Bulge test specimens aspect ratio	0.4	0.63	0.8	0.9	1.0*		
codes	B1, B2, B12	B3	B4, B5, B11	B6, B10	B7, B9		
Tensile test specimens notch radius, mm	∞†	66	30	20	10		
codes	T1, T2, T7	T3	T4	T5	T6		

* Equibiaxial.
† Normal tensile test specimen.

$d\bar{\varepsilon}$ is calculated from Eq. (11.52) by introducing the strain increment $d\varepsilon_1$ from Eq. (11.56) and also the anisotropy parameters r_i. In calculating $d\varepsilon_1$, a small step in the increment $d\varepsilon_2$ can be used to ensure that the increments describe the curves accurately enough [11.9].

The limiting strain is the optimum localized or diffused strain that is developed in the stressed specimen at the time that the limit criterion is reached, whether localized necking or fracture. Since limit strains depend on a number of factors such as the (1) strain path, (2) strain rate, (3) strain gradient, (4) punch curvature, (5) friction and lubrication involved, (6) grid size, etc., considerable amount of scatter may occur in the measurement of the limit strain, which would partially explain the marginal zone in Fig. 11.29. Comparisons of diagrams obtained by different methods and under different conditions are usually not possible.

11.2.6   Calculation of Limit Diagrams for Localized Necking and Fracture

11.2.6.1   PROCEDURE FOR CALCULATION. Embury and LeRoy [11.10] have given a good illustration as to the way that localized necking and fracture limit diagrams (maps) in stress space can be obtained by calculation. Their calculations relate stress to strain for different conditions of anisotropy, deformed in proportional-loading, plane-stress forming processes. They simplified and summarized some of the equations and procedures presented in the foregoing as follows [11.10]:

1. *Choice of an equivalent stress function.* Hill's analysis of anisotropy leads to a function of the form

$$\left\{ \begin{array}{c} \bar{\sigma}^2 = \sigma_1^2 + a\sigma_1\sigma_2 + b\sigma_2^2 \\ \sigma_3 = 0 \end{array} \right\} \tag{11.57}$$

where a and b are constants which can be obtained from the strain ratios measured in uniaxial tests in the rolling and transverse directions of the sheet, respectively. In this theory, it is assumed that hydrostatic stress does not influence yielding

2. *Associated flow rule.* The normality rule

$$d\varepsilon_{ij} = d\lambda \left(\frac{\partial \bar{\sigma}}{\partial \sigma_{ij}} \right)$$

can be written, using the condition of volume constancy

$$d\varepsilon_1 + d\varepsilon_2 + d\varepsilon_3 + 0 \tag{11.58}$$

as

$$\frac{d\varepsilon_1}{2\sigma_1 + a\sigma_2} = \frac{d\varepsilon_2}{2b\sigma_2 + a\sigma_1} = \frac{d\varepsilon_3}{-(2+a)\sigma_1 - (2b+a)\sigma_2} = \frac{d\bar{\varepsilon}}{2\bar{\sigma}} \tag{11.59}$$

3. *Derivation of the equivalent strain function.* The expression of $d\varepsilon$ can be obtained from Eq. (11.59) and from the definition of $\bar{\sigma}$, Eq. (11.57), resulting in

$$(d\varepsilon)^2 = \frac{4}{4b - a^2}(b\, d\varepsilon_1^2 - a\, d\varepsilon_1\, d\varepsilon_2 + d\varepsilon_2^2) \qquad (11.60)$$

4. *Straining condition.* For proportional straining, it is assumed

$$\frac{d\varepsilon_1}{d\varepsilon_2} = \frac{\varepsilon_1}{\varepsilon_2} = l \qquad (11.61)$$

Equation (11.59) gives the proportional loading condition with a slope m defined by

$$m = \frac{\sigma_1}{\sigma_2} = \frac{a - 2bl}{al - 2} \qquad (11.62)$$

The introduction of l and m into Eqs. (11.59) and (11.60) leads to the simplified expressions

$$\bar{\sigma} = \left(1 + \frac{a}{m} + \frac{b}{m^2}\right)^{1/2} \sigma_1 \qquad (11.63)$$

and

$$\bar{\varepsilon} = \frac{4}{4b - a^2}\left(b - \frac{a}{l} + \frac{1}{l^2}\right)^{1/2} \varepsilon_1 \qquad (11.64)$$

5. *Choice of a material law.* An appropriate relationship such as the power law can be used:

$$\bar{\sigma} = K\bar{\varepsilon}^n \qquad (3.5)\ (11.65)$$

6. *Mapping of strain and stress states.* From strain measurements, which can be made directly from the measurements of the deformed part, the corresponding stress values can be calculated as shown in the flowchart in Fig. 11.44.

11.2.6.2 RELATIONSHIPS FOR THREE EXAMPLE MATERIALS.

1. *Isotropic materials.* In this case, the von Mises criterion can be written

$$\bar{\sigma}^2 = \sigma_1^2 - \sigma_1\sigma_2 + \sigma_2^2 \qquad (11.66)$$

so that in Eq. (11.57), $a = -1$ and $b = +1$. Replacing a and b with -1 and 1, respectively, in Eqs. (11.63), (11.64), and (11.65), one obtains

$$\bar{\sigma} = \left(1 + \frac{1}{m^2} - \frac{1}{m}\right)^{1/2} \sigma_1 \qquad (11.67)$$

$$\bar{\varepsilon} = \frac{2}{\sqrt{3}}\left(1 + \frac{1}{l^2} + \frac{1}{l}\right)^{1/2} \varepsilon_1 \qquad (11.68)$$

$$m = \frac{2l + 1}{l + 2} \qquad (11.69)$$

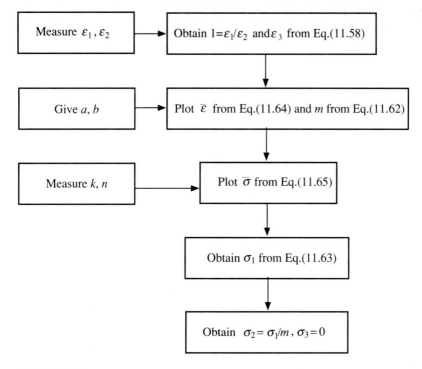

FIGURE 11.44
Flowchart for calculating σ_1 and σ_2 [11.10].

2. *Planar isotropic materials.* Assuming that the normal anisotropic plastic strain ratio R is constant during straining, one can use the expression proposed by Hill. (Note the special use of R in this section.)

$$\bar{\sigma}^2 = \sigma_1^2 - \frac{2R}{1+R}\sigma_1\sigma_2 + \sigma_2^2 \qquad (11.70)$$

so that in Eq. (11.57), $a = 2R/(1+R)$ and $b = +1$. By replacing a and b by $-2R/(1+R)$ and 1, respectively, in Eqs. (11.63), (11.64), and (11.69), one obtains

$$\bar{\sigma} = \left(1 - \frac{2R}{1+R}\frac{1}{m} + \frac{1}{m^2}\right)^{1/2}\sigma_1 \qquad (11.71)$$

$$\bar{\varepsilon} = \frac{1+R}{\sqrt{1+R}}\left(1 + \frac{2R}{1+R}\frac{1}{l} + \frac{1}{l^2}\right)^{1/2}\varepsilon_1 \qquad (11.72)$$

$$m = \frac{(1+R)l+R}{Rl+(1+R)} \qquad (11.73)$$

3. *Anisotropic materials.* For anisotropic materials, the constants a and b can be related to the strain ratio $\varepsilon_w/\varepsilon_t$, measured in the rolling (R_0) and transverse (R_{90}) directions, as follows:

$$\bar{\sigma}^2 = \sigma_1^2 - \frac{2}{C}\,\sigma_1\sigma_2 + \frac{B}{C}\,\sigma_2^2 \tag{11.74}$$

where $B = (1 + R_{90})/R_{90}$, and $C = (1 + R_0)/R_0$.

The following relations can then be written:

$$\bar{\sigma} = \left(1 - \frac{2}{C}\cdot\frac{1}{m} + \frac{B}{C}\cdot\frac{1}{m^2}\right)^{1/2}\sigma_1 \tag{11.75}$$

$$\bar{\varepsilon} = \left(\frac{C}{BC-1}\right)^{1/2}\left(B + \frac{2}{l} + \frac{C}{l^2}\right)^{1/2}\varepsilon_1 \tag{11.76}$$

and

$$m = \frac{Bl+1}{l+C} \tag{11.77}$$

11.2.6.3 EXAMPLES OF CALCULATED LIMIT AND FRACTURE MAPS. Embury and LeRoy gave an example for the use of the above calculations for an annealed 5154 aluminum alloy [11.10]. Figure 11.45 shows an experimentally determined limit diagram showing both the limit strain states for localized necking and for ductile fracture for this alloy. The linearly proportional strain path assumed for

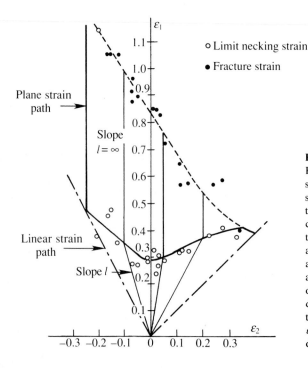

FIGURE 11.45
Forming limit curve and fracture strain curve in principal strain space. The limit strain curve and the fracture strain curve in the case of an Al-Mg alloy (5154) tested at room temperature in the annealed condition. ε_1 and ε_2 are, respectively, the major strain and the minor strain in the plane of the sheet. (Note the sharp decrease in fracture strains about the balanced biaxial axis (ε_1 and ε_2), where the limit and fracture data coincide.) [11.10].

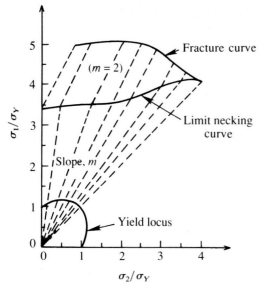

FIGURE 11.46

Limit map and fracture map corresponding to the limit strain curve and fracture curve, respectively, in axes normalized to the yield stress σ_Y. The limit curve represents the locus of stress states at which flow ceases to be uniform. The fracture curve represents the locus of stress states at fracture. The dashed lines show the loading paths chosen for the calculations [11.10].

the limit strain curve and the plane strain path assumed for necking to fracture are also shown.

The necking limit and fracture curves in stress space for this aluminum alloy, using the above calculating procedure, are shown in Fig. 11.46. Very approximate limit curves for necking for a broader range of stress space are plotted in Fig. 11.47, which are calculated from experimental strain data obtained for six materials.

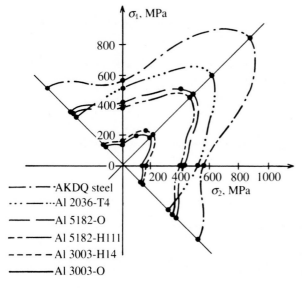

FIGURE 11.47

Limit-maps-to-failure for five different aluminum alloys and one aluminum-killed drawing quality (AKDQ) steel. (Note that in general the failure surface is not an expanded yield surface but it connects points on various expanded yield surfaces.) [11.10].

The fracture curves might be used to help relate the relative fracture behavior of these materials to their microstructure and to help select the operative fracture criteria and fracture modes.

11.2.6.4 WORKHARDENING CAPACITY DIAGRAMS. If one represents the isotropic strainhardening of a material as a uniform expansion of the initial yield locus as shown in Fig. 2.22(*b*), instability (necking) and fracture occur at different levels of strainhardening capacity as a function of loading. The plots of the strainhardening rate $d\sigma/d\varepsilon$, after any imposed strain for the 5154 alloy versus σ and ε are shown in Figs. 11.48 and 11.49, respectively. The difference between the point of instability and this limiting value of $d\sigma/d\varepsilon$ determines the rate at which the neck develops and is reflected in the relative position of the limit and failure curves in Fig. 11.46 [11.22].

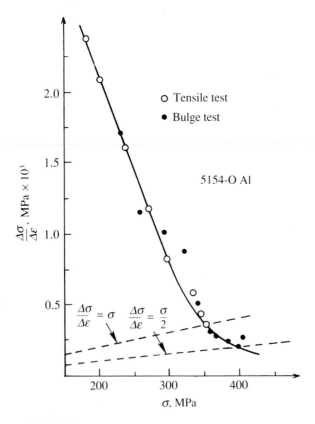

FIGURE 11.48
A diagram showing the variation in workhardening capacity with stress for a 5154-O alloy. The data are derived from a simple tension test and bulge test. The dashed lines correspond to the condition for diffuse ($\Delta\sigma/\Delta\varepsilon = \sigma$) and localized necking ($\Delta\sigma/\Delta\varepsilon = \sigma/2$) given by isotropic theories [11.22].

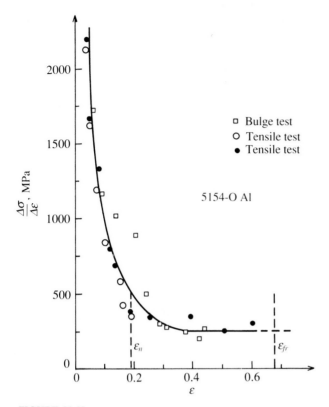

FIGURE 11.49
A graph showing the variation in workhardening capacity as a function of strain, for both tensile and bulge tests [11.22].

11.2.7   Superimposition of Severity Curves on an FLD

Severity curves may be superimposed on the FLD as shown in Fig. 11.50 to indicate the amount of strain, less than that required for failure, that may exist or be expected in a formed part. The severity curve, representing the extent of maximum strain that a particular grade and thickness of sheet steel (such as SAE 1008, 20 gauge or 0.036 in thick) can withstand without localized necking (failure), is the FLC described above. A series of lines paralleling the FLC, each representing a particular increase in the surface area of a unit square grid on the surface of the sheet under various combinations of engineering strains e_1 and e_2, can be constructed to represent the boundaries of ranges of conditions typically encountered in forming of steel sheet. The difference in area increase between the curves is usually taken as 25 percent as shown in Fig. 11.50, which is equivalent approximately to a 20 percent reduction in thickness.

Some years ago, the Society of Automotive Engineers (SAE) established a 25 percent increase in area criterion to differentiate between commercial quality

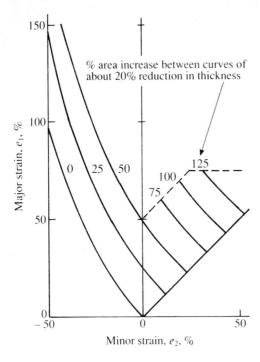

FIGURE 11.50

Relationship of e_1 strain, e_2 strain, and area increase [11.23].

(CQ) and drawing quality (DQ) steels. Although this standard was based on a 1 in (25.4 mm) grid square scribed on the surface, it also applies to one based on the gauge length of 0.1 in (2.54 mm) of a circular grid. In most deep-drawing operations, the local area increase is about 25 percent.

11.2.8 Strain Distribution Developed in Forming a Part

The limiting strain as obtained from an FLD is only one consideration of the overall formability of a production part. Another consideration is the distribution of the strain throughout the part. In actual practice, a large number of external variables, such as the shape of the part, blankholding pressure, lubrication, etc., exert very strong influences on the strain distribution and the state of strain at failure.

In case of the dome-height test as shown in Fig. 11.30, the most critical strain condition does not occur at the pole or apex of the dome, but at some location away from the pole which shifts with punch penetration (dome-height). An arbitrary line, that is drawn on the surface of the part along which the strain severity condition is determined, is called an *analysis line*. In a dome-shaped part, this line may be drawn along the great circle of the part as shown in Fig. 11.51. The major and minor strains can be obtained from the elliptically distorted grid circles. The major and the minor strains may then be plotted versus the distance from the pole as shown in Fig. 11.52.

FIGURE 11.51
Deformed punch specimen showing circle grid and directions of strain measurement. *RD* and *TD* denote rolling and transverse directions [2.14, p. 152].

Both the radial strain (left side), e_1, and circumferential strain (right side), e_2, distributions are shown in Fig. 11.52 as a function of position from the pole for various stretch dome (cup) heights for (a) aluminum-killed, low-carbon steel, (b) α-brass, and (c) 2036-T4 aluminum alloy. The limit strain level taken from the FLD is also shown for each material.

Plotting strain e_1 as a function of e_2 for different stretched dome heights, one obtains the strain paths at any cup location as shown in Fig. 11.53. (Also, see Fig. 11.43.) For example, for a 200 mm (7.87 in.) diameter blank of aluminum-killed (AK) steel, deformed dry, i.e., without lubrication, the strain path at a location 25.4 mm (1 in) from the pole as shown in Fig. 11.52 would have the following coordinates for runs Nos. 2, 4, 5, 6, 7, and 8: (14, 7), (19, 9), (25, 11), (34, 12), (41.5, 12.5), and (51, 14) as approximated by the curve labeled 200 mm— *D* in Fig. 11.53.

The strain peak, developed during rigid punch stretching, can move toward the edge during deformation, as shown in Fig. 11.52. This movement is enhanced by increasing the strainhardening exponent *n*, because a better transmittal of strainhardening throughout the material occurs, while frictional effects tend to retard deformation over the punch surface.

From Fig. 11.54 it can be seen that, the greater the strainhardening exponent *n*, the more uniform in the strain distribution throughout the stamping. The ability of a material to distribute strain is reflected by the width of the strain peaks of a strain distribution curve: the wider the peak, the better the strain distribution and the more efficient the deformation during forming.

The good correlation between the dome (cup) height at maximum load or fracture and *n* for low-carbon steel is shown in Fig. 11.55. However, there is no such correlation among different materials such as steel, brass, and aluminum.

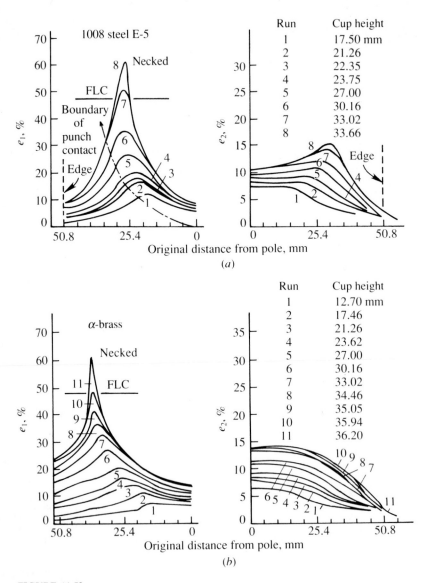

FIGURE 11.52.
Strain distribution (left major and right minor strain) as a function of the distance from the pole or blank center for various cup heights. FLC denotes onset of local necking. (*a*) Aluminum-killed low-carbon steel, E-5. Boundary of punch contact is shown. (*b*) 70-30 α-brass. (*c*) 2036-T4 aluminum alloy. The distribution of the different stages (runs) of forming were obtained by varying the length of the punch travel. Most of the deformation is in the final stages [2.14, p. 180].

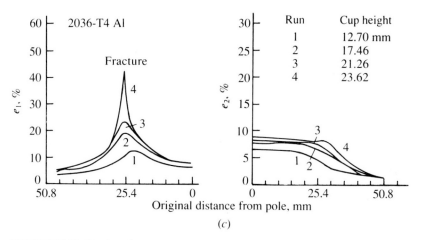

(c)

FIGURE 11.52. Continued

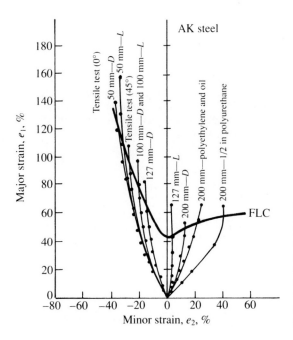

FIGURE 11.53

Strain paths for tensile specimens taken at 0° and 45° to the direction of rolling, and punch stretch specimens of different widths and different lubricants. FLC denotes the onset of local necking. Specimen widths are noted in mm; lubricated specimens by *L*, dry; unlubricated specimens by *D* [2.14, p. 163].

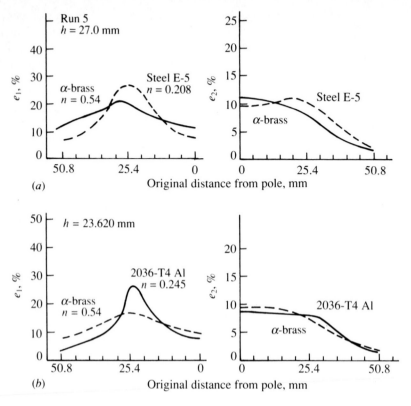

(a)

(b)

Original distance from pole, mm

FIGURE 11.54
Comparison of the strain distributions at specific cup heights, h. (a) E-5 steel versus α-brass for Run 5 of Fig. 11.52. (b) 2036-T4 Al versus α-brass for Run 4. Since the depth (height) of the stamping is proportional to the area under the strain distribution curve, a greater depth of stamping can be achieved with a material having a uniform strain distribution. Therefore, the α-brass would form to a greater depth than either the steel or the aluminium alloy [2.14, p. 164].

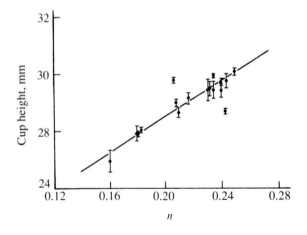

FIGURE 11.55
Dome (cup) height obtained by loading to maximum load or fracture plotted as a function of n, the strainhardening exponent, for low-carbon steel [11.27].

An increase in the anisotropic plastic strain ratio r can produce an increase in friction forces over the punch in biaxial stretching, which may reduce the influence of strainhardening exponent n to shift the peak strain location away from the pole. Small changes in the strain rate sensitivity m can also cause significant effects on strain distribution. The role of r in the biaxial punch stretch test will be discussed in the next section.

The FLC defines the maximum or peak strain that any element in a stamping can withstand without failure by localized necking (or fracture). A wide difference in formability may be observed even for a stamping of a given shape, blank size, and material. In each case the limit strain is identical but the strain peak and strain distribution may be quite different. The FLD by itself, therefore, provides insufficient information to specify the formability of a stamping completely. A stamping that has a uniform strain distribution throughout the part will represent potentially a more efficient deformation operation than one in which the deformation is all localized in one area.

The control of the strain distribution in an actual production situation is a challenging undertaking. The final strain distribution results from a complex, and usually not too well-known, interaction of four primary variables: (1) bulk material characteristics, (2) interface characteristics including surface roughness and lubrication, (3) die design including stamping shape, and (4) press parameters.

Any good forming limit analysis must, therefore, include both (1) the limit or permissible peak strain in the form of an FLD, and (2) a description of the strain distribution for a given set of operating conditions.

Data are available for the strain distribution obtained by stretching a 152 mm (6 in) minimum diameter blank over a 101.6 mm (4 in) diameter hemispherical punch and with no lubricant, as shown in Figs. 11.30 and 11.51. The meridional (radial) strain e_1, and the circumferential strain e_2, are measured.

The forming of a part such as a simple dome with a rigid hemispherical punch involves two features: (1) the level of the peak strain, and (2) the distribution of the strain surrounding the peak. Both of these features must be considered to obtain the required stamping configuration.

For example, let us assume that three different materials are used to form a dome and have the strain distribution curves as shown schematically in Fig. 11.56(a). Material A has been formed to a greater depth than B and C and utilizes its optimum formability as indicated by the greater area under its strain distribution curve. Materials B and C have been drawn to the same depth, but material C has been underutilized. It could either be drawn to a greater depth if so desired or be replaced by a cheaper, lower-grade material. The geometry of the punch may be modified so as possibly to yield a deeper cup, if so desired. However, for a nonuniform permissible peak-strain distribution due to a variation in strainhardening and the strain rate because of a nonuniform strain gradient as shown in Fig. 11.56(b), material D would form to a greater stamping depth and its forming capability would be more efficiently utilized than material E.

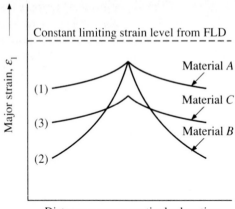

Constant limiting strain level from FLD

Material A

Material C

Material B

(1)

(3)

(2)

Major strain, ε_1

Distance across a particular location

(a)

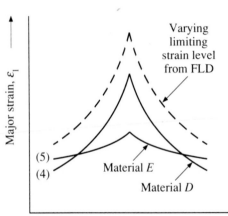

Varying
limiting
strain level
from FLD

Material E

Material D

(5)

(4)

Major strain, ε_1

Distance across a particular location

(b)

FIGURE 11.56
Schematic curves showing idealized distributions of strain with respect to (a) constant and (b) variable strain levels obtained from FLDs. (a) Curve (1) shows a broad, high peaked curve showing the strain distribution for material A for an equal critical strain but a greater depth of cup than material B. Curve (2) for material B shows a narrow, peaked curve having the same critical severity but a lesser depth of cup. Curve (3) for material C shows a broad, low peaked curve having a lower severity than material B, but an equal depth of draw. (b) Curve (4), having a non-uniform distribution of strain for material D, would have the optimum distribution as compared to that of curve (5) for material E. The strainhardening exponent n would be higher for material C than for A. (See Figs. 11.52 and 11.54.)

The basic difficulty in describing the ability of sheetmetal to be formed into specific shapes is to define some formability limit, which relates to a particular end condition associated with the straining process, and to correlate this failure criterion with the important parameters of the material such as r, n, m, etc. mentioned above [11.10].

Since each material-process-shape system has its own set of requirements, an FLD derived from laboratory tests will not apply unless it simulates accurately the system that will be used to form the part in production. There is, therefore, a need to predict the formability of the actual production parts prior to the construction of the production dies. Shape analysis was developed for this purpose.

11.2.9 Tensile Anisotropy Ratio r versus Biaxial Stretching [11.11]

If Hill's anisotropy criterion as expressed by Eq. (2.108) is applied to pure biaxial stretching where $\sigma_x = \sigma_y = \sigma$, and $\sigma_z = 0$ as occurs at the pole of the punch stretch (bulge) test in Figs. 11.30 and 11.51, then the strains, by use of Eqs. (2.113) become

$$d\varepsilon_x = d\lambda\, G\sigma \qquad (11.78a)$$

$$d\varepsilon_y = d\lambda\, F\sigma \qquad (11.78b)$$

$$d\varepsilon_z = -d\lambda\,(F+G)\sigma \qquad (11.78c)$$

Then, in the above biaxial test, it can be shown by use of Eqs. (2.115), (2.116), and (11.78) that

$$\frac{d\varepsilon_x}{d\varepsilon_y} = \frac{G}{F} = \frac{H/r_0}{H/r_{90}} = \frac{r_{90}}{r_0} \qquad (11.79)$$

Therefore, if the increments in strain are measured at the pole, i.e., on the axis of symmetry, in an axisymmetric punch (bulge) test it can be shown that Eq. (11.79) is valid in the biaxial test for anisotropy ratios r_0 and r_{90}, determined from the tension test shown in Figs. 2.70 and 10.2.

The r values can be obtained from the tension test by plotting the negative width strain versus the axial strain. The resulting curve is a straight line, the slope of which is equal to $r/(1+r)$. To avoid measuring small thickness, the width is used from the constancy of volume relation.

The test results obtained from a punch stretch (bulge) test similar to that shown in Figs. 11.30 and 11.51 showed that the strain ratio, $\varepsilon_0/\varepsilon_{90}$, for stainless steel under the test conditions was 1.196. This result compared favorably with the ratio of r_{90}/r_0, taken from the tension test of 1.149 in good agreement with Eq. (11.79). Equivalent values obtained from aluminum-killed steel and 70-30 cartridge brass are 1.276 versus 1.405 and 0.991 versus 0.990, respectively. These results show that Hill's yield criterion for an anisotropic material as expressed by Eq. (2.108), with the use of the uniaxial r values r_0 and r_{90}, is essentially valid in the case of the pure biaxial stress state, where $\sigma_1 = \sigma_2$. However, small nonuniform secondary stresses, resulting from nonuniform clamping of the blank, as shown in Fig. 11.51, may affect the results.

11.2.10 Computer-Aided Control of Sheetmetal Forming [11.12]

11.2.10.1 INTRODUCTION. The ultimate in the design of a sheetmetal forming process would be to compute and plot the forming limit diagram (FLD), and then compute the strain in the critical locations of the part to be formed to determine if the part can be safely formed without failure. Just such a computer software package has been developed, which is capable of predicting the success or the failure of sheetmetal parts being formed at the design stage. One of the important features of the software system is that it provides a quick representation of the computed major and minor strains at all nodal points of the formed parts. The computed strains are then directly superimposed on the forming limit diagram for the particular material to be used. With this information a design engineer may either proceed with the particular design and manufacturing method or make changes in the process variables such as the geometry of the part, material, loading method, boundary conditions, die design, etc., until a satisfactory condition is established.

Important elements of the analysis portion of the computer program consist of the constitutive relations and the description of the limiting FLD based on material parameters derived from laboratory experiments. Strain and stress distributions obtained for the particular formed part are computed by a finite element analysis (FEA) method, and the results are graphically superimposed on the computed FLD. In this way, all the relevant information is made available to a design engineer and metallurgist, so that they can decide whether or not to proceed with the production of the particular part in question.

The deepdrawing of a simple, partially drawn, axisymmetric cup is used here as an example.

To achieve the basic objective of predicting at the computer terminal whether or not a particular sheetmetal part can be formed requires several data bases and analysis programs.

The conceptional diagram illustrating the main elements, which consist of an analysis program, a computer-aided design (CAD) program, and the computer terminal, is shown in Fig. 11.57. The analysis program consists of (1) a constitutive relations program, (2) an FLD analysis program, and (3) a finite element analysis program. The CAD program contains all the information necessary for a full geometric description of the part, which may be obtained from engineering drawings. In addition, the material database as well as details of the loading condition are specified.

The three components of the analysis program: (1) the plastic and constitutive relations, (2) the prediction of the FDLs, and (3) the FEA methods, are discussed below.

11.2.10.2 REVIEW OF PLASTICITY AND CONSTITUTIVE RELATIONS. The background for this section is given in Secs. 3.12.2 and 3.12.3. If one assumes an anisotropic, inelastic, and rate-dependent material under a general state of stress, the inelastic strain-rate $\dot{\varepsilon}_i$ may be expressed in terms of the flow potential or the yield function f, and of the scalar multiplier $\dot{\lambda}$, by use of Eq. (3.99):

$$\dot{\varepsilon}_i = \dot{\lambda} \left[\frac{\partial f}{\partial \sigma_i} \right]_{\lambda} \tag{3.99}$$

where f stands for the simplified form of the generalized yield function [Eq. (3.99)] that has been presented elsewhere, and the scalar multiplier $\dot{\lambda}$ is equal to $3\dot{\bar{\varepsilon}}/2\bar{\sigma}$ where $\dot{\bar{\varepsilon}}$ and $\bar{\sigma}$ represent the equivalent strain rate and equivalent stress, respectively. For example, the yield function can be written in terms of the anisotropy or distortion matrix [Eq. (3.94)] which describes the variation of the

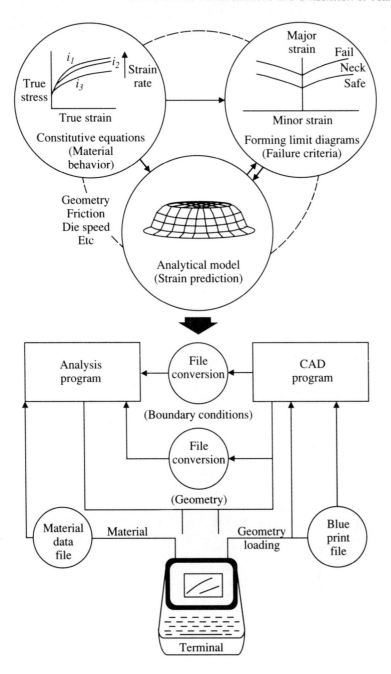

FIGURE 11.57
Diagram showing the major elements of the computer-aided sheetmetal formability prediction system [11.12].

flow stress with orientation as follows:

$$f = M_{ij}\sigma_i\sigma_j \tag{11.80}$$

where σ_i and σ_j denote the stress vectors corresponding to the appropriate tensor counterparts, σ_{ij}. Therefore, it follows that the equivalent stress $\bar{\sigma}$ can be expressed as $\bar{\sigma} = (M_{ij}\sigma_i\sigma_j)^{1/2}$ [Eq. (3.97)]. For the case of a plane-stress loading condition ($\sigma_3 = 0$) and for materials with planar isotropy ($M_{11} = M_{22}$), it can be shown that the well-known anisotropy parameter R is related to M_{33} by $R = 2/(M_{33} - 1)$ [Eq. (3.105)]. (Note the special use of R in this section.)

In order to describe the strainhardening and strain-rate hardening behavior of the material, the equivalent strain-rate $\dot{\bar{\varepsilon}}$ may be expressed in terms of the equivalent stress $\bar{\sigma}$ by Equation (3.109):

$$\dot{\bar{\varepsilon}} = \dot{\varepsilon}_0 \left[\frac{\bar{\sigma}}{k}\right]^{1/m} \tag{11.81}$$

where $m =$ the strain-rate sensitivity of the flow stress
$k = k_0(\varepsilon_0 + \bar{\varepsilon})^n =$ the effective reference flow stress
$\dot{\varepsilon}_0 =$ the reference strain rate
$k_0 =$ the reference strength coefficient
$n =$ the strainhardening exponent

The material constants k_0 and ε_0, and n, can be obtained by tensile testing as explained elsewhere.

The tension-test data for the material used in this example, drawing-quality enameling iron (DQEI or IEDQ), obtained by a uniaxial tension test at an initial strain rate of $2.78 \times 10^{-4}/s$ are as follows: $k_0 = 90.0$ ksi (62 MPa), $\dot{\varepsilon}_0 = 0.19$, $n = 0.50$, and $m = 0.0067$ at large plastic strains. The traverse strain ratio R had a value of about 1.0 at a plastic strain of 0.20.

The effect of temperature can be included by including an Arrhenius-type expression such as Eq. (2.158).

11.2.10.3 PREDICTION OF THE FORMING LIMIT DIAGRAM (FLD). Most of the forming limit diagrams in Chap. 11 have been determined experimentally by the circular grid method as shown in Fig. 11.27. The method of calculation of the limit diagrams for both localized necking and fracture as shown in Figs. 11.45 and 11.46 are discussed in Sec. 11.2.6.

The generation of a forming limit diagram by neck growth simulation was presented in Sec. 3.12.4 and shown in Fig. 3.37. The concept of a marginal zone is shown in Fig. 11.29. The system presented here not only plots the computed FLD but also plots the experimental or "shop" data.

There are several methods that can be used to compute the FLDs: (1) one method is to treat the onset of failure as the condition that leads to plastic instability, (2) another approach incorporates J_2 deformation theory into a classical bifurcation analysis (bifurcation occurs when localized deformation occurs from a homogeneous deformation state) and (3) still another approach, which is based on the idea that necking develops from local regions of initial, geometric nonuniformity, and which is the one used here. In this case, the test specimen is assumed to have an initial, geometric nonuniformity in the form of a band of reduced section.

A uniform strain-rate state is then imposed on the specimen containing the initial nonuniformity. While assuming that the states of stress and strain are uniform in the width direction of initial nonuniformity, the equation describing the rate of thickness reduction is integrated starting from the initial geometric and material conditions. The growth of initial nonuniformity is described by simultaneously integrating a series of equations at different but prescribed locations in the neck. A rate-dependent flow theory of plasticity is used, and the computation of the detailed neck growth is repeated over a wide range of proportional loading conditions to establish the limiting strain FLDs. The input material parameters, as mentioned above, that are required for the calculation of FLD, are m, n, ε_0, M_{33}, and η, the nonuniformity index, which is defined in Sec. 3.12.3 and is given by

$$\eta = 1 - \frac{h|_0^0}{h|_1^0} \tag{11.82}$$

where $h|_0^0$ is the minimum thickness at the reduced section and $h|_1^0$ is the thickness at the uniform section. (See Eq. (3.48) and Fig. 3.36.)

A computed limiting strain FLD and experimental data are compared for aluminum-killed (AK) steel in Fig. 11.58. The η value of 0.008 was obtained from the measurement of sheet thickness variations. Since the limiting strain refers to ultimate level of strain in the uniform section while the neck growth has taken place, it is safe to conclude that the material has failed when the state of limiting strain is reached. For this reason, another set of FLDs is necessary to specify the onset of failure, which may either be the point of plastic instability or represent the beginning of the diffuse and/or localized necking. (See Fig. 3.18 for diffuse and localized necking.) Since the specification of the boundary that separates the "safe" from the "necking" regions by an analytical method is difficult and is also dependent on the product application, a new lower bound may be established based on the shop experience on the particular product. Such a lower bound is also shown in Fig. 11.58 by the dashed lines which separate the safe from the marginal regions, taken from an applicance-business, manufacturing practice. An added advantage of specifying such as lower bound is that it incorporates the empirical relationship which accounts for the effects associated with sheet thickness and materials properties on the onset of necking.

11.2.10.4 FINITE ELEMENT ANALYSIS METHOD. To be able to identify the critical design and processing parameters efficiently while at the same time being cost-effective, a simplified one-dimensional finite element analysis (FEA) code is used. A full two-dimensional multielement FEA is used only when necessary. A typical three-dimensional finite element code to generate a mesh, to analyze

AK steel

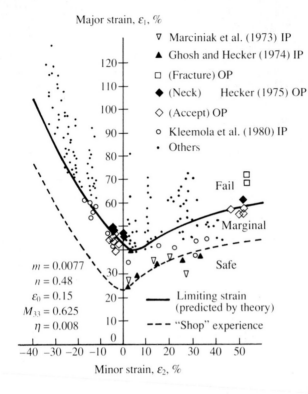

Major strain, ε_1, %

▽ Marciniak et al. (1973) IP
▲ Ghosh and Hecker (1974) IP
□ (Fracture) OP
◆ (Neck)　Hecker (1975) OP
◇ (Accept) OP
○ Kleemola et al. (1980) IP
· Others

Fail

Marginal

$m = 0.0077$
$n = 0.48$
$\varepsilon_0 = 0.15$
$M_{33} = 0.625$
$\eta = 0.008$

Safe

—— Limiting strain
　　(predicted by theory)
--- "Shop" experience

Minor strain, ε_2, %

FIGURE 11.58
Comparison of calculated limiting strain and "shop" experience forming limit diagrams (FLD) for aluminum-killed (AK) steel with experimental data. Experimental data are distinguished between those tested under the in-plane (IP) and the out-of-plane (OP) loading conditions [11.12].

the problem, and to postprocess the output would require too many worker-hours and too much computer time.

The simple finite element analysis code used here utilizes a one-dimensional element model, in which the nodal point coordinates are specified along a line representing the inner surface contour of the particular axisymmetric part. For nonaxisymmetric problems, the elements are described in the manner used to construct a shell element. No thickness elements are present in the construction of the nodal points describing the particular geometry. Aside from using the flow theory of time-independent plasticity, the computational method involves determining the nodal locations by the strain energy minimization process.

Under certain conditions, where the deformation is localized and needs to be determined accurately, a general purpose structural analysis code developed at MIT, called Automatic Dynamic Incremental Nonlinear Analysis (ADINA), may be used [11.13].

11.2.10.5 COMPUTER FLOW DIAGRAM. The simplified flowchart for processing and controlling the flow of information is outlined in Fig. 11.59.

Briefly, the simple finite element analysis program obtains the necessary input material data, geometry of the part, boundary conditions, and conditions

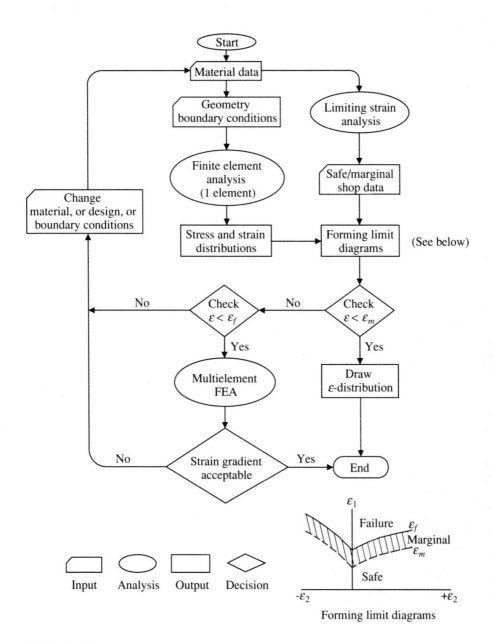

FIGURE 11.59
Flow diagram illustrating various points of input, analysis, output, and decision for the formability analysis [11.12].

of loading, from which it computes the stress and strain distributions on the formed part. Branching to the right of the diagram in Fig. 11.59, the computer program reads the necessary material parameters from the material database and computes the theoretical limiting FLD for the particular material. Since necking may occur below the limiting strain region, a boundary depicting the safe and marginal regions obtained from shop experience is also specified on the computed FLD as shown in Fig. 11.60. Finally, the computed major and minor strains in the formed part are plotted directly on the composite FLD. If all the computed strains in the formed part fall in the safe zone, the program terminates with a comment that indicates that the particular part can be formed without any difficulty. If, however, any computed strain falls in the area defined as marginal, the program asks whether the neck profile should be determined to ascertain if the strain gradient may still be satisfactory for a specific application. If the result of the multielement finite element analysis at the bottom of Fig. 11.59 indicates that the strain gradient is within an acceptable range, the program also terminates at this point. On the other hand, if the computed strain levels are well in the

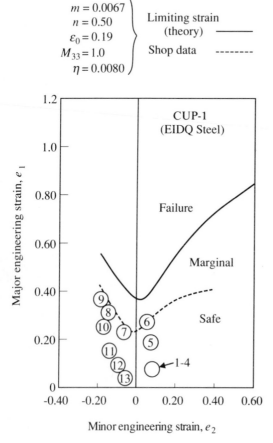

$$m = 0.0067$$
$$n = 0.50$$
$$\varepsilon_0 = 0.19$$
$$M_{33} = 1.0$$
$$\eta = 0.0080$$

Limiting strain (theory) ———

Shop data --------

FIGURE 11.60
Comparison of computed major and minor strains at each node point with FLD for CUP-1. The diagram for CUP-3 is quite similar [11.12].

y

x

z

FIGURE 11.61
Finite element model for CUP [11.12].

failure zone, the program requests that either the material or the geometry or the loading condition be changed as indicated by the loop on the left side of Fig. 11.59. The entire routine is repeated until a satisfactory or safe condition is achieved.

11.2.10.6   PROCESSING OF AN EXAMPLE PART. The example part is a partially drawn cup, whose finite element model is shown in Fig. 11.61. The coordinates for the nodal points for the cup drawn under two different conditions of friction, $\mu = 0.14$ (measured) and $\mu = 0.02$ (assumed), are shown in Fig. 11.62. The normal loads F_n shown in Fig. 11.62 are applied, and the relative motion of the sheetmetal with respect to the die surface is accounted for by the sign of the friction coefficient, i.e., when the metal flow is away from the origin ($r = 0$), the sign of μ is considered to be positive, and vice versa. In this example, the sheet was clamped at node 13, and the lower friction coefficient of 0.03 was found to be appropriate at the clamping area.

If the material properties, the geometry file, and the loading boundary conditions are given, the next step in the flow diagram in Fig. 11.59 is to compute the strain distributions when the cups have been formed. Results of the radial

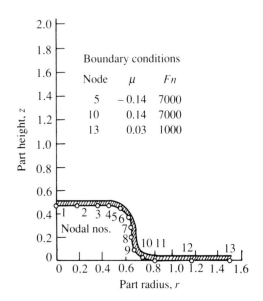

Boundary conditions

Node	μ	F_n
5	-0.14	7000
10	0.14	7000
13	0.03	1000

Part height, z

Nodal nos.

Part radius, r

FIGURE 11.62
Description of the final geometry and boundary conditions for CUP. (The units of the height and radius are in in and of the punch load in lbf. [11.12].

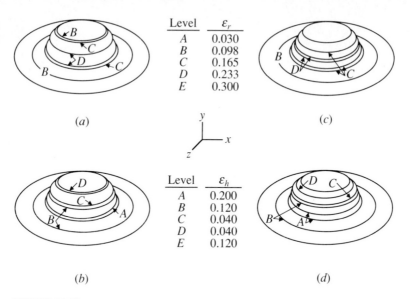

Level	ε_r
A	0.030
B	0.098
C	0.165
D	0.233
E	0.300

(a)

(c)

Level	ε_h
A	0.200
B	0.120
C	0.040
D	0.040
E	0.120

(b)

(d)

FIGURE 11.63
Computed strain distribution contour diagrams for (a) radial strain ε_r distributions in CUP-1, (b) hoop strain ε_h distributions in CUP-1, (c) radial strain ε_r distributions in CUP-3, and (d) hoop strain ε_h distributions in CUP-3 [11.12].

and hoop strain distributions in CUP-1 and CUP-3, respectively, are shown in Fig. 11.63. A graphics software package called MOVIE BYU (developed at Brigham Young University) is used for the display of the strain contours in Fig. 11.63. The FLD is computed, and the shop FLD is superimposed on the computed FLD as described above. The strain distribution for the particular cup is compared to the failure criteria in the composite FLD shown in Fig. 11.60. The computed radial (major) and hoop (minor) strains at each nodal point are identified in the composite FLD by the corresponding nodal point number contained in Fig. 11.62. All the information is now available to make a decision regarding the safe performance of the operation. The deep drawing of CUP-1 may be marginal, whereas that of CUP-3 is entirely safe as far as excessive necking or fracture is concerned. Failure by some other mode, such as wrinkling as shown in Fig. 11.4, etc., may still have to be evaluated.

A comparison of the computed thickness strain ε_t, where $\varepsilon_t = -\varepsilon_r - \varepsilon_h$, obtained from the FEA with the measured thickness strain along the length of the generator, is summarized in Fig. 11.64. Localized necking occurs near nodal point 6 in Fig. 11.62, where the computed thickness strain underestimated the experimental data. This discrepancy is probably due to the oversimplified, one-dimensional method of formulating the FEA problem. The indicated point is obtained by the multielement FEA solution, utilizing the ADINA code, which uses 80 isoparametric 8-noded elements. The analytical model tends to develop an abrupt neck, thereby overestimating the limiting strain. One of the reasons for this discrepancy between the two models is that the stress distribution becomes

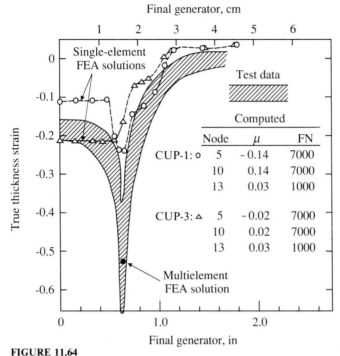

FIGURE 11.64

Comparison of computed thickness strain along new generator with experimental data in CUP. (The units of the punch load are in lbf.) [11.12].

nonuniform as the neck develops. The analytical model assumes that the stress is uniform throughout the specimen.

In summary, a computer-aided predictive method, as opposed to a diagnostic method, is here described, which is capable of providing an instantaneous graphic representation of the success or failure in the formability of sheetmetal parts at the engineering drawing stage. Key elements of the analysis program consist of constitutive equations, computed and shop-data FLDs, and FEA computer programs.

One of the reasons for using such a computer software system is to introduce a straightforward engineering method to the material processing technology. In this way, not only can the design engineering cost be reduced, but also a traditional trial-and-error method can be partially, if not entirely, eliminated. An added advantage of using such an integrated system is that it provides the design engineer with some of the critical information that is useful in making changes before the design and construction of the dies, or when it becomes desirable.

11.2.11 Simulative Cup Tests

11.2.11.1 INTRODUCTION. Simulative cup tests have been widely used to analyze sheetmetal formability as partially summarized in Fig. 11.65. If the deformation

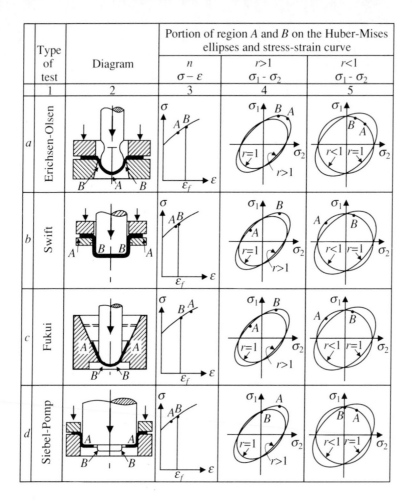

FIGURE 11.65

Configuration and characteristics of (*a*) the Erichsen-Olsen, (*b*) the Swift, (*c*) the Fukui, and (*d*) the Siebel-Pomp simulative cup tests, showing the conditions at the flow region, *A*, and the fracture region, *B*. Normal anisotropy and a constant strainhardening exponent, *n*, are assumed [11.15].

within the region *A* in Fig. 11.65 is smaller than in the region *B*, then the strainhardening capacity of the metal as indicated by *n* enhances the drawability. When the stress condition within region *A* increases, approaching biaxial tension, then a normal plastic anisotropic ratio greater than one ($r > 1$) has a beneficial effect on the drawability because, in such cases, the ratio of the limiting force-to-fracture and the drawing force increases, resulting in a greater factor of safety.

Also, much experimental analyses have been done such as by Kasper [11.14] to determine the correlation of the various drawability indices and the test and material parameters such as sheet thickness, mechanical properties such as percent elongation, composition, plastic anisotropic strain ratio, lubrication, etc. These simulative cup tests appear to be very attractive, because they attempt to simulate the modes of deformation in the actual forming of parts from sheetmetal. The two principal cup-forming actions, mentioned in Section 11.1.2, that simulative cup tests attempt to duplicate to varying degree are (1) biaxial stretching over a hemispherical punch, in which both principal strains are tensile, and (2) drawing-in of a flange into a die cavity, in which one principal strain is tensile and the other is compressive.

Special equipment has been made commercially available such as the Hille-Wallace Universal Sheet Metal Tester consisting of a 30 tonf (2.67 kN) press with different die accessories and controls to facilitate performing certain common tests.

Simulative cup tests are now losing favor because of the scatter and irreproducibility of the data and the lack of correlation either with other properties of the material or with production experience. For these reasons only a brief discussion of only a few of the tests and experimental results will be covered. The three tests that will be covered primarily are (1) the Swift cup test involving drawing-in primarily (using a flat-bottomed punch with a radius on the bottom edge as shown in Fig. 11.65(b)), (2) Olsen (or Erichsen) cup test involving stretching primarily (using a hemispherical punch as shown in Fig. 11.65(a)), and (3) the Fukui conical cup test involving both drawing-in and stretching (using a hemispherical punch and a conical die as shown in Fig. 11.65(c)). (The Siebel-Pomp test in Fig. 11.65(d) is used as a hole expansion test mentioned in Chapter 3 and in conjunction with edge condition analyses discussed in Section 11.2.12.6.) Variation in the test procedure and tooling exist among the various standards and practices proposed and used by different laboratories and organizations such as the International Deep Drawing Group. These tests incorporate various amounts of stretchability and drawing-in.

The Olsen cup test has been standardized in customary English units as the "ball deformation test" as described in ASTM Designation E643-84. The cross section of the die and its dimensions are shown in Fig. 11.66. Ideally this test involves biaxial stretching, and no drawing-in of the flange should occur. The modified Erichsen test has been standardized in Europe in SI units. The main difference between the ball punch deformation test and the Erichsen are the diameters of the penetrator ($\frac{7}{8}$ in versus 20 mm) and the dies.

11.2.11.2 SWIFT CUP TEST. In the Swift cup test procedure used by Kasper [11.14], the limiting drawing ratio (LDR) is obtained as follows: The blank is cut to a size smaller than that at which it will fracture due to overload when drawn. The blank is drawn to the maximum punch load which occurs before the cup is fully drawn. The flange that remains in the blankholder is then clamped by the serrated clamping ring, and the punch stroke is restarted until the maximum load occurs again and the cup fractures. From these two maximum loads, the limiting blank diameter D_c is calculated as follows:

$$D_c = \frac{L_f}{L_d}(D_s - D_0) + D_0 \qquad (11.83)$$

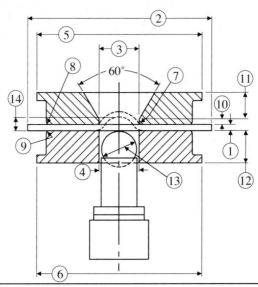

Key	Dimensions	
	in	mm
① Thickness of test piece	Full thickness	Full thickness
② Width of test piece (minimum)	3.5	90
③ Bore diameter of top die	B	B
④ Bore diameter of bottom die	1 ± 0.004	25.4 ± 0.1
⑤ External diameter of top die (approximate)	3.5	90
⑥ External diameter of bottom die (approximate)	3.5	90
⑦ Corner radius of interior of top die	0.032 ± 0.002	0.81 ± 0.05
⑧ Corner radius of exterior of top die	0.032	0.8
⑨ Corner radius of exterior of bottom die	0.032	0.8
⑩ Depth of bore of top die	0.197 ± 0.010	5 ± 0.2
⑪ Thickness of top die (minimum)	0.78	20
⑫ Thickness of bottom die (minimum)	0.78	20
⑬ Diameter of spherical end of penetrator [1]	0.875 ± 0.002	22.22 ± 0.04
⑭ Depth of cup	Depth of cup	Depth of cup

[1] "Olsen" Ball, 22.22 mm (7/8 in); "Erichsen" Ball, 20 mm
B For $t_①$ = 0.060 in (1.5 mm), $d_③$ = 1.000 in (25.40 mm)
B For $t_① \geq 0.060$ in (1.5 mm) ≤ 0.080 in (2.0 mm), $d_③$ = 1.125 in (28.58 mm)

FIGURE 11.66
ASTM ball punch deformation test tooling [11.25].

Then, the limiting drawing ratio (LDR) is calculated as follows:

$$\text{LDR} = \frac{D_c}{D_p} = \frac{(L_f/L_d)(D_s - D_0) + D_0}{D_p} \tag{11.84}$$

where D_c = critical blank diameter
L_f = fracture load
L_d = draw load
D_s = blank diameter
D_0 = die throat diameter
D_p = punch diameter

The punch diameter is 1.97 in (50 mm), and the die lip radius and the die throat diameter vary with the thickness of the sheetmetal used. Typically for sheetmetal 0.025–0.036 in (0.635–0.914 mm) thick, the die throat diameter is 2.07 in (52.6 mm) and the die lip radius is 0.360 in (9.14 mm). Discs of polyethylene 0.003 in (0.08 mm) thick, oiled with SAE 20 oil, are used as a lubricant.

An alternate Swift cup test also used by Kasper, which requires more material and time, may be used. In this test circular blanks are accurately cut in 0.50 in (12.7 mm) increments of diameter, so as to have a sequence extending from below to above the expected critical (maximum) diameter. The blanks are cleaned and oiled polyethylene discs are used as a lubricant. Blanks of increasing size are loaded until a blank breaks. Additional specimens are tested between the largest blank that drew and the smallest blank that broke in order to determine the critical size at which one-half of the blanks would draw. The LDR is then calculated as follows where D_c and D_p are defined above:

$$\text{LDR} = \frac{D_c}{D_p} \tag{11.85}$$

11.2.11.3 OLSEN CUP TEST. The Olsen cup test value is the height of the cup in thousandths of an inch (or in millimeters) at the instant that the punch load starts to drop off.

In the test used by Kasper [11.14], a $\frac{7}{8}$ in (22 mm) diameter ball-end punch and a 1 in (25.4 mm) die throat diameter are used for sheets below $\frac{1}{16}$ in (1.6 mm) thick. A $1\frac{1}{4}$ in (31.75 mm) diameter die is used for sheets up to $\frac{1}{8}$ in (3.2 mm). The die lip radius is 0.025 in (0.635 mm). Discs 0.003 in (0.008 mm) thick of oiled polyethylene are placed between the punch nose and specimen and between the die ring and specimen to provide a standard low-friction lubricant.

11.2.11.4 ERICHSEN CUP TEST. Sometimes the Erichsen cup test, which is quite similar to the Olsen test, is used in lieu of it. In one investigation [11.15], a 20 mm diameter ball-punch was used, and the drawability index JE is the depth of penetration within 0.01 mm of the depth of fracture.

11.2.11.5 FUKUI CUP TEST. In the test used by Kasper [11.14], a tooling configuration that was used had an $\frac{11}{16}$ in (17.5 mm) diameter ball-end punch and a conical

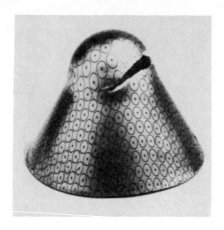

FIGURE 11.67
A Fukui cup test used to predict the formability of sheetmetal. No blankholder is needed, and wrinkles can be avoided by proper attention to the dimensions ratios in the test disc. (*Courtesy Institut de Recherches de la Siderurgie Francaise.*)

die with a 0.786 in (20 mm) diameter throat. A drawn Fukui cup is shown in Fig. 11.67. These dimensions are used for sheetmetal thicknesses of 0.030–0.040 in (0.762–1.016 mm). High viscosity lubricating oil is used. No blankholding pressure is required, although a minimum of pressure may be applied to bring the blank in contact with the conical die. A punch speed of 3 in/min (1.27 mm/s) is used at the start and then it is reduced to 0.1 in/min (0.042 mm/s). In this case the cup depth at the maximum load is used as the formability index.

Fukui conical cup tests have also been made while using punches from 8 to 27 mm in diameter and dies of throat diameters from 9.4 to 32 mm as well as blanks of diameters from 23 to 79 mm [11.15]. These parameters have been selected on the basis of material thickness. The drawability index has been determined in this case as follows:

$$\eta_F = \frac{D}{D_f}(100)\% \tag{11.86}$$

where $D =$ the blank diameter
$D_f =$ the cup OD at the point (moment) of fracture

11.2.11.6 REGRESSION EQUATIONS FOR CUP TEST RESULTS. The planar, regression equation giving the general relationship between the limiting drawing ratio (LDR) or the cup depth z, and the average elongation in percent, $\bar{E}$, and the average anisotropy parameter $\bar{r}$, is

$$z = A + B\bar{E} + C\bar{r} \tag{11.87}$$

In the investigation cited above by Kasper [11.14], the equations relating the various formability indices to the average total elongation $\bar{E}$ in percent, and the average plastic strain ratio r, are as follows:

1. $\text{LDR} = F_s = 1.93 + 0.00216\bar{E} + 0.226\bar{r}$
    with a correlation coefficient of 0.835 $\hfill (11.88)$

2. Olsen cup depth (in) $= F_0 = 0.217 + 0.00474\bar{E} + 0.00392\bar{r}$ (11.89)
with a correlation coefficient of 0.925

3. Fukui cup depth (in) $= F_f = 0.525 + 0.0134\bar{E} + 0.207\bar{r}$ (11.90)
with a correlation coefficient of 0.757

    The above three relationships are equations of planes as shown in Figs. 11.68, 11.69, and 11.70.

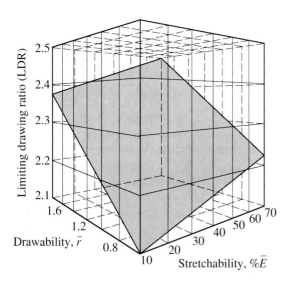

FIGURE 11.68
Computer analysis of results for the Swift cup test indicated that the limiting drawing ratio (LDR) conforms to Eq. (11.88). In this test, a sheet's drawability, in terms of plastic anisotropy, has more effect on the LDR than does its stretchability [11.14].

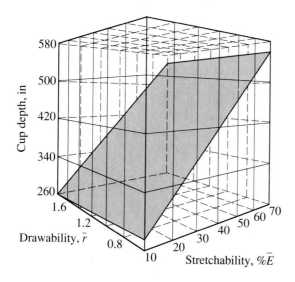

FIGURE 11.69
Computer analysis showed that the depths of Olsen cups vary mainly with the sheet's stretchability given in terms of tensile elongation, as expressed by Eq. (11.89) [11.14].

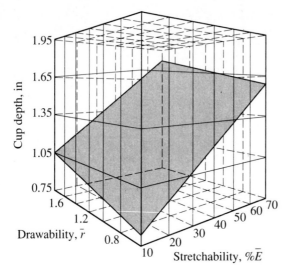

FIGURE 11.70
Depths of Fukui test cups vary with both drawability and stretchability, especially the latter as expressed by Eq. (11.90) [11.14].

They have been found to be essentially independent of the material. They have been obtained from the experimental data of 48 different materials including low-carbon steels, stainless steels, and some aluminum alloys.

The data in Fig. 11.71 show that the Fukui test data fall between those of the Swift and Olsen tests. A few production stamping measurements are also plotted on this graph, which has dashed lines representing the forming limits as related to the percentage of blank utilization.

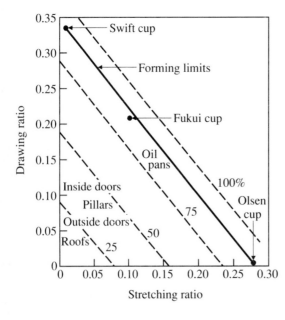

FIGURE 11.71
Forming limits for parts made from sheetmetal can be related to those of typical cup tests by this graph. As can be seen from the graph, most components are formed by a combination of stretching and drawing. Dashed lines indicate the percentage of blank utilization, in which plastic deformation extends more uniformly through the sheet [11.14].

When stampings are analyzed by the grid circle analysis method and large variations in strain are encountered from one area to another, forming limits are moved toward the origin, i.e., down to the left, of Fig. 11.71. These limits can be raised through proper lubrication by spreading the plastic deformation over a larger area of the sheet.

Formability analysis of a stamping design must therefore take into account a measure of the percentage of the blank utilization. Many production parts have a very small portion of the total area involved in plastic deformation. Steps that spread the plastic strain to a greater area are generally more beneficial in reducing the severity of draw than are the minor improvements that can be achieved through use of a more ductile material.

In the investigation cited by Gronostajski and Banasiak [11.15], the simplified equation relating the drawability indices for low-carbon steels of varying composition to various parameters obtained by fitting the equations to the data are as follows:

1. $LDR = 1.816 + 0.307\bar{r} \pm 0.002$ $\hspace{3cm}$ (11.91)
   with a correlation coefficient of 0.734

2. $JE = 7.534 + 1.788t + 4.65\bar{n} \pm 0.047$ $\hspace{2cm}$ (11.92)
   with a correlation coefficient of 0.853

3. $\eta_F = 117.675 + 11.023\bar{r} \pm 0.110$ $\hspace{2.3cm}$ (11.93)
   with a correlation coefficient of 0.785

The symbols used in the above empirical equations are as follows: $JE =$ the depth of the punch in mm up to fracture in the Erichsen test, $LDR =$ the limiting drawing ratio for the Swift test using a 32 mm in diameter flat-bottomed punch, $\eta_F =$ the ratio in percent of the blank to cup diameter at fracture, $t =$ the thickness in mm, $\bar{n} =$ the minimum strainhardening exponent, and $\bar{r} =$ the average value of the anisotropic plastic strain ratio

$$\bar{r} = \frac{(r_0 + 2r_{45} + r_{90})}{4} \hspace{2cm} (11.3)(11.94)$$

11.2.12 Shape Analysis of Stampings

11.2.12.1 DEFINITION AND SCOPE. *Shape analysis* is the process of predicting the severity of forming a specific sheetmetal into a desired shape by use of laboratory tests such as simulation cup tests. This method recognizes the interaction of die and material variables in making a shape of a production part. The shape of the part is the most important factor affecting severity. Once the shape has been determined, the necessary tooling can be discerned for forming the part from a particular material; or conversely for a specific die set, the feasibility of making a part from various materials can be determined. Whereas the determination of the FLD is oriented toward the laboratory-type test specimens, shape analysis is oriented toward the production parts themselves.

Such analysis is applied to those critically formed areas of the stamping that establish its overall formability. Generally, critical locations are those that involve combinations of stretch and draw whose strain state approaches the limiting strain. An arbitrary line drawn on the surface of the part through the critical location is called an *analysis line* to be discussed in more detail later. In shape analysis, these stretch-draw formations (shapes) are broken down into combinations of spherical and cylindrical sections whose formabilities can be estimated from the results of optimized laboratory forming tests of similar shapes. Forming ratios that describe the shapes of these spherical and cylindrical sections can be readily calculated and then combined to give an overall severity rating.

Production stampings usually contain a wide range of stretch-draw combinations. The *forming ratio* is the sum of the stretch forming fraction and the draw forming fraction. The stretch forming fraction, *Stretch*, is the height-to-width of the stretch portion multiplied by the strain along the analysis line which is due to stretching. The draw forming fraction, *Draw*, is the blank-to-width ratio for the draw portion of the part multiplied by the strain along the analysis line which is due to drawing. In other words, since Stretch + Draw = 1, the foregoing may be stated as

$$R_s \left(\frac{\%\text{Stretch}}{100} \right) + R_d \left(\frac{\%\text{Draw}}{100} \right) = 1 \tag{11.95}$$

where R_s is the height-to-diameter ratio as obtained by the Olsen cup test, and R_d is the Swift limiting draw ratio of blank diameter-to-cup diameter; and the %Stretch/100 is the fraction of forming contributed by stretching, and %Draw/100 is the fraction of forming contributed by drawing-in. The foregoing parameters will be defined more specifically later. [See Eqs. (11.98), (11.100), and (11.101).]

Different parts exhibit different combinations of stretch and draw, ranging from complete stretch to complete draw. If the Olsen and Swift cup test ratios are taken as the quantitative representations of the two extreme cases, a plot showing the forming performance of the material can be constructed as shown in Fig. 11.72 by joining the two forming ratio points for the Olsen and Swift cup tests with a straight line. The former is assumed to be 100 percent stretch and the latter 100 percent draw. The assumed linear function represented is defined by Eq. (11.95).

In the event that the Olsen and/or Swift cup data are not available, tensile test data might be substituted with the aid of previously obtained planar equations (11.89) and (11.88) [11.14]. Equation (11.89) relates the average tensile total elongation $\bar{E}$, and the average plastic strain ratio $\bar{r}$ to the stretch forming ratio R_s, and Eq. (11.88) relates the foregoing parameters to the Swift limiting drawing ratio R_d in Eq. (11.95).

The shape analysis technique involving some combination of stretching and drawing involves the optimization of the interaction between the material, shape, and dies. The problem can be formulated as an optimization problem, in which the overall severity of the part or design (SEV), subject to certain constraints put on the different variables, is minimized. The variables involved can be classified

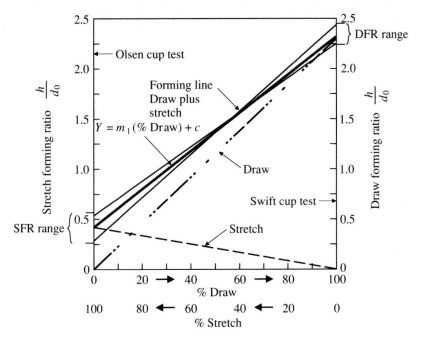

FIGURE 11.72
Stretch-draw (SD) chart for the construction of a material forming line based on the Olsen and Swift test ratios. The forming line shown is for drawing quality special killed steel (DQSK) (SAE 1006). The braces on the graph define the zone, in which the forming lines having different slopes fall of typical sheetmetals used for forming. A linear relationship is assumed [11.5].

into three categories: (1) material variables, (2) shape variables, and (3) die variables.

11.2.12.2 STEPS IN THE APPLICATION OF SHAPE ANALYSIS. The steps in the application of the shape-analysis approach in evaluating the formability of a specific sheetmetal for a specific desired shape are (1) evaluating of the formability capability of the sheetmetal by the construction of a modified stretch-draw (SD) diagram or chart similar to Fig. 11.72 by use of simulative cup or substituted tensile data, (2) locating the critical area of plastic deformation on the formed part, and drawing a convenient analysis line, (3) locating the stretch-draw boundary between biaxial stretching and tensile-compressive drawing on the surface of the part, (4) calculating the shape analysis severity (SEV), (5) locating the SEV value on the modified SD chart to see if it falls below the forming limit line or optimizing as desired, and (6) modifying the tooling, if necessary, so that the severity of the part (SEV) falls below the forming line, or optimum formability is obtained.

11.2.12.3 MODIFICATION OF THE SD DIAGRAM. The SD chart shown in Fig. 11.72 can be modified after Johnson and Stine [11.16] as shown in Fig. 11.73 to

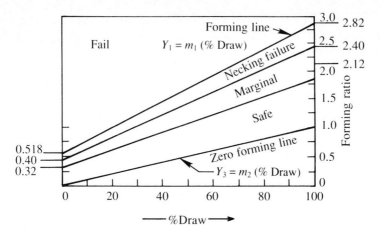

FIGURE 11.73
Modified stretch-draw (SD) chart after Johnson and Stine to include the onset of necking (marginal zone), fracture (necking-failure), and the zero forming line [11.16].

include the onset of necking (marginal zone), fracture (necking failure), and the zero forming line. The basic information needed for these calculations includes the forming line endpoint values obtained from the Olsen and Swift cup tests, Kasper's shape analysis severity equation, and the severity values (SEV) of 1.3 for the top of the necking-failure band and 0.8 for the bottom of the marginal band. These values are calculated by use of the following severity relation expressed in terms of the forming ratios R:

$$SEV = \frac{R_C - R_0}{R_L - R_0} \qquad (11.96)$$

where R_C is the calculated forming ratio of the endpoints of the top of the necking failure and the bottom of the marginal bands, R_L is the forming ratio of the endpoints of the forming line at 0 or 100%Draw, and R_0 is the endpoints of the zero forming line at 0 or 100%Draw.

Since for 100%Draw, $R_L = 2.4$ and $R_0 = 1.0$, R_C for the top of the necking-failure band at 100%Draw is $R_C = 2.82$, and R_C for the bottom of the marginal band is 2.12. Since for 0%Draw, $R_L = 0.4$ and $R_0 = 0$, R_C for the top of the necking-failure band at 0%Draw is $R_C = 0.518$ and the bottom of the marginal band, $R_C = 0.32$. Using the foregoing values, one can plot the modified SD diagram as shown in Fig. 11.73.

The significant severity-rating distribution for a stretch-draw forming operation may be obtained by first locating the most severely deformed area, or a potential fracture-prone area, on the stamping. This area is usually located at a sharp change in contour such as a corner. This may be done in the die tryout stage by forming the part to failure using the least favorable conditions. The punch stroke may then be reduced so that the part is strained to a critical condition without failure. A convenient analysis line is drawn across the stamping through the most severely deformed area in such a manner that a symmetric strain distribution exists on either side of the line. In case of a cup, the analysis line would lie on the intercept of a plane through the axis of the cup as shown in Fig. 11.74(a). In case of the fuel tank upper stamping that has been analyzed by the shape analysis technique, the analysis line is drawn diagonally across the

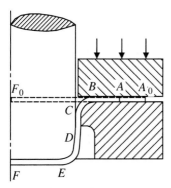

Intermediate stage in drawing

$A_0 F_0$	Blank
AB	Zone of simple radial drawing
B	Die profile radius
C	Die throat
CD	Cup
DE	Zone of profile radius of punch
FF_0	Centerline of punch

(a)

Stretch-draw (SD) boundary

$$L_{ds} = L_d + L_s$$

$$L_0 = \frac{D_0}{2}$$

(b)

FIGURE 11.74
Configuration of the cup deep-drawing process [11.17].

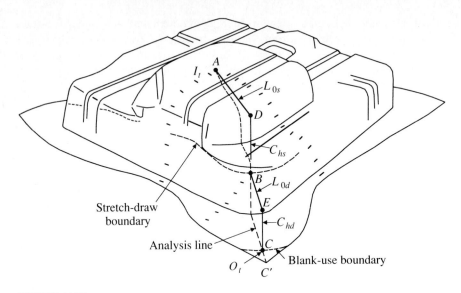

FIGURE 11.75

Upper half of an automobile fuel tank stamping first made of terne-coated steel and subjected to shape analysis to optimize forming conditions. The part was then reanalyzed to determine if it could be made successfully from 5182-O aluminum alloy. I_t at point A is chosen as the effective cup center. Point B is the intersection of the analysis line with the stretch-draw line. L_s is the curved distance AB, and L is the curved distance BC. (These and the other dimensions shown are given in Table 11.6 to be discussed later.) [10.13], [11.5].

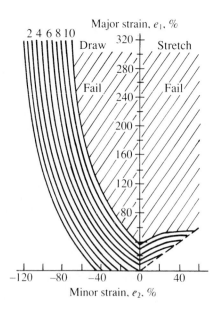

FIGURE 11.76

This modified Keeler-Goodwin FLD for AISI 1008-type, 20-gauge sheet steel shows the critical strain combinations for large negative minor strains. The hatched section represents strain combinations for which onset of localized thinning or visible necking is probable. Zones 1 to 10 are a means of indicating relative severity (RS) of different strain combinations. Severity zones 9 and 10 are considered critical, zones 6 to 8 optimum, and zones 5 or less under utilization. (*From D. A. Chatfield and S. P. Keeler, "Designing for Formability," Metal Progress, Vol. 99, No. 5, 1971, p. 116.*)

stamping from the corner to the crest, as shown in Fig. 11.75. These two examples of analysis lines will be discussed later. The major and minor strains are calculated for each deformed grid circle lying on the analysis line through the potential failure area. The major and minor strain values for each point on the line may be translated into a severity zone rating by use of Fig. 11.76.

Two examples of shapes mentioned above will be used to illustrate the solution of an analysis line and the shape analysis technique. One involves the computer optimization of a simple drawn cup as shown in Fig. 11.74 and the other involves the experimental optimization of an automobile fuel tank upper-stamping, shown in Fig. 11.75. The simple cup shape will be used to illustrate shape analysis as a computer optimization problem. The fuel tank stamping will be used to outline the experimental approach. As mentioned in the foregoing, three categories of variables are involved: (1) material variables, (2) shape variables, and (3) die variables.

11.2.12.4 COMPUTER OPTIMIZATION IN SHAPE ANALYSIS OF A DRAWN CUP

[11.17]. The material variables are expressed in terms of a forming line whose equation can be written as

$$Y_1 = m_1 \, (\%\text{Draw}) + C \tag{11.97}$$

where m_1 and C, the slope and intercept, respectively, are fixed material parameters, which can be obtained from the SD diagram such as Fig. 11.72. %Draw in Eq. (11.97) is the percentage draw defined as

$$\%\text{Draw} = \frac{(L_d - L_{0d})(100)}{L_{ds} - L_0} \tag{11.98}$$

where L_0 is the original radius of the blank, L_d is the length of the drawn portion of the cup from the top edge to the stretch-draw boundary, L_{ds} is the final formed length of the drawn cup from the center of the bottom to the top edge, and L_{0d} is the original distance from the edge of the blank to the die ring, since drawing takes place outside the die ring and stretching inside. In terms of the other dimensions shown in Fig. 11.74(b), it can be expressed as

$$L_{0d} = \frac{D_0 - D_d}{2.0} - r_2 \tag{11.99}$$

The percentage stretch is defined as

$$\%\text{Stretch} = \frac{(L_s - L_{0s})}{L_{ds} - L_0} (100) \tag{11.100}$$

where L_s is the length of the stretched portion of the cup, L_{0s} is the original distance from the cup centerline to the die ring or the die radius [10.13, p. 155]. By substitution and manipulation, both %Draw and %Stretch can be expressed in terms of D_0 (the blank diameter), D_d (the die throat diameter), L_d (the drawing length), L_s (the stretch length), and r_2 (the die radius).

The shape variables are given by the forming ratio, Y_2, as follows:

$$Y_2 = \left[\frac{H_s}{D_p}(\%\text{Stretch})\right] + \left[\frac{D_0}{D_d}(\%\text{Draw})\right] \qquad (11.101)$$

where H_s is the height of the cup to the SD boundary, and D_p is the diameter of the punch. The other variables are defined above. H_s is expressed in terms of L_s, D_p, r_1, and t_0, if only the cylindrical cup wall thickness is reduced to t and the other portions remain at t_0 [11.17].

The overall severity of the part (SEV) can be calculated from

$$\text{SEV} = \frac{Y_2 - Y_3}{Y_1 - Y_3} \qquad (11.102)$$

where Y_3 is given by $Y_3 = m_2$ (%Draw), which is the equation for the zero forming line in Fig. 11.73 (where m_2 is the slope), Y_1 is the equation for the forming line ($Y_1 = m_1$ (%Draw + c)), and Y_2 is Eq. (11.101) for the forming ratio. (m_1 is the slope and c is the Y-intercept of the forming line in Fig. 11.72).

This problem can now be formulated as an optimization problem, in which the overall part severity, SEV, is minimized subject to certain constraints put on certain variables. In this case, a Fortran computer program DEEPDR has been used to solve this problem, utilizing the optimization package OPTISEP to obtain the optimum [11.17].

From the above optimization procedure for certain constraints, the following general, expected conclusions were obtained: (1) for an increase in the percentage draw, %Draw, the severity decreases, i.e., the drawability of the material improves, (2) as the initial diameter of the blank D_0 decreases, the severity also decreases, i.e., the drawing operation becomes safer, (3) as the die radius r_2 increases, the severity decreases, i.e., drawing operation becomes safer, (4) as the drawing length L_d increases by adjusting the blankholding system, the severity decreases, (5) as the punch radius r_1 increases, there is a small decrease in severity, and (6) as the stretch length L_s increases, the severity increases, that is, L_s should be made as small as possible.

11.2.12.5 EXPERIMENTAL OPTIMIZATION IN THE SHAPE ANALYSIS OF A FUEL TANK STAMPING [10.13, pp. 184–185].

A more complex stamping, the upper half of an automobile fuel tank as shown in Fig. 11.75, is used in this example. Review of the part shape indicated that the critical forming area is located in one of the corners, which might be considered to be one-quarter of a deep-drawn circular cup. A diagonal analysis line is drawn from the effective corner to the crest from C to A, as shown in Fig. 11.75. The region from C to the edge of the drawn blank at the right-front corner, C', has no significant effect on the forming operation.

The stretch-draw boundary is the boundary on the part between biaxial stretching and drawing. It is the boundary between the metal initially suspended over the die cavity that is stretched over the punch and the metal in the flange that moves into the die cavity over the die ring. If the dimensions L_d, L_s, L_0, and L_{ds} are defined as before, L_{0s}, and L_{0d} are determined by the horizontal projection of the appropriate sections of the analysis line. C_{hs}, the stretch cup height, and C_{hd}, the draw cup height, are the vertical projections of these sections. The draw fraction D and the stretch fraction S are given by Eqs. (11.98) and (11.100), respectively.

The cup-forming ratios in stretch, R_s, and in draw, R_d, are given by

$$R_s = \frac{C_{hs}}{C_{ws}} \quad \text{and} \quad R_d = \frac{E_{bw}}{C_{wd}} \tag{11.103}$$

where C_{hs} is the stretch cup height, C_{ws} is the stretch cup width at the stretch-draw boundary, E_{bw} is the effective blank width, and C_{wd} is the draw width at the ring die.

The forming severity of the part may be calculated as follows:

$$\text{SEV} = \frac{[(R_s(S) + R_d)(D) - D]}{[D(\text{LDR} - O_d) + O_d - D]} \tag{11.104}$$

where LDR is Swift's limiting drawing ratio, S is the stretch fraction, D the draw fraction, and O_d is the Olsen cup-test value.

TABLE 11.6
Identification of symbols used in shape analysis of fuel tank stamping (Fig. 11.75) and their values [10.13, p. 185]

Symbol	Identification	Value	
I_t	Analysis-line inner terminal		
O_t	Analysis-line outer terminal		
L_s	Final analysis-line length in stretch	10.75 in (273.1 mm)	
L_d	Final analysis-line length in draw	10.35 in (262.9 mm)	
L_{0s}	Original analysis-line length in stretch	9.60 in (243.8 mm)	
L_{0d}	Original analysis-line length in draw	8.43 in (214.1 mm)	
C_{hs}	Stretch cup height	3.34 in (84.8 mm)	
C_{hd}	Draw cup height		
L_{ds}	Final analysis-line length	21.10 in (535.4 mm)	
L_0	Original analysis-line length	18.03 in (438.0 mm)	
S	Amount of forming contributed by stretching	0.375	
D	Amount of forming contributed by drawing	0.625	
C_{ws}	Stretch cup width at stretch/draw boundary	17.48 in (444.0 mm)	
C_{wd}	Draw cup width at die ring	19.80 in (503.0 mm)	
E_{bw}	Effective blank width	37.02 in (940.3 mm)	
R_s	Stretch cup ratio	0.191	
R_d	Draw cup ratio	1.81	
		(a)	(b)
O_d	Olsen cup-test value	0.375	0.346
LDR	Swift limiting draw ratio	2.28	2.09
SEV	Forming severity	0.45	0.76

(a) Terne-coated steel.
(b) 5182-O aluminum.

Using the parameters for terne- (alloy of tin and lead) coated steel and 5182-O aluminum alloy shown in Table 11.6, one obtains a forming severity, SEV, for the steel of 0.65 and for the Al of 0.76. For these values to be comparable such variables as the blank hold-down pressure and lubrication would have to be adjusted so that the stretch-draw boundary would be in the same location. Otherwise, a new set of calculations would have to be made on the basis of the new boundary. These calculations would indicate the change in the severity due to the change in tooling variables. From these calculations it would appear to be highly probable that the aluminum alloy would be suitable for forming the fuel tank stamping shown in Fig. 11.75.

11.2.12.6   EDGE CONDITION ANALYSIS. The ability of a sheetmetal to be deformed without failure by fracture or excessive thinning at a sheared edge or hole is termed *edge formability* [11.18]. Since high-strength steels are notch-sensitive, edge formability will be of growing importance as the use of these steels increases in the future.

Edge condition analysis may be of concern in (1) edge formability (simulative) testing, and (2) edge forming analysis of production parts containing formed stretch-flanged holes or reentrant angles, in which the formed edge is subjected to tension. The hole expansion test, mentioned in Chap. 3, is a well-known test to simulate edge formability. One such test is the Siebel-Pomp test shown in Fig. 11.65(d). A circular blank 80 mm (3.15 in) in diameter or a 80 mm square with a central hole 12 mm (0.473 in) in diameter is stretched by deep-drawing with a flat-bottomed punch as shown in Fig. 11.65(d), until the first crack appears at the edge of the hole. In the edge formability test, the formability index may be determined as follows:

$$\varepsilon_{sp} = \frac{(d_0 - \Delta d)(100)}{d_0}\% \qquad (11.105)$$

where d_0 is the hole diameter before drawing and Δd is the difference between the maximum and minimum diameters of the hole at the moment of fracture.

The objections to this technique as a formability test is that the results depend on (1) the method of machining and finishing of the hole, (2) the ratio of the initial hole and punch diameters, (3) thickness of the sheetmetal, and (4) the tooling used.

The objective of the foregoing hole-expansion test is to evaluate the formability of a given sheetmetal material for a given condition of hole preparation and metal thickness. Edge condition analysis can also be used to evaluate whether a given material with a certain edge condition can be used to produce a part containing a stretch flanged hole or reentrant angles.

The procedure used in edge condition analysis is as follows:

1. Characterize the material being used
2. Obtain the flange stretch limit of the material from Table 11.7

TABLE 11.7
Flange stretch limits with zero burr [11.18]

Material	Stretch limit
Hot-rolled low-carbon steel (DQSK)†	65%
Cold-rolled low-carbon steel (DQSK)†	55%
Cold-rolled low-carbon steel (commercial quality)	50%
High-strength low alloy steel	40%
Aluminum (less than 1.78 mm (0.07 in)	25%

† DQSK = Drawing quality special killed steel.

3. Determine the burr height by measuring the metal thickness at the edge and away from it. The difference is the burr height
4. Calculate the burr height to metal thickness ratio
5. Obtain the percent remaining stretchability left in the metal at the edge by use of the empirical curve in Fig. 11.77
6. Calculate the percent stretchability remaining in the burred metal by multiplying the flange stretch limit from step 2 by the percent of remaining stretchability obtained in step 5
7. Measure the radius of curvature of the blank internal edge before flanging, R_1, and the flange edge after flanging, R_2

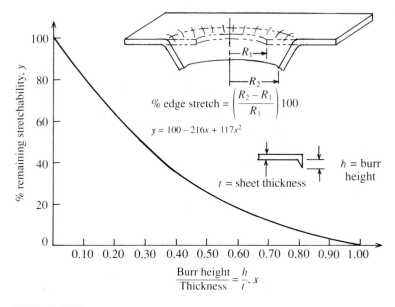

FIGURE 11.77
Graph used to estimate the percentage stretchability remaining in a part with a burred edge. The regression equation for this line is $Y = 100 - 216x + 117x^2$ [11.18].

8. Calculate the percentage of edge stretch required by forming, such as for the simple flanged shape shown in Fig. 11.77, as follows:

$$\%\text{Edge stretch} = \left(\frac{R_2}{R_1} - 1\right)100 \qquad (11.106)$$

9. Compare the percentage of edge stretch required from step 8 to the percentage of stretchability remaining in the burred metal from step 6. If the required stretch is less than the stretchability of the metal, then the probability is favorable that the flange can be made without cracking. If the required stretch is greater than the available stretch, then a change must be made either to the metal used, the edge condition of the metal, or the design, that is, R_1 or R_2

ACKNOWLEDGMENT

The material and most of the illustrations in this chapter were adapted from the references as indicated in the text and in the legends by the numbers of the references enclosed in square brackets pursuant to all copyrights.

REFERENCES

11.1. Hosford, W. F., "The Effect of Anisotropy and Work Hardening on Cup Drawing, Redrawing, and Ironing," *Formability: Analysis, Modeling, and Experimentation*, S. S. Hecker, A. K. Ghosh, and H. L. Gegel (eds.), *Proc. Symp.* October 1977, AIME, New York, pp. 78-95.

11.2. Hasek, V. V., and K. Lange, "Use of the Slip-line Method in Deep Drawing of Large Irregular Shaped Components," in *7th NAMRC*, 1979, SME, pp. 65-71.

11.3. Gloeckl, H., and K. Lange, "Computer Aided Design for Deep Drawn Irregular Shaped Components," in *11th NAMRC*, 1983, SME, pp. 243-251.

11.4. Nagpal, V., "Analysis of Thickness Reduction in Deep Drawing with Simultaneous Ironing," *6th NAMRC*, 1978, SME, Dearborn, Michigan, pp. 158-165.

11.5. Kasper, A. S., D. G. Adams, and J. A. Dicello, "Sheet Metal Forming Limits with Manufacturing Applications," presented at the Twenty-First Sagamore Army Materials Conference on Advances in Deformation Processing, Aug. 13-16, 1974.

11.6. McCandless, A. J., and A. S. Bahrani, "Strain Paths, Limit Strains and Forming Limit Diagram," *7th NAMRC*, 1979, SME, pp. 184-190.

11.7. Ghosh, A. K., "How to Rate Stretch Formability of Sheet Metals," *Metal Progress*, ASM, May 1975, pp. 52-54.

11.8. Ghosh, A. K., "The Effect of Lateral Drawing-In on Stretch Formability," *Metal Engr. Quarterly*, ASM, Aug. 1975, pp. 53-61.

11.9. Kleemola, H. J., and J. O. Kumpulainen, "Factors Influencing the Forming Limit Diagram: Part 1—The Experimental Determination of the Forming Limits of Sheet Steel," *Jour. of Mech. Working Tech.*, vol. 3, 1980, pp. 289-302.

11.10. Embury, J. D., and G. H. LeRoy, "Failure Maps Applied to Metal Deformation Processes," *Fracture 1977*, vol. 1, ICF4, 1977, pp. 15-42.

11.11. Gerdeen, J. C. et al. "The Validity of the Tensile Anisotropy Ratio in Biaxial Stretching of Sheet Metal," *15th NAMRC*, 1987, SME, pp. 353-357.

11.12. Lee, D., "Computer-Aided Control of Sheet Metal Forming Processes," *Journal of Metals*, vol. 34, no. 10, November 1982, pp. 20-29.

11.13. Bathe, K., *ADINA, A Finite Element Program for Automatic Dynamic Incremental Nonlinear Analysis*, MIT, Cambridge, Massachusetts, December 1978.

11.14. Kaspar, A. S., "How We Will Predict Sheet Metal Formability," *Metal Progress*, ASM, Oct. 1969, pp. 159–160.

11.15. Gronostajski, J., and C. Banasiak, "The Effect of Anisotropic Plasticity and Work-Hardening on the Sheet Metal Drawability," Sheet Metal Forming and Energy Conservation, 9th Biennial Congress, IDDRG, 1976, ASM, pp. 81–96.

11.16. Johnson, W. E., and P. A. Stine, "Application of Sheetmetal Research to High Production Fabrication Shops," ibid, p. 235.

11.17. Badawy, A., "Cup Deep Drawing, An Optimization Problem," Process Modeling Tools, Proceedings of ASM Materials and Processes Congress, 1980, p. 75.

11.18. Dinda, S., H. F. James, S. P. Keeler, and P. A. Stine, "How to Use Circle Grid Analysis for Die Tryout," ASM, Metals Park, Ohio 1981, pp. 7-1 to 7-10.

11.19. Guy, A. G., *Elements of Physical Metallurgy*, Addison-Wesley, Reading, Mass., 1959, p. 421.

11.20. *ASM Metals Handbook*, 9th Ed., Vol. 1, Properties and Selection: Irons and Steels, Metals Park, Ohio, pp. 550 and 554.

11.21. Duncan, J. L., and T. Altan, "New Directions in Sheet Metal Forming Research," *CIRP*, vol. 291, 1980, pp. 153–156.

11.22. LeRoy, G., and J. D. Embury, "The Utilization of Failure Maps to Compare the Fracture Modes Occurring in Aluminum Alloys," *Formability Analysis Modeling and Experimentation, AIME/ASM Symposium*, 1977, pp. 204 and 206.

11.23. Newby, J. R., "Strain Analysis of Formed Sheet Metal Parts," *Metals Engineering Quarterly*, vol. 15, May 1975, pp. 10–17.

11.24. Hecker, S. S., "Experimental Studies of Sheet Stretchability," Formability: Analysis Modeling, and Experimentation, *Proc. of Symp.*, Oct. 1977. S. S. Hecker, A. K. Ghosh, and H. L. Gegel (eds.), Pub. of AIME, pp. 150–176.

11.25. ASTM Standard E643, Vol. 03.01, *1986 Annual Book of ASTM Standards*, p. 703.

11.26. Keeler, S. P., "Forming Limit Criteria—Sheets," in Advances in Deformation Processing, J. J. Burke and V. Weiss (eds.), Plenum Press, 1978, p. 133.

11.27. Hecker, S. S., "A Cup Test for Assessing Stretchability," *Metals Engr. Quart.*, ASM, Nov. 1974, p. 34.

PROBLEMS

11.1. If the average elongation of a material is 40 percent and the average anisotropy ratio is 1.2, what are the formability indices for the following cup tests: (1) Swift, (2) Olsen, and (3) Fukui? Compare the LDR obtained by Eq. (11.88) to those obtained from Eq. (11.91). Compare the formability indices obtained from Eqs. (11.88), (11.89), and (11.90) to those obtained from Figs. 11.68, 11.69, and 11.70. What conclusion may be drawn regarding the usefulness of the graphs?

11.2. By use of the data in Table 11.6, calculate the severity of forming the terne coated steel.

11.3. Calculate the percent draw and the percent stretch for a solution treated rimmed steel from the following data: $D_0 = 4.664$ in, $L_d = 0.818$ in, $r_2 = 0.444$ in, $t_0 = 0.0499$, $L_s = 2.474$ in, and $D_d = 3.01$ in.

11.4. Evaluate whether or not a part can be made of a commercial quality, cold-rolled, low-carbon steel, in which a hole flange is formed. The steel is 0.027 in thick, the punched hole in the part is 2.0 in in diameter before forming, and the flange radius is 2.7 in. Measurements at the edge of the hole and away from it after punching, indicates that the burr height is 0.003 in.

CAD/CAM
OF
SHEETMETAL
DRAWING

12.1 GENERAL COVERAGE

12.1.1 Computer Modeling of Sheetmetal
Forming Processes [12.1]

The shapes of sheetmetal parts can be divided into two categories, (1) those whose surface is developable and singly curved and (2) those (stampings and pressings) formed by stretching the sheet so that it becomes nondevelopable and doubly curved. The former can be described by straight-line generators and are single parameter surfaces. The latter are irregular and highly complex shapes and cannot be fitted by primitive solids such as cones, toroids, and ellipsoids.

The use of elemental shapes or a myriad of surface points to approximate a surface is rather unsuited to describe the surface of metal formed part. Any three-dimensional surface can be described in two-dimensional form by use of parametric surface patches as shown in Fig. 12.1, which greatly condenses the information that must be stored. (A parametric surface patch is a portion of a curved surface bounded only by curves that are a function of parametric equations, in which the change of one parameter changes the curvature of the surface.)

Instead of using "clay" models, the style designer can generate shapes by use of a computer, the resulting standardized information can then be used to machine a model and/or dies by use of a computer-controlled metal-cutting machine.

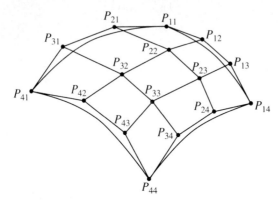

FIGURE 12.1
A three-dimensional surface
described in two-dimensional form
by use of parametric surface patches.
The control points define the surface
of a Bezier patch [12.1].

The use of a grid of small circles, discussed in the foregoing, is a useful but not too convenient method for measuring strains over the surface of a part. It is preferable to use a regular array of points such as of a square grid for this purpose. After deformation, the location of these points can be determined with a coordinate measuring machine and the deformed mesh can be plotted by a computer graphics system as shown in Fig. 12.2. The strain at a point can be determined by comparing the displacement of the mesh before and after deformation.

Some methods for mathematical modeling of the deformation process in sheetmetal forming are by use of (1) shell theory, in which the surface is divided into a number of shell elements of spherical, cylindrical, or toroidal shapes to develop a flexible modeling system, (2) finite element method, which has been discussed very briefly in Chap. 4 and will be discussed subsequently very briefly as applied to stretch forming of sheetmetal, (3) method of characteristics, which utilizes numerical methods of computation of slip-line fields represented by equations of characteristics for the α and β slip-lines of maximum shear, (4)

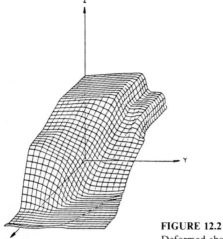

FIGURE 12.2
Deformed shape of a square grid marked on a flat sheet [12.1].

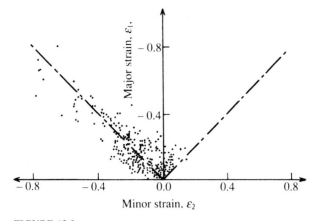

FIGURE 12.3

Nodal strains measured in a rectangular deep-drawn pan showing that the significant strain path is scattered about the constant thickness one, where the major and minor strains are equal and opposite [12.1].

kinematic models, which are based on the assumption that the only significant strain path is the constant thickness one in which the major and minor strains are equal and opposite as shown in Fig. 11.28 and Fig. 12.3. This model, in which the forming process becomes a kinematic rather than a continuum mechanics problem, is amenable to analysis by an approach called geometric modeling discussed in the appendix of this chapter. The other methods of mathematical modeling will not be discussed here.

A number of examples are reported in the literature for use of mathematical, geometric modeling in sheetmetal forming. Some of these will be used here as illustrations.

12.1.2 Finite Element Modeling of a Simple Stretch-Formed Part [12.2]

12.1.2.1 INTRODUCTION. The finite element method (FEM) was discussed in general in Sec. 4.5 and its application to sheetmetal forming in Sec. 10.8. An example, of modeling of a stretch-formed automotive panel using an elastic-plastic, *membrane*-type, finite element formulation, which includes consideration of friction between the punch and the sheet being formed will be discussed here [12.2].

It is very desirable to assess a design of a sheetmetal deep drawing early in the design process as shown in Fig. 12.4 by computer modeling rather than by tryout of actual constructed dies. (See Section 11.2.1.)

12.1.2.2 COMPUTATIONAL CONSIDERATIONS OF THE FEM MODEL [12.3]. To model sheetmetal formability, three primary characteristics must be described analytically (1) die geometry, (2) sheetmetal properties, and (3) die-sheetmetal frictional parameters. (See Section 11.2.1.)

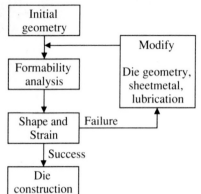

FIGURE 12.4

Flowchart for a computerized die tryout system [12.2].

12.1.2.3 DESCRIPTION OF A FEM CODE [12.3]. If all the elemental stiffness equations in rate form are assembled in the usual way, the following stiffness equation is obtained:

$$\mathbf{K}\dot{\mathbf{U}} = \dot{\mathbf{F}} \tag{12.1}$$

where $\mathbf{K}$ is the global stiffness matrix, $\dot{\mathbf{U}}$ and $\dot{\mathbf{F}}$ are the global nodal velocity vector and the corresponding force-rate vector, which are defined by

$$\dot{\mathbf{U}}^T = (\dot{U}_1^{(1)}, \dot{U}_2^{(1)}, \dot{w}^{(1)}, \dot{U}_1^{(2)}, \ldots) \tag{12.2}$$

$$\dot{\mathbf{F}}^T = (\dot{T}_1^{(1)}, \dot{T}_2^{(1)}, \dot{Q}^{(1)}, \dot{T}_1^{(2)}, \ldots) \tag{12.3}$$

where U_1, U_2, and w are components of the displacement vector $\mathbf{U}$; $\dot{U}$, and $\dot{W}$, the horizontal and vertical velocities, are common vectors defined by

$$\dot{\mathbf{U}}^T = (\dot{U}_1^{(1)}, \dot{U}_2^{(1)}, \dot{U}_1^{(2)}, \dot{U}_2^{(2)}, \dot{U}_1^{(3)}, \dot{U}_2^{(3)}),$$

and

$$\dot{\mathbf{W}}^T = (\dot{w}^{(1)}, \dot{w}^{(2)}, \dot{w}^{(3)}),$$

where the superscripts refer to the node numbers of the elements and $(\ )^T$ denotes the transpose; and each $\dot{T}_\alpha^{(j)}$ and $\dot{Q}^{(j)}$ is the sum of the elemental $\dot{t}_\alpha^{(j)}$ and $\dot{q}^{(j)}$ associated with the elements sharing node j, and $\dot{w}^{(j)}$ is the vertical displacement rate at node j.

For the nodes, in which the punch and sheetmetal are in contact during penetration, the relative velocity of slip between the punch and the sheet is

$$\mathbf{v}_{rel} = \mathbf{v}_s - \mathbf{v}_p \tag{12.4}$$

where $\mathbf{v}_s$ and $\mathbf{v}_p$ are the sheet and punch velocities, respectively. This relative velocity is tangential to the punch surface, so that

$$\mathbf{v}_{rel} \cdot \mathbf{n} = 0 \tag{12.5}$$

where $\mathbf{n}$ is the local unit normal to the punch.

For the nodes in contact with the punch the above constraining equation (12.5) requires

$$\dot{w} - S_{,\alpha}\dot{U}_{\alpha} = 1 \qquad (12.6)$$

where $\dot{w}$ = vertical displacement rate

$S_{,\alpha}$ = slope of the punch surface, which is evaluated at the current nodal coordinates.

During slip, the horizontal and vertical components of the relative velocities are $\dot{U}_{\alpha}$ and $S_{,\alpha}\dot{U}_{\alpha}$, respectively, and the corresponding components of the nodal force may be expressed by use of equation (12.6) as

$$\begin{pmatrix} T_{\alpha} \\ Q \end{pmatrix} = \begin{pmatrix} -S_{,\alpha}/N - \mu\dot{U}_{\alpha}/V \\ 1/N - \mu S_{,\alpha}\dot{U}_{\alpha}/V \end{pmatrix} P \qquad (12.7)$$

where $N = [1 + S_{,\alpha}S_{,\alpha}]^{1/2}$

$V \equiv \|\mathbf{v}_{\text{rel}}\| = [\dot{U}_{\alpha}\dot{U}_{\alpha} + (S_{,\alpha}\dot{U}_{\alpha})^2]^{1/2}$

$P \equiv$ normal component of the external nodal force

A typical schematic of an FEM code for solving a sheetmetal forming problem is shown in Fig. 12.5 [12.4].

During an increment of punch travel into the die cavity, the forces at each node in contact with the punch surface are calculated by Wang and Budiansky in their classic paper [12.3] as shown by the following equation, which is obtained by differentiating Eq. (12.7) and using $S_{,\alpha} = S_{,\alpha\beta}\dot{U}_{\beta}$:

$$\begin{pmatrix} \dot{T}_{\alpha} \\ \dot{Q} \end{pmatrix} = \left\{ \begin{pmatrix} S_{,\alpha}/N \\ -1/N \end{pmatrix} \dot{P} + P \begin{pmatrix} S_{,\alpha\rho}/N - S_{,\alpha}S_{,\beta}S_{,\beta\rho}/N^3 \\ S_{,\alpha}S_{,\alpha\rho}/N^3 \end{pmatrix} \dot{U}_{\rho} \right\}$$

$$- \mu \left\{ \begin{pmatrix} \dot{U}_{\alpha}/V \\ S_{,\alpha}\dot{U}_{\alpha}/V \end{pmatrix} \dot{P} + \frac{P}{V^3} \begin{pmatrix} -\dot{U}_{\alpha}\dot{U}_{\beta}\dot{U}_{\gamma}S_{,\beta}S_{,\gamma\rho} \\ \dot{U}_{\alpha}\dot{U}_{\alpha}\dot{U}_{\gamma}S_{,\gamma\rho} \end{pmatrix} \dot{U}_{\rho} \right\}$$

$$- \mu \frac{P}{V^3} \varepsilon_{\alpha\beta}\varepsilon_{\rho\eta} \begin{pmatrix} \dot{U}_{\beta} + S_{,\beta}S_{,\gamma}\dot{U}_{\gamma} \\ \dot{U}_{\beta}S_{,\alpha} \end{pmatrix} \dot{U}_{\eta}\dot{U}_{\rho} \qquad (12.8)$$

where $\dot{T}_{\alpha}$ and $\dot{Q}$ are the time rate of change of the nodal forces in the horizontal and vertical directions, respectively. The term U_{α} is the horizontal nodal displacement vector. $S_{,\alpha}$ and $S_{,\alpha\beta}$ are, respectively, the first and second derivatives of the punch surface, and $\varepsilon_{\alpha\beta}$ is the alternating tensor defined by $\varepsilon_{11} = \varepsilon_{22} = 0$, $\varepsilon_{12} = -\varepsilon_{21} = 1$ [12.3].

The solution to Eq. (12.8) may be made more obvious by substituting the symbols A, B, C, etc. for the complex terms within the brackets to give the following equation:

$$\begin{pmatrix} \dot{T}_{\alpha} \\ \dot{Q} \end{pmatrix} = -\left\{ \begin{pmatrix} A \\ B \end{pmatrix} \dot{P} + P \begin{pmatrix} C \\ D \end{pmatrix} \dot{U}_{\rho} \right\}$$

$$- \mu \left\{ \begin{pmatrix} E \\ F \end{pmatrix} \dot{P} + \frac{P}{V^3} \begin{pmatrix} G \\ H \end{pmatrix} \dot{U}_{\rho} \right\} - \mu \frac{P}{V^3} \varepsilon_{\alpha\beta}\varepsilon_{\rho\eta} \begin{pmatrix} I \\ J \end{pmatrix} \dot{U}_{\eta}\dot{U}_{\rho} \qquad (12.9)$$

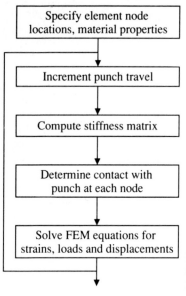

FIGURE 12.5
Schematic of FEM code for solving sheetmetal forming problems [12.4].

The solution, therefore, would have the following form

$$\dot{T} = -\{A \cdot \dot{P} + P \cdot C \cdot \dot{U}_\rho\} - \mu\left\{E \cdot P + \frac{P}{V^3} \cdot G \cdot \dot{U}_\rho\right\} - \mu\frac{P}{V^3}\varepsilon_{\alpha\beta}\varepsilon_{\rho\nu} \cdot I \cdot \dot{U}_\eta\dot{U}_\rho \quad (12.10)$$

$$\dot{Q} = -\{B \cdot \dot{P} + P \cdot D \cdot \dot{U}_\rho\} - \mu\left\{F \cdot \dot{P} + \frac{P}{V^3} \cdot H \cdot \dot{U}_\rho\right\} - \mu\frac{P}{V^3}\varepsilon_{\alpha\beta}\varepsilon_{\rho\eta} \cdot J \cdot \dot{U}_\eta\dot{U}_\rho \quad (12.11)$$

The terms in Eq. (12.8) have simple interpretations. The terms proportional to $\dot{P}$ give the changes in $\dot{T}_\alpha$ and $\dot{Q}$ due to change in the normal force magnitude; the term containing $\dot{U}_\rho$ reflects the change of the frictional force vector associated with its rotation about the current normal to the sheet; and the remaining terms give the nodal force changes due to the directional changes in the normal and frictional forces due to rotation of the current normal to the sheet. It can also be noted that the terms containing $\dot{U}_\rho$ vanish identically whenever the horizontal direction of the relative slip remains unchanged [12.3].

Introduction of Eq. (12.8) into the right-hand side of the global stiffness equation (12.1) for each contacting, slipping node introduces the extra unknown $\dot{P}$ at each of these nodes. But then the augmentation of Eq. (12.1) by the constraining equations (12.6) at the contacting, slipping nodes brings the number of equations up to the total number of unknowns. It should be noted here that Eq. (12.8) introduces nonlinearities in the velocities, as well as a term in $\dot{U}_\rho$ [12.3].

By using the finite element procedure discussed in the preceding section, numerical results have been obtained for the hemispherical punch stretching of a circular sheets shown in Fig. 12.6, having a grid of triangular elements as shown in the pie-shaped mesh shown in Fig. 12.7. In obtaining the foregoing results,

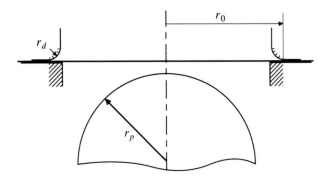

FIGURE 12.6
Punch and die geometry used in hemispherical punch stretching. (Lock bead is not shown. See Fig. 11.51.) [12.3]

the following uniaxial true stress–true strain relation was assumed:

$$\varepsilon = \frac{\sigma}{E} + \left(\frac{\sigma}{K}\right)^{1/n} \tag{12.12}$$

where E is Young's modulus, n is the strainhardening exponent, and K is the strength coefficient. The familiar power law can be obtained by dropping the term σ/E [12.3].

The equation of the hemispherical punch is

$$S = [r_p^2 - (x_1^2 + x_2^2)]^{1/2} - r_p \tag{12.13}$$

where r_p is the radius of the punch, and the sheet is clamped at a radius of r_0 where the radius of the die is r_d.

If, for *hemispherical punch stretching* with $r_0 = r_p$ and $r_d = 0$, and for the material parameters $E = 206.8$ GPa, $K = 500$ MPa, $n = 0.2$, and $R = 1$ with $\mu = 0.2$, the results in Fig. 12.8 were obtained in comparison with axisymmetric rigid-plastic solutions. Figure 12.9 shows the comparison of the numerical results with experimental results for the radial and circumferential strain distributions at three punch travel distances.

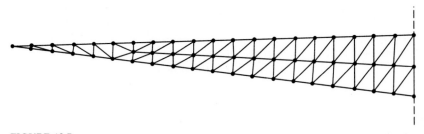

FIGURE 12.7
A pie-shaped sector of a circle of a finite element mesh used· to study sheetmetal deformation of a circular blank by a hemispherical punch [12.4].

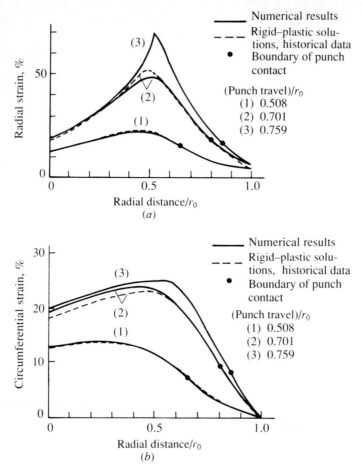

FIGURE 12.8

Comparison of finite element results presented here with existing axisymmetric rigid–plastic solutions for (a) radial, and (b) circumferential strain distributions for $n = 0.2$, $R = 1$, $r_p = r_0$, and $r_d = 0$ [12.3].

As can be seen in Eq. (12.8), the nodal forces depend on the punch surface in a complicated manner. The dependence becomes a matter of concern when parametric surface descriptions are used, because these descriptions may introduce oscillations in the punch surface which in turn perturb the FEM solution. The magnitude and nature of this perturbation is not easily inferred by inspection of Eq. (12.8). It may therefore be necessary to compare solutions using analytic and parametric surface representations to determine the severity of the problem [12.4].

The FEM code written by Wang and Budiansky is for a material which assumes an elastic–plastic, rate-insensitive (Hollomon) isotropic strainhardening sheetmetal, possessing normal anisotropy. It assumes Coulomb friction, i.e., friction proportional to the contact pressure, and deals with both material and

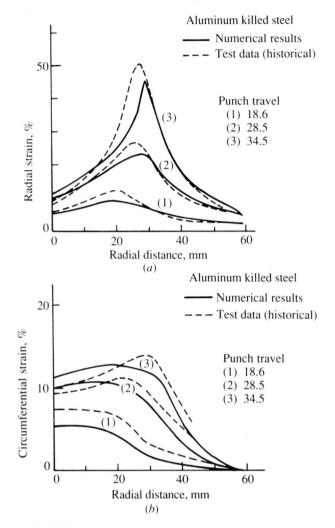

FIGURE 12.9
Comparison of numerical results presented here with experimental data for (a) radial (major) strain and (b) circumferential (minor) strain distributions for AK steel. The coefficient of friction used in the calculations is 0.17 (see Fig. 11.52(a)) [12.3].

geometric nonlinearities. To reduce the computer running time by a factor of about 1/40 from hundreds of hours to a matter of hours, in this example, the above program was completely recoded to a vectorized Gauss elimination scheme in Cray machine language for us on a CRAY 1-S/2000 superspeed computer [12.2].

The part in one example was designed to be stretch-formed from a "flat" sheet by clamping tightly around the outer perimeter, so as to allow no drawing-in [12.2].

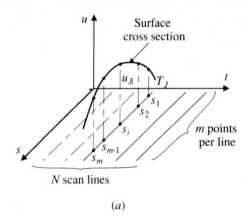

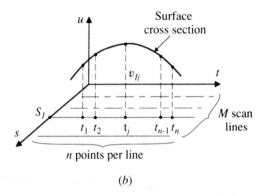

(a)

(b)

FIGURE 12.10
Location of data used to define a
surface $U(s, t)$, from (a) N scan lines,
parallel to the s axis with s coordinates
and (b) M scan lines parallel to the
t-axis with t coordinates [12.4].

12.1.2.4 DESCRIPTION OF A PARAMETRIC SURFACE. The method of describing
a punch (or die) surface such as of a "clay" model may be done by use of data
obtained from two sets of scan line as shown in Fig. 12.10 [12.4].

In this example (of a Camaro lift window outer), the analysis began by
obtaining scan lines in two directions from a plastic cast as shown of a rectangular
panel in Fig. 12.11. The actual number of lines is much greater than shown in
the figure. There were 50 equally spaced lines running the length of the part and
75 running the width with 225 and 150 equally spaced data points respectively.
The data lines are fitted by a cubic B-spline representation. (See the appendix

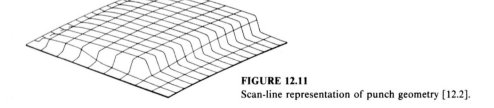

FIGURE 12.11
Scan-line representation of punch geometry [12.2].

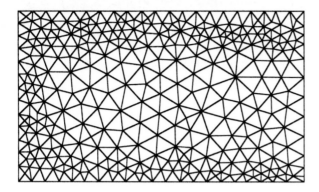

FIGURE 12.12
FEM mesh for the panel shown
in Fig. 12.11 [12.2].

of this chapter.) The fitting parameters, in the form of a long table of coefficients, serve as input to the main code for evaluating rapidly and efficiently the punch and die positions, slopes, and curvature [12.2].

The finite element mesh as shown in Fig. 12.12 is generated by a computer with regions of rapidly varying strain requiring a large number of elements such as the edge of the panel whose model is shown in Fig. 12.11. The mechanical properties of the sheetmetal, including Hollomon strainhardening, and Coulomb friction are incorporated in the computer code. Strain-rate sensitivity is not included as it is considered less critical in biaxial, slow-speed, room-temperature stretching. The parameters used are given in Table 12.1 [12.2].

12.1.2.5 FEM OUTPUT. In this example, the program prints out monitoring data every 20 punch increments of penetration. For the sample part used, 500 punch increments are used from a flat sheet to the full part depth.

The results of this example will not be discussed here. As expected as in Fig. 12.12, the forming strains are very low across the top of the part, moderately high in the steep side walls, and the highest at the corners.

In spite of the amount of high-speed computer time required, much time and expense may be saved in the die-tryout stage. Because the overall procedure is still in the design stage when the design is evaluated, radical modifications of the die can still be made. Also, this computer system presents a convenient way to evaluate various choices of materials for a particular part and the effect of friction at various points in the die to determine the amount of lubrication

TABLE 12.1
The Example Part Parameters

Number of nodes	332
Number of elements	595
Coefficient of friction	0.15
R-value	1.8
Young's modulus	210 GPa
Strainhardening exponent	0.21

required. Factors such as the foregoing make this system worthwhile. This computer system would be more applicable for sheetmetal parts requiring areas of localized deformation containing regions of rapidly varying strain. For simpler formed parts, a less rigorous, more approximate system, discussed elsewhere, would be used.

12.1.3   CAD/CAM Systems for Die and Mold Design [12.5]

Computer-aided design and manufacturing (CAD/CAM) was discussed in Chap. 7 in regard to extrusion and in Chap. 9 in conjunction with closed-die forging, both of which are bulk deformation processes. Here it will be discussed in relation to the design of dies or molds for use in sheetmetal forming such as for body parts in the automobile industry as an example. This industry worldwide is, of course, a very large user of sheetmetal formed parts.

A CAD/CAM system is, in a narrow sense, software that processes the input data of product specifications consistently from planning to manufacturing of the product, and in a broad sense, it includes the hardware that runs on the software and provides the output processed data. A CAD/CAM system is most often not generally intended for the production of all types of products, but is usually intended for one specialized product such as for the aircraft, automobile, or electronic industries. This approach leads to the problem of the independency of a CAD/CAM system, i.e., whether it is better to use a CAD/CAM general-purpose system for the design and manufacture of dies (and molds) for the production of different products or a specialty system for one specialized product. A number of CAD/CAM systems have been introduced chiefly for the production of dies (or molds). This approach indicates that a CAD/CAM system for die (or mold) design may be a subsystem of a larger system for the design and manufacture of production of tools and dies for a final product. In view of the actual state of the die (and mold) manufacturing industry, a CAD/CAM die and mold system should exist independently of the overall production system with the exception of large automobile and home electric appliance manufacturers that produce dies and molds for themselves [12.5].

Figure 12.13 depicts present-day production flow from design to manufacture of an industrial product that uses a die (or mold) for use in sheetmetal forming. Most die and mold shops are of small size, specialized according the intended use of the die (or mold), and produce the dies (or molds) according to the drawings and specifications of the users. On the other hand, about 40 percent of the dies for sheetmetal press working are made in-house in a captive shop.

12.1.4   Computer-Aided Design of Irregular Blanks for Deep Drawing for a Slip-Line Field Solution [11.3]

12.1.4.1   INTRODUCTION. The computer program system mentioned in Sec. 11.1.7.5, used in the computer-aided design of blanks for deep drawing of irregular shaped parts that is discussed here, is called PLATIN2 [11.3]. The solution

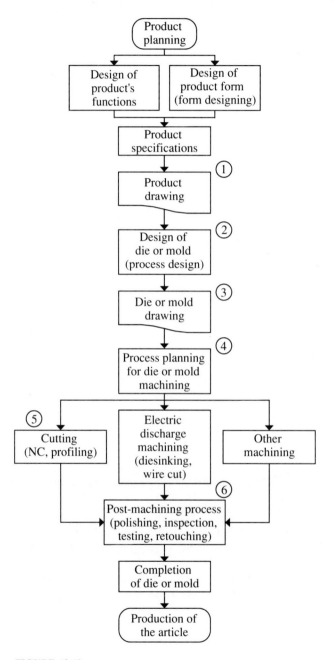

FIGURE 12.13
Chart showing the overall production flow of a part from the planning stage to production including die design and manufacture [12.5].

Range of parts : Parallel bottom and flange

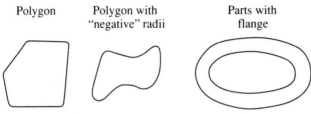

Prismatic   Conical ($\alpha_{max} \approx 20°$)

α

Polygon   Polygon with   Parts with
             "negative" radii   flange

Combined shapes

Compound   Parts with   Parts with
                different   domed bottom
              bottom heights

ca.20°

FIGURE 12.14
Outlines of the range of parts that can be designed by the PLATIN2 CAD program package utilizing
the slip-line field solution [11.3].

method used is based on the deformation theory of plasticity using the slip-line
field method. The three-dimensional deep drawing process is reduced to a plane
strain working model. The fundamental plasticity equations for use with the
slip-line field method were presented in Sec. 11.1.7.2. The same five-sided shaped
part shown in Fig. 11.16 is used here. The range of parts that can be analyzed
with this program is shown in outline form in Fig. 12.14.

12.1.4.2 THE PLATIN2 COMPUTER PROGRAM SYSTEM. The program package
PLATIN2, which is written in Fortran IV and which runs in the interactive mode,
provides for the automatic generation of the complete slip-line field for a variety
of simple irregular shaped parts. Its main features include: (1) the preparation
and the 3D-check of the input data, (2) the generation of the slip-line field

according to the given boundary conditions, (3) the determination of the optimized shape of the blank, (4) the computation of the drawing force, (5) the analysis of the state of stress and strain, and (6) the velocity distribution and strain path-lines with distribution of equivalent strain.

The program's structure and sequence of operations is shown in Fig. 12.15. The program will be discussed module by module in what follows. Modules 2, 6, 7, and 8 are optional and can be omitted during execution.

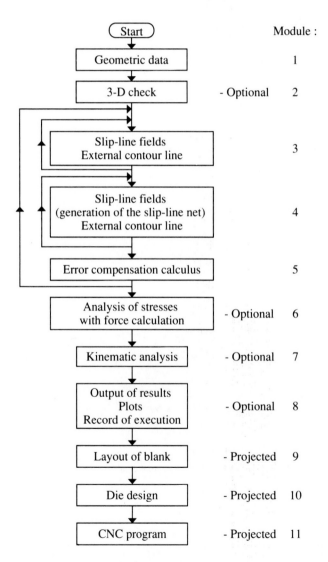

FIGURE 12.15
Flowchart showing the structure of the CAD program package PLATIN2 [11.3].

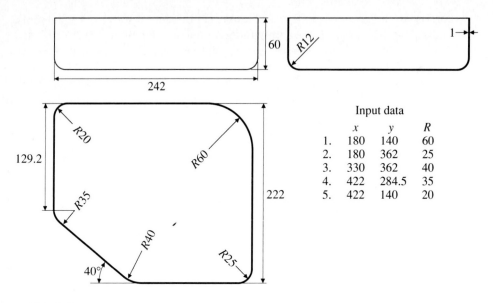

Input data			
	x	y	R
1.	180	140	60
2.	180	362	25
3.	330	362	40
4.	422	284.5	35
5.	422	140	20

FIGURE 12.16

Drawing and the input data for the example part for use of PLATIN2. The dimensions are in mm. The coordinates are of the vertices of the pentagon and not of the radii center points [11.3].

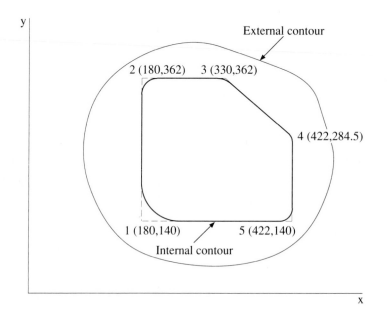

FIGURE 12.17

Computer plot of the internal and external contours of the blank for the example part designed by the PLATIN2 computer package. The coordinates of the vertices of the pentagon have been added [11.3].

1. *Module 1*. This module is designed for the input and the preparation of all needed information, i.e., the data describing the part and involved with the selection of a suitable material. Only coordinates and radii of the corners and the height have to be input to identify the part. The drawing of the example part and the input dimensions are shown in Fig. 12.16. The shape of the blank and the vertices of the internal surface are shown in Fig. 12.17.

2. *Module 2*. This module provides a graphic check as shown in Fig. 11.16 of the input data, which is needed because errors often occur in inputting the data which lead to incorrect shapes or to difficulties during execution of the program. Various isometric views can be produced, such as rotating the part to any desired position.

3. *Module 3*. This module is designed for computing a single point such as point M in Fig. 11.17 on the external contour line located opposite a circular element of the internal contour line. Its position is dependent on the height, radius, and width of the flange. The computed point serves as a starting point for the generation of the whole external contour. The slip-line net can now be constructed, which can be done by computing the coordinates of the intersection points of the slip-lines. The external contour line, i.e., the shape of the blank, is determined by a line which cuts the slip-lines at an angle of 45°.

4. *Module 4*. This module computes the slip-lines of the tertiary slip-line fields. (Primary fields consist of homogeneous lines adjacent to the internal contour, and the secondary fields border the primary ones.) The computed slip-lines, that are not exact solutions of the basic equation set, are approximated by numerical integration of the equations.

5. *Module 5*. This module smooths the external contour line by balancing the errors caused by the empirical calculation of the external contour starting-point or by approximation in the computation of the tertiary slip-lines. Steps in the contour line have to be found and then balanced by use of the least squares method. The balanced calculation is terminated when the errors are within a certain limit.

6. *Module 6*. This module calculates the stresses within the flange and the drawing force as shown in Fig. 11.18. Equation (11.40) allows the computation of the behavior of the mean stresses under certain boundary conditions. The behavior of any kind of stress can be determined, using the yield condition equation (11.36) and Eqs. (11.37):

$$\frac{|\sigma_1 - \sigma_2|}{2} = k \tag{11.36}$$

$$\sigma_x = 2k\omega + k \sin 2\phi \tag{11.37a}$$

$$\sigma_y = 2k\omega - k \sin 2\phi \tag{11.37b}$$

$$\tau_{xy} = -k \cos 2\phi \tag{11.37c}$$

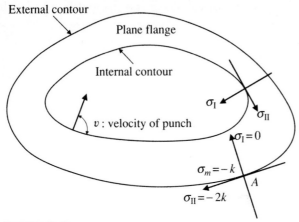

FIGURE 12.18
Description of the working model of the blank for the example part [11.3].

The boundary conditions are described in Fig. 12.18:
(1) The principal stress σ_1 is defined as the normal to the internal contour, since the shear stresses are equal to zero along this line.
(2) Another boundary condition must be assumed at the external surface. Since the external contour line represents a free surface and deep drawing is a tension-compression process, the principal stress σ_1 must be equal to zero, and hence $\sigma_{11} = -2k$, and the mean stress equals $-k$ according to Eq. (11.36) for the yield condition and that for the mean stress $\sigma_m = \frac{1}{2}(\sigma_1 + \sigma_2)$.

If the state of stress in the flange is analyzed certain discrepancies arise, for example, different values may be computed for the state of stress at the same point on the external slip-line. An approximate solution is used to deal with this problem.

Starting from a point on the internal contour line, the boundary condition for stress as shown in Fig. 12.18 is adhered to strictly. By use of Eq. (11.40)

$$\sigma_{m1} - \sigma_{mA} = 2k \, \partial\phi, \tag{12.14}$$

the means stress σ_{m1} on the internal contour line is computed and the distribution of stresses of the external contour line is determined. After a correction operation and the analysis of the state of stress are carried out, the results are displayed as small crosses indicating the amount and directions of principal stresses as shown in Fig. 12.19. The deformation forces (taking friction and bending into consideration by use of a formula) are then calculated using the normal stresses at the internal contour line and are shown in Fig. 11.21.

7. *Module 7.* This module analyzes (*a*) the flow velocity, and (*b*) the state of strain.
  (*a*) The kinematic analysis utilizes the Geiringer equations (11.41) and radial flow velocity equation (11.45) to determine the flow velocity in the flange. The assumed normal speed at the internal contour line serves as a kinematic

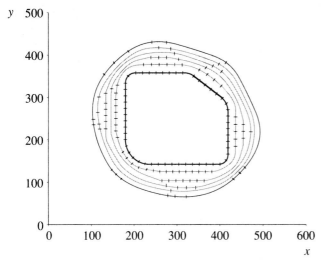

FIGURE 12.19
Representation of the magnitude and directions of the principal stresses by means of small crosses as plotted by PLATIN2 [11.3].

boundary condition, which is satisfied over the whole flange. The fact that the velocity distribution is continuous without jumps or lines of discontinuity lends validity to the solution. A plotted diagram of small vectors shown in Fig. 12.20 indicates the magnitude and direction of the flow velocity distribution.

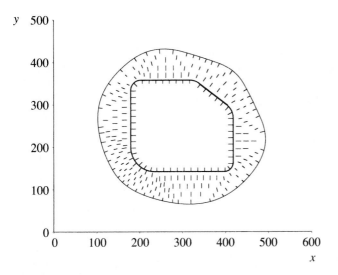

FIGURE 12.20
Small vectors plotted by PLATIN2 showing the magnitude and direction of the flow velocity distribution [11.3].

(b) Starting with the flow velocity distribution, the program analyzes the strain rate, equivalent strain rate, and the equivalent strain by use of the relationships that follow.

The strain rate under valid conditions of incompressibility is defined as

$$\dot{\varepsilon} = \sqrt{\tfrac{2}{3}(\dot{\varepsilon}_1^2 + \dot{\varepsilon}_2^2 + \dot{\varepsilon}_3^2)} \tag{12.15}$$

For plane strain with $\dot{\varepsilon}_3 = 0$ and $\dot{\varepsilon}_1 = -\dot{\varepsilon}_2$, the equivalent strain rate is

$$\dot{\bar{\varepsilon}}_v = \frac{2}{\sqrt{3}}\,\dot{\varepsilon}_1 \tag{12.16}$$

and the equivalent strain is

$$\bar{\varepsilon}_v = \int_{t_0}^{t_1} \dot{\bar{\varepsilon}}_v \, dt \tag{12.17}$$

The strain of the internal contour line is numerically computed, element by element, in accordance with the program structure. Points of the external contour line move inward toward the internal contour line according to the flow velocity distribution.

A finite line element in direction of the principal strain has at its beginning and ending points a velocity which is given by the velocity distribution as shown in Fig. 12.21. At the starting point at time t_0 this element has a resulting mean velocity of v_0 and the final length of l_0.

After a finite small time interval of $\Delta t = t_1 - t_0$, we get v_1, l_1 and the strain values according to the velocity distribution. Then a difference relation for the strain rate can be developed as follows:

$$\dot{\varepsilon} = \frac{\partial v}{\partial l} = \frac{v_1 - v_0}{l_1 - l_0} \tag{12.18}$$

Subsequently the equivalent strain rate according to Eq. (12.16) and the equivalent strain according to Eq. (12.17) yield

$$\bar{\varepsilon}_v = \int_{t_0}^{t_1} \dot{\bar{\varepsilon}}_v \, dt \cong \dot{\bar{\varepsilon}}_v \, \Delta t \tag{12.19}$$

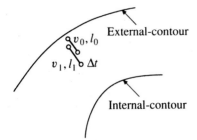

External-contour

v_0, l_0

v_1, l_1 Δt

Internal-contour

FIGURE 12.21
Finite line elements drawn in the direction of the principal strains toward the internal contour showing the velocity and length at time t_0 and at time t_1 [11.3].

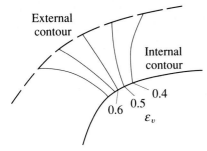

External
contour

Internal
contour

0.4

0.6 0.5

ε_v

FIGURE 12.22
Equivalent strain rates and flow paths as computed and
plotted by PLATIN2. Three of the equivalent strains of
the strain distribution are entered along the internal
boundary [11.3].

This procedure is repeated until the internal contour line is reached and
the whole part is traversed. The computed equivalent strain rates and flow
paths are plotted as shown in Fig. 12.22.

8. *Module 8.* This module is designed only for organization of the execution of
the computer program, and it is distributed over the whole program package.
It serves primarily for the preparation and the control of the various outputs
and for recording the program sequence data.

In review, if all of the options in the foregoing computer program are used,
five plots are produced showing (1) the slip-line field as in Fig. 12.23, (2) the
blank shape as in Fig. 12.17, (3) the analysis of stresses as displayed by small
crosses in Fig. 12.19 indicating the amount and direction of the principal stresses,
(4) the distribution of the velocities as in Fig. 12.20, and (5) the strain-path lines
as in Fig. 12.24 showing the distribution of the equivalent strains.

In closing, very satisfactory agreement is obtained between the computed
and the measured results; however, with increased depth of the deep-drawn part,
the agreement drops off. Errors may be caused by the approximation involved
with numerical calculations and by such assumptions as plane strain, rigid–plastic
material behavior, and the concept that the principal directions of the strain axes
coincide with those of the stress axes at any point, i.e., the deformation theory
of plasticity applies.

12.2 AN INTEGRATED, MODULAR CAD/CAM SYSTEM FOR SHEETMETAL FORMING [12.6]

12.2.1 Introduction

In Chapter 10, blank layout and the operations of blanking and piercing were
covered from the point of view of the press shop, the ultimate of which is the
flexible manufacturing system, such as is described in Sec. 10.4. In the foregoing
case, blank size, shape, and layout were done more or less manually. In this
section we are going up one big step in sophistication to the application of a
CAD/CAM system to these tasks.

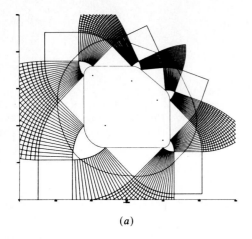

(a)

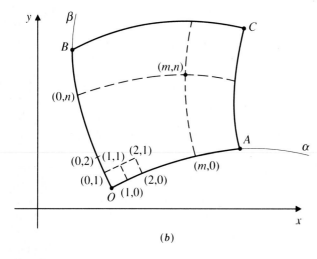

(b)

FIGURE 12.23
(a) Slip-line field for the example deep-drawn part as plotted by PLATIN2. (b) Coordinate system for a slip-line field net. (a) [11.3], (b) [12.19].

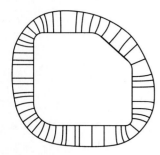

FIGURE 12.24
Flow paths with equivalent strains (which are not discernible on the reduced figure) as plotted by PLATIN2 [11.3].

The application of CAD/CAM is a relatively new development in sheetmetal forming as it has been considered to be an area of empirical engineering which was too difficult to computerize. However, the advantages to be gained by the application of methods of computer-aided engineering are so significant to metalforming that it can no longer be ignored.

An intensive research project has been in progress at the Dept. of Mechanical Engineering, Technical University of Heavy Industry in Miskolc, Hungary, to develop an integrated, modular CAD/CAM system for sheetmetal forming. This elaborate CAD/CAM system, that is still in the process of being developed, will be briefly discussed here [12.6].

12.2.2   The Requirements of the CAD/CAM System

The requirements placed on this integrated, modular sheetmetal forming and production CAD/CAM system are as follows:

1. Each module should be independently applicable
2. The modules should provide the feasibility of their integration into the total system and should contain the necessary input/output connection points
3. The system should be easily applied, i.e., it should be compatible with conventional engineering practice
4. All the routine tasks should be carried out by the computer
5. The flexibility of the system and the intuition and the creativity of the engineering should be provided for by an interactive mode of operation
6. The total system should be built on an unified data-base, which requires the standardization of a high level to ensure the regular maintenance, enlargement, and modification of the data base

The general structure of this computer integrated system that meets the above requirements is shown in Fig. 12.25.

12.2.3   Modules of the CAD/CAM system

The principle of the modular construction of the system, which ensures the independent applicability of each module, and the hierarchical relation between them is shown in Fig. 12.25. The elaborate system software provides a considerable amount of accessibility of the designer not only at the connection points but within the modules themselves.

Each module connects with the unified database, which contains a great amount of information regarding the forming machines, the tools, the technological processes, the raw materials, etc. The steps in the computer-aided processing of a component to be manufactured in a progressive die is shown on the right side of Fig. 12.25. Similar steps for deep drawing are shown in Fig. 12.26.

In the following, the function of each module shown in Fig. 12.25 will be described briefly.

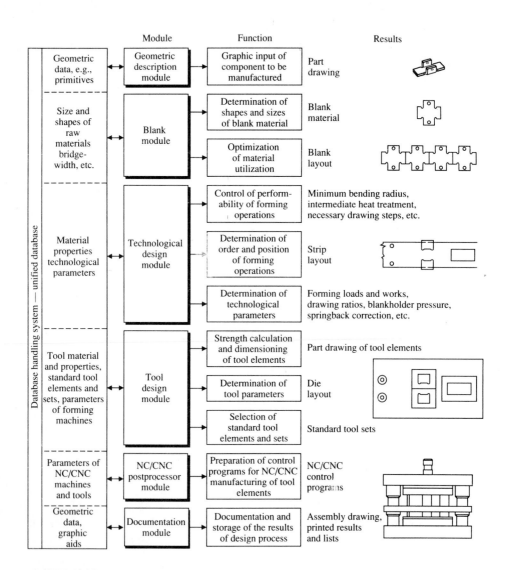

Module	Function	Results

Database handling system — unified database

Geometric data, e.g., primitives — Geometric description module — Graphic input of component to be manufactured — Part drawing

Size and shapes of raw materials bridge-width, etc. — Blank module — Determination of shapes and sizes of blank material — Blank material

Optimization of material utilization — Blank layout

Material properties technological parameters — Technological design module — Control of performability of forming operations — Minimum bending radius, intermediate heat treatment, necessary drawing steps, etc.

Determination of order and position of forming operations — Strip layout

Determination of technological parameters — Forming loads and works, drawing ratios, blankholder pressure, springback correction, etc.

Tool material and properties, standard tool elements and sets, parameters of forming machines — Tool design module — Strength calculation and dimensioning of tool elements — Part drawing of tool elements

Determination of tool parameters — Die layout

Selection of standard tool elements and sets — Standard tool sets

Parameters of NC/CNC machines and tools — NC/CNC postprocessor module — Preparation of control programs for NC/CNC manufacturing of tool elements — NC/CNC control programs

Geometric data, graphic aids — Documentation module — Documentation and storage of the results of design process — Assembly drawing, printed results and lists

FIGURE 12.25
General scheme of an integrated, modular CAD/CAM system for sheetmetal forming [12.6].

Results

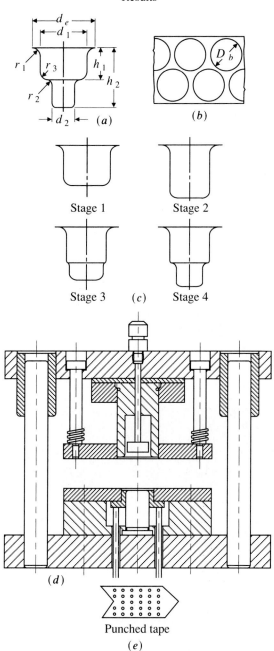

Stage 1

Stage 2

Stage 3 (c) Stage 4

(d)

Punched tape

(e)

FIGURE 12.26
Results for deep drawing of the output of the integrated CAD/CAM shown in Fig. 12.25: (a) design of the final, drawing punch, (b) blank layout, (c) successive stages in the deep-drawing operation, (d) cross-sectional drawing of the die assembly, and (e) punched NC tape for use in machining die components [12.18].

12.2.3.1 THE GEOMETRIC DESCRIPTION MODULE. The purpose of this program is to provide the total and unambiguous geometric input of the components as simply as possible. It also provides for the storage of geometric information both graphically and alphanumerically for further processing.

The main graphic input menu offers several possibilities depending on whether the component is (1) a two-dimensional plane configuration containing only blanking and piercing operations, or (2) a three-dimensional spatial configuration involving bent, deep-drawn and/or flanged elements.

One of the applied graphic input modes for a complicated cross section is based on the decomposition of the component into simple surface or volume elements, such as is shown in Fig. 12.27, called "primitives." The program first inquires about the number of constituent elements of the component. It selects the proper number of elements from the graphic input menu and requests the dimensions of the selected surface elements. The graphic construction of the

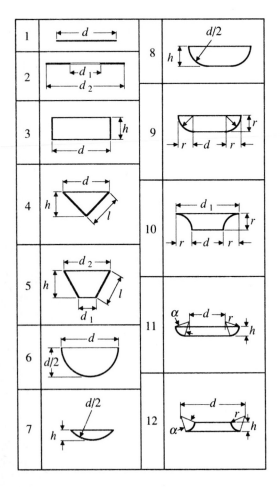

FIGURE 12.27
Possible graphic input, geometrical primitives used to decompose complicated, deep-drawn shapes into simple surface and volume elements [12.18].

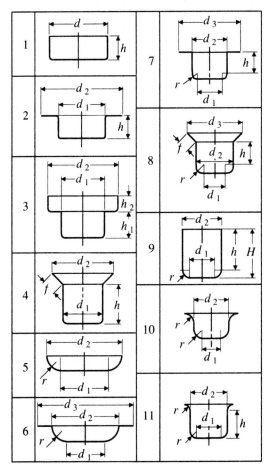

FIGURE 12.28
Complicated axisymmetric components defined as blocks from geometric primitives as shown in Fig. 12.27 [12.18].

component is continuously displayed and may be corrected by the designer, if necessary. Complicated axisymmetric components, defined as *blocks from geometric primitives*, are shown in Fig. 12.28.

Another interactive graphic-input module converts the geometrical shape of a component into coordinates as shown in Fig. 12.29. The neutral axis of the meridian section of the component can be divided into either straight lines or circular arcs. Starting, for example, from the point of intersection of the neutral and the symmetrical axis at point O in Fig. 12.29, one can represent each section of the meridian curve by the coordinates (r_i, z_i) as well as by the radius r_i attached to the point. For straight lines, it is necessary to define $R_i = \infty$. For the unambiguous determination of the circular arcs, it is also necessary to define the central angle α_i belonging to the arc, as well as the rotational direction, such as by use of the conventionally accepted positive sign.

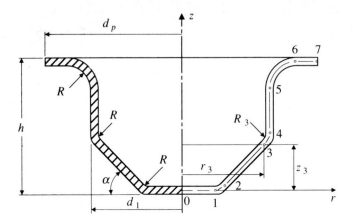

FIGURE 12.29
Graphic input-mode using coordinate geometric description for converting the geometric shape of a component into coordinates [12.6].

12.2.3.2 DETERMINATION OF THE SHAPE AND SIZE OF THE BLANK. These modules are needed only in those cases in which the components have bent, drawn, and/or flanged parts. In these cases, the shape and size of the blank are determined by well known equations obtained from the technical literature. In these modules, different submodules can be called upon depending on the component to be manufactured. For example, in the case of bent components, the size of the blank can be calculated by taking into consideration the displacement of the neutral axis. For deep-drawn parts different shape and sizes can be determined. For example, the program module is capable of handling 18 different types of blanks for components of rectangular cross section depending on the specific geometric ratio.

12.2.3.3 MODULES FOR OPTIMIZING MATERIAL UTILIZATION. The optimization of material utilization is an important consideration in most sheetmetal operations. The optimization calculations depend on the type of material and whether sheets or strips are used. The system is suitable for designing for production by use of conventional forming machines and by the use of NC/CNC shearing machines and manufacturing centers. In the former case coiled strip is usually used and in the latter, flat sheets.

The optimizing subsystem offers two different alternatives depending on further processing of the strip or sheet:

1. A prescribed number of blanks, of different materials, belonging to a given production run, with the least amount of material waste, and meeting certain requirements, may be specified. For example, the following requirements may be specified: (1) the number of blank types that can be placed on a single strip or sheet, (2) the maximum length to be cut, (3) the rotatability of the components, (4) the minimum distance between cuts, etc.

The program based on the foregoing requirements and on the application of linear programming and heuristic principles, provides layout alternatives, of which the most favorable solution from the viewpoint of material utilization is selected by mathematical methods. The results may be printed and/or plotted and stored on a magnetic disk for further data processing, such as for the preparation of a control tape for an NC sheet shear, for example.

2. The subprogram for generating optimum layout for an NC manufacturing center is capable of handling special cutting processes such as plasma and laser cutting in addition to the more conventional mechanical blanking and piercing. It is also capable of handling displacement, rotation, and reflection of blank configurations. Moreover, because of the clamping devices used, turning of sheets may also be included in the program. The optimal version of the blank layout may also be documented graphically as shown in Fig. 12.30. In the conventional process, using strip coils, the optimum blank layout may be generated by interactive manipulation of the drawing of the blank by displacement, rotation, and reflection as shown in Fig. 12.30.

12.2.3.4 TECHNOLOGICAL DESIGN MODULE. This module is regarded as one of the most important modules. It can be applied to both conventional and NC/CNC manufacturing. It is capable of handling single and complex planning of the following main forming processes: (1) material processing by cutting such as blanking, piercing, shearing, cropping, etc., and (2) shape forming such as bending, deep drawing, hole-flanging, etc.

Within the scope of the data provided by the datafiles created by the geometric description module, the program carries out the checking of performability of selected operations from the viewpoint of limit deformability such as

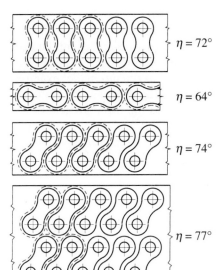

$\eta = 72°$

$\eta = 64°$

$\eta = 74°$

$\eta = 77°$

FIGURE 12.30
Computer generation of blank layout alternatives for progressive die blanking. The efficiency of utilization of the surface area of the blank is shown at the right of each layout (see Fig. 10.19). (See Fig. 10.17.) [12.6].

the minimum bending radius, minimum diameter to be punched or flanged, etc. Then, the technological parameters such as the forming load and energy, the steps of operation, intermediate heat treatment, etc., are determined.

The possibilities offered by this CAD/CAM system can be fully utilized during the complex design involving the forming procedures carried out in progressive dies such as in the blank layout performed by the module for optimizing the material utilization. In its application, the strip layout is determined interactively. The order of the various operations is defined by the designer, and the layout of the strip is performed by use of the interactive graphic menu method producing the strip layout design as shown in Fig. 12.31. The strip layout design process simultaneously produces the layout of the die. Variations of the layout can be displayed, plotted, or stored for future processing. After the design of the strip and die layout are completed, the technological parameters such as the forming loads and energy, the drawing ratios, blankholder pressure, springback correction, etc., can be determined.

The technological design module may be used to simulate the technological procedures performed on NC/CNC machines and manufacturing centers. The computer simulation program (TRUMF) is written for a specific type of sheetmetal manufacturing center; however, its modular structure allows easy adaptability to other control systems. An NC/CNC postprocessing module is being developed using the information stored in the databank on NC/CNC machines and manufacturing centers, which will be capable of producing interactively the NC/CNC control programs and the operational sequence of processing, thus eliminating the time-consuming, error-prone manual method of programming.

12.2.3.5 TOOL DESIGN MODULE. This module is regarded as one of the most important parts of the elaborate CAD/CAM system, which frees the designer from most manual, routine tasks and makes it possible for him to use his creativeness in other stages of the design process, where it is most needed.

The tool design module, similar to the technological module, can be used for both individual and complex designs. By "individual design" is meant that the tool design task is carried out for only a single-forming operation. For example, in the design of a single-forming-operation die for deep drawing, the results of the geometric input module, the blank-calculating and the technological design modules are used. The tool design module determines the geometric shapes, dimensions, and tolerances of the punch and die, while taking into consideration

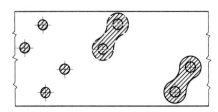

FIGURE 12.31
Strip layout for progressive dies for producing the double-rowed blank layout shown in Fig. 12.30 [12.6].

the requirements of the component to be manufactured. The strength of the component may be calculated, and the materials for the components of the tooling may also be selected. The part drawings of the tool elements can be shown graphically on the computer display screen and/or drawn out on a plotter and stored for further processing. By use of the blank and die dimensions, a standard dieset can be selected from the information stored in the database, and the tool components drawn into it. The assembly drawing prepared in this way may be plotted and/or stored in a datafile. Essentially the same procedure is followed, with some modification, for progressive dies as for single-forming operation dies.

It is often necessary to select a suitable forming machine on the basis of the results obtained in the technological and tool design modules, especially in the case of conventional forming operations. This task is carried out on the basis of (1) the geometric parameters, such as the maximum enclosing dimensions of the tool, the opened and closed heights of the tool, and the length of stroke, and (2) the "power" parameters, such as the forming force and energy, and the power demands.

12.2.3.6 NC/CNC POSTPROCESSOR MODULE. One of the objectives of this module is to work out the control programs for manufacturing the active tool elements, i.e., the punches, dies, etc., on NC/CNC manufacturing machines. It uses the results of the geometric, technological and the tool design modules and also the data on machines and tools stored in the databank. This module also includes the postprocessing of NC control programs for use with different sheet-metal forming machines.

12.2.4 The Database Handling System and the Unified Database

The large, unified database is readily accessed by each module of the elaborate CAD/CAM system by use of the database handling system. Moreover, this system provides for the storage of new data, and for its modification and cancellation.

The database as can be seen on the left side of Fig. 12.25 consists of the following:

1. The geometric information used by the geometric describing module such as geometric primitives, graphic data, etc.
2. The sizes and mechanical properties of the raw material such as the width, thickness, and tolerance of the sheets and strips, its strength and deformation characteristics, etc.
3. Technological parameters of the forming processes
4. The fundamental data for tool design, standard tool components, and tool sets
5. The geometric, kinematic, and kinetic parameters of forming and manufacturing machines, etc.

12.2.5   Advantages

The advantages of this system are

1. The time and labor required for design and manufacture can be greatly reduced
2. The system provides for more flexibility in design and production
3. As compared to the conventional design process, it produces a more optimal design, provides for the consideration of many more options, and provides for quick analysis of a great number of alternatives
4. It frees the designer from the labor- and the time-consuming routine work such as drawing, calculation, etc., and provides more time for creative work, which he does best

12.3   BODY ENGINEERING IN THE AUTOMOTIVE INDUSTRY—THE BIG PICTURE

12.3.1 Conventional Process [12.7]

Before the CAD/CAM processes are discussed, the *conventional* body engineering processes will be described.

Figure 12.32 shows the flow of a conventional process, which involves the production of a full-size "clay" model based on design ideas generated in the style design stage, and then the clay model is modified as required. The model is then measured to obtain geometric data for input to the computer. The point data are then smoothed using a graphics terminal and the results are represented as full-size external drawings [12.7].

Based on these drawings, the structural components and flanges required for the body panels are then added in the body structural design process. Finally, full-size master drawings and production drawings for each part are produced for mass production of the parts.

The next phase involves the design of the stamping dies. The initial stage in this process is the digitizing of the external and full-size master drawings. The part is subsequently investigated in various tipped positions with the graphics terminal. "Plaster" molds are then produced to investigate various points, which in turn is followed by the design of the die-face shapes and the production of the drawings of the dies.

In the next stage, the master models are used as the basis for further work. In the stamping die manufacturing process, the stamping dies are produced by copy milling with models duplicated for the master models or by machining with an NC machine from data points obtained by measuring the master models. The finishing process uses checker models, such as spotting models, for final finishing. Welding jigs and fixtures are then produced for resistance welding the panels together to make the car body assembly. The jigs and fixtures are frames containing some small pads on which the different parts are located and clamped for welding. The pads must be accurate enough to locate properly the stamped parts.

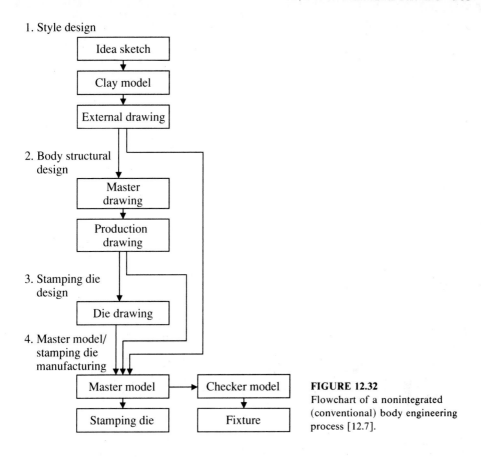

1. Style design

Idea sketch

Clay model

External drawing

2. Body structural design

Master drawing

Production drawing

3. Stamping die design

Die drawing

4. Master model/ stamping die manufacturing

Master model → Checker model

Stamping die

Fixture

FIGURE 12.32
Flowchart of a nonintegrated (conventional) body engineering process [12.7].

In the conventional engineering process described above, a number of models and drawings are produced, which requires a considerable number of worker-hours and a lengthy lead-time. Also, this process involves an accumulation of errors resulting from the repeated reproduction of the drawings and models. To overcome these difficulties, an *integrated CAD/CAM* system was introduced, which will be described next.

12.3.2 An Integrated CAD/CAM System in the Body Engineering Process —An Overview

12.3.2.1 INTRODUCTION. Four major CAD/CAM systems have been developed at the Toyota Motor Corporation: (1) COSMOS, which stands for the Compound Surface Modeling Systems supports styling design and die-face design; (2) CADETT, which stands for Computer Aided Design and Engineering Tool for Toyota, supports body structural design and welding tool design; (3) TINCA, which stands for Toyota Integrated Numerical Approach, supports manufacturing master models and stamping dies; (4) VESTA, which stands for Vehicle Structural Toyota Analysis system, supports structural analysis using the finite element method. The above four systems provide a highly efficient CAD/CAM system through all the processes—from style design to the manufacture of the stamping—because the geometric data base constructed in each process can be transferred freely among each other [12.8]. One should differentiate between the computer-aided design (CAD) and the computer-aided manufacturing (CAM) domains as shown in Fig. 12.33 [12.9].

Figure 12.34 is a flowchart that shows the following stages of an *integrated CAD/CAM* car body engineering process: (1) styling design, (2) body structural design, (3) stamping die design, (4) master model and stamping die manufacture, and (5) checker (inspection fixture) and welding fixture manufacture. An overview of this integrated process is given below. A greater detailed discussion of the design and evaluation of the die-face CAD system will be given later.

It should be noted in Fig. 12.34 that in the first three steps the drawings (hard copies) can be made by use of the numerical database and the CADETT system [12.7].

The CADETT system is the computer system that mainly supports the body engineering process. It is used to assist the design and drafting work of the body engineers by use of computers. The designers use it to do the structural design of the outer and inner panels of car bodies by using the styling design data received from the styling design process. The resultant body structure data and

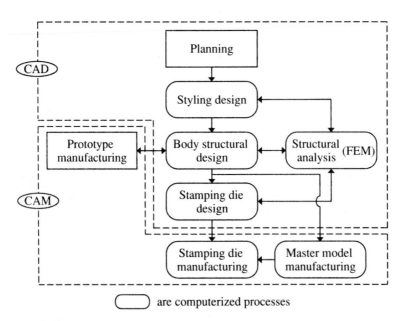

are computerized processes

FIGURE 12.33
Flowchart of the process of an automobile body development showing the CAD and the CAM domains. (See Figs. 9.77 and 9.78.) [12.9].

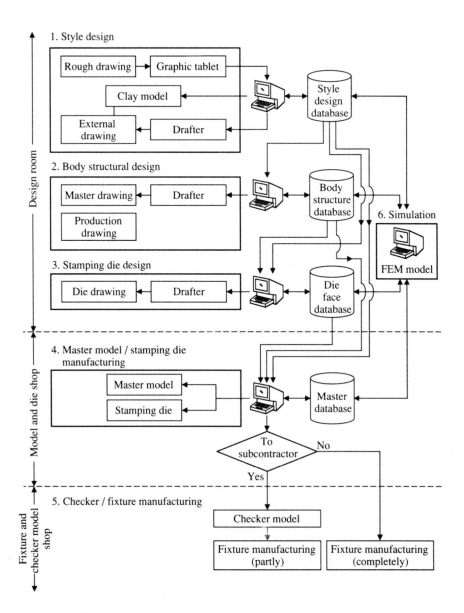

FIGURE 12.34
Flowchart of an integrated CAD/CAM body engineering process [12.7].

drafting data are stored in the databases. If necessary, they issue master and product drawings such as is shown in Fig. 12.35 by means of drafting machines using the data in the database [12.9].

The CADETT system also offers such functions as the definition, display, and calculation of geometrical elements using graphic displays. The operators can design and do engineering work by conventional drafting methods on the graphics display screen instead of using manual drafting tools. They can quickly draft three-dimensional geometrical elements using the large data storage capacity and high calculating speed of the computer [12.9].

Figure 12.36 shows the process chart of the CADETT system, Figs. 12.37, 12.38, and 12.39 show the hardware, the software, and the database configurations. The latter consists of about 1000 subroutines written mainly in PL/1 [12.9].

Figure 12.34 gives stages of the integrated CAD/CAM system as follows:

12.3.2.2 STYLING DESIGN PROCESS. In the *conventional* styling process (see Section 12.3.1), clay models are produced first and then measured to obtain the point sequence of data to produce the curves, from which the wire-frame models and finally the free surface models are produced. (Figure 12.40 shows a wire-frame model of an automobile.) The foregoing procedure requires many worker-hours and presents problems in relation to the smoothness of the curves and curved surfaces. To overcome these problems in the computerized system, the curves and curved surfaces, as seen by the designer, are first precisely defined mathematically and then generated directly with the aid of the database stored in the

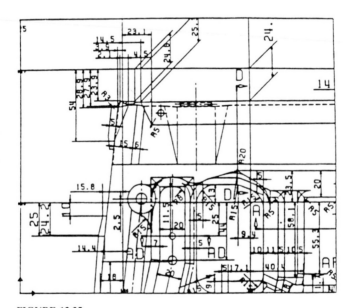

FIGURE 12.35
An example of a product drawing made with a drawing machine by use of numerical data found in the database [12.9].

Styling design department

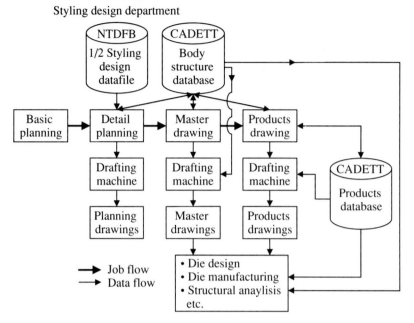

FIGURE 12.36
Process chart of the CADETT (computer-aided design and engineering tool for Toyota) system [12.9].
(The styling design data is contained in the NTDFB file which stands for new Toyota data file base
for a system of body design and manufacture.)

computer. The clay models are then produced, based on the database. This
method has enabled the designer to perform such operations as modification and
evaluation with the aid of the graphics terminal just as with the clay model and
has resulted in a considerable reduction in the worker-hours and lead-time
required, with an increase in the quality of the data for later processes [12.7].

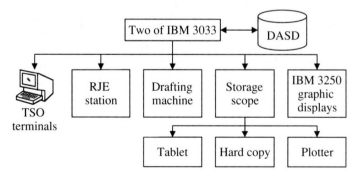

FIGURE 12.37
Hardware configuration for the CADETT (computer-aided design and engineering tool for Toyota)
system showing the TSO (time sharing option) that allows the user to share computer time and
resources, RJE (remote job entry) station, and the DASD (direct access storage device) [12.9].

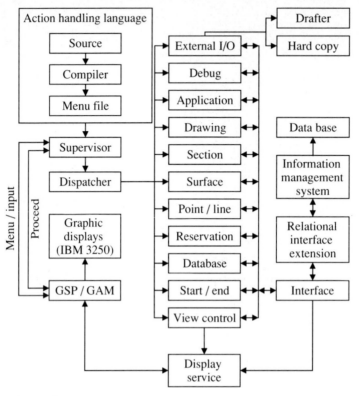

FIGURE 12.38

Software configuration of the CADETT (computer-aided design and engineering tool for Toyota) system [12.9].

At the *styling design* stage, the outer shapes of the car body are created on a graphics terminal. Input data for the CAD system are characteristic lines read from the designer's sketch. The quality of the geometric model is quantitatively evaluated on the terminal. The criteria of the evaluation are the smoothness of the highlight lines and the curvature distribution. The highlight lines are simulated as images reflected on a clay model by parallel fluorescent lamps as shown in Fig. 12.41, and the curvature distribution on all section shapes corresponds to the touching test of the stamping dies [12.10].

12.3.2.3 BODY DESIGN PROCESS. In the conventional method (see Section 12.3.1), the body design process is such that it requires the production of a large number of drawings, in particular, full-size master drawings, in a relatively short space of time. For this reason, a large number of designers are required at one time. The situation is further complicated by the increase in the number of cars and models under development and by the continual reduction in the lead-time. The use of CAD technology has enabled the generation of accurate data in short

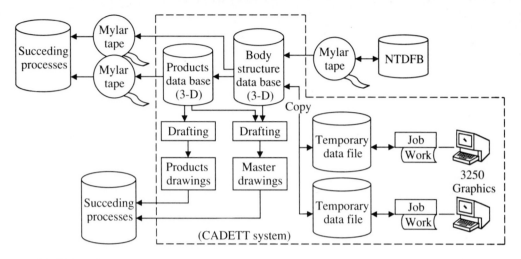

FIGURE 12.39
Database configuration of the CADETT (computer-aided design and engineering tool for Toyota system and NTDFB stands for new Toyota data file base) [12.9].

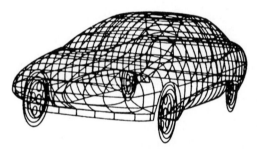

FIGURE 12.40
Wire-frame model of the outer surface of an automobile used for a proportion check with a perspective view [12.13].

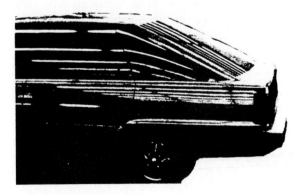

FIGURE 12.41
Highlight lines on a "clay" model simulated by reflected images by parallel fluorescent bulbs [12.13].

periods of time with the use of a database stored in the computer. This situation has also enabled simulation of performance-related characteristics such as strength, stiffness, vibration, and noise which was previously impossible to do because of the time required. Such simulation employs the finite element method (FEM) and permits a number of investigations to be performed in earlier stages of the body design process [12.7].

The CADETT system, mentioned in the foregoing, can quickly generate finite element analysis models as shown in Fig. 12.42. Triangular, quadrilateral, and beam elements can be generated automatically from the data in the products database, using the automatic mesh generation, the modification, and the check functions [12.9].

For the *body structural design* evaluations, the body structure is defined on the basis of the above geometric model. Characteristics such as strength, stiffness, and vibration of the body components are evaluated using the finite element structural analysis system. The geometric model of the body structure is then modified so as to reflect the results of the analysis [12.10].

12.3.2.4 STAMPING DESIGN PROCESS. Die-face shapes are next generated in the *stamping die design* process based on the product shapes supplied from the preceding CAD processes. Press forming severity of these shapes is evaluated at this point since the die-face shapes strongly govern the formability.

This process is involved with the design of the die-face for panel surfaces and die structural design. The shape of the die-face for the forming of panels of complex shape is of considerable importance. Incorrect die-face shape may cause imperfect highlight lines, rough surfaces, dimensional inaccuracies, and fractures. Since dynamic mathematical design is practically impossible in conventional design, one must depend on the intuitive decisions of experienced designers. In conventional die-design practice, a repeated process of trial-and-error is used, so that a considerable amount of time is required for the production of the final die. This trial-and-error process is one of the largest obstacles to a reduction of the lead-time required for the development of new cars [12.7].

A system has been developed in which a skilled experienced designer is able to predict, with good accuracy, the occurrence of surface distortions and fractures at different points of the stroke on the basis of historical data. The introduction of CAD/CAM technology to the die design process enables the deficiencies in the die-face design to be fed back immediately to the designer and the resulting improvements stored in the system.

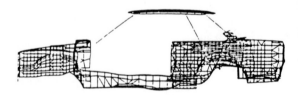

FIGURE 12.42
Example of a finite element model generated by the CADETT system (computer-aided design and engineering tool for Toyota) system. (See stage 6 at right-hand side of Fig. 12.34.) [12.9].

12.3.2.5 MASTER MODEL AND STAMPING DIE MANUFACTURING PROCESS. The master model is the standard used for checking the shape of the stamping die-face and of the stamped parts. It may be made of an ensemble of separate blocks, each of which is related to one of the parts of the body: fenders, hood, top, side-panels, doors, trunk, grille, etc. The shape of the die-face must duplicate the shape of the part that it is supposed to produce with compensation for springback [12.11].

In the final step, the *stamping dies are manufactured* by NC machines based on the geometric models representing the product shapes and the die-face shapes which are supplied by the preceding CAD system [12.10].

The manufacture of stamping dies has *conventionally* required the initial production of a master model from which the final stamping dies were manufactured. As this method requires a number of models, considerable time and effort is expended in their production. As already mentioned, the repeated process of transferring data from one model to another necessarily results in a reduction in the accuracy and changes in model shape over long periods of time. The introduction of CAD/CAM technology into the body design process has resulted in the replacement of drawings with a highly accurate database and the consequent direct production of dies by numerical or computer controlled machining without use of a master model [12.7].

12.3.2.6 CHECKER AND FIXTURE MANUFACTURING PROCESS. The introduction of CAD/CAM technology to the main process of body engineering has also affected greatly the process of design and manufacture of checkers and fixtures. For example, conventionally the selection of the type and shape of welding guns has been determined by studying the drawings. In some cases, the interference between the welding guns and components and between components can be only determined by investigations made on prototypes of the cars. The use of CAD/CAM technology permits the early investigation of these points on a graphics terminal and has resulted in appreciable reductions in lead-time and in improvements in quality [12.7].

12.3.3 An Integrated CAD/CAM System in the Body Engineering Process — Details

12.3.3.1 NUMERICAL MODELS FOR MANUFACTURING STAMPING DIES IN THE INTEGRATED CAD/CAM SYSTEM [12.12]. A system for stamping dies and welding fixtures has been developed as a part of an integrated CAD/CAM system. The implementation of this system has been based on the premise that master models employed in the conventional processes should be replaced by highly accurate numerical models and by taking into account effective transfer of data from the existing CAD systems.

The new computer-aided manufacturing (CAM) system can resolve the following shortcomings involved in the conventional manufacturing processes for stamping dies based on master models. Figure 12.43 schematically compares

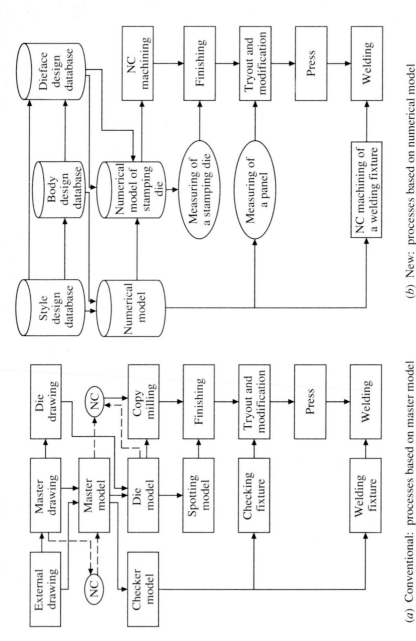

(a) Conventional: processes based on master model   (b) New: processes based on numerical model

FIGURE 12.43

Flowcharts of the stamping die and welding fixture manufacturing processes (a) by the conventional method with the processes based on master models, and (b) by the CAM method with processes based on numerical models obtained from the various data bases (see Figs. 12.32 and 12.34) [12.12].

the conventional processes with the new ones. In the former, several physical models such as a die model, a spotting model, and a checker model are to be manufactured by copying a master model for use in various processes. In the machining process, a die model is used, for example, for copy milling. In the finishing process, finishing of die surface shape is performed so that it coincides with a spotting model. Finally, in the tryout and modification process, panels are inspected with checking fixtures, whose manufacture is based on a checker model, and modifications are continued until the panel shapes satisfy the required accuracy. These processes based on the master models have had serious shortcomings as follows: (1) Many worker-hours and much time are required for the manufacturing of a master model and its duplicates, and (2) duplicate models inevitably involve inaccuracies in shapes caused by repeated duplication and structural and material changes over long periods of time, which makes it difficult to satisfy the required quality in each process. The time consumed in manual labor of skilled workers in the finishing, trying out, and modification of the models and parts becomes prohibitive.

The main objectives therefore, for the application of CAD/CAM systems in the automotive industries have been to reduce the worker-hours and the lead-time in the new product development and to improve the quality of design.

12.3.3.2 REQUIREMENTS FOR REALIZING THE NEW CAM SYSTEM BASED ON NUMERICAL MODELS [12.12]. The generation of highly accurate numerical models and the consistent use of them are essential in the manufacturing system for stamping dies and welding fixtures based on numerical models. As shown in Fig. 12.43(b), the numerical model of the product is generated at first by combining the style design information and the body design information. The numerical model of the stamping die is produced, in the next step, by combining the numerical model of the product and the die-face design information. These numerical models are referenced in the NC machining, finishing, tryout, and modification processes as the standard data. Therefore, the following three requirements must be met to realize the new CAD system: (1) the creation of an accurate numerical model, (2) a machining system based on the numerical model, and (3) a finishing system based on the numerical model.

The shape data received from the CAD systems are incomplete for use in the machining and finishing process, so they are automatically supplemented or corrected to produce the numerical model fully representing the final product shape and quality.

12.3.3.3 CREATION OF AN ACCURATE NUMERICAL MODEL [12.12]. Two technologies have been established for the creation of an accurate numerical model: (1) one for the receiving of CAD information from the three kinds of CAD systems and combining them, and (2) the other for supplementing missing or incorrect shapes in the data received and for completing the numerical model consistent with the final product shape by correcting inaccurate portions such as irregular highlight lines or uneven surface shapes.

Three kinds of information are involved: (1) the Style CAD information representing outer shapes of a car body, which consists of high quality aesthetic free-form surfaces, (2) the Body CAD information, representing body structural (inner) shapes, which consists of wire-frame data since most of them are expressed with ruled surfaces, and (3) the Die-face CAD information, representing die-face shapes, which consists of both free-form surfaces and ruled surfaces.

Interface functions for receiving free-form curves and surfaces from the CAD systems have to be implemented to provide proper match-up automatically as shown in Fig. 12.44.

Several techniques have been developed (1) for detecting and supplementing incomplete or inaccurate information contained in the data received from the CAD systems, and (2) for checking and correcting the quality of the surface data.

Several functions have been implemented for detecting incorrect information, such as missing topological information between curves, among the large amount of CAD information. Several functions for showing the qualitative nature of the data on the graphics display have also been implemented. Highlight lines are displayed for checking for their smoothness, inflection points for checking the existence of unevenness, and curvature distribution for confirming the smoothness of surfaces as shown in Fig. 12.45. In some cases, the repositioning of points is not effective such as for a corner shape where a number of surfaces meet. A

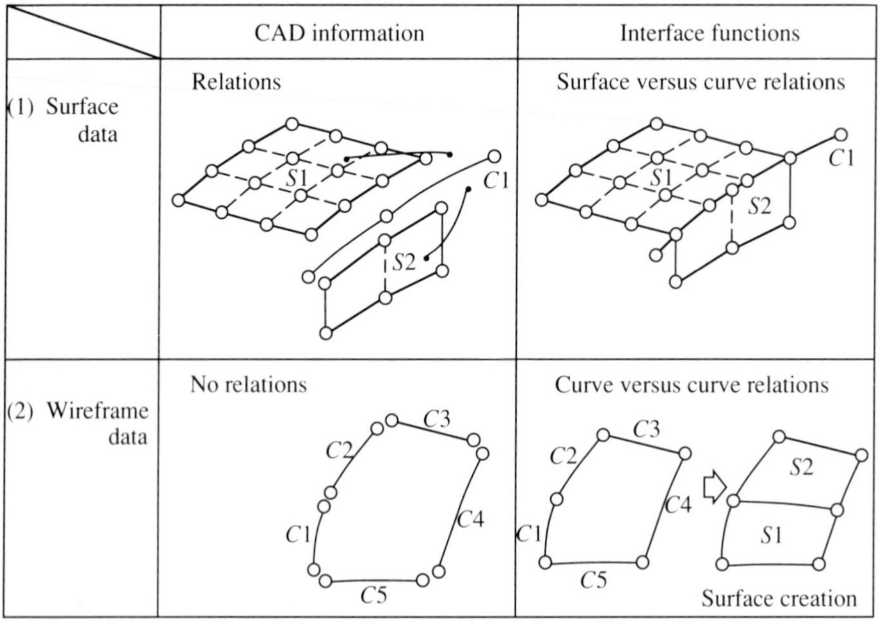

	CAD information	Interface functions
(1) Surface data	Relations	Surface versus curve relations
(2) Wireframe data	No relations	Curve versus curve relations

FIGURE 12.44
Chart depicting the use of interface functions for establishing the relation between surfaces and curves and the connection between curves [12.12].

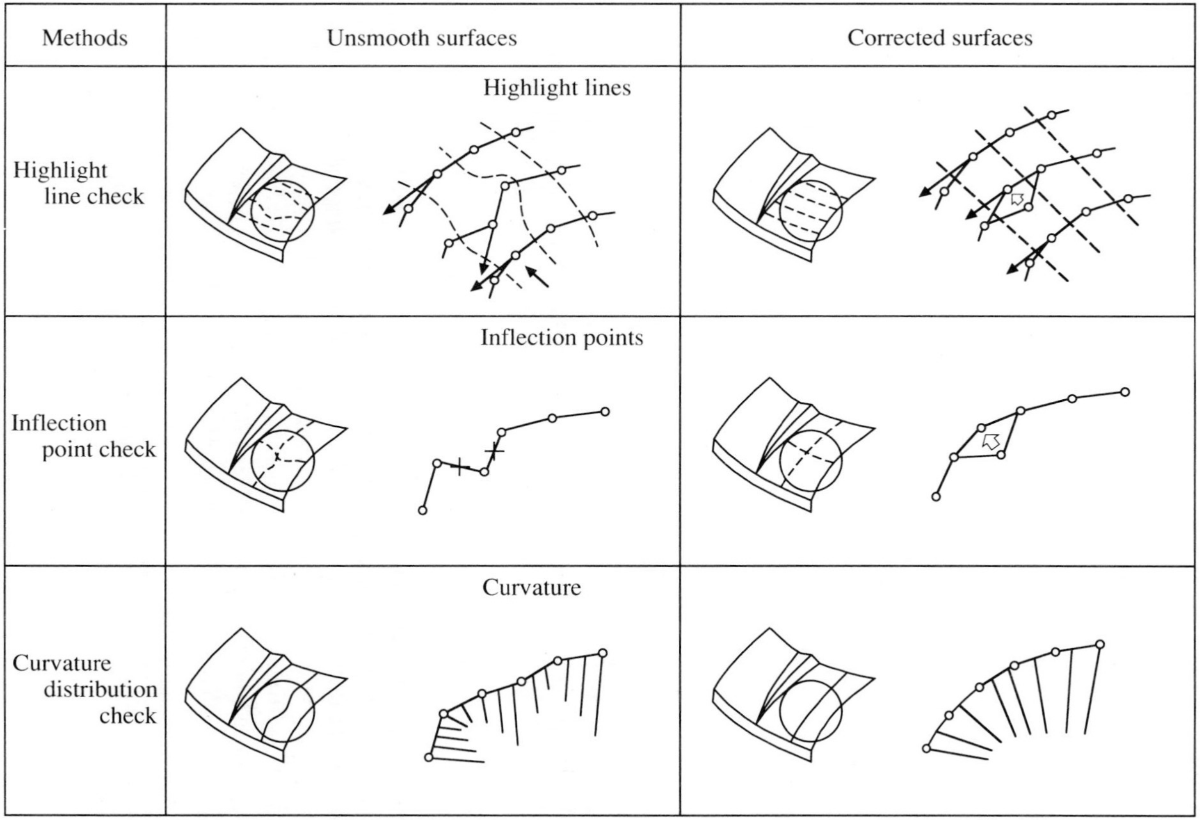

Methods	Unsmooth surfaces	Corrected surfaces
Highlight line check	Highlight lines	
Inflection point check	Inflection points	
Curvature distribution check	Curvature	

FIGURE 12.45
Chart showing the methods for checking the smoothness of surfaces involving highlight lines, inflections points, and curvature distribution. (See Fig. 12.41 for highlight lines.) [12.12]

917

function for regenerating a corner surface smoothly connected with neighboring surfaces takes precedence over the repositioning of points.

By use of the above techniques for examining and correcting of inaccurate information, highly accurate numerical model data have been realized. The final product based on such a generated numerical model possesses acceptable quality. Highlight lines generated by numerical model data are quite smooth, and the surface unevenness is below 0.005 mm.

The processes for generating a numerical model of a stamping die described here are shown in the flowchart in Fig. 12.46, which is for a right front fender of a Toyota VISTA as an example. The styling CAD information and the body CAD information are combined to produce a numerical model of a panel and, in the next step, the die-face CAD information is merged to it to produce a numerical model of the stamping die.

12.3.3.4 MACHINING AND FINISHING BASED ON THE NUMERICAL MODEL

[12.12]. Two technologies as described below for realizing easy and accurate NC machining of the die-face are (1) the automatic calculation of cutter locations which eases the need to generate a large quantity of NC machining information, and (2) a method of administrating a machining process for guaranteeing the required machining accuracy.

Machining of indicated areas of the die-face by milling with a ball-end cutter is an essential function of machining free-form surfaces. High accuracy, where possible error is below 0.05 mm, is realized (1) by regulating all phases of the machining process, which takes into account the thermal expansion of the NC machine and the cutting tool wear, and (2) by using a new mechanism for adjusting cutter positions.

In order to perform finishing based on the numerical model, the coordinates of enough points indicated on the surfaces and the characteristic lines are first extracted from the numerical model. Next the product is measured automatically at the indicated points by a three-dimensional measuring machine. Then the operators finish the product interactively by comparing the data obtained in the first step with those obtained in the second on a graphics display terminal. The system for supporting this capability is realized as an on-line system, in which a host computer, a microcomputer, a three-dimensional measuring machine, and a color graphics display terminal are combined.

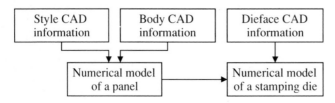

FIGURE 12.46
Flow chart of the CAD information and final numerical models of a right front fender of a Toyota VISTA [12.12].

Generation of numerical models
and NC machining information

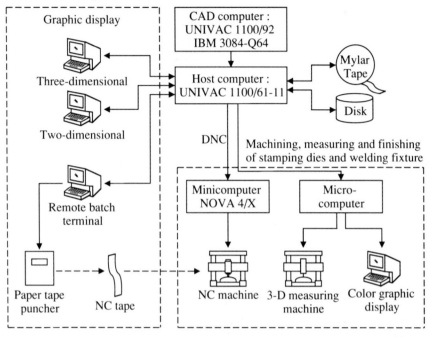

FIGURE 12.47
Hardware configuration of the CAM system involving the domains of (1) generation of numerical models of NC machining information and the production of NC tapes, and (2) direct numerical control of machining, measuring, and finishing of stamping dies and welding fixtures [12.12].

Figure 12.47 shows the hardware configuration of the CAM system involved. As shown in the figure, CAD information is transferred from other computers (UNIVAC 1100/92 and IBM 3084-064). Numerical models, machining, and finishing information are transferred from the host computer to the NC machines and the measuring machines by means of a telephone line or by paper tapes. The software was obtained by enhancing an existing NC system called the Toyota Integrated Numerical Control Approach (TINCA), which has been used since 1973 and which now is composed of about 450,000 Fortran statements. This CAM system has been put into practical use since the 1980s model of a small Toyota VISTA.

12.3.4 Die-Face Design with a CAD System and Computer Computation Aspects

12.3.4.1 PROCEDURE FOR DESIGNING THE DIE-FACE SHAPE.
Figure 12.48 shows a flowchart for the new design procedure, that is followed for evaluating the press forming severity of each feature of the die-face shape. The die-face

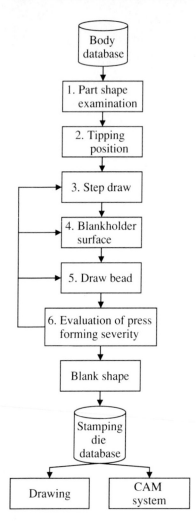

FIGURE 12.48
Flowchart showing the steps in the design of die cavity using the "Die-Face CAD system" [12.10].

designer of the stamping die performs the various tasks as follows [12.10]:

1. Receives initially the topological surface data representing the outer shape of a product from the styling design database and the curve data, which represents the body structure from the body structural design database.
2. Examines the product shape for various favorable views such as in the tipping edge position as shown in Fig. 12.49(a), a photograph of the terminal display screen. (Examples of other photographs of the display screen are also shown in Fig. 12.49(b) to (e)).
3. Designs the characteristic sections such as the shape of the step-draw, interpolates between the sections, and determines the trim line along which the sheetmetal will be sheared off in the trimming process.

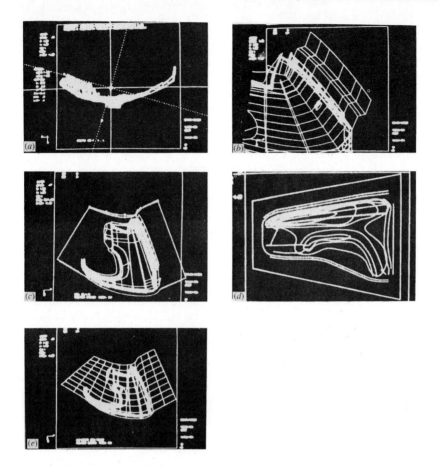

FIGURE 12.49
Photographs of a graphics display screen showing various examples of the images obtained [12.10].

4. Designs the blankholder surface, using the front and rear side curves of the part.
5. Designs the drawbead shape, as explained elsewhere, to control the flow of the sheetmetal over the blankholder surface.
6. Evaluates the press forming severity of the proposed die-face design. (If the results of the various evaluation functions, as discussed below, indicate the occurrence of any imperfections, the required modifications of the geometric model will be made. If, on the other hand, the proposed design is found to be satisfactory, the designer proceeds to the next step.)
7. Determines the blank shape taking the yield ratio of the sheetmetal into account.
8. Transmits finally the completed geometric model of the die-face to the database for use by the CAM system for the manufacturing of the stamping dies.

12.3.4.2 CAD EVALUATING FUNCTIONS [12.10]

1. *Functions for generating die-face shapes.* The functions for interactively generating the geometric model of the die-face shapes, which correspond to the plaster model in the conventional approach, includes basic functions as shown in Table 12.2 and the applications functions as shown in Table 12.3. The basic functions are (1) those required for generating individual geometric entities such as shown in Table 12.2, while (2) the application functions are those required for generating a set of geometric entities in stylized shapes such as step-draw shapes and blankholder surfaces, etc., as shown in Table 12.3.

    Using the application functions, the designer can create compound surfaces representing the step-draw shapes by sliding a section curve along a guide curve. The designer can also create a compound surface representing a blankholder shape by sliding lines along two guide curves. The designer directs the lines to lie either on a cylindrical or conical surface. The trim line is created by developing a specified flange curve of the product shape onto the step-draw surfaces.

2. *Functions for evaluating the press forming severity.* Several kinds of characteristic values, which are mainly obtained from geometrical calculations, of the die-face shapes are used in this method instead of the more detailed numerical

TABLE 12.2
Basic Functions [12.10]

	Intersection	Projection	Polyline	Tangent line
Point, line				
	Offset	Projection	Fillet boundary	Controlling curve
Curve				
	2 curves ×1 section	1 curve ×1 section	4 curves	Surface trimming
Surface				
Other	Section, grouping, standardized geometry			

TABLE 12.3
Application Functions [12.10]

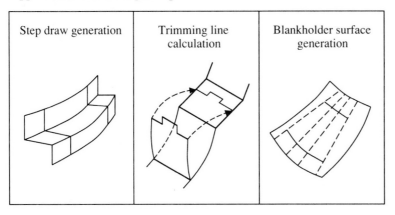

Step draw generation	Trimming line calculation	Blankholder surface generation

analysis. This approach gives a simplified simulation of the press forming process with the advantage of providing a quick indication of the forming severity. As shown in Table 12.4, the characteristic values are classified into two groups: those based on geometrical calculations only, that is, (a), (b), (c), and (d), and those based on both the geometry and the mechanics of materials, that is, (e) and (f).

The data inputs and method of computation are described below.

1. *Estimation of the blank shape in the die cavity* [see Table 12.4(e)]. The estimated blank shape in the die cavity is calculated by the FEM, which assumes that the deformation of the sheetmetal held in the blankholder is elastic. The required data inputs are mesh points, Young's modulus, Poisson's ratio, and the sheet thickness. The system calculates the displacements of the mesh points by solving the following equilibrium equation:

$$[K]\mathbf{u} = \mathbf{f} \qquad (12.20)$$

where $[K]$ = stiffness matrix
$\mathbf{u}$ = displacement vector
$\mathbf{f}$ = load vector (see Eq. (12.1))

All functions for evaluating the press forming severity are based on the estimated blank shape.

2. *Calculation of the mean section length ratio* [see Table 12.4(d)]. The designer first specifies the section planes which coincide with the directions of metal flow for obtaining section curves on the product surfaces; then specifies a position on the blank shape where the punch first makes contact. With this information, the ratio of the section length on the blank shape to that on the

TABLE 12.4
Evaluation Functions [12.10]

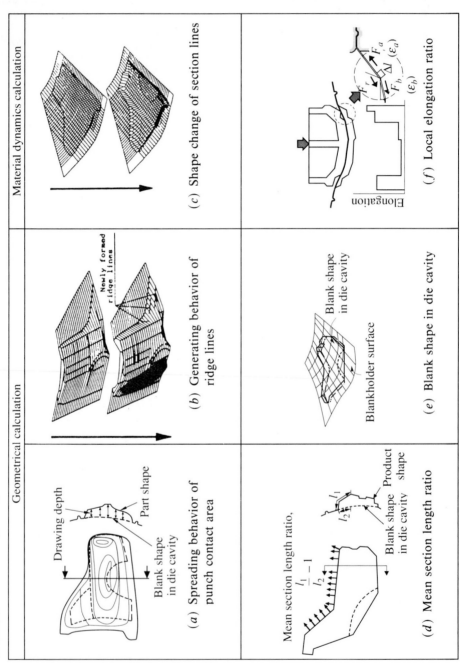

Geometrical calculation		Material dynamics calculation
(a) Spreading behavior of punch contact area	(b) Generating behavior of ridge lines	(c) Shape change of section lines
(d) Mean section length ratio	(e) Blank shape in die cavity	(f) Local elongation ratio

product shape is calculated and displayed graphically. Based on the distribution of these ratios, the designer can predict the occurrence of fracture and surface distortion.

3. *Calculation of local elongation ratios* [see Table 12.4(f)]. The local elongation ratios are calculated for predicting the occurrence of fracture. Based on the section geometry shown in Table 12.4(c), sheetmetal movement is calculated so that the resisting force at the contact point of the panel and of the die balances with the forces on both sides of the point. The accompanying strain changes are then calculated using the stress-strain curve and the predetermined friction data. By comparing the formed section with its initial configuration, the ratio of sheetmetal elongation is obtained. These calculations are repeated at each forming step for areas where the application of the local elongation ratios are useful for predicting the occurrence of localized fracture in the areas formed by the punch and the counter die.

The above methods of evaluation are preferred for practical use, because they are based not on the plastic deformation of the sheet but mainly on geometric calculations. However, sheetmetal flows in shear only with no change in thickness, and the material properties are taken into account in the calculations. The basic idea common in all such calculations is that the characteristic values are easily obtained on section curves of the product shape and of the formed shape.

12.3.4.3 TECHNIQUES FOR INCREASING COMPUTATION EFFICIENCY [12.10]. The techniques of efficiently computing the functions described in the foregoing are those concerning (1) the *data structure design* for efficient access such as creation, addition, modification, and retrieval of data, (2) the *mathematical expressions for curves and surfaces*, and (3) *the structure of the data base management system*, which must be designed for effectively administrating the mass data and for ensuring the required response time for data access.

Details of the above three techniques are described as follows:

1. *Data structure design* [12.10]. The data structure for defining the curve and surface entities for facilitating the creation and modification of the geometrical model is shown in Fig. 12.50. A curve entity is one which contains the smallest unit of curved lines. A surface is defined by a pair of two entities: (1) an elemental surface entity, which contains information about the surface geometry and (2) a topological surface entity containing the boundary information of the surface. The information of the surface is preserved even if the surface is trimmed.

A section curve entity and a surface-versus-curve relation were introduced for calculating the characteristic values. These values are computed using the section curves of the product shapes and the formed shapes defined in the same cutting plane. The following three requirements must be met for efficient calculation: (1) the calculations of the section curves must be fast, (2) section

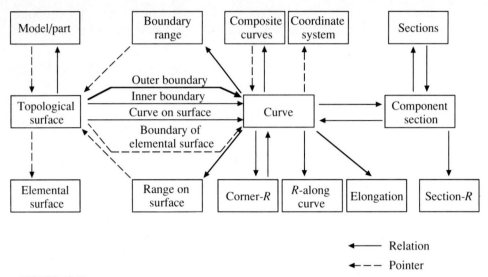

← Relation

←— — Pointer

FIGURE 12.50
The data structure for defining the curve and surface entities for facilitating the creation and modification of the geometrical model [12.10].

curves on a specified portion of the model, such as the blankholder surfaces, must be easily recognizable, and (3) the section curves in the same cutting plane should be quickly retrievable. In order to satisfy the first condition, for example, computation time can be greatly shortened by attaching fillet radii on the appropriate curves instead of actually creating the surface. In order to satisfy the second condition, "portion boundary curves," which separate various portions of a geometric model such as step draw, blankholder, etc., as shown in Fig. 12.51 and which are specified by the designer, can be

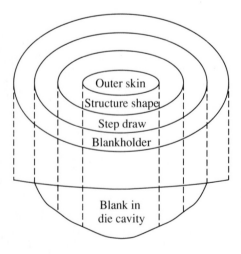

FIGURE 12.51
Illustration of the die-face portions that separate various portions of a geometric model such as step draw, blankholder, etc. [12.10].

automatically recognized. In order to satisfy the third condition, a section curve entity has been implemented to connect all component section curves in the same cutting plane.

2. *Mathematical expressions of curves and surfaces* [12.10]. The designer evaluates the surfaces from the "clay" model in terms of style and of surface smoothness. Human perception is necessary for the former, but the CAD system must include a function for determining smoothness, which is a function of unevenness and of highlight lines that represent surface variation.

It is difficult to produce in a single step a complicated surface as envisioned by the designer, so the surfaces are broken down into simple surfaces, which are used to assemble the desired surfaces. The problem of dividing a *surface* into units is solved by dividing *curves* into units. Also, methods must be available for inputting unit curves, for curve generation, for numerical handling of the generation of three-dimensional space curves, for generating unit surfaces, and for combining unit surfaces. Some of these topics will be discussed below.

3. *Methods of inputting unit curves and curve generation* [12.13]. Curve scales have been used to input unit curves. Curve scales have been standardized in this illustration, so that a curve can be input and positioned at the desired location by specifying its number and either three points on the curve or two points and the connecting curve. This means that curves with a perfectly smooth distribution of curvature can be generated, which is not possible by connecting measured point sequences and then smoothing.

If a curve cannot be handled by means of curve scales, an interval can be interactively specified on the graphics display for a curve input from a point sequence and the curve then processed as a parametric curve segment by the method of least squares. The designer can then join unit curves, create different unit curves, and synthesize unit curves into space curves.

Cubic spline formulas are used for the internal expression of curves, so as to avoid the occurrence of unexpected shapes such as fourth-degree and higher order curves. (See the appendix of this chapter for a discussion of spline curves.) A unit curve, that has just been input, is a single, cubic segment. However, once a space curve is synthesized and any other such work is performed, the curve must be approximated with multiple splines in order to express it. When a space curve is synthesized from two projection drawings, the numerical formulas must not be changed so as to alter the distribution of curvature of the original curves. Therefore, the connection between adjacent segments, which has not been sufficiently elucidated with the existing spline method, must be correctly determined. The problem is how to determine the ratio, k, of the sizes of the tangential vectors of adjacent segments. The ratio of the cord lengths has conventionally been used for k in the case of spline curves using k as proposed by Hosaka.

The B-spline form proposed by Hosaka [12.14] is used here for expressing curves and surfaces. This form permits both a compact expression and easy geometric processing, and it also utilizes a scale factor instead of a knot vector used in the original B-spline form [12.15]. The scale factor is defined as the ratio of the tangential vector lengths of adjacent curve segments, the parameter of each segment being normalized in [0, 1]. The C^2 curve in the Hosaka form is expressed as follows:

$$(1+k_i)P_i = \frac{[Q_{i-1}+k_i(1+k_{i-1})Q_i]}{[1+k_i(1+k_{i-1})]} + \frac{[k_i(1+k_{i+1})Q_i+k_i^2 k_{i+1}Q_{i+1}]}{[1+k_{i+1}(1+k_i)]} \quad (12.21)$$

where k_i = scale factor at the ith segment p_i
$\qquad Q_i$ = ith B-spline control point [12.10]

As explained by Hosaka, the transformation between the B-spline form and the Bezier form [12.16] can be carried out quite easily by use of Fig. 12.52. In the B-spline form the required number of control points for n curve segments is $(n+3)$ as compared to $(3n+1)$ in the Bezier form. This implies that the B-spline form is preferable in view of the volume of data involved. On the other hand, the Bezier form is preferable to the B-spline form for geometric calculations since segmentwise manipulation is easier. Both forms are used to advantage in this CAD/CAM system [12.10].

k_i is found as the ratio of the tangential vectors after the curve shape has been decided upon, but consideration must be given beforehand, when deciding on the curve shape, to use a k_i that will yield a smooth distribution of curvature. With this method, a curve estimated as suitable in terms of the desired boundary conditions is found, and k_i for that curve is used as the scale for the spline curve to be determined subsequently [12.13].

In deriving a space curve, the magnitudes of the curvature of two 2-dimensional curves at their end points are used as the boundary conditions and a fifth-degree curve with a smooth distribution of curvature is used as the estimated curve. Hosaka's method is used to find this curve as a fourth-degree curve, and a fifth-degree curve is obtained here by adding the condition of minimal sum of the squares of its second derivatives. This method provides stability of solutions and a smooth distribution of curvature with excellent results [12.13].

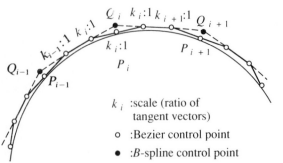

k_i :scale (ratio of tangent vectors)

o :Bezier control point

● :B-spline control point

FIGURE 12.52
Example of the use of Bezier and B-spline control points. (See Appendix to Chap. 12.) [12.10].

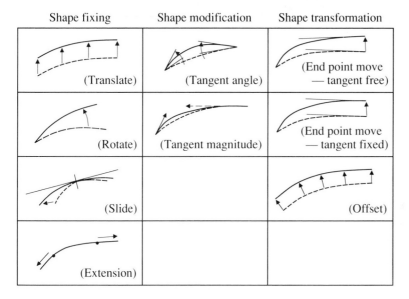

Shape fixing	Shape modification	Shape transformation
(Translate)	(Tangent angle)	(End point move — tangent free)
(Rotate)	(Tangent magnitude)	(End point move — tangent fixed)
(Slide)		(Offset)
(Extension)		

FIGURE 12.53
Three methods for controlling the shape of curves by interactively changing them on a graphics display terminal by shape fixing, shape modification, and shape transformation [12.13].

4. *Method of changing curves* [12.13]. The designer must be able to modify freely the curves initially input by dynamic changing on the graphics display, which is sometimes called *curve control.* This method is broken down into shape fixing, modification, and transformation as shown in Fig. 12.53.

  Fixing consists of moving, rotating, or extending the curve without changing its shape. *Modification* involves changing the distribution of curvature. The curve is controlled by the direction and magnitude of the tangents at its end points. This modification can be made regardless of the number of segments involved. *Transformation* is the changing of the curve shape so as to maintain the original distribution of its curvature as much as possible.

  The foregoing operations are used for controlling a curve as a whole, but *B*-spline control points can also be specified individually for local modifications, so that provision has been made for the free insertion or deletion of control points.

  Unit input curves in this method can be connected and unified. *Connecting* consists of transforming the indicated curves so that their tangents will be continuous; while *unifying* involves transforming two curves to obtain continuous curvature.

5. *Methods of surface construction* [12.13]. If the baseline is made to run along the guidelines, the surface can be categorized according to baseline movement into three types: cross (+), H type, and rectangular (□) as shown in Fig. 12.54. With cross-type surfaces the baseline moves along one guideline, with H-type

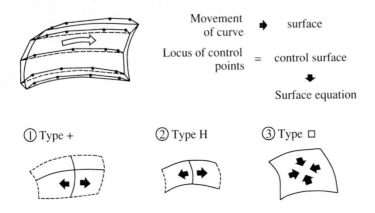

Movement of curve ➡ surface

Locus of control points = control surface

⬇

Surface equation

① Type +   ② Type H   ③ Type □

FIGURE 12.54
Scheme for generation of surfaces into three types: (1) cross type, (2) H type, and rectangular type [12.13].

surfaces, the baseline moves along two guidelines, and with rectangular types a surface with four boundary lines is bent in toward the middle.

A surface equation amounts to the expression, with Eq. (12.21), of the locus of control points of the baselines as curves. These curves are known as the *controlling curves of the surface.* Surface equations using these curves correspond to B-spline surface equations. With them, twist vectors are derived automatically, and the continuity between them is ensured. A B-spline surface equation can easily be converted to patch equations just as with a curve, and it is well to use patch equations for calculating the intersecting curves of surfaces.

Forming car surfaces is a matter of combining and joining unit surfaces. The complicated combining of surfaces begins with the determination of a large base surface. Next, peripheral approach surfaces are prepared. Fillet surfaces are then made along the edge.

The highlight lines and section curves are used to check whether or not a surface that is constructed is as smooth as intended. This system enables evaluation on the graphics display corresponding to that of an actual model. It can be checked on the screen whether the highlight lines are positioned and as smooth as intended and whether the distribution of curvature of the section curves is smooth.

The highlight lines are simulated on the display screen as a representation of how infinitely distant parallel lines would be reflected on the surface. That is, they are represented as curves consisting of the point along specified sections having a constant tangential angle. Mathematically, this means that they consist of points with constant direction for the outer product of the normals of the surface and specified plane. The functions required of CAD for the above construction and evaluation of surfaces are shown in Fig. 12.55.

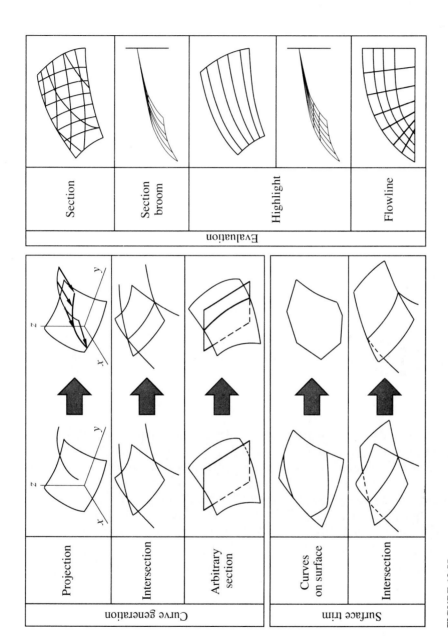

FIGURE 12.55
Functions required of CAD for the generation of curves, and the trimming and the evaluation of surfaces [12.13].

931

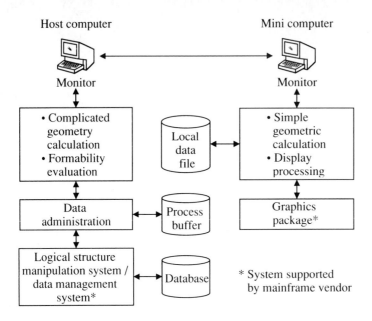

FIGURE 12.56
Database system for geometric modeling techniques for interactively creating, evaluating, and modifying die-face shapes showing the division of load between the host and minicomputers [12.10].

12.3.4.4 STRUCTURE OF THE DATA BASE MANAGEMENT SYSTEM [12.10]. The structure of the database system as shown in Fig. 12.56 is designed to ensure an easy management of the mass data, rapid recovery from system failures, and quick response to command execution. It has been incorporated into a general purpose *data base management system.*

A local data file compatible with the database in the host computer is used in a minicomputer to achieve a quick response to execution commands. The purpose of this feature is to share properly the processing of the load between the host computer and the minicomputer with respect to their computing capacities. Calculations of surface evaluation functions, which require extensive computation, are being done in the host computer. On the other hand, the drafting functions and display control functions which require little computation time are carried out in the minicomputer. With this arrangement, the response time for the graphics displays becomes practical.

In order to shorten the response time for geometric calculations, an intermediate file, called the *process buffer,* is located between the geometric processing module and the database. It is used to decrease the database access time and also to facilitate several time-saving features such as issuing a new command while the results of the preceding command are still being transmitted.

12.3.4.5 HARDWARE CONFIGURATION [12.10]. Figure 12.57 shows the hardware configuration of this system. The host computer is a UNIVAC 1100/92, and the

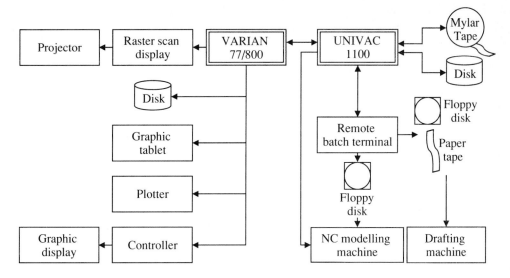

FIGURE 12.57
Hardware configuration for geometric modeling [12.13].

minicomputer is a VARIAN 77/800. Four AGS4145 graphics display terminals are connected to the minicomputer. Other peripheral equipment such as large tablets, plotters, and hard copy devices are also connected to the minicomputer. Some practical examples of the output of this system are shown in Fig. 12.49.

12.3.5 Evaluation of Press-Forming Severity in an Integrated CAD/CAM System

12.3.5.1 EVALUATION OF PRESS-FORMING SEVERITY USING THE CONVENTIONAL METHOD [12.17]. Prior to discussing the integrated CAD/CAM system, the conventional method, as shown in Fig. 12.58(a), with its attendant problems, will be reviewed very briefly: (1) production design begins with the rough drawings of the die-face; (2) a plaster model, based on the rough drawings, is molded and the shapes of the details are built into the model; (3) the forming capability of the stamping die is checked by making a plaster mold of the model; (4) the stamping die is manufactured by NC machining, using the measurements of the plaster model; (5) after the die is finished and mounted in a press, its performance is tried out.

At the tryout stage, defects such as surface unevenness, wrinkles, dimensional inaccuracies, and fractures often appear, which are caused by the inferior quality of the design as represented by the drawings and the plaster model. Numerous modifications of the stamping die must be made on a trial-and-error basis, which requires many worker-hours.

Experimental analyses as shown in Fig. 12.59 have been made in this example in an effort to prevent the formation of the above defects. For example,

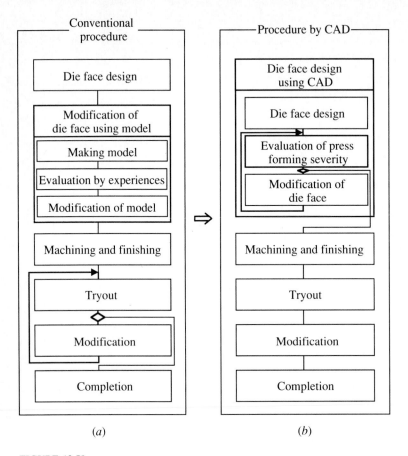

Conventional procedure | Procedure by CAD

FIGURE 12.58
Flowcharts for the evaluation of die-face shape from the standpoint of press-forming severity (*a*) by the conventional method during die tryout, and (*b*) by the CAD method in the design stage. The former is giving way to the latter as shown by the open arrow [12.17].

for the analysis of the fracture as shown in Fig. 12.59(*a*), the panel deformation was evaluated by using the *scribed circle test* (SCT). The mechanisms of the generation and disappearance of surface deflection induced in the press-forming stroke were analyzed as shown in Fig. 12.59(*b*), which included an investigation of the distribution of the strain over the formed panel. The distribution of the strain was explored by classifying the strain into the six deformation areas, *A* to *F*, in terms of the amount and the ratio of strain. The relationship of the die-face shape to the strain distribution and the spreading of the punch contact area were then analyzed in order to determine how the die-face should be modified. These analyses were usually effective in removing the press forming defects occurring during the tryout stage. However, when these defects cannot be eliminated, material of a better quality at increased cost might have to be used, the production

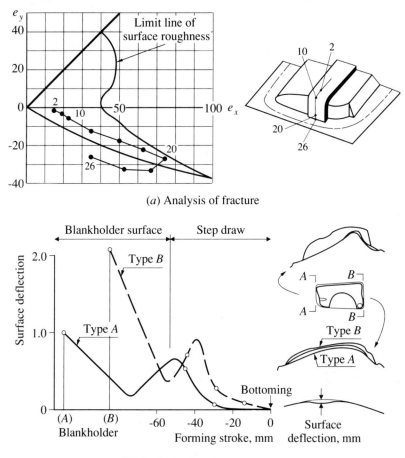

(*a*) Analysis of fracture

(*b*) Analysis of surface deflection

FIGURE 12.59
Experimental analysis techniques used to eliminate forming defects occurring during the die tryout state in the conventional method: (*a*) forming limit diagram, (*b*) surface deflection versus stroke analysis. (Note that in (*a*) surface roughness serves as the forming limit.) [12,17].

rate may have to be reduced, and sometimes the part shape itself has to be modified.

12.3.5.2   EVALUATION OF PRESS-FORMING SEVERITY USING CAD [12.17]. With the newer CAD system as shown in Fig. 12.58(*b*), the most important thing is that the press-forming defects can be predicted before manufacturing the die rather than be removed afterward. In other words, as shown in Fig. 12.58(*b*), the die-face shape must be evaluated from the standpoint of press-forming severity at the design stage and the necessary modifications must be made before transmitting the die information to the subsequent step.

Defects	Cause \ Analytical "means" using CAD	a. Blank shape in die cavity	b. Spreading behaviour of punch contact area	c. Shape change of section lines	d. Generating behaviour of ridge lines	e. Mean section length ratio	f. Local elongation ratio	g. Movement of sheet
Surface deflection / Wrinkling	1. Unsuitable blank shape in die cavity	○						
Surface deflection / Wrinkling	2. Unsuitable contact between punch and sheet		○	○	○			
Surface deflection / Wrinkling	3. Non uniform stretch		○			○		○
Surface deflection / Wrinkling	4. Non uniform deformation by drawing					○		○
Surface deflection / Wrinkling	5. Non uniform deformation with counter die			○	○		○	○
Fracture	6. Elastic recovery after taking off					○		
Fracture	7. Whole elongation							
Fracture	8. Local elongation						○	
Fracture	9. Stretch flanging							○
Method of calculation	Linear FEM							
Method of calculation	Geometrical calculation	●	●	●	●	●		●
Method of calculation	Plasticity calculation	●					●	●

(b)

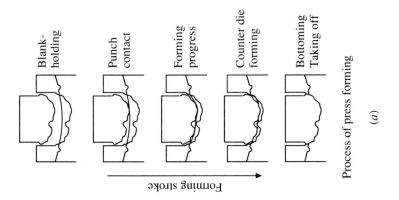

Blank-holding

Punch contact

Forming progress

Counter die forming

Bottoming
Taking off

Forming stroke

Process of press forming

(a)

The key to resolving the problems encountered in the conventional method and, at the same time, to obtain a high quality geometric model of the die-face shapes is interactively to create, evaluate, and modify the geometric model in the design stage rather than in the tryout stage as with the conventional method.

This approach is becoming increasingly more necessary because of the greater demands placed on automobiles such as low aerodynamic drag, low noise and vibration generation, high crash resistance, and weight reduction. Also, with the anticipated development of new materials, etc., past experience may not be sufficient to meet future requirements, so that the analytical approach will become increasingly important.

12.3.5.3 METHODS FOR ANALYZING PRESS-FORMING DEFECTS [12.17]. Analytical means, that relate to the press-forming defects, are summarized in Fig. 12.60.

Here, the press-forming defects, caused by inappropriate die-face design, are divided into two groups as shown in column 1 in Fig. 12.60(b): (1) one group consists of geometrical surface inaccuracies such as surface deflection and wrinkling, and (2) the other consists of fracture. The causes of the first group are categorized into six subgroups, (1) to (6), as shown in the second column in Fig. 12.60(b). This subgroup category is based on the previously mentioned analyses of surface deflection in terms of sheetmetal behavior during the press-forming processes. The second group is categorized into three subgroups, (7) to (9), also as shown in Fig. 12.60(b), according to the type of fracture.

The deformation of a panel was analyzed in the process of designing the dies to evaluate these defects as shown in Fig. 12.60(b). A nonlinear FEM was also applied in addition to the linear FEM shown by the black bullet for method (a) in Fig. 12.60(b). It was concluded however, that automobile panels were too complicated in shape to use FEM with the available computers. Therefore, geometrical functions for curved lines and surfaces were used for press-forming evaluations, which are indispensable for drawing a die-face and which are discussed in Section 12.3.4. Plasticity calculation methods were used for methods (f) and (g).

12.3.5.4 FUNCTIONS FOR EVALUATING PRESS-FORMING SEVERITY [12.17]. Functions for evaluating the press-forming severity are shown in Figs. 12.61 and 12.62 as discussed below. The characteristics of these functions are the simulations of simplified press-forming processes and the interactive designing with the computer. The calculated results can be used by the designers to evaluate the appropriateness of the designs.

FIGURE 12.60
(a) Stages occurring during the course of the forming stroke in a sheetmetal drawing operation. (b) A chart correlating the press-forming defects and the methods of calculation (column 1) with the cause of the defects and the CAD "means" (methods) of analysis. (See Figs. 12.43 and 12.44 and Sec. 12.2.5.3.) [12.17].

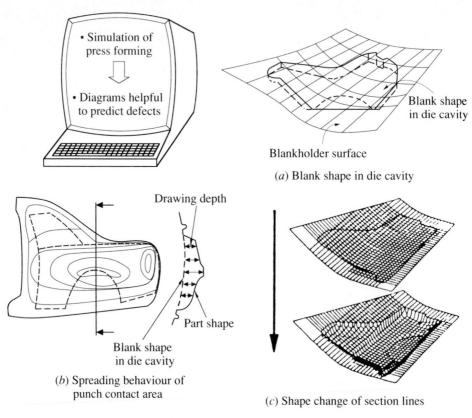

(a) Blank shape in die cavity

(b) Spreading behaviour of punch contact area

(c) Shape change of section lines

FIGURE 12.61
Evaluation functions for press-forming severity (part 1) [12.17].

1. *Blank shape in die cavity* (see Fig. 12.61(a)). A linear FEM for steel sheet bending is built in to predict the blank shape in the die cavity. A nonlinear FEM was not used because of the enormous computer processing time that was required.

2. *Spreading behavior of punch contact area* (see Fig. 12.61(b)). The depth of drawing is calculated for the whole area of the die cavity, and the equivalent depth is traced to make a contour map. By use of the contour map, the spreading behavior of the punch contacting area with the sheet can be estimated during the forming process.

3. *Shape change of section lines* (see Fig. 12.61(c)). The section lines of a sheet are figure-processed when they are deformed with the punch and die. The sheet deformation can be estimated by this diagram during the forming process.

FIGURE 12.62
Evaluation functions for press-forming severity (part 2). (Note the black spot in (d) and in Table 12.4(b) is a photographic artifact.) [12.17]

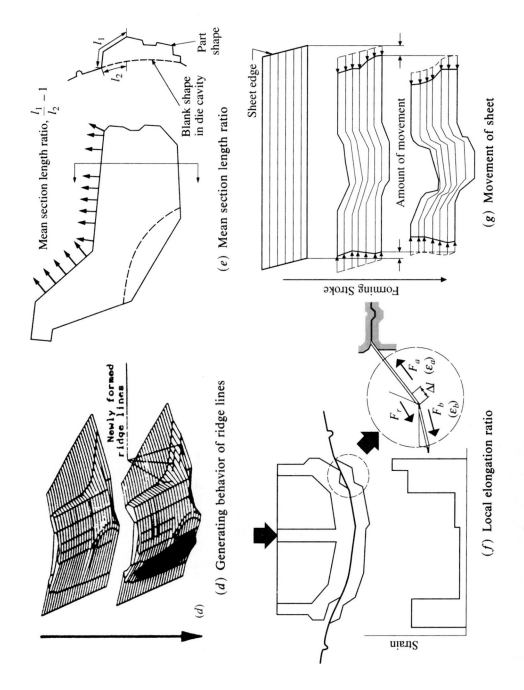

Mean section length ratio, $\dfrac{l_1}{l_2} - 1$

Blank shape in die cavity

Part shape

(e) Mean section length ratio

Newly formed ridge lines

(d) Generating behavior of ridge lines

Sheet edge

Amount of movement

Forming Stroke

(g) Movement of sheet

Movement of sheet

F_a (ε_a)

Δl

F_r

F_b (ε_b)

Strain

(f) Local elongation ratio

939

The calculation is done on the assumption that there is no force acting between the neighboring sections and no bending moment at the section lines.

4. *Generating behavior of ridge lines* (see Fig. 12.62(*d*)). This information combines the ridge lines created by the contacting points of the punch and die. This calculation is made after the calculation of the shape change of section lines on several sections with function (*c*) above. This information allows one to estimate the generation of the ridge lines during the forming process.

5. *Mean section length ratio* (see Fig. 12.62(*e*)). This information is obtained by calculating the section length ratio between predetermined section lines before and after forming, which is equivalent to the average elongation of the panel. It is assumed that large differences in the mean elongation ratio between neighboring sections lead to nonuniform forming.

6. *Local elongation ratio* (see Fig. 12.62(*f*)). As shown in Fig. 12.62(*f*), a fracture is induced by local elongation when the sheet is deformed with both punch and die. This function uses the calculation of the local elongation ratio in these areas. It is designed for the shaded areas in Fig. 12.63 where plane-stretching occurs.

7. *Movement of the sheet* (see Fig. 12.62(*g*)). This function is used for finding how a specific point on the section moves during the forming process. Since elongation ratios can also be input in this calculation, a precise calculation can be made if they are given. The movement of the line drawn on the sheet can be simulated by carrying out the operation for several sections and tracing the moving points on each section.

12.3.6 Application of the CAD/CAM System [12.17]

12.3.6.1 DESIGNING PROCESS USING DIE-FACE CAD SYSTEM. The designing process of die faces using this CAD system is shown in Fig. 12.48, and Fig.

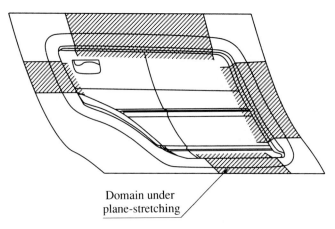

Domain under
plane-stretching

FIGURE 12.63
Crosshatched areas show where the local elongation ratio can be applied [12.17].

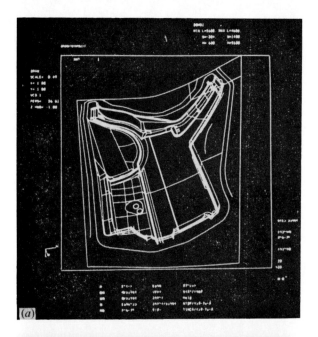

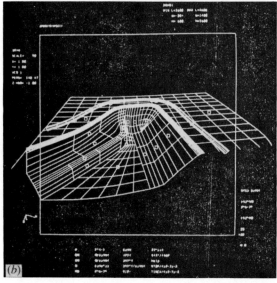

FIGURE 12.64
Photographs of the display screen
images of the die-face design (*a*)
plan view of the entire quarter
panel, and (*b*) tipped enlarged
view of the upper right end of the
die cavity [12.8].

12.64(*a*) shows a photograph of the display screen of a completed die-face design
for a quarter panel. At this stage the die-face shape is stored in the database as
a numerical model containing the curved surface information. With this system
any section can be displayed and the die-face shape can be displayed at any
angle as shown in Fig. 12.64(*b*). Thus, a die-face shape can be evaluated precisely

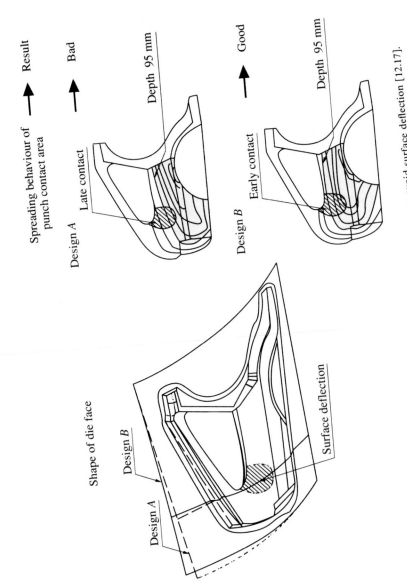

Spreading behaviour of
punch contact area → Result

→ Bad

Design A   Late contact

Depth 95 mm

Design B   Early contact

→ Good

Depth 95 mm

Shape of die face

Design B

Design A

Surface deflection

FIGURE 12.65
Example of the application of the spreading behavior of punch contact are to avoid surface deflection [12.17].

on a graphic display without manufacturing any actual model such as a plaster model. Also, the data of the die-face shape can be transmitted to the CAM system to produce a die-face by NC machining. Thus, the manufacturing process of the die is greatly expedited.

12.3.6.2 APPLICATION OF THE "SPREADING BEHAVIOR OF THE PUNCH CONTACT AREA" TO AVOID SURFACE DEFLECTION [12.17]. Figure 12.49(d) and Fig. 12.65 show examples of contour maps applied to the die-face design of a quarter panel.

Surface deflection tends to occur in the shaded corner area when forming the window of the quarter panel as shown in Fig. 12.65. From experience, it is known that the punch must contact this area as soon as possible to avoid surface deflection.

As shown in Fig. 12.65, two die-face designs A and B were evaluated in this example. From viewing the contour map formation on the display screen, the designer could readily see that B would have the punch contact the window corner earlier than A. B would, therefore, be expected to have less surface deflection and a greater depth of draw at the window corner than A. About 300 worker-hours were saved at the tryout in this case with this method.

12.3.6.3 APPLICATION OF THE "MEAN SECTION LENGTH RATIO" TO AVOID SURFACE DEFLECTION [12.17]. Figure 12.66 shows an example of the application of the mean section length ratio approach to two die-faces having different ratios. As shown in Fig. 12.66, the base of the pillar on the quarter panel is prone to nonuniform forming and surface deflection because of the saddle shape. This investigation showed that the mean section length ratio is an effective index to evaluate nonuniform forming, which is the prime cause of surface deflection. The step-draw shape of B was, therefore, adopted with a gradual distribution of the mean section length ratio. About 200 worker-hours were saved at tryout with this method.

12.3.6.4 APPLICATION OF VARIOUS FUNCTIONS TO AVOID WRINKLING [12.17]. In the application, the shape change of section lines, generating behavior of ridge lines, and movement of the sheet, shown in Fig. 12.61(c) and Fig. 12.62(d) and (g), were used to avoid wrinkling in the center pillar shown in Fig. 12.67, which is prone to wrinkling because of the complexity in shape.

In this study, it was noticed, that in comparison with "the bottom" in Fig. 12.67(b), the sheet deformation tended to occur in area B in Fig. 12.67(a). This was caused by excessive drawing-in of area A, because the forming of the ridge lines had not yet occurred. It was presumed that excess metal caused by too much drawing-in induced buckling which resulted in wrinkling. Wrinkling was avoided by incorporating a certain shape in the panel as shown in Fig. 12.67(b). About 200 worker-hours were saved at the tryout stage by this method.

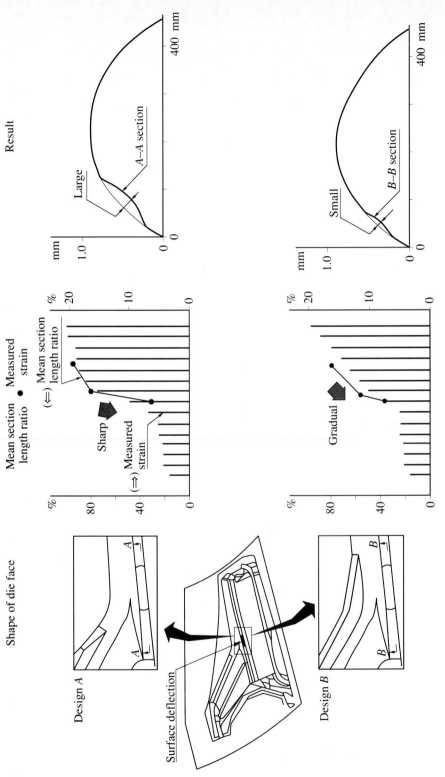

FIGURE 12.66
Example of the mean section length ratio to avoid surface deflection [12.17].

944

B. Area without ridge lines   *A*. Area with excessive
draw-in

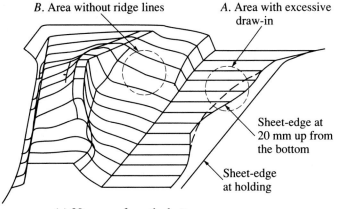

Sheet-edge at
20 mm up from
the bottom

Sheet-edge
at holding

(*a*) 20 mm up from the bottom

Shape for absorbing wrinkling

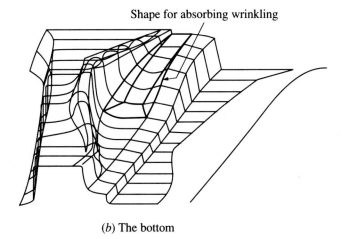

(*b*) The bottom

FIGURE 12.67
Example of the evaluation functions to avoid wrinkling [12.17].

**12.3.6.5 APPLICATION OF "LOCAL ELONGATION RATIO" TO AVOID FRAC-
TURE AND TO IMPROVE THE YIELD RATE** [12.17]. Figure 12.68 shows an
example of the progressive design of a die-face where fracture is avoided as much
as possible and the yield rate is maximized.

In the first stage (1) shown in Fig. 12.68, a conventional die-face was used,
where the local elongation ratio is much lower than the deformation limit. In the
second stage (2) in Fig. 12.68, the die-face was reduced by 10 mm to save material,
where the ratio exceeded the deformation limit. Then in the third stage (3), the
radius of the step-draw was modified as shown in Fig. 12.68, where the strain
was maintained 7 percent below the limit.

In this case, 1 percent of the material was saved because 10 mm was
eliminated out of the total length of 1000 mm.

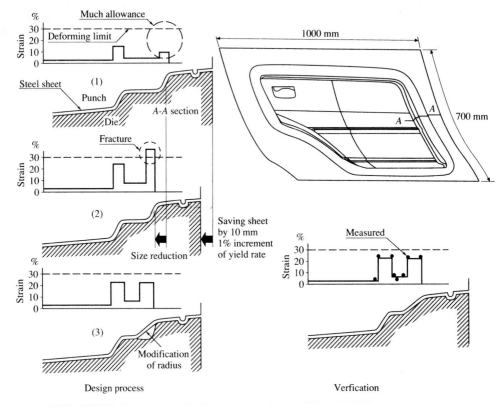

FIGURE 12.68
Example of the application of local elongation ratio to avoid fracture and improve the yield rate [12.17].

12.3.7   Conclusions [12.17]

By use of the die-face CAD system, the press forming severity can be evaluated on a graphics display terminal and the necessary modification of the die-face can be made to obtain a high quality design.

With this system, 30 percent of the total worker-hours and 30 percent of the total lead-time for die tryout were saved. At the same time the utilization of the material was improved, the designing time of the die-faces was reduced by 50 percent and the worker-hours for manufacturing the dies were reduced by 30 percent. The significant saving in time and money would not be possible without the use of metalworking engineering in place of the shop craft approach.

ACKNOWLEDGMENT

The material and the illustrations in this chapter were adapted from the references as indicated in the text and in the legends by the numbers of the references enclosed in square brackets pursuant to all copyrights.

REFERENCES

12.1. Duncan, D. L., R. Sowerby, and E. Chu, "The Development of Sheet Metal Modelling," *Computer Modeling of Sheet Metal Forming Process*, N.-M. Wang and S. C. Tang (eds.), Proc. Symposium Met. Soc. and TMS Detroit Sec., 12th Automotive Mat. Symp., Ann Arbor, Michigan, April 29-30, 1985, Met. Soc., Inc., Warrendale, Pennsylvania, pp. 1-20.

12.2. Arlinghaus, F. J., W. H. Frey, T. B. Stoughton, and B. K. Murthy, "Finite Element Modeling of a Stretch-Formed Part," ibid., pp. 51-66.

12.3. Wang, N.-M., and Bernard Budiansky, "Analysis of Sheet Metal Stamping by a Finite Element Method," *Journal of Applied Mechanics*, vol. 45 (1978), pp. 73-82.

12.4. Stoughton, T. B., "Parametric Punch Descriptions in Modeling Sheet Metal Formability," *12th NAMRC*, 1984, pp. 214-218.

12.5. Suzuki, H., "The CAD/CAM System for Die and Mold and an Example of its Application," *Bull. of the Japan Soc. of Precision Engg.*, vol. 18, no. 2, June 1984, pp. 198-206.

12.6. Romvári, P., M. Tisza, and P. Rácz, "A Complete CAD/CAM Package for Sheet Metal Forming," *Proceedings of the Twenty-Sixth International Machine Tool Design and Research Conference*, Sept. 1986, B. J. Davies (ed.), Dept. of M.E., Univ. of Man. Inst. of Sc. and Tech. and MacMillan Publishers Ltd., Hampshire, pp. 33-39.

12.7. Ohara, M., "CAD/CAM in the Automotive Industry," *Bull. Japan Soc. Prec. Eng.*, vol. 18, no. 2, June 1984, pp. 193-197.

12.8. Ohara, M., and M. Higashi, "Integration of CAD/CAM Systems in Automotive Body Engineering," *Computer Graphics*, vol. 7, no. 3, 4, 1983, pp. 307-314.

12.9. Sakai, Y., and Y. Kuranaga, "The development of CADETT System," Paper No. 36, *Proc. ISTATA*, 1981.

12.10. Higashi, M., T. Mori, H. Taniguchi, and J. Yoshimi, "Geometric Modelling for Efficient Evaluation," *Computer Modeling of Sheet Metal Forming Processes*, N.-M. Wang and S. C. Tang (eds.), Proc. Symposium Met. Soc. and TMS Detroit Sec., 12th Automotive Mat. Symp., Ann Arbor, Michigan, April 29-30, 1985, Met. Soc., Inc., Warrendale, Pennsylvania, pp. 21-35.

12.11. Bezier, P. E., "UNISURF, From Styling to Tool-Shop," *Computer Applications in Production and Engineering*, E. A. Warman (ed.), CAPE '83, North-Holland Pub. Co., New York, pp. 275-287.

12.12. Araki, H., et al., "Replacement of Physical Models by Highly Accurate Numerical Models for Manufacturing Stamping Dies in the Integrated CAD/CAM System", Software for Discrete Manufacturing, Proc. of 6th Inter. IFIP/FAC Conf., PROLAMAT 85, Paris, June, 1985, pp. 47-60.

12.13. Higashi, M. I. Kohzen, and J. Nagasaka, "An Interactive CAD System for Construction of Shapes with High-Quality Surface," *Computer Applications in Production and Engineering*, E. A. Warman (ed.), CAPE '83, North-Holland Pub. Co., New York, pp. 371-390.

12.14. Hosaka, M., and F. Kimura, "A Theory and Methods for Three Dimensional Free Form Shape Construction," *Journal of Inf. Proc.*, vol. 3 (1980), pp. 140-151.

12.15. Reisenfeld, R. F., "Applications of *B*-Spline Approximation to Geometric Problems of Computer Aided Design," Univ. of Utah, UTEC-CSC-73-126, 1973.

12.16. Bezier, P. E., *Numerical Control—Mathematics and Applications*, John Wiley and Sons, London, 1972, pp. 222-227.

12.17. Takahashi, A, T. Okamoto, T. Hiramatsu, and N. Yamada, "Evaluation Methods of Press Forming Severity in CAD Applications," *Computer Modeling of Sheet Metal Forming Processes*, N.-M. Wang and S. C. Tang (eds.), Proc. Symposium Met. Soc. and TMS Detroit Sec., 12th Automotive Mat. Symp., Ann Arbor, Michigan, April 29-30, 1985, Met. Soc., Inc., Warrendale, Pennsylvania, pp. 37-50.

12.18. Tiza, M., "A CAD/CAM System for Deep-Drawing Processes", in *Advanced Technology of Plasticity*, Vol. 1, K. Lange (ed.), Springer-Verlag, New York, 1987, pp. 145-155.

12.19. Kachanov, L. M., *Foundations of the Theory of Plasticity*, North-Holland, London, 1971.

A12.1 GEOMETRIC MODELING

A model is a substitute or representation of something. Geometric modeling refers to a collection of methods used to define the shape and other geometric characteristics of an object such as the properties of its material. It is used to construct a precise mathematical description of the shape of a real object such as a deep-drawn part or to simulate some process such as a deep-drawing operation. The construction of a geometric model is usually a computer-aided operation, with the model stored in, and analyzed by, a digital computer. Without the computational power of a computer, often a very large and high-speed one, one would not be able to construct and analyze sophisticated models of any practical importance. [A12.1]

A12.2 PARAMETRIC EQUATIONS

Equations can be classified as parametric or nonparametric. The latter can be expressed in explicit form as $y = f(x)$ or in implicit form as $f(x, y) = 0$. Both are axis dependent. A general second-degree implicit form equation is

$$ax^2 + 2bxy + cy^2 + 2dx + 2cy + f = 0 \qquad (A12.1)$$

If this curve passes through the origin, $f = 0$.

Parametric equations are useful for expressing intrinsic properties of a curve or shape. An intrinsic property is one that depends only on the figure and not on its frame of reference. The fact that a rectangle has four equal angles is intrinsic to the rectangle. The directions of the sides are extrinsic, because they require a frame of reference.

A curve as in Fig. A12.1 requires two intrinsic equations, one to express the curvature $1/\rho$, and one the torsion t and the arc length s, of the curve. A natural equation of a curve can be expressed as

$$f\left(\frac{1}{\rho}, t, s\right) = 0. \qquad (A12.2)$$

For ease of programming and computability and for ease of drawing by a plotter or on a computer graphic display screen, the predominant means of representing shapes in geometric modeling is with parametric equations. For example, a two-dimensional curve is expressed not by a single ordinary function like $y = f(x)$ but by a set of two functions $x = x(u)$, $y = y(u)$ of a parameter u. A point on such a two-dimensional curve is represented as

$$\boldsymbol{p} = [x(u), y(u)] \qquad (A12.3)$$

A point on a space curve is given by the vector

$$\boldsymbol{p} = [x(u), y(u), z(u)] \qquad (A12.4)$$

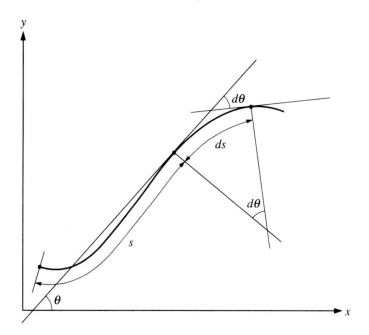

FIGURE A12.1
Intrinsic definition of a plane curve, which is defined completely by the variation of θ with arc length
s. (θ is the angle subtended by the tangent to the curve with the x axis.) [A12.1]

and a point on a surface is represented by

$$p = [x(u, w), y(u, w), z(u, w)] \tag{A12.5}$$

In the above equations, the multiplying matrix $[i, j, k]^T$ was omitted for convenience from the representation of a point p by

$$p = p_x i + p_y j + p_z k = [p_x \ p_y \ p_z][i \ j \ k]^T \tag{A12.6}$$

Parametric equations have many advantages over nonparametric forms for
expressing curves and surfaces such as more degrees of freedom, ease of transformation, for expressing infinite slopes, representation of variables, ease of expressing in the form of vectors and matrices, and many others.

It is not desirable or often possible to plot a curve for all values of the
parametric variable, say, u from $-\infty$ to $+\infty$. It is convenient to normalize the
parametric variable by limiting its value as in Fig. A12.2 to, say, between -1 and
$+1$, which may be expressed symbolically as $u \in [-1, 1]$. This point-bounded
collection of points is called a *curve segment* whose coordinates are given by
continuous, one-parameter, single-valued mathematical functions of the form
$x = x(u)$, $y = y(u)$, and $z = z(u)$.

Any point on a parametric curve can be treated as the components of a
vector $p(u)$ as shown in Fig. A12.3. Here, $p(u)$ is the vector to the point $x(u)$,
$y(u)$, and $p^u(u)$ is the tangent vector to the curve at the same point and is

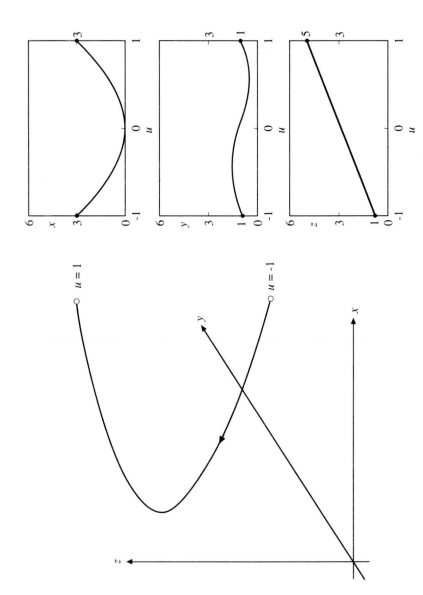

FIGURE A12.2

Example of a parametric curve plotted for the interval on u of $u \in [-1, +1]$ for which $x = 3u^2$, $y = u^3 - u + 1$ and $z = 2u + 3$ as shown on the right [A12.1].

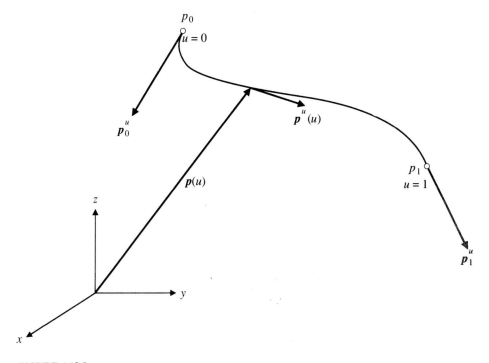

FIGURE A12.3
Vector elements of a parametric curve bounded by the end point $p(0)$ at $u = 0$ and by end point $p(1)$ at $u = 1$. (Any point on the curve can be defined as components of vector $p(u)$.) [A12.1]

sometimes written as $p'(u)$. It is found by differentiating $p(u)$ with respect to u as follows:

$$p''(u) = p'(u) = \frac{dp(u)}{du} \tag{A12.7}$$

The vector components are

$$x^u = \frac{dx(u)}{du} \qquad y^u = \frac{dy(u)}{du} \qquad z^u = \frac{dx(u)}{dy} \tag{A12.8}$$

Often the functional notation is omitted for simplicity, so that

$$p = p(u) \qquad p^u = p' = p^u(u) \tag{A12.9}$$

$$x^u = x^u(u) \tag{A12.10}$$

A12.3 BEZIER CURVES [A12.1]

Some curve-defining techniques interpolate a given set of points, which means that the curve produced passes exactly through the points. Interpolation techniques have certain disadvantages when used in an interactive CAD program.

An alternate approach defines a curve that only approximates or approaches the given points. For example, if the shape of a spline-interpolated curve is changed by moving one or more of the interpolated points, perturbations and inflections may be produced, both locally and remotely.

Bezier started with the principle that any point on a curve segment must be given a parametric function of the following form:

$$p(u) = \sum_{i=0}^{n} p_i f_i(u) \qquad u \in [0, 1] \tag{A12.11}$$

where the vectors p_i represent the $n+1$ vertices of a characteristic polygon such as shown in Fig. A12.4. These vertices are also called *control points*. He then set forth certain properties that the $f_i(u)$ blending functions must have and then looked for specific functions to meet these requirements.

Bezier chose a family of functions called Bernstein polynomials to satisfy these requirements. The functions that Bezier selected depend on the number of

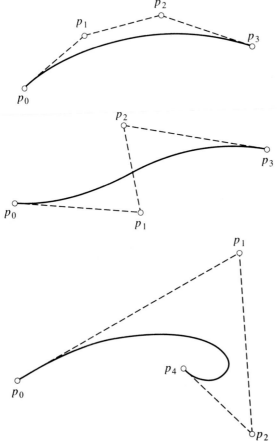

FIGURE A12.4
Bezier curves showing control points, p_i, whose movement controls the shape of the curves. Note that the reverse curvature as in (c) is possible [A12.1].

vertices used to specify a particular curve. To indicate this dependence, Eq. (A12.11) can be rewritten

$$p(u) = \sum_{i=0}^{n} p_i B_{i,n}(u) \qquad u \in [0, 1] \tag{A12.12}$$

where

$$B_{i,n}(u) = C(n, i) u^i (1 - u)^{n-i} \tag{A12.13}$$

and where $C(n, i)$ is the familiar binomial coefficient

$$C(n, i) = \frac{n!}{i!(n-1)!} \tag{A12.14}$$

It should be observed that for $(n+1)$ vertices, the blending function, $B_{i,n}(u)$, yields an nth degree polynomial. Figure A12.5(a) and (b) shows cubic Bezier curves uninflected and reflected, respectively. Figure A12.6(a) and (b) shows blending function curves $B_{i,n}$ for $n = 2$ and 3, respectively.

A12.4 SPLINE CURVES [A12.2]

There are two types of splines: (1) physical and (2) mathematical. A physical spline is a thin lath of metal or wood that is bent elastically around movable magnetic pins or weights placed at points chosen to give the desired curve as shown in Fig. A12.7(a). They are used in the design of ship hulls, aircraft fuselages, and automobile bodies. A mathematical spline is a mathematical analogy [A12.2]. A physical spline assumes a shape for which its internal strain energy is a minimum. This can be expressed mathematically by requiring that the following integral, when integrated over the entire length of the spline, is a minimum:

$$B \int K^2 \, ds = \text{minimum} \tag{A12.15}$$

where B = constant expressing the stiffness of the spline
K = curvature of the spline
s = arc length, having limits $0 \le \sigma \le L$, where L is the total length of the spline

In Cartesian coordinates, the integral can be written as

$$\int \frac{y''^2 \, dx}{(1+y^2)^{5/2}} = \text{minimum} \tag{A12.16}$$

If $y' = dy/dx$ is everywhere sufficiently small, that is $y' \ll 1$, the problem reduces to minimizing the integral

$$\int y''^2 \, dx = \text{minimum} \tag{A12.17}$$

Solving the variational problem of minimizing Eq. (A12.16) subject to the spline passing through specified points or "knots" as shown in Fig. A12.7(b),

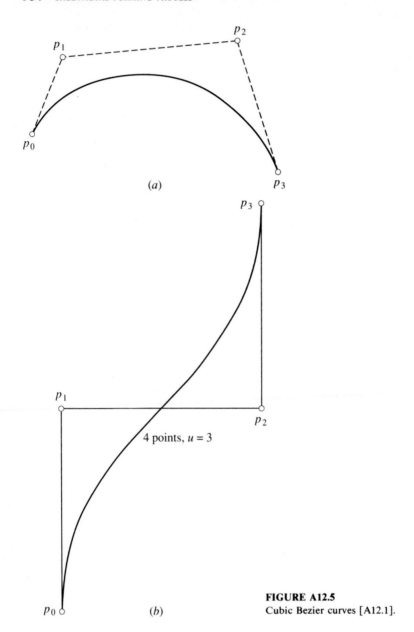

p_1
p_2
p_0
(a)
p_3

p_3

p_1
p_2

4 points, $u = 3$

p_0
(b)

FIGURE A12.5
Cubic Bezier curves [A12.1].

one finds that the resultant curve or mathematical spline is composed of a series of cubic curves joined at the points. The mathematical spline is a good approximation of the physical spline provided that the slopes are not too large.

Parametric (vector) methods may be used to compute a spline which is a function of t for each component of the vector $p(t)$. By writing the following

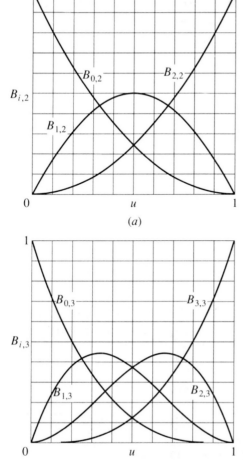

FIGURE A12.6
Bezier blending functions. (a) Three points, $n = 2$. (b) Four points, $n = 3$ [A12.1].

equation for the ith span in Fig A12.7(b),

$$p_i(t) = p_{i-1}(1 - 3t^2 + 2t^3) + p_i(3t^2 - 2t^3) + p'_{i-1}(t - 2t^2 + t^3) + p'_i(-t^2 + t^3) \quad \text{(A12.18)}$$

and by differentiating twice, one can obtain the equations

$$p''_i(0) = -6p_{i-1} + 6p_i - 4p'_{i-1} - 2p'_i \quad \text{(A12.19)}$$

and

$$p''_i(1) = 6p_{i-1} - 6p_i + 2p'_{i-1} + 4p'_i \quad \text{(A12.20)}$$

If the span $p_i(t)$ is to be continuous in the second derivative with the adjacent span $p_{i+1}(t)$ at the point p_i by equating Eqs. (A12.19) and (A12.20), dividing by 2, and rearranging, one can obtain

$$p'_{i-1} + 4p'_i + p'_{i+1} = -3p_{i-1} + 3p_{i+1} \quad \text{(A12.21)}$$

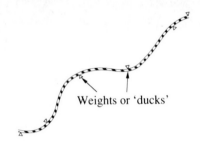

Weights or 'ducks'

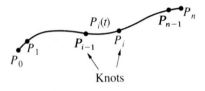

Knots

FIGURE A12.7
(a) Sketch of a physical spline curve. (b) Plot of a mathematical (parametric) spline curve whose ith span $p_i(t)$ ($0 \le t \le 1$) runs from $p_i(0) = p_{i-1}$ to $p_i(1) = p_i$ [A12.2]

Using $n-1$ equations (A12.21) and two additional equations for end conditions shown in Fig. A12.8, one can construct a matrix as follows:

$$A p'_i = B p_i \qquad (A12.22)$$

where A is an $(n+1) \times (n+1)$ matrix and B is a matrix with $(n+1)$ rows. In the case where a tangent vector is specified at a knot, the column vector of vectors p_i also includes the specified tangent vector.

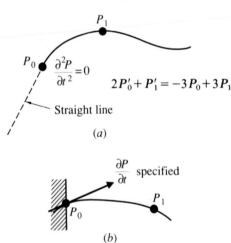

$$2P'_0 + P'_1 = -3P_0 + 3P_1$$

Straight line

(a)

$\dfrac{\partial P}{\partial t}$ specified

(b)

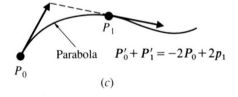

Parabola $\qquad P'_0 + P'_1 = -2P_0 + 2p_1$

(c)

FIGURE A12.8
End conditions. (a) Free end, no bending moment at the end of the spline; (b) built-in or cantilevered ends with a specified first derivative at the end $p'_0 = t_0$; and (c) parabolic end span [A12.2].

A four-span spline curve with one end built in and the other free has the following matrix equation:

$$
\begin{bmatrix}
1 & 0 & 0 & 0 & 0 \\
1 & 4 & 1 & 0 & 0 \\
0 & 1 & 4 & 1 & 0 \\
0 & 0 & 1 & 4 & 1 \\
0 & 0 & 0 & 1 & 2
\end{bmatrix}
\begin{bmatrix}
p_0' \\ p_1' \\ p_2' \\ p_3' \\ p_4'
\end{bmatrix}
=
\begin{bmatrix}
1 & 0 & 0 & 0 & 0 & 0 \\
0 & -3 & 0 & 3 & 0 & 0 \\
0 & 0 & -3 & 0 & 3 & 0 \\
0 & 0 & 0 & -3 & 0 & 3 \\
0 & 0 & 0 & 0 & -3 & 3
\end{bmatrix}
\begin{bmatrix}
t_0 \\ p_0 \\ p_1 \\ p_2 \\ p_3 \\ p_4
\end{bmatrix}
\qquad (A12.23)
$$

One can solve for the tangent vectors p_i' by inverting the matrix A and premultiplying B by the inverse

$$p_i = A^{-1} B p_i \qquad (A12.24)$$

Each span of the spline is then specified by use of Eq. (A12.18).

A12.5   B-SPLINE CURVES [A12.1]

Most curve-defining techniques do not provide for local control of shape. Consequently, local changes tend to be strongly propagated throughout the entire curve. This effect is sometimes described as a global propagation of change. The B-spline curve avoids this problem by using a special set of blending functions that has only a local influence and depends on only a few neighboring control points.

B-spline curves are similar to Bezier curves in that a set of blending functions combines the effects of $n+1$ control points p_i given by

$$p(u) = \sum_{i=0}^{n} p_i N_{i,k}(u) \qquad (A12.25)$$

The most important difference between Eqs. (A12.25) and (A12.12) is the way the blending functions, $N_{i,k}(u)$ are formulated. For Bezier curves, the number of control points determines the degree of the blending function polynomials. For B-spline curves, the degree of these polynomials is specially controlled by a parameter k and is usually independent of the number of control points, except as limited by the following equation [A12.1]

$$0 \le u \le n - k + 2 \qquad (A12.26)$$

REFERENCES

A12.1 Mortenson, M. E., *Geometric Modeling*, John Wiley & Sons, New York, 1985.
A12.2 Bezier, P., *Numerical Control—Mathematics and Applications*, John Wiley & Sons, New York, 1972.

ANSWERS
TO
SELECTED
QUESTIONS

Chapter 2

2.1. $\sigma_m = 5$, and $D_{ii} = 0$ is always true for any stress state.

2.3. (1) By use of the Mohr stress circle: $\sigma_1 = 90$ MPa and $\tau_{max} = 60$ MPa.
(2) Analytically: $\sigma_1 = 89$ MPa, $\tau_{max} = 61.5$ MPa, and $\phi = 13.3°$.

2.5. (a) $\sigma_1 = 890$ MPa, $\sigma_2 = 110$ MPa, and $\alpha = 19.9°$.
(b) $\tau = 390$ MPa. According to the Tresca criterion, $\sigma_Y = 780$ MPa or 890 MPa. According to the von Mises criterion, $\sigma_Y = 840$ MPa.

2.6. (a) $\varepsilon_1 = 0.1$, $\varepsilon_2 = 0.0308$, $\varepsilon_3 = -0.1308$, and $\tau_{max} = 500$ MPa.
(b) $\gamma_{max} = 0.2308$.

2.10. $\sigma_2/\sigma_1 = 0.333$.

2.12. $Q = 278$ kJ/mol.

2.14. $A'' = 2.1 \times 10^{-8}$ s^{-1}. Comparing 2.1×10^{-8} s^{-1} to $1.47 \times 10^{-8} \times$ s^{-1} at 977 K, one can conclude that the agreement is good.

Chapter 3

3.1. $\sigma_1 = 40$ MPa, $\sigma_2 = 100$ MPa, and $\sigma_3 = -100$ MPa.

3.3. $\sigma_f = 574.6$ MPa. It is assumed that the true stress–true strain curves in tension and compression are the same.

3.5. (a) $\sigma_d = 12.83$ MPa.
(b) $\sigma_{actual} = 19.74$ MPa.

3.7. $Z_l = 1.103$.

3.9. For $\varepsilon = 0.4$, 0.6, 0.8, and 1.0, $B = 0.956$, 0.918, 0.884, and 0.855, respectively, and $\sigma_{corr} = 163.5$, 174.4, 183.9, and 189.0, respectively.

3.11. $\sigma_f = 277$ MPa and $\dot{\varepsilon} = 120\ \text{s}^{-1}$.

3.13. $r = 1.5$. Yes.

3.15. $\bar{\sigma} = 27.5$ MPa and $\bar{\varepsilon} = 0.56$.

Chapter 4

4.1. (a) $p_{max} = 805$ MPa.
  (b) (1) By Eq. (4.19), $p_m = 468.8$ MPa.
      (2) By Eq. (4.25), $p_m = $ about 388.0 MPa.
  (c) $p_{max} = 969.9$ MPa and $p_m = 606$ MPa.

4.7. $\Delta T_f = 2.75°$ per time increment.

4.8. $\Delta T_D = 0.258°$ per time increment.

4.9. $\Delta T = 1.28\ °\text{C}$ for element 2.

Chapter 6

6.2. (a) $P = 4725$ kN.
  (b) The assumption of homogeneity is not too good, since $w/\sqrt{R\,\Delta h} = 12$ versus 1 to 4.
  (c) Since the strain rate increases with the speed of rolling and since the strain rate in rolling is high, it is a factor especially for hot rolling which is strain rate sensitive.

6.3. (a) $R'' = 306.4$ mm.
  (b) $h_{min} = 0.451$ mm.

6.5. $R_{max} = 19.5\%$ for hot rolling and $R_{max} = 0.50\%$ for cold rolling. The maximum reduction per pass for $D = 500$ mm and for $D = 1000$ mm would be the same.

6.7. $A = 19.1$ N rad/m, and $P = 861$ kN.

Chapter 7

7.1. $D_0 = 0.707$ mm.

7.3. (a) $P_1 = (V/l_1)\bar{\sigma}_Y \ln (l_1/l_0)$.
  (b) $P_1 = 427$ N.

7.5. $p = 795$ MPa.

7.7. $R(\theta, z) = 1 + \left[1\sqrt{\dfrac{0.00879}{0.0625 \cos^2 \theta + 0.141 \sin^2 \theta}} \right] \left\{ \left(\dfrac{1}{4}\right) z^3 - \left(\dfrac{3}{4}\right) z^2 \right\}$

Chapter 8

8.1. $l = 2.32$ in.

8.3. $P_a = 6.88$ MN.

8.5. $P = 1144$ kips.

8.7. $\bar{\varepsilon}_c = 1.46$.

Chapter 9

9.1. (1) $P_{fa} = 106,724$ lbf and $P_{ca} = 267,614$ lbf.

(2) $P_{fp} = 33,264$ lbf and $P_{cp} = 859,607$ lbf.

(3) $P_{fa} = 64,380$ lbf and $P_{ca} = 74,338$ lbf.

9.3. (*a*) $\Delta T = 53.3°F$ or 29.6 K.

(*b*) $T = 1039°C$.

9.5. (*a*) $w/t = 7.16$ and $w = 10.65$ mm.

(*b*) $P_f = 530.1$ kN and $P_b = 301$ kN.

Chapter 10

10.1. $P = 19.9$ N/mm.

Chapter 11

11.1. (1) For the Swift cup test: (*a*) $LDR_1 = F_s = 2.28$ calculated by Eq. (11.88) $\cong 2.31$ from Fig. 11.68. (*b*) $LDR_2 = 2.18$ by Eq. 11.91.

(2) For Olsen cup test: $F_o = 0.411$ in calculated $\cong 0.430$ in from Fig. 11.69.

(3) For Fukui cup test: $F_f = 1.31$ in calculated $\cong 1.39$ in from Fig. 11.70.

The conclusion is that it is hard to read the values from the graphs, so that they are useful only for illustrative purposes.

11.3. Draw = 50% and stretch = 50%.

INDEX